Oregon Burial Site Guide

Oregon Burial Site Guide

Compiled by: Dean H. Byrd
Co-Compiled by: Stanley R. Clarke and Janice M. Healy

Binford & Mort Publishing
Portland, Oregon

Front Cover Photo: **Walsh Mausoleum at Calvary Cemetery in Marion County**
Janice M. Healy (1991)

Back Cover Photo: **Walsh Mausoleum at Calvary Cemetery in Marion County**
Looking through the front glass door at the stained glass window.
Janice M. Healy (1991)

Oregon Burial Site Guide

Copyright © 2001
by: Ruth C. Bishop, Dean H. Byrd, Stanley R. Clarke and Janice M. Healy

Printed in the United States of America

Library of Congress Catalog Card Number: 2001090795

ISBN 0-8323-0546-4 hb
0-8323-0547-2 pb

First Edition 2001

Dedicated to the late
Darlene Dickson Albert

Oregon Burial Site Guide

Table of Contents

Acknowledgements

The compiler now wishes to acknowledge the assistance of the following: Gloria Aagaard, Richard and Ava AuFranc, George Bent, Jacques Bergman, Jo Bollman, Sudie Boyce, Mr. and Mrs. Henry Cupper, Pat Doerner, Anita Drake, Maynard Drawson, Norma Eid, Warren T. Faulkner, Stephanie Flora, Jack Fosmark, Cheryl Gage, Lucille Geigle, Judy Goldmann, Christy Hanson, Alice Godsey Harris, Carla Healy, Dallas Helsley, Ken and Phyllis Hoggatt, Arlie Holt, Margaret Hunter, Jim Johnson, Katherine Johnson, Verlie Johnston, Judy Juntunen, Sherry Kaseberg, Robert Marsh, Tom McAllister, Grace McKinney, Richard E. Meyer, Mary Muller, James Nelson, Mrs. Russel Nelson, Karen Olson, Evelyn Parry, Liisa Penner, Perry Powers, Rod Purdy, Raymond M. Ramsay, Sam and Dorothy Randle, Addie Dyal Rickey, Jeanne Robinson, Jim and Evelyn Rogers, Jack Rowland, Leroy Rush, Wilma Stahl, Lester Steckley, George Strozut, Daraleen Wade, Rudy Wellbrock, Bill and Myra Weston. If by chance I have missed anyone it was not intentional.

With a very special thanks to: Ruth C. Bishop, Stanley R. Clarke, Janice M. Healy, and the late Lois L. Lehl.

Dean H. Byrd
January 2001

This guide has been a labor of love by four people and the dream of many others. It would never have been started without Dean Byrd presenting his work at the Sleuthing the Burials conference held in Portland in March of 1987. A group of us promised Dean that it would be published. Little did we know at the time that this final product would be nothing like the survey the Oregon Department of Transportation published, which was the basis for this guide. I take my hat off to Dean Byrd who pored over maps, visited and photographed many cemeteries; Janice M. Healy who has spent so many hours inputting information, researching, filing data and traveling to many burial sites with Dean, Ruth Bishop and myself; Ruth Bishop for her constant encouragement in the project; and to my mother, Florence H. Clarke who spent many hours in libraries, archives and on the road touring cemeteries with me.

Stanley R. Clarke
January 2001

I wish to thank my father Harry H. Hammerly for teaching me patience; that any job worth doing is worth doing well; and that I could do any thing that I set my mind to. Thank you Ruth C. Bishop, Dean H. Byrd, Stanley R. Clarke and the late Lois L. Lehl for having the faith in my being able to take on the task of putting this into a condition for publishing. Thank you Zane H. Healy, son, for all of your computer technical support. Thank you Ruth C. Bishop, Dean H. Byrd, Stanley R. Clarke and Christy Hanson for all of the help with proofreading. I take sole credit for any and all typographical errors. Thank you Edmund A. Healy, husband, for your patience with late meals, never knowing where I was off to half the time and all of your encouragement when the going got tough. Last but not least I want to thank my mother Ethel Wade Hammerly Paschal and all of the rest of the family and friends who said I was crazy and that I would never finish this. You are the ones who kept my determination going all of these years. The greatest pleasure in life is doing something others say you cannot do.

Janice M. Healy
30 January 2001

I became involved in this project later than the other four. However, I do think my knowledge of cemeteries, map reading, and the beautiful state of Oregon has been greatly enriched. Many thanks to Dean H. Byrd for starting this project, which has become a "labor of love". I would like to thank Stanley R. Clarke for his attentiveness, especially when I got overly exuberant in a cemetery and he had to help me back to the car from a point of no return. I would like to thank Janice M. Healy for the numerous trips for photography; for instruction in the learn-as-you-ride topographical map reading; and for showing me back roads, side roads, and non-roads of Oregon. Many thanks to Lois L. Lehl, whose courageous spirit enriched all of our lives and encouraged us to continue this guide. Finally to Eloise C. Bishop, my mother, who has weathered the ups and downs of life with me, as I take one final photograph, visit one final county, or meet for one final edit --- which, by the way, never happens. All of you have influenced my life the twelve years I've been on this project. You all have made these years exciting and memorable.

Ruth C. Bishop
4 February 2001

Introduction

This book had its genesis in the publication of the *Oregon Cemetery Survey*. The Survey was authorized by the 1977 state legislature by Senate Bill 598 and was mandated to the Oregon Department of Transportation (ODOT).

ODOT was to list the names of all cemeteries in the state of Oregon by size, number of interments, current condition of the grounds, the year of establishment, and its geographic location by Township, Range and Section. In addition the Survey included a line or two giving the name of the caretaker, the cemetery address and how to travel to it. To help locate any cemetery the Survey included a small map of each of the 36 Oregon counties outlining the major roads and the Townships. The Survey depended upon replies from funeral directors, county historical organizations and Genealogical Societies. The result was published in December 1978 for the legislature in the following month.

The *Oregon Cemetery Survey* was the first state-wide listing of cemeteries. Each of the 36 counties was listed in alphabetical order, and within each county each cemetery was supposed to be listed in alphabetical order. Unfortunately that alpha listing often broke down. Late arrival of information for Josephine County, for example, placed Hillcrest Memorial Park after the listing of Wonder Cemetery. After listing Hillcrest, then came Laurel, and then Perrydale, and then No Name and then Croxton and so on. There was little time to check out the names with the result that the Survey, admirable on the whole, is marred by omissions, duplications and wrong locations.

The principal compiler was then employed in the ODOT mapping department. He was told by his boss to spend a minimum amount of time checking cemetery information for the *Oregon Cemetery Survey*, but he was aware of some of the omissions and the misspellings.

After the 1978 publication the principal compiler gradually added a few corrections to the *Oregon Cemetery Survey*, then after his retirement in December 1983 he considered compiling enough for a second edition to the Survey. To cut a long story short, ODOT decided not to publish a second edition. After all, cemeteries are usually of no importance to a highway department unless a cemetery abuts directly with a highway right-of-way. So the compiler decided to go ahead with another state-wide cemetery survey based on ODOT"s 1978 publication but expanded. Needless to say the compiler did not realize what he was getting into.

A major turning point came around Memorial Day in 1987. The late Darlene Dickson Albert, along with her husband, persuaded the compiler into escorting them on a photography visit to Fairfield Cemetery. This was so enjoyable that we drove to St. Louis Cemetery nearby for more pictures. The upshot was that the compiler bought a camera and continued field trips which eventually resulted in personal visits at least once to 437 cemeteries/burial sites in Oregon.

Dean H. Byrd at Neer City Cemetery in Columbia County

Janice M. Healy (1991)

Foreword

The purpose of this book is to preserve the historical information on the locations of these burial sites. It also makes it easier for those looking for family and lost cemeteries to be able to locate the burial sites found in historical records. In some cases where the site is on private property, we have listed who is buried at the site with their dates, if we have the information. This was done to keep the curious from bothering the current land owners.

The primary name we list may or may not be what you know it as. This is because we used the name on the sign, if there was one and we had visited the site, or the name listed on the maps and land records. If this was not available we used what was published in other historical writings. This is why we can not stress enough the importance of putting up a sign at a burial site so that everyone knows what it is called. The sign doesn't have to be expensive. Some of the best signs we have seen were just scrap steel with the letters cut out or a bead from the welders torch naming the site and placed very high on a tree.

The compilers have found there is all too much duplication of names. Mountain View appears in one form or another at least 15 times. Someone wishing to search out information on one particular Mountain View Cemetery can do so by using the State-wide index. Each Mountain View is listed by county and by Township, Range and Section. In the case of Multnomah County, the reader will note there are two separate Mountain View Cemeteries distinguished by their different locations. If you are searching for Mountain View Cemetery in Benton County, the index will tell you that it is now headed by its present name of Mt. Union Cemetery.

We at first had no idea that there was so much duplication of names of cemeteries or even less notion that any cemetery could have so many bygone or alternative names. The principal cemetery for the town of Junction City is now called Restlawn Memorial Park. It has had at least seven different names in the past: hence the use of county name and Township, Range, and Section in all indices. (See the article on Restlawn Memorial Park in the Lane County chapter.)

Next are the cemeteries belonging to the fraternal orders. They were very much a part of American society. The fraternal orders have been gradually fading away since the 1930s and many of their cemeteries have been taken over by cities or counties or special associations. The Independent Order of Odd Fellows, an offshoot of the Masonic Lodges, established more cemeteries in Oregon than any other fraternal society. They are listed here under the primary heading of "I.O.O.F.", followed by the name of the town or the name of the particular lodge. Occasionally the Odd Fellows established two cemeteries for the same town (Eugene, Bandon). The female auxiliary is the Rebekahs.

The next most numerous cemeteries of the fraternal orders are Masonic. We have retained the same system of listing them under "Masonic" followed by the name of the town or the name of the particular lodge. The female auxiliary is the Order of the Eastern Star.

Much less numerous are cemeteries for the Knights of Pythias, an organization dating from 1864. The female auxiliary is the Pythian Sisters.

The Noble Order of Redmen founded a number of cemeteries in Clatsop, Columbia and other Counties. Their lodges were known as Wickiups. The large cemetery at Jacksonville included an area used by the Noble Order of Redmen and a smaller area for the German Order of Redmen.

The Benevolent and Protective Order of Elks (1868) and the Loyal Order of Moose were both popular. The visitor can note the lodge emblems on tombstones in cemeteries. We are unaware of any cemeteries established by the Elks or Moose.

The Woodmen of the World is a fraternal organzation with a life insurance society affiliation (1890). They apparently had no separate cemeteries of their own, but the compilers mention them here because of the unique monuments found in many cemeteries. The cement and white marble simulated tree trunks and stumps can not be mistaken for any but a Woodmen of the World monument.

There are monuments for the A.O.U.W., the Ancient Order of United Workmen in many cemeteries. Their emblem is a shield in front of an anchor. The only cemetery the compilers know that was established by them is Alford in Linn County.

The Grange (1867) is an organization to defend the interests of farmers. The compilers know of only two cemeteries established by the Grange, in Lane County and Clatsop County, but Grange monuments are found in many cemeteries. They are marked with the Patron of Husbandry emblem.

Church-oriented cemeteries are numerous. Except in the French Prairie area of northern Marion County which were Roman Catholic, virtually all of the first-generation pioneer American settlers were Protestant of Calvinist or Methodist derivation. Lutheran cemeteries were established for German and Scandinavian immigrants. Roman Catholic settlers from Ireland, Germany, Switzerland and even the Czech Republic and other immigrants from eastern and southern Europe (Italy, Greece, Yugoslavia, etc.) also established cemeteries. Jewish cemeteries are almost exclusively in or near Portland. The only "working" Jewish cemetery outside of the Portland area is the Waverly Jewish Cemetery at Albany in Linn County. There are bygone Jewish burial grounds in Jacksonville and The Dalles.

Chinese cemeteries were in a class by themselves. Chinese immigrants arrived early in the settlement period and consisted almost entirely of male laborers and miners. They were so numerous and so "foreign" that the Chinese Exclusion Act of 1882 closed the United States to legal immigration until 1942. There were Chinese cemeteries in the gold-mining centers in Oregon as well as the larger cities. Chinese culture required that burials in this country should eventually be returned to their home burial ground in China. There remain many Chinese portions of established cemeteries in Oregon but they often appear empty of monuments. The long war with China and Japan that began in the summer of 1937 and lasting for eight years seems to be the time when Chinese burials in America stopped being returned to China. Present day Chinese burials can appear in almost any cemetery and usually the monuments are very similar to the surrounding monuments except for the ideograms.

Japanese immigrants arrived starting a generation after the Chinese and were not as numerous. They did not have the tradition of returning their burials to Japan. They established at least one cemetery in Oregon.

The compilers know of only one cemetery, a small one, exclusively for Muslims. It is in Benton County. Other ethnic groups are now establishing new burial sites throught out Oregon.

Family cemeteries were numerous at the time of the first generation of American settlers. If they are still maintained, they are by definition small, or they may have become the starting point of what are now larger public cemeteries. Many have fallen out of use and later generations are trying to clean them up. Acquiring access for family members can run into opposition from present day landowners. This is why legal easements and deeds which were or were not filed at the county court house come into play. Many an old family plot has been later destroyed by farming or logging practices and development. If stout fences are not kept up, cattle will enter a graveyard. Cattle like to rub against the monuments, eventually knocking them over and breaking them up. Given time cattle will vandalize any burial ground as effectively as human vandals.

Military burial grounds in Oregon were established around the temporary forts during the time of the first white settlers. These were not only forts manned by regulars, but the militia forts which were briefly in use in southern Oregon. Most known burials of regulars of these temporary forts were eventually removed to the Presidio in

San Francisco. The only long-lasting fort in Oregon was Fort Stevens at the mouth of the Columbia River in Clatsop County. The graveyard for this fort is still maintained. (See the article entitled U. S. Army Fort Stevens.)

In addition there are, in Oregon, three National Cemeteries for veterans and their families. One of these, Roseburg National, is now closed for further burials, except for widows whose husbands are buried here. The National Veterans Cemetery at Eagle Point and Willamette National Cemetery in Portland are both active today. The latter is currently the most active in the state as the World War II generation comes to its close.

There are standardized military monuments which are in use in any cemetery whether it is a Veterans Cemetery or not. These standardized markers were apparently first used for veterans of the American Civil War of 1861-1865. There were no battles in the then-remote new state of Oregon, but many veterans of the war settled later in the state. Occasionally, one finds the same man has a military marker naming his regiment and company and also a civilian monument.

The Grand Army of the Republic (G.A.R.) was an organization of veterans of the Union Army in the Civil War. There were five of these cemeteries in Oregon, plus a number of "G.A.R. circles" in other cemeteries, often embellished with life-size statues of soldiers. As that generation died out, at least some G.A.R. cemeteries were used for burials of veterans and their families of later wars and some are now open to any one.

Although many Confederate veterans also settled in Oregon, the compilers do not know of any cemetery established primarily for them. Although Oregon was far removed from the main theaters of the Civil War, visitors to cemeteries can catch glimpses of the passions it stirred. For example, in Salem there is a monument to a Confederate veteran of General Nathan Bedford Forrest's "Git thar the fustest with the mostest" forces. This monument is conspicuously out of alignment with its neighbors. The monument is deliberately turned with its back to the G.A.R. circle of Union veterans. In Fernwood Cemetery at Newberg there is a monument to one Stonewall J.[Jackson] Everest who is pointedly buried next to but not within the neighboring G.A.R. Cemetery.

Oregon was settled several years after the end of the Revolutionary War. The compilers have learned of a known veteran of this war buried in Oregon. A marker dedicated to William Cannon, Revolutionary War Veteran, has been place in St. Paul [Old] Cemetery in Marion County.

Neglected in both senses of the word are cemeteries or burials for the poor, the unlucky, and the failures in life. Call them Paupers, Potters Fields or whatever, sometimes they are the entire burial ground or they are allotted portions of some cemeteries. If the word "County" is part of the cemetery's name, the visitor may well find standardized small ground-hugging cement squares labelled "unknown" or "John Doe" and burials in chronological order. Many counties also at one time had what were called Poor Farms and some neglected burial sites remain from these bygone institutions. There are also cemeteries associated with state institutions. By far the most numerous burials and cremations are associated with the State of Oregon's institutions for the mentally deranged or unfit. (See the articles on "Asylum" and "Penitentiary" in Marion County and Umatilla County.)

For better or worse the compilers have retained the name Indian instead of the newly favored title of Native American. Before white settlement the various tribes, in what is now Oregon, disposed of their dead in different ways, all sacred to them. This book contains few references to those times because they are the province of various tribes and their customs. We can not stress enough the importance of honoring the sacredness of these sites. Many pre-white settlement burial sites on the Columbia River Islands were removed to other sites during the time of dam construction on the river beginning in the 1930s.

The compilers have decided to include articles about Indian cemeteries only if they appear on USGS Quad. maps or are published elsewhere and if they are post-white settlement. Many of these latter are on current or past Indian Reservations with a few along side state highways. Some Indian burials are by their nature not written about or marked with written monuments and the compilers have deliberately not said anything about them. Those who are not of Indian heritage would do well to avoid all of these burial sites unless accompanied by some who are of that heritage.

There are numerous references to "Unknown". Sometimes these are "Unknown" to the compilers and sometimes they refer to the real "Unknowns" who are unlikely to be identified. Who will ever identify the man struck and killed by a train in 1902 near Kent in Sherman County?

In the listing of cemeteries nothing has been more vexing than how to list the "Pioneer" Cemeteries. The term Pioneer evolved from its military origin in European armies. Pioneers built bridges, trenches and fortifications there. But in America the term, especially in the west, was applied to Americans who arrived by wagon trains or on horseback. Cemeteries using the word Pioneer sometimes were in or near a town (Eugene, Lebanon, Vale) and sometimes named for a person or family (Henderson, Herbert, Trask), sometimes even a religion (Pioneer Catholic) or even a single person (Pioneer Woman). Persons searching through obituaries can find references to an ancestor being buried in the "Pioneer Cemetery." Unless the newspaper is identified and dated the researcher could well be lost. The compiler has been to Brooks Pioneer Cemetery near Salem and to Jordan Pioneer Cemetery in Linn County. Both were signed simply as "Pioneer Cemetery."

Finally, we would encourage visits to the public cemeteries. There on display are the final statements on leaving life in all their varying temperaments. "Pappy" depicted as panning Gold; "Pardon me for not standing" (Waverly Memorial); The man on a bucking bronco: "ain't no horse can't be rode. Ain't no man can't be throwed" (Hilltop); Vince Shamburg: "Went to Heaven in Eighty Seven" (Hubbard); for a 23-year old man whose death leaves the family bitter,"why hopes are crushed and castles fall. Up there sometime we'll understand." (Hopewell Mennonite). The visitor can note the change of fashion for naming babies. Who currently names a girl Sarepta or Minerva? Nowadays it would be Brittany which would baffle a person from the 19th Century. Why name a girl for a French Province? Brittany will be out of fashion a century hence and there will be different names, unheard of now, in use.

Dads named boys for Presidents, especially for George Washington and including such as Warren Gamaliel [Harding]. Even the candidates who did not make it to the White House have had their names bestowed by politically-conscious new fathers. William Jennings Bryan seems to be the favorite in that category. Also Revolutionary war hero Lafayette. How about Marquis De Lafayette Remington (Miller Cemetery)?

The cemetery visitor can always be surprised by the style of the monuments or the depictions on the monuments, (why do we occasionally see the winged horse Pegasus on graves of deceased adolescent girls?) We can even occasionally educate the young. A cemetery custodian once heard a little girl visiting with her father: "Look, Daddy," she pointed to a military marker, "He was in World War Eleven." The child was then introduced to the mysteries of Roman numerals.

We hope the photos in this book will encourage you to visit some of these burial sites which one of the compilers likes to refer to as "history parks". They are truly resources of art, cultural trends, indications of world tragedies, epidemics, disasters, extravagances, customs and more. You will find Clergy, poets, politicians, firemen and ladies of the night in residence next to each other. Also, there will be monuments that do not always portray the status or notoriety of the individual they memorialize. Virgil Earp, the gunslinger has a simple marker while a lady of the night has a beautiful six foot or taller cross. They are gardens and sanctuaries of peace and quiet for humans and wildlife. They are often the only places left for the birds, squirrels and other creatures. They are sacred treasures to visit. We hope you enjoy your visits.

How To Use This Book

This book includes as many cemeteries in the state of Oregon as are known to the compilers at this time. There are also many known scattered single and multiple burials which cannot be classified as an organized cemetery. Hence the title of this work: *Oregon Burial Site Guide.*

Be aware that there are many of these scattered burial sites not listed in this book due to lack of information. Genealogists and local historians also should be aware that there are numerous cemeteries just over the boundaries of Oregon in the adjacent states of Washington, Idaho, Nevada and California which can affect their research.

The 36 counties are arranged in alphabetical order. Within each county the articles are in alphabetical order. The also known as names (AKA) within each site are listed in alphabetical order of each in the burial sites.

In the indices of cemetery names, each name is followed by the county name and the cemetery's location as expressed by Township, Range and Section (T,R,S). This is the standard way to locate the cemetery on a map.

An example is the Masonic Cemetery in the town of Sheridan in Yamhill county. Since it is one of the many cemeteries in Oregon established by the Masonic Order, the reader should turn to the Yamhill County chapter in the book, find the Yamhill County index; noting that there is a Masonic Cemetery for the Yamhill County towns of Lafayette and McMinnville and then, at last, Masonic (Sheridan). Now the reader can turn the pages of the Yamhill County chapter to the proper alphabetical location of the Masonic (Sheridan) Cemetery.

The endless additions of new sites to the cemetery names have made it impossible to make an index by page number. If the reader knows only the name of a cemetery or burial site but has no idea of the location, turn to the State-wide Index. The reader may be suprised (as were the compilers) about how many cemeteries use identical names.

The article on the Sheridan Masonic Cemetery informs the reader of the approximate number of burials, the acreage, the condition of the grounds, the date of establishment and the T,R,S. Then follows a description of how to drive to the cemetery. The statement that it is within the Absalom Faulconer DLC #43, OC #2564 (explained below). Next comes a date within parentheses, for example, {29 September 1989}, the date when a compiler personally visited the cemetery.

Maps: Each cemetery or burial site is located by T,R,S if known and therefore can be identified or placed on a map. No map that is familiar to the compilers are satisfactory in all respects. The compilers have selected USGS Quadrangle maps (United States Department of the Interior Geological Survey 7.5 Minute Topographic) as the series used to locate Oregon's cemeteries and burial sites. They are drawn to show Township, Range and Sections as well as showing any access roads and streets.

Section numbers run from 1 to 36 in each Township but the USGS Quads. show precedence to another mapping system in some areas. These are the Donation Land Claims (DLC). There were more than 7000 DLCs established between 1850 and 1855. They are mostly located in the Willamette Valley in western Oregon with only a very few in eastern Oregon. These were considered as prime agricultural lands by the first American settlers. Since there are 36 Sections to a Township, the DLC numbers start with 37 and run upwards. Sheridan Masonic Cemetery is shown to be in Absalom Faulconer's DLC #43. The USGS Quad. map of Sheridan (1970) shows the cemetery in a tract numbered #43. The compilers added the Federal file number of Absalom Faulconer's DLC #43 which is OC #2564, meaning it was filed in Oregon City and is #2564 of the 7000-odd Donation Land Claims. These niceties are necessary in tracking real estate ownership and to some extent are necessary for some genealogical or historical research.

Besides using the Sheridan USGS Quad. map to locate the Sheridan Masonic Cemetery, it would be more convenient for the visitor who is unfamiliar with the town of Sheridan to use a smaller map of the area. The Oregon Department of Transportation (ODOT) has maps of all incorporated towns. These are particularly useful for towns such as Sheridan which are too small for maps by commercial publishers. Cemeteries in or near Portland are shown on commercially produced maps available in bookstores. ODOT also puts out maps of the 36 counties which show the road names as well as many of the cemeteries.

Oregon Department of Transportation Geographic Information Services Unit
555 13th Street Northeast, Suite 2
Salem, Oregon 97301-4178
Web site: <http://www.odot.state.or.us>

The compilers have tried to use the most up-to-date road and street names in the directions to all burial sites, but the reader should be aware that county commissioners and city leaders can and do change such names.

The listing indicates that Sheridan Masonic Cemetery is indeed shown on the Sheridan USGS Quad. map. But the reader soon finds that many cemeteries are not shown. All maps consulted by the compilers omit some cemeteries, locate some of them wrongly, misspell the name, or use an obsolete name.

No mapping agency has solved one especially vexing cemetery problem. Bandon Pioneer Cemetery is a prime example. Bandon is a small town in Coos County at the mouth of the Coquille River. The Pioneer Cemetery actually consists of three distinct entities. The Old I.O.O.F., the Grand Army of the Republic (GAR) and the Bandon Catholic (Holy Trinity) are all here. When visiting it is possible to see the three different burial grounds, but it is not possible for the Bandon USGS Quad. map to show all three. This situation of two or more cemeteries abutting each other shows up in a considerable number of places.

Number of Burials: A = 0-25; B = 25-100; C = 100-500; D = 500-2,000; and E = over 2,000 is used. Where records have been lost or destroyed, estimates are the best we can do.

Acreage: Again, in many instances this is an estimate taken by scaling from maps which sometimes are exaggerated. Some cemeteries have purchased acreage that is not yet utilized and thus the burial area is clearly smaller in size than the dedicated area.

Condition of the cemetery: If the lawn is manicured and there is a sprinkler system the cemetery is clearly condition 1 and if it is in a jungle that is obviously condition 5. But conditions 2 to 4 leads to many gradations. Some cemeteries are condition 2 where the burials are located and condition 4 over where nobody is yet buried. If a cemetery only gets maintenance once or twice a year it will probably look its best around Memorial Day weekend in late May.

The compilers have seen a surprising number of cemeteries where new interments are no longer being made, but there are still real or artificial flowers visable. So it was worthwhile to create a condition 13 for such. Incidentally two of these condition 13 cemeteries each had a headstone for a dog, Curly and Aaron. Early on the compilers decided to omit listing pet cemeteries. So far as the compilers know there are pet cemeteries at Portland, Medford and Salem. There are reports of a pet cemetery out of Sweet Home on the road to Quartzville also.

Date of establishment: This is not easy to establish in many cases. Many public cemeteries began as private family burial grounds. The date of establishment often refers to filing a legal document at the county courthouse quite some time after the first burial. In addition, private family burial grounds or individual burials are sometimes transferred at a later date to larger nearby public cemeteries. This also means there are older burials in any given public cemetery which do not reflect the date of establishment.

<u>Who is the caretaker of a particular cemetery?</u> This proved to be an insuperable problem on a state-wide basis. Many burial sites have no one in charge; others are on an ad hoc basis year to year. Caretakers tend to change too often. Reluctantly the compilers gave up providing such a list.

Finally we hope this book can be carried into the field and used for noting observations. The compilers and all those who helped them have not by any means visited all the cemeteries and burial sites. Some we have visited earlier may have obsolete information now. This is an ongoing project and we are seeking information on all sites, we have listed and especially those which have not been noted do to lack of information. Please copy and use the form provided for submiting information for future updates.

NOTES

Oregon State Revised Statutes

We are including a section of the 1999 Oregon Revised Statutes. For the most current version go to the World Wide Web at: http://www.leg.state.or.us/ors/home.html

Indian Graves and Protected Objects

97.740 Definitions for ORS 97.740 to 97.760. For the purposes of ORS 97.740 to 97.760:

(1) "Burial" has the meaning given that term in ORS 358.905.

(2) "Funerary object" has the meaning given that term in ORS 58.905.

(3) "Human remains" has the meaning given that term in ORS 358.905.

(4) "Indian tribe" means any tribe of Indians recognized by the Secretary of the Interior or listed in the Klamath Termination Act, 25 U.S.C. 3564 et seq., or listed in the Western Oregon Indian Termination Act, 25 U.S.C. 3691 et seq., if the traditional cultural area of the tribe includes Oregon lands.

(5) "Object of cultural patrimony" has the meaning given that term in ORS 358.905.

(6) "Professional archaeologist" means a person who has extensive formal training and experience in systematic, scientific archaeology.

(7) "Sacred object" has the meaning given that term in ORS 358.905. [1977 c.647 s.1; 1981 c.442 s.3; 1985 c.198 s.2; 1993 c.459 s.9; 1997 c.249 s.34]

97.745 Prohibited acts; application; notice. (1) Except as provided in ORS 97.750, no person shall willfully remove, mutilate, deface, injure or destroy any cairn, burial, human remains, funerary object, sacred object or object of cultural patrimony of any native Indian. Persons disturbing native Indian cairns or burials through inadvertence, including by construction, mining, logging or agricultural activity, shall at their own expense reinter the human remains or funerary object under the supervision of the appropriate Indian tribe.

(2) Except as authorized by the appropriate Indian tribe, no person shall:

(a) Possess any native Indian artifacts, human remains or funerary object having been taken from a native Indian cairn or burial in a manner other than that authorized under ORS 97.750.

(b) Publicly display or exhibit any native Indian human remains, funerary object, sacred object or object of cultural patrimony.

(c) Sell any native Indian artifacts, human remains or funerary object having been taken from a native Indian cairn or burial or sell any sacred object or object of cultural patrimony.

(3) This section does not apply to:

(a) The possession or sale of native Indian artifacts discovered in or taken from locations other than native Indian cairns or burials; or

(b) Actions taken in the performance of official law enforcement duties.

(4) Any discovered human remains suspected to be native Indian shall be reported to the state police, the State Historic Preservation Officer, the appropriate Indian tribe and the Commission on Indian Services. [1977 c.647 s.2; 1979 c.420 s.1; 1981 c.442 s.4; 1985 c.198 s.1; 1993 c.459 s.10]

97.750 Permitted acts; notice. (1) Any proposed excavation by a professional archaeologist of a native Indian cairn or burial shall be initiated only after prior written notification to the State Historic Preservation Officer and the state police, as defined in ORS 358.905, and with the prior written consent of the appropriate Indian tribe in the vicinity of the intended action. Failure of a tribe to respond to a request for permission within 30 days of its mailing shall be deemed consent. All associated material objects, funerary objects and human remains removed during such an excavation shall be reinterred at the archaeologist's expense under the supervision of the Indian tribe.

(2) In order to determine the appropriate Indian tribe under this section and ORS 97.745, a professional archaeologist or other person shall consult with the Commission on Indian Services which shall designate the appropriate tribe. [1977 c.647 s.3; 1979 c.420 s.2; 1981 c.442 s.5; 1993 c.459 s.11]

97.760 Civil action by Indian tribe or member; time for commencing action; venue; damages; attorney fees.
(1) Apart from any criminal prosecution, an Indian tribe or enrolled member thereof shall have a civil action to secure an injunction, damages or other appropriate relief against any person who is alleged to have violated ORS 97.745. The action must be brought within two years of the discovery of the violation by the plaintiff. The action may be filed in the circuit court of the county in which the subject grave, cairn, remains or artifacts are located, or within which the defendant resides.
(2) Any conviction pursuant to ORS 97.990 (5) shall be prima facie evidence of a violation of ORS 97.745 in an action brought under this section.
(3) If the plaintiff prevails:
(a) The court may grant injunctive or such other equitable relief as is appropriate, including forfeiture of any artifacts or remains acquired or equipment used in the violation. The court shall order the disposition of any items forfeited as it sees fit, including the reinterment of any human remains in accordance with ORS 97.745 (1);
(b) The plaintiff shall recover imputed damages in an amount not to exceed $10,000 or actual damages, whichever is greater. Actual damages include special and general damages, which include damages for emotional distress;
(c) The plaintiff may recover punitive damages upon proof that the violation was willful. Punitive damages may be recovered without proof of actual damages. All punitive damages shall be paid by the defendant to the Commission on Indian Services for the purposes of Indian historic preservation; and
(d) An award of imputed or punitive damages may be made only once for a particular violation by a particular person, but shall not preclude the award of such damages based on violations by other persons or on other violations.
(4) The court may award reasonable attorney fees to the prevailing party in an action under this section. [1981 c.442 s.2; 1995 c.543 s.1; 1995 c.618 s.55]

Additional applicable Statutes

166.076 Abuse of a memorial to the dead. (1) A person commits the crime of abuse of a memorial to the dead if the person intentionally:
(a) Destroys, mutilates, defaces, injures or removes any:
(A) Tomb, monument, gravestone or other structure or thing placed as or designed for a memorial to the dead; or
(B) Fence, railing, curb or other thing intended for the protection or for the ornamentation of any structure or thing listed in subparagraph (A) of this paragraph; or
(b) Destroys, mutilates, removes, cuts, breaks or injures any tree, shrub or plant within any structure listed in paragraph (a) of this subsection.
(2) Abuse of a memorial to the dead is a Class A misdemeanor.
(3) This section does not apply to a person who is the burial right owner or that person's representative, an heir at law of the deceased, or a person having care, custody or control of a cemetery by virtue of law, contract or other legal right, if the person is acting within the scope of the person's legal capacity and the person's actions have the effect of maintaining, protecting or improving the tomb, monument, gravestone or other structure or thing placed as or designed for a memorial to the dead. [1995 c.261 s.1; 1999 c.731 s.12]

See Oregon revised statutes for more detailes on the following.

166.085 and 166.087 Abuse of corpse.

97.310, 97.320, 97,330, 97.340, and 97.360 Platting and dedication of cemeteries.

97.440, 97.445, 97.450 Removal of dedication of cemeteries.

97.770 through 97.779 Pioneer Cemetery Commission.

List Of Abbreviations Used In This Book

AKA = Also known as.

D.A.R. = Daughters of the American Revolution.

DLC = Donation Land Claims. From the time of the Donation Land Claim Laws 1850-1855. They are generally the lands most attractive for farming by the first American settlers. Many cemeteries and burial sites are keyed to DLC's.

G.A.R. = Grand Army of the Republic.

I.O.O.F. = Independent Order of Odd Fellows.

K.P. = Knights of Pythias.

ODOT = Oregon Department of Transportation. Their maps of the 36 counties, the incorporated towns of Oregon and road names maps of the 36 counties are also useful in locating cemeteries. ODOT mileage records for county roads are spotty because some county roadmasters do record mileposts for entrances to cemeteries and other roadmasters ignore cemeteries. Some counties (Clatsop, Lane, Lincoln, Multnomah, Tillamook and Washington) cannot or will not give mileage on any one road.

OR. Hwy. = Oregon Route shields that the traveling public sees for example, Oregon Highway 99.

T, R, S = Township Range and Section. Used for land surveys and the location of properties, including cemeteries. Townships usually consist of 36 square miles and with each of the 36 Sections is one square mile. Some mountainous parts of Oregon are still unsurveyed.

USGS = United States Geological Survey. Uncle Sam's mapping agency. The quadrangle maps are very useful for locating cemeteries and burial sites.

U.S. Hwy. = Federal Route shield that the travelling public sees for example, U.S. Highway 26.

V.F.W. = Veterans of Foreign Wars.

This listing is showing what the codes in the top highlighted bar of each burial site listing means.

Name of Cemetery

Number of Burials

(A) 0-25
(B) 25-100
(C) 100-500
(D) 500-2000
(E) Over 2000

Size of Cemetery In Acres

Conditions of Cemeteries

1 = Fully tended.
2 = Moderately tended.
3 = Overgrown.
4 = Densely overgrown.
5 = Abandoned to nature.
6 = Moved.
7 = Moved & site now built over.
8 = Moved & site now underwater.
9 = Underwater. We don't know if burials were moved.
10 = Now used for a park. Some burials remain.
11 = Site not moved, but now built over.
12 = Farmed over.
13 = No longer used, but still has maintenance.

Date Established or Earliest Known Burial.

Location by Township, Range, Section

Glossary

Black Glass: Engraved black glass about eight inches by ten inches set in concrete. Manufactured by Memorial Arts in Portland, Oregon in the 1940's.

Burial: 1. the act or ceremony of burying. 2. the place of burying; grave.

Burial ground: a tract of land for burial of the dead; a cemetery, often a small or primitive one.

Casket: a coffin.

Cemetery: an area set apart for or containing graves, tombs, or funeral urns, esp. one that is not a churchyard; burial ground; graveyard.

Cenotaph: a sepulchral monument erected in memory of a deceased person whose body is buried elsewhere.

Churchyard: The yard or ground adjoining a church, often used as a graveyard.

Coffin: the box or case in which the body of a dead person is placed for burial; casket.

Colonial Tablet: Similar to Monolith but with a curved top.

Columbarium: a sepulchral vault or other structure with recesses in the walls to receive the ashes of the dead.

Cremains: the ashes of a cremated corpse.

Cremate: to reduce (a dead body) to ashes by fire, esp. as a funeral rite.

Crypt: a Subterranean chamber or vault, esp. one beneath the main floor of a church, used as a burial place.

Epitaph: a commemorative inscription on a tomb or mortuary monument about the person buried at the site.

Footstone: a stone placed at the foot of a grave.

Funeral: the ceremonies for a dead person prior to burial or cremation.

Grave Box or Liner: A concrete or other impervious container placed in the grave first. Then the casket or urn are placed in it for burial.

Grave Marker: a marker used to mark the grave.

Graveyard: a burial ground, often associated with smaller rural churches, as distinct from a larger urban or public cemetery.

Headstone: a stone marker set at the head of a grave; gravestone.

Interment: the act or ceremony of interring; burial.

Inurn: 1. To put into an urn, esp. ashes after cremation. 2. to bury; inter.

Ledger Stone: A marker that covers most or all of the grave. Usually contains a great deal of information.

Mausoleum: 1. a stately and magnificent tomb. 2. a burial place for the bodies or remains of many individuals, often of a single family, usually in the form of a small building.

Monolith: Vertical marker of various designs.

Monument: something erected in memory of a person.

Pillow: A one foot by two foot raised flat marker.

Plot: a small piece or area of ground; *burial plot.*

Roll: A round granite marker like a turned piece of wood set in a concrete cradle.

Sarcophagus: a stone coffin, esp. one bearing sculpture, inscriptions, etc., often displayed as a monument.

Sepulchral: 1. of, pertaining to, or serving as a tomb. 2. of or pertaining to burial. 3. proper to or suggestive of a tomb; funeral or dismal.

Sexton: an official of a church charged with taking care of the edifice and its contents, ringing the bell, etc., and sometimes burying the dead.

Site: 1. the position or location of a town, building, etc., esp. as to its environment. 2. the area or exact plot of ground on which anything is, has been, or is to be located.

Tomb: 1. an excavation in earth or rock for the burial of a corpse; grave. 2. a mausoleum, burial chamber, or the like. 3. a monument for housing or commemorating a dead person. 4. any sepulchral structure.

Tombstone: a stone marker, usually inscribed, on a tomb or grave.

Urn: a vase for holding the ashes of the cremated dead.

Vault: a burial chamber.

White Bronze: A cast metal monument made to resemble monoliths. Made of mostly Zinc.

Symbolism of Tombstone Art

Anchor: Hope for resurrection and eternal life.

Anchor and ships: Hope or seafaring profession.

Angel carrying soul: Heavenly guide.

Angel with trumpet: Resurrection.

Angels: God's messengers.

Arches: Victory in death.

Archways, pillars, and gates: Passageway into the next life.

Arrow with heart: The conjunction of heaven and earth to produce supreme peace and eternal rest.

Arrows: Mortality.

Asphodel: Means the deceased is in fact dead. Is meant to remind viewers of their own mortality. It is a genus of the lily family but also includes the narcissus and daffodil.

Bat: The evil of the temporal world. Often used in conjunction with the eagle, illustrating the escape of the soul from earthly wickedness.

Bible-open: If deceased was a minister, open Bible often identifies text of last sermon. Also represents the "book of life".

Bible-closed: Indicates the end of earthly life.

Birds: From earliest times a symbol of the soul.

Bouquets of flowers: Condolences, grief, sorrow.

Broken column: Loss of head of family.

Broken ring: Family circle is broken.

Broken rosebud: Death of a young person.

Broken tree stump or pillar: Life cut short.

Buds and Rosebuds: Morning of life or renewal of life.

Bugles: Resurrection and the military profession.

Butterfly: Short-lived; early death; resurrection.

Candle being snuffed: Time, mortality.

Chain: Often in the form of a circle with one link broken. Indicates the continuity of the family has been broken.

Chain links, three: International Order of Oddfellows (I.O.O.F.)

Chalices: Wine, the divine fluid of communion.

Cherub: Angelic.

Cherub - winged: Innocence, spirituality. Often used for young persons.

Cherubim: Regarded as guardians of a sacred place and as servants of God. Symbolize divine wisdom or justice.

Clasped hands: Until we meet again. Represents both a farewell to those left behind and the meeting of the soul with God.

Clover: Represents the Trinity.

Coffin: Mortality, reminder of our ultimate death.

Cocks: Symbolize man's fall from grace and his resurrection.

Columns: Similar to a ladder or path. Because of vertical nature, implies ascension.

Completed pillar or column: A complete and full life.

Corn: Ripe old age.

Cornucopia: A symbol of the joys awaiting in heaven.

Cross: Emblem of faith. A symbol of agony, struggle, existence.

Cross and Crown: Kingship of Christ.

Crossed Swords: High-ranking military person.

Crown: Symbol of pre-eminence and spiritual enlightenment.

Crowns: Glory and righteousness.

Cypress: A reminder of mortality. A symbol of death.

Darts: Mortality.

Dove: Used alone, a symbol to the constancy of the deceased. A symbol of gentleness, affection, purity, the soul, innocence and peace. In conjunction with Christian symbolism, generally represents the Holy Ghost.

Doves: The soul, purity, children, Holy Spirit.

Dragon: Satan.

Drape: Symbolizes the closing off of earthly life.

Draperies: Grief.

Eagle: A high-flying bird to symbolize the ascension of the soul. A messenger from heaven. Dante called the eagle "the bird of God."

Father time: Mortality, the grim reaper, nearness of death.

Festoon: May be garland of leaves, fruits, flowers, or ribbon draped between two points.

Fig: The deceased was happy and/or prosperous or those left behind like to think the deceased in now prosperous and happy in heaven. In the Bible the fig is a symbol of the Oneness of the universe. Was one of the earliest fruit trees cultivated by primitive man.

Figure clutching cross: A symbol of hope of redemption.

Fish: Savior.

Flame Rising from urn: The soul rising from its mortal ashes.

Flowers: Sorrow, brevity of life. Symbol of rewards of heaven which the deceased now enjoys. Symbol of impermanence.

Flying birds: Flight of the soul. Fruits, gourds, vines; Immortality.

Fruits: Eternal plenty.

Full-blown rose: Prime of life.

G.A.R. star: Grand Army of the Republic.

Garlands: Victory in death.

Gates of heaven: Eternal life. Usually both of the gates are open. Represents Christian salvation.

Globe or sphere: Represents soul waiting for resurrection.

Gold star mother: One who lost a child during World War I.

Gourds: Deliverance from grief.

Grapes: Wine, the divine fluid of communion.

Grapevine: The symbol of Jesus and his protection. Also used as a symbol of the rewards of heaven.

Half carved, half unfinished marker: Transition from life to death.

Hand forefinger pointing up: Soul has gone to heaven.

Hand forefinger pointing down: God reaching down for the soul.

Hand of God: Pointing the way.

Hand of God Chopping: Sudden death.

Hands - clasped: Represents a farewell to those left behind or the meeting of the soul with God.

Handshake: God's welcome to heaven or handshake of matrimony.

Handshakes: Farewell to earthly existence.

Harp: Praise to the maker. A bridge between heaven and earth.

Heart: Life, children, soul in bliss, romantic love, center or soul of man.

Hearts: Soul in bliss or love of Christ.

Horn: Generally a trumpet. A symbol of a spiritual call.

Horns: The resurrection.

Hourglass: Passing of time or swiftness of time. The impermanence of life.

Hourglass with wings of time: Time flying; short life.

Imps: Mortality.

Ivy: Friendship and immortality.

Lamb: Innocence. Often used on graves of children. Also represents the resurrection to become the "Lamb of God."

Lambs: Purity, gentleness, innocence, Christ.

Laurel: Fame or victory.

Laurel wreath: A spiritual victory over the negative and dissipative influence of base forces.

Lily: Purity, the flower of the Virgin.

Lily of the valley: Emblem of innocence and purity.

Lion: Christ called "Lion of the tribe of Judah."

Mermaid: Half fish, half woman, a symbol of the dualism of Christ, who is half God, half man.

Morning glory: Beginning of life.

Oak leaf: A symbol of Faith.

Oak leaves and acorn: Maturity, ripe old age.

Open Bible or book: Resurrection through Scripture. Deceased teacher, minister, etc.

Palm: A symbol of the soul's victory over death.

Palm branch: Signifies victory and rejoicing.

Palm leaves and lilies: Resurrection.

Peacocks: Eternal life, immortality.

Phoenix: Resurrection.

Picks and shovels: Mortality.

Pickax: Reminder of our ultimate end.

Poppy: Sleep.

Portals: Passageway to eternal journey, a symbol of the House of the Dead, death as a passageway to the unknown, a shrine or temple, a portal through which the soul passes into immortality.

Rope: A representation of Ascension and eternity. Steps, a ladder, or a path have same meaning.

Rose: Motherhood and beauty. A reminder that the soul achieves its most perfect state after physical death. Probably the most often used flower as a symbol of life, death, love and religion. A symbol of the blood of Christ.

Roses: Brevity of earthly existence or brevity of human existence.

Rosettes: Life.

Scales: Equality and justice.

Serpent: Satan.

Shaft - broken: Represents the "shaft of Life"; If broken near top the person was young at time of death.

Shafts: Similar to a ladder or path. Because of vertical nature, implies ascension.

Sheaf of wheat: Ripe for harvest, divine harvest time. The deceased was an elderly person.

Sheaves of wheat: Time, the divine harvest.

Shell or shells: Pilgrimage of life, rebirth, birth and resurrection.

Ship: Faithful carried over "Sea of Life." The seafaring profession.

Shovels: Mortality.

Skeleton: Death.

Skull and Crossbones: Mortal remains of the deceased.

Skull raised on a pillar: Triumph of death.

Skulls: Remainder of our ultimate end.

Soul effigy: Flight of soul, the immortal soul.

Sphere: Represents soul waiting for resurrection.

Spires: Similar to a ladder or path. Because of vertical nature, implies ascension.

Stag: Soul thirsting for baptism.

Stars and stripes around an eagle: Eternal vigilance, liberty.

Sun or suns: The resurrection.

Sun - rising: The resurrection of the soul.

Sun - setting: The deceased was an elderly person.

Thistles: Remembrance.

Tombs: Mortality.

Torch inverted: Life extinct.

Tree stump with ivy: Head of family; immortality.

Trees: Life.

Trees - twin: A representation of marriage or unity. Almost always found on stones that mark the graves of two people. If one of the trees has fallen, it represents the fact that the stone was erected while one of the couple still lives.

Trefoil: Represents the Trinity.

Triangle: A symbol of the Trinity. A symbol of God -- a protection for the deceased.

Trumpeting angelic figures: Accompanying the soul heavenward and announcing the arrival of the departed's soul in heaven.

Trumpeters: Heralds of the resurrection.

Urn: Mortality, occupied grave, death of the flesh. The soul waits here for resurrection.

Urn with blaze: Undying friendship.

Urn with drape: Mourning.

Urn with flame: The soul rising from its mortal ashes.

Urn with wreath: Mourning.

Veil: Symbolizes the closing off of earthly life.

Vines: Wine, the divine fluid of communion.

Weeping Willow: Emblem of sorrow.

Willow: Earthly sorrow, mourning.

Willows: Earthly sorrow.

Winged death head: Mortal remains of the deceased.

Winged effigies: Flight of the soul.

STATE

HIGHWAY NUMBE

Prepc
OREGON DEPARTME
HIGHW
PLANN

OREGON

AND ROUTES

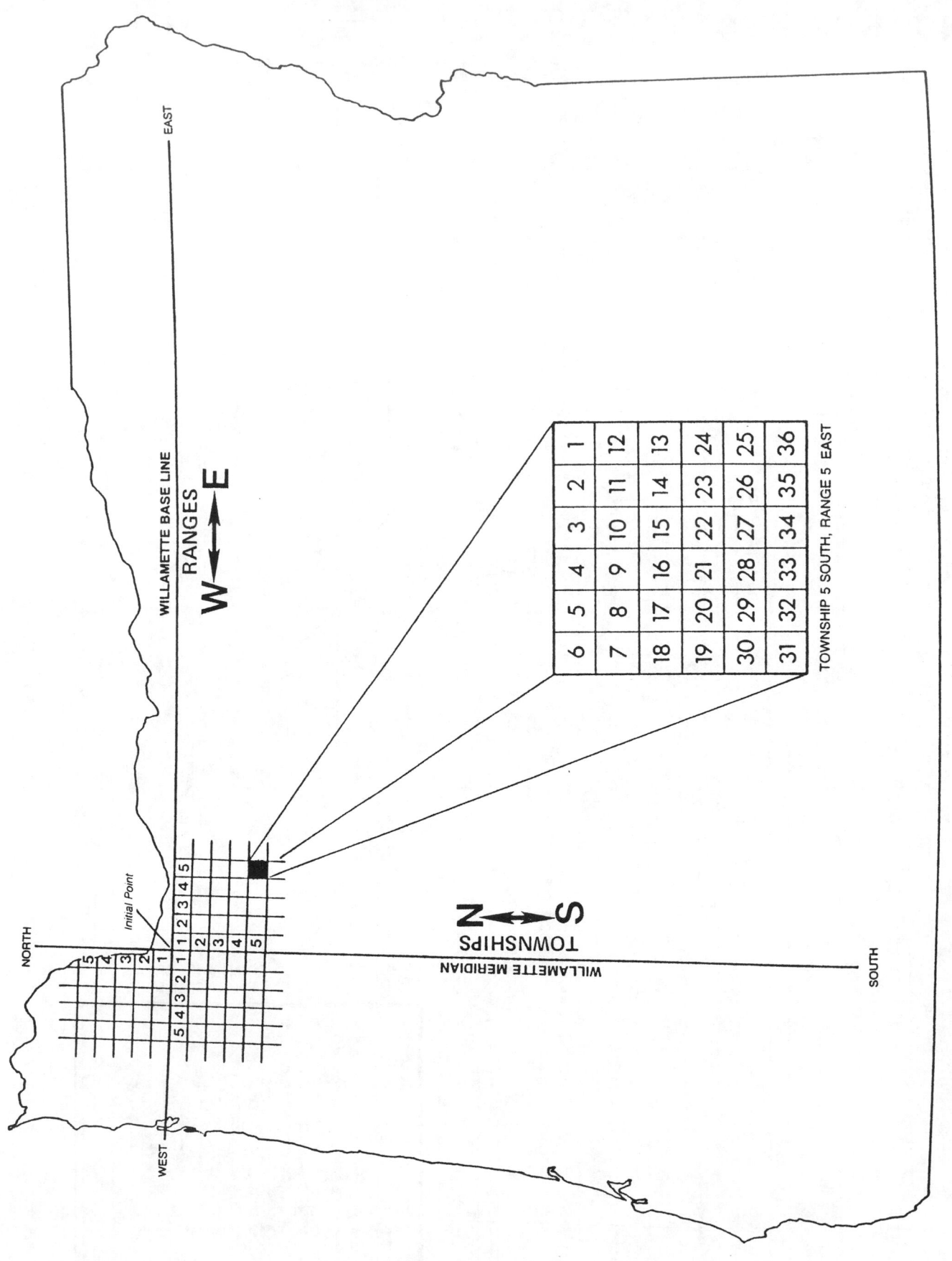

Oregon

Area: 98,386 square miles
Approximately: 360 miles wide west to east,
261 miles long north to south and 296 miles
of coastline on the Pacific Ocean side.
Population (1998): 3,281,974
State Capital: Salem, Population 120,835

After the Louisiana Purchase in 1803 from France by the United States, and as a result of the Lewis and Clark expedition through the Louisiana Territory to the Pacific Ocean to what is now Oregon (1804-1806) Americans laid claims to this region west of the Rocky Mountains. European powers had claims as well: Spain, Russia, and Great Britain.

The first boundary to be established and recognized came from the Florida Treaty of February 1819 between Spain and the United States. Spain, struggling to recover from the years of French invasions and simultaneously trying to suppress revolts in the Spanish Empire in Mexico and South America, was compelled to cede Florida to the United States. The Florida Treaty also provided that Spain abandon any claims in North America north of the 42nd parallel. At the time neither Spain nor America had any settlements near this parallel. The 42nd parallel later became the boundary between the future states of California and Nevada on the south and Oregon and Idaho on the north.

A convention between Great Britain and the United States in October 1818 established the 49th parallel as the boundary between the United States and Canada east of the crest of the Rocky Mountains. Between the Rockies and the Pacific both powers were allowed joint occupation north of 42° and south 54° 40' (Russian Alaska).

On 2 May 1843 a convention of about 100 settlers was held at Champoeg to establish a provisional government. The membership was split almost evenly between the French Canadian and American settlers. An American style government won out and governed the Oregon Country into 1846.

In June 1846 with the Oregon Treaty, Great Britain and the United States divided their respective claims by extending the 49th parallel west to the Pacific with the United States yielding its claims on Vancouver Island.

The 1846 treaty left the Oregon Territory with 286,541 square miles. Congress granted territorial status on 14 August 1848. But on 2 March 1853 the territory north of the lower Columbia River was detached to become the future state of Washington and on 3 March 1863 the territory east of the Snake River and the 117° parallel of longitude was detached from Oregon to become the future state of Idaho. With this congressional act Oregon attained is present boundaries. Congress admitted Oregon as a state on 14 February 1859 the 33rd State in the Union and the last to be admitted before the Civil War.

I.O.O.F. [Huntington]
Janice M. Healy (2000)

Mt. Hope
Janice M. Healy (2000)

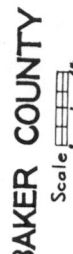

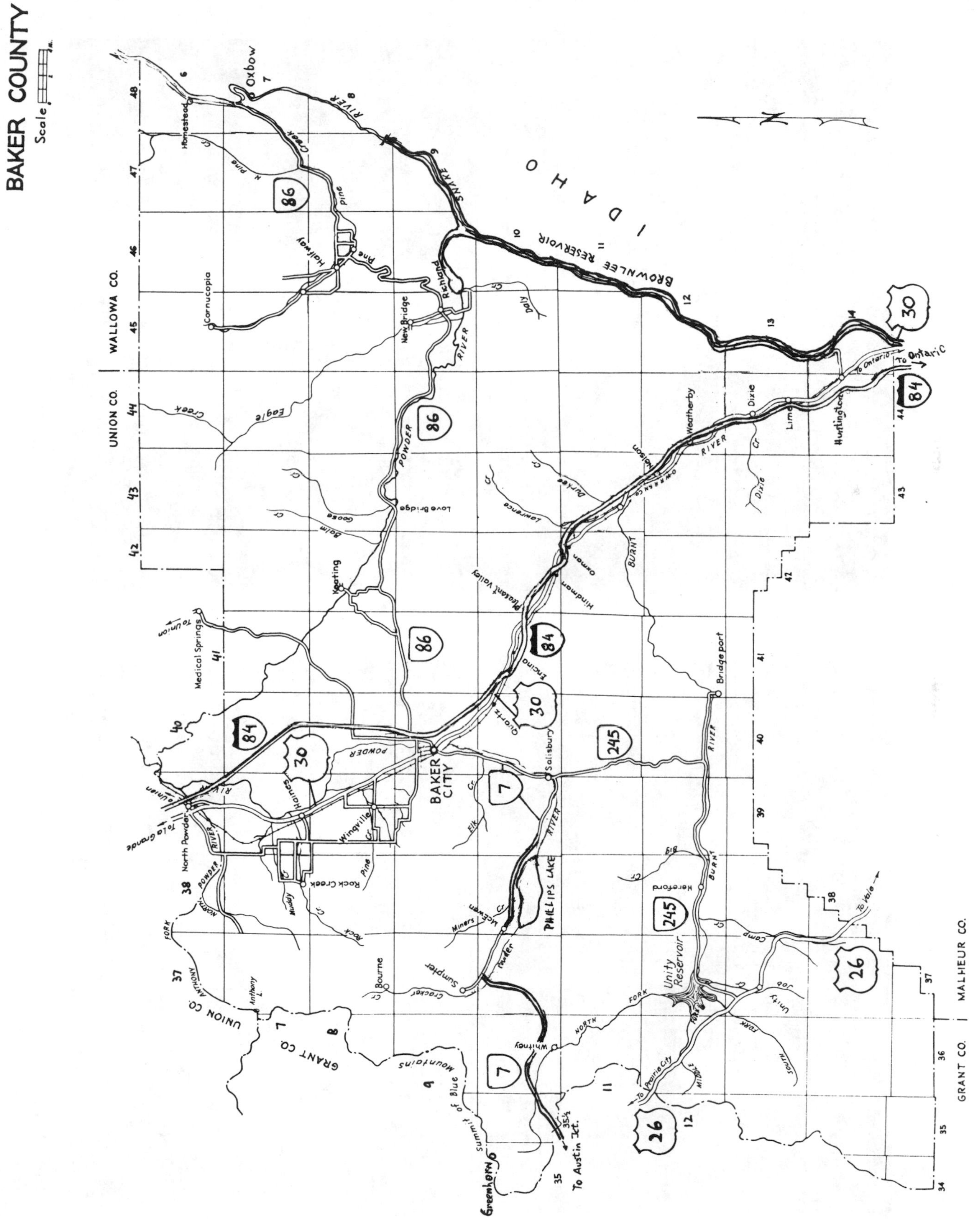
BAKER COUNTY
Scale
WALLOWA CO.
UNION CO.
UNION CO.
GRANT CO.
GRANT CO.
MALHEUR CO.
IDAHO
BROWNLEE RESERVOIR
SNAKE RIVER
Oxbow
Homestead
Halfway
Cornucopia
Richland
New Bridge
Love Bridge
Keating
Medical Springs
North Powder
Haines
Wingville
Rock Creek
BAKER CITY
Salisbury
Pleasant Valley
Durkee
Weatherby
Dixie
Lime
Huntington
To Ontario
Bridgeport
Hereford
Unity Reservoir
PHILLIPS LAKE
Sumpter
McEwen
Bourne
Whitney
Greenhorn
Summit of Blue Mountains
To Austin Jct.
To Prairie City
To Union
To La Grande
To Vale
POWDER RIVER
BURNT RIVER
86
84
30
7
245
26

I.O.O.F. [Huntington]
Janice M. Healy (2000)

Eagle Valley
Janice M. Healy (2000)

Area: 3,089 square miles
Population (1998) 16,448
County Seat: Baker City, Population: 9,870
County Established: 22 September 1862

The Oregon Trail crossed what is now Baker County. Cemeteries were not established until after gold was discovered in 1861. The cemeteries of the boom town of Auburn were apparently the first public cemeteries. There were a number of short-lived mining towns that had cemeteries. Chinese miners started cemeteries for their dead. In the 1870's livestock ranchers arrived and established most of the present day public cemeteries.

Eagle Valley
Janice M. Healy (2000)

Hibbard Creek
Janice M. Healy (2000)

Hibbard Creek
Janice M. Healy (2000)

Name of Cemetery and also known as	Number of burials	Acres	Condition	Date started or earliest known burial	Township	Range	Section

ALDER CREEK
AKA: 1. PLEASANT
VALLEY

B   0.5   ?   Circa 1892   T10S R41E   S35
Leave U.S. 30 at the south Baker City Interchange. Continue ahead on Old U.S. 30, (now a county road) for 10 miles, passing under the I-84 Freeway. Turn right on Alder Creek Road, again passing under the I-84 Freeway, for 3.2 miles. Turn right on Dry Creek Cutoff, crossing Alder Creek, and go 0.25 of a mile up to the top of the ridge, where the cemetery is. There are 26 known graves, as per *Yesterdays Roll Call*, Published by the Genealogical Forum of Portland Oregon, Inc. (1970). (Encina 1967-84 USGS Quad. map.)

ASHBY CHILD

A   ?   ?   ?   ?   R47E   ?
This could be in Township 7 South or Township 8 South, and in Section 3 or 34. A child of Bill Ashby that drowned in Pine Creek and was buried on the Ashby Homestead. The burial is just west of the confluence of Fish Creek with Pine Creek. NOTE: This site is on private property. (Not shown on McLain Gulch 1987 USGS Quad. map.)

AUBURN

B   0.5   5   1862   T10S R39E   S8
Located at the site of Auburn. Originally there were 2 Chinese cemeteries and 1 for whites. The Chinese were moved back to China. Only 5 graves in the white cemetery are visible today 1910-1960's. (Blue Canyon 1967-84 USGS Quad. map.)

AUNT POLLY

A   0.01   ?   ?   T12S R38E   ?
Possibly located in Section 29, in the Hereford area on a hill above the old Butts Place. Her name has been lost. NOTE: No other information was given with the report. (Not shown on Hereford 1972 USGS Quad. map.)

BASTIAN FAMILY

A   ?   ?   ?   T12S R45E   ?
The father and sister of Mary D. Bastian were buried at their homestead in the Hibbard Creek area. They may have later been reburied in Mt. Hope Cemetery in Baker City.

Name of Cemetery and also known as	Number of burials	Acres	Condition	Date started or earliest known burial	Township	Range	Section

NOTE: No other information was given with the report. (Not shown on Connor Creek 1987 USGS Quad. map.)

BIG CREEK
AKA: 1. BEAGLE CREEK

B	?	?	**Sep 1878**	T7S	R41E	S2

Located 0.25 of a mile off OR. Hwy. 203 and 2 or 3 miles south of Medical Springs, on a hill on the east side of the highway. The land was donated by Jim Sams. There are 54 known burials; 3 unknown burials (1970); with 14 markers, 1880-1914. Could this cemetery be in Union County? (Not shown on Keating Northwest 1967 or Medical Springs 1965-84 USGS Quad. maps.)

BIG FLAT
AKA: 1. AUDREY

?	0.6	?	**Circa 1905**	T12S	R37E	S10

Go 5 miles west of Hereford on OR. Hwy. 245, and then 3.25 miles north on Big Flat Road. This site is located on the east side, 400 feet south of the school (in the area served by the old Audrey P.O.). This is on the homestead of Dr. Ulysses Grant Strieby, who donated 2 acres for a cemetery, and donated land 400 feet north of the cemetery for a school. There are 3 adults and 4 children known to be buried here. This site was fenced in 1969. (Unity Reservoir 1972-84 USGS Quad. map.)

BOBBINGTON, THOMAS

A	0.01	?	**2 June 1894**	T6S	R45E	S34

A 79 year-old miner who died of a heart attack is buried on the bank of Pine Creek one eighth of a mile south of Cornucopia. (Not shown on Cornucopia 1990 USGS Quad. maps.)

BOOT HILL

A	?	5	**1860'S**	T8S	R44E	?

Located near Sparta. There are 3 graves on a hill south of the townsite of Sparta. The men were killed in a gunfight. This is separate from the Sparta Cemetery. (Not shown on Sparta 1988 USGS Quad. map.)

Name of Cemetery and also known as	Number of burials	Acres	Condition	Date started or earliest known burial	Township	Range	Section

BOURNE

A ? 5 ? T8S R37E ?

Possibly found in Section 32 or 33. Three graves were located in this ghost town, no markers of any kind remain. (Not shown on Bourne 1972-84 USGS Quad. map.)

BOYER FAMILY

A 0.25 5 Circa 1890 T12S R38E ?

Perhaps located in Section 28 or 29 along Hereford Loop. Thomas Boyer donated the land for this small cemetery. It was fenced in 1970 and cared for by family members. There are 5 known burials on the Fred Boyer Ranch (1969). NOTE: This site is on private property. (Not shown on Hereford 1972 USGS Quad. map.)

BRIDGEPORT

C 0.5 5 1878-1931 T12S R41E S30

Located on the north side of Burnt River, 0.4 of a mile north of Bridgeport and about 0.25 of a mile north of the bridge over Burnt River, on the left side of the road. There are 18 known burials. The bodies were moved 1877-1884 from Clarksville, as that cemetery was mined out. This cemetery is on the Dave Ennis Homestead. The land was donated by the Wendt brothers. (Bridgeport 1990 USGS Quad. map.)

BURKEMONT

? ? ? Circa 1909 T7S R42E S28

Burkemont was a gold-mining community approximately 20 miles northeast of Baker City. The platted site occupied the Southeast 1/4 of Section 28. There was a post office for Burkemont from October 1900 to August 1957. Baker County death certificate #576 for 28 August 1909 records the death of Ezra VanDeventer, aged about 45, and his burial the next day at the cemetery. (Not shown on Sawtooth Ridge 1967-1984 USGS Quad. map)

CHINESE [BAKER CITY]

? 0.2 5 ? T9S R40E S15

Go east from down town on Campbell Street under the I-84 Freeway and on the east side of the interchange the cemetery site is on the left (north) side of Campbell Street.

Name of Cemetery and also known as	Number of burials	Acres	Condition	Date started or earliest known burial	Township	Range	Section

Presumably all or most of the remains were later shipped back to China as was the custom. (Not shown on Baker City 1994 USGS Quad. map.)

CHINESE [SPARTA]   ?   ?   5   ?   **T8S R44E**   ?
Perhaps located in Section 15. There was formerly a Chinese cemetery on a hill just east of Sparta. The remains were shipped back to China. (Not shown on Sparta 1988 USGS Quad. map.)

CLARK CHILDREN   A   ?   5   ?   **T8S R46E**   ?
Perhaps located in Section 9 or 10 on the north side of OR. Hwy. 86, 1.5 miles east of Halfway. There are 2 or 3 of the Clark children buried on the Ed Greener Place (1966) in Pine Valley. The graves are now lost, or perhaps were removed to the Pine Haven Cemetery. NOTE: This site is on private property. (Not shown on Halfway 1987 USGS Quad. map.)

CLARKSVILLE   ?   0.15   ?   ?   **T12S R41E**   **S34**
Located 0.35 of a mile south of Clarksville on a hill by Towne Gulch. (Bridgeport 1990 USGS Quad. map.)

CLAWSON BABIES   A   0.01   ?   **29 May 1916**   ?   ?   ?
Baker County death certificates #82 and #83 for 1916 report the deaths of two unnamed male premature infants. They are buried "at home 12 miles south of Baker." The parents were Ellis L. Clawson and Martha Lucile Stam.

COLT, ISAAC   A   0.01   ?   **1890**   **T13S R37E**   **S5**
Isaac Colt was killed in a snow slide. He is buried on the ranch of his brother, Porter Colt, about 9 miles west of Hereford and just to the right (west) of OR. Hwy. 245. The grave is on a height surrounded by a steel fence and is plainly visible from the highway (1966). NOTE: This site is on private property. (Not shown on Unity 1972-84 USGS Quad. map.)

Name of Cemetery and also known as	Number of burials	Acres	Condition	Date started or earliest known burial	Township	Range	Section

CONNOR CREEK

? ? ? ?   T11S R45E   S34

Drive 17 miles from Huntington via Snake River Road. Turn inland on Connor Creek Road. This old burial ground contains a "good many" miners, including Chinese, at an old mining camp about 3 miles from the Snake River. NOTE: No other information was given in the report. {12 September 2000, Found this to be a one lane road with a creek to ford in several spots, we do not recommend this for the average passenger car, the road is closed by a big steel gate at 3.1 miles signed "NO PUBLIC ACCESS". We saw no sign of a cemetery in this very narrow canyon, but lots of mining activity from different time periods, with active prospecting still being carried on. Beware of the jumbo poison oak.} (Not shown on Connor Creek 1987 USGS Quad. map.)

COOPER, J. F. J.

A 0.01 2 ?   T12S R44E   S19

Leave the I-84 Freeway at the Weatherby interchange, exit #335. Head for Gales Road on the west side of the freeway. Gales Road runs westerly and then sharply northerly crossing the Burnt River twice and then the Union Pacific tracks. After crossing the tracks the road continues ahead northerly parallel to the tracks. About 0.5 of a mile from the interchange legs there is a single government marker about 200 yards to the left upslope in the brush. It is the grave of J. F. J. Cooper, Sergeant of Co. M., 2nd Colo. Cav. (no dates). Someone has planted rosebushes here and the grave is best located when the yellow roses are in bloom. (Not shown on Big Lookout Mtn. 1988 USGS Quad. map.)

COPPERFIELD-HOMESTEAD
AKA: 1. HOMESTEAD

B 0.25 5 Circa 1903 T6S R48E   S33

This cemetery is located about halfway between Copperfield and Homestead on the Snake River. Leave the tunnel and go north another 0.43 of a mile. Turn off the main road onto a side road to the left. Go 0.55 of a mile to the cemetery, which is on the bluff above the south bank of Bob Creek. There is an airport between the river road

Name of Cemetery and also known as	Number of burials	Acres	Condition	Date started or earliest known burial	Township	Range	Section

and cemetery access road. There were about 40 known burials in 1966. (Homestead 1990 USGS Quad. map.)

CORNUCOPIA	A	?	? ?		T6S	R45E	?

Possibly located in Section 35, 0.25 of a mile below Schneider's cabin (1894). One known marker. NOTE: No other information was given in the report. (Not shown on Jimtown 1987 USGS Quad. map.)

DEVIN, GRANDMA	A	0.01	?	1878/1879	T12S	R38E	?

Located in Section 28 or 29, in the vicinity of Hereford and a short distance from the Boyer Ranch. NOTE: No other information was given in the report. (Not shown on Hereford 1972 USGS Quad. map.)

DURKEE	C	2.9	4	Late 1890's	T11S	R43E	S18

Located about 2.5 miles northwest of Durkee, on old U.S. Hwy. 30, then right and back on an unnamed road 0.34 of a mile to the ridgetop. The cemetery was deeded to the community by Mr. T.B. Moore in the late 1890's. Some of the unmarked burials probably date from the 1850's. It is believed there are about 150 burials here. Most are unmarked, and there are no known records. (Durkee 1988 USGS Quad. map.)

EAGLE VALLEY AKA: 1. I.O.O.F. [RICHLAND]	C	4.5	1	1870	T9S	R45E	S26

Located 1 mile south of Richland. January 1871 is the first recorded burial. This includes the I.O.O.F. section. (Richland 1987 USGS Quad. map.)

EBENGER FAMILY	A	?	9	?	T12S	R45E	S14

A little girl was buried here. The grave was marked by a thin flat stone at each end. Located at the mouth of Connor Creek, presumably now flooded by Brownlee Reservoir. NOTE: No other information was given in the report. (Not shown on Connor Creek 1987 USGS Quad. map.)

Name of Cemetery and also known as	Number of burials	Acres	Condition	Date started or earliest known burial	Township	Range	Section

EMIGRANT GRAVES

? ? ? 1841-1849 T14S R45E S20

Located 2.25 miles north of Farewell Bend. NOTE: No other information was given in the report. (Not shown on Olds Ferry 1952-74 USGS Quad. map.)

FLEETWOOD FAMILY, ASA

A 0.25 5 1891 T12S R38E S20

Located 2 miles west of Hereford, on the south (left) side of OR. Hwy. 245. It is on the homestead of Asa Fleetwood, who donated the land for this cemetery at the time of a scarlet fever epidemic in the 1890's. There are 5 family members buried here. NOTE: Not to be confused with the Jim Fleetwood Family Cemetery. This site is on private property. (Beaverdam Creek 1972-84 USGS Quad. map.)

FLEETWOOD FAMILY, JIM

A ? ? ? T12S R38E S25

Two infants are buried on the old Jim Fleetwood Ranch along the Burnt River approximately 3 miles east of Hereford on OR. Hwy. 245. The graves are about 400 feet north of the highway on a narrow ridge and about 800 feet northeast of the bridge over Big Creek. [A baby of Jim Fleetwood's, and a baby of Fleetwood's daughter Alice Tetreau.] The graves are marked by a layer of rocks. NOTE: Not to be confused with the Asa Fleetwood Family Cemetery. This site is on private property. (Not shown on Devils Heel 1990 USGS Quad. map.)

GOLD RIDGE MINE
AKA: 1. CORD, OTTO

A ? 5 ? T12S R43E S16

A few miles up Shirttail Creek and French Creek is the Gold Ridge Mine. There are 2 infants and a child named Otto Cord buried here, apparently during the late 19th century. NOTE: No other information was given in the report. (Not shown on Durkee 1988 USGS Quad. map.)

GOOSE CREEK
AKA: 1. KEATING

? 0.2 2 Circa 1874 T8S R43E S29

Go to Milepost 20.8 on OR. Hwy. 86, then north 1.9 miles on Middle Bridge Road, then go northeast 0.5 of a mile on Duby Road over Goose Creek Bridge to a ranch. The cemetery

Name of Cemetery and also known as	Number of burials	Acres	Condition	Date started or earliest known burial	Township	Range	Section

is 300 yards from the house. There are 3 known burials here. NOTE: This site is on private property. (Glasgow Butte 1988 USGS Quad. map.)

GORDON, FRANK

| | A | 0.01 | 5 | ? | T10S | R36E | ? |

Frank Gordon died at his mine above Whitney and is buried there. The headboard on his grave was indecipherable in 1966. NOTE: No other information was given in the report. (Not shown on Whitney 1972-84 USGS Quad. map.)

GREENHORN

| | ? | ? | 5 | ? | T10S | R35E | S9 |

Located in the southeast part of the near-ghost town of Greenhorn. Leave OR. Hwy. 7 southwest of Sumpter and turn northwesterly onto Greenhorn Road, go about 10 miles to the one-time mining town of Greenhorn. In the mid-1960's the cemetery had no markers and only traces of 3 graves. (Greenhorn 1972-84 USGS Quad. map.)

HAINES
  AKA: 1. ELKS
        2. MAXWELL

| | C | 7 | 1 | 1899 | T7S | R39E | S21 |

Located about 1.5 miles north on U.S. Hwy. 30, out of Haines. (Haines 1967 USGS Quad. map.)

HAMLIN, NATHANIEL

| | A | 0.01 | 2 | Circa 1905 | T7S | R39E | S27 |

The burial site is located about 1.5 miles northeast of Haines, and it is on the west side of Haines Dump Road, a few hundred feet north of Conroes Pig Ranch: one grave, fenced, with a stone marker. Nathaniel Hamlin was a Union Pacific worker who wished to be buried at the summit of Coyote Point, however the road was too icy at the time of the burial. (Not shown on Haines 1967 USGS Quad. map.)

HARDMAN GIRLS

| | A | 0.01 | ? | 9 Apr 1894 | T11S | R37E | S31 |

Located about 8 miles southeast of Whitney, near the locale of Audrey on the North Fork of the Burnt River. This is a private fenced cemetery, about 3 miles northwest of Big Flat

Name of Cemetery and also known as	Number of burials	Acres	Condition	Date started or earliest known burial	Township	Range	Section

Cemetery on the original Franklin Lincoln Hardman Homestead (property was bought in 1892 for a homestead). Buried are 2 girls: Grace, age 6, died: 9 April 1894, daughter of Frank Hardman, and an infant daughter (died circa 1900) of Joseph Bart Hardman, a brother of Frank Hardman's. NOTE: This site is on private property. See *An illustrated History of Baker, Grant, Malheur and Harney Counties State of Oregon*, by Western Historical Publishing Company 1902, pages 334 and 335. (Not shown on Unity Reservoir 1984 USGS Quad. map.)

HASKINS YARD

? ? ? ?   T13S R37E   ?
Possibly located in Section 18. There is a Haskins Gulch about 2 miles west of Unity, perhaps this cemetery is in this vicinity. NOTE: No other information other than the name and county was given with the report. (Not shown on Unity 1972-84 USGS Quad. map.)

HEATH, TOM

A   0.01   4   1877   T8S R47E   ?
Possibly located in Section 25 or 36, near Brownlee Reservoir. The grave is neglected, but is marked with a stone marker. We are uncertain if this is above the current waterline of the Brownlee Reservoir. (Not shown on Brownlee Dam 1987 USGS Quad. map.)

HIBBARD CREEK
AKA: 1. HOME
     2. SNAKE RIVER

A   0.1   2   1882-1934   T12S R45E   S27
Leave U.S. Hwy. 30 at Huntington onto Snake River Road for 14.2 miles. Go 0.3 of a mile north of junction with Hibbard Creek Road. The cemetery is down on the bank of Brownlee Reservoir, it has a cement breakwater on the river side. The road down to this site is steep and rough, not suitable for modern passenger cars, best for a pick up or 4-wheel drive. One fenced in grave lot was totally covered with large poison oak, (2000). It has about 14 markers and was fenced a few years prior to 1970, according to *Yesterday's Roll Call*, Published by the Genealogical Forum of Portland Oregon, Inc. (1970). {12 September 2000} (Connor Creek 1987 USGS Quad. map.)

Name of Cemetery and also known as	Number of burials	Acres	Condition	Date started or earliest known burial	Township	Range	Section

HOOPINGGARDNER CHILDREN

A   ?   ?   ?   T7S R45E   ?
Three children are buried on Walt Blacker's place (1966) near Carson. NOTE: No other information was given in the report. This site is on private property. (Not shown on Jimtown 1987 USGS Quad. map.)

HUNTINGTON, [OLD]

A   0.2   4   1883-1898   T14S R44E   S13
Turn off U.S. Hwy. 30 onto 1st Street and go uphill 0.2 of a mile to a fork in the road. Turn right, the old burial ground is on the left, a total of 0.25 of a mile from the highway. There were 11 markers. (Huntington 1988 USGS Quad. map.)

I.O.O.F. [HUNTINGTON]
  AKA: 1. HUNTINGTON
        [NEW]

C   2   2   1890   T14S R45E   S19
Land was donated by the lodge, 0.5 mile east of Huntington, on U.S. Hwy. 30. {12 September 2000} (Huntington 1988 USGS Quad. map.)

KOONTZ FAMILY

A   ?   3   1868-1900   T12S R40E   ?
Possibly located on Section 29, 5 miles west of Bridgeport on the south side of Burnt River; 0.5 of a mile west from where Bridgeport Road joins OR. Hwy. 245. NOTE: This site is on private property. (Not shown on Wendt Butte 1990 USGS Quad. map.)

LIME-DIXIE
  AKA: 1. DIXIE
      2. DURBIN
      3. LANGLEY
      4. LIME

B   2.4   5   Circa 1878   T13S R44E   S22
Located about 1 mile north of Lime via Old U.S. Hwy. 30 and an unnamed road to the right at Bragg Creek. (Lime 1988 USGS Quad. map.)

LOVE FAMILY

A   0.2   5   1865   T8S R43E   S32
This is located on the homestead of Avon S. Love, 0.5 of a mile north of OR. Hwy. 86. The burials are past Love Bridge (Powder River), on the west side of Middle Bridge Road and 0.15 of a mile via a driveway. NOTE: This site is on private property. (Glasgow Butte 1988 USGS Quad. map.)

Name of Cemetery and also known as	Number of burials	Acres	Condition	Date started or earliest known burial	Township	Range	Section

McEWEN

A   0.2   5   1897-1904   T10S R38E   S18
Located 0.25 of a mile north of OR. Hwy. 7 at McEwen. The cemetery has 15 known burials, with 5 identified; but only 2 stones according to *Yesterday's Roll Call*, Published by the Genealogical Forum of Portland Oregon, Inc. (1970). (Phillips Lake 1972-84 USGS Quad. map.)

MINERAL

A   ?   ?   19 Jul 1910 T12S R45E   S12
Baker County death certificate #4036 reports the death of Earnest William Lockard. Born 16 October 1900, aged 9 years, 9 months, 3 days, died of a gun shot wound at Copperfield. The body was shipped to the railway station of Mineral on the Snake River. NOTE: The actual burial may have been across the river in the mining settlement of Mineral, Idaho. (Not shown on Connor Creek 1987 USGS Quad. map.)

MT. HOPE
  AKA: 1. CATHOLIC
       2. CLEAVER
       3. EAGLES
       4. FAIR VIEW
       5. FAIRVIEW
       6. I.O.O.F.
         [BAKER CITY]
       7. MASONIC
         [BAKER CITY]
       8. MAUSOLEUM
         [BAKER CITY]
       9. PIONEER
         [BAKER CITY]

E 100   1   1876   T9S R40E   S21
Found in Baker City on South Bridge Street. Take U.S. Hwy. 30 from downtown, crossing over the North Powder River Bridge. Turn left at the substation off of U.S. Hwy 30 and onto South Bridge Street. Go past the State Police station to the cemetery. {13 September 2000} (Baker City 1994 USGS Quad. map.)

PARKINSON, JOHN T.

A   0.01 5 7 Oct 1862 T8S ?   ?
Probably located in Range 38 East or Range 39 East. Parkinson died enroute to western Oregon. He is buried in an unknown grave somewhere in the Willow Creek area. The grave was marked with the end gate of a wagon, with name and date carved on it; however nobody has ever located it again. (Not shown on Haines 1967 USGS Quad. map.)

Name of Cemetery and also known as	Number of burials	Acres	Condition	Date started or earliest known burial	Township	Range	Section

PINE HAVEN
AKA: 1. HALFWAY
     2. PINE CREEK
     3. PINE VALLEY

C 5 1 1885   T8S R46E   S17

Located at Halfway, at the junction of Pine Creek Road and Fairgrounds Road. (Halfway 1987 USGS Quad. map.)

POCAHONTAS

? ? 5 ?   T9S R39E   S5

Located close to the old Nelson Placer Mine on Salmon Creek. No marked graves remain [correspondence, March 1966.] NOTE: Pocahontas is a locale west of Baker City. (Not shown on Wingville 1993 USGS Quad. map.)

ROBINETTE

? ? ? ?   T9S R46E   S25

Located on the Snake River at the mouth of Robinette Creek and about a mile downstream from the mouth of the Powder River. There was a railway station established about 1909 and a post office. Apparently there was also a Robinette Cemetery as at least two death certificates so state. Pvt. Harold J. McKinnon who died of Spanish Flu at South Beach Camp near Newport, Lincoln County on 14 December 1918 was sent to Robinette. Mary E. Wilcox died 16 January 1929 is also buried at Robinette. The compiler does not know if the cemetery is now under Brownlee Reservoir or if the burials were removed elsewhere. (Not shown on Posy Valley or Sturgill Creek 1987 USGS Quad. maps.)

ROCK CREEK
AKA: 1. HEARING

B 10 3 1895   T7S R38E   S36

Located 3.1 miles southwest of Haines on South Rock Creek Road. Take 4th Street westerly out of Haines, where the name changes to Anthony Lakes Highway. At 1.7 miles from downtown Haines, turn left (south) onto South Rock Creek Road. At 2 miles turn right (east) and continue to 3.1 miles. The cemetery is adjacent to the Rock Creek School, now a residence. The cemetery was deeded in June 1895, but reburials dating back to 1862 may have been made. The water table here is high, and some burials were moved to Haines Cemetery when it was opened. However Rock Creek remains open for burials,

Name of Cemetery and also known as	Number of burials	Acres	Condition	Date started or earliest known burial	Township	Range	Section

the latest being in 1982. There were 73 known burials as of August, 1992. (Haines 1967 USGS Quad. map.)

ROSENBERG HILL	A ?	5	Sept. 1876	T8S	R46E	S13

This is the oldest cemetery in Pine Valley, September 1876. Physical evidence is now lost. It was located 4 miles east of Halfway on OR. Hwy. 86. On the right hand side going east is a marker set up in 1953. It is a heavy steel plate affixed to a railroad iron post. (Not shown on Halfway 1987 USGS Quad. map.)

RYE VALLEY	B 0.3	5	Mid 1860'S	T13S	R43E	S5

Located one mile northwest of Rye Valley. Take the Dixie Interchange (Exit #340) from the I-84 Freeway and cross over the railroad on Dixie Creek Road to Rye Valley, past the junction of Mormon Basin Road; turn left 8.4 miles at "Y", from the railroad crossing, 0.3 of a mile beyond 2nd "Y" leg is a track to the right, at 0.5 of a mile it dead ends at the cemetery. Or you can take Shirttail Creek Road, which is not as good a road: Take Nelson Point Interchange from I-84 Freeway, Milepost 330, 0.75 of a mile, on a connection from the interchange. Go west across railroad tracks and Burnt River Bridge on the west side of I-84 Freeway and 7.85 miles to the junction of Dixie Creek Road. Turn left on Dixie Creek Road, then 0.7 of a mile on Dixie Creek Road to the same cemetery track junction and turn left. There are 2 markers, 1884-1895, for 1 adult and 2 infants. (Rye Valley 1988 USGS Quad. map.)

ST. FRANCIS DeSALES CATHOLIC	A 2.5	5	?	T9S	R40E	S8

Located at the north end of College Street, in Baker City. Abandoned, with 1 grave left; the rest were moved to Mt. Hope Cemetery. (Baker City 1994 USGS Quad. map.)

SISLEY FAMILY	A ?	9	?	T12S	R45E	S15

The Sisley family had 2 or 3 graves on a bench north of Fox Creek and south of Home.

Name of Cemetery and also known as	Number of burials	Acres	Condition	Date started or earliest known burial	Township	Range	Section

The cemetery is now flooded by Brownlee Reservoir. The grave of Frank Sisley was relocated. Whether the other graves were moved we do not know at this time. (Not shown on Connor Creek 1987 USGS Quad. map.)

SPARTA

B   0.7   5   Circa 1870   T8S   R44E   S16
Go 22 miles on OR. Hwy. 86 from the I-84 Freeway, 7.6 miles on Sparta Road, and 0.25 of a mile west of Sparta Butte Road junction. This site is about 60 yards north of the county road. There were 33 known burials in 1966. (Sparta 1988 USGS Quad. map.)

SPEAK RANCH

A   ?   ?   11 Sep 1913   ?   R45E   ?
Baker County death certificate #3377 reports Thomas Huffman was a miner and rancher. Born 20 May 1833, and single. Huffman died in the hospital at Huntington and was buried the next day at the Speak Ranch, "13 miles north of Huntington on the Snake River." Further research shows a Thomas Huffman, died 11 September 1918 is buried at Hibbard Creek Cemetery, along with three other Huffman family members. See page 13 of *Yesterdays Roll Call*, published by the Genealogical Forum of Portland, Oregon Inc. This burial and the other three may have been moved in from the Speak Ranch to Hibbard Creek Cemetery. More information is needed to prove this out. (Not shown on Henley Basin 1976 USGS Quad. map.)

STURGILL CHILDREN, EFFIE AND ESTHER

A   ?   ?   6 Jan 1871   T9S   R40E   S19
The children are buried where Baker City Reservoir is located and near the Kolb Ranch (1966). Effie Lenora died 6 January 1871, aged 18 months. Esther Elizabeth died 7 February 1878 aged 2 years, 10 months. They were the daughters of William R. and Adeline Talley Sturgill. (Not shown on Baker City 1994 USGS Quad. map.

STURGILL CHILDREN, HILDA AND LOUIE

A   ?   ?   30 Oct 1893   T8S   R43E   ?
Located about 25 miles northeast of Baker City off of OR. Hwy. 86, on the Roy Hunt

Oregon Burial Site Guide
Baker County

| Name of Cemetery and also known as | Number of burials | Acres | Condition | Date started or earliest known burial | Township | Range | Section |

Place (1966) near the old Gilkinson Sawmill. Hilda, aged 8, and Louie, aged 10 died of diphtheria. They were the children of Lewis and Carrie Jones Sturgill. NOTE: This site is on private property. (Not shown on Glasgow Butte 1988 USGS Quad. map.)

SUMPTER
AKA: 1. BLUE
MOUNTAIN
2. MASONIC
3. McEWEN
MASONIC
LODGE
#125 A.F.
AND A.M.

C 2.5 2 Circa 1895 T9S R37E S33
Located at Sumpter. (*Sumpter Miner*, July 1985.) "Sumpter Cemetery tract is 10 acres total, 2 1/2 acres are fenced. The Masonic Cemetery is 60 by 660 feet adjoining the old cemetery on the south. The old cemetery originally was called Blue Mountain Cemetery. The records and map were lost in the fire of 1917. A still earlier cemetery in Sumpter was near northeast corner of Auburn and Ibex Streets. Those graves were all moved in 1900 to the present Sumpter Cemetery (Blue Mountain Cemetery). 1895 was the earliest known burial, and was probably moved in 1900. The Sumpter Cemetery burials as of October 1961; there are 98 known, with 79 unknown for a total of 177." (This apparently includes the Masonic burials too.) 15 additional burials to July 1985, all in the Masonic portion. {12 July 1995} (Sumpter 1972-84 USGS Quad. map.)

TRIMBLE FAMILY

A 0.25 5 1 Mar 1919 T12S R38E S18
Located in the Hereford area. This site is not visible from the highway, it·is a short distance north of OR. Hwy. 245 and was donated by John Trimble. Trimble was a 73 year-old widower so there are probably earlier burials than his on 1 March 1919. NOTE: This site is on private property. (1933 Metsker map Section 18. Not shown on Beaverdam Creek 1972-84 USGS Quad. map.)

UNITY
AKA: 1. BURNT RIVER

B 2 2 1893 T13S R36E S12
Go about 2 miles west of Unity on South Fork Burnt River Road, then turn right on Cemetery Road for 1.5 mile. This cemetery is on the

Name of Cemetery and also known as	Number of burials	Acres	Condition	Date started or earliest known burial	Township	Range	Section

left (west) side of the road. There were 81 known graves in July 1982. (Unity 1972-84 USGS Quad. map.)

UNKNOWN

? ? ? ? ? ? ?

This unknown graveyard north of Baker City might be in Township 8 South and Range 40 East. NOTE: This is NOT the St. Francis DeSales Cemetery, but an earlier one. Most of the graves of both were moved to Mt. Hope Cemetery. (Not shown on Baker City 1994 USGS Quad. map.)

UNKNOWN

? ? ? **Circa 1890 T8S R39E** ?

An unknown graveyard near where the city reservoir now stands. It is in the Lone Pine District, 13 miles northwest of Baker City. NOTE: Lone Pine refers to a bygone school. (Not shown on Wingville 1993 USGS Quad. map.)

UNKNOWN INFANT

A 0.01 ? 1900 **T6S R45E S34**

This grave is one-eighth of a mile south of Thomas Bobbington's burial site on the bank of Pine Creek. It contains an unknown infant who died in 1900. (Not shown on Cornucopia 1990 USGS Quad. map.)

UNKNOWN MAN

A 0.01 ? ? **T11S R46E** ?

"A lone grave is at the junction of Soda Creek with Connor Creek." This was a man who accidentally shot himself while trapping otter. The given location is impossible as Soda Creek is entirely separate from Connor Creek. Soda Creek enters the Snake River 7 miles north of the mouth of Connor Creek. (Not shown on Connor Creek 1987 USGS Quad. map. There is no Soda Creek shown flowing into Connor Creek.)

UTTER PARTY

A 0.01 ? 13 Oct 1860 **T14S R45E** ?

Reportedly the site was marked by a white cross "on the left side of the road between Farewell Bend and Huntington." This is Huntington Highway, the old alignment of I-84. The Utter party massacre occurred at

Name of Cemetery and also known as	Number of burials	Acres	Condition	Date started or earliest known burial	Township	Range	Section

Sinker Creek near present-day Murphy, Idaho. More of the survivors starved to death along the Owyhee River. See also the article Owyhee River in Malheur County, 6 more of the party were killed by Indians almost at the site of Huntington. Presumably these graves are not the same as those in the article entitled "Emigrant Graves", but the compiler cannot be certain. (Not shown on Olds Ferry Idaho-Oreg. 1952-74 or Huntington Ore. 1988 USGS Quad. maps.)

VAN CLEAVE, CHARLES AND EDWIN

A 0.01 ? Circa 1900 T12S R38E ?
A small fenced cemetery about 0.75 mile south of OR. Hwy. 245 Hereford Loop, west of Hereford, for Edwin and Charles, the sons of Tom Van Cleave. The boys died of diphtheria. NOTE: This site is on private property. (Not shown on Hereford 1972 USGS Quad. map.)

WAGON BOX BURIAL

A 0.01 ? ? T14S R45E S32
Located 0.5 of a mile west of Farewell Bend. NOTE: No other information was given in the report. (Not shown on Olds Ferry 1952-74 USGS Quad. map.)

WEATHERBY

A 0.01 ? ? T12S R44E ?
Two children. NOTE: No further information was given, and the markers are reportedly illegible. (Not shown on Big Lookout Mountain or Lime 1988 USGS Quad. maps.)

WHEELOCK, HATTIE

A 0.01 ? Apr 1888 T8S R46E ?
Possibly located in Section 1 or 2 about 7 miles northeast of Halfway via OR. Hwy. 86 and Buchanan Road, on the ranch of Don Haight, Jr. (1966). She was the 4 year-old daughter of J. B. Wheelock and who died of croup. The grave is fenced, but now is uncared for. NOTE: This site is on private property. (Not shown on Halfway 1987 USGS Quad. map.)

Name of Cemetery and also known as	Number of burials	Acres	Condition	Date started or earliest known burial	Township	Range	Section

WHITNEY

A 0.25 5 Before 1905 T10S R36E S27
Located 0.75 of a mile east of Whitney on a point of land on the north side of OR. Hwy. 7. (Whitney 1972-84 USGS Quad. map.)

WILLIAMS, REES AND JANE

A 0.01 5 1873 & 1888 T8S R38E ?
Perhaps found in Section 25. They are buried on the Williams Farm 4 miles west of Wingville. Mrs. Williams died in 1873, her husband died on 9 April, 1888. They were buried just below the big house on the right hand side in the field. In 1900 the markers were plowed over as the Williams' had requested. NOTE: No other information was given in the report. (Not shown on Wingville 1993 or Elkhorn Peak 1972-84 USGS Quads. maps.)

WINGVILLE
AKA: 1. I.O.O.F.

C 12.5 3 1871 T8S R39E S29
Located northwest of Baker City. Leave U.S. Hwy. 30 at Milepost 46.4 north of town, turning left (west) onto Wingville Road and drive 2 miles to Wingville Grange. Continue another 2.3 miles westerly on Cemetery Road to the cemetery on the right (north). Although it is now closed for burials, there are still requests for burials at Wingville Cemetery. However, the locations of so many of the graves are now unknown, due to several range fires, the Wingville Grange Chapter has not granted these requests. Deeded in 1878 but the earliest recorded burial is 1871. (Wingville 1993 USGS Quad. map.)

ALDER CREEK	BAKER CO.	T10S	R41E	S35
ASHBY, BILL see **ASHBY CHILD**	BAKER CO.	?	R47E	?
ASHBY CHILD	BAKER CO.	?	R47E	?
AUBURN	BAKER CO.	T10S	R39E	S8
AUDREY see **BIG FLAT**	BAKER CO.	T12S	R37E	S10
AUNT POLLY	BAKER CO.	T12S	R38E	?
BASTIAN FAMILY	BAKER CO.	T12S	R45E	?
BASTIAN, MARY D. see **BASTIAN FAMILY**				
	BAKER CO.	T12S	R45E	?
BEAGLE CREEK see **BIG CREEK**	BAKER CO.	T7S	R41E	S2
BIG CREEK	BAKER CO.	T7S	R41E	S2
BIG FLAT	BAKER CO.	T12S	R37E	S10
BLACKER'S PLACE, WALT see **HOOPINGGARDNER CHILDREN**				
	BAKER CO.	T7S	R45E	?
BLUE MOUNTAIN see **SUMPTER**	BAKER CO.	T9S	R37E	S33
BOBBINGTON, THOMAS	BAKER CO.	T6S	R45E	S34
BOBBINGTON, THOMAS see **UNKNOWN INFANT**				
	BAKER CO.	T6S	R45E	S34
BOOT HILL	BAKER CO.	T8S	R44E	?
BOURNE	BAKER CO.	T8S	R37E	?
BOYER FAMILY	BAKER CO.	T12S	R38E	?
BOYER RANCH, FRED see **BOYER FAMILY**				
	BAKER CO.	T12S	R38E	?
BOYER RANCH, FRED see **DEVIN, GRANDMA**				
	BAKER CO.	T12S	R38E	?
BOYER, THOMAS see **BOYER FAMILY**	BAKER CO.	T12S	R38E	?
BRIDGEPORT	BAKER CO.	T12S	R41E	S30
BURKEMONT	BAKER CO.	T7S	R42E	S28
BURNT RIVER see **UNITY**	BAKER CO.	T13S	R36E	S12
CATHOLIC see **MT. HOPE**	BAKER CO.	T9S	R40E	S21
CHINESE [BAKER CITY]	BAKER CO.	T9S	R40E	S15
CHINESE [SPARTA]	BAKER CO.	T8S	R44E	?
CLARK CHILDREN	BAKER CO.	T8S	R46E	?
CLARKSVILLE	BAKER CO.	T12S	R41E	S34
CLAWSON BABIES	BAKER CO.	?	?	?
CLAWSON, ELLIS L. see **CLAWSON BABIES**				
	BAKER CO.	?	?	?
CLAWSON, MARTHA LUCILE STAM see **CLAWSON BABIES**				
	BAKER CO.	?	?	?
CLEAVER see **MT. HOPE**	BAKER CO.	T9S	R40E	S21
COLT, ISAAC	BAKER CO.	T13S	R37E	S5
COLT RANCH, PORTER see **COLT, ISAAC**				
	BAKER CO.	T13S	R37E	S5
CONNOR CREEK	BAKER CO.	T11S	R45E	S34
CONROE'S PIG RANCH see **HAMLIN, NATHANIEL**				
	BAKER CO.	T7S	R39E	S27
COOPER, J. F. J.	BAKER CO.	T12S	R44E	S19
COPPERFIELD-HOMESTEAD	BAKER CO.	T6S	R48E	S33
CORD, OTTO see **GOLD RIDGE MINE**	BAKER CO.	T12S	R43E	S16
CORNUCOPIA	BAKER CO.	T6S	R45E	?
DEVIN, GRANDMA	BAKER CO.	T12S	R38E	?
DIXIE see **LIME-DIXIE**	BAKER CO.	T13S	R44E	S22

DURBIN see **LIME-DIXIE**	BAKER CO.	T13S	R44E	S22
DURKEE	BAKER CO.	T11S	R43E	S18
EAGLE VALLEY	BAKER CO.	T9S	R45E	S26
EAGLES see **MT. HOPE**	BAKER CO.	T9S	R40E	S21
EBENGER FAMILY	BAKER CO.	T12S	R45E	S14
ELKS see **HAINES**	BAKER CO.	T7S	R39E	S21
EMIGRANT GRAVES	BAKER CO.	T14S	R45E	S20
ENNIS HOMESTEAD, DAVE see **BRIDGEPORT**				
	BAKER CO.	T12S	R41E	S30
FAIR VIEW see **MT. HOPE**	BAKER CO.	T9S	R40E	S21
FAIRVIEW see **MT. HOPE**	BAKER CO.	T9S	R40E	S21
FLEETWOOD FAMILY, ASA	BAKER CO.	T12S	R38E	S20
FLEETWOOD FAMILY, JIM	BAKER CO.	T12S	R38E	S25
FLEETWOOD HOMESTEAD, ASA see **FLEETWOOD FAMILY, ASA**				
	BAKER CO.	T12S	R38E	S20
FLEETWOOD RANCH, JIM see **FLEETWOOD FAMILY, JIM**				
	BAKER CO.	T12S	R38E	S25
GILKINSON SAWMILL see **STURGILL CHILDREN, HILDA AND LOUIE**				
	BAKER CO.	T8S	R43E	?
GOLD RIDGE MINE	BAKER CO.	T12S	R43E	S16
GOOSE CREEK	BAKER CO.	T8S	R43E	S29
GORDON, FRANK	BAKER CO.	T10S	R36E	?
GREENER PLACE, ED see **CLARK CHILDREN**				
	BAKER CO.	T8S	R46E	?
GREENHORN	BAKER CO.	T10S	R35E	S9
HAIGHT, JR. RANCH, DON see **WHEELOCK, HATTIE**				
	BAKER CO.	T8S	R46S	?
HAINES	BAKER CO.	T7S	R39E	S21
HALFWAY see **PINE HAVEN**	BAKER CO.	T8S	R46E	S17
HAMLIN, NATHANIEL	BAKER CO.	T7S	R39E	S27
HARDMAN, FRANK see **HARDMAN GIRLS**				
	BAKER CO.	T11S	R37E	S31
HARDMAN GIRLS	BAKER CO.	T11S	R37E	S31
HARDMAN, GRACE see **HARDMAN GIRLS**				
	BAKER CO.	T11S	R37E	S31
HARDMAN HOMESTEAD, FRANKLIN LINCOLN see **HARDMAN GIRLS**				
	BAKER CO.	T11S	R37E	S31
HARDMAN, JOSEPH BART see **HARDMAN GIRLS**				
	BAKER CO.	T11S	R37E	S31
HASKINS YARD	BAKER CO.	T13S	R37E	?
HEARING see **ROCK CREEK**	BAKER CO.	T7S	R38E	S36
HEATH, TOM	BAKER CO.	T8S	R47E	?
HIBBARD CREEK	BAKER CO.	T12S	R45E	S27
HOME see **HIBBARD CREEK**	BAKER CO.	T12S	R45E	S27
HOMESTEAD see **COPPERFIELD-HOMESTEAD**				
	BAKER CO.	T6S	R48E	S33
HOOPINGGARDNER CHILDREN	BAKER CO.	T7S	R45E	?
HUFFMAN, THOMAS see **SPEAK RANCH**	BAKER CO.	?	R45E	?
HUNT PLACE, ROY see **STURGILL CHILDREN, HILDA AND LOUI**				
	BAKER CO.	T8S	R43E	?
HUNTINGTON [NEW] see **I.O.O.F. [HUNTINGTON]**				
	BAKER CO.	T14S	R45E	S19

HUNTINGTON [OLD]	BAKER CO.	T14S	R44E	S13
I.O.O.F. see WINGVILLE	BAKER CO.	T8S	R39E	S29
I.O.O.F. [BAKER CITY] see MT. HOPE				
	BAKER CO.	T9S	R40E	S21
I.O.O.F. [HUNTINGTON]	BAKER CO.	T14S	R45E	S19
I.O.O.F. [RICHLAND] see EAGLE VALLEY				
	BAKER CO.	T9S	R45E	S26
KEATING see GOOSE CREEK	BAKER CO.	T8S	R43E	S29
KOLB RANCH see SRURGILL CHILDREN, EFFIE AND ESTER				
	BAKER CO.	T9S	R40E	S19
KOONTZ FAMILY	BAKER CO.	T12S	R40E	?
LANGLEY see LIME-DIXIE	BAKER CO.	T13S	R44E	S22
LIME see LIME-DIXIE	BAKER CO.	T13S	R44E	S22
LIME-DIXIE	BAKER CO.	T13S	R44E	S22
LOCKARD, EARNEST WILLIAM see MINERAL				
	BAKER CO.	T12S	R45E	S12
LOVE, AVON S. see LOVE FAMILY	BAKER CO.	T8S	R43E	S32
LOVE FAMILY	BAKER CO.	T8S	R43E	S32
MASONIC see SUMPTER	BAKER CO.	T9S	R37E	S33
MASONIC [BAKER CITY] see MT. HOPE				
	BAKER CO.	T9S	R40E	S21
MAUSOLEUM [BAKER CITY] see MT. HOPE				
	BAKER CO.	T9S	R40E	S21
MAXWELL see HAINES	BAKER CO.	T7S	R39E	S21
McEWEN	BAKER CO.	T10S	R38E	S18
McEWEN MASONIC LODGE #125 A.F. AND A.M. see SUMPTER				
	BAKER CO.	T9S	R37E	S33
McKINNON, PVT. HAROLD J. see ROBINETTE				
	BAKER CO.	T9S	R46E	S25
MINERAL	BAKER CO.	T12S	R45E	S12
MOORE, MR. T. B. see DURKEE	BAKER CO.	T11S	R43E	S18
MT. HOPE	BAKER CO.	T9S	R40E	S21
PARKINSON, JOHN T.	BAKER CO.	T8S	?	?
PINE CREEK see PINE HAVEN	BAKER CO.	T8S	R46E	S17
PINE HAVEN	BAKER CO.	T8S	R46E	S17
PINE VALLEY see PINE HAVEN	BAKER CO.	T8S	R46E	S17
PIONEER [BAKER CITY] see MT. HOPE				
	BAKER CO.	T9S	R40E	S21
PLEASANT VALLEY see ALDER CREEK	BAKER CO.	T10S	R41E	S35
POCAHONTAS	BAKER CO.	T9S	R39E	S5
ROBINETTE	BAKER CO.	T9S	R46E	S25
ROCK CREEK	BAKER CO.	T7S	R38E	S36
ROSENBERG HILL	BAKER CO.	T8S	R46E	S13
RYE VALLEY	BAKER CO.	T13S	R43E	S5
ST. FRANCIS DeSALES CATHOLIC	BAKER CO.	T9S	R40E	S8
SAMS, JIM see BIG CREEK	BAKER CO.	T7S	R41E	S2
SCHNEIDER'S CABIN see CORNUCOPIA				
	BAKER CO.	T6S	R45E	?
SISLEY FAMILY	BAKER CO.	T12S	R45E	S15
SISLEY, FRANK see SISLEY FAMILY	BAKER CO.	T12S	R45E	S15
SNAKE RIVER see HIBBARD CREEK	BAKER CO.	T12S	R45E	S27
SPARTA	BAKER CO.	T8S	R44E	S16

SPEAK RANCH   BAKER CO.   ?   R45E   ?
STRIEBY HOMESTEAD, DR. ULYSSES GRANT see **BIG FLAT**
                                       BAKER CO.   T12S   R37E   S10
STURGILL, ADELINE TALLEY see **STURGILL CHILDREN, EFFIE AND ESTHER**
                                       BAKER CO.   T9S   R40E   S19
STURGILL, CARRIE JONES see **STURGILL CHILDREN, HILDA AND LOUIE**
                                       BAKER CO.   T8S   R43E   ?
STURGILL CHILDREN, EFFIE AND ESTHER
                                       BAKER CO.   T9S   R40E   S19
STURGILL CHILDREN, HILDA AND LOUIE
                                       BAKER CO.   T8S   R43E   ?
STURGILL, EFFIE LENORA see **STURGILL CHILDREN, EFFIE AND ESTHER**
                                       BAKER CO.   T9S   R40E   S19
STURGILL, ESTHER ELIZABETH see **STURGILL CHILDREN, EFFIE AND ESTHER**
                                       BAKER CO.   T9S   R40E   S19
STURGILL, LEWIS see **STURGILL CHILDREN, HILDA AND LOUIE**
                                       BAKER CO.   T8S   R43E   ?
STURGILL, WILLIAM R. see **STURGILL CHILDREN, EFFIE AND ESTHER**
                                       BAKER CO.   T9S   R40E   S19
SUMPTER   BAKER CO.   T9S   R37E   S33
TETREAU, ALICE see **FLEETWOOD FAMILY, JIM**
                                       BAKER CO.   T12S   R38E   S25
TRIMBLE FAMILY   BAKER CO.   T12S   R38E   S18
TRIMBLE, JOHN see **TRIMBLE FAMILY**
                                       BAKER CO.   T12S   R38E   S18
UNITY   BAKER CO.   T13S   R36E   S12
UNKNOWN   BAKER CO.   ?   ?   ?
UNKNOWN   BAKER CO.   T8S   R39E   ?
UNKNOWN INFANT   BAKER CO.   T6S   R45E   S34
UNKNOWN MAN   BAKER CO.   T11S   R46E   ?
UTTER PARTY   BAKER CO.   T14S   R45E   ?
VAN CLEAVE, CHARLES AND EDWIN   BAKER CO.   T12S   R38E   ?
VAN CLEAVE, TOM see **VAN CLEAVE, CHARLES AND EDWIN**
                                       BAKER CO.   T12S   R38E   ?
VANDEVENTER, EZRA see **BURKEMONT** BAKER CO.   T7S   R42E   S28
WAGON BOX BURIAL   BAKER CO.   T14S   R45E   S32
WEATHERBY   BAKER CO.   T12S   R44E   ?
WENDT BROTHERS see **BRIDGEPORT** BAKER CO.   T12S   R41E   S30
WHEELOCK, **HATTIE**   BAKER CO.   T8S   R46E   ?
WHEELOCK, J. B. see **WHEELOCK, HATTIE**
                                       BAKER CO.   T8S   R46E   ?
WHITNEY   BAKER CO.   T10S   R36E   S27
WILCOX, MARY E. see **ROBINETTE** BAKER CO.   T9S   R46E   S25
WILLIAMS, REES AND JANE   BAKER CO.   T8S   R38E   ?
WINGVILLE   BAKER CO.   T8S   R39E   S29

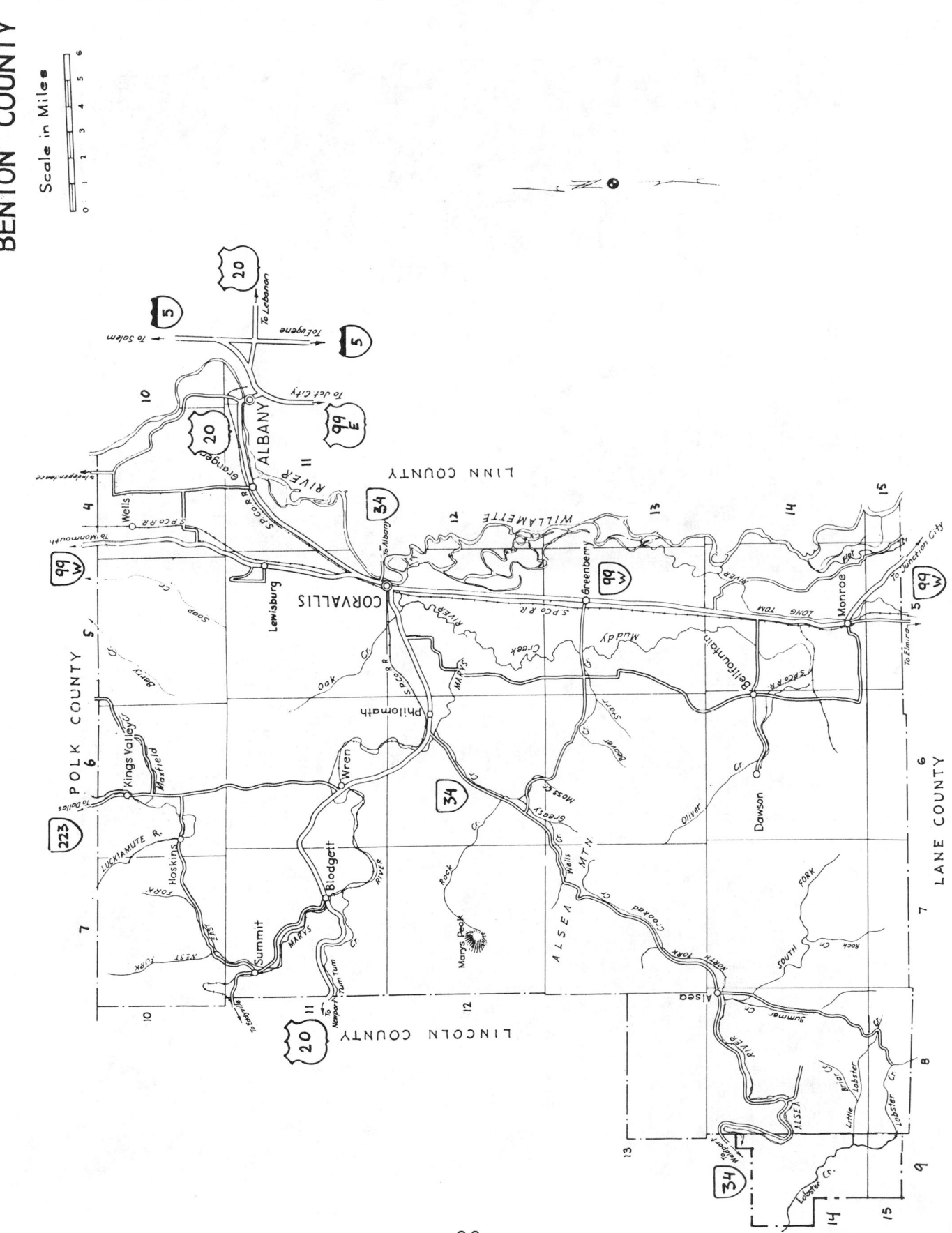

BENTON COUNTY

Scale in Miles

Benton County

Oak Ridge
Dean H. Byrd (1993)

Monroe
Dean H. Byrd (1991)

Area: 679 square miles
Population (1998): 77,755
County seat: Corvallis, Population: 49,275
County established: 23 December 1847

Benton County in the Willamette Valley was a goal for the earliest settlers seeking farmlands. Many public cemeteries were established by 1849-1850, but Locke in 1846 was apparently the earliest public cemetery to be established near Corvallis. In 1992 a small Islamic Cemetery was established near Corvallis, the first for that faith in Oregon.

Kings Valley Pioneer
Dean H, Byrd (1991)

Kings Valley Pioneer
Dean H. Byrd (1994)

Crystal Lake
Dean H. Byrd (1991)

Name of Cemetery and also known as	Number of burials	Acres	Condition	Date started or earliest known burial	Township	Range	Section

ALPINE
AKA: 1. GOODMAN
    2. SIMPSONS
       CHAPEL

C 3.86 2 Circa 1850 T14S R6W   S24
Located to the west of the crossroads at Alpine. Go west on Alpine Road for 0.2 of a mile past the school on the left and Alpine Park on the right and then right (north) up the hill. The earliest dated stone is 2 March 1851. This is on the Jesse Belknap D.L.C. #41, OC #185, on tax lot #1700. {30 August 1991} (Monroe 1969-75 USGS Quad. map.)

ALSEA

D 8   1   1858   T14S R8W   S1
Located on the right (north) side of OR. Hwy. 34, 0.5 of a mile west of Alsea. At present (1990) 2.6 acres are occupied by burials; 875 marked burials as of May 1979. On tax lot #800. (Alsea 1985 USGS Quad. map.)

ARMSTRONG

A 0.5 3 1869-1934 T12S R5W   S31
Go south of Philomath on Bellfountain Road to its junction with Airport Avenue. Continue 0.5 of a mile farther south on Bellfountain Road to a driveway on the right (west). The cemetery is 0.1 of a mile off of Bellfountain Road on the Jacob and Evaline Martin's D.L.C. #66, OC #186, tax lot #600. {4 September 1992} (Greenberry 1969-75 USGS Quad. map.)

BELLFOUNTAIN

D 11   2 Circa 1850 T14S R5W   S7
Go east from Bellfountain Road onto Dawson Road. At 0.6 of a mile turn left (north) up the hill to the cemetery. 1859 was the earliest death date found on a stone. On the Jonas Belknap D.L.C. #39, RB #1550, tax lot #1200. NOTE: The fenced area containing the burials is perhaps two acres in size. {14 September 1990} (Monroe 1969-75 USGS Quad. map.)

BENTON
AKA: 1. OAK LAWN
      MEMORIAL
      PARK
    2. OAKLAWN
      MEMORIAL
      PARK

? ?   ? ?   T12S R5W   S10
This now forms the western portion of Oak Lawn Memorial Park. (Shown as Oak Lawn Memorial Park on Corvallis 1969-86 USGS Quad. map.)

Name of Cemetery and also known as	Number of burials	Acres	Condition	Date started or earliest known burial	Township	Range	Section

BENTON COUNTY POOR FARM ? ? ? 18 Feb 1904 T14S R6W ?
Benton County death certificate #239 for Andrew Hanson reports that he was 67 years old, widowed and a former resident of Fisher, Lincoln County. He died on 18 February and was buried on 19 February "at the poor farm." It was said to be 3 miles Southwest of Bellfountain. (NOT shown on Glenbrook 1984 or Monroe 1969-75 USGS Quad. maps)

BLODGETT C 0.5 2 Late 1860's T11S R7W S23
Just east of Philomath is the junction of the Alsea Highway (OR. Hwy. 34), with the highway to Newport (U.S. Hwy. 20). Drive westerly on U.S. Hwy. 20 towards Newport for 8.2 miles to the unmarked driveway uphill on the left (south) that leads to the cemetery, which is not visible from the highway. The driveway is about 50 yards west beyond the west junction with Davis Road on the left. Davis Road is a portion of Old U.S. Hwy 20. This is about 1.3 miles short of the community of Blodgett. The cemetery driveway goes past a house and ends about 0.2 of a mile at the parking area. The Blodgett Cemetery is almost entirely surrounded by second-growth fir timber, and indeed there are several towering firs within the fenced enclosure. At least one of these fir trees is marked with its own brass plaque noting it was planted in 1914. The Blodgett Community Cemetery Association, incorporated 18 November 1974, has thoughtfully provided many brass markers for bygone or non-existent monuments. This cemetery is also distinguished by mounding over the earlier graves of the Blodgett family. The earliest dated stone was for 1876, but it is believed that Blodgett family members were buried in the 1860's. On the William Blodgett D.L.C. #40, OC #5060, tax lot #101. {9 March 1994} (Wren 1984 USGS Quad. map.)

CRYSTAL LAKE D 20 1 Circa 1850 T12S R5W S11
AKA: 1. HAVEN OF ST. JOHN
Located south of the Marys River in Corvallis at 1945 Southeast Crystal Lake Drive. On the

Name of Cemetery and also known as	Number of burials	Acres	Condition	Date started or earliest known burial	Township	Range	Section

       MAUSOLEUM
2. MASONIC
      LODGE #14

Joseph Alexander D.L.C. #46, OC #848; deeded in 1860. {1 June 1991} (Corvallis 1969-86 USGS Quad. map.)

CUTSFORTH FAMILY

| | A | 0.01 | 1 | 20 Feb 1989 | ? | ? | ? |

Two family members: Delbert Lee Cutsforth, died 20 February 1989, and Florence M. Cutsforth, died 24 February 1989 are buried on the Cutsforth Ranch. NOTE: This site is on private property. No other information was given in the report.

DAVIDSON
 AKA: 1. PEAK

| | A | 0.04 | 2 | 1887-1942 | T12S | R7W | S8 |

Located on the northwest side of Marys Peak and on the south side of Shotpouch Road, 2 miles east of its junction with Shotpouch Trail. It is on the Harrison Davidson Homestead, which was settled in 1885. This is on tax lot #102. Just to the east of the cemetery is the townsite of Peak, which had a post office from 1899 to 1917. The name referred to Marys Peak. There were 13 recorded burials found in March of 1991. NOTE: This site is on private property. (Marys Peak 1984 USGS Quad. map.)

DOW, OSCAR A.

| | A | 0.01 | 3 | 11 Jan 1879 | T13S | R5W | S28 |

Located in the Southeast 1/4 of Section 28. This is a fenced grave in a grove of trees on the Finley Wildlife Refuge, about 2 miles from the south boundary and 0.13 of a mile from the east boundary of the refuge. Oscar was the 6 year-old son of William Dow and Eliza Jane Stark. William W. Dow's D.L.C. was some distance away, to the east of OR. Hwy. 99W; the Wildlife Refuge is west of OR. Hwy. 99W. (Not shown on Greenberry 1969-75 USGS Quad. map.)

DUNN FAMILY
 AKA: 1. WILKINSON--
     DUNN FAMILIES

| | ? | 0.05 | 5 | Pre-1866 | T13S | R6W | S11 |

Located in the Southeast 1/4 of Section 11, on a private drive 0.65 of a mile east off of Beaver Creek Road and on the south side of Decker Road. There are no gravestones and no known records. The cemetery was plowed over and is now planted with Christmas trees. On

Name of Cemetery and also known as	Number of burials	Acres	Condition	Date started or earliest known burial	Township	Range	Section

the William Wilkinson D.L.C. #53, OC #2876, tax lot #1200. NOTE: This site is on private property. (Not shown on Flat Mountain 1984 USGS Quad. Quad. map.)

EMERICK FAMILY
AKA: 1. EMERICK AND
ALLIED
FAMILIES

A 0.5 3 Circa 1863 T12S R6W S27
Located off of the south side of Southwest Airport Road and about 1 mile west of the junction of Peterson Road. From the address of 24602 Southwest Airport Road, it is on a steep private drive up the hill. The cemetery is not visible from the county road. There were 16 marked graves out of 18 known graves and probable graves (1978). On the Clement Barker D.L.C. #60, OC #5186, tax lot #1600. NOTE: This site is on private property. (Flat Mountain 1984 USGS Quad. map.)

FOLKS, B. A.

A ? 8 1848-1860 T10S R5W S10
Four members of the Daniel D. Davis family were originally buried in the B. A. Folks Cemetery located in the east half of Section 10. This is on Smith Hill in what is now the Paul Dunn State Forest northeast off of Tampico Road. On 29 September 1942 the graves with their markers were removed to what is now English [New] Cemetery near Monmouth; see Polk County. (Not shown on Airlie South 1984 USGS Quad. map.)

GINGLES
AKA: 1. SCHOOL
DISTRICT
#1

B 0.75 5 1852 T10S R4W S15
Located about 0.5 of a mile east of the Independence Highway (a county road), just north of the Camp Adair Road junction. It is no longer accessible by road; access is by private drive and by foot across fields. This cemetery is marked by tall fir trees and was deeded to the School District in 1886. Gingles fell into disuse after Palestine Cemetery was started in the 1880's. On the James Gingles D.L.C. #44, OC #3509. (Lewisburg 1970-86 USGS Quad. map.)

Name of Cemetery and also known as	Number of burials	Acres	Condition	Date started or earliest known burial	Township	Range	Section

HENDERSON FAMILY

A 0.5 3 Circa 1885 T12S R6W S36

From the east side of Peterson Road just south of Ervin Road junction, this is located on a 0.75 of a mile-long private drive going east and north; up a high steep hill through a Christmas tree farm. This family cemetery probably contains burials prior to 1885, the earliest on record. It includes the unmarked grave of William Dixon, the co-founder of Corvallis. On the Sanford White D.L.C. #61, OC #5187, tax lot #100. NOTE: This site is on private property. (Not shown on Flat Mountain 1984 USGS Quad. map.)

HERBERT PIONEER
AKA: 1. HERBERT FAMILY

A 0.01 2 1851-1866 T13S R5W S17

Located about 8 miles south of Corvallis via OR. Hwy. 99W and then 2 miles west on Greenberry Road. Turn left (south) from Greenberry Road onto Bellfountain Road and drive a little more than one mile to a side driveway left (east) at an electric substation. From here there is a gated private driveway due east a few hundred feet into a Christmas tree farm marked with a giant Douglas fir. The Herbert family has rededicated the small burial site on 26 June 1997 with four new headstones. They are for Joshua Herbert 1801-1851, wife Elizabeth Herbert 1811-1866. Of their five sons and two daughters, two of the sons are buried here: Adam 1838-1859 and James 1845-early 1860s. This is on the Elizabeth Herbert D.L.C. #41, OC #2911, tax lot #700. NOTE: This site is on private property. {26 June 1997} (Not shown on Greenberry 1969-75 USGS Quad. map.)

HORN, COLUMBIA
AKA: 1. SHEPHARD, MATTIE

A ? 6 10 Aug 1855 ? ? ?

Columbia Horn, infant daughter of J. M. and M. J. Horn was buried within an 8-foot square iron fence on land owned by Mattie Shephard. When the U. S. Government bought the land for the Camp Adair Military Base in 1942, the grave and monument were removed 29 September 1942 to the English [New] Cemetery near Monmouth; see Polk County.

Name of Cemetery and also known as	Number of burials	Acres	Condition	Date started or earliest known burial	Township	Range	Section

I.O.O.F. [CORVALLIS]
AKA: 1. BARNUM LODGE
#7
2. ODD FELLOWS
CEMETERY OF
CORVALLIS

D 3 2 Circa 1855 T11S R5W S28
Located at 4343 Witham Road in Corvallis, near the top of the hill. There were 635 marked burials noted by a D.A.R. survey in 1947. The cemetery was chartered in April of 1860, but the earliest death date found on a monument was 1858. This cemetery is very near the St. Mary's Catholic Cemetery, on the Alfred M. Witham D.L.C. #55, OC #906. {15 Feb. 1991} (Corvallis 1969-86 USGS Quad. map.)

IRWIN FAMILY
AKA: 1. FIR GROVE

A ? 3 1850's T13S R5W S22
Located about 6 miles south of Corvallis on the east side of OR. Hwy. 99W. This small fenced plot is located in a fir grove at the southwest base of the smaller of the two Wagner (formerly Winkle) Buttes. The Winkle and McBee Cemeteries are close by. On the Richard Irwin D.L.C. #51, OC #3865, tax lot #101. NOTE: This site is on private property. (Greenberry 1969-75 USGS Quad. map.)

ISLAMIC CEMETERY OF OREGON
AKA: 1. DAR MAKKAH
2. MUSLIM

A 0.5 2 1992 T12S R5W S5
Located in the Northwest 1/4 of Section 5. The cemetery is on the north (left) side of West Hills Road coming from Philomath towards Corvallis. It is about 300 yards from Reservoir Road and the railway crossing, towards the junction with Winding Way. The compiler found the gateway locked and curious sightseers will not find anything to attract attention. The mosque is in Corvallis and the name Dar Makkah reportedly translates as "House of Mecca." Located on the Abiathar Newton D.L.C. #42, OC #843. {11 November 1993} (Not shown on Corvallis 1969-86 USGS Quad. map.)

KING FAMILY, ISAAC

A ? 5 1857 T10S R6W S28
Located on a hill east of OR. Hwy. 223 and 0.25 of a mile south of the Hoskins Road intersection. There are 4 known burials located northeast of the Isaac King house in a small fenced plot. This is on the Isaac

Name of Cemetery and also known as	Number of burials	Acres	Condition	Date started or earliest known burial	Township	Range	Section

King D.L.C. #39, OC #2181, tax lot #900. NOTE: This site is on private property. (Not shown on Kings Valley 1984 USGS Quad. map.)

KINGS VALLEY PIONEER
AKA: 1. I.O.O.F.

D   4.46   2   Circa 1850   T10S R6W   S28
Located 1.3 miles south of Kings Valley Church and School on OR. Hwy. 223. Turn right (west) on a dirt road for 0.25 of a mile to the cemetery. This is 0.2 of a mile north of the junction with Hoskins Road. 1850 was the earliest death date found on a monument. On the Charles Allen D.L.C. #42, OC #2766, tax lot #200. {20 July 1991} (Kings Valley 1984 USGS Quad. map.)

LOBSTER VALLEY
AKA: 1. HENDRIX--
        LOBSTER VALLEY
     2. HENDRIX
        MEMORIAL
        GARDEN,
        CHARLES

A   1   2   Circa 1917   T15S R8W   S4
Located southwest of Alsea. At the south end of the Alsea-Deadwood Highway turn right onto Lobster Valley Road and go a short distance. Just before reaching the Church of Christ on the left, there is a road to the right up the hill to the cemetery, which is on tax lot #101. The Hendrix stone, 30 July 1906, is a reburial. Not to be confused with the Lone Fir Cemetery which is also sometimes referred to as Lobster Valley, and is about 3 miles west of here. (Digger Mountain 1984 USGS Quad. map.)

LOCKE
AKA: 1. LEWISBURG

D   3.2   2   1846   T11S R5W   S12
Located about 4.5 miles north of Corvallis on OR. Hwy. 99W to Lewisburg. Turn left (west) onto Lewisburg Avenue and go 0.3 of a mile and then turn left (south) again for 0.2 of a mile, up a steep hill to the cemetery. On A. N. Locke D.L.C. #41, OC #171, tax lot #2000. Locke deeded the cemetery 21 August 1855. {27 June 1991} (Lewisburg 1970-86 USGS Quad. map.)

LONE FIR
AKA: 1. LOBSTER
        VALLEY OLD
     2. LONE PINE

B   1.72   2   Circa 1891   T15S R8W   S6
Not to be confused with the other cemetery known as Lobster Valley. This cemetery is on the right (north) side of Lobster Valley Road, about 3 miles west of the south end of Alsea-Deadwood Highway and less than a mile

Name of Cemetery and also known as	Number of burials	Acres	Condition	Date started or earliest known burial	Township	Range	Section

from the junction with Preacher Creek Road. The cemetery is up the hill and not visible from the county road. Established on the Sapp Family Homestead, tax lot #400. There were 85 interments as of October 1988. (Digger Mountain 1984 USGS Quad. map.)

MAYS-STROUTS
AKA: 1. MAYS
2. STROUTS

B 0.5 2 Circa 1860 T11S R7W S6
The cemetery is about a 0.75 of a mile northwest of Summit and off the right (north) side of the Eddyville-Blodgett Highway. The access road is about 200 feet west of the railroad trestle. The cemetery is on top of a knoll and not visible from the highway, tax lot #200. There were an estimated 50-100 known burials as of November 1984. (Summit 1984 USGS Quad. map.)

McBEE FAMILY
AKA: 1. BIG BUTTE

A 0.01 3 1865 & 1893 T13S R5W S23
Located about 6 miles south of Corvallis on the east side of OR. Hwy. 99W. The 2 marked graves of William and Elizabeth McBee are on top of the higher of the 2 Wagner (formerly Winkle) Buttes. The Winkle and Irwin Cemeteries are close by. On the Isaac W. Winkle D.L.C. #47, OC #3233, tax lot #200. NOTE: This site is on private property. (Greenberry 1969-75 USGS Quad. map.)

MONROE

C 5.41 2 Circa 1850 T14S R5W S28
Located west off of OR. Hwy. 99W, about 0.75 of a mile north of downtown Monroe, tax lot #300. {11 October 1991} (Monroe 1969-75 USGS Quad. map.)

MT. UNION
AKA: 1. MOUNTAIN VIEW
2. NEWTON
3. SHIPLEY

D 68.16 2 1852 T12S R5W S7
This is the principal cemetery of Philomath. Leave Philomath Boulevard (U.S. Hwy. 20/ OR. Hwy. 34) and go south on 53rd Street, past the Country Club Drive intersection. Leave 53rd Street and turn right onto Plymouth Drive and go west 1.2 miles towards Philomath. The cemetery is visible on the right, up the hill off of Plymouth Drive at Mt. Union Avenue. This cemetery was established by Reuben Shipley, a landowner

Name of Cemetery and also known as	Number of burials	Acres	Condition	Date started or earliest known burial	Township	Range	Section

here. The cemetery was deeded to the county in 1861. On the Charles Bales D.L.C. #53, OC #839, tax lot #900. NOTE: The actual burial area of Mt. Union is only 2 or 3 acres. {9 June 1991} (Corvallis 1969-86 USGS Quad. map.)

NIBLER, WILLIAM J.

A   0.01 1   26 Mar 1990 ?   ?   ?
William J. "Jerry" Nibler is buried near Beldon Creek. NOTE: This site is on private property. No other information was given in the report. There is no Beldon Creek listed in Oregon by USGS.

OAK LAWN MEMORIAL PARK
AKA: 1. BENTON
     2. OAKRIDGE

E   35   1   1935   T12S R5W   S10
Located in Corvallis on Southwest Whiteside Drive. It is on the James A. Bennett D.L.C. #45, OC #847. The secondary name Oakridge must not be confused with Oak Ridge Cemetery to the south, see that article. {12 July 1991} (Corvallis 1969-86 USGS Quad. map.)

OAK RIDGE
AKA: 1. OAKRIDGE
        PRESBYTERIAN
        CHURCH

B   0.86 2   Circa 1880   T13S R5W   S6
Located on the east side of Bellfountain Road, about 0.2 of a mile north of Llewellyn Road junction. The earliest death date found on a monument was 1881, the latest was 1935. There are about 50 burials. The Oak Ridge Presbyterian Church was situated on the north side of the cemetery from 1878 to 1938. This cemetery is located on tax lot #1500. NOTE: This site is on private property. {24 June 1993} (Greenberry 1969-75 USGS Quad. map.)

PALESTINE
AKA: 1. NORTH
        PALESTINE
     2. PALESTINE
        MEMORIAL
        CHURCH

C   3.12 2   1879   T10S R4W   S22
Located on Northwest Palestine Avenue about 0.75 of a mile east of Independence Highway (a county road). The North Palestine Baptist church is no longer used as a church and is next to the cemetery. The cemetery was donated by Tolbert Carter in 1884, on the Tolbert Carter D.L.C. #45, OC #4058, tax lot #2000. The earliest death date found on a monument was 1879. {28 August 1989} (Lewisburg 1970-86 USGS Quad. map.)

Name of Cemetery and also known as	Number of burials	Acres	Condition	Date started or earliest known burial	Township	Range	Section

PHILOMATH [OLD]

A ? 7 1852-1853 T12S R6W S12

There were about a dozen burials at the top of the hill at "B" and North Streets; now known as 9th and Pioneer Streets, respectively. The burials were reputedly near the E. B. Harris house. The United Brethren purchased the cemetery as part of the grounds for Philomath College. The burial grounds remained uncultivated as late as the 1930's or early 1940's. We do not know if any or all of the burials have or have not been moved, at this writing. On the David Henderson D.L.C. #46, OC #3063. {15 September 1993} (Not shown on Corvallis 1969-86 USGS Quad. map.)

PLEASANT VALLEY

C 4.8 2 1854 T12S R6W S21

Located just west of Philomath on U.S. Hwy. 20 is the junction with the Alsea Highway (OR. Hwy. 34). Take the Alsea Highway and drive 3 miles. Then take the short unmarked driveway on the right off of OR. Hwy. 34 to a knoll and the cemetery, which is not visible from the highway. Earliest dated stone is 1856. On the John and Charity Ann Rexford D.L.C., OC #4105, tax lot #500. {6 August 1993} (Wren 1984 USGS Quad. map.)

POWELL FAMILY
AKA: 1. HOMEPLACE

A 0.25 3 Circa 1880 T13S R6W S3

Located on a private drive west from the west end of Llewellyn Road. This cemetery is on a knoll in a Douglas fir forest. There are no gravestones, only some temporary markers. On the Levi E. Penland D.L.C. #47, OC #4997, tax lot #100: 11 known burials 1985. NOTE: This site is on private property. (Flat Mountain 1984 USGS Quad. map.)

REEVES FAMILY
AKA: 1. EDWARDS

A 0.25 3 Circa 1849 T14S R5W S7

Located about 2 miles northeast of Bellfountain, and north off of McFarland Road at a point about 0.8 of a mile northeast of the intersection of McFarland and Dawson Roads. The cemetery is on a knoll at the foot of a larger hill, is crowned with fir trees and surrounded by small Christmas trees. On the Thomas Reeves D.L.C. #40, OC

Name of Cemetery and also known as	Number of burials	Acres	Condition	Date started or earliest known burial	Township	Range	Section

#190, tax lot #400, 15 marked graves and at least 4 or 5 unmarked burials. This cemetery was superseded by the Bellfountain Cemetery. NOTE: This site is on private property. {4 September 1992} (Monroe 1969-75 USGS Quad. map.)

RIDDERS PIONEER
AKA: 1. RIDDER

A   0.21   2   Circa 1880   T10S R4W   S9
Located on the west side of Independence Highway (a county road), about 0.5 of a mile north of the Spring Hill Road junction and 0.1 of a mile south of the Polk County Line. Dedicated and platted in 1904: on the Croghan Rhodes D.L.C. #68, OC #3141, tax lot #200. {28 August 1989} (Lewisburg 1970-86 USGS Quad. map.)

ROBINSON FAMILY

A   0.01   4   1869 & 1885 T11S R5W   S10
Located on the Southwest 1/4 of Section 10, northwest of Corvallis via Belhaven Drive. The burials are to the east of 5392 Belhaven Drive on a knoll in the Huntington subdivisions. The graves of Benaiah and Jane Robinson are on the Benaiah Robinson D.L.C., OC #2924, tax lot #1400. NOTE: This site is on private property. (Not shown on Corvallis 1969-86 or Airlie South 1984 USGS Quad. maps.)

ST. MARY'S CATHOLIC

C   2.5   1   1873   T11S R5W   S27
Located in Corvallis, at 4300 Witham Hill Road at the intersection with Grant Street. Corvallis I.O.O.F. Cemetery is nearby. There were 3 burials 1866-1867 on the grounds before the cemetery was purchased. Later, some 1863-1867 burials were reburied here. On the Joseph P. Friedley D.L.C. #62, OC #1025. {1 June 1991} (Corvallis 1969-86 USGS Quad. map.)

ST. ROSE CATHOLIC

B   2.09   2   Circa 1885   T14S R5W   S32
Located on Coon Road about 0.8 of a mile west and southwest of Monroe, on tax lot #1100, with about 100 burials as of February 1984. {11 October 1991} (Monroe Quad. 1969-75 USGS map.)

43

Name of Cemetery and also known as	Number of burials	Acres	Condition	Date started or earliest known burial	Township	Range	Section

SMITH, JOSEPH
AKA: 1. SHEARER

A   ?   6   ?   T10S R5W   S9

Located in the Northeast 1/4 of the Northeast 1/4 of Section 9. This cemetery, now gone, was apparently along the right (northeasterly) side of Tampico Road, going north from Adair Village and only 300 feet short of the Polk County line. On 29 September 1942, 4 bodies were removed; 3 to Harmony Cemetery, and 1 to Willamina Cemetery. This area had been bought by the U. S. Government for the Camp Adair Military base. The site was on the Green B. Smith D.L.C. #53, OC #2322. (Not shown on the Airlie South 1984 USGS Quad. map.)

SUMMIT

C   0.76   2   Circa 1870   T11S R7W   S8

Leave U.S. Hwy. 20 at Blodgett onto the Summit Highway, also known as the Eddyville-Blodgett Highway. Drive 3.9 miles on Summit Highway to Burtonwood Drive on the right (east). There is another sign at this junction which names the Summit Cemetery, located on tax lot #1000. The community of Summit is about 0.9 of a mile further on. The earliest dated monument in this cemetery was 1874. {18 April 1994} (Summit 1984 USGS Quad. map.)

UNKNOWN

A   0.01   ?   ?   ?   R5W   ?

"Just outside the State Forestry Building." This could be in the McDonald State Forest and is apparently somewhere along Sulphur Springs Road, which goes northwest off of Northwest Lewisburg Avenue. (Not shown on Airlie South 1984 USGS Quad. map.)

VALHALLA MEMORIAL PARK

?   ?   7   1932-1940'S   T12S R5W   S4

This cemetery was platted in February of 1932. It was located on the north side of Philomath Boulevard (U.S. Hwy. 20), on the east side of 53rd Street and the south side of Hillview Avenue. The cemetery was sold for suburban development and the graves removed to Oak Lawn Memorial Park in the 1940's. Blueberry Drive is entirely within

Name of Cemetery and also known as	Number of burials	Acres	Condition	Date started or earliest known burial	Township	Range	Section

the onetime cemetery, which is on the Albert G. Hovey D.L.C. #43, OC #835. (Not shown on Corvallis 1969-86 USGS Quad. map.)

WILLIAMSON FAMILY

A ? 3 ?   T10S R4W   S17
An abandoned family burial ground on the former Camp Adair Military base and what is now the E. E. Wilson Game Management Area. It is in the woods north of Camp Adair Road. (Not shown on Lewisburg 1970-86 USGS Quad. map.)

WILSON FAMILY

A 0.01 ? 1912-1938 T11S R7W   S34
Southwest of Blodgett on the road to Thompson Lake, located on land owned by the Oregon Department of Forestry. Leave Blodgett going west on Blodgett Road (old U.S. Hwy. 20) for 0.32 of a mile, to the school. Turn left (south) onto Tumtum Road and drive another 1.6 miles to a road junction to the right. Turn right (westerly) and go about 0.15 of a mile down to a creek bottom. The grave is on the right. Captain Frederick Bacon Powell Wilson, his wife Carrie and baby are buried here. ("Grave" is marked on Marys Peak 1984 USGS Quad. map.)

WINKLE FAMILY
  AKA: 1. SMALL BUTTE

A ? 3 1867-1875 T13S R5W   S22
Located about 6 miles south of Corvallis on the east side of OR. Hwy. 99W, almost on top of the northwest side of the smaller of the 2 Wagner (formerly Winkle) Buttes. There are 6 marked graves of the Winkle family; on the Isaac Winkle D.L.C. #47, OC #3233, tax lot #101. The Irwin and McBee Cemeteries are nearby. NOTE: This site is on private property. (Greenberry 1969-75 USGS Quad. map.)

WREN
  AKA: 1. WRENN
        MEMORIAL,
        GEORGE P.

C 2.52 4 1857-1970's T11S R6W   S28
Located on the west side of OR. Hwy. 223, which separates the cemetery from the community church. George P. Wrenn deeded 5 acres for a cemetery and United Brethren Church. The town of Wren (minus the final "n") was named for him. 52 graves were

Name of Cemetery and also known as	Number of burials	Acres	Condition	Date started or earliest known burial	Township	Range	Section

located in 1973, and there are perhaps 100 in all: on the George P. Wrenn D.L.C. #54, OC #4594, tax lot #1200. (Wren 1984 USGS Quad. map.)

ZION LUTHERAN   C   1.5   2   1910   T11S R5W   S23
Located north of Corvallis to the left (west) off of Highland Way, and just north of intersection with Conifer Boulevard: on the Heman Lewis D.L.C. #47, OC #177. {1 June 1991} (Corvallis 1969-86 USGS Quad. map.)

Blodgett
Dean H, Byrd (1994)

ALEXANDER D.L.C., JOSEPH see **CRYSTAL LAKE**

	BENTON CO.	T12S	R5W	S11

ALLEN D.L.C., CHARLES see **KINGS VALLEY PIONEER**

	BENTON CO.	T10S	R6W	S28
ALPINE	BENTON CO.	T14S	R6W	S24
ALSEA	BENTON CO.	T14S	R8W	S1
ARMSTRONG	BENTON CO.	T12S	R5W	S31

BALES D.L.C., CHARLES see **MT. UNION**

	BENTON CO.	T12S	R5W	S7

BARKER D.L.C., CLEMENT see **EMERICK FAMILY**

	BENTON CO.	T12S	R6W	S27

BARNUM LODGE #7 see **I.O.O.F. [CORVALLIS]**

	BENTON CO.	T11S	R5W	S28

BELKNAP D.L.C., JESSE see **ALPINE**

	BENTON CO.	T14S	R6W	S24

BELKNAP D.L.C., JONAS see **BELLFOUNTAIN**

	BENTON CO	T14S	R5W	S7
BELLFOUNTAIN	BENTON CO.	T14S	R5W	S7

BENNETT D.L.C., JAMES A. see **OAK LAWN MEMORIAL PARK**

	BENTON CO.	T12S	R5W	S10
BENTON	BENTON CO.	T12S	R5W	S10

BENTON see **OAK LAWN MEMORIAL PARK**

	BENTON CO.	T12S	R5W	S10
BENTON COUNTY POOR FARM	BENTON CO.	T14S	R6W	?
BIG BUTTE see **McBEE FAMILY**	BENTON CO.	T13S	R5W	S23
BLODGETT	BENTON CO.	T11S	R7W	S23

BLODGETT D.L.C., WILLIAM see **BLODGETT**

	BENTON CO.	T11S	R7W	S23
BLODGETT FAMILY see **BLODGETT**	BENTON CO.	T11S	R7W	S23

CARTER D.L.C., TOLBERT see **PALESTINE**

	BENTON CO.	T10S	R4W	S22
CARTER, TOLBERT see **PALESTINE**	BENTON CO.	T10S	R4W	S22
CRYSTAL LAKE	BENTON CO.	T12S	R5W	S11

CUTSFORTH, DELBERT LEE see **CUTSFORTH FAMILY**

	BENTON CO.	?	?	?
CUTSFORTH FAMILY	BENTON CO.	?	?	?

CUTSFORTH, FLORENCE M. see **CUTSFORTH FAMILY**

	BENTON CO.	?	?	?

CUTSFORTH RANCH see **CUTSFORTH FAMILY**

	BENTON CO.	?	?	?

DAR MAKKAH see **ISLAMIC CEMETERY OF OREGON**

	BENTON CO.	T12S	R5W	S5
DAVIDSON	BENTON CO.	T12S	R7W	S8

DAVIDSON HOMESTEAD, HARRISON see **DAVIDSON**

	BENTON CO.	T12S	R7W	S8

DAVIS FAMILY, DANIEL D. see **FOLKS, B. A.**

	BENTON CO.	T10S	R5W	S10

DIXON, WILLIAM see **HENDERSON FAMILY**

	BENTON CO.	T12S	R6W	S36

DOW D.L.C., WILLIAM W. see **DOW, OSCAR A.**

	BENTON CO.	T13S	R5W	S28
DOW, OSCAR A.	BENTON CO.	T13S	R5W	S28

DOW, WILLIAM see **DOW, OSCAR A.**	BENTON CO.	T13S	R5W	S28
DUNN FAMILY	BENTON CO.	T13S	R6W	S11
EDWARDS see **REEVES**	BENTON CO.	T14S	R5W	S7
EMERICK AND ALLIED FAMILIES see **EMERICK FAMILY**				
	BENTON CO.	T12S	R6W	S27
EMERICK FAMILY	BENTON CO.	T12S	R6W	S27
FIR GROVE see **IRWIN FAMILY**	BENTON CO.	T13S	R5W	S22
FOLKS, B. A.	BENTON CO.	T10S	R5W	S10
FRIEDLEY D.L.C., JOSEPH P. see **ST. MARY'S CATHOLIC**				
	BENTON CO.	T11S	R5W	S27
GINGLES	BENTON CO.	T10S	R4W	S15
GINGLES D.L.C., JAMES see **GINGLES**				
	BENTON CO.	T10S	R4W	S15
GOODMAN see **ALPINE**	BENTON CO	T14S	R6W	S24
HANSON, ANDREW see **BENTON COUNTY POOR FARM**				
	BENTON CO.	T14S	R6W	?
HARRIS HOUSE, E. B. see **PHILOMATH [OLD]**				
	BENTON CO.	T12S	R6W	S12
HAVEN OF ST. JOHN MAUSOLEUM see **CRYSTAL LAKE**				
	BENTON CO.	T12S	R5W	S11
HENDERSON D.L.C., DAVID see **PHILOMATH [OLD]**				
	BENTON CO.	T12S	R6W	S12
HENDERSON FAMILY	BENTON CO.	T12S	R6W	S36
HENDRIX-LOBSTER VALLEY see **LOBSTER VALLEY**				
	BENTON CO.	T15S	R8W	S4
HENDRIX MEMORIAL GARDEN, CHARLES see **LOBSTER VALLEY**				
	BENTON CO	T15S	R8W	S4
HERBERT, ADAM see **HERBERT PIONEER**				
	BENTON CO.	T13S	R5W	S17
HERBERT D.L.C., ELIZABETH see **HERBERT PIONEER**				
	BENTON CO.	T13S	R5W	S17
HERBERT, ELIZABETH see **HERBERT PIONEER**				
	BENTON CO.	T13S	R5W	S17
HERBERT FAMILY see **HERBERT PIONEER**				
	BENTON CO.	T13S	R5W	S17
HERBERT, JAMES see **HERBERT PIONEER**				
	BENTON CO.	T13S	R5W	S17
HERBERT, JOSHUA see **HERBERT PIONEER**				
	BENTON CO.	T13S	R5W	S17
HERBERT PIONEER	BENTON CO.	T13S	R5W	S17
HOMEPLACE see **POWELL FAMILY**	BENTON CO.	T13S	R6W	S3
HORN, COLUMBIA	BENTON CO.	?	?	?
HORN, J. M. see **HORN, COLUMBIA**	BENTON CO.	?	?	?
HORN, M. J. see **HORN, COLUMBIA**	BENTON CO.	?	?	?
HOVEY D.L.C., ALBERT G. see **VALHALLA MEMORIAL PARK**				
	BENTON CO.	T12S	R5W	S4
I.O.O.F. see **KINGS VALLEY PIONEER**				
	BENTON CO.	T10S	R6W	S28
I.O.O.F. [CORVALLIS]	BENTON CO.	T11S	R5W	S28
IRWIN D.L.C., RICHARD see **IRWIN FAMILY**				
	BENTON CO.	T13S	R5W	S22
IRWIN FAMILY	BENTON CO.	T13S	R5W	S22

ISLAMIC CEMETERY OF OREGON	BENTON CO.	T12S	R5W	S5
KING D.L.C., ISAAC see **KING FAMILY, ISAAC**				
	BENTON CO.	T10S	R6W	S28
KING FAMILY, ISAAC	BENTON CO.	T10S	R6W	S28
KINGS VALLEY PIONEER	BENTON CO.	T10S	R6W	S28
LEWIS D.L.C., HEMAN see **ZION LUTHERAN**				
	BENTON CO.	T11S	R5W	S23
LEWISBURG see **LOCKE**	BENTON CO.	T11S	R5W	S12
LOBSTER VALLEY	BENTON CO.	T15S	R8W	S4
LOBSTER VALLEY OLD see **LONE FIR**				
	BENTON CO.	T15S	R8W	S6
LOCKE	BENTON CO.	T11S	R5W	S12
LOCKE D.L.C., A. N. see **LOCKE**	BENTON CO.	T11S	R5W	S12
LONE FIR	BENTON CO.	T15S	R8W	S6
LONE PINE see **LONE FIR**	BENTON CO.	T15S	R8W	S6
MARTIN'S D.L.C., JACOB AND EVALINE see **ARMSTRONG**				
	BENTON CO.	T12S	R5W	S31
MASONIC LODGE #14 see **CRYSTAL LAKE**				
	BENTON CO.	T12S	R5W	S11
MAYS see **MAYS-STROUTS**	BENTON CO.	T11S	R7W	S6
MAYS-STROUTS	BENTON CO.	T11S	R7W	S6
McBEE, ELIZABETH see **McBEE FAMILY**				
	BENTON CO.	T13S	R5W	S23
McBEE FAMILY	BENTON CO.	T13S	R5W	S23
McBEE, WILLIAM see **McBEE FAMILY**	BENTON CO.	T13S	R5W	S23
MONROE	BENTON CO.	T14S	R5W	S28
MT. UNION	BENTON CO.	T12S	R5W	S7
MOUNTAIN VIEW see **MT. UNION**	BENTON CO.	T12S	R5W	S7
MUSLIM see **ISLAMIC CEMETERY OF OREGON**				
	BENTON CO.	T12S	R5W	S5
NEWTON see **MT. UNION**	BENTON CO.	T12S	R5W	S7
NEWTON D.L.C., ABIATHAR see **ISLAMIC CEMETERY OF OREGON**				
	BENTON CO.	T12S	R5W	S5
NIBLER, WILLIAM J.	BENTON CO.	?	?	?
NORTH PALESTINE see **PALESTINE**	BENTON CO.	T10S	R4W	S22
OAK LAWN MEMORIAL PARK	BENTON CO.	T12S	R5W	S10
OAK LAWN MEMORIAL PARK see **BENTON**				
	BENTON CO.	T12S	R5W	S10
OAKLAWN MEMORIAL PARK see **BENTON**				
	BENTON CO.	T12S	R5W	S10
OAK RIDGE	BENTON CO.	T13S	R5W	S6
OAKRIDGE see **OAKLAWN MEMORIAL PARK**				
	BENTON CO.	T12S	R5W	S10
OAKRIDGE PRESBYTERIAN CHURCH see **OAK RIDGE**				
	BENTON CO.	T13S	R5W	S6
ODD FELLOWS CEMETERY OF CORVALLIS see **I.O.O.F. [CORVALLIS]**				
	BENTON CO.	T11S	R5W	S28
PALESTINE	BENTON CO.	T10S	R4W	S22
PALESTINE MEMORIAL CHURCH see **PALESTINE**				
	BENTON CO.	T10S	R4W	S22
PEAK see **DAVIDSON**	BENTON CO.	T12S	R7W	S8

PENLAND D.L.C., LEVI E. see **POWELL FAMILY**				
	BENTON CO.	T13S	R6W	S3
PHILOMATH [OLD]	BENTON CO.	T12S	R6W	S12
PLEASANT VALLEY	BENTON CO.	T12S	R6W	S21
POWELL FAMILY	BENTON CO.	T13S	R6W	S3
REEVES D.L.C., THOMAS see **REEVES FAMILY**				
	BENTON CO.	T14S	R5W	S7
REEVES FAMILY	BENTON CO.	T14S	R5W	S7
REXFORD D.L.C., JOHN AND CHARITY ANN see **PLEASANT VALLEY**				
	BENTON CO.	T12S	R6W	S21
RHODES D.L.C., CROGHAN see **RIDDERS PIONEER**				
	BENTON CO	T10S	R4W	S9
RIDDER see **RIDDERS PIONEER**	BENTON CO.	T10S	R4W	S9
RIDDERS POINEER	BENTON CO.	T10S	R4W	S9
ROBINSON, BENAIAH see **ROBINSON FAMILY**				
	BENTON CO.	T11S	R5W	S10
ROBINSON D.L.C., BENAIAH see **ROBINSON FAMILY**				
	BENTON CO.	T11S	R5W	S10
ROBINSON FAMILY	BENTON CO.	T11S	R5W	S10
ROBINSON, JANE see **ROBINSON FAMILY**				
	BENTON CO.	T11S	R5W	S10
ST. MARY'S CATHOLIC	BENTON CO.	T11S	R5W	S27
ST. ROSE CATHOLIC	BENTON CO.	T14S	R5W	S32
SAPP FAMILY HOMESTEAD see **LONE FIR**				
	BENTON CO.	T15S	R8W	S6
SCHOOL DISTRICT #1 see **GINGLES**	BENTON CO.	T10S	R4W	S15
SHEARER see **SMITH, JOSEPH**	BENTON CO.	T10S	R5W	S9
SHEPHARD, MATTIE see **HORN, COLUMBIA**				
	BENTON CO.	?	?	?
SHIPLEY see **MT. UNION**	BENTON CO	T12S	R5W	S7
SHIPLEY, REUBEN see **MT. UNION**	BENTON CO	T12S	R5W	S7
SIMPSONS CHAPEL see **ALPINE**	BENTON CO.	T14S	R6W	S24
SMALL BUTTE see **WINKLE FAMILY**	BENTON COUNTY	T13S	R5W	S22
SMITH D.L.C., GREEN B. see **SMITH, JOSEPH**				
	BENTON CO.	T10S	R5W	S9
SMITH, JOSEPH	BENTON CO.	T10S	R5W	S9
STARK, ELIZA JANE see **DOW, OSCAR A.**				
	BENTON CO.	T13S	R5W	S28
STROUTS see **MAYS-STROUTS**	BENTON CO.	T11S	R7W	S6
SUMMIT	BENTON CO.	T11S	R7W	S8
UNKNOWN	BENTON CO.	?	R5W	?
VALHALLA MEMORIAL PARK	BENTON CO.	T12S	R5W	S4
WHITE D.L.C., SANFORD see **HENDERSON FAMILY**				
	BENTON CO.	T12S	R6W	S36
WILKINSON D.L.C., WILLIAM see **DUNN FAMILY**				
	BENTON CO.	T13S	R6W	S11
WILKINSON-DUNN FAMILIES see **DUNN FAMILY**				
	BENTON CO.	T13S	R6W	S11
WILLIAMSON FAMILY	BENTON CO.	T10S	R4W	S17
WILSON, BABY see **WILSON FAMILY**	BENTON CO.	T11S	R7W	S34
WILSON, CAPTAIN FREDERICK BACON POWELL see **WILSON FAMILY**				
	BENTON CO.	T11S	R7W	S34

WILSON, CARRIE see **WILSON FAMILY**				
	BENTON CO.	T11S	R7W	S34
WILSON FAMILY	BENTON CO.	T11S	R7W	S34
WILSON GAME MANAGEMENT AREA, E. E. see **WILLLIAMSON FAMILY**				
	BENTON CO.	T10S	R4W	S17
WINKLE D.L.C., ISAAC W. see **McBEE FAMILY**				
	BENTON CO.	T13S	R5W	S23
WINKLE D.L.C., ISAAC W. see **WINKLE FAMILY**				
	BENTON CO.	T13S	R5W	S22
WINKLE FAMILY	BENTON CO.	T13S	R5W	S22
WITHAM D.L.C., ALFRED M. see **I.O.O.F. [CORVALLIS]**				
	BENTON CO.	T11S	R5W	S28
WREN	BENTON CO.	T11S	R6W	S28
WRENN D.L.C., GEORGE P. see **WREN**				
	BENTON CO.	T11S	R6W	S28
WRENN, GEORGE P. see **WREN**	BENTON CO.	T11S	R6W	S28
WRENN MEMORIAL, GEORGE P. see **WREN**				
	BENTON CO.	T11S	R6W	S28
ZION LUTHERAN	BENTON CO.	T11S	R5W	S23

Benton County

Crystal Lake
Dean H, Byrd (1991)

Bellfountain
Dean H. Byrd (1990)

Crystal Lake
Dean H. Byrd (1991)

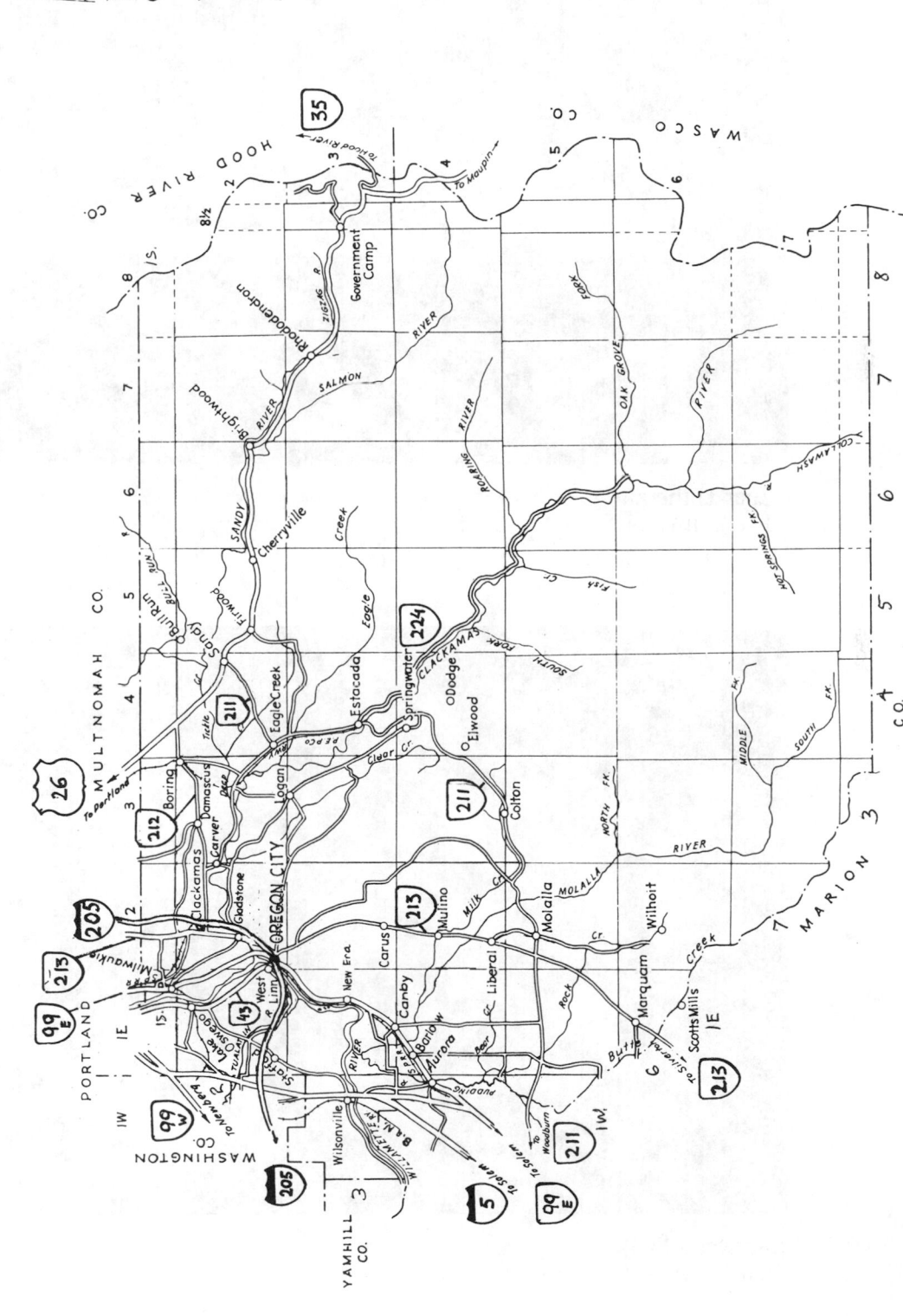

CLACKAMAS COUNTY
Scale

Clackamas County

Zoar Lutheran
Janice M. Healy (1992)

Oswego Pioneer
Dean H. Byrd (1990)

Area: 1,879 square miles
Population (1998): 334,732
County seat: Oregon City, Population: 20,410
County established: 5 July 1843

Starting in 1842 what is now Clackamas County received the first wagon trains of immigrants from the mid-west. Oregon City, located at the falls of the Willamette River had for centuries been an Indian trading post. The town of Oregon City was laid out in 1842. It was the territorial capital from 1844-1851, when the capital was moved to Salem. The first organized cemeteries were in or near Oregon City; 1840 Canemah; 1847 three at Oregon City itself and Lewthwaite, 1850 Milwaukie a mile or so downstream. Immigrants rapidly settled to establish farmlands and by 1851 there were at least 9 additional public cemeteries.

Pleasant View [West]
Dean H. Byrd (1988)

Springwater, Stanley R. Clarke
Janice M. Healy (1991)

Oswego Pioneer
Dean H. Byrd (1990)

Name of Cemetery and also known as	Number of burials	Acres	Condition	Date started or earliest known burial	Township	Range	Section

ADAMS

D 3.5 2 Circa 1850 T5S R2E S22

This is the principal cemetery for the town of Molalla. At the east end of town where OR. Hwy. 211 turns left, leave the highway, turning right (south) on Mathas Road. This is County Road #52006 and you can stay on #52006 directly to the cemetery, despite the sharp changes of directions and names. After about 1.1 miles; #52006 turns hard left and is named Claim Road. At 1.75 miles there is Adams Road from the left, but turn right and drive to the cemetery, 2.5 miles from OR. Hwy. 211. A plaque on the entrance gate says: Established 1865. {18 January 1992} (Molalla 1954-85 and Wilhoit 1955-85 USGS Quad. maps.)

BAKER PRAIRIE
AKA: 1. BAKERS
         PRAIRIE
      2. CANBY
         PIONEER
      3. OLD CANBY

D 1 2 1863-1928 T3S R1E S33

Leave OR. Hwy. 99E in Canby at the signalized intersection with Grant Street. Turn northerly, crossing the railway tracks, for a total of 8 blocks from the highway. Then turn left (westerly) onto Northwest Knights Bridge Road and go a short distance to the cemetery on the left (south). Older than the town of Canby, Baker Prairie was completely full by June 1955, except for 3 or 4 plots. It has been superseded by Zion Memorial Park as the principal Protestant burial ground. {11 October 1989} (Canby 1961-85 USGS Quad. map.)

BARLOW PIONEER
AKA: 1. BARLOW

B 0.4 1 1856 T4S R1E S6

Leave OR. Hwy. 99E at the signalized intersection with Barlow Road less than 2 miles southwest of downtown Canby. Turn north onto Barlow Road, passing the town of Barlow and at the cemetery is on the left at 0.4 of a mile from OR. Hwy. 99E. {31 Oct. 1989} (Canby 1961-85 USGS Quad. map.)

BARTON

? 0.94 ? ? T2S R3E S14

Reportedly located 0.25 of a mile west of Barton on the north side of OR. Hwy. 224. NOTE: A search by the compilers failed to find this cemetery, 10 Febuary 1991. (Not shown on Damascus 1961-84 USGS Quad. map.)

Name of Cemetery and also known as	Number of burials	Acres	Condition	Date started or earliest known burial	Township	Range	Section

BATTY FAMILY

A ? ? 1874 T2S R3E ?

Perhaps located in Section 36, north of Estacada and northwest of Currinsville. The cemetery is supposedly just southeast of the confluence of Eagle Creek with the Clackamas River. This is near Dowty Road and Bonnie Lure State Park. NOTE: A search party from the Committee on 10 February 1991 could not locate this cemetery. (Not shown on Redland 1961-85 USGS Quad. map.)

BATY FAMILY
AKA: 1. BEATTIE

A ? 5 1850 T5S R2E S14

Located off of Wright Road near the intersection with Fernwood Road: On the Andrew J. Baty D.L.C. #54, OC #4428. NOTE: This site is on private property. (Not shown on Molalla 1954-85 USGS Quad. maps.)

BEAR CREEK
AKA: 1. MOSHBERGER

B 0.5 2 1859 T5S R1E S2

Located about 3.5 miles west of Molalla on OR. Hwy. 211. Turn north off of OR. Hwy. 211 at Milepost 9.1 at the Dryland Road intersection. Go north 1.2 miles on Dryland Road to the junction of Toliver Road. The cemetery is at the junction. Access is by a set of steps on the Toliver Road side. {19 October 1988} (Yoder 1955-85 USGS Quad. map.)

BEAVERCREEK MEMORIAL

C 1.8 1 1879 T3S R2E S26

Leave OR. Hwy. 213 in Oregon City at Milepost 3 and turn onto Beavercreek Road. Go 3.7 miles on Beavercreek Road to the community of Beavercreek and continue ahead south onto Kamrath Road. The cemetery is on the left (east) side of Kamrath Road about 0.5 of a mile from Beavercreek. {Spring 1991} (Oregon City 1961-85 USGS Quad. map.)

BIRD, ROBERT

C 2 2 1855 T2S R1E S31

Located between Wilsonville and Lake Oswego. Stafford Road is the main road between these two cities. The cemetery is on Gage Road at its junction with Newland Road. Both of these two roads intersect Stafford Road from the right, when driving from Wilsonville

Name of Cemetery and also known as	Number of burials	Acres	Condition	Date started or earliest known burial	Township	Range	Section

towards Stafford community and Lake Oswego. NOTE: Robert Bird Cemetery directly adjoins the separate Stafford Baptist Church Cemetery. See that article. {7 December 1989} (Canby Quad. 1961-85 USGS Quad. map.)

BLOSSER
AKA: 1. AMISH
     2. BLASSER
     3. ERB
     4. MENNONITE
     5. MILLER

A 0.15 5 1882-1901 T4S R1W   S36
Take Meridian Road south from its intersection with Whiskey Hill Road (Ninety-One School is at the northeast corner). Go 0.17 of a mile on Meridian and turn right (west), onto a private driveway. The cemetery is on the right (north) of the driveway, just before it heads down to the Pudding River bottomlands. There are 15 known burials remaining and 5 have been known to be reburied in Zion Mennonite Cemetery. NOTE: This site is on private property. (Yoder 1955-85 USGS Quad. map.)

BONNEY
AKA: 1. CANYON CREEK
     2. DIX
     3. PUTZ

C 2 1 1882   T4S R3E   S35
Take OR. Hwy. 211 to Colton, and then 1.5 miles east of Colton, at Milepost 22.6, turn left (northeast) off of OR. Hwy. 211 onto Baurer Road. Drive uphill 0.3 of a mile to the cemetery on the left (west) side of Baurer Road, just beyond the junction with Girard Road. {21 January 1991} (Colton 1955-85 USGS Quad. map.)

BROUSSARD JR., ELDRIDGE J.

A 0.01 ? 7 Sep. 1991 T2S R5E   ?
Perhaps located in Section 23. The founder and leader of the Ecclesia Athletic Association, died of diabetes and is buried on the farm property of the Association near Sandy. (Not shown on Bull Run 1985 USGS Quad. map.)

CALLAHAN FAMILY

A ? ? ?   T5S R2E   S24
This cemetery is supposed to be on the south side of Callahan Road, just west of the intersection with Wright Road in the Dickey Prairie area: on the Clifton R. Callahan D.L.C. #50, OC #1130. (Not shown on Wilhoit 1955-85 USGS Quad. map.)

Name of Cemetery and also known as	Number of burials	Acres	Condition	Date started or earliest known burial	Township	Range	Section

CANEMAH

C 2.5 2 Circa 1840 T3S R1E S1
Canemah (accent on the second syllable) was an early community, now within Oregon City. The cemetery is outside of the present city limits. Leave OR. Hwy. 99E southerly, beyond the Falls Viewpoint, on any of the 4 block-long side streets going uphill. Use 3rd or 4th Avenues and Blanchard Street to reach 5th Avenue. There is a gate at the end of 5th Avenue. The cemetery road ahead can be walked, but the cemetery itself is usually locked shut. There are many burials, but only about 298 are known (1984). The only burial spaces left here are for some reserved plots. This is on the Absalom F. Hedges D.L.C. #40, OC #99. {Spring 1991} (Not shown on Canby 1961-85 USGS Quad. map.)

CARUS

D 2.75 1 1851 T3S R2E S27
The locale of Carus, with a school and a church, is at the crossroads of Carus Road and the Cascade Highway (OR. Hwy. 213) at Milepost 7.1, between Oregon City and Mulino. Go north towards Oregon City on OR. Hwy. 213 from Carus for 0.35 of a mile. Turn right (east) onto Kirk Road and go 0.9 of a mile to the cemetery. 518 monuments were noted in Febuary of 1961. {9 September 1991} (Oregon City 1961-85 USGS Quad. map.)

CASE, CHARLES LAFERTY

A 0.01 ? 23 Jan 1911 T2S R1E S36
Charles Laferty Case, born 14 January 1873, died 23 January 1911, was cremated. The ashes were placed under a tree in the yard of the family home at Oregon City and overlooking the Falls of the Willamette River. The site is supposedly on one of the streets leading off of the present OR. Hwy. 99E. This is from a June 1967 report. (Not shown on Oregon City 1961-85 USGS Quad. map.)

CASON, REBECCA

A 0.01 ? 1877 T2S R2E S20
Rebecca Cason, 1803-1877, wife of John Cason is buried on the grounds of the original house. The present address is 260 82nd Drive, Gladstone: at the intersection of 82nd

Name of Cemetery and also known as	Number of burials	Acres	Condition	Date started or earliest known burial	Township	Range	Section

Drive and Arlington Street, on the Fendall Cason D.L.C. #50, OC #92. NOTE: This site is on private property. (Not shown on Gladstone 1961-84 USGS Quad. map.)

CHASE BURIAL	A	0.01	5	?	T4S	R4E	?

Located near OR. Hwy. 211 south of Estacada, on the Perry Place. NOTE: It could be on any of 4 different D.L.C.'s. No other information was given in the report. (Not shown on Estacada 1961-85 USGS Quad. maps.)

CHERRYVILLE	B	2.3	3	1888	T2S	R6E	S30

Drive 6 miles east of Sandy on Mt. Hood Highway (U.S. Hwy. 26). Turn off to the left (north) from U.S. Hwy. 26 at Milepost 30.4 onto Southeast Cherryville Road. Drive 1.7 miles on Cherryville Road to a driveway, on the left (north), at 52235 Southeast Cherryville Road. NOTE: This cemetery is landlocked, so one must get permission from property owners to cross their land in order to get into the cemetery. {18 Febuary 1991} (Not shown on Wildcat Mtn. 1985 USGS Quad. map.)

CHRIST CHURCH PARISH	?	?	1	?	T2S	R1E	S10

Christ Church Parish - Episcopal maintains both a memorial garden and a columbarium for members of the congregation. Christ Church Parish is located at 1060 Chandler Road in Lake Oswego. This information has come from obituaries published in The Oregonian. (The church is shown on Lake Oswego 1961-84 USGS Quad. map)

CLACKAMAS	D	2	1	1850	T2S	R2E	S4

AKA: 1. CLACKAMAS PIONEER
2. MARSHFIELD
3. MATLOCK FAMILY

Located a mile north of the community of Clackamas. Drive north on 82nd Drive from the community; cross the viaduct over the I-205 Freeway and immediately turn right (north) onto Ambler Road. Drive another 0.25 of a mile and the cemetery is on the left. The old burial ground is now surrounded by the I-205 Freeway, 82nd Avenue (OR. Hwy. 213), Clackamas Highway (OR. Hwy. 224) and

Name of Cemetery and also known as	Number of burials	Acres	Condition	Date started or earliest known burial	Township	Range	Section

the Southern Pacific railway tracks: on the William T. Matlock D.L.C. #37, OC #1070. {Spring 1991}   (Gladstone 1961-84 USGS Quad. map.)

CLARKES PIONEER
AKA: 1. CLARKS
     2. RINGO

C 1   2   1861   T4S   R3E   S29
Located 11.5 miles southeast of Oregon City via South Beavercreek Road and about 1 mile south of Clarkes Four Corners on the right (west) side of Beavercreek Road. The cemetery is on a low ridgeback and features a long flight of steps. {18 Feb. 1991} (Colton 1955-85 USGS Quad. map.)

CLAUSEN, NICK

A   0.01   5   ?   T4S   R4E   ?
The lone grave of Nick Clausen is at the east end of Skinner Road. NOTE: This site is on private property. (Not shown on Elwood 1986 USGS Quad. map.)

CLIFFSIDE

C   2   1   1889   T2S   R5E   S7
Located 2 miles northeast of Sandy. Leave U.S. Hwy. 26 at Milepost 24.6 onto Ten Eyck Road, crossing the Sandy River on the Revenue Bridge at 1.9 miles. About 0.25 of a mile farther is the cemetery on the left (west) side of the road. There are about 150 graves here. {7 Febuary 1991} (Bull Run 1985 USGS Quad. map.)

COLTON LUTHERAN
AKA: 1. SWEDE

C   1   1   1912   T5S   R3E   S3
At the main intersection in Colton turn south off of OR. Hwy. 211 onto Wall Street South. Go 0.13 of a mile and then turn left (east) and proceed 0.15 of a mile to the cemetery. {21 January 1991} (Colton 1955-85 USGS Quad. map.)

COOK, RONALD PETER

?   ?   ?   29 Apr 1926 ?   ?   ?
Ronald Peter Cooke, the five day old son of T. H. Cooke of Illinois and Annie Keillor of Canada, was buried 29 April 1926 "On My Place" per Oregon Death Certificate #147. The undertaker was D. S. Webster. The death occurred 3 miles Northeast of Sandy, Oregon

Name of Cemetery and also known as	Number of burials	Acres	Condition	Date started or earliest known burial	Township	Range	Section

on 27 April 1926. The child was born 22 April 1926. The informant was Thomas H. Cooke. No further information is known by the compiler.

CRISTILLA PIONEER
AKA: 1. CHRISTILDA
2. DEARDORFF
FAMILY

A   0.5   2   1852-1932   T1S   R2E   S36

Leave Sunnyside Road just east of the town of Happy Valley onto Southeast 147th Avenue and go north on Southeast 147th Avenue: turn right (northeast) on Boy Scout Lodge Road. The cemetery is in the Scout camp on Scouter Mountain. The Deardorff family referred to Happy Valley as Cristilla Valley. In 1969 there were 23 known burials and 2 to 4 unknown burials: on the John M. Deardorff D.L.C. #63, OC #3172. NOTE: This is private property, you must get permission from the camp director. (Gladstone 1961-84 USGS Quad. map.)

CURRIN FAMILY
AKA: 1. CURRINSVILLE

A   0.5   1   1855   T3S   R4E   S8

Drive north from Estacada on Eagle Creek Road (old alignment of OR. Hwy. 211) to Currinsville. The cemetery is 0.2 of a mile north of Duuss Road on the left (west) side of Eagle Creek Road. The burials are on the site of the Currin cabin built in 1845: on the Hugh Currin D.L.C. #40, OC #4177. NOTE: This site is fenced and you must cross private property to get to it. {7 Febuary 1991} (Not shown on Estacada 1961-85 USGS Quad. map.)

CURRINSVILLE
AKA: 1. LONE OAK

?   1   11   ?   T3S   R4E   S7

Take the Clackamas Highway (OR. Hwy. 211), between Eagle Creek and Estacada, to the intersection of Heiple Road. Turn west onto Heiple Road and drive about 0.75 of a mile to where the cemetery was and which is now the Shady Oaks Airpark: on the George Currin D.L.C. #41, OC #4591. {7 Febuary 1991} (Not shown on Estacada 1961-85 USGS Quad. map. Clearly shown in the 1951 and 1966 Metsker Landownership Atlas.)

Name of Cemetery and also known as	Number of burials	Acres	Condition	Date started or earliest known burial	Township	Range	Section

CUTTING FAMILY

A ? 2 ?   T4S R2E   S36

Leave Molalla on OR. Hwy. 211 northeasterly toward Estacada. About one mile after crossing the Molalla River is the Four Corners Road intersection where OR. Hwy. 211 turns sharply to the right (east). Continue ahead on South Beavercreek Road very soon crossing Milk Creek and then going uphill. About 0.3 of a mile from Four Corners is a private road right (east) called South Hallbacka Lane. Turn onto this lane and go about 0.15 of a mile. The small cemetery is on the left (north) along the north line of the Charles Cutting D.L.C. #47, OC #3684 on Tax Lot #2401 and also on Savon Garden Tax Lot #109. There are graves of Charles and Abigail Cutting and of a baby. NOTE: This is on private property. The informant believes the Cutting family graves may also be the site of the Indian graves referred to as being somewhere near Molalla. See that article. (Not shown on Molalla 1954-85 USGS Quad. map.)

DAMASCUS PIONEER
AKA: 1. CHITWOOD
      2. DAMASCUS

C 3.1+ 2 1855   T2S R3E   S8

This cemetery is near the community of Damascus. It is located 0.25 of a mile west of the junction of Sunnyside Road with the Clackamas-Boring Highway (OR. Hwy. 212) and at the junction of OR. Hwy. 212 with Chitwood Road from the right (south). The cemetery is on your right about 100 feet east of the highway. {Spring 1991} (Damascus 1961-84 USGS Quad. map.)

DICKEY FAMILY
AKA: 1. DECKEY

A ? ? ?   T5S R2E   S23

Located in Dickey Prairie, southeast of Molalla, at a point about 0.25 of a mile east of Dickey Prairie Road and 0.25 of a mile south of Callahan Road. It is in a field: on the John K. Dickey D.L.C. #49, OC #1119. NOTE: This site is on private property. (Not shown on Wilhoit 1955-85 USGS Quad. map.)

Name of Cemetery and also known as	Number of burials	Acres	Condition	Date started or earliest known burial	Township	Range	Section

DRAPER FAMILY

? ? ? ?   T3S   R1E   S1

In January 1985 it was reported that the Draper family house in Canemah has a small cemetery in the backyard. This is located at 707 Fourth Avenue and was the home of George and Martha Draper, built circa 1876. Canemah is that portion of Oregon City along OR. Hwy. 99E going towards Canby. (Not shown on Oregon City or Canby 1961-85 USGS Quad. maps.)

FELLOWS
AKA 1. HIGHLAND
     2. LOWER HIGHLAND

C 1 2 1848   T4S   R3E   S3

Located about 8 miles southeast of Beaver Creek community via Beavercreek Road and Lower Highland Road. The cemetery is just east of 21895 Lower Highland Road, the old North Highland School building, and 0.4 of a mile west of the junction of Lower Highland Road with Fellows Road. It is on the Hiram Fellows D.L.C., OC #4906. {1 January 1991} (Redland 1961-85 USGS Quad. map.)

FERGUSON FAMILY

? ? 6 ?   T2S   R2E   ?

Perhaps located in Section 28. This was on the home place of Ephraim Ferguson on Holcomb Road. All graves were moved to Clackamas Cemetery. {Spring 1991} (Not shown on Oregon City 1961-85 USGS Quad. map.)

FERN HILL
AKA: 1. BOYER, DUDLEY
     2. BOYER FAMILY
     3. FERNHILL

A 1 2 Pre-1907   T5S   R3E   S21

In the center of the Southwest 1/4 of the Northwest 1/4 of Section 21 and north of Red House Road. NOTE: This is located on private property and there is no public access. The present landowner reports {13 March 1991} that the only remaining marker is for Elizabeth J. Pendleton, 1875-1907. (The cemetery is shown on a 1966 Metsker Land Ownership Map but it is not shown on the Fernwood 1986 USGS Quad. map.)

FEYRER

? 0.01 ? ?   T5S   R3E   S19

Located in the Southeast 1/4 of the Southwest 1/4 of Section 19. The burial is south of Callahan Road and west of Ball Road, southeast of Molalla and east of Dickey

Prairie. It is on the Clifton R. Callahan D.L.C. #37, OC #1130. NOTE: This burial site is on private property. (Not shown on Fernwood 1986 USGS Quad. map.)

FIELDS

A   ?   4   ?   T2S R1E   S34

This old cemetery was located by the Fields Bridge over the Tualatin River at the western edge of the town of West Linn. It was at the sharp turn to the right of Dollar Road, which in turn leaves Borland Road right by the bridge. The site is now a nursery. There were several burials, all of them removed to Mountain View Cemetery in Oregon City. This was located on the Joseph A. Fields D.L.C., OC #324. {23 March 1995} (Not shown on Canby 1961-85 USGS Quad. map.)

FIR HILL
AKA: 1. FIR LAWN
     2. FIR MEMORIAL
     3. HOOD LOOP
     4. MT. HOOD
        LOOP
     5. SANDY HOOD
        LOOP
     6. SANDY PIONEER

D 2+   1   1889   T2S R4E   S14

Located at the western edge of the town of Sandy. Turn north off of Mt. Hood Highway (U.S. Hwy. 26) into the driveway between the two cemeteries. Fir Hill is north and east of the adjacent Scandinavian Cemetery. The only sign we found on our visit was for Fir Hill Cemetery on the right (east) side of the driveway between the two cemeteries. {7 February 1991} (Sandy 1961-85 USGS Quad. map. The 2 cemeteries are not shown separated on the Quad. map.)

FISCHER BABY

?   ?   ? 1 Oct 1922 ?   ?   ?

Oregon State Death Certificate #151 reports that the baby daughter of Wm. F. Fischer and Pearl Carson died on 30 September 1922 and was buried 1 October 1922 at home place in Firwood.

FORRESTER
AKA: 1. DOUGLAS
        RIDGE
     2. JUDD

C 0.5 1   1860   T2S R4E   S29

Take the Eagle Creek-Sandy Highway (OR. Hwy. 211) and drive 1.5 miles northeast from Eagle Creek. The cemetery is on the left (west) side of the highway opposite the junction with Howlett Road. {7 February 1991} (Estacada 1961-85 USGS Quad. map.)

Name of Cemetery and also known as	Number of burials	Acres	Condition	Date started or earliest known burial	Township	Range	Section

FOSTER PIONEER

B 1 1 1850-1935 T2S R4E S31
Located at Eagle Creek. Inquire at the Eagle Creek Store for key to the cemetery (Fall 1999). From the junction of Eagle Creek-Sandy Highway (OR. Hwy. 211) with Southeast Eagle Creek Road, drive a short distance on the latter to the east end of the shops; turn left (east) uphill on a private road past several gates for 0.2 of a mile to the end of the road. From there it is a short walk to the cemetery: on the Philip Foster D.L.C. #37, OC #4719. {17 August 1996} (Not shown on Estacada 1961-85 USGS Quad. map.)

G. W. W.

? 0.01 ? 5 May 1875 T3S R2E S4
This is a rock with the engraved date of 5 May 1875 and the initials G. W. W. It is in the northwest corner of a 25-acre farm owned by C. J. Montague in 1958. Leave OR. Hwy. 213 at Milepost 3 onto Beavercreek Road to the southeast. After 0.15 of a mile, turn left (northeast) onto Maple Lane Road and go 0.56 of a mile farther. Turn left again onto Holly Lane and drive about 0.25 of a mile to the left (northwest): on the Lyman D. Latourette D.L.C. #39, OC #1009. NOTE: This site is on private property. (Not shown on Oregon City 1961-85 USGS Quad. map.)

GARDEN OF REVERENCE
AKA: 1. MT. HOOD
        MEMORIAL

A 1.08 ? ? T1S R4E S28
Located at the east end of Southeast Altman Road, east of the junction with Southeast 327th Avenue and southeast of Pleasant Home. The cemetery was apparently never used. It is now (1991) the Schmidt Nursery: on the Leander Williams D.L.C. #37, OC #4731. {18 February 1991} (Not shown on Sandy 1961-85 USGS Quad. map.)

GEER PIONEER
AKA: 1. LADD HILL
        2. WEST
            BUTTEVILLE

A 0.1 2 1847-1926 T3S R1W S31
This burial ground is on an embankment on the northeast corner of the intersection of Ladd Hill Road and Wilsonville Road. It is near the Willamette River opposite the town of Butteville, on private land and on the edge of a filbert orchard. A D.A.R. survey of 1935 reported 13 known burials but there

Name of Cemetery and also known as	Number of burials	Acres	Condition	Date started or earliest known burial	Township	Range	Section

could have been others unmarked. In October 1991 the compiler found a single shattered obelisk with 3 names for the Weeks family, a fallen slab for Mary Geer, and a metal War of 1812 marker for Josph C. Geer. It is on the Frederick W. Geer D.L.C. #41, OC #499. {7 October 1991} (Not shown on Sherwood 1961-85 USGS Quad. map.)

GEORGE
AKA: 1. GEORGE PROTESTANT
2. PRESBYTERIAN
3. SUTTER CREEK

B 1.82 1 1881 T3S R5E S19

Located about 9.5 miles east of Estacada. Leave Estacada on Coupland Road at the Coupland and Cemetery Road junction. Turn left (north) onto Currin Road after going 1.4 miles. At 2.8 miles, turn right (east) off of Currin Road and onto Snuffin Road. Drive down Eagle Creek Canyon, crossing Eagle Creek, and at 6.1 miles turn hard right onto George Road. Drive on George Road, past the junction with Clausen Road, to about 9.5 miles from the start at Coupland and Cemetery Roads. The cemetery is on the left (north) side of the road. George Community Church is about 500 yards east of the cemetery on the right (south) side of the road. {10 February 1991} (Cherryville 1985 USGS Quad. map.)

GETHSEMANI
AKA: 1. GETHSEMANE

D 26 1 1959 T1S R2E S33

Located at 11166 Southeast Stevens Road, on the east side of the road. Leave the I-205 Freeway at the Exit 14, going east onto Sunnyside Road. Take the first road to the left (north), which is Stevens Road, and go about 0.4 of a mile to Gethsemani. NOTE: On some maps Gethsemani is incorrectly labelled Little Chapel of the Chimes Memorial: that is a separate cemetery on the west side of Stevens Road. There were approximately 3,485 burials at Gethsemani as of 5 January 1991. {Spring 1991} (Gladstone 1961-84 USGS Quad. map.)

GIBSON
AKA: 1. DOUGLAS
2. HOWLETT

B 0.5 2 1883-1952 T3S R4E ?

Perhaps located in the Southeast 1/4 of Section 2. It is 2.5 miles east of the Eagle Creek Grange, north of Wildcat Mountain Road by way of a bulldozed road into a clearing in

Name of Cemetery and also known as	Number of burials	Acres	Condition	Date started or earliest known burial	Township	Range	Section

heavy timber: dry weather access only. There were about 32 known burials in 1965: on the William J. Howlett D.L.C., OC #4436. NOTE: This site is on private property. {February 1991} (Not shown on Estacada 1961-85 USGS Quad. map.)

GITHENS FAMILY

A   0.25   1   1869   T3S   R4E   S5

Located on a hilltop east of Eagle Creek Road and north of Currin Road. The access is through a farmer's field, from the house on Currin Road: owned by Ted Kiggens at the junction of Currin Road and Eagle Creek Road. It is about 2 miles south of the locale of Eagle Creek. See also the article about the adjacent Kiggens burial. 5 markers were found in the Githens Family Cemetery (1991): on the Henrietta Knight D.L.C. #44, OC #4415. NOTE: You must obtain permission to go to this site as it is on private property. {7 February 1991} (Not shown on Estacada 1961-85 USGS Quad. map.)

GLEASON
  AKA: 1. GLEASON,
     PARSON

B   1   5   1876-1940   T4S   R   S

Located in Township 4 South, Range 1 West, Section 36 and Township 4 South, Range 1 East, Section 31. This one is very difficult to visit as it is not visible from the roadway and is in dense brush and trees. Leave OR. Hwy. 99E in Hubbard, in Marion County, and go east on Whiskey Hill Road, crossing the Pudding River into Clackamas County. Continue a short distance to the crossroads with Meridian Road at Ninety-One School. Turn left (north) onto Meridian Road, past a flight strip and at about 0.75 of a mile from the crossroads, on a slight curve and downslope, park your vehicle. You must search on foot for the faint footpath on the right (east) in the brush. There is one tombstone showing on the low ridgetop from the footpath entry. Once inside the brush there are a fair number of tombstones and no vandalism was evident. NOTE: This site is on private property. Watch out for poison oak and blackberry vines. On their visit Mrs. Lucille Geigle and Nadiene Miln found 31

Name of Cemetery and also known as	Number of burials	Acres	Condition	Date started or earliest known burial	Township	Range	Section

markers and they estimate nearly 80 are buried here, see *Walking Through The Cemeteries, Vol. 1. 1991.* {26 June 1989} (Yoder 1955-85 USGS Quad. map.)

GRAY, MRS. ELIZA JANE

A 0.01 ? 31 Jan 1914 T6S R2E S16

Wilhoit was a spa that was fashionable in the late 19th and early 20th centuries. The compiler was unaware of any burials here. However there is a 1914 Clackamas County Death Certificate #1121 for a Mrs. Eliza Jane Gray, born 19 February 1883, died 31 January 1914 who died of pulmonary tuberculosis. She was buried the following day at Wilhoit and her widower resided at Wilhoit. (Not shown on the Wilhoit 1955-85 USGS Quad. map.)

GRIBBLE

B 2 2 1858 T4S R1E S21

Located about 5 miles south of Canby, either via the Canby-Marquam Highway (Kropf Road) or Barlow Road. Leave the latter to the left (east) on Zimmerman Road and proceed to Oglesby Road. Go left (north) for about 0.75 of a mile to Gribble Road, turn right (east). After leaving Oglesby Road you cross Gribble Creek almost immediately and about 200 feet beyond the bridge is the large cemetery sign (established in 1858) on the right (south) side of Gribble Road. There are 2 separate burial areas here; one is apparently for the Gribble family and its connections and the other for non-family members. You can leave by continuing east on Gribble Road for about a mile to the Canby-Marquam Highway (Kropf Road). It is on the Andrew E. Gribble D.L.C. #41, OC #896. {21 September 1989} (Not shown on Yoder 1955-85 USGS Quad. map.)

HABELT, MRS.

A 0.01 5 ? T4S R4E S26

The April 1928 *Metsker Land Ownership Atlas* shows the Habelt family owned the Northeast 1/4 of Section 26. Leave OR. Hwy. 211 at Milepost 28.8 northeast of Elwood by turning right (southerly) onto Hillockburn Road. Pass through the locale of Dodge after driving 1.15 miles, and turn right (south) onto Habelt Road at 1.65 miles. The grave is

| Name of Cemetery and also known as | Number of burials | Acres | Condition | Date started or earliest known burial | Township | Range | Section |

supposed to be at the end of Habelt Road, 3 miles from OR. Hwy. 211. NOTE: This site is on private property. (Not shown on Elwood 1986 USGS Quad. map.)

HAZELWOOD
AKA: 1. CEMETERY
       ASSOCIATION

B   3.42   4   1856   T2S R3E   S13
Located southwest of Boring and northeast of Barton. Leave the Clackamas Highway (OR. Hwy. 224) east of Boring and turn left (northeast) onto Aemisegger Hill Road. Go towards Boring, but turn off of Aemisegger Hill Road to the left (west) onto Rebman Road. Proceed about 0.25 of a mile to a roadway left (south). There is no public access the last 0.5 of a mile to the cemetery, which is in a grove of evergreens at the south edge of a field. {18 February 1991} (Not shown on Damascus 1961-84 USGS Quad. map.)

HODGE, GERTRUDE

A   0.01   ?   27 Dec 1897 T3S R1E   ?
Located somewhere off of Mountain Road in the area of Stafford. Gertrude, born 12 October 1896, the daughter of Andrew and Cora Hodge died of diphtheria. (Not shown on Canby 1961-85 USGS Quad. map)

HOLLAND

B   1   7   1845   T1S R1E   S36
Located at 11687 Southeast 33rd Avenue, Milwaukie, at the northwest corner of the intersection with Wister Street. This was on one of Lot Whitcomb's cemeteries; and all other bodies but these two were removed to other locations prior to 1928. In about 1961, the owner had removed but safely stored the monuments for Eliza Holland, wife of William Holland; died 30 November 1852, and a stone marked Willie; no date or surname. See also the *Oregon Journal*, 9 December 1968, Section 3, page 12; on the Lot Whitcomb D.L.C. #38, OC #90. (Not shown on Lake Oswego 1961-84 USGS Quad. map.)

Name of Cemetery and also known as	Number of burials	Acres	Condition	Date started or earliest known burial	Township	Range	Section

HOLY NEW MARTYRS RUSSIAN ORTHODOX CHURCH

A ? ? ? T4S R2E ?

An obituary for Aaron Tesch reports the burial on 16 July 1994 at the Holy New Martyrs Russian Orthodox Church in the vicinity of Mulino. The compiler does not know the exact location of the church. As far as the compiler knows this is the only burial ground exclusively dedicated to the Russian Orthodox Church. There are Russian Orthodox burials in various cemeteries. (Not shown on Molalla 1954-85 USGS Quad. map.)

HOWARD FAMILY

A 0.01 2 1861-1896 T4S R2E S17

Drive north from Mulino on OR. Hwy. 213 from the junction with South Mulino Road. Go 0.5 of a mile, crossing Milk Creek Bridge to Alder Creek Lane on the right (east). There are 4 known burials in a small fenced area between the highway and the house. There are said to be an estimated 20 graves in all west of the house, plus 3 white children and 10 or 12 Indians buried under the house. The old road passed behind (east) of the house. There has been a highway widening project in 1991 which may have altered the burials still more. (Not shown on Molalla 1954-85 USGS Quad. map.)

I.O.O.F. [ESTACADA]
AKA: 1. ESTACADA
2. ESTACADA ODD FELLOWS
3. LONE OAK

D 4 1 1858 T3S R4E S21

Leave the Clackamas Highway (OR. Hwy. 211 and OR. Hwy. 224) and turn north on Main Street in Estacada. Go past the schools to 6th Avenue and turn right (east), cross Wade Creek, and at the junction of Coupland Road turn left (north) onto Cemetery Road. The cemetery is on the left (west) and opposite Foothills Drive. See also the article on Philip E. Linn, which adjoins Estacada Odd Fellows: on the William N. and Sarah Wade D.L.C. #39, OC #5027. {7 Feburary 1991} (Estacada 1961-85 USGS Quad. map.)

I.O.O.F. [OREGON CITY]
AKA: 1. I.O.O.F. PIONEER

E 60 1 1847 T3S R2E S5

This now constitutes the easternmost portion of Mountain View Cemetery. The entrance is from 500 Hilda Street, east off of Molalla Avenue. There are no signboards

Name of Cemetery and also known as	Number of burials	Acres	Condition	Date started or earliest known burial	Township	Range	Section

delineating the I.O.O.F. Cemetery from the Masonic, adjoining to the west. The visitor can assume the boundary by observing the lodge emblems on the monuments: on the William Holmes D.L.C. #38, OC #94. {26 July 1990} (Oregon City 1961-85 USGS Quad. map. shows only the name Mountain View.)

ILERS PEAK
AKA: 1. EILER PEAK
    2. EILERS PEAK

A   ?   ?   1861   T2S R3E   S18

Located on top of Ilers Peak not far to the northeast of Carver. Take the Carver Highway (OR. Hwy. 224 and 212) east from the town of Clackamas. At Rock Creek Corner, turn right (south) on OR. Hwy. 224 towards Carver. Go about 0.5 of a mile and turn off the highway to the left (east). This road goes uphill for about 0.44 of a mile. There you must climb up to the top of Ilers Peak on foot. This roadway towards the peak is about 0.6 of a mile north of Carver. There are only 4 depressions where boulders marked the burial sites of 3 adults and a child drowned in the Clackamas River during the November 1861 flood. As long ago as March 1970 the 4 boulders were missing. (Not shown on Damascus 1961-84 USGS Quad. map. The peak is shown but is not named.)

INDIAN BURIAL

? ?   ? ?   T2S R2E   S30

In West Linn there is reportedly an Indian burial site underneath the old Ralph Milln house. This house is the fifth house on the east (river) side of River Street going northerly from the Holly Street junction. Holly Street leaves OR. Hwy. 43 very close to the interchange legs of I-205 with OR. Hwy.43. (Not shown on Oregon City 1961-85 USGS Quad. map.)

INDIAN GRAVES

? ?   ? ?   T5S R2E   ?

Located somewhere in or near Molalla. NOTE: No other information was given in the report. See the article on the Cutting Family. (Not shown on Molalla 1954-85 USGS Quad. map.)

Name of Cemetery and also known as	Number of burials	Acres	Condition	Date started or earliest known burial	Township	Range	Section

IRVIN FAMILY
AKA: 1. BRACKETT
     2. IRWIN FAMILY

A 0.6 4 1851-1930 T4S R1E S18
Leave OR. Hwy. 99E at Milepost 24.5 onto Lone Elder Road, just before OR. Hwy. 99E crosses the Pudding River into Aurora. Follow Lone Elder Road for 0.3 of a mile; the cemetery is on the right, in a conspicuous grove of fir trees in a field of tree seedlings. The land is owned by the Weyerhaeuser Timber Co., so apply at the office for permission to visit this cemetery. There are 9 graves, 3 unmarked, and the markers spell the name: Irvin. It is on the George and Mary Ann Irvin D.L.C., OC #297. {26 June 1989} (Yoder 1955-85 USGS Quad. map.)

JACKSON FAMILY
AKA: 1. AUSTIN FAMILY
     2. DIBBLE FAMILY
     3. LARKINS FAMILY

B 1.55 2 1850 T5S R2E S7
Located a mile west of the main intersection in Molalla: on the left (south) side of OR. Hwy. 211, located in the woods south of the Church of Jesus Christ of Latter-Day Saints. There is limited access on foot from the southeast corner of the church parking lot. There has been extensive vandalism. It is on the Rachel Larkins D.L.C. #43, OC #1132. {21 January 1991} (Not shown on Molalla 1954-85 USGS Quad. map.)

JOHNSON FAMILY
AKA: 1. FERNWOOD
     2. JOHNSON, ANDREW

A 0.01 ? 1891-1892 T5S R3E S18
Located in the Southeast 1/4 of the Southeast 1/4 of Section 18. Go easterly on Callahan Road 0.23 of a mile from the bridge over Woodcock Creek. Leave Callahan Road to the left (north) on Bud Smith Road. The cemetery is somewhere to the left (west) of Bud Smith Road on a bank above Woodcock Creek. 2 children are buried here and the graves were enclosed by a picket fence at one time. (Not shown on Colton 1955-85 USGS Quad. map.)

KELLOGG FAMILY

? ? 7 1848-1897 T2S R2E S7
This burial ground was about 0.25 of a mile east of Oatfield Road and left (northerly) from View Acres Road. It was closed in 1897 and the bodies were removed to Greenwood, in Multnomah County. There are 14 known burials

Name of Cemetery and also known as	Number of burials	Acres	Condition	Date started or earliest known burial	Township	Range	Section

and many unknowns. The site was marked in 1959; on the Orrin Kellogg D.L.C. #55, OC #1421. (Not shown on Gladstone 1961-84 USGS Quad. map.)

KIGGENS, PATRICK LEROY

A 0.1 1 25 Aug 1986 T3S R4E S5

This recent burial is fenced and separate from, but adjacent to, the Githens Family Cemetery. It is located on a hilltop east of Eagle Creek Road and north of Currin Road. The access is through a farmer's field, from the house owned by Ted Kiggens (1991) on Currin Road at its junction with Eagle Creek Road. it is about 2 miles south of the locale of Eagle Creek. See also the article on Githens Family Cemetery. Located on the Henrietta Knight D.L.C. #44, OC #4415. NOTE: This site is on private property. Please get permission before going to either of these sites. {7 February 1991} (Not shown on Estacada 1961-85 USGS Quad. map.)

KLINGLER MEMORIAL
AKA: 1. KLINGER
2. KLINGLER
3. LATOURETTE WOODS

A 0.5 2 1856 T4S R1E S24

Drive east from the locale of Macksburg on Macksburg Road. After going 1.85 miles turn right (south) onto Klinger Road and drive another 0.45 of a mile to the top of the hill. There is a driveway on the right (west),which leads back to the cemetery. The county road is signed Klinger and the cemetery is signed Klingler Memorial and dated 11 June 1890. There were 20 markers for 21 persons noted 19 November 1992. Due to the spacing there probably are considerably more interred here. It is on the John L. Klingler D.L.C. #46, OC #443. {18 January 1992} (Not shown on the Molalla 1954-85 USGS Quad. map.)

KLINKER

? ? ? ? T3S R5E ?

Perhaps located in the Southeast 1/4 of Section 18. This is supposed to be in the area of George and is possibly Lutheran. No other information was given in the report. (Not shown on Cherryville 1985 USGS Quad. map.)

Name of Cemetery and also known as	Number of burials	Acres	Condition	Date started or earliest known burial	Township	Range	Section

KOWALL, THERESA

A   0.01   2   1898   T3S R5E   S18
This single burial is on private land at the end of Southeast Kowall Road in the vicinity of George. It is in the Northwest 1/4 of the Southwest 1/4 of Section 18 on the family farm which was homesteaded in 1884. The 8 foot by 10 foot plot is fenced and marked, Mrs. Kowall, born in 1839, wished to be buried on this site. Kowall Road branches off to the left (Northwest) about 0.3 of a mile along Clausen Road on the way to the Scheel Family Cemetery. See that article for directions. (Not shown on Cherryville 1985 USGS Quad. map.)

LARKINS, MONROE AND ELIZABETH V.

A   0.01   ?   1868-1898   T4S R2E   ?
This could be located in Section 26 or 35. Two graves of Monroe and Elizabeth V. Larkins were found about 0.25 of a mile "off the road" in a logged-off area, surrounded by a deteriorated iron fence. The date of the report was 1961. This appears to be in the vicinity of Windy City Road and Salo Road, just northeast of Union Mills: on the Monroe and Elizabeth Larkins D.L.C., OC #13. (Not shown on Molalla 1954-85 USGS Quad. map.)

LEISMAN, FAMILY

A   0.01   ?   ?   T4S R3E   ?
Perhaps located in Section 34. Go east of the Colton Post Office on OR. Hwy. 211. Turn right (east) after about 0.3 of a mile onto Schieffer Road. Cross the bridge and about 0.1 of a mile beyond is a side road to the left (north). This leads through a Christmas tree farm about 1,000 feet down to the bottom of the property. The unmarked graves of Joseph and Annie Jackson Leisman are here. NOTE: This site is on private property. (Not shown on Colton 1955-85 USGS Quad. map.)

LEWTHWAITE
 AKA: 1. PARK PLACE

A   1   5   1847   T2S R2E   S20
Take OR. Hwy. 213 from Exit 10 off of the I-205 Freeway. Take the first exit left (northerly) onto Clackamas River Drive. Go 0.5 of a mile on Clackamas River Drive, then turn right (east) onto Forsythe Road. Proceed only 0.1 of a mile on Forsythe Road

Name of Cemetery and also known as	Number of burials	Acres	Condition	Date started or earliest known burial	Township	Range	Section

and then turn left (north) onto Harley Avenue. Drive about 200 yards to Abernethy Grange and turn right (east) onto a driveway to 3 houses. The cemetery is on private property behind the middle house. The cemetery is fenced with only one headstone remaining; there are a total of 9 known burials, with many unknowns. The cemetery was established by Captain W. H. Smith on the Hiram and Susan Straight D.L.C. #42, OC #95. (Not shown on Gladstone 1961-84 USGS Quad. maps.)

LINCOLN MEMORIAL PARK
AKA: 1. MT. SCOTT
      PARK

E 443   1   1911   T1S R2E   S22

The address of the office is 10500 Southeast Mt. Scott Boulevard, in Multnomah County. See the article in the Multnomah County section of this book. Some of the cemetery acreage is in Clackamas County. {Summer 1991} (Gladstone 1961-84 USGS Quad. map.)

LINN, PHILIP E.
AKA: 1. PIONEER
      MEMORIAL
   2. WADE
   3. WADE FAMILY
   4. WADE
      MEMORIAL

C 0.5 1 1865   T3S R4E   S21

This is a separate cemetery which adjoins the Estacada Odd Fellows Cemetery. Leave the Clackamas Highway (OR. Hwy. 211 and OR. Hwy 224) and turn north on Main Street in Estacada. Go past the schools to 6th Avenue and turn right (east), cross Wade Creek and at the junction of Coupland Road turn left (north) onto Cemetery Road. The cemetery is on the left (west) opposite Foothills Drive. The Philip E. Linn Cemetery adjoins the larger cemetery on the north side of Estacada Odd Fellows Cemetery and on the west side of Cemetery Road. Only the descendants of Philip E. Linn may be buried here. William N. and wife Sarah Wade are also buried here. This cemetery was deeded in October of 1905 by W. H. H. Wade under the name of Pioneer Memorial Cemetery: on the William N. and Sarah Wade D.L.C. #39, OC #5027. In December of 1983 it was deeded to Clackamas County under the maintenance of the Estacada Cemetery District. Until the present signboard was erected in June of 1986, it was usually referred to as the Wade or Wade

| Name of Cemetery and also known as | Number of burials | Acres | Condition | Date started or earliest known burial | Township | Range | Section |

Memorial Cemetery. {7 February 1991}
(Estacada 1961-85 USGS Quad. map. The map
does not distinguish between the two
cemeteries.)

**LITTLE CHAPEL OF
THE CHIMES MEMORIAL
GARDEN**
AKA: 1. EASTLAWN
MEMORIAL
GARDENS
2. ETERNAL
MEMORIAL
GARDENS
3. SUNNYSIDE
CHIMES MEMORIAL
GARDENS
4. TERRACE LAWN
MEMORIAL PARK

D   2   1   Circa 1950   T1S   R2E   S33
Located at 11167 Southeast Stevens Road,
across the road from Gethsemani Cemetery.
Leave the I-205 Freeway at Exit 14, going
east onto Sunnyside Road. Take the first
road to the left (north), which is Stevens
Road, and go about 0.4 of a mile to the
cemetery on the left (west) side of the road.
(Not shown on Gladstone 1961-84 USGS Quad.
map.)

LOWE FAMILY
AKA: 1. AIMS
2. PULLEY-LOWE
FAMILY

A   ?   ?   ?   T1S   R5E   S30
In east Multnomah County, leave Springdale on
Hurlburt Road and then turn right
(southeasterly) onto Gordon Creek Road.
Follow the winding Gordon Creek Road until
turning right (south) onto Groce Road and go
0.3 of a mile to the Multnomah-Clackamas
county line. Ahead the road is not
maintained by either county. It dead ends
0.7 of a mile from the junction of Gordon
Creek Road. The graves are somewhere along
this road in Clackamas County on private
property. There are 14 known burials. (Not
shown on Bull Run 1985 USGS Quad. map.)

MAPLEWOOD
AKA: 1. I.O.O.F.
[SCOTTS MILLS]
2. MAPLE GROVE
3. SCOTTS MILLS

C   4   2   1866   T6S   R1E   S14
Located in the Northwest 1/4 of the Southeast
1/4 of Section 14, in what was Lot #130 of
the Friends Oregon Colony. From Scotts
Mills, cross Butte Creek into Clackamas
County onto Nowlen Bridge Road, drive about
0.27 of a mile to the cemetery road on the
right (east) and go 0.4 of a mile to the
grounds. The cemetery is aptly named; all of
the numerous trees appear to be maples.
Maplewood is sometimes mistakenly listed as a

Marion County cemetery, since the town of Scotts Mills is in Marion County; on the Joshua Bowman D.L.C., OC #4635. {21 May 1989} (Scotts Mills 1954-85 USGS Quad. map.)

MARK MEMORIAL PARK
AKA: 1. MARK FAMILY
2. MARKS
3. MARKS PRAIRIE

A 2 2 1948 T4S R1E S20

Leave OR. Hwy. 99E at the signalized intersection onto Barlow Road. Drive south on Barlow Road about 2.4 miles and then turn left (east) onto Mark Road. Drive another 0.5 of a mile and the gated road on the right (south) leads to the park. It is signed; Mark Memorial. The park is a 2-acre tract including the old school house and a picnic area. The burials are arranged around a single monument that contains 7 tombstones for 6 adults and 4 children, whose deaths ranged from January 1859 to November 1905. The burials were reburied here from another site. The plaque in their honor is dated 25 July 1948; on the John and Fanny Marks D.L.C. #39, OC #63. {11 October 1989} (Yoder 1955-85 USGS Quad. map.)

MARQUAM FAMILY

A 0.52 4 1853-1975 T6S R1E S10

Located about a mile southeast of Marquam, as the crow flies. One must have guidance from the landowner as the vehicle must traverse a gated farm road (off of Wildcat Road) and then through open fields. Wait until after harvest time and hope for fair weather. The cemetery is on a hillside surrounded by fields. It was fenced and cleaned up by Dorothy Barber, but after her death on 13 September 1975, there has been no further upkeep. Reportedly there are records of 22 burials; the landowner estimated 19 burials. The compiler found 11 stones for 12 people, but there is so much vegetation there could be more. It is on the Alfred Marquam D.L.C. #46, OC #1693. NOTE: This site is on private property. {26 August 1989} (Not shown on Scotts Mills 1954-85 USGS Quad. map, but it is shown in the 1928 Metsker Atlas of Clackamas County Landowners.)

Name of Cemetery and also known as	Number of burials	Acres	Condition	Date started or earliest known burial	Township	Range	Section

MASONIC [OREGON CITY]   E 60   1   1847   T3S R2E   S5

This was once a separate cemetery between the I.O.O.F. Cemetery adjoining to the east and the more recent Mountain View Cemetery adjoining to the west. The entrance is from 500 Hilda Street, east off of Molalla Avenue. There are no signboards delineating the Masonic cemetery from the adjacent I.O.O.F. and Mountain View, but the visitor can assume the boundaries by observing the lodge emblems on the monuments; on the William Holmes D.L.C. #38, OC #94. {1 August 1990} (Oregon City 1961-85 USGS Quad. map shows only the name Mountain View.)

McLOUGHLIN FAMILY   A 0.01 1   1948   T2S R2E   S31

The graves of Doctor John McLoughlin and his wife, Marguerite McKay McLoughlin, are now located adjacent to the McLoughlin House Museum in Oregon City. The house was moved to its present site at the northwest corner of 7th Street and Center Street on 23 July 1909. He died in September of 1857, she in February of 1860; they were originally buried under St. John the Apostle Catholic Church. The unused crypt for the McLoughlins exists under the bell tower of the present church. {Summer 1991} (Not shown on Oregon City 1961-85 USGS Quad. map.)

McNEIL, FRED H.   A 0.01 ?   1958   T2S UNSURVEYED

Although the area is unsurveyed the Mt. Hood National Forest Map projects the marker to be in Township 2 South, Range 8 East, and Section 19. The burial and marker are in McNeil Forest Camp. To reach the camp, leave the Mt. Hood Highway (U.S. Hwy. 26) at Zigzag. Turn north on Forestry Road #18, crossing the Zigzag River and continuing northeasterly past Old Maid Flat. Enter the Mt. Hood Wilderness and almost immediately turn right onto Forestry Road #1828. Proceed about 0.5 of a mile and turn right (east), onto Forest Road #1825, crossing the Sandy River and into McNeil Forest Camp. McNeil Point, high up on the northwest slope of Mt. Hood, was named for Fred H. McNeil. The marker is for the burial of Fred H. McNeil,

Name of Cemetery and also known as	Number of burials	Acres	Condition	Date started or earliest known burial	Township	Range	Section

born 1893 in Illinois, died 28 December 1958. For more information see *Oregon Journal*, 29 December 1958 and 13 July 1959. (Bull Run Lake 1962 USGS Quad. map shows the camp. A Mt. Hood National Forest Map however, is preferable.)

MEINIG PARK

? ? ? ?   T2S   R4E   S13

This is a city of Sandy park. It is 0.1 of a mile south of Pioneer Avenue (U.S. Hwy. 26) on Meinig Avenue. There have been unverified rumors of a horse thief hung and buried here. (Not shown on Sandy 1961-85 USGS Quad. map.)

MERIDIAN [OLD]
AKA 1. DEUTSCHE
           EVANGELISCHE
           REFORMIERTE
           MERIDIAN CHURCH
     2. FROG POND
           CHURCH
     3. MERIDIAN UNITED
           CHURCH OF
           CHRIST

?   0.25   ?   1882-1895   T3S   R1W   S13

Leave the I-5 Freeway at exit 283 at Wilsonville and start from the junction on the interchange legs with Wilsonville Road on the east side of the freeway. Drive easterly and northerly for 2 miles to the junction of Wilsonville and Boeckman Roads. The church is on the left at the junction. Turn left (west) onto Boeckman Road for a short distance to the entry into the church parking lot. This gravelled parking lot on the west side of the church was the site of the original cemetery. The church was erected in 1880 and the cemetery was used until 1895 when the burials were removed to the present Meridian Cemetery about 1.5 miles north and on S.W. 65th Avenue in Washington County. {23 March 1995} (the church is shown on the Canby 1961-85 USGS Quad. map.)

MILWAUKIE PIONEER
AKA: 1. MILWAUKIE
      2. SELLWOOD
      3. WAVERLY

D   1.77   1   1850   T1S   R1E   S26

Located on the west side of Southeast 17th Avenue at Waverly Drive and just north of McLoughlin Boulevard (OR. Hwy. 99E) between Milwaukie and the Sellwood district of Portland. The cemetery has been filled since 1943 except for some reserved spaces for some pioneer families: on the William Meek D.L.C. #60, OC #636. {5 January 1991} (Lake Oswego 1961-84 USGS Quad. map.)

Name of Cemetery and also known as	Number of burials	Acres	Condition	Date started or earliest known burial	Township	Range	Section

MOEHNKE
AKA: 1. LOWER SCHUEBEL
     2. MINK
     3. ST. PETER'S
        LUTHERAN CHURCH

B 0.3 2 1897 T3S R3E S31

Located about 0.5 of a mile north of Schuebel School. Cross Lower Highland Road and continue north on the road now known as Carus Road, for about 0.2 of a mile from Lower Highland Road. The large sign and cemetery are on the right (east). 0.25 of an acre was donated by Michael Moehnke to construct St. Peter's Lutheran Church. The church (torn down in the 1950's) site is now vacant. The name Moehnke is pronounced Mink. {Spring 1991} (Redland 1961-85 USGS Quad. map.)

MOLALLA MEMORIAL
AKA: 1. DART
     2. I.O.O.F. [OLD]
     3. MEMORIAL
     4. MOLALLA PRAIRIE
     5. MULLALLA (Sic)
        PRAIRIE
     6. ODD FELLOWS
     7. TEASEL CREEK

C 2.5 2 Circa 1870 T5S R2E S20

Located about 2 miles south of Molalla on the left (east) side of Wilhoit Road. {20 November 1989} (Wilhoit 1955-85 USGS Quad. map.)

MORGAN, BABY

A 0.01 2 24 Oct 1847 T3S R8 1/2E S25

Located in Summit Meadows and evidently near the other graves. (See the article on Summit Meadows.) The Morgan infant girl was born in June 1847, her mother dying on 21 June 1847 near Independence Rock. The babys' father, Daniel Morgan, and 3 other children continued on the trail. The baby was fatally injured at the White River Camp, but survived another 3 weeks, dying at Summit Meadows. She was buried under a huge boulder which was marked with a plaque in 1957. (Not shown on Mount Hood South 1962-80 USGS Quad. map)

MT. HOME
AKA: 1. ELWOOD
     2. MT. HOMES
     3. MOUNTAIN HOME

C 1 2 1890 T4S R4E S19

Leave Foothill Boulevard (OR. Hwy. 211) east of Colton at Milepost 26.65 and turn onto Elwood Road. Go east past the fire station and turn uphill to a crossroads about 0.4 of a mile from the highway. At this crossroads you will find the cemetery, Mountain Home Church (1903), and the Elwood Community Hall, a former schoolhouse. {2 October 1991} (Elwood 1986 USGS Quad. map.)

Name of Cemetery and also known as	Number of burials	Acres	Condition	Date started or earliest known burial	Township	Range	Section

MT. ZION
AKA: 1. GARFIELD
2. PALMATEER
3. ZION [ESTACADA]

C 2.4 1 1877 T3S R4E S22

Leave Estacada via Main Street, 6th Avenue, and then Coupland Road, the principal route to the east. Go about 1.4 miles on Coupland Road from its junction with Cemetery Road (the route to Estacada Odd Fellows Cemetery) to the junction with Currin Road. Turn left (north) off of Coupland Road onto Currin Road and proceed 0.9 of a mile to Lucky Lane. The cemetery is at the northwest corner of that intersection: on the Thomas Lee D.L.C. #64, OC #3129. {10 February 1991} (Estacada 1961-85 USGS Quad. map.)

MOUNTAIN VIEW
AKA: 1. CITY OF OREGON CITY
2. MOUNT VIEW
3. OLD CITY
4. OLD OREGON CITY
5. OREGON CITY

E 53.76 1 31 Dec 1847 T3S R2E S5

This cemetery was established later than the Masonic Cemetery which adjoins it to the east, and the I.O.O.F. Cemetery, beyond the Masonic. There are no boundaries now demarcating the three cemeteries and all receive the same care under the name Mountain View. The entrance is from 500 Hilda Street, east off of Molalla Avenue. The I.O.O.F. and Masonic Lodges deeded their cemeteries to Mountain View in the 1970's: on the William Holmes D.L.C. #38, OC #94. {Spring 1991} (Oregon City 1961-85 USGS map.shows only the name Mountainview.)

OSWEGO PIONEER
AKA: 1. I.O.O.F. #93
2. PIONEER

D 5.14 2 1872 T2S R1E S16

Now within the city limits, it is 2 miles from the older downtown of Lake Oswego (formerly Oswego). Drive south and westerly via State Street, McVey Avenue, and Stafford Road. The Sacred Heart Cemetery adjoins Oswego Pioneer immediately to the north. In 1938, the Odd Fellows took over the cemetery. There are an estimated 1,400 burials (1995). Located on the Jesse Bullock D.L.C. #46, OC #1267. {26 October 1990} (Lake Oswego 1961-84 USGS Quad. map.)

PENDLETON FAMILY

A 0.25 7 1857-1900 T3S R1E S32

This burial site was on the right bank of the Molalla River, on the highest ridge and downstream from Canby. A housing development at Northwest 12th Avenue is now on the site

Clackamas County

and 3 of the 5 graves were removed to Zion Memorial Park in November of 1965. This site was on the Champing Pendleton D.L.C. #58, OC #1462. (Not shown on Canby 1961-85 USGS Quad. map.)

PERRIN, MARSHALL K.　　A　0.01　?　?　　T3S　R1E　S2

Located in West Linn. At Willamette Falls Drive and 14th Street intersection. The burial plot of Marshall K. Perrin is off the north side of Willamette Falls Drive opposite the Methodist church which is on the south side. (The church but not the grave is shown on Canby 1961-85 USGS Quad. map.)

PERSHALL, JOSEPH　　?　?　?　9 Dec 1922　?　?　?

Joseph Pershall widower age 89 was buried 9 December 1922 "on home place" in Sandy Township, Clackamas County per Oregon Death Certificate #377. He was born 29 June 1833 in Bohemia and died 7 December 1922. His father was Joseph Pershall of Bohemia, mother not known. A Mrs. Pershall was the informant. No further information is known by the compiler.

PIONEER WOMAN'S GRAVE　　A　0.01　2　Circa 1845　T3S　R9E　S29

Drive 3 miles east of Government Camp towards Barlow Pass and leave U.S. Hwy. 26 to take OR. Hwy. 35. About 0.2 of a mile past this major interchange, leave OR. Hwy. 35 to the right, onto the Old Barlow Pass·Road (Forestry Road #3531). Go about 0.4 of a mile on Forestry Road #3531: the grave is on the right (west), and marked by a large sign. Located in the Mount Hood National Forest. (Mount. Hood South 1962-80 USGS Quad. map shows "grave".)

PLEASANT VIEW [EAST]　　C　2　1　1854　T2S　R3E　S19
AKA: 1. ARTHUR
　　　2. LOGAN
　　　3. LOWER LOGAN
　　　4. PLEASANT VALLEY

Located southeast of Carver. From the junction of Bakers Ferry Road with Springwater Road, continue southerly on Springwater for 0.45 of a mile. Turn right

Name of Cemetery and also known as	Number of burials	Acres	Condition	Date started or earliest known burial	Township	Range	Section

(west) at the cemetery: on the William Arthur D.L.C. #38, OC #2306. {Spring 1991} (Damascus 1961-84 USGS Quad. map.)

PLEASANT VIEW [WEST]
AKA: 1. HOODVIEW
2. PLEASANT HILL

D 3.2 2 1865   T3S R1W   S9
Located between Wilsonville and Sherwood. Start at Wilsonville Road on the west side of the I-5 Freeway interchange and drive westerly on Wilsonville Road. At 0.8 of a mile turn right (north) onto Brown Road. At 2 miles from your starting point turn left (west) onto Tooze Road. At 2.6 miles the road forks, but continue ahead on Westfall Road to the cemetery, a total of about 3.7 miles from your starting point. The name of the cemetery was altered to avoid confusion with Pleasant Hill Cemetery, near Sheridan in Polk County, but in the process duplicated another such name in Clackamas County itself. See that article. The cemetery was donated 15 May 1886 by Moses Matthew Baker. {10 March 1991} (Sherwood 1961-85 USGS Quad. map.)

POTTER FAMILY

? ? ? ?   T2S R2E   ?
This could be in Section 25 or 36. These lost burials are reported to be at the end of Potter Road, in a field by some trees. Take Redland Road 4.6 miles easterly from Oregon City towards Redland, turn left (north) onto Potter Road. Potter Road goes due north and then turns due west to intersect Bradley Road, so it is difficult to determine what is meant by a "field at the end of Potter Road". A father, mother and 2 children are buried here. NOTE: This site is on private property. (Not shown on Oregon City 1961-85 USGS Quad. map.)

RATH

? ? ? ?   T3S R5E   ?
This is supposed to be in the area of George and is possibly Catholic. No other information was given in the report. (Not shown on Cherryville 1985 USGS Quad. map.)

Clackamas County

Name of Cemetery and also known as	Number of burials	Acres	Condition	Date started or earliest known burial	Township	Range	Section

REDLAND PIONEER
AKA: 1. REDLAND HILLS

D   3   1   1858   T3S   R3E   S16

Located in both Sections 16 and 17. Leave Washington Street at the northern end of Oregon City onto Redland Road. Drive 8.7 miles on Redland Road to the cemetery at the junction with Lyons Road. Begun as a cemetery for the Richardson and Cutting families, they turned it over to an association in 1899 and it is now a perpetual care property; on the Matthew Richardson D.L.C. #57, OC #4647 and Mary Cutting D.L.C. #56, OC #3949. {1 January 1991} (Redland 1961-85 USGS Quad. map.)

REIMER

? ?   ? ?   T3S   R5E   ?

This is supposed to be in the area of George and is possibly Lutheran. No other information was given in the report. (Not shown on Cherryville 1985 USGS Quad. map.)

REVENUE FAMILY
AKA: 1. CABBAGE HILL

A   0.25   4   1853-1953   T2S   R5E   S7

Located northeast of Sandy, on the right (east) side of Ten Eyck Road. At the east end of the town of Sandy where the one-way highway couplet ends turn left (northeasterly) onto Ten Eyck Road and drive 0.6 of a mile to the junction of Coalman Road from the right. Continue 0.9 of a mile north of the junction of Coalman Road and just north of a driveway. Located on Cabbage Hill, before you descend to Revenue Bridge over the Sandy River. Two giant old maples are in the cemetery and a row of cedars (Thuja) marks the east line of the burial ground. On the Francis Revenue D.L.C. #37, OC #3798. (Not shown on Bull Run 1985 USGS Quad. map.)

RISLEY FAMILY

A   ?   7   1876-1917   T2S   R1E   S12

These 6 or 8 burials were located 300 feet west of River Road, between Risley Avenue and Oak Shore Lane. In 1917 all of the bodies were removed to Riverview Cemetery in Portland, but artifacts were found and a stone wall was removed in 1969. See The *Oregonian* and *Oregon Journal* articles, both 9

Name of Cemetery and also known as	Number of burials	Acres	Condition	Date started or earliest known burial	Township	Range	Section

April 1969, page 21, and Section 2, page 7, respectively. It was on the Jacob S. Risley D.L.C. #51, OC #1261. (Not shown on Lake Oswego 1961-84 USGS Quad. map.)

ROCK CREEK

C 2 2 1852 T5S R1E S5

Drive about 6.25 miles on South Barlow Road from OR. Hwy. 99E at Barlow. At the South Sconce Road crossroads turn left (east) and go about 0.4 of a mile. The old Rock Creek Church and Cemetery are on the left (north) and near the junction of Stuwe Road. The Smyrna Cemetery is less than 2 miles distant by Sconce Road to the east. {17 October 1988} (Yoder 1955-85 USGS Quad. map.)

RUSSELLVILLE
AKA: 1. I.O.O.F. [OLD]
     2. RUSSELVILLE

B 0.8 2 1884 T6S R2E S2

Located about 6.9 miles southeast of Molalla town center. Leave Molalla to the south on Wilhoit Road, at 1.1 miles turn left (easterly) onto Sawtell Road. Follow Sawtell Road southerly and then due east, to the junction with Trout Creek Road 6.9 miles ahead from your starting point. The cemetery is on your left at that junction. The signboard spells the name "Russelville", however the family tombstones say "Russell" and there is a Russell Creek nearby. {10 August 1989 and spring of 1991} (Wilhoit 1955-85 USGS Quad. map.)

RUU, FREDRICK

? ? ? 22 May 1926 ? ?· ?

Oregon Death Certificate #296 states that Fredrick Ruu born 10 May 1926 and died 22 may 1926 was buried "on farm at Mulina" [Sic]. There was no Undertaker. The parents were Wm. Ruu and Eva Rodmacher both of Romainia. No further information is known by the compiler.

SACRED HEART
AKA: 1. OSWEGO
        CATHOLIC

C 5.1 2 Circa 1850 T2S R1E S16

Now within the city limits, it is 2 miles from the older downtown part of Lake Oswego (formerly Oswego). Drive south and westerly via State Street, McVey Avenue and Stafford Road. Sacred Heart Cemetery immediately

Name of Cemetery and also known as	Number of burials	Acres	Condition	Date started or earliest known burial	Township	Range	Section

adjoins Oswego Pioneer Cemetery, which is to the south. The actual burial area in Sacred Heart is much smaller than the cemetery acreage: on the Jesse Bullock D.L.C. #46, OC #1267. {2 February 1992} (Lake Oswego 1961-84 USGS Quad. map.)

ST. AGNES BABY HOME ? ? 7 1890-1954 T2S R2E S20

This was located at Park Place, between Oregon City and Gladstone. The site is now underneath the Park Place Interchange of the I-205 Freeway. In 1954 all known burials were removed to Mt. Calvary Cemetery in Multnomah County. A separate section was not created there: on the Hiram Straight D.L.C. #42, OC #95. (Not shown on Gladstone 1961-84 USGS Quad. map.)

ST. JOHANN A 2 4 1866 T3S R1E S36
AKA: 1. GERMAN EVANGELICAL
2. NEW ERA
3. ST. JOHANN LUTHERAN
4. ST. JOHN LUTHERAN

Leave OR. Hwy. 99E at the traffic signals at Ivy Street in Canby, turning southeasterly on Ivy Street for about 0.3 of a mile to the junction of Township Road, turn left (east). Drive the length of Township Road for 3 miles, to its junction with Central Point Road, passing Zion Memorial Park on your left (north). Turn left (north) onto Central Point Road, drive past the junction of Carus Road on the right (east) and you will soon see a roadsign saying "500 feet to Bremer Road." About 100 feet past this sign is a private gated driveway to the left (west) into a nursery. This is your destination, which is about 4 miles from the starting point in Canby. You will need permission to visit the cemetery, hidden from view from Central Point Road. The tallest fir tree in the area is within the cemetery. The compiler found 16 monuments to 18 persons, all of whom had German names. Death dates ranged from 24 November 1886 to 1944. St. Johann church has been demolished. Although no longer used, there are family visits and modest maintenance. NOTE: The AKA New Era is a confusion with the present St. Patrick's Cemetery, AKA New Era. {14 April 1993} (Not shown on Canby 1961-85 USGS Quad. map.)

Name of Cemetery and also known as	Number of burials	Acres	Condition	Date started or earliest known burial	Township	Range	Section

ST. JOHN THE EVANGELIST

? ? ? ? ? ? ?

This was the earliest Catholic Cemetery at Oregon City. There is a record of the burial of Doctor James Long in June or July of 1846, and Doctor John McLoughlin was buried here 5 September 1857. We do not know the location of this early cemetery which was evidently near the river. It has been superseded by St. John's Catholic, AKA: St. John the Apostle Cemetery, please see that article.

ST. JOHN THE EVANGELIST EPISCOPAL CHURCH

? ? 1 ? T1S R1E S36

St. John the Evangelist Episcopal Church is located at 2036 Southeast Jefferson in Milwaukie. A Columbarium is maintained for members of the congregation. This information has come from obituaries published in *The Oregonian*. (The church is shown on Lake Oswego 1961-84 USGS Quad. map.)

ST. JOHN'S CATHOLIC
AKA: 1. ST. JOHN THE APOSTLE

E 10.2 1 1887 T3S R2E S5

Located at 451 Warner Street, Oregon City, 3 blocks west of Molalla Avenue. There are about 2,500 burials (1991): on the William Holmes D.L.C. #38, O.C. #94. {2 February 1991} (Oregon City 1961-85 USGS Quad. map wrongly labels this as St. Paul's Cemetery.)

ST. PATRICK'S
AKA: 1. NEW ERA CATHOLIC
     2. ST. JAMES
     3. ST. PATRICK

C 2 1 1870 T3S R1E S23

Located between Canby and Oregon City, near the site of New Era. Drive 2.5 miles on OR. Hwy. 99E from the signalized Ivy Street intersection in Canby northerly towards Oregon City. Turn off of OR. Hwy. 99E to the right (east) at a new intersection (1995) and then immediately turn left (north) onto New Era Road. The gated entrance to St. Patrick's is on the right 0.3 of a mile from leaving OR. Hwy. 99E. The St. James Church here was in use between 1883 and 1942. St. Patrick's, in Canby, now has charge of this cemetery: on the Joseph Parrott D.L.C. #43, OC #890. {31 Oct. 1989} (Canby 1961-85 USGS Quad. map.)

Name of Cemetery and also known as	Number of burials	Acres	Condition	Date started or earliest known burial	Township	Range	Section

SANDERS FAMILY
AKA: 1. SAUNDERS
        FAMILY
     2. SWEIGEL FAMILY

A   1   5   1886-1933   T5S R2E   S4
Located 0.9 of a mile north of the main intersection in Molalla, on the right (east) side of Molalla Avenue. The cemetery is just north of Jim Drive and 0.1 of a mile south of Vick Road, in a grove of trees. The fenced burial area is far smaller than 1 acre: on the Matthias Swegle D.L.C. #45, OC #1129. {30 Sept. 1992} (Not shown on Molalla 1954-85 USGS Quad. map. It is shown on a 1955 Metskers Land Ownership Atlas of Clackamas County.)

SANDY RIDGE

C   2   1   1862   T2S R4E   S27
In the northwest corner of Section 27, located along the Eagle Creek-Sandy Highway (OR. Hwy. 211). It is 3.1 miles southwest of Sandy and 3 miles northeast of Eagle Creek, on the south side of the highway. {7 February 1991} (Not shown on Estacada 1961-85 USGS Quad. map.)

SAWTELL FAMILY
AKA: 1. MOORE

A 0.25 5 Circa 1850 T5S R2E   S30
This abandoned cemetery is located about 3 miles southwest of Molalla. Take Wilhoit Road out of town and turn right (westerly) on Thomas Road. The cemetery is off of the right (north) side of Thomas Road on the Albert Mautz farm. It is a fenced area about 100 feet square, in a dense thicket just north of the barn. There were 8 markers for 11 people noted in November 1992. NOTE: This is on private property. {14 November 1992} (Not shown on Wilthoit 1955-85 USGS Quad. map.)

SCANDINAVIAN

C   1   1   1907   T2S R4E   S14
Located at the western edge of the town of Sandy. Turn north off of Mt. Hood Highway (U.S. Hwy. 26) into the driveway between the two cemeteries. Scandinavian is south and west of the adjacent Fir Hill Cemetery. The only sign we found on our visit was for Fir Hill Cemetery, on the right side of the driveway (east). {7 February 1991} (Sandy 1961-85 USGS Quad. map. The two cemeteries are not shown separated on the Quad. map.)

Name of Cemetery and also known as	Number of burials	Acres	Condition	Date started or earliest known burial	Township	Range	Section

SCHEEL FAMILY
AKA: 1. EAGLE CREEK
2. LUTHERAN--
CATHOLIC
3. SHEEL

| | B | 1 | 4 | 1888 | T3S | R5E | S18 |

Located on the southeast corner of Gruber Road and Clausen Road and 0.5 of a mile from George Road. There is a set of 5 concrete steps leading from Gruber Road to the cemetery. {10 February 1991} (Not shown on Cherryville 1985 USGS Quad. map.)

SCHUEBEL
AKA: 1. SHUBEL
2. SHUBEL HILL

| | B | 0.25 | 3 | 1880-1968 | T3S | R2E | S36 |

Located about 3.5 miles southeast of the locale of Beaver Creek along South Beavercreek Road (note the variant spellings). Although it is at roadside, the cemetery is not easily spotted when driving northerly towards Oregon City, so it is best to be travelling southeasterly. The cemetery is about 0.2 of a mile beyond the junction of Lower Highland Road and before reaching Larkin Road. There was once an Evangelical Church on the opposite side of the road. The land was donated by John Gard (Circa 1880). There are about 68 burials, of whom 46 are known. {30 September 1988} (Oregon City 1961-85 USGS Quad. map.)

SISTERS OF THE HOLY NAMES
AKA: 1. HOLY NAMES
2. MARYLHURST CONVENT

| | C | 1 | 1 | 1911 | T2S | R1E | S14 |

Located on the east side of OR. Hwy. 43 between Lake Oswego and West Linn, on the southwest corner of the Marylhurst campus. There are some graves dating from 1900: on the Gabriel Walling D.L.C. #63, OC #3225. {19 January 1991} (Lake Oswego 1961-84 USGS Quad. map.)

SMITH PLACE

| | A | ? | 5 | 2 Sept 1866 | T2S | R4E | S30 |

Located on private property at 28312 Southeast Glover Road, Eagle Creek. Near the Suter Farm Cemetery in the same section but on the John P. Glover D.L.C. #40, OC #308. There are four tombstones left for the following people: C. L. Eggers, died 31 July 1872 aged 30 years, 6 months, 23 days; Our Mother Mrs. Jane A. Eggers, died 15 January 1873 aged 59 years, 10 months, 21 days; Mrs. Rachel N. Lake, born Fulton Co. Illinois 10 Dec. 1838, died 24 June 1876; Edmund Walkey, died 2 September 1866, aged 33 years, 5

Name of Cemetery and also known as	Number of burials	Acres	Condition	Date started or earliest known burial	Township	Range	Section

months, 7 days. The property is currently owned by Bill Barger (1999). See *Clackamas Legacy*, Vol. 12, Number 1, March 1999. (Not shown on Estacada 1961-85 USGS Quad. map.)

SMYRNA
AKA: 1. SMYRNA UNITED CHURCH OF CHRIST
2. YODER

C 1 2 1897 T5S R1E S9

Located 7.3 miles south of Canby, west of Molalla, and north of Marquam. Leave OR. Hwy. 211 at Milepost 7.6, turn north onto Canby-Marquam Highway (a county road) and drive 0.4 of a mile to the church on the left (west). The cemetery is behind the church. A plaque states the church was established in April 1891, the first burial noted by the compiler was from June 1897. There are 298 known burials, and 3 unknown burials. {19 October 1988} (Yoder 1955-85 USGS Quad. map.)

SPRAGUE FAMILY

A 0.19 3 1867 T3S R3E S18

Located in the Southeast 1/4 of the Southeast 1/4 of Section 18. It is 1.25 miles west from Redland Cemetery, on the left (south) side of Lyons Road and on the Warner property (1991). It is on the Alfred Sprague D.L.C., OC #4985. NOTE: This site is on private property. (Redland 1961-85 USGS Quad. map.)

SPRINGWATER

C 2.7 1 1894 T4S R4E S8

Leave OR. Hwy. 211 at Milepost 29.6 south of Estacada and go west on South Springwater Road for about 0.5 of a mile. Turn left (south) off of Springwater Road onto Metzler Park Road and go 0.35 of a mile to a driveway, turn right (northwest), down to the cemetery which is out of sight from Metzler Park Road. On the Elison B. Lewellen D.L.C. #40, OC #3252. {2 Oct 1991} (Elwood 1986 USGS Quad. map.)

STAFFORD BAPTIST CHURCH
AKA: 1. GERMAN BAPTIST
2. STAFFORD

C 1.7 2 1880 T2S R1E S31

Leave Stafford Road at Stafford and drive south on Newland Road about 0.3 of a mile to the junction with Gage Road, on the right (southwest). The church is on the right and the cemetery is across Gage Road from the

Name of Cemetery and also known as	Number of burials	Acres	Condition	Date started or earliest known burial	Township	Range	Section

church. The Robert Bird Cemetery immediately adjoins Stafford Baptist on the south side. (See that article.) The burial area at Stafford Baptist appears smaller than the stated acreage, which perhaps includes the church grounds. {6 July 1988} (Canby 1961-85 USGS Quad. map.)

STRAIGHT FAMILY
AKA: 1. PARK PLACE

B   0.1   1   1840's   T2S R2E   S29
Located at 16038 Clackamas River Drive, on the right (east) side of the road and 0.2 of a mile north of the intersection of Clackamas River Drive with Cascade Highway (OR. Hwy. 213). The cemetery is at the east end of Depot Street. It is fenced with a white picket fence; a tall cyclone fence was put around that in 1991. It has also been marked with a state historical marker. The cemetery was dedicated in 1892. There are an estimated 40-50 burials with 15 known burials: on the Hiram Straight D.L.C. #42, OC #95. {Spring 1991} (Not shown on Oregon City 1961-85 USGS Quad. map.)

SUMMIT MEADOWS
AKA: 1. BARCLAY, BABY

A   0.01 2   1880's   T3S R8 1/2E   S25
Located 1.5 miles east of Government Camp and 1.1 miles south of the Mt. Hood Highway (U.S. Hwy. 26), on the right (west) side of Forest Road #2650, which leads to Trillium Lake. The 25' x 25' graveyard is near the site of Perry Vickers' cabin and trading post of 1868. In the Mt. Hood National Forest. There are 3 known burials: Vickers, a Barclay baby, and a person now unknown. (Mount Hood South 1962-80 USGS Quad. map.)

SUNNYSIDE PIONEER

B   0.35 2   1882   T2S R2E   S2
Leave the I-205 Freeway at Exit 14 and drive easterly on Sunnyside Road for 1.9 miles. Turn left (north) onto Southeast 132nd Avenue and drive through the residential subdivision for 0.35 of a mile to the cemetery on the left (west). Donated by Seth Johnson. {1 January 1991} (Gladstone 1961-84 USGS Quad. map.)

Name of Cemetery and also known as	Number of burials	Acres	Condition	Date started or earliest known burial	Township	Range	Section

SUTER FARM
AKA: 1. TWO GIRLS

A   0.01   1   Circa 1853   T2S   R4E   S30
Located on the Suter Century Farm. Leave Clackamas Highway (OR. Hwy. 224) about 0.65 of a mile northwest of Eagle Creek. Turn onto Glover Road, southwest off of the highway, and go a short distance. Two graves for nine year old pioneer girls are on the left (south) side of the road: on the James W. Foster D.L.C. #38, OC #4934. (Not shown on Estacada 1961-85 USGS Quad. map.)

SWAILS CEDARS

A   0.01   ?   24 Jul 1972   T3S   R3E   ?
Donald A. Schreiber, born 9 September 1950, died 24 July 1972 is buried on private property behind the home on a Christmas tree farm. The address is 18737 Redland Road, apparently in the vicinity of the locale of Redland itself. NOTE: This site is on private property. (Not shown on Redland 1961-85 USGS Quad. map.)

TEN O'CLOCK
AKA: 1. BEAVERCREEK
        UNITED CHURCH
        OF CHRIST
     2. ST. PETER'S
        CHURCH

C   2   1   1859   T3S   R2E   S35
The church is southeast of Oregon City on Beavercreek Road, 1.6 miles south of the Carus Road intersection and just before the junction with Spangler Road. The church is on the right (west) side of the road and the cemetery is on the hill south of the church parking lot. There are 397 known burials. {30 September 1988} (Oregon City 1961-85 USGS Quad. map.)

TRULLINGER FAMILY

A   0.5   ?   1865-1905   T4S   R2E   S27
Leave Cascade Highway (Or. Hwy. 213) just north of Wrights Bridge over the Molalla River south of Mulino. Go easterly on Union Mills Road, passing through the locale of Union Mills to the next crossroads. Turn right (south) onto Jordan Road. The cemetery is said to be on the left (east) side of the road on private property and in dense timber. There are 11 known burials. (Not shown on Molalla 1954-85 USGS Quad. map.)

Name of Cemetery and also known as	Number of burials	Acres	Condition	Date started or earliest known burial	Township	Range	Section

TUCKER CHILDREN

A ? 5 ? T4S R4E S9

Four Tucker children are buried on the Branch Tucker D.L.C. #48, OC #4363, south of Estacada. NOTE: This site is on private property. (Not shown on Elwood 1986 USGS Quad. map.)

UNKNOWN

? ? ? ? T5S R3E S5

Located about 1.4 miles west of Colton. Leave OR. Hwy 211 at Milepost 19.8, at the Dhooghe Road intersection. Go south about 0.25 of a mile on Dhooghe Road: the burial or burials are on the left (east) side of the road. NOTE: This site is on private property. (Not shown on Colton 1955-85 USGS Quad. map.)

VIOLA PIONEER

C 1.4 2 1850 T3S R3E S23

Located 1.5 miles northeast of Viola. Take Redland Road out of Oregon City, past the community of Redland, towards Estacada. Continue on Redland Road out of Viola towards Estacada and at 1 mile past Viola turn right (south) onto Jubb Road. Continue on Jubb Road just past the junction with Bluegrass Lane and at 0.2 of a mile from Redland Road turn hard right off of Jubb Road onto the driveway to the cemetery. It is on the Asa Stone D.L.C. #49, OC #1500. {Spring 1991} (Redland 1961-85 USGS Quad. map.)

WEHRHEIM FAMILY

A ? 5 ? T3S R4E S9

Located off of South Currin Road, north of Estacada and on the Henry Wehrheim D.L.C. #48, OC #4141. NOTE: This site is on private property. (Not shown on Estacada 1961-85 USGS Quad. map.)

WHITCOMB

A 1 7 1850 T1S R1E S36

This was the second cemetery that Lot Whitcomb established in Milwaukie. Some of the graves were removed to Lone Fir in Portland. It was south of Monroe Street, west of 28th Avenue and north of Washington

Name of Cemetery and also known as	Number of burials	Acres	Condition	Date started or earliest known burial	Township	Range	Section

Street: on the Lot Whitcomb D.L.C. #38, OC #90. (Not shown on Lake Oswego 1961-84 USGS Quad. map.)

WILLAMETTE NATIONAL   E 268   1   1951   T1S   R2E   S22

The address for the office is 11800 Southeast Mt. Scott Boulevard, Portland. That office is in Multnomah County, but some of the acreage is in Clackamas County. See the article on Willamette National in the Multnomah County section of this book. {Summer 1991} (Gladstone 1961-84 USGS Quad. map.)

WILSON   A   1   3   1857   T3S   R2E   S1

Take Redland Road from Washington Street east out of Oregon City. At 4.9 miles from Washington Street turn right (south) onto Grasle Road and go about 0.5 of a mile. The cemetery is about 500 feet to the left (east), on the edge of a canyon that is tributary to Abernethy Creek. It is bounded by a stone wall. There are 14 graves, 12 marked, with 2 unknowns and reportedly one Indian. NOTE: This site is on private property with no public access. {18 February 1991} (Not shown on Oregon City 1961-85 USGS Quad. map.)

WISE FAMILY, GEORGE   A   0.3   ?   1886   T2S   R2E   S5

The land was deeded for a cemetery and family burying plot by George Wise on 24 February 1886. This was described as near the county road leading from Oregon City to Portland. The plot appears to be to the northeast of what is now Lake Road and immediately north of what is now the Milwaukie Expressway (OR. Hwy. 224). Clackamas High School is a short distance south and North Clackamas County Park is close by to the west. The area is now filled with industrial sites and parking lots and probably the cemetery site is obliterated. The compiler recalls some Wise family burials in Clackamas Cemetery about a mile to the east. Located on the Joseph Eagon D.L.C., OC #3575. (Not shown on Gladstone 1961-84 USGS Quad. map.)

Name of Cemetery and also known as	Number of burials	Acres	Condition	Date started or earliest known burial	Township	Range	Section

WYLAND FAMILY

A 0.5 3 1870'S T5S R1E S4

Located in the Southeast 1/4 of Section 4, just west of the Canby-Marquam Highway (South Kropf Road) and on the north side of Sconce Road. This lost burial ground contains 5 or 6 graves of relatives of Daniel Wyland. The burials appear to be on private property. (Not shown on Yoder 1955-85 USGS Quad. map.)

YODER, CLAYTON
AKA: 1. I.O.O.F.
[AURORA]

B 0.75 2 1898 T4S R1E S18

Leave OR. Hwy. 99E at Milepost 24.5 onto Lone Elder Road, just before OR. Hwy. 99E crosses the Pudding River into Aurora. Follow Lone Elder Road (passing at 0.3 of a mile the fir grove containing the Irvin Cemetery) to the junction with Meridian Road at 0.46 of a mile. Turn right (south) onto Meridian Road and proceed about 500 feet to the house at 26050: their driveway and the cemetery driveway are one and the same. Head left (east), where the cemetery is behind a new home and a screen of arbor vitae. Established by the Aurora I.O.O.F. in 1898, and the plat was filed 24 May 1899. The cemetery was deeded to the Canby I.O.O.F. in 1965. The Canby lodge sold it to private owners in 1971. Originally three acres in size, the burial area is now only about 0.75 of an acre and contains about 100 graves. Clayton Yoder was the longtime caretaker of this cemetery, and two different cemetery caretakers separately told the compiler this cemetery is now known as Clayton Yoder. There was, however, no sign here: {27 June 1992} (Yoder 1955-85 USGS Quad. map.)

ZIMMERMAN

B 0.5 1 1868-1941 T4S R1E S32

From OR. Hwy. 211 at Milepost 6.6 west of Molalla, turn north onto South Needy Road, heading towards Canby. Go 2.3 miles on Needy Road and then turn left (west) onto Three-Gait Lane. The cemetery is out of sight, on a high bank, on the right (north) of Three-Gait Lane at the first private driveway after leaving Needy Road. There are 38 known burials and 23 unknowns; on the James Shirley

D.L.C. #45, OC #898. NOTE: This site is on private property. {21 September 1989} (Not shown on the Yoder 1955-85 USGS Quad. map.)

ZION MEMORIAL PARK
AKA: 1. CANBY
         LUTHERAN
      2. MT. ZION
      3. ZION [CANBY]
      4. ZION LUTHERAN

D 14   1   1892   T3S   R1E   S34

Leave OR. Hwy. 99E in Canby at the signalized intersection of South Ivy Street. Proceed southerly on South Ivy Street past 3rd Avenue, then turn left (east) onto Township Road. Go about a mile to the main entrance of the cemetery on the left (north), where there is a large archway. {1 December 1989} (Canby 1961-85 USGS Quad. map.)

ZION MENNONITE
AKA: 1. NEEDY
      2. SINE *[Sic]*
      3. YODERVILLE
      4. ZION
         [HUBBARD]

C 5   1   1897   T4S   R1E   S31

Located east of Hubbard, in Marion County, and south of Barlow, in Clackamas County. Drive 5.25 miles south of OR. Hwy. 99E from the signalized intersection with Barlow Road. Leave South Barlow Road at Ninety One crossroads, turning right (west) onto Whiskey Hill Road. Go about 0.8 of a mile on Whiskey Hill Road to the church and cemetery on a low hill to the left (south). There is an adjacent duckpond. {26 March 1990} NOTE: There is a Hopewell Mennonite Church east of Hubbard, also on Whiskey Hill Road. It has a cemetery too, and is about 2 miles west of Zion Mennonite in Marion County. See that article in the Marion County section of this book. (Yoder 1955-85 USGS Quad. map.)

ZOAR LUTHERAN
AKA: 1. ZOAR
      2. ZOAR LUTHERAN
         [EAST]

C 0.5   2   1892   T3S   R1E   S34

Leave OR. Hwy. 99E in Canby at the signalized intersection of South Ivy Street. Proceed southerly on South Ivy, past 3rd Avenue; then turn left (east) onto Township Road, passing Zion Memorial Park on the left, to Walnut Street. Turn left (north) onto Walnut Street and it is about 0.7 of a mile to the cemetery on the left (west). There are about 100 graves: on the Philander Lee D.L.C. #56, OC #2795. NOTE: The reader should be aware that there is another cemetery about 6 miles away that is also signed "Zoar Lutheran Cemetery."

| Name of Cemetery and also known as | Number of burials | Acres | Condition | Date started or earliest known burial | Township | Range | Section |

Established 1892." See that article. {17 October 1988} (Canby 1961-85 USGS Quad. map.)

ZOAR LUTHERAN [BARLOW ROAD]

C 0.8 2 1900 T4S R1E S7

AKA:
1. AURORA
2. BARLOW
3. BARLOW CORNER
4. FOUR CORNERS
5. NORWAY [BARLOW]
6. NORWEGIAN [BARLOW]
7. NORWEGIAN [CANBY]
8. NORWEGIAN LUTHERAN
9. OAK HILL
10. ZION LUTHERAN
11. ZOAR LUTHERAN [WEST]

From the signalized intersection of OR. Hwy. 99E with Barlow Road, less than 2 miles southwest of Canby, turn south onto South Barlow Road. Go 1.25 miles on South Barlow Road to the crossroads with South Lone Elder Road: the cemetery is on the northwest corner. Here, there is a new signboard saying "Zoar Lutheran Cemetery Established 1892." NOTE: The reader should be aware that there is another cemetery about 6 miles away that is also signed "Zoar Lutheran Cemetery. Established 1892." See that article. 30 November 1991} (Yoder 1955-85 USGS Quad. map.)

Carus
Black glass
Dean H. Byrd (1991)

Mt. Home
Dean H. Byrd (1991)

St. John's Catholic
Dean H. Byrd (1992)

_____, WILLIE see **HOLLAND**	CLACKAMAS CO.	T1S	R1E	S36
ADAMS	CLACKAMAS CO.	T5S	R2E	S22
AIMS see **LOWE FAMILY**	CLACKAMAS CO.	T1S	R5E	S30
AMISH see **BLOSSER**	CLACKAMAS CO.	T4S	R1W	S36
ARTHUR see **PLEASANT VIEW [EAST]**	CLACKAMAS CO.	T2S	R3E	S19
ARTHUR D.L.C., WILLIAM see **PLEASANT VIEW [EAST]**				
	CLACKAMAS CO.	T2S	R3E	S19
AURORA see **ZOAR LUTHERAN [BARLOW ROAD]**				
	CLACKAMAS CO.	T4S	R1E	S7
AUSTIN FAMILY see **JACKSON FAMILY**				
	CLACKAMAS CO.	T5S	R2E	S7
BAKER, MOSES MATTHEW see **PLEASANT VIEW [WEST]**				
	CLACKAMAS CO.	T3S	R1W	S9
BAKER PRAIRIE	CLACKAMAS CO.	T3S	R1E	S33
BAKERS PRAIRIE see **BAKER PRAIRIE**				
	CLACKAMAS CO.	T3S	R1E	S33
BARBER, DOROTHY see **MARQUAM FAMILY**				
	CLACKAMAS CO.	T6S	R1E	S10
BARCLAY, BABY see **SUMMIT MEADOWS**				
	CLACKAMAS CO.	T3S	R8 1/2E	S25
BARGER, BILL see **SMITH PLACE**	CLACKAMAS CO.	T2S	R4E	S30
BARLOW see **BARLOW PIONEER**	CLACKAMAS CO.	T4S	R1E	S6
BARLOW see **ZOAR LUTHERAN [BARLOW ROAD]**				
	CLACKAMAS CO.	T4S	R1E	S7
BARLOW CORNER see **ZOAR LUTHERAN [BARLOW ROAD]**				
	CLACKAMAS CO.	T4S	R1E	S7
BARLOW PIONEER	CLACKAMAS CO.	T4S	R1E	S6
BARTON	CLACKAMAS CO.	T2S	R3E	S14
BATTY FAMILY	CLACKAMAS CO.	T2S	R3E	?
BATY D.L.C., ANDREW J. see **BATY FAMILY**				
	CLACKAMAS CO.	T5S	R2E	S14
BATY FAMILY	CLACKAMAS CO.	T5S	R2E	S14
BEAR CREEK	CLACKAMAS CO.	T5S	R1E	S2
BEATTIE see **BATY FAMILY**	CLACKAMAS CO.	T5S	R2E	S14
BEAVERCREEK MEMORIAL	CLACKAMAS CO.	T3S	R2E	S26
BEAVERCREEK UNITED CHURCH OF CHRIST see **TEN O'CLOCK**				
	CLACKAMAS CO.	T3S	R2E	S35
BIRD, ROBERT	CLACKAMAS CO.	T2S	R1E	S31
BLASSER see **BLOSSER**	CLACKAMAS CO.	T4S	R1W	S36
BLOSSER	CLACKAMAS CO.	T4S	R1W	S36
BONNEY	CLACKAMAS CO.	T4S	R3E	S35
BOWMAN D.L.C., JOSHUA see **MAPLEWOOD**				
	CLACKAMAS CO.	T6S	R1E	S14
BOYER, DUDLEY see **FERN HILL**	CLACKAMAS CO.	T5S	R3E	S21
BOYER FAMILY see **FERN HILL**	CLACKAMAS CO.	T5S	R3E	S21
BRACKETT see **IRVIN FAMILY**	CLACKAMAS CO.	T4S	R1E	S18
BROUSSARD JR., ELDRIDGE J.	CLACKAMAS CO.	T2S	R5E	?
BULLOCK D.L.C., JESSE see **OSWEGO PIONEER**				
	CLACKAMAS CO.	T2S	R1E	S16
BULLOCK D.L.C., JESSE see **SACRED HEART**				
	CLACKAMAS CO.	T2S	R1E	S16
CABBAGE HILL see **REVENUE FAMILY**	CLACKAMAS CO.	T2S	R5E	S7

CALLAHAN D.L.C., CLIFTON R. see **CALLAHAN FAMILY**				
	CLACKAMAS CO.	T5S	R2E	S24
CALLAHAN D.L.C., CLIFTON R. see **FEYRER**				
	CLACKAMAS CO.	T5S	R3E	S19
CALLAHAN FAMILY	CLACKAMAS CO.	T5S	R2E	S24
CANBY LUTHERAN see **ZION MEMORIAL PARK**				
	CLACKAMAS CO.	T3S	R1E	S34
CANBY PIONEER see **BAKER PRAIRIE**	CLACKAMAS CO.	T3S	R1E	S33
CANEMAH	CLACKAMAS CO.	T3S	R1E	S1
CANYON CREEK see **BONNEY**	CLACKAMAS CO.	T4S	R3E	S35
CARUS	CLACKAMAS CO.	T3S	R2E	S27
CASE, CHARLES LAFERTY	CLACKAMAS CO.	T2S	R1E	S36
CASON D.L.C., FENDALL see **CASON, REBECCA**				
	CLACKAMAS CO.	T2S	R2E	S20
CASON, JOHN see **CASON, REBECCA**	CLACKAMAS CO.	T2S	R2E	S20
CASON, REBECCA	CLACKAMAS CO.	T2S	R2E	S20
CEMETERY ASSOCIATION see **HAZELWOOD**				
	CLACKAMAS CO.	T2S	R3E	S13
CHASE BURIAL	CLACKAMAS CO.	T4S	R4E	?
CHERRYVILLE	CLACKAMAS CO.	T2S	R6E	S30
CHITWOOD see **DAMASCUS PIONEER**	CLACKAMAS CO.	T2S	R3E	S8
CHRIST CHURCH PARISH	CLACKAMAS CO.	T2S	R1E	S10
CHRISTILDA see **CRISTILLA PIONEER**				
	CLACKAMAS CO.	T1S	R2E	S36
CITY OF OREGON CITY see **MOUNTAIN VIEW**				
	CLACKAMAS CO.	T3S	R2E	S5
CLACKAMAS	CLACKAMAS CO.	T2S	R2E	S4
CLACKAMAS PIONEER see **CLACKAMAS**	CLACKAMAS CO.	T2S	R2E	S4
CLARKES see **CLARKES PIONEER**	CLACKAMAS CO.	T4S	R3E	S29
CLARKES PIONEER	CLACKAMAS CO.	T4S	R3E	S29
CLAUSEN, NICK	CLACKAMAS CO.	T4S	R4E	?
CLIFFSIDE	CLACKAMAS CO.	T2S	R5E	S7
COLTON LUTHERAN	CLACKAMAS CO.	T5S	R3E	S3
COOKE, RONALD PETER	CLACKAMAS CO.	?	?	?
CRISTILLA PIONEER	CLACKAMAS CO.	T1S	R2E	S36
CURRIN D.L.C., GEORGE see **CURRINSVILLE**				
	CLACKAMAS CO.	T3S	R4E	S7
CURRIN D.L.C., HUGH see **CURRIN FAMILY**				
	CLACKAMAS CO.	T3S	R4E	S8
CURRIN FAMILY	CLACKAMAS CO.	T3S	R4E	S8
CURRINSVILLE	CLACKAMAS CO.	T3S	R4E	S7
CURRINSVILLE see **CURRIN FAMILY**	CLACKAMAS CO.	T3S	R4E	S8
CUTTING, ABIGAIL see **CUTTING FAMILY**				
	CLACKAMAS CO.	T4S	R2E	S36
CUTTING, BABY see **CUTTING FAMILY**				
	CLACKAMAS CO.	T4S	R2E	S36
CUTTING, CHARLES see **CUTTING FAMILY**				
	CLACKAMAS CO.	T4S	R2E	S36
CUTTING D.L.C., CHARLES see **CUTTING FAMILY**				
	CLACKAMAS CO.	T4S	R2E	S36
CUTTING D.L.C., MARY see **REDLAND PIONEER**				
	CLACKAMAS CO.	T3S	R3E	S16

CUTTING FAMILY	CLACKAMAS CO.	T4S	R2E	S36
CUTTING FAMILY see **REDLAND PIONEER**				
	CLACKAMAS CO.	T3S	R3E	S16
DAMASCUS see **DAMASCUS PIONEER**	CLACKAMAS CO.	T2S	R3E	S8
DAMASCUS PIONEER	CLACKAMAS CO.	T2S	R3E	S8
DART see **MOLALLA MEMORIAL**	CLACKAMAS CO.	T5S	R2E	S20
DEARDORFF D.L.C., JOHN M. see **CRISTILLA PIONEER**				
	CLACKAMAS CO.	T1S	R2E	S36
DEARDORFF FAMILY see **CRISTILLA PIONEER**				
	CLACKAMAS CO.	T1S	R2E	S36
DECKEY see **DICKEY FAMILY**	CLACKAMAS CO.	T5S	R2E	S23
DEUTSCHE EVANGELISCHE REFORMIETE MERIDIAN CHURCH see **MERIDIAN [OLD]**				
	CLACKAMAS CO.	T3S	R1W	S13
DIBBLE FAMILY see **JACKSON FAMILY**				
	CLACKAMAS CO.	T5S	R2E	S7
DICKEY D.L.C., JOHN K. see **DICKEY FAMILY**				
	CLACKAMAS CO.	T5S	R2E	S23
DICKEY FAMILY	CLACKAMAS CO.	T5S	R2E	S23
DIX see **BONNEY**	CLACKAMAS CO.	T4S	R3E	S35
DOUGLAS see **GIBSON**	CLACKAMAS CO.	T3S	R4E	?
DOUGLAS RIDGE see **FORRESTER**	CLACKAMAS CO.	T2S	R4E	S29
DRAPER FAMILY	CLACKAMAS CO.	T3S	R1E	S1
DRAPER, GEORGE see **DRAPER FAMILY**				
	CLACKAMAS CO.	T3S	R1E	S1
DRAPER, MARTHA see **DRAPER FAMILY**				
	CLACKAMAS CO.	T3S	R1E	S1
EAGLE CREEK see **SCHEEL FAMILY**	CLACKAMAS CO.	T3S	R5E	S18
EAGON D.L.C., JOSEPH see **WISE FAMILY, GEORGE**				
	CLACKAMAS CO.	T2S	R2E	S5
EASTLAWN MEMORIAL GARDENS see **LITTLE CHAPEL OF THE CHIMES MEMORIAL**				
GARDEN	CLACKAMAS CO.	T1S	R2E	S33
EGGERS, C. L. see **SMITH PLACE**	CLACKAMAS CO.	T2S	R4E	S30
EGGERS, JANE A. see **SMITH PLACE**	CLACKAMAS CO.	T2S	R4E	S30
EILER PEAK see **ILERS PEAK**	CLACKAMAS CO.	T2S	R3E	S18
EILERS PEAK see **ILERS PEAK**	CLACKAMAS CO.	T2S	R3E	S18
ELWOOD see **MT. HOME**	CLACKAMAS CO.	T4S	R4E	S19
ERB see **BLOSSER**	CLACKAMAS CO.	T4S	R1W	S36
ESTACADA see **I.O.O.F. [ESTACADA]**				
	CLACKAMAS CO.	T3S	R4E	S21
ESTACADA ODD FELLOWS see **I.O.O.F. [ESTACADA]**				
	CLACKAMAS CO.	T3S	R4E	S21
ETERNAL MEMORIAL GARDENS see **LITTLE CHAPEL OF THE CHIMES MEMORIAL**				
GARDEN	CLACKAMAS CO.	T1S	R2E	S33
FELLOWS	CLACKAMAS CO.	T4S	R3E	S3
FELLOWS D.L.C., HIRAM see **FELLOWS**				
	CLACKAMAS CO.	T4S	R3E	S3
FERGUSON, EPHRAIM see **FERGUSON FAMILY**				
	CLACKAMAS CO.	T2S	R2E	?
FERGUSON FAMILY	CLACKAMAS CO.	T2S	R2E	?
FERN HILL	CLACKAMAS CO.	T5S	R3E	S21
FERNHILL see **FERN HILL**	CLACKAMAS CO.	T5S	R3E	S21
FERNWOOD see **JOHNSON FAMILY**	CLACKAMAS CO.	T5S	R3E	S18

FEYRER	CLACKAMAS CO.	T5S	R3E	S19
FIELDS	CLACKAMAS CO.	T2S	R1E	S34
FIELDS D.L.C., JOSEPH A. see **FIELDS**				
	CLACKAMAS CO.	T2S	R1E	S34
FIR HILL	CLACKAMAS CO.	T2S	R4E	S14
FIR LAWN see **FIR HILL**	CLACKAMAS CO.	T2S	R4E	S14
FIR MEMORIAL see **FIR HILL**	CLACKAMAS CO.	T2S	R4E	S14
FISCHER, BABY	CLACKAMAS CO.	?	?	?
FORRESTER	CLACKAMAS CO.	T2S	R4E	S29
FOSTER D.L.C., JAMES W. see **SUTER FARM**				
	CLACKAMAS CO.	T2S	R4E	S30
FOSTER D.L.C., PHILIP see **FOSTER PIONEER**				
	CLACKAMAS CO.	T2S	R4E	S31
FOSTER PIONEER	CLACKAMAS CO.	T2S	R4E	S31
FOUR CORNERS see **ZOAR LUTHERAN [BARLOW ROAD]**				
	CLACKAMAS CO.	T4S	R1E	S7
FROG POND CHURCH see **MERIDIAN [OLD]**				
	CLACKAMAS CO.	T3S	R1W	S13
G. W. W.	CLACKAMAS CO.	T3S	R2E	S4
GARD, JOHN see **SCHUEBEL**	CLACKAMAS CO.	T3S	R2E	S36
GARDEN OF REVERENCE	CLACKAMAS CO.	T1S	R4E	S28
GARFIELD see **MT. ZION**	CLACKAMAS CO.	T3S	R4E	S22
GEER D.L.C., FREDERICK W. see **GEER PIONEER**				
	CLACKAMAS CO.	T3S	R1W	S31
GEER, JOSPH C. see **GEER PIONEER**	CLACKAMAS CO.	T3S	R1W	S31
GEER, MARY see **GEER PIONEER**	CLACKAMAS CO.	T3S	R1W	S31
GEER PIONEER	CLACKAMAS CO.	T3S	R1W	S31
GEORGE	CLACKAMAS CO.	T3S	R5E	S19
GEORGE PROTESTANT see **GEORGE**	CLACKAMAS CO.	T3S	R5E	S19
GERMAN BAPTIST see **STAFFORD BAPTIST CHURCH**				
	CLACKAMAS CO.	T2S	R1E	S31
GERMAN EVANGELICAL see **ST. JOHANN**				
	CLACKAMAS CO.	T3S	R1E	S36
GETHSEMANE see **GETHSEMANI**	CLACKAMAS CO.	T1S	R2E	S33
GETHSEMANI	CLACKAMAS CO.	T1S	R2E	S33
GIBSON	CLACKAMAS CO.	T3S	R4E	?
GITHENS FAMILY	CLACKAMAS CO.	T3S	R4E	S5
GLEASON	CLACKAMAS CO.	T4S	R	S
GLEASON, PARSON see **GLEASON**	CLACKAMAS CO.	T4S	R	S
GLOVER D.L.C., JOHN P. see **SMITH PLACE**				
	CLACKAMAS CO.	T2S	R4E	S30
GRAY, MRS. ELIZA JANE	CLACKAMAS CO	T6S	R2E	S16
GRIBBLE	CLACKAMAS CO.	T4S	R1E	S21
GRIBBLE D.L.C., ANDREW E. see **GRIBBLE**				
	CLACKAMAS CO.	T4S	R1E	S21
HABELT, MRS.	CLACKAMAS CO.	T4S	R4E	S26
HAZELWOOD	CLACKAMAS CO.	T2S	R3E	S13
HIGHLAND see **FELLOWS**	CLACKAMAS CO.	T4S	R3E	S3
HODGE, ANDREW see **HODGE, GERTRUDE**				
	CLACKAMAS CO.	T3S	R1E	?
HODGE, CORA see **HODGE, GERTRUDE**	CLACKAMAS CO.	T3S	R1E	?

HODGE, GERTRUDE	CLACKAMAS CO.	T3S	R1E	?
HOLLAND	CLACKAMAS CO.	T1S	R1E	S36
HOLLAND, ELIZA see **HOLLAND**	CLACKAMAS CO.	T1S	R1E	S36
HOLLAND, WILLIAM see **HOLLAND**	CLACKAMAS CO.	T1S	R1E	S36
HOLMS D.L.C., WILLIAM see **I.O.O.F. [OREGON CITY]**				
	CLACKAMAS CO.	T3S	R2E	S5
HOLMS D.L.C., WILLIAM see **MASONIC [OREGON CITY]**				
	CLACKAMAS CO.	T3S	R2E	S5
HOLMS D.L.C., WILLIAM see **MOUNTAIN VIEW**				
	CLACKAMAS CO.	T3S	R2E	S5
HOLMS D.L.C., WILLIAM see **ST. JOHN'S CATHOLIC**				
	CLACKAMAS CO.	T3S	R2E	S5
HOLY NAMES see **SISTERS OF THE HOLY NAMES**				
	CLACKAMAS CO.	T2S	R1E	S14
HOLY NEW MARTYRS RUSSIAN ORTHODOX CHURCH				
	CLACKAMAS CO.	T4S	R2E	?
HOOD LOOP see **FIR HILL**	CLACKAMAS CO.	T2S	R4E	S14
HOODVIEW see **PLEASANT VIEW [WEST]**				
	CLACKAMAS CO.	T3S	R1W	S9
HOWARD FAMILY	CLACKAMAS CO.	T4S	R2E	S17
HOWLETT see **GIBSON**	CLACKAMAS CO.	T3S	R4E	?
HOWLETT D.L.C., WILLIAM J. see **GIBSON**				
	CLACKAMAS CO.	T3S	R4E	?
I.O.O.F. [AURORA] see **YODER, CLAYTON**				
	CLACKAMAS CO.	T4S	R1E	S18
I.O.O.F. [ESTACADA]	CLACKAMAS CO.	T3S	R4E	S21
I.O.O.F. [OLD] see **MOLALLA MEMORIAL**				
	CLACKAMAS CO.	T5S	R2E	S20
I.O.O.F. [OLD] see **RUSSELLVILLE**				
	CLACKAMAS CO.	T6S	R2E	S2
I.O.O.F. [OREGON CITY]	CLACKAMAS CO.	T3S	R2E	S5
I.O.O.F. [SCOTTS MILLS] see **MAPLEWOOD**				
	CLACKAMAS CO.	T6S	R1E	S14
I.O.O.F. #93 see **OSWEGO PIONEER**	CLACKAMAS CO.	T2S	R1E	S16
I.O.O.F. PIONEER see **I.O.O.F. [OREGON CITY]**				
	CLACKAMAS CO.	T3S	R2E	S5
ILERS PEAK	CLACKAMAS CO.	T2S	R3E	S18
INDIAN BURIAL	CLACKAMAS CO.	T2S	R2E	S30
INDIAN GRAVES	CLACKAMAS CO.	T5S	R2E	?
IRVIN D.L.C., GEORGE AND MARY ANN see **IRVIN FAMILY**				
	CLACKAMAS CO.	T4S	R1E	S18
IRVIN FAMILY	CLACKAMAS CO.	T4S	R1E	S18
IRWIN FAMILY see **IRVIN FAMILY**	CLACKAMAS CO.	T4S	R1E	S18
JACKSON FAMILY	CLACKAMAS CO.	T5S	R2E	S7
JOHNSON, ANDREW see **JOHNSON FAMILY**				
	CLACKAMAS CO.	T5S	R3E	S18
JOHNSON FAMILY	CLACKAMAS CO.	T5S	R3E	S18
JOHNSON, SETH see **SUNNYSIDE PIONEER**				
	CLACKAMAS CO.	T2S	R2E	S2
JUDD see **FORRESTER**	CLACKAMAS CO.	T2S	R4E	S29
KELLOGG D.L.C., ORRIN see **KELLOGG FAMILY**				
	CLACKAMAS CO.	T2S	R2E	S7

KELLOGG FAMILY	CLACKAMAS CO.	T2S	R2E	S7
KIGGENS, PATRICK LEROY	CLACKAMAS CO.	T3S	R4E	S5
KIGGENS, TED see **GITHENS FAMILY**	CLACKAMAS CO.	T3S	R4E	S5
KIGGENS, TED see **KIGGENS, PATRICK LEROY**				
	CLACKAMAS CO.	T3S	R4E	S5
KLINGER see **KLINGLER MEMORIAL**	CLACKAMAS CO.	T4S	R1E	S24
KLINGLER see **KLINGLER MEMORIAL**	CLACKAMAS CO.	T4S	R1E	S24
KLINGLER D.L.C., JOHN L. see **KLINGLER MEMORIAL**				
	CLACKAMAS CO.	T4S	R1E	S24
KLINGLER MEMORIAL	CLACKAMAS CO.	T4S	R1E	S24
KLINKER	CLACKAMAS CO.	T3S	R5E	?
KNIGHT D.L.C., HENRIETTA see **GITHENS FAMILY**				
	CLACKAMAS CO.	T3S	R4E	S5
KNIGHT D.L.C., HENRIETTA see **KIGGENS, PATRICK LEROY**				
	CLACKAMAS CO.	T3S	R4E	S5
KOWALL, THERESA	CLACKAMAS CO.	T3S	R5E	S18
LADD HILL see **GEER PIONEER**	CLACKAMAS CO.	T3S	R1W	S31
LAKE, RACHEL N. see **SMITH PLACE**	CLACKAMAS CO.	T2S	R4E	S30
LARKINS D.L.C., MONROE AND ELIZABETH V. see **LARKINS, MONROE AND**				
ELIZABETH V.	CLACKAMAS CO.	T4S	R2E	?
LARKINS D.L.C., RACHEL see **JACKSON FAMILY**				
	CLACKAMAS CO.	T5S	R2E	S7
LARKINS FAMILY see **JACKSON FAMILY**				
	CLACKAMAS CO.	T5S	R2E	S7
LARKINS, MONROE AND ELIZABETH V.				
	CLACKAMAS CO.	T4S	R2E	?
LATOURETTE D.L.C., LYMAN D. see **G. W. W.**				
	CLACKAMAS CO.	T3S	R2E	S4
LATOURETTE WOODS see **KLINGLER MEMORIAL**				
	CLACKAMAS CO.	T4S	R1E	S24
LEE D.L.C., PHILANDER see **ZOAR LUTHERAN**				
	CLACKAMAS CO.	T3S	R1E	S34
LEE D.L.C., THOMAS see **MT. ZION**	CLACKAMAS CO.	T3S	R4E	S22
LEISMAN, ANNIE JACKSON see **LEISMAN, FAMILY**				
	CLACKAMAS CO.	T4S	R3E	?
LEISMAN, FAMILY	CLACKAMAS CO.	T4S	R3E	?
LEISMAN, JOSEPH see **LEISMAN, FAMILY**				
	CLACKAMAS CO.	T4S	R3E	?
LEWELLEN D.L.C., ELISON B. see **SPRINGWATER**				
	CLACKAMAS CO.	T4S	R4E	S8
LEWTHWAITE	CLACKAMAS CO.	T2S	R2E	S20
LINCOLN MEMORIAL PARK	CLACKAMAS CO.	T1S	R2E	S22
LINN, PHILIP E.	CLACKAMAS CO.	T3S	R4E	S21
LINN, PHILIP E. see **I.O.O.F. [ESTACADA]**				
	CLACKAMAS CO.	T3S	R4E	S21
LITTLE CHAPEL OF THE CHIMES MEMORIAL GARDEN				
	CLACKAMAS CO.	T1S	R2E	S33
LOGAN see **PLEASANT VIEW [EAST]**	CLACKAMAS CO.	T2S	R3E	S19
LONE OAK see **CURRINSVILLE**	CLACKAMAS CO.	T3S	R4E	S7
LONE OAK see **I.O.O.F. [ESTACADA]**				
	CLACKAMAS CO.	T3S	R4E	S21

LONG, DOCTOR JAMES see **ST. JOHN THE EVANGELIST**

	CLACKAMAS CO.	?	?	?
LOWE FAMILY	CLACKAMAS CO.	T1S	R5E	S30
LOWER HIGHLAND see **FELLOWS**	CLACKAMAS CO.	T4S	R3E	S3
LOWER LOGAN see **PLEASANT VIEW [EAST]**				
	CLACKAMAS CO.	T2S	R3E	S19
LOWER SCHUEBEL see **MOEHNKE**	CLACKAMAS CO.	T3S	R3E	S31
LUTHERAN-CATHOLIC see **SCHEEL FAMILY**				
	CLACKAMAS CO.	T3S	R5E	S18
MAPLE GROVE see **MAPLEWOOD**	CLACKAMAS CO.	T6S	R1E	S14
MAPLEWOOD	CLACKAMAS CO.	T6S	R1E	S14
MARK FAMILY see **MARK MEMORIAL PARK**				
	CLACKAMAS CO.	T4S	R1E	S20
MARK MEMORIAL PARK	CLACKAMAS CO.	T4S	R1E	S20
MARKS see **MARK MEMORIAL PARK**	CLACKAMAS CO.	T4S	R1E	S20
MARKS D.L.C., JOHN AND FANNY see **MARK MEMORIAL PARK**				
	CLACKAMAS CO.	T4S	R1E	S20
MARKS PRAIRIE see **MARK MEMORIAL PARK**				
	CLACKAMAS CO.	T4S	R1E	S20
MARQUAM D.L.C., ALFRED see **MARQUAM FAMILY**				
	CLACKAMAS CO.	T6S	R1E	S10
MARQUAM FAMILY	CLACKAMAS CO.	T6S	R1E	S10
MARSHFIELD see **CLACKAMAS**	CLACKAMAS CO.	T2S	R2E	S4
MARYLHURST CONVENT see **SISTERS OF THE HOLY NAMES**				
	CLACKAMAS CO.	T2S	R1E	S14
MASONIC [OREGON CITY]	CLACKAMAS CO.	T3S	R2E	S5
MATLOCK D.L.C., WILLIAM T. see **CLACKAMAS**				
	CLACKAMAS CO.	T2S	R2E	S4
MATLOCK FAMILY see **CLACKAMAS**	CLACKAMAS CO.	T2S	R2E	S4
MAUTZ FARM, ALBERT see **SAWTELL FAMILY**				
	CLACKAMAS CO.	T5S	R2E	S30
McLOUGHLIN, DOCTOR JOHN see **McLOUGHLIN FAMILY**				
	CLACKAMAS CO.	T2S	R2E	S31
McLOUGHLIN, DOCTOR JOHN see **ST. JOHN THE EVANGELIST**				
	CLACKAMAS CO.	?	?	?
McLOUGHLIN FAMILY	CLACKAMAS CO.	T2S	R2E	S31
McLOUGHLIN, MARGUERITE McKAY see **McLOUGHLIN FAMILY**				
	CLACKAMAS CO.	T2S	R2E	S31
McNEIL, FRED H.	CLACKAMAS CO.	T2S	UNSURVEYED	
MEEK D.L.C., WILLIAM see **MILWAUKIE PIONEER**				
	CLACKAMAS CO.	T1S	R1E	S26
MEINIG PARK	CLACKAMAS CO.	T2S	R4E	S13
MEMORIAL see **MOLALLA MEMORIAL**	CLACKAMAS CO.	T5S	R2E	S20
MENNONITE see **BLOSSER**	CLACKAMAS CO.	T4S	R1W	S36
MERIDIAN [OLD]	CLACKAMAS CO.	T3S	R1W	S13
MERIDIAN UNITED CHURCH OF CHRIST see **MERIDIAN [OLD]**				
	CLACKAMAS CO.	T3S	R1W	S13
MILLER see **BLOSSER**	CLACKAMAS CO.	T4S	R1W	S36
MILLN HOUSE, RALPH see **INDIAN BURIAL**				
	CLACKAMAS CO.	T2S	R2E	S30
MILWAUKIE see **MILWAUKIE PIONEER**	CLACKAMAS CO.	T1S	R1E	S26
MILWAUKIE PIONEER	CLACKAMAS CO.	T1S	R1E	S26

MINK see **MOEHNKE**	CLACKAMAS CO.	T3S	R3E	S31
MOEHNKE	CLACKAMAS CO.	T3S	R3E	S31
MOEHNKE, MICHAEL see **MOEHNKE**	CLACKAMAS CO.	T3S	R3E	S31
MOLALLA MEMORIAL	CLACKAMAS CO.	T5S	R2E	S20
MOLALLA PRAIRIE see **MOLALLA MEMORIAL**				
	CLACKAMAS CO.	T5S	R2E	S20
MONTAQUE, C. J. see **G. W. W.**	CLACKAMAS CO.	T3S	R2E	S4
MOORE see **SAWTELL FAMILY**	CLACKAMAS CO.	T5S	R2E	S30
MORGAN, BABY	CLACKAMAS CO.	T3S	R8 1/2E	S25
MORGAN, DANIEL see **MORGAN, BABY**	CLACKAMAS CO.	T3S	R8 1/2E	S25
MOSHBERGER see **BEAR CREEK**	CLACKAMAS CO.	T5S	R1E	S2
MT. HOME	CLACKAMAS CO.	T4S	R4E	S19
MT. HOMES see **MT. HOME**	CLACKAMAS CO.	T4S	R4E	S19
MT. HOOD LOOP see **FIR HILL**	CLACKAMAS CO.	T2S	R4E	S14
MT. HOOD MEMORIAL see **GARDEN OF REVERENCE**				
	CLACKAMAS CO.	T1S	R4E	S28
MT. SCOTT PARK see **LINCOLN MEMORIAL PARK**				
	CLACKAMAS CO.	T1S	R2E	S22
MT. ZION	CLACKAMAS CO.	T3S	R4E	S22
MT. ZION see **ZION MEMORIAL PARK**	CLACKAMAS CO.	T3S	R1E	S34
MOUNT VIEW see **MOUNTAIN VIEW**	CLACKAMAS CO.	T3S	R2E	S5
MOUNTAIN HOME see **MT. HOME**	CLACKAMAS CO.	T4S	R4E	S19
MOUNTAIN VIEW	CLACKAMAS CO.	T3S	R2E	S5
MULLALLA *[Sic]* PRAIRIE see **MOLALLA MEMORIAL**				
	CLACKAMAS CO.	T5S	R2E	S20
NEEDY see **ZION MENNONTE**	CLACKAMAS CO.	T4S	R1E	S31
NEW ERA see **ST. JOHANN**	CLACKAMAS CO.	T3S	R1E	S36
NEW ERA CATHOLIC see **ST. PATRICK'S**				
	CLACKAMAS CO.	T3S	R1E	S23
NORWAY [BARLOW] see **ZOAR LUTHERAN [BARLOW ROAD]**				
	CLACKAMAS CO.	T4S	R1E	S7
NORWEGIAN [BARLOW] see **ZOAR LUTHERAN [BARLOW ROAD]**				
	CLACKAMAS CO.	T4S	R1E	S7
NORWEGIAN [CANBY] see **ZOAR LUTHERAN [BARLOW ROAD]**				
	CLACKAMAS CO.	T4S	R1E	S7
NORWEGIAN LUTHERAN see **ZOAR LUTHERAN [BARLOW ROAD]**				
	CLACKAMAS CO.	T4S	R1E	S7
OAK HILL see **ZOAR LUTHERAN [BARLOW ROAD]**				
	CLACKAMAS CO.	T4S	R1E	S7
ODD FELLOWS see **MOLALLA MEMORIAL**				
	CLACKAMAS CO.	T5S	R2E	S20
OLD CANBY see **BAKER PRAIRIE**	CLACKAMAS CO.	T3S	R1E	S33
OLD CITY see **MOUNTAIN VIEW**	CLACKAMAS CO.	T3S	R2E	S5
OLD OREGON CITY see **MOUNTAIN VIEW**				
	CLACKAMAS CO.	T3S	R2E	S5
OREGON CITY see **MOUNTAIN VIEW**	CLACKAMAS CO.	T3S	R2E	S5
OSWEGO CATHOLIC see **SACRED HEART**				
	CLACKAMAS CO.	T2S	R1E	S16
OSWEGO PIONEER	CLACKAMAS CO.	T2S	R1E	S16
PALMATEER see **MT. ZION**	CLACKAMAS CO.	T3S	R4E	S22
PARK PLACE see **LEWTHWAITE**	CLACKAMAS CO.	T2S	R2E	S20
PARK PLACE see **STRAIGHT FAMILY**	CLACKAMAS CO.	T2S	R2E	S29

PARROTT D.L.C., JOSEPH see **ST. PATRICK'S**				
	CLACKAMAS CO.	T3S	R1E	S23
PENDLETON D.L.C., CHAMPING see **PENDLETON FAMILY**				
	CLACKAMAS CO.	T3S	R1E	S32
PENDLETON, ELIZABETH J. see **FERN HILL**				
	CLACKAMAS CO.	T5S	R3E	S21
PENDLETON FAMILY	CLACKAMAS CO.	T3S	R1E	S32
PERRIN, MARSHALL K.	CLACKAMAS CO.	T3S	R1E	S2
PERSHELL, JOSEPH	CLACKAMAS CO.	?	?	?
PIONEER see **OSWEGO PIONEER**	CLACKAMAS CO.	T2S	R1E	S16
PIONEER MEMORIAL see **LINN, PHILIP E.**				
	CLACKAMAS CO.	T3S	R4E	S21
PIONEER WOMAN'S GRAVE	CLACKAMAS CO.	T3S	R9E	S29
PLEASANT HILL see **PLEASANT VIEW [WEST]**				
	CLACKAMAS CO.	T3S	R1W	S9
PLEASANT VALLEY see **PLEASANT VIEW [EAST]**				
	CLACKAMAS CO.	T2S	R3E	S19
PLEASANT VIEW [EAST]	CLACKAMAS CO.	T2S	R3E	S19
PLEASANT VIEW [WEST]	CLACKAMAS CO.	T3S	R1W	S9
POTTER FAMILY	CLACKAMAS CO.	T2S	R2E	?
PRESBYTERIAN see **GEORGE**	CLACKAMAS CO.	T3S	R5E	S19
PULLEY-LOWE FAMILY see **LOWE FAMILY**				
	CLACKAMAS CO.	T1S	R5E	S30
PUTZ see **BONNEY**	CLACKAMAS CO.	T4S	R3E	S35
RATH	CLACKAMAS CO.	T3S	R5E	?
REDLAND HILLS see **REDLAND PIONEER**				
	CLACKAMAS CO.	T3S	R3E	S16
REDLAND PIONEER	CLACKAMAS CO.	T3S	R3E	S16
REIMER	CLACKAMAS CO.	T3S	R5E	?
REVENUE D.L.C., FRANCIS see **REVENUE FAMILY**				
	CLACKAMAS CO.	T2S	R5E	S7
REVENUE FAMILY	CLACKAMAS CO.	T2S	R5E	S7
RICHARDSON FAMILY see **REDLAND PIONEER**				
	CLACKAMAS CO.	T3S	R3E	S16
RICHARDSON, MATTHEW see **REDLAND PIONEER**				
	CLACKAMAS CO.	T3S	R3E	S16
RINGO see **CLARKES PIONEER**	CLACKAMAS CO.	T4S	R3È	S29
RISLEY D.L.C., JACOB S. see **RISLEY FAMILY**				
	CLACKAMAS CO.	T2S	R1E	S12
RISLEY FAMILY	CLACKAMAS CO.	T2S	R1E	S12
ROCK CREEK	CLACKAMAS CO.	T5S	R1E	S5
RUSSELLVILLE	CLACKAMAS CO.	T6S	R2E	S2
RUSSELVILLE see **RUSSELLVILLE**	CLACKAMAS CO.	T6S	R2E	S2
RUU, FREDRICK	CLACKAMAS CO.	?	?	?
SACRED HEART	CLACKAMAS CO.	T2S	R1E	S16
ST. AGNES BABY HOME	CLACKAMAS CO.	T2S	R2E	S20
ST. JAMES see **ST. PATRICK'S**	CLACKAMAS CO.	T3S	R1E	S23
ST. JOHANN	CLACKAMAS CO.	T3S	R1E	S36
ST. JOHANN LUTHERAN see **ST. JOHANN**				
	CLACKAMAS CO.	T3S	R1E	S36
ST. JOHN LUTHERAN see **ST. JOHANN**				
	CLACKAMAS CO.	T3S	R1E	S36

ST. JOHN THE APOSTLE see **ST. JOHN'S CATHOLIC**				
	CLACKAMAS CO.	T3S	R2E	S5
ST. JOHN THE EVANGELIST	CLACKAMAS CO.	?	?	?
ST. JOHN THE EVANGELIST EPISCOPAL CHURCH				
	CLACAMAS CO.	T1S	R1E	S36
ST. JOHN'S CATHOLIC	CLACKAMAS CO.	T3S	R2E	S5
ST. PATRICK see **ST. PATRICK'S**	CLACKAMAS CO.	T3S	R1E	S23
ST. PATRICK'S	CLACKAMAS CO.	T3S	R1E	S23
ST. PETER'S CHURCH see **TEN O'CLOCK**				
	CLACKAMAS CO.	T3S	R2E	S35
ST. PETER'S LUTHERAN CHURCH see **MOEHNKE**				
	CLACKAMAS CO.	T3S	R3E	S31
SANDERS FAMILY	CLACKAMAS CO.	T5S	R2E	S4
SANDY HOOD LOOP see **FIR HILL**	CLACKAMAS CO.	T2S	R4E	S14
SANDY PIONEER see **FIR HILL**	CLACKAMAS CO.	T2S	R4E	S14
SANDY RIDGE	CLACKAMAS CO.	T2S	R4E	S27
SAUNDERS FAMILY see **SANDERS FAMILY**				
	CLACKAMAS CO.	T5S	R2E	S4
SAWTELL FAMILY	CLACKAMAS CO.	T5S	R2E	S30
SCANDINAVIAN	CLACKAMAS CO.	T2S	R4E	S14
SCHEEL FAMILY	CLACAMAS CO.	T3S	R5E	S18
SCHMIDT NURSERY see **GARDEN OF REVERENCE**				
	CLACKAMAS CO.	T1S	R4E	S28
SCHREIBER, DONALD A. see **SWAILS CEDARS**				
	CLACKAMAS CO.	T3S	R3E	?
SCHUEBEL	CLACKAMAS CO.	T3S	R2E	S36
SCOTTS MILLS see **MAPLEWOOD**	CLACKAMAS CO.	T6S	R1E	S14
SELLWOOD see **MILWAUKIE PIONEER**	CLACKAMAS CO.	T1S	R1E	S26
SHEEL see **SCHEEL FAMILY**	CLACKAMAS CO.	T3S	R5E	S18
SHIRLEY D.L.C., JAMES see **ZIMMERMAN**				
	CLACKAMAS CO.	T4S	R1E	S32
SHUBEL see **SCHUEBEL**	CLACKAMAS CO.	T3S	R2E	S36
SHUBEL HILL see **SCHUEBEL**	CLACKAMAS CO.	T3S	R2E	S36
SINE *[Sic]* see **ZION MENNONITE**	CLACKAMAS CO.	T4S	R1E	S31
SISTERS OF THE HOLY NAMES	CLACKAMAS CO.	T2S	R1E	S14
SMITH, CAPTAIN W. H. see **LEWTHWAITE**				
	CLACKAMAS CO.	T2S	R2E	S20
SMITH PLACE	CLACKAMAS CO.	T2S	R4E	S30
SMYRNA	CLACKAMAS CO.	T5S	R1E	S9
SMYRNA UNITED CHURCH OF CHRIST see **SMYRNA**				
	CLACKAMAS CO.	T5S	R1E	S9
SPRAGUE D.L.C., ALFRED see **SPRAGUE FAMILY**				
	CLACKAMAS CO.	T3S	R3E	S18
SPRAGUE FAMILY	CLACKAMAS CO.	T3S	R3E	S18
SPRINGWATER	CLACKAMAS CO.	T4S	R4E	S8
STAFFORD see **STAFFORD BAPTIST CHURCH**				
	CLACKAMAS CO.	T2S	R1E	S31
STAFFORD BAPTIST CHURCH	CLACKAMAS CO.	T2S	R1E	S31
STONE D.L.C., ASA see **VIOLA PIONEER**				
	CLACKAMAS CO.	T3S	R3E	S23
STRAIGHT D.L.C., HIRAM see **ST. AGNES BABY HOME**				
	CLACKAMAS CO.	T2S	R2E	S20

STRAIGHT D.L.C., HIRAM see **STRAIGHT FAMILY**

CLACKAMAS CO.	T2S	R2E	S29

STRAIGHT D.L.C., HIRAM AND SUSAN see **LEWTHWAITE**

CLACKAMAS CO.	T2S	R2E	S20
STRAIGHT FAMILY CLACKAMAS CO.	T2S	R2E	S29
SUMMIT MEADOWS CLACKAMAS CO.	T3S	R8 1/2E	S25

SUNNYSIDE CHIMES MEMORIAL GARDENS see **LITTLE CHAPEL OF THE CHIMES**

MEMORIAL GARDEN CLACKAMAS CO.	T1S	R2E	S33
SUNNYSIDE PIONEER CLACKAMAS CO.	T2S	R2E	S2

SUTER CENTURY FARM see **SUTER FARM**

CLACKAMAS CO.	T2S	R4E	S30
SUTER FARM CLACKAMAS CO.	T2S	R4E	S30
SUTTER CREEK see **GEORGE** CLACKAMAS CO.	T3S	R5E	S19
SWAILS CEDARS CLACKAMAS CO.	T3S	R3E	?
SWEDE see **COLTON LUTHERAN** CLACKAMAS CO.	T5S	R3E	S3

SWEGLE D.L.C., MATTHIAS see **SANDERS FAMILY**

CLACKAMAS CO.	T5S	R2E	S4

SWEIGEL FAMILY see **SANDERS FAMILY**

CLACKAMAS CO.	T5S	R2E	S4

TEASEL CREEK see **MOLALLA MEMORIAL**

CLACKAMAS CO.	T5S	R2E	S20
TEN O'CLOCK CLACKAMAS CO.	T3S	R2E	S35

TERRACE LAWN MEMORIAL PARK see **LITTLE CHAPEL OF THE CHIMES**

MEMORIAL GARDEN CLACKAMAS CO.	T1S	R2E	S33

TESCH, AARON see **HOLY NEW MARTYRS RUSSIAN ORTHODOX CHURCH**

CLACKAMAS CO.	T4S	R2E	?
TRULLINGER FAMILY CLACKAMAS CO.	T4S	R2E	S27
TUCKER CHILDREN CLACKAMAS CO.	T4S	R4E	S9

TUCKER D.L.C., BRANCH see **TUCKER CHILDREN**

CLACKAMAS CO.	T4S	R4E	S9
TWO GIRLS see **SUTER FARM** CLACKAMAS CO.	T2S	R4E	S30
UNKNOWN CLACKAMAS CO.	T5S	R3E	S5

VICKERS' CABIN, PERRY see **SUMMIT MEADOWS**

CLACKAMAS CO.	T3S	R8 1/2E	S25
VIOLA PIONEER CLACKAMAS CO.	T3S	R3E	S23
WADE see **LINN, PHILIP E.** CLACKAMAS CO.	T3S	R4E	S21

WADE D.L.C., WILLIAM N. AND SARAH see **I.O.O.F. [ESTACADA]**

CLACKAMAS CO.	T3S	R4E	S21

WADE D.L.C., WILLIAM N. AND SARAH see **LINN, PHILIP E.**

CLACKAMAS CO.	T3S	R4E	S21
WADE FAMILY see **LINN, PHILIP E.** CLACKAMAS CO.	T3S	R4E	S21

WADE MEMORIAL see **LINN, PHILIP E.**

CLACKAMAS CO.	T3S	R4E	S21
WADE, SARAH see **LINN, PHILIP E.** CLACKAMAS CO.	T3S	R4E	S21

WADE, W. H. H. see **LINN, PHILIP E.**

CLACKAMAS CO.	T3S	R4E	S21

WADE, WILLIAM N. see **LINN, PHILIP E.**

CLACKAMAS CO.	T3S	R4E	S21
WALKEY, EDMUND see **SMITH PLACE** CLACKAMAS CO.	T2S	R4E	S30

WALLING D.L.C., GABRIEL see **SISTERS OF THE HOLY NAMES**

CLACKAMAS CO.	T2S	R1E	S14
WAVERLY see **MILWAUKIE PIONEER** CLACKAMAS CO.	T1S	R1E	S26

WEEKS FAMILY see **GEER PIONEER**	CLACKAMAS CO.	T3S	R1W	S31
WEHRHEIM D.L.C., HENRY see **WEHRHEIM FAMILY**				
	CLACKAMAS CO.	T3S	R4E	S9
WEHRHEIM FAMILY	CLACKAMAS CO.	T3S	R4E	S9
WEST BUTTEVILLE see **GEER PIONEER**				
	CLACKAMAS CO.	T3S	R1W	S31
WHITCOMB	CLACKAMAS CO.	T1S	R1E	S36
WHITCOMB D.L.C., LOT see **HOLLAND**				
	CLACKAMAS CO.	T1S	R1E	S36
WHITCOMB D.L.C., LOT see **WHITCOMB**				
	CLACKAMAS CO.	T1S	R1E	S36
WHITCOMB, LOT see **WHITCOMB**	CLACKAMAS CO.	T1S	R1E	S36
WILLAMETTE NATIONAL	CLACKAMAS CO.	T1S	R2E	S22
WILLIAMS D.L.C., LEANDER see **GARDEN OF REVERENCE**				
	CLACKAMAS CO.	T1S	R4E	S28
WILSON	CLACKAMAS CO.	T3S	R2E	S1
WISE FAMILY, GEORGE	CLACKAMAS CO.	T2S	R2E	S5
WISE, GEORGE see **WISE FAMILY, GEORGE**				
	CLACKAMAS CO.	T2S	R2E	S5
WYLAND, DANIEL see **WYLAND FAMILY**				
	CLACKAMAS CO.	T5S	R1E	S4
WYLAND FAMILY	CLACKAMAS CO.	T5S	R1E	S4
YODER see **SMYRNA**	CLACKAMAS CO.	T5S	R1E	S9
YODER, CLAYTON	CLACKAMAS CO.	T4S	R1E	S18
YODERVILLE see **ZION MENNONITE**	CLACKAMAS CO.	T4S	R1E	S31
ZIMMERMAN	CLACKAMAS CO.	T4S	R1E	S32
ZION [CANBY] see **ZION MEMORIAL PARK**				
	CLACKAMAS CO.	T3S	R1E	S34
ZION [ESTACADA] see **MT. ZION**	CLACKAMAS CO.	T3S	R4E	S22
ZION [HUBBARD] see **ZION MENNONITE**				
	CLACKAMAS CO.	T4S	R1E	S31
ZION LUTHERAN see **ZION MEMORIAL PARK**				
	CLACKAMAS CO.	T3S	R1E	S34
ZION LUTHERAN see **ZOAR LUTHERAN [BARLOW ROAD]**				
	CLACKAMAS CO.	T4S	R1E	S7
ZION MEMORIAL PARK	CLACKAMAS CO.	T3S	R1E	S34
ZION MENNONITE	CLACKAMAS CO.	T4S	R1E	S31
ZOAR see **ZOAR LUTHERAN**	CLACKAMAS CO.	T3S	R1E	S34
ZOAR LUTHERAN	CLACKAMAS CO.	T3S	R1E	S34
ZOAR LUTHERAN [BARLOW ROAD]	CLACKAMAS CO.	T4S	R1E	S7
ZOAR LUTHERAN [EAST] see **ZOAR LUTHERAN**				
	CLACKAMAS CO.	T3S	R1E	S34
ZOAR LUTHERAN [WEST] see **ZOAR LUTHERAN [BARLOW ROAD]**				
	CLACKAMAS CO.	T4S	R1E	S7

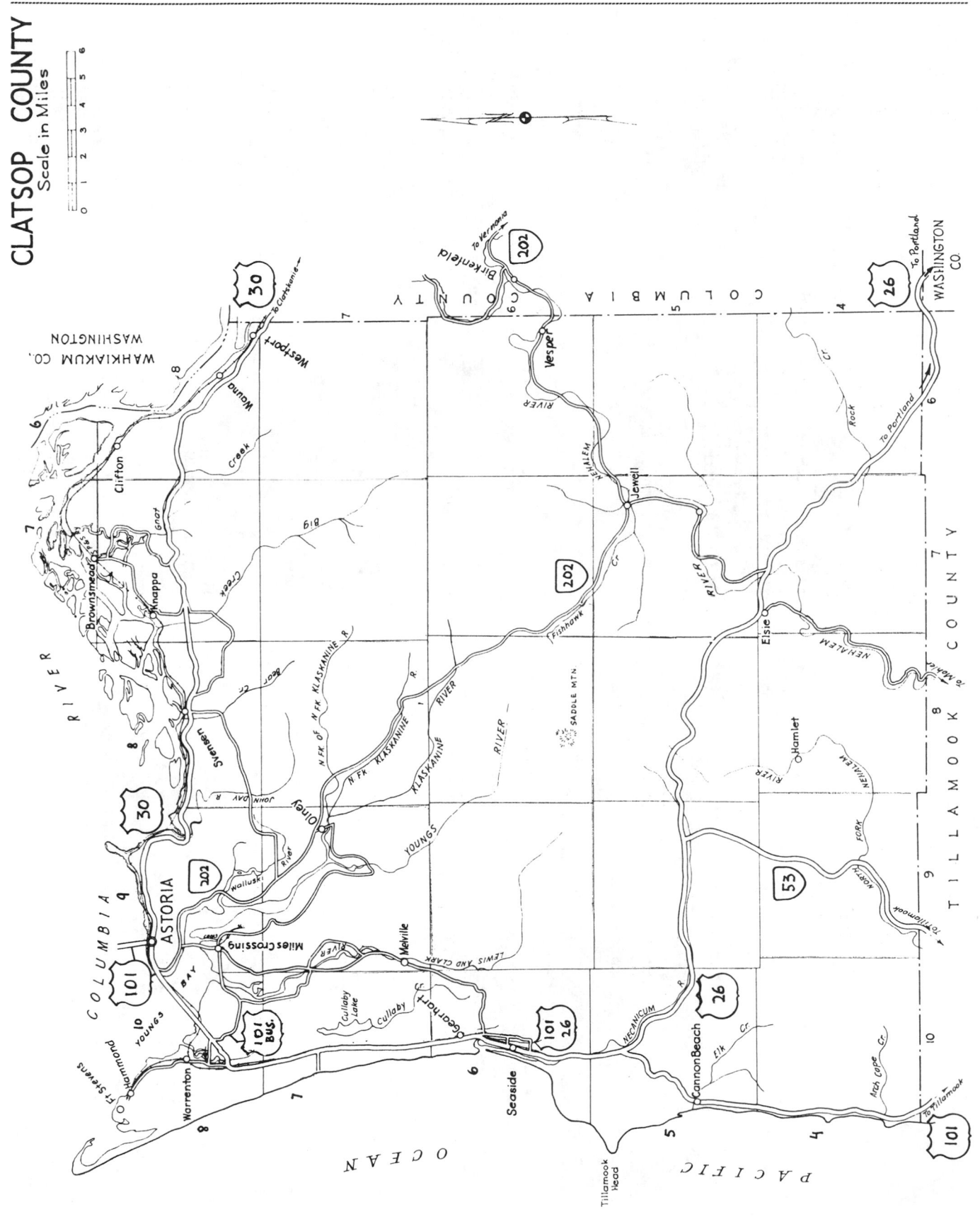

CLATSOP COUNTY
Scale in Miles

U. S. Army Fort Stevens, Ruth C. Bishop
Janice M. Healy (1992)

Knappa Prairie
Dean H. Byrd (1992)

Area: 873 square miles
Population (1998): 35,424
County seat: Astoria, Population: 10,130
County established: 22 June 1844

Located on the south bank of the lower Columbia River where it enters the Pacific Ocean. Clatsop County was the site of the first white trading post in Oregon and therefore the earliest established cemetery. This was Fort Astoria founded in the spring of 1811 for the fur trade. It was occupied by the British in the fall of 1813 during the War of 1812 and was renamed Fort George. Returned to the Americans in 1818 and once again called Fort Astoria, the name was gradually transferred to a small civilian settlement as Astoria. The earliest burials after 1811 and those dating from the 1850's to about 1878 are now built over. Eventually most of Astoria's known burials were transferred to Ocean View which was established in 1872. The Clatsop Plains Pioneer Cemetery was begun in 1846 and is the earliest organized cemetery outside of Astoria. By the 1870's there were at least four other organized cemeteries. There were many family burial sites and still some Indian burials sites and a United States Military cemetery begun as early as 1868 at Fort Stevens. The most prominent ethnic nationalities from Europe were Finns and Swedes who are scattered through many cemeteries and family burial sites.

Clatsop Plains Pioneer
Dean H. Byrd (1996)

Ocean View
Dean H. Byrd (1996)

Evergreen
Dean H. Byrd (1996)

Name of Cemetery and also known as	Number of burials	Acres	Condition	Date started or earliest known burial	Townshp	Range	Section

AHLERS, DORTHEA
AKA: 1. NECANICUM
POST OFFICE

A 0.01 ? 15 Nov 1915 T5N R9W S22

The grave site is located about 1.5 miles west of Necanicum Junction along the right (north) side of U.S. Hwy. 26 and just before the bridge over Little Humbug Creek. This is about 15 miles south and east of Seaside. She and her huband Herman Ahlers (1859-1944) were German immigrants who settled here in 1886. The Ahlers house served as a post office from 1896-1916 and was variously known as Ahlers, Push and lastly Necanicum. (Not shown on Necanicun Junction 1985 USGS Quad. map.)

ASTORIA [OLD]
AKA: 1. CATHOLIC
[ASTORIA]
2. POTTERS FIELD
3. SHIVELY
FAMILY

? ? 9 Circa 1850 T8N R9W S8

This was the second cemetery used in Astoria in the early 1850's; Fort Astoria Cemetery being the first. This site was formally donated about March 1865 by John M. Shively but was used as much as a decade previously. Shively donated to the city, Block #55 (now Block #255) bounded by Irving and Jerome Streets and 14th and 15th Streets. Most burials seem to have been around 14th and Irving. The cemetery was also known as Catholic because the church was near by. Located on the John Shively D.L.C., OC #1052. Around 1878 removals were begun to rebury the graves farther up hill to Hillside Cemetery, now Astoria Pioneer. See the article on the latter. (Not shown on Astoria 1949-84 USGS Quad. map.)

ASTORIA PIONEER
AKA: 1. CITY
2. HILLSIDE
3. HILLTOP
4. PIONEER
[ASTORIA]

D 5 2 1865-1903 T8N R9W S17

Located at the intersection of 15th and Niagara Streets in the city of Astoria: Block #93 of the Shively Addition. The city maintains this old cemetery as a park. There is a historical marker which records some of the history. It is now signed as Astoria Pioneer but was most often referred to as Hillside Cemetery in earlier times. The cemetery was deeded on 12 April 1865, the third of the city cemeteries. Around 1878 the graves from the Astoria [OLD] Cemetery were reburied here. In 1897 a city ordinance forbade any more burials within the city limits and ordered reburials to what is now

Name of Cemetery and also known as	Number of burials	Acres	Condition	Date started or earliest known burial	Townshp	Range	Section

Ocean View Cemetery in Warrenton. Burials continued in Hillside until 1903 and in 1904 the removals to Ocean View were carried out. More than 700 burials had been made in Hillside. There are still some old monuments remaining in Astoria Pioneer Park and pre-dating the establishment of this cemetery. This is on the John Shively D.L.C., OC #1052. {9 May 1992} (Not shown as a cemetery on the Astoria 1949-84 USGS Quad. Map.)

BAYNEY CREEK
AKA: 1. BARNEY CREEK

A   0.01   5   Circa 1900   T6N   R9W   ?
Perhaps found in Section 2. A logger was killed during a tree-felling accident and was buried nearby with a wooden marker and picket fence. It is near a concrete bridge over Bayney Creek on the Youngs River Mainline Road. This road follows the left (west) bank of Youngs River between Saddle Mountain Road and Youngs River Loop. (Not shown on Olney 1949-73-81 USGS Quad. map.)

BITTERLING FAMILY

A   ?   6   1887-1902   T7N   R10W   S24
The homestead and burial site was located in the Southwest 1/4 of Section 24. Julius Bitterling was a German immigrant and Anna Louise Ottinger a Swiss immigrant who met in Astoria where both were employed in a restaurant. After marriage they settled in 1875 on this homestead near the bygone settlement of Melville. Louise was born in 1851 and died 23 August 1887 giving birth to their sixth child. Julius was born in 1842 and died 28 November 1902. The graves have been removed to Clatsup Plains Pioneer Cemetery. The date for Julius on the monument is incorrect. (Not shown on Gearhart 1949-73 or Olney 1949-73-81 USGS Quad. maps.)

CASEY FAMILY, ROSE

A   ?   5   ?   T7N   R9W   ?
These could be located on Section 11 or 14, probably on Section 11. There are 16 to 20 Indian graves on the Lilli Watson Farm, 0.2 of a mile northwest of Youngs River Loop

Name of Cemetery and also known as	Number of burials	Acres	Condition	Date started or earliest known burial	Townshp	Range	Section

junction on OR. Hwy. 202 near Olney. Land owner noted in *Metsker Landownership Atlases* 1930 and 1956. (Not shown on Olney 1949-73-81 USGS Quad. map, but is on 1936 ODOT map.)

CLATSOP INDIANS   ?   ?   11 ?   T6N R10W   S28

Located in the south part of Seaside along the west bank of the Necanicum River from the northwest end of the Avenue 'U' Bridge. The burial ground was about 100 feet wide and extended northerly several hundred feet to a point about east of the old Seaside Hospital, now the School Administration building. The area was noted as still being used as late as 1852-1860 and probably later than that. It was mostly of canoe burials. Any interments were shallow because this was on an old beach line and large boulders underlay the ground surface. Some graves were later marked with wooden crosses. After the area was subdivided in 1909 much of the cemetery was covered over: on Elizabeth Lattie D.L.C. #37, OC #3256. (Not shown on Tillamook Head 1949-73 USGS Quad. map.)

CLATSOP PLAINS PIONEER   C   2   2   1846-1957   T7N R10W   S4
AKA: 1. ASTORIA

Access to the cemetery is from U.S. Hwy. 101 South of Astoria and Warrenton. Take the road to the right (west) marked by the sign for Camp Rilea, Oregon National Guard. Almost immediately after turning off of U.S. Hwy. 101 is the the driveway to the left (south) to the Clatsop Plains Pioneer Presbyterian Church. Parking is limited to the church parking lot but you are free to enter the cemetery on foot. Five acres were deeded to the church in 1851, 2.5 extra acres deeded in 1888 for additional cemetery use, but only about 2 acres are enclosed by the fence. There are 245 known burials (20 November 1975) but undoubtedly more have been interred since then; on the Robert Morrison D.L.C., OC #720. {25 June 1996} (Gearhart 1949-73 USGS Quad. map.)

Clatsop County

Name of Cemetery and also known as	Number of burials	Acres	Condition	Date started or earliest known burial	Townshp	Range	Section

COMCOMLY'S GRAVE
AKA: 1. CONCOMLY

A   0.01   ?   Circa 1835   T8N   R9W   S8
Chief Comcomly is said to be buried under the old Taylor House near 15th and Exchange Streets in Astoria. Originally buried near Point Ellice on the north side of the Columbia River, the date of transfer to Astoria is unknown to the compiler. The chief's skull was stolen by an English doctor and taken to Portsmouth, England, where it remained from 1836 to 1961 when it was returned to Astoria and reburied in Ilwaco Cemetery across the Interstate Bridge in 1972. (Not shown on Astoria 1948-84 USGS Quad. map.)

CRAZY VALLEY

?   ?   ?   ?   T5N   R9W   ?
Located in Section 16 or 21. "Past the fish hatchery near the old C.C.C. (Civilian Conservation Corps) camp was an old cemetery" was the vague description. The fish hatchery was on U.S. Hwy. 26 on the North Fork Necanicum River between Necanicum Junction and Cannon Beach Junction. The site of the C.C.C. camp is now ocupied by an Oregon Department of Transportation maintenance station. The compiler wonders if the "old cemetery" could perhaps be the Dorthea Ahlers burial site about a mile east. See that article. (Not shown on the Necanicum Junction 1985 USGS Quad. map)

DUNKIN, GEORGE
AKA: 1. INDIAN GEORGE

?   ?   5   1886   T7N   R8W   ?
Located in section 20 or 29, 2.5 miles east of Lex Norman's home in Olney; a 160-acre homestead in 1870, near Barth Road. George was an Indian, 7 of his dogs were shot and buried with him. (Not shown on Green Mountain 1949-73-81 USGS Quad. map.)

ELSIE
AKA: 1. SUNNY HILL
         CEMETERY OF
         NEHALEM

B   1   2   1889   T4N   R7W   S5
Located 0.25 of a mile from Elsie, on U.S. Hwy. 26 about halfway between Elsie and Jewell Junction. Halfway between Milepost 20 and Milepost 21 and on top of the ridge is the obscure driveway on the right (south) called Elsie Cemetery Road. Drive 0.3 of a mile to the cemetery which is not visible

from the highway. The visitor must approach
eastbound on U.S. Hwy. 26 towards Portland
because of the volume of traffic. The
cemetery was incorporated 10 May 1927 and
there were 94 known burials in 1992. (Elsie
1984 USGS Quad. map.)

**ETERNITY AT SEA
COLUMBARIUM**
AKA: 1. TILLAMOOK
ROCK
LIGHTHOUSE

A   ?   1   1980   T5N R11W   S-0
Located on an acre-sized rock 1.2 miles off
shore from Tillamook Head. This lighthouse
was built in 1879-81 but is no longer used as
such: it was closed down 2 September 1957.
This became privately owned in 1979 by Kron
and Waid and was added to the National
Register of Historic Places 9 January 1981.
It has been adapted for use as a columbarium
and has space for 300,000 niches. The rock
is now a Federal Wildlife Refuge for seabirds
and is almost entirely inaccessible for
boats. Pontoon-equipped helicopter flights
are made annually or on other suitable
occasions. A good view of this can be had
from Cape Meares lighthouse {29 May 1998}
with binoculars or a spotting scope.
Tillamook Head 1949-73 USGS Quad. map.)

EVERGREEN
AKA: 1. EVERGREEN
LODGE #137
2. MASONIC
[SEASIDE]
3. SEASIDE

D 17.8 1 1913   T6N R10W   S34
Located south of Seaside off of U.S. Hwy.
101; go 2.5 miles from the intersection of
Broadway with U.S. Hwy. 101 to Milepost 23.2
and then turn left (east) on Beerman Creek
Road, and go 0.5 of a mile to the cemetery on
the left. Only about 5 acres is currently
open. The earliest dated monument is 1909;
the Masons took over the cemetery in 1913 and
as of Memorial Day 1987 there were 1090
recorded burials. There is also an infant
burial located just outside of the cemetery
at the northeast corner near a large alder
tree. {26 June 1996} (Tillamook Head 1949-73
USGS Quad. map.)

FITCHA HOMESTEAD
AKA: 1. ESTOOS
2. LILLENAS

B 0.15 ? Circa 1880 T8N R8W   S31
Located on the Southwest 1/4 of the Southwest
1/4 of Southeast 1/4 of Section 31. Access
is from Labiske Road off of OR. Hwy. 202, two
miles south of the Fitcha Homestead. It is

Clatsop County

Name of Cemetery and also known as	Number of burials	Acres	Condition	Date started or earliest known burial	Townshp	Range	Section

on a ridge overlooking the valley; 26 known burials. NOTE: This site is on private property. (Not shown on Cathlamet Bay 1949-84 USGS Quad. map.)

FORT ASTORIA
AKA: 1. FORT GEORGE

| | ? | ? | 11 | Circa 1811 | T8N | R10W | S8 |

This was the first cemetery in the Pacific Northwest for burials of whites. It was a "stone's throw" from the fort itself, which was where 15th Street and Exchange intersects. A plat map published in 1834 defined the cemetery as occupying Block #120 bounded by Duane, Exchange, 16th and 17th Streets and partly under 16th Street. The cemetery was then along the Columbia River shoreline. Since then landfills have been extended into the river. Fort Astoria was established in 1811. During the British occupation between 1813 and 1818 it was known as Fort George. There are no remaining records of this cemetery which may have been in use as late as the 1850's when it was superseded by the Astoria [OLD] Cemetery, see that article. (Not shown on Astoria 1949-84 USGS Quad. map.)

FORT STEVENS [OLD]

| | A | 0.4 | 6 | 1868-1898 | T8N | R10W | S5 |

A small cemetery 165' x 104' in size was constructed 0.25 of a mile south of the post on the east side of the road on a sandy ridge. The first burial was in May of 1868. By December of 1869 the post surgeon reported that there had been 3 deaths, "all due to inebriation." In August of 1898 it was decided to move the cemetery as its site was needed for building sites. At the end of that year 20 bodies were removed to the present cemetery site. Why 20 were moved from a reported 21 graves (Aug. 1898) was not explained. From *Fort Stevens*, by Marshall Hanft, 1980. Oregon State Printer, page 67. See the article on U.S. Army Fort Stevens, for the later history. (Not shown on Warrenton 1953-84 USGS Quad. map.)

Name of Cemetery and also known as	Number of burials	Acres	Condition	Date started or earliest known burial	Townshp	Range	Section

GREEN MOUNTAIN ROAD

A 0.01 5 ? T7N R8W ?
Perhaps located in Section 30. A man died and was buried on land owned by Israel Kallio. NOTE: No other information was given in the report. (Not shown on Green Mountain 1949 USGS Quad. map.)

GREENWOOD
AKA: 1. CRESTVIEW

E 30 2 1891 T8N R9W S33
Take OR. Hwy. 202 to 1 mile south of the Wallooskee River Bridge; turn left up the hill. {10 May 1992} (Astoria 1949-84 USGS Quad. map.)

GRONNELL FAMILY
AKA: 1. GRONNEL

? ? ? 1881-1902 T4N R7W ?
Most likely located within Section 4. Leave U.S. Hwy. 26 at Jewell Junction at Milepost 21.8 onto the Fishhawk Falls Highway. Go only about 0.1 of a mile on that highway and turn left onto Gronnel Road before this county road passes underneath U.S. Hwy. 26. The cemetery is somewhere off of Gronnel Road (the Clatsop County Road Dept. spelling) which goes southerly along the left bank of the Nehalem River. NOTE: This site is on private property. (Not shown on Elsie 1984 USGS Quad. map.)

HAMLET

A 1 2 Circa 1891 T4N R8W S6
Located near Hamlet: 4 miles southeast, off of Necanicum Highway (OR. Hwy. 53). Go 3.64 miles on Hamlet Road to Hill Road; turn right (south) onto Hill Road. The cemetery is on the right, before the North Fork Nehalem River Bridge crossing 0.2 of a mile from the main road. The cemetery was incorporated in 1916. This was a Finnish/Bohemian settlement. There are many burials of the Hill/Maki family. Hill is a literal translation of the Finnish surname Maki. (Not shown on Hamlet 1984 USGS Quad. map.)

HECKARD FAMILY

? 0.3 ? 1870's T7N R9W S18
Located on the Lewis and Clark Road about 6 miles from Astoria, on tax lot 700: are the Heckard children burials. NOTE: No other information was given in the report. There

Name of Cemetery and also known as	Number of burials	Acres	Condition	Date started or earliest known burial	Townshp	Range	Section

were other marked graves here but no markers are now visible. (Not shown on Astoria 1949-84 or Olney 1949-73-81 USGS Quad. map.)

HOLY INNOCENTS EPISCOPAL

?	?	11	1874	T8N	R9W	S9

This was near 34th and Grand Avenue on the south side of Grand Avenue, before Harrison Drive. The site is now a parking lot for the First Lutheran Church in Astoria. General John Adair the first U.S. customs collector of Astoria started construction of the Episcopal Church 27 March 1874. The graves were relocated to Ocean View Cemetery about 1924: on the John Adair D.L.C., OC #3872. (NOT on Astoria 1948-84 USGS Quad. map.)

JEWELL

C	0.75	3	?	T5N	R7W	S11

Located at Jewell: 0.2 of a mile north from OR. Hwy. 202 at Milepost 29, and on Beneke Road. (Vinemaple 1984 USGS Quad. map.)

JEWELL [OLD]

?	?	?	?	T5N	R7W	S12

The old cemetery at Jewell is reportedly not maintained. It is near Jewell High School less than 0.5 of a mile south of OR. Hwy. 202, on the road to Vinemaple. (Not shown on Vinemaple 1984 USGS Quad. map.)

JOHANSON FAMILY

A	?	5	?	?	?	?

Located on Green Mountain Road on land owned by Jim and Jacquie Hyde (1987). It has been reported that some Johanson babies possibly are buried here. NOTE: This site is on private property. (Not shown on Olney Quad. 1949-73-81 or Green Mountain 1949 USGS Quad. maps.)

KNAPPA PRAIRIE
AKA: 1. KNAPPA
    2. PRAIRIE

C	1.7	2	1878	T8N	R7W	S17

Leave U.S. Hwy. 30 at Milepost 82 onto Old Hwy. 30 and go 0.12 of a mile; then turn right (north) onto Knappa Dock Road and go another 0.31 of a mile. The cemetery is on the left on land donated in 1878 and the

Name of Cemetery and also known as	Number of burials	Acres	Condition	Date started or earliest known burial	Townshp	Range	Section

first burial was in 1880: on the Daniel C. Ramey D.L.C. #42, OC #3553. {9 May 1992} (Knappa 1986 USGS Quad. map.)

LATTIE-CLOUTRIE FAMILY　　A　1　11　1853　　T6N　R10W　　S21
This bygone cemetery in Seaside was located along the east side of South Franklin Street at the jog north of Avenue 'S' and the west bank of the Necanicum River. The cemetery was established for the family and descendants of Elizabeth Lattie whose Clatsop tribal name was Sikkas. She was born about 1813 and died 13 May 1868. She married Alexandre Lattie a Scottish-born pilot for the Hudsons Bay Company. Their daughter Helen married a well-known mountain man Antoine J. Cloutrie (originally Cloutier). She died 23 May 1882. The gravesites of mother and daughter are the only ones which can possibly be located. Three more members of the family are known to be buried including William Lattie, son of Elizabeth. He died in 1900. Others are probably buried here. After this area was subdivided in 1909 some parts of the cemetery were built over and other parts abandoned. On the Elizabeth Lattie D.L.C. #37, OC #3256. (Not shown on Tillamook Head 1949-73 USGS Quad. map.)

LEWIS AND CLARK　　D　3　2　1897　　T7N　R9W　　S6
　AKA: 1. RIVERVIEW
Located approximately 7.8 miles south of Astoria and 3.1 miles south of U.S. Hwy. 101 Business Route, on Lewis and Clark Road. On the Preston W. Gillett D.L.C., OC #2942. (Olney 1949-73-81 USGS Quad. map.)

LUPATIA CREW　　A　?　?　3 Jan 1881　T5N　R11W　　S1
The British bark "Lupatia" ran ashore in a storm on the night of 3 January 1881. The nearby Tillamook Rock Lighthouse was not quite completed at the time. A burial party on 10 January 1881 found two sets of bodies and buried them at or near two small coves between Tillamook Head and Bird Point in what is now Ecola State Park. The sites are dangerous to reach and probably no traces now remain. Either 10 or 12 were buried. One

| Name of Cemetery and also known as | Number of burials | Acres | Condition | Date started or earliest known burial | Townshp | Range | Section |

other "Lupatia" crewman's body was washed ashore on 18 January 1881 about 6 miles north of Seaside House. It was buried in the sand nearby and is no doubt long lost. (Not shown on Tillamook Head 1949-73 USGS Quad. map.)

MAPLEWOOD
  AKA: 1. KALANDER
       FAMILY, EMIL

A   1.5   3   1943   T8N R7W   S16
Located on the road to Brownsmead, about 0.5 to 0.75 of a mile northerly from U.S. Hwy. 30; on the left (west) side of Brownsmead Hill Road. The actual burial area is only 90' X 30' and with a single monument to four persons of the Emil Kalander Family. {9 May 1992} (Knappa 1986 USGS Quad. map.)

McTAVISH, DONALD

A   0.01   ?   22 May 1814 T8N R9W   S8
Located at the northwest corner of 15th and Exchange Streets in Astoria, immediately west of the site marking Old Fort Astoria. Donald McTavish was one of seven men who drowned when their longboat was swamped in the Columbia River. He was Chief Factor at Fort Astoria, called Fort George, at the time of the British occupation. Originally, he was buried with this marker at the Fort's burial ground. Some time during the 1870's these bones and the marker were removed to the Astoria Pioneer Cemetery. About 1904, the monument was removed and eventually was placed at 15th and Exchange Streets. In the 1970's the tombstone was once again moved: this time to the Heritage Center. But where McTavish's bones are, who knows? (Not shown on Astoria 1949-84 USGS Quad. map.)

MESCHELLE, JENNIE
  AKA: 1. MARCHINO,
          MESCHELLE
       2. MARTINEAU,
          MICHEL
       3. TSIN-IS-TUM

A   0.01   1   18 Feb 1905 T6N R10W   S15
This graveyard plaque is located in the northern part of Seaside. Take Holladay Drive north past Seaside High School. Turn left (northwesterly) onto Indian Street which is the last street before 24th Avenue. The plaque is by a small patch of woods on the right (north) on private property of the last house on the street. Born about 1815 as Tsin-is-tum she was married to a Nehalem chief who died in 1860. About 1863 she married a French Canadian Michel Martineau

Name of Cemetery and also known as	Number of burials	Acres	Condition	Date started or earliest known burial	Townshp	Range	Section

whose name has usually been rendered as Meschelle Marchino. He died in 1902 and Jennie is buried next to his unmarked grave. There are/were other Indian burials in the vicinity. The existing plaque was dedicated 3 June 1988. {24 June 1996} (Not shown on Gearhart 1949-73 USGS Quad. map.)

MICKELSON FAMILY
AKA: 1. MICKELSON, EDITH
2. OJA, SOPHIA

A   ?   ?   1900-1901 T8N R7W   S11
Located in the Northeast 1/4 of Section 11. On Aldrich Point Road turn off onto Anderson Road; go east on Anderson Road to a hill on the right. Two cousins are buried in this small cemetery: Edith Mickelson and Sophia Oja. (Not shown on Knappa 1986 USGS Quad. map.)

NORMAN'S HILL

A 0.01 5 ?   T7N ?   ?
A burial somewhere near Smiley's Hole, off of Green Mountain Road and apparently also near Norman's Road, which goes northeasterly towards OR. Hwy. 202. NOTE: No other information was given in the report. (Not shown on Green Mountain 1949 USGS Quad. maps.)

OCEAN VIEW
AKA: 1. CLATSOP

E 100   1   1872   T8N R10W   S28
Located in the south part of Warrenton. Leave Fort Stevens Highway (Main Street) just south of Warrenton High School and take 18th Street up the ridge to the northwest. It is 0.28 of a mile to the main entrance to the largest cemetery in Clatsop County. Although more than 40 acres are not currently in use there have been close to 16,000 burials as of June 1996. Land for this cemetery was purchased by the city of Astoria in the early 1880's but the present caretaker reports burials on the site as early as 1872. Most earlier burials in Astoria have been reburied here. The Warrenton Pauper Cemetery is now a part of Ocean View, see that article: on the William H. Grey D.L.C., OC #4192. {25 June 1996} (Warrenton 1953-84 USGS Quad. map.)

Name of Cemetery and also known as	Number of burials	Acres	Condition	Date started or earliest known burial	Townshp	Range	Section

PAUPER [WARRENTON]
AKA: 1. CLATSOP COUNTY
2. COUNTY

C 4.5 5 20 Apr 1885 T8N R10W S21

This cemetery is located about 0.5 of a mile west of Main Street in Warrenton on the ridgetop and along the south line of 9th Street. It is now a part of Ocean View Cemetery but the caretaker told the compiler that the "Pauper Cemetery is not now in use." There is an interesting Article in the Winter 1982 edition of *Cumtux*, Vol. 3, No. 1, by Lloyd Ferrell which tells some of the history. Clatsop County purchased about 4.5 acres but only a portion was ever used. The first recorded burial was on 10 November 1885. Only 26 burials, including 2 women, were buried by 18 July 1893 when the surviving records end. There were burials for a total of about 30 years and indeed there are two death certificates for "County Cemetery" for burials on 9 January and 29 March 1915. Chinese burials were separate and were located northeast of the present Ocean View Mausoleum. The caretaker has an old map of the Pauper Cemetery with some of the burials marked in ink and some in pencil. (Not shown as a separate cemetery from Ocean View on Warrenton 1953-84 USGS Quad. map.)

RED-HEADED MAN
AKA: 1. RAMSEY, JACK

? ? ? ? ? ? ?

A great deal has been written about a red-headed white man (Ramsey) supposedly wrecked on shore a generation before Lewis and Clark arrived. This gentleman has been described as a Spaniard or an Englishman, the latter with the name Jack Ramsey tattooed on his arm. Whatever his nationality, he is supposed to have left descendants noted by early white visitors. In 1955, construction workers near Fort Stevens uncovered a grave identified as that of the red-headed man. Then it was covered up again. The compiler wonders if there was a store of red hair in this grave which presumably predates 1805. On this unsatisfactory note, this lost grave is consigned to future archeology.

RYAN FAMILY

? ? 5 ? T7N R8W ?

Perhaps located in Section 30 or 31. The supposition is based upon the name of a Ryan

Name of Cemetery and also known as	Number of burials	Acres	Condition	Date started or earliest known burial	Townshp	Range	Section

Road. This road leads south from the right hand side of Green Mountain Road and is located between the North fork and the South Fork of the Klaskanine River. However an article by Jean McKinney entitled *The Walluski-Labiske Neighborhood*, Cumtux Vol. 12, No. 3, Summer 1992, page 20 says their homestead (Certificate #455) was near the Old Military Road. The compiler cannot identify the homestead site. (Not shown on Green Mountain 1949 USGS Quad. maps.)

SADDLE MOUNTAIN ROAD

A   0.01   5   ?   T6N   R8W   ?

A baby named Niemi was buried on the ridge at the end of Saddle Mountain Road, supposedly about 0.5 of a mile short of the highway. (Not shown on Green Mountain 1949 USGS Quad. map.)

SIMMONS FAMILY
  AKA: 1. SIMMONDS
          FAMILY
       2. SIMONDS FARM

A   ?   5   Circa 1880   T7N   R8W   ?

Perhaps located in Section 27. It is supposed to be off of OR. Hwy. 202 somewhere between Cooperage Road and the Klaskanine Summit southeast of Olney. There is a Simmons Ridge Road to the left (northeasterly) off of OR. Hwy 202 about one mile short of the bridge over the North Fork Klaskanine River. Perhaps the Simmons Family Cemetery is in that vicinity. The cemetery has burials from the 1880's until the 1900's (Not on Green Mountain 1949 USGS Quad. map.)

SVENSEN PIONEER
  AKA: 1. FINNISH
       2. FOREST HILL
       3. INDEPENDENT
          ORDER OF
          REDMEN;
          WICKIUP
          TRIBE #21

C   1   3   Circa 1919   T8N   R8W   S23

Leave U.S. Hwy. 30 at Milepost 85.75, at Svensen, turning right (south) onto Svensen Market Road for 0.12 of a mile. Then turn left onto Old U.S. Hwy. 30 and go 0.47 of a mile; turn right (south) onto Simonson Loop and continue for 0.36 of a mile, going 350 feet past the powerlines. The cemetery is off of the road 400 feet and behind some houses. (Not shown on Cathlamet Bay 1985 USGS Quad. map.)

Clatsop County

Name of Cemetery and also known as	Number of burials	Acres	Condition	Date started or earliest known burial	Townshp	Range	Section

UNKNOWN FAMILY

A ? 5 ? ? ? ?

"Past the end of Saddle Mountain Road." About 1962 Mr. Vernon stumbled across a family burial ground at an abandoned farm. NOTE: No other information was given in the report. (Not shown on Green Mountain 1949 USGS Quad. map.)

UNKNOWN SAILORS

A 0.01 6 25 Apr 1865 T6N R10W S28

Two or three shipwrecked sailors were buried on the ocean side of what is now called Sunset Boulevard. This is just outside of the south city limits of Seaside and just past the convergence of South Edgewood Drive and Ocean Vista Way by the golf course. The burials were for a time under the roadway but about 1926 the bones were moved to the ocean side of the road. The burials are within a concrete square about 12' X 12' which has the wording: "found on the beach 25 April 1865." Within the square is a boulder with the wording: "known only to God." A 20' flagpole also marks the monument. On the William Lattie D.L.C. #38, OC #3158 {10 September 1996} (Not shown on Tillamook Head 1949-73 USGS Quad. map.)

U.S. ARMY
  FORT STEVENS
AKA: 1. FORT STEVENS
     2. MILITARY
     3. SOLDIERS

C 1.2 1 1898 T8N R10W S8

Take the Fort Stevens Highway from downtown Warrenton and follow the main route through Hammond (annexed to Warrenton in December of 1991) to the end of the highway. Continue ahead a short distance; turn left on 7th Drive, which ends at Russell Drive. Turn left (south) on Russell Drive for a short distance to the cemetery. The Enlisted Mans Cemetery of Fort Stevens served 3 forts; Stevens, Canby, and Columbia. See the article on Fort Stevens for the earlier history of the cemetery. 20 bodies were moved to this, the present cemetery site at the end of 1898. In 1913 the burials were realigned and the 50 known burials from Fort Canby and Fort Columbia, across the Columbia River from Fort Stevens, were brought to this cemetery. Fort Columbia never had a cemetery and those who died there had been included in the Fort Canby cemetery

Name of Cemetery and also known as	Number of burials	Acres	Condition	Date started or earliest known burial	Townshp	Range	Section

which was closed in 1913. There is also a civilian section for the families of the military personnel. It was closed in 1942, but reopened for Vietnam War dead. There are also burials for Coast Guardsmen, Airforce and civilian workers. {29 May 1992} (Warrenton 1953-84 USGS Quad. map.)

WALLUSKI AREA

? ? ? ?   T8N R9W   S27

Perhaps as early as 1850, it was located on an island in the Walluski (now Wallooskee) River and was the predecessor of Greenwood Cemetery. NOTE: No other information was given in the report. (Not shown on Astoria 1949-84 USGS Quad. map.)

WALLUSKI ROAD

A 0.01 5 ?   T8N R9W   S34

Located near the Moffit Landing on the Wallooskee River. A tombstone was buried in the ground because the housewife didn't wish to be reminded of the grave. On the John W. and Orrilla Moffit D.L.C., OC #4204. NOTE: This site is on private property. (Not shown on Astoria 1949-84 USGS Quad. map.)

WARREN FAMILY, DANIEL K.

A 0.01 ? 1903-1922 T8N R10W   ?

These are at Warrenton on the Warren estate "1000 feet from the old home." NOTE: This site is on private property. (Not shown on Warrenton 1953-84 USGS Quad. map.)

WESTPORT

C 1 2 1870   T8N R6W   S36

Turn south off U.S. Hwy. 30 toward Westport school for 0.5 of a mile, then turn left to the cemetery, 0.1 of a mile. The cemetery was incorporated in 1909. Vandalized in March of 1992. (Cathlamet, Washington Quad. 1985 USGS Quad. map.)

YOUNGS RIVER
AKA: 1. GRANGERS
     2. YOUNG, ANDY

B 1.3 5 1874   T7N R9W   S10

Located on the right bank of Youngs River, 0.38 of a mile due south of OR. Hwy. 202. Go 0.5 of a mile southeast on OR. Hwy. 202 from the junction of the south end of Walluski Loop Road. There appears to be no road

Name of Cemetery and also known as	Number of burials	Acres	Condition	Date started or earliest known burial	Townshp	Range	Section

access to the cemetery and most of the burials were moved to Greenwood. On the Enoch Blodgett D.L.C., OC #4187 and Luke Taylor D.L.C., OC #4255. NOTE: This site is on private property. (Not shown on Olney 1949-73-81 USGS Quad. map. The 1956 Metsker Atlas does show this site.)

Eternity At Sea Columbarium (Tillamook Rock Lighthouse)
Courtesy of Eternity at Sea Columbarium (1991)

ADAIR D.L.C., JOHN see **HOLY INNOCENTS EPISCOPAL**				
	CLATSOP CO.	T8N	R9W	S9
AHLERS, DORTHEA	CLATSOP CO.	T5N	R9W	S22
AHLERS HOUSE see **AHLERS, DORTHEA**				
	CLATSOP CO.	T5N	R9W	S22
ASTORIA see **CLATSOP PLAINS PIONEER**				
	CLATSOP CO.	T7N	R10W	S4
ASTORIA [OLD]	CLATSOP CO.	T8N	R9W	S8
ASTORIA PIONEER	CLATSOP CO.	T8N	R9W	S17
BARNEY CREEK see **BAYNEY CREEK**	CLATSOP CO.	R6N	R9W	?
BAYNEY CREEK	CLATSOP CO.	T6N	R9W	?
BITTERLING FAMILY	CLATSOP CO.	T7N	R10W	S24
BITTERLING, JULIUS see **BITTERLING FAMILY**				
	CLATSOP CO.	T7N	R10W	S24
BLODGETT D.L.C., ENOCH see **YOUNGS RIVER**				
	CLATSOP CO.	T7N	R9W	S10
CASEY FAMILY, ROSE	CLATSOP CO.	T7N	R9W	?
CATHOLIC see **ASTORIA [OLD]**	CLATSOP CO.	T8N	R9W	S8
CHIEF CONCOMLY see **COMCOMLY'S GRAVE**				
	CLATSOP CO.	T8N	R9W	S8
CITY see **ASTORIA PIONEER**	CLATSOP CO.	T8N	R9W	S17
CLATSOP see **OCEAN VIEW**	CLATSOP CO.	T8N	R10W	S28
CLATSOP COUNTY see **PAUPER [WARRENTON]**				
	CLATSOP CO.	T8N	R10W	S21
CLATSOP INDIANS	CLATSOP CO.	T6N	R10W	S28
CLATSOP PLAINS PIONEER	CLATSOP CO.	T7N	R10W	S4
CLOUTIER see **LATTIE-CLOUTRIE FAMILY**				
	CLATSOP CO.	T6N	R10W	S21
CLOUTRIE, ANTOINE J. see **LATTIE-CLOUTRIE FAMILY**				
	CLATSOP CO.	T6N	R10W	S21
CLOUTRIE, HELEN see **LATTIE-CLOUTRIE FAMILY**				
	CLATSOP CO.	T6N	R10W	S21
COMCOMLY'S GRAVE	CLATSOP CO.	T8N	R9W	S8
CONCOMLY see **COMCOMLY'S GRAVE**	CLATSOP CO.	T8N	R9W	S8
COUNTY see **PAUPER [WARRENTON]**	CLATSOP CO.	T8N	R10W	S21
CRAZY VALLEY	CLATSOP CO.	T5N	R9W	?
CRESTVIEW see **GREENWOOD**	CLATSOP CO.	T8N	R9W	S33
DUNKIN, GEORGE	CLATSOP CO.	T7N	R8W	?
ELSIE	CLATSOP CO.	T4N	R7W	S5
ESTOOS see **FITCHA HOMESTEAD**	CLATSOP CO.	T8N	R8W	S31
ETERNITY AT SEA COLUMBARIUM	CLATSOP CO.	T5N	R11W	S-0
EVERGREEN	CLATSOP CO.	T6N	R10W	S34
EVERGREEN LODGE #137 see **EVERGREEN**				
	CLATSOP CO.	T6N	R10W	S34
FERRELL, LLOYD see **PAUPER [WARRENTON]**				
	CLATSOP CO.	T8N	R10W	S21
FINNISH see **SVENSEN PIONEER**	CLATSOP CO.	T8N	R8W	S23
FITCHA HOMESTEAD	CLATSOP CO.	T8N	R8W	S31
FOREST HILL see **SVENSEN PIONEER**	CLATSOP CO.	T8N	R8W	S23
FORT ASTORIA	CLATSOP CO.	T8N	R10W	S8
FORT GEORGE see **FORT ASTORIA**	CLATSOP CO.	T8N	R10W	S8

FORT STEVENS see **U.S. ARMY FORT STEVENS**				
	CLATSOP CO.	T8N	R10W	S8
FORT STEVENS [OLD]	CLATSOP CO.	T8N	R10W	S5
GILLETT D.L.C., PRESTON W. see **LEWIS AND CLARK**				
	CLATSOP CO.	T7N	R9W	S6
GRANGERS see **YOUNGS RIVER**	CLATSOP CO.	T7N	R9W	S10
GRAY D.L.C., WILLIAM H. see **OCEAN VIEW**				
	CLATSOP CO.	T8N	R10W	S28
GREEN MOUNTAIN ROAD	CLATSOP CO.	T6N	R8W	?
GREENWOOD	CLATSOP CO.	T8N	R9W	S33
GRONNEL see **GRONNELL FAMILY**	CLATSOP CO.	T4N	R7W	?
GRONNELL FAMILY	CLATSOP CO.	T4N	R7W	?
HAMLET	CLATSOP CO.	T4N	R8W	S6
HECKARD FAMILY	CLATSOP CO.	T7N	R9W	S18
HILL FAMILY see **HAMLET**	CLATSOP CO.	T4N	R8W	S6
HILLSIDE see **ASTORIA PIONEER**	CLATSOP CO.	T8N	R9W	S17
HILLTOP see **ASTORIA PIONEER**	CLATSOP CO.	T8N	R9W	S17
HOLY INNOCENTS EPISCOPAL	CLATSOP CO.	T8N	R9W	S9
HYDE, JACQUIE see **JOHANSON FAMILY**				
	CLATSOP CO.	?	?	?
HYDE, JIM see **JOHANSON FAMILY**	CLATSOP CO.	?	?	?
INDEPENDENT ORDER OF REDMEN; WICKIUP TRIBE #21 see **SVENSEN PIONEER**				
	CLATSOP CO.	T8N	R8W	S23
INDIAN GEORGE see **DUNKIN, GEORGE**				
	CLATSOP CO.	T7N	R8W	?
JEWELL	CLATSOP CO.	T5N	R7W	S11
JEWELL [OLD]	CLATSOP CO.	T5N	R7W	S12
JOHANSON BABIES see **JOHANSON FAMILY**				
	CLATSOP CO.	?	?	?
JOHANSON FAMILY	CLATSOP CO.	?	?	?
KALANDER FAMILY, EMIL see **MAPLEWOOD**				
	CLATSOP CO.	T8N	R7W	S16
KALLIO, ISRAEL see **GREEN MOUNTAIN ROAD**				
	CLATSOP CO.	T6N	R8W	?
KNAPPA see **KNAPPA PRAIRE**	CLATSOP CO.	T8N	R7W	S17
KNAPPA PRAIRIE	CLATSOP CO.	T8N	R7W	S17
LATTIE, ALEXANDRE see **LATTIE-CLOUTRIE FAMILY**				
	CLATSOP CO.	T6N	R10W	S21
LATTIE-CLOUTRIE FAMILY	CLATSOP CO.	T6N	R10W	S21
LATTIE D.L.C., ELIZABETH see **CLATSOP INDIANS**				
	CLATSOP CO.	T6N	R10W	S28
LATTIE D.L.C., ELIZABETH see **LATTIE-CLOUTRIE FAMILY**				
	CLATSOP CO.	T6N	R10W	S21
LATTIE D.L.C., WILLIAM see **UNKNOWN SAILORS**				
	CLATSOP CO.	T6N	R10W	S28
LATTIE, ELIZABETH see **LATTIE-CLOUTRIE FAMILY**				
	CLATSOP CO.	T6N	R10W	S21
LATTIE, WILLIAM see **LATTIE-CLOUTRIE FAMILY**				
	CLATSOP CO.	T6N	R10W	S21
LEWIS AND CLARK	CLATSOP CO.	T7N	R9W	S6
LILLENAS see **FITCHA HOMESTEAD**	CLATSOP CO.	T8N	R8W	S31
LUPATIA CREW	CLATSOP CO.	T5N	R11W	S1

MAKI FAMILY see **HAMLET**	CLATSOP CO.	T4N	R8W	S6
MAPLEWOOD	CLATSOP CO.	T8N	R7W	S16
MARCHINO, MESCHELLE see **MESCHELLE, JENNIE**				
	CLATSOP CO.	T6N	R10W	S15
MARTINEAU, MICHEL see **MESCHELLE, JENNIE**				
	CLATSOP CO.	T6N	R10W	S15
MASONIC [SEASIDE] see **EVERGREEN**	CLATSOP CO.	T6N	R10W	S34
McKINNEY, JEAN see **RYAN FAMILY**	CLATSOP CO.	T7N	R8W	?
McTAVISH, DONALD	CLATSOP CO.	T8N	R9W	S8
MESCHELLE, JENNIE	CLATSOP CO.	T6N	R10W	S15
MICKELSON, EDITH see **MICKELSON FAMILY**				
	CLATSOP CO.	T8N	R7W	S11
MICKELSON FAMILY	CLATSOP CO.	T8N	R7W	S11
MILITARY see **U.S. ARMY FORT STEVENS**				
	CLATSOP CO.	T8N	R10W	S8
MOFFIT D.L.C., JOHN W. AND ORRILLA see **WALLUSKI ROAD**				
	CLATSOP CO.	T8N	R9W	S34
MORRISON D.L.C., ROBERT see **CLATSOP PLAINS PIONEER**				
	CLATSOP CO.	T7N	R10W	S4
NECANICUM POST OFFICE see **AHLERS, DORTHEA**				
	CLATSOP CO.	T5N	R9W	S22
NIEMI, BABY see **SADDLE MOUNTAIN ROAD**				
	CLATSOP CO.	T6N	R8W	?
NORMAN'S HILL	CLATSOP CO.	T7N	?	?
NORMAN'S HOME, LEX see **DUNKIN, GEORGE**				
	CLATSOP CO.	T7N	R8W	?
OCEAN VIEW	CLATSOP CO.	T8N	R10W	S28
OJA, SOPHIA see **MICKELSON FAMILY**				
	CLATSOP CO.	T8N	R7W	S11
OLD TAYLOR HOUSE see **COMCOMLY'S GRAVE**				
	CLATSOP CO.	T8N	R9W	S8
OTTINGER, ANNA LOUISE see **BITTERLING FAMILY**				
	CLATSOP CO.	T7N	R10W	S24
PAUPER [WARRENTON]	CLATSOP CO.	T8N	R10W	S21
PIONEER see **ASTORIA PIONEER**	CLATSOP CO.	T8N	R9W	S17
POTTERS FIELD see **ASTORIA [OLD]**	CLATSOP CO.	T8N	R9W	S8
PRAIRIE see **KNAPPA PRAIRIE**	CLATSOP CO.	T8N	R7W	S17
RAMEY D.L.C., DANIEL C. see **KNAPPA PRAIRIE**				
	CLATSOP CO.	T8N	R7W	S17
RAMSEY, JACK see **RED HEADED MAN**	CLATSOP CO.	?	?	?
RED HEADED MAN	CLATSOP CO.	?	?	?
RIVERVIEW see **LEWIS AND CLARK**	CLATSOP CO.	T7N	R9W	S6
RYAN FAMILY	CLATSOP CO.	T7N	R8W	?
SADDLE MOUNTAIN ROAD	CLATSOP CO.	T6N	R8W	?
SEASIDE see **EVERGREEN**	CLATSOP CO.	T6N	R10W	S34
SHIVELY D.L.C., JOHN see **ASTORIA [OLD]**				
	CLATSOP CO.	T8N	R9W	S8
SHIVELY D.L.C., JOHN see **ASTORIA PIONEER**				
	CLATSOP CO.	T8N	R9W	S17
SHIVELY FAMILY see **ASTORIA [OLD]**				
	CLATSOP CO.	T8N	R9W	S8

SHIVELY, JOHN M. see **ASTORIA [OLD]**				
	CLATSOP CO.	T8N	R9W	S8
SIMMONDS FAMILY see **SIMMONS FAMILY**				
	CLATSOP CO.	T7N	R8W	?
SIMMONS FAMILY	CLATSOP CO.	T7N	R8W	?
SIMONDS FARM see **SIMMONS FAMILY**	CLATSOP CO.	T7N	R8W	?
SOLDIERS see **U.S. ARMY FORT STEVENS**				
	CLATSUP CO.	T8N	R10W	S8
SUNNY HILL CEMETERY OF NEHALEM see **ELSIE**				
	CLATSOP CO.	T4N	R7W	S5
SVENSEN PIONEER	CLATSOP CO.	T8N	R8W	S23
TAYLOR D.L.C., LUKE see **YOUNGS RIVER**				
	CLATSOP CO.	T7N	R9W	S10
TILLAMOOK ROCK LIGHTHOUSE see **ETERNITY AT SEA COLUMBARIUM**				
	CLATSOP CO.	T5N	R11W	S-0
TSIN-IS-TUM see **MESCHELLE, JENNIE**				
	CLATSOP CO.	T6N	R10W	S15
UNKNOWN FAMILY	CLATSOP CO.	?	?	?
UNKNOWN SAILORS	CLATSOP CO.	T6N	R10W	S28
U.S. ARMY FORT STEVENS	CLATSOP CO.	T8N	R10W	S8
VERNON, MR. see **UNKNOWN FAMILY**	CLATSOP CO.	?	?	?
WALLUSKI AREA	CLATSOP CO.	T8N	R9W	S27
WALLUSKI ROAD	CLATSOP CO.	T8N	R9W	S34
WARREN FAMILY, DANIEL K.	CLATSOP CO.	T8N	R10W	?
WATSON FARM, LILLI see **CASEY FAMILY, ROSE**				
	CLATSOP CO.	T7N	R9W	?
WESTPORT	CLATSOP CO.	T8N	R6W	S36
YOUNG, ANDY see **YOUNGS RIVER**	CLATSOP CO.	T7N	R9W	S10
YOUNGS RIVER	CLATSOP CO.	T7N	R9W	S10

Ocean View
Dean H. Byrd (1996)

COLUMBIA COUNTY

Scale

Neer City, Dean H. Byrd
Janice M. Healy (1991)

Area: 687 square miles
Population (1998): 44,416
County seat: St. Helens, Population: 8,300
County established: 16 January 1854

After the fur traders, other emigrants settled along the Columbia River in the late 1840's. St. Helens was founded as early as 1845 but did not have a public cemetery until 1853. By the mid-1870's four additional public cemeteries had been opened in communities along the Columbia River, plus one cemetery at Vernonia in the Nehalem River Valley. Private family burial sites were more common outside of the towns. As in Clatsop County there was a considerable infusion of Finnish immigrants into Columbia County.

Mayger-Downing Family
Dean H. Byrd (1991)

Columbia County

Bayview Memorial

Janice M. Healy (1991)

Name of Cemetery and also known as	Number of burials	Acres	Condition	Date started or earliest known burial	Township	Range	Section

APIARY

C 1.4 1 1893   T6N R3W   S14

Leave Rainier at the traffic light at "B" Street (U.S. Hwy. 30) and 1st Street; turn and drive south, uphill on 1st Street, to "C" Street. Turn right onto "C" Street and go 6 blocks, cross the narrow bridge and turn left at 7th Street, which is also Fern Hill Road. Drive on Fern Hill Road to the Apiary Cemetery sign, which is 8 miles from the starting point. Turn left (south) and drive 0.15 of a mile to the cemetery. 1894 was the earliest burial date noted. {24 June 1991} (Delena 1985 USGS Quad. map.)

BAYVIEW MEMORIAL
AKA: 1. I.O.O.F.
      [ST. HELENS]

E 3.7 2 1893   T4N R1W   S17

Located 3 miles south of St. Helens at Warren. Leave Columbia River Highway (U.S. Hwy. 30) at Milepost 25.5, at Warren, onto Church Road. Turn east towards the river, cross the railway tracks and then turn left onto Old Portland Road. Drive 0.6 of a mile towards St. Helens and the cemetery is on the left. The St. Helens Odd Fellows Lodge #117 was organized in July of 1892. They soon started the cemetery which was surveyed in January of 1893. Earlier burials have been relocated here. On the Samuel C. Achilles D.L.C. #57, OC #2922. {24 June 1991} (St. Helens 1990 USGS Quad. map.)

BEAVER HOMES
AKA: 1. BARKER ROAD

? ? ? ?   T6N R2W   ?

Perhaps located in Section 16 or 17. Beaver Homes was an area along the middle reaches of Goble Creek and Baker Road which is a short county road northwesterly from Goble Creek. Robert Thomas notes that an unnamed cemetery was reported in the vicinity of Red Town, a company logging town. The compiler wonders if this could be Kobel (NOT Goble) Cemetery about a mile to the southwest as the crow flies. (Not shown on Trenholm 1990 USGS Quad. map.)

BETHANY MEMORIAL
AKA: 1. LUTHERAN
     2. WARREN

E 2 1 1915   T4N R1W   S19

Located at Warren about halfway between Scappoose and St. Helens. Leave U.S. Hwy. 30 at Milepost 25.5 and turn west (inland) onto

Name of Cemetery and also known as	Number of burials	Acres	Condition	Date started or earliest known burial	Township	Range	Section

Church Road. Go 0.15 of a mile on Church Road to the cemetery driveway on the right (north), next to the church. {16 September 1991} (St. Helens 1990 USGS Quad. map.)

BLANCHARD'S
AKA: 1. BLANCHARD, DEAN
2. INDIAN BURIALS
3. POTTERS

? ? 5 ? T7N R2W S16

Located in Rainier. There were burials uncovered by a bulldozer during some construction for a new residence. It has been reported that this was a potter's cemetery and that seven people were buried here two of which were Indians. For more information see *Portland Reporter*, Wednesday, October 16, 1963. (Not shown on Rainier 1953-70 USGS Quad. map.)

BRYANT
AKA: 1. CEDAR HILL

C 0.6 1 1878 T7N R4W S9

Located in Clatskanie. Leave U.S. Hwy. 30 at the traffic light and drive north on Nehalem Street, the old highway, for four blocks (0.23 of a mile) and turn right onto 5th Street (or Swedetown Road). Go 0.13 of a mile to Haven Acres Road, turn left. On Haven Acres Road drive two blocks to Wood Lane and turn right. The cemetery is on the left side of Wood Lane, 0.75 of a mile from the starting point. Although the establishment of the cemetery is given as 1878, Nancy C. wife of E. G. Bryant, is buried here: she died 29 November 1859. The cemetery was dedicated 12 May 1905 as Cedar Hill. In 1967 the cemetery was deeded to the city of Clatskanie. Located on the Henry B. Hastings D.L.C. #38, OC #1522. {18 November 1991} (Clatskanie 1985 USGS Quad. map.)

CEDAR CREEK ROAD

? ? ? 1918-1919 T4N R2W S18

Drive about 8.25 miles from U.S. Hwy. 30 at Scappoose via the Scappoose-Vernonia Highway, a county road. Cedar Creek Road intersects on the right (north) about halfway between Spitzenberg and Chapman. Kass Bradley reports there were several unmarked family graves of victims of the Spanish flu epidemic at the end of World War I. The compiler could find no death certificates on file in

Name of Cemetery and also known as	Number of burials	Acres	Condition	Date started or earliest known burial	Township	Range	Section

the State Archives of deaths from Spanish flu or any other cause in this area in 1918 or 1919. (Not shown on Chapman 1990 USGS Quad. map.)

COLUMBIA MEMORIAL GARDENS
AKA: 1. SACRED HEART CATHOLIC

D 20   1   1957   T4N R2W   S36
Located on Columbia River Highway (U.S. Hwy. 30), on the river side of the highway at about Milepost 22.5, between Scappoose and St. Helens. It is about 2 miles north of Scappoose. Although there is no principal signboard, there is a separate sign designating the Sacred Heart Catholic area of Columbia Memorial Gardens. The cemetery includes Good Shepherd Mausoleum (1959), another mausoleum and 2 columbariums: on the David A. Coninger D.L.C. #37, OC #2922. {24 June 1991} (Not shown on St. Helens 1990 USGS Quad. map.)

CRAIG, HENRY CLAY

A ?   ?   11 Jul 1919 ?   ?   ?
There is a Columbia County death certificate #61 for the year 1919 which reports the death of Henry Clay Craig on 11 July 1919 and his burial on the following day "near Scappoose." He was born 10 June 1840 and was survived by his widow Martha. Neither is listed in any Columbia County Cemetery publications.

DIBBLEE HOUSE

A 0.01 ?   1873   T7N R2W   S16
Located at 313 "B" Street East, Rainier ("B" Street is U.S. Hwy. 30). John and Sarah Blanchard Dibblee purchased what is now known as the Dibblee House in 1869. Their 5 year-old son Merrill died in 1873. In 1875, Sarah's 20 year-old brother, Merrill Blanchard died two days after being stabbed in a tavern brawl. Both Merrill Dibblee and Merrill Blanchard are buried west of the house, in the yard under a present day apple tree. The graves are unmarked and on private property. (Not shown on Rainier 1953-70 USGS Quad. map.)

| Name of Cemetery and also known as | Number of burials | Acres | Condition | Date started or earliest known burial | Township | Range | Section |

FAIRVIEW
AKA: 1. PROTESTANT
2. SCAPPOOSE
PIONEER

D 5 1 1871   T3N R2W   S24
Located at the south edge of Scappoose, on the west side of U.S. Hwy. 30. Although there is access to U.S. Hwy. 30, because of the traffic it is best to use Old Portland Road, which is more or less parallel to the highway and west of it. Leave U. S. Hwy. 30 onto Old Portland Road at highway Milepost 19.1 at the south edge of Scappoose go north. It is on the Thomas J. Jackson D.L.C. #44, OC # 3587. (Dixie Mountain 1961-85 and USGS Quad. map.)

FISHHAWK

C 1.6 2 1886   T6N R5W   S17
Located near Birkenfeld. From the junction of OR. Hwy. 47 with OR. Hwy. 202 at Mist, drive westerly towards Birkenfeld and Astoria on OR. Hwy. 202. After driving about 4.2 miles, turn right (northerly) off of OR. Hwy. 202 onto Fishhawk Road and cross the Nehalem River. At 0.3 of a mile from the highway is a road junction; stay left and go up the hill. The cemetery is on the left at 0.8 of a mile from the highway. A bonus is a fine view of the Nehalem Valley below. {12 August 1991} (Marshland 1985 USGS Quad. map.)

GILBREATH-MOECK FAMILY
AKA: 1. STENNICK
FARM

B 0.01 ? ?   T7N R2W   S18
Located west of Rainier on private property, at 28414 Parkdale Road. This is on the south side of the road, at the second house west of Parkdale Road junction with Meserve Road. As of January 1992, Judith Whipple reports only two stones remain: Sarah Ann, wife of J. C. Gilbreath, died 19 February 1865; Louise B., daughter of G.F. and M. J. Moeck died 23 June 1878. There were reportedly 20 or 30 burials of people of the Hudson community here. NOTE: This site is on private property. (Not shown on Rainier 1953-70 USGS Quad. map.)

GIRGENSON FAMILY

A ? ? 1948   T6N R3W   S14
Located in the Southwest 1/4 of Section 14, near Apiary. Starting at the traffic light at "B" Street (U.S. Hwy. 30) and 1st Street in Rainier, turn and drive south, uphill on

Name of Cemetery and also known as	Number of burials	Acres	Condition	Date started or earliest known burial	Township	Range	Section

1st Street, to "C" Street. Then turn right onto "C" Street and go 6 blocks, crossing the narrow bridge and turning left at 7th Street, which is also Fern Hill Road. Drive southerly on Fern Hill Road 8.6 miles to Apiary Road. Turn left onto Apiary Road and go 0.85 of a mile to Meissner Road. Turn left onto Meissner Road and drive 0.2 of a mile. This is about 9.5 miles from the starting point. The cemetery is on the left after walking through a field. Reportedly there are 3 graves here, one is for Bertha Christina Girgenson who died before 1912 and John Girgenson born 1860, died 29 June 1948. NOTE: This site is on private property. (Not shown on Delena 1985 USGS Quad. map.)

GORE FAMILY

A	?	5	1900	T5N	R2W	S10	

From the locale of Deer Island on U.S. Hwy. 30 about 5 miles north of Saint Helens turn inland to the west on Canaan Road. Drive about 3.7 miles from the highway to the mailbox with the address 31810 Canaan Road on the right (north). On the opposite side of the road is a small red house with a large green metal barn. The burial site is about 200 yards from Canaan Road behind that barn and in the remains of a holly orchard. NOTE: this is on private property. Mr. Robert M. Thomas of Columbia City reported a large tombstone for Henry C. Gore, 1858-1922, and his wife Mary C. 1865-1922; plus two small stones for Isaac Gray, died 28 April 1900 and Anna C. Gray, died 10 December 1910. In addition two children, ages 6 and 8, of the Seidel family who drowned are reportedly buried here also. (Not shown on Trenholm 1990 USGS Quad. map.)

GREEN MOUNTAIN
AKA: 1. GREEN MOUNTAIN
    SOUTH

D	2	1	1906	T7N	R3W	S13	

From the traffic signals at "B" Street (U.S. Hwy. 30) Milepost 47, and 1st Street in Rainier, drive westerly on U.S. Hwy. 30, past the Longview Bridge, for 3.25 miles. At Milepost 50.3 turn left (southerly) onto Larson Road. Drive past Beaver Valley Grange and Woodbine Cemetery on the left and at the right curve, about 0.25 of a mile down Larson

Name of Cemetery and also known as | Number of burials | Acres | Condition | Date started or earliest known burial | Township | Range | Section

Road, is Green Mountain Cemetery on the left. The new Hudson Cemetery is across Larson Road from the other two. (29 July 1991} (Rainier 1953-70 USGS Quad. map.)

HALL, JESSE W.

A 0.01 ? 12 Jun 1993 ?   ?   ?
Jesse "Jack" W. Hall is buried at 32682 Scappoose-Vernonia Highway in the area of Scappoose. (Not shown on Chapman 1990 USGS Quad. Map.)

HALL-TIPTON FAMILY

A 0.15 5 31 Oct 1918 T4N R4W   S3
This abandoned cemetery is located at the east end of Vernonia. Take Bridge Street (OR. Hwy. 47) east from downtown and cross the bridge over the Nehalem River. Turn right off of OR. Hwy. 47 onto Pebble Creek Road and drive south 0.2 of a mile. The cemetery is on the left (east) side of the road and to the left of the gravel pit. This is opposite the house at 523 Pebble Creek Road. The cemetery has never been known to have a name. It is tentatively suggested here to name it Hall-Tipton for the two families found here on the five monuments, dating from 31 Oct. 1918 to 1936. NOTE: This site is on private property. {14 September 1991} (Vernonia 1979 USGS Quad. map.)

HAVLIK PLACE

? ?   ? ?   T3N R2W   ?
Long-ago unverified reports state that Jesse Miles, his wife, daughter, grandson and three people named Hines are buried on the Havlik Place at Scappoose; on Jesse Miles D.L.C. #39, OC #1434. (Not shown on Dixie Mountain 1961-85 USGS Quad. map.)

HERWICK JR., FRED WM.

A 0.01 5 1934   T4N R3W   S35
Located on what was the Herwick Homestead near Pisgah Home. Leave U.S. Hwy. 30 and take the Scappoose-Vernonia Highway for about 8 miles. Turn left (south) onto Chapman Grange Road. After 1.5 miles take the right fork on Pisgah Main Line Road and drive 2 miles passing three houses on the right side

Name of Cemetery and also known as	Number of burials	Acres	Condition	Date started or earliest known burial	Township	Range	Section

of the road. After the third house turn right and drive 0.2 of a mile. The grave is on the right side of the road on an elevation in a small wooded area in logged terrain. Young Herwick was walking home from football practice along the tracks of a logging railroad when he apparently grabbed for a passing rail car and fell under the wheels. (Not shown on Bacona 1979 USGS Quad. map.)

| HILLCREST AKA: 1. YANKTON-- HILLCREST | D 3 | 1 | | 1954 | T5N | R2W | S36 |

This new cemetery is very close to the old Yankton Cemetery, now called Union Cemetery. Leave U.S. Hwy. 30 in St. Helens at Milepost 29 and drive 3.1 miles west on Pittsburg Road. The old Yankton Cemetery is on the left (south). The driveway on the right (north) leads to the Yankton Baptist Church and parking lot, and also to Hillcrest Cemetery. {16 September 1991} (Not shown on Chapman 1990 USGS Quad. map.)

| HUDSON AKA: 1. HUDSON PARK | C 3 | 1 | | 1964 | T7N | R3W | S13 |

From the traffic signals at "B" Street (U.S. Hwy. 30) Milepost 47 and 1st Street in Rainier, drive westerly on U.S. Hwy. 30, past the Longview Bridge, for 3.25 miles. At Milepost 50.3 turn left (southerly) onto Larson Road. Drive past Beaver Valley Grange and Woodbine Cemetery on the left; at 0.2 of a mile on Larson Road, Hudson Cemetery is on the right, opposite Woodbine Cemetery. A third cemetery, Green Mountain, is also adjacent to Hudson and Woodbine. Woodbine Cemetery was earliest known as Hudson, after the Samuel K. Hudson family. The name was revived in 1964 when 3 acres were purchased and called Hudson Cemetery. The name Hudson Park properly belongs to a nearby county park. {29 June 1991} (Rainier 1953-70 USGS Quad. map.)

| JOHNSON PLACE, LOREN | ? ? | ? | ? | ? | T3N | R1W | ? |

Long-ago unverified reports state that there are burials from the families of Jim Gosa, Tom Jackson and Henry Miller, all early white

Name of Cemetery and also known as	Number of burials	Acres	Condition	Date started or earliest known burial	Township	Range	Section

settlers. Supposedly located east of Fairview Cemetery and "next to the railroad fence." (Not shown on Sauvie Island 1990 USGS Quad. map.)

JONES FAMILY
  AKA: 1. JONES
       2. SHILOH BASIN

B   0.25 1   1902   T6N R2W   S33
Leave U.S. Hwy. 30 between Deer Island and Goble at Milepost 36.5 and turn inland (westerly) onto Tide Creek Road. Drive 6 miles to the cemetery, on the left, at the junction with Nicolai and Bishop Creek Roads. Shiloh Basin Community Church is within sight and Kobel Cemetery is not much more than a mile distant. {24 June 1991} (Trenholm 1990 USGS Quad. map.)

KEASEY
  AKA: 1. CARROLL
       2. UNKNOWN
       [KEASEY]

?   0.5   5   ?   T5N R5W   S27
Located in the Southeast 1/4 of Section 27. This unnamed cemetery lies about 5.3 miles west of Vernonia Pioneer Cemetery on Rock Creek Road, going towards Keasey. It lies a very short distance west of the mailboxes on the left (south): 13882 and 13890. The location is readily identified because of the remaining fir trees standing therein, while the surrounding area was logged off in 1986. There is no ready access and you must climb the steep embankment above the road. It is fenced, with 2 Civil War military monuments found: Brice Hacker, Co. D 23rd Iowa Inf. and Edward D. Webster, Co. D, 24th Mich. Inf., died 1892. {27 August 1991} (Not shown on Birkenfeld 1979 USGS Quad. map.)

KENTUCKY FLAT

B   ?   5   ?   T7N R2W   S16
The cemetery was in the western part of Rainier, in the area of West 8th Street between "B" and "C" Streets. Old-timers reported to Judith Whipple, in January 1992, that settlers from Kentucky, who arrived about 1910, found many bones and Indian trinkets. A 1966 report stated the burial ground was formerly enclosed by a white picket fence containing an estimated 30 graves, thought to be mostly of Indians plus

Name of Cemetery and also known as	Number of burials	Acres	Condition	Date started or earliest known burial	Township	Range	Section

2 white children. NOTE: This site is on private property. (NOT shown on Rainier 1953-70 USGS Quad. map.)

KINDER
AKA: 1. DEER ISLAND

C   1   2   1892   T5N   R1W   S16
Located in sections 16 and 17, at about Milepost 32.6 of U.S. Hwy. 30 and on the right (east) when driving from Columbia City toward Deer Island community. There is a railroad signboard "Reichhold" and the cemetery is directly opposite the large chemical plant on the left side of the highway. There is a short driveway from the highway over the railway tracks and under the archway sign of the cemetery. 1877 was the earliest dated monument found, probably a reburial from Merrill Lake Cemetery. There is a fine American chestnut tree on the grounds: on the Charles C. Caples D.L.C. #40, OC #1560. {29 July 1991} (Deer Island 1990 USGS Quad. map.)

KNIGHTS OF PYTHIAS [RAINIER]
AKA: 1. K.P.

C   1.5   1   1883   T7N   R2W   S21
Located near Rainier. Leave "B" Street (U.S. Hwy. 30) at the traffic light, turning uphill on 1st Street for 3 blocks. Turn left onto "E" Street and continue past the school as the street curves to become "F" Street. Turn right on 10th Street, continue uphill and out into the country. The road name changes to Neer or Neer City Road. The cemetery is on the right (west) about 1 mile from the starting point. The Knights of Pythias established the cemetery circa 1895. There is a splendid view of the Columbia River and of Mt. St. Helens. {29 July 1991} (Rainier 1953-70 USGS Quad. map.)

KOBEL
AKA: 1. ANLIKER

B   0.85 2   1901   T6N   R2W   S20
This cemetery name is easily confused with Goble. Leave the Columbia River Highway (U.S. Hwy. 30) at Goble, at Milepost 40.5, and turn inland on Nicolai Road. Drive 5.7 miles on Nicolai Road to Clark Road. Turn right (west) onto Clark Road and go 0.15 of a

Name of Cemetery and also known as	Number of burials	Acres	Condition	Date started or earliest known burial	Township	Range	Section

mile to Whitney Road. Turn right (northerly), uphill for 0.35 of a mile to the cemetery. {24 June 1991} (Trenholm 1990 USGS Quad. map.)

LACEY, CHARLES S.

A 0.01 ? 4 Feb 1899 T3N R2W ?

Perhaps located in Section 17. This lone unmarked grave is below the city water works dam in the city of Scappoose watershed in upper Dutch Canyon. (Not shown on Dixie Mountain 1961-85 USGS Quad. map.)

LAMBERSON FAMILY

A 0.01 5 12 Jan 1852 T3N R2W S1

From Scappoose, drive north on U.S. Hwy. 30 to Milepost 22.5, the junction with West Lane Road. Turn right (easterly) onto West Lane Road and go about 0.5 of a mile to the junction with North Honeyman Road. Turn right again (southerly) and continue on West Lane Road for another 0.4 of a mile. There are three graves of Sarah Lamberson and two sons, now unmarked. There are four very large oak trees here also, at the site of the William West home, which burned in 1921. West bought out the Lamberson claim in 1868. The compiler does not know on which side of the road are the four oak trees: on the Timothy Lamberson D.L.C. #42, OC #2850. NOTE: This site is on private property. {Sept. 1992} (Not shown on Chapman or St. Helens 1990 USGS Quad. maps.)

MAPLEWOOD

C 0.8 1 1878 T7N R4W S8

Located in Clatskanie. Leave U.S. Hwy. 30 at the traffic light and turn southerly on Nehalem Street, uphill. Go 0.16 of a mile and turn left onto Southeast 4th Street; go one block on 4th Street and turn right on Conyers Street for one more block. Jog to the left on Bellflower a very short distance and then turn right (south) again on Conyers Street. The cemetery is about 0.3 of a mile from the starting point. Mary Tichenor, who died 12 February 1876, was the earliest monument found: on the Enoch W. Conyers D.L.C. #39, OC #3488. {18 November 1991} (Clatskanie 1985 USGS Quad. map.)

Name of Cemetery and also known as	Number of burials	Acres	Condition	Date started or earliest known burial	Township	Range	Section

MARSHLAND

A ? 5 ?   T7N R5W   S11

This abandoned cemetery was a short distance east of Marshland, on the south (right) side of the old highway (U.S. Hwy. 30), now known as Colvin Road. Drive west from the traffic light at U.S. Hwy. 30 and Nehalem Street in Clatskanie for 2.2 miles to the Marshland crossroads and Milepost 66. Turn left (south) off of the highway and go 0.17 of a mile to Colvin Road. Turn left onto Colvin Road and drive to 14099 Colvin Road. The cemetery is across the road from this address about 100 feet inland into the woods. In a 1980's conversation in Clatskanie, an old-timer, Mr. Salmi, told Rudy Wellbrock that the 4 or 5 markers were all wooden and that the school children used to decorate the graves. Mr. Salmi believed there had been no burials for many years. NOTE: This site is on private property. {July 1992} (Not shown on Marshland 1985 USGS Quad. map.)

MASONIC [ST. HELENS]
AKA: 1. EVERGREEN
     2. GERMANY HILL
     3. LIBERTY HILL
     4. NEER FAMILY
     5. OLD MASONIC
     6. ST. HELENS
        PIONEER
        MASONIC

C 9.5 1 1853   T5N R1W   S33

Leave U.S. Hwy. 30 at Milepost 29.4 at the north edge of St. Helens. Drive uphill on Liberty Hill Road for about 0.4 of a mile to a locked gate with a sign: Masonic Cemetery. A key is available at the Fire Station; otherwise walk up slope for about 0.5 of a mile to the cemetery. In 1847 Caleb Neer donated one acre for a family cemetery. In 1853 the first Masonic burial was held here, and in 1872 the Saint Helens Masonic Lodge purchased the cemetery plus more acreage. Because the Neer family was of German origin the area was known as Germany Hill. During World War I that name was changed to Liberty Hill. At present only the original acre has been used; other acreage remains in grass: on the Abraham Neer D.L.C. #56, OC #3361. {16 September 1991} (Not shown on Deer Island 1990 USGS Quad. map.)

MAYGER-DOWNING FAMILY
AKA: 1. DOWNING-MAYGER
        FAMILY

C 1.25 1 1870   T8N R3W   S19

Leave Rainier at the traffic light at 1st and "B" Streets (U.S. Hwy. 30) and drive westerly past the Longview Bridge for 5.35 miles. Leave U.S. Hwy. 30 at Milepost 52.3, the

Name of Cemetery and also known as	Number of burials	Acres	Condition	Date started or earliest known burial	Township	Range	Section

Alston-Mayger exit, on the right (north). Drive 0.3 of a mile to the intersection at the Alston country store. Stay right on the Alston-Mayger Road and go 5.75 miles from Alston to Life Lane and the cemetery and church, built in 1904, on the right (east). {18 November 1991} (Coal Creek 1985 USGS Quad. map.)

McKAY, THOMAS A 0.01 1 1849 T4N R1W S31
Located north and east of Scappoose. Drive north on West Lane Road past the airport; turn right onto Honeyman Road and then off of Honeyman Road onto Freeman Road. The monument, installed in 1967 by the D.A.R., is at the south end of Freeman Road. Located at 54176 Freeman Road. This area is now covered by a large mobile home park. Thomas McKay, born in Canada in 1797, arrived at Astoria in 1811: His first wife and son may also be buried here. Perhaps on the Malcolm McKay D.L.C. #30, OC #4373. NOTE: This site is on private property. (NOT shown on St. Helens 1990 USGS Quad. map.)

McNULTY FAMILY A 0.5 2 1858-1902 T4N R1W S8
Located west of St. Helens. Leave U.S. Hwy. 30 in St. Helens at Milepost 28.6 onto Columbia Boulevard. Drive westerly and the name of the road changes to Bachelor Flat Road; continue to the junction with Childs Road from the left (south), about 1.6 miles from U.S. Hwy. 30. Originally 0.5 of an acre in extent with 6 known graves, there is now a single monument standing with the names of 4 people. The small area around the monument has been paved over by the present landowner to protect the monument from being hit by the traffic: on the John McNulty D.L.C. #50, OC #2910. NOTE: this site is on private property. See: Vol. XIII, 1974 *Columbia County History*, page 32. (Not shown on St. Helens 1990 USGS Quad. map.)

McPHERSON, JOHN A 0.01 5 6 Sep 1877 T4N R1W S31
A single grave 40 yards from the Thomas McKay grave: east of the south end of Freeman

Road. Located at 54176 Freeman Road. John McPherson, 1816-1877 was a Hudson Bay man. NOTE: This site is on private property. (Not shown on St. Helens 1990 USGS Quad. map.)

MERRILL
AKA: 1. MERRILL LAKE

A ? 5 1874 T5N R1W ?

Perhaps located in Section 6. This cemetery was 0.5 of a mile north of the locale of Deer Island on on the west side of U.S. Hwy. 30. According to a sketch by Edwin J. Barnes made in 1958 the cemetery was on the west side of the highway next to Merrill Lake and just south of the Merrill Creek Bridge and the school. After the Merrill family sold this land in 1909, they had their own kin reburied in Kinder Cemetery, 2 miles to the south. However other burials remain but there are no longer any monuments. In 1966, Blythe Gaittens Carey reported that at least 11 known burials remain, dating from 1874 to 1894. (*Genealogical Forum of Portland Oregon, Bulletin* Vol. 16, page 8, 9, 13, September 1966.) It is on the Joseph Merrill D.L.C. #37, OC #3508. NOTE: This site is on private property. (Not shown on Deer Island 1990 USGS Quad. map.)

MERRIMAN, BABY GIRL

A 0.01 5 Circa 1945 T4N R2W S35

At the north edge of Scappoose turn off of U.S. Hwy 30 onto the Scappoose-Vernonia Highway (a county road) to the northwest. Drive about 2 miles to Apple Valley Road to the left (southerly). Go on Apple Valley Road to Flint Drive to the left (south). The burial is on private property at 53279 Flint Drive and there is no marker. (Not shown on Chapman 1990 USGS Quad. map)

MIST

C 1 2 1898 T6N R5W S13

The locale of Mist is 12 miles south of Clatskanie via OR. Hwy. 47. The cemetery is adjacent to the south side of the church at Mist and is 0.4 of a mile short of the junction of OR. Hwy. 47 with OR. Hwy 202. {12 August 1991} (Clatskanie Quad. 1985 USGS map.)

Name of Cemetery and also known as	Number of burials	Acres	Condition	Date started or earliest known burial	Township	Range	Section

MOUNTAIN VIEW
AKA: 1. BITTE

A   ?   ?   1890's   T6N   R3W   S2

In the Southeast 1/4 of Section 2, located on private property at 71023 Fern Hill Road; permission is needed to visit as this is on private property. Leave "B" Street (U.S. Hwy. 30) at the traffic light with 1st Street, in Rainier, turning south uphill on 1st Street for one block, to "C" Street. Turn right on "C" Street and drive 6 blocks, crossing the narrow bridge to Fern Hill Road. Turn left onto Fern Hill Road and go 5.15 miles to the junction of Hammond Road. Continue another 1.5 miles on Fern Hill Road to 71023 and Mauris Road on the right (west). You are now 6.65 miles from your starting point. On the driveway, drive past the house on the left and then take the left fork, past an old barn, uphill, on a one-lane rough road through the trees, 0.4 of a mile to a house with a turnaround. The cemetery is behind the trees to the right of the house and is about 1100 feet in elevation above Fern Hill Road. There are 9 known burials. (Not shown on Delena 1985 USGS Quad. map.)

MURRAY HILL

D   7   1   1932   T7N   R4W   S17

Located in Clatskanie. Leave U.S. Hwy. 30 at the traffic light and turn southerly on Nehalem Street uphill. Drive 0.55 of a mile to Conyers Creek Road, turn right. At 0.8 of a mile from the starting point turn right again onto Hall Road and go about a block to the cemetery on the right: on the Enoch W. Conyers D.L.C. #39, OC #3488. {18 November 1991} (Clatskanie 1985 USGS Quad. map.)

NEER CITY
AKA: 1. GOBLE
2. NEER

C   1.25   1   1888   T6N   R2W   S2

Located in Sections 2 and 11. Drive the Columbia River Highway (U.S. Hwy. 30) through the townsite of Goble, going north across the Goble Creek Bridge. At Milepost 40.8 turn left (inland) onto Neer Road. Drive 0.75 of a mile to the junction with Terry Road on the right. Proceed uphill 0.15 of a mile on Terry Road to an unnamed junction; turn hard right and go further uphill a final 0.13 of a mile to the cemetery. Commenced with a 0.5 of an acre tract in 1888, enlarged by 0.34 of an acre in 1890 and lastly by 0.4 of an acre in 1923. There are I. O. R. monuments here, as Neer City was the site of Umptats Tribe #24, Improved Order of Redmen Lodge, which was well-known throughout Oregon. {24 June 1991} (Rainier 1953-70 USGS Quad. map.)

NORTH CEMETERY OF CLEAR CREEK
AKA: 1. CLEAR CREEK
      2. KIST

B   1.37 2   1892   T4N R5W   S27
The cemetery is named for the North family, not a direction of the compass. South of Vernonia, leave OR. Hwy. 47 at Milepost 64.3 onto Timber Road. Follow Timber Road for 5.15 miles to the west and south before turning right (west) onto Clear Creek Road. Continue 0.9 of a mile on Clear Creek Road to the driveway right, turn up slope to the cemetery. The older name of Kist is not to be confused with the better-known locale of Mist. The post office of Kist was in operation between January 1899 through May 1912. {12 August 1991} (Clear Creek 1979 USGS Quad. map.)

OWEN, LEVI B.

A   0.01 ? 26 Jun 1985 ?   ?   ?
Levi B. Owen, born 29 November 1959 died 26 June 1985 was buried on the Owen Ranch in the area of Vernonia.

PALM PIONEER, AUGUST

A   0.1 5   1880'S   T7N R3W   S18
Drive about 2 miles on U.S. Hwy. 30 from the Delena crossroads towards Clatskanie. Leave the highway to the left (south) an a short connection to Lindberg Road. Turn right (west) onto the winding Lindberg Road and drive about 0.65 of a mile to the driveway on the left (south) side of 22530 Lindberg Road. The abandoned cemetery is about 200-300 feet south on this driveway and about 75-100 feet left (east), in an area that was logged in the mid-1980's. August Palm took up a homestead here about 1880, after immigrating from Sweden via Nebraska. There are approximately 6 known burials, mostly his children. NOTE: This site is on private property. (Not shown on Delena 1985 USGS Quad. map.)

Name of Cemetery and also known as	Number of burials	Acres	Condition	Date started or earliest known burial	Township	Range	Section

PERRY FAMILY

A ? ? ?   ?   R1W   ?

These burials could be in Township 4 North Section 5 or in Township 5 North in Section 32. There are said to be 2 graves a mile or so west of US. Hwy. 30, from St. Helens: on the Francis Perry D.L.C. #55, OC #4760. NOTE: This site is on private property. (Not shown on Deer Island or St. Helens 1990 USGS Quad. map.)

PISGAH HOME

? 0.4 5 1919-1938 T4N R3W   S36

From Scappoose on U.S. Hwy. 30 turn inland on the Scappoose-Vernonia Highway (a county road). Then turn left (westerly) onto Siercks Road after about 3 miles. Leave Siercks County Road to the left (westerly) uphill on Pisgah Home Road. It is about 5.5 miles to the site of the Pisgah Home from the Scappoose-Vernonia Highway. The cemetery was about 0.6 of a mile northeast of the Pisgah Home. Pisgah Home was a large 3-story building established in 1919 for the down-and-out elderly men from the Portland city streets. It was abandoned in 1938 and burned some time after 1961. The cemetery had wooden grave markers. (Chapman 1990 USGS Quad. map.)

POTTERS FIELD

A ? 5 ?   T7N R2W   S17

Located on private property in the area around 75311 Fern Hill Road, in the vicinity of its junction with Townsend Road. This is about 0.75 of a mile from West "B" Street and 7th Street, Rainier. This cemetery was in the southwest part of Rainier and no longer exists. It was established by Dean Blanchard, perhaps in the 1890's. Judith Whipple, January 1992, reports that several residents remember hearing a story that a Chinese laundry owner was buried here. Another story reported that two men, decapitated in an accident, are also buried here. (NOT shown on Rainier 1953-70 USGS Quad. map.)

Name of Cemetery and also known as	Number of burials	Acres	Condition	Date started or earliest known burial	Township	Range	Section

ST. JOSEPH POLISH CATHOLIC

| ? | 1.5 | 5 | 1896 | T5N R3W | S27 |

From U.S. Hwy. 30 at Milepost 29 in north Saint Helens take the Pittsburg Road to the east for 13.4 miles at which point there is a three-way junction. Pittsburg Road continues ahead, Schaeffer Road is to the right and the unmarked Wilark Main Line Road to the left (southwest). Robert M. Thomas in January 1991 passed through the gate onto Wilark Main Line Road (the gate is closed in the fire season) and drove another 2 miles to a large ditch and mound of dirt which blocks a vehicle. Walk across the ditch and go about 100 yards to the Section Line Marker for Section 27 and with Camp 9 Extension Road ahead. The cemetery is on the right (northeast) side of Wilark Main Line Road. There is a walk of about another 145 yards through scotch broom to the two 30-foot alder trees in the middle of the graveyard. Five Polish immigrant families deeded land on 2 December 1891 for a school, church and cemetery. The church burned from a slash fire on 4 August 1899 and was not rebuilt. The Oregon Cemetery Survey, 1978, reported a No Name Cemetery of 1912 with "many children buried" at Township 5 North, Range 3 West, Section 25 or 26. The compiler believes this to be the St. Joseph Cemetery. Especially since the 1928 *Columbia County Metsker Landownership Atlas* shows the Archdiocese of Oregon City owned 1.5 acres in Section 27. Only two stones were found in November 1993. (Baker Point 1979 USGS Quad. map.)

ST. WENCESLAUS
AKA: 1. SCAPPOOSE CATHOLIC

| D | 0.7 | 2 | 1907 | T3N R2W | S13 |

Located behind St. Wenceslaus Church on the west side of Old Portland Road. The church was built in 1910-1911 and 1 acre was donated for a cemetery in 1910. These were Czech (Bohemian) settlers: on the Jesse Miles D.L.C. #39, OC #1434. (Dixie Mountain 1961-85 USGS Quad. map.)

SCHIEVE, AUGUST

| A | 0.01 | 5 | 2 July 1902 | T5N R2W | ? |

There is a single grave in the Trenholm area. August Schieve was found guilty of murdering Joseph Schulkowski, a miner at the Bunker

Name of Cemetery and also known as	Number of burials	Acres	Condition	Date started or earliest known burial	Township	Range	Section

Hill coal mines 7 miles west of St. Helens. Schieve was duly hanged in St. Helens on 2 July 1902. He was buried next to the barn on his parent's place. Reportedly years later, John Schieve, August's father, on his own deathbed confessed that it was he who had murdered Schulkowski. (Not shown on Trenholm 1990 USGS Quad. map.)

SCHOOLMASTER'S GRAVE
AKA: 1. STRONG

A 0.01 5 1858 T7N R2W S16
Located at the junction of 5th Street West and U.S. Hwy. 30, in Rainier. Schoolmaster Riley (or William) Strong was buried here at the site now (January 1992) occupied by a former service station: Dennis Auto Body, 506 "B" Street West. (Not shown on Rainier 1953-70 USGS Quad. map.)

SELDERS, ANTHONY

A 0.01 5 25 Dec 1884 T5N R5W S32
Anthony Selders was found dead in the snow and was buried on the spot. This is on now what is know as Sander's Ranch up Rock Creek in the area of Vernonia. There is a Selders Creek which flows into Rock Creek at Keasey. (The creek is shown on Clear Creek 1979 USGS Quad. map, but no gravesite is indicated.)

STEWART CREEK
AKA: 1. INGLES
     2. INGLIS
     3. QUINCY
     4. STEWART HILL
     5. STEWER CREEK

D 4 1 Circa 1886 T7N R4W S3
Located on a low rise to the right of Shepard Road, 0.1 of a mile east from its junction with Rutter Road. Leave Clatskanie at the traffic light on Nehalem Street and drive north on Nehalem and 5th Street Northwest (Old U.S. Hwy. 30) out of town. At 3.2 miles, the junction with Mayger Road, continue left and ahead towards Quincy, but after about 0.4 of a mile on Mayger Road turn hard right and back onto Rutter Road. Drive about 0.4 of a mile on Rutter Road, crossing Stewart Creek and turn left (east) onto Shepard Road at the "Luther Church." The cemetery driveway is directly ahead. There are many Finnish families interred here. {18 November 1991} (Oak Point 1985 USGS Quad. map.)

Name of Cemetery and also known as	Number of burials	Acres	Condition	Date started or earliest known burial	Township	Range	Section

STEWART'S POINT

A 0.01 5 Before 1882 T8N R4W ?

A Mrs. Stewart is buried in a lone grave where Stewart's Point juts out into the bottomlands near Quincy. Mrs. Stewart fell victim to bizarre circumstances. She and another lady had each pulled up a fresh turnip, but had no way to peel them. They happened to meet a trapper whom both knew, and asked to borrow his knife. The trapper had been skinning animals and his knife was partially coated with arsenic, which inadvertantly poisoned the turnips as they were peeled. Mrs. Stewart died, but the other lady recovered. NOTE: See *Columbia County History*, Vol. V, 1966, Bertha Fogel, page 16. (Not shown on Oak Point 1985 USGS Quad. map.)

TURPIN, ANNIE

A 0.01 ? 28 Feb 1892 T6N R5W ?

Perhaps located in Section 30. 17 year-old Annie Turpin, who died of diphtheria, is buried on the highest knoll on the farm of her father, John S. Turpin. This is in the Nehalem Valley along OR. Hwy. 202, west of Birkenfeld. The farm was closer to Vesper, which is just over the county line in Clatsop County. The Turpins lived here from 1875 to 1897. NOTE: This site is on private property. (Not shown on Birkenfeld 1979 USGS Quad. map.)

UNITED BRETHREN
AKA: 1. OLD MIST
     2. UNITED LUTHERAN

? 0.75 5 1895 T6N R5W S36

Located in the territory known as The Burn, near Mist. Mist is at the junction of OR. Hwy. 47 and OR. Hwy. 202. Go westerly towards Birkenfeld on OR. Hwy. 202 from that junction. Turn left onto Burn Road and cross the bridge over the Nehalem River. At the junction at the west end of the bridge turn left (south), still on Burn Road. At 0.5 of a mile from OR. Hwy. 202 is the end of county maintenance; the road ahead is still Burn Road, but is a private road for Longview Fiber Co. Continuing southerly at about 1.6 mile from the highway is a crossroads. The Barnhardt Main Line Road comes in from the right. Continue ahead (south) on what is now Barnhardt Main Line Road past the junctions

Name of Cemetery and also known as	Number of burials	Acres	Condition	Date started or earliest known burial	Township	Range	Section

of Roads 191 (to the left) and 445 (to the right). At this latter point you are about 1.9 miles from OR. Hwy. 202. The cemetery entrance is marked between two orange and blue gas markers on the left side of the left fork. The entry 500 feet to the east is deeply rutted with truck tracks. The surrounding land is owned by a timber company. 9 stones are readable and recorded as of 1992. The October 1928 *Columbia County Metsker Landownership Atlas* shows a United Lutheran Church here. (Birkenfeld 1979 USGS Quad. map.)

UNKNOWN	A	0.01	?	?	T4N	R2W	S16

Kass Bradley of Saint Helens reported in 1992 two unidentified unmarked burials behind the first house on the right (east) on Cater Road at Spitzenberg. Cater Road leads north from the Scappoose-Vernonia Highway (a county road). (Not shown on Chapman 1990 USGS Quad. map.)

UNKNOWN	A	0.01	?	?	T5N	R4W	S5

Located in the north half of the Southwest 1/4 of Section 5. Leave the Nehalem Highway (OR. Hwy. 47) at Milepost 49.9 and cross the Nehalem River at the Natal Bridge on Burris Road. The county maintenance ends 1 mile south of the bridge and Crown-Zellerbach's private logging roads continue in the area. Turn to the right on the logging road, still called Burris Road and go another 2 miles to the southwest. The grave is about 200 feet west of Burris Road, which is called Road 284 here. Road 294, on the left of Road 284, is about 300 feet to the south of the point opposite the grave. It is advisable to have a guide or a good map of the logging roads. In October 1928, the *Columbia County Metsker Landownership Atlas* shows that Earl L. Smith owned the land where the grave is situated. (Pittsburg 1979 USGS Quad. map.)

UNKNOWN CHILD	A	0.01	?	?	T5N	R1W	?

There is said to be a child's grave just north of the mobile home park, which is

Name of Cemetery and also known as	Number of burials	Acres	Condition	Date started or earliest known burial	Township	Range	Section

itself just north of Deer Island Village along U.S. Hwy. 30. This was a report made in the mid-1950's. On the Leonard Harris D.L.C. #38, OC #3153. NOTE: This site is on private property. (Not shown on Deer Island 1990 USGS Quad. map.)

VERNONIA

| | ? | ? | 5 | 1874-1900 | T4N | R4W | ? |

This was the first cemetery for Vernonia and was located on Capitol Hill adjacent to a garbage fill (1978). The bodies were reburied in 1900 at the Vernonia Pioneer Cemetery. (Not shown on Vernonia 1979 USGS Quad. map.)

VERNONIA MEMORIAL
AKA: 1. CITY OF
      VERNONIA
      MEMORIAL

| D | 10 | 1 | | 1917 | T4N | R4W | S5 |

Located on a hill at the west end of town. Leave Bridge Street at the junction of Rose Avenue (this is the Nehalem Highway, OR. Hwy. 47) and continue westerly uphill, still on Bridge Street. Go past the school and the cemetery entrance is on the right, 0.5 of a mile from OR. Hwy. 47. {12 August 1991} (Vernonia 1979 USGS Quad. map.)

VERNONIA PIONEER
AKA: 1. ROCK CREEK

| C | 1.32 | 2 | | 1900 | T5N | R4W | S33 |

Leave Bridge Street (OR. Hwy. 47) in Vernonia and turn north onto State Avenue, which becomes Rock Creek Road when it leaves the north city limits. The cemetery is on the left about 1.25 miles from the highway. The oldest dated monument found was 1889. {12 August 1991} (Vernonia 1979 USGS Quad. map.)

VETERAN'S GRAVE

| A | 0.01 | ? | | ? | T6N | R5W | S24 |

On 9 May 1991, Betty Davis reported that there is a veteran's grave located about a mile south of Mist. It is on the south side of OR. Hwy. 47 and 50 to 100 feet from the Nehalem River. NOTE: This site is on private property. (Not shown on Pittsburg 1979 USGS Quad. map.)

Name of Cemetery and also known as	Number of burials	Acres	Condition	Date started or earliest known burial	Township	Range	Section

WATTS FAMILY

A 0.02 5 19 Aug 1854 T3N R2W ?

Perhaps located in Section 12. There are 3 graves of the Watts family somewhere in Scappoose: on the William Watts D.L.C. #40, OC #1358. (Not shown on Chapman or St. Helens 1990 USGS Quad. maps.)

WELTER FAMILY
AKA: 1. PRESCOTT

A 1.43 2 1906 T6N R2W S2

Leave U.S. Hwy. 30 about 50 yards south of the visitors access road to the now closed Trojan Nuclear Plant. The cemetery is on a short stretch of abandoned highway and angles sharply backwards if approached from the south, as from St. Helens. There is a gate about halfway into the cemetery, with a further walk of about 2 blocks. The site of the house is marked by locust trees and there is also a nearby waterfall of Neer Creek. The burial area is quite small. NOTE: This site is on private property. {29 May 1992} (Rainier 1953-70 USGS Quad. map.)

WHITTIG

B 0.5 2 1900 T6N R5W S20

The cemetery was described in 1978 as being "behind the Olympic Products Mill at Birkenfeld." There are 16 markers. The 1928 Metsker Landownership Atlas of Columbia County shows that the Whittig family owned a block of the plat of Birkfenfeld community. This block was on the northwest side of the Nehalem Highway (OR. Hwy. 202). The compiler does not know if the cemetery was within that block. NOTE: This site is on private property. (Not shown on Birkenfeld 1979 USGS Quad. map.)

WOODBINE
AKA: 1. BEAVER
VALLEY
2. GREEN
MOUNTAIN
[NORTH]
3. HUDSON [OLD]

D 2 1 1870's T7N R3W S13

From the traffic signals at "B" Street (U.S. Hwy. 30) Milepost 47 and 1st Street in Rainier, drive westerly on U.S. Hwy 30, past the Longview Bridge, for 3.25 miles. At Milepost 50.3 turn left (southerly) onto Larson Road. The Beaver Valley Grange is on the left at 0.2 of a mile on Larson Road and Woodbine Cemetery is on your left immediately afterwards. Hudson Cemetery is across Larson Road from Woodbine; Green Mountain Cemetery

Name of Cemetery and also known as	Number of burials	Acres	Condition	Date started or earliest known burial	Township	Range	Section

directly adjoins Woodbine on the left as Larson Road curves to the right. In the 1870's Samuel K. Hudson donated an acre of land for a cemetery for the Hudson community; later, it was named Woodbine. An adjacent cemetery started about 1906 on the Franklin Rice estate and was known as Green Mountain or Green Mountain South, while Woodbine was also known as Green Mountain North. After 1964 the name Hudson Cemetery was revived for a third adjoining cemetery. Although confusing to write about, the three cemeteries are readily distinguishable when you are there. 1879 was the earliest dated monument found in Woodbine, the oldest of the three cemeteries. {29 July 1991} (Rainier 1953-70 USGS Quad. map.)

YANKTON [OLD]
AKA: 1. UNION

D 0.8 2 1888 T4N R2W S1

This cemetery is directly across Pittsburg Road from the Baptist Church. Leave U.S. Hwy. 30 in St. Helens at Milepost 29 and drive 3.1 miles west. The cemetery is on the left (south) side of the road. NOTE: The church driveway on the right (north) leads to the church parking lot and also the new cemetery. Please see the article on Hillcrest. {16 September 1991} (Chapman 1990 USGS Quad. map.)

Neer City
Janice M. Healy (1991)

163

North Cemetery of Clear Creek
Dean H. Byrd (1991)

Kinder
Dean H. Byrd (1991)

ACHILLES D.L.C., SAMUEL C. see **BAYVIEW MEMORIAL**				
	COLUMBIA CO.	T4N	R1W	S17
ANLIKER see **KOBEL**	COLUMBIA CO.	T6N	R2W	S20
APIARY	COLUMBIA CO.	T6N	R3W	S14
BARKER ROAD see **BEAVER HOMES**	COLUMBIA CO.	T6N	R2W	?
BARNES, EDWIN J. see **MERRILL**	COLUMBIA CO.	T5N	R1W	?
BAYVIEW MEMORIAL	COLUMBIA CO.	T4N	R1W	S17
BEAVER HOMES	COLUMBIA CO.	T6N	R2W	?
BEAVER VALLEY see **WOODBINE**	COLUMBIA CO.	T7N	R3W	S13
BETHANY MEMORIAL	COLUMBIA CO.	T4N	R1W	S19
BITTE see **MOUNTAIN VIEW**	COLUMBIA CO.	T6N	R3W	S2
BLANCHARD, DEAN see **BLANCHARD'S**	COLUMBIA CO.	T7N	R2W	S16
BLANCHARD, MERRILL see **DIBBLEE HOUSE**				
	COLUMBIA CO.	T7N	R2W	S16
BLANCHARD'S	COLUMBIA CO.	T7N	R2W	S16
BRADLEY, KASS see **UNKNOWN**	COLUMBIA CO.	T4N	R2W	S16
BRYANT	COLUMBIA CO.	T7N	R4W	S9
BRYANT, E. G. see **BRYANT**	COLUMBIA CO.	T7N	R4W	S9
BRYANT, NANCY C. see **BRYANT**	COLUMBIA CO.	T7N	R4W	S9
CAPLES D.L.C., CHARLES C. see **KINDER**				
	COLUMBIA CO.	T5N	R1W	S16
CAREY, BLYTHE GAITTENS see **MERRILL**				
	COLUMBIA CO.	T5N	R1W	?
CARROLL see **KEASEY**	COLUMBIA CO.	T5N	R5W	S27
CEDAR CREEK ROAD	COLUMBIA CO.	T4N	R2W	S18
CEDAR HILL see **BRYANT**	COLUMBIA CO.	T7N	R4W	S9
CITY OF VERNONIA MEMORIAL see **VERNONIA MEMORIAL**				
	COLUMBIA CO.	T4N	R4W	S5
CLEAR CREEK see **NORTH CEMETERY OF CLEAR CREEK**				
	COLUMBIA CO.	T4N	R5W	S27
COLUMBIA MEMORIAL GARDENS	COLUMBIA CO.	T4N	R2W	S36
CONINGER D.L.C., DAVID A. see **COLUMBIA MEMORIAL GARDENS**				
	COLUMBIA CO.	T4N	R2W	S36
CONYERS D.L.C., ENOCH W. see **MAPLEWOOD**				
	COLUMBIA CO.	T7N	R4W	S8
CONYERS D.L.C., ENOCH W. see **MURRAY HILL**				
	COLUMBIA CO.	T7N	R4W	S17
CRAIG, HENRY CLAY	COLUMBIA CO.	?	?	?
CRAIG, MARTHA see **CRAIG, HENRY CLAY**				
	COLUMBIA CO.	?	?	?
DAVIS, BETTY see **VETERAN'S GRAVE**				
	COLUMBIA CO.	T6N	R5W	S24
DEER ISLAND see **KINDER**	COLUMBIA CO.	T5N	R1W	S16
DIBBLEE HOUSE	COLUMBIA CO.	T7N	R2W	S16
DIBBLEE, JOHN see **DIBBLEE HOUSE**	COLUMBIA CO.	T7N	R2W	S16
DIBBLEE, MERRILL see **DIBBLEE HOUSE**				
	COLUMBIA CO.	T7N	R2W	S16
DIBBLEE, SARAH BLANCHARD see **DIBBLEE HOUSE**				
	COLUMBIA CO.	T7N	R2W	S16
DOWNING-MAYGER FAMILY see **MAYGER-DOWNING FAMILY**				
	COLUMBIA CO.	T8N	R3W	S19

```
EVERGREEN see MASONIC [ST. HELENS]
                                COLUMBIA CO.      T5N     R1W       S33
FAIRVIEW                        COLUMBIA CO.      T3N     R2W       S24
FISHHAWK                        COLUMBIA CO.      T6N     R5W       S17
FOGEL, BERTHA see STEWART'S POINT
                                COLUMBIA CO.      T8N     R4W       ?
GERMANY HILL see MASONIC [ST. HELENS]
                                COLUMBIA CO.      T5N     R1W       S33
GILBREATH, J. C. see GILBREATH-MOECK FAMILY
                                COLUMBIA CO.      T7N     R2W       S18
GILBREATH, SARA ANN see GILBREATH-MOECK FAMILY
                                COLUMBIA CO.      T7N     R2W       S18
GILBREATH-MOECK FAMILY          COLUMBIA CO.      T7N     R2W       S18
GIRGENSON, BERTHA CHRISTINA see GIRGENSON FAMILY
                                COLUMBIA CO.      T6N     R3W       S14
GIRGENSON FAMILY                COLUMBIA CO.      T6N     R3W       S14
GIRGENSON, JOHN see GIRGENSON FAMILY
                                COLUMBIA CO.      T6N     R3W       S14
GOBLE see NEER CITY             COLUMBIA CO.      T6N     R2W       S2
GORE FAMILY                     COLUMBIA CO.      T5N     R2W       S10
GORE, HENRY C. see GORE FAMILY  COLUMBIA CO.      T5N     R2W       S10
GORE, MARY C. see GORE FAMILY   COLUMBIA CO.      T5N     R2W       S10
GOSA, JIM see JOHNSON PLACE, LOREN
                                COLUMBIA CO.      T3N     R1W       ?
GRAY, ANNA C. see GORE FAMILY   COLUMBIA CO.      T5N     R2W       S10
GRAY, ISAAC see GORE FAMILY     COLUMBIA CO.      T5N     R2W       S10
GREEN MOUNTAIN                  COLUMBIA CO.      T7N     R3W       S13
GREEN MOUNTAIN [NORTH] see WOODBINE
                                COLUMBIA CO.      T7N     R3W       S13
GREEN MOUNTAIN SOUTH see GREEN MOUNTAIN
                                COLUMBIA CO.      T7N     R3W       S13
HACKER, BRICE see KEASEY        COLUMBIA CO.      T5N     R5W       S27
HALL, JESSE "JACK" W. see HALL, JESSIE W.
                                COLUMBIA CO.      ?       ?         ?
HALL, JESSE W.                  COLUMBIA CO.      ?       ?         ?
HALL-TIPTON FAMILY              COLUMBIA CO.      T4N     R4W       S3
HARRIS D.L.C., LEONARD see UNKNOWN CHILD
                                COLUMBIA CO.      T5N     R1W       ?
HASTINGS D.L.C., HENRY B. see BRYANT
                                COLUMBIA CO.      T7N     R4W       S9
HAVLIK PLACE                    COLUMBIA CO.      T3N     R2W       ?
HERWICK HOMESTEAD see HERWICK JR., FRED WM.
                                COLUMBIA CO.      T4N     R3W       S35
HERWICK JR., FRED WM.           COLUMBIA CO.      T4N     R3W       S35
HILLCREST                       COLUMBIA CO.      T5N     R2W       S36
HINES see HAVLIK PLACE          COLUMBIA CO.      T3N     R2W       ?
HUDSON                          COLUMBIA CO.      T7N     R3W       S13
HUDSON [OLD] see WOODBINE       COLUMBIA CO.      T7N     R3W       S13
HUDSON PARK see HUDSON          COLUMBIA CO.      T7N     R3W       S13
HUDSON, SAMUEL K. see HUDSON    COLUMBIA CO.      T7N     R3W       S13
HUDSON, SAMUEL K. see WOODBINE  COLUMBIA CO.      T7N     R3W       S13
```

I.O.O.F. [ST. HELENS] see **BAYVIEW MEMORIAL**				
	COLUMBIA CO.	T4N	R1W	S17
INDIAN BURIALS see **BLANCHARD'S**	COLUMBIA CO.	T7N	R2W	S16
INGLES see **STEWART CREEK**	COLUMBIA CO.	T7N	R4W	S3
INGLIS see **STEWART CREEK**	COLUMBIA CO.	T7N	R4W	S3
JACKSON D.L.C., THOMAS J. see **FAIRVIEW**				
	COLUMBIA CO.	T3N	R2W	S24
JACKSON, TOM see **JOHNSON PLACE, LOREN**				
	COLUMBIA CO.	T3N	R1W	?
JOHNSON PLACE, LOREN	COLUMBIA CO.	T3N	R1W	?
JONES see **JONES FAMILY**	COLUMBIA CO.	T6N	R2W	S33
JONES FAMILY	COLUMBIA CO.	T6N	R2W	S33
K. P. see **KNIGHTS OF PYTHIAS [RAINIER]**				
	COLUMBIA CO.	T7N	R2W	S21
KEASEY	COLUMBIA CO.	T5N	R5W	S27
KENTUCKY FLAT	COLUMBIA CO.	T7N	R2W	S16
KINDER	COLUMBIA CO.	T5N	R1W	S16
KIST see **NORTH CEMETERY OF CLEAR CREEK**				
	COLUMBIA CO.	T4N	R5W	S27
KNIGHTS OF PYTHIAS [RAINIER]	COLUMBIA CO.	T7N	R2W	S21
KOBEL	COLUMBIA CO.	T6N	R2W	S20
LACEY, CHARLES S.	COLUMBIA CO.	T3N	R2W	?
LAMBERSON D.L.C., TIMOTHY see **LAMBERSON FAMILY**				
	COLUMBIA CO.	T3N	R2W	S1
LAMBERSON FAMILY	COLUMBIA CO.	T3N	R2W	S1
LAMBERSON, SARAH see **LAMBERSON FAMILY**				
	COLUMBIA CO.	T3N	R2W	S1
LIBERTY HILL see **MASONIC [ST. HELENS]**				
	COLUMBIA CO.	T5N	R1W	S33
LUTHERAN see **BETHANY MEMORIAL**	COLUMBIA CO.	T4N	R1W	S19
MAPLEWOOD	COLUMBIA CO.	T7N	R4W	S8
MARSHLAND	COLUMBIA CO.	T7N	R5W	S11
MASONIC [ST. HELENS]	COLUMBIA CO.	T5N	R1W	S33
MAYGER-DOWNING FAMILY	COLUMBIA CO.	T8N	R3W	S19
McKAY D.L.C., MALCOLM see **McKAY, THOMAS**				
	COLUMBIA CO.	T4N	R1W	S31
McKAY, THOMAS	COLUMBIA CO.	T4N	R1W	S31
McKAY, THOMAS see **McPHERSON, JOHN**				
	COLUMBIA CO.	T4N	R1W	S31
McNULTY D.L.C., JOHN see **McNULTY FAMILY**				
	COLUMBIA CO.	T4N	R1W	S8
McNULTY FAMILY	COLUMBIA CO.	T4N	R1W	S8
McPHERSON, JOHN	COLUMBIA CO.	T4N	R1W	S31
MERRIL D.L.C., JOSEPH see **MERRILL**				
	COLUMBIA CO.	T5N	R1W	?
MERRILL	COLUMBIA CO.	T5N	R1W	?
MERRILL FAMILY see **MERRILL**	COLUMBIA CO.	T5N	R1W	?
MERRILL LAKE see **MERRILL**	COLUMBIA CO.	T5N	R1W	?
MERRIMAN, BABY GIRL	COLUMBIA CO.	T4N	R2W	S35
MILES D.L.C., JESSE see **HAVLIK PLACE**				
	COLUMBIA CO.	T3N	R2W	?

MILES D.L.C., JESSE see **ST. WENCESLAUS**				
	COLUMBIA CO.	T3N	R2W	S13
MILES, JESSE see **HAVLIK PLACE**	COLUMBIA CO.	T3N	R2W	?
MILLER, HENRY see **JOHNSON PLACE, LOREN**				
	COLUMBIA CO.	T3N	R1W	?
MIST	COLUMBIA CO.	T6N	R5W	S13
MOEK, G. F. see **GILBREATH-MOECK FAMILY**				
	COLUMBIA CO.	T7N	R2W	S18
MOEK, LOUISE B. see **GILBREATH-MOECK FAMILY**				
	COLUMBIA CO.	T7N	R2W	S18
MOEK, M. J. see **GILBREATH-MOECK FAMILY**				
	COLUMBIA CO.	T7N	R2W	S18
MOUNTAIN VIEW	COLUMBIA CO.	T6N	R3W	S2
MURRAY HILL	COLUMBIA CO.	T7N	R4W	S17
NEER see **NEER CITY**	COLUMBIA CO.	T6N	R2W	S2
NEER, CALEB see **MASONIC [ST. HELENS]**				
	COLUMBIA CO.	T5N	R1W	S33
NEER CITY	COLUMBIA CO.	T6N	R2W	S2
NEER D.L.C., ABRAHAM see **MASONIC [ST. HELENS]**				
	COLUMBIA CO.	T5N	R1W	S33
NEER FAMILY see **MASONIC [ST. HELENS]**				
	COLUMBIA CO.	T5N	R1W	S33
NORTH CEMETERY OF CLEAR CREEK	COLUMBIA CO.	T4N	R5W	S27
OLD MASONIC see **MASONIC [ST. HELENS]**				
	COLUMBIA CO.	T5N	R1W	S33
OLD MIST see **UNITED BRETHREN**	COLUMBIA CO.	T6N	R5W	S36
OWEN, LEVI B.	COLUMBIA CO.	?	?	?
PALM, AUGUST see **PALM PIONEER, AUGUST**				
	COLUMBIA CO.	T7N	R3W	S18
PALM PIONEER, AUGUST	COLUMBIA CO.	T7N	R3W	S18
PERRY D.L.C., FRANCIS see **PERRY FAMILY**				
	COLUMBIA CO.	?	R1W	?
PERRY FAMILY	COLUMBIA CO.	?	R1W	?
PISGAH HOME	COLUMBIA CO.	T4N	R3W	S36
POTTERS see **BLANCHARD'S**	COLUMBIA CO.	T7N	R2W	S16
POTTERS FIELD	COLUMBIA CO.	T7N	R2W	S17
PRESCOTT see **WELTER FAMILY**	COLUMBIA CO.	T6N	R2W	S2
PROTESTANT see **FAIRVIEW**	COLUMBIA CO.	T3N	R2W	S24
QUINCY see **STEWART CREEK**	COLUMBIA CO.	T7N	R4W	S3
RICE, FRANKLIN see **WOODBINE**	COLUMBIA CO.	T7N	R3W	S13
ROCK CREEK see **VERNONIA PIONEER**	COLUMBIA CO.	T5N	R4W	S33
SACRED HEART CATHOLIC see **COLUMBIA MEMORIAL GARDENS**				
	COLUMBIA CO.	T4N	R2W	S36
ST. HELENS PIONEER MASONIC see **MASONIC [ST. HELENS]**				
	COLUMBIA CO.	T5N	R1W	S33
ST. JOSEPH POLISH CATHOLIC	COLUMBIA CO.	T5N	R3W	S27
ST. WENCESLAUS	COLUMBIA CO.	T3N	R2W	S13
SALMI, MR. see **MARSHLAND**	COLUMBIA CO.	T7N	R5W	S11
SANDER'S RANCH see **SELDERS, ANTHONY**				
	COLUMBIA CO.	T5N	R5W	S32
SCAPPOOSE CATHOLIC see **ST. WENCESLAUS**				
	COLUMBIA CO.	T3N	R2W	S13

SCAPPOOSE PIONEER see **FAIRVIEW**	COLUMBIA CO.	T3N	R2W	S24
SCHIEVE, AUGUST	COLUMBIA CO.	T5N	R2W	?
SCHIEVE, JOHN see **SCHIEVE, AUGUST**				
	COLUMBIA CO.	T5N	R2W	?
SCHOOLMASTER'S GRAVE	COLUMBIA CO.	T7N	R2W	S16
SCHULKOWSKI, JOSEPH see **SCHIEVE, AUGUST**				
	COLUMBIA CO.	T5N	R2W	?
SEIDEL FAMILY see **GORE FAMILY**	COLUMBIA CO.	T5N	R2W	S10
SELDERS, ANTHONY	COLUMBIA CO.	T5N	R5W	S32
SHILOH BASIN see **JONES FAMILY**	COLUMBIA CO.	T6N	R2W	S33
SMITH, EARL L. see **UNKNOWN**	COLUMBIA CO.	T5N	R4W	S5
STENNICK FARM see **GILBREATH-MOECK FAMILIES**				
	COLUMBIA CO.	T7N	R2W	S18
STEWART CREEK	COLUMBIA CO.	T7N	R4W	S3
STEWART HILL see **STEWART CREEK**	COLUMBIA CO.	T7N	R4W	S3
STEWART, MRS. see **STEWART'S POINT**				
	COLUMBIA CO.	T8N	R4W	?
STEWART'S POINT	COLUMBIA CO.	T8N	R4W	?
STEWER CREEK see **STEWART CREEK**	COLUMBIA CO.	T7N	R4W	S3
STRONG see **SCHOOLMASTER'S GRAVE**	COLUMBIA CO.	T7N	R2W	S16
STRONG, RILEY see **SCHOOLMASTER'S GRAVE**				
	COLUMBIA CO.	T7N	R2W	S16
STRONG, WILLIAM see **SCHOOLMASTER'S GRAVE**				
	COLUMBIA CO.	T7N	R2W	S16
THOMAS, MR. ROBERT M. see **GORE FAMILY**				
	COLUMBIA CO.	T5N	R2W	S10
THOMAS, ROBERT see **BEAVER HOMES**	COLUMBIA CO.	T6N	R2W	?
THOMAS, ROBERT M. see **ST. JOSEPH POLISH CATHOLIC**				
	COLUMBIA CO.	T5N	R3W	S27
TICHENOR, MARY see **MAPLEWOOD**	COLUMBIA CO.	T7N	R4W	S8
TURPIN, ANNIE	COLUMBIA CO.	T6N	R5W	?
TURPIN, JOHN S. see **TURPIN, ANNIE**				
	COLUMBIA CO.	T6N	R5W	?
UNION see **YANKTON [OLD]**	COLUMBIA CO.	T4N	R2W	S1
UNITED BRETHREN	COLUMBIA CO.	T6N	R5W	S36
UNITED LUTHERAN see **UNITED BRETHREN**				
	COLUMBIA CO.	T6N	R5W	S36
UNKNOWN	COLUMBIA CO.	T4N	R2W	S16
UNKNOWN	COLUMBIA CO.	T5N	R4W	S5
UNKNOWN [KEASEY] see **KEASEY**	COLUMBIA CO.	T5N	R5W	S27
UNKNOWN CHILD	COLUMBIA CO.	T5N	R1W	?
VERNONIA	COLUMBIA CO.	T4N	R4W	?
VERNONIA MEMORIAL	COLUMBIA CO.	T4N	R4W	S5
VERNONIA PIONEER	COLUMBIA CO.	T5N	R4W	S33
VETERAN'S GRAVE	COLUMBIA CO.	T6N	R5W	S24
WARREN see **BETHANY MEMORIAL**	COLUMBIA CO.	T4N	R1W	S19
WATTS D.L.C., WILLIAM see **WATTS FAMILY**				
	COLUMBIA CO.	T3N	R2W	?
WATTS FAMILY	COLUMBIA CO.	T3N	R2W	?
WEBSTER, EDWARD D. see **KEASEY**	COLUMBIA CO.	T5N	R5W	S27
WELTER FAMILY	COLUMBIA CO.	T6N	R2W	S2

WEST HOME, WILLIAM see **LAMBERSON FAMILY**

	COLUMBIA CO.	T3N	R2W	S1
WHITTIG	COLUMBIA CO.	T6N	R5W	S20
WHITTIG FAMILY see **WHITTIG**	COLUMBIA CO.	T6N	R5W	S20
WOODBINE	COLUMBIA CO.	T7N	R3W	S13
YANKTON [OLD]	COLUMBIA CO.	T4N	R2W	S1
YANKTON-HILLCREST see **HILLCREST**	COLUMBIA CO.	T5N	R2W	S36

Bayview Memorial
Janice M. Healy (1991)

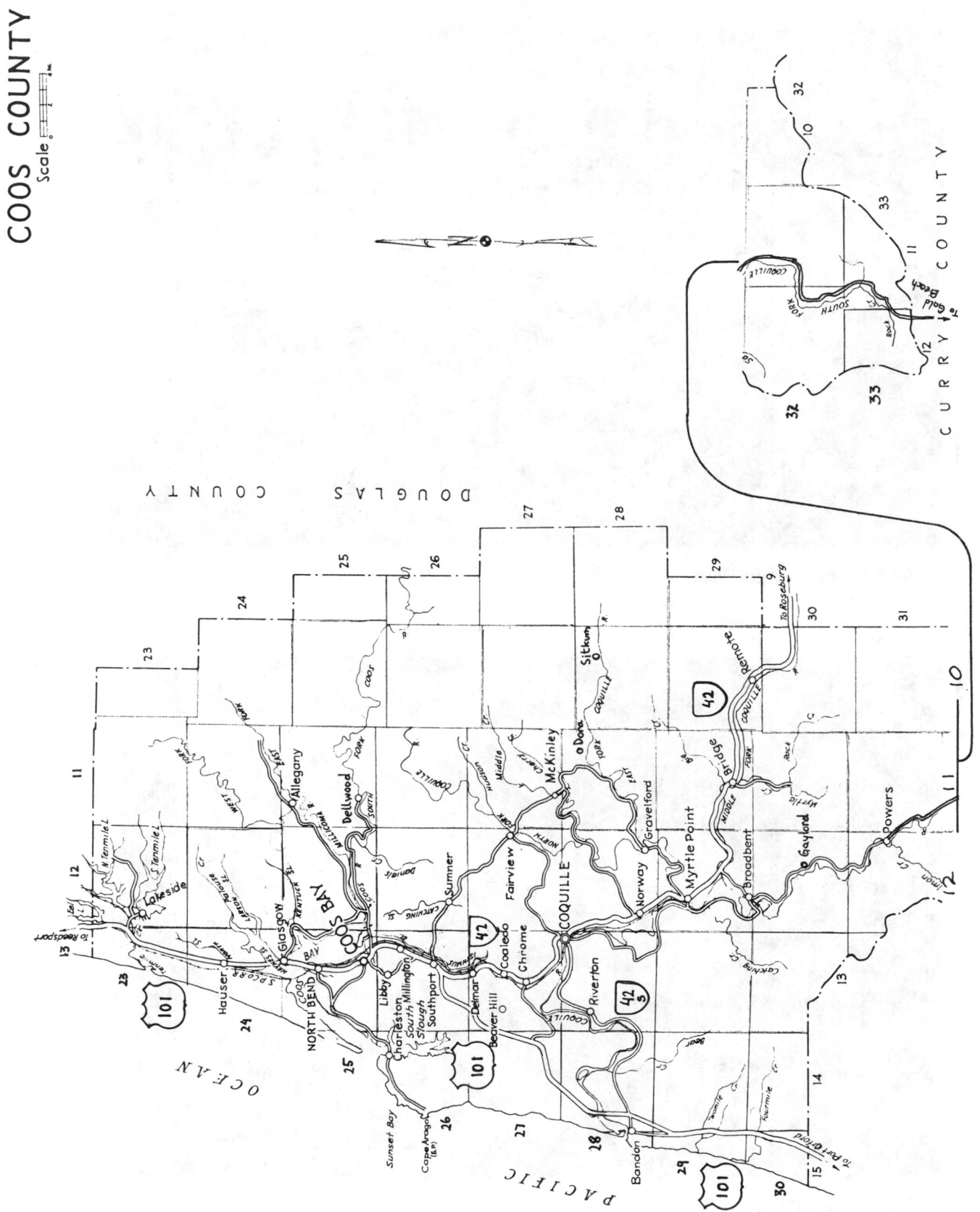

COOS COUNTY

Scale

Veterans of Foreign Wars
Dean H. Byrd (1996)

Veterans of Foreign Wars
Dean H. Byrd (1996)

Area: 1,629 square miles
Population (1998): 62,162
County seat: Coquille, Population: 4,225
County established: 16 January 1854

Permanent white settlement in Coos County began in the early and mid-1850's with gold rushes along certain ocean beaches. About the same time settlement also began along the shores of Coos Bay. The first public cemetery was apparently that at Empire in 1866. Coos County featured agriculture in the Coquille (pronounced Co-KEEL) River Valley, lumbering, fishing and working Oregon's few productive coal mines.

Bandon Pioneer
G.A.R. Section
Dean H. Byrd (1996)

173

Veterans of Foreign Wars
Dean H. Byrd (1996)

I.O.O.F. [Old Bandon]
Dean H. Byrd (1996)

Name of Cemetery or also known as	Number of burials	Acres	Condition	Date started or earliest known burial	Township	Range	Section

ALLEGANY
AKA: 1. ALLEGHANY

B 0.2 3 1887-1954 T25S R11W S5
Located 15 miles from Coos Bay, at Allegany, and 0.5 mile uphill from the community of Allegany. Access is on foot: 38 graves listed. (Allegany 1971 USGS Quad. map.)

ARCHER
AKA: 1. OLD RED BARN
2. RED BARN

A 0.15 1 1888-1935 T26S R13W S1
Located 1.4 miles from Eastside, and 800 feet east of Olive Barber Road. Go through the ranch yard and 200 yards up hill. There are 5 known burials. NOTE: This site is on private property. Eastside has since been annexed to Coos Bay. (Coos Bay 1971-75 USGS Quad. map.)

BANDON PIONEER
AKA: 1. CATHOLIC
2. G.A.R.
3. I.O.O.F.
[OLD BANDON]

D 1 2 1883 T28S R14W S30
Located on the left (west) side of Harlem Street in Bandon and on a bluff overlooking the Coquille River estuary. Harlem Street runs north off of U.S. Hwy. 101 about 0.5 of a mile west of the junction of U.S. Hwy. 101 with OR. Hwy. 42S. NOTE: This is a group of three cemeteries. The I.O.O.F., Catholic and Grand Army of the Republic Cemeteries (G.A.R.) which are separated only by driveways. The three cemeteries are often designated all together as Bandon Pioneer Cemetery. See individual articles. {24 May 1996} (Bandon 1970 USGS Quad. map.)

BARKER-MORRIS FAMILIES
AKA: 1. MORRIS-BARKER FAMILIES

A 0.15 3 1872 T27S R12W S14
From Coquille take the road to Fairview. At the Four Corners store in Fairview turn left (northwesterly) onto the Fairview-Sumner Road and drive towards Sumner. About 1.6 miles from Fairview turn off to the right (northeasterly) onto Woodward Creek Road for about 200 yards. The cemetery is on the right (east) on a hilltop. There were 16 or more graves reported in 1957. NOTE: This site is on private property. (McKinley 1971 USGS Quad. map.)

BEAR CREEK

B 0.1 3 1886 T28S R14W S35
Located on the left (east) side of Bear Creek Road, 2.5 miles up Bear Creek Road off OR.

Name of Cemetery or also known as	Number of burials	Acres	Condition	Date started or earliest known burial	Township	Range	Section

Hwy. 42S between Coquille and Bandon. NOTE: This site is on private property. (Not shown on Bill Peak 1971 USGS Quad. map.)

BEAVER HILL

| ? | ? | ? | ? | | T27S | R13W | S17 |

Mine accidents listed in the *Myrtle Point Enterprise:* 22 Jan. 1898; 1 Dec. 1905; 23 Nov. 1906. (Not shown on Riverton 1971-75 USGS Quad. map.)

BRACK FAMILY

| A | ? | ? | 1910 | T29S | R12W | S26 |

Located 5 miles east of Myrtle Point on OR. Hwy. 42 above the road and in a field in back of a barn. NOTE: This site is on private property. No other information was given in the report. (Not shown on Bridge 1971 USGS Quad. map.)

BREEN, BABY

| A | 0.01 | ? | ? | T25S | R13W | ? |

Across from Empire, Oregon, in the sand dunes near the site of the old Life Saving Service Station, is the Breen grave: an infant of Annie Wasson Breen. NOTE: Empire is now a part of the town of Coos Bay. No other information was given in the report. (Not shown on Empire 1970 USGS Quad. map.)

BREUER

| A | 0.25 | 5 | 1890 | T29S | R12W | S36 |

Located 5 miles east of Myrtle Point on OR. Hwy. 42. At Mile Post 25.5 turn right on Indian Creek Road through a privately owned road of Albert Breuer's (1978). Most graves have been removed to Norway Cemetery. (Bridge 1971 USGS Quad. map.)

BROWN

| A | ? | ? | ? | ? | ? | ? |

Located on the George Hall Farm (1978), and deeded. The information was given by Francis Floyd of Myrtle Point, who died in 1965; and was also given by Clarence Strong. NOTE: No other information was given in these reports.

Name of Cemetery or also known as	Number of burials	Acres	Condition	Date started or earliest known burial	Township	Range	Section

BULLARD FAMILY
AKA: 1. HAMBLOCH
     2. HAMBLOCK

A   0.2   1   1874-1941   T28S R14W   S7
Located north of Bandon on a knoll in Bullards Beach State Park. Take the trail from the RV campground dump station. There are 10 known burials. Originally this was known as Hambloch, *Coos Bay World*, 16 Jan. 1967. {September 1991} (Bullards 1970 USGS Quad. map.)

CATCHING CREEK

C   0.5   2   1883   T29S R13W   S35
Located in the Myrtle Point area, 6.1 miles southwest up Dement Creek Road, from its junction with West Side Road; on the right hand side of West Side Road and just past Getty Creek Bridge. The cemetery was in back of the Marsters Memorial United Brethren Chapel. (Myrtle Point 1971 USGS Quad. map.)

CATHOLIC [BANDON]
AKA: 1. HARLEM
     2. HOLY TRINITY
     3. PIONEER

C   1.5   2   1870'S   T28S R14W   S30
Located in the town of Bandon off of Harlem Street. See the article entitled Bandon Pioneer for a description of the access. The G.A.R. and the Catholic Cemeteries adjoin the I.O.O.F. [Old Bandon] Cemetery and all three are called Bandon Pioneer Cemetery. {24 May 1996} (Bandon 1970 USGS Quad. map.)

COLLVER, BENHAM B.

A   0.01   ?   20 Oct 1897   T26S R14W   ?
Located 0.75 mile to 1 mile east of Cape Arago Park, on a hill overlooking South Cape towards Bandon. Benham B. Collver was born 31 March 1894 and died 20 October 1897. (Not shown on Cape Arago or Charleston 1970 USGS Quad. maps.)

COOK, CHRIS

A   0.01   5   1918   T30S R10W   S3
The Cook grave is located about 0.25 mile up Upper Rock Creek, which drains into the Middle Fork of the Coquille River. "Chris Cook, 1886-1918, Brother." NOTE: This site is on private property. It is uncared for at this time. (Not shown on Bone Mountain 1990 USGS Quad. map.)

Name of Cemetery or also known as	Number of burials	Acres	Condition	Date started or earliest known burial	Township	Range	Section

COOS RIVER PIONEER
AKA: 1. SOUTH FORK

D 2.3 1 1870   T25S R12W   S25
This is located on Sections 25 and 26. At the eastern approach to Anson Rogers Bridge over the South Fork of the Coos River is the junction of South Fork Coos River Road and Landrith Road. Take Landrith Road and drive 1.5 miles to the cemetery on the right. (Allegany 1971 USGS Quad. map.)

COUNTY POOR FARM

? 0.5 ? ?   T27S R12W   S29
Leave Central Blvd. formerly OR. Hwy. 42 in Coquille, turn onto Fairview Road and drive about 2.6 miles from the highway. The cemetery is on the left (northerly) side of the road just before the road crosses Dye Creek. The cemetery borders the creek and is on the easterly slope of a hill. The northwest quarter of Section 29 was owned by the county as late as 1929, this was the site of the Coos County Poor Farm. (Coquille 1971-75 USGS Quad. map.)

DANS CREEK

? ? ? ?   ? ?   ?
The name refers to Daniels Creek, a tributary of the South Fork of Coos River. The confluence is in Township 25 South, Range 12 West, Section 35. NOTE: It is unclear to the compiler just which is Dans Creek Cemetery; perhaps an AKA for Coos River Cemetery or Masters Cemetery, or a previously unlocated burial ground. NOTE: No other information was given in the report. (Daniels Creek 1971 USGS Quad. map.)

DAVIS

A 0.2 ? 1898   T29S R10W   S28
Located near Remote on Sandy Creek, 0.12 mile uphill past the Fetter Road junction; the cemetery is on the left. NOTE: The Fetter Cemetery is nearby. (Remote 1990 USGS Quad. map.)

DEMENT FAMILY
AKA: 1. ECKLEY

A 0.15 2 1867   T30S R12W   S7
Located on Wallace Dement Ranch (1978) on Dement Creek Road 0.25 of a mile northwest and uphill from the farm buildings. On the

Name of Cemetery or also known as	Number of burials	Acres	Condition	Date started or earliest known burial	Township	Range	Section

Samuel Dement D.L.C. #41, OC #1949. NOTE: This is located on private property. (Dement Creek 1986 USGS Quad. map.)

DIETRICH, W.
  AKA: 1. IRON MOUNTAIN
          GRAVE

A   0.01   ?   13 Apr 1936   T33S R12W   S33
Located in the Siskiyou National Forest off of Forestry Road #5325. The grave of W. Dietrich was reported as being on the Smith Claim. (Not shown on Ophir Mtn. 1989 USGS Quad. map.)

DORA
  AKA: 1. McKINLEY

C   1.4   2   1885   T28S R11W   S10
Located 2.8 miles west and south of Dora and 0.2 mile north of Dora Chapel. (Dora 1990 USGS Quad. map.)

EDEN VALLEY

A   ?   ?   1933   T32S R11W   S12
Located in the Siskiyou National Forest. Take Forest Road #33 south out of Powers and then Forest Road #3348 to the left (east), following the South Fork of Coquille River. The burials were behind the schoolhouse. This is now on the site of Wooden Rock Campground. (Not shown on Eden Valley 1990 USGS Quad. map.)

EMANUEL EPISCOPAL
CHURCH COLUMBARIUM
  AKA: 1. ALL SAINTS
          COLUMBARIUM

?   ?   1   1989   T25S R13W   S26
Located at 4th and Highland in Coos Bay. (Church building is shown on Coos Bay 1971-75 USGS Quad. map.)

EMPIRE
  AKA: 1. OLD COUNTY
          ROAD
       2. OLD EMPIRE

B   1   11   1866-1926   T25S R13W   S17
Located in Coos Bay, near Empire Lakes, northwest of the county road between North Bend and Empire. It is on the north side of Lakeshore Drive, between Chickses Avenue and John Avenue. There were 54 graves listed in late 1920's, and 45 graves listed in 1932. NOTE: Empire has since been annexed into Coos Bay. By April 1996 the cemetery has reportedly been bulldozed and houses are being built on the site. (Empire 1970 USGS Quad. map.)

Name of Cemetery or also known as	Number of burials	Acres	Condition	Date started or earliest known burial	Township	Range	Section

ENCHANTED PRAIRIE   B   0.8   3   ?   T29S R11W   S35

This is 0.5 mile north of OR. Hwy. 42 and 5 miles west of Remote. Leave OR. Hwy. 42 at about Mile Post 32.5 to go uphill to the cemetery. NOTE: This site is on private property, with 79 known burials as of 1961. (Remote 1990 USGS Quad. map.)

ENGLEWOOD   ?   ?   6   Circa 1880   T25S R13W   ?

Perhaps located in Section 34. The location of this cemetery is no longer known. It was established in the mid-1880's and used until about 1915. The bodies were moved to Coos Bay I.O.O.F. Cemetery. This may have been the same as Libby; see entry under Libby. (Not shown on Coos Bay 1971-75 USGS Quad. map.)

FAIRVIEW   C   0.5   3   1884   T27S R12W   S26

Located 0.5 mile southwest of Fairview on the road to Coquille; then go right (west) on a side road for 0.5 mile. NOTE: This site is on private property. (McKinley 1971 USGS Quad. map.)

FETTER
 AKA: 1. REMOTE   A   0.2   ?   1885   T29S R10W   S28

Located on John Fetter Creek, east of Myrtle Point and 0.8 mile off of OR. Hwy. 42 at Mile Post 37.3 on Sandy Creek Road; turn left and go another 0.13 mile. The cemetery is on the right on land owned by L. B. Jennings (1978) of Remote. (Remote 1990 USGS Quad. map.)

FISHTRAP
 AKA: 1. ARAGO
      2. LOWER
         FISHTRAP
      3. ROBISON   B   0.5   2   1888   T28S R13W   S23

Leave Myrtle Point to the west, crossing the South Fork Coquille River. Very soon turn right (north) towards Arago and Coquille. After passing through Arago continue ahead to the junction with the Fishtrap Landing Road. Turn right (northerly) towards Coquille. The cemetery is along the first fence line on the left. It is accessed by a trail going steeply uphill along this fence to the graveyard about an eighth of a mile from the county road. Located on private property, so please get permission from the property

Name of Cemetery or also known as	Number of burials	Acres	Condition	Date started or earliest known burial	Township	Range	Section

owner. There were about 30 graves in July, 1957 but no records are known to exist. One can continue on Fishtrap Landing Road another 5.5 miles to Coquille. (Myrtle Point 1971 USGS Quad. map.)

FOX BRIDGE   B   0.3   2   1887   T28S R12W   S15
Located northeast of Myrtle Point on Summerlin Road and 0.1 of a mile north of the junction with Fox Bridge. (McKinley 1971 USGS Quad. map.)

G. A. R. [GRAND ARMY OF THE REPUBLIC; OLD BANDON]
AKA: 1. BANDON PIONEER

   B   1   2   Circa 1880   T28S R14W   S30
Located in the town of Bandon off of Harlem Street. See the article entitled Bandon Pioneer for a description of the access. G. A. R. and the Catholic Cemeteries adjoin the I.O.O.F. [Old Bandon] Cemetery and all three are called Bandon Pioneer Cemetery. The G. A. R. cemetery is easily distinguished by the tallest column of all. It was erected 22 July 1912 in honor of the Union Veterans of the Civil War. {24 May 1996} (Bandon 1970 USGS Quad. map.)

GARRETT
AKA: 1. FERRY, HENRIETTA

   A   0.01   5   1889   T29S R12W   ?
Located in Section 21 or 22. 2.5 miles to 3 miles east of Myrtle Point on OR. Hwy. 42, on the Garrett Ranch (1978). The grave of Henrietta Ferry, born 2 September 1888, died 21 December 1889, was located across the highway from the present house on a bluff, and was completely destroyed by vandals. NOTE: This is located on private property. (Not shown on Bridge or Myrtle Point 1971 USGS Quad. map.)

GRAVELFORD   A   0.8   3   Circa 1881   T28S R12W   S26
Take Brady Road 0.8 mile west and north of Gravelford Junction. There was a church here in 1936. (NOTE: Hansen Cemetery is mis-labeled as Gravelford Cemetery on Bridge 1971 USGS Quad. map. The real Gravelford Cemetery is unlabeled on Bridge 1971 USGS Quad. map.)

| Name of Cemetery or also known as | Number of burials | Acres | Condition | Date started or earliest known burial | Township | Range | Section |

GREEN, JAMES

A 0.01 ? ? T28S R13W S30
Go 0.5 mile up Lampa Road from OR. Hwy. 42S. James Green was a bachelor who committed suicide. He is buried in back of a barn belonging to George Albertson (1978). (Not shown on Bill Peak 1971 USGS Quad. map.)

GREENE
AKA: 1. BIGELOW
        FAMILY
      2. DEER PARK

A 1 ? 1888 T32S R12W S8
Located in the Eckley area, on Upper Salmon Creek at Powers Ranch (1986). NOTE: No other information was given in the report. (Barklow Mountain 1986 USGS Quad. map.)

HANSEN
AKA: 1. CULBERTSON

A 0.2 ? 1892 T28S R12W S25
Traveling from Myrtle Point to Dora, go 8.5 miles to Gravelford Bridge. Go past Gravelford Bridge 0.25 of a mile and it is on the left, just off of the road, up on a ridge. NOTE: This site is on private property. (This cemetery is mis-labeled as Gravelford Cemetery on Bridge 1971 USGS Quad. map.)

HAYES

A 1.6 3 1886 T31S R11W S19
Located 0.84 of a mile south of Powers city limits, just south of Hayes Creek, on the left (east) side of the road. There was a church here in 1936. (China Flat 1986 USGS Quad. map.)

HAYNES, CHARLES T.

A 0.01 ? 18 Sep 1876 T26S R13W S25
The Haynes grave is located near the club house of the Coos Country Club on Sumner Road, in a clump of trees. Deeded. Charles T. Haynes was aged 12 years, 10 months, and 12 days. (Coos Bay 1971-75 USGS Quad. map.)

HERMANN

B 0.25 2 21 Dec 1862 T30S R12W S5
Located in the Broadbent area. Leave the Powers Highway at Milepost 2.4, turn right (west), go through Broadbent, cross the bridge, and go 0.2 of a mile on West Side Road northwest from its junction with Dement Creek Road. You are 0.85 of a mile from the Powers Highway. On a private driveway and on

Name of Cemetery or also known as	Number of burials	Acres	Condition	Date started or earliest known burial	Township	Range	Section

private property. There were 32 known burials in 1972. (Myrtle Point 1971 USGS Quad. map.)

HILL, RICHARD

A   0.01 ?   Circa 1907 T32S R11W   ?

This is probably in Section 18. A single grave located at the intersection of the line fence for Clarence Butler and Walter Krueger Farms (1978) on Hall Creek. This is now within the Siskiyou National Forest, adjacent to Forestry Road #33 and at or near to Myrtle Grove Campground. Richard was the infant son of Russel J. and Dollie Hill. (Not shown on China Flat 1986 USGS Quad. map.)

HOFFMAN

A   0.25 ?   1860   T29S R12W   S22

This is near the junction of OR. Hwy. 42 and Powers Highway, on a hill above the road on the old Hoffman Homestead: owned by Robert E. Powrie (1978). Near Hoffman Memorial State Wayside. (Bridge 1971 USGS Quad. map.)

HULTIN
  AKA: 1. THRUSH

A   0.18 5   1 Feb. 1890 T28S R14W   S3

Located 0.5 mile east of Randolph on North Bank Road; at its junction with Sevenmile Slough Road, and on the old Thrush Farm. NOTE: This site is on private property. (Riverton 1971-75 USGS Quad. map.)

I.O.O.F. [COOS BAY]
  AKA: 1. OLD PIONEER

D   4   3   1891   T25S R13W   S34

Located at Ingersoll Avenue and 7th Street in the town of Coos Bay, opposite Marshfield High School. There were 785 burials listed in 1962. (Coos Bay 1971-75 USGS Quad. map.)

I.O.O.F. [NEW BANDON]
  AKA: 1. BANDON ODD
       FELLOWS

D   3.4   2   1958   T28S R14W   S29

From the junction of U.S. Hwy. 101 with OR. Hwy. 42S at the eastern edge of Bandon drive east 0.25 of a mile. The cemetery is on the left (north) side of OR. Hwy. 42S. NOTE: Drive another 0.25 of a mile easterly on OR. Hwy 42S and you will see the Veterans of Foreign Wars Cemetery also on the left. See that article. {24 May 1996} (Bandon 1970 USGS Quad. map.)

Name of Cemetery or also known as	Number of burials	Acres	Condition	Date started or earliest known burial	Township	Range	Section

I.O.O.F. [NEW COQUILLE]   C   3   1   1930   T28S R13W   S1
Located in the town of Coquille, on Northwest 6th Street at Birch Street, one block west of Central Boulevard. {Septmber 1991} (Coquille 1971-75 USGS Quad. map.)

I.O.O.F. [OLD BANDON]   D   2   2   1883   T28S R14W   S30
AKA: 1. BANDON
       PIONEER
Located in the town of Bandon, on Harlem Street. It abuts upon the Catholic and G.A.R. Cemeteries. See the article on Bandon Pioneer for a description of the access. {24 May 1996} (Bandon 1970 USGS Quad. map.)

I.O.O.F. [OLD COQUILLE]   C   0.5   2   1885   T27S R13W   S36
AKA: 1. COQUILLE
       PIONEER
Located in the town of Coquille, just north of Central Blvd. formerly OR. Hwy. 42 on Northwest Fir Street. This cemetery adjoins the Masonic Cemetery. {September 1991} (Coquille 1971-75 USGS Quad. map.)

JEFFERSON, THOMAS   A   0.01   ?   1909   T31S R11W   S31
South of Powers and south of the Tom Hayes Ranch and west of the South Fork Coquille River. A footbridge over the river which gave access is now gone and access is now round about. Local assistance will be needed. Thomas Jefferson was born about 1823 and died a few days before 7 July 1909. The grave is fenced and is near Jefferson Creek, on land owned by Ellis Dement. NOTE: Jefferson Creek is not listed by the USGS. This creek now appears to be known as Upper Land Creek. Information was given by Mrs. Ruby Huntly, granddaughter of Thomas Jefferson. This site is on private property. (Not shown on China Flat 1986 USGS Quad. map.)

JUNGLEBANK   A   ?   ?   31 Oct 1924   T28S R10W   S6
AKA: 1. EASTON FAMILY
Probably located in the Northeast 1/4 of Section 6. Reportedly this small burial ground is about 20 miles from Myrtle Point via the Myrtle Point-Sitkum Road. Drive past Dora Cemetery, Frona County Park and the locale of Dora itself. Continue ahead towards Sitkum and entering Brewster Canyon.

Name of Cemetery or also known as	Number of burials	Acres	Condition	Date started or earliest known burial	Township	Range	Section

About 2 miles from Dora is the mouth of Bills Creek which here joins the right bank of the East Fork Coquille River. The burials should be in this vicinity. They are of three new-born daughters of Theodore and Mildred Neely Easton who died between 31 October 1924 and 27 October 1938 plus the ashes of Robert A. Easton, the babies' grandfather who died in 1946. (Not shown on Dora 1990 USGS Quad. map.)

KENTUCK INLET
AKA: 1. KENTUCK SLOUGH
2. THOMAS FAMILY

A ? 2 Circa 1903 T25S R12W ?
Perhaps in Section 6, 1.5 miles from the junction off of East Bay Drive and what is apparently the north side of Kentuck Way Road. Located on the Otto Witt Ranch in the backyard of the house (1978): 10 gravestones (1967). NOTE: This site is on private property. (Not shown on North Bend 1971 USGS Quad. map.)

LAKESIDE

B 1.1 2 1902 T23S R13W S13
Located about 3 blocks south of U.S. Hwy. 101. Leave U.S. Hwy. 101 at Lakeside Junction with the Old Highway; go to the Archery Club House, and the cemetery is behind that. There are 24 graves listed, plus 12 unmarked and 1 unknown. (Lakeside 1985 USGS Quad. map.)

LAMPA CREEK

A ? 5 1882 T28S R13W ?
This may be in Section 30 or 31. Located at the junction of Lampa Creek and Lampa Mountain Road and OR. Hwy. 42S, between Coquille and Bandon, on the southwest corner on top of the mountain. (Not shown on Bill Peak 1971 USGS Quad. map.)

LEE VALLEY
AKA: 1. LEE

? 0.15 ? Circa 1892 T28S R12W S1
Located northeast of Myrtle Point. Go 0.73 of a mile on Lee-McKinley Road over Hervey Bridge; then turn left, going 0.4 of a mile up and back onto a hill. (McKinley 1971 USGS Quad. map.)

Name of Cemetery or also known as	Number of burials	Acres	Condition	Date started or earliest known burial	Township	Range	Section

LETT CHILDREN   A ? ? ?   T30S R11W   S9

The graves for three of the Lett children (all under the age of 6) are on a bluff above Camp Myrtlewood, which was once the Lett Farm. The camp is located 3.3 miles up Myrtle Creek Road, 11 miles east of Myrtle Point. NOTE: This site is probably on private property. No other information was given in the report. (Not shown on Powers 1986 USGS Quad. map.)

LIBBY   ? ? 6 Circa 1880 T26S R13W   ?

Perhaps this is in Section 3. The location of this cemetery is no longer known. It was established in the mid-1880's and used until about 1915. The bodies then were moved to Coos Bay I.O.O.F. Cemetery. This site may have been the same as Englewood. (Not shown on Coos Bay 1971-75 USGS Quad. map.)

MARSHFIELD
  AKA: 1. TELEGRAPH
        HILL   ? ? 6 1875-1915 T25S R13W   S26

Located at the south extremity of Telegraph Hill. A few marble tombstones were still standing in 1967 near the old Marshfield Public Library (in 1967 this was the Coos County Art Museum); on North 5th Street off of West Commercial Street. The Chinese had a plot here; the bones were sent back to China, circa 1915. Non-Chinese were moved to the Coos Bay I.O.O.F. Cemetery. NOTE: By 1986 all traces of the cemetery were built over. (Not shown on Coos Bay 1971-75 USGS Quad. map.)

MASONIC [COQUILLE]   D 3 2 1879   T27S R13W   S36

Located in the town of Coquille, on Northwest Fir Street. This cemetery adjoins the old I.O.O.F. Cemetery. {September 1991} (Coquille 1971-75 USGS Quad. map.)

MAST FAMILY   B ? 2 23 May 1885 T27S R11W   ?

This could be in Section 32 or 33. Located in the McKinley district about 12 miles northeast of Myrtle Point, on the Mast Farm

Name of Cemetery or also known as	Number of burials	Acres	Condition	Date started or earliest known burial	Township	Range	Section

(1991), and requires a four-wheel drive vehicle in bad weather to reach this site. NOTE: This is on private property. (Not shown on McKinley 1971 USGS Quad. map.)

MASTERS

A	?	?		1881-1952	T26S	R12W	S6

Located 1.1 miles from the junction of Coos River Road and Catching Slough Road on a farm formerly owned by Fred Conliff (1978). There are 5 known burials. NOTE: This is on private property. (Not shown on Coos Bay 1971-75 USGS Quad. map.)

MILLER FAMILY

A	0.01	?	Circa 1907	T29S	R12W	S33

These 3 graves are located 2 miles from the junction of OR. Hwy. 42 and Powers Highway, toward Powers, on the Ralph Gibbs property (1978). This is along Rhoda Creek north of Broadbent, about 0.3 of a mile southeast of Powers Highway and just beyond a gravel pit. The burials are for Conrad Miller, who died 4 January 1907 and two small daughters. NOTE: This is on private property. (Marked as "Grave" on Myrtle Point 1971 USGS Quad. map.)

MORRIS FAMILY

A	?	?	1903-1936	T31S	R12W	S12

This family burial ground is located on the old homestead near Rural, (now Powers). This may now be a part of Powers City Cemetery. (Not shown on Powers 1986 USGS Quad. map.)

MYRTLE CREEK
  AKA: 1. BANCROFT
       2. FISH
       3. RICE

B	?	?	1875	T30S	R11W	S16

Take Myrtle Creek Road out of the community of Bridge, for 6.2 miles. Leave the county road, turn left up the hill and go 0.6 mile to the cemetery. (Powers 1986 USGS Quad. map.)

MYRTLE CREST MEMORIAL GARDENS

D	8	1	1958	T28S	R12W	S7

Located on Rink Creek Road just east of OR. Hwy. 42, near Coquille. (Coquille 1971-75 USGS Quad. map.)

Name of Cemetery or also known as	Number of burials	Acres	Condition	Date started or earliest known burial	Township	Range	Section

MYRTLE POINT
  AKA: 1. OLD MYRTLE
       POINT

D 6.4 3 1893   T29S R12W   S15
Located at the end of Maple Street near the reservoir in the town of Myrtle Point. (Bridge 1971 USGS Quad. map.)

NEAL

B 0.1 ? 1882   T30S R12W   S15
Located 8.8 miles from the junction of OR. Hwy. 42 and the Powers Highway, 2 miles north of Gaylord. Turn off Powers Highway onto a winding road uphill for 0.4 of a mile. The cemetery is off to the right about 200 yards on a ridge point. NOTE: This site is on private property. (Powers 1986 USGS Quad. map.)

NELSON FAMILY

A 0.1 2 1928-1948   T28S R12W   S32
The burials for Frank A. and Amelia Ann Nelson were located outside of the fence of the Norway Cemetery, on property owned by the Nelson family. NOTE: In 1963 these graves were included in the Norway Cemetery. {September 1991} (Myrtle Point 1971 USGS Quad. map shows Norway Cemetery.)

NOAH, MR.

A 0.01 ? ?   T30S R11W   S9
Mr. Noah is buried at Noah's Prairie near the present site of Camp Myrtlewood. NOTE: Probably on private property. No other information was given in the report. (Not shown on Powers 1986 USGS Quad. map.)

NORWAY

D 8.9 2 1858   T28S R12W   S32
Located 3 miles north of Myrtle Point on OR. Hwy. 42. {September 1991} (Myrtle Point 1971 USGS Quad. map.)

**OCEAN VIEW MEMORIAL
GARDENS**

D 17 1 1941   T25S R13W   S20
Located at 1525 Ocean Boulevard, Coos Bay. (Empire 1970 USGS Quad. map.)

PALLASKE FAMILY
  AKA: 1. PULASKI FAMILY

A ? ? 1880   T28S R13W   S3
Located on Fat Elk Road west of Coquille. Go 0.3 mile south from the junction of the Coquille-Bandon Highway (OR. Hwy. 42S) and

Name of Cemetery or also known as	Number of burials	Acres	Condition	Date started or earliest known burial	Township	Range	Section

Fat Elk Road. Reportedly on the Ithamar Robison Farm in the 1970's and very near the Smith Family Cemetery. There is also confusion regarding the name Pallaske with the nearby Pulaski Creek. (Not shown on Coquille 1971-75 USGS Quad. map.)

PARKERSBURG
  AKA: 1. KRONENBERG

A 0.12 5 1883   T28S R14W   S15

Go 3 or 4 miles east of Bandon on OR. Hwy. 42S, and 0.7 of a mile north up Parkersburg Road. Located in Judah Parker County Park. {September 1991} (Riverton 1971-75 USGS Quad. map.)

PLEASANT HILL

? 0.01 ? ?   T29S R12W   S7

A Joseph Taylor is supposed to be buried here. The compiler is quite uncertain of the location of this Pleasant Hill, unless the site has some connection with Pleasant Valley. This latter is about 1 mile northwest of Myrtle Point as the crow flies. (Not shown on Myrtle Point 1971 USGS Quad. map.)

POWERS
  AKA: 1. BINGHAM
       2. MASONIC

B 2 ? 1920   T31S R12W   S12

Located at the north end of Powers: on the left (west) side of Powers Highway on a hill, near property owned by a mill. (Powers 1986 USGS Quad. map.)

RACKLEFF

A ? ? 1870   T29S R12W   ?

This could be on Section 5 or 8, located 1.5 miles west of Myrtle Point on the Arago Road: 9 burials were reported. NOTE: No other information was given in the report. (Not shown on Myrtle Point 1971 USGS Quad. map.)

RANDOLPH

A ? ? 1877   T28S R14W   S3

Leave the North Bank Road at Randolph and go north 0.25 of a mile toward U.S. Hwy. 101 on the Randolph-Whisky Run Road. Turn hard right and then back southerly on a driveway for 100 yards. The graves are on the left in back of the schoolhouse. (Riverton 1971-75 USGS Quad. map.)

| Name of Cemetery or also known as | Number of burials | Acres | Condition | Date started or earliest known burial | Township | Range | Section |

RIVERTON A ? ? 1903 T28S R13W ?
Possibly located in Section 8. A note from Mrs. Alice Wooldridge lists Urquhart Allen died about 3 April 1903, aged 65 years. NOTE: No other information was given in the report. (Not shown on Riverton 1971-75 USGS Quad. map.)

ROBBINS FAMILY A 0.01 ? 30 Oct.1898 T30S R12W S4
Located off of the Powers Highway south of Broadbent at about Milepost 3.8, driving towards Powers. Four children of the Robbins family are reportedly buried near a barn on private property in this area. (Not shown on Dement Creek 1986 USGS Quad. map.)

ROLAND-POLAND FAMILIES A ? 5 Early 1880 T29S R13W ?
AKA: 1. POLAND FAMILY
     2. ROLAND FAMILY
Perhaps located in Section 35. From the bridge over the Coquille River, at Myrtle Point drive south on West Side Road, and then turning right (southwesterly) onto Catching Creek Road. The burials are supposed to be on the right hand side of Catching Creek Road and about 7 miles from the Myrtle Point Bridge. All markers have been destroyed. William Roland was clawed by a bear. Jane Poland found him in the woods and carried him to her home and nursed him. Later they were married. NOTE: This information was given by Mrs. Pearl Poland. (Not shown on Myrtle Point 1971 USGS Quad. map.)

RUSSELL A 0.15 ? 1887 T28S R14W S3
Located 1 mile northeast of Randolph on Sevenmile Road. Then west and south 0.5 of a mile on a private road on the Russell Ranch (1980's). NOTE: This site is on private property. (Riverton 1971-75 USGS Quad. map.)

SACCHI A 0.01 5 ? T26S R14W S32
This burial site appears to be somewhere off of the Seven Devils Road between Bandon and Charleston and near to Sacchi Beach. Located on the old Sacchi Ranch (1978) near the beach

Name of Cemetery or also known as	Number of burials	Acres	Condition	Date started or earliest known burial	Township	Range	Section

north of Bandon.   NOTE: This site is on private property. (Not shown on Cape Arago or Charleston 1970 USGS Quad. maps.)

SKAGGS, MARTHA J. A 0.01 ? 1 Mar 1872 T28S R10W S10
The Skaggs grave is on the Kenneth Laird Ranch at Sitkum (1978). NOTE: This site is on private property. (Dora 1990 USGS Quad. map.)

SMALLEY, EVELYN A 0.01 ? 1895 T29S R13W S11
Located northwest of Myrtle Point. This grave is on Hall Creek Road, on property that was owned by Albert Tomlinson (1978). Evelyn Smalley: born 25 March 1892, died 1895 aged 3. NOTE: This site is on private property. (Not shown on Myrtle Point 1971 USGS Quad. map.)

SMITH FAMILY A ? 4 1880 T28S R13W S3
Located on Fat Elk Road, west of Coquille. Go 0.3 of a mile south from the junction of the Coquille-Bandon Highway (OR. Hwy. 42S) and Fat Elk Road. Reportedly on the Oran Shull Farm, on a hill past the barn. Be aware that this is exactly the same directions as was given to the Pallaske Family burials, so they must be very close by. NOTE: This site is on private property. (Not shown on Coquille 1971-75 USGS Quad. map.)

SOUTH SLOUGH
  AKA: 1. GRAVEYARD
        POINT A 0.4 ? Before 1901 T26S R14W S15
Located about 2.5 miles south off of Cape Arago Highway and southeast off of Seven Devils Road, near Hayward Creek. It was reported that there are no longer any stones left at this site. NOTE: This site is on private property. (Charleston 1970 USGS Quad. map.)

STEWARD FAMILY A ? 5 1881-1887 T28S R13W ?
Possibly located in Section 19 or 30, across the Coquille River from Lampa Creek on the North Bank Road and up a steep bank. Four

Name of Cemetery or also known as	Number of burials	Acres	Condition	Date started or earliest known burial	Township	Range	Section

children that died of diphtheria in 1881 and Stephen Steward 1835-1887. NOTE: This site is on private property. No other information was given in the report. (Not shown on Bill Peak 1971 or Riverton 1971-75 USGS Quad. map.)

SUMNER [OLD]
AKA: 1. PIONEER
3. SUMNER PIONEER
2. WILSON FAMILY

C   0.6   2   1888   T26S R12W   S33
Located 11 miles southeast of Coos Bay. Go 0.75 of a mile southeast of Sumner on Sumner Road and turn left uphill. (Coos Bay 1971-75 USGS Quad. map.)

SUMNER SCHOOL
AKA: 1. SUMNER
PLOT

A   ?   ?   ?   T26S R12W   S17
Located north of Sumner Grade School under some locust trees (1978) about 2.25 miles north of Sumner and on the west side of the Eastside-Sumner Road. This is an earlier site of Sumner School. It has been reported that the six monuments that were at this site have been destroyed by vandals. (Not shown on Coos Bay 1971-75 USGS Quad. map.)

SUNSET MEMORIAL PARK

E 120   1   1915   T26S R13W   S2
Located at 2450 U.S. Hwy. 101 at the south end of the town of Coos Bay. (Coos Bay 1971-75 USGS Quad. map.)

TEMPLETON
AKA: 1. PIONEER

B   0.5   2   1895   T23S R12W   S26
Located 10 miles east of old U.S. Hwy. 101 (now Wildwood Drive) on Shutters Landing Road and Templeton Road; on the north side of the road, 0.5 of a mile east of Templeton. (Trail Butte 1985 USGS Quad. map.)

TURNER FAMILY

A   ?   5   ?   T30S R14W   S18
Located in the Northeast 1/4 of Section 18. There is no convenient access from Bethel Hill Road, the nearest county road. The nearest road had already been abandoned by the time of the 1936 O.D.O.T. field survey. (Shown on Langlois 1986 USGS Quad. map as "Graves" and shown as a cemetery in the 1958 Metsker Coos County Landownership Atlas.)

Name of Cemetery or also known as	Number of burials	Acres	Condition	Date started or earliest known burial	Township	Range	Section

UNKNOWN

A   0.01   ?   ?   T26S R14W   S15
A lone grave adjacent to Farley Creek near its mouth with Hayward Creek and near South Slough Cemetery. NOTE: No other information was given in the report. (Charleston 1970 USGS Quad. map.)

UPPER FISHTRAP
 AKA: 1. UPPER FISH
         TRAP [Sic]

A   ?   ?   1881   T28S R13W   S34
Drive westerly and northerly from Arago on the Myrtle Point-Lampa Road for about 2.2 miles to the junction of Fishtrap Landing Road to the right and ahead. Turn left, still on Fishtrap-Lampa Road which follows the narrow valley of Upper Fishtrap Creek. Drive southwesterly passing the power lines for about another 1.4 miles from the junction of Myrtle Point-Lampa Road with Fishtrap Landing Road from Arago. At this point there is a steep winding driveway on the right (northwest) for about 300 yards to the cemetery. There were 28 known graves in 1957, with no known records left. The cemetery and the driveway were both donated. (Myrtle Point 1971 USGS map.)

VETERANS OF FOREIGN WARS
 AKA: 1. KNIGHTS OF THE
         PYTHIAS
         [BANDON]
      2. V.F.W.

D   2.3   2   1906   T28S R14W   S29
Located 0.5 of a mile east of the junction of OR. Hwy.42S with U.S. Hwy. 101 at Bandon. The Veterans of Foreign Wars Cemetery is on the left (north) side of OR. Hwy. 42S and on the west side of Bates Road. NOTE: Do not confuse this cemetery with the Bandon I.O.O.F. Cemetery about 0.25 of a mile distant towards town. See that article. {24 May 1996} (Bandon 1970 USGS Quad. Map.)

WARNER, CALVIN
 AKA: 1. WARNER

A   0.6   3   1882-1952   T29S R12W   S28
This burial is located south on Powers Highway 1.1 miles from its junction with OR. Hwy. 42. Then turn right 0.25 of a mile northwest from Powers Highway. Calvin Warner died in 1882. NOTE: This site is on private property. (Myrtle Point 1971 USGS Quad. map.)

Name of Cemetery or also known as	Number of burials	Acres	Condition	Date started or earliest known burial	Township	Range	Section

WARNER, WILLIAM N.
AKA: 1. ROWLAND

A   0.01   ?   19 Aug 1898   T30S R12W   S34
This lone grave is 1.75 miles from Gaylord Bridge between Gaylord and Powers, about 400 feet west of Gaylord Road. On Robert Y. Philips D.L.C., RB #1168. NOTE: This site is on private property. (Powers 1986 USGS Quad. map.)

WASSON

A   ?   ?   1910   T26S R14W   ?
Perhaps located in Section 35, on the old Wasson Ranch. Go out Seven Devils Road from Charleston; located at the head of South Slough Road, in the area of Wasson Creek. NOTE: No other information was given in the report. This is probably on private property. (Not shown on Charleston 1970 USGS Quad. map.)

WATERMAN
AKA: 1. BANCROFT

A   0.2   ?   1873   T30S R11W   S33
Located south of Bancroft. Turn off of OR. Hwy. 42 at the community of Bridge, onto Myrtle Creek Road. Keep on Myrtle Creek Road, just past the one-time community of Bancroft, to the bridge over Cole Creek. The bridge is the terminus of the county road. Ahead to the south are private roads, one of which crosses Myrtle Creek and doubles back north towards Bancroft. The cemetery lies between this private road and the west (left) bank of Myrtle Creek. This is all private property. (Powers 1986 USGS Quad. map.)

WHEELER, ANNIE R.

A   0.01   ?   13 Aug 1880   T25S R12W   S5
This burial is on the south side of Kentuck Creek and south off of Kentuck Way. Located on the Arnold Brelage Ranch (1978), about 2.25 miles above where the slough enters Coos Bay. It is across the valley on a bare hill and above an old house. (Not shown on North Bend 1971 USGS Quad. map.)

WHITTINGTON

A   ?   ?   1891   T29S R12W   S32
Go on Broadbent Road 3.1 miles past the junction of Catching Creek Road with Broadbent Road, out of Myrtle Point. Located on the right hand (north) side of the road,

Name of Cemetery or also known as	Number of burials	Acres	Condition	Date started or earliest known burial	Township	Range	Section

but not visible from the road. There is evidence of many graves, but no markers are left. The land was owned by Kenneth Laird (1978). NOTE: This is on private property. (Not shown on Myrtle Point 1971 USGS Quad. map.)

WIGENT FAMILY
AKA: 1. WIGERT FAMILY

	A	?	?	1883	T29S	?	?

On Middle Fork of Coquille River. NOTE: No other information was given with the report.

WISE

	A	0.15	2	1 Nov. 1908	T30S	R12W	S34

Located 6 miles north of Powers and 0.1 of a mile left (west) of Powers Highway on the property of Jack McLeod (1978); on William Rowland D.L.C. #37, RB #496. NOTE: This site is on private property. (Powers 1986 USGS Quad. map.)

YOAKAM FAMILY

	A	?	?	14 Jul 1853	?	R13W	?

Located about 6 miles south of Empire toward Libby on Camman Road. NOTE: Camman Road is shown as a pack trail on the USGS Quad. map. No other information was given in the report. (Not shown on Charleston 1970 USGS Quad. map.)

Veterans of Foreign Wars
Dean H. Byrd (1996)

Bandon Pioneer
G.A.R. Monument
Dean H. Byrd (1996)

ALBERTSON, GEORGE see **GREEN, JAMES**

	COOS CO.	T28S	R13W	S30

ALL SAINTS COLUMBARIUM see **EMANUAL EPISCOPAL CHURCH COLUMBARIUM**

	COOS CO.	T25S	R13W	S26
ALLEGANY	COOS CO.	T25S	R11W	S5
ALLEGHANY see **ALLEGANY**	COOS CO.	T25S	R11W	S5
ALLEN, URQUHART see **RIVERTON**	COOS CO.	T28S	R13W	?
ARAGO see **FISHTRAP**	COOS CO.	T28S	R13W	S23
ARCHER	COOS CO.	T26S	R13W	S1
BANCROFT see **MYRTLE CREEK**	COOS CO.	T30S	R11W	S16
BANCROFT see **WATERMAN**	COOS CO.	T30S	R11W	S33

BANDON ODD FELLOWS see **I.O.O.F. [NEW BANDON]**

	COOS CO.	T28S	R14W	S29
BANDON PIONEER	COOS CO.	T28S	R14W	S30

BANDON PIONEER see **G.A.R. [GRAND ARMY OF THE REPUBLIC; OLD BANDON]**

	COOS CO.	T28S	R14W	S30

BANDON PIONEER see **I.O.O.F. [OLD BANDON]**

	COOS CO.	T28S	R14W	S30
BARKER-MORRIS FAMILIES	COOS CO.	T27S	R12W	S14
BEAR CREEK	COOS CO.	T28S	R14W	S35
BEAVER HILL	COOS CO.	T27S	R13W	S17
BIGELOW FAMILY see **GREENE**	COOS CO.	T32S	R12W	S8
BINGHAM see **POWERS**	COOS CO.	T31S	R12W	S12
BRACK FAMILY	COOS CO.	T29S	R12W	S26

BREEN, ANNIE WASSON see **BREEN, BABY**

	COOS CO.	T25S	R13W	?
BREEN, BABY	COOS CO.	T25S	R13W	?

BRELAGE RANCH, ARNOLD see **WHEELER, ANNIE R.**

	COOS CO.	T25S	R12W	S5
BREUER	COOS CO.	T29S	R12W	S36
BREUER, ALBERT see **BREUER**	COOS CO.	T29S	R12W	S36
BROWN	COOS CO.	?	?	?
BULLARD FAMILY	COOS CO.	T28S	R14W	S7

BUTLER FARM, CLARENCE see **HILL, RICHARD**

	COOS CO.	T32S	R11W	?
CATCHING CREEK	COOS CO.	T29S	R13W	S35
CATHOLIC see **BANDON PIONEER**	COOS CO.	T28S	R14W	S30
CATHOLIC [BANDON]	COOS CO.	T28S	R14W	S30
COLLVER, BENHAM B.	COOS CO.	T26S	R14W	?
CONLIFF, FRED see **MASTERS**	COOS CO.	T26S	R12W	S6
COOK, CHRIS	COOS CO.	T30S	R10W	S3
COOS RIVER PIONEER	COOS CO.	T25S	R12W	S25

COQUILLE PIONEER see **I.O.O.F. [OLD COQUILLE]**

	COOS CO.	T27S	R13W	S36
COUNTY POOR FARM	COOS CO.	T27S	R12W	S29
CULBERTSON see **HANSEN**	COOS CO.	T28S	R12W	S25
DANS CREEK	COOS CO.	?	?	?
DAVIS	COOS CO.	T29S	R10W	S28
DEER PARK see **GREENE**	COOS CO.	T32S	R12W	S8

DEMENT D.L.C., SAMUAL see **DEMENT FAMILY**

	COOS CO.	T30S	R12W	S7

DEMENT, ELLIS see **JEFFERSON, THOMAS**				
	COOS CO.	T31S	R11W	S31
DEMENT FAMILY	COOS CO.	T30S	R12W	S7
DEMENT RANCH, WALLACE see **DEMENT FAMILY**				
	COOS CO.	T30S	R12W	S7
DIETRICH, W.	COOS CO.	T33S	R12W	S33
DORA	COOS CO.	T28S	R11W	S10
EASTON FAMILY see **JUNGLEBANK**	COOS CO.	T28S	R10W	S6
EASTON, MILDRED NEELY see **JUNGLEBANK**				
	COOS CO.	T28S	R10W	S6
EASTON, ROBERT A. see **JUNGLEBANK**				
	COOS CO.	T28S	R10W	S6
EASTON, THEODORE see **JUNGLEBANK**	COOS CO.	T28S	R10W	S6
ECKLEY see **DEMENT FAMILY**	COOS CO.	T30S	R12W	S7
EDEN VALLEY	COOS CO.	T32S	R11W	S12
EMANUEL EPISCOPAL CHURCH COLUMBARIUM				
	COOS CO.	T25S	R13W	S26
EMPIRE	COOS CO.	T25S	R13W	S17
ENCHANTED PRAIRIE	COOS CO.	T29S	R11W	S35
ENGLEWOOD	COOS CO.	T25S	R13W	?
FAIRVIEW	COOS CO.	T27S	R12W	S26
FERRY, HENRIETTA see **GARRETT**	COOS CO.	T29S	R12W	?
FETTER	COOS CO.	T29S	R10W	S28
FETTER CREEK, JOHN see **FETTER**	COOS CO.	T29S	R10W	S28
FISH see **MYRTLE CREEK**	COOS CO.	T30S	R11W	S16
FISHTRAP	COOS CO.	T28S	R13W	S23
FLOYD, FRANCIS see **BROWN**	COOS CO.	?	?	?
FOX BRIDGE	COOS CO.	T28S	R12W	S15
G. A. R. [GRAND ARMY OF THE REPUBLIC] see **BANDON PIONEER**				
	COOS CO.	T28S	R14W	S30
G. A. R. [GRAND ARMY OF THE REPUBLIC; OLD BANDON]				
	COOS CO.	T28S	R14W	S30
GARRETT	COOS CO.	T29S	R12W	?
GARRETT RANCH see **GARRETT**	COOS CO.	T29S	R12W	?
GIBBS PROPERTY, RALPH see **MILLER FAMILY**				
	COOS CO.	T29S	R12W	S33
GRAVELFORD	COOS CO.	T28S	R12W	S26
GRAVEYARD POINT see **SOUTH SLOUGH**				
	COOS CO.	T26S	R14W	S15
GREEN, JAMES	COOS CO.	T28S	R13W	S30
GREENE	COOS CO.	T32S	R12W	S8
HALL FARM, GEORGE see **BROWN**	COOS CO.	?	?	?
HAMBLOCH see **BULLARD FAMILY**	COOS CO.	T28S	R14W	S7
HAMBLOCK see **BULLARD FAMILY**	COOS CO.	T28S	R14W	S7
HANSEN	COOS CO.	T28S	R12W	S25
HARLEM see **CATHOLIC [BANDON]**	COOS CO.	T28S	R14W	S30
HAYES	COOS CO.	T31S	R11W	S19
HAYES RANCH, TOM see **JEFFERSON, THOMAS**				
	COOS CO.	T31S	R11W	S31
HAYNES, CHARLES T.	COOS CO.	T26S	R13W	S25
HERMANN	COOS CO.	T30S	R12W	S5
HILL, DOLLIE see **HILL, RICHARD**	COOS CO.	T32S	R11W	?

HILL, RICHARD	COOS CO.	T32S	R11W	?
HILL, RUSSEL J. see **HILL, RICHARD**				
	COOS CO.	T32S	R11W	?
HOFFMAN	COOS CO.	T29S	R12W	S22
HOFFMAN HOMESTEAD see **HOFFMAN**	COOS CO.	T29S	R12W	S22
HOLY TRINITY see **CATHOLIC [BANDON]**				
	COOS CO.	T28S	R14W	S30
HULTIN	COOS CO.	T28S	S14W	S3
HUNTLY, RUBY see **JEFFERSON, THOMAS**				
	COOS CO.	T31S	R11W	S31
I.O.O.F. [COOS BAY]	COOS CO.	T25S	R13W	S34
I.O.O.F. [NEW BANDON]	COOS CO.	T28S	R14W	S29
I.O.O.F. [NEW COQUILLE]	COOS CO.	T28S	R13W	S1
I.O.O.F. [OLD BANDON]	COOS CO.	T28S	R14W	S30
I.O.O.F. [OLD BANDON] see **BANDON PIONEER**				
	COOS CO.	T28S	R14W	S30
I.O.O.F. [OLD COQUILLE]	COOS CO.	T27S	R13W	S36
IRON MOUNTAIN GRAVE see **DIETRICH, W.**				
	COOS CO.	T33S	R12W	S33
JEFFERSON, THOMAS	COOS CO.	T31S	R11W	S31
JENNINGS, L. B. see **FETTER**	COOS CO.	T29S	R10W	S28
JUNGLEBANK	COOS CO.	T28S	R10W	S6
KENTUCK INLET	COOS CO.	T25S	R12W	?
KENTUCK SLOUGH see **KENTUCK INLET**				
	COOS CO.	T25S	R12W	?
KNIGHTS OF PYTHIAS [BANDON] see **VETERANS OF FOREIGN WARS**				
	COOS CO.	T28S	R14W	S29
KRONENBERG see **PARKERSBURG**	COOS CO.	T28S	R14W	S15
KRUEGER FARM, WALTER see **HILL, RICHARD**				
	COOS CO.	T32S	R11W	?
LAIRD, KENNETH see **WHITTINGTON**	COOS CO.	T29S	R12W	S32
LAIRD RANCH, KENNETH see **SKAGGS, MARTHA J.**				
	COOS CO.	T28S	R10W	S10
LAKESIDE	COOS CO.	T23S	R13W	S13
LAMPA CREEK	COOS CO.	T28S	R13W	?
LEE see **LEE VALLEY**	COOS CO.	T28S	R12W	S1
LEE VALLEY	COOS CO.	T28S	R12W	S1
LETT CHILDREN	COOS CO.	T30S	R11W	S9
LETT FARM see **LETT CHILDREN**	COOS CO.	T30S	R11W	S9
LIBBY	COOS CO.	T26S	R13W	?
LOWER FISHTRAP see **FISHTRAP**	COOS CO.	T28S	R13W	S23
MARSHFIELD	COOS CO.	T25S	R13W	S26
MASONIC see **POWERS**	COOS CO.	T31S	R12W	S12
MASONIC [COQUILLE]	COOS CO.	T27S	R13W	S36
MAST FAMILY	COOS CO.	T27S	R11W	?
MASTERS	COOS CO.	T26S	R12W	S6
McKINLEY see **DORA**	COOS CO.	T28S	R11W	S10
McLEOD, JACK see **WISE**	COOS CO.	T30S	R12W	S34
MILLER, CONRAD see **MILLER FAMILY**				
	COOS CO.	T29S	R12W	S33
MILLER FAMILY	COOS CO.	T29S	R12W	S33
MORRIS FAMILY	COOS CO.	T31S	R12W	S12

MORRIS-BARKER FAMILIES see **BARKER-MORRIS FAMILIES**

	COOS CO.	T27S	R12W	S14
MYRTLE CREEK	COOS CO.	T30S	R11W	S16
MYRTLE CREST MEMORIAL GARDENS	COOS CO.	T28S	R12W	S7
MYRTLE POINT	COOS CO.	T29S	R12W	S15
NEAL	COOS CO.	T30S	R12W	S15
NELSON, AMELIA ANN see **NELSON FAMILY**				
	COOS CO.	T28S	R12W	S32
NELSON FAMILY	COOS CO.	T28S	R12W	S32
NELSON, FRANK A. see **NELSON FAMILY**				
	COOS CO.	T28S	R12W	S32
NOAH, MR.	COOS CO.	T30S	R11W	S9
NORWAY	COOS CO.	T28S	R12W	S32
OCEAN VIEW MEMORIAL GARDENS	COOS CO.	T25S	R13W	S20
OLD COUNTY ROAD see **EMPIRE**	COOS CO.	T25S	R13W	S17
OLD EMPIRE see **EMPIRE**	COOS CO.	T25S	R13W	S17
OLD MYRTLE POINT see **MYRTLE POINT**				
	COOS CO.	T29S	R12W	S15
OLD PIONEER see **I.O.O.F. [COOS BAY]**				
	COOS CO.	T25S	R13W	S34
OLD RED BARN see **ARCHER**	COOS CO.	T26S	R13W	S1
PALLASKE FAMILY	COOS CO.	T28S	R13W	S3
PARKER COUNTY PARK, JUDAH see **PARKERSBURG**				
	COOS CO.	T28S	R14W	S15
PARKERSBURG	COOS CO.	T28S	R14W	S15
PHILIPS D.L.C., ROBERT Y. see **WARNER, WILLIAM N.**				
	COOS CO.	T30S	R12W	S34
PIONEER see **CATHOLIC [BANDON]**	COOS CO.	T28S	R14W	S30
PIONEER see **SUMNER [OLD]**	COOS CO.	T26S	R12W	S33
PIONEER see **TEMPLETON**	COOS CO.	T23S	R12W	S26
PLEASANT HILL	COOS CO.	T29S	R12W	S7
POLAND FAMILY see **ROLAND-POLAND FAMILIES**				
	COOS CO.	T29S	R13W	?
POLAND, JANE see **ROLAND-POLAND FAMILIES**				
	COOS CO.	T29S	R13W	?
POLAND, MRS. PEARL see **ROLAND-POLAND FAMILIES**				
	COOS CO.	T29S	R13W	?
POWERS	COOS CO.	T31S	R12W	S12
POWRIE, ROBERT E. see **HOFFMAN**	COOS CO.	T29S	R12W	S22
PULASKI see **PALLASKE FAMILY**	COOS CO.	T28S	R13W	S3
RACKLEFF	COOS CO.	T29S	R12W	?
RANDOLPH	COOS CO.	T28S	R14W	S3
RED BARN see **ARCHER**	COOS CO.	T26S	R13W	S1
REMOTE see **FETTER**	COOS CO.	T29S	R10W	S28
RICE see **MYRTLE CREEK**	COOS CO.	T30S	R11W	S16
RIVERTON	COOS CO.	T28S	R13W	?
ROBBINS FAMILY	COOS CO.	T30S	R12W	S4
ROBISON see **FISHTRAP**	COOS CO.	T28S	R13W	S23
ROBISON FARM, ITHAMAR see **PALLASKE FAMILY**				
	COOS CO.	T28S	R13W	S3
ROLAND D.L.C., WILLIAM see **WISE**	COOS CO.	T30S	R12W	S34

ROLAND FAMILY see **ROLAND-POLAND FAMILIES**				
	COOS CO.	T29S	R13W	?
ROLAND, WILLIAM see **ROLAND-POLAND FAMILIES**				
	COOS CO.	T29S	R13W	?
ROLAND-POLAND FAMILIES	COOS CO.	T29S	R13W	?
ROWLAND see **WARNER, WILLIAM N.**	COOS CO.	T30S	R12W	S34
RUSSEL RANCH see **RUSSELL**	COOS CO.	T28S	R14W	S3
RUSSELL	COOS CO.	T28S	R14W	S3
SACCHI	COOS CO.	T26S	R14W	S32
SACCHI RANCH see **SACCHI**	COOS CO.	T26S	R14W	S32
SHULL FARM, ORAN see **SMITH FAMILY**				
	COOS CO.	T28S	R13W	S3
SKAGGS, MARTH J.	COOS CO.	T28S	R10W	S10
SMALLEY, EVELYN	COOS CO.	T29S	R13W	S11
SMITH CLAIM see **DIETRICH, W.**	COOS CO.	T33S	R12W	S33
SMITH FAMILY	COOS CO.	T28S	R13W	S3
SOUTH FORK see **COOS RIVER PIONEER**				
	COOS CO.	T25S	R12W	S25
SOUTH SLOUGH	COOS CO.	T26S	R14W	S15
STEWARD FAMILY	COOS CO.	T28S	R13W	?
STEWARD, STEPHEN see **STEWARD FAMILY**				
	COOS CO.	T28S	R13W	?
STRONG, CLARENCE see **BROWN**	COOS CO.	?	?	?
SUMNER [OLD]	COOS CO.	T26S	R12W	S33
SUMNER PIONEER see **SUMNER [OLD]**	COOS CO.	T26S	R12W	S33
SUMNER PLOT see **SUMNER SCHOOL**	COOS CO.	T26S	R12W	S17
SUMNER SCHOOL	COOS CO.	T26S	R12W	S17
SUNSET MEMORIAL PARK	COOS CO.	T26S	R13W	S2
TAYLOR, JOSEPH see **PLEASANT HILL**				
	COOS CO.	T29S	R12W	S7
TELEGRAPH HILL see **MARSHFIELD**	COOS CO.	T25S	R13W	S26
TEMPLETON	COOS CO.	T23S	R12W	S26
THOMAS FAMILY see **KENTUCK INLET**	COOS CO.	T25S	R12W	?
THRUSH see **HULTIN**	COOS CO.	T28S	R14W	S3
THRUSH FARM see **HULTIN**	COOS CO.	T28S	R14W	S3
TOMLINSON, ALBERT see **SMALLEY, EVELYN**				
	COOS CO.	T29S	R13W	S11
TURNER FAMILY	COOS CO.	T30S	R14W	S18
UNKNOWN	COOS CO.	T26S	R14W	S15
UPPER FISH TRAP *[Sic]* see **UPPER FISHTRAP**				
	COOS CO.	T28S	R13W	S34
UPPER FISHTRAP	COOS CO.	T28S	R13W	S34
V. F. W. see **VETERANS OF FOREIGN WARS**				
	COOS CO.	T28S	R14W	S29
VETERANS OF FOREIGN WARS	COOS CO.	T28S	R14W	S29
WARNER see **WARNER, CALVIN**	COOS CO.	T29S	R12W	S28
WARNER, CALVIN	COOS CO.	T29S	R12W	S28
WARNER, WILLIAM N.	COOS CO.	T30S	R12W	S34
WASSON	COOS CO.	T26S	R14W	?
WASSON RANCH see **WASSON**	COOS CO.	T26S	R14W	?
WATERMAN	COOS CO.	T30S	R11W	S33
WHEELER, ANNIE R.	COOS CO.	T25S	R12W	S5

WHITTINGTON	COOS CO.	T29S	R12W	S32
WIGENT FAMILY	COOS CO.	T29S	?	?
WIGERT FAMILY see **WIGENT FAMILY**	COOS CO.	T29S	?	?
WILSON FAMILY see **SUMNER [OLD]**	COOS CO.	T26S	R12W	S33
WISE	COOS CO.	T30S	R12W	S34
WITT RANCH, OTTO see **KENTUCK INLET**				
	COOS CO.	T25S	R12W	?
YOAKAM FAMILY	COOS CO.	?	R13W	?

Bandon Pioneer
Dean H. Byrd (1996)

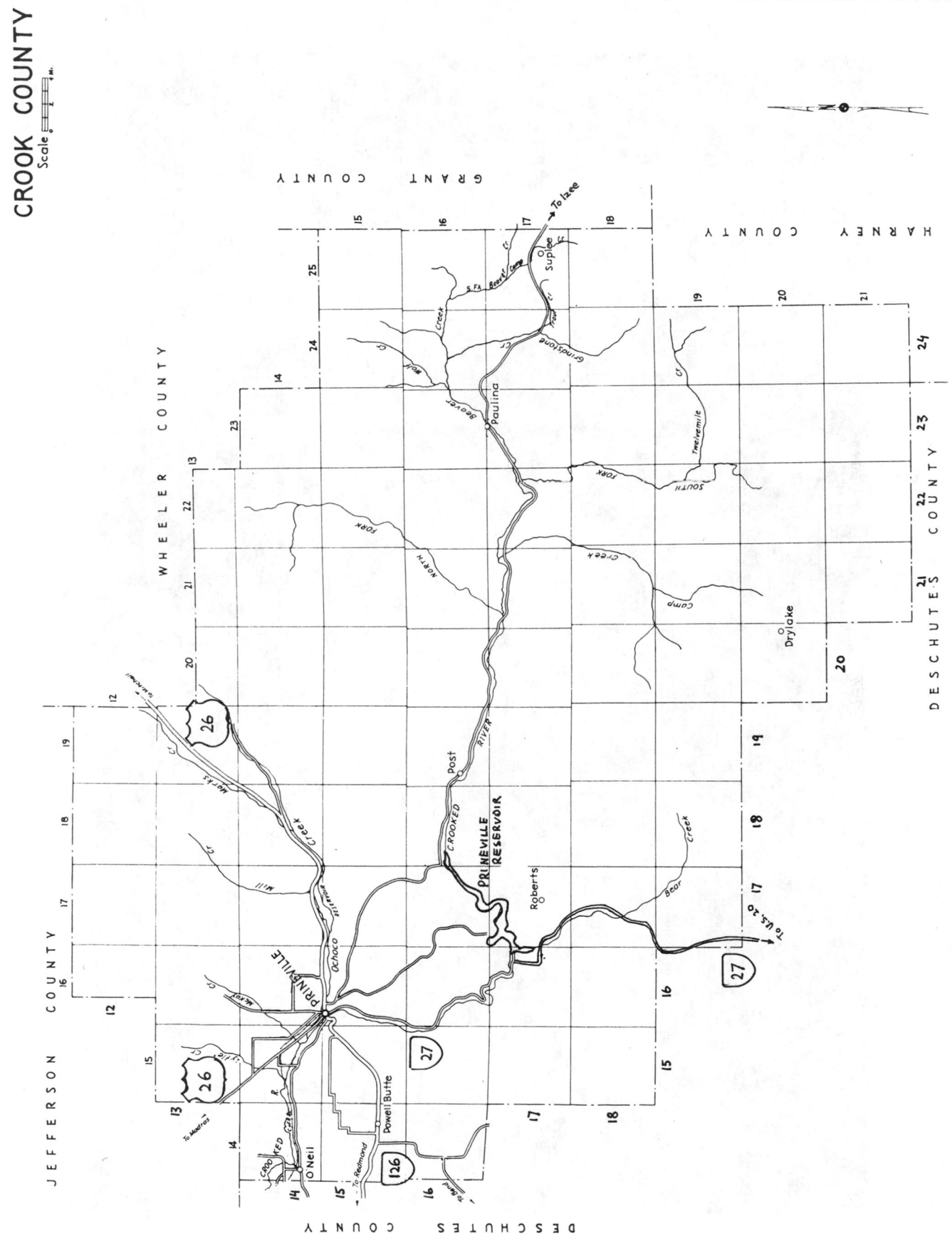

Pilgrim's Rest

Janice M. Healy (2000)

Area: 2,991 square miles
Population (1998): 17,236
County seat: Prineville, Population: 6,230
County established: 24 October 1882

Crook County was not settled by emigrants until around 1870. The first organized public cemetery was started in that year at Prineville, soon followed by Mill Creek Cemetery in 1872. Seven more were created by the mid-1890s. Crook County had livestock ranches and many families used family cemeteries.

Pilgrim's Rest
Janice M. Healy (2000)

Pilgrim's Rest
Janice M. Healy (2000)

Pilgrim's Rest
Janice M. Healy (2000)

Name of Cemetery or also known as	Number of burials	Acres	Condition	Date started or earliest known burial	Township	Range	Section

BARNES
AKA: 1. CAMP CREEK
    2. DEMARIS

A   0.25 5   1888   T18S R20E   S35
Go 31 miles south from Prineville on OR. Hwy. 27. Turn left (east) on Bear Creek-Fife Road and go 27 miles. The cemetery is about 30 yards off of the road on the right. The site of Barnes School is 0.5 of a mile further on. There are about 8 graves, with 2 markers reported in 1980. [October 1999] (Logan Butte 1983 USGS Quad. map.)

BEAVER CREEK
AKA: 1. LISTER
    2. PAULINA

C   1   1   1883   T16S R24E   S15
Located on the former Lister Ranch about 10 miles northeast of Paulina. Go 4.7 miles east of Paulina on the Paulina-Suplee Road, then turn left onto Beaver Creek Road and go 3.4 miles. Turn right onto Lister Road and go another 1.4 miles. The cemetery is on the north (left) side of the road. There are 74 graves, with 4 unidentified (1980). (Mud Spring 1983 USGS Quad. map.)

DEEDS BABIES

A   ?   ?   ?   T17S R25E   S11
Two babies of the Deeds family are reported to be buried on the Henry Bernard Ranch (1966). Leave the Paulina-Suplee Road east of Paulina at the Suplee junction. Turn left (north) onto Bernard Road and drive about 2 miles to the Bernard Ranch on Miners Flat. NOTE: The graves are on private property. (The ranch but not the graves are shown on Suplee 1981 USGS Quad. map.)

DELORE
AKA: 1. ROBERTSON
    2. SUPLEE

A   ?   3   1887   T18S R25E   S13
Located 4 miles south of the Paulina-Suplee Road and 0.25 of a mile west of Weberg Road. There were 25 known graves in 1980, mostly descendants of French-Canadians from French Prairie in Marion County, via French Cemetery in Wasco County. See the article for French Cemetery in Wasco County. {Sept. 1994} (Suplee 1981 USGS Quad. map.)

DRY LAKE
AKA: 1. CUNNINGHAM
      RANCH

A   ?   ?   ?   T20S R20E   S14
Located in the Northwest corner of the Northwest 1/4 of Section 24. Eight graves

Name of Cemetery or also known as	Number of burials	Acres	Condition	Date started or earliest known burial	Township	Range	Section

2. HAMMACK RANCH, VERLE

are reported on the old Cunningham Ranch now owned by Verle Hammack. Access is by way of Central Oregon Highway (U.S. 20), going east out of Bend towards Burns. Once past Brothers continue on about 11 miles. Turn off left (northeasterly) on Van Lake Road. Go about 4.2 miles to the Crook County Line. Continue ahead another 4.5 miles to the ranch road right (east). The cedar grave markers have been burnt. NOTE: This site is on private property. {1999} (Not shown on Hampton Butte 1983 USGS Quad. map.)

GRANT

?   ?   ?   ?   T13S R19E   S1

There are some burials reported in this area of the Ochoco Mountains near Grant Butte and/or Grant Meadows. No further information was given in the report. (Not shown on Whistler Point 1990 USGS Quad. map.)

HELD

?   ?   ?   ?   T19S R19E   S4

Reportedly there is an old cemetery for the bygone community of Held. Leave Prineville to the south by the way of the Crooked River Highway (OR. Hwy. 27). Drive 27 miles to the junction with Bear Creek-Fife Road to the left (east). Proceed easterly on this county road for about 17.5 miles to the site of Held. As of 1976 there were no buildings left here. One can continue ahead on Bear Creek-Fife Road for 0.4 of a mile to the junction with Pringle Flat Road right (south). Turn onto Pringle Flat Road and drive 18 miles to the locale of Brothers on Central Oregon Highway, U.S. Hwy. 20 and thence one can drive to Bend. Held was important enough to have had a post office from May 1909 to May 1919. (The site of Held is shown but no graveyard is shown on Pringle Flat 1992 USGS Quad. map.)

HOWARD
AKA: 1. OCHOCO

A   0.25 2   1892   T14S R19E   S8

Located in Sections 8 and 9. Go 16 miles east of Prineville on U.S. Hwy. 26. Turn right onto Ochoco Creek Road and go another 5.4 miles. The cemetery is on the right,

Name of Cemetery or also known as	Number of burials	Acres	Condition	Date started or earliest known burial	Township	Range	Section

0.28 of a mile past the Ochoco Creek Bridge. It is within the Ochoco National Forest. {30 Sept. 1995} (Gerow Butte 1990 USGS Quad. map.)

JUNIPER HAVEN
AKA: 1. CITY
2. CROOK COUNTY
3. I.O.O.F. [PRINEVILLE]
4. MASONIC [PRINEVILLE]
5. PIONEER [PRINEVILLE]
6. UNION

E 36 1 1870 T14S R16E S31
Located 0.8 of a mile north of U.S. Hwy. 26 on North Main Street, Prineville. Numbers 3, 4 and 5 were three separate cemeteries at one time and have since been merged into one. There are about 3,000 graves, with 86 unidentified (1980). (Prineville 1962 USGS Quad. map.)

KNOX FAMILY, E. B.
AKA: 1. NEWSOME CREEK

A 1 3 1887-1935 T17S R19E S8
Located south of Post on the old E. B. Knox Ranch on Newsome Creek. It was on the Owen Panne Place (1978). There are 18 graves, with 8 unmarked (1980). A visit by Jim and Evelyn Rogers in Sept. 1994 found only 8 markers with 7 unmarked graves, plus records of two cremations. Vandalized by cattle breaking in and repair work has resulted in markers being moved about. NOTE: This is on private property. {Sept. 1994} (Mule Deer Ridge 1990 USGS Quad. map.)

MAURY MOUNTAIN
AKA 1. MAURY

B 1.5 3 1885 T17S R21E S11
Located southwest of Paulina approximately 12 miles, off the south side of the Paulina Highway along the Crooked River near Milepost 41, by Camp Creek. There are 37 graves (1980). {Sept. 1994} (Arrowwood Point 1982 USGS Quad. map.)

MILL CREEK

B 1 2 1872 T14S R17E S26
Located out of Prineville: 8.7 miles east of the junction of U.S. Hwy. 26, Ochoco Highway and the Paulina Highway, on the east side of Mill Creek. Go 0.28 of a mile past Mill Creek. A road to the left (north) for 0.25

Name of Cemetery or also known as	Number of burials	Acres	Condition	Date started or earliest known burial	Township	Range	Section

of a mile leads to the cemetery on the left. There are 92 graves, with 10 unidentified (1980). (Ochoco Reservoir 1990 USGS Quad. map.)

PILGRIM'S REST
 AKA: 1. POWELL BUTTE

C 2 1 1905   T16S R14E   S11

At 0.8 of a mile west of the community of Powell Butte leave OR. Hwy. 126, and go south 2.8 miles on the road to Alfalfa. At the sharp curve to the right (west) turn to your left (east) onto Bussett Road, at 1 mile you will come to a "T" intersection, at this turn right (south) on Cemetery Road. Travel 1.76 miles more and on your left (east) is the cemetery. {30 September 2000} (Powell Butte 1962 USGS Quad. map.)

ROBERTS

A 0.5 3 1888   T17S R17E   S22

Located south of the Prineville Reservoir, near the abandoned townsite of Roberts. Go 28.3 miles south of Prineville on OR. Hwy. 27. Then turn left onto Salt Creek Road and go 4.3 miles to Roberts. The cemetery is 0.5 of a mile southwest of Roberts, on the tip of a ridge, about 400 feet southeast of a driveway and in the trees. There are 21 graves, with 2 unidentified (1980). (Alkali Flat 1990 USGS Quad. map.)

UNKNOWN

A 0.01 ? ?   T14S R14E   ?

A single grave in the community of O'Neil. NOTE: No other information was given in the report. (Not shown on O'Neil 1962 USGS Quad. map.)

UNKNOWN

A 0.01 ? ?   T15S R25E   S33

A single grave at the Rager Ranger Station out of Paulina in the Ochoco National Forest. NOTE: No other information was given in the report. (Not shown on Powell Mountain 1981 USGS Quad. map.)

WEEVER

A 0.01 ? 1890   T14S R14E   S23

Located in Section 23 or 24. The Weever grave is located near the Crooked River on

Name of Cemetery or also known as	Number of burials	Acres	Condition	Date started or earliest known burial	Township	Range	Section

the old Montgomery Place. NOTE: This site is on private property. (Not shown on O'Neil 1962 or Huston Lake 1975 USGS Quad. maps.)

Pilgrim's Rest
Janice M. Healy (2000)

Pilgrim's Rest
Front of Monument
Janice M. Healy (2000)

Pilgrim's Rest
Back of same Monument
Janice M. Healy (2000)

BARNES	CROOK CO.	T18S	R20E	S35
BEAVER CREEK	CROOK CO.	T16S	R24E	S15
BERNARD RANCH, HENRY see **DEEDS BABIES**				
	CROOK CO.	T17S	R25E	S11
CAMP CREEK see **BARNES**	CROOK CO.	T18S	R20E	S35
CITY see **JUNIPER HAVEN**	CROOK CO.	T14S	R16E	S31
CROOK COUNTY see **JUNIPER HAVEN**	CROOK CO.	T14S	R16E	S31
CUNNINGHAM RANCH see **DRY LAKE**	CROOK CO.	T20S	R20E	S14
DEEDS BABIES	CROOK CO.	T17S	R25E	S11
DEEDS FAMILY see **DEEDS BABIES**	CROOK CO.	T17S	R25E	S11
DELORE	CROOK CO.	T18S	R25E	S13
DEMARIS see **BARNES**	CROOK CO.	T18S	R20E	S35
DRY LAKE	CROOK CO.	T20S	R20E	S14
GRANT	CROOK CO.	T13S	R19E	S1
HAMMACK RANCH, VERLE see **DRY LAKE**				
	CROOK CO.	T20S	R20E	S14
HAMMACK, VERLE see **DRY LAKE**	CROOK CO.	T20S	R20E	S14
HELD	CROOK CO.	T19S	R19E	S4
HOWARD	CROOK CO.	T14S	R19E	S8
I.O.O.F. [PRINEVILLE] see **JUNIPER HAVEN**				
	CROOK CO.	T14S	R16E	S31
JUNIPER HAVEN	CROOK CO.	T14S	R16E	S31
KNOX FAMILY, E. B.	CROOK CO.	T17S	R19E	S8
KNOX RANCH, E. B. see **KNOX FAMILY, E. B.**				
	CROOK CO.	T17S	R19E	S8
LISTER see **BEAVER CREEK**	CROOK CO.	T16S	R24E	S15
LISTER RANCH see **BEAVER CREEK**	CROOK CO.	T16S	R24E	S15
MASONIC [PRINEVILLE] see **JUNIPER HAVEN**				
	CROOK CO.	T14S	R16E	S31
MAURY see **MAURY MOUNTAIN**	CROOK CO.	T17S	R21E	S11
MAURY MOUNTAIN	CROOK CO.	T17S	R21E	S11
MILL CREEK	CROOK CO.	T14S	R17E	S26
MONTGOMERY PLACE see **WEEVER**	CROOK CO.	T14S	R14E	S23
NEWSOME CREEK see **KNOX FAMILY, E. B.**				
	CROOK CO.	T17S	R19E	S8
OCHOCO see **HOWARD**	CROOK CO.	T14S	R19E	S8
PANNE PLACE, OWEN see **KNOX FAMILY, E. B.**				
	CROOK CO.	T17S	R19E	S8
PAULINA see **BEAVER CREEK**	CROOK CO.	T16S	R24E	S15
PILGRIM'S REST	CROOK CO.	T16S	R14E	S11
PIONEER [PRINEVILLE] see **JUNIPER HAVEN**				
	CROOK CO.	T14S	R16E	S31
POWELL BUTTE see **PILGRIM'S REST**	CROOK CO.	T16S	R14E	S11
ROBERTS	CROOK CO.	T17S	R17E	S22
ROBERTSON see **DELORE**	CROOK CO.	T18S	R25E	S13
SUPLEE see **DELORE**	CROOK CO.	T18S	R25E	S13
UNION see **JUNIPER HAVEN**	CROOK CO.	T14S	R16E	S31
UNKNOWN	CROOK CO.	T14S	R14E	?
UNKNOWN	CROOK CO.	T15S	R25E	S33
WEEVER	CROOK CO.	T14S	R14E	S23

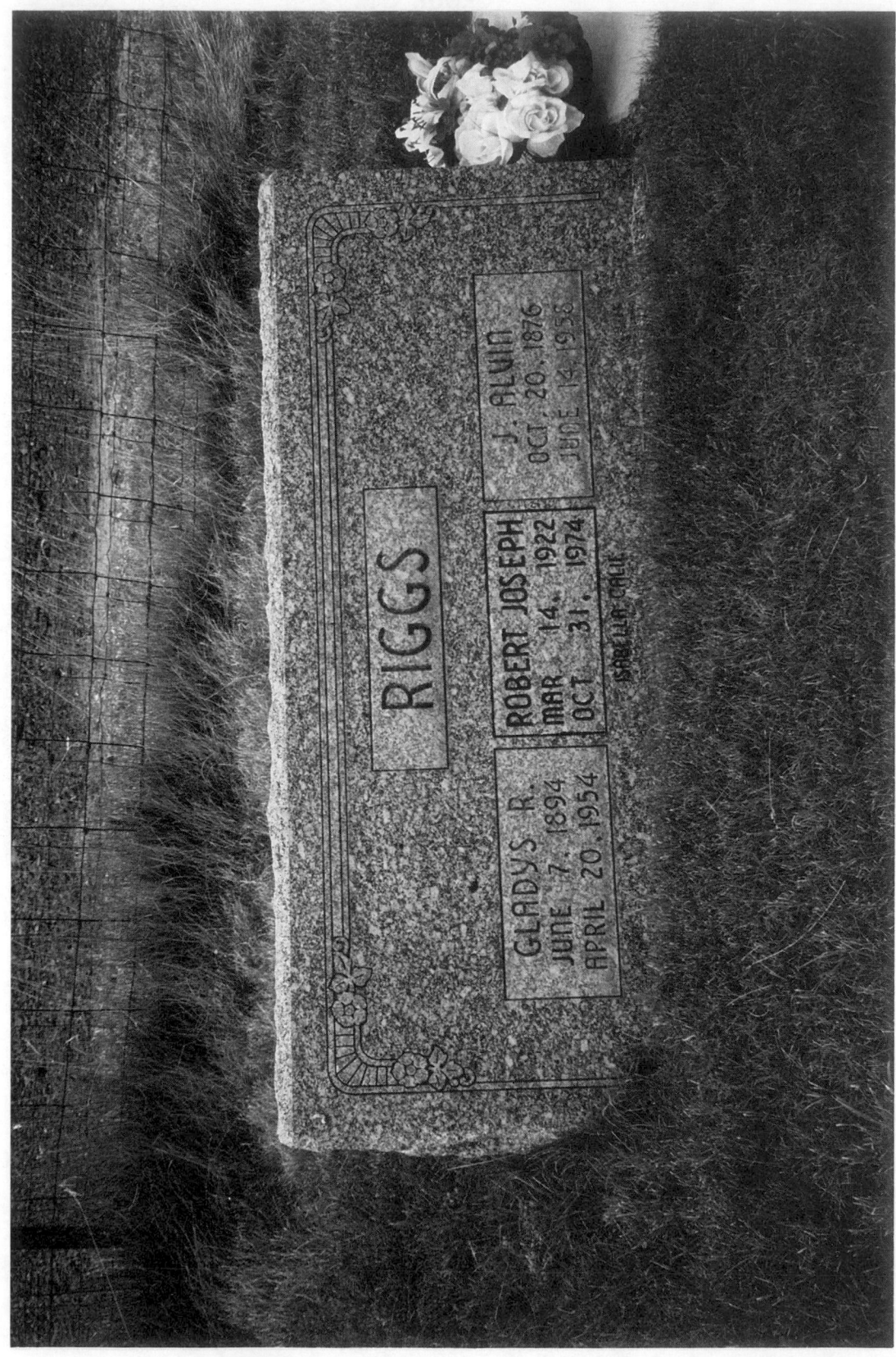

Pilgrim's Rest
Janice M. Healy (2000)

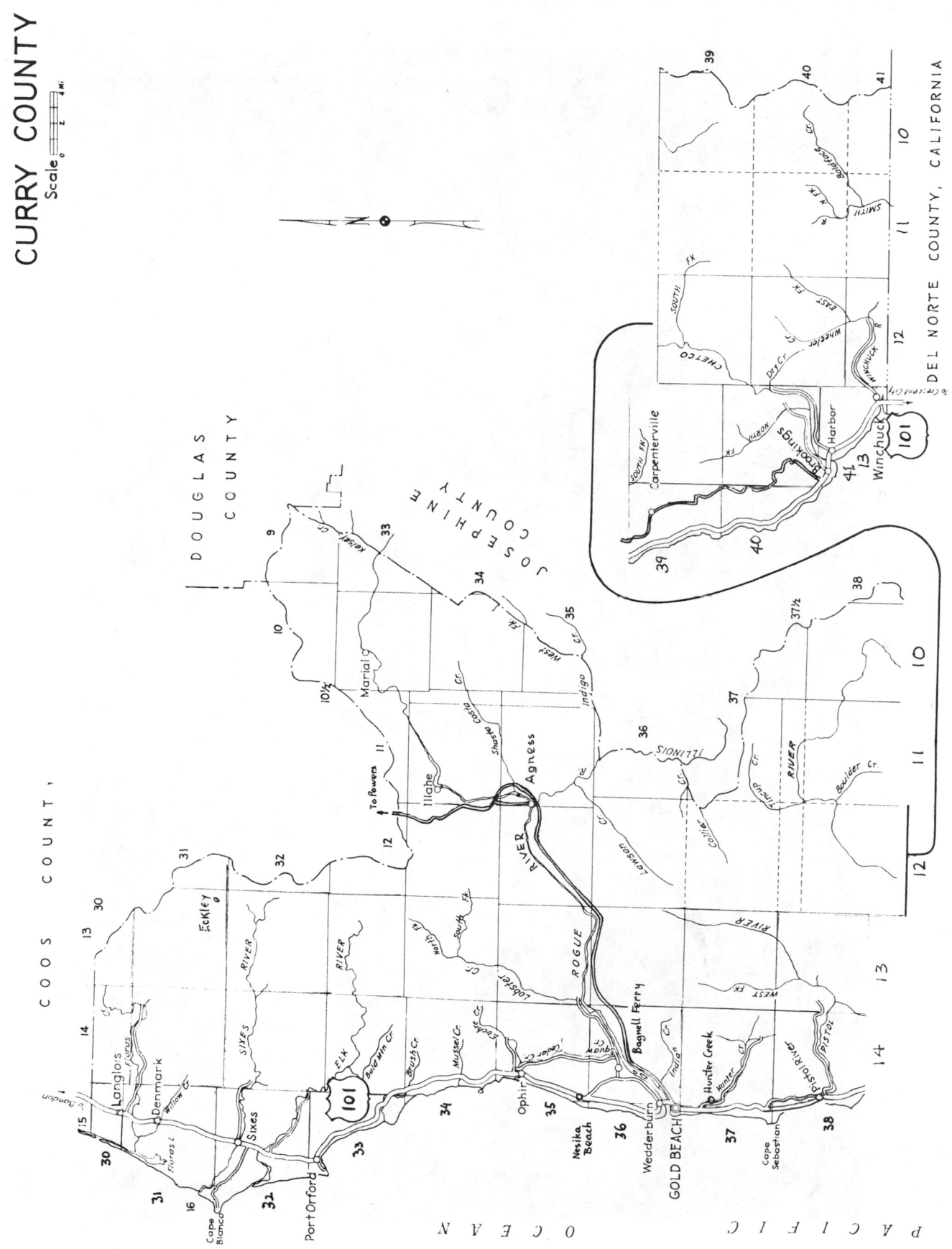

Port Orford
Dean H. Byrd (1996)

Area: 1,648 square miles
Population (1998): 21,157
County seat: Gold Beach, Population: 2,115
County established: 18 December 1855

Cemeteries were established after permanent settlement began in 1854. Public cemeteries were established at Port Orford (1854) and the Pioneer Cemetery at Gold Beach (1859). Settlement was slow until the 1930s.

Rogue River
Dean H. Byrd (1996)

Curry County

Tichenor
Dean H. Byrd (1996)

Name of Cemetery and also known as	Number of burials	Acres	Condition	Date started or earliest known burial	Township	Range	Section

ARMPRIEST FAMILY

A ? 5 1880 T36S R12W UNS

This section is unsurveyed but is projected as Section 13. The Armpriest family is supposed to be located at Armpriest Prairie. NOTE: There is no Armpriest Prairie listed by USGS. There is a camp known as Brandon Camp shown in this area however. The camp is within the Siskiyou National Forest and is reached by Trail #1169. No other information was given in the report. (Not shown on Horse Sign Butte 1989 USGS Quad. map.)

BALD RIDGE
AKA: 1. CRITESER, MAY

A ? 5 1917 T33S R9W S8

Mrs. Wooldridge reported at least two known burials near the airstrip. There are some ruins about 700 feet southeast of this airstrip in land owned by the Criteser Family according to the 1932 *Curry County Metsker Land Ownership Atlas*. May Criteser, born 1 November 1863, died 21 June 1934 is one of these burials. This may be reached by the Mule Creek-Marial Road (B.L.M. Road 32-9-142) east of Marial. (Not shown on Kelsey Peak 1989 USGS Quad. map.)

BARLOW, JIM

A 0.01 ? ? T33S R10W ?

Perhaps in Section 2, located near Marial [Old] Cemetery in an unmarked grave. NOTE: No further information was given in the report. (Not shown on Kelsey Peak 1989 USGS Quad. map.)

BATTLE ROCK
AKA: 1. SUMMERS
        FAMILY

A 0.01 1 1969 T33S R15W S4

Located on the rock in the State Park at Port Orford. In May of 1969, the 3 graves of the Summers family were reburied here. Ralph Summers, died 1909. He had participated in the battle of Battle Rock. {September 1991} (Port Orford 1986 USGS Quad. map.)

BIG MEADOWS
AKA: 1. BILLINGS

A ? 5 Circa 1908 T32S R10W S36

Located on the Rogue River Trail about 15 miles above Illahe in the Rogue River Wilderness Area. Reportedly there are no

Name of Cemetery and also known as	Number of burials	Acres	Condition	Date started or earliest known burial	Township	Range	Section

markers. This cemetery is close to the Frye or Fry Cemetery. NOTE: There is another Billings Cemetery. (Not shown on Kelsey Peak 1989 USGS Quad. map.)

BILLINGS

A   0.01   3   ?   T34S R11W   S7
Located on a hill on the Big Bend Ranch near the Foster Creek Bridge, between Agness-Illahe Road and Billings Road (private). There are 8 known graves of the Billings and Fry families, but only 2 markers were there in the mid. 1960's. (Not shown on Illahe 1989 USGS Quad. map.)

CAPE BLANCO PIONEER
AKA: 1. CAPE BLANCO
         CATHOLIC
     2. HUGHES
         FAMILY

A   0.5   6   1878   T31S R16W   S36
Located in Cape Blanco State Park. The old cemetery is about 1 mile short of the Cape Blanco lighthouse and about 200 feet to the left (south) of the Cape Blanco Highway as it climbs up onto the plateau that overlooks the Sixes River. In a field there remain 6 headstones, but the bodies were removed to Mt. Calvary Cemetery in Portland in 1938. {September 1991} (Cape Blanco 1986 USGS Quad. map.)

CARPENTER
AKA: 1. SNODGRASS
         FAMILY

A   ?   ?   ?   T39S R14W   ?
There are 4 graves at the Snodgrass Farm at Carpenterville. This is located on the old alignment of U.S. Hwy. 101, now called Carpenterville Frontage Road 18 miles north of Brookings NOTE: This site is on private property. No other information was given in the report. (Carpenterville 1986 USGS Quad. map shows 1 grave in Section 3.)

CLARNO SPRINGS

A   ?   ?   22 Feb 1856 T36S R14W   S9
Leave U.S. Hwy. 101 at Wedderburn and drive up river on North Bank Rogue River Road. At the junction with Edson Creek Road ahead, turn right still on North Bank Rogue River Road for another 0.7 of a mile. The mass grave of 12 whites killed by Indians is

Name of Cemetery and also known as	Number of burials	Acres	Condition	Date started or earliest known burial	Township	Range	Section

located in a meadow near a small creek from Clarno Springs: on the north side of the Rogue River opposite of Jerrys Flat. (Not shown on Signal Buttes 1986 USGS Quad. map.)

CLAY HILL
AKA: 1. THOMAS,
      ETHEL

A   0.01   ?   ?   T34S R11W   S2
Located above the Clay Hill Rapids of the Rogue River, on the north bank and about 800 feet west of Clay Hill Creek. This is a mother and infant burial. Reportedly one of these burials is Ethel Thomas. (Marial 1989 USGS Quad. map.)

COLVIN GRAVE

A   ?   1   ?   T37S R14W   ?
Perhaps located in Section 20, up Hunter Creek on the Leith Place (1978). NOTE: This site is on private property. No other information was given in the report. (Not shown on Cape Sebastian 1986 USGS Quad. map.)

COOLEY FAMILY

A   0.01   5   3 Oct. 1897 T41S R13W   S9
Near Harbor, west of U.S. Hwy. 101 and somewhere near Pedrioli Lane there is a 12 foot by 14 foot fenced plot with 3 graves. Reported by Mrs. Wooldridge. On the Thomas Sharp D.L.C. #41, RB #1908. NOTE: This site is on private property. (Not shown on Mt. Emily 1989 USGS Quad. map.)

COOPER M.D., ARTHUR
AKA: 1. COOPER'S,
      DOCTOR

A   0.01   5   18 Aug 1903 T40S R14W   S10
Doctor Cooper's grave is along the north side of Cape Ferrelo Road, 0.75 of a mile from U.S. Hwy.101. Doctor Cooper was 63. (Not shown on Carpenterville 1986 USGS Quad. map.)

COSTELLOE, EDMOND

A   0.01   ?   18 Nov 1912 T41S R12W   S5
Located about 5.5 miles up the Winchuck River Road, in a field near the riverbank and about 0.6 of a mile inside the Siskiyou National Forest. Edmond Costelloe was 36. (Not shown on Mt. Emily 1989 USGS Quad. map.)

Curry County

Name of Cemetery and also known as	Number of burials	Acres	Condition	Date started or earliest known burial	Township	Range	Section

CREW FAMILY

A ? 3 1884-1888 T32S R15W S9

Located about 0.25 of a mile downstream on the Sixes River from the locale of Sixes. This was located on the Piercy Sweet Ranch in 1962. The monument for Mr. and Mrs. Crew was found on the north side of the Sixes River NOTE: This is located on private property. (Not shown on Sixes 1986 USGS Quad. map.)

DAVIS'S PLACE, JIMMY

A ? 5 ? ? ? ?

An old burial site was reported as being on the road going up to Walton Miller's Place. NOTE: No other infomation was given with the report.

DENMARK
 AKA: 1. FLORAS CREEK
 2. LANGLOIS
 3. WILLOW CREEK

C 3 2 1880 T31S R15W S10

Located about 0.5 of a mile north of Denmark and about 3 miles south of Langlois on Floras Lake Loop. If travelling north on U.S. Hwy. 101 from Denmark turn left (west) off of the highway for 0.4 of a mile to a 90-degree turn right (north). The cemetery is on the left. One can continue ahead for a mile, turn right to the highway and then left (north) to Langlois. {26 May 1996} (Langlois 1986 USGS Quad. map.)

EDDY, HARRIET
 AKA: 1. MORRELL [?]

A ? 5 1914 T30S R14W ?

Perhaps located in Section 26. Go 12 miles east of Langlois: it is on the H.E. Morrell Place on the East Fork of Floras Creek. Harriet aged 16, was the daughter of Frank and Fanny Eddy. NOTE: This site is on private property. A "Herb Morrill burial on Upper Floras Creek" may be in the same burial ground. Note the variant spelling. No other information was given in the report. (Not shown on Calf Ranch Mountain 1985 USGS Quad. map.)

EDGERTON FAMILY

A ? ? ? T35S R12W S12

Located in the vicinity of Agness. Go north from the boat landing on the Rogue River along the main road to Illahe for about 0.5 of a mile. Turn left (westerly) onto a road which skirts the north edge of the Agness

Name of Cemetery and also known as	Number of burials	Acres	Condition	Date started or earliest known burial	Township	Range	Section

Flight Strip, crossing Rilea Creek about 0.25 of a mile from the main road. Continue another 0.25 of a mile past Rilea Creek to the junction of Siskiyou Forest trail #1171 turn right, up hill. It is about 0.35 of a mile along this trail to the graves, which are about 40 yards to the left of the trail. (Agness 1989 USGS Quad. map.)

EDSON, HARRIET G.   A   0.01   5   11 Jun 1878   T36S R14W   S6

Located on Edson Creek Road (Old Coast Highway) across from the power station and 400 feet west of Edson Creek Road. There is one tombstone in an old orchard for Harriet G. Edson; born 2 December 1825, died 11 June 1878, wife of A. J. Edson. NOTE: This site is on private property. (Gold Beach 1986 USGS Quad. map.)

ELEPHANT ROCK   A   ?   5   ?   T32S R14W   S11

Located near Sixes River and Elephant Rock Creek. NOTE: No other information was given in the report. (Not shown on Mount Butler 1986 USGS Quad. map.)

FORT HILL   A   ?   5   1855   T32S R15W   S5

Reportedly two soldiers are buried near Port Orford. There may be some confusion here. The two blockhouses built at Fort Point, by Captain William Tichenor's second expedition in July 1851, was not the same as Fort Orford, established in November 1851 by the U.S. Army. Fort Orford was a few hundred feet northwest of the civilian Fort Orford on Fort Point. It seems more probable that soldiers would be buried near the Army's fort. The military Fort Orford was garrisoned until 1856. Both block houses were destroyed by fire on 10 October 1868. This is close to the Tichenor Cemetery. (Not shown on Port Orford 1986 USGS Quad. map.)

FOSTER BAR   A   ?   5   1856   T34S R11W   S18

Located on top of a knoll between Foster Creek and the road to Powers at Big Bend. 300 yards up the hill is the burial site of 6

| Name of Cemetery and also known as | Number of burials | Acres | Condition | Date started or earliest known burial | Township | Range | Section |

soldiers who died in the battle of Big Bend. NOTE: This is in the same section that the Illahe Cemetery AKA: Foster Creek Cemetery is in, but apparently they are 2 separate burial sites. (Not shown on Illahe 1989 USGS Quad. map.)

FOX HILL

A   0.2   5   1892-1917   T35S R14W   S8
This cemetery is at Ophir; on the west side of U.S. Hwy. 101 and north of the mouth of Euchre Creek on a hill. NOTE: This site is on private property and the stones are now gone. (Ophir 1986 USGS Quad. map.)

FRYE FAMILY
  AKA: 1. FRY

A   0.01   ?   ?   T33S R10W   ?
Located very close to the quarter corner between Sections 1 and 2. The cemetery is located on the C. J. Frye Homestead about 300 feet below the site of Fort Lamerick. Lewis McArthur's *Oregon Geographic Names* and *Metsker Landownership Atlas* spell the name Frye. Mrs. Wooldridge spells it Fry. (Not shown on Kelsey Peak 1989 USGS Quad. map.)

GEISEL FAMILY

A   0.1   1   22 Feb 1856   T36S R15W   S1
Located near U.S. Hwy. 101 in the Geisel State Wayside a mile south of Nesika Beach. John Geisel and three sons were killed by Indians. {September 1991} (Gold Beach 1986 USGS Quad. map.)

GIBBS FAMILY

A   ?   ?   1889   T31S R13W   ?
There are five known burials at Eckley, perhaps in Section 36. NOTE: No other information given in the report. (Not shown on Barklow Mtn. 1986 USGS Quad. map.)

HAINES

A   0.1   ?   1890   T31S R13W   S36
Located in the Eckley area: Haines Creek at South Sixes River, on the Dement Ranch (1986) where there are six known burials. NOTE: This site is on private property. No other information was given in the report. (Barklow Mtn. 1986 USGS Quad. map.)

Name of Cemetery and also known as	Number of burials	Acres	Condition	Date started or earliest known burial	Township	Range	Section

HALF MOON BAR

A   ?   5   1947   T33S R11W   S25
Located across from Paradise Bar, along the left bank of the Rogue River less than a mile downstream from Paradise Bar. (Not shown on Marial 1989 USGS Quad. map.)

HANZICKER, AL

A   0.1   ?   23 Jan 1933 T41S R11W   S9
A single grave is located at Packsaddle Mountain in the Siskiyou National Forest. One mile south of the Packsaddle trail on top of a ridge, it is reached by Trail #1114. Hanzicker was a 63-year old miner. (Fourth of July Creek 1989 USGS Quad. map.)

HAWKINS PLACE, ANGIE

A   ?   5   ?   T35S R13W   S33
Located immediately downstream on the south bank of the Rogue River from the mouth of Quosatana Creek. NOTE: This site is on private property. An Angie Hawkins, 20 November 1876-1 January 1960, is buried in the Rogue River Cemetery at Gold Beach according to Mrs. Wooldridge. (Not shown on Quosatana Butte 1989 USGS Quad. map.)

HIGGINS AND MAHONEY

A   ?   ?   1947-1951   T33S R10W   S9
Located across the Rogue River from Marial. NOTE: No other information was given in the report. (Not shown on Marial 1989 USGS Quad. map.)

HUCKLEBERRY KNOLL
  AKA: 1. HUCKLEBERRY
        KNOB

A   ?   5   1870   T32S R13W   S22
Located along the Upper South Fork of the Sixes River, along a trail following the right bank of the Upper South Fork of the Sixes River, between Bear Paw Flat and Russian Mike Creek. NOTE: No other information was given in the report. (Barklow Mtn. 1986 USGS Quad. map.)

HUCKTILL

A   0.01   5   ?   ?   ?   ?
One unmarked grave is located somewhere along Floras Creek. NOTE: No other information was given with the report.

Name of Cemetery and also known as	Number of burials	Acres	Condition	Date started or earliest known burial	Township	Range	Section

ILLAHE
AKA: 1. FOSTER CREEK

A 0.1 3 1895   T34S R11W   S18
Located on the Billings' Place (1978) on Foster Creek, about 1 mile north of Illahe and 500 feet north of Foster Creek, on the west side of Agness-Illahe Road. NOTE: This site is on private property. (Illahe 1989 USGS Quad. map.)

JACK CREEK

A ? 5 ?   T40S R13W   ?
Perhaps located in Section 2, south of the Chetco River. NOTE: No other information was given in the report. (Not shown on Mt. Emily 1989 USGS Quad. map.)

LOWERY

? ? ? 1902   T36S R13W   S1
There are seven known burials located on the north side of the Rogue River near Billy Southerlin's Place; on the Rogue River Trail below Agness. The cemetery appears to be about opposite the mouth of Bradford Creek. NOTE: This site is on private property. (Not shown on Quosatana Butte 1989 USGS Quad. map.)

LUCAS, MARCELLUS

A ? 5 1911   T35S R11W   S6
This burial is on the heights above Shasta Costa Riffle of the Rogue River and 1,000 feet north of the mouth of Shasta Costa Creek on the north side. Marcellus Lucas was age 40 and his grave is covered by a huge rock. (Agness 1989 USGS Quad. map.)

MACFARLAND
AKA: 1. QUOSATANA
CREEK

A ? 5 ?   T35S R13W   S34
There is a grave on the north bank of the Rogue River just downstream from Silver Creek and opposite Quosatana Creek. NOTE: No other information was given in the report. (Not shown on Soldier Camp Mtn. 1989 USGS Quad. map.)

MARIAL [OLD]

? ? ? 1900-1949   T33S R10W   S2
Located at the old site of Marial away from the Rogue River. NOTE: The present site of Marial is on the right bank of the Rogue

Name of Cemetery and also known as	Number of burials	Acres	Condition	Date started or earliest known burial	Township	Range	Section

River. This may be in the vicinity of the Frye Cemetery. No other information was given in the report. (Not shown on Kelsey Peak 1989 USGS Quad. map.)

McGLONE GRAVES

	A	?	?	?	T31S	R12W	S31

Old Jimmy and young Jimmy McGlone, bachelors, are buried across a creek and on the top of a ridge east of the Sam Dement House. NOTE: No further information was given in the report. (Not shown on Barklow Mountain 1986 USGS Quad. map.)

MERRIMAN
  AKA: 1. JERRYS FLAT
       2. MERRIAM
       3. MILLER

	?	0.1	?	1889-1902	T36S	R14W	S16

Leave U.S. Hwy. 101 at Gold Beach on Jerrys Flat Road and go for 3.7 miles. Then turn right onto a public roadway for 0.25 of a mile. Turn right again and go for another 0.3 of a mile, then turn left into a driveway and go 100 yards to the cemetery. The cemetery is on a ridge south of U.S. Plywood Mill at Jerrys Flat. (Signal Buttes 1986 USGS Quad. map.)

MESERVEY FAMILY

	A	?	?	?	T35S	R12W	S16

Located on the north bank of the Rogue River opposite the mouth of Nail Keg Creek and about 7 miles downstream from Agness. There are 7 known burials. (Not shown on Soldier Camp Mtn. 1989 USGS Quad. map.)

MORRILL RANCH, HERB

	A	?	5	?	?	?	?

Located on Upper Floras Creek, near an old windmill (1978). See entry for Eddy Cemetery this is possibly one and the same. NOTE: No other information was given in the report.

MULE CREEK

	A	0.1	3	Circa 1940	T33S	R10W	S16

Located in the Mule Creek Canyon of the Rogue River above the right bank and about 0.3 of a mile downstream from Marial, near the one-time Mule Creek Guard Station. It is about 50 yards inland from the road. (Marial 1989 USGS Quad. map.)

| Name of Cemetery and also known as | Number of burials | Acres | Condition | Date started or earliest known burial | Township | Range | Section |

MUNSEY, COLONEL

A   0.01   ?   ?   T37S R13W   ?

Perhaps located in Section 6. There is 1 grave in the Signal Buttes area east of Gold Beach, in the Siskyou National Forest near a mine. NOTE: No other information was given in the report. (Not shown on Signal Buttes 1986 USGS Quad. map.)

NAVY MONUMENT
AKA: 1. AIRMEN, 8

A   ?   4   30 Jan. 1945   **UNSURVEYED**

Although the area is unsurveyed, the U.S. Forest Service projects that the site would be in Township 39 South, Range 11 West, Section 33. The *Oregon Journal* reports in a later newspaper article on 31 January 1972: A Catalina Amphibious Patrol Bomber (PBY-5A) flying from Terminal Island, San Pedro, to Sand Point, Seattle, crashed about 3:00 P.M. and all 8 men were killed. The plane struck trees on a mountainside at about 2000 feet elevation. The bodies were buried about half way down in the canyon. An 8-foot concrete monument was erected in 1957." This is 36 miles east of Brookings and in the present Kalmiopsis Wilderness Area. Take Chetco River Road to Forest Service Road #1909 and then Spur Road #261 for another 1.3 miles at the South Fork of the Chetco and Quail Prairie Creek. Go up Quail Prairie Creek to the end of the road at Vulcan Lake/Vulcan Peak turnaround. Take Trail #1210 for 1.3 miles south on ridgetop. Then turn off onto Trail #1105 and then to the right again onto Trail #1105-A. The burials should be downhill to the right, in the canyon of the South Fork of the Chetco River, after a short but steep walk. NOTE: The site is marked on the Siskiyou National Forest map, 1984, about 1.5 miles downstream from Cottonwood Camp. Please check with the Forestry Service before visiting this site. (Not shown on Quail Prairie Mtn. 1989 USGS Quad. map.)

OAK FLATS
AKA: 1. INDIAN
     2. OAK GROVE

B   0.75   2   1893   T35S R11W   S20

Located 3.1 miles from Agness on Oak Flat Road, 200 yards south and east off of Oak Flat Road. (Agness 1989 USGS Quad. map.)

Name of Cemetery and also known as	Number of burials	Acres	Condition	Date started or earliest known burial	Township	Range	Section

OCEAN VIEW
AKA: 1. SMITH, NORMAN

A ? 3 13 Mar 1893 T30S R14W S21
Access is from U.S. Hwy 101, 3 miles north of Langlois and in Coos County. Leave U.S. Hwy. 101 at Milepost 284.6 onto Bethel Mountain Road. Go 3.4 miles to the Curry County Line, then another 0.5 of a mile to the graves on the right (west) side of the road. NOTE: This site is on private property. (Calf Ranch Mtn. 1985 USGS Quad. map.)

OLD BROOKINGS
AKA: 1. NO NAME
2. OLD CEMETERY

B 0.5 5 1915-1930 T41S R13W S5
Located in the city limits of Brookings, west off of Old County Road. (Brookings 1986 USGS Quad. map.)

PARADISE BAR

A 0.01 1 ? T33S R10W S18
A miners grave is located on the right bank of the Rogue River less than a mile upstream from Half Moon Bar. (Not shown on Marial 1989 USGS Quad. map.)

PAYNE FAMILY

A ? ? ? T39S R12W ?
Perhaps located in Section 9, which was owned by the Payne Family as shown in the 1932 *Metsker Land Ownership Atlas*. Drive 8 miles from Brookings on the North Bank Chetco River Road into Alfred Loeb State Park. Turn onto Siskiyou Forestry Road #1376 and perhaps Forestry Road #1909, although the section is not within the Siskiyou National Forest. The burials may be near the site of Upper Chetco School. (Not shown on Bosley Butte 1989 USGS Quad. map.)

PIONEER [GOLD BEACH]
AKA: 1. ROGUE

C 1.3 2 1859 T36S R15W S36
Located one block west of U.S. Hwy. 101 in Gold Beach. Take Hillcrest Street and at the right turn (north) is the cemetery with the Presbyterian Church adjoining on the north. Reportedly there are only two vacant plots remaining and they are reserved. {25 May 1996} (Gold Beach 1986 USGS Quad. map.)

Curry County

Name of Cemetery and also known as	Number of burials	Acres	Condition	Date started or earliest known burial	Township	Range	Section

PIONEER [HARBOR]
AKA: 1. BENHAM

C ? 4 Circa 1860 T40S R13W S9
Located in the community of Harbor, south of Brookings. Cross the Chetco River Bridge from Brookings on U.S. Hwy. 101 and drive 1.25 miles from the south end of the bridge to the Benham Street intersection. Turn left (east) onto East Benham Street and proceed about 0.15 of a mile to a point where the road begins to curve to the right. The cemetery is ahead beneath the water tower. There are perhaps as many as 100 graves, Indians as well as whites, but only one grave was visible; that of W. W. Hatfield, 1883-1912. (Mt. Emily 1989 USGS Quad. map.)

PISTOL RIVER

B 0.9 2 1897 T38S R14W S18
Located 1.6 miles north of the Pistol River Store and 0.3 of a mile from Pistol River Junction on U.S. Hwy. 101. Turn into narrow lane through a gate, and go another 0.2 of a mile. (Cape Sebastian 1986 USGS Quad. map.)

PLUM TREE
AKA: 1. PLUM TREES

A ? 5 ? T32S R14W S3
Located on the Hale Place, which is on the Sixes River. NOTE: This site is on private property. No other information was given in the report. (Not shown on Mount Butler 1986 USGS Quad. map.)

PORT ORFORD
AKA: 1. MASONIC
     2. PIONEER

D 5 1 1854 T32S R15W S4
Located southeast of Port Orford on the old highway that turns inland from the present U.S. Hwy. 101. Take the old highway now called Cemetery Loop at the south end of town. The cemetery is on the left (north) after about 0.5 of a mile from U.S. Hwy. 101. The cemetery was deeded in March of 1912. {September 1991} (Port Orford 1986 USGS Quad. map.)

PUGH'S PLACE, DICK

A ? 5 ? T35S R13W S34
There is or was a grave just upstream from the mouth of Quosatana Creek, on the south bank of the Rogue River opposite the mouth of Silver Creek. The Quosatana Campground is

Name of Cemetery and also known as	Number of burials	Acres	Condition	Date started or earliest known burial	Township	Range	Section

now on the site. (The campground is shown but no grave on the Quosatana Butte 1989 USGS Quad. map.)

QUILHAUGH, MAUD A 0.01 ? ? T33S R9W ?
Perhaps in Section 6 or 7, the grave is located in the Rogue River Wilderness Area near Bald Ridge. (Not shown on Kelsey Peak 1989 USGS Quad. map.)

RALPH AND CLARNO BABIES
AKA: 1. CLARNO AND RALPH BABIES
A 0.01 2 ? T39S R14W S2
Located on the Ray Passley Place at Carpenterville, located 0.4 of a mile north of Carpenterville State Frontage Road (Old U.S. 101). It is thought that "Ralph" may refer to Ralph Passley. NOTE: No other information was given in the report. This site is located on private property. (Carpenterville 1986 USGS Quad. map.)

RAT HOLE A ? 5 ? T35S R11W S5
Located up Shasta Costa Creek 1 mile, on the Frye Homestead. NOTE: No other information was given in the report. (Not shown on Agness 1989 USGS Quad. map.)

RILEA FAMILY A 0.2 ? ? T35S R12W S12
Located in the area of Agness. From the boat landing on the Rogue River, take the road north towards Illahe. About 0.4 of a mile from the landing turn left (west) on the road to the school, cross the Agness Flight Strip. At 0.1 of a mile from the main road turn right (northerly) towards the hangar and go another 0.2 of a mile, where you will cross Rilea Creek. Go another 0.25 of a mile past Rilea Creek to the junction with a trail to the right, up hill. The cemetery is about 0.1 of a mile up the trail and on the right. (Agness 1989 USGS Quad. map.)

ROGUE RIVER
AKA: 1. GOLD BEACH
D 4 1 1932 T37S R15W S12
This is the present principle cemetery for the town of Gold Beach and it is located a short distance south of town. Leave U.S.

Curry County

Name of Cemetery and also known as	Number of burials	Acres	Condition	Date started or earliest known burial	Township	Range	Section

Hwy. 101 at Milepost 330.3 and turn inland on Hunter Creek Loop. The cemetery access road is only 0.1 of a mile east of U.S. Hwy. 101 and leads up a hill to the left (north). The owner told the compiler that this cemetery is already mostly reserved and he plans to start a new cemetery at Nesika Beach north of Gold Beach. {25 May 1996} (Gold Beach 1986 USGS Quad. map.)

RUMLEY HILL
AKA: 1. BAGNELL
      FERRY

B   0.25   2   ?   T36S R14W   S9
Leave U.S. Hwy. 101 at Wedderburn; go 5 miles on North Bank Rogue River Road. Turn left onto Squaw Valley Road for 0.9 of a mile, then turn left uphill for 0.3 of a mile to the cemetery. It overlooks the Rogue River. There are 20 graves. NOTE: This site appears to be on private property. (Signal Buttes 1986 USGS Quad. map.)

SIXES

A   ?   5   1870   T32S R14W   S7
Located on Dry Creek, where a slide buried alive some Chinese miners. This was probably on the east bank of Dry Creek at its confluence with the Sixes River. A mining company still owned land there, in 1932, on the south bank of the Sixes River. The Sixes River Road runs along the north bank. (Not shown on Sixes 1986 USGS Quad. map.)

SKOOKUMHOUSE

A   0.01   ?   ?   T36S R13W   ?
There are 2 burials on the John Ingleman Place, along the Rogue River, but it is unclear to the compiler on which side. NOTE: This is on private property. No other information was given in the report. (Not shown on Quosatana Butte 1989 USGS Quad. map.)

SMITH FAMILY

A   ?   5   1900   T35S R12W   S13
Located in the vicinity of Agness on the south side of the Rogue River. Leave the west end of the bridge over the Illinois River opposite Agness and go about 0.35 of a mile west to cross Tom Fry Creek. Continue on this Siskiyou Forest Road #33 another 0.2

Name of Cemetery and also known as	Number of burials	Acres	Condition	Date started or earliest known burial	Township	Range	Section

of a mile and turn off to the right on a side road towards the river. Go about 0.25 of a mile and the graves are about 40 yards to the left. (Agness 1989 USGS Quad. map.)

SMITH FAMILY

A 0.15 2 1821-1959 T37S R14W S7

Located south of Gold Beach on the old highway on the east side of Hunter Creek Loop, at a trailer park. There are 14 names on 1 stone. It is believed that 1821 is too early of a death date. {September 1991} (Gold Beach 1986 USGS Quad. map.)

SMITH, SERGEANT

A 0.01 5 ? T41S R13W S7

Sergeant Smith was a soldier; his grave is located at Brady Park in Brookings, at the seaward end of Tanbark Road. On the Augustus F. Miller D.L.C. #37, RB #1932. (Not shown on Brookings 1986 USGS Quad. map.)

SNYDER'S LODGE

? 0.01 ? ? ? ? ?

Located in a meadow near a turnout from the Powers-Illahe Road is the burial of a Mrs. White, mother of Rolly White. NOTE: No other information was given in the report.

THOMPSON FLAT
  AKA: 1. TOMPKINS
       FLAT

A ? 5 ? T32S R13W S22

Located on the Upper South Fork of the Sixes River, about 0.5 of a mile or 0.75 of a mile upstream from Huckleberry Knoll. (Barklow Mtn. 1986 USGS Quad. map.)

THRIFT RANCH

A ? 3 1855 T32S R15W ?

This is in Section 19 or 20, south of Elk River and west of U.S. Hwy. 101; now owned by L. Knapp, Langlois, Oregon (1978). NOTE: This site is on private property. (Not shown on Cape Blanco 1986 USGS Quad. maps.)

TICHENOR

B 0.5 5 1880 T33S R15W S5

This private cemetery is located on top of a hill in the western part of Port Orford. Take 9th Street west off of U.S. Hwy. 101 for two blocks. Then turn left (southerly) onto

| Name of Cemetery and also known as | Number of burials | Acres | Condition | Date started or earliest known burial | Township | Range | Section |

Coast Guard Road. Turn right (north) after about another 0.25 of a mile to the cemetery at the top of the hill. There is a fenced lot and a curbed lot plus some scattered markers. In October 1962 researchers tallied 24 known burials. The compiler found 3 more recent markers and more may have been hidden in the tall grass. {26 May 1996} (Port Orford 1986 USGS Quad. map.)

TRUAX BABY

A 0.01 ? ? T30S R14W S23

This is an unmarked grave, 0.25 of a mile off of Langlois Mountain Road at the Truax Place in the Floras Creek district. NOTE: This is on private property. No other information was given in the report. (Not shown on Calf Ranch Mountain 1985 USGS Quad. map.)

UNKNOWN

A ? ? ? T39S R14W S9

Located in Boardman State Park at the mouth of Hooskanaden Creek, on U.S. Hwy. 101. (Not shown on Carpenterville 1986 USGS Quad. map.)

UNKNOWN

A 0.01 5 1855 T39S R14W S28

This burial is near Thomas Creek Bridge on U.S. Hwy. 101, in Boardman State Park. (Not shown on Carpenterville 1986 USGS Quad. map.)

VAN PELT

A 0.1 5 1895 T41S R13W S4

Leave Brookings, heading south on U.S. Hwy. 101. Cross the Chetco River Bridge into the community of Harbor. Drive 0.7 of a mile from the south end of the bridge to the Hoffeldt Lane intersection. Turn left (east) onto East Hoffeldt Lane, driving 0.25 of a mile to the end of the county maintenance; continue ahead on a one-lane driveway for another 0.15 of a mile to the end. The cemetery is at the end and just above the north bank of Tuttle Creek. On Hiram Tuttle D.L.C. #38, RB #2070. NOTE: this site is on private property. (Mt. Emily 1989 USGS Quad. map.)

Name of Cemetery and also known as	Number of burials	Acres	Condition	Date started or earliest known burial	Township	Range	Section

WARD MEMORIAL

C 15   1   1936   T40S R13W   S31
Located west off of 7th Street along the north city limits of Brookings. This is the principle cemetery for the city. (Brookings 1986 USGS Quad. map.)

WELLS, GRANDMA

A 0.01   ?   ?   T31S R13W   ?
Perhaps located in Section 36. Grandma Wells died sometime between 1900 and 1905 and is buried at Eckley. (Not shown on Barklow Mtn. 1986 USGS Quad. map.)

WEST, WILLIAM ROBERT

A 0.01 5   14 Nov 1923 T30S R14W   ?
Located about 12 miles east of Langlois. The West grave is unmarked; on the West Place on the North Fork of Floras Creek. NOTE: This site is on private property. (Not shown on Calf Ranch Mtn. 1985 USGS Quad. map.)

WHEELER CREEK

A ?   5   ?   T41S R12W   S3
Located near the Winchuck River: at Ludlum House Campground on Wheeler Creek Road (Forestry Road #1108) in the Siskiyou National Forest. (Not shown on Fourth of July Creek 1989 USGS Quad. map.)

WHEELER, JAMES P.

A 0.01 2   1903   T41S R12W   S10
Cross the Chetco River Bridge from Brookings to Harbor and drive south 3.1 miles on U.S. Hwy. 101. Turn left (east) onto Winchuck River Road and drive to the end of the paving at Elk Creek. Continue about 0.6 of a mile and about 50 yards past the junction of Elk Mountain Trail; the grave is on the right (south). You are about 7.5 miles from U.S. Hwy. 101 and a mile short of Winchuck Forest Camp. {September 1991} (Fourth of July Creek 1989 USGS Quad. map.)

WILSON RANCH, BEVERLY

A ?   ?   30 Jul 1865 T14S R13W   ?
This ranch is south of Brookings between the Chetco and Winchuck Rivers and facing the ocean. The overloaded steamship "Brother Jonathan" out of San Fransisco was caught in a storm on 30 July 1865. The captain tried

Name of Cemetery and also known as	Number of burials	Acres	Condition	Date started or earliest known burial	Township	Range	Section

to turn back to Crescent City but 8 miles northwest of that port the ship struck a rock and sank in high seas. 19 survivors in one boat made it to shore approximately 200 perished. Six or eight bodies washed ashore in Curry County and are buried on what is now (1980) the Beverly Wilson Ranch. The cemetery at Crescent City in Del Norte County, California is known as the Brother Jonathan Cemetery. (Not shown on Mt. Emily 1989 USGS Quad. map.)

WINKLE BAR
A   0.01 5   1908   T33S R9W   S18
On the north side of the Rogue River there is a miners grave. (Not shown on Kelsey peak 1989 USGS Quad. map.)

WOODRUFF, LYMAN
A   ?   5   24 Dec 1886 T35S R14W   S31
Located 0.5 of a mile north of Nesika Beach Junction between U.S. Hwy. 101 and Frontage Road. Lyman Woodruff was 60 years old.
NOTE: No other information was given in the report. (Not shown on Ophir 1986 USGS Quad. maps.)

Denmark
Dean H. Byrd (1996)

236

AIRMEN, 8 see **NAVY MONUMENT**	CURRY CO.	UNSURVEYED		
ARMPRIEST FAMILY	CURRY CO.	T36S	R12W	UNS
BAGNELL FERRY see **RUMLEY HILL**	CURRY CO.	T36S	R14W	S9
BALD RIDGE	CURRY CO.	T33S	R9W	S8
BARLOW, JIM	CURRY CO.	T33S	R10W	?
BATTLE ROCK	CURRY CO.	T33S	R15W	S4
BENHAM see **PIONEER [HARBOR]**	CURRY CO.	T40S	R13W	S9
BIG MEADOWS	CURRY CO.	T32S	R10W	S36
BILLINGS	CURRY CO	T34S	R11W	S7
BILLINGS see **BIG MEADOWS**	CURRY CO.	T32S	R10W	S36
BILLINGS FAMILY see **BILLINGS**	CURRY CO	T34S	R11W	S7
BILLINGS' PLACE see **ILLAHE**	CURRY CO.	T34S	R11W	S18
CAPE BLANCO CATHOLIC see **CAPE BLANCO PIONEER**				
	CURRY CO.	T31S	R16W	S36
CAPE BLANCO PIONEER	CURRY CO.	T31S	R16W	S36
CARPENTER	CURRY CO.	T39S	R14W	?
CLARNO AND RALPH BABIES see **RALPH AND CLARNO BABIES**				
	CURRY CO.	T39S	R14W	S2
CLARNO SPRINGS	CURRY CO.	T36S	R14W	S9
CLAY HILL	CURRY CO.	T34S	R11W	S2
COLVIN GRAVE	CURRY CO.	T37S	R14W	?
COOLEY FAMILY	CURRY CO.	T41S	R13W	S9
COOPER MD, ARTHUR	CURRY CO.	T40S	R14W	S10
COOPER'S, DOCTOR see **COOPER MD, ARTHUR**				
	CURRY CO.	T40S	R14W	S10
COSTELLOE, EDMOND	CURRY CO.	T41S	R12W	S5
CREW FAMILY	CURRY CO.	T32S	R15W	S9
CREW, MR. see **CREW FAMILY**	CURRY CO.	T32S	R15W	S9
CREW, MRS. see **CREW FAMILY**	CURRY CO.	T32S	R15W	S9
CRISTESER FAMILY see **BALD RIDGE**	CURRY CO.	T33S	R9W	S8
CRITESER, MAY see **BALD RIDGE**	CURRY CO.	T33S	R9W	S8
DAVIS'S PLACE, JIMMY	CURRY CO.	?	?	?
DEMENT HOUSE, SAM see **McGLONE GRAVES**				
	CURRY CO.	T31S	R12W	S31
DEMENT RANCH see **HAINES**	CURRY CO.	T31S	R13W	S36
DENMARK	CURRY CO.	T31S	R15W	S10
EDDY, FANNY see **EDDY, HARRIET**	CURRY CO.	T30S	R14W	?
EDDY, FRANK see **EDDY, HARRIET**	CURRY CO.	T30S	R14W	?
EDDY, HARRIET	CURRY CO.	T30S	R14W	?
EDGERTON FAMILY	CURRY CO.	T35S	R12W	S12
EDSON, A. J. see **EDSON, HARRIET G.**				
	CURRY CO.	T36S	R14W	S6
EDSON, HARRIET G.	CURRY CO.	T36S	R14W	S6
ELEPHANT ROCK	CURRY CO.	T32S	R14W	S11
FLORAS CREEK see **DENMARK**	CURRY CO.	T31S	R15W	S10
FORT HILL	CURRY CO.	T32S	R15W	S5
FOSTER BAR	CURRY CO.	T34S	R11W	S18
FOSTER CREEK see **ILLAHE**	CURRY CO.	T34S	R11W	S18
FOX HILL	CURRY CO.	T35S	R14W	S8
FRY see **FRYE FAMILY**	CURRY CO.	T33S	R10W	?
FRY FAMILY see **BILLINGS**	CURRY CO	T34S	R11W	S7
FRYE FAMILY	CURRY CO.	T33S	R10W	?

Curry County

FRYE HOMESTEAD see **RAT HOLE**   CURRY CO.   T35S   R11W   S5

FRYE HOMESTEAD, C. J. see **FRYE FAMILY**

    CURRY CO.   T33S   R10W   ?

GEISEL FAMILY   CURRY CO.   T36S   R15W   S1

GEISEL, JOHN see **GEISEL FAMILY**   CURRY CO.   T36S   R15W   S1

GIBBS FAMILY   CURRY CO.   T31S   R13W   ?

GOLD BEACH see **ROGUE RIVER**   CURRY CO.   T37S   R15W   S12

HAINES   CURRY CO.   T31S   R13W   S36

HALE PLACE see **PLUM TREE**   CURRY CO.   T32S   R14W   S3

HALF MOON BAR   CURRY CO.   T33S   R11W   S25

HANZICKER, AL   CURRY CO.   T41S   R11W   S9

HATFIELD, W. W. see **PIONEER [HARBOR]**

    CURRY CO.   T40S   R13W   S9

HAWKINS, ANGIE see **HAWKINS PLACE, ANGIE**

    CURRY CO.   T35S   R13W   S33

HAWKINS PLACE, ANGIE   CURRY CO.   T35S   R13W   S33

HIGGINS AND MAHONEY   CURRY CO.   T33S   R10W   S9

HUCKLEBERRY KNOB see **HUCKLEBERRY KNOLL**

    CURRY CO.   T32S   R13W   S22

HUCKLEBERRY KNOLL   CURRY CO.   T32S   R13W   S22

HUCKTILL   CURRY CO.   ?   ?   ?

HUGHES FAMILY see **CAPE BLANCO PIONEER**

    CURRY CO.   T31S   R16W   S36

ILLAHE   CURRY CO.   T34S   R11W   S18

INDIAN see **OAK FLATS**   CURRY CO.   T35S   R11W   S20

INGLEMAN PLACE, JOHN see **SKOOKUMHOUSE**

    CURRY CO.   T36S   R13W   ?

JACK CREEK   CURRY CO.   T40S   R13W   ?

JERRYS FLAT see **MERRIMAN**   CURRY CO.   T36S   R14W   S16

KNAPP, L. see **THRIFT RANCH**   CURRY CO.   T32S   R15W   ?

LANGLOIS see **DENMARK**   CURRY CO.   T31S   R15W   S10

LEITH PLACE see **COLVIN GRAVE**   CURRY CO.   T37S   R14W   ?

LOEB STATE PARK, ALFRED see **PAYNE FAMILY**

    CURRY CO.   T39S   R12W   ?

LOWERY   CURRY CO.   T36S   R13W`   S1

LUCAS, MARCELLUS   CURRY CO.   T35S   R11W   S6

MACFARLAND   CURRY CO.   T35S   R13W   S34

MARIAL [OLD]   CURRY CO.   T33S   R10W   S2

MASONIC see **PORT ORFORD**   CURRY CO.   T32S   R15W   S4

McGLONE GRAVES   CURRY CO.   T31S   R12W   S31

McGLONE, OLD JIMMY see **McGLONE GRAVES**

    CURRY CO.   T31S   R12W   S31

McGLONE, YOUNG JIMMY see **McGLONE GRAVES**

    CURRY CO.   T31S   R12W   S31

MERRIAM see **MERRIMAN**   CURRY CO.   T36S   R14W   S16

MERRIMAN   CURRY CO.   T36S   R14W   S16

MESERVEY FAMILY   CURRY CO.   T35S   R12W   S16

MILLER see **MERRIMAN**   CURRY CO.   T36S   R14W   S16

MILLER D.L.C., AUGUSTUS F. see **SMITH, SERGEANT**

    CURRY CO.   T41S   R13W   S7

MILLER'S PLACE, WALTON see **DAVIS'S PLACE, JIMMY**

    CURRY CO.   ?   ?   ?

MORRELL [?] see **EDDY, HARRIET**	CURRY CO.	T30S	R14W	?
MORRELL PLACE, H. E. see **EDDY, HARRIET**				
	CURRY CO.	T30S	R14W	?
MORRILL, HERB see **EDDY, HARRIET**	CURRY CO.	T30S	R14W	?
MORRILL RANCH, HERB	CURRY CO.	?	?	?
MULE CREEK	CURRY CO.	T33S	R10W	S16
MUNSEY, COLONEL	CURRY CO.	T37S	R13W	?
NAVY MONUMENT	CURRY CO.	UNSURVEYED		
NO NAME see **OLD BROOKINGS**	CURRY CO.	T41S	R13W	S5
OAK FLATS	CURRY CO.	T35S	R11W	S20
OAK GROVE see **OAK FLATS**	CURRY CO.	T35S	R11W	S20
OCEAN VIEW	CURRY CO.	T30S	R14W	S21
OLD BROOKINGS	CURRY CO.	T41S	R13W	S5
OLD CEMETERY see **OLD BROOKINGS**	CURRY CO.	T41S	R13W	S5
PARADISE BAR	CURRY CO.	T33S	R10W	S18
PASSLEY, RALPH see **RALPH AND CLARNO BABIES**				
	CURRY CO.	T39S	R14W	S2
PAYNE FAMILY	CURRY CO.	T39S	R12W	?
PIONEER see **PORT ORFORD**	CURRY CO.	T32S	R15W	S4
PIONEER [GOLD BEACH]	CURRY CO.	T36S	R15W	S36
PIONEER [HARBOR]	CURRY CO.	T40S	R13W	S9
PISTOL RIVER	CURRY CO.	T38S	R14W	S18
PLUM TREE	CURRY CO.	T32S	R14W	S3
PLUM TREES see **PLUM TREE**	CURRY CO.	T32S	R14W	S3
PORT ORFORD	CURRY CO.	T32S	R15W	S4
PUGH'S PLACE, DICK	CURRY CO.	T35S	R13W	S34
QUILHAUGH, MAUD	CURRY CO.	T33S	R9W	?
QUOSATANA CREEK see **MACFARLAND**	CURRY CO.	T35S	R13W	S34
RALPH AND CLARNO BABIES	CURRY CO.	T39S	R14W	S2
RAT HOLE	CURRY CO.	T35S	R11W	S5
RILEA FAMILY	CURRY CO.	T35S	R12W	S12
ROGUE see **PIONEER [GOLD BEACH]**	CURRY CO.	T36S	R15W	S36
ROGUE RIVER	CURRY CO.	T37S	R15W	S12
RUMLEY HILL	CURRY CO.	T36S	R14W	S9
SHARP D.L.C., THOMAS see **COOLEY FAMILY**				
	CURRY CO.	T41S	R13W	S9
SIXES	CURRY CO.	T32S	R14W	S7
SKOOKUMHOUSE	CURRY CO.	T36S	R13W	?
SMITH FAMILY	CURRY CO.	T35S	R12W	S13
SMITH FAMILY	CURRY CO.	T37S	R14W	S7
SMITH, NORMAN see **OCEAN VIEW**	CURRY CO.	T30S	R14W	S21
SMITH, SERGEANT	CURRY CO.	T41S	R13W	S7
SNODGRASS FAMILY see **CARPENTER**	CURRY CO.	T39S	R14W	?
SNODGRASS FARM see **CARPENTER**	CURRY CO.	T39S	R14W	?
SNYDER'S LODGE	CURRY CO.	?	?	?
SOUTHERLIN'S PLACE, BILLY see **LOWERY**				
	CURRY CO.	T36S	R13W`	S1
SUMMERS FAMILY see **BATTLE ROCK**	CURRY CO.	T33S	R15W	S4
SUMMERS, RALPH see **BATTLE ROCK**	CURRY CO.	T33S	R15W	S4
SWEET RANCH, PIERCY see **CREW FAMILY**				
	CURRY CO.	T32S	R15W	S9
THOMAS, ETHEL see **CLAY HILL**	CURRY CO.	T34S	R11W	S2

THOMPSON FLAT	CURRY CO.	T32S	R13W	S22
THRIFT RANCH	CURRY CO.	T32S	R15W	?
TICHENOR	CURRY CO.	T33S	R15W	S5
TICHENOR, CAPTAIN WILLIAM see **FORT HILL**				
	CURRY CO.	T32S	R15W	S5
TOMPKINS FLAT see **THOMPSON FLAT**	CURRY CO.	T32S	R13W	S22
TRUAX BABY	CURRY CO.	T30S	R14W	S23
TRUAX PLACE see **TRUAX BABY**	CURRY CO.	T30S	R14W	S23
TUTTLE D.L.C., HIRAM see **VAN PELT**				
	CURRY CO.	T41S	R13W	S4
UNKNOWN	CURRY CO.	T39S	R14W	S9
UNKNOWN	CURRY CO.	T39S	R14W	S28
VAN PELT	CURRY CO.	T41S	R13W	S4
WARD MEMORIAL	CURRY CO.	T40S	R13W	S31
WELLS, GRANDMA	CURRY CO.	T31S	R13W	?
WEST PLACE see **WEST, WILLIAM ROBERT**				
	CURRY CO.	T30S	R14W	?
WEST, WILLIAM ROBERT	CURRY CO.	T30S	R14W	?
WHEELER CREEK	CURRY CO.	T41S	R12W	S3
WHEELER, JAMES P.	CURRY CO.	T41S	R12W	S10
WHITE, MRS. see **SNYDER'S LODGE**	CURRY CO.	?	?	?
WHITE, ROLLY see **SNYDER'S LODGE**	CURRY CO.	?	?	?
WILLOW CREEK see **DENMARK**	CURRY CO.	T31S	R15W	S10
WILSON RANCH, BEVERLY	CURRY CO.	T14S	R13W	?
WINKLE BAR	CURRY CO.	T33S	R9W	S18
WOODRUFF, LYMAN	CURRY CO.	T35S	R14W	S31

Rogue River
Dean H. Byrd (1996)

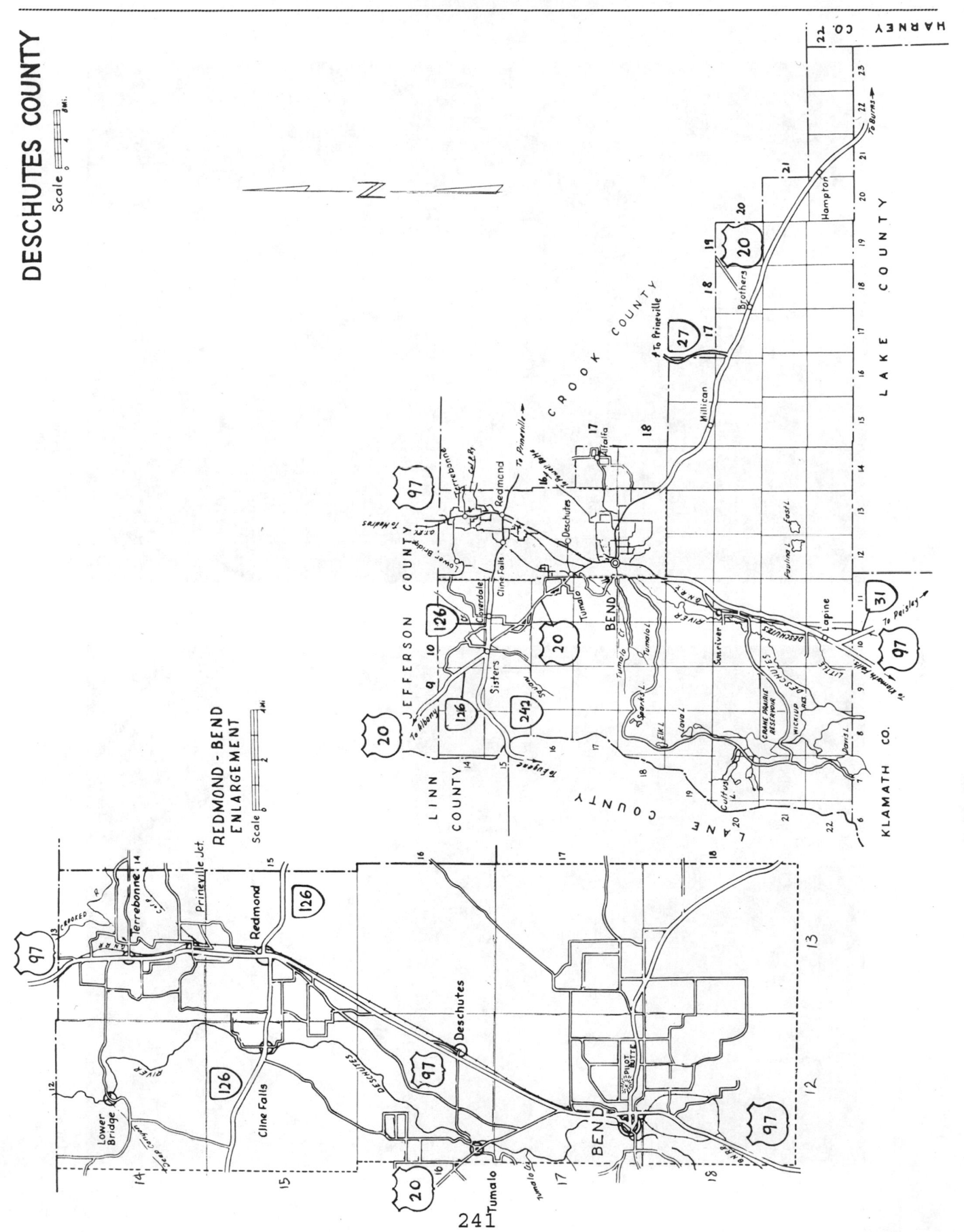

DESCHUTES COUNTY

Scale

REDMOND - BEND
ENLARGEMENT
Scale

Deschutes County

Greenwood Memorial
Janice M. Healy (2000)

Greenwood Memorial
Janice M. Healy (2000)

Area: 3,055 square miles
Population (1998): 105,640
County seat: Bend, Population: 32,220
County established: 13 December 1916

Deschutes County was detached from Crook County when it was given over to lumbering, ranching and irrigated farming. In the past 30 years the county has been transformed by resort and retirement communities. The earliest organized public cemetery was at Camp Polk near Sisters. By 1906 there were six additional public cemeteries.

Camp Polk
Janice M. Healy (2000)

Deschutes County

Pilot Butte
Janice M. Healy (2000)

Pilot Butte
Janice M. Healy (2000)

Name of Cemetery or also known as	Number of burials	Acres	Condition	Date started or earliest know burial	Township	Range	Section

ALLEN RANCH
AKA: 1. HARPER

| A | 0.25 | 3 | 1880 | T20S R11E | S8 |

Located south of the Harper Bridge, west of the closed Harper Airstrip and west of the old Bend-La Pine Road, now called Huntington Road. Homesteaded in 1871, the first burials were in 1880. The La Pine Genealogical Society reports 5 known burials up to 1942, not all of which are marked. NOTE: This site is on private property. It is now reported to be surrounded by a golf course (1999). (Anns Butte 1963-81 USGS Quad. map.)

BREESE
AKA: 1. OLD REASE
2. REASE

| A | 0.1 | 3 | 1910 | T21S R11E | S29 |

About 22 miles south of Bend on U.S. Hwy. 97 is the junction left (southeast) of the road to Newberry Crater, Paulina and East Lakes. Take this road for about 1.3 miles; then turn right (south) onto a paved road and go about 0.5 of a mile to the north edge of Paulina Prairie. There, turn left (east) onto private property for about 0.5 of a mile to the cemetery. It is on a small hill bordered by a pine forest and just above Paulina Prairie. There are 5 known burials of the period 1910-1918. The cemetery donor, Guy Rease, has an unmarked grave here. A descendant says the name should be spelled Breese. (Finley Butte 1963-81 USGS Quad. map.)

CAMP POLK
AKA: 1. HINDMAN
2. OLD FORT
3. SISTERS

| C | 2 | 2 | 1875 | T14S R10E | S27 |

Located 6.7 miles northeast of Sisters on Locust which changes to Camp Polk Road. At the "Y" intersection Camp Polk Road makes a sharp right turn, continue to Cemetery Road to the left, go to the end which is 0.3 of a mile and you are at the cemetery gate. The cemetery is on the Camp Polk parade ground. [Camp Polk, Sept. 1865 through Spring 1866, with a post office and store in 1875.] There are over 205 burials (2000). {30 September 2000} (Sisters 1959 USGS Quad. map. NOT shown on Sisters 1988 USGS Quad. map.)

CULTUS MOUNTAIN

| A | ? | ? | ? | UNSURVEYED |

Located in projected Township 20 South, Range 7 East, Section 23 in the unsurveyed lands within the Deschutes National Forest. Cultus Mountain is an old volcano between Cultus and Little Cultus Lakes, Northwest of Crane Prairie Reservoir and west off of the Cascade Lakes Highway. Persistent stories report that 19 Indians were buried at the summit of the mountain. A visitor in 1906 reported the sites and this visitor repeated his report as late as January 1955 for the *Deschutes Pioneer Gazette* (Reprinted in *Deschutes County Yester-Year*, No. 2 Fall 1986; Deschutes County Historical Society, Bend Oregon). The mountain top is 2,100 feet in elevation above Cultus Lake and it is difficult to understand how 19 bodies would be transported up the steep slopes. Were horses available? Be that as it may the compiler has found that the story persists, but with no confirmation. (Not shown on Crane Prairie Reservoir 1963-81 USGS Quad. map.)

DESCHUTES MEMORIAL GARDENS   D 40   1   1954   **T17S R12E**   S9
Located along US. Hwy. 97 north of Bend. This is 3.8 miles north of the intersection of Northeast 3rd Street (U.S. Hwy. 97) and Northeast Greenwood Avenue (U.S. Hwy. 20). (Bend 1962-81 USGS Quad. map.)

GREENWOOD MEMORIAL   E 10   1   1924   **T17S R12E**   S33
Located in Bend. From Northeast Greenwood Avenue (U.S. Hwy. 20) turn south to Pilot Butte Road and Forbes Road junction. The cemetery is on Forbes Road. Greenwood Cemetery adjoins Pilot Butte Cemetery. (Bend 1962-81 USGS Quad. map.)

LA PINE COMMUNITY
AKA: 1. IMPROVED ORDER OF REDMEN
2. REDMEN-LA PINE
C 40   2   Circa 1900   **T22S R11E**   S7
This occupies the Southwest 1/4 of the Southeast 1/4 of Section 7. Only a small portion of this acreage is occupied by burials. It is located 2.2 miles east from U.S. Hwy. 97 at the north edge of La Pine. There were a few burials, most of them unmarked until 1938. From 1938 to 1979 the cemetery was bypassed in favor of burials in cemeteries at Bend. Since the Redmen

Name of Cemetery or also known as	Number of burials	Acres	Condition	Date started or earliest know burial	Township	Range	Section

fraternal organization had become inactive, the American Legion Auxiliary took over in 1979 and burials have been resumed. NOTE: The community name was usually spelled Lapine from 1910 to 1951, and La Pine since 1951. (Finley Butte 1963-81 USGS Quad. map.)

MASTEN
AKA: 1. MASTER   [Sic]

A ?   2   1901   T22S R9E   S25
Drive about 2 miles south of La Pine immediately past the junction of OR. Hwy. 31 with U.S. Hwy. 97. Leave U.S. Hwy. 97 to the right (west) on Masten Road; drive about 2.75 miles to the intersection of the old stage road to Crescent and turn left (south) on this paved road. When the pavement ends, continue straight ahead past the site of the Masten School on the right (west). About 0.5 of a mile past this school site is the "Masten Homestead, Mill, School site, and Cemetery" Turn right (west) onto private property. The cemetery is on a bluff overlooking the Little Deschutes River. There are 14 known burials, with 1948 being the most recent. (Not shown on La Pine 1963-81 USGS Quad. map.)

MELLIN FAMILY

? ?   ?   11 Sep 1976 T19S R15E   ?
Mrs. Mellin and a daughter were buried near Millican. When another child died in California Mr. Mellin decided to move the whole family to the Pilot Butte Cemetery in Bend. (Not shown on Millican 1967 USGS Quad. map.)

MILLICAN

A 0.01 3   1910   T19S R15E   S34
There are 2 graves; at Millican. (Not shown on Millican 1967 or Pine Mountain 1967-81 USGS Quad. maps.)

PILOT BUTTE

E 10   1   1906   T17S R12E   S33
Located on Pilot Butte in Bend. Take Northeast Greenwood Street (U.S. Hwy. 20) to 10th Street, then turn right (south) on 10th Street. Pilot Butte Cemetery adjoins Greenwood Cemetery. (Bend 1962-81 USGS Quad. map.)

Deschutes County

Name of Cemetery or also known as	Number of burials	Acres	Condition	Date started or earliest know burial	Township	Range	Section

PIONEER [TERREBONNE]
AKA: 1. I.O.O.F.
　　　 [TERREBONNE]
　　2. TERREBONNE

C　3　1　Circa 1900　T14S R13E　S22
Leave U.S. Hwy. 97 at Terrebonne, then go 1.5 miles east on Smith Rock Road to the cemetery. (Redmond 1962-75 USGS Quad. map.)

QUINN, BILLY

A　0.01　3　1894　T21S R7E　S1
A lone grave, located on the banks of the Quinn River on the west side of Crane Prairie Reservoir, at Quinn River Campground. Billy Quinn, aged 25, was accidentally shot. His parents are buried in Grizzly Cemetery in Jefferson County. (Crane Prairie Reservoir 1963-81 USGS Quad. map.)

REDMOND MEMORIAL
AKA: 1. REDMOND

D　20　1　Circa 1900　T15S R13E　S29
Located 1.5 miles south of Redmond on Old Bend-Redmond Highway; city owned. (Forked Horn Butte 1962 USGS Quad. map.)

TUMALO
AKA: 1. I.O.O.F.
　　2. LAIDLAW
　　3. LAIDLAW
　　　 ODD FELLOWS

C　5　2　Circa 1900　T16S R12E　S29
The cemetery is located on the right side of Cline Falls Highway, 1.8 miles north of the Tumalo Community Church. (Tumalo 1962-75 USGS Quad. map.)

VANDEVERT, GRACE CLARK
AKA: 1. VANDEVERT,
　　　 KATHERINE
　　　 GRACE

A　0.01　?　3 Nov. 1918　T20S R11E　S20
This lone grave is located across a pasture due south of the Vandevert house, 0.2 of a mile west of the junction of Vandervert Road with Century Drive. She died in the epidemic of Spanish flu. NOTE: This burial is on private property. (Not shown on Anns Butte 1963-81 USGS Quad. map.)

ALLEN RANCH	DESCHUTES CO.	T20S	R11E	S8
BREESE	DESCHUTES CO.	T21S	R11E	S29
CAMP POLK	DESCHUTES CO.	T14S	R10E	S27
CULTUS MOUNTAIN	DESCHUTES CO.	UNSURVEYED		
DESCHUTES MEMORIAL GARDENS	DESCHUTES CO.	T17S	R12E	S9
GREENWOOD MEMORIAL	DESCHUTES CO.	T17S	R12E	S33
HARPER see ALLEN RANCH	DESCHUTES CO.	T20S	R11E	S8
HINDMAN see CAMP POLK	DESCHUTES CO.	T14S	R10E	S27
I.O.O.F. see TUMALO	DESCHUTES CO.	T16S	R12E	S29
I.O.O.F. [TERREBONNE] see PIONEER [TERREBONNE]				
	DESCHUTES CO.	T14S	R13E	S22
IMPROVED ORDER OF REDMEN see LA PINE COMMUNITY				
	DESCHUTES CO.	T22S	R11E	S7
LA PINE COMMUNITY	DESCHUTES CO.	T22S	R11E	S7
LAIDLAW see TUMALO	DESCHUTES CO.	T16S	R12E	S29
LAIDLAW ODD FELLOWS see TUMALO	DESCHUTES CO.	T16S	R12E	S29
MASTEN	DESCHUTES CO.	T22S	R9E	S25
MASTEN HOMESTEAD see MASTEN	DESCHUTES CO.	T22S	R9E	S25
MASTER [Sic] see MASTEN	DESCHUTES CO.	T22S	R9E	S25
MELLIN FAMILY	DESCHUTES CO.	T19S	R15E	?
MELLIN, MRS. see MELLIN FAMILY	DESCHUTES CO.	T19S	R15E	?
MILLICAN	DESCHUTES CO.	T19S	R15E	S34
OLD FORT see CAMP POLK	DESCHUTES CO.	T14S	R10E	S27
OLD REASE see BREESE	DESCHUTES CO.	T21S	R11E	S29
PILOT BUTTE	DESCHUTES CO.	T17S	R12E	S33
PIONEER [TERREBONNE]	DESCHUTES CO.	T14S	R13E	S22
QUINN, BILLY	DESCHUTES CO.	T21S	R7E	S1
REASE see BREESE	DESCHUTES CO.	T21S	R11E	S29
REASE, GUY see BREESE	DESCHUTES CO.	T21S	R11E	S29
REDMEN-LA PINE see LA PINE COMMUNITY				
	DESCHUTES CO.	T22S	R11E	S7
REDMOND see REDMOND MEMORIAL	DESCHUTES CO.	T15S	R13E	S29
REDMOND MEMORIAL	DESCHUTES CO.	T15S	R13E	S29
SISTERS see CAMP POLK	DESCHUTES CO.	T14S	R10E	S27
TERREBONNE see PIONEER [TERREBONNE]				
	DESCHUTES CO.	T14S	R13E	S22
TUMALO	DESCHUTES CO.	T16S	R12E	S29
VANDEVERT, GRACE CLARK	DESCHUTES CO.	T20S	R11E	S20
VANDEVERT HOUSE see VANDEVERT, GRACE CLARK				
	DESCHUTES CO.	T20S	R11E	S20
VANDEVERT, KATHERINE GRACE see VANDEVERT, GRACE CLARK				
	DESCHUTES CO.	T20S	R11E	S20

Deschutes County

Camp Polk

Stanley R. Clarke (2000)

250

Oregon Burial Site Guide
Douglas County

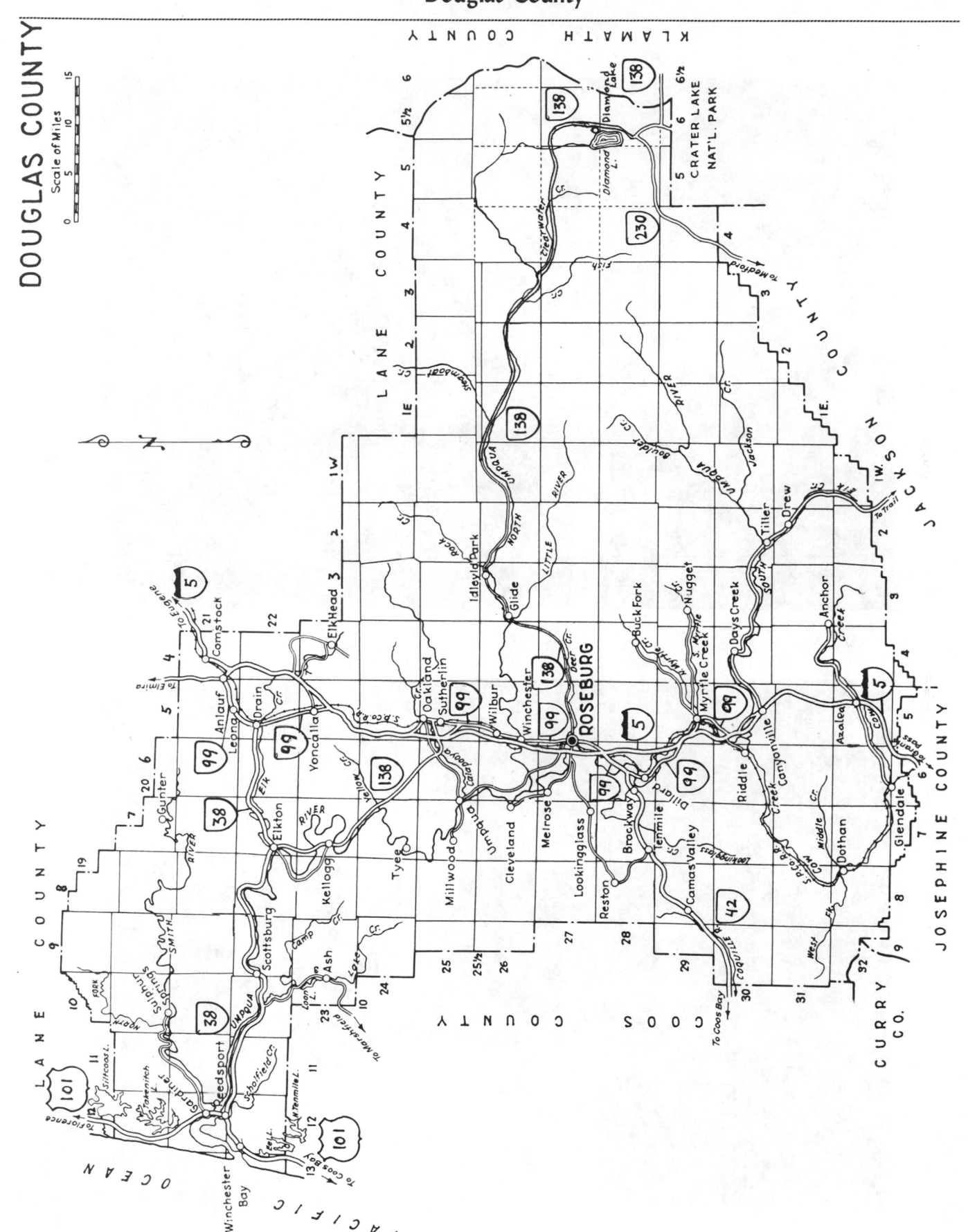

Douglas County

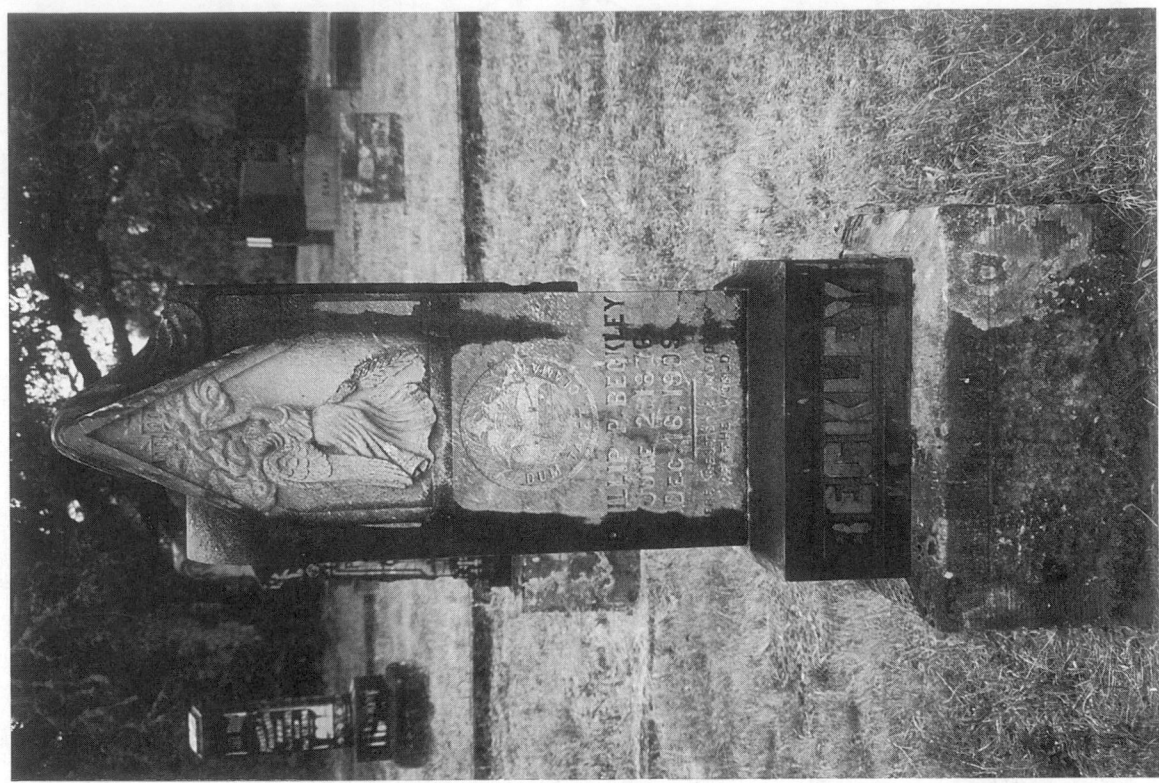

Cedar Hill
Janice M. Healy (2000)

Cedar Hill
Janice M. Healy (2000)

Area: 5,071 square miles
Population (1998): 101,837
County seat: Roseburg, Population: 19,720
County established: 7 January 1852

Douglas County occupies the Umpqua River basin. Settlement began in earnest in 1850 by settlers arriving by ship up the Umpqua River and by land from the Willamette Valley. The compiler lacks dates for cemeteries at early settlements such as Yoncalla, Drain and Roseburg; but early public cemeteries were established at Melrose (1854), Coles Valley (1854), Wilbur (1855), Kellogg (1857), Oak Creek (1857), and Scottsburg (1858). Riddle (1855) is the site of a cemetery for an unusually long-lived mining settlement, until recently it was the only producing nickel mine in the United States.

Cedar Hill
Janice M. Healy (2000)

Wells Family
Rudy Wellbrook (1993)

I.O.O.F. [Roseburg]
Dean H. Byrd (1991)

Name of Cemetery and also known as	Number of burials	Acres	Condition	Date started or earliest known burial	Township	Range	Section

ABBOTT GRAVE

A   0.01   ?   ?   ?   ?   ?

The Abbott grave has been reported as being somewhere along the Smith River. The compiler has no further information.

APPLEGATE FAMILY

A   0.8   2   ?   T22S R5W   S28

A little over a mile north of Yoncalla, on Drain-Yoncalla Highway, (OR. Hwy. 99, Co. Rd. #389) is the Jesse Applegate Historic Marker on the left (west) side of the highway. The family cemetery is on the west by private access: on the Jesse Applegate D.L.C. #38, RB #103. NOTE: This site is on private property. The reader should be aware that the larger Applegate Pioneer Cemetery AKA: Yoncalla Pioneer Cemetery, is a much larger burial ground and is located in Yoncalla. This has members of the family also, as well as numerous burials for the public at large. (Drain 1987 USGS Quad. map.)

APPLEGATE PIONEER
AKA: 1. PIONEER
       [YONCALLA]

?   4.82   3   1856   T23S R5W   S4

Enter Yoncalla on the Drain-Yoncalla Highway (OR. Hwy. 99, Co. Rd. #389)on Front Street. Leave Front Street and turn right (west) on Applegate Avenue; turn left (south) onto Douglas Street, right onto Elm Street and right (south) to the cemetery. The same turnaround at the end of the street serves both the Applegate Pioneer Cemetery on the right and the Masonic [Yoncalla] Cemetery on the left. Applegate Pioneer Cemetery was deeded 25 May 1880. This sizable cemetery in town should not be confused with the Applegate Family's private cemetery about a mile north of town. {23 June 1991} (Yoncalla 1987 USGS Quad. map.)

ARCHAMBEAUX FAMILY

A   0.1   3   ?   T26S R6W   S31

Leave the I-5 Freeway on Garden Valley Road (Co. Rd. #6) and go west from Roseburg to Melrose Road (Co. Rd. #167 and #13). Turn right (north) on Melqua Road (Co. Rd. #13-A) and go 0.91 of a mile. This family cemetery is on the right, in the yard of the Joel R. Fenn Ranch (1978). This is on the Francis

Name of Cemetery and also known as	Number of burials	Acres	Condition	Date started or earliest known burial	Township	Range	Section

Archambeaux D.L.C. #65, RB #199; in Douglas County the family name was pronounced Shambo. NOTE: This site is on private property. (Garden Valley 1987 USGS Quad. map.)

AZALEA

| ? | ? | ? | ? | | T32S | R5W | S14 |

One woman and two children are buried here reported Berl Oar of the Douglas County Water Survey Office (1978). NOTE: No other information was given in the report. (Not shown on Quines Creek 1986 USGS Quad. map.)

BAKER, DORSEY

| A | ? | 5 | ? | | T24S | R5W | S32 |

Located north of Oakland, on the west side of Old Highway 99 North (Co. Rd. #388). Unmarked, this family burial may have been destroyed by construction of the I-5 Freeway. The compiler found no reference to this cemetery in the relevant I-5 Freeway construction projects records. (Not shown on Sutherlin 1988 USGS Quad. map.)

BARRETT FAMILY

| ? | ? | ? | ? | | T21S | R12W | S19 |

Located on the right bank of the Umpqua estuary about 4 miles downstream from Gardiner. The river light and Barretts Landing are here. (Not shown on Winchester Bay 1985 USGS Quad. map.)

BELL FAMILY

| A | ? | 3 | ? | | T22S | R7W | S29 |

From Elkton, go south on OR. Hwy. 138 and take off to the left on the old highway, now Azalea Drive (Co. Rd. #10). About 0.75 of a mile from Elkton turn left (southeasterly) on the road to Bell Mountain Lookout. The Bell Family Cemetery was on the Moore property (1978). NOTE: This site is on private property. (Not shown on Kellogg 1990 USGS Quad. map.)

BETHEL

| ? | 0.1 | ? | ? | | T26S | R7W | S36 |

Leave the community of Melrose on Melrose Road (Co. Rd. #13). Turn north onto Cleveland Hill Road (Co. Rd. #59) for about a mile. The cemetery is on the left (west) of

Name of Cemetery and also known as	Number of burials	Acres	Condition	Date started or earliest known burial	Township	Range	Section

Cleveland Hill Road. Located on the Augustine Foisy D.L.C. #48, RB #534. NOTE: There was a Bethel Mission Church for about 10 years, beginning in the late 1920's. A 1936 Oregon Department of Transportation General Highway Series map shows the church. (Garden Valley 1987 USGS Quad. map.)

BIG CAMAS RANGER STATION
AKA: 1. GARWOOD GRAVE

A   0.01 5   ?   T27S R3E   ?
This could be in Sections 9 or 10, in the Umpqua National Forest. Go east from Roseburg on OR. Hwy. 138 to just past Eagle Rock Camp. Turn off the highway, to the right, on Big Camas Road (Forest Service Rd. #28) and drive to Big Camas Ranger Station. There is one grave for a Mr. Garwood on the south side of the pasture. (Grave is not shown on Fish Creek Desert 1989 USGS Quad. map.)

BLAND MOUNTAIN
AKA: 1. BLAND
     2. DAYS CREEK [?]

B   0.28 ?   1867   T30S R4W   S24
From Canyonville, drive east on Tiller-Trail Highway (Co. Rd. #1). About 3.6 miles beyond the community of Days Creek and about Milepost 14.45, there is a lane on the left (northerly) going 0.4 of a mile to the cemetery. (Days Creek 1986 USGS Quad. map.)

BOGGESS FAMILY
AKA: 1. BOGGUS
     2. SOUTH DEER CREEK

A   0.15 2   1880-1939   T28S R5W   S1
Go east of Roseburg on OR. Hwy. 138 to Buckhorn Road (Co. Rd. #4-C) and then turn right (south) onto Dixonville Road (Co. Rd. #16-E), going south of the Dixonville substation about 2.9 miles. This family cemetery is on the left: 11 marked burials were found in May 1988. The stones spelled the name Boggess. Located on Matthew Adams D.L.C. #51, RB #991. NOTE: This site is on private property. (Dixonville 1987 USGS Quad. map.)

BOUNDS

?   ?   ?   ?   T28S R6W   S35
A Bounds Cemetery has been reported as being located at Round Prairie between Dillard and

| Name of Cemetery and also known as | Number of burials | Acres | Condition | Date started or earliest known burial | Township | Range | Section |

Myrtle Creek. NOTE: The compiler has no other information. (Not shown on Winston 1987 USGS Quad. Map.)

BOURNE, CHARLES F.

A   0.01   5   19 Sep 1856   T22S R9W   S8
Located east of Scottsburg and near Scottsburg Cemetery. The Bourne burial is off the right bank of Golden Creek, whereas Scottsburg Cemetery is off of the left bank. The grave is about 0.27 of a mile left (northeast), off of the highway (OR. Hwy. 38) from Scottsburg and behind a house. A marble headstone, in the timber on a knoll, marks the spot. Bourne, overheated from unloading a vessel, drank cold water and died of shock. NOTE: This burial is on private property. (Scottsburg 1985 USGS Quad. map.)

BRIGGS, SAMUEL
  AKA: 1. BRADLEY,
        WM. D.
      2. PARDEE

A   0.4   3   1872-1972   T30S R5W   S20
Leave the I-5 Freeway at Exit #101, just south of Fords Bridge and north of Canyonville. Take Stanton Park Road (Co. Rd. #1-B) to the South Douglas Guard Station. There were 20 known burials and possibly 2 more behind the buildings in April of 1971. On the William Preston D.L.C. #44, RB #885. NOTE: The compiler does not know which name has priority. (Canyonville 1986 USGS Quad. map.)

BROWN FAMILY, H. G.

A   ?   4   1868   T22S R8W   S21
From Drain take OR. Hwy. 38 westerly, passing through Elkton. Near Sawyers Rapids of the Umpqua River at Milepost 32. This family cemetery is directly north of the Milepost and up the hill. NOTE: This site is on private property. (Not shown on Devils Graveyard 1990 USGS Quad. map.)

BROWN, O. C.

A   ?   5   ?   T27S R5W   S24
Perhaps located in what is now the O. C. Brown County Park. Go east from Roseburg on OR. Hwy. 138 and Buckhorn Road (Co. Rd. #4-C) to the park. There are 3 known undated graves of a Mrs. Tom Whitsett, a child and a

Name of Cemetery and also known as	Number of burials	Acres	Condition	Date started or earliest known burial	Township	Range	Section

man. NOTE: No other information was given in the report. (Not shown on Dixonville 1987 USGS Quad. map.)

BRYANT FAMILY

A 0.3 ? ?   T29S R4W   S21

From Myrtle Creek, via 3rd and Division Streets onto South Myrtle Road (Co. Rd. #18), go a total of 6.75 miles to a logging road and turn left. This logging road turns hard right about 400 feet from County Road #18. The cemetery is about 100 feet west of the gate to J. Bryant's Ranch (1978) on this logging road. On Benjamin Stephens D.L.C. #38, RB #413. NOTE: This site is on private property. (Dodson Butte 1987 USGS Quad. map.)

BUCKHEAD CAMP

A 0.01 5 ?   T27S R2E   S31

From Roseburg, go east on OR. Hwy. 138 to just east of Eagle Rock Camp in the Umpqua National Forest. Turn off of OR. Hwy. 138 to the right on Big Camas Road (Forest Service Rd. #28), go to the fork with Rhododendron Road. Take that road to the right, which is still Forest Service Road #28, along Rhododendron Ridge southerly to French Junction. At French Junction turn right (west) on Forest Service Road #2715 to Buckhead Camp. A Forest Service map is advisable. While a party was travelling from Fort Klamath to Roseburg, a woman, who is now unknown, died and was buried here. (Grave is not shown on Twin Lakes Mountain 1989 USGS Quad. map.)

BURNETT FAMILY
AKA: 1. DOLE

A 1.1 3 1854-1957 T29S R6W   S12

Leave the I-5 Freeway south of Roseburg at the Clarks Branch Exit (Exit #113) on the west side of the freeway. Go about 2 blocks south and turn right (westerly) onto Weigle Road (Co. Rd. #14-A). Go to the first gate on the left side. The cemetery is on a timbered knoll; on John S. Burnett D.L.C. #42, RB #408. (Myrtle Creek 1987 USGS Quad. map.)

Douglas County

Name of Cemetery and also known as	Number of burials	Acres	Condition	Date started or earliest known burial	Township	Range	Section

BURT

C ? 2 1857 T27S R5W S14

Go about 2.2 miles east of Roseburg on OR. Hwy. 138; turn left (northerly) onto Temple Brown Road (Co. Rd. #137). The cemetery is at the top of the hill behind the mill. The gate is locked, but a key may be obtained at Boyer Meats across OR. Hwy. 138 from the mill. About 125 graves were found in April of 1988. (Not shown on Roseburg East 1987 USGS Quad. map.)

CAMAS VALLEY

A 0.01 5 ? T31S R8W S5

Go southwesterly about 5 miles from the community of Camas Valley via OR. Hwy. 42. Turn left (southerly) on B.L.M. Road #30-9-11. Cross the Middle Fork Coquille River and continue on Twelvemile Creek Road; turn left onto Dice Creek Road on the way towards Dutchman Butte. An unknown prospector was buried in an unmarked grave, on a ridge in the southwest 1/4 of Section 5. (Not shown on Chipmunk Ridge 1990 USGS Quad. map.)

CANNON, SARAH

A 0.01 5 ? T22S R4W S20

Leave the I-5 Freeway at Scotts Valley Exit (Exit #154) near Yoncalla, taking Anlauf Road (Co. Rd. #25) on the west side of the I-5 Freeway. Go northerly and turn right (east) onto Cox Road (Co. Rd. #196); cross over the I-5 Freeway. This burial is a single grave off of Cox Road. NOTE: This site is on private property. (Not shown on Curtin 1987 USGS Quad. map.)

CANYONVILLE
AKA: 1. I.O.O.F.
2. MASONIC

C 4 1 1882 T30S R5W S27

Just north of Canyonville, on Main Street, on the right (east) side of the street. It can also be easily reached from the I-5 Freeway via the North Canyonville Exit (Exit #99) and taking Stanton Park Road (Co. Rd. #1-B) towards Canyonville. This was originally two separate cemeteries for the I.O.O.F. and Masonic Lodge. There are monuments dated as early as 1863. Located on the James G. Clark D.L.C. #51, RB #792.

Name of Cemetery and also known as	Number of burials	Acres	Condition	Date started or earliest known burial	Township	Range	Section

NOTE: The Rose Hill Memorial adjoins this cemetery, see that article. {27 October 1995} (Canyonville 1986 USGS Quad. map.)

CANYONVILLE PIONEER

A   0.1   5   1860   T30S R5W   S34
Located in Canyonville, west of the I-5 Freeway. It is in back of Canyonville Hospital, on a hill. The cemetery can also be reached by leaving the I-5 Freeway at Canyonville Exit (Exit #98). Located on the Joseph Roberts D.L.C. #59, RB #1070.5. (Canyonville 1986 USGS Quad. map.)

CEDAR HILL
AKA: 1. I.O.O.F.
      [OAKLAND, 2ND]
    2. OAKLAND

?   6+   1   1890   T25S R5W   S5
Take Old Highway 99 North (Co. Rd. #388) north from Oakland, cross the bridge a mile from town and turn left (west) onto Green Valley Road (Co. Rd. #23-A) continue until you reach the intersection with Manning Road. On your left is the cemetery on the south side of the road, the oldest monument found was for 1869. Located on the Reason Reid [Sic] D.L.C. #58, RB #249. {17 September 2000} (Sutherlin 1988 USGS Quad. map.)

CHAMPAIGN FAMILY
AKA: 1. CHAMPAGNE

A   0.1   5   1860   T27S R6W   S6
From Roseburg take Garden Valley Road (Co. Rd. #6) westerly. Turn left onto Melrose Road (Co. Rds.#167 and #13). At Melrose turn right (north) onto Melqua Road (Co. Rd. # 13-A) and go about 0.3 of a mile north of the store. This family cemetery is on the right (east) about 200 yards on top of a knoll above Champagne Creek (as USGS spells it): Champaign is the tombstones spelling. The name is locally pronounced Champine as in pine tree. French, as spoken in Douglas County, differs from French as spoken in Paris: on the Joseph Champaign D.L.C. #57, RB #521. NOTE: This site is on private property. (Garden Valley 1987 USGS Quad. map.)

CHINESE [GARDINER?]

?   ?   ?   ?   T21S R12W   ?
A Chinese cemetery has been reported at or near Gardiner. The compiler has no other

Douglas County

Name of Cemetery and also known as	Number of burials	Acres	Condition	Date started or earliest known burial	Township	Range	Section

information. (Not shown on Reedsport 1985 USGS Quad. map.)

CIVIL BEND
AKA: 1. BROCKWAY
     2. WINSTON

| | D | 2.9 | 2 | 1877 | T28S R6W | | S21 |

From OR. Hwy. 42 in Winston, turn left (south) onto Civil Bend Avenue. Access from the I-5 Freeway is at the Winston Exit (Exit #119); on the James Belieu D.L.C. #52, RB #223. (Winston 1987 USGS Quad. map.)

CLARK GRAVE

| | A | 0.01 | ? | ? | ? | ? | ? |

There is a grave of a person named Clark buried near Scottsburg. No other information was given to the compiler. (Not shown on Scottsburg 1985 USGS Quad. map.)

CLEVELAND
AKA: 1. CLEVELAND
       HILL
     2. UNITED
       BRETHREN

| | C | 1.5 | 2 | 1877 | T26S R7W | | S24 |

Go westerly from Roseburg on Garden Valley Road (Co. Rd. #6), turn left onto Melrose Road (Co. Rd. #167 and #13); at Melrose turn right (northerly) onto Cleveland Hill Road (Co. Rd. #59). The cemetery is on the right at the site of a church: on the John B. Gilham D.L.C. #46, RB #2122. (Garden Valley 1987 USGS Quad. map.)

COFFEE CREEK

| | A | 0.15 | 5 | ? | T30S R2W | | S18 |

From Canyonville take the Tiller-Trail Highway (Co. Rd. #1) through Days Creek and past the turnout to Milo Academy. About 2.5 miles east of that turnout is Coffee Creek Road (B.L.M. Rd. 30-2-30) to the left (northerly). The cemetery is about 3.5 miles up this road, on the right just before the road crosses Ruby Creek. This was a mining district. (Tiller 1989 USGS Quad. map.)

COLE FAMILY, DR. JAMES

| | A | 0.1 | 2 | 1864 | T25S R6W | | S8 |

Leave Sutherlin, going westerly on OR. Hwy. 138 and then Fort McKay Road (Co. Rd. #9). Turn right (north) onto Cole Road (Co. Rd. #91) for 5 or 6 miles. The access is from Cole Road, 0.1 of a mile south of the junction with Murdock Road. Turn left (east and southeast) on a private four-wheel drive road for 0.75 of a mile, then hike 100 yards

Name of Cemetery and also known as	Number of burials	Acres	Condition	Date started or earliest known burial	Township	Range	Section

uphill. This family cemetery is on a hillside above Coon Creek Valley. NOTE: This site is on private property. (Tyee Mountain 1987 USGS Quad. map.)

COLES VALLEY

| | C | 3 | 1 | 1854 | T25S | R7W | S35 |

From Sutherlin going westerly on OR. Hwy. 138. Turn left (west) onto Fort McKay Road (Co. Rd. #9) to Umpqua, cross the Umpqua River and continue west another mile. Turn left (south) onto Melqua Road (Co. Rd. #13-A). The cemetery is about another mile on the right (west): on the William Churchill D.L.C. #46, RB #190. There are also 8 known Indian graves here. (Garden Valley 1987 USGS Quad. map.)

COLVIN
AKA: 1. EUREKA
    VALLEY

| | A | 0.2 | ? | ? | T22S | R5W | S6 |

Go west on OR. Hwy. 38 from Drain, turning right (north) off of the highway onto Hardscrabble Road (Co. Rd. #65). About 2.5 miles from OR. Hwy. 38 turn right (east) off of Hardscrabble Road. There are 4 graves on the old Earl Frier Place; in 1978 this was owned by the Woolley family. NOTE: This site is on private property. (Drain 1987 USGS Quad. map.)

COMSTOCK
AKA: 1. ANLAUF
    2. CURTIN

| | ? | 2 | 2 | 1871 | T21S | R4W | S20 |

Take Exit #163 off of the I-5 Freeway to Curtin. Turn right (north) onto Curtin Road (Co. Rd. #212) and follow it for a mile with the railway on the right. Turn right, crossing the tracks and passing underneath the I-5 Freeway. Go 0.6 of a mile from Curtin Road, up the hill to the cemetery. (Curtin 1987 USGS Quad. map.)

COX FAMILY

| | ? | ? | ? | ? | ? | ? | ? |

A Cox Family Cemetery on the old Cox Place has been reported as being somewhere along the Smith River. The compiler has no further information. This Cox Family Cemetery is not to be confused with the bygone John Cox Cemetery near Brockway.

Name of Cemetery and also known as | Number of burials | Acres | Condition | Date started or earliest known burial | Township | Range | Section

COX, JOHN

? ? ? **2 Jan 1856 T28S R6W** ?
Perhaps located in Section 20. This almost
forgotten cemetery was located just north of
Brockway and west of Winston. Young Tom Gage
and another youth were killed in the Cow
Creek Canyon by Indians, Gage dying on
2 January 1856. He was buried on the John
Cox D.L.C. #49, RB #900 rather than in the
D.L.C. of his father Joseph Gage which
adjoins the south edge of the Cox D.L.C..
Lewis Kent was buried here on 2 or 22 January
1857 and then other members of the Kent
Family later on. Cox Cemetery was closed in
December 1877 with most of the burials
removed to Civil Bend Cemetery at Winston.
(Not shown on Winston 1987 USGS Quad. map.)

COX, SARAH

A 0.01 ? ? **T22S R4W** S20
Located in Section 20 or 29. No further
information was given in the report. (Curtin
1987 USGS. quad. map)

DAY FAMILY
  AKA: 1. DENN

A 0.5 5 ? **T29S R9W** S26
Take OR. Hwy. 42 to Camas Valley. Continue
southwesterly on the highway, then turn hard
right (north) onto Westside Camas Road (Co.
Rd. #129). After less than a mile turn left
(west) onto Denn Road (Co. Rd. #210) for
about 1.5 miles to the cemetery, which is 250
feet off to the left of the road. In 1960
the D.A.R. reported 5 known burials, which
included William P. Day and wife Phoebe; on
the William P. Day D.L.C. #44, RB #971.
NOTE: This site is on private property.
(Reportedly (1978) the graves had been plowed
over, however the cemetery is shown on the
Camas Valley 1990 USGS Quad. map.)

DIMMICK FAMILY

B 0.7 2 **1867 T23S R7W** S20
Located south of Elkton and near Kellogg.
Take OR. Hwy. 138 south from Elkton to a road
just before the north end of the Kellogg
Bridge over the Umpqua River. Turn left
(east) off of OR. Hwy. 138 onto Maupin Road
(Co. Rd. #57-B) for about 100 feet; turn left
(north) onto the old OR. Hwy. 138, now
Kellogg Drive (Co. Rd. #10-C), and go north

Name of Cemetery and also known as	Number of burials	Acres	Condition	Date started or earliest known burial	Township	Range	Section

about 120 yards. Here there is a private road on the right, with a locked gate, which goes easterly for 0.4 of a mile to a bench where the cemetery overlooks the river on the Ziba Dimmick D.L.C. #45, RB #358. NOTE: This site is on private property. (Kellogg 1990 USGS Quad. map.)

DIXON FAMILY

A 0.15 3 1858-1971 T26S R5W S26
Go east from Roseburg on OR. Hwy. 138 and turn left (northerly) onto Sunshine Road (Co. Rd. #58). After 5.1 miles on Sunshine Road, turn left onto Rio Nes Lane at the fork and proceed about 0.45 of a mile to the Dixon Family Cemetery on the left; on the Hiram Dixon D.L.C. #41, RB #229. NOTE: This site is on private property. The Douglas County Genealogical Society inventoried 22 graves in August 1988. (Winchester 1987 USGS Quad. map.)

DOUGLAS COUNTY BROOKSIDE
AKA: 1. PAUPER'S
[ROSEBURG]
2. POTTERS
FIELD
[ROSEBURG]

C ? 2 1930-1942 T27S R5W S17
This county-owned cemetery is located on the north side of Diamond Lake Boulevard (OR. Hwy. 138), east of the Champion International Corporation Forest Products plant and west of the Douglas County Shops. Only one grave is known to have been moved to Roseburg Memorial Gardens, about 120 burials remain here. Located on the William T. Perry D.L.C. #38, RB #174. (Not shown on Roseburg East 1987 USGS Quad. map.)

DOUGLAS COUNTY POOR FARM

? 0.1 ? ? T26S R6W S30
This small cemetery is in Section 30, the same as LaBrie Cemetery and about 0.25 of a mile northwest of the latter. Like LaBrie, it is also west off of Melqua Road on the slopes of Cleveland Hill. The County Poor Farm was once located nearby along the road. There are no markers; on the George Shambrook D.L.C. #57, RB #383. NOTE: This site is on private property. (Garden Valley 1987 USGS Quad. map.)

Douglas County

Name of Cemetery and also known as	Number of burials	Acres	Condition	Date started or earliest known burial	Township	Range	Section

DRAIN [NORTH]
AKA: 1. CITIZENS
     2. CITY
     3. NORTH

? 1 ? ?   T22S R5W   S8
Located off of OR. Hwy. 99 in the north part of Drain. Watch for the sign on the east side of the highway, turn on Rogers Avenue and go back up the hill. (Drain 1987 USGS Quad. map.)

DRIVER FAMILY

A ? 4 ?   T24S R4W   S22
Leave Oakland to the east on Driver Valley Road (Co. Rd. #22) to the upper reaches of Oldham Creek. This family cemetery is on a private road with a locked gate; on the Samuel Driver D.L.C. #41, RB #819. NOTE: This site is on private property. (Nonpareil 1987 USGS Quad. map.)

DUMONT, AUGUST
AKA: 1. DUMOND,
      AUGUST

A 0.01 ? Feb 1868   T30S R4W   S9
Alexander Dumont settled on the right (north) bank of the South Umpqua River, upstream from Canyonville and just downstream from the present community of Days Creek. From Canyonville, drive east on Tiller-Trail Highway (Co. Rd. #1) to the bridge over the South Umpqua River. Just beyond the bridge, about 10.5 miles from Canyonville, is the community church. Turn left (west) at the church and take the one-lane gravel road west along the right (north) bank of the river for about a mile to the farm. The grave of August Dumont, and possibly others of the family, are somewhere on this private property. The compiler prefers the spelling in the Catholic church records to the D.L.C. spelling which is Alexander Dumond D.L.C. #46, RB #328. (Not shown on Days Creek 1986 USGS Quad. map.)

DUNES MEMORIAL MAUSOLEUM

? ? ? ?   T22S R12W   S4
In Reedsport. At 2300 Frontage Road. Take 22nd Street under U.S. Hwy. 101 at the south end of town and turn right onto the Frontage Road which parallels U.S. Hwy. 101. The mausoleum is opposite the Reedsport Cemetery. (Not shown on Winchester Bay 1985 USGS Quad. map.)

Name of Cemetery and also known as	Number of burials	Acres	Condition	Date started or earliest known burial	Township	Range	Section

EAST GARDINER

? ? ? ? ? ? ?

There is a Death Certificate #208 for Coos County 1924 for Mervin Donald Henderson of Reedsport, born 4 Augest 1913, died 11 October 1924. Young Henderson, the son of Harry and Edna Waggoner Henderson, died of appendicitis in a North Bend hospital. He was reported buried in East Garndiner on 11 October 1924. The site is unknown to the compiler. (Not shown on Reedsport 1985 USGS Quad. map.)

EDEN
AKA: 1. EDEN LUTHERAN CHURCH
2. ELGAROSE

C 1.4 1 1913 T27S R7W S2

From Roseburg go westerly on Garden Valley Road (Co. Rd. #6) and left onto Melrose Road (Co. Rd. #167 and #13). Continue westerly from Melrose still on Melrose Road (now Co. Rd. #51-B). Turn off to the right (due west) onto Doerner Road (Co. Rd. #90). Then turn right (north) onto Elgarose Loop Road (Co. Rd. #53). After about 0.75 of a mile on Elgarose Loop Road (Co. Rd. #53), turn left at the next fork, still on Elgarose Loop Road (Co. Rd. #53), and you will soon see the cemetery at the next corner. 1914 was the earliest death date found on a monument. Eden Lutheran Church burned in 1964. (Garden Valley 1987 USGS Quad. map.)

ELKTON

C 2 2 1875 T22S R7W S29

Just south of Elkton. Take OR. Hwy. 138 across Elk Creek. Turn left onto the old highway, now Azalea Drive (Co. Rd. #10-E) and continue south for about a mile. The cemetery is on the right (west) side of Azalea Drive. Located on the Zacheus Levens D.L.C. #39, RB #1068. (Elkton 1990 USGS Quad. map.)

ELLIOTT-PERKINS FAMILY

? ? ? ? T21S R12W ?

Near Gardiner. NOTE: No other information was given in the report. (Not shown on Reedsport 1985 USGS Quad. map.)

Name of Cemetery and also known as	Number of burials	Acres	Condition	Date started or earliest known burial	Township	Range	Section

ELLIS

A 0.01 ? ? ? ? ?
A burial of an unknown person on the Ellis property (1978) in the Camas Valley area. NOTE: This site is on private property. No other information was given in the report. (Not shown on Camas Valley 1990 USGS Quad. map.)

ENSLEY FAMILY

A 0.1 ? ? T22S R6W S2
From Drain go west on OR. Hwy. 38; turn right (north) onto Schoen Road (Co. Rd. #66). Go about 1.8 miles north of the highway on Schoen Road. The Ensley Family and Farmer Family cemeteries are on the left about 150 feet from the road. See entry for Farmer Family. NOTE: This site is on private property. (Putnam Valley 1987 USGS Quad. map.)

FAIR OAKS
AKA: 1. HUNTS MEMORIAL
2. NONPAREIL

D 5.1 1 1857 T25S R4W S7
From Sutherlin go easterly on Central Avenue (OR. Hwy. 138). Continue on Central Avenue to the eastern city limits where the name changes to Nonpareil Road (Co. Rd. #19) to a crossroads; turn left (north) on Fair Oaks Road (Co. Rd. #22-A) for about 0.5 of a mile, and the cemetery is close by to the right on the south bank of Calapooya Creek. On the William Hoskins D.L.C. #46, RB #1149. (Nonpareil 1987 USGS Quad. map.)

FARMER FAMILY

? 0.1 ? ? T22S R6W S2
Follow the same directions from Drain as to the Ensley cemetery; see the entry for Ensley. The Ensley and Farmer family cemeteries are side by side in an east-west alignment about 150 feet to the left (west) of the road. On the James Farmer D.L.C. #40, RB #545. The compiler does not know which cemetery is which. NOTE: This site is on private property. (Putnam Valley 1987 USGS Quad. map.)

FORT UMPQUA [NEW]

? ? ? July 1856 T21S R12W S31
The fort was located on the right bank of the Umpqua River upstream about two miles from

its mouth. The military burials at the fort presumably were removed to the Presidio at San Francisco some time after July 1862. See the article on Umpqua City Cemetery for civilian burials near the fort. (Not shown on Winchester Bay 1985 USGS Quad. map.)

FORT UMPQUA [OLD]
AKA: 1. McKAY

A ? 6 ? T22S R7W S30
Fort Umpqua was a Hudsons Bay trading post and Jean Baptiste Desportes McKay operated from here. The site of the fort was at the west end of the present Beckley Bridge spanning the Umpqua River, immediately upstream from Elkton. The previous bridge was swept away in the Christmas Eve flood of December 1964 and the present bridge location built over the fort's site on the left bank. The graves of Jonathan McKay and his wife are here somewhere. Jonathan was the son of Jean Baptiste Desportes McKay. NOTE: There were two different Fort Umpquas far apart. See the article on Fort Umpqua [new]. (Not shown on Elkton 1990 USGS Quad. map.)

FORTUNE BRANCH GRAVES
AKA: 1. BURCH
       FAMILY [?]

? ? ? ? T32S R5W S20
Four miles west of Azalea on the Azalea-Glen Road (Co. Rd. #12) at Fortune Branch 0.13 of a mile past the Fortune Branch Bridge. Turn right (north) onto a side road and go about 500 feet. The graves are on the right. NOTE: This site is on private property. (Quines Creek 1986 USGS Quad. map.)

FREEMAN FAMILY

A 0.01 ? 1864-1901 T28S R7W ?
This family cemetery is on Section 25 or 26, most likely the former. Go about 4.75 miles southwest of Winston on OR. Hwy. 42. The cemetery is about 0.25 of a mile to the right (north) off of the highway on a steep knoll west of Richards Cemetery. On the John Freeman D.L.C. #49, RB #669 and was on the Stutzman property (1978). Six gravestones were found in 1978 but there are probably many more burials here. NOTE: This site is on private property. (Not shown on Winston 1987 USGS Quad. map.)

Douglas County

Name of Cemetery and also known as	Number of burials	Acres	Condition	Date started or earliest known burial	Township	Range	Section

FRENCH CREEK

? ? 5 ? T32S R3W S4

Leave the I-5 Freeway at the Azalea Exit (Exit #88), and proceed easterly on Upper Cow Creek Road (Co. Rd. #36) for about 15 miles and into the Umpqua National Forest. The construction of Galesville Reservoir since 1978 may have altered this mileage figure. Ike French and wife and an uncertain number of others were buried near Cow Creek and near its tributary, French Creek. (Not shown on Cedar Springs Mountain 1986 USGS Quad. map.)

FRIER FAMILY

? ? ? ? T22S R6W S1

From Drain turn west on OR. Hwy. 38; turn right (north) onto Hardscrabble Road (Co. Rd. #65). This family cemetery is in Eureka Valley on the Carl Frier Ranch (1978). NOTE: This site is on private property. (Not shown on Drain 1987 USGS Quad. map.)

FROZEN CREEK

A ? ? ? T28S R4W ?

This could be in Section 31 or 32. Leave Myrtle Creek by Division Street and then turn left to the northeast on North Myrtle Road (Co. Rd. #15). Go past North Myrtle Creek County Park about 0.4 of a mile and turn left (northeasterly) onto Frozen Creek Road (Co. Rd. #104). This unmarked cemetery was on the Dority Place (1978). NOTE: This site is on private property. (Not shown on Dodson Butte 1987 USGS Quad. map.)

GARDINER
AKA: 1. AURORA
     MASONIC
     LODGE #59
     [GARDINER]
   2. MASONIC
     [GARDINER]

C 1.5 2 1872 T21S R12W S22

Go north of Reedsport on U.S. Hwy. 101 through the community of Gardiner. Leave U.S. Hwy. 101 at the fork at the north end of Gardiner taking off to the right on Old Highway 101 (Co. Rd. #49-K). This cemetery is up the hill on the right (east) side of the road. 365 known burials as of 1981. (Reedsport 1985 USGS Quad. map.)

GARDNER
AKA: 1. BLACKFORD

? ? ? ? T22S R6W ?

This cemetery could be in Sections 3, 4, 9, or 10. It is unclear to the compiler if these are two separate cemeteries for the

Name of Cemetery and also known as	Number of burials	Acres	Condition	Date started or earliest known burial	Township	Range	Section

Gardner and Blackford families or two names for the same cemetery. Both (or it, alone) are listed as being on the Rydell Ranch in 1978. In the Sunnydale area west of Drain and off of OR. Hwy. 38. NOTE: This site is on private property. No other information was given in the report. (Not shown on Putnam Valley 1987 USGS Quad. map.)

GERHARD PLACE, LOREN	?	?	?	?	T21S	R11W	S9

One or more burials of persons unknown to this compiler have been reported on the Loren Gerhard Place. The 1932 *Metsker Land Ownership Atlas* of Douglas County shows a Gerhardt owning land on the left bank of Smith River between Gardiner and North Fork. There are two different spellings of the same name, Gerhardt being the original German spelling. (Not located on Fivemile Creek 1984 USGS Quad. map.)

GILMORE FAMILY	B	?	4	1858	T28S	R5W	S11

Go east from Roseburg on OR. Hwy. 138 and then right onto Buckhorn Road (Co. Rd. #4-C) to Dixonville. Turn right (south) onto Dixonville Road (Co. Rd. #16-E) and go 3.2 miles to the fork. Turn right onto Roberts Creek Road (Co. Rd. #16-C) and go west and south 1.1 miles. The cemetery is on the right. On the James P. Gilmore D.L.C. #41, RB #875. 62 known burials (May of 1988). NOTE: This site is on private property. (Not shown on Roseburg East 1987 USGS Quad. map.)

GLENDALE AKA: 1. AZALEA LODGE 2. MASONIC	?	6.5	?	?	T33S	R6W	S5

Leave the I-5 Freeway at the Glendale Exit (Exit #80). Go past the elementary school on 1st Street to the cemetery which is at the end of the street. (Glendale 1986 USGS Quad. map.)

GOFF FAMILY	A	?	3	1882-1930	T25S	R5W	S30

Just south of Sutherlin. Leave the I-5 Freeway at the Deady Exit (Exit #135), to the west side of the freeway. Turn right (north) on the Frontage Road and go up the hill.

This family cemetery is behind the house in the trees; on Joseph Holdman D.L.C. #37, RB #1026. There were 15 burials noted in the summer of 1973. NOTE: This site is on private property. (Not shown on Winchester 1987 USGS Quad. map.)

GREEN VALLEY
  AKA: 1. METZ HILL

B   0.5   2   1855   T24S R6W   S25
Leave the I-5 Freeway at the Metz Hill Exit (Exit #142), north of Oakland. Go west on Metz Hill Road (Co. Road #74) for 1.5 miles. Just over the top of the hill on the left (south) side of the road is the cemetery. On the Nathan W. Allen D.L.C. #42, RB #583. (Sutherlin 1988 USGS Quad. map.)

GUNTER
  AKA: 1. WOOLLEY

A   0.05   2   ?   T20S R7W   S27
Leave OR. Hwy. 99 north of Drain and southwest of Anlauf. Take Upper Smith River Road (Co. Rd. #37) for 20 miles to the locale of Gunter. Continue westerly 0.5 of a mile past the Haney Creek Bridge, and the cemetery is on the left (south) side of the road. {January 1992} (Gunter 1984 USGS Quad. map.)

HAINES FAMILY

A   0.1   3   1864-1879   T22S R7W   S32
Go south from Elkton on the old alignment of OR. Hwy. 138, now Azalea Drive (Co. Rd. #10-E). 2 miles south of Elkton turn left off of Azalea Drive on a road for about 1 mile. A D.A.R. visit in 1960 disclosed 3 marked graves, with possibly other unmarked ones; On the Thomas Levens D.L.C. #38, RB #548. NOTE: This site is on private property. (Not shown on Kellogg 1990 USGS Quad. map.)

HAMACHER FAMILY

?   ?   ?   ?   ?   ?   ?
A burial plot presumably for the family has been reported as being located at the Hamacher Place, it is supposed to be somewhere in the vicinity of Drain. The compiler has no other information.

Name of Cemetery and also known as	Number of burials	Acres	Condition	Date started or earliest known burial	Township	Range	Section

HARDY FAMILY, THEOTINE

A ? 4 1854 T27S R6W S6

Leave Roseburg on Garden Valley Road (Co. Rd. #6) westerly. Turn left (west) onto Melrose Road (Co. Rd. #167 and #13), then right (north) onto Melqua Road (Co. Rd. #13-A). This family cemetery is to the right (east) of Melqua Road; on the Theotine Hardy D.L.C. #59, RB #666. NOTE: This site is on private property. (Not shown on Roseburg West 1987 USGS Quad. maps.)

HARRIS, DR.

A ? 5 ? T24S R4W ?

This could be in Section 5 or 6. Leave Oakland to the northeast on Driver Valley Road (Co. Rd. #22). Turn left (north) onto Elkhead Road (Co. Rd. #50) continuing northerly past Kanipe Memorial Park to a place just south of the intersection of Hogan Road (Co. Rd. #190). On the right (east) side of Elkhead Road about 0.25 of a mile back of the present (1978) ranch house is the grave of a Dr. Harris and a few others; on the Jonathan Cozad D.L.C. #37, RB #124. NOTE: This site is on private property. (Not shown on Scotts Valley 1987 USGS Quad. map.)

HARVEY FAMILY

A ? 4 ? T24S R4W S30

Leave Oakland to the northeast on Driver Valley Road (Co. Rd. #22). Just before the road crosses Oldham Creek you will find this family cemetery, it is on the right in a field. NOTE: This site is on private property. (Nonpareil 1987 USGS Quad. map.)

HASKELL FAMILY

? ? ? ? ? ? ?

A cemetery has been reported on the Haskell Place. This is supposedly somewhere near Gardiner. The compiler has no other information.

HEDRICK FAMILY

? 0.1 ? ? T21S R6W S35

Leave Drain to the west on OR. Hwy. 38; turning right (north) onto Schoen Road (Co. Rd. #66); beyond county maintenance the name changes to Jack Creek Road. Continue on this road beyond the end of county maintenance for

Name of Cemetery and also known as	Number of burials	Acres	Condition	Date started or earliest known burial	Township	Range	Section

about 2.5 or 3 miles from the highway. This family cemetery is located on a knoll about 700 feet to the right; on the Andrew J. Swearinger D.L.C. #37, RB #577. Ahead is gate of private road to Woolley Ranch (1978). NOTE: This site is on private property. (Putnam Valley 1987 USGS Quad. map.)

HEDRICK FAMILY — ? ? ? ? T22S R6W S1

Leave Drain to the west on OR. Hwy. 38 turning right (north) onto Hardscrabble Road (Co. Rd. #65). This is on the Woolley Ranch (1978). NOTE: This site is on private property. It is not clear to the compiler if these are actually 2 separate cemeteries for the Hedrick Family. (In any event, this particular cemetery is not shown on Drain 1987 USGS Quad. map.)

HEFTY FAMILY — A 0.01 ? ? T20S R6W S34

One grave for a member of the Hefty Family has been reported. The grave is probably near where Hefty Creek joins the right bank of the Smith River. This is along Upper Smith River Road between Gunter and the Gunter Recreation Site, not enough information was given in the report to be sure of the location. (The creek is shown on Beaver Creek 1984 USGS Quad. map.)

HENDERER FAMILY — A 0.15 ? ? T22S R8W S23

Located west of Elkton and south of the left bank of the Umpqua River. Leave Elkton to the south on OR. Hwy. 138, turning right (west) on Mehl Creek Road (Co. Rd. #11), crossing the Umpqua River on Beckley Bridge. Very soon turn right (westerly) onto Henderer Road (Co. Rd. #118) and go 2.3 miles further. The cemetery of the Henderer Family is on the left (south) side of the road; on the Edward Griffin D.L.C. #42, RB #650. NOTE: This site is on private property. (Elkton 1990 USGS Quad. map.)

| Name of Cemetery and also known as | Number of burials | Acres | Condition | Date started or earliest known burial | Township | Range | Section |

HURST FAMILY   A   0.05   5   ?   T25S R6W   S22

Leave Sutherlin to the west on OR. Hwy. 138, then turn left (west) onto Fort McKay Road (Co. Rd. #9) to just short (east) of the bridge over Calapooya Creek. The Hurst Family Cemetery was about 1,000 feet left (south) of Fort McKay Road on the left bank of Calapooya Creek and just south of an unnamed tributary. There is no ready access to the unmarked graves; on the David Hurst D.L.C. #56, RB #689. NOTE: This site is on private property. This is also the site of the early post office of Stephens. (Tyee Mountain 1987 Quad. map.)

I.O.O.F. [DRAIN]   ?   4.3   ?   ?   T22S R5W   S16
 AKA: 1. DRAIN [EAST]

From Drain at OR. Hwy. 99 turn east on "B" Avenue, crossing the railway tracks, to South Main Street. Turn right (south), follow South Main Street to Alto Vista Avenue where you turn left (west) and proceed to Cemetery Road; then turn right (southeast) up the hill to the cemetery. (Drain 1987 USGS Quad. map.)

I.O.O.F. [MYRTLE CREEK]   ?   5.3   ?   1861   T29S R5W   S22

In the northeast part of town at Craig Street. (Myrtle Creek 1987 USGS Quad. map.)

I.O.O.F. [OAKLAND]   ?   ?   7   ?   T25S R5W   S4

Located just east of the southeast edge of the town of Oakland, off of 8th Street. Most of the graves were moved to Cedar Hill Cemetery. NOTE: This site is on private property now. (Not shown on Sutherlin 1988 USGS Quad. map.)

I.O.O.F. [ROSEBURG]   D   5.9   2   ?   T27S R5W   S19

Take Southeast Douglas Avenue easterly, past the courthouse over the hill. The cemetery is on the right (south) side of the street. The Roseburg I.O.O.F. and St. Joseph's Catholic Cemeteries adjoin and are not separated by any barrier; on the Thomas Stevens D.L.C. #39, RB #868. {21 June 1991} (Roseburg East 1987 USGS Quad. map.)

Douglas County

Name of Cemetery and also known as	Number of burials	Acres	Condition	Date started or earliest known burial	Township	Range	Section

INDIAN

? 6.3 ? ? T22S R4W S18
Leave the I-5 Freeway at Exit #159, onto the west side of the freeway and onto Anlauf Road (Co. Rd. #25). Go left (south) parallel to the freeway about 2 miles; four-wheel drive access right (westerly), into the hills onto private property. NOTE: This Quad. map conspicuously shows an unnamed cemetery of about 500 X 550 feet in size; in other words about 6.3 acres in area. One source suggested the Indian burial is on the John Letsom D.L.C. #40, RB #314 which overlaps sections 17, 18, 19 and 20. This seems credible, but no burials are indicated there on the said Curtin USGS Quad. NOTE: Two Death Certificates for 1918 and 1919 do confirm burials of Indians in "Indian burial ground near Anlauf". (Curtin 1987 USGS Quad. map.)

INDIAN

A ? 5 ? T25S R4W ?
Possibly located in Sections 15 or 22. Leave Sutherlin to the east on Nonpareil Road (Co. Rd. #19). Turn right (south) onto Banks Creek Road (Co. Rd. #45) and then left (easterly) onto Markham Creek Road for a short distance. NOTE: This unmarked grave or graves is on private property; on the David Markham D.L.C. #39, RB #1230. (Not shown on Nonpareil 1987 USGS map.)

INDIAN BOY

A 0.01 5 **Before 1890** T26S R7W S13
From Melrose, proceed northerly on Cleveland Hill Road (Co. Rd. #59) past Cleveland Cemetery. Turn left (west) onto Heydon Road (Co. Rd. #143). Go 0.28 of a mile to a farm on the right; turn right on a private driveway for 0.36 of a mile. The grave is in the woods 450 feet to the right. A six-year old boy was refused burial in Cleveland Cemetery by the settlers. A Mr. McBeth, who lived nearby, then gave permission for the burial on his property. NOTE: This site is on private property. (Garden Valley 1987 USGS Quad. map.)

Name of Cemetery and also known as	Number of burials	Acres	Condition	Date started or earliest known burial	Township	Range	Section

INDIAN BURIAL GROUNDS

? ? ? ?   T22S R12W   ?

Possibly in Range 12 West or Range 13 West: located in the vicinity of Winchester Bay, and is both pre-and-post contact with whites. NOTE: No further information was given in the report. (Not shown on Winchester Bay 1985 USGS Quad. map.)

JAMES, SAMUEL M.

A   0.01   5   7 Jun 1867   T23S R4W   S22

Leave the I-5 Freeway at Scotts Valley Exit (Exit #154); go southeast onto Elkhead Road (Co. Rd. #7) soon turning left (east) onto Scotts Valley Road (Co. Rd. #8), going east and southeasterly past the Elkhead mines. The grave is located opposite the mine (left side of Scotts Valley Road) on top of a hill known as Turkey Hill. The stone lists: Born 27 Dec. 1818, Indiana, Died 7 June 1867. He was killed in a hunting accident. NOTE: The Turkey Hill referred to in this text is not the same hill as the one written up as Turkey Hill Cemetery; please see that article. NOTE: This site is on private property. (Not shown on Scotts Valley 1987 USGS Quad. map.

JOHANNSEN FAMILY
AKA: 1. JOHNSON
        FAMILY

A   ?   ?   Circa 1916   T22S R11W   S11

Go 5.75 miles east from Reedsport on the Umpqua Highway (OR. Hwy. 38), then turn right (south) onto Deans Creek Road (Co. Rd. #64). Continue for 1.6 miles up Deans Creek Road and turn left (east) onto Johnson Creek Road. Go about 0.5 of a mile on Johnson Creek Road. The 2 marked graves are on the left between the road and the creek: Andreas or Andrew, Johannsen or Johnson, who died in 1916, and his wife, Marie Sophia Ansama, whose death date is unknown. In addition there are 2 unmarked graves, believed to be for children. NOTE: This site is on private property. (Deer Head Point 1985 USGS Quad. map.)

JOHNSON, HERMAN

A   0.01   ?   Circa 1900   T27S R6W   S25

This lone grave is located in Umpqua Park (Fairgrounds) south of Roseburg and is presently unmarked, but family members reportedly know the exact spot where he is buried. Leave the I-5 Freeway at Exit 123,

Name of Cemetery and also known as	Number of burials	Acres	Condition	Date started or earliest known burial	Township	Range	Section

the exit to the Douglas County Fairgrounds and Umpqua Park. Turn right (south) on Frear Street and go about 0.4 of a mile to the parking area; on the John Kelly D.L.C. #41, RB #155. (The Fairgrounds and park are shown on the Roseburg East 1987 USGS Quad. map.)

JONES FAMILY   B   0.5   2   1853   T27S R6W   S10
From Roseburg, go westerly on Garden Valley Road (Co. Rd. #6) for about 2 miles to the Pacific Power and Light substation. This family cemetery is off to the left on a hill in back of the substation; on the Jacob Jones D.L.C. #43, RB #204. NOTE: This site is on private property and is fenced with locked gates. (Roseburg West 1987 USGS Quad. map.)

KANIPE, MILDRED   A   0.01   1   13 Jul 1983   T24S R4W   S18
Located in Kanipe Memorial County Park. Northeast of Oakland via Driver Valley Road (Co. Rd. #22) turn left (north) onto Elkhead Road (Co. Rd. #50). This new county park is on the left side of Elkhead Road. The fenced enclosure and the grave of Mildred Kanipe (1907-1983) is within the park. (Not shown on Nonpareil 1987 USGS Quad. map.)

KELLOGG   C   2   2   1857   T23S R7W   S29
Take OR. Hwy. 138 northwesterly from Sutherlin about 18 miles or southerly from Elkton about 7.5 miles, near the locale of Kellogg on the Umpqua River. Go about 0.6 of a mile south of the Kellogg Bridge over the Umpqua and opposite the grange hall. Go down a lane 200 yards from the west side of OR. Hwy. 138; on the John Kellogg D.L.C. #41, RB #664. (Kellogg 1990 USGS Quad. map.)

KINGERY FAMILY   ?   ?   ?   Circa 1918   T23S R5W   ?
There is a Death Certificate #29 for John Wesley Kingery, born 10 September 1862, died 15 February 1918, occupation farmer. He was reported buried in a family graveyard in the vicinity of Yoncalla. Probably this is in Section 11 or 12. The 1932 *Metsker Atlas of Landowners* shows Kingery ownership east of

Name of Cemetery and also known as	Number of burials	Acres	Condition	Date started or earliest known burial	Township	Range	Section

Yoncalla, east of the present I-5 Freeway and on the eastern slopes above Pleasant Valley. (Not shown on Scotts Valley 1987 USGS Quad. map.)

KREWSON

A 0.01 ? ?   T22S R5W   S4

About 2 miles north of Drain via OR. Hwy. 99 crossing Pass Creek at Johnson Creek. This burial is on or near an old mill site east of OR. Hwy. 99 and off of Laurel Hill Drive (Co. Rd. #68). (Not shown on Drain 1987 USGS Quad. map.)

LaBRIE FAMILY

A 0.1 5 ?   T26S R6W   S30

Go westerly from Roseburg via Garden Valley Road (Co. Rd. #6) then turn left (west) on Melrose Road (Co. Rd. #167 and #13). LaBrie Cemetery is 2.75 miles north on Melqua Road from Melrose Road and 300 feet left (west) on a driveway on the side of Cleveland Hill. The 5 or so monuments were removed in a family dispute but have lately been rediscovered and will be restored (July 1991). This cemetery is located on George Shambrook D.L.C. #57, RB #383. NOTE: This site is on private property. A separate small cemetery about 0.25 of a mile farther northwest, also off of Melqua Road, was a paupers burial ground; see Douglas County Poor Farm entry. (Garden Valley 1987 USGS Quad. map.)

LAVADOURE
  AKA: 1. PERDUE
       2. VAN NORMAN
       3. WRIGHT FAMILY

B 0.4 ? 1857   T30S R3W   S29

Leave Canyonville east on Tiller-Trail Highway (Co. Rd. #1), going through Days Creek. 6 miles east of Days Creek community and 0.13 of a mile east of Lavadoure Creek is a road; turn left (B.L.M. Road #30-3-17) northerly for 0.3 of a mile. The cemetery is on the left uphill 50 yards from the road. This was on the Ray Wright property (1978); on Leonard Stinger D.L.C. #37, RB 354. NOTE: This site is on private property. (Milo 1986 USGS Quad. map.)

Douglas County

| Name of Cemetery and also known as | Number of burials | Acres | Condition | Date started or earliest known burial | Township | Range | Section |

LEONA

B 1 3 1863 T21S R5W S34

Located off of OR. Hwy. 99 southwest of Curtin and northeast of Drain. Turn off of OR. Hwy. 99 onto Sandy Creek Road (Co. Rd. #178). Go about 100 yards on Sandy Creek Road and the cemetery is on the right. NOTE: the USGS map calls it Sand Creek Road but the county refers to it as Sandy Creek Road. This was the cemetery for the bygone community of Leona. {January 1992} (Drain 1987 USGS Quad. map.)

LETITIA
 AKA: 1. TISH

? ? ? ? T29S R3W S20

From Myrtle Creek go easterly on South Myrtle Road (Co. Rd. #18) for 11.6 miles to Letitia (Tish) Creek. NOTE: This cemetery location is quite uncertain to the compiler as there was no other information given in the report. (Not shown on White Rock 1987 USGS Quad. map.)

LEVENS GRAVE, ALBERT

A 0.01 ? ? T32S R5W S21

This lone grave is about 2.75 miles west of Azalea on the Azalea-Glen Road (Co. Rd. #12) on the right (northerly) about 800 feet from the county road and 250 feet left of a four-wheel drive road. It is on the Daniel H. Levens D.L.C. #38, RB #418 at Galesville. NOTE: This site is on private property. (Quines Creek 1986 USGS Quad. map.)

LIVINGSTON FAMILY
 AKA: 1. DIXON
   2. DIXONVILLE

A 0.15 3 1861-1898 T27S R4W S7

Go east of Roseburg and onto Buckhorn Road (Co. Rd. #4C and #17) through Dixonville. 0.25 of a mile past the Dixonville Store turn left (north) at the Roseburg Mill and go 2 miles northerly. The cemetery is on the right and downslope, about 100 feet west of the powerline. Fenced but overgrown, 14 markers in this family cemetery were found in 1988; on the Thomas Livingston D.L.C. #48 RB, #195. NOTE: This site is on private property. (Dixonville 1987 USGS Quad. map.)

Name of Cemetery and also known as	Number of burials	Acres	Condition	Date started or earliest known burial	Township	Range	Section

LONG FAMILY, JOHN

A ? ? 1871   T23S R5W   ?

This could be located in Sections 15, 16, 21, or 22, but it is thought to be in Section 16. Located somewhere off of Crest Road about 0.5 of a mile west and south of the I-5 Freeway interchange for Yoncalla (Exit #150), or about 2 miles south of Yoncalla as the crow flies. John and Minerva Long settled their 640 acre donation land claim 17 September 1850. The first 3 burials took place in 1871 for 3 of John and Minerva's children. It is unclear in what order the 3 died: Marquis Long, born 1857, died 1871; Emma M. Long, born 1859, died 1871; and Minerva A. Long, born 1865, died 1871. Next came the death of John Long, born 26 February 1810 in Tennessee, died 23 March 1890; then Minerva Jane Smith Long, his wife, died 3 April 1908. Then Robert Long, born 1862, died 1924 and Mary Jane Long Aldridge wife of M. C. S. Aldridge, born 1854, died 1929. Our source states that the 5 youngest of their 9 children are buried here. Our information was taken from *Historic Douglas County Oregon 1982*, published by Douglas County Historical Society. See the article on the John Long family on pages 204 and 205, written by Margaret Underwood Lofquist. The cemetery is on the John Long D.L.C. #46, RB #481. NOTE: This site is on private property. Total number of burials are unknown to the compiler. (Not shown on Yoncalla 1987 USGS Quad. map.)

LOOKINGGLASS
AKA: 1. I.O.O.F.

D 3.7 2 1871   T27S R7W   S35

In Roseburg from OR. Hwy 99 (Stephens Street) cross the South Umpqua River, going underneath the I-5 Freeway along Harvard Avenue for 2 miles from OR. Hwy. 99. Turn left off of Harvard Avenue onto Lookingglass Road (Co. Rd. #5-D) and go southwesterly about 6 miles, turning left (south) for 0.25 of a mile at Lookingglass. Turn right (west) onto Coos Bay Wagon Road (Co. Rd. #5-B) for a short distance. The cemetery is behind the community church. (Roseburg West 1987 USGS Quad. map.)

Douglas County

Name of Cemetery and also known as | Number of burials | Acres | Condition | Date started or earliest known burial | Township | Range | Section
---

LOST CREEK
AKA: 1. HARRIS, MR.

A 0.01 5 ? T25S R7W S12

Take OR. Hwy. 138 south from Elkton about 14 miles or go from Sutherlin northwesterly about 11 miles. Leave OR. Hwy. 138 to the west on Tyee Road (Co. Rd. #33). About 3.5 miles down Tyee Road cross Lost Creek and on the far side is B.L.M. Road #24-7-22 on the left. Take this four-wheel drive road inland and uphill. At the head of Rock Creek and Lost Creek where you will find one marked grave for a Mr. Harris, who requested burial at his favorite hunting grounds on Tyee Mountain. (Not shown on Tyee Mountain 1987 USGS Quad. map.)

MACEY FAMILY

? ? ? ? T22S R11W S2

Reportedly this family cemetery is located off of the Umpqua Highway (OR. Hwy. 38) at East Canyon, about 6.5 miles east of Reedsport (about 0.65 of a mile east of Deans Creek Road) and about 1 mile west of the Echo Resort. NOTE: This is all the information that was given in the report in 1979. (Not shown on Deer Head Point 1985 USGS map.)

MARTINDALE

C 1 ? 1882 T29S R8W S20

Located in Camas Valley, southwest of the community of Camas Valley. Leave OR. Hwy. 42 turning right (north) onto Main Camas Road (Co. Rd. #131-W). The cemetery is on the left only 100 feet further on Main Camas Road; on the Alston Martindale D.L.C. #42, RB #972. (Camas Valley 1990 USGS Quad. map.)

MASONIC [OAKLAND]

C 1 2 1865 T24S R5W S33

Travel north from Oakland on Old Highway 99 North (Co. Rd. #388) for about one mile, turn right (east) onto Old Town Road (Co. Rd. #152-A) crossing the railway tracks. At 0.5 of a mile from the highway turn hard left (northerly) onto Old Town Cemetery Road (Co. Rd. #152-B) and go 0.33 of a mile to the cemetery entrance. There are actually two distinct cemeteries here. The front (north) cemetery is the Masonic Cemetery, the back (south) is the Old Town Oakland Cemetery which belongs to the city of Oakland. See

Name of Cemetery and also known as	Number of burials	Acres	Condition	Date started or earliest known burial	Township	Range	Section

that article. {25 November 1997} (Sutherlin 1988 USGS Quad. map shows the Masonic Cemetery but omits the Old Town Oakland Cemetery.)

MASONIC [OLD ROSEBURG]
AKA: 1. CHINESE
2. DOUGLAS COUNTY
3. EARLY
I.O.O.F.
4. EARLY
MASONIC

? 1 2 1859 T27S R5W S19

Travel east on Douglas Avenue past the courthouse and over the hill, past Roseburg I.O.O.F. and St. Joseph Catholic cemeteries; turn right (south) onto Eastwood Street, then left onto California Street. The unmarked cemetery was in an old orchard (1977), but is now an open field on the south side of California Street. There are now no visible markers or headstones. The cemetery was deeded to the Masonic Laurel Lodge #13 on 8 November 1859. In 1897 the Laurel Lodge and the I.O.O.F. #8 donated it to the county, and it is unclear, now, how the I.O.O.F. was involved. Although it is commonly referred to as the Chinese Cemetery, there is no proof that any Chinese were ever buried here. {21 June 1991} (Roseburg East 1987 USGS Quad. map.)

MASONIC [YONCALLA]

? 4.13 2 ? T23S R5W S4

This cemetery is adjacent to Applegate Cemetery on the east. Access is from Front Street to Applegate Avenue, turning left (south) onto Douglas Street, right onto Elm Street and right (south) to the cemetery. {23 June 1991} (Yoncalla 1987 USGS Quad. map.)

McCULLOCH FAMILY

? 0.3 ? ? T29S R7W S6

Take OR. Hwy. 42 southwesterly from Winston past the Tenmile Store. Just past the store cross Tenmile Creek, then turn left (south) off of OR. Hwy. 42 onto Benedict Road (Co. Rd. #141) and go 0.6 of a mile to the cemetery on the right (west); on the William McCulloch D.L.C. #37, RB #641. (Tenmile 1990 USGS Quad. map.)

Douglas County

Name of Cemetery and also known as	Number of burials	Acres	Condition	Date started or earliest known burial	Township	Range	Section

McGUIRE FAMILY A 0.3 5 1856-1895 T28S R7W S34

Take OR. Hwy. 42 southwesterly from Winston. Leave OR. Hwy. 42, turning left (southwest) onto Olalla Road (Co. Rd. #38) and go about 1.4 miles. The cemetery is about 200 yards west of the road, across Pearon Creek, on land owned by Winifred Swift (1978). It is unfenced and the cattle have knocked over the stones. There were 8 known burials as of 1967 and it is just about on the line between Thomas J. McGuire D.L.C. #52, RB #892 and the John Olmstead D.L.C. #53, RB #674. NOTE: This site is on private property. (Tenmile 1990 USGS Quad. map.)

MELROSE C 2.6 2 1854 T27S R7W S1
AKA: 1. FRENCH
         SETTLEMENT

Leave Roseburg to the west on Garden Valley Road (Co. Rd. #6) then turn left (west) onto Melrose Road (Co. Rds. #167 and #13) to the Melrose Store; continue west another 0.4 of a mile, still on Melrose Road (now Co. Rd. #51-B). The cemetery is up the hill on the left (south) side of the road. (Roseburg West 1987 USGS Quad. map.)

MOUNTAIN VIEW ? ? ? ? T29S R5W S28
  CREMATORIUM
AKA: 1. MOUNT VIEW

Located in Myrtle Creek at 428 North Old Pacific Highway. (Not shown on Myrtle Creek 1987 USGS Quad. map.)

MURPHY FAMILY ? ? ? ? ? ? ?

A Murphy Family Cemetery has been reported on the Murphy Place on Smith River. The compiler has no other information.

MURRY B 0.5 ? 1862 T29S R8W S18
AKA: 1. MURRAY

Located in Camas Valley. Leave OR. Hwy. 42 westerly on Upper Camas Road (Co. Rd. #128), turn hard right (north) and go 0.6 of a mile. This cemetery is 800 feet to the left (west). There were 25 known burials (1960). NOTE: Murry is the USGS spelling. (Camas Valley 1990 USGS Quad. map.)

Name of Cemetery and also known as	Number of burials	Acres	Condition	Date started or earliest known burial	Township	Range	Section

MYRTLE CREEK PIONEER
AKA: 1. ADAMS

C   0.9   ?   1857   T29S R5W   S28

Take South Main Street, the old Pacific Highway (OR. Hwy. 99), crossing Myrtle Creek Bridge. Turn right (southwest) onto Pioneer Way, to the cemetery at the end of the street; on the John Adams D.L.C. #41, RB #851. (Myrtle Creek 1987 USGS Quad. map.)

NICHOLS
AKA: 1. BROCKWAY
     2. DAVLIN

A   0.15   ?   ?   T28S R6W   S20

Located just south and west of Winston at Brockway and north (right) off of OR. Hwy. 42. The cemetery is about 100 feet behind Douglas High School; on the Joseph Gage D.L.C. #51, RB #763. NOTE: This site is possibly on private property or school property. (Winston 1987 USGS Quad. map.)

NOAH

C   1.3   ?   1882   T29S R8W   S7

Located in Camas Valley. Leave OR. Hwy. 42 to the west on Upper Camas Road (Co. Rd. #128), turn hard right, still on Upper Camas Road and go north for about 0.75 of a mile. The cemetery is on the right (east), just before the Dancer Road junction (Co. Rd. #218) on the right; on Frank J. Higginson D.L.C. #50, RB #690. The property for this cemetery was donated by the Noah family. (Camas Valley 1990 USGS Quad. map.)

NOEL FAMILY

A   ?   5   1896-1898   T21S R11W   S3

From Reedsport go north on U.S. Hwy. 101, crossing the Umpqua River. Turn right (northeasterly) onto Lower Smith River Road (Co. Rd. #48) and continue along the right bank of the Smith River to Noel Creek, about 7.5 miles northeast of U.S. Hwy. 101. This family burial ground is about 0.23 of a mile north of the county road and across Noel Creek from the Lyle Earl Ranch (1978). There were 3 known burials as of June of 1973. NOTE: This site is on private property. (North Fork 1984 USGS Quad. map.)

NOFOG

?   ?   ?   ?   T28S R3W   ?

This could possibly be in Section 2. A small cemetery was reported in 1966 to be almost

Douglas County

Name of Cemetery and also known as	Number of burials	Acres	Condition	Date started or earliest known burial	Township	Range	Section

returned to a primitive state; at the bygone community of Nofog. NOTE: No further information was given with the report. (Not shown on Lane Mountain 1987 USGS Quad. map.)

NORTH FORK
  AKA: 1. LOWER SMITH
         RIVER
       2. SHERRETT--
         LYSTER

A	?	?		1875-1908	T20S	R10W	S31

Leave Reedsport to the north on U.S. Hwy. 101 and cross the Umpqua River. Turn right (northeasterly) onto Lower Smith River Road (Co. Rd. #48) and go about 15 miles up this road to the LeRoy Stemmerman Ranch (1978). The cemetery had at least 18 burials, but only 2 markers bearing 6 names were found in 1973. NOTE: This site is on private property. (North Fork 1984 USGS Quad. map.)

OAK CREEK

D	4.5	2	1857	T26S	R4W	S29

Leave Roseburg on OR. Hwy. 138 (easterly and northeasterly). The cemetery, is just beyond Milepost 10, 0.2 of a mile off to the left on Oak Creek Drive (Co. Rd. #4-K) and on a hill. It is now reported to be larger than the 4.5 acre size given in 1978. 548 known burials were found in March of 1988 in a survey by the Douglas County Genealogical Society. (Oak Creek Valley 1987 USGS Quad. map.)

OLD TOWN OAKLAND
  AKA:1. OAKLAND CITY
       2. PIONEER
          [OAKLAND]

C	1	2	1865	T24S	R5W	S33

Travel north from Oakland on Old Highway 99 North (Co. Rd. #388) for about one mile, turn right (east) onto Old Town Road (Co. Rd. #152-A) crossing the railway tracks. At 0.5 of a mile from the highway turn hard left (northerly) onto Old Town Cemetery Road (Co. Rd. #152-B) and go 0.33 of a mile to the cemetery entrance. There are actually two distinct cemeteries here. The front (north) cemetery is the Masonic Cemetery, the back (south) is the Old Town Oakland Cemetery which belongs to the city of Oakland. When the railroad reached this area in 1872 most folks moved to the present townsite of Oakland leaving Old Town behind. {25 November 1997} (Sutherlin 1988 USGS Quad. map shows the Masonic Cemetery but omits the Old Town Oakland Cemetery.)

Name of Cemetery and also known as	Number of burials	Acres	Condition	Date started or earliest known burial	Township	Range	Section

OTEY FAMILY

A   0.15   ?   ?   T26S R6W   S1
Leave Old Highway 99 North (Co. Rd. #388) in the Wilbur area north of Winchester. Go northwest on Oak Hill Road (Co. Rd. #32), underneath the I-5 Freeway, for about 1.5 miles from Old Highway 99 North. The family cemetery is about 300 yards on the left, up the hillside behind the Miller home (1978); on the Edwin W. Otey D.L.C. #48, RB #995. NOTE: This site is on private property. (Winchester 1987 USGS Quad. map.)

PANTHER CREEK

A   0.01   ?   ?   T20S R7W   S26
One grave of an unknown person has been reported at Panther Creek. This is most likely near the confluence of that creek with the right bank of Smith River at Gunter. Very possibly the grave in question has been removed to the nearby Gunter Cemetery. (Not shown on Gunter 1984 USGS Quad. map.)

PATTERSON FAMILY

A   0.5   ?   1852-1930   T29S R8W   S17
Located in Camas Valley. Leave OR. Hwy. 42 onto Upper Camas Road (Co. Rd. #128), going west. Soon turn right (north) at the crossroads onto Kirkendahl Road (Co. Rd. #128-A) and go 0.5 of a mile from Upper Camas Road. The cemetery is 700 feet to the left (west) of Kirkendahl Road; on the Abraham Patterson D.L.C. #40, RB #484. Five graves were reported from a 1930 D.A.R. visit. NOTE: This site is on private property. (Camas Valley 1990 USGS Quad. map.)

PAUPER'S [WINSTON]

A   ?   ?   ?   T28S R6W   S21
Reportedly there are 6 paupers' graves next to the south border of the Civil Bend Cemetery. Civil Bend Cemetery is located off of OR. Hwy. 42 in Winston; turn left (south) onto Civil Bend Avenue. Access from the I-5 Freeway is at the Winston Exit (Exit #119). (Not shown on Winston 1987 USGS Quad. map.)

PEEL

A   ?   ?   Circa 1917   T27S R3W   S11
Drive 6.75 miles up Little River Road from Glide to the old site of Peel at the

Name of Cemetery and also known as	Number of burials	Acres	Condition	Date started or earliest known burial	Township	Range	Section

confluence of Jim Creek with the Little River. Peel rated a post office from January 1888 until December 1921. Douglas County Death Certificate #21 in 1917 reports the death of J. H. Everts, born 14 August 1841, died 8 February 1917 and his burial at Peel the following day. (Not shown on Lane Mountain 1987 USGS Quad. map.)

QUINES CREEK
AKA: 1. GILLAM
    2. GILLIAMS

? 0.5 ? ? T32S R5W S15
Go about 0.75 of a mile west of Azalea on Azalea-Glen Road (Co. Rd. #12). The cemetery is on the left (south) side of the road; on the Carrick S. Mynott D.L.C. #37, RB #826. (Quines Creek 1986 USGS Quad. map.)

RAINVILLE

? 0.2 ? ? T31S R2W S3
Located in the Umpqua National Forest. Take the Tiller-Trail Highway (Co. Rd. #1) southeast from Tiller towards Drew. Go about 1.75 miles from the bridge over the South Umpqua River at Tiller; turn left (east) off of the main road and then curve back northerly, for a total of 0.6 of a mile from the main road. The cemetery is on the left and on top of a knob before you reach the powerline. NOTE: This is probably a four-wheel drive road. (Tiller 1989 USGS Quad. map.)

RED HILL
AKA: 1. DAGAN, THEOPHILUS
    2. DR. DUTCH
    3. SMITH HILL

A 0.01 5 18 Feb 1882 T23S R5W S34
Leave the I-5 Freeway at the Metz Hill Exit (Exit #142) to the east, taking Goodrich Highway (Co. Rd. #29) and going north towards Rice Hill. There is a single granite headstone to Dr. Dagan placed by the Oregon Pioneer Association in a glade near his house. It is not easy to find. It is said to be 0.25 of a mile south of the road and on the south side of Red Hill (or Smith Hill?). Doctor Theophilus Dagan, was born in Germany in 1814, he emigrated to America at an unknown date. He came to Oregon with the Gilliam wagon train in 1844, eventually settling in Douglas County between Oakland and Yoncalla. Dagan was a colorful character; among other traits each of his

Name of Cemetery and also known as	Number of burials	Acres	Condition	Date started or earliest known burial	Township	Range	Section

horses was named "Rachel". He also appears somewhat fictionalized in Honore Wilson Morrow's novel *On to Oregon* (1926), the story of the Sager children in that wagon train. See the *Statesman-Journal* 12 April 1998, page 6D. NOTE: This site is on private property. (Not shown on Yoncalla 1987 USGS Quad. map.)

REED FAMILY, REASON

A 0.1 4 ?   T25S R5W   S5

Take Old Highway 99 North (Co. Rd. #388) north of Oakland, cross the bridge a mile from town and turn left (west) onto Green Valley Road (Co. Rd. #23-A). Go west past Cedar Hill Cemetery 0.38 mile, almost to the overpass over the I-5 Freeway. The Reed Family Cemetery is on the left (south), 0.23 of a mile from Green Valley Road, on the right hand side of the driveway on top of a hill. It is on the Reason Reid [*Sic*] D.L.C. #58, RB #249. NOTE: This site is on private property. (Sutherlin 1988 USGS Quad. map.)

REED-HILL FAMILY

B 1 2 1861   T26S R5W   S7

The Reed-Hill Cemetery for these families adjoins the Wilbur Cemetery but is a separate entity. This cemetery is reached by Old Highway 99 North (Co. Rd. #388) north from Roseburg or south from Sutherlin. Just north of the locale of Wilbur turn right (east) onto Wilbur Cemetery Road (Co. Rd. #170), crossing the railway tracks and go 0.1 of a mile to the cemetery. Wilbur Cemetery itself adjoins Reed-Hill Cemetery ahead to the north; on the Samuel Gardniner D.L.C. #43, RB #1982. (Winchester 1987 USGS Quad. map.

REEDSPORT
AKA: 1. AURORA
     MASONIC
     LODGE #59
  2. MASONIC

? 3.7 ? ?   T22S R12W   S4

Located at the west end of town on the north side of Longwood Drive, in sight of U.S. Hwy. 101. (Winchester Bay 1985 USGS Quad. map.)

RICE CREEK

? ? ? ?   T29S R6W   ?

There is perhaps a Rice Creek Cemetery, or perhaps it is an A.K.A. for Willis Creek

Name of Cemetery and also known as	Number of burials	Acres	Condition	Date started or earliest known burial	Township	Range	Section

Cemetery. Rice and Willis Creeks are parallel, about a mile apart here. (Not shown on Winston 1987 USGS Quad. map.)

RICE FAMILY   A   ?   ?   ?   T24S R5W   S5

These two grave sites of the Rice family are on the old Rice Place at Rice Hill. They are both just east of the I-5 Freeway Exit #146 and apparently on the left (east) side of North Cabin Creek Road (Co. Rd. #279), between the road and the railway tracks. Each site contains 2 or 3 graves. NOTE: This site is on private property. (Not shown on Yoncalla 1987 USGS Quad. map.)

RICE-MARSH FAMILY   A   ?   ?   ?   T23S R5W   S31

Located on the west side of the I-5 Freeway, on a hill on the G. N. Colvin Ranch, formerly the Ervin Rice Ranch. Access is probably via four-wheel drive northwesterly from Rice Valley Road South (Co. Rd. #30-A). There is a Marsh Creek in this section also. NOTE: This site is on private property. (Not shown on Yoncalla 1987 USGS Quad. map.)

RICHARDS FAMILY   A   0.1   ?   1873-1907   T28S R7W   S25

Take OR. Hwy. 42 westerly from Winston for about 3.25 miles. Turn right (north), off the highway, for 0.25 of a mile to this family cemetery. There are 9 known burials (1970) on the John A. Richards D.L.C. #58, RB #754. NOTE: This site is on private property. (Not shown on Winston 1987 USGS Quad. map.)

RIDDLE   ?   6.2   1   1855   T30S R6W   S23

Leave the town of Riddle from the intersection of Main Street and Sixth Avenue; turn southwest, with the railway tracks on the left. Go southwesterly on Cow Creek Road (Co. Rd. #39) about a mile from Main and Sixth and turn right (north) onto Riddle Cemetery Road (Co. Rd. #183) to the cemetery. (Nickel Mountain 1986 USGS Quad. map.)

Name of Cemetery and also known as	Number of burials	Acres	Condition	Date started or earliest known burial	Township	Range	Section

RITCHEY FAMILY

?   1.2   ?   ?   T21S R5W   S31

Go west from Drain on OR. Hwy. 38 and turn right (north) onto Hardscrabble Road (Co. Rd. #65). As the county road swings right (easterly), leaving the valley of Hardscrabble Creek, this family cemetery is off to the right (south). NOTE: There is no ready access through this private property. It is on the old Ritchey Ranch. (Drain 1987 USGS Quad. map.)

RONDEAU
  AKA: 1. TILLER

?   0.4   ?   ?   T30S R2W   S24

Take the Tiller-Trail Highway (Co. Rd #1) easterly, 24 miles to Tiller from Canyonville. At Tiller turn left (northeast) onto South Umpqua Road (Co. Rd. #46) and go about 3.5. miles. The cemetery is on the left (north) side of the road. (Tiller 1989 USGS Quad. map.)

ROSE HILL MEMORIAL
  AKA: 1. CANYONVILLE
         BIBLE ACADEMY

B   ?   1   ?   T30S R5W   S27

This is located along the south border of the Canyonville Cemetery, just north of Canyonville, on Main Street, on the right (east) side of the street. It can also be easily reached from the I-5 Freeway via the North Canyonville Exit (Exit #99) and taking Stanton Park Road (Co. Rd. #1-B) towards Canyonville. There is a fence between the two cemeteries. Located on the James G. Clark D.L.C. #51, RB #792. {27 October 1995} (Not shown as a separate cemetery on Canyonville 1986 USGS Quad. map.)

ROSEBURG

A   0.01   5   ?   T27S R5W   S18

Take Diamond Lake Boulevard (OR. Hwy. 138) easterly; turn left (north) onto Fulton Street and go about 2 blocks to the junction of Commercial Avenue, formerly 6th Street. On the right (east) there was once a small wooden marker and a rosebush which marked the grave of "Baby Girl." The grave is now lost, having been covered with debris from the mills. (Not shown on Roseburg East 1987 USGS Quad. map.)

Douglas County

Name of Cemetery and also known as	Number of burials	Acres	Condition	Date started or earliest known burial	Township	Range	Section

ROSEBURG MEMORIAL GARDENS
AKA: 1. MASONIC

E 16.5 1 1865   T27S R6W   S13
Take Stephens Street (OR. Hwy. 99) north from downtown. Turn left (west) onto Garden Valley Boulevard, cross the railway tracks, turn left (south) on Hicks Street to the cemetery at the end of the street. {21 June 1991} (Roseburg East 1987 USGS Quad. map.)

ROSEBURG NATIONAL
AKA: 1. OLD SOLDIERS
     2. OREGON SOLDIERS HOME
     3. ROSEBURG VETERANS
     4. VETERANS ADMINISTRATION

E 3.2 1 1897   T27S R6W   S14
Take Harvard Avenue westerly from the I-5 Freeway Exit #124. Drive 0.7 of a mile from the freeway exit, turning right (north) onto the cemetery driveway at the west edge of Stewart Park. As of 1996 the number of burials stood at 5,200. {21 June 1991} (Roseburg East 1987 USGS Quad. map.)

RUTERS FAMILY

A ? 4 ?   T24S R7W   ?
Possibly located in Section 14 or 15. Take OR. Hwy. 138 northwesterly from Sutherlin for 11 miles, then turn left (westerly) onto Tyee Road (Co. Rd. #33). The distance along Tyee Road is vague: "several miles." There is a marker and the graves are near a ranch house, by some myrtle trees and near the banks of the Umpqua River. NOTE: This family cemetery was on the private property of L. R. Ocumpaugh in 1977. (Not shown on Tyee or Tyee Mountain 1990 USGS Quad. maps.)

ST. GEORGE'S EPISCOPAL CHURCH COLUMBARIUM

? ? ? ?   T27S R5W   S19
Located at 1024 Southeast Cass Avenue, Roseburg. (Not shown on Roseburg East 1987 USGS Quad. map.)

ST. JOSEPH CATHOLIC
AKA: 1. ROSEBURG CATHOLIC
     2. ST. STEPHEN'S

C 1 1 1877   T27S R5W   S19
Take Southeast Douglas Avenue easterly past the courthouse, over the hill and just past the I.O.O.F. Cemetery. The Catholic Cemetery is also on the right; on the Thomas Stevens D.L.C. #39, RB #868. {21 June 1991} (Roseburg East 1987 USGS Quad. map.)

Name of Cemetery and also known as	Number of burials	Acres	Condition	Date started or earliest known burial	Township	Range	Section

SCOTTSBURG
AKA: 1. I.O.O.F.
     2. LONG PRAIRIE

C   3.2   1   1858   T22S R9W   S8

As the head of navigation on the Umpqua, Scottsburg was an important place in the early days of settlement. Go about 3 miles east of Scottsburg on OR. Hwy. 38. Turn left (northwest) and go 0.3 of a mile to the cemetery. There are 2 sections to this cemetery; on the William Golden D.L.C. #40, RB #1244. (Scottsburg 1985 usgs Quad. map.)

SHEPHERD, INA

A   0.01   ?   ?   T27S R5W   ?

A single grave located in the Roseburg area. NOTE: No further information was given in the report.

SHOESTRING
AKA: 1. ELKHEAD CHURCH

A   1   3   Circa 1850   T23S R4W   S10

Located about 3 miles north of Elkhead in the hills west of Shoestring Valley and on a ridgetop of the watershed between Walker Creek and Elk Creek. The county road to the church and cemetery was vacated in 1925 and there is now a four-wheel drive road leading northwest from Scotts Valley Road (Co. Rd. #8). The church was 150/200 feet north of the cemetery and burned early in the 1930's: *Roseburg News-Review*, 10 June 1990. (Not shown on Scotts Valley 1987 USGS Quad. map.)

SINGLETON FAMILY

A   ?   ?   ?   T26S R4W   ?

Possibly located in Section 34 or 35. From Roseburg go east on OR. Hwy. 138, turning right onto Buckhorn Road (Co. Rds. #4-C and 17). Go 2.6 miles past the Dixonville substation and turn left (north) onto Strader Road (Co. Rd. #136). The cemetery is to the left, on a hill, 3.2 miles from Buckhorn Road. A September 1988 visit by the Genealogical Society of Douglas County reported that at least 13 burials were known, but only a single stone marker remains (with an 1899 date). It is unknown if any of the Singleton family is actually buried here; on the William R. Singleton D.L.C. #50, RB #251. NOTE: This site is on private property. (Not shown on Oak Creek Valley 1987 USGS Quad. map.)

Name of Cemetery and also known as	Number of burials	Acres	Condition	Date started or earliest known burial	Township	Range	Section

STORES FAMILY   ?   ?   ?   ?   T22S R6W   ?

Perhaps located in Section 10. Leave Drain and go west on OR. Hwy. 38, turning right (north) onto Schoen Road (Co. Rd. #66). NOTE: The location of this family cemetery which includes McClellan burials is very uncertain to the compiler. (Not shown on Putnam Valley 1987 USGS Quad. map.)

STOWEL FAMILY
  AKA: 1. WINCHESTER   ?   0.14   5   1887   T26S R6W   S36

Located 0.57 of a mile south of the bridge over the North Umpqua River at Winchester, along the west side of the I-5 Freeway, near the southbound lanes. In this area, the west line of the John Akin D.L.C. #53, RB #128 is also the west line of the cemetery and of the freeway right-of-way, but the cemetery is excluded from state ownership. On a knoll and grown over with ivy, there were 2 gravestones and at least one other burial (1977). Access is unclear except perhaps informally by highway maintenance crews. (Not shown on Winchester 1987 USGS Quad. map.)

STRADER FAMILY   A   ?   5   Circa 1871   T27S R4W   ?

Perhaps located in Section 9 or 10. Norma Hatfield of Dixonville reports (December 1991) that there are 3 unmarked graves on a hill overlooking Strader Road. Go east of the Dixonville crossroads on Buckhorn Road for 2.75 miles then turn left (north) onto Strader Road (Co. Rd. #136). The graves may be on a hillside, on the right (east) of the road about 2.5 miles from Buckhorn Road, as Strader owned land here in 1928. The burials are of Jane Worthington Strader, first wife of John Strader; her brother Chester; and an infant of John Strader and his second wife, Martha. NOTE: This appears to be on private land. (Not shown on Dixonville 1987 USGS Quad. map.)

SUNNYDALE
  AKA: 1. PUTNAM FAMILY
        2. SUNSET   ?   1   4   ?   T22S R6W   S16

Take OR. Hwy. 38 west from Drain towards Elkton. Drive 5.1 miles and then turn left (south) onto Snell Road South, which

Name of Cemetery and also known as	Number of burials	Acres	Condition	Date started or earliest known burial	Township	Range	Section

parallels the highway. The cemetery is on the left (south) only 0.1 of a mile after leaving the highway; on the Joseph Putnam D.L.C. #38, RB #412. (Putnam Valley 1987 USGS Quad. map.)

SUTHERLIN [OLD]

| | ? | ? | ? | ? | T25S | R5W | S15 |

Travel easterly out of Sutherlin via Central Avenue and Nonpareil Road (Co. Rd. #19). Turn left (north) onto North Side Road (Co. Rd. #120-A). It may be on the Thomas Sutherlin D.L.C. #40, RB #1032. NOTE: This old cemetery is on private property. (Not shown on Sutherlin 1988 USGS Quad. maps.)

TENMILE

| | ? | 2 | ? | 1886 | T28S | R7W | S31 |

Go southwesterly from Winston on OR. Hwy. 42 for 9 miles. Turn right (northerly) onto Coats Road (Co. Rd. #109-A) for a short distance; then left (westerly) onto Tenmile Valley Road (Co. Rd. #109) to the cemetery, which is about 0.5 of a mile from OR. Hwy. 42. (Tenmile 1990 USGS Quad. map.)

THIELE FAMILY

| | ? | ? | ? | ? | T24S | R5W | S4 |

The Thiele Family Cemetery is near the Rice Family Cemeteries. The latter are west of the railway tracks, the former is east of the tracks. Leave the I-5 Freeway at Metz Hill Exit (Exit #142) to the east and take the Goodrich Highway (Co. Rd. #29) easterly and northerly to Rice Valley. The graves are on the west side of the Old Thiele Ranch; 6 known burials. NOTE: This site is on private property. (Not shown on Yoncalla 1987 USGS Quad. map.)

THRUSH

| | A | 1.3 | ? | 1894 | T29S | R8W | S7 |

Located in Sections 7 and 8. Here is still another cemetery in Camas Valley. Turn west off of OR. Hwy. 42 onto Upper Camas Road (Co. Rd. #128). Turn hard right (north), still on Upper Camas Road, passing Murry and Noah Cemeteries; turn right (east) onto Baldwin Road (Co. Rd. #130). This cemetery, donated by Abraham Thrush, is at the end of Baldwin

Douglas County

Name of Cemetery and also known as	Number of burials	Acres	Condition	Date started or earliest known burial	Township	Range	Section

Road (Co. Rd. #130). A 1960 D.A.R. visit reported 21 known graves. (Camas Valley 1990 USGS Quad. map.)

TIPTON, MACE
 AKA: 1. INDIAN

| | B | ? | ? | ? | T26S R3W | | S1 |

Take OR. Hwy. 138 east from Roseburg to Idleyld Park: located just east of the Idleyld Store and on the property of Dr. Frank Moore in 1978. The graveyard, with one brass plaque to Mace Tipton "the last of the Umpquas" (died 1932), is on the hillside overlooking the North Umpqua River between the mouth of Rock Creek and King Creek. There are 28 others of his family known to be buried here. NOTE: This site is on private property. (Not shown on Glide 1987 USGS Quad. map.)

TISON
 AKA: 1. DREW
    2. TISON RANCH
    3. TYSON

| | A | ? | 5 | ? | T31S R1W | | S19 |

Located in the northwest 1/4 of Section 19. Take the Tiller-Trail Highway (Co. Rd. #1) from Tiller, to the southeast, past Drew. Joe Hall Creek is on the left very soon after the highway reenters the Umpqua National Forest. The cemetery was in back of a house (1978) on the left side of the highway. NOTE: This site is on private property. (Not shown on Richter Mountain 1989 USGS Quad. map.)

TULLER

| | A | ? | ? | 1895-1907 | T32S R7W | | ? |

Possibly located on Section 28. Go west of Glendale via Reuben Road (Co. Rd. #27), which becomes Cow Creek Road (Co. Rd. #321), for 7.4 miles. There is a wooden marker on the left, which reads: "Pioneer Graves. In this vicinity are buried - Jeremiah G. Tuller, born in Ohio 1822, who came to Oregon in 1844, served in the Cayuse Indian War in 1847 and 1848. He died in 1895. His wife Miriam, born in Illinois in 1826, came to Oregon in 1845, via the Barlow Road, and died in 1907. Their daughter, Clementine Bell M.D., born in 1852, graduated from the University Medical School in 1899, and died in 1901. Another daughter, Edith Tuller, known locally as "the Hermit Lady", tended

| Name of Cemetery and also known as | Number of burials | Acres | Condition | Date started or earliest known burial | Township | Range | Section |

the family graves until her death in 1931.
She is buried in the Glendale Cemetery. The
Tuller home was destroyed by fire shortly
after Edith's death." SEE: *In Search of
Western Oregon*, by Ralph Friedman 1990.
{1998} (Not shown on Rabbit Mountain 1990
USGS Quad. map.)

TURKEY HILL

A ? ? ?   T24S R5W   S17
Leave the I-5 Freeway at Metz Hill Exit (Exit
#142), to the east. Turn left (north) and
stay parallel to the east side of the
freeway, past the junction with Goodrich
Highway (Co. Rd. #29). Continue northerly on
South Cabin Creek Road (Co. Rd. #285) for
1.25 miles, to a house. The cemetery is
about 0.25 of a mile east of the house on the
south side of Turkey Hill. There are several
graves. NOTE: This site is on private
property. (Not shown on Sutherlin 1988 USGS
Quad. map.)

UMPQUA CITY
  AKA: 1. UMPQUA

? ? ? 1850-1867   T21S R12W   S31
A cemetery called Umpqua has been reported as
being in the vicinity of the present
community of that name. The compiler
suspects that this cemetery was at the bygone
town of Umpqua City which was far downstream
near Fort Umpqua #2 and about two miles from
the Pacific Ocean, *Oregon Geographic Names*,
by Lewis A. McArthur reports that Umpqua City
existed between 1850 and 1867. The present
community of Umpqua he says was originally
called Umpqua Ferry until about 1905. The
cemetery needs of the present Umpqua
community would be served by Coles Valley
Cemetery about three miles distant. (Umpqua
City graveyard is not shown on the Winchester
Bay 1985 USGS Quad. map.)

UNKNOWN

? 0.15 ? ?   T21S R11W   S35
This cemetery has no roadway access. The
most convenient route appears to be by boat,
from the Echo Resort on the Umpqua River,
about 7.5 miles east of Reedsport via OR.
Hwy. 38. Leave the dock and head downstream
about 0.6 of a mile; go ashore on the north

Name of Cemetery and also known as	Number of burials	Acres	Condition	Date started or earliest known burial	Township	Range	Section

bank of the Umpqua River at the mouth of an unnamed canyon, about 300 yards upstream from a hill with a quarry. Walk inland about 300 yards to the cemetery on the right (eastern) slope of the canyon. It is within the Siuslaw National Forest. (Deer Head Point 1985 USGS Quad. map.)

VALLEY VIEW
AKA: 1. SUTHERLIN

| | ? | 8 | ? | ? | T25S R5W | | S13 |

Travel easterly out of Sutherlin via Central Avenue and Nonpareil Road (Co. Rd. #19). Turn right (south) onto Plat "I" road (Co. Rd. #70) for about 0.5 of a mile, then left (east) onto Valley View Road (Co. Rd. #199); the cemetery is on the right. (Nonpareil 1987 USGS Quad. map.)

WELKER GIRLS

| | A | ? | ? | ? | T26S R4W | | ? |

Possibly located on Section 13. Take OR. Hwy. 138 east and northeast from Roseburg, almost to Glide. Turn left (north) onto North Bank Road (Co. Rd. #200), cross the North Umpqua River; then turn right (east) from the county road and find the Updegrave Place. The Welker girls are buried near an old stone farm building (1978). The graves may be unmarked. NOTE: This site is on private property. (Not shown on Glide 1987 USGS Quad. map.)

WELLS FAMILY

| | B | 0.2 | 2 | Circa 1851 | T22S R7W | | S31 |

Take OR. Hwy. 138 south from Elkton for about 1.75 miles; turn right (west) at the crossroads, onto Wells Road (Co. Rd. #203), and go about 0.8 of a mile. The Wells Family Cemetery is 50 yards on the right, on a ridgetop; just outside of Ira Wells D.L.C. #56, RB #1058. NOTE: This site is on private property. {23 February 1993} (Kellogg 1990 USGS Quad. map.)

WEST-WINNIFORD FAMILIES
AKA: 1. WEST FAMILY, CALVIN B.

| | ? | 0.1 | ? | 1862 | T26S R6W | | S7 |

Located 10 miles northwest from Roseburg via Garden Valley Road (Co. Rd. #6). This small family cemetery is about 1.5 miles beyond the junction of Lower Garden Valley Road (Co. Rd.

Name of Cemetery and also known as	Number of burials	Acres	Condition	Date started or earliest known burial	Township	Range	Section

#191) with Garden Valley Road. After crossing a small stream, the cemetery is on top of a hill in the fields, in back of fir trees on the left side of the road, towards the Umpqua River. It is on the Calvin Burnside West D.L.C., RB #1248. There were 3 unmarked graves of children; 2 of the West family and later a Winniford child, according to a 1970 D.A.R. report. NOTE: This site is on private property. (Garden Valley 1987 USGS Quad. map.)

WILBUR [NEW]

C 3 2 1861 T26S R5W S7

This cemetery adjoins but is distinct from the Reed-Hill Cemetery. The visitor encounters the latter first. Both cemeteries are reached by Old Highway 99 North (Co. Rd. #388) north from Roseburg or south from Sutherlin. Just north of the locale of Wilbur turn right (east) onto Wilbur Cemetery Road (Co. Rd. #170), crossing the railway tracks and go 0.1 mile to the entrance which is for Reed-Hill and Wilbur Cemetery is beyond. Located on the Samuel Gardiner D.L.C. #43, RB #1982. (Winchester 1987 USGS Quad. map.)

WILBUR [OLD]
AKA: 1. UMPQUA
ACADEMY

? ? 5 1855 T26S R5W S18

From Old Highway 99 North (Co. Rd. #388) at Wilbur, turn east on North Bank Road (Co. Rd. #200) for a mile or less. This cemetery was located on a hill shaped like a half an egg that runs east-west, on the right (south) of the county road. Most of the graves were moved to the present Wilbur Cemetery. A visit in the summer of 1973 disclosed the remains of 9 markers; on the James H. Wilbur D.L.C. #48, RB #631. NOTE: This site is on private property. (The half-egg hill is shown on the Winchester 1987 USGS Quad. map, but no cemetery is indicated.)

WILLIS CREEK
AKA: 1. DILLARD

C 1 2 Jan 1857 T29S R6W S9

From Winston go south on Old Highway 99 South (Co. Rd. #387) to Dillard, turn right and cross the South Umpqua River. Turn left onto Willis Creek Road (Co. Rd. #43) and continue

Name of Cemetery and also known as	Number of burials	Acres	Condition	Date started or earliest known burial	Township	Range	Section

southeasterly near the river bank. At the next road fork continue ahead on Willis Creek Road (Co. Rd. #43 is now #88); turn right (south) up Willis Creek Valley. This cemetery is on the right (west), was deeded in January 1948; on the Stephen D. Willis D.L.C. #41, RB #860. (Winston 1987 USGS Quad. map.)

WILLIS FAMILY, WILLIAM A.
AKA: 1. HAHN

A 0.01 5 1858-1891 T27S R4W S19

From Roseburg take OR. Hwy. 138 and Buckhorn Road (Co. Rd. #4-C) past the Dixonville crossroads. Continue easterly on Buckhorn Road (now Co. Rd. #17) another 1.6 miles. The cemetery is on the right (south) in the middle of a field; on William A. Willis D.L.C. #45, RB #221. There are 3 graves enclosed in an iron fence, of members of the Willis family (August 1988 visit for the Douglas Co. Genealogical Society). NOTE: This site is on private property. (Not shown on Dixonville 1987 USGS Quad. map.)

WIMBERLY
AKA: 1. GLIDE

? 0.75 ? 1852 T26S R3W S19

Leave OR. Hwy. 138 just before crossing the bridge over Little River and just before entering Glide. Drive south on Little River Road (Co. Rd. #17-A) for 0.75 of a mile and then turn right (west) onto Schloeman Lane for 700 feet to a fork. Take the road on the right, the cemetery is ahead another 700 feet through a gate. It is on the site of Fort Wimberly. There were 117 marked burials noted in Sept. 1987. (Glide 1987 USGS Quad. map.)

WINCHESTER SCHOOL
AKA: 1. LANE FAMILY

A ? 2 1859-1871 T26S R6W S25

Located at the Winchester Elementary School, in the schoolyard. The school is in the community of Winchester on Page Road (Co. Rd. #115-A). There were 3 known burials; 2 Lanes and a Gilliam (1960 D.A.R. visit); on the John Akin D.L.C. #53, RB #128. (Winchester 1987 USGS Quad. map.)

Name of Cemetery and also known as	Number of burials	Acres	Condition	Date started or earliest known burial	Township	Range	Section

WOLFE VALLEY
  AKA: 1. DURNAME, MR.

A   ?   ?   1910   T25S R7W   S8

West from Sutherlin by Fort McKay Road (Co. Rd. #9), to Umpqua. Turn right onto Tyee Road (Co. Rd. #33), following the Umpqua River downstream past Mack Brown and James Woods County Parks. About a mile past the latter is the Johnson Place (a frame house in 1978). An earlier owner, a Mr. Durname, is buried here in an unmarked grave. NOTE: This site is on private property. (Not shown on Tyee 1990 USGS Quad. map.)

YOCUM
  AKA: 1. YOKUM

A   ?   ?   ?   T30S R5W   S19

Leave the I-5 Freeway at Exit #102 and turn westerly, towards Riddle, on Yokum Road (Co. Rd. #20-A). After crossing the Cow Creek Bridge take a driveway on the right, go up the hill for 0.2 of a mile, where there are 3 known graves; on the John Yokum D.L.C. #61, RB #787. NOTE: USGS shows only one grave. NOTE: This site is on private property. (Canyonville 1986 USGS Quad. map.)

Cedar Hill
Janice M. Healy (2000)

Cedar Hill
Janice M. Healy (2000)

I.O.O.F. [Roseburg]
Dean H. Byrd (1991)

ABBOTT GRAVE	DOUGLAS CO.	?	?	?
ADAMS see **MYRTLE CREEK PIONEER**	DOUGLAS CO.	T29S	R5W	S28
ADAMS D.L.C., JOHN see **MYRTLE CREEK PIONEER**				
	DOUGLAS CO.	T29S	R5W	S28
ADAMS D.L.C., MATTHEW see **BOGGESS FAMILY**				
	DOUGLAS CO.	T28S	R5W	S1
AKIN D.L.C., JOHN see **STOWEL FAMILY**				
	DOUGLAS CO.	T26S	R6W	S36
AKIN D.L.C., JOHN see **WINCHESTER SCHOOL**				
	DOUGLAS CO.	T26S	R6W	S25
ALDRIDGE, M. C. S. see **LONG FAMILY, JOHN**				
	DOUGLAS CO.	T23S	R5W	?
ALDRIDGE, MARY JANE LONG see **LONG FAMILY, JOHN**				
	DOUGLAS CO.	T23S	R5W	?
ALLEN D.L.C., NATHAN W. see **GREEN VALLEY**				
	DOUGLAS CO.	T24S	R6W	S25
ANLAUF see **COMSTOCK**	DOUGLAS CO.	T21S	R4W	S20
ANSAMA, MARIE SOPHIA see **JOHANNSEN FAMILY**				
	DOUGLAS CO.	T22S	R11W	S11
APPLEGATE D.L.C., JESSE see **APPLEGATE FAMILY**				
	DOUGLAS CO.	T22S	R5W	S28
APPLEGATE FAMILY	DOUGLAS CO.	T22S	R5W	S28
APPLEGATE, JESSE see **APPLEGATE FAMILY**				
	DOUGLAS CO.	T22S	R5W	S28
APPLEGATE PIONEER	DOUGLAS CO.	T23S	R5W	S4
ARCHAMBEAUX D.L.C., FRANCIS see **ARCHAMBEAUX FAMILY**				
	DOUGLAS CO.	T26S	R6W	S31
ARCHAMBEAUX FAMILY	DOUGLAS CO.	T26S	R6W	S31
AURORA MASONIC LODGE #59 see **GARDINER**				
	DOUGLAS CO.	T21S	R12W	S22
AURORA MASONIC LODGE #59 see **REEDSPORT MASONIC**				
	DOUGLAS CO.	T22S	R12W	S4
AZALEA	DOUGLAS CO.	T32S	R5W	S14
AZALEA LODGE see **GLENDALE**	DOUGLAS CO.	T33S	R6W	S5
BAKER, DORSEY	DOUGLAS CO.	T24S	R5W	S32
BARRETT FAMILY	DOUGLAS CO.	T21S	R12W	S19
BELIEU D.L.C., JAMES see **CIVIL BEND**				
	DOUGLAS CO.	T28S	R6W	S21
BELL FAMILY	DOUGLAS CO.	T22S	R7W	S29
BELL MD., CLEMENTINE see **TULLER**	DOUGLAS CO.	T32S	R7W	?
BETHEL	DOUGLAS CO.	T26S	R7W	S36
BETHEL MISSION CHURCH see **BETHEL**				
	DOUGLAS CO.	T26S	R7W	S36
BIG CAMAS RANGER STATION	DOUGLAS CO.	T27S	R3E	?
BLACKFORD see **GARDNER**	DOUGLAS CO.	T22S	R6W	?
BLACKFORD FAMILY see **GARDNER**	DOUGLAS CO.	T22S	R6W	?
BLAND see **BLAND MOUNTAIN**	DOUGLAS CO.	T30S	R4W	S24
BLAND MOUNTAIN	DOUGLAS CO.	T30S	R4W	S24
BOGGESS FAMILY	DOUGLAS CO.	T28S	R5W	S1
BOGGUS see **BOGGESS FAMILY**	DOUGLAS CO.	T28S	R5W	S1
BOUNDS	DOUGLAS CO.	T28S	R6W	S35
BOURNE, CHARLES F.	DOUGLAS CO.	T22S	R9W	S8

BRADLEY, WM. D. see **BRIGGS, SAMUEL**

	DOUGLAS CO.	T30S R5W	S20
BRIGGS, SAMUEL	DOUGLAS CO.	T30S R5W	S20
BROCKWAY see **CIVIL BEND**	DOUGLAS CO.	T28S R6W	S21
BROCKWAY see **NICHOLS**	DOUGLAS CO.	T28S R6W	S20
BROWN FAMILY, H. G.	DOUGLAS CO.	T22S R8W	S21
BROWN, O. C.	DOUGLAS CO.	T27S R5W	S24
BRYANT FAMILY	DOUGLAS CO.	T29S R4W	S21

BRYANT RANCH, J. see **BRYANT FAMILY**

	DOUGLAS CO.	T29S R4W	S21
BUCKHEAD CAMP	DOUGLAS CO.	T27S R2E	S31

BURCH FAMILY [?] see **FORTUNE BRANCH GRAVES**

	DOUGLAS CO.	T32S R5W	S20

BURNETT D.L.C., JOHN S. see **BURNETT FAMILY**

	DOUGLAS CO.	T29S R6W	S12
BURNETT FAMILY	DOUGLAS CO.	T29S R6W	S12
BURT	DOUGLAS CO.	T27S R5W	S14
CAMAS VALLEY	DOUGLAS CO.	T31S R8W	S5
CANNON, SARAH	DOUGLAS CO.	T22S R4W	S20
CANYONVILLE	DOUGLAS CO.	T30S R5W	S27

CANYONVILLE BIBLE ACADEMY see **ROSE HILL MEMORIAL**

	DOUGLAS CO.	T30S R5W	S27
CANYONVILLE PIONEER	DOUGLAS CO.	T30S R5W	S34
CEDAR HILL	DOUGLAS CO.	T25S R5W	S5
CHAMPAGNE see **CHAMPAIGN FAMILY**	DOUGLAS CO.	T27S R6W	S6

CHAMPAIGN D.L.C., JOSEPH see **CHAMPAIGN FAMILY**

	DOUGLAS CO.	T27S R6W	S6
CHAMPAIGN FAMILY	DOUGLAS CO.	T27S R6W	S6
CHINESE [GARDINER ?]	DOUGLAS CO.	T21S R12W	?

CHINESE see **MASONIC [OLD ROSEBURG]**

	DOUGLAS CO.	T27S R5W	S19

CHURCHILL D.L.C., WILLIAM see **COLES VALLEY**

	DOUGLAS CO.	T25S R7W	S35
CITIZENS see **DRAIN [NORTH]**	DOUGLAS CO.	T22S R5W	S8
CITY see **DRAIN [NORTH]**	DOUGLAS CO.	T22S R5W	S8
CIVIL BEND	DOUGLAS CO.	T28S R6W	S21

CLARK D.L.C., JAMES G. see **CANYONVILLE**

	DOUGLAS CO.	T30S R5W	S27

CLARK D.L.C., JAMES G. see **ROSE HILL MEMORIAL**

	DOUGLAS CO.	T30S R5W	S27
CLARK GRAVE	DOUGLAS CO.	? ?	?
CLEVELAND	DOUGLAS CO.	T26S R7W	S24
CLEVELAND HILL see **CLEVELAND**	DOUGLAS CO.	T26S R7W	S24
COFFEE CREEK	DOUGLAS CO.	T30S R2W	S18
COLE FAMILY, DR. JAMES	DOUGLAS CO.	T25S R6W	S8
COLES VALLEY	DOUGLAS CO.	T25S R7W	S35
COLVIN	DOUGLAS CO.	T22S R5W	S6

COLVIN RANCH, G. N. see **RICE-MARSH FAMILY**

	DOUGLAS CO.	T23S R5W	S31
COMSTOCK	DOUGLAS CO.	T21S R4W	S20
COX D.L.C., JOHN see **COX, JOHN**	DOUGLAS CO.	T28S R6W	?
COX FAMILY	DOUGLAS CO.	? ?	?

COX, JOHN	DOUGLAS CO.	T28S	R6W	?
COX PLACE see **COX FAMILY**	DOUGLAS CO.	?	?	?
COX, SARAH	DOUGLAS CO.	T22S	R4W	S20
COZAD D.L.C., JONATHAN see **HARRIS, DR.**				
	DOUGLAS CO.	T24S	R4W	?
CURTIN see **COMSTOCK**	DOUGLAS CO.	T21S	R4W	S20
DAGAN, DR. see **RED HILL**	DOUGLAS CO.	T23S	R5W	S34
DAGAN, DOCTOR THEOPHILUS see **RED HILL**				
	DOUGLAS CO.	T23S	R5W	S34
DAGAN, THEOPHILUS see **RED HILL**	DOUGLAS CO.	T23S	R5W	S34
DAVLIN see **NICHOLS**	DOUGLAS CO.	T28S	R6W	S20
DAY D.L.C., WILLIAM P. see **DAY FAMILY**				
	DOUGLAS CO.	T29S	R9W	S26
DAY FAMILY	DOUGLAS CO.	T29S	R9W	S26
DAY, PHOEBE see **DAY FAMILY**	DOUGLAS CO.	T29S	R9W	S26
DAY, WILLIAM P. see **DAY FAMILY**	DOUGLAS CO.	T29S	R9W	S26
DAYS CREEK [?] see **BLAND MOUNTAIN**				
	DOUGLAS CO.	T30S	R4W	S24
DENN see **DAY FAMILY**	DOUGLAS CO.	T29S	R9W	S26
DILLARD see **WILLIS CREEK**	DOUGLAS CO.	T29S	R6W	S9
DIMMICK D.L.C., ZIBA see **DIMMICK FAMILY**				
	DOUGLAS CO.	T23S	R7W	S20
DIMMICK FAMILY	DOUGLAS CO.	T23S	R7W	S20
DIXON see **LIVINGSTON**	DOUGLAS CO.	T27S	R4W	S7
DIXON D.L.C., HIRAM see **DIXON FAMILY**				
	DOUGLAS CO.	T26S	R5W	S26
DIXON FAMILY	DOUGLAS CO.	T26S	R5W	S26
DIXONVILLE see **LIVINGSTON**	DOUGLAS CO.	T27S	R4W	S7
DR. DUTCH see **RED HILL**	DOUGLAS CO.	T23S	R5W	S34
DOLE see **BURNETT FAMILY**	DOUGLAS CO.	T29S	R6W	S12
DORITY PLACE see **FROZEN CREEK**	DOUGLAS CO.	T28S	R4W	?
DOUGLAS COUNTY see **MASONIC [OLD ROSEBURG]**				
	DOUGLAS CO.	T27S	R5W	S19
DOUGLAS COUNTY BROOKSIDE	DOUGLAS CO.	T27S	R5W	S17
DOUGLAS COUNTY POOR FARM	DOUGLAS CO.	T26S	R6W	S30
DRAIN [EAST] see **I.O.O.F. [DRAIN]**				
	DOUGLAS CO.	T22S	R5W	S16
DRAIN [NORTH]	DOUGLAS CO.	T22S	R5W	S8
DREW see **TISON**	DOUGLAS CO.	T31S	R1W	S19
DRIVER D.L.C., SAMUEL see **DRIVER FAMILY**				
	DOUGLAS CO.	T24S	R4W	S22
DRIVER FAMILY	DOUGLAS CO.	T24S	R4W	S22
DUMOND, AUGUST see **DUMONT, AUGUST**				
	DOUGLAS CO.	T30S	R4W	S9
DUMONT, ALEXANDER see **DUMONT, AUGUST**				
	DOUGLAS CO.	T30S	R4W	S9
DUMONT, AUGUST	DOUGLAS CO.	T30S	R4W	S9
DUMONT D.L.C., ALEXANDER see **DUMONT, AUGUST**				
	DOUGLAS CO.	T30S	R4W	S9
DUNES MEMORIAL MAUSOLEUM	DOUGLAS CO.	T22S	R12W	S4
DURNAME, MR. see **WOLF VALLEY**	DOUGLAS CO.	T25S	R7W	S8

EARL RANCH, LYLE see **NOEL FAMILY**

	DOUGLAS CO.	T21S	R11W	S3

EARLY I.O.O.F. see **MASONIC [OLD ROSEBURG]**

	DOUGLAS CO.	T27S	R5W	S19

EARLY MASONIC see **MASONIC [OLD ROSEBURG]**

	DOUGLAS CO.	T27S	R5W	S19

Name	County	Township	Range	Section
EAST see **I.O.O.F. [DRAIN]**	DOUGLAS CO.	T22S	R5W	S16
EAST GARDINER	DOUGLAS CO.	?	?	?
EDEN	DOUGLAS CO.	T27S	R7W	S2
EDEN LUTHERAN CHURCH see **EDEN**	DOUGLAS CO.	T27S	R7W	S2
ELGAROSE see **EDEN**	DOUGLAS CO.	T27S	R7W	S2
ELKHEAD CHURCH see **SHOESTRING**	DOUGLAS CO.	T23S	R4W	S10
ELKTON	DOUGLAS CO.	T22S	R7W	S29
ELLIOTT-PERKINS FAMILIES	DOUGLAS CO.	T21S	R12W	?
ELLIS	DOUGLAS CO.	?	?	?
ELLIS PROPERTY see **ELLIS**	DOUGLAS CO.	?	?	?
ENSLEY FAMILY	DOUGLAS CO.	T22S	R6W	S2
EUREKA VALLEY see **COLVIN**	DOUGLAS CO.	T22S	R5W	S6
EVERTS, J. H. see **PEEL**	DOUGLAS CO.	T27S	R3W	S11
FAIR OAKS	DOUGLAS CO.	T25S	R4W	S7

FARMER D.L.C., JAMES see **FARMER FAMILY**

	DOUGLAS CO.	T22S	R6W	S2

FARMER FAMILY	DOUGLAS CO.	T22S	R6W	S2

FENN RANCH, JOEL R. see **ARCHAMBEAUX FAMILY**

	DOUGLAS CO.	T26S	R6W	S31

FOISY D.L.C., AUGUSTINE see **BETHEL**

	DOUGLAS CO.	T26S	R7W	S36

FORT UMPQUA [NEW]	DOUGLAS CO.	T21S	R12W	S31
FORT UMPQUA [OLD]	DOUGLAS CO.	T22S	R7W	S30
FORTUNE BRANCH GRAVES	DOUGLAS CO.	T32S	R5W	S20

FREEMAN D.L.C., JOHN see **FREEMAN FAMILY**

	DOUGLAS CO.	T28S	R7W	?

FREEMAN FAMILY	DOUGLAS CO.	T28S	R7W	?
FRENCH CREEK	DOUGLAS CO.	T32S	R3W	S4

FRENCH, IKE AND WIFE see **FRENCH CREEK**

	DOUGLAS CO.	T32S	R3W	S4

FRENCH SETTLEMENT see **MELROSE**	DOUGLAS CO.	T27S	R7W	S1
FRIER FAMILY	DOUGLAS CO.	T22S	R6W	S1
FRIER PLACE, EARL see **COLVIN**	DOUGLAS CO.	T22S	R5W	S6

FRIER RANCH, CARL see **FRIER FAMILY**

	DOUGLAS CO.	T22S	R6W	S1

FROZEN CREEK	DOUGLAS CO.	T28S	R4W	?
GAGE D.L.C., JOSEPH see **NICHOLS**	DOUGLAS CO.	T28S	R6W	S20
GAGE, JOSEPH see **COX, JOHN**	DOUGLAS CO.	T28S	R6W	?
GAGE, TOM see **COX, JOHN**	DOUGLAS CO.	T28S	R6W	?
GARDINER	DOUGLAS CO.	T21S	R12W	S22

GARDINER D.L.C., SAMUEL see **WILBUR [NEW]**

	DOUGLAS CO.	T26S	R5W	S7

GARDNER	DOUGLAS CO.	T22S	R6W	?
GARDNER FAMILY see **GARDNER**	DOUGLAS CO.	T22S	R6W	?

GARDNINER D.L.C., SAMUEL see **REED-HILL FAMILY**

	DOUGLAS CO.	T26S	R5W	S7

GARWOOD GRAVE see **BIG CAMAS RANGER STATION**
                                                   DOUGLAS CO.   T27S   R3E   ?

GARWOOD GRAVE see **BIG CAMAS RANGER STATION**				
	DOUGLAS CO.	T27S	R3E	?
GARWOOD, MR. see **BIG CAMAS RANGER STATION**				
	DOUGLAS CO.	T27S	R3E	?
GERHARD PLACE, LOREN	DOUGLAS CO.	T21S	R11W	S9
GILHAM D.L.C., JOHN B. see **CLEVELAND**				
	DOUGLAS CO.	T26S	R7W	S24
GILLAM see **QUINES CREEK**	DOUGLAS CO.	T32S	R5W	S15
GILLIAM see **WINCHESTER SCHOOL**	DOUGLAS CO.	T26S	R6W	S25
GILLIAMS see **QUINES CREEK**	DOUGLAS CO.	T32S	R5W	S15
GILMORE D.L.C., JAMES P. see **GILMORE FAMILY**				
	DOUGLAS CO.	T28S	R5W	S11
GILMORE FAMILY	DOUGLAS CO.	T28S	R5W	S11
GLENDALE	DOUGLAS CO.	T33S	R6W	S5
GLIDE see **WIMBERLY**	DOUGLAS CO.	T26S	R3W	S19
GOFF FAMILY	DOUGLAS CO.	T25S	R5W	S30
GOLDEN D.L.C., WILLIAM see **SCOTTSBURG**				
	DOUGLAS CO.	T22S	R9W	S8
GREEN VALLEY	DOUGLAS CO.	T24S	R6W	S25
GRIFFIN D.L.C., EDWARD see **HENDERER FAMILY**				
	DOUGLAS CO.	T22S	R8W	S23
GUNTER	DOUGLAS CO.	T20S	R7W	S27
HAHN see **WILLIS FAMILY, WILLIAM A.**				
	DOUGLAS CO.	T27S	R4W	S19
HAINES FAMILY	DOUGLAS CO.	T22S	R7W	S32
HAMACHER FAMILY	DOUGLAS CO.	?	?	?
HARDY D.L.C., THEOTINE see **HARDY FAMILY, THEOTINE**				
	DOUGLAS CO.	T27S	R6W	S6
HARDY FAMILY, THEOTINE	DOUGLAS CO.	T27S	R6W	S6
HARRIS, DR.	DOUGLAS CO.	T24S	R4W	?
HARRIS, MR. see **LOST CREEK**	DOUGLAS CO.	T25S	R7W	S12
HARVEY FAMILY	DOUGLAS CO.	T24S	R4W	S30
HASKELL FAMILY	DOUGLAS CO.	?	?	?
HASKELL PLACE see **HASKELL FAMILY**				
	DOUGLAS CO.	?	?	?
HATFIELD, NORMA see **STRADER FAMILY**				
	DOUGLAS CO.	T27S	R4W	?
HEDRICK FAMILY	DOUGLAS CO.	T21S	R6W	S35
HEDRICK FAMILY	DOUGLAS CO.	T22S	R6W	S1
HEFTY FAMILY	DOUGLAS CO.	T20S	R6W	S34
HENDERER FAMILY	DOUGLAS CO.	T22S	R8W	S23
HENDERSON, EDNA WAGGONER see **EAST GARDINER**				
	DOUGLAS CO.	?	?	?
HENDERSON, HARRY see **EAST GARDINER**				
	DOUGLAS CO.	?	?	?
HENDERSON, MERVIN DONALD see **EAST GARDINER**				
	DOUGLAS CO.	?	?	?
HIGGINSON D.L.C., FRANK J. see **NOAH**				
	DOUGLAS CO.	T29S	R8W	S7
HOLDMAN D.L.C., JOSEPH see **GOFF FAMILY**				
	DOUGLAS CO.	T25S	R5W	S30

HOSKINS D.L.C., WILLIAM see **FAIR OAKS**				
	DOUGLAS CO.	T25S	R4W	S7
HUNTS MEMORIAL see **FAIR OAKS**	DOUGLAS CO.	T25S	R4W	S7
HURST D.L.C., DAVID see **HURST FAMILY**				
	DOUGLAS CO.	T25S	R6W	S22
HURST FAMILY	DOUGLAS CO.	T25S	R6W	S22
I.O.O.F. see **CANYONVILLE**	DOUGLAS CO.	T30S	R5W	S27
I.O.O.F. see **LOOKINGGLASS**	DOUGLAS CO.	T27S	R7W	S35
I.O.O.F. see **SCOTTSBURG**	DOUGLAS CO.	T22S	R9W	S8
I.O.O.F. [DRAIN]	DOUGLAS CO.	T22S	R5W	S16
I.O.O.F. [MYRTLE CREEK]	DOUGLAS CO.	T29S	R5W	S22
I.O.O.F. [OAKLAND]	DOUGLAS CO.	T25S	R5W	S4
I.O.O.F. [OAKLAND], 2ND see **CEDAR HILL**				
	DOUGLAS CO.	T25S	R5W	S5
I.O.O.F. [ROSEBURG]	DOUGLAS CO.	T27S	R5W	S19
INDIAN	DOUGLAS CO.	T22S	R4W	S18
INDIAN	DOUGLAS CO.	T25S	R4W	?
INDIAN see **TIPTON, MACE**	DOUGLAS CO.	T26S	R3W	S1
INDIAN BOY	DOUGLAS CO.	T26S	R7W	S13
INDIAN BURIAL GROUNDS	DOUGLAS CO.	T22S	R12W	?
JAMES, SAMUEL M.	DOUGLAS CO.	T23S	R4W	S22
JOHANNSEN, ANDREAS see **JOHANNSEN FAMILY**				
	DOUGLAS CO.	T22S	R11W	S11
JOHANNSEN, ANDREW see **JOHANNSEN FAMILY**				
	DOUGLAS CO.	T22S	R11W	S11
JOHANNSEN FAMILY	DOUGLAS CO.	T22S	R11W	S11
JOHNSON, ANDREAS see **JOHANNSEN FAMILY**				
	DOUGLAS CO.	T22S	R11W	S11
JOHNSON, ANDREW see **JOHANNSEN FAMILY**				
	DOUGLAS CO.	T22S	R11W	S11
JOHNSON FAMILY see **JOHANNSEN FAMILY**				
	DOUGLAS CO.	T22S	R11W	S11
JOHNSON, HERMAN	DOUGLAS CO.	T27S	R6W	S25
JOHNSON PLACE see **WOLFE VALLEY**	DOUGLAS CO.	T25S	R7W	S8
JONES D.L.C., JACOB see **JONES FAMILY**				
	DOUGLAS CO.	T27S	R6W	S10
JONES FAMILY	DOUGLAS CO.	T27S	R6W	S10
KANIPE MEMORIAL COUNTY PARK see **KANIPE, MILDRED**				
	DOUGLAS CO.	T24S	R4W	S18
KANIPE, MILDRED	DOUGLAS CO.	T24S	R4W	S18
KELLOGG	DOUGLAS CO.	T23S	R7W	S29
KELLOGG D.L.C., JOHN see **KELLOGG**				
	DOUGLAS CO.	T23S	R7W	S29
KELLY D.L.C., JOHN see **JOHNSON, HERMAN**				
	DOUGLAS CO.	T27S	R6W	S25
KENT FAMILY see **COX, JOHN**	DOUGLAS CO.	T28S	R6W	?
KENT, LEWIS see **COX, JOHN**	DOUGLAS CO.	T28S	R6W	?
KINGERY FAMILY	DOUGLAS CO.	T23W	R5W	?
KINGERY, JOHN WESLEY see **KINGERY FAMILY**				
	DOUGLAS CO.	T23W	R5W	?
KREWSON	DOUGLAS CO.	T22S	R5W	S4
LaBRIE FAMILY	DOUGLAS CO.	T26S	R6W	S30

```
LANE FAMILY see WINCHESTER SCHOOL
                              DOUGLAS CO.     T26S    R6W     S25
LAVADOURE                     DOUGLAS CO.     T30S    R3W     S29
LEONA                         DOUGLAS CO.     T21S    R5W     S34
LETITIA                       DOUGLAS CO.     T29S    R3W     S20
LETSOM D.L.C., JOHN see INDIAN DOUGLAS CO.    T22S    R4W     S18
LEVENS D.L.C., DANIEL H. see LEVENS GRAVE, ALBERT
                              DOUGLAS CO.     T32S    R5W     S21
LEVENS D.L.C., THOMAS see HAINES FAMILY
                              DOUGLAS CO.     T22S    R7W     S32
LEVENS D.L.C., ZACHEUS see ELKTON
                              DOUGLAS CO.     T22S    R7W     S29
LEVENS GRAVE, ALBERT          DOUGLAS CO.     T32S    R5W     S21
LIVINGSTON D.L.C., THOMAS see LIVINGSTON FAMILY
                              DOUGLAS CO.     T27S    R4W     S7
LIVINGSTON FAMILY             DOUGLAS CO.     T27S    R4W     S7
LOFQUIST, MARGARET UNDERWOOD see LONG FAMILY, JOHN
                              DOUGLAS CO.     T23S    R5W     ?
LONG D.L.C., JOHN see LONG FAMILY, JOHN
                              DOUGLAS CO.     T23S    R5W     ?
LONG, EMMA M. see LONG FAMILY, JOHN
                              DOUGLAS CO.     T23S    R5W     ?
LONG FAMILY, JOHN             DOUGLAS CO.     T23S    R5W     ?
LONG, JOHN see LONG FAMILY, JOHN
                              DOUGLAS CO.     T23S    R5W     ?
LONG, MARQUIS see LONG FAMILY, JOHN
                              DOUGLAS CO.     T23S    R5W     ?
LONG, MINERVA see LONG FAMILY, JOHN
                              DOUGLAS CO.     T23S    R5W     ?
LONG, MINERVA A. see LONG FAMILY, JOHN
                              DOUGLAS CO.     T23S    R5W     ?
LONG, MINERVA JANE SMITH see LONG FAMILY, JOHN
                              DOUGLAS CO.     T23S    R5W     ?
LONG PRAIRIE see SCOTTSBURG   DOUGLAS CO.     T22S    R9W     S8
LONG, ROBERT see LONG FAMILY, JOHN
                              DOUGLAS CO.     T23S    R5W     ?
LOOKINGGLASS                  DOUGLAS CO.     T27S    R7W     S35
LOST CREEK                    DOUGLAS CO.     T25S    R7W     S12
LOWER SMITH RIVER see NORTH FORK
                              DOUGLAS CO.     T20S    R10W    S31
MACEY FAMILY                  DOUGLAS CO.     T22S    R11W    S2
MARKHAM D.L.C., DAVID see INDIAN
                              DOUGLAS CO.     T25S    R4W     ?
MARSH-RICE see RICE-MARSH FAMILY
                              DOUGLAS CO.     T23S    R5W     S31
MARTINDALE                    DOUGLAS CO.     T29S    R8W     S20
MARTINDALE D.L.C., ALSTON see MARTINDALE
                              DOUGLAS CO.     T29S    R8W     S20
MASONIC see CANYONVILLE       DOUGLAS CO.     T30S    R5W     S27
MASONIC see GARDINER          DOUGLAS CO.     T21S    R12W    S22
MASONIC see GLENDALE          DOUGLAS CO.     T33S    R6W     S5
MASONIC see REEDSPORT         DOUGLAS CO.     T22S    R12W    S4
```

MASONIC see **ROSEBURG MEMORIAL GARDENS**				
	DOUGLAS CO.	T27S	R6W	S13
MASONIC [OAKLAND]	DOUGLAS CO.	T24S	R5W	S33
MASONIC [OLD ROSEBURG]	DOUGLAS CO.	T27S	R5W	S19
MASONIC, [YONCALLA]	DOUGLAS CO.	T23S	R5W	S4
McBETH, MR. see **INDIAN BOY**	DOUGLAS CO.	T26S	R7W	S13
McCLELLAN BURIALS see **STORES FAMILY**				
	DOUGLAS CO.	T22S	R6W	?
McCULLOCH D.L.C., WILLIAM see **McCULLOCH FAMILY**				
	DOUGLAS CO.	T29S	R7W	S6
McCULLOCH FAMILY	DOUGLAS CO.	T29S	R7W	S6
McGUIRE D.L.C., THOMAS J. see **McGUIRE FAMILY**				
	DOUGLAS CO.	T28S	R7W	S34
McGUIRE FAMILY	DOUGLAS CO.	T28S	R7W	S34
McKAY see **FORT UMPQUA [OLD]**	DOUGLAS CO.	T22S	R7W	S30
McKAY, JEAN BAPTISTE DESPORTES see **FORT UMPQUA [OLD]**				
	DOUGLAS CO.	T22S	R7W	S30
McKAY, JONATHAN AND WIFE see **FORT UMPQUA [OLD]**				
	DOUGLAS CO.	T22S	R7W	S30
MELROSE	DOUGLAS CO.	T27S	R7W	S1
METZ HILL see **GREEN VALLEY**	DOUGLAS CO.	T24S	R6W	S25
MILLER HOME see **OTEY FAMILY**	DOUGLAS CO.	T26S	R6W	S1
MOORE, DR. FRANK see **TIPTON, MACE**				
	DOUGLAS CO.	T26S	R3W	S1
MOORE PROPERTY see **BELL FAMILY**	DOUGLAS CO.	T22S	R7W	S29
MORROW, HONORE WILSON see **RED HILL**				
	DOUGLAS CO.	T23S	R5W	S34
MOUNT VIEW see **MOUNTAIN VIEW CREMATORIUM**				
	DOUGLAS CO.	T29S	R5W	S28
MOUNTAIN VIEW CREMATORIUM	DOUGLAS CO.	T29S	R5W	S28
MURPHY FAMILY	DOUGLAS CO.	?	?	?
MURPHY PLACE see **MURPHY FAMILY**	DOUGLAS CO.	?	?	?
MURRAY see **MURRY**	DOUGLAS CO.	T29S	R8W	S18
MURRY	DOUGLAS CO.	T29S	R8W	S18
MYNOTT D.L.C., CARRICK S. see **QUINES CREEK**				
	DOUGLAS CO.	T32S	R5W	S15
MYRTLE CREEK PIONEER	DOUGLAS CO.	T29S	R5W	S28
NICHOLS	DOUGLAS CO.	T28S	R6W	S20
NOAH	DOUGLAS CO.	T29S	R8W	S7
NOAH FAMILY see **NOAH**	DOUGLAS CO.	T29S	R8W	S7
NOEL FAMILY	DOUGLAS CO.	T21S	R11W	S3
NOFOG	DOUGLAS CO.	T28S	R3W	?
NONPAREIL see **FAIR OAKS**	DOUGLAS CO.	T25S	R4W	S7
NORTH see **DRAIN [NORTH]**	DOUGLAS CO.	T22S	R5W	S8
NORTH FORK	DOUGLAS CO.	T20S	R10W	S31
OAK CREEK	DOUGLAS CO.	T26S	R4W	S29
OAKLAND see **CEDAR HILL**	DOUGLAS CO.	T25S	R5W	S5
OAKLAND CITY see **OLD TOWN OAKLAND**				
	DOUGLAS CO.	T24S	R5W	S33
OCUMPAUGH, L. R. see **RUTERS FAMILY**				
	DOUGLAS CO.	T24S	R7W	?
OLD RICE PLACE see **RICE FAMILY**	DOUGLAS CO.	T24S	R5W	S5

OLD RITCHEY RANCH see **RITCHEY FAMILY**

	DOUGLAS CO.	T21S	R5W	S31

OLD SOLDIERS see **ROSEBURG NATIONAL**

	DOUGLAS CO.	T27S	R6W	S14

OLD THIELE RANCH see **THIELE FAMILY**

	DOUGLAS CO.	T24S	R5W	S4

OLD TOWN OAKLAND — DOUGLAS CO. — T24S — R5W — S33

OLMSTEAD D.L.C., JOHN see **McGUIRE FAMILY**

	DOUGLAS CO.	T28S	R7W	S34

OREGON SOLDIERS HOME see **ROSEBURG NATIONAL**

	DOUGLAS CO.	T27S	R6W	S14

OTEY D.L.C., EDWIN W. see **OTEY FAMILY**

	DOUGLAS CO.	T26S	R6W	S1

OTEY FAMILY — DOUGLAS CO. — T26S — R6W — S1

PANTHER CREEK — DOUGLAS CO. — T20S — R7W — S26

PARDEE see **BRIGGS, SAMUEL** — DOUGLAS CO. — T30S — R5W — S20

PATTERSON D.L.C., ABRAHAM see **PATTERSON FAMILY**

	DOUGLAS CO.	T29S	R8W	S17

PATTERSON FAMILY — DOUGLAS CO. — T29S — R8W — S17

PAUPER'S [ROSEBURG] see **DOUGLAS COUNTY BROOKSIDE**

	DOUGLAS CO.	T27S	R5W	S17

PAUPER'S [WINSTON] — DOUGLAS CO. — T28S — R6W — S21

PEEL — DOUGLAS CO. — T27S — R3W — S11

PERDUE see **LAVADOURE** — DOUGLAS CO. — T30S — R3W — S29

PERKINS-ELLIOTT see **ELLIOTT-PERKINS**

	DOUGLAS CO.	T21S	R12W	?

PERRY D.L.C., WILLIAM T. see **DOUGLAS COUNTY BROOKSIDE**

	DOUGLAS CO.	T27S	R5W	S17

PIONEER [OAKLAND] see **OLD TOWN OAKLAND**

	DOUGLAS CO.	T24S	R5W	S33

PIONEER [YONCALLA] see **APPLEGATE**

	DOUGLAS CO.	T23S	R5W	S4

POTTERS FIELD see **DOUGLAS COUNTY BROOKSIDE**

	DOUGLAS CO.	T27S	R5W	S17

PRESTON D.L.C., WILLIAM see **BRIGGS, SAMUEL**

	DOUGLAS CO.	T30S	R5W	S20

PUTNAM D.L.C., JOSEPH see **SUNNYDALE**

	DOUGLAS CO.	T22S	R6W	S16

PUTNAM FAMILY see **SUNNYDALE** — DOUGLAS CO. — T22S — R6W — S16

QUINES CREEK — DOUGLAS CO. — T32S — R5W — S15

RAINVILLE — DOUGLAS CO. — T31S — R2W — S3

RED HILL — DOUGLAS CO. — T23S — R5W — S34

REED FAMILY see **REED FAMILY, REASON**

	DOUGLAS CO.	T25S	R5W	S5

REED FAMILY, REASON — DOUGLAS CO. — T25S — R5W — S5

REED-HILL FAMILY — DOUGLAS CO. — T26S — R5W — S7

REEDSPORT — DOUGLAS CO. — T22S — R12W — S4

REID *[Sic]* D.L.C., REASON see **CEDAR HILL**

	DOUGLAS CO.	T25S	R5W	S5

REID *[Sic]* D.L.C., REASON see **REED FAMILY, REASON**

	DOUGLAS CO.	T25S	R5W	S5

RICE CREEK — DOUGLAS CO. — T29S — R6W — ?

RICE FAMILY	DOUGLAS CO.	T24S	R5W	S5
RICE-MARSH FAMILY	DOUGLAS CO.	T23S	R5W	S31
RICE RANCH, ERVIN see **RICE-MARSH FAMILY**				
	DOUGLAS CO.	T23S	R5W	S31
RICHARDS D.L.C., JOHN A. see **RICHARDS FAMILY**				
	DOUGLAS CO.	T28S	R7W	S25
RICHARDS FAMILY	DOUGLAS CO.	T28S	R7W	S25
RIDDLE	DOUGLAS CO.	T30S	R6W	S23
RITCHEY FAMILY	DOUGLAS CO.	T21S	R5W	S31
ROBERTS D.L.C., JOSEPH see **CANYONVILLE PIONEER**				
	DOUGLAS CO.	T30S	R5W	S34
RONDEAU	DOUGLAS CO.	T30S	R2W	S24
ROSE HILL MEMORIAL	DOUGLAS CO.	T30S	R5W	S27
ROSEBURG	DOUGLAS CO.	T27S	R5W	S18
ROSEBURG CATHOLIC see **ST. JOSEPH CATHOLIC**				
	DOUGLAS CO.	T27S	R5W	S19
ROSEBURG MEMORIAL GARDENS	DOUGLAS CO.	T27S	R6W	S13
ROSEBURG NATIONAL	DOUGLAS CO.	T27S	R6W	S14
ROSEBURG VETERANS see **ROSEBURG NATIONAL**				
	DOUGLAS CO.	T27S	R6W	S14
RUTERS FAMILY	DOUGLAS CO.	T24S	R7W	?
RYDELL RANCH see **GARDNER**	DOUGLAS CO.	T22S	R6W	?
SAGER CHILDREN see **RED HILL**	DOUGLAS CO.	T23S	R5W	S34
ST. GEORGE'S EPISCOPAL CHURCH COLUMBARIUM				
	DOUGLAS CO.	T27S	R5W	S19
ST. JOSEPH CATHOLIC	DOUGLAS CO.	T27S	R5W	S19
ST. STEPHENS see **ST. JOSEPH CATHOLIC**				
	DOUGLAS CO.	T27S	R5W	S19
SCOTTSBURG	DOUGLAS CO.	T22S	R9W	S8
SHAMBROOK D.L.C., GEORGE see **DOUGLAS COUNTY POOR FARM**				
	DOUGLAS CO.	T26S	R6W	S30
SHAMBROOK D.L.C., GEORGE see **LaBRIE FAMILY**				
	DOUGLAS CO.	T26S	R6W	S30
SHEPHERD, INA	DOUGLAS CO.	T27S	R5W	?
SHERRETT-LYSTER see **NORTH FORK**	DOUGLAS CO.	T20S	R10W	S31
SHOESTRING	DOUGLAS CO.	T23S	R4W	S10
SINGLETON D.L.C., WILLIAM R. see **SINGLETON FAMILY**				
	DOUGLAS CO.	T26S	R4W	?
SINGLETON FAMILY	DOUGLAS CO.	T26S	R4W	?
SMITH HILL see **RED HILL**	DOUGLAS CO.	T23S	R5W	S34
SOUTH DEER CREEK see **BOGGESS FAMILY**				
	DOUGLAS CO.	T28S	R5W	S1
STEMMERMAN RANCH, LEROY see **NORTH FORK**				
	DOUGLAS CO.	T20S	R10W	S31
STEPHENS D.L.C., BENJAMIN see **BRYANT FAMILY**				
	DOUGLAS CO.	T29S	R4W	S21
STEVENS D.L.C., THOMAS see **I.O.O.F. [ROSEBURG]**				
	DOUGLAS CO.	T27S	R5W	S19
STEVENS D.L.C., THOMAS see **ST. JOSEPH CATHOLIC**				
	DOUGLAS CO.	T27S	R5W	S19
STINGER D.L.C., LEONARD see **LAVADOURE**				
	DOUGLAS CO.	T30S	R3W	S29

STORES FAMILY	DOUGLAS CO.	T22S	R6W	?
STOWEL FAMILY	DOUGLAS CO.	T26S	R6W	S36
STRADER FAMILY	DOUGLAS CO.	T27S	R4W	?
STRADER, JANE WORTHINGTON see **STRADER FAMILY**				
	DOUGLAS CO.	T27S	R4W	?
STRADER, JOHN see **STRADER FAMILY**				
	DOUGLAS CO.	T27S	R4W	?
STRADER, MARTHA see **STRADER FAMILY**				
	DOUGLAS CO.	T27S	R4W	?
SUNNYDALE	DOUGLAS CO.	T22S	R6W	S16
SUNSET see **SUNNYDALE**	DOUGLAS CO.	T22S	R6W	S16
SUTHERLIN [OLD]	DOUGLAS CO.	T25S	R5W	S15
SUTHERLIN see **VALLEY VIEW**	DOUGLAS CO.	T25S	R5W	S13
SUTHERLIN D.L.C., THOMAS see **SUTHERLIN [OLD]**				
	DOUGLAS CO.	T25S	R5W	S15
SWEARINGER D.L.C., ANDREW J. see **HEDRICK FAMILY**				
	DOUGLAS CO.	T21S	R6W	S35
SWIFT, WINIFRED see **McGUIRE FAMILY**				
	DOUGLAS CO.	T28S	R7W	S34
TENMILE	DOUGLAS CO.	T28S	R7W	S31
THIELE FAMILY	DOUGLAS CO.	T24S	R5W	S4
THRUSH	DOUGLAS CO.	T29S	R8W	S7
THRUSH, ABRAHAM see **THRUSH**	DOUGLAS CO.	T29S	R8W	S7
TILLER see **RONDEAU**	DOUGLAS CO.	T30S	R2W	S24
TIPTON, MACE	DOUGLAS CO.	T26S	R3W	S1
TISH see **LETITIA**	DOUGLAS CO.	T29S	R3W	S20
TISON	DOUGLAS CO.	T31S	R1W	S19
TISON RANCH see **TISON**	DOUGLAS CO.	T31S	R1W	S19
TULLER	DOUGLAS CO.	T32S	R7W	?
TULLER, EDITH see **TULLER**	DOUGLAS CO.	T32S	R7W	?
TULLER, JEREMIAH G. see **TULLER**	DOUGLAS CO.	T32S	R7W	?
TURKEY HILL	DOUGLAS CO.	T24S	R5W	S17
TYSON see **TISON**	DOUGLAS CO.	T31S	R1W	S19
UMPQUA see **UMPQUA CITY**	DOUGLAS CO.	T21S	R12W	S31
UMPQUA ACADEMY see **WILBUR [OLD]**	DOUGLAS CO.	T26S	R5W	S18
UMPQUA CITY	DOUGLAS CO.	T21S	R12W	S31
UNITED BRETHREN see **CLEVELAND**	DOUGLAS CO.	T26S	R7W	S24
UNKNOWN	DOUGLAS CO.	T21S	R11W	S35
UPDEGRAVE PLACE see **WELKER GIRLS**				
	DOUGLAS CO.	T26S	R4W	?
VALLEY VIEW	DOUGLAS CO.	T25S	R5W	S13
VAN NORMAN see **LAVADOURE**	DOUGLAS CO.	T30S	R3W	S29
VETERANS ADMINISTRATION see **ROSEBURG NATIONAL**				
	DOUGLAS CO.	T27S	R6W	S14
WELKER GIRLS	DOUGLAS CO.	T26S	R4W	?
WELLS D.L.C., IRA see **WELLS FAMILY**				
	DOUGLAS CO.	T22S	R7W	S31
WELLS FAMILY	DOUGLAS CO.	T22S	R7W	S31
WEST D.L.C., CALVIN BURNSIDE see **WEST-WINNIFORD FAMILIES**				
	DOUGLAS CO.	T26S	R6W	S7
WEST FAMILY, CALVIN B. see **WEST-WINNIFORD FAMILIES**				
	DOUGLAS CO.	T26S	R6W	S7

WEST-WINNIFORD FAMILIES	DOUGLAS CO.	T26S	R6W	S7
WHITSETT, MRS. TOM see **BROWN, O. C.**				
	DOUGLAS CO.	T27S	R5W	S24
WILBUR [NEW]	DOUGLAS CO.	T26S	R5W	S7
WILBUR [OLD]	DOUGLAS CO.	T26S	R5W	S18
WILBER D.L.C., JAMES H. see **WILBUR [OLD]**				
	DOUGLAS CO.	T26S	R5W	S18
WILLIS CREEK	DOUGLAS CO.	T29S	R6W	S9
WILLIS D.L.C., STEPHEN D. see **WILLIS CREEK**				
	DOUGLAS CO.	T29S	R6W	S9
WILLIS D.L.C., WILLIAM A. see **WILLIS FAMILY, WILLIAM A.**				
	DOUGLAS CO.	T27S	R4W	S19
WILLIS FAMILY see **WILLIS FAMILY, WILLIAM A.**				
	DOUGLAS CO.	T27S	R4W	S19
WILLIS FAMILY, WILLIAM A.	DOUGLAS CO.	T27S	R4W	S19
WIMBERLY	DOUGLAS CO.	T26S	R3W	S19
WINCHESTER see **STOWEL FAMILY**	DOUGLAS CO.	T26S	R6W	S36
WINCHESTER SCHOOL	DOUGLAS CO.	T26S	R6W	S25
WINNIFORD CHILD see **WEST-WINNIFORD FAMILIES**				
	DOUGLAS CO.	T26S	R6W	S7
WINSTON see **CIVIL BEND**	DOUGLAS CO.	T28S	R6W	S21
WOLFE VALLEY	DOUGLAS CO.	T25S	R7W	S8
WOOLLEY see **GUNTER**	DOUGLAS CO.	T20S	R7W	S27
WOOLLEY FAMILY see **COLVIN**	DOUGLAS CO.	T22S	R5W	S6
WOOLLEY RANCH see **HEDRICK FAMILY**				
	DOUGLAS CO.	T21S	R6W	S35
WRIGHT FAMILY see **LAVADOURE**	DOUGLAS CO.	T30S	R3W	S29
WRIGHT PROPERTY, RAY see **LAVADOURE**				
	DOUGLAS CO.	T30S	R3W	S29
YOCUM	DOUGLAS CO.	T30S	R5W	S19
YOKUM see **YOCUM**	DOUGLAS CO.	T30S	R5W	S19
YOKUM D.L.C., JOHN see **YOCUM**	DOUGLAS CO.	T30S	R5W	S19

GILLIAM COUNTY

Scale

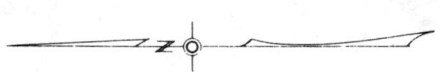

Map of Gilliam County showing Arlington, Shutler, Blalock, Quinton, Rockcreek, Mikkalo, Olex, Glem, Gwendolen, Condon, Mayville, Alville, Lonerock, and surrounding areas. Bordered by Washington, Morrow County, Wheeler County, and Sherman County. Routes 30, 84, 74, 19, 206 shown.

Cecil Children
Janice M. Healy (2000)

Cecil Children
Janice M. Healy (2000)

Area: 1,223 square miles
Population (1998): 2,023
County seat: Condon, Population: 790
County established: 25 February 1885

The earliest established public cemetery in Gilliam County was apparently Blalock in 1880. This was during the construction of the trans-continental railway to Portland. Gilliam County then began to be populated by settlers who engaged in wheat and livestock ranching. There was some lumbering in the far south of the county. The 1880's saw the establishment of most of the public cemeteries.

Cecil Children
Janice M. Healy (2000)

Cecil Children (Looking East)
Janice M. Healy (2000)

Cecil Children (Looking West)
Janice M. Healy (2000)

Cecil Children

Janice M. Healy (2000)

Name of Cemetery and also known as	Number of burials	Acres	Condition	Date started or earliest known burial	Township	Range	Section

ARLINGTON
AKA: 1. MASONIC

| D | 3.38 | 1 | | 1882 | T3N | R21E | S28 |

Leave the I-84 Freeway and turn onto OR. Hwy. 19 (Locust Street) into town. Turn right off of Locust Street onto Main Street, go about 0.6 of a mile up the hill to the cemetery below the water tower. You will pass the Elementary and High Schools. (Arlington 1971 USGS Quad. map.)

BLALOCK

| ? | 8.75 | 8 | | 1880-1895 | T3N | R19E | S36 |

Now underwater in Lake Umatilla. In 1960 all known graves (16) were moved to the Arlington Cemetery as the John Day Dam was being constructed. (Not shown on Sundale N. W. 1971 USGS Quad. map.)

BROWN, FAMILY
AKA: 1. DEVILS GAP

| A | 2 | 5 | | 1881 | T3S | R22E | S10 |

Go 7 miles north of Condon on OR. Hwy. 19 at Milepost 29, turn right (southeast) on Cayuse Canyon Road for 5.1 miles, then turn right (south) onto a private road. Go 1 mile to the confluence of Rock Creek and South Fork of Rock Creek. There were 20 known burials 1972. NOTE: This site is thought to be on private property. (Devils Gap 1970 USGS Quad. map. Metsker Land Ownership Atlas 1934 lists H. G. Brown Ranch.)

CECIL CHILDREN,
ANNA LAURA AND WALTER

| A | ? | ? | | 13 Feb 1877 | T3N | R22E | S12 |

This small burial ground is located in the Northwest 1/4 of the Northwest 1/4 of Section 12. It is on the heights above the left (west) bank of the valley of Willow Creek, upstream from its mouth with the Columbia River. The burial ground is about half a mile to the northeast from the nearest point on the new alignment of OR. Hwy. 74; at 2.2 miles south of Heppner Junction. It is out of sight of the road and access is on foot through a farm field, possibly private property. A range fire has cleared the sage and grass this fall (2000) so we were able to locate it. There are only three tombstones left here. They are for Walter Cecil aged 5 years, 7 months, 21 days died 13 February 1877. Anna Laura Cecil aged 7 years, 11 months, 5 days died 17 February 1877. Who

Name of Cemetery and also known as	Number of burials	Acres	Condition	Date started or earliest known burial	Township	Range	Section

were the children of William Y. Cecil and Mary Ellen Cecil who settled in 1862 starting the hamlet of Cecil in what is now Morrow County. Elizabeth M. Shippy Died 12 December 1879 aged 32 years, 7 months and 13 days. There is evidence of other graves here as well as holes doug that were not fully filled back in. With the site having being totally burned over a few days before, we could not tell if they were recent or not. When Gilliam and Morrow Counties were created in February 1885 the graves were then in Gilliam County. {2 September 2000} (Heppner Junction 1962 USGS Quad. map)

CLEM   ?   0.15   ?   ?   T1S R21E   S32

Leave OR. Hwy 19 at Milepost 23.1 and turn right (west), go 1.2 miles to Clem. Turn right (northerly) onto Clem Road and drive another 1.7 miles to a driveway, turn left (west) to the cemetery, which is about 70 yards off of the county road. (Mikkalo 1970 USGS Quad. map.)

CYRUS CHILDREN   A   0.01   2   1877   T1N R20E   S15

Go 0.35 of a mile east of the railway overpass over Middle Rock Creek Lane and 0.45 of a mile east of Rock Creek community. The grave is about 500-600 feet southwest of the road on a low ridge overlooking the valley. Go 9.6 miles northwest of OR. Hwy. 19 at Olex via Middle Rock Creek Lane. A rock-enclosed grave for the three children of Lawson and Martha H. Milkey Cyrus is located about 0.25 of a mile upstream from the Rock Creek School, near the Don Ramsay home (1990). The children: George W. Cyrus, died 28 May 1877, aged 4 years, 6 months, 6 days; Lillia May Cyrus, died 28 May 1877, aged 1 year, 8 months, 28 days; and Wayman Cyrus, died 4 June 1877, age 9 years, 4 months, 15 days. (Turner Butte 1964-75 USGS Quad. map.)

DEEN, TOMMY   A   0.3   2   10 Apr 1885 T1N R22E   S26
AKA: 1. DEAN

Located 18.7 miles southeast of Arlington. Drive 4 miles south of Arlington on OR. Hwy. 19. Turn left (east) onto Fourmile Road;

Name of Cemetery and also known as	Number of burials	Acres	Condition	Date started or earliest known burial	Township	Range	Section

after driving 4.8 miles on Fourmile Road, turn right (southerly) onto Eightmile Canyon Road and go 8.6 miles (incidentally you will pass by Eightmile Cemetery). Turn right (south) onto Davidson Road and drive another 1.5 miles. The cemetery is on the left. There are 11 known burials. {14 July 1990} (Hickland Butte 1964 USGS Quad. map.)

EIGHTMILE
AKA: 1. MONTAGUE

B   0.3   1   1880'S   T1N R22E   S5
Located 12 miles from Arlington in Eightmile Canyon. Go 4 miles south of Arlington on OR. Hwy. 19, then left (southeast) 4.8 miles on Fourmile Road before turning right (south) and going 3.3 miles on Eightmile Canyon Road. The cemetery is located in the Eightmile Canyon Valley. {14 July 1990} (Hickland Butte 1964 USGS Quad. map.)

EWING FAMILY

A   0.01   ?   ?   T3N R22E   S34
Reportedly Harvey Ewing's wife and sister are buried in this section, about two miles southwest of OR. Hwy. 74 at Rhea. This is a mile or so southwest of the bygone railway stop of Rhea, within the Willow Creek Valley and up Eightmile Canyon. (Not shown on Horn Butte 1964 USGS Quad. map.)

FLETT

A   0.08   ?   1903   T2S R22E   S9
This cemetery is on the lower slope of a ridge overlooking Rock Creek Valley. Leave OR. Hwy. 19 at Milepost 17, (at Olex), and go southeast past Olex Cemetery via Upper Rock Creek Road 8.7 miles and then 200 yards right on the (southwest) side of road, up slope behind a ranch house. It was fenced when visited in 1971. There were 12 known burials at that time. NOTE: This site is on private property. (Wolf Hollow Falls 1970 USGS Quad. map.)

Name of Cemetery and also known as	Number of burials	Acres	Condition	Date started or earliest known burial	Township	Range	Section

I.O.O.F. [CONDON]
AKA: 1. DOWNING
    2. KING OF
       PEACE
    3. KNIGHTS OF
       PYTHIAS
    4. MASONIC
       [CONDON]

C 10.7 1 16 Dec 1886 T4S R21E S2
Found in Sections 2 and 3. In the northeast corner of Condon. {1 September 2000} (Condon 1970-87 USGS Quad.map.)

I.O.O.F. [MAYVILLE]
AKA: 1. MAYVILLE

B 5 1 1901 T5S R21E S28
Located near Mayville. Go 11.6 miles south of Condon on OR. Hwy. 19 to Milepost 50, turn a hard right and back onto Wehrli Canyon Loop where the highway climbs out of the Dyer Canyon onto a broad ridgetop. Drive 0.6 of a mile west to the cemetery on the right (north). (Fossil North 1970 USGS Quad. map.)

IGO
AKA: 1. ALVILLE
    2. IGO GRANGE

C 2 1 18 Jul 1888 T3S R20E S21
Located west of Condon about 10 miles. Go 8.9 miles northwest of Condon on OR. Hwy. 206, and then 2.3 miles west and south on Alville Lane. {Nov. 1987} (Igo Butte 1970 USGS Quad. map.)

LONEROCK

B 3 1 1922 T6S R24E S4
Drive 4.7 miles east from Condon on OR. Hwy. 206. At Milepost 45.6 turn right (south) onto Lonerock Road, going 16.5 miles to the old town of Lonerock. Turn right (south) of the town, still on Lonerock Road for an additional 1.9 miles. Then turn left (east) onto Campbell Lane, driving about 0.9 of a mile along the Wheeler County Line, and lastly a hard left up a ridge and back 0.3 of a mile to the cemetery. (Lefevre Prairie 1969-83 USGS Quad. map.)

LOST VALLEY

? 0.1 5 Circa 1879 T6S R23E S4
Go 4.7 miles east of Condon on OR. Hwy. 206 to Milepost 45.6, then go 6.1 miles southeast on Lonerock Road and then a further 8.1 miles south on Lost Valley Road. The cemetery is about 200 feet on the right (west) down slope in Lost Valley. It is on the Earl Hardie Ranch, just inside the gate. Only one

Name of Cemetery and also known as	Number of burials	Acres	Condition	Date started or earliest known burial	Township	Range	Section

readable marker remains: Duane Y. Baily, 22 March 1864-11 April 1885. The marker is inside the barn. (Lonerock 1969-83 USGS Quad. map.)

MARICK FAMILY   ? ? ? ?   T1N R20E   ?

Perhaps located in Section 13 or 24. Reportedly this family cemetery is several miles upstream (southwest) from the locale of Rock Creek. (Not shown on Turner Butte 1964-75 USGS Quad. map)

MARVEL GIRL   A 0.01 ? ?   T1N R22E   S7

This is a single grave surrounded by a pipe fence situated on a hill. Take the route to Eightmile Cemetery (see that article) and continue south past Eightmile Cemetery on Eightmile Road about 2 miles to the junction with Cameron Road to the right (west). Proceed on Cameron Road a mile or less to the property of Bill and Barbara West. The grave is off on the right (north). The 15 year-old Marvel girl was killed when a horse fell on her. NOTE: This site is on private property. (Not shown on Hickland Butte 1964 USGS Quad. map.)

MILLER, FRANK   A 0.01 ? 7 Jan 1896 T5S R24E   ?

"Located about 5 miles south[west] of Hardman is the burial for Frank Miller, born 11 September 1879, died 7 January 1896." No further information was given in the report. (Not shown on Lefevre Prairie USGS Quad. map.)

OLEX   C 0.75 2 1870'S   T1S R21E   S11

Leave OR. Hwy. 19 at Milepost 17, at Olex, then go 0.6 of a mile southeast on Upper Rock Creek Road. The cemetery is on the left (east) side of road and is fenced. (Mikkalo 1970 USGS Quad. map.)

Name of Cemetery and also known as	Number of burials	Acres	Condition	Date started or earliest known burial	Township	Range	Section

PAPERSACK
AKA: 1. TRAIL FORK
2. WHITE
FAMILY

A   0.07   5   1882   T5S   R22E   S16
Located in Papersack Canyon. Go 1.3 miles on a private road east, off of Trail Fork Road. This private road junction is 6.9 miles via Trail Fork Lane from OR. Hwy. 19 at Milepost 43.7. Follow the private road to the left (easterly) at the ranch for 1.3 miles from Trail Fork Canyon, over 2 ridges to Papersack Canyon. The cemetery is between the road and the stream bed, fenced, with no easy access. There are 15 known burials, with only 4 stones remaining. NOTE: This site most likely is on private property. (Matney Flat 1970 USGS Quad. map.)

POTTER'S
AKA: 1. MT. MORIAH

A   0.2   2   14 Jul 1911 T1S   R20E   S29
Located northwest of Condon via OR. Hwy. 206 at Milepost 24.1, then go 6.3 miles north on Devils Butte Road to the cemetery on the left (west) side of road. The cemetery is fenced with 9 known burials. (Devils Backbone 1970 USGS Quad. map.)

ST. JOSEPH
AKA: 1. CATHOLIC

B   0.87   1   1891   T4S   R21E   S10
Located on the south side of Cottonwood Road across from the I.O.O.F. [Condon] Cemetery; just northeast of Condon and next to the Fairgrounds. {1 September 2000} (Condon 1970-87 USGS Quad.map.)

UNKNOWN

A   0.01   5   1880   T1N   R21E   S18
A lone grave, possibly located on the breaks of the plateau above Rock Creek. Leave OR. Hwy. 19 at Milepost 7.2 and turn right (westerly) onto Cedar Springs Lane. Go 2.4 miles to Berthold Lane on the left (southerly). Continue on Berthold Lane; the county jurisdiction ends at 2.9 miles with a private road continuing ahead to the south. The grave is presumably about 1.5 miles, as the crow flies, due west of here. No known access other than on foot. NOTE: This site is on private property. (Not shown on Shutler Flat 1964 USGS Quad. map.)

Name of Cemetery and also known as	Number of burials	Acres	Condition	Date started or earliest known burial	Township	Range	Section

UNKNOWN

? ? ? ?   T5S R22E   S28

This cemetery is on the eastern slope of a ridge above an unnamed tributary of Trail Fork Canyon. Noted on a field log, taken by a State Highway crew on 8 July 1936, as a cemetery 0.25 of a mile off of a county road. This county road has since been abandoned. The cemetery is 0.9 of a mile, as the crow flies, southwest of the abandoned Trail Fork School. Trail Fork School is 8.9 miles from OR. Hwy. 19 at Milepost 43.7, via Trail Fork Lane. (Salmon Fork 1970 USGS Quad. map.)

UNKNOWN MAN

A 0.01 ? ?   T1N R20E   ?

Located in Section 7 or 18. This unknown man was reportedly killed by Indians and is buried in an unmarked grave in a field on the Marick Ranch north of Rock Creek and downstream several miles from the locale of Rock Creek. (Not shown on Turner Butte 1964-75 USGS Quad. map.)

WASHBURN, ROYAL ARTHUR

A 0.01 ? 9 Oct 1898 T6S R23E   S4

The single gravestone of a 15 year-old boy was last reported to be broken into three pieces and lying in a field. That report appears to be from the 1960's. The site was on the David Hardie Ranch and is apparently just west of the Lost Valley Cemetery. (Not shown on Lonerock 1983 USGS Quad. map.)

WILSON, D. J.

A 0.01 ? 10 Jul 1907 ?   ?   ?

An article in the *Community Press* of 22 March 1978, page 11 reports a visit to this lonely grave. It is about "20 miles outside of Condon and five miles down a canyon." Apparently this refers to OR. Hwy. 206 for about 15 miles and then turn off for five miles towards the John Day River via a dusty road. There was a black iron gate with a granite tombstone inside and inscribed D. J. Wilson, 20 August 1871 to 10 July 1907: "A kind wife mourns in thee a husband lost." (Not shown on Devils Backbone or Esau Canyon 1970 USGS Quad. maps.)

I.O.O.F. [Condon]
Ruth C. Bishop (2000)

I.O.O.F. [Condon]
Janice M. Healy (2000)

ALVILLE see **IGO**	GILLIAM CO.	T3S	R20E	S21
ARLINGTON	GILLIAM CO.	T3N	R21E	S28
BAILY, DUANE Y. see **LOST VALLEY**	GILLIAM CO.	T6S	R23E	S4
BLALOCK	GILLIAM CO.	T3N	R19E	S36
BROWN FAMILY	GILLIAM CO.	T3S	R22E	S10
CATHOLIC see **ST. JOSEPH**	GILLIAM CO.	T4S	R21E	S10
CECIL CHILDREN, ANNA LAURA AND WALTER				
	GILLIAM CO.	T3N	R22E	S12
CECIL, MARY ELLEN see **CECIL CHILDREN, ANNA LAURA AND WALTER**				
	GILLIAM CO.	T3N	R22E	S12
CECIL, WILLIAM Y. see **CECIL CHILDREN, ANNA LAURA AND WALTER**				
	GILLIAM CO.	T3N	R22E	S12
CLEM	GILLIAM CO.	T1S	R21E	S32
CYRUS CHILDREN	GILLIAM CO.	T1N	R20E	S15
CYRUS, GEORGE W. see **CYRUS CHILDREN**				
	GILLIAM CO.	T1N	R20E	S15
CYRUS, LAWSON see **CYRUS CHILDREN**				
	GILLIAM CO.	T1N	R20E	S15
CYRUS, LILLIA MAY see **CYRUS CHILDREN**				
	GILLIAM CO.	T1N	R20E	S15
CYRUS, MARTHA H. MILKEY see **CYRUS CHILDREN**				
	GILLIAM CO.	T1N	R20E	S15
CYRUS, WAYMAN see **CYRUS CHILDREN**				
	GILLIAM CO.	T1N	R20E	S15
DEAN see **DEEN, TOMMY**	GILLIAM CO.	T1N	R22E	S26
DEEN, TOMMY	GILLIAM CO.	T1N	R22E	S26
DEVILS GAP see **BROWN FAMILY**	GILLIAM CO.	T3S	R22E	S10
DOWNING see **I.O.O.F. [CONDON]**	GILLIAM CO.	T4S	R21E	S2
EIGHTMILE	GILLIAM CO.	T1N	R22E	S5
EWING FAMILY	GILLIAM CO.	T3N	R22E	S34
EWING, HARVEY see **EWING FAMILY**	GILLIAM CO.	T3N	R22E	S34
FLETT	GILLIAM CO.	T2S	R22E	S9
HARDIE RANCH, DAVID see **WASHBURN, ROYAL ARTHUR**				
	GILLIAM CO.	T6S	R23E	S4
HARDIE RANCH, EARL see **LOST VALLEY**				
	GILLIAM CO.	T6S	R23E	S4
I.O.O.F. [CONDON]	GILLIAM CO.	T4S	R21E	S2
I.O.O.F. [MAYVILLE]	GILLIAM CO.	T5S	R21E	S28
IGO	GILLIAM CO.	T3S	R20E	S21
IGO GRANGE see **IGO**	GILLIAM CO.	T3S	R20E	S21
KING OF PEACE see **I.O.O.F. [CONDON]**				
	GILLIAM CO.	T4S	R21E	S2
KNIGHTS OF PYTHIAS see **I.O.O.F. [CONDON]**				
	GILLIAM CO.	T4S	R21E	S2
LONEROCK	GILLIAM CO.	T6S	R24E	S4
LOST VALLEY	GILLIAM CO.	T6S	R23E	S4
MARICK FAMILY	GILLIAM CO.	T1N	R20E	?
MARICK RANCH see **UNKNOWN MAN**	GILLIAM CO.	T1N	R20E	?
MARVEL GIRL	GILLIAM CO.	T1N	R22E	S7
MASONIC see **ARLINGTON**	GILLIAM CO.	T3N	R21E	S28
MASONIC [CONDON] see **I.O.O.F. [CONDON]**				
	GILLIAM CO.	T4S	R21E	S2

MAYVILLE see **I.O.O.F.** [MAYVILLE]

	GILLIAM CO.	T5S	R21E	S28
MILLER, FRANK	GILLIAM CO.	T5S	R24E	?
MONTAGUE see **EIGHTMILE**	GILLIAM CO.	T1N	R22E	S5
MT. MORIAH see **POTTER'S**	GILLIAM CO.	T1S	R20E	S29
OLEX	GILLIAM CO.	T1S	R21E	S11
PAPERSACK	GILLIAM CO.	T5S	R22E	S16
POTTER'S	GILLIAM CO.	T1S	R20E	S29
RAMSAY HOME, DON see **CYRUS CHILDREN**				
	GILLIAM CO.	T1N	R20E	S15
ST. JOSEPH	GILLIAM CO.	T4S	R21E	S10
TRAIL FORK see **PAPERSACK**	GILLIAM CO.	T5S	R22E	S16
UNKNOWN	GILLIAM CO.	T1N	R21E	S18
UNKNOWN	GILLIAM CO.	T5S	R22E	S28
UNKNOWN MAN	GILLIAM CO.	T1N	R20E	?
WASHBURN, ROYAL ARTHUR	GILLIAM CO.	T6S	R23E	S4
WHITE FAMILY see **PAPERSACK**	GILLIAM CO.	T5S	R22E	S16
WILSON, D. J.	GILLIAM CO.	?	?	?

I.O.O.F. [Condon]
Janice M. Healy (2000)

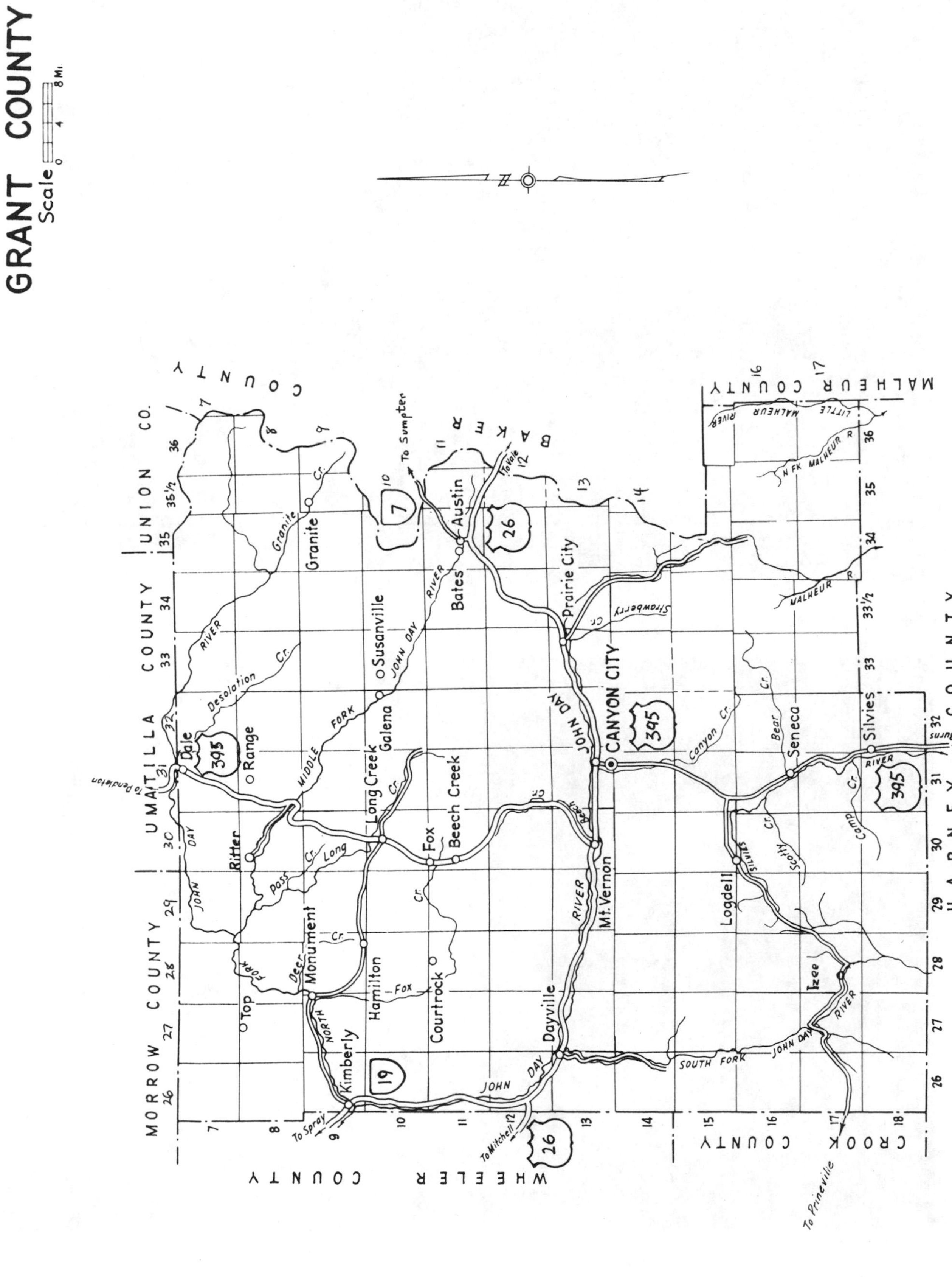

GRANT COUNTY

Scale 0 4 8 Mi.

Canyon City
Dean H. Byrd (1993)

St. Andrews Catholic
Dean H. Byrd (1993)

Area: 4,528 square miles
Population (1998): 8,075
County seat: Canyon City, Population: 705
County established: 14 October 1864

Placer gold mining beginning in late 1861 was the first attraction for white settlers in what is now Grant County. Canyon City in the 1860s was a sizable bonanza town rivalling Auburn in Baker County. Canyon City had the first organized cemetery but the compiler has no firm date for its establishment. There were at least 12 public cemeteries by 1890 after ranching settlement spread. Family burial sites was the usual practice outside the towns.

Boot Hill
Dean H. Byrd (1993)

Grant County

Canyon City
Dean H. Byrd (1993)

St. Andrews Catholic
Dean H. Byrd (1993)

Name of Cemetery and also known as	Number of burials	Acres	Condition	Date started or earliest known burial	Township	Range	Section

ALDRICH, ELMER OLIVER A 0.01 ? 29 Jun 1878 T13S R27E S10
Located on the south side of the John Day River, east of Aldrich Creek and about 5 miles east of Dayville. Aldrich was a soldier killed by Indians. He was born in Augest 1859. There are 5 or 6 graves located here. NOTE: This site is on private property. (Aldrich Mtn. North 1972-83 USGS Quad. map.)

AUSTIN
AKA: 1. BATES-AUSTIN   A ? 7 ? T11S R35E S21
Located outside of Austin, southeast of town, on the Henry Ricco Ranch (1978). The cemetery has been trampled by cattle according to a May 1998 report. Mostly children are buried here. (Not shown on Austin 1972-83 USGS Quad. map.)

BOOT HILL   A 0.1 2 ? T13S R31E S36
Take East Main Street which continues on as Marysville Road and go uphill; turn left on the road to Canyon City Cemetery. Boot Hill Cemetery is reached first. There are 4 burials, reportedly two prostitutes and two horse thieves. {9 July 1993} (John Day 1972-83 USGS Quad. map.)

CABELL CITY
AKA: 1. CABELL
        FAMILY   A 0.2 ? Circa 1878 T8S R35 1/2E S1
Located 2.5 miles west by road from La Bellevue Mine at the site of Cabell City. These are the graves of Johanna Camilla Cabell about 6 years old, Fred Cabell died 1915, and Mrs. Cabell died 5 May 1924 aged 74 years. Access is northerly from Granite by National Forest Road #73, past Crane Flat Ranger Station. Turn right (east) and go onto National Forest Road #7335 within the Wallowa-Whitman National Forest to the Cabell City site. The cemetery is on the left across Onion Creek. (Crawfish Lake 1972-84 USGS Quad. map.)

CANYON CITY
AKA: 1. I.O.O.F.
     2. MASONIC   D 12 1 1875 T13S R31E S35
Located northeast of Canyon City. Take East Main Street, which continues on as Marysville Road, uphill; turn left, passing Boot Hill

Name of Cemetery and also known as	Number of burials	Acres	Condition	Date started or earliest known burial	Township	Range	Section

Cemetery before reaching Canyon City Cemetery. As of 1970 there were 36 marked graves of unknowns. {9 July 1993} (John Day 1972-83 USGS Quad. map.)

CHILD'S GRAVE

| | A | 0.01 | ? | ? | T9S | R31E | S14 |

This grave is along the Middle Fork John Day River downstream from Galena towards U.S. Hwy. 395. It is in the area of the right bank of Slide Creek, near its mouth with the Middle Fork John Day River. (Not shown on Wildcat Point 1990 USGS Quad. map.)

COCHRAN, WALLACE

| | A | 0.01 | ? | 8 May 1886 | T9S | R27E | S5 |

Wallace Cochran born 7 April 1835; died 8 May 1886 and is buried on a ranch now owned by the Silva brothers (1991). Located in the Northwest 1/4 of the Southeast 1/4 of Section 5. Cochran Creek enters the river from the south here. NOTE: This site is on private property. (Not shown on Monument 1990 USGS Quad. map.)

CUMMINGS

| | A | ? | 5 | 1891-1951 | T13S | R28E | ? |

These could be on Section 15 or 16. The burials are beside the Earl Valade Ranch (1978) at Cummingsville. There was a school called Cummingsville in the Southeast 1/4 of Section 15. There are 6 known burials. NOTE: This site is on private property. (Not shown on Shop Gulch 1972-83 USGS Quad. map.)

CUPPER FAMILY

| | A | 0.01 | 2 | 1890-1893 | T8S | R27E | S33 |

Leave the highway between Monument and Kimberly and turn north on Cupper Creek Road for about 2 miles. The graves are west of the ranch house 300-400 yards and under an old locust tree; Nora Alice Cupper born 17 September 1880, died 22 July 1890; Harry Charles Adams Cupper born 13 July 1873, died 31 May 1893, are buried here. This information comes from the old family bible of Henry Cupper. NOTE: This site is on private property. (Not shown on Monument 1990 USGS Quad. map.)

Name of Cemetery and also known as	Number of burials	Acres	Condition	Date started or earliest known burial	Township	Range	Section

DALE BURIALS

? ? ? ?   **T7S R31E**   ?
Perhaps the burials are located in Sections 1 and 2. Several burials are reported in the area of the Dale Ranger Station along U.S. Hwy. 395. This is 26 miles north of the town of Long Creek. Some burials may also be located in Umatilla County. (Not shown on Dale 1990 or Bridge Creek 1967-83 USGS Quad. maps.)

DAYVILLE
AKA: 1. VALLEY VIEW

C 0.5 2 1887   **T12S R26E**   S34
Located about 2.4 miles west of Dayville, several hundred feet south of U.S. Hwy. 26. There are 248 known graves and 6 unknown burials (1970). (Dayville 1972-85 USGS Quad. map.)

DICKERSON RANCH

A 0.2 5 1890   **T8S R30E**   S8
Located about a block from Ritter Hot Springs in a pasture: There are 7 burials. NOTE: This site is on private property. (Ritter 1990 USGS Quad. map.)

FLETCHER
AKA: 1. LEMONS GROVE

? 0.9 ? ?   **T13S R30E**   S28
Leave Main Street (U.S. Hwy. 26) in Mt. Vernon and turn south on Ingle Street. Leave Ingle Street at Milepost 1.13 and turn right onto a driveway to the cemetery. It is on the Byron Lemons Ranch (1978). NOTE: This site is on private property. (Mount. Vernon 1972-83 USGS Quad. map.)

FOX
AKA: 1. FOX VALLEY

B 2.5 3 1914   **T11S R30E**   S6
Leave U.S. Hwy. 395 at Milepost 99.47. Located 0.5 of a mile west of U.S Hwy. 395, in a valley near the Justice Ranch (1978), 1.2 miles southwest of Fox. There are 9 markers "unknown". (Fox 1990 USGS Quad. map.)

GALENA
AKA: 1. SUSANVILLE

B 0.3 1 1870'S   **T10S R32E**   S12
Leave U.S. Hwy. 395 and drive up the Middle Fork Road to the old mining town of Galena within the Malheur National Forest. The

Name of Cemetery and also known as	Number of burials	Acres	Condition	Date started or earliest known burial	Township	Range	Section

cemetery is about 0.33 of a mile by 4-wheel drive from Middle Fork Road to the northeast above Galena. (Susanville 1990 USGS Quad. map.)

GRANITE

B ? 5 Circa 1880 T9S R35 1/2E S4
Located about 300 feet north northwest from the intersection of Center Street and Main Streets in Granite. There were 57 known burials as of July 1985. (Granite 1972-83 USGS Quad. map.)

GRANT COUNTY POOR FARM
AKA: 1. HOG FLAT
     STAGE STATION
   2. MOUNTAIN REST
     STAGE STATION

? ? ? ? T12S R30E S12
Located in the Southeast 1/4 of the Southeast 1/4 of Section 12 and situated on the west side of U.S. Hwy.395, 11 miles north of Mt. Vernon. This was first known as Hog Flat Stage Station and was later the site of a county poor farm; it is usually denoted on maps as Mountain Rest. The compiler is uncertain if there were any burials on the site, but it would not be surprising, as most counties buried any one who died at the poor farms on the poor farm. (The site is shown on the Johnson Saddle 1990 USGS Quad. map.)

HAMILTON

C 0.9 1 1886 T9S R28E S35
Located 300 yards north of the Kimberly-Long Creek Highway and 0.5 of a mile west of Hamilton. There are 134 known burials (1970). (Hamilton 1990 USGS Quad. map.)

HANKINS
AKA: 1. SILVIES

A 0.25 3 1906 T18S R32E S7
Located near Silvies. Drive one mile south of Silvies on U.S. Hwy. 395 to a crossroads. Turn left (east) onto Bridge Creek Road, Forestry Road #3930. Drive about 0.7 of a mile to the east and north. At that point the cemetery is about 300 yards to the left (west), on top of a low hill and above the valley of Bridge Creek. There appears to be no driveway access. There were 7 graves known in 1970. (Silvies 1990 USGS Quad. map.)

Name of Cemetery and also known as	Number of burials	Acres	Condition	Date started or earliest known burial	Township	Range	Section

HOWELL HOMESTEAD

A 0.01 ? ? T9S ? ?

Perhaps located in Range 29 East or Range 30 East, Round Basin. There were 3 known burials reported in 1970. NOTE: No other information was given in the report. This is probably on private property. (Not shown on Fox 1990 USGS Quad. map.)

INGLE
AKA: 1. FLETCHER

A 0.2 2 1918 T13S R30E S27

Located on a hill in a field southeast of Mt. Vernon on the Dennis Lemons Ranch (1978). There are 19 unknown burials. NOTE: This site is on private property. (Mount Vernon 1972-83 USGS Quad. map.)

IZEE

B 1 2 1881 T17S R28E S29

Go 0.2 of a mile west of the school on the main road. Turn right (north) onto a driveway for 200 yards to the cemetery. Located on E. P. Smith Ranch at Izee (1978): 9 unknown burials. NOTE: This site is on private property. (Izee 1990 USGS Quad. map.)

KENNEDY, SUSAN

A 0.01 ? 1863 T13S R32E ?

This lone grave is located on Dog Creek on the Carl Sheedy property (1978); perhaps in Section 29, about 2.5 miles east of John Day. NOTE: This site is on private property. (Not shown on John Day 1972-83 USGS Quad. map.)

LEMCKE RANCH
AKA: 1. 96 RANCH

A 1 2 1895 T16S R30E S28

Leave the town of Seneca on U.S. Hwy. 395 and go northwesterly and west on Scotty Creek Road for about 9.5 miles to the 96 Ranch. The cemetery is about 0.6 of a mile on a low hill overlooking Bear Valley. There were only 6 burials as of 1978. NOTE: this site is on private property. (The cemetery is shown on the Logdell 1990 USGS Quad. map. The ranch buildings are shown on the Scotty Creek 1990 USGS Quad. map.)

Name of Cemetery and also known as	Number of burials	Acres	Condition	Date started or earliest known burial	Township	Range	Section

LOGDELL

A ? ? 2 Feb 1920 T15S R30E S33

Grant County Death Certificate #2, states that an unnamed male infant died 2 February 1920 and is buried at "Logdell". He was the child of Edwin A. and Ella R. Duncan Rhodes. No other information is known by the compiler. (Not shown on Logdell 1990 USGS Quad. map.)

LONG CREEK

C 2.7 1 1879 T10S R30E S11

This cemetery is about 1.5 miles east of the town of Long Creek. Turn left off of Keeney Forks Road at the first 90 degree turn east of Long Creek. (Long Creek 1990 USGS Quad. map.)

MANN GROVE

? ? ? ? ? ? ?

NOTE: The only information given in the report was the name and county. (Not shown on John Day 1972-83 USGS Quad. map.)

McHALEY

A 0.04 3 1877-1953 T13S R33E S3

Located 0.5 of a mile west of Prairie City on the Gene Ricco Ranch (1978), on top of a hill which overlooks the town. It is fenced: with 6 burials. George McHaley wanted a plot there. "On resurrection day I want to get up and look over the entire valley," he is quoted as saying. NOTE: This site is on private property. (Prairie City 1988 USGS Quad. map.)

MONUMENT [NEW]

C 2.5 1 1899 T9S R27E S1

Located about 0.3 of a mile to the northwest of Monument see Quad. map. (Monument 1990 USGS Quad. map.)

MONUMENT [OLD]

A 0.25 2 1874-1891 T9S R27E S12

Located 1.5 miles south of Monument and across Cottonwood Creek overlooking Monument on the Murphy Ranch (1978). A lot of vandalism was noted in 1970. No ready access. NOTE: This site is on private property. (Monument 1990 USGS Quad. map.)

Name of Cemetery and also known as	Number of burials	Acres	Condition	Date started or earliest known burial	Township	Range	Section

MOON CREEK
AKA: 1. FIELDS
    2. FIELDS CREEK

C   1   ?   ?   **T13S R29E**   **S20**
This cemetery is west of Mt. Vernon on Moon Creek, on the north side of the John Day River, 0.2 of a mile north and west of John Day on U.S. Hwy. 26 at Moon Creek Bridge. There are 86 known burials. (Wolfinger Butte 1972-83 USGS Quad. map.)

PRAIRIE CITY

D   5   1   1874   **T13S R33E**   **S11**
Located at Prairie City. Take Main Street south from U.S. Hwy. 26 and cross the John Day River. Turn left and the cemetery is on the right. (Prairie City 1988 USGS Quad. map.)

RANGE [NEW]

A   0.1   1   1984   **T8S R31E**   **S17**
Located on the Southwest 1/4 of the Southwest 1/4 of section 17; 15 miles north of Long Creek, just west of U.S. Hwy. 395 on the Walton property. The two burials are: Mrs. Walton, May 1984; Monsignor George A. Murphy, July 1984. Monsignor George A. Murphy, a Catholic priest, who from 1938 to 1955 was the head of the Diocese of John Day; he lived the last 10 years of his life at Ben Walton's Ranch. NOTE: This site is on private property. (Flowers Gulch 1990 USGS Quad. map.)

RANGE [OLD]

B   2   1   1870'S   **T8S R31E**   **S10**
Located in McGrews pasture northeast of Long Creek (1978), 3 miles southeast of U.S. Hwy. 395 on Trout Road. NOTE: This site is on private property. (The locale of Range is shown on Dale 1990 USGS Quad. map. The cemetery is not shown.)

RESTLAWN
AKA: 1. GROVE
    2. JOHN DAY

C   2   1   Sept 1923   **T13S R31E**   **S22**
Located in John Day. Leave U.S. Hwy. 26 and go north on Bridge Street, cross the John Day River, going past the Forestry buildings to the cemetery. There were 103 known burials and 2 unknown burials (1970). {10 July 1993} (John Day 1972-83 USGS Quad. map.)

Grant County

Name of Cemetery and also known as	Number of burials	Acres	Condition	Date started or earliest known burial	Township	Range	Section

RICCO
A 0.5 3 1906   T12S R34E   ?
Perhaps located in Section 19, 4 miles up Dixie Creek on the Ernest Ricco Ranch (1978) out of Prairie City. There are 4 known burials. NOTE: This site is on private property. (Not shown on Dixie Meadows 1988 USGS Quad. map.)

RITTER
B 0.75 1 1870'S   T7S R30E   S31
Located on a high plateau on the farm of Earl Burnett (1978), 7 miles from Ritter. Leave Ritter on the Ritter-Dale Road and go 3.6 miles; turn left on Bone Point-Nelson Road and go 2.6 miles. Turn left on the cemetery driveway and travel 0.78 of a mile to the cemetery. There are 9 unknown burials. (Ritter 1990 USGS Quad. map.)

ST. ANDREW'S CATHOLIC
C 3 1 Late 1800'S T13S R31E   S35
Located on a hillside above Canyon City, just below the larger Canyon City Cemetery, which is on top of the hill. Take East Main Street, turn left up the hill on Patterson Drive. There are 11 unknown burials. (John Day 1972-83 USGS Quad. map.)

SOUTHWORTH RANCH
A 0.5 2 Late 1800'S T16S R31E   S15
Leave Seneca from the schoolhouse on U.S. Hwy. 395 and drive northerly for 3.25 miles close to the bridge over Van Aspen Creek. Turn off to the right (east) on a private road and go east and north for about 1.25 miles. The cemetery is about 200 feet off to the left (west). There were 2 known and 9 unknown burials here in 1978. NOTE: This site is on private property. (Seneca 1990 USGS Quad. map.)

UNKNOWN
A 0.01 ? ?   T13S R30E   ?
Perhaps located in Section 20. An unknown pioneer grave on the Byron Lemons Ranch (1959). This grave is apparently separate from the Fletcher Cemetery. NOTE: No other information was given in the report. This site is on private property. (Not shown on Mt. Vernon 1972-83 USGS Quad. map.)

Name of Cemetery and also known as | Number of burials | Acres | Condition | Date started or earliest known burial | Township | Range | Section

VARDIMAN GRAVE, JAMES
AKA: 1. VERDAMAN

A   0.01   ?   1878   T10S ?   ?
Located in the Galena-Susanville area. NOTE:
This could be Range 32 East or Range 33 East
and Section 13 or 18. NOTE: Not enough
information was given in the report to be
able to give directions on how to find this
burial site. Verdiman and another man were
killed by Bannock Indians. (Not shown on
Susanville 1990 USGS Quad. map.)

WEBERG FAMILY
AKA: 1. SWICK

?   ?   ?   Circa 1890   T18S R26E   ?
Perhaps in Section 19, it is located on the
Weberg Ranch about a mile east of the ranch
house in a meadow and on private property.
The ranch is best reached from Crook County
from the Paulina-Izee Road. Turn south from
that road on the county road variously called
Suplee or Weberg Road. At 4 miles from the
Paulina-Izee Road is the junction to the
right to Delore Cemetery. Continue southerly
about another 1.5 miles to the Weberg Ranch
on the left (east). At this point the road
runs along the county line between Crook and
Grant Counties. (Weberg Ranch is shown on
the Suplee 1981 USGS Quad. map, but the
cemetery is not.)

WILLOW CREEK

?   1   ?   ?   T8S   R31E   S28
This cemetery is accessible only by
roundabout routes, and partly by 4-wheel
drive only. Leave U.S. Hwy. 395 to the
southeast on Middle Fork John Day Road, going
upstream. Somewhere off to the left and back
to the northwest is the miles-long 4-wheel
drive road to the cemetery. NOTE: No other
instructions on how to find this was given by
the informant to the compiler. (Wildcat
Point 1990 USGS Quad. map.)

Grant County

96 RANCH see **LEMCKE RANCH**	GRANT CO.	T16S	R30E	S28
ALDRICH, ELMER OLIVER	GRANT CO.	T13S	R27E	S10
AUSTIN	GRANT CO.	T11S	R35E	S21
BATES-AUSTIN see **AUSTIN**	GRANT CO.	T11S	R35E	S21
BOOT HILL	GRANT CO.	T13S	R31E	S36
CABELL CITY	GRANT CO.	T8S	R35 1/2E	S1
CABELL FAMILY see **CABELL CITY**	GRANT CO.	T8S	R35 1/2E	S1
CABELL, FRED see **CABELL CITY**	GRANT CO.	T8S	R35 1/2E	S1
CABELL, JOHANNA CAMILLA see **CABELL CITY**				
	GRANT CO.	T8S	R35 1/2E	S1
CABELL, MRS. see **CABELL CITY**	GRANT CO.	T8S	R35 1/2E	S1
CANYON CITY	GRANT CO.	T13S	R31E	S35
CHILD'S GRAVE	GRANT CO.	T9S	R31E	S14
COCHRAN, WALLACE	GRANT CO.	T9S	R27E	S5
CUMMINGS	GRANT CO.	T13S	R28E	?
CUPPER FAMILY	GRANT CO.	T8S	R27E	S33
CUPPER, HARRY CHARLES ADAMS see **CUPPER FAMILY**				
	GRANT CO.	T8S	R27E	S33
CUPPER, HENRY see **CUPPER FAMILY**	GRANT CO.	T8S	R27E	S33
CUPPER, NORA ALICE see **CUPPER FAMILY**				
	GRANT CO.	T8S	R27E	S33
DALE BURIALS	GRANT CO.	T7S	R31E	?
DAYVILLE	GRANT CO.	T12S	R26E	S34
DICKERSON RANCH	GRANT CO.	T8S	R30E	S8
FIELDS see **MOON CREEK**	GRANT CO.	T13S	R29E	S20
FIELDS CREEK see **MOON CREEK**	GRANT CO.	T13S	R29E	S20
FLETCHER	GRANT CO.	T13S	R30E	S28
FLETCHER see **INGLE**	GRANT CO.	T13S	R30E	S27
FOX	GRANT CO.	T11S	R30E	S6
FOX VALLEY see **FOX**	GRANT CO.	T11S	R30E	S6
GALENA	GRANT CO.	T10S	R32E	S12
GRANITE	GRANT CO.	T9S	R35 1/2E	S4
GRANT COUNTY POOR FARM	GRANT CO	T12S	R30E	S12
GROVE see **RESTLAWN**	GRANT CO.	T13S	R31E	S22
HAMILTON	GRANT CO.	T9S	R28E	S35
HANKINS	GRANT CO.	T18S	R32E	S7
HOG FLAT STAGE STATION see **GRANT COUNTY POOR FARM**				
	GRANT CO.	T12S	R30E	S12
HOWELL HOMESTEAD	GRANT CO.	T9S	?	?
I.O.O.F. see **CANYON CITY**	GRANT CO.	T13S	R31E	S35
INGLE	GRANT CO.	T13S	R30E	S27
IZEE	GRANT CO.	T17S	R28E	S29
JOHN DAY see **RESTLAWN**	GRANT CO.	T13S	R31E	S22
KENNEDY, SUSAN	GRANT CO.	T13S	R32E	?
LEMCKE RANCH	GRANT CO.	T16S	R30E	S28
LEMONS GROVE see **FLETCHER**	GRANT CO.	T13S	R30E	S28
LEMONS RANCH, BYRON see **FLETCHER**				
	GRANT CO.	T13S	R30E	S28
LEMONS RANCH, BYRON see **UNKNOWN**	GRANT CO.	T13S	R30E	?
LEMONS RANCH, DENNIS see **INGLE**	GRANT CO.	T13S	R30E	S27
LOGDELL	GRANT CO.	T15S	R30E	S33
LONG CREEK	GRANT CO.	T10S	R30E	S11

Grant County

MANN GROVE	GRANT CO.	?	?	?
MASONIC see **CANYON CITY**	GRANT CO.	T13S	R31E	S35
McGREWS PASTURE see **RANGE [OLD]**	GRANT CO.	T8S	R31E	S10
McHALEY	GRANT CO.	T13S	R33E	S3
McHALEY, GEORGE see **McHALEY**	GRANT CO.	T13S	R33E	S3
MONUMENT [NEW]	GRANT CO.	T9S	R27E	S1
MONUMENT [OLD]	GRANT CO.	T9S	R27E	S12
MOON CREEK	GRANT CO.	T13S	R29E	S20
MOUNTAIN REST STAGE STATION see **GRANT COUNTY POOR FARM**				
	GRANT CO.	T12S	R30E	S12
MURPHY, MONSIGNOR GEORGE A. see **RANGE [NEW]**				
	GRANT CO.	T8S	R31E	S17
MURPHY RANCH see **MONUMENT [OLD]**	GRANT CO.	T9S	R27E	S12
PRAIRIE CITY	GRANT CO.	T13S	R33E	S11
RANGE [NEW]	GRANT CO.	T8S	R31E	S17
RANGE [OLD]	GRANT CO.	T8S	R31E	S10
RESTLAWN	GRANT CO.	T13S	R31E	S22
RHODES, EDWIN A. see **LOGDELL**	GRANT CO.	T15S	R30E	S33
RHODES, ELLA R. DUNCAN see **LOGDELL**				
	GRANT CO.	T15S	R30E	S33
RICCO	GRANT CO.	T12S	R34E	?
RICCO RANCH, ERNEST see **RICCO**	GRANT CO.	T12S	R34E	?
RICCO RANCH, GENE see **McHALEY**	GRANT CO.	T13S	R33E	S3
RICCO RANCH, HENRY see **AUSTIN**	GRANT CO.	T11S	R35E	S21
RITTER	GRANT CO.	T7S	R30E	S31
ST. ANDREWS CATHOLIC	GRANT CO.	T13S	R31E	S35
SHEEDY, CARL see **KENNEDY, SUSAN**	GRANT CO.	T13S	R32E	?
SILVA RANCH, see **COCHRAN, WALLACE**				
	GRANT CO.	T9S	R27E	S5
SILVIES see **HANKINS**	GRANT CO.	T18S	R32E	S7
SMITH RANCH, E. P. see **IZEE**	GRANT CO.	T17S	R28E	S29
SOUTHWORTH RANCH	GRANT CO.	T16S	R31E	S15
SUSANVILLE see **GALENA**	GRANT CO.	T10S	R32E	S12
SWICK see **WEBERG FAMILY**	GRANT CO.	T18S	R26E	?
UNKNOWN	GRANT CO.	T13S	R30E	?
VALADE RANCH, EARL see **CUMMINGS**	GRANT CO.	T13S	R28E	?
VALLEY VIEW see **DAYVILLE**	GRANT CO.	T12S	R26E	S34
VARDIMAN GRAVE, JAMES	GRANT CO.	T10S	?	?
VERDAMAN see **VARDIMAN GRAVE, JAMES**				
	GRANT CO.	T10S	?	?
WALTON, MRS. see **RANGE [NEW]**	GRANT CO.	T8S	R31E	S17
WALTON PROPERTY see **RANGE [NEW]**	GRANT CO.	T8S	R31E	S17
WALTON RANCH, BEN see **RANGE [NEW]**				
	GRANT CO.	T8S	R31E	S17
WEBERG FAMILY	GRANT CO.	T18S	R26E	?
WEBERG RANCH see **WEBERG FAMILY**	GRANT CO.	T18S	R26E	?
WILLOW CREEK	GRANT CO.	T8S	R31E	S28

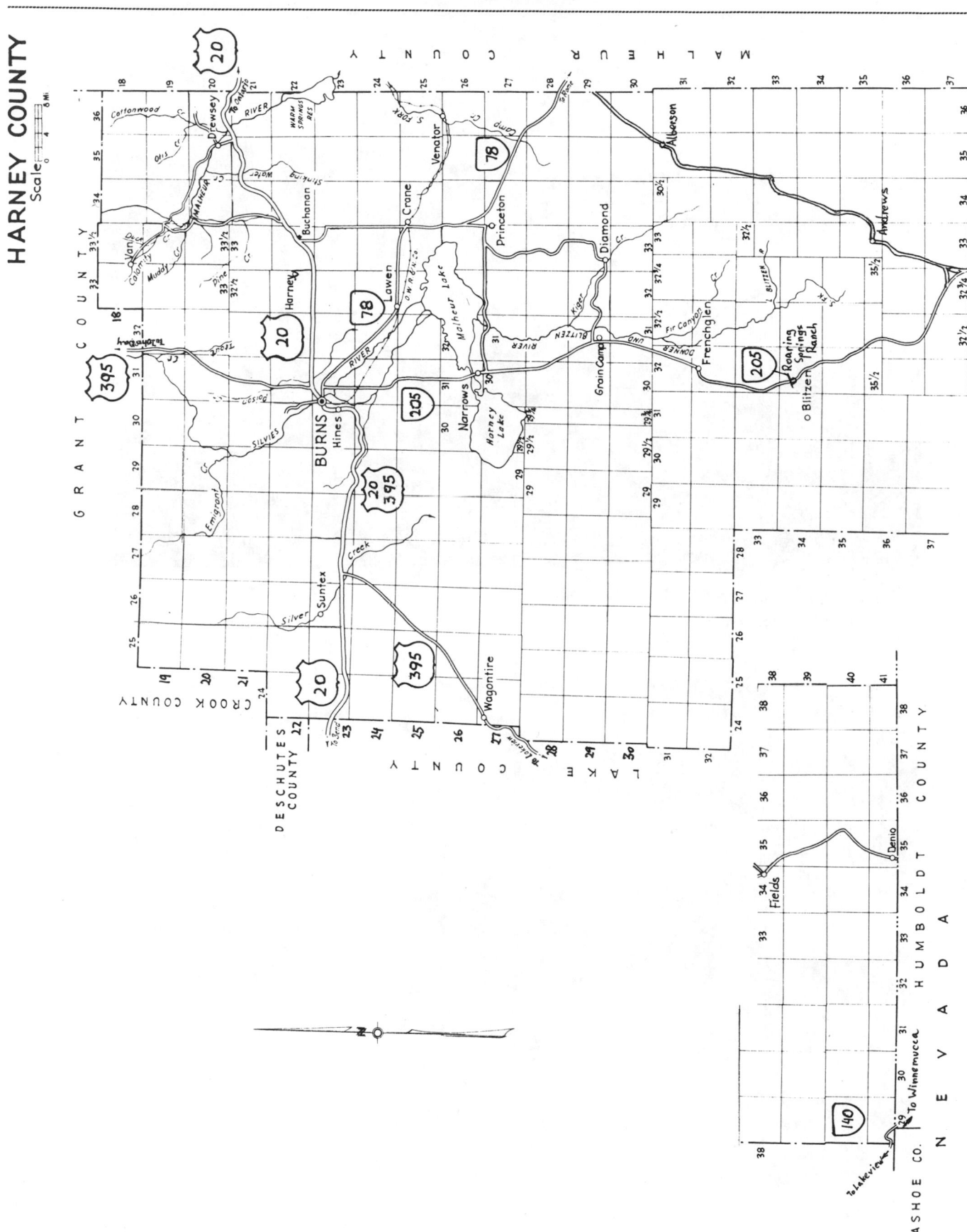

347

Sunset Valley, Janice M. Healy
What some won't do to get to a cemetery.
Ruth C. Bishop (2000)

Sunset Valley
Janice M. Healy (2000)

Oregon Burial Site Guide
Harney County

Area: 10,228 square miles
Population (1998): 7,198
County seat: Burns, Population: 2,935
County established: 25 February 1889

Harney County is Oregon's largest. It is given over mostly to livestock ranching but there are large areas in the north that are timbered. Other than military cemeteries around old forts, the earliest organized public cemeteries appear to be Silver Creek and Happy Valley Cemeteries, both from 1881. The 1880's and 1890's saw most of the public cemeteries established. In addition there are two Paiute Indian Cemeteries near Burns.

Sunset Valley
Janice M. Healy (2000)

Crane
Janice M. Healy (2000)

Crane
Janice M. Healy (2000)

Name of Cemetery and also known as	Number of burials	Acres	Condition	Date started or earliest known burial	Township	Range	Section

ANDREWS

A   0.5   5   1902   T35S R33E   S22
Located near the Penland Ranch at Andrews. Go 1.1 miles north of the Andrews Store on the main road, then 0.2 of a mile further north on a private road. There are 16 burials; 12 known and 4 unmarked graves (1977). (Andrews 1971-79 USGS Quad. map.)

BABY'S GRAVE

A   ?   ?   ?   T20S R25E   S9
Located in the Ochoco National Forest, in the Snow Mountain Ranger District. Leave Central Oregon Highway (U.S. Hwy. 20) at Milepost 103.15, just west of Riley. Turn north onto Silver Creek Market Road, drive north and northwesterly past Suntex and Silver Creek Cemetery. At 14.74 miles from U.S. Hwy. 20 the county road ends. Turn left onto Forestry Road #45 going west and northwesterly to Sawmill Creek; keep on Forestry Road #45 almost to the head of Sawmill Creek. The grave is on the right. (Buck Spring 1990 USGS Quad. map and 1993 Ochoco National Forest map.)

BUNYARD, WILLARD

A   0.01   4   1 Nov 1897   T37S R36E   S12
Drive from Burns south on Frenchglen Highway (OR. Hwy. 206) to Roaring Springs Ranch. Continue southerly and southeasterly to Fields. Drive south 8 miles from Fields and then turn left (east and northeasterly) onto Whitehorse Ranch Road. It is another 28 miles to the road the ranch headquarters are on; turn left. A short distance beyond is a road, on the left (north), to the site of Camp C. F. Smith. Drive about 0.5 of a mile north on the Camp C. F. Smith Road where there are 3 graves to the left (west), through a gate about 100 yards from the road. The site of Camp C. F. Smith is a very short distance north. You may return to Whitehorse Ranch Road and drive another 21 miles to U.S. Hwy. 95. Willard Bunyard was a ranch hand; the other two burials were not identified in the report. (Whitehorse Ranch 1982 USGS Quad. map.)

Name of Cemetery and also known as	Number of burials	Acres	Condition	Date started or earliest known burial	Township	Range	Section

BURNS
AKA: 1. I.O.O.F.

D 16   3   Circa 1887   T23S R30E   S13
The cemetery is on the left, on the hillside, when entering Burns from Hines on U.S. Hwys. 20 and 395. (Burns 1960 USGS Quad. map.)

CALL MEADOW GRAVE

A   0.01   ?   Circa 1865   T20S R33E   S29
Located in the Malheur National Forest. NOTE: No other information was given in the report. (Not shown on Telephone Butte 1990 USGS Quad. map.)

CAMP CURREY

A   ?   ?   1865-1866   T22S R25E   S25
According to a correspondent, in January of 1944 there were 3 graves at this military camp which was occupied from September of 1865 to May of 1866. From *Oregon Geographic Names*, by Lewis L. McArthur, 4th edition, page 110. (Camp Currey Spring 1981 USGS Quad. map.)

CATLOW, JOHN AND MARGARET FINN

A   ?   ?   1901   T40S R31E   S4
Located about 10 miles south of Fields and 10 miles north of Denio is the old Catlow Ranch along the Fields-Denio Road. John Catlow, born 5 November 1824 in England settled here in 1872. He died in 1901, and his wife Margaret Finn Catlow, also English born in 1852 died in 1925. Both are buried about 0.5 of a mile up Catlow Creek from the ranch house. Catlow Valley covers a large area of southern Harney County and there was a post office named Catlow which operated from December 1914 to January 1923. This post office is about 60 miles northwest of the Catlow Ranch house which gives an idea of the size of the ranch holdings. In addition a Harney County death certifcate #19 for 6 September 1923 reports the death of an unknown man. He was buried in Catlow Cemetery. (Not shown on Tumtum Lake 1981 USGS Quad. map, which shows the ranch house but not the burial site.)

CRANE

B   2.3   3   1917   T25S R33E   S12
One mile west of Crane, cross OR. Hwy. 78 onto Crane Dump Road. The cemetery is 0.5 of

Name of Cemetery and also known as	Number of burials	Acres	Condition	Date started or earliest known burial	Township	Range	Section

a mile west of OR. Hwy. 78. The town was founded in 1916. {3 September 2000} (Crane 1990 USGS Quad. map.)

CUMMINGS FIELD
AKA: 1. DIAMOND
    2. OTLEY FIELD

A   0.01 ? ?   T29S R33E   S31

This single grave is just south of the Diamond School at Diamond. Go west from Diamond on Diamond Lane about 1 mile, Diamond School and burial are on the left. (Not shown on Diamond 1967 USGS Quad. map.)

DENIO

B   1.1 4 1907   T41S R35E   S20

Located 0.6 of a mile north of the Nevada State Line, on the west side of the road at Denio. There are 72 known burials, 32 marked and 40 unmarked (1977). (Van Horn Basin 1981 USGS Quad. map.)

DREWSEY
AKA: 1. I.O.O.F.

C   4 4 1893   T20S R35E   S23

At the main intersection in Drewsey take the Drewsey Market Road to the west 0.4 of a mile. The cemetery is on the right. This cemetery once consisted of two separate but adjoining cemeteries. The I.O.O.F. portion was filed 17 March 1902; the "Drewsey Cemetery" adjoining on the north was defined by an act of the town council at an unrecorded later date. The present fenced area is considerably smaller than the combined area of the plats. {18 June 1991} (Drewsey 1990 USGS Quad. map.)

DREWSEY FIELD

A   ? ? ?   T20S R35E   ?

On the possibility that the word "field" refers to the Drewsey Airfield this would be in Section 21 or 28. The Airfield is 2.5 miles west of Drewsey Cemetery and over the ridge and down into the valley. A D.A.R. survey reported three graves. Possibly these burials and the Gus Horton burial may now be included within the fenced area of the main Drewsey Cemetery. There are some much smaller burial areas on the upper portion of that cemetery and well separated from the lower portions which have numerous burials. (The airfield is shown but with no burial site shown near it on the Drewsey 1990 USGS Quad. map.)

FIELDS [#1]

A 0.5 5 1894-1972 T38S R34E S24

There are 3 graves at the Fields Airstrip. (Not shown on Fields 1971-80 USGS Quad. map.)

FIELDS [#2]

A 0.01 4 1897-1910 T38S R34E S24

At Fields, there are 2 graves that are fenced and at the back of the store. (Not shown on Fields 1971-80 USGS Quad. map.)

FORT HARNEY

? ? ? 1867-1880 T22S R32 1/2E S18

Located 2.4 miles north of Harney on the east side of Rattlesnake Road. This fort was occupied August 1867-June 1880. (The Cemetery is not shown but the site of Fort Harney is shown on Harney 1990 USGS Quad. map.)

HAPPY VALLEY
AKA: 1. SMYTH

A 0.5 4 1881 T29S R33E S12

Located near the Happy Valley Road to Diamond, and near the Happy Valley Ranch. (Happy Valley 1967-80 USGS Quad. map.)

HARNEY
AKA: 1. HARNEY CITY

B 3.7 4 1886 T22S R32E S24

Located on the Reed Ranch (1978), at the mouth of Rattlesnake Canyon. Go 2 miles north from U.S. Hwy. 20 to Harney; then turn left (west) onto North Harney Road and drive 0.5 of a mile to a bend to the left in the road. Continue ahead on a driveway upslope for 0.3 of a mile to the cemetery. NOTE: This site is on private property. (Harney 1990 USGS Quad. map.)

HINES
AKA: 1. CATHOLIC
[OLD]
2. HOLY FAMILY
CHURCH

? ? 1 1855 T23S R30E S24

Located on the southeasterly side of U.S. Hwy. 395 at Hines and next to Valley Golf Course buildings. Most of the bodies were removed to the Burns Cemetery in 1936. The cemetery was dedicated again on Memorial Day, 1992. (Not shown on Burns 1960 USGS Quad. map.)

HORTON, GUS

? 0.01 ? ?   T20S R35E   ?
Possibly located in Section 26: 1 grave, in a field in Drewsey (1977 D.A.R. survey). This may be in the same burial ground as Drewsey Field. (Not shown on Drewsey or Drinkwater Pass 1990 USGS Quad. maps.)

McLAUGHLIN, NETTIE

A 0.01 5 15 Jun 1887 T28S R31E   S27
Located in the Malheur National Wildlife Refuge. Drive 34.8 miles south of Burns into the refuge. Just beyond Milepost 33 turn left off of OR. Hwy. 205 onto Rockford Lane. Go east 2.7 miles to Central Patrol Road and turn right (south), driving another 1.8 miles to the lone grave on the right. {15 June 1991} (Diamond Swamp 1967 USGS Quad. map.)

MOFFITT MILL

? ? ? ?   T19S R34E   ?
Two graves were found (in 1977 D.A.R. survey.) NOTE: No other information was given in the report. (Not shown on Moffit Table 1990 USGS Quad. map. Note variant spelling.)

MULLER

A 0.1 5 1886-1942 T20S R34E   S3
Take the Van-Drewsey Road from Drewsey, crossing the Malheur River and turning left (westerly) towards Van. Drive about 9.1 miles from Drewsey to a driveway on the left (southwest). Take this driveway for about 0.5 of a mile to a gate. Turn left and go on foot about 700 feet to a knoll where the cemetery overlooks the Malheur River. Eight graves were found by D.A.R. in 1977. (House Butte 1990 USGS Quad. map.)

NARROWS
  AKA: 1. ELLIOTT,
      THEODOSIA
      MILLER

A 0.01 5 25 Aug 1892 T26S R30E   S26
Theodosia Miller Elliott wife of Henderson Elliott she was born 5 March 1855; died 25 August 1892. The other undated burial is thought to be the Reineman child, both lived

Name of Cemetery and also known as	Number of burials	Acres	Condition	Date started or earliest known burial	Township	Range	Section

at the Narrows. These are on an unnamed butte on the south side of the Narrows; on the east side of Frenchglen Highway (OR. Hwy. 205), 0.25 of a mile from the townsite of Narrows. There is no ready access. {15 June 1991} (The Narrows 1990 USGS Quad. map.)

PAIUTE [NEW]
AKA: 1. INDIAN [NEW]
    2. NEW CAMP

B   1.5   4   1938   T23S R30E   S1
Located near Burns, on a hill above Paiute Village. D.A.R, in 1977, noted 37 known burials; 22 marked and 15 unmarked. (Burns 1960 USGS Quad. map.)

PAIUTE [OLD]
AKA: 1. BURNS PAIUTE
    2. INDIAN [OLD]
    3. OLD CAMP

?   0.23   ?   ?   T23S R30E   S14
The compiler was not given any other information on this site. (Burns 1960 USGS Quad. map.)

RICKERT RANCH

?   ?   ?   ?   T19S R33 1/2E   S13
Located in the area of Van. Go up river from Drewsey, then turn right (north) off of Van-Drewsey Road; go about a total of 14.2 miles from Drewsey and 0.66 of a mile from the bridge over the Malheur River. Go right (north) on a side road about 0.75 of a mile. There are three graves about 400 feet off to the left (west) side of road (1977 D.A.R. survey). (Moffit Table 1990 USGS Quad. map.)

ROCK CREEK

A   0.15   4   1918-1933   T34S R30E   S4
Go 7 miles south of Frenchglen, then turn right (west) on the main county road to Hart Mountain. Go 13.5 miles on this county road, across the north Catlow Valley. Turn left (southwest) on a side road, over a ridge, for 2 miles. On the down slope, the cemetery is about 200 yards to the right. 2 miles south of Rock Creek Ranch (1978). There are 2 graves. (Blitzen N. W. 1971 USGS Quad. map.)

SADDLE BUTTE

B   0.4   4   1890   T25S R32 1/2E   S1
Located between OR. Hwy. 78 and Saddle Butte. Go 5.6 miles east of Lawen on OR. Hwy. 78; turn right (south) off of OR. Hwy. 78 and go

Name of Cemetery and also known as	Number of burials	Acres	Condition	Date started or earliest known burial	Township	Range	Section

0.75 of a mile to the cemetery. The cemetery is on the east side of a large pond (which could be dry) north of Malheur Lake. (Warm Springs Butte 1990 USGS Quad. map.)

SILVER CREEK
AKA: 1. RILEY
2. SILVER CREEK VALLEY
3. SUNTEX

B 1 4 1881 T23S R26E S5

Located in the area of Suntex. Leave Central Oregon Highway (U.S. Hwy. 20) 1.6 miles west of Riley. Turn north onto Silver Creek Road and go 1.6 miles; then turn left at the intersection and go another 5.1 miles (6.7 miles from the highway) to the cemetery. The cemetery is on the left, about 500 feet from the road. (Riley 1981 USGS Quad. map.)

SMITH, SILVESTER

A 0.1 4 9 Apr 1923 T28S R33E S26

This is on the Southeast 1/4 of the Northwest 1/4 of Section 26. This is on a hill on the west side of a north-south road near Happy Valley. It is several miles southeast of the famous round barn. There are 4 known burials, 1 person "died of sour beans". (Not shown on Happy Valley 1967-80 USGS Quad. map.)

SUNSET VALLEY
AKA: 1. DOG MOUNTAIN
2. HENNEY
3. LOMA [?]
4. NARROWS

A 0.3 4 1913 T25S R31E S27

Leave Burns on OR. Hwy. 78, at milepost 1.75 turn right (south) on OR. Hwy. 205. The cemetery is on the left 17 miles from Burns. The burials are confined to a fenced area about 20 feet square with 9 visible burials. To reach this cemetery you must first go under a four strand tightly strung barbed wire fence. The cemetery is fenced with a gate. This cemetery has been mistakenly referred to in the past as Narrows Cemetery, so see the article under that heading also. {3 September 2000} (Redess 1990 USGS Quad. map.)

VAN

A 0.15 4 1890-1937 T18S R33 1/2E S30

Located up-river from Drewsey. Go 21 miles from Drewsey, turn left (west) on Calamity Road, cross Wolf Creek and go 0.34 of a mile.

Name of Cemetery and also known as	Number of burials	Acres	Condition	Date started or earliest known burial	Township	Range	Section

Take the road to the left (south) 0.1 of a mile, to the cemetery on the left. There are 8 known burials. (Van 1990 USGS Quad. map.)

VOLTAGE GRAVES

? ? ? ?   T27S R31E   S1

Located on the south side of the Narrows-Princeton Road, 1 mile east of the Blitzen River Bridge. (Malheur Lake West 1990 USGS Quad. map.)

WINDY POINT

A ? 4 1917   T26S R33E   S11

Located between the easternmost edge of Malheur Lake and at the foot of the western end of Windy Point Table. Leave OR. Hwy. 78 about 3 miles north of New Princeton and go about 2.5 miles, on private roads, around the south and west base of Windy Point Table. There are 5 known burials. (New Princeton 1990 USGS Quad. map.)

WRIGHT POINT
  AKA: 1. CAMP WRIGHT
       2. MACKEY, JOHN

A 0.01 2 1866   T24S R31E   ?

This is on Section 33 or 34, on the east side of OR. Hwy. 205 at Wright Point, at the top of the hill. There is one known burial: John Mackey, killed by Indians. (Not shown on Dog Mountain 1990 USGS Quad. map.)

Crane

Janice M. Healy (2000)

ANDREWS	HARNEY CO.	T35S	R33E	S22
BABY'S GRAVE	HARNEY CO.	T20S	R25E	S9
BUNYARD, WILLARD	HARNEY CO.	T37S	R36E	S12
BURNS	HARNEY CO.	T23S	R30E	S13
BURNS PAIUTE see **PAIUTE [OLD]**	HARNEY CO.	T23S	R30E	S14
CALL MEADOW GRAVE	HARNEY CO.	T20S	R33E	S29
CAMP C. F. SMITH see **BUNYARD, WILLARD**				
	HARNEY CO.	T37S	R36E	S12
CAMP CURREY	HARNEY CO.	T22S	R25E	S25
CAMP WRIGHT see **WRIGHT POINT**	HARNEY CO.	T24S	R31E	?
CATHOLIC [OLD] see **HINES**	HARNEY CO.	T23S	R30E	S24
CATLOW, JOHN AND MARGARET FINN	HARNEY CO.	T40S	R31E	S4
CATLOW RANCH see **CATLOW, JOHN AND MARGARET FINN**				
	HARNEY CO.	T40S	R31E	S4
CRANE	HARNEY CO.	T25S	R33E	S12
CUMMINGS FIELD	HARNEY CO.	T29S	R33E	S31
DENIO	HARNEY CO.	T41S	R35E	S20
DIAMOND see **CUMMINGS FIELD**	HARNEY CO.	T29S	R33E	S31
DOG MOUNTAIN see **SUNSET VALLEY**	HARNEY CO.	T25S	R31E	S27
DREWSEY	HARNEY CO.	T20S	R35E	S23
DREWSEY FIELD	HARNEY CO.	T20S	R35E	?
ELLIOTT, HENDERSON see **NARROWS**	HARNEY CO.	T26S	R30E	S26
ELLIOTT, THEODOSIA MILLER see **NARROWS**				
	HARNEY CO.	T26S	R30E	S26
FIELDS [#1]	HARNEY CO.	T38S	R34E	S24
FIELDS [#2]	HARNEY CO.	T38S	R34E	S24
FORT HARNEY	HARNEY CO.	T22S	R32 1/2E	S18
HAPPY VALLEY	HARNEY CO.	T29S	R33E	S12
HAPPY VALLEY RANCH see **HAPPY VALLEY**				
	HARNEY CO.	T29S	R33E	S12
HARNEY	HARNEY CO.	T22S	R32E	S24
HARNEY CITY see **HARNEY**	HARNEY CO.	T22S	R32E	S24
HENNEY see **SUNSET VALLEY**	HARNEY CO.	T25S	R31E	S27
HINES	HARNEY CO.	T23S	R30E	S24
HOLY FAMILY CHURCH see **HINES**	HARNEY CO.	T23S	R30E	S24
HORTON, GUS	HARNEY CO.	T20S	R35E	?
HORTON, GUS see **DREWSEY FIELD**	HARNEY CO.	T20S	R35E	?
I.O.O.F. see **BURNS**	HARNEY CO.	T23S	R30E	S13
I.O.O.F. see **DREWSEY**	HARNEY CO.	T20S	R35E	S23
INDIAN [NEW] see **PAIUTE [NEW]**	HARNEY CO.	T23S	R30E	S1
INDIAN [OLD] see **PAIUTE [OLD]**	HARNEY CO.	T23S	R30E	S14
LOMA [?] see **SUNSET VALLEY**	HARNEY CO.	T25S	R31E	S27
MACKEY, JOHN see **WRIGHT POINT**	HARNEY CO.	T24S	R31E	?
McLAUGHLIN, NETTIE	HARNEY CO.	T28S	R31E	S27
MOFFITT MILL	HARNEY CO.	T19S	R34E	?
MULLER	HARNEY CO.	T20S	R34E	S3
NARROWS	HARNEY CO.	T26S	R30E	S26
NARROWS see **SUNSET VALLEY**	HARNEY CO.	T25S	R31E	S27
NEW CAMP see **PAIUTE [NEW]**	HARNEY CO.	T23S	R30E	S1
OLD CAMP see **PAIUTE [OLD]**	HARNEY CO.	T23S	R30E	S14
OTLEY FIELD see **CUMMINGS FIELD**	HARNEY CO.	T29S	R33E	S31
PAIUTE [NEW]	HARNEY CO.	T23S	R30E	S1

PAIUTE [OLD]	HARNEY CO.	T23S	R30E	S14
PENLAND RANCH see **ANDREWS**	HARNEY CO.	T35S	R33E	S22
REED RANCH see **HARNEY**	HARNEY CO.	T22S	R32E	S24
REINEMAN CHILD see **NARROWS**	HARNEY CO.	T26S	R30E	S26
RICKERT RANCH	HARNEY CO.	T19S	R33 1/2E	S13
RILEY see **SILVER CREEK**	HARNEY CO.	T23S	R26E	S5
ROCK CREEK	HARNEY CO.	T34S	R30E	S4
ROCK CREEK RANCH see **ROCK CREEK**	HARNEY CO.	T34S	R30E	S4
SADDLE BUTTE	HARNEY CO.	T25S	R32 1/2E	S1
SILVER CREEK	HARNEY CO.	T23S	R26E	S5
SILVER CREEK VALLEY see **SILVER CREEK**				
	HARNEY CO.	T23S	R26E	S5
SMITH, SILVESTER	HARNEY CO.	T28S	R33E	S26
SMYTH see **HAPPY VALLEY**	HARNEY CO.	T29S	R33E	S12
SUNSET VALLEY	HARNEY CO.	T25S	R31E	S27
SUNTEX see **SILVER CREEK**	HARNEY CO.	T23S	R26E	S5
VAN	HARNEY CO.	T18S	R33 1/2E	S30
VOLTAGE GRAVES	HARNEY CO.	T27S	R31E	S1
WHITEHOURSE RANCH see **BUNYARD, WILLARD**				
	HARNEY CO.	T37S	R36E	S12
WINDY POINT	HARNEY CO.	T26S	R33E	S11
WRIGHT POINT	HARNEY CO.	T24S	R31E	?

Crane

Janice M. Healy (2000)

360

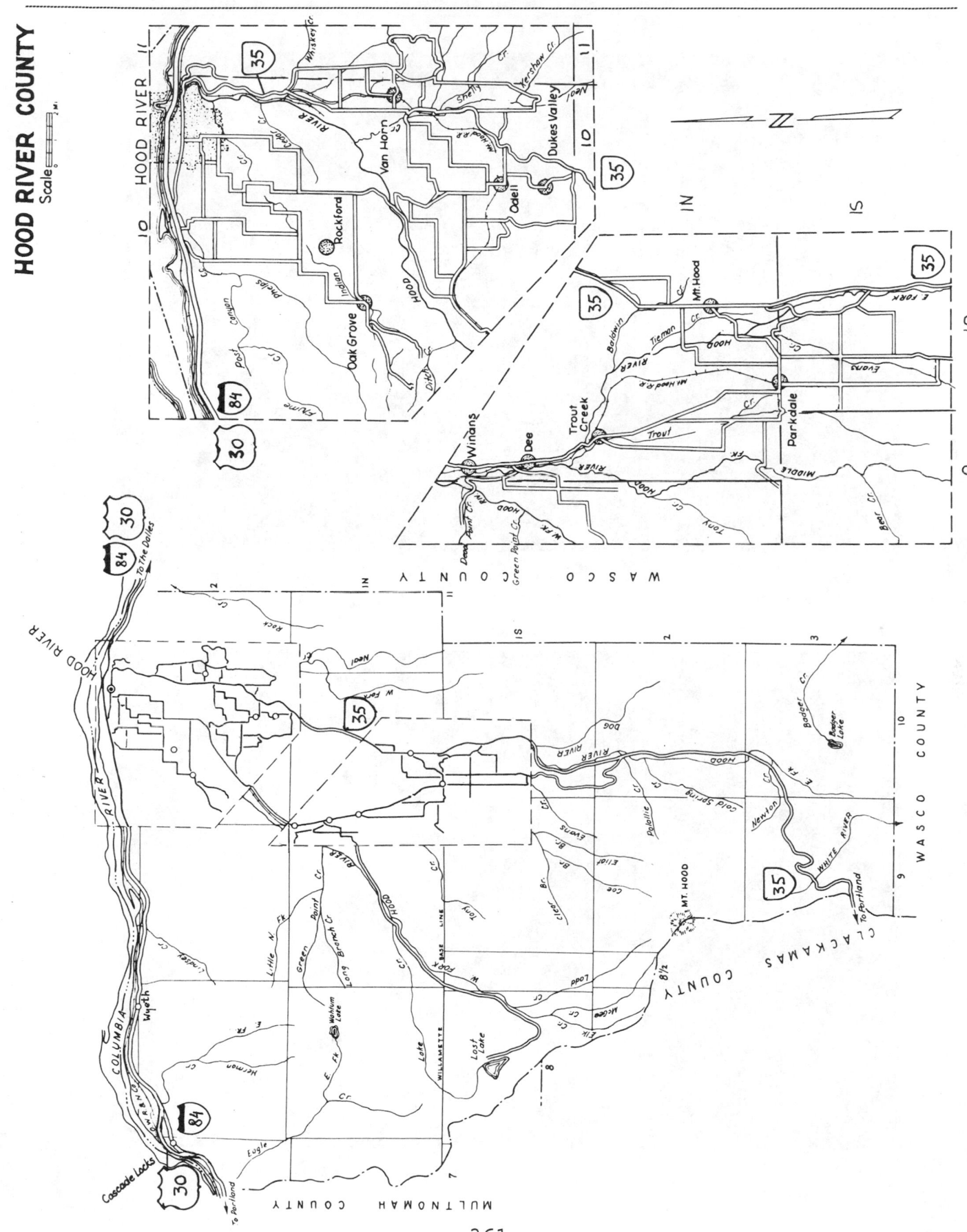

Idlewild

Janice M. Healy (2001)

Idlewild

Janice M. Healy (2001)

Area: 533 square miles
Population (1998): 19,553
County seat: Hood River, Population: 5,110
County established: 23 June 1908

This small county was detached from Wasco County to accommodate the boom in orchards in the Hood River Valley. Reportedly Frankton Cemetery was the first organized public cemetery in the county, however the compiler does not know the date of its establishment. Pine Grove Butte Cemetery (1869) appears to be the next earliest cemetery.

Pine Grove Butte
Janice M. Healy (1992)

Idlewild
Janice M. Healy (2001)

Idlewild
Janice M. Healy (2001)

Name of Cemetery and also known as	Number of burials	Acres	Condition	Date started or earliest known burial	Township	Range	Section

CASCADE LOCKS
AKA: 1. CASCADES

C 1.5 2 1875   T2N R7E   S12
Located north off of U.S. Hwy. 30 at Cascade Locks, on Lakeside Drive. The driveway, on the northeast side of the intersection across from the Texaco gas station, goes to a locked gate. There are 94 known burials (1987). {2 April 1992} (Bonneville Dam 1994 USGS Quad. map.)

CUSHMAN'S PASTURE

? ? ? ?   T3N R10E   ?
Located in Section 26 or 27. Reportedly 4 graves dating from 1881 to 1890 were in a fenced enclosure, somewhere along what is now Westcliff Drive westerly out of Hood River. The fence has since been torn down. (Not shown on Hood River 1979 USGS Quad. map.)

FISCHER, JOHN G.

A 0.01 5 ?   T1N R10E   S31
Located in the North 1/2 of Southeast 1/4 of Section 31. Go 0.75 of a mile west on Baseline Road from Parkdale and then right (north) onto the Mount Hood Highway for 0.4 of a mile to the front of the old McIsaac House. The grave had no marker but was enclosed by a white picket fence (1950's information). Mr. Fischer was thrown from his horse. NOTE: This site is on private property. (Not shown on Parkdale 1994 USGS Quad. map.)

FRANKTON
AKA: 1. BACKUS
2. OLD PIONEER
3. SMITH BURIAL GROUND

A 0.3 2 ?   T3N R10E   S27
This was the first white cemetery in the county. Located in the Frankton area, on the right bank of Phelps Creek, west of Frankton Road very near its junction with Country Club Road. There are 27 known burials (1987). The cemetery was badly vandalized in 1973. (Hood River 1979 USGS Quad. map.)

HOMESTEADER GRAVE

A 0.01 ? ?   T1N R10E   S21
Located in the South 1/2 of Northeast 1/4 of Section 21, 100 feet north and 100 feet west from the junction of OR. Hwy. 35 and Leasure Drive, 1.5 miles north of the community of Mount Hood. Two homesteaders filed land

Name of Cemetery and also known as	Number of burials	Acres	Condition	Date started or earliest known burial	Township	Range	Section

claims while "batching". One died from botulism or ptomaine, from eating poison beans, and his partner sold out to Robert Leasure. (Not shown on Parkdale 1994 USGS Quad. map.)

IDLEWILD
AKA 1. A.O.U.W. RIVERSIDE #68 [HOOD RIVER]
    2. IDELWILDE
    3. IDLEWOOD
    4. I.O.O.F IDLEWILDE #107 [HOOD RIVER]
    5. MASONIC, HOOD RIVER #105 [HOOD RIVER]

D 18 1 1894 T2N R10E S2
Located 2 miles south of Hood River, at 980 Tucker Road. Since 1971 this has been controlled by the Masons. There were about 6,500 burials as of 1986. Idlewood is a misspelling. It is on the James M. Benson D.L.C. #37. OC #4046. {2 April 1992} (Hood River 1979 USGS Quad. map.)

JACKSON FAMILY

A 0.25 2 1885 T2N R11E S30
This cemetery is on the west side of Fir Mountain Road, 0.5 of a mile south of the junction with Wells Drive. There were 11 or 12 graves (1987). {2 April 1992} (White Salmon 1978 USGS Quad. map.)

MASTERSON, FREDDIE

A 0.01 ? Circa 1878 T2N R7E S12
At Cascade Locks at or near the residence of J. Alfred Masterson and Martha Gay Masterson. Freddie their young son, died and was buried near where he played. No further information was given in the report. See: *One Woman's West*, Edited by Lois Barton, page 126. (Not shown on Bonneville Dam 1994 USGS Quad. map.)

McISAAC RANCH

A 0.01 5 ? T1N R10E S29
In the late 1950's someone reported 3 old graves near Parkdale, on the McIsaac Ranch. NOTE: This site is on private property. (NOT shown on Parkdale 1994 USGS Quad. map.)

MT. HOOD COMMUNITY
AKA: 1. FREDENBURG
    2. FRIEDENBURG

A 1 5 1891-1895 T1N R10E S21
Located in the South 1/2 of the Southeast 1/4 of Section 21, it is 0.25 of a mile west on Leasure Drive. Walk south another 0.25 of a

Name of Cemetery and also known as	Number of burials	Acres	Condition	Date started or earliest known burial	Township	Range	Section

mile to an irrigation ditch and to the cemetery, which is on the northeast corner of the Avery Friedenburg Homestead (in 1986, was the northeast corner of the Lavern Hatfield Farm). There are 4 known burials. NOTE: This site is on private property. (Not shown on Parkdale 1994 USGS Quad. map.)

MOUNTAIN VIEW MEMORIAL
AKA: 1. HOOD RIVER
     COUNTY
  2. KNIGHTS OF
     PYTHIAS
     [HOOD RIVER]

D	2.2	1	1870'S		T2N	R10E	S2

Located 2.5 miles southwest of Hood River at 1235 Tucker Road, adjacent to and south of St. Mary's Cemetery. There are 518 burials (1987). (Hood River 1979 USGS Quad. map.)

OAK GROVE

?	?	?	1906		T2N	R10E	?

Located in Section 16 or 17 near the present Oak Grove School. Country Club Road, Portland Drive, Reed Road, and Binns Hill Drive converge here about 5 miles southwest of Hood River. See Wasco County death certificate #355 for 1906. Tilman H. Smith, a farmer, died 18 February 1906, place of burial Oak Grove Cemetery, Hood River. (The locale is shown but no cemetery on Hood River 1979 USGS Quad. map.)

PINE GROVE BUTTE
AKA: 1. BUTTE
  2. NEAL FAMILY
  3. PINE GROVE

D	7	1	1869		T2N	R10E	S13

This cemetery straddles two Ranges in east and west direction: Range 10 East and 11 East. It is also in Sections 13 and 18. Go about 6 miles south of Hood River on OR. Hwy. 35 to the Pine Grove area, then go 0.3 of a mile east of OR. Hwy. 35 on Van Horn Drive to Paasch Drive; it is at 2651 Paasch Drive. The cemetery is on the edge of the butte and below the main road on the right. {3 April 1992} (Hood River 1979 USGS Quad. map.)

ST. MARK THE EVANGELIST CHURCH COLUMBARIUM

B	0.01	1	1992		T3N	R10E	S36

The church is located in Hood River on Eugene Street, at the corner of 11th. A columbarium was established with 48 spaces of which a

Hood River County

Name of Cemetery and also known as	Number of burials	Acres	Condition	Date started or earliest known burial	Township	Range	Section

single space was filled as of February 1994.
(The church itself is on the Hood River 1979
USGS Quad. map.)

ST. MARY'S
 AKA: 1. CATHOLIC

C 1.5 1 1875   T2N R10E   S2
Located just north and adjacent to Mt.
View Cemetery on Tucker Road. In 1906 St.
Mary's Cemetery was separated from a portion
of what was then the Knights of Pythias
Cemetery (the present-day Mountain View
Memorial). However pre-1906 burials remained
with St. Mary's. There were 288 burials
(1986). (Hood River 1979 USGS Quad. map.)

SHELLEY FAMILY

A 1 4 1910-1928 T2N R10E   S25
Leave OR. Hwy. 35 on Sunday Drive, to the
southeast and east for 0.4 of a mile, then
turn right on Scott Road, go southwest
0.25 of a mile; the cemetery is on the
right. There are 7 known burials plus
several unknown infants (1987). NOTE:
This site is on private property.
(Parkdale 1994 USGS Quad. map.)

UPPER VALLEY
 AKA: 1. I.O.O.F.
       [PARKDALE]
    2. McKAMEY
    3. MT. HOOD
    4. PARKDALE

D 1.14 1 1896/1897 T1N R10E   S33
Travel north 0.5 of a mile from Parkdale
on Allen Road, then east 0.25 of a mile on
Parkdale Cemetery Road. There were 367
known burials as of Feb. 1987. (Parkdale
1994 USGS Quad. map.)

VIENTO

? ? ? 3 Jul 1906 T3N R9E   S34
Viento was a railway stop between Hood River
and Wyeth. An unknown man, aged about 25,
was found drowned in the Columbia River. He
was buried at Viento 3 July 1906. See Wasco
County death certificate #1187 for 1906.
(Not shown on Mount. Defiance 1979-93 USGS
Quad. map.)

WEART, GEORGE W.

A 0.01 5 ?   T1N R10E   S8
Located in the Southwest 1/4 of the Northeast
1/4 of Section 8, at the summit of Middle
Mountain, on his homestead. Take Gilhouley
Road and continue on it beyond the end of

county maintenance. This route probably requires a 4-wheel drive vehicle, but continue to a road junction and keep left. The vague description of the region in 1956 is probably not valid in 2000. Good luck! NOTE: This site is probably on private property. (Not shown on Parkdale 1994 USGS Quad. map.)

WOLLAM, HARRY   A   0.01   ?   ?   T2N R10E   S3
From Hood River, drive south on Hood River Highway (Tucker Road) to Windmaster Corner (Milepost 3.8) turn right (west) onto Barrett Drive towards Rockford. Go 0.4 of a mile on Barrett Drive, and then turn right (north) onto Alameda Road. This road turns right and then left. At this last turn, at 0.5 of a mile from Barrett Drive, is a grave on the right (east) side of Alameda Road. The Wollam farm and orchard was on the opposite side of the road. You may continue north on Alameda Road to Belmont Drive and turn right (east) back to Hood River. NOTE: This site is on private property. (Not shown on Hood River 1979 USGS Quad. map.)

WYETH   ?   0.15   ?   ?   T2N R8E   S2
This cemetery is located on the north side of Wyeth Road, 1 mile west of the Wyeth Interchange with the I-84 Freeway. Leave the freeway at Exit 51 turning right (south), and then turn right again onto Wyeth Road, which parallels the east-bound (south) side of the I-84 Freeway. There are 14 known burials, it was last used in the 1920's. (Carson 1979 USGS Quad. map.)

Hood River County

Cascade Locks
Dean H. Byrd (1995)

Jackson Family
Janice M. Healy (1992)

A.O.U.W. RIVERSIDE #68 [HOOD RIVER] see **IDLEWILD**

	HOOD RIVER CO.	T2N	R10E	S2
BACKUS see **FRANKTON**	HOOD RIVER CO.	T3N	R10E	S27

BENSON D.L.C., JAMES M. see **IDLEWILD**

	HOOD RIVER CO.	T2N	R10E	S2
BUTTE see **PINE GROVE BUTTE**	HOOD RIVER CO.	T2N	R10E	S13
CASCADE LOCKS	HOOD RIVER CO.	T2N	R7E	S12
CASCADES see **CASCADE LOCKS**	HOOD RIVER CO.	T2N	R7E	S12
CATHOLIC see **ST. MARY'S**	HOOD RIVER CO.	T2N	R10E	S2
CUSHMAN'S PASTURE	HOOD RIVER CO.	T3N	R10E	?
FISCHER, JOHN G.	HOOD RIVER CO.	T1N	R10E	S31

FISCHER, MR. see **FISCHER, JOHN G.**

	HOOD RIVER CO.	T1N	R10E	S31
FRANKTON	HOOD RIVER CO.	T3N	R10E	S27

FREDENBURG see **MT. HOOD COMMUNITY**

	HOOD RIVER CO.	T1N	R10E	S21

FRIEDENBURG see **MT. HOOD COMMUNITY**

	HOOD RIVER CO.	T1N	R10E	S21

FRIEDENBURG HOMESTEAD, AVERY see **MT. HOOD COMMUNITY**

	HOOD RIVER CO.	T1N	R10E	S21

HATFIELD FARM, LAVERN see **MT. HOOD COMMUNITY**

	HOOD RIVER CO.	T1N	R10E	S21
HOMESTEADER GRAVE	HOOD RIVER CO.	T1N	R10E	S21

HOOD RIVER COUNTY see **MOUNTAIN VIEW MEMORIAL**

	HOOD RIVER CO.	T2N	R10E	S2

I.O.O.F. [PARKDALE] see **UPPER VALLEY**

	HOOD RIVER CO.	T1N	R10E	S33

I.O.O.F. IDLEWILDE #107 [HOOD RIVER] see **IDLEWILD**

	HOOD RIVER CO.	T2N	R10E	S2
IDELWILDE see **IDLEWILD**	HOOD RIVER CO.	T2N	R10E	S2
IDLEWILD	HOOD RIVER CO.	T2N	R10E	S2
IDLEWOOD see **IDLEWILD**	HOOD RIVER CO.	T2N	R10E	S2
JACKSON FAMILY	HOOD RIVER CO.	T2N	R11E	S30

KNIGHTS OF PYTHIAS [HOOD RIVER] see **MOUNTAIN VIEW MEMORIAL**

	HOOD RIVER CO.	T2N	R10E	S2

LEASURE, ROBERT see **HOMESTEADER GRAVE**

	HOOD RIVER CO.	T1N	R10E	S21

MASONIC, HOOD RIVER #105 [HOOD RIVER] see **IDLEWILD**

	HOOD RIVER CO.	T2N	R10E	S2
MASTERSON, FREDDIE	HOOD RIVER CO.	T2N	R7E	S12

MASTERSON, J. ALFRED see **MASTERSON, FREDDIE**

	HOOD RIVER CO.	T2N	R7E	S12

MASTERSON, MARTHA GAY see **MASTERSON, FREDDIE**

	HOOD RIVER CO.	T2N	R7E	S12
McISAAC RANCH	HOOD RIVER CO.	T1N	R10E	S29
McKAMEY see **UPPER VALLEY**	HOOD RIVER CO.	T1N	R10E	S33
MT. HOOD see **UPPER VALLEY**	HOOD RIVER CO.	T1N	R10E	S33
MT. HOOD COMMUNITY	HOOD RIVER CO.	T1N	R10E	S21
MOUNTAIN VIEW MEMORIAL	HOOD RIVER CO.	T2N	R10E	S2

NEAL FAMILY see **PINE GROVE BUTTE**

	HOOD RIVER CO.	T2N	R10E	S13
OAK GROVE	HOOD RIVER CO.	T2N	R10E	?

OLD PIONEER see **FRANKTON**	HOOD RIVER CO.	T3N	R10E	S27
PARKDALE see **UPPER VALLEY**	HOOD RIVER CO.	T1N	R10E	S33
PINE GROVE see **PINE GROVE BUTTE**	HOOD RIVER CO.	T2N	R10E	S13
PINE GROVE BUTTE	HOOD RIVER CO.	T2N	R10E	S13
ST. MARK THE EVANGELIST CHURCH COLUMBARIUM				
	HOOD RIVER CO.	T3N	R10E	S36
ST. MARY'S	HOOD RIVER CO.	T2N	R10E	S2
SHELLEY FAMILY	HOOD RIVER CO.	T2N	R10E	S25
SMITH BURIAL GROUND see **FRANKTON**				
	HOOD RIVER CO.	T3N	R10E	S27
SMITH, TILMAN H. see **OAK GROVE**	HOOD RIVER CO.	T2N	R10E	?
UPPER VALLEY	HOOD RIVER CO.	T1N	R10E	S33
VIENTO	HOOD RIVER CO.	T3N	R9E	S34
WEART, GEORGE W.	HOOD RIVER CO.	T1N	R10E	S8
WOLLAM, HARRY	HOOD RIVER CO.	T2N	R10E	S3
WYETH	HOOD RIVER CO.	T2N	R8E	S2

Idlewild

Janice M. Healy (2001)

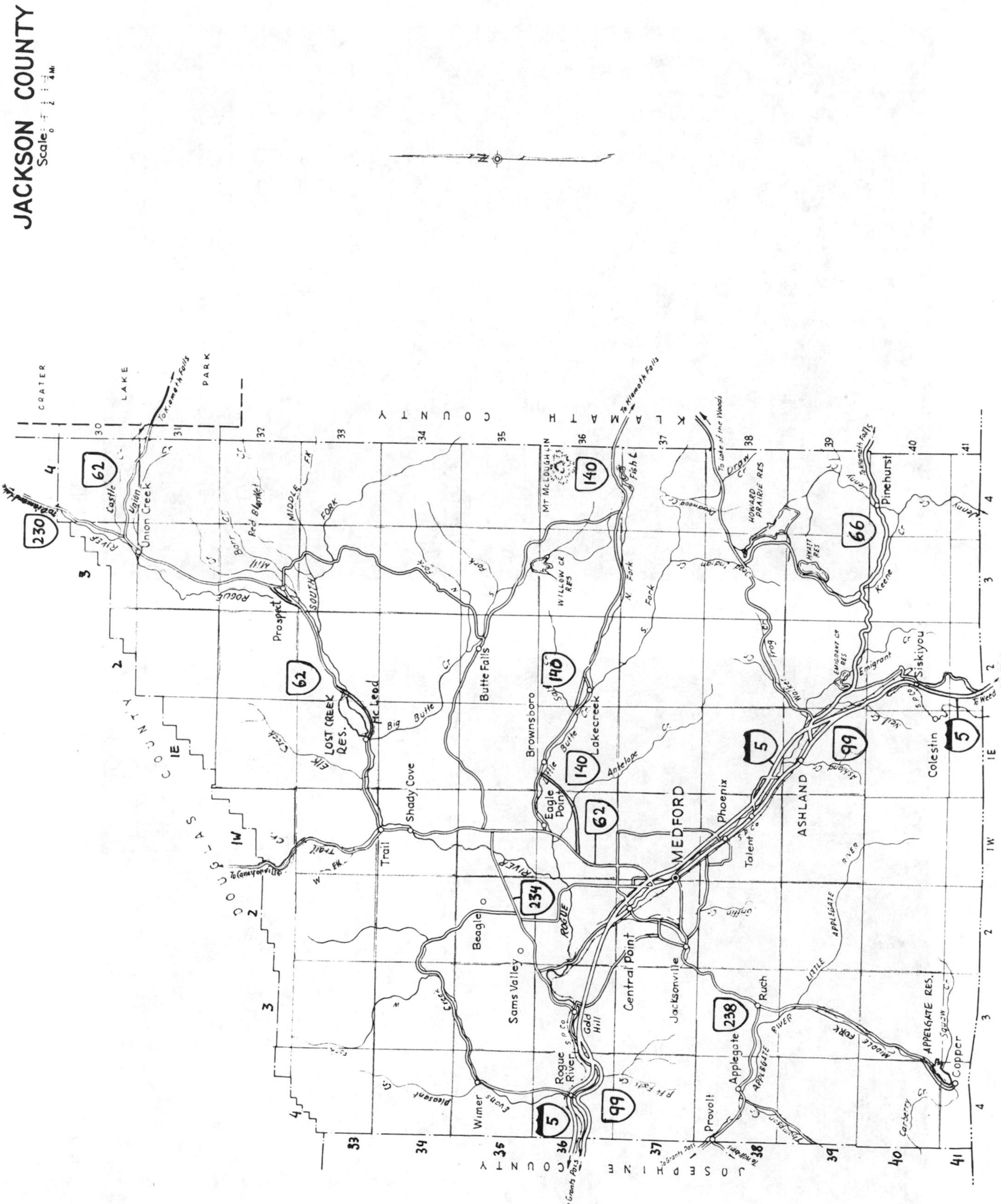

JACKSON COUNTY
Scale

Woodville
Dean H. Byrd (1995)

Central Point
Dean H. Byrd (1995)

Area: 2,801 square miles
Population (1998): 173,123
County seat: Medford, Population: 57,155
County established: 12 January 1852

The discovery of gold in 1851 brought an influx of settlers as well as gold-seekers. The earliest public cemetery is listed as Hargadine (1850) in Ashland. Which seems a bit too early to the compiler as Ashland was not named until 1852. Be that as it may early cemeteries are Antelope (1853), Hill-Dunn (1853), Brownsboro (1854), Phoenix (1856) and Stearns (1857). Jacksonville Cemetery is by far the largest of the early cemeteries was not formally organized until 1859 but has many burials dating from 1852 and is well worth a visit.

Jacksonville
Dean H. Byrd (1995)

Jackson County

Central Point

Dean H. Byrd (1995)

Woodville

Dean H. Byrd (1995)

Name of Cemetery and also known as	Number of burials	Acres	Condition	Date started or earliest known burial	Township	Range	Section

AIKIN FAMILY
AKA: 1. AIKEN
       FAMILY

? ? ? 1905   T32S R3E   ?

This is possibly in Section 27 or 28. Follow Red Blanket Road, out of Prospect, turn right down a lane. The cemetery is at the end of this lane. (Not shown on Prospect North 1989 USGS Quad. map.)

ANTELOPE
AKA: 1. ANTELOPE
       CREEK
     2. EAGLE POINT

C 1.7 3 1853-1937   T36S R1W   S14

From Medford take OR. Hwy. 62 to OR. Hwy. 140, then follow OR. Hwy. 140 for 3.6 miles to Riley Road on the left. Follow Riley Road 1.2 miles, go past Alta Vista Road and the cemetery is on the right. The earliest date is June 1853; latest date is January 1937. There are 64 known burials (1972). The Veterans Cemetery is another 1.5 miles north on Riley Road. (Eagle Point 1983 USGS Quad. map.)

ANTIOCH
AKA: 1. BEAGLE

C 2.9 3 1867   T35S R2W   S23

From Medford take Table Rock Road 7.5 miles to Modoc Road. Follow Modoc Road 1.8 miles to Antioch Road. Follow Antioch Road 3.7 miles, then cross over OR. Hwy. 234 and go another mile on Antioch Road. The cemetery is on the right. (Boswell Mountain 1983 USGS Quad. map.)

APPLEGATE CHURCH

A ? ? ?   T38S R4W   S22

Located at OR. Hwy. 238 and Missouri Flat Road. A 1953 D.A.R. investigation reported burials of 2 Knutzen family infants, and 2 forgotten hired men; all were unmarked. (Applegate 1983 USGS Quad. map shows the church but no cemetery.)

ASHLAND CITY
AKA: 1. ASHLAND

E 5 1 1870   T39S R1E   S9

Located 2 blocks past East Main and Siskiyou Boulevard (OR. Hwy. 99) intersection, on the south side of East Main Street. (Ashland 1983 USGS Quad. map.)

BAILEY GULCH

A 0.1 3 ?   T37S R4W   S22

On old OR. Hwy. 99, go 2.6 miles southeast of the Rogue River town bridge. Turn right on

Name of Cemetery and also known as	Number of burials	Acres	Condition	Date started or earliest known burial	Township	Range	Section

Foots Creek Road, go 0.9 of a mile to Foots Creek Cemetery, then turn right on a road up the right fork of Foots Creek. Go 3.4 miles, turn right onto a lane up Bailey Gulch and go about 0.3 of a mile further. Two grave stones, inside a wire fence, are on U.S. land near some mining claims. (Not on Applegate 1983 USGS Quad. map, but Bailey Gulch is.)

BARNEBURG HILL ? ? 7 ? T37S R1W S32

This is in sections 32 and 33. These graves were all moved to Siskiyou Memorial Park before the building of Rogue Valley Manor. (Not shown on Medford East 1983 USGS Quad. map.)

BLACK, CLIFTON A 0.01 5 16 Mar 1867 T34S R1W S28

The exact site of this burial is now lost, but it was on the west side of Crater Lake Highway (OR. Hwy. 62), just short of the south city limits of Shady Cove. John M. and Mary Louisa Black settled here in 1866, where 2 year-old Clifton died of diphtheria. The family buried him at the edge of a field below the house. The site was later inundated several times by the Rogue River. After the major flood of 1890, the Rogue River cut a new channel a quarter of a mile further west, leaving the Blacks with a field that was a swamp with a few acres of rock bar. John and Mary Louisa are themselves buried at the I.O.O.F. Cemetery at Central Point. (Not shown on Shady Cove 1983 USGS Quad. map.)

BRADLEY FAMILY ? ? ? 1875 ? ? ?

Located somewhere out of Lakecreek. NOTE: No further information was given to the compiler.

BRISTO ? ? ? ? ? ? ?

The location is unknown to the compiler. Just the name and the county were given with no other information in the report.

Name of Cemetery and also known as	Number of burials	Acres	Condition	Date started or earliest known burial	Township	Range	Section

BROWNSBORO

C 0.66 3 1854 T36S R1E S4

From OR. Hwy. 62 take OR. Hwy. 140 and go 8.5 miles to Obenchain Road, then 0.13 of a mile on Obenchain Road; turn left onto a lane and go 0.4 of a mile. The cemetery is on the left (west) side 700 feet from the lane. (Brownsboro 1988 USGS Quad. map.)

BUTTE FALLS

C 8 1 1868 T35S R2E S5

Located 13.8 miles from OR. Hwy 62 on Butte Falls Road, then turn right for 0.5 of a mile on Obenchain Road. There were 300 known burials (1971). (Butte Falls 1988 USGS Quad. map.)

CENTRAL POINT
AKA: 1. I.O.O.F.
  2. I.O.O.F. #193
  3. MASONIC
     LODGE #135

D 8.5 2 1866 T37S R2W S1

From OR. Hwy. 99 in Central Point, turn off on East Pine Street and go northeast, crossing over the I-5 Freeway and Bear Creek. Turn left (north) onto Hamrick Road and drive north on Hamrick Road. The cemetery is on the right (east) just as Hamrick Road curves to the right (east) and its name changes into West Vilas Road. {27 October 1995} (Sams Valley 1983 USGS Quad. map.)

CLIMAX GRAVES

B ? 3 1890 T38S R2E S5

From Medford take OR. Hwy. 62 to Lake of the Woods Highway (OR. Hwy. 140). Turn right (easterly) and follow OR. Hwy. 140 to Milepost 3.6, the intersection of Riley and Antelope Roads. Turn right (south) onto Antelope Road. Drive 1.5 miles on Antelope Road and turn right 90 degrees, at 2 miles turn left 90 degrees; and at 2.5 miles turn right 90 degrees, drive south up the narrow valley of Antelope Creek. The end of county maintenance is at 14.5 miles from OR. Hwy. 140, at Climax. Go up hill to the left about 0.2 of a mile, to the old site of Climax; the graves are somewhere in the vicinity. (Not shown on Grizzly Peak 1988 USGS Quad. map.)

COLLINGS GRAVES
AKA: 1. SQUAW CREEK
  2. WATKINS

? ? 8 Circa 1888 T40S R4W S36

This burial site was located at Watkins, at the confluence of Squaw Creek with the

Name of Cemetery and also known as	Number of burials	Acres	Condition	Date started or earliest known burial	Township	Range	Section

Applegate River near the California Line. A survey by the D.A.R. in 1953 reported 9 known burials but no markers. In 1980, the burials were removed to Logtown Cemetery prior to the creation of Applegate Lake by dam construction. (Not shown on Carberry Creek or Squaw Lakes 1983 USGS Quad. maps.)

CRATER — ? ? ? ? T35S R2E ?

There is, or was, a Crater Cemetery in Jackson County. This is possibly an AKA for Butte Falls Cemetery as there was a Crater Lake School less than a mile southwest of that cemetery. The compiler was given no other information in the report. (Not shown on Butte Falls or Obenchain Mtn. 1988 USGS Quad. maps.)

DEADMANS POINT — ? ? ? ? T40S R2W S27

This is a pronounced "point" directed to the northwest separating the watersheds of uppermost Squaw Creek and uppermost Yale Creek. The location is deep within the Rogue River National Forest. Drive south from Ruch up the Valley of the Applegate River to the vicinity of McKee Bridge Campground. Turn left (easterly) onto the Siskiyou Summit Forestry Road up the valley of Beaver Creek. You will need a Rogue River National Forest Road map. A number of graves have been reported but no other information was given in the report. (Not shown on Dutchman Peak 1983 USGS Quad. map.)

DODGE BRIDGE — A 0.01 3 ? T35S R1W S17

Dodge Bridge is on OR. Hwy. 234, crossing the Rogue River 1.5 miles west of the junction with OR. Hwy. 62 and north of Eagle Point. There are 1 or 2 graves, possibly in Dodge Bridge County Park. (Not shown on Shady Cove 1983 USGS Quad. map.)

Name of Cemetery and also known as	Number of burials	Acres	Condition	Date started or earliest known burial	Township	Range	Section

DOWNING PLACE

? ? ? ? ? ? ?

Reported to be somewhere near Butte Falls. NOTE: No other information was given in the report. (Not shown on Willow Lake or Big Butte Springs 1988 USGS Quad. maps.)

DUNKARD
AKA: 1. CHURCH OF
       BRETHREN

B 1.7 3 1888-1933 T38S R1W S23

Located on Old Hwy. 99 at Talent, just before entering Talent from the north. The cemetery is on the right, set off of the highway behind a power substation, at the edge of an orchard and down a gravel path (1978). There were 25 known and 2 unmarked burials (D.A.R. 1939). On the Nelson D. Smith D.L.C. #59, RB #147. (Not shown on Medford East 1983 USGS Quad. map.)

EVANS VALLEY

? ? ? ? T35S R4W ?

Presumably this cemetery is, or was, between the towns of Rogue River and Wimer. NOTE: No other infomation was given in the report. (Not shown on Wimer 1983 USGS Quad. map.)

FOOTS
AKA: 1. FOOTS CREEK
       CHAPEL

? ? ? ? T36S R4W S35

From the town of Rogue River, cross the bridge to OR. Hwy. 99, the Rogue River Highway. Turn left (easterly) and go 2.7 miles to Foots Creek Road at Bolt, turn right (south) for another 0.9 of a mile to the cemetery driveway. Then turn right (east) again for 0.1 mile to the cemetery behind a house. (Rogue River 1983 USGS Quad. map.)

FRINK FAMILY

? ? 11 ? T36S R1W ?

A cemetery for the Frink Family had been reported from Jackson County, but the compiler had no idea where within the county. Now it appears to have been within the boundaries of Camp White, the World War II military base. An article in the *Medford Mail Tribune*, 29 May 1994, quotes a family member who recalls that the cemetery and its wooden markers, were buried by the military. (Not shown on Eagle Point 1983 USGS Quad. map.)

Jackson County

Name of Cemetery and also known as	Number of burials	Acres	Condition	Date started or earliest known burial	Township	Range	Section

GRIFFIN CREEK
  AKA: 1. GRIFFIN
         FAMILY

B 1 3 1859 T38S R2W S9

From OR. Hwy. 99, between Medford and Phoenix, turn west on South Stage Road. At Voorhies go west 3.5 miles on South Stage Road to Griffin Road; turn left (south) on Griffin Road for 1.25 miles. Turn right (west) on West Griffin Creek Road and keep on the main West Griffin Creek Road for 1.6 miles. On the right, between two buildings, is a small road north over an irrigation canal; follow this small road 0.3 of a mile, then turn right, on a path uphill, 0.2 of a mile to the cemetery. (Not shown on Medford West 1983 USGS Quad. map.)

HARGADINE
  AKA: 1. CITY OF
         ASHLAND

D 1.4 3 1850 T39S R1E S5

Leave OR. Hwy. 99 at the north edge of Ashland and turn west onto Sheridan Street. The cemetery is at the top of Sheridan Street on the right side of the street; on the William Chase D.L.C. #38, RB #908. (Ashland 1983 USGS Quad. map.)

HAYS
  AKA: 1. GALL

B 0.8 3 1856 T36S R3W S20

From Medford, take the I-5 Freeway to the Gold Hill exit. Turn left, go over the overpass of the I-5 Freeway and immediately after turn right (westerly) onto the Old Stage Road, which parallels the freeway on the right. Follow this frontage road for 1.6 miles. Turn left onto Hodson Road and go 0.2 of a mile south: the cemetery is on the right. (Gold Hill 1983 USGS Quad. map.)

HILL-DUNN FAMILY
  AKA: 1. DUNN FAMILY
       2. DUNN-HILL
          FAMILY
       3. HILL FAMILY
       4. KINGSBURY
       5. KINGSBURY
          SODA SPRINGS

D 3 3 1853 T39S R2E S30

From Ashland, take OR. Hwy. 66 past the Emigrant Lake entrance, then take the next road on the left toward the lake. The Kingsbury portion of the cemetery was moved up the hill when the lake was enlarged in 1958. 17 Indian War heroes were buried in this cemetery; 135 graves were moved. The original Kingsbury cemetery site is now under the waters of Emigrant Lake. On the Isaac Hiatt D.L.C. #45. (Emigrant Lake 1983 USGS Quad. map.)

| Name of Cemetery and also known as | Number of burials | Acres | Condition | Date started or earliest known burial | Township | Range | Section |

HILLCREST MEMORIAL PARK AND MAUSOLEUM

E   14   1   1959   T38S R1W   S3
From Medford, take Barnett Road to North Phoenix Road; follow North Phoenix Road south to the cemetery. The cemetery will be on the left at about 2.6 miles, at 2201 North Phoenix Road; on the John F. Gray D.L.C. #84, RB #153. (Medford East 1983 USGS Quad. map.)

I.O.O.F., EASTWOOD [MEDFORD]
AKA: 1. EASTWOOD I.O.O.F.

E   20   2   1908   T37S R1W   S29
In Medford, take Barnett Road to Highland Drive; turn north onto Siskiyou Boulevard and go one block. The cemetery is on a small knoll to the right of the road. Siskiyou Memorial Park is on the south side of Siskiyou Boulevard in this area; on the William Berneburg D.L.C. #52, RB #117. The first burials at this site were for members of the Berneburg family 1878 and 1883. {27 October 1995} (Medford East 1983 USGS Quad. map.)

I.O.O.F. [GOLD HILL]
AKA: 1. SARDINE CREEK

D   5.12   2   1864   T36S R3W   S17
Take OR. Hwy 99 westerly through the town of Gold Hill and past the junction of Sardine Creek Road. Go 0.3 of a mile past that junction, turn right and cross the railway tracks into the cemetery. The I.O.O.F. Cemetery is separated, by a lane, from Rock Point Cemetery. {27 October 1995} (Gold Hill 1983 USGS Quad. map.)

INDIAN RANCHERIA TRAIL MASSACRE
AKA: 1. RANCHERIA

A   ?   ?   1856   T35S R4E   S18
There are 5 marked graves of men in the Rogue River National Forest, on Rancheria Prairie Road south of Butte Falls. (Not shown on Big Butte Springs 1988 USGS Quad. map.)

JACKSONVILLE
AKA: 1. CATHOLIC
2. CITY
3. GERMAN ORDER OF RED MEN
4. I.O.O.F.
5. JACKSONVILLE PIONEER

E   30   2   1859   T37S R2W   S29
This cemetery contains sections for Masonic, Catholic (2.5 acres in 1860), Jewish, Order of the Red Men, and a City section. Follow California Street to Oregon Street in Jacksonville, then turn left on Oregon Street at the cemetery sign and follow the road to the top of the hill. The original cemetery

Name of Cemetery and also known as	Number of burials	Acres	Condition	Date started or earliest known burial	Township	Range	Section

6. JEWISH
7. MASONIC
8. ORDER OF RED
   MEN

was donated by J. N. T. Miller. Several burials from 1852 were moved up from the base of the hill to the present area. The I.O.O.F. section is the lower part of this cemetery. This cemetery is one of the most interesting in the state. {28 October 1995} (Medford West 1983 USGS Quad. map.)

JOHNSON FAMILY
AKA: 1. JOHNSON,
         CAROLINE
     2. SHADY COVE
     3. WEEKS (?)

B 1   3   1908   T34S R1W   S15
This family cemetery is between the bridge over Indian Creek and the bridge over the Rogue River: on OR. Hwy. 62, to the left as one enters Shady Cove from Medford. (Shady Cove 1983 USGS Quad. map.)

KANE CREEK

?   ?   ?   ?   T36S R3W   ?
Reportedly located near a mine in the vicinity of Gold Hill. NOTE: No other information was given in the report. (Not shown on Gold Hill 1983 USGS Quad. map.)

LAKECREEK
AKA: 1. PECK FAMILY

A 0.1   ?   ?   T37S R2E   S4
Leave OR. Hwy. 62 onto OR. Hwy. 140 for 12.5 miles; then turn right (southeast) onto Old Hwy. 140 for 1.6 miles, to the community of Lakecreek. Continue on South Little Butte Creek Road for 3.6 miles, to a bridge over the South Fork of Little Butte Creek. Take a driveway to the left 0.8 of a mile beyond the bridge. This driveway immediately forks: keep to the right for 0.15 of a mile around the side of the hill, to another fork. Turn hard left, go up the hill 200 feet. The cemetery is on top of this hill. (Lakecreek 1988 USGS Quad. map.)

LAURELHURST

?   ?   6   ?   T33S ?   ?
Most of the graves were moved to the I.O.O.F. Eastwood Cemetery in Medford, in 1974, when Lost Creek Dam was built. (Not shown on McLeod or Cascade Gorge 1988 USGS Quad. maps.)

Name of Cemetery and also known as	Number of burials	Acres	Condition	Date started or earliest known burial	Township	Range	Section

LILYGLEN

A   ?   ?   5 Sep 1914   T38S R3E   S14

Jackson County Death Certificate #2269 for 1914 states that Charles E. Butterworth, born 21 April 1889, died 5 September 1914 and was buried 7 September 1914 at Lillie Glenn [sic.]. He was the son of Charles and Margret Gerhart. Lewis A. McArthur in *Oregon Geographic Names* spells the place Lilyglen. At the east edge of Ashland near the airport take Dead Indian Road off of OR. Hwy. 66. At Milepost 17.20 on Dead Indian Road turn right (southeast) onto Howard Prairie Lake Road and drive about 0.7 of a mile to the Lindsay Ranch on the left. The burial[s] may be in this vicinity. NOTE: This site is on private property. The above information is from latest O.D.O.T. field log of the area. (Not shown on Robinson Butte 1988 USGS Quad. map.)

LOGTOWN
  AKA: 1. FOREST
          CREEK
       2. LAUREL GROVE
       3. RUCH

D   2.8   3   1862   T38S R3W   S14

The cemetery is within Sections 14 and 23. It is 6 miles southwest of downtown Jacksonville via OR. Hwy. 238. The cemetery is on the left at the confluence of Poorman Creek with Forest Creek. (Mt. Isabelle 1983 USGS Quad. map.)

MATTHEWS FAMILY

A   0.3   3   1857-1906   T35S R1W   S27

From Eagle Point take OR. Hwy. 62 to the north, going about 1.65 miles from the Linn Road intersection. The cemetery is on the right (east), at the canal crossing of the highway. The cemetery is about 0.25 of a mile from the highway in a field. There is no direct access and 20 known burials. (Not shown on Eagle Point 1983 USGS Quad. map. It is shown on the 1932 Metsker Atlas of Jackson County.)

MEADOWS GRAVES
  AKA: 1. WALKER BURIAL
          PLOT

?   ?   ?   1894-1900   T34S R3W   S25

Located on Ramsey Road 8.3 miles north of OR. Hwy. 234, just short of junction with Evans Creek Road. A few graves are in the Spikenard area where the Meadows School was located: 3 identified. (Not shown on McConville Peak 1983 USGS Quad. map.)

Name of Cemetery and also known as	Number of burials	Acres	Condition	Date started or earliest known burial	Township	Range	Section

MEMORY GARDENS MEMORIAL PARK AND MAUSOLEUM

E 32   1   1956   T37S R2W   S34
Located on the corner of Bellinger Lane and Arnold Lane, west of Medford. Go west on OR. Hwy. 238, from downtown Medford, 3.3 miles and turn south on Arnold Lane. This cemetery is located at 1395 Arnold Lane; on the Abram Tenbrook D.L.C. #78, RB #111. {25 October 1995} (Medford West 1983 USGS Quad. map.)

MERRIMAN FAMILY

A ?   ?   19 Sep 1865 T38S R2W   ?
An article in the "Accent" column by Susan Stanley in the *Oregon Journal*, 26 July 1977 reports her visit to the Merriman Family Cemetery. Stanley locates it "high on a hill above Jacksonville." There were ten monuments in the small graveyard ringed with rocks. Four were for infants of Artemisia and William H. Merriman who died between 1865 and 1875. Another infant died in 1921 and the remaining five were adults with 1950 as the latest date. The compiler has no other information on this site. (Not shown on Medford West 1983 USGS Quad. map.)

MILLER FAMILY

? 0.1 ? ?   T36S R1E   S5
Leave OR. Hwy. 62 at OR. Hwy. 140, go 7.4 miles on OR. Hwy. 140, then turn left and go 0.1 of a mile to Brownsboro-Meridian Road. Turn right onto Brownsboro-Meridian Road, then go 0.3 of a mile to a farm road. The road to the cemetery is to the left. (Not shown on Brownsboro 1988 USGS Quad. map.)

MISSOURI FLAT
AKA: 1. APPLEGATE
    2. WILLIAMS
      CREEK (?)

D 1.7 3 1864   T38S R4W   S6
From Medford, take OR. Hwy. 238 to Applegate Store (1978); take North Applegate Road and go 4.5 miles. The cemetery is on the left. Upper River Road continues into Josephine County to Grants Pass. The land for this cemetery was donated by William M. Miller. (Applegate 1983 USGS Quad. map.)

MORSE FAMILY

A 0.5 3 1921   T38S R1E   S30
Take Valley View Road and OR. Hwy. 99 at Talent, then go east over the I-5 Freeway, 2

Name of Cemetery and also known as	Number of burials	Acres	Condition	Date started or earliest known burial	Township	Range	Section

miles to Staples Road. Turn left on Staples Road and go 0.45 of a mile to the cemetery, which is fenced; on the Nathaniel Myer D.L.C. #43, RB #157. (Ashland 1983 USGS Quad. map.)

MOUNTAIN VIEW AND RESTHAVEN MAUSOLEUM

| | E | 13 | 1 | 1904 | T39S | R1E | S10 |

Located in Ashland on OR. Hwy. 66, on the left (north) side of the road just past Normal Avenue. Some earlier graves have been moved into this cemetery. (Ashland 1983 USGS Quad. map.)

MOUNTAIN VIEW I.O.O.F. AND MAUSOLEUM
AKA: 1. I.O.O.F. [ASHLAND]
2. MOUNT VIEW

| | D | 2 | 1 | 1904 | T39S | R1E | S15 |

Located in Ashland on the right (south) side of OR. Hwy. 66 and Normal Avenue, just opposite Mountain View Cemetery. (Ashland 1983 USGS Quad. map.)

MYER FAMILY
AKA: 1. BUTLER-- THOMPSON FAMILY
2. MEYERS FAMILY
3. THOMPSON FAMILY

| | B | 0.14 | 3 | 1853 | T38S | R1E | S30 |

Take Valley View Road From OR. Hwy. 99 northwest of Ashland; go north over the I-5 Freeway for 0.65 of a mile. At this point there is a driveway to the right (east) that takes you up to the cemetery on top of a small hill. There was a trailer at the edge of the cemetery (1978). Quite a number of stones are broken, it is not fenced and had been used as a pasture (1978); on the William C. Myer D.L.C. #45, RB #158. (Ashland 1983 USGS Quad. map.)

NATIONAL VETERANS ADMINISTRATION
AKA: 1. EAGLE POINT NATIONAL
2. VETERANS
3. WHITE CITY

| | E | 34 | 1 | 1952 | T36S | R1W | S2 |

Take Main Street in Eagle Point and go across a bridge to the southeast, then east on Stevens Road a distance of 0.9 of a mile, to Riley Road. Turn right on Riley Road and go 0.25 of a mile. The cemetery is on the left. There were 6,700 total burials here in 1996. (Eagle Point 1983 USGS Quad. map.)

Jackson County

Name of Cemetery and also known as	Number of burials	Acres	Condition	Date started or earliest known burial	Township	Range	Section

NICHOLS FAMILY

A 0.1 3 1868   T35S R1W   S25

Leave OR. Hwy. 62 onto Royal Street and go through Eagle Point; go on Eagle Point-Brownsboro Road for 2.9 miles, to Brophy Road. Turn left on Brophy Road and go 1.6 miles. Turn left, into a private driveway of the St. Laurent Land and Cattle Company and go past 2 barns, 2 houses, on down a lane through 2 gates, crossing a creek (Nichols Branch). The cemetery is on a hill, 200 feet on the right (north)(1978). This is on John M. Nichols D.L.C. RB#938. There were 11 known graves 1969. The fence was down, and cattle were roaming among the tombstones which were knocked over. (Not shown on Eagle Point 1983 USGS Quad. map.)

NYE FAMILY
AKA: 1. FLOUNCE
     ROCK

? 0.4 ? ?   T33S R2E   S10

The Nye family cemetery is located on Ulrich Road, off of OR. Hwy. 62, just past Cascade Gorge. Turn left off of OR. Hwy. 62 onto Ulrich Road. Go past another cemetery (name unknown) at 0.45 of a mile to Nye Cemetery which is on the right about 0.6 of a mile from the highway. (Cascade Gorge 1988 USGS Quad. map.)

PANKEY PARK
AKA: 1. PANKEY
    2. ROCK CREEK
      METHODIST
      CHURCH
    3. SAMS VALLEY

C 3.15 3 1863   T35S R2W   S30

Take OR. Hwy. 234 from Gold Hill for 4.9 miles to Sams Valley; then turn left onto Ramsey Road for 1.6 miles and the cemetery is on the right. (Sams Valley 1983 USGS Quad. map.)

PHOENIX [NEW]

E 6 3 1874   T38S R1W   S9

Leave Main Street (OR. Hwy. 99), go west on 5th Street and turn right onto Pine Street, which leads to the cemetery. The land was donated by Lewellyn and Jemima Colver, after 24 Oct. 1874. Several graves were moved to this cemetery from a hill south of Phoenix and other areas; on the John Thurber D.L.C. #44, RB #407 and Samuel Colver D.L.C. #42, RB 383. (Medford East 1983 USGS Quad. map.)

Name of Cemetery and also known as	Number of burials	Acres	Condition	Date started or earliest known burial	Township	Range	Section

PHOENIX [OLD]

? ? ? 1856   T38S R1W   S15

The old cemetery for the town of Phoenix was on the unnamed hill about 0.66 of a mile, as the crow flies, southeasterly from the present cemetery. The hill rises about 120 feet above the surrounding area and is accessed by Elm Street and Amerman Drive. The present cemetery was established after 1874 and some, but not all, of the graves were moved to it. (Medford East 1983 USGS Quad. map shows the hill, but does not indicate any cemetery on it.)

PINEHURST
  AKA: 1. EDSALL
      2. GREEN
         SPRINGS
      3. LINCOLN [?]

? ? ? ?   T40S R4E   S5

Located north off of OR. Hwy. 66 and east of Round Prairie. The cemetery is about 0.5 of a mile northwest of Pinehurst, as the crow flies. It is just east of Beaver Creek and has no ready access. (Not shown on Parker Mtn. 1988 USGS Quad. map. NOTE: The county line is miss labled on the map.)

PROSPECT
  AKA: 1. DEAN HILL

A 1 3 1886-1906   T32S R3E   S31

There are 6 early burials by the Pacific Power and Light Canal. These were marked by P.P.L. crews in 1973. They are 2.5 miles northeast of the locale of Cascade Gorge on OR. Hwy. 62. Cross the OR. Hwy. 62 bridge over the canal at Milepost 42.19. Turn left off of OR. Hwy. 62 at the east end of the bridge and follow the road parallel to the canal for 0.23 of a mile to the cemetery. See 28 October 1973 *Oregonian* article "On A Hill". (Cascade Gorge 1988 USGS Quad. map.)

RED ROCK CANYON GRAVES

? ? ? ?   T33S R2E   ?

Thought to be on the Northeast 1/4 of Section 26. Cascade Gorge is at the mouth of Red Rock Canyon on the right; it takes an 8-mile hike up Red Rock Canyon to get to the graves. There are 13 graves of soldiers; no dates. (Not shown on Cascade Gorge 1988 USGS Quad. map.)

Name of Cemetery and also known as	Number of burials	Acres	Condition	Date started or earliest known burial	Township	Range	Section

REESE CREEK — ? ? ? ? — T35S R1W — S14

Take OR. Hwy. 62 north of Eagle Point to Butte Falls Road. Then turn right onto Butte Falls Road and go 0.9 of a mile. A church is on the right, and the cemetery is probably there. Reese Creek School was also in this vicinity; on the Lewis Reese, [Reed or Rees] D.L.C. #41, RB #993, which is the correct surname we do not know, it is listed different ways in different sources. (Church is on Shady Cove 1983 USGS Quad. map, but the cemetery is not shown.)

ROCK POINT
AKA: 1. SARDINE CREEK — ? 17 3 1865 — T36S R3W — S17

Located 1.2 miles west of Gold Hill and usually considered as part of the Gold Hill I.O.O.F. Cemetery. It is just across the lane from the latter. {27 October 1995} (Gold Hill 1983 USGS Quad. map.)

SCENIC HILLS MEMORIAL PARK — D 18 1 1964 — T39S R1E — S11

Go northwest off of OR. Hwy. 66 on East Main Street, drive for 0.7 of a mile then turn right (north) onto East Hills. Located 0.6 of a mile east of Ashland, near the airport; on the Henry C. Willis D.L.C. #48, RB #16. (Ashland 1983 USGS Quad. map.)

SISKIYOU MEMORIAL PARK AND MAUSOLEUM — E 54 1 1932 — T37S R1W — S29

Located at the corner of Highland and Siskiyou Boulevard, in Medford. This is on the south side of Siskiyou Boulevard; Eastwood I.O.O.F. is on the north side of Siskiyou Boulevard in this area; on David Ball D.L.C. #78, RB #962. {27 October 1995} (Medford East 1983 USGS Quad. map.)

SMITH DAUGHTER — A 0.01 3 Nov. 1859 — T39S R1E — S24

The burial of a 2 year-old daughter of Thomas and Margaret Harrison Smith is reportedly on the present Clayton Creek Mobile Estates. This is off of the Clayton Creek Frontage Road and near OR. Hwy. 99, southeast of Ashland. See 6 June 1967 *Ashland Daily*

Name of Cemetery and also known as	Number of burials	Acres	Condition	Date started or earliest known burial	Township	Range	Section

Tidings; on the Thomas Smith D.L.C. #55, RB #9. (Not shown on Ashland 1983 USGS Quad. map.)

STEAMBOAT
AKA: 1. CARBERRY
     2. COPPER

| B | 0.5 | 3 | 1896 | T40S R4W | | S20 |

From Medford, follow OR. Hwy. 238 to the community of Ruch. From Ruch, follow Applegate Road 18.4 miles to Copper. Past Copper, take Carberry Road (Rogue River National Forest Road #10) to the right (west) for 7.6 miles. The cemetery will be on the right. There are 14 known burials (1989). (Carberry Creek 1983 USGS Quad. map.)

STEARNS FAMILY
AKA: 1. GRAVE HILL
     2. TALENT
     3. WAGNER
       CREEK

| D | 1.25 | 3 | 1857 | T38S R1W | | S34 |

This cemetery is on Sections 34 and 35. From OR. Hwy. 99 in Talent, take Main Street to the southwest; then head south on Wagner Creek Road for 1.5 miles, to Anderson Road. Turn right on Anderson Road for 0.15 of a mile to the cemetery on the left on the hilltop. This cemetery was deeded in 1889. The section in front of the cemetery belongs to Ashland I.O.O.F; on the David E. Stearns D.L.C. #67, RB #134. (Talent 1983 USGS Quad. map.)

STERLINGVILLE
AKA: 1. STERLING

| C | 1.43 | 3 | 1863 | T38S R2W | | S33 |

Located 8.5 miles southeast of Jacksonville. From OR. Hwy. 238, take Southwest Oregon Street southwest 0.2 of a mile; then turn left onto Applegate Street, going 1.7 miles to Sterling Creek Road. Go 6.6 miles further to the cemetery on the left of Sterling Creek Road. It is on top of a rise and is not visible from the road. Old-timers said that there were about 150 burials here in 1953, but only 46 were identified at that time. (Sterling Creek 1983 USGS Quad. map.)

THOMPSON CREEK

| ? | ? | ? | ? | ? | ? | ? |

This could be in Township 38 South Range 4 West in Section 21, 22 or 32 or it could be in Township 39 South Range 4 West Section 5, 7, or 18. There is a reference to a Thompson

Name of Cemetery and also known as	Number of burials	Acres	Condition	Date started or earliest known burial	Township	Range	Section

Creek Cemetery, but the compiler has no other information. (Not shown on Tallowbox Mtn. or Applegate 1983 USGS Quad. maps.)

TOLO ? ? ? ? **T36S R2W** ?

This could be in Section 19 or 20. There is a reference to a cemetery at the bygone site of Tolo. NOTE: no other information was given in the report. (Not shown on Sams Valley 1983 USGS Quad. map.)

TRAIL ? 2.3 ? ? **T33S R1W** S33

Leave OR. Hwy. 62 at the community of Trail. Go northwest 0.6 of a mile on Old Trail Creek Road; the cemetery is on the left. (Trail 1983 USGS Quad. map.)

UNION CREEK ? ? ? ? **T31S R3E** ?

Perhaps located in Section 3. There is a vague undated reference to a cemetery at Union Creek along OR. Hwy. 62. (Not shown on Union Creek 1989 USGS Quad. map.)

UNIONTOWN A ? ? **Circa 1874 T38S R3W** S34

A 1953 D.A.R. report placed this cemetery 1.2 miles south of Ruch, off of Upper Applegate Road at its junction with a lane on the right, on land owned by Lance Offenbacher. Three burials were identified in 1953: Haskins, Cameron and Sanders, one dated 1874. Warning: There are two or more suggested sites a mile or two apart. (Not shown on Ruch 1983 USGS Quad. map.)

UNKNOWN ? 0.25 ? ? **T32S R1E** S23

Go 0.75 of a mile beyond Trail towards Crater Lake on OR. Hwy. 62 and turn left (northerly) onto Elk Creek Road. Proceed 10.5 miles on Elk Creek Road to the junction with a road to the left. The cemetery is at this junction, but as it is about 50 to 60 feet above Elk Creek Road, the cemetery access is more likely from the side road about 50 yards from Elk Creek Road. The cemetery perhaps

Name of Cemetery and also known as	Number of burials	Acres	Condition	Date started or earliest known burial	Township	Range	Section

contains the burials of the Sturgis and Trusty families. (Sugarpine Creek 1989 USGS Quad. map.)

UNKNOWN   ?   0.2   ?   ?   T33S R2E   S10

Very close to Nye Cemetery is another cemetery that is shown on Cascade Gorge 1988 USGS Quad. map. It is off of Ulrich Road and north off of OR. Hwy. 62. At Cascade Gorge, Ulrich Road makes a sharp 90 degree curve left before crossing Nye Ditch. This cemetery is shown on the north side of Nye Ditch. Nye Cemetery is about 0.15 of a mile farther up the road and also on the right. (Cascade Gorge 1988 USGS Quad. map.)

UNKNOWN   A   ?   3   ?   T35S R2W   ?

An article in the *Medford Mail Tribune* of 29 May 1994 reports an unnamed cemetery, west of Antioch Road a mile north of OR. Hwy. 234, in Sams Valley. It is reported to be on a small knoll under three oak trees, on the west side of Antioch Road. This cemetery is not to be confused with Antioch Cemetery which is on the east side of Antioch Road and 1.8 miles north of OR. Hwy 234. This knoll is possibly one of three in the Southeast 1/4 of Section 22. (Not shown on Boswell Mtn. 1983 USGS Quad. map.)

UNKNOWN   ?   ?   ?   ?   T36S R2E   S22

Located in the Southwest 1/4 of Section 22. Take OR. Hwy 140 easterly, to the easterly junction of Lake Creek Loop at OR. Hwy. 140 Milepost 14.76. Continue easterly for another 1.44 miles to about Milepost 16.2. The graves are on the left (northerly) about 200 feet from the highway and just across the North Fork of Little Butte Creek. (Lakecreek 1988 USGS Quad. map.)

UNKNOWN   ?   0.1   ?   ?   T37S R2E   S7

Located about 5.6 miles south of the locale of Lakecreek. Starting at Medford take the Crater Lake Highway (OR. Hwy. 62) north for 6 miles. Turn right (east) onto the Lake Of

Jackson County

The Woods Highway (OR. Hwy. 140) to Milepost 12.6 and turn right (southeasterly) onto Lake Creek Loop. Go another 1.1 miles to the South Fork Little Butte Creek Road continuing to the right (southeast). Another 1.9 miles takes you across the creek and to the locale of Lakecreek itself. Continue ahead another 2.1 miles to the junction with Lake Creek Road on the right (south). Drive on Lake Creek Road and at 5.3 miles from the locale is a side road to the right (southwest). Drive this side road for about 0.25 of a mile where you are about 5.6 miles from Lakecreek. The cemetery is due right (northwest) about 250 feet and an additional 100 feet in altitude above the road. It is on top of a wooded promontory and probably accessible only by foot. (Rio Canyon 1988 USGS Quad. map.)

Name	Burials	Acres	Condition	Date	Township	Range	Section
UNKNOWN	?	?	?	?	T37S	R2E	S8

Leave Lake of the Woods Highway (OR. Hwy. 140) at Milepost 12.6 to the right (southeast), to the locale of Lakecreek and the store. Continue southerly on Lake Creek Road past the reservoir. County maintenance ends about 5.2 miles from the store at a marker noting sections 7, 8, 17, and 18. Continue ahead, upslope, for about another 0.3 of a mile. The graves are about 300 yards to the left (east) and you must go on foot. The 1932 *Metsker Land Ownership Atlas* indicates that Andrew J. Grissom then owned the land. (Grizzly Peak 1988 USGS Quad. map.)

Name	Burials	Acres	Condition	Date	Township	Range	Section
UNKNOWN [DRAPER?]	?	0.15	?	?	T37S	R4W	S15

Perhaps this is Draper Cemetery. Draper was a mining community in the area and had a post office from 1882 to 1912. From the town of Rogue River, cross the bridge to OR. Hwy. 99, Rogue River Highway. Turn left (easterly) and drive 2.7 miles to Milepost 11.5, at Bolt turn right (south) onto Foots Creek Road. At 0.9 of a mile on Foots Creek Road pass Foots Church and Cemetery (see that article). After driving 1.5 miles on Foots Creek Road, turn right onto Right Fork Foots Creek Road.

Name of Cemetery and also known as	Number of burials	Acres	Condition	Date started or earliest known burial	Township	Range	Section

Pass the junction of Foots Creek Road on the left (west) at 3.4 miles. Finally, at 3.8 miles from OR. Hwy.99, the cemetery lies on the left (west) across the tailings of the Right Fork of Foots Creek, on the hillside about 50 feet in altitude above the creek. There appears to be no access except on foot. This was goldmining territory. (Applegate 1983 USGS Quad. map.)

WELLS FAMILY

A   0.01   1   1894-1911   **T39S R1E**   **S13**
There are 4 graves just to the right off of the fourth green in the Oak Knoll Golf Course in Ashland . They are bounded by Crowson Road, OR. Hwy. 66, and a circular carpet of greens; on the Giles Wells D.L.C. #53, RB #73. (Ashland 1983 USGS Quad. map.)

WELLSVILLE
  AKA: 1. WELLESVILLE

?   ?   ?   ?   **T39S R3W**   **S15**
A 1953 D.A.R. report placed this cemetery 4.5 miles south of Ruch, on a flat spot on a hillside, on the left (east) side of East Side Road; between the Grange Hall and Cameron Bridge. The report stated the size of the cemetery was unknown, as were the numbers and dates of burials; there were 7 whites who were killed by Indians plus other burials. No other information was given in the report. (Not shown on Ruch 1983 USGS Quad. map.)

WOODVILLE
  AKA: 1. ROGUE RIVER
       2. WARD CREEK

C   6   2   1886   **T36S R4W**   **S15**
Take the overpass off of the I-5 Freeway at Rogue River. At 0.75 of a mile from the I-5 Freeway cross over the railroad tracks to East Main Street, turn right; go another 0.35 of a mile, then turn left onto Ward Creek Road for 0.13 of a mile. The cemetery is on the left. {27 October 1995} (Rogue River 1983 USGS Quad. map.)

WRIGHT FAMILY

?   ?   ?   ?   **T41S R4E**   **S6**
Located at Agate Flat in southeast Jackson County. Access is from Jenny Creek Road in California. It is in the Jenny Creek area in the Siskiyous, close to the California State

Jackson County

Name of Cemetery and also known as	Number of burials	Acres	Condition	Date started or earliest known burial	Township	Range	Section

Line. NOTE: No other information was given
to the compiler. The 1932 *Metsker
Landownership Atlas* shows the Wright family
owned the Southeast 1/4 of Section 6.
("Graves" are shown on Soda Mtn. 1988 USGS
Quad. map.)

Woodville

Dean H. Byrd (1995)

AIKEN FAMILY see **AIKIN FAMILY**	JACKSON CO.	T32S	R3E	?
AIKIN FAMILY	JACKSON CO.	T32S	R3E	?
ANTELOPE	JACKSON CO.	T36S	R1W	S14
ANTELOPE CREEK see **ANTELOPE**	JACKSON CO.	T36S	R1W	S14
ANTIOCH	JACKSON CO.	T35S	R2W	S23
APPLEGATE see **MISSOURI FLAT**	JACKSON CO.	T38S	R4W	S6
APPLEGATE CHURCH	JACKSON CO.	T38S	R4W	S22
ASHLAND see **ASHLAND CITY**	JACKSON CO	T39S	R1E	S9
ASHLAND CITY	JACKSON CO	T39S	R1E	S9
BAILEY GULCH	JACKSON CO.	T37S	R4W	S22
BALL D.L.C., DAVID see **SISKIYOU MEMORIAL PARK AND MAUSOLEUM**				
	JACKSON CO.	T37S	R1W	S29
BARNEBURG HILL	JACKSON CO.	T37S	R1W	S32
BEAGLE see **ANTIOCH**	JACKSON CO.	T35S	R2W	S23
BERNEBURG D.L.C., WILLIAM see **I.O.O.F., EASTWOOD [MEDFORD]**				
	JACKSON CO.	T37S	R1W	S29
BLACK, CLIFTON	JACKSON CO.	T34S	R1W	S28
BLACK, JOHN M. see **BLACK, CLIFTON**				
	JACKSON CO.	T34S	R1W	S28
BLACK, MARY LOUISA see **BLACK, CLIFTON**				
	JACKSON CO.	T34S	R1W	S28
BRADLEY FAMILY	JACKSON CO.	?	?	?
BRISTO	JACKSON CO.	?	?	?
BROWNSBORO	JACKSON CO.	T36S	R1E	S4
BUTLER-THOMPSON FAMILY see **MYER FAMILY**				
	JACKSON CO.	T38S	R1E	S30
BUTTE FALLS	JACKSON CO.	T35S	R2E	S5
BUTTERWORTH, CHARLES E. see **LILYGLEN**				
	JACKSON CO.	T38S	R3E	S14
CAMERON see **UNIONTOWN**	JACKSON CO.	T38S	R3W	S34
CARBERRY see **STEAMBOAT**	JACKSON CO.	T40S	R4W	S20
CATHOLIC see **JACKSONVILLE**	JACKSON CO.	T37S	R2W	S29
CENTRAL POINT	JACKSON CO.	T37S	R2W	S1
CHASE D.L.C., WILLIAM see **HARGADINE**				
	JACKSON CO.	T39S	R1E	S5
CHURCH OF BRETHREN see **DUNKARD**	JACKSON CO.	T38S	R1W	S23
CITY see **JACKSONVILLE**	JACKSON CO.	T37S	R2W	S29
CITY OF ASHLAND see **HARGADINE**	JACKSON CO.	T39S	R1E	S5
CLIMAX GRAVES	JACKSON CO.	T38S	R2E	S5
COLLINGS GRAVES	JACKSON CO.	T40S	R4W	S36
COLVER D.L.C., SAMUEL see **PHOENIX [NEW]**				
	JACKSON CO.	T38S	R1W	S9
COLVER, JEMIMA see **PHOENIX [NEW]**				
	JACKSON CO.	T38S	R1W	S9
COLVER, LEWELLYN see **PHOENIX [NEW]**				
	JACKSON CO.	T38S	R1W	S9
COPPER see **STEAMBOAT**	JACKSON CO.	T40S	R4W	S20
CRATER	JACKSON CO.	T35S	R2E	?
DEADMANS POINT	JACKSON CO.	T40S	R2W	S27
DEAN HILL see **PROSPECT**	JACKSON CO.	T32S	R3E	S31
DODGE BRIDGE	JACKSON CO.	T35S	R1W	S17
DOWNING PLACE	JACKSON CO.	?	?	?

DUNKARD	JACKSON CO.	T38S	R1W	S23
DUNN FAMILY see **HILL-DUNN FAMILY**				
	JACKSON CO.	T39S	R2E	S30
DUNN-HILL FAMILY see **HILL-DUNN FAMILY**				
	JACKSON CO.	T39S	R2E	S30
EAGLE POINT see **ANTELOPE**	JACKSON CO.	T36S	R1W	S14
EAGLE POINT NATIONAL see **NATIONAL VETERANS ADMINISTRATION**				
	JACKSON CO.	T36S	R1W	S2
EASTWOOD I.O.O.F. see **I.O.O.F., EASTWOOD [MEDFORD]**				
	JACKSON CO.	T37S	R1W	S29
EDSALL see **PINEHURST**	JACKSON CO.	T40S	R4E	S5
EVANS VALLEY	JACKSON CO.	T35S	R4W	?
FLOUNCE ROCK see **NYE FAMILY**	JACKSON CO.	T33S	R2E	S10
FOOTS	JACKSON CO.	T36S	R4W	S35
FOOTS CREEK CHAPEL see **FOOTS**	JACKSON CO.	T36S	R4W	S35
FOREST CREEK see **LOGTOWN**	JACKSON CO.	T38S	R3W	S14
FRINK FAMILY	JACKSON CO.	T36S	R1W	?
GALL see **HAYS**	JACKSON CO.	T36S	R3W	S20
GERHART, CHARLES see **LILYGLEN**	JACKSON CO.	T38S	R3E	S14
GERHART, MARGRET see **LILYGLEN**	JACKSON CO.	T38S	R3E	S14
GERMAN ORDER OF RED MEN see **JACKSONVILLE**				
	JACKSON CO.	T37S	R2W	S29
GRAVE HILL see **STEARNS FAMILY**	JACKSON CO.	T38S	R1W	S34
GRAY D.L.C., JOHN F. see **HILLCREST MEMORIAL PARK AND MAUSOLEUM**				
	JACKSON CO.	T38S	R1W	S3
GREEN SPRINGS see **PINEHURST**	JACKSON CO.	T40S	R4E	S5
GRIFFIN CREEK	JACKSON CO.	T38S	R2W	S9
GRIFFIN FAMILY see **GRIFFIN CREEK**				
	JACKSON CO.	T38S	R2W	S9
GRISSOM, ANDREW J. see **UNKNOWN**	JACKSON CO.	T37S	R2E	S8
HARGADINE	JACKSON CO.	T39S	R1E	S5
HASKINS see **UNIONTOWN**	JACKSON CO.	T38S	R3W	S34
HAYS	JACKSON CO.	T36S	R3W	S20
HIATT D.L.C., ISAAC see **HILL-DUNN FAMILY**				
	JACKSON CO.	T39S	R2E	S30
HILL-DUNN FAMILY	JACKSON CO.	T39S	R2E	S30
HILL FAMILY see **HILL-DUNN FAMILY**				
	JACKSON CO.	T39S	R2E	S30
HILLCREST MEMORIAL PARK AND MAUSOLEUM				
	JACKSON CO.	T38S	R1W	S3
I.O.O.F. see **CENTRAL POINT**	JACKSON CO.	T37S	R2W	S1
I.O.O.F. see **JACKSONVILLE**	JACKSON CO.	T37S	R2W	S29
I.O.O.F. [ASHLAND] see **MOUNTAIN VIEW I.O.O.F. AND MAUSOLEUM**				
	JACKSON CO.	T39S	R1E	S15
I.O.O.F. [GOLD HILL]	JACKSON CO.	T36S	R3W	S17
I.O.O.F. #193 see **CENTRAL POINT**	JACKSON CO.	T37S	R2W	S1
I.O.O.F., EASTWOOD [MEDFORD]	JACKSON CO.	T37S	R1W	S29
INDIAN RANCHERIA TRAIL MASSACRE	JACKSON CO.	T35S	R4E	S18
JACKSONVILLE	JACKSON CO.	T37S	R2W	S29
JACKSONVILLE PIONEER see **JACKSONVILLE**				
	JACKSON CO.	T37S	R2W	S29
JEWISH see **JACKSONVILLE**	JACKSON CO.	T37S	R2W	S29

JOHNSON, CAROLINE see **JOHNSON FAMILY**				
	JACKSON CO.	T34S	R1W	S15
JOHNSON FAMILY	JACKSON CO.	T34S	R1W	S15
KANE CREEK	JACKSON CO.	T36S	R3E	?
KINGSBURY see **HILL-DUNN FAMILY**	JACKSON CO.	T39S	R2E	S30
KINGSBURY SODA SPRINGS see **HILL-DUNN FAMILY**				
	JACKSON CO.	T39S	R2E	S30
KNUTSEN FAMILY see **APPLEGATE CHURCH**				
	JACKSON CO.	T38S	R4W	S22
LAKECREEK	JACKSON CO.	T37S	R2E	S4
LAUREL GROVE see **LOGTOWN**	JACKSON CO.	T38S	R3W	S14
LAURELHURST	JACKSON CO.	T33S	?	?
LILYGLEN	JACKSON CO.	T38S	R3E	S14
LINCOLN [?] see **PINEHURST**	JACKSON CO.	T40S	R4E	S5
LOGTOWN	JACKSON CO.	T38S	R3W	S14
MASONIC see **JACKSONVILLE**	JACKSON CO.	T37S	R2W	S29
MASONIC LODGE #135 see **CENTRAL POINT**				
	JACKSON CO.	T37S	R2W	S1
MATTHEWS FAMILY	JACKSON CO.	T35S	R1W	S27
MEADOWS GRAVES	JACKSON CO.	T34S	R3W	S25
MEMORY GARDENS MEMORIAL PARK AND MAUSOLEUM				
	JACKSON CO.	T37S	R2W	S34
MERRIMAN, ARTINECIA [ARTEMISIA?] see **MERRIMAN FAMILY**				
	JACKSON CO.	T38S	R2W	?
MERRIMAN FAMILY	JACKSON CO.	T38S	R2W	?
MERRIMAN, WILLIAM H. see **MERRIMAN FAMILY**				
	JACKSON CO.	T38S	R2W	?
MEYERS FAMILY see **MYER FAMILY**	JACKSON CO.	T38S	R1E	S30
MILLER FAMILY	JACKSON CO.	T36S	R1E	S5
MILLER, J. N. T. see **JACKSONVILLE**				
	JACKSON CO.	T37S	R2W	S29
MILLER, WILLIAM M. see **MISSOURI FLAT**				
	JACKSON CO.	T38S	R4W	S6
MISSOURI FLAT	JACKSON CO.	T38S	R4W	S6
MORSE FAMILY	JACKSON CO.	T38S	R1E	S30
MORRISON, RILEY see **MOONVILLE**	JACKSON CO.	?	?	?
MOUNT VIEW see **MOUNTAIN VIEW I.O.O.F. AND MAUSLEUM**				
	JACKSON CO.	T39S	R1E	S15
MOUNTAIN VIEW AND RESTHAVEN MAUSOLEUM				
	JACKSON CO.	T39S	R1E	S10
MOUNTAIN VIEW I.O.O.F. AND MAUSOLEUM				
	JACKSON CO.	T39S	R1E	S15
MYER D.L.C., NATHANIEL see **MORSE FAMILY**				
	JACKSON CO.	T38S	R1E	S30
MYER D.L.C., WILLIAM C. see **MYER FAMILY**				
	JACKSON CO.	T38S	R1E	S30
MYER FAMILY	JACKSON CO.	T38S	R1E	S30
NATIONAL VETERANS ADMINISTRATION				
	JACKSON CO.	T36S	R1W	S2
NICHOLS D.L.C., JOHN M. see **NICHOLS FAMILY**				
	JACKSON CO.	T35S	R1W	S25
NICHOLS FAMILY	JACKSON CO.	T35S	R1W	S25

NYE FAMILY	JACKSON CO.	T33S	R2E	S10
OFFENBACHER, LANCE see **UNIONTOWN**				
	JACKSON CO.	T38S	R3W	S34
ORDER OF RED MEN see **JACKSONVILLE**				
	JACKSON CO.	T37S	R2W	S29
PANKEY see **PANKEY PARK**	JACKSON CO.	T35S	R2W	S30
PANKEY PARK	JACKSON CO.	T35S	R2W	S30
PECK FAMILY see **LAKECREEK**	JACKSON CO.	T37S	R2E	S4
PHOENIX [NEW]	JACKSON CO.	T38S	R1W	S9
PHOENIX [OLD]	JACKSON CO.	T38S	R1W	S15
PINEHURST	JACKSON CO.	T40S	R4E	S5
PROSPECT	JACKSON CO.	T32S	R3E	S31
RANCHERIA see **INDIAN RANCHERIA TRAIL MASSACRE**				
	JACKSON CO.	T35S	R4E	S18
RED ROCK CANYON GRAVES	JACKSON CO.	T33S	R2E	?
REED D.L.C., LEWIS see **REESE CREEK**				
	JACKSON CO.	T35S	R1W	S14
REES D.L.C., LEWIS see **REESE CREEK**				
	JACKSON CO.	T35S	R1W	S14
REESE D.L.C., LEWIS see **REESE CREEK**				
	JACKSON CO.	T35S	R1W	S14
ROCK CREEK METHODIST CHURCH see **PANKEY PARK**				
	JACKSON CO.	T35S	R2W	S30
ROCK POINT	JACKSON CO.	T36S	R3W	S17
ROGUE RIVER see **WOODVILLE**	JACKSON CO.	T36S	R4W	S15
RUCH see **LOGTOWN**	JACKSON CO.	T38S	R3W	S14
SAMS VALLEY see **PANKEY PARK**	JACKSON CO.	T35S	R2W	S30
SANDERS see **UNIONTOWN**	JACKSON CO.	T38S	R3W	S34
SARDINE CREEK see **I.O.O.F. [GOLD HILL]**				
	JACKSON CO.	T36S	R3W	S17
SARDINE CREEK see **ROCK POINT**	JACKSON CO.	T36S	R3W	S17
SCENIC HILLS MEMORIAL PARK	JACKSON CO.	T39S	R1E	S11
SHADY COVE see **JOHNSON FAMILY**	JACKSON CO.	T34S	R1W	S15
SISKIYOU MEMORIAL PARK AND MAUSOLEUM				
	JACKSON CO.	T37S	R1W	S29
SMITH D.L.C., NELSON D. see **DUNKARD**				
	JACKSON CO.	T38S	R1W	S23
SMITH D.L.C., THOMAS see **SMITH DAUGHTER**				
	JACKSON CO.	T39S	R1E	S24
SMITH DAUGHTER	JACKSON CO.	T39S	R1E	S24
SMITH, MARGARET HARRISON see **SMITH DAUGHTER**				
	JACKSON CO.	T39S	R1E	S24
SMITH, THOMAS see **SMITH DAUGHTER**				
	JACKSON CO.	T39S	R1E	S24
SQUAW CREEK see **COLLINGS GRAVES**	JACKSON CO.	T40S	R4W	S36
STANLEY, SUSAN see **MERRIMAN FAMILY**				
	JACKSON CO.	T38S	R2W	?
STEAMBOAT	JACKSON CO.	T40S	R4W	S20
STEARNS D.L.C., DAVID E. see **STEARNS FAMILY**				
	JACKSON CO.	T38S	R1W	S34
STEARNS FAMILY	JACKSON CO.	T38S	R1W	S34
STERLING see **STERLINGVILLE**	JACKSON CO.	T38S	R2W	S33

STERLINGVILLE	JACKSON CO.	T38S	R2W	S33
STURGIS FAMILY see **UNKNOWN**	JACKSON CO.	T32S	R1E	S23
TALENT see **STEARNS FAMILY**	JACKSON CO.	T38S	R1W	S34
TENBROOK D.L.C., ABRAM see **MEMORY GARDENS MEMORIAL PARK AND MAUSOLEUM**				
	JACKSON CO.	T37S	R2W	S34
THOMPSON CREEK	JACKSON CO.	?	?	?
THOMPSON FAMILY see **MYERS FAMILY**				
	JACKSON CO.	T38S	R1E	S30
THURBER D.L.C., JOHN see **PHOENIX [NEW]**				
	JACKSON CO.	T38S	R1W	S9
TOLO	JACKSON CO.	T36S	R2W	?
TRAIL	JACKSON CO.	T33S	R1W	S33
TRUSTY FAMILY see **UNKNOWN**	JACKSON CO.	T32S	R1E	S23
UNION CREEK	JACKSON CO.	T31S	R3E	?
UNIONTOWN	JACKSON CO.	T38S	R3W	S34
UNKNOWN	JACKSON CO.	T32S	R1E	S23
UNKNOWN	JACKSON CO.	T33S	R2E	S10
UNKNOWN	JACKSON CO.	T35S	R2W	?
UNKNOWN	JACKSON CO.	T36S	R2E	S22
UNKNOWN	JACKSON CO.	T37S	R2E	S7
UNKNOWN	JACKSON CO.	T37S	R2E	S8
UNKNOWN [DRAPER?]	JACKSON CO.	T37S	R4W	S15
VETERANS see **NATIONAL VETERANS ADMINISTRATION**				
	JACKSON CO.	T36S	R1W	S2
WAGNER CREEK see **STEARNS FAMILY**	JACKSON CO.	T38S	R1W	S34
WALKER BURIAL PLOT see **MEADOWS GRAVES**				
	JACKSON CO.	T34S	R3W	S25
WARD CREEK see **WOODVILLE**	JACKSON CO.	T36S	R4W	S15
WATKINS see **COLLINGS GRAVES**	JACKSON CO.	T40S	R4W	S36
WEEKS [?] see **JOHNSON FAMILY**	JACKSON CO.	T34S	R1W	S15
WELLESVILLE see **WELLSVILLE**	JACKSON CO.	T39S	R3W	S15
WELLS D.L.C., GILES see **WELLS FAMILY**				
	JACKSON CO.	T39S	R1E	S13
WELLS FAMILY	JACKSON CO.	T39S	R1E	S13
WELLSVILLE	JACKSON CO.	T39S	R3W	S15
WHITE CITY see **NATIONAL VETERANS ADMINISTRATION**				
	JACKSON CO.	T36S	R1W	S2
WILLIAMS CREEK [?] see **MISSOURI FLAT**				
	JACKSON CO.	T38S	R4W	S6
WILLIS D.L.C., HENRY C. see **SCENIC HILLS MEMORIAL PARK**				
	JACKSON CO.	T39S	R1E	S11
WOODVILLE	JACKSON CO.	T36S	R4W	S15
WRIGHT FAMILY	JACKSON CO.	T41S	R4E	S6

Jacksonville

Dean H. Byrd (1995)

JEFFERSON COUNTY
Scale 0 2 4 Mi
WASCO COUNTY
WHEELER COUNTY
CROOK COUNTY
DESCHUTES COUNTY
MARION CO.
LINN CO.
MADRAS
Willowdale
Ashwood
Horse Heaven
Gateway
Hay Creek
Grizzly
Lamonta
Metolius
Culver
Opal City
Grandview
Geneva
Warm Springs
Camp Sherman
To The Dalles
To Gov't Camp
To Prineville
To Redmond
To Sisters
To Albany
JOHN DAY R.
Trout Creek
Wilson Cr.
Hay Cr.
Little Willow Cr.
Willow Creek
Mud Spring Cr.
DESCHUTES RIVER
CROOKED RIVER
METOLIUS RIVER
Seekseequa Cr.
Shitike Creek
WHITEWATER RIVER
Jefferson Cr.
Canyon Cr.
Jack Cr.
Lake Cr.
Fly Cr.
Squaw Cr.
Suttle L.
Blue L.
97
26
20
126

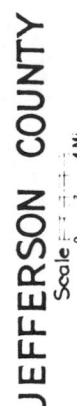

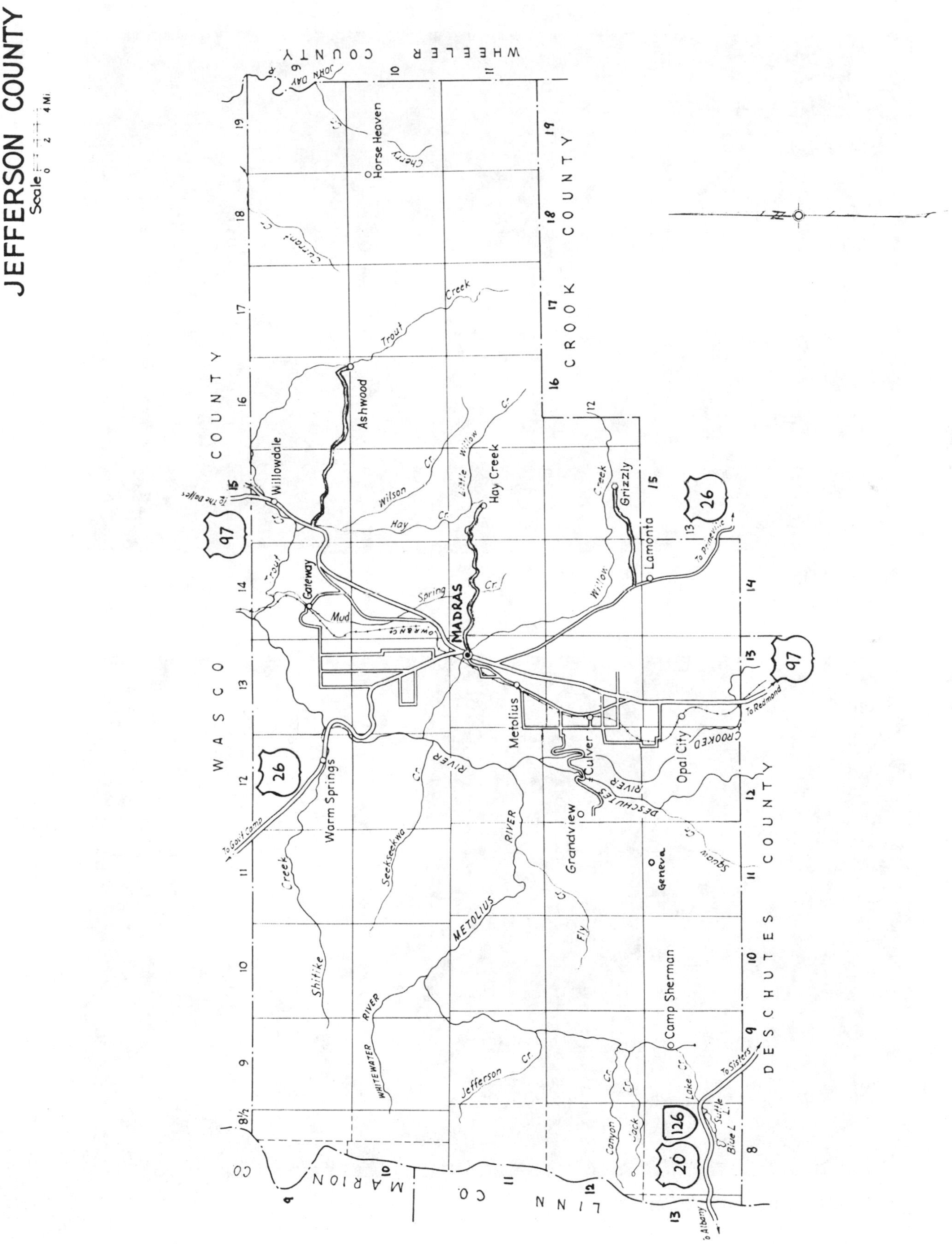

Gard, Milo
Janice M. Healy (2000)

Mt. Jefferson Memorial Park
Unusual-Highway-type sign of reflective blue and white.
Janice M. Healy (2000)

Area: 1,791 square miles
Population (1998): 16,627
County seat: Madras, Population: 4,770
County established: 12 December 1914

Detached from Crook County, Jefferson County was an area of irrigation agriculture, dry land farming and ranching. The earliest organized public cemeteries were at Hay Creek and Grizzly, both in 1874. By 1905 there were nine public cemeteries. There are also seven cemeteries on the Warm Springs Indian Reservation.

Mt. Jefferson Memorial Park
Dean H. Byrd (1988)

Mt. Jefferson Memorial Park
Janice M. Healy (2000)

Mt. Jefferson Memorial Park
Janice M. Healy (2000)

Name of Cemetery and also known as	Number of burials	Acres	Condition	Date started or earliest known burial	Township	Range	Section

BABY [HAY CREEK]

A 0.01 ? ? T11S R15E S9

M. D. Morgan who worked on the Hay Creek Ranch reports that there is a baby's tombstone a short distance to the west of Hay Creek Cemetery in the trees. The infant was not buried in the nearby Hay Creek Pioneer Cemetery for fear of some infection. (Not shown on Teller Butte 1969-85 USGS Quad. map.)

BROWNHILL CHILDREN

A 0.01 12 Circa 1917 T9S R13E S24

In the village of Gateway start at the railway crossing of Juniper Lane. Drive westerly climbing the bluff onto Agency Plains. At about 2.25 miles from the railway is a field road to the right (north) which runs along the township line and through wheat fields. Almost a mile into the fields is a large juniper tree on the left (west). Two infant boys of the Brownhill Family are buried under the juniper which is not to be disturbed. There are no markers. The parents are buried in Mt. Jefferson Memorial Park. NOTE: This site is on private property. {November 1997} (Not shown on Gateway 1962-93 USGS Quad. map.)

BRUNO
AKA: 1. WARM SPRINGS
      AGENCY

D 10 3 ? T9S R12E S23

Located just north of Warm Springs on the Warm Springs Reservation. This is one of three separate cemeteries in this area. (Warm Springs 1963 USGS Quad. map.)

CULVER I.O.O.F.
AKA: 1. CORWIN
     2. HALE
     3. HALE I.O.O.F.
     4. HALE, MINERVA
     5. I.O.O.F.

B 0.5 2 Circa 1899 T12S R13E S16

Located 4 miles south of Madras on U.S. Hwy. 97 and 0.25 of a mile east of U.S. Hwy. 97 on Highland Road. {September 1997} (Culver 1985-93 USGS Quad. map.)

DRY CREEK

B 0.9 3 ? T9S R12E S12

Located on the Warm Springs Reservation. Leave U.S. Hwy. 26 at Warm Springs and go 2.6 miles to the northeast on the road to Kah-

Name of Cemetery and also known as	Number of burials	Acres	Condition	Date started or earliest known burial	Township	Range	Section

Nee-Ta. At a road junction, turn left (northwest) and go 0.6 of a mile to the cemetery. (Eagle Butte 1962 USGS Quad. map.)

GARD, MILO
AKA: 1. AGENCY PLAINS
    2. BIG AGENCY PLAINS
    3. BIG PLAINS

A   0.5   2   1903   **T10S R13E**   **S9**
Located 5 miles northwest of Madras on the Warm Springs Highway (U.S. Hwy. 26) and 1 mile west of U.S. Hwy. 26, on Northwest Fir Lane. The first burial was for Caroline Gard, 1855 - 1903, wife of Milo Gard. They homesteaded this property in July of 1902. There was not a cemetery in the area so Milo donated land for one at this time. Milo Gard passed away on 13 February 1907 and is buried here beside his wife. {30 September 2000} (Madras West 1963-93 USGS Quad. map.)

GRANDVIEW
AKA: 1. GENEVA

?   0.8   2   ?   **T12S R11E**   **S36**
This cemetery is 22 miles from Madras. Take the Culver Highway south out of Madras for 7.3 miles; turn off to the right onto Gem Road and left onto Frazier Drive 1.7 miles, turn right onto Jordan Road. Go down Crooked River Canyon, across the bridge and up the other side 12.9 miles to the cemetery on the left. (Steelhead Falls 1985 USGS Quad. map.)

GRAY BUTTE
AKA: 1. GRAY'S

C   1   2   1891   **T13S R14E**   **S6**
Located 11.5 miles south of Madras on U.S. Hwy. 26, then 3 miles west on Southeast Laurel Lane. There are 172 graves and 11 unmarked graves (1980). {September 1997} (Gray Butte 1985 USGS Quad. map.)

GRIZZLY
AKA: 1. LAMONTA
    2. WILLOW CREEK

B   0.5   3   1874   **T12S R15E**   **S33**
Located on Northeast 1/4 of Section 33: at Grizzly, 17.9 miles southeast of Madras. Take U.S. Hwy. 97 in Madras. Go south to the junction with U.S. Hwy. 26 and the highway to Prineville. Turn left onto U.S. Hwy. 26, go southeast 10 miles and turn left onto Southeast Ramms Road at the junction. Go 5.8 miles to Hay Creek Road; turn right onto Hay Creek Road and go 0.6 of a mile to Newbill Creek Bridge. The cemetery is 500 yards due south of Newbill Creek Bridge on an abandoned

Name of Cemetery and also known as	Number of burials	Acres	Condition	Date started or earliest known burial	Township	Range	Section

ranch. NOTE: This site is on private land and is difficult to access. {September 1997} (Grizzly Mountain 1988 USGS Quad. map.)

HAY CREEK PIONEER

| | B | 0.5 | 3 | 1874 | T11S | R15E | S9 |

Located on a hill near Hay Creek Ranch House, 11 miles east of Madras via Ashwood Road to Hay Creek Road. Turn right 0.5 of a mile southeast of the junction with Ashwood Road. The cemetery is on a ridge and on the right (south) northwest of the ranch headquarters. You must walk uphill to the cemetery. There are possibly as many as 150 burials: 39 markers (1968). NOTE: This site is on private property. {September 1997} (Teller Butte 1969-85 USGS Quad. map.)

KALAMA

| | B | 0.25 | 3 | ? | T9S | R12E | S35 |

Located 1 mile south of Warm Springs on the Warm Springs Indian Reservation. (Not shown on Seekseequa Junction 1985-93 USGS Quad. maps.)

KAMPFER FAMILY
AKA: 1. GATEWAY

| | A | ? | ? | 1878 | T9S | R14E | S11 |

Gateway is a small community in northern Jefferson County; it had a post office and was a railway stop. A woman named Emma Kampfer, age 46, and wife of Godfrey Kampfer, died 19 July 1921 in a Pendleton hospital. The body was reportedly sent to Gateway for burial. Umatilla County Death Certificate #161 for 1921. There are 9 burials, 7 marked and 2 unmarked. NOTE: This site is on private property. {October 1999} (Not shown on Gateway 1962-93 USGS Quad. map.)

LITTLE PLAINS

| | ? | ? | ? | ? | T11S | R13E | ? |

"A few graves" in the area of Metolius. NOTE: This is apparently not an alternate name for the Methodist Hill, or German Cemetery. No other information was given with the report. (Not shown on Culver 1985-93 USGS Quad. map.)

Name of Cemetery and also known as	Number of burials	Acres	Condition	Date started or earliest known burial	Township	Range	Section

MAUPIN
AKA: 1. FRIENDS RANCH

B   0.2   3   1887   T9S   R16E   S24
Located near Wood Cemetery, 27 miles east of Madras. It is 2.5 miles north of Wood Cemetery on Trout Creek Road, on the east side of Trout Creek. There are 37 known burials. (Degner Canyon 1987 USGS Quad. map.)

METHODIST HILL
AKA: 1. GERMAN
     2. METOLIUS

B   2   2   1905   T11S   R13E   S32
Drive about 1.5 miles south of the town of Metolius on the Culver Highway. Turn right (west) off of the highway onto Southwest Franklin Lane and drive 0.5 of a mile to the intersection with Southwest Elbe Drive. The cemetery is at the intersection with the entrance from Elbe Drive. {14 June 1988} (Culver 1985-93 USGS Quad. map.)

MT. JEFFERSON MEMORIAL PARK
AKA: 1. I.O.O.F. #196
     2. MADRAS

D   7   1   1902   T11S   R14E   S6
Located 1 mile northeast of Madras off of U.S. Hwy. 97: 0.75 of a mile east of U.S. Hwy. 97 on Northeast Loucks Road and Northeast Bean Drive. {30 September 2000} (Madras East 1985 USGS Quad. map.)

PEARCE, JOHN
AKA: 1. PEARCE, JOSHUA [Sic]

A   0.01   2   14 Aug. 1875   T10S   R15E   S32
Drive east out of Madras via Ashwood Road for about 10 miles. Upon turning down into the canyon of Hay Creek turn left (north) onto the road to Willowdale. Drive about 1.7 miles and off to the right (east) about 25 yards is the grave of John Pearce in an iron fenced plot. This is on what was the Chas. McPherson Ranch. John Pearce was the father of Mrs. McPherson. John Pearce was born 1810, died 1875 aged 65 years. NOTE: This site is on private property. {September 1997} (Teller Butte 1969-85 USGS Quad. map)

RAJNEESH CREMATORIUM

?   ?   ?   ?   T9S   R18E   S1
Located about 1 mile west and south from "downtown" Rajneeshpuram, across Currant Creek and up Arrastra Canyon. (Arrastra Butte 1987 USGS Quad. map.)

Name of Cemetery and also known as	Number of burials	Acres	Condition	Date started or earliest known burial	Township	Range	Section

ROUND BUTTE PIONEER
A 0.5 2 1916   T11S R13E   S6
Located on the southeast 1/4 of Section 6. Leave Madras on Culver Highway and at the south edge of town turn left onto Southwest Belmont Lane for 4.3 miles. Turn right on Southwest Elbe Drive for 1 mile and the cemetery is on the left at the end of the county road. {13 June 1988} (Madras West 1963-93 USGS Quad.map.)

SEEKSEEQUA [NORTH]
C 2 3 ?   T10S R12E   S28
Located on the Warm Springs Indian Reservation. One of two cemeteries called Seekseequa which are about a mile apart as the crow flies. This one is on the north side of the road, on the north side of Seekseequa Creek 1 mile west (upstream) from Seekseequa Junction. Seekseequa Juction is 11 miles south of Warm Springs. (Seekseequa Junction 1985-93 USGS Quad. map.)

SEEKSEEQUA [SOUTH]
C 1 3 ?   T10S R12E   S27
Located on the Warm Springs Indian Reservation. This cemetery is south of Seekseequa Creek. Go southeast about 0.85 of a mile from Seekseequa Junction to a side road on the right (west). Turn on that road for 0.5 of a mile to the cemetery. (Seekseequa Junction 1985-93 USGS Quad. map.)

SMITH, WHISTLING
A 0.01 ? 1885   T10S R13E   S7
In the spring of 1885, Whistling Smith was found frozen to death; he was buried where he was found, about 0.5 of a mile up the canyon from Negro Brown Ranch. This is in the center of Section 7, off of U.S. Hwy. 26 and due east of Pelton Dam in the area of Vanora. A range fire in 1941 destroyed his marker. (Not shown on Madras West 1963-93 USGS Quad. map.

TENINO
C 1 3 ?   T9S R12E   S27
Located 1 mile southwest of Warm Springs on the Warm Springs Indian Reservation. NOTE:

Name of Cemetery and also known as	Number of burials	Acres	Condition	Date started or earliest known burial	Township	Range	Section

No other information was given to the compiler. (Warm Springs 1963 USGS Quad. map.)

UNKNOWN   **A   0.01   ?   ?   T11S R15E   ?**

The compiler has received two slightly different reports for this area. We do not know if they refer to the same burial site or to two different burial sites. One report is "there is a lone grave south of Hay Creek Ranch." The other report is "there is a lone grave 4 miles south of the Hay Creek Ranch." Unfortunately there was no other information given in either report. (Not shown on Brewer Reservoir 1969-85 USGS Quad. map.)

UPPER WARM SPRINGS   **B   0.25   3   ?   ?   ?   ?**
RIVER

Located on the Warm Springs Indian Reservation and said to be about 5 miles northeast of Warm Springs on the road to Kah-Nee-Ta. Perhaps Hot Springs Cemetery is intended, which is in Wasco County. NOTE: No other information was given to the compiler. (No cemetery is indicated 5 miles northeast of Warm Springs on the Eagle Butte 1962 USGS Quad. map.)

WOODS   **B   0.2   2   1901   T9S   R16E   S36**
AKA: 1. ASHWOOD

Located 27 miles east of Madras, 0.5 of a mile north of Ashwood and west off of Trout Creek Road near the Maupin Cemetery. There are 18 known burials. NOTE: This site is on private property. {September 1997} (Ashwood 1987 USGS Quad. map.)

AGENCY PLAINS see **GARD, MILO**	JEFFERSON CO.	T10S	R13E	S9
ASHWOOD see **WOODS**	JEFFERSON CO.	T9S	R16E	S36
BABY [HAY CREEK]	JEFFERSON CO.	T11S	R15E	S9
BIG AGENCY PLAINS see **GARD, MILO**				
	JEFFERSON CO.	T10S	R13E	S9
BIG PLAINS see **GARD, MILO**	JEFFERSON CO.	T10S	R13E	S9
BROWN RANCH, NEGRO see **SMITH, WHISTLING**				
	JEFFERSON CO.	T10S	R13E	S7
BROWNHILL CHILDREN	JEFFERSON CO.	T9S	R13E	S24
BRUNO	JEFFERSON CO.	T9S	R12E	S23
CORWIN see **CULVER I.O.O.F.**	JEFFERSON CO.	T12S	R13E	S16
CULVER I.O.O.F.	JEFFERSON CO.	T12S	R13E	S16
DRY CREEK	JEFFERSON CO.	T9S	R12E	S12
FRIENDS RANCH see **MAUPIN**	JEFFERSON CO.	T9S	R16E	S24
GARD, MILO	JEFFERSON CO.	T10S	R13E	S9
GATEWAY see **KAMPFER FAMILY**	JEFFERSON CO.	T9S	R14E	S11
GENEVA see **GRANDVIEW**	JEFFERSON CO.	T12S	R11E	S36
GERMAN see **METHODIST HILL**	JEFFERSON CO.	T11S	R13E	S32
GRANDVIEW	JEFFERSON CO.	T12S	R11E	S36
GRAY BUTTE	JEFFERSON CO.	T13S	R14E	S6
GRAY'S see **GRAY BUTTE**	JEFFERSON CO	T13S	R14E	S6
GRIZZLY	JEFFERSON CO.	T12S	R15E	S33
HALE see **CULVER I.O.O.F.**	JEFFERSON CO.	T12S	R13E	S16
HALE I.O.O.F. see **CULVER I.O.O.F.**				
	JEFFERSON CO.	T12S	R13E	S16
HALE, MINERVA see **CULVER I.O.O.F.**				
	JEFFERSON CO.	T12S	R13E	S16
HAY CREEK PIONEER	JEFFERSON CO.	T11S	R15E	S9
HAY CREEK RANCH see **HAY CREEK PONEER**				
	JEFFERSON CO.	T11S	R15E	S9
HAY CREEK RANCH see **UNKNOWN**	JEFFERSON CO.	T11S	R15E	?
I.O.O.F. see **CULVER I.O.O.F.**	JEFFERSON CO.	T12S	R13E	S16
I.O.O.F. #196 see **MT. JEFFERSON MEMORIAL PARK**				
	JEFFERSON CO.	T11S	R14E	S6
KALAMA	JEFFERSON CO.	T9S	R12E	S35
KAMPFER, EMMA see **KAMPFER FAMILY**				
	JEFFERSON CO.	T9S	R14E	S11
KAMPFER FAMILY	JEFFERSON CO.	T9S	R14E	S11
KAMPFER, GODFREY see **KAMPFER FAMILY**				
	JEFFERSON CO.	T9S	R14E	S11
LAMONTA see **GRIZZLY**	JEFFERSON CO.	T12S	R15E	S33
LITTLE PLAINS	JEFFERSON CO.	T11S	R13E	?
MADRAS see **MT. JEFFERSON MEMORIAL PARK**				
	JEFFERSON CO.	T11S	R14E	S6
MAUPIN	JEFFERSON CO.	T9S	R16E	S24
McPHERSON, MRS. see **PEARCE, JOHN**				
	JEFFERSON CO.	T10S	R15E	S32
McPHERSON RANCH, CHAS. see **PEARCE, JOHN**				
	JEFFERSON CO.	T10S	R15E	S32
METHODIST HILL	JEFFERSON CO.	T11S	R13E	S32
METOLIUS see **METHODIST HILL**	JEFFERSON CO.	T11S	R13E	S32

MORGAN, M. D. see **BABY [HAY CREEK]**

	JEFFERSON CO.	T11S	R15E	S9
MT. JEFFERSON MEMORIAL PARK	JEFFERSON CO.	T11S	R14E	S6
PEARCE, JOHN	JEFFERSON CO.	T10S	R15E	S32
PEARCE, JOSHUA *[Sic]* see **PEARCE JOHN**				
	JEFFERSON CO.	T10S	R15E	S32
RAJNEESH CREMATORIUM	JEFFERSON CO.	T9S	R18E	S1
ROUND BUTTE PIONEER	JEFFERSON CO.	T11S	R13E	S6
SEEKSEEQUA [NORTH]	JEFFERSON CO.	T10S	R12E	S28
SEEKSEEQUA [SOUTH]	JEFFERSON CO.	T10S	R12E	S27
SMITH, WHISTLING	JEFFERSON CO.	T10S	R13E	S7
TENINO	JEFFERSON CO.	T9S	R12E	S27
UNKNOWN	JEFFERSON CO.	T11S	R15E	?
UPPER WARM SPRINGS RIVER	JEFFERSON CO.	?	?	?
WARM SPRINGS AGENCY see **BRUNO**	JEFFERSON CO.	T9S	R12E	S23
WILLOW CREEK see **GRIZZLY**	JEFFERSON CO.	T12S	R15E	S33
WOODS	JEFFERSON CO.	T9S	R16E	S36

Gard, Milo
Stanley R. Clarke (2000)

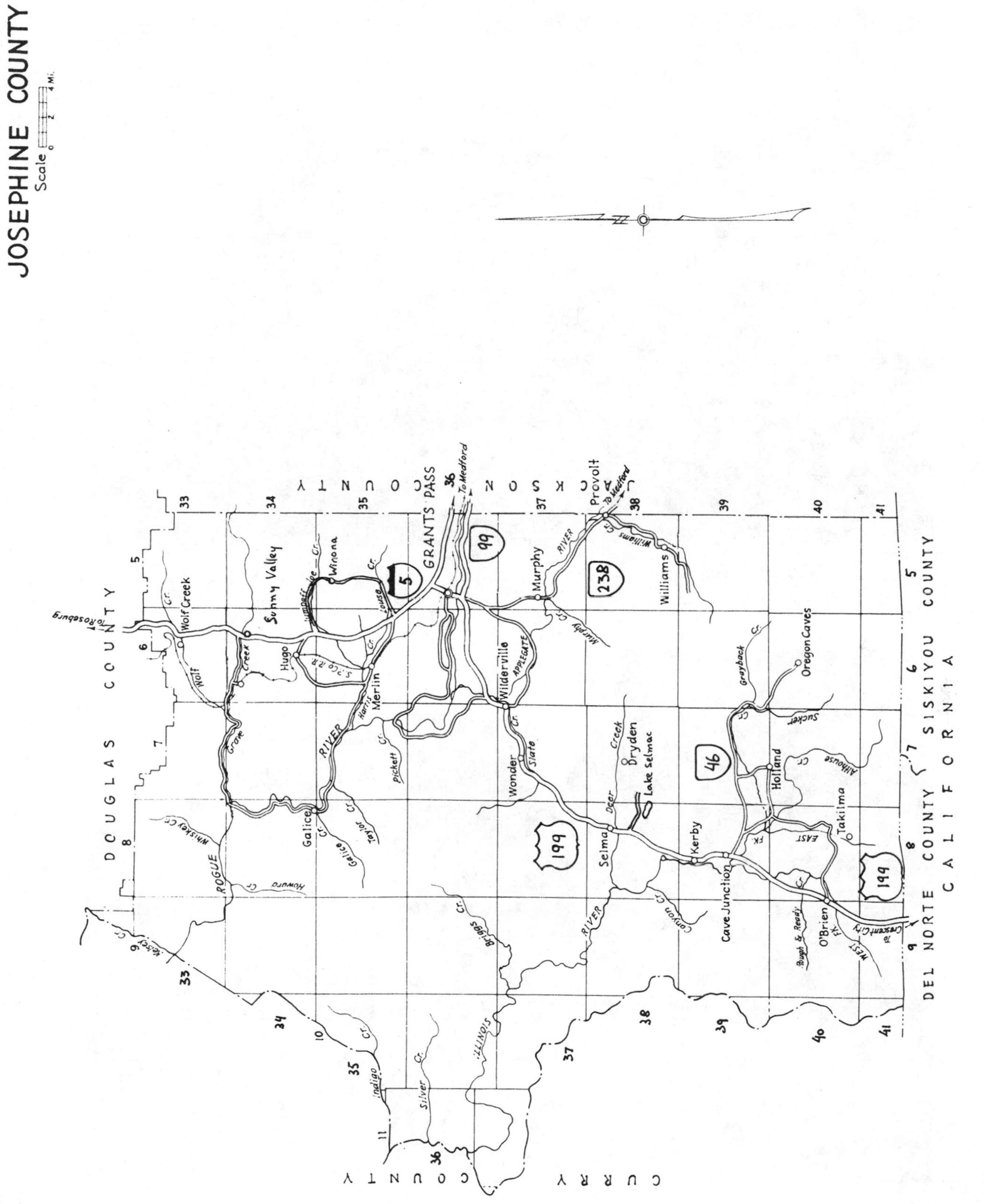

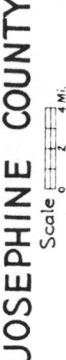

JOSEPHINE COUNTY

Scale

415

I.O.O.F. [Grants Pass]
Janice M. Healy (2000)

Masonic, Pioneer [Grants Pass]
Janice M. Healy (2000)

Area: 1,641 square miles
Population (1998): 74,377
County seat: Grants Pass, Population: 20,255
County established: 22 January 1856

The present area of Josephine County remained "Indian Country" until gold was discovered in 1852. The inevitable Indian wars then erupted which forced the remaining tribes onto distant reservations. There were numerous short-lived mining centers. Sloan Cemetery (1853) is apparently the oldest public cemetery. At least four more were established by 1856 including Croxton now in Grants Pass. Granite Hill (1881) near Grants Pass indicates the later settlement as the gold fever faded.

I.O.O.F. [Grants Pass]
Janice M. Healy (2000)

Masonic, Pioneer [Grants Pass]
Janice M. Healy (2000)

I.O.O.F. [Grants Pass]
Janice M. Healy (2000)

Name of cemetery and also known as	Number of burials	Acres	Condition	Date started or earliest known burial	Township	Range	Section

BOOT HILL   ? ? ? ?   T38S R5W   ?

From the interchange at the south end of the bridge at Grants Pass take OR. Hwy. 238 for Murphy and Provolt. Drive about 14 miles to the junction of Williams Highway at Provolt. Turn right (south) and go about 6 miles to Williams. Boot Hill Cemetery was described as being on top of a hill south of and above the "old town of Williams." This does not suit the topography. The compiler wonders if Boot Hill Cemetery is instead above the site of the old town of Williamsburg, not Williams. Williamsburg was about 3 miles from Provolt. See the article on Williamsburg. (Not shown on Applegate 1983 USGS Quad. map.)

BUTLER, CHARLES   A 0.01 ? 15 Sep 1897 T39S R9W   S10

The marker for Charles Butler is thought to be in the Northeast 1/4 of Section 10 where the USGS Quad map shows a "ruin" just east of the confluence of Hansen Gulch with Canyon Creek. Charles Butler, a Prussian, was born in 1823 or 1826 and died 15 September 1897. NOTE: See also the article for Sebastopol Flats. (Not shown on Cave Junction 1989 USGS Quad. map.)

CORSE, HERMANN HEINRICH   A 0.01 ? 28 Jan 1860 T39S R9W   S10

Located in the Southeast 1/4 of Section 10. This is the site of the lone grave of Hermann Corse, on the west side of Sebastopol Creek near its confluence with Canyon Creek and within the Siskiyou National Forest. *The Grants Pass Daily Courier*, 2 April 1960 reported: Corse, a gold miner, left enough gold to pay for a monument of Italian marble. It was inscribed "Hermann Heinrich Corse, native of Barcelona, Hanover. Died 28 January 1860, age 28 years." The compiler suggests that Barcelona is a misunderstanding for Barsinghausen, a town 16 miles from the city of Hanover, Germany. NOTE: see also the article for Sebastopol Flats. (Not shown on Cave Junction 1989 USGS Quad. map.)

Name of cemetery and also known as	Number of burials	Acres	Condition	Date started or earliest known burial	Township	Range	Section

CROXTON PIONEER MEMORIAL PARK
AKA: 1. OLD INDIAN
     2. PIONEER

| A | 1.82 | 1 | | 1856-1915 | T36S | R5W | S8 |

This cemetery was located at 1001 Memorial Drive, Grants Pass. This is at the east end of Memorial Drive, east of Lincoln School and now a city park. Most of the graves were moved to the I.O.O.F. Cemetery, but some of the remaining markers are emplaced in a concrete border. (Grants Pass 1986 USGS Quad. map.)

DEER CREEK
AKA: 1. DRYDEN
     2. SELMA [NEW]

| C | 5 | 2 | | 1856 | T38S | R7W | S18 |

Leave Redwood Highway, U.S. Hwy.199, at Selma and drive east on Upper Deer Creek Road past Lake Selmac to Lakeshore Drive, 3 miles from the highway. The first recorded burial was that of William Guest, killed by an Indian on 10 March 1856. As of spring of 1994, Kendell Phillips reports there are 445 known burials in Deer Creek Cemetery, plus 4 burials of unknown persons. (Selma 1989 USGS Quad. map.)

DOG CREEK

| A | 0.5 | 5 | | 1850'S | T34S | R6W | S8 |

Leave Interstate I-5 at Sunny Valley Exit 71 onto Sunny Valley Road on the east side of I-5. Drive north on Sunny Valley Road 0.6 of a mile, turn left (west) onto Leland Road, which goes back underneath I-5. Continue on Leland Road for 2.3 miles from Sunny Valley Road, then turn off to the left (southerly) onto Dog Creek Road. Cross Grave Creek and go through the mine tailings. At 0.3 miles from Leland Road is a junction with a private road from the left; the road ahead is also private. The cemetery is on the right (west) 0.4 of a mile from Leland Road. (Glendale 1986 USGS Quad. map.)

ELLIOTT FAMILY

| A | ? | ? | | 1877 | T37S | R7W | ? |

This could be in Sections 10 or 15 about 8 miles south of Grants Pass, on a former stage route, now called Hidden Valley Road. It is located on a pine-covered slope on the property of Walter House. There are burials of Luther Elliott, 1870-1877, and John T. Elliott, 1821-1880, plus other unmarked graves: 15 to 20 in all. Perhaps

Name of cemetery and also known as	Number of burials	Acres	Condition	Date started or earliest known burial	Township	Range	Section

this is in the vicinity of Elliott Creek near Wonder. Elliott Creek Road leaves OR. Hwy. 199 at Highway Milepost 11.30: this is on the left (southerly) when driving from Grants Pass. (Not shown on Selma 1989 USGS Quad. map.)

FERRYDALE

A   0.2   2   1900   T36S R7W   S1

Located at the end of Ferry Road, near the Rogue River opposite Griffin Park, on the old Baumgartner Place. (Not shown on Wilderville 1986 USGS Quad. map.)

FORT BRIGGS

A   0.01   11   1855   T39S R8W   S35

Located in the Northeast 1/4 of Section 35. It is east off of Holland Loop Road a mile or so from OR. Hwy. 38, on a hill that was logged in 1963 and 1964 without noticing any cemetery. However, some apparently human bones were uncovered and reburied on the site next to a well house that was constructed in 1965. The 2 known victims of Indian attacks died on 30 October 1855 and were buried on the hill northeast of Fort Briggs. It is on private property and on the George E. Briggs D.L.C. RB #136. (Not shown on Holland 1989 USGS Quad. map.)

FORT HAYES
  AKA: 1. SELMA [OLD]

A   ?   ?   1856   T37S R8W   S35

Located in the Northwest 1/4 of the Northwest 1/4 of the Northwest 1/4 of the Southwest 1/4 of the Southwest 1/4 of the Northeast 1/4 of Section 35. It is on a knoll behind and to the south of what was first known as Fort Hayes and later as Anderson Station, a stage stop. Drive Redwood Highway, U.S. Hwy. 199, from Grants Pass. At Highway Milepost 17.8 is Draper Valley Road on the left, continue another 720 feet to the intersection of Circle West on the right. Leave U.S. Hwy. 199 onto Circle West and drive northwesterly and north for 0.25 of a mile to a road on the left (west). Turn left (west) and drive about 100 yards to the site of the fort on the left (south). Various dates from 1850 to 1853 have been given for the fort's construction. A skirmish between Indians and

Name of cemetery and also known as	Number of burials	Acres	Condition	Date started or earliest known burial	Township	Range	Section

Co. "E" of the Southern Battalion of the Oregon Mounted Volunteers took place on 24 and 25 March 1856 in which 4 of the volunteers were killed. In addition, Pedro, who helped in the pack train, was also killed. We are indebted to Kendell Phillips for this information. (Not shown on Selma 1989 USGS Quad. map.)

GOTCHER	C	2.5	2	1891	T38S	R5W	S22

Go 4.3 miles south of OR. Hwy. 238 on Water Gap Road; the cemetery is on the west side of the road opposite Sparlin Cemetery. (Williams 1986 USGS Quad. map.)

GRANITE HILL AKA: 1. COUNTY	D	36	2	1881	T36S	R6W	S13

This is located in both Sections 13 and 14, off of Upper River Road before Pinecrest Drive, Grants Pass. The county first purchased 5 acres in February 1895 and another 23.3 acres in December 1912. (Grants Pass 1986 USGS Quad. map.)

GRAVE CREEK AKA: 1. SUNNY VALLEY	A	?	3	1850'S	T34S	R6W	?

This is in Section 2 or 11. Leave the I-5 Freeway at Exit 71 onto Sunny Valley Loop on the east side of the freeway. Proceed north on Sunny Valley Loop for 0.6 of a mile before Leland Road passes under I-5 is, or was, the Frank Price Farm, where the cemetery is located. On the James H. Twogood D.L.C. #37, RB #896. NOTE: This site is on private property. (Not shown on Glendale Quad. 1986 USGS map.)

GUNTER MEMORIAL, CLYDE M.	?	?	?	28 Jun 1937	T36S	R6W	?

"In memory of Clyde M. Gunter who nearby on 28 June 1937 gave his life to save a child from drowning. Dedicated by his brother Elks Lodge #1584." Located somewhere off of Lower River Road. NOTE: This marker is not an actual grave site. Mr. Gunter, a 36 year-old florist, was buried in Hillcrest Memorial Park. (Not shown on Grants Pass or Wilderville 1986 USGS Quad. maps.)

Name of cemetery and also known as	Number of burials	Acres	Condition	Date started or earliest known burial	Township	Range	Section

HALL, J. G.

A   0.01   ?   22 Sep 1867   T35S R6W   S13
Located about 8 miles north of Grants Pass via Highland Avenue Frontage Road. At the north end of state jurisdiction the county road, Gun Club Road, continues ahead along the east side of the I-5 Freeway. The grave is on a 10-foot bank on the right side of Gun Club Road, just within the grounds of the club. NOTE: This site is on private property. (Sexton Mtn. 1986 USGS Quad. map.)

HARRINGTON, LEONARD

A   0.01   1   1904   T38S R8W   S14
This small burial ground is located between Rogue Drive and Redwood Highway (U.S. Hwy. 199) at Selma. Although less than 75 feet west of the highway, it is screened from view by trees and brush. Leonard Harrington was a Civil War veteran and his was a lone grave until the present property owner buried 2 family members in 1989 and 1992. NOTE: This site is on private property. (Not shown on Selma 1989 USGS Quad. map.)

HARRIS CABIN

A   0.01   ?   9 Oct 1855   T35S R6W   S24
A marker for 3 burials is located 6 miles north of Grants Pass at the Manzanita Rest Area at Milepost 63. George Harris was reburied in Jacksonville Cemetery. (The rest area but NOT the marker is on Sexton Mountain 1986 USGS Quad. map.)

HARTLEY
  AKA: 1. METHODIST
       2. WILLIAMS
       3. WILLIAMS
          CREEK

B   2.3   2   1885   T39S R5W   S4
From the interchange at the south end of the bridge at Grants Pass take OR. Hwy. 238 for Murphy and Provolt. Drive about 14 miles to the junction of Williams Highway and go about 6 miles to the Williams Store. Continue ahead on the highway another 1.6 miles to the cemetery on the right (northwest). NOTE: Not to be confused with Williamsburg and Boot Hill cemeteries in this vicinity. See those articles. (Williams 1986 USGS Quad. map.)

HAWTHORNE MEMORIAL GARDENS

D   50   1   1954   T36S R6W   S13
Located off of Upper River Road, before Pinecrest Drive, at 2500 Upper River Road,

Name of cemetery and also known as	Number of burials	Acres	Condition	Date started or earliest known burial	Township	Range	Section

Grants Pass. It is on the south side of the road opposite the Granite Hill Cemetery. (Grants Pass 1986 USGS Quad. map.)

HILLCREST MEMORIAL PARK AND CREMATORY
AKA: 1. JOSEPHINE MEMORIAL PARK

E 45   1   1933   T36S R5W   S8

Located on Northeast 9th and Hillcrest Drive, Grants Pass. (Grants Pass 1986 USGS Quad. map.)

HOLLAND SCHOOL

A   ?   12   1883   T39S R7W   S33

Drive east out of Cave Junction on OR. Hwy. 46 for about 6.2 miles; turn right (south) onto Holland Loop Road. The school was about 1.8 miles from the highway on the left (east) side of Holland Loop Road. Kendell Phillips says nothing remains of this small cemetery which old-timers say had "four or five graves". There were 3 known burials of Kitterman children and a known burial of A. Judd Ganiard, 1852-1894. His marker was removed to the Ashland City Cemetery, but not his body. (Not shown on Holland 1989 USGS Quad. map.)

HOLTON CREEK
AKA: 1. KERBY [OLD]
     2. KERBYVILLE

?   ?   12   1859   T39S R8W   S9

Located in the Northeast 1/4 of Section 9. The old cemetery cannot now be precisely located, but it is off the eastern side of the Redwood Highway (U.S. Hwy. 199) and near the intersection of Holton Creek Road. This is about 27 miles southwest of Grants Pass. There is a church on the west side of the highway here. As late as 1931 this cemetery was still recognizable. A D.A.R. survey in April 1935 identified 10 markers, with the oldest date of 1859 and the latest date of 1868. Some time after 1935 the area was logged and bulldozed over and the cemetery destroyed. Some reburials were made to Laurel Cemetery after 1935, but Kendell Phillips reports that records indicate 12 known burials from 1859 to 1869 still remain somewhere here. It is on the James Kerby D.L.C., RB #1872. (Not shown on Cave Junction 1989 USGS Quad. map.)

Name of cemetery and also known as	Number of burials	Acres	Condition	Date started or earliest known burial	Township	Range	Section

HUNGRY HILL

? ? ? 1855 ? ? ?

31 October-1 November 1855: there are burials of 5 soldiers who were killed by Indians. Located north of Galice and west of Wolf Creek "some miles west of the railway" in Grave Creek Hills. This site was lost even before 1879.

I.O.O.F. [GRANTS PASS]
AKA: 1. GOLDEN RULE
I.O.O.F.
LODGE #73
[GRANTS PASS]
2. TOKAY HEIGHTS

C 6 2 1891 T36 R5W S16

Exit I-5 Freeway from the south at exit #55 onto State Hwy. 199 to Foothill Boulevard. Turn left onto Foothill Boulevard traveling less the 0.5 of a mile to the two cemeteries on your right. The first that you come to is Pioneer Masonic and the second is I.O.O.F. Cemetery. {16 September 2000} (Grants Pass 1986 USGS Quad. Map.)

IDA MINE

? ? 7 ? T35S R5W S26

According to Dan Hager, who was born and raised near here, there was a good-sized cemetery at the Ida Mine at Granite Hill; there also was a post office there in years gone by. It was up Winona Road, northeast of Grants Pass. Mr. Hager was also in charge of Granite Hill Cemetery, on Upper River Road in Grants Pass, at the time of this report in 1978. NOTE: The old locale of Granite Hill, where the Ida Mine is located, is many miles from the present Granite Hill Cemetery. (Ida Mine is shown but no cemetery is shown on the Grants Pass 1986 USGS Quad. map.)

LAUREL
AKA: 1. I.O.O.F. LODGE
#55 OF KERBY
2. KERBY
3. LAUREL HILL
4. MASONIC
[CAVE JUNCTION]

D 35 1 1862 T39S R8W S15

This is the cemetery for Cave Junction and indeed, the principal cemetery in the Illinois Valley. Leave Redwood Highway (U.S. Hwy. 199) just north of Cave Junction, taking Laurel Road to the southeast. The cemetery is on the right, on a hill, after 0.9 of a mile. The first known burial was of an infant on 10 November 1862. Kendell Phillips reports that there are 1,815 documented burials as of early 1994, plus 73 documented unknown burials. Because of the lack of

Name of cemetery and also known as	Number of burials	Acres	Condition	Date started or earliest known burial	Township	Range	Section

records in the first decades of the cemetery there are probably still more burials. (Cave Junction 1989 USGS Quad. map.)

LELAND

? ? ? ? T34S R6W S32

Located south of Wolf Creek, north of the locale of Leland. (Glendale 1986 USGS Quad. map.)

LEONARD FAMILY

A 0.01 2 1874 T40S R7W S4

Located in the Northwest 1/4 of the Northeast 1/4 of Section 4 and situated about 150 yards up the hillside on the northeast side of Browntown Road, about 0.5 of a mile southeast of the townsite of Holland. To reach Holland, leave Cave Junction on the Oregon Caves Highway (OR. Hwy. 38) and drive 1.7 miles; turn right (southerly) onto Holland Loop Road and drive another 5.4 miles to Holland. Turn right (southeasterly) onto Browntown Road. Kendell Phillips reports the enclosed area contains a single red granite marker with 8 names and death dates from 1874 to 1894. (Not shown on Takilma 1989 USGS Quad. map.)

LOWER WOLF CREEK

A 0.01 5 1850'S T33S R6W S30

Leave the I-5 Freeway at Exit 76 from either the north or the south Wolf Creek Exits. Go into the community of Wolf Creek, leaving the interchange connections and take Lower Wolf Creek Road to the north. Pass under the railway overpass and turn hard left (west). You will soon pass Glendale Road on the right (north) which leads to the principal Wolf Creek Cemetery. Continue on Lower Wolf Creek Road for about 4 miles from the interchange connections. There are 3 or 4 graves on the left, between the road and Wolf Creek (the stream), about 100 feet short of Water Tank Gulch. (Glendale 1986 USGS Quad. map.)

LUCKY QUEEN

? ? ? 6 Apr 1914 T34S R5W S32

This bygone mining settlement, named for a nearby gold mine, is east of I-5 Freeway and north of Winona. Leave I-5 on the Jumpoff

Name of cemetery and also known as	Number of burials	Acres	Condition	Date started or earliest known burial	Township	Range	Section

Joe interchange and take Jumpoff Joe Creek Road to the east towards Winona. Drive about 2.5 miles. Turn left (northeasterly) onto Jack Creek Road and go about 0.6 of a mile to the site. The burial ground is probably in this vicinity. Josephine County Death Certificate #1008 for 6 April 1914 reports the death of an unnamed infant of W. H. Pollock and Evabell Kenniston. There were surely other burials. Lucky Queen was important enough to have a post office from Dec 1876 to July 1896 and again from November 1908 to March 1913 under the name of Mountain. (Not shown on Sexton Mtn. 1986 USGS Quad. map.)

MASONIC, PIONEER [GRANTS PASS]
AKA: 1. TOKAY HEIGHTS

C 6 2 1891 T36 R5W S16

Exit I-5 Freeway from the south at exit #55 onto State Hwy. 199 to Foothill Boulevard. Turn left onto Foothill Boulevard traveling less the 0.5 of a mile to the two cemeteries on your right. The first that you come to is Pioneer Masonic and the second is I.O.O.F. Cemetery. {16 September 2000} (Grants Pass 1986 USGS Quad. Map.)

PLACER

A 0.5 3 1850'S T34S R5W S8

Leave the I-5 Freeway at Exit 71 onto the east side of the freeway onto Sunny Valley Loop. At 0.4 of a mile on Sunny Valley Loop turn right (east) onto Placer Road. After going 3.4 miles on Placer Road the driver reaches the crossroads that is signed "Placer". Continue ahead another 100 yards; turn left (north) onto John Street. Go on one-lane John Street for 300 yards to the cemetery on the right (east). (Golden 1986 USGS Quad. map.)

PLEASANT VALLEY
AKA: 1. MERLIN

C 20 2 1870 T35S R6W S11

Located north of Grants Pass on the I-5 Freeway. Leave the freeway at Louse Creek Interchange Exit 61, go north on Monument Drive 3.6 miles; turn east on School Creek Road for 0.1 of a mile. (Merlin 1986 USGS Quad. map.)

Name of cemetery and also known as	Number of burials	Acres	Condition	Date started or earliest known burial	Township	Range	Section

POTTERVILLE

? ? ? ?   T34S R6W   ?

Said to be in Sunny Valley which is located in Section 2. NOTE: No other information was given in the report. (Not shown on Glendale or Golden 1986 USGS Quad. maps.)

ST. LUKE'S PARISH COLUMBARIUM

? ? ? ?   T36S R5W   S18

224 Northwest "D" Street, Grants Pass. (The church is show on the Grants Pass 1986 USGS Quad. map.)

ST. PATRICK'S
AKA: 1. ALLEN GULCH
       2. CATHOLIC

? ? 2 Circa 1860 T40S R8W   S34

This cemetery lies in the upper reaches of Allen Gulch above the bygone mining settlement of Allentown. Although not much more than a mile southeast of Waldo Cemetery as the crow flies, St. Patrick's and Waldo Cemeteries are much farther apart by road. Kendell Phillips reports that a new access road has been built since 1988, but the compiler cannot say whether this access is from the Sanger Peak Road or the Bridgeview-Takilma Road. A church once stood on the grounds but has long since been torn down. During the 1960's and 1970's persons from the counter-cultural settlement at Takilma almost totally destroyed the remaining monuments in St. Patrick's as they did at Waldo Cemetery. Since then a wrought iron fence has been put in place and homemade concrete markers placed on 21 documented burials. There are an additional 29 unknown graves. (O'Brien 1989 USGS Quad. map.)

SEBASTOPOL FLATS
AKA: 1. CANYON CREEK

? ? ? ?   T39S R9W   S15

The marker of a Chinese youth has been lost or stolen. This was a mining area and Kendell Phillips suggests that 25 to 50 additional burials are scattered throughout the area. NOTE: See also the articles for Charles Butler and Hermann Heinrich Corse which are also buried in this general vicinity. (Not shown on Cave Junction 1989 USGS Quad. map.)

Name of cemetery and also known as	Number of burials	Acres	Condition	Date started or earliest known burial	Township	Range	Section

SLATE CREEK

A   0.01   7   ?   T37S R7W   ?
Possibly located in Section 17 or 18. There are graves of 2 West family babies. NOTE: This site is on private property, on the Slate Creek Ranch (1978). (Not shown on Selma 1989 USGS Quad. map.)

SLOAN
  AKA: 1. RIVER BANK
           FARM

C   1.2   2   1853   T36S R6W   S30
Leave U.S. Hwy. 199 between Grants Pass and Cave Junction just after crossing the Applegate River. Turn right (northerly) onto Rogue River Loop and drive about 1.6 miles. The cemetery is tree-covered and on the right (east), several hundred yards from the road. Access appears to be by private driveway or on foot. There were 52 known burials (1966). (Wilderville 1986 USGS Quad. map.)

SPARLIN
  AKA: 1. SPARLING

C   3   4   1861   T38S R5W   S22
Located 4.3 miles south of OR. Hwy. 238, on Water Gap Road. This cemetery is on the east side of the road opposite Gotcher Cemetery. (Williams 1986 USGS Quad. map.)

SPENCE FAMILY

A   0.01   ?   1883   T40S R8W   S2
Located in the Northwest 1/4 of Section 2. This small fenced burial ground is on private property at 3862 Takilma Road. Take OR. Hwy. 46 from Cave Junction for about 2 miles; turn right (southerly) on Holland Loop Road for about 1.9 miles to the junction with Takilma Road to the right (south) at Bridgeview. This junction was once called Spence Corners and a Spence School was nearby. The cemetery is on the right (west) about 75 feet from the road and apparently before the bridge over Althouse Creek. There are two markers to the daughters of Dr. James C. Spence and Susan Higgins. Both girls died of diphtheria. Eva Louse Spence, born 17 September 1873, died 10 September 1883; Laurie Eldora Spence, born 11 June 1877, died 14 August 1883. In addition there is a monument for Daniel Allen, a neighbor who died 31 May 1891. (Not shown on Takilma 1989 USGS Quad. map.)

Name of cemetery and also known as	Number of burials	Acres	Condition	Date started or earliest known burial	Township	Range	Section

UNKNOWN
? 0.5 ? ?   T33S R5W   S29

Might this cemetery be called Bear Gulch or Golden? Reportedly, a "Boot Hill" Cemetery was constructed for a movie, made in the 1950's and then left in place. Is this so? As you can see this one has us puzzled. To reach this site leave the I-5 Freeway at the South Wolf Creek Interchange at Milepost 76, going to the right (east). Turn right (south) onto Coyote Creek Road, which parallels the freeway for aways before turning inland to the east. At 3.5 miles from the freeway is a sign: "Down Town Golden." Before that, at 3.3 miles, is a road to the right, downhill, known as Bill Lane. It crosses Coyote Creek and the maintenance of the road stops at 0.4 of a mile from Coyote Creek Road. The driveway continues ahead, crosses Bear Gulch and then climbs the hillside on the east side of the gulch to the cemetery, which is about a mile from Coyote Creek Road. (Golden 1986 USGS Quad. map.)

UNKNOWN
? ? ? ?   T36S R8W   S18

This is possibly the Briggs family burial, in the Briggs Valley Picnic Area at the confluence of Briggs Creek and Horse Creek. (Chrome Ridge 1989 USGS Quad. map.)

UNKNOWN
A 0.2 5 1874   T37S R6W   ?

Located in Section 13 or 14 on the D. Bud Combe Farm (1999), at 6211 New Hope Road, Grants Pass near the hills. This is very close to New Hope School at the Junction of New Hope and Hidden Valley Roads. NOTE: This site is on private property. (Not shown on Murphy 1986 USGS Quad. map.)

VANNOY
? ? ? ?   T36S R6W   ?

Possibly located in Section 16 or 17. A very small cemetery, within the boundaries of a mint field adjoining Riverbanks Road. NOTE: This site is on private property. (Not shown on Wilderville 1986 USGS Quad. map.)

Name of cemetery and also known as	Number of burials	Acres	Condition	Date started or earliest known burial	Township	Range	Section

WALDO

C   0.5   2   1858   T40S R8W   S28

Drive south from Cave Junction on OR. Hwy. 199 towards the California State line for about 7 miles. Turn right (east) onto Waldo Road. Drive about 2.65 miles, turn right (southerly) off of Waldo Road and head for the small butte known as Waldo Hill. The cemetery, on top of the hill is reached after driving about 0.4 of a mile from Waldo Road. 213 marked graves were noted in December 1957, with many more unmarked. Kendell Phillips reports that in 1993 only a few gravestones remain and only 33 burials can be documented. 40 more are documented but the locations are unknown. In the 1960's and early 1970's a counter-culture settlement was established at Takilma and the residents desecrated this cemetery, hauling away gravestones for hearths and even for walkway stones. Waldo Cemetery is now cleaned up annually by the Illinois Valley Historical Society. The land is owned by the Bureau of Land Management. (O'Brien 1989 USGS Quad. map.)

WALKER GULCH
  AKA: 1. BROWNTOWN
        2. GRASS FLAT
        3. TIGERTOWN

? ? ? ?   T40S R7W   S15

Walker Gulch itself is a short tributary to Althouse Creek. The road in this area is the Althouse Creek Road. The county road runs for about 3 miles south from Holland and then the Siskiyou National Forest Road continues. Browntown was located at the mouth of Walker Gulch and the cemetery was about "one mile up the hill from the site of Browntown." This presumably means to the east, up Walker Gulch. This was mining country; the sites of Grass Flat and Tigertown are not known to the compiler. Kendell Phillips records of 5 burials between 1859 and 1902. Show James Althouse, died between 1870/1880 at Browntown; Joseph Delaney, died 1 January 1873, at Browntown; John Ghirardelli born 1839 Genova, Soglio, Italy died 1902 on Althouse Creek, near Browntown; _____ Hubert died 3 January 1873 on East Fork of Althouse Creek; Samuel Hurd died 1859 at Browntown. (Not shown on Takilma 1989 USGS Quad. map.)

431

Name of cemetery and also known as	Number of burials	Acres	Condition	Date started or earliest known burial	Township	Range	Section

WILDERVILLE   C 9   2   1903   T37S R6W   S6

1.1 miles southeast of U.S. Hwy. 199 via Wilderville Frontage Road and Fish Hatchery Road; it is on a hill to the right (south). (Wilderville 1986 USGS Quad. map.)

WILLIAMSBURG   ? ?   ?   ?   T38S R5W   S24

R. F. Lewman, an old time resident said that Williamsburg was in the north half of the Northeast 1/4 of Section 24 and was located on a rise just east (left) of Williams Highway. See the article on Williamsburg in Lewis L. McArthur's: *Oregon Geographic Names*. From the interchange at the south end of the bridge at Grants Pass take OR. Hwy. 238 for Murphy and Provolt. Turn right (south) onto Williams Highway and go about 3 miles, about halfway to the present locale of Williams. Boot Hill Cemetery was reported as being on top of a hill above Williams, but it seems to the compiler that the description better suits Williamsburg. The latter settlement was active in the later 1850's and early 1860's a generation prior to Williams. However the compiler cannot be certain. See the article on Boot Hill Cemetery. (Not shown on Applegate 1983 USGS Quad. map.)

WOLF CREEK   C 1.4   2   1856   T33S R6W   S15

Leave the (southbound) I-5 Freeway at the North Wolf Creek Exit 76. Go 0.3 of a mile on a connection and then turn right (northerly) onto Lower Wolf Creek Road. Cross under the railway overpass and turn hard left; at 0.5 of a mile from the freeway turn right (north) onto Glendale Road. Continue to the cemetery on the left (west), 0.65 of a mile from the freeway. There were 241 marked graves (D.A.R.); 1922 was the latest date noted. (Glendale 1986 USGS Quad. map.)

WONDER   ? ?   ?   ?   T37S R7W   ?

The locale of Wonder is in section 9. This cemetery might be in Section 9 or 10. Perhaps Wonder is an A.K.A. for Elliott

Name of cemetery and also known as	Number of burials	Acres	Condition	Date started or earliest known burial	Township	Range	Section

Cemetery; see that article. NOTE: No other information was given in the report. (Not shown on Selma 1989 USGS Quad. map.)

I.O.O.F. [Grants Pass]
Janice M. Healy (2000)

I.O.O.F. [Grants Pass]
Janice M. Healy (2000)

I.O.O.F. [Grants Pass]
Janice M. Healy (2000)

ALLEN, DANIEL see **SPENCE FAMILY**	JOSEPHINE CO.	T40S	R8W	S2
ALLEN GULCH see **ST. PATRICKS**	JOSEPHINE CO.	T40S	R8W	S34
ALTHOUSE, JAMES see **WALKER GULCH**				
	JOSEPHINE CO.	T40S	R7W	S15
BAUMGARTNER PLACE see **FERRYDALE**	JOSEPHINE CO.	T36S	R7W	S1
BOOT HILL	JOSEPHINE CO.	T38S	R5W	?
BRIGGS D.L.C., GEORGE E. see **FORT BRIGGS**				
	JOSEPHINE CO.	T39S	R8W	S35
BRIGGS FAMILY see **UNKNOWN**	JOSEPHINE CO.	T36S	R8W	S18
BROWNTOWN see **WALKER GULCH**	JOSEPHINE CO.	T40S	R7W	S15
BUTLER, CHARLES	JOSEPHINE CO.	T39S	R9W	S10
CANYON CREEK see **SABASTOPOL FLATS**				
	JOSEPHINE CO.	T39S	R9W	S15
CATHOLIC see **ST. PATRICKS**	JOSEPHINE CO.	T40S	R8W	S34
COMBE FARM, D. BUD see **UNKNOWN**	JOSEPHINE CO.	T37S	R6W	?
CORSE, HERMANN see **CORSE, HERMANN HEINRICH**				
	JOSEPHINE CO.	T39S	R9W	S10
CORSE, HERMANN HEINRICH	JOSEPHINE CO.	T39S	R9W	S10
COUNTY see **GRANITE HILL**	JOSEPHINE CO.	T36S	R6W	S13
CROXTON PIONEER MEMORIAL PARK	JOSEPHINE CO.	T36S	R5W	S8
DEER CREEK	JOSEPHINE CO.	T38S	R7W	S18
DELANEY, JOSEPH see **WALKER GULCH**				
	JOSEPHINE CO.	T40S	R7W	S15
DOG CREEK	JOSEPHINE CO.	T34S	R6W	S8
DRYDEN see **DEER CREEK**	JOSEPHINE CO.	T38S	R7W	S18
ELLIOTT FAMILY	JOSEPHINE CO.	T37S	R7W	?
ELLIOTT, JOHN T. see **ELLIOTT FAMILY**				
	JOSEPHINE CO.	T37S	R7W	?
ELLIOTT, LUTHER see **ELLIOTT FAMILY**				
	JOSEPHINE CO.	T37S	R7W	?
FERRYDALE	JOSEPHINE CO.	T36S	R7W	S1
FORT BRIGGS	JOSEPHINE CO.	T39S	R8W	S35
FORT HAYES	JOSEPHINE CO.	T37S	R8W	S35
GANIARD, A. JUDD see **HOLLAND SCHOOL**				
	JOSEPHINE CO.	T39S	R7W	S33
GHIRARDELLI, JOHN see **WALKER GULCH**				
	JOSEPHINE CO.	T40S	R7W	S15
GOLDEN RULE I.O.O.F. LODGE #78 [GRANTS PASS] see **I.O.O.F. [GRANTS PASS]**				
	JOSEPHINE CO.	T36S	R5W	S16
GOTCHER	JOSEPHINE CO.	T38S	R5W	S22
GRANITE HILL	JOSEPHINE CO.	T36S	R6W	S13
GRASS FLAT see **WALKER GULCH**	JOSEPHINE CO.	T40S	R7W	S15
GRAVE CREEK	JOSEPHINE CO.	T34S	R6W	?
GUEST, WLLIAM see **DEER CREEK**	JOSEPHINE CO.	T38S	R7W	S18
GUNTER, CLYDE M. see **GUNTER MEMORIAL, CLYDE M.**				
	JOSEPHINE CO.	T36S	R6W	?
GUNTER MEMORIAL, CLYDE M.	JOSEPHINE CO.	T36S	R6W	?
HAGER, DAN see **IDA MINE**	JOSEPHINE CO.	T35S	R5W	S26
HALL, J. G.	JOSEPHINE CO.	T35S	R6W	S13
HARRINGTON, LEONARD	JOSEPHINE CO.	T38S	R8W	S14
HARRIS CABIN	JOSEPHINE CO.	T35S	R6W	S24
HARRIS, GEORGE see **HARRIS CABIN**	JOSEPHINE CO.	T35S	R6W	S24

HARTLEY	JOSEPHINE CO.	T39S	R5W	S4
HAWTHORNE MEMORIAL GARDENS	JOSEPHINE CO.	T36S	R6W	S13
HIGGINS, SUSAN see **SPENCE FAMILY**				
	JOSEPHINE CO.	T40S	R8W	S2
HILLCREST MEMORIAL PARK AND CREMATORY				
	JOSEPHINE CO.	T36S	R5W	S8
HOLLAND SCHOOL	JOSEPHINE CO.	T39S	R7W	S33
HOLTON CREEK	JOSEPHINE CO.	T39S	R8W	S9
HUBERT, _____ see **WALKER GULCH**				
	JOSEPHINE CO.	T40S	R7W	S15
HUNGRY HILL	JOSEPHINE CO.	?	?	?
HURD, SAMUEL see **WALKER GULCH**	JOSEPHINE CO.	T40S	R7W	S15
I.O.O.F. [GRANTS PASS]	JOSEPHINE CO.	T36	R5W	S16
I.O.O.F. LODGE #55 OF KERBY see **LAUREL**				
	JOSEPHINE CO.	T39S	R8W	S15
IDA MINE	JOSEPHINE CO.	T35S	R5W	S26
JOSEPHINE MEMORIAL PARK see **HILLCREST MEMORIAL PARK AND CREMATORY**				
	JOSEPHINE CO.	T36S	R5W	S8
KERBY see **LAUREL**	JOSEPHINE CO.	T39S	R8W	S15
KERBY D.L.C., JAMES see **HOLTON CREEK**				
	JOSEPHINE CO.	T39S	R8W	S9
KERBY [OLD] see **HOLTON CREEK**	JOSEPHINE CO.	T39S	R8W	S9
KERBYVILLE see **HOLTON CREEK**	JOSEPHINE CO.	T39S	R8W	S9
KITTERMAN CHILDREN see **HOLLAND SCHOOL**				
	JOSEPHINE CO.	T39S	R7W	S33
LAUREL	JOSEPHINE CO.	T39S	R8W	S15
LAUREL HILL see **LAUREL**	JOSEPHINE CO.	T39S	R8W	S15
LELAND	JOSEPHINE CO.	T34S	R6W	S32
LEONARD FAMILY	JOSEPHINE CO.	T40S	R7W	S4
LEWMAN, R. F. see **WILLIAMSBURG**	JOSEPHINE CO.	T38S	R5W	S24
LOWER WOLF CREEK	JOSEPHINE CO.	T33S	R6W	S30
LUCKY QUEEN	JOSEPHINE CO.	T34S	R5W	S32
MASONIC, PIONEER [GRANTS PASS]	JOSEPHINE CO.	T36S	R5W	S16
MASONIC [CAVE JUNCTION] see **LAUREL**				
	JOSEPHINE CO.	T39S	R8W	S15
MERLIN see **PLEASANT VALLEY**	JOSEPHINE CO.	T35S	R6W	S11
METHODIST see **HARTLEY**	JOSEPHINE CO.	T39S	R5W	S4
OLD INDIAN see **CROXTON PIONEER MEMORIAL PARK**				
	JOSEPHINE CO.	T36S	R5W	S8
PEDRO see **FORT HAYES**	JOSEPHINE CO.	T37S	R8W	S35
PIONEER see **CROXTON PIONEER MEMORIAL PARK**				
	JOSEPHINE CO.	T36S	R5W	S8
PLACER	JOSEPHINE CO.	T34S	R5W	S8
PLEASANT VALLEY	JOSEPHINE CO.	T35S	R6W	S11
POLLOCK, EVABELL KENNISTON see **LUCKY QUEEN**				
	JOSEPHINE CO.	T34S	R5W	S32
POLLOCK INFANT see **LUCKY QUEEN**	JOSEPHINE CO.	T34S	R5W	S32
POLLOCK, W. H. see **LUCKY QUEEN**	JOSEPHINE CO.	T34S	R5W	S32
POTTERVILLE	JOSEPHINE CO.	T34S	R6W	?
PRICE FARM, FRANK see **GRAVE CREEK**				
	JOSEPHINE CO.	T34S	R6W	?
RIVER BANK FARM see **SLOAN**	JOSEPHINE CO.	T36S	R6W	S30

ST. LUKE'S PARISH COLUMBARIUM	JOSEPHINE CO.	T36S	R5W	S18
ST. PATRICK'S	JOSEPHINE CO.	T40S	R8W	S34
SEBASTOPOL FLATS	JOSEPHINE CO.	T39S	R9W	S15
SELMA [NEW] see **DEER CREEK**	JOSEPHINE CO.	T38S	R7W	S18
SELMA [OLD] see **FORT HAYES**	JOSEPHINE CO.	T37S	R8W	S35
SLATE CREEK	JOSEPHINE CO.	T37S	R7W	?
SLATE CREEK RANCH see **SLATE CREEK**				
	JOSEPHINE CO.	T37S	R7W	?
SLOAN	JOSEPHINE CO.	T36S	R6W	S30
SPARLIN	JOSEPHINE CO.	T38S	R5W	S22
SPARLING see **SPARLIN**	JOSEPHINE CO.	T38S	R5W	S22
SPENCE, DR. JAMES C. see **SPENCE FAMILY**				
	JOSEPHINE CO.	T40S	R8W	S2
SPENCE, EVA LOUSE see **SPENCE FAMILY**				
	JOSEPHINE CO.	T40S	R8W	S2
SPENCE FAMILY	JOSEPHINE CO.	T40S	R8W	S2
SPENCE, LAURIE ELDORA see **SPENCE FAMILY**				
	JOSEPHINE CO.	T40S	R8W	S2
SUNNY VALLEY see **GRAVE CREEK**	JOSEPHINE CO.	T34S	R6W	?
TIGERTOWN see **WALKER GULCH**	JOSEPHINE CO.	T40S	R7W	S15
TOKAY HEIGHTS see **I.O.O.F. [GRANTS PASS]**				
	JOSEPHINE CO.	T36S	R5W	S16
TOKAY HEIGHTS see **MASONIC, PIONEER [GRANTS PASS]**				
	JOSEPHINE CO.	T36S	R5W	S16
TWOGOOD D.L.C., JAMES H. see **GRAVE CREEK**				
	JOSEPHINE CO.	T34S	R6W	?
UNKNOWN	JOSEPHINE CO.	T33S	R5W	S29
UNKNOWN	JOSEPHINE CO.	T36S	R8W	S18
UNKNOWN	JOSEPHINE CO.	T37S	R6W	?
VANNOY	JOSEPHINE CO.	T36S	R6W	?
WALDO	JOSEPHINE CO.	T40S	R8W	S28
WALKER GULCH	JOSEPHINE CO.	T40S	R7W	S15
WEST FAMILY BABIES see **SLATE CREEK**				
	JOSEPHINE CO.	T37S	R7W	?
WILDERVILLE	JOSEPHINE CO.	T37S	R6W	S6
WILLIAMS see **HARTLEY**	JOSEPHINE CO.	T39S	R5W	S4
WILLIAMS CREEK see **HARTLEY**	JOSEPHINE CO.	T39S	R5W	S4
WILLIAMSBURG	JOSEPHINE CO.	T38S	R5W	S24
WOLF CREEK	JOSEPHINE CO.	T33S	R6W	S15
WONDER	JOSEPHINE CO.	T37S	R7W	?

I.O.O.F. [Grants Pass]
Janice M. Healy (2000)

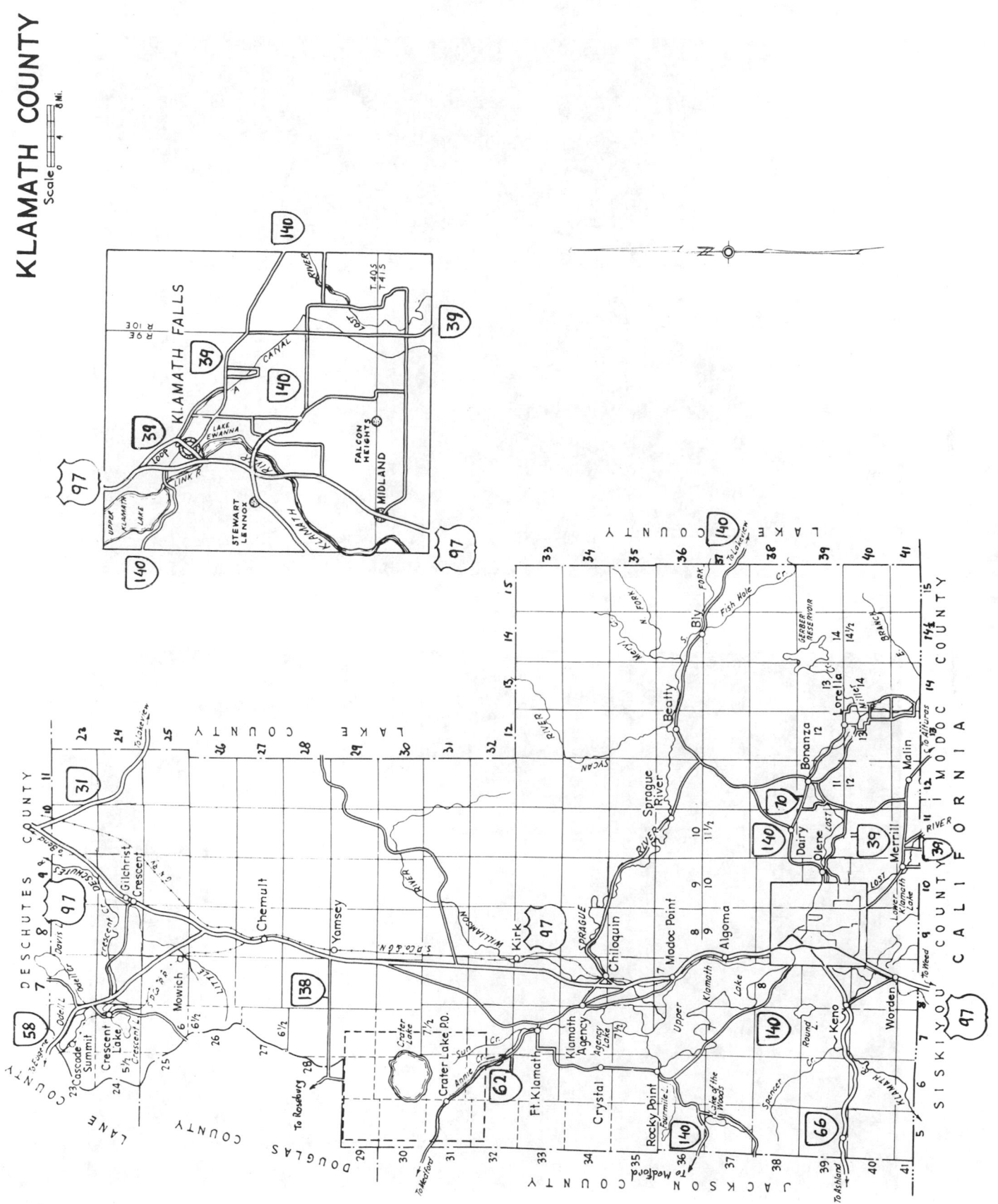

Brown
Janice M. Healy (2000)

Brown
Janice M. Healy (2000)

Area: 6,135 square miles
Population (1998): 63,185
County seat: Klamath Falls,
Population: 18,765
County established: 17 October 1882

Klamath County has more Indian cemeteries, at least 13, than any other county in Oregon. Linkville Cemetery (1872) in Klamath Falls was the earliest sizable burial ground for whites. Eight more public cemeteries were in use by 1900. Malin (1910) marks one of the two Czech settlements in Oregon known to the compiler.

Brown
Janice M. Healy (2000)

Unknown

Ruth C. Bishop (2000)

Name of Cemetery and also known as	Number of burials	Acres	Condition	Date started or earliest known burial	Township	Range	Section

BEDFIELD
AKA: 1. POE VALLEY

C 1 2 1886 **T40S R11E** **S1**
Go 6.7 miles south and southwest of Bonanza via Harpold Road; it is located on the east side of Bedfield Cemetery Road in Poe Valley. (Bonanza and Malin 1988 USGS Quad. maps.)

BENSINGER, ESSIE
AKA: 1. BENZINGER, ESSIE

A 0.01 ? 20 Jun 1907 **T37S R10E** **S19**
The lone grave of this 5-year old child, born 25 Aug. 1902, who was the daughter of A. E. and Carrie Bensinger (also spelled Benzinger). The burial is marked by a field stone and is west of the old home on Sunnyside Ranch. It is located about 0.5 or 0.75 of a mile north of Coleman Road and south of Swan Lake Road (1985). (Whiteline Reservoir 1985 USGS quad. map.)

BLY [NEW]
AKA: 1. CARTWRIGHT PLACE
2. PARKER PLACE

A ? ? 1901-1945 **T36S R14E** **S28**
There are 2 separate cemeteries known as Bly. The new Bly Cemetery was first used in 1901 and abandoned about 1945 (undated statement in a letter). This new cemetery was about 2 miles west of Bly, on the north side of OR. Hwy. 140 near the Ivory Pine Road junction. It was on the edge of a pine grove on the Monte Cline Ranch. (Not shown on Bly 1988 USGS Quad. map.)

BLY [OLD]

A ? ? 1874-1901 ? ? ?
The old Bly Cemetery was described as being "on a hill close to Bly settlement." Six or seven burials were known and most, but not all, were reburied about 1902 in the new Bly Cemetery. (Not shown on Bly 1988 USGS Quad. map.)

BONANZA MEMORIAL PARK
AKA: 1. LOST RIVER

D 5.4 1 1882 **T39S R12E** **S10**
Located on sections 10 and 15. Go 0.5 of a mile east of the bridge over Lost River, east of Bonanza. (Bonanza 1988 USGS Quad. map.)

BROWN
AKA: 1. BIG BELLY
2. MASCASKET
3. MASEKESKET

C 3 2 Circa 1876 **T36S R12E** **S13**
The earliest visible date was 1876. At Beatty on OR. Hwy. 140, turn north on Dowa Springs Road. Going north about 2 miles turn

Klamath County

| Name of Cemetery and also known as | Number of burials | Acres | Condition | Date started or earliest known burial | Township | Range | Section |

4. MO-GHEN-KAS-
   KET
5. YAINAX

right (east) on Sycan Road, at the end of the black top veer to the right. At about 0.4 of a mile you will see the old rail road switching yard and the end of the rail road tracks. Also on the right at the end of the rail road is an old house, house #25750 about opposite of this turn to your left (east), and then again to your right (south). Go about 0.3 of a mile the road forks again take the left fork to the cemetery which is about 0.1 of a mile up hill from the last fork. The site is fenced and gated. {16 September 2000} (Ferguson Mountain 1988 USGS Quad. map.)

CASEY FAMILY

A ? ? 1897-1901 T39S R11 1/2E ?
Probably in Section 32. Burials of J. T. Casey, died 16 Sept. 1897 and wife Jennie, died 5 Nov. 1901, are on what was the Casey Place, on a hill on the west side of Poe Valley. Leave OR. Hwy. 140 onto South Poe Valley Road. Go 6 miles, then turn right (west) onto Webber Road at a 90 degree turn. Go west on Webber Road 1.3 miles to its end. (Not shown on Dairy 1985 USGS Quad. map.)

COPPERFIELD FAMILY

? ? ? ? ? ? ?
Reportedly this family cemetery is near Chiloquin. No other information was given in the report. (Not shown on Chiloquin 1988 or Agency Lake 1985 USGS Quad. maps.)

CRUME FAMILY

? ? ? ? T36S R12E ?
An Indian family buried at Beatty. (1960's information.) NOTE: No other information was given in the report. (Not shown on Beatty 1988 USGS Quad. map.)

CRYSTAL

A ? 11 1904-1918 T34S R6E ?
This could be in section 26 or 35 on the west side of Upper Klamath Lake. There are 3 known burials now covered over by the Crystal Creek Lodge parking lot on the west side of the road. (Not shown on Crystal Spring 1985 USGS Quad. map.)

Name of Cemetery and also known as	Number of burials	Acres	Condition	Date started or earliest known burial	Township	Range	Section

DAIRY
AKA: 1. ROBERTS

A ? 5 1892   T38S R11 1/2E ?

The exact location for this cemetery is now unknown. There are 4 known burials, one dating from 1892: Henry and Billy Roberts, Mrs. McCurdy and a Callahan baby. (Not shown on Dairy 1985 USGS Quad. map.)

DANFORTH, BABY GIRL

A ? ? ?   T34S R6E   S23

Located on the site of the Dodge family home on the west side of the road, in the area of Crystal. The daughter of F. J. and Mary Jane Brown Danforth. NOTE: This site is on private property. (Not shown on Crystal Spring 1985 USGS Quad. map.)

EGGSMAN

A ? ? ?   T36S R7E   S15

Indian children are buried just north of Modoc Point, east of U.S. Hwy. 97. There are no markers in a fenced area which contains about 10 burials. (Not shown on Modoc Point 1985 USGS Quad. map.)

**ETERNAL HILLS
MEMORIAL GARDENS**

D 20.4 1 ?   T39S R10E   S18

Located east of Klamath Falls, at 4711 Highway 39; 1 mile south of the junction with OR. Hwy. 140, on the left side. (Altamont 1985 USGS Quad. map.)

FORT KLAMATH MEMORIAL

C 1.1 2 1863   T33S R7 1/2E   S22

Near Fort Klamath Junction on OR. Hwy. 62, just west of the junction with Sun Mountain Highway and on the south side of the road. The earliest existing marker is 1876. The military occupied Fort Klamath from 1863-1889. There were 59 soldiers buried here: all were supposed to have been moved to the Presidio in San Francisco, but bones are still found here. (Fort Klamath 1985 USGS Quad. map.)

FRIENDSHIP
AKA: 1. FRIENDS

C 1.13 3 1870   T34S R7E   S34

This is mostly an Indian cemetery located at Chiloquin. From the Chiloquin Highway junction in town, turn south onto 1st Street and go 1 block to Schonchin Street. Drive 3

Name of Cemetery and also known as	Number of burials	Acres	Condition	Date started or earliest known burial	Township	Range	Section

blocks on Schonchin Street and turn left (north) onto Valley Street. The cemetery is on the right, on the slope. NOTE: The city map lists this as Friendship. (Chiloquin 1988 USGS Quad. map.)

GABRIEL FAMILY

A 0.25 5 1929-1947 T37S R9E S25
This is located on the northwest edge of Swan Valley. Take a public road 0.75 of a mile south off of Swan Lake Road. Turn left (east), go up a draw and over the ridge top for about 1 mile. Three burials are behind a house on the hill (5 Oct. 1985). NOTE: This site is on private property. (Whiteline Reservoir 1985 USGS Quad. map.)

GOODMAN CHILDREN

A ? ? ? T39S R12E ?
Perhaps in Section 30, 6 miles east of Bonanza on the Sanford Jones Place. Drive 4.7 miles from Bonanza on the East Langell Valley Road, then turn hard right onto Jones Lane and continue another 0.5 of a mile. The graves are probably on the left (south). Two children are buried here. NOTE: This site is on private property. No further information was given in the report. (Not shown on Lorella 1988 USGS Quad. map.)

HALL
AKA: 1. HAYNESVILLE
    2. LORELLA
    3. NOBLE
    4. OLD LORELLA

A 0.15 ? 1882-1915 T39S R14E S32
Travel 2 miles east and northeast of Lorella on Gerber Reservoir Road, then turn south 0.5 of a mile and east 400 feet. The cemetery is closed to further burials. There were 9 graves in 1968, with some reburials to the Bonanza Cemetery. (Goodlow Mountain 1988 USGS Quad. map.)

HIBBERT
AKA: 1. SWAN LAKE

A 0.25 ? 1907-1927 T38S R10E S8
This cemetery is located on the west side of Swan Lake Road, 5.8 miles northwest of its junction with Klamath Falls-Lakeview Highway, (OR. Hwy. 140). There were 3 burials (5 Oct. 1985). (Whiteline Reservoir 1985 USGS Quad. map.)

Name of Cemetery and also known as	Number of burials	Acres	Condition	Date started or earliest known burial	Township	Range	Section

HILL, DAVID
AKA: 1. HILL

C 7.4 2 1911   T35S R7E   S32
Located near the Williamson River on the south side of Day School Road; 1.4 miles west of the junction with U.S. Hwy. 97 and 0.2 of a mile east of the junction of Modoc Point Highway, about 5 miles north of Modoc Point. This is an Indian cemetery. (Shoalwater Bay 1985 USGS Quad. map.)

HODSON

A ?   ? 1921-1923   T38S R11 1/2E ?
Located in Section 9 or 10. Leave OR. Hwy. 140 to the left just east of Dairy onto Hildebrand Road. Go north 3.4 miles to Drews Ranch, where Hildebrand Road makes a 90-degree turn to the right (east). The burials, however, are about 1 mile west of this 90-degree turn. There are 2 known burials on the Parker Place (1923). NOTE: This site is on private property. (Not shown on Swan Lake 1985 USGS Quad. map.)

I.O.O.F. [MERRILL]

D 5.7 1 1924   T40S R10E   S33
Travel 1.75 miles northwest of the center of town on OR. Hwy. 39, to a crossroads. Turn left (west) on I.O.O.F. Cemetery Road and cross the railway tracks. Then turn right (north) at 1 mile; the cemetery is on your left. (Lost River 1986 USGS Quad. map.)

JACKSON FAMILY, HENRY
AKA: 1. COBURN
         FAMILY

? ?   ? 1929   T36S R11E   S29
Located 4 miles southeast of the community of Sprague River, 1.5 miles south of Sprague River Road and south of the Yainax Agency site approximately 0.5 of a mile. Henry Jackson was an Indian. There are mainly just 2 families buried here; the Jackson family and Coburn family. (Not shown on Sprague River East 1988 USGS Quad. map.)

KENO

C 2.2 3 1882   T40S R8E   S6
Located at Keno, on the east side of road. Go 0.25 of a mile south of OR. Hwy. 66 on the road to Worden. (Hamaker Mountain 1986 USGS Quad. map.)

Klamath County

Name of Cemetery and also known as	Number of burials	Acres	Condition	Date started or earliest known burial	Township	Range	Section

KLAMATH COUNTY POOR FARM

? ? ? ? ? ? ?

The Klamath County Poor Farm was described as "one mile south of Klamath Falls." Death Certificate #124 for 17 January 1910 states that John Brown, a 28 year old laborer died of typhoid and was buried at the Poor Farm. The compiler does not know exactly where the location is or how many more burials there were. (Not shown on Klamath Falls 1985 USGS Quad. map.)

KLAMATH MEMORIAL PARK

E 10 1 1946 T39S R9E S8

Turn off of U.S. Hwy. 97 on Fountain Avenue and Memorial Drive junction, take Memorial Drive and go 0.5 of a mile to 2680 Memorial Drive. (Klamath Falls 1985 USGS Quad. map.)

LINKVILLE
AKA: 1. I.O.O.F. [KLAMATH FALLS]

E 16 1 1872 T38S R9E S29

Closed, circa 1958, except for those with reserved plots. There are 4,000 graves with over 300 unknown burials (1958). The entrance is from Upham Street. This site was originally two cemeteries which are now combined as one. (Klamath Falls 1985 USGS Quad. map.)

LOBERT

? 2.4 2 ? T34S R7E S31

This is an Indian cemetery accessible from two different state highways. From Crater Lake Hwy. (OR. Hwy. 62), at its junction with U.S. Hwy. 97 north of Klamath Falls, drive north about 0.63 of a mile to a crossroads. Turn off of OR. Hwy. 62 to the left (west) and drive 100 yards to a junction; the driveway on the right leads to the Modoc Point Hwy., but continue ahead 0.2 of a mile to the cemetery. The access from Modoc Point Hwy. is 2 miles south of its junction with OR. Hwy. 62, with access to Lobert Cemetery on the right (east). (Agency Lake 1985 USGS Quad. map.)

MALIN COMMUNITY
AKA: 1. MALIN
2. TURKEY HILL

D 6.4 1 1910 T41S R12E S10

Located 0.5 of a mile northwest of downtown Malin. Leave OR. Hwy. 39 at 6th Street, go north to the end of 6th Street at

Name of Cemetery and also known as	Number of burials	Acres	Condition	Date started or earliest known burial	Township	Range	Section

Washington Avenue. Turn right (east) onto Washington and follow to Malin Cemetery Road. Turn left (north and west) up the hill to the cemetery. (Malin 1988 USGS Quad. map.)

MODOC WARRIORS
AKA: 1. FORT KLAMATH
     2. MILITARY
       POST

A ? 2 3 Oct. 1873 T33S R7 1/2E S23
Old Fort Klamath is now a county park and museum (1972). This cemetery is located at the west end of the park, which is 0.25 of a mile south of the junction of Sun Mountain Highway and the west side of OR. Hwy. 62. Modoc warriors are buried here. (Fort Klamath 1985 USGS Quad. map.)

MT. CALVARY MEMORIAL PARK

? 15 1 1932 T39S R10E S8
Located east of Klamath Falls and Altamont. Go east from the junctions of OR. Hwy. 39 (to Merrill) and OR. Hwy 140. After traveling 1.9 miles east, on OR. Hwy 140, from that junction you are at Milepost 7.4. Turn left (north) onto Pine Grove Road and drive 0.25 of a mile to the cemetery on the right (east) side of the road. (Altamont 1985 USGS Quad. map.)

MT. LAKI
AKA: 1. FAIRVIEW
     2. HENLEY

D 5.7 1 1909 T40S R9E S2
Take U. S. Hwy. 97 south from Klamath Falls, going a mile past Midland. At Milepost 283.3 turn left (southeast) off of the highway onto Cross Road. Continue southeast for 1.75 miles, then turn left (east); keep going for a total of 4.10 miles from U. S. Hwy. 97 to the cemetery on the left (north) side of the road. (Lost River 1986 USGS Quad. map.)

OLD MERRILL
AKA: 1. MERRILL
       TOWN
     2. OLD TULELAKE

? ? ? 1896 T41S R10E S12
Located at the southeast edge of town, in back of the St. Augustine Catholic Church on Lost River. Leave OR. Hwy. 39 about opposite Willow Street and turn right (south), towards the river. (Merrill 1986 USGS Quad. map.)

Name of Cemetery and also known as	Number of burials	Acres	Condition	Date started or earliest known burial	Township	Range	Section

PAIUTE

? 2.75 2 1911   T35S R12E   S35

This is an Indian cemetery. Go north from OR. Hwy. 140 at Beatty for 3.1 miles on Godowa Road; then go 0.25 of a mile on Godowa Road to the cemetery access road on the right (east). (Beatty 1988 USGS Quad. map.)

ROCK CREEK
AKA: 1. YAINAX
      AGENCY

? 0.15 ? ?   T36S R11E   S20

Located about 3 miles east of the locale of Sprague River, about 0.85 of a mile southwest of Sprague River Road and 0.34 of a mile northwest of the site of Old Yainax Agency on the right. (Sprague River East 1988 USGS Quad. map.)

SCHONCHIN, CHIEF AND WINEMA

D 1 3 ?   T36S R11E   S25

Located southwest of Beatty approximately 5.5 miles. Leave OR. Hwy. 140 at Milepost 35.9 onto Sprague River Road. Go 1.15 miles on Sprague River Road; turn right (northerly) onto the access road and go another 0.7 of a mile to the cemetery. The graves of Indian Chief Schonchin and Winema are on the southeast foot of Bug Butte. (Beatty 1988 USGS Quad. map.)

SPENCER

C 0.4 5 1871-1905   T39S R7E   S30

Go west from Keno on the Green Springs Highway (OR. Hwy. 66) for 6.6 miles, crossing the Spencer Bridge over the Klamath River. Turn right (northwest) off of the highway onto the Keno B. L. M. Road and drive northerly 0.9 of a mile to a crossroads. Turn right (northeast) and go 0.82 of a mile; then turn right again, towards the reservoir, for 0.2 of a mile to the cemetery. 10 gravesites are visible and 16 others known (D.A.R. visit, 1967). (Spencer Creek 1986 USGS Quad. map.)

UNKNOWN

A 0.01 ? ?   T37S R15E   S8

This lone grave is in Section 8 on the Southeast 1/4 of the Southeast 1/4. Go northeast off of OR. Hwy. 140 then turn off at the Sprague River Picnic Area exit. Turn right at a fork within 400 yards of the

Name of Cemetery and also known as	Number of burials	Acres	Condition	Date started or earliest known burial	Township	Range	Section

highway. Go another 0.2 of a mile to a locked gate and the remains of an old building, this is private property clearly signed "No Trespassing". The grave is reported to be on the south bank of the river about 600 feet east of the gate. The area has been logged over the old road in is very steep with very little room for turning around. {16 September 2000} (Paradise Mountain 1988 USGS Quad. map.)

WAY

B 0.34 ? 1884-1932 T41S R6E S8

Located 13 miles south of OR. Hwy. 66 from Topsy Park, near Frain Ranch (1978). This is on Topsy Road, 0.75 of a mile from the California State Line and 0.1 of a mile north of the county road. About 30 graves are on the Thomas Way Place; 11 known burials and 17 or 18 unmarked burials (1985), with 1889 being the earliest dated marker. NOTE: This site is on private property. (Mule Hill 1985 USGS Quad. map.)

WILSON

C 10 5 ? T35S R7E S16

This is an Indian cemetery, located 1 mile southeast of Chiloquin Highway on Wilson Cemetery Road. (Agency Lake 1985 USGS Quad. map.)

WOODLAWN

? 40.5 ? 1928-1930 T39S R9E S5

In use from April 1928 to May 1930, located along OR. Hwy. 66. NOTE: Presumably the burials here were removed to other cemeteries. (Not shown on Klamath Falls 1985 USGS Quad. map.)

WORDEN
 AKA: 1. GORDON

B 0.2 5 1903-1948 T40S R8E S34

Drive south from Klamath Falls on U.S. Hwy. 97 to Worden, about 3.5 miles short of the California State Line. Continue southerly to the junction with the county road to Keno on the right. Cross over the railway tracks, turn right and head back northerly parallel to the railway. The cemetery is on the left about 0.9 of a mile from the junction with U.S. Hwy. 97 and about due west of the locale

Name of Cemetery and also known as	Number of burials	Acres	Condition	Date started or earliest known burial	Township	Range	Section

of Worden. There are 26 known burials within the enclosure and one grave outside of the fence. (Worden 1986 USGS Quad. map.)

Brown

Janice M. Healy (2000)

BEDFIELD	KLAMATH CO.	T40S	R11E	S1
BENSINGER, A. E. see **BENSINGER, ESSIE**				
	KLAMATH CO.	T37S	R10E	S19
BENSINGER, CARRIE see **BENSINGER, ESSIE**				
	KLAMATH CO.	T37S	R10E	S19
BENSINGER, ESSIE	KLAMATH CO.	T37S	R10E	S19
BENZINGER, ESSIE see **BENSINGER, ESSIE**				
	KLAMATH CO.	T37S	R10E	S19
BIG BELLY see **BROWN**	KLAMATH CO.	T36S	R12E	S13
BLY [NEW]	KLAMATH CO.	T36S	R14E	S28
BLY [OLD]	KLAMATH CO.	?	?	?
BONANZA MEMORIAL PARK	KLAMATH CO.	T39S	R12E	S10
BROWN	KLAMATH CO.	T36S	R12E	S13
BROWN, JOHN see **KLAMATH COUNTY POOR FARM**				
	KLAMATH CO.	?	?	?
CALLAHAN BABY see **DAIRY**	KLAMATH CO.	T38S	R11 1/2E	?
CARTWRIGHT PLACE see **BLY [NEW]**	KLAMATH CO.	T36S	R14E	S28
CASEY FAMILY	KLAMATH CO.	T39S	R11 1/2E	?
CASEY, J. T. see **CASEY FAMILY**	KLAMATH CO.	T39S	R11 1/2E	?
CASEY, JENNIE see **CASEY FAMILY**	KLAMATH CO.	T39S	R11 1/2E	?
CASEY PLACE see **CASEY FAMILY**	KLAMATH CO.	T39S	R11 1/2E	?
CLINE RANCH, MONTE see **BLY [NEW]**				
	KLAMATH CO.	T36S	R14E	S28
COBURN FAMILY see **JACKSON FAMILY, HENRY**				
	KLAMATH CO.	T36S	R11E	S29
COPPERFIELD FAMILY	KLAMATH CO.	?	?	?
CRUME FAMILY	KLAMATH CO.	T36S	R12E	?
CRYSTAL	KLAMATH CO.	T34S	R6E	?
DAIRY	KLAMATH CO.	T38S	R11 1/2E	?
DANFORTH, BABY GIRL	KLAMATH CO.	T34S	R6E	S23
DANFORTH, F. J. see **DANFORTH, BABY GIRL**				
	KLAMATH CO.	T34S	R6E	S23
DANFORTH, MARY JANE BROWN see **DANFORTH, BABY GIRL**				
	KLAMATH CO.	T34S	R6E	S23
DREWS RANCH see **HODSON**	KLAMATH CO.	T38S	R11 1/2E	?
EGGSMANN	KLAMATH CO.	T36S	R7E	S15
ETERNAL HILLS MEMORIAL GARDENS	KLAMATH CO.	T39S	R10E	S18
FAIRVIEW see **MT. LAKI**	KLAMATH CO.	T40S	R9E	S2
FORT KLAMATH see **MODOC WARRIORS**	KLAMATH CO.	T33S	R7 1/2E	S23
FORT KLAMATH MEMORIAL	KLAMATH CO.	T33S	R7 1/2E	S22
FRIENDS see **FRIENDSHIP**	KLAMATH CO.	T34S	R7E	S34
FRIENDSHIP	KLAMATH CO.	T34S	R7E	S34
GABRIEL FAMILY	KLAMATH CO.	T37S	R9E	S25
GOODMAN CHILDREN	KLAMATH CO.	T39S	R12E	?
GORDON see **WORDEN**	KLAMATH CO.	T40S	R8E	S34
HALL	KLAMATH CO.	T39S	R14E	S32
HAYNESVILLE see **HALL**	KLAMATH CO.	T39S	R14E	S32
HENLEY see **MT. LAKI**	KLAMATH CO.	T40S	R9E	S2
HIBBERT	KLAMATH CO.	T38S	R10E	S8
HILL see **HILL, DAVID**	KLAMATH CO.	T35S	R7E	S32
HILL, DAVID	KLAMATH CO.	T35S	R7E	S32
HODSON	KLAMATH CO.	T38S	R11 1/2E	?

I.O.O.F. [KLAMATH FALLS] see **LINKVILLE**				
	KLAMATH CO.	T38S	R9E	S29
I.O.O.F. [MERRILL]	KLAMATH CO.	T40S	R10E	S33
JACKSON FAMILY, HENRY	KLAMATH CO.	T36S	R11E	S29
JACKSON, HENRY see **JACKSON FAMILY, HENRY**				
	KLAMATH CO.	T36S	R11E	S29
KENO	KLAMATH CO.	T40S	R8E	S6
KLAMATH COUNTY POOR FARM	KLAMATH CO.	?	?	?
KLAMATH MEMORIAL PARK	KLAMATH CO.	T39S	R9E	S8
LINKVILLE	KLAMATH CO.	T38S	R9E	S29
LOBERT	KLAMATH CO.	T34S	R7E	S31
LORELLA see **HALL**	KLAMATH CO.	T39S	R14E	S32
LOST RIVER see **BONANZA MEMORIAL PARK**				
	KLAMATH CO.	T39S	R12E	S10
MALIN see **MALIN COMMUNITY**	KLAMATH CO.	T41S	R12E	S10
MALIN COMMUNITY	KLAMATH CO.	T41S	R12E	S10
MESCASKET see **BROWN**	KLAMATH CO.	T36S	R12E	S13
MASEKESKET see **BROWN**	KLAMATH CO.	T36S	R12E	S13
McCURDY, MRS. see **DAIRY**	KLAMATH CO.	T38S	R11 1/2E	?
MERRILL TOWN see **OLD MERRILL**	KLAMATH CO.	T41S	R10E	S12
MILITARY POST see **MODOC WARRIORS**				
	KLAMATH CO.	T33S	R7 1/2E	S23
MO-GHEN-KAS-KET see **BROWN**	KLAMATH CO.	T36S	R12E	S13
MODOC WARRIORS	KLAMATH CO.	T33S	R7 1/2E	S23
MT. CALVARY MEMORIAL PARK	KLAMATH CO.	T39S	R10E	S8
MT. LAKI	KLAMATH CO.	T40S	R9E	S2
NOBLE see **HALL**	KLAMATH CO.	T39S	R14E	S32
OLD LORELLA see **HALL**	KLAMATH CO.	T39S	R14E	S32
OLD MERRILL	KLAMATH CO.	T41S	R10E	S12
OLD TULELAKE see **OLD MERRILL**	KLAMATH CO.	T41S	R10E	S12
PAIUTE	KLAMATH CO.	T35S	R12E	S35
PARKER PLACE see **BLY [NEW]**	KLAMATH CO.	T36S	R14E	S28
PARKER PLACE see **HODSON**	KLAMATH CO.	T38S	R11 1/2E	?
POE VALLEY see **BEDFIELD**	KLAMATH CO.	T40S	R11E	S1
ROBERTS see **DAIRY**	KLAMATH CO.	T38S	R11 1/2E	?
ROBERTS, BILLY see **DAIRY**	KLAMATH CO.	T38S	R11 1/2E	?
ROBERTS, HENRY see **DAIRY**	KLAMATH CO.	T38S	R11 1/2E	?
ROCK CREEK	KLAMATH CO.	T36S	R11E	S20
SCHONCHIN, CHIEF AND WINEMA	KLAMATH CO.	T36S	R11E	S25
SPENCER	KLAMATH CO.	T39S	R7E	S30
SWAN LAKE see **HIBBERT**	KLAMATH CO.	T38S	R10E	S8
TURKEY HILL see **MALIN COMMUNITY**	KLAMATH CO.	T41S	R12E	S10
UNKNOWN	KLAMATH CO.	T37S	R15E	S8
WAY	KLAMATH CO.	T41S	R6E	S8
WAY PLACE, THOMAS see **WAY**	KLAMATH CO.	T41S	R6E	S8
WILSON	KLAMATH CO.	T35S	R7E	S16
WOODLAWN	KLAMATH CO.	T39S	R9E	S5
WORDEN	KLAMATH CO.	T40S	R8E	S34
YAINAX see **BROWN**	KLAMATH CO.	T36S	R12E	S13
YAINAX AGENCY see **ROCK CREEK**	KLAMATH CO.	T36S	R11E	S20

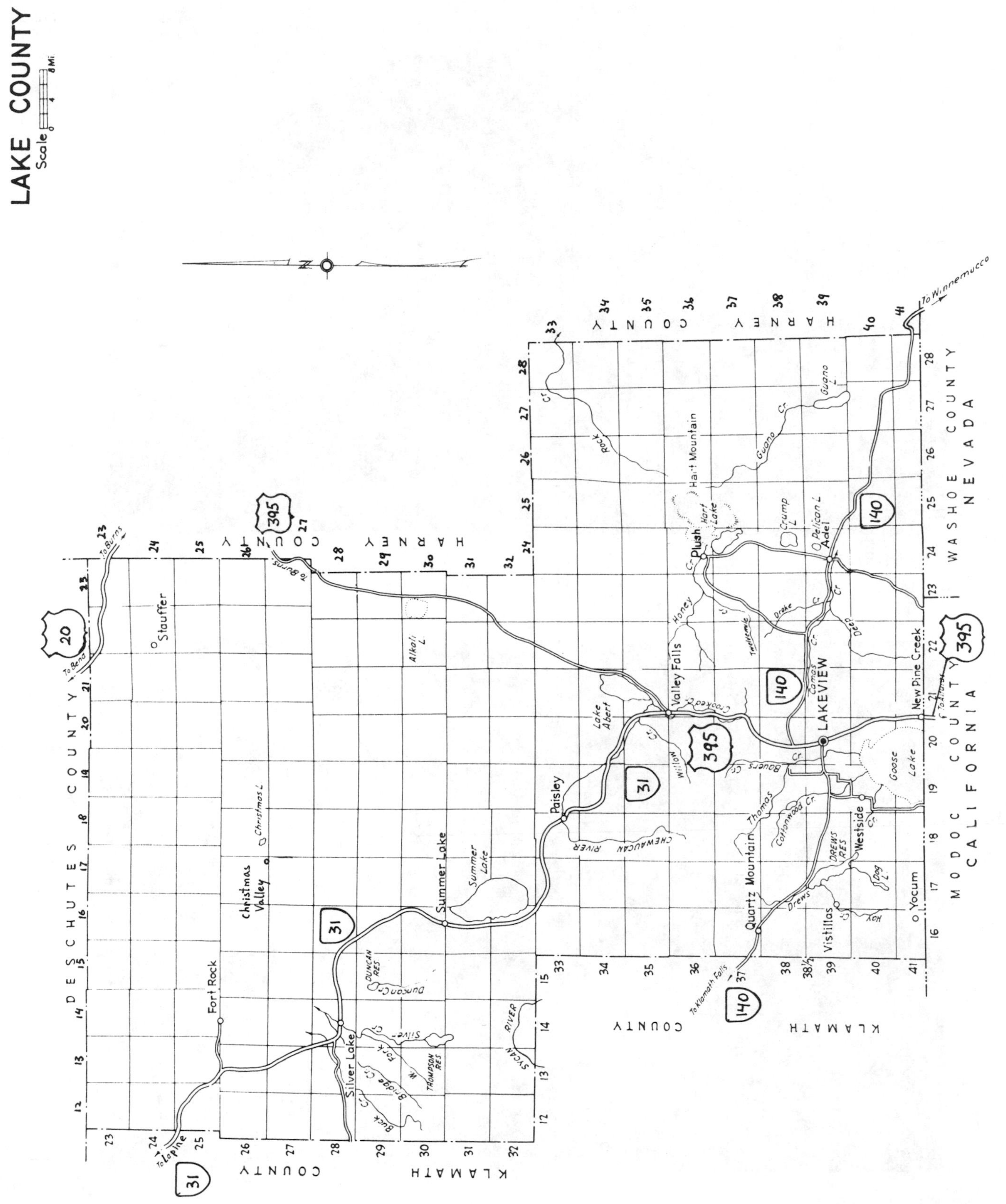

LAKE COUNTY

Scale 0 4 8 Mi.

Fort Rock
Ruth C. Bishop (2000)

Fort Rock
Janice M. Healy (2000)

Area: 8,359 square miles
Population (1998): 7,152
County seat: Lakeview, Population: 2,655
County established: 24 October 1874

Lake County was occupied by settlers for livestock ranching and by homesteaders of dry-land agriculture. The latter more often failed after the boom years of 1908-1914. The first organized public cemetery was the I.O.O.F. at Lakeview in 1879. Six more public cemeteries were established by 1909.

Silver Lake
Janice M. Healy (2000)

Lake County

Mitchell Monument
Janice M. Healy (2000)

Name of Cemetery and also known as	Number of burials	Acres	Condition	Date started or earliest known burial	Township	Range	Section

ADEL [NEW]

? ? 1 1988   T39S R24E   S21

Located on top of a small hill on the left off of OR. Hwy. 140 when coming from Lakeview just before reaching the Adel store. It has a chain link fence and about half of it is under irrigation and grass. (Not shown on Adel 1968 USGS Quad. map.)

ADEL [OLD]

? ? 5 ?   T39S R24E   ?

Located south of Adel about 0.75 of a mile and west of the road to Fort Bidwell, California. This site is overgrown but fenced and there are no markers left. Reportedly the burials are of Indians and MC Ranch hands. There are no known records. (Not shown on Adel 1968 USGS Quad. map.)

ADEL AREA

? ? ? ?   T39S R24E   ?

This locale has scattered burials. (Not shown on Adel 1968 USGS Quad. map.)

CAMP WARNER
AKA: 1. FORT WARNER

A ? 8 1867   T36S R22E   S33

The military occupied Camp Warner from 1 September 1867 until its abandonment on 3 September 1874. The first post in this area was known as Old Camp Warner; see that article. The *Dalles Chronicle* of 20 June 1900 reports that "the remains of the soldiers buried for over thirty years in the military cemetery at Fort Warner are now being exhumed and it is understood they will be shipped to the Presidio in San Francisco." The site of Camp Warner is on private property and is not easily reached. (Little Honey Creek 1968 USGS Quad. map.)

CHEWAUCAN

A 0.03 3 1878   T34S R19E   S33

Leave Paisley on OR. Hwy. 31 towards Valley Falls and Lakeview. Go about 7.5 or 8 miles to the junction of Clover Flat Road to the right and south. Drive about 4.5 or 5 miles almost to Schoolhouse Road. The cemetery is on the right (west) from Clover Flat Road on private property, currently owned by J-Spear Ranch. It is on a hill top within a 12 foot by 12 foot metal fence. Four graves are

459

known but only the tombstone of Absalom Bringle, died 8 April 1878 remains. {July 1998} (Not shown on Tucker Hill 1966 USGS Quad map.)

CHRISTMAS VALLEY   A   5   ?   Jan. 1987   T27S R17E   S28
In the Northeast 1/4 of the Northwest 1/4 of Section 28; located about 2.5 miles southwesterly from the center of Christmas Valley as the crow flies, on the lower eastern slope of Sevenmile Ridge. By road the distance is about 6 miles, go about 3 miles due south on Old Lake Road and then turn right (west, and northwesterly) and right (due north) to the cemetery. There are 3 burials at this new cemetery as of January 1992. (Not shown on Christmas Valley 1986 USGS Quad. map.)

FORT ROCK   B   1.1   2   1909   T25S R14E   S29
  AKA: 1. FORT ROCK
       PIONEER
Go 1 mile north of the locale of Fort Rock and then 0.5 of a mile west; it is at the base of Fort Rock. In June 1965, there were 13 stones found with 20 unreadable markers. In September 1972, a visitor found 37 markers, plus 2 illegible markers and several unmarked graves, with 2 burials in 1965. A great majority of the burials are 1910-1919. Our visit found new burials, the site is fenced and gated. {15 September 2000} (Fort Rock 1981 USGS Quad. map.)

HESS, DOC.   ?   ?   ?   Circa 1912   T39S R24E   S16
Located in the Adel area, he was buried in a field in back of Charlie Crump's Ranch House, 0.25 of a mile north of Adel. Reportedly Hess was of questionable character because of his keen interest in liquor. "The women of Adel hated him because their men hung out too often at the Hess Place." NOTE: This site appears to be on private property. (Not shown on Adel 1968 USGS Quad. map.)

Name of Cemetery and also known as	Number of burials	Acres	Condition	Date started or earliest known burial	Township	Range	Section

I.O.O.F. [LAKEVIEW]
AKA: 1. CATHOLIC

D 25   2   1879   T39S R20E   S10
This cemetery is located on "J" Street North at the north end of Lakeview, on U.S. Hwy. 395. {15 September 2000} (Lakeview N.E. 1964 USGS Quad. map.)

INDIAN

? ?   ? Circa 1920 T39S R24E   S20
There are a number of unmarked burials southwest of Adel at the mouth of Deep Creek Canyon; on the south side of the creek, which is on the south side of OR. Hwy. 140, 0.75 of a mile west of Adel. (Not shown on Adel 1968 USGS Quad. map.)

JOHNSON, DOCTOR

A   0.01 ? Circa 1912 T39S R24E   ?
This burial is located somewhere in Adel. Doctor Johnson was a dentist; the exact location of his burial is unknown. NOTE: No other information was given in the report. (Not shown on Adel 1968 USGS Quad. map.)

LONE GRAVE [UNKNOWN]

A   0.01 ? ?   T37S R28E   S34
Go 25.7 miles east from Adel on the Warner Highway (OR. Hwy. 140). Just before leaving the Guano Valley and ascending the Doherty Slide, turn left (north) off of OR. Hwy. 140 onto Beatys Butte Road. Follow this road for about 20.5 miles passing the east side of Guano Lake. This lone grave is about a mile north of Lone Grave Waterhole, on the east side of Lone Grave Butte and about 100 yards to the right (east) of Beatys Butte Road. NOTE: The compiler does not know the identity or date of the burial. (Lone Grave Butte 1971 USGS Quad. map.)

MITCHELL MONUMENT

? 0.1 1 1950   T36S R16E   S19
This is on Section 19 and 20. Leave OR. Hwy. 140, 1.4 miles east of Bly, at Milepost 55.3 in Klamath County, turning left onto Campbell Road. Go 0.5 of a mile north on Campbell Road, then turn right (easterly) onto Forestry Road #34 and enter the Fremont National Forest. This is about 7 miles from OR. Hwy. 140, a mile inside of Lake County, near Salt Spring and Leonard Creek. The

Name of Cemetery and also known as	Number of burials	Acres	Condition	Date started or earliest known burial	Township	Range	Section

monument reads: "In Memory Of: Elsie Mitchell age 26, Dick Patzke age 14, Jay Gifford age 13, Edward Engen age 13, Joan Patzke age 13, Sherman Shoemaker age 11, who died here May 5, 1945 by Japanese bomb explosion, only place on the American continent where death resulted from enemy action dudring WWII." Rev. Archie Mitchell of Bly and wife Elsie, who was 5 months pregnant, took the 5 children for a picnic. While Mitchell was parking their vehicle and speaking with some timber company employees, Mrs. Mitchell and the children got out and were about 100 yards distant. She called out "Look what I found, dear." There was a big explosion. The object had been a high-explosive fragmentation bomb delivered by a hydrogen-filled paper balloon that had floated from Japan. Mrs. Mitchell died in a few minutes; the children were killed instantly. Mitchell remarried and was a missionary in, of all places, the highlands of Vietnam. The mission was overrun in about 1964 by the Viet Cong and he and his second wife were never seen again. The present monument was erected by the Weyerhaeuser Company in 1950. There are no burials at this site. {16 September 2000} (Gearhart Mountain 1988 USGS Quad. map.)

NEW PINE CREEK

C 3.8 ? 1904 T41S R21E S19
This cemetery is located 0.25 of a mile north of the California Line on U.S. Hwy. 395, then east 0.3 of a mile. (Crane Creek 1964-79 USGS Quad. map.)

OLD CAMP WARNER

A ? 8 1867 T36S R25E S24
The site of this military establishment is less than 0.25 of a mile downstream from the Blue Sky Hotel Camp in the Hart Mountain Antelope Refuge. The military occupied this site from 15 July 1866 to 1 September 1867 when it was removed to a different location many miles to the west and was named Camp Warner. See the article under that heading. Presumably any burials at this site were also moved. (Warner Peak 1967 USGS Quad. map.)

Name of Cemetery and also known as	Number of burials	Acres	Condition	Date started or earliest known burial	Township	Range	Section

PAISLEY
AKA: 1. I.O.O.F.

C 3.7 2 1881 T33S R18E S24
This cemetery is fenced and on a hill just south of Paisley. (Paisley 1966-80 USGS Quad. map.)

PARTIN FAMILY

A 0.01 2 ? T30S R16E S23
Located about 1.5 miles south of the community of Summer Lake, west of OR. Hwy. 31. It is on private property on the southwest side of Jacks Lake; four known burials. (Not shown on Summer Lake 1966-80 USGS Quad. map.)

PLUSH

? ? ? ? T36S R24E ?
Possibly located on Section 29. The locale of Plush did have a cemetery, but the last markers were picked up about 1965 (1966 information). Six people were buried "back of Plush" and 2 miners were buried farther back on a hill. (Not shown on Plush 1967 USGS Quad. map.)

ROUSCOE, MRS. DAVE

? 0.01 ? Circa 1912 T39S R24E S16
Located 0.25 of a mile north and 0.75 of a mile east of Adel. This unmarked grave is on the O'Keefe Ranch. Mrs. Rouscoe is buried with her baby daughter; reportedly she is best remembered as the aunt of 2 brothers serving life for murder in Nevada. NOTE: This site is on private property. (Not shown on Adel 1968 USGS Quad. map.)

SHIRK RANCH

A ? ? 1887 T38S R27E ?
This is on Section 26 or Section 35. There are two graves of a horse thief and a companion, who were shot. These graves are located at the Hart Mountain Antelope Refuge, which included the old Shirk Ranch. (NOT shown on Guano Lake 1968 USGS Quad. map.)

SILVER LAKE

C 2 1 1881 T28S R14E S22
Located approximately 0.3 of a mile east of 9th Street on the Fremont Highway (OR. Hwy. 31) in Silver Lake. There is a massive monument with the names and ages of the 44

Name of Cemetery and also known as	Number of burials	Acres	Condition	Date started or earliest known burial	Township	Range	Section

victims of a fire in an upstairs hall 24
December 1894. {15 September 2000}
(Silver Lake 1968 USGS Quad. map.)

SUMMER LAKE

B   0.6   2   1885   T31S R16E   S10

Go 5.8 miles south of the locale of Summer
Lake. It is located on the east side of OR.
Hwy. 31, beside a grove of cottonwood trees
with a red barn. {15 September 2000}
(Summer Lake 1966-80 USGS Quad. map.)

SUNSET
  AKA: 1. SUNSET PARK

D   3.9   2   1919   T39S R20E   S10

Located adjacent to the I.O.O.F. Cemetery on
"J" Street, at the north end of Lakeview on
U.S. Hwy. 395. (Lakeview N.E. 1964 USGS
Quad. map.)

UNKNOWN

A   0.2   3   1845   T29S R23E   S35

Go 2 miles north of the Alkali Maintenance
Station on U.S. Hwy. 395 and turn right at
Leehman Cow Camp onto Big Juniper Road. Go
2.3 miles on Big Juniper Road to a fork; turn
right, go uphill past the gravel pit another
0.3 of a mile. The graves are about 100
yards south of the road on the right. There
is a 100-foot square plot with 3 graves that
are outlined; possibly 2 adults and 1 child.
These are more burials from the Lost Wagon
Train of 1845. (Venator Canyon 1984 USGS
Quad. map.)

WESTSIDE
  AKA: 1. NICKELS
          FAMILY

C   2   1   1896   T40S R19E   S6

Go west 7.3 miles from Lakeview on OR. Hwy.
140 to Five Corners at Milepost 91.7. Turn
south and west on West Side Road, go another
7.3 miles to Dog Lake Road; turn right (west)
go another 1.5 miles. The cemetery is on the
north side of Dog Lake Rd. This cemetery was
begun as a burial ground for the Nickels
family and was incorporated 2 March 1896.
(Fitzwater Point 1964-80 USGS Quad. map.)

XL RANCH
  AKA: 1. ABERT LAKE

A   0.01   ?   1845   T33S R21E   S31

There is one grave: either a young woman and
her baby, or a young woman and an unborn

Name of Cemetery and also known as	Number of burials	Acres	Condition	Date started or earliest known burial	Township	Range	Section

child.   Located along Abert Lake Road on the
northwest side of Lake Abert. The burial is
several miles south of the old "XL" Ranch
House.   The burial is reported to be one of
the immigrants of the Lost Wagon Train.
NOTE: This site is on private property.   (Not
shown on Coglan Buttes N.E. 1966-80 USGS
Quad. map.)

Fort Rock
Red, White and Blue Ribbons
Janice M. Healy (2000)

Lake County

Silver Lake
Monument for the 44 victims of the 24 December 1894 fire. 466
Janice M. Healy (2000)

ABERT LAKE see **XL RANCH**	LAKE CO.	T33S	R21E	S31
ADEL [NEW]	LAKE CO.	T39S	R24E	S21
ADEL [OLD]	LAKE CO.	T39S	R24E	?
ADEL AREA	LAKE CO.	T39S	R24E	?
BRINGLE, ABSALOM see **CHEWAUCAN**	LAKE CO.	T34S	R19E	S33
CAMP WARNER	LAKE CO.	T36S	R22E	S33
CATHOLIC see **I.O.O.F.** [LAKEVIEW]				
	LAKE CO.	T39S	R20E	S10
CHEWAUCAN	LAKE CO.	T34S	R19E	S33
CHRISTMAS VALLEY	LAKE CO.	T27S	R17E	S28
CRUMP'S RANCH HOUSE, CHARLIE see **HESS, DOC.**				
	LAKE CO.	T39S	R24E	S16
FORT ROCK	LAKE CO.	T25S	R14E	S29
FORT ROCK PIONEER see **FORT ROCK**	LAKE CO.	T25S	R14E	S29
FORT WARNER see **CAMP WARNER**	LAKE CO.	T36S	R22E	S33
HESS, DOC.	LAKE CO.	T39S	R24E	S16
HESS PLACE see **HESS, DOC.**	LAKE CO.	T39S	R24E	S16
I.O.O.F. see **PAISLEY**	LAKE CO.	T33S	R18E	S24
I.O.O.F. [LAKEVIEW]	LAKE CO.	T39S	R20E	S10
INDIAN	LAKE CO.	T39S	R24E	S20
J-SPEAR RANCH see **CHEWAUCAN**	LAKE CO.	T34S	R19E	S33
JOHNSON, DOCTOR	LAKE CO.	T39S	R24E	?
LEEHMAN COW CAMP see **UNKNOWN**	LAKE CO.	T29S	R23E	S35
LONE GRAVE [UNKNOWN]	LAKE CO.	T37S	R28E	S34
MITCHELL, ELSIE see **MITCHELL MONUMENT**				
	LAKE CO.	T36S	R16E	S19
MITCHELL MONUMENT	LAKE CO.	T36S	R16E	S19
MITCHELL, MRS. see **MITCHELL MONUMENT**				
	LAKE CO.	T36S	R16E	S19
MITCHELL, REV. ARCHIE see **MITCHELL MONUMENT**				
	LAKE CO.	T36S	R16E	S19
NEW PINE CREEK	LAKE CO.	T41S	R21E	S19
NICKELS FAMILY see **WESTSIDE**	LAKE CO.	T40S	R19E	S6
O'KEEFE RANCH see **ROUSCOE, MRS. DAVE**				
	LAKE CO.	T39S	R24E	S16
OLD CAMP WARNER	LAKE CO.	T36S	R25E	S24
PAISLEY	LAKE CO.	T33S	R18E	S24
PARTIN FAMILY	LAKE CO.	T30S	R16E	S23
PLUSH	LAKE CO.	T36S	R24E	?
ROUSCOE BABY see **ROUSCOE, MRS. DAVE**				
	LAKE CO.	T39S	R24E	S16
ROUSCOE, MRS. DAVE	LAKE CO.	T39S	R24E	S16
SHIRK RANCH	LAKE CO.	T38S	R27E	?
SILVER LAKE	LAKE CO.	T28S	R14E	S22
SUMMER LAKE	LAKE CO.	T31S	R16E	S10
SUNSET	LAKE CO.	T39S	R20E	S10
SUNSET PARK see **SUNSET**	LAKE CO.	T39S	R20E	S10
UNKNOWN	LAKE CO.	T29S	R23E	S35
WESTSIDE	LAKE CO.	T40S	R19E	S6
XL RANCH	LAKE CO.	T33S	R21E	S31

Lake County

Fort Rock
Janice M. Healy (2000)

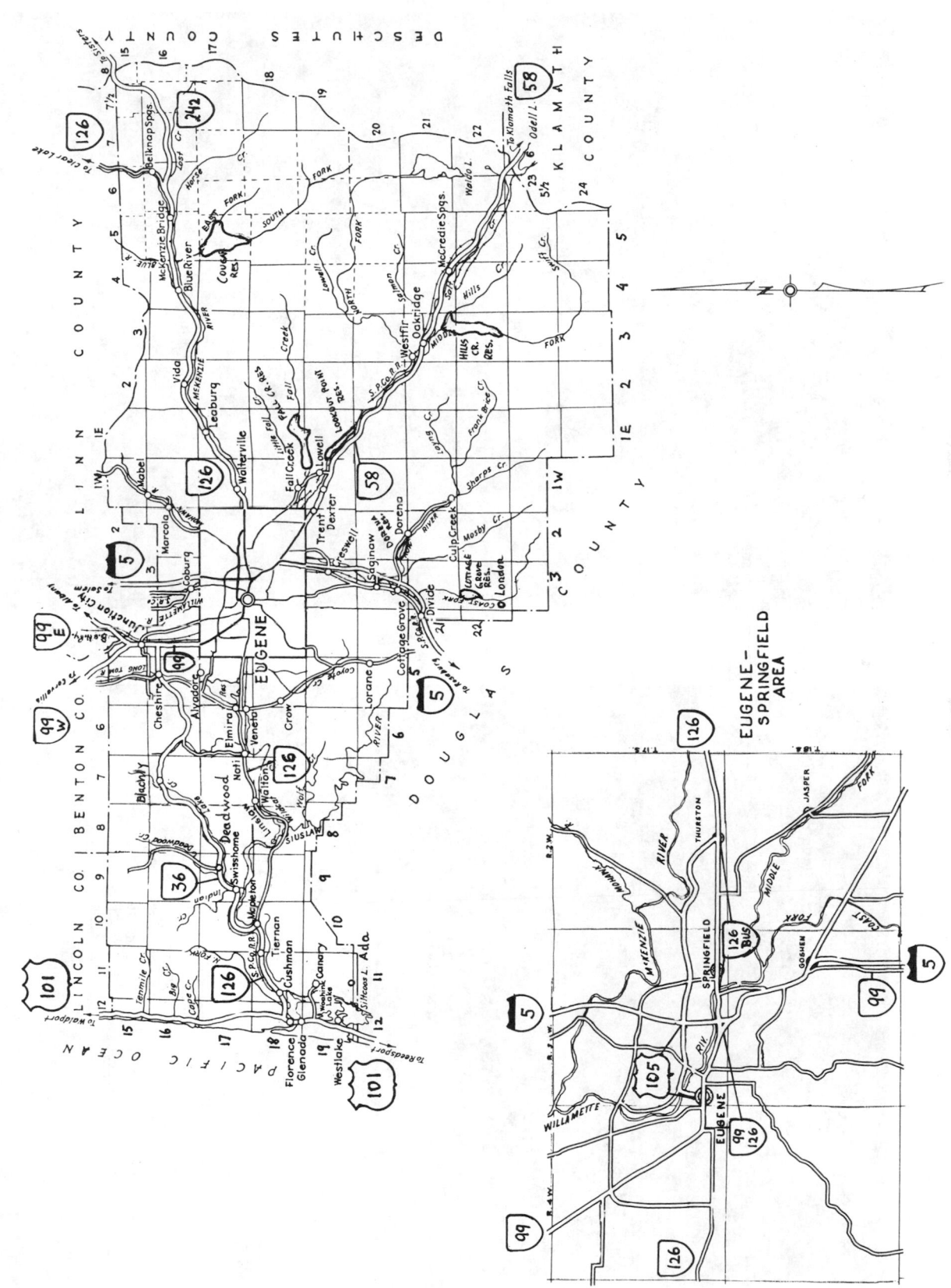

Laurel Grove
Dean H. Byrd (1992)

Laurel Grove
Dean H. Byrd (1992)

Area: 4,620 square miles
Population (1998): 314,068
County seat: Eugene, Population: 126,325
County established: 18 January 1851

Lane County consists of the uppermost Willamette River basin and the basin of the Siuslaw River which flows directly into the Pacific Ocean. Fur traders were the first whites to traverse the area. When immigration by wagon train commenced, especially after 1843, the prairies and hill sides of the upper Willamette Valley were prime goals for those seeking farmlands. As far as the compiler can determine Fir Grove and Gates, both established 1850, were the earliest public cemeteries. Not far behind are I.O.O.F. [Coburg] in 1850's, Pioneer Memorial Park and Creswell (1852), Pleasant Hill, Sears and young (1853), Gillespie and Masonic [Eugene] in (1854). Numerous cemeteries were started in the later 1850's and 1860's. Although the Lorane Grange Cemetery in the uppermost reaches of the Siuslaw River was begun in 1861, most of the cemeteries in that river basin date from the mid-1880's to mid-1890's. There is still an Indian Cemetery (Drew Memorial) in the Siuslaw Basin. The most prominent ethnic cemetery in Lane County is the Danish Cemetery (1902) near Junction City.

Jenkins Family
Dean H. Byrd (1996)

Lane County

Gates
Dean H. Byrd (1991)

Oak Hill
Dean H. Byrd (1996)

Name of Cemetery and also known as	Number of burials	Acres	Condition	Date started or earliest known burial	Township	Range	Section

ADA
AKA: 1. CANARY
    2. FIR GROVE

B   1   2   1899   T20S R11W   S5
Not to be confused with Fir Grove at Cottage Grove. Located south of Florence and east of Siltcoos Lake near the Douglas County Line. Leave U.S. Hwy. 101, turn east on Canary Road and then south on South Canary Road to Ada. Then turn right (west) onto Lower Fiddle Creek Road and go about 0.9 of a mile to the cemetery. (Fivemile Creek 1984 USGS Quad. map.)

ALLEN, WILLIAM P.

A   0.01   ?   1898   ?   ?   ?
Somewhere in or near Oakridge is the grave of William P. Allen. It was located on the Donald Walker Place. We have no further information at this time.

ALMA
AKA: 1. LAYNE
    2. MOUND
    3. PETTIT

B   0.1   2   1891   T19S R8W   S3
Leave Route "F" (OR. Hwy. 126) between Walton and Mapleton and turn southeasterly onto Siuslaw River Road, following the river upstream. Go about 10 miles to the junction with Esmond Creek Road, on the right. Go 0.1 of a mile further to the cemetery on a hill, on the left (north). Alma School was adjacent in 1936; Alma and Mound were separate migratory lumber settlements. Layne Creek enters the Siuslaw east of Alma and west of Mound: the alternate name of Layne is wrongly applied to Alma Cemetery. There were 26 known and one illegible burials in 1987. (Roman Nose Mountain 1984 USGS Quad. map.)

ALPHA

?   ?   ?   ?   T16S R8W   ?
The settlement of Alpha migrated between Sections 19 in the south to Section 7 in the north. Reportedly there was a cemetery at one time, which seems reasonable, since Alpha was important enough to maintain a post office for 50 years between 1890 and 1940. Leave OR. Hwy. 36 at Deadwood, going north on Deadwood Creek Road. The present site of Alpha is placed at about Milepost 7.5 on Deadwood Creek Road in Section 19. (No cemeteries are shown in Section 19 or 7 on the Windy Peak 1984 USGS Quad. map.)

| Name of Cemetery and also known as | Number of burials | Acres | Condition | Date started or earliest known burial | Township | Range | Section |

ANDERSON'S HAVEN OF REST

A 0.25 2 15 Dec 1974 T15S R5W S30
A private burial ground at 94731 Turnbow Lane. Leave Territorial Road and go west on High Pass Road for 3.4 miles, then turn right (north) onto Turnbow Lane. Drive 0.6 of a mile to 94731, turn right (east) onto a gravel lane and go 0.4 of a mile to the house. The burial is 0.2 of a mile up the hill near an old oak tree. Ruth Rogers Anderson is buried there. NOTE: This site is on private property you must have permission to visit. (Not shown on Cheshire 1984 USGS Quad. map.)

BEMIS

A 0.9 3 1860 T22S R3W S32
Located south of Cottage Grove off of London Road, about 1.7 miles south of London and just beyond the bridge over the Coast Fork Willamette River. The cemetery is uphill on the left, on the William Rouse Homestead. NOTE: This site is on private property. Stop at 72076 Rouse Road, about 0.1 of a mile short of the cemetery access driveway, and ask permission and make sure to close the gates behind you on the cemetery driveway. (Harness Mtn. 1987 USGS Quad. map.)

BETHESDA DANISH EVANGELICAL LUTHERAN

C 0.67 1 1901 T17S R4W S33
Located at 225 South Danebo Road and north off of West 11th Avenue, Eugene. It is now a part of West Lawn Memorial Park (see that article), not to be confused with Danish Cemetery west of Junction City. (Eugene West 1967-86 USGS Quad. map.)

BLACHLY
AKA: 1. LAKEVIEW CEMETERY ASSOCIATION
2. TRIANGLE LAKE

C 2 3 1894 T16S R7W S9
Located off of OR. Hwy. 36, on the hill behind the church. The cemetery access road is off of Post Road, which is about a mile west of Blachly on OR. Hwy. 36. Turn left onto Post Road and go about 0.2 of a mile. The driveway goes left, uphill, but is usually closed off by a locked gate. Information from October 1980. NOTE: The Quad. map does show the Taylor Burials (see

that article) in the same Section 9 on Post Road. (Not shown on Triangle Lake 1984 USGS Quad. map.)

BRAY
AKA: 1. STONEFIELD
BEACH
BURIALS

A   0.25   1   1892-1909   T15S R12W   S27

Two graves for a mother and infant daughter are located in Stonefield Beach State Wayside, soon after entering the park there is an opening on the left to park in, the wooden fence nearby surrounds the burials. Located north of Florence at Ten Mile Creek on the west side of U.S. Hwy. 101, one half mile north of Milepost 172, the wayside is plainly marked on the highway. Buried here are Georgiania Starr Bray, born 7 November 1860, died 19 October 1909; Katie Myrth Bray, born 17 December 1889 in sight of beach, died 16 October 1892. (Heceta Head 1984 USGS Quad. map.)

BRUMBAUGH
AKA: 1. BLUE
MOUNTAIN
2. MOSBY

C   1   2   1878   T21S R2W   S18

Located on a hillside, approximately 6 miles southeast of Cottage Grove via Mosby Creek and Blue Mountain Roads. Located on the left (west) side of the road. (Blue Mountain 1986 USGS Quad. map.)

CALDWELL

A   1   3   1864   T16S R5W   S24

This abandoned cemetery has been reduced to a small brush-covered mound surrounded by cultivated fields and is on private property. It can be readily noticed by 2 tall firs on the mound. It is located about 3.5 miles southwest of Junction City. Leave OR. Hwy. 99 just south of town and turn west onto OR. Hwy. 36 and then turn left (south) onto Vogt Lane for another 1.5 miles to the end at Milliron Road. Turn right (west) on Milliron Road for a very short distance to the Huston Farm at the junction of Milliron and Purkerson roads. The cemetery must be reached through the farm yard and fields on the Huston Farm, to the southwest of the house. The remaining monuments, 11 in number, were cast down by a previous landowner decades ago. The death dates run from April 1859 to November 1884. Some burials were relocated

Name of Cemetery and also known as	Number of burials	Acres	Condition	Date started or earliest known burial	Township	Range	Section

many years ago to Rest Lawn Memorial Park. NOTE: This site is on private property. {1 September 1994} (Not shown on Junction City 1967-86 USGS Quad. map.)

CAMP CREEK

C 1.5 4 1868 T17S R1W S19

Take Camp Creek Road east of Springfield along the north bank of the McKenzie River. Turn left onto Upper Camp Creek Road; go to Worth Road, turn right (east) and drive up the hill to the cemetery. It was described as well kept in the 1940 D.A.R. survey; on James Worth D.L.C. #43, RB #1271. (Walterville 1967-86 USGS Quad. map.)

CENTRAL SCHOOL
AKA: 1. AMERICAN BOTTOM
2. CENTRAL GRANGE
3. DRISKELL
4. FERN RIDGE
5. JONES SCHOOL
6. LANE SCHOOL DISTRICT #28J

C 0.25 5 1868 T18S R5W S4

Drive west from Eugene on Route "F" (OR. Hwy. 126) to Fern Ridge Reservoir. Turn left (south) onto Central Road and continue past Perkins Road intersection for 0.6 of a mile. Turn left off of Central Road at 87320 Central Road onto a driveway and go 0.5 of a mile to the mobile home; ask permission, as the cemetery is in the tree farm owned by the Stapleton family. The cemetery is 0.2 of a mile beyond the mobile home on the right about 30 feet off the driveway. There were 3 standing stones to the Jones family found in September 1980, but 2 years later they had been badly vandalized. There were many reburials to other cemeteries and in 1940 the D.A.R. survey found only 3 stones left, all members of the Jones family. NOTE: This site is on private property. (Veneta 1984 USGS Quad. map.)

CHICKAHOMINY

B 0.2 2 1890 T17S R7W S20

Leave Route "F" (OR. Hwy. 126) at Walton onto Nelson Mountain-Chickahominy Road, toward the Nelson Mountain summit. Go about 4.3 miles from Route "F" to where the road crosses Haynes Creek, 0.3 of a mile beyond the creek is the cemetery, on the right above the road. It is necessary to walk up the hill to the cemetery. (Walton 1984 USGS Quad. map.)

| Name of Cemetery and also known as | Number of burials | Acres | Condition | Date started or earliest known burial | Township | Range | Section |

CLOVERDALE
AKA 1. KNOX HILL
2. LOWER
3. PETTY

C 2.08 2 1856   T19S R2W   S18
Take Cloverdale Road east out of Creswell and turn right onto Bear Creek Road. Go about 0.15 of a mile on Bear Creek Road and turn right onto South Bradford Road. Drive 0.3 of a mile up South Bradford to the cemetery on the right. NOTE: The name Knox Hill is sometimes misapplied to Shields Cemetery at Cottage Grove. Also, the name Lower (rhymes with "power") is a family name; on the Daniel Locke D.L.C. #56, RB #499. {24 March 1995} (Jasper 1986 USGS Quad. map.)

COGSWELL
AKA: 1. GAY
2. GAY-MASTERSON
3. GAY PIONEER, MARY
4. KAY, MARY

B 2 2 1852   T19S R3W   S5
Located on Sections 5 and 8. Leave Creswell to the west on Oregon Street and Camas Swale Road. Then turn right (north) onto Sher Khan Road for about 0.9 of a mile. A road or driveway on the left (northwesterly) off of Sher Khan Road leads uphill under the powerlines about 0.7 of a mile to the cemetery. About 2 dozen stones were visible November 1980: on the Martin B. Gay D.L.C. #68, RB #1070. NOTE: This site is on private property. Permission is needed at 31999 East Camas Swale Road as the access from Sher Khan Road is mostly for foot traffic. (Creswell 1984 USGS Quad. map.)

CRAIG MEMORIAL
AKA: 1. GRAIG GRAVE

A 0.01 1 Dec. 1877 T15S R7 1/2E UNS
There is no Section number as the McKenzie Lava Beds have never been surveyed. Located about Milepost 74.3 on McKenzie Highway (OR. Hwy. 242) and about 2.25 miles west of the summit. John Templeton Craig was a mail carrier who froze to death. (North Sister 1988 USGS Quad. map.)

CRESWELL PIONEER
AKA: 1. HOWE

C 3.5 1 1853   T19S R3W   S21
Leave Creswell to the west on Oregon Street and Camas Swale Road. Turn left (south) onto Howe Lane and drive 0.6 of a mile. The cemetery driveway is on the right (west) up the hill; on the Elizabeth Miller D.L.C. #55, RB #1923. (Creswell 1984 USGS Quad. map.)

Lane County

Name of Cemetery and also known as	Number of burials	Acres	Condition	Date started or earliest known burial	Township	Range	Section

CROW FAMILY
AKA: 1. CROWE *[Sic]*

A   0.5   5   1860   T20S R5W   S13

Not to be confused with McCulloch Cemetery, which is also known as Crow I.O.O.F. Cemetery. The spelling Crowe is erroneous. The cemetery is just east of Lorane, on a hillside 0.75 of a mile south off of Cottage Grove-Lorane Road. There are 13 or 14 known burials with the last one in 1936 (November 1980 information); on the John Crow D.L.C. #41, RB #625. NOTE: Please obtain permission at Lorane at 80299 Old Lorane Road as this is a private burial ground. (Lorane 1984 USGS Quad. map.)

CULP CREEK
AKA: 1. HUNT
2. OLD PIONEER
3. WILDWOOD FALLS

A   0.5   5   1878   T21S R1W   S33

This cemetery is on private property at 38659 Lower Brice Creek Road. Drive 15.9 miles from the I-5 Freeway overpass in Cottage Grove on Row River Road to the junction with Lower Brice Creek Road. Turn left onto Lower Brice Creek Road and drive a mile to the driveway at 38659. It is necessary to walk from the house up a steep hill about 0.25 of a mile to the cemetery on the right about 30-40 feet in the brush and trees. 10 markers for 12 graves were found in June of 1981. (Culp Creek 1986 USGS Quad. map.)

DANISH
AKA: 1. DANISH LUTHERAN CHURCH

C   3.4   2   1902   T16S R5W   S4

Located about 5 miles west of Junction City via High Pass Road. Go west of Territorial Road junction on High Pass Road about 0.7 of a mile to the power sub-station on the left. The driveway up the hill to the cemetery passes under a lich-gate which says "Kampen er til ende bragt." (The English translation given on a bronze plaque reads "The struggle is ended.") {15 August 1990} (Cheshire 1984 USGS Quad. map.)

DEADWOOD
AKA: 1. DEADWOOD CHURCH

C   2   2   1889   T17S R9W   S15

Leave Or. Hwy. 36 at Deadwood, going west; turn right (northerly) onto Lower Deadwood Creek Road. Go only 0.1 of a mile and turn right, uphill, to the cemetery and the church

Name of Cemetery and also known as	Number of burials	Acres	Condition	Date started or earliest known burial	Township	Range	Section

site on the left; 211 known burials
(December 1991). (Mapleton 1984 USGS Quad.
map.)

DERKATSCH, JOHANN

A   0.01 ?   1 Dec. 1979 T17S R12W   S36
Buried on Tax Lot #1200 on a "summer place"
near Mercer Lake. NOTE: No further
information was available to the compiler.
This site is on private property. (Not shown
on Mercer Lake 1984 USGS Quad. map.)

DOOLITTLE FAMILY

A   0.4   5   1905   T20S R2W   S21
There is no direct access off of Row River
Road to this site northeast of Dorena Dam,
Cerro Gordo and west of Rat Creek. (Dorena
Lake 1986 USGS Quad. map.)

DOWNS, JAMES

A   0.01 ?   9 Dec 1852 T16S R4W   ?
Located somewhere in Sections 9, 10, 15 or 16
on the William H. Brice D.L.C. #50, OC #2605.
The 640-acre D.L.C. straddles the present day
River Road between Eugene and Junction City.
River Road runs for 1.1 miles through Brices'
D.L.C. between Hayes Lane on the north and
Riverview Drive on the south. Downs was a
native of Leeds, England and was presumably
buried near the Brice house. (NOT shown on
Junction City 1967-86 USGS Quad. map.)

DREW MEMORIAL
  AKA: 1. COOS
       2. DREW, CHIEF
          FRANK
       3. INDIAN TOWN
       4. LOWER
          UMPQUA
       5. SIUSLAW
          INDIAN

C   1.1   2   1897   T18S R12W   S24
Drive about 2 miles east of Florence on
OR. Hwy. 126 and turn left (north) onto
North Fork Road. Go about 0.55 of a mile
to the cemetery on the left. There were 51
marked graves in 1987. NOTE: Chief Frank
Drew (died 1931) was himself of the Coos
tribe. After 1875, when white settlers were
allowed into the Yachats area of the Siletz
Indian Reservation, Chief Drew and some
members of the Coos, Umpqua and Siuslaw
tribes settled on the North Fork of the
Siuslaw River. (Florence 1984 USGS Quad.
map.)

Name of Cemetery and also known as	Number of burials	Acres	Condition	Date started or earliest known burial	Township	Range	Section

EMIGRANT

? ? 5 ? T18S R2W S3

Located at 36191 Jasper Road, southeast of Springfield. Drive southerly along Jasper Road for 0.8 of a mile from the junction with Mt. Vernon Road, turn left (east) onto a driveway into what was the Mt. June Lumber Company. NOTE: At 0.2 of a mile uphill along this driveway is the house 36191, where you must ask permission to visit the site. The cemetery is in an open field about 200 yards north of the house and to the west of a fence. A previous owner plowed it under at some time prior to 1947. The Smith Family burial is only a few yards distant see that article. The title "Emigrant" has been bestowed to this unnamed cemetery on the John Smith D.L.C. #48, RB #1791. (Not shown on Springfield 1967-86 USGS Quad. map, which does however show the fence lines.)

EUGENE PIONEER
AKA: 1. I.O.O.F. SPENCER BUTTE
2. ODD FELLOWS
3. PIONEER
4. PIONEER MEMORIAL PARK
5. SPENCER BUTTE I.O.O.F. LODGE #9

D 15 2 1873 T17S R3W S32

Located at East 18th Avenue and University Street at the University of Oregon; on the Hilyard Shaw D.L.C. #56, RB #1694. (Eugene East 1967-86 USGS Quad. map.)

EVERGREEN HILL
AKA: 1. CHURCH OF THE CHRISTIANS
2. EVERGREEN

B 0.5 1 1913 T17S R3W S14

Take Coburg Road north out of Eugene and cross the McKenzie River, turning right on the north bank onto McKenzie View Drive. Go east about 1.7 miles, turn left onto Douthit Road and head up the hill, keeping to the right. NOTE: Permission is needed to see the cemetery. From the home, which is about 0.5 of a mile from McKenzie View Drive. The cemetery is about 0.1 of a mile from the house, is fenced and usually locked. (Not shown on Eugene East 1967-86 USGS Quad. map.)

Name of Cemetery and also known as	Number of burials	Acres	Condition	Date started or earliest known burial	Township	Range	Section

FALL CREEK
AKA: 1. CHURCH
2. FALL CREEK CHRISTIAN
3. NEET
4. STEWART
5. WARNER

B 1 5 1854-1965 T18S R1W S33

At the time of Daniel Hays visit in January 1981, access was through private property from 38739 Jasper-Lowell Road, approximately 0.9 of a mile west of the locale of Fall Creek. The cemetery is reached on foot about 0.25 of a mile from the house, on a knoll in a stand of medium-growth firs. Right-of-way for a road has been granted for a possible road from Fall Creek Church. In November 1991 it was reported to the compiler that the access road was still not built; on the Frederick Warner D.L.C. #43, OC #1630. (Lowell 1986 USGS Quad. map.)

FERGUESON FAMILY
AKA: 1. FERGUSON FAMILY

B 0.5 1 1877-1949 T15S R5W S22

This family cemetery is on top of a hill. Drive north from Cheshire on Territorial Road towards Monroe. At 0.25 of a mile north past the intersection with Ferguson Road is a driveway on the right (east), up the hill to the house adjacent to the cemetery. The cemetery is fenced and well-cared for. This cemetery is sometimes confused with the Richardson Family Cemetery which is on the next hill to the east. The family always spells their name Fergueson on the markers; however Ferguson Road and Ferguson Creek at the foot of the hill use the variant spelling; on the John B. Fergueson D.L.C., RB #1340. NOTE: This site is on private property. {22 July 1992} (Not shown on Monroe 1969-75 USGS Quad. map.)

FIR GROVE
AKA: 1. COTTAGE GROVE
2. I.O.O.F. [COTTAGE GROVE]
3. MASONIC LODGE #51 [COTTAGE GROVE]

E 25 1 1850 T20S R3W S29

Leave Cottage Grove to the west on Main Street. At the fork where Cottage Grove-Lorane Road veers left, continue ahead to the cemetery. The Odd Fellows portion is in the south and is the oldest; the Masons established a cemetery to the north. The name was changed to Fir Grove in 1952. The I.O.O.F. portion is on the George Small D.L.C. #60, RB #755. (Cottage Grove 1984 USGS Quad. map.)

Name of Cemetery and also known as	Number of burials	Acres	Condition	Date started or earliest known burial	Township	Range	Section

FOREST VALE MEMORIAL PARK
AKA: 1. HIGH PRAIRIE
2. OAKRIDGE
3. UPPER WILLAMETTE
4. VALE MEMORIAL PARK

C 5.47 1 1911   T21S R3E   S10
Drive from Oakridge east to High Prairie Road. Go 1.15 miles on High Prairie Road past the golf course and turn right onto McFarland Road. Drive 1.4 miles on McFarland Road to the cemetery. (Westfir East 1986 USGS Quad. map.)

FOTHERGILL, JOHN
AKA: 1. FATHERGILL [Sic], JOHN

A 0.01 2 16 Sep 1855 T18S R1W   S33
This single grave is about 900 yards south southeast of Fall Creek Christian Cemetery. Park at the Fall Creek Christian Church, 39025 Jasper-Lowell Road. Above and behind the church is the old Fall Creek School, now a residence. Please ask permission there to walk to the cemetery, as there are several fences in the way and the site is on private property. Walk about 220 yards due north and then you will see a very large oak tree on the right (east) another 220 yards. The grave is at the base of the tree in a small fenced area. The spelling Fathergill is wrong; on the John Stuart D.L.C. #37, RB #1754. (Lowell 1986 USGS Quad. map.)

FRANKLIN
AKA: 1. CHESHIRE
2. FRANKLIN GRANGE
3. SMITHFIELD

D 3 2 1897   T16S R5W   S21
Located about 3 miles southwest of Cheshire, going west on OR. Hwy. 36 and then left (south) on Territorial Road. The cemetery is on the left before reaching Franklin with its two side-by-side churches. It is on the James B. Southworth D.L.C. #50, OC #866; land donated Jan. 1897. The earliest grave is dated 1898. The cemetery address is 92385 Territorial Road. {25 July 1990} (Cheshire 1984 USGS Quad. map.)

GARBER NURSING HOME

                    T18S R3W   S5
This was strictly a nursing home located at 2815 Potter Street in Eugene. Somehow it has gotten on an L.D.S. list for burials as the site of a cemetery. Deaths are listed from the 1930's into the 1950's, but it was definitely not a cemetery and should be removed from consideration as a cemetery. This list of deaths are in one person's

| Name of Cemetery and also known as | Number of burials | Acres | Condition | Date started or earliest known burial | Township | Range | Section |

handwriting, they are not listed alphabetically or in chronological order by death dates. This list contains 28 death records. SEE: Family History Library Locality Catalog under "*Oregon, Lane, Eugene Cemeteries, Garbers Nursing Home Cemetery records, Eugene, Lane County Oregon*/compiled by the Genealogical Committee of the L.D.S. Church---Salt Lake City: Filmed by the Genealogical Society of Utah, 1956. Film no. 0002114 item 20. Typescript (2p.)"

GATES

C   1   2   1850   T18S R5W   S19
Go about 0.3 of a mile south of Crow on Territorial Road and just past the athletic field of Crow-Lane High School. A driveway leads about 700 feet to the left (west), to the cemetery. NOTE: Although the driveway to the cemetery is a public access, there are 2 gates and cattle guards to pass, so it is best to ask permission at the farm house. It is on the Hiram Rowe D.L.C. #53, OC #818. {30 October 1991} (Crow 1984 USGS Quad. map.)

GATES OF HEAVEN
  AKA: 1. CARMELITE
         NUNNERY

A   1   1   1965   T18S R4W   S5
The Sisters of Carmel of Maria Regina, located at 87609 Green Hill Road. There is 1 burial. (Eugene West 1967-86 USGS Quad. map.)

GILLESPIE
  AKA: 1. GILESPI *[Sic]*

C   1.5   1   1854   T17S R3W   S19
Located on the north slope of Gillespie Butte in Eugene. Across the Willamette River from downtown, take Country Club Road northwest past Valley River Interchange. Continue north on Willagillespie Road, turn right onto Clinton Drive, uphill to Debrick Road; turn left onto Debrick Road and then turn right onto Crenshaw Road, to a barricade. Then turn hard left and keep left around the west side of the butte; on the Jacob Gillespie D.L.C. #70, RB #1637. (Eugene East 1967-86 USGS Quad. map.)

Name of Cemetery and also known as	Number of burials	Acres	Condition	Date started or earliest known burial	Township	Range	Section

GOSHEN
AKA: 1. GOSHEN
     GRANGE #561
   2. I.O.O.F.
   3. PISGAH
     LODGE

B   0.5   5   1870   T18S R3W   S24

Located on a hilltop just east of the I-5 Freeway and west (right) off of Dillard Access Road. The cemetery is reached off of Goshen Interchange of the I-5 Freeway and Willamette Highway (OR. Hwy. 58). Soon after leaving the interchange turn right off of OR. Hwy. 58 and cross the Coast Fork of the Willamette River; then turn right onto Mathews Road and soon turn right (south) onto Dillard Access Road, AKA: Peebles Road. Go about 0.5 of a mile futher to the old grange hall and the cemetery is on the right, on the hilltop; on the Milton Riggs D.L.C. #57, RB #1807. (Creswell 1984 USGS Quad. map.)

GRAY, FRED W.

A   0.01   8   ?   T19S R1E   S19

Fred Gray was originally cremated and buried about 20 feet from his house. On 11 August 1952, the burial was disinterred and reburied to the new location of Middle Fork Cemetery, now a part of Mt. Vernon Cemetery. The move was made before Lookout Point Dam was completed. The Fred Gray marker in Mt. Vernon has since disappeared. (Not shown on the Fall Creek Lake 1986 USGS Quad. map.)

GREENWOOD
AKA: 1. GLENWOOD
   2. LEABURG
   3. PEPIOT

D   4   2   1894   T17S R1E   S12

The cemetery lies between the McKenzie Highway (OR. Hwy. 126) and its old alignment, now named Greenwood Drive. The cemetery is about 1.5 or 2 miles east of Leaburg. It was begun as the Pepiot Family Cemetery in 1894 and in June 1922 was established as Greenwood Cemetery. The name Glenwood in this context is a mistake. Glenwood is a suburban area between Eugene and Springfield. (Leaburg 1988 USGS Quad. map.)

HANSEN, DAVID W.

A   0.01   1   1986   T15S R6W   S35

Located in the Southeast 1/4 of Section 35 on private property. The grave is under a large oak tree on the lower slopes of a hill and off of a private driveway, which in turn is off the western end of Lavell Road near its junction with High Pass Road. David W.

Name of Cemetery and also known as	Number of burials	Acres	Condition	Date started or earliest known burial	Township	Range	Section

Hansen, born 8 October 1964, died 24 June 1986 intended to be married under this, his favorite tree. He was killed on his first flight in an ultra-light aircraft and so is buried under that tree. {22 September 1993} (Not shown on Cheshire 1984 USGS Quad. map.)

HARING PIONEER
AKA: 1. NORTH FORK

B   0.5   2   1883   T18S R11W   S7
Leave Florence on OR. Hwy. 126, to the east. Turn left (north) onto North Fork Road and drive about 4.8 miles from OR. Hwy. 126. The cemetery is on the left; with 34 known burials in 1993. {26 Octeober 1996} (Mercer Lake 1984 USGS Quad. map.)

HAWLEY
AKA: 1. DIVIDE
     2. VEATCH

B   1.5   2   1860   T21S R4W   S12
Leave Cottage Grove, to the south, on OR. Hwy. 99. Turn off of OR. Hwy. 99 to the right on Kenady Lane; go 0.25 of a mile on Kenady, turn left (west) onto Valley View Drive. Drive up the hill about 0.4 of a mile to the last house, where the road forks and a gate is in front. Go through this public gate and drive to the right for 0.1 of a mile. The cemetery is on the left on a hill; on the Ira Hawley D.L.C., RB #493. (Cottage Grove 1984 USGS Quad. map.)

HEATHERLY FAMILY

A   0.01   5   1877   T19S R5W   S10
Drive southerly from Crow on Territorial Road for a total of 5.3 miles, passing the junction (on the left) of Briggs Hill Road. At about 0.68 of a mile southerly from the Briggs Hill junction, the cemetery is about 1,000 feet due east of Territorial Road, on a hillside. NOTE: There is no ready access. This ruined cemetery stands in the middle of a field in a plum thicket. Permission is needed at the farmhouse to cross the field. There are 4 known burials on the James Heatherly D.L.C. #39, RB #1120. (Crow 1984 USGS Quad. map.)

HELFRICH, PRINCE E.

A   0.01   2   ?   T16S R3E   S31
Located east of Springfield and off of the McKenzie Highway (OR. Hwy 126). About 0.5 of

Lane County

Name of Cemetery and also known as	Number of burials	Acres	Condition	Date started or earliest known burial	Township	Range	Section

a mile past Milepost 30, turn left (north) at the driveway of 47611 McKenzie Highway. The signboard says "Rail Creek Ranch". NOTE: This site is on private property; ask permission to visit the grave. It is on a rock outcropping above the gravel road less than 220 yards from the house. Helfrich was a river guide, wilderness expert and a writer. {March 1981} (Not shown on Mt. Hagan 1989 USGS Quad. map.

HILL MEMORIAL, JOHN
AKA: 1. HILLS CREEK
    2. UPPER
       WILLAMETTE

B 1   2   1890's-1929 T21S R3E   S26
Take Willamette Highway (OR. Hwy. 58) past Oakridge, beyond the Ranger Station, burned in 1996. Turn right off of OR. Hwy. 58 onto Kitson Springs Road. Go about 1.1 miles on Kitson Springs Road to the cemetery on the left. The cemetery is about 200 feet above Kitson Springs Road and about 50 feet to the left of the dirt driveway. There were 18 marked graves in February 1981. (Not shown on Oakridge 1986 USGS Quad. map.)

HOLY CROSS

-   -   -   1955   T18S R5W   S3
Land was purchased for a cemetery, but was eventually sold without ever having been used for burials.

HOPE ABBEY

? ?   ?   1913   T18S R3W   S5
The name of a mausoleum built in the Masonic Cemetery in Eugene. See Masonic [Eugene]. (Hope Abbey is not shown on Eugene East 1967-86 USGS Quad. map.)

HULBERT LAKE BURIALS
AKA: 1. ZUMWALT

A 0.01 5 ?   T15S R4W   ?
Perhaps in Section 18, located about 0.75 of a mile north of Ferguson Road and just off of Hulbert Lake Road. Ask permission at 95902 Hulbert Lake Road. The burial site is reached from a gate on the right side of the road near an old barn; walk through the gate and about 50 feet up onto a small hill, to the site under a tree. These were probably 2 members of the Zumwalt family. {November 1980} (Not shown on Harrisburg 1969 USGS Quad. map.)

Name of Cemetery and also known as	Number of burials	Acres	Condition	Date started or earliest known burial	Township	Range	Section

I.O.O.F. [COBURG]
AKA: 1. COBURG
2. WEST POINT LODGE #62

C   4   2   1850'S   T17S R3W   S4

Located about 1.3 miles south of Coburg, via Coburg Road. Turn left (west) into driveway to the cemetery. The cemetery signboard gives a date of 1882. This cemetery was platted on Sept. 1909; on the Jacob C. Spores D.L.C. #38, OC #1325. {21 January 1991} (Eugene East 1967-86 USGS Quad. map.)

I.O.O.F. [GLENADA]
AKA: 1. HECETA LODGE #111
2. I.O.O.F. [FLORENCE]
3. SEVERY HILL

C   5   2   1893   T19S R12W   S2

This cemetery consists of two pieces of property owned by the I.O.O.F., but separated by a walkway which is the only access to both. Leave U.S. Hwy. 101 at Glenada just south of Florence, 0.3 of a mile south of the Siuslaw Bridge. Turn left (east) off of U.S. Hwy. 101 onto Glenada Road, go east 0.3 of a mile and turn right (south) 0.8 of a mile to the cemetery which you must walk: 135 known burials in 1991. (Florence 1984 USGS Quad. map.)

I.O.O.F. [LORANE]
AKA: 1. INDEPENDENT ORDER OF GOOD TEMPLARS

B   2   3   1884   T20S R5W   S24

Located a mile south of Lorane on Territorial Road, on a hillside to the right (west). Jointly operated by I.O.O.F. and Masons, it has been taken over by the former; on the Daniel Lucas D.L.C. #48, RB #550. (Lorane 1984 USGS Quad. map.)

I.O.O.F. [MAPLETON]
AKA: 1. MAPLE LODGE #139
2. MAPLETON

C   4.5   2   6 Oct 1906   T18S R10W   S11

Located in Mapleton, just west of the junction of OR. Hwy. 36 and OR. Hwy. 126. A road leading uphill 0.3 of a mile to the cemetery is about opposite the Siuslaw National Forest headquarters. The first known urial here was in 1906 but there are five known burials earlier, as far back as 1880 which were reburied here from Knowles and Sweet Creek Cemeteries. This Mapleton Cemetery was dedicated 24 February 1913; 436 known burials in 1993. (Mapleton 1984 USGS Quad. map.)

Lane County

Name of Cemetery and also known as	Number of burials	Acres	Condition	Date started or earliest known burial	Township	Range	Section

I.O.O.F. SPENCER BUTTE LODGE #9

? ? ? 1923   T17S R4W   S33

This was the second cemetery established by the same I.O.O.F. lodge. Combined with Bethesda Danish Evangelical Lutheran Cemetery into West Lawn Memorial Park (See those articles). (Eugene West 1967-86 USGS Quad. map.)

INDIAN

? ? ? ?   T17S R1W   ?

Located east of the Walterville area. NOTE: No other information was given in the report. (Not shown on Walterville 1967-86 USGS Quad. Map.)

INDIAN BURIAL

? ? ? ?   T20S R2W   S31

Located on a little mound, on west side of Dorena Dam near the tree farm. NOTE: No other information was given in the report. (Not shown on Dorena Lake 1986 USGS Quad. map.)

INDIAN BURIALS

A 0.01 ? ?   ? ?   ?

Possibly located in Township 21 South, Range 3 East, Section 31. Charlie Tufi's wife and two of his children are buried on the Charles Dunning place. Dunning occupied the site after 1908. This is somewhere in or near Oakridge. (Not shown on Oakridge 1986 USGS Quad. map.)

INDIAN CREEK
AKA: 1. BEERS
      2. HOPELAND

B 1 2 17 Dec 1891 T16S R10W   S36

Located in the Siuslaw National Forest. Turn off of OR. Hwy. 36 at Indiola which is about halfway between Deadwood and Swisshome, onto Indian Creek Road (Co. Rd. #5130), about 7 miles to the bridge over the West Fork of Indian Creek. Just past the bridge turn left and go 0.2 of a mile from Indian Creek Road on County Road #5134, past the closed schoolhouse. The cemetery is on the right: There were 74 known burials in 1993. (Herman Creek 1984 USGS Quad. map.)

Name of Cemetery and also known as	Number of burials	Acres	Condition	Date started or earliest known burial	Township	Range	Section

INDIAN LIZA

A 0.01 1 ? T17S R3W ?

Perhaps located in Section 30. There is a concrete plate on the sixth fairway at the Eugene Country Club. (Not shown on Eugene East 1967-86 USGS Quad. map.)

INMAN
  AKA: 1. ELMIRA
       2. INMAN FAMILY

C 2 2 1859 T17S R5W S8

Located on a peninsula at the northwest shore of Fern Ridge Reservoir, 3 miles north of Elmira, on Territorial Road. The cemetery is 0.25 of a mile east of Territorial Road on Inman Road, behind the Inman residence; on the Joel C. Inman D.L.C. #43, RB #1350. NOTE: This site is on private property. {25 July 1990} (Veneta 1984 USGS Quad. map.)

JACKSON FAMILY

A 0.2 5 1853 T19S R3W S34

Drive 2.5 miles south of Creswell, on OR. Hwy. 99 to West Tate Road. Turn to the right (west) on West Tate Road to a fork; taking the road on the right uphill (northerly and westerly) about 200 yards. The cemetery is behind a farm house, nearly inaccessible and covered with poison oak: on the George W. Harper D.L.C. #65, RB #1086. NOTE: This site is on private property. (Creswell 1984 USGS Quad. map.)

JENKINS FAMILY
AKA: 1. FORD

A 0.2 5 23 May 1862 T18S R5W S22

Located 2 miles east of Territorial Road near the junction of Crow Road and Doane Road. At a point 0.25 of a mile south of the junction, go up a hill on driveway about 0.35 of a mile, behind a cattle farm (1978); on the Stephen Jenkins D.L.C. #44, RB #1528. NOTE: This site is on private property. Please stop and ask permission to visit the cemetery. {17 October 1996.} (Crow Quad. 1984 USGS Quad. map.)

JOHNSON FAMILY, GEORGE

? ? ? ? ? ? ?

There reportedly are family burials at the Johnson place somewhere out of Florence. No other information as been given to the compiler. (Not shown on the Florence 1984 USGS Quad. map.)

Name of Cemetery and also known as	Number of burials	Acres	Condition	Date started or earliest known burial	Township	Range	Section

JONES FAMILY

A 1 4 1890-1895 T16S R5W S16

Located on a hilltop 0.65 of a mile west of Cheshire. Jones Cemetery and Kime-Brown Cemetery have mistakenly been considered to be a single cemetery, see the article on the Kime-Brown Family Cemetery. They are not the same cemetery. Jones is south of OR. Hwy. 36, Kime-Brown is north of OR. Hwy. 36. Drive west on OR. Hwy. 36 from Cheshire. Go past the junction with Territorial Road on the right (north), which leads to Monroe. Continue westerly another 0.35 of a mile, to a road on the left (south) off of the highway. It is a posted driveway which goes uphill through a Christmas tree farm. At a fork, take the driveway to the right to the summit where there is a large oak tree. There are only 3 monuments standing (4 were noted in December of 1980) in a small patch of Vinca major ("myrtle" or "periwinkle"). The burials are unfenced and there are no visible reminders of other burials; on the William H. McAtee D.L.C. #49, OC #674. NOTE: This site is on private property. {22 July 1992} (Cheshire 1984 USGS Quad. map.)

KEENEY FAMILY
  AKA: 1. SELLERS

A 0.6 5 1851 T19S R2W S5

Turn off of OR. Hwy. 58 onto Cloverdale Road, going about 2 miles south on Cloverdale Road; turn left (east) into the farm driveway and go 0.65 of a mile to the house. It is necessary to ask for permission and directions to the cemetery as the site is on private property. The cemetery is off to the left (east), on top of Sellers Butte; on the Eli Keeney D.L.C. #49, RB #2089. (Jasper 1986 USGS Quad. map.)

KERR GIRL

A 0.01 5 ? T21S R1W S33

A 6-year old girl was buried under a lilac bush on Row River Road between Culp Creek and Bryce Creek. NOTE: The location given for the Kerr burial is the same Township, Range, and Section as the Culp Creek Cemetery which is shown on the Quad. map. One suspects therefore that possibly the burial was in that cemetery. (Not shown on Culp Creek 1986 USGS Quad. map.)

Name of Cemetery and also known as	Number of burials	Acres	Condition	Date started or earliest known burial	Township	Range	Section

KIME-BROWN FAMILY
AKA: 1. HISE

B   1   4   ?   T16S R5W   S17

This is an abandoned cemetery 2.4 miles west of Cheshire. It is near the Jones Cemetery, and the two cemeteries have been mistakenly considered to be a single cemetery, which they are not. Jones is south of OR. Hwy 36 and Kime-Brown is north (see the article on Jones Cemetery). Take OR. Hwy. 36 west from the junction with Territorial Road, which goes south to Veneta. Drive about 0.7 of a mile and leave OR. Hwy. 36, turning right (northerly) onto a private driveway. This driveway passes under an overhead gateway and skirts around the base of a low hill. Drive 0.6 of a mile to the house and ask permission to visit this site. Walk from there to the top of the hill where there have been a few traces of burials. The compiler found what had been the trench to hold an upright marble slab. The last remaining stone was stolen in 1973; on the Jesse Cox D.L.C. #52, OC #665. {22 July 1992} (Not shown on Cheshire 1984 USGS Quad. map.)

KNOWLES
AKA: 1. KNOWLES CREEK
2. MAPLETON
   MEMORIAL
   CEMETERY
   ASSOCIATION

A   ?   5   Circa 1880   T18S R10W   S1

This cemetery was abandoned and supposedly all of the bodies except one were removed to the I.O.O.F. Mapleton Cemetery in 1937 and 1938. The remaining body is that of a female Knowles, variously said to have been 13 or an infant. It is supposedly at the foot of a cedar tree and most likely in Section 1. The 1931 *Metsker Land Ownership Atlas* shows the Knowles family owning lands in both Sections 1 and 2 on both sides of what is now Route "F" (OR. Hwy. 126). This site is east of Mapleton. (Not shown on Mapleton 1984 USGS Quad. map.)

LANE MEMORIAL GARDENS

D   79   1   1964   T17S R4W   S32

This is on Sections 32 and 33, located at 5300 West 11th Street, Eugene. (Eugene West 1967-86 USGS Quad. map.)

LAUREL GROVE
AKA: 1. I.O.O.F.
   SPRINGFIELD

D   4   2   1878   T18S R3W   S3

Turn off of the I-5 Freeway at Exit #191 onto Glenwood Boulevard and then left

LODGE #70
2. LAUREL HILL

(westerly), onto Judkins Road up the hill. After 1913 there were many reburials from the Pioneer Memorial Cemetery Park (see that entry). This cemetery has, until recently, been known as Laurel Hill. However, research showed that the legal name was Laurel Grove and a large signboard has now been erected with that designation. The term "Laurel" actually refers to the madrone trees which are numerous on this hill. It is on the Zara Sweet D.L.C. #44, RB #1798. {13 August 1992} (Eugene East 1967-86 USGS Quad. map.)

LAYNE, MRS. MINNIE

A   0.01   5   ?   T19S R7W   S22
The Minnie Layne burial is under an old tall cedar stump, not far from the present road (Siuslaw River Road) and just west of Layne Creek. Mrs. Layne was the postmistress of either Mound or Alma. NOTE: The name Layne is wrongly applied as an alternate name for the Alma Cemetery. (Not shown on Clay Creek 1984 USGS Quad. map.)

LILES
AKA 1. LYLE

B   5   2   1867   T18S R5W   S16
Leave Crow and go northeasterly on Central Road; turn right on Petzold Road for 1.8 miles, then turn right again (southerly) onto Boehringer Road and go about 0.2 of a mile uphill to the top. NOTE: This site is on private property so permission is needed. (Crow 1984 USGS Quad. map.)

LINSLAW PIONEER

B   0.55   2   1901   T18S R8W   S17
Turn off of Route "F" (OR. Hwy. 126) onto the Richardson Bridge over the Siuslaw River; drive about 1.7 miles easterly and upstream on old Stagecoach Road. The cemetery is on the left, uphill. The cemetery is reached through a gated rough gravel road and is about 220 yards from the county road. There were 22 known burials in 1992. The burial area is within a 40 foot by 100 foot fenced area. (Greenleaf 1984 USGS Quad. map.)

Name of Cemetery and also known as	Number of burials	Acres	Condition	Date started or earliest known burial	Township	Range	Section

LITTLE LAKE
AKA: 1. JAY BURIALS

A   0.2   5   Circa 1903   T16S R7W   S18
Turn off of OR. Hwy. 36 onto Triangle Lake Resort Road. Little Lake itself is in Section 19. (The burials are entirely abandoned and are not shown on Triangle Lake 1984 USGS Quad. map.)

LORANE GRANGE
AKA: 1. GRANGE
     2. GRANGER
     3. SIUSLAW
       GRANGE
     4. SIUSLAW
       PRECINCT

B   2   5   1861-1966   T20S R5W   S2
This is located 1.5 miles northwest of Lorane on a hill on a farm and difficult to find without a guide. The grange itself was at the foot of the hill and has long since burned. It is on the John W. Thompson D.L.C. #37, RB #1717. NOTE: This site is on private property. (Cemetery is split between the Lorane and Letz Creek 1984 USGS Quad. maps.)

LOWELL
AKA: 1. HOWE
     2. HYLAND

B   1.5   3   1880   T19S R1W   S15
Located about 0.4 of a mile west from the center of Lowell on Pengra Road. The cemetery is on the left. (Lowell 1986 USGS Quad. map.)

LUPER
AKA: 1. BAKER
     2. BAKER FAMILY
     3. I.O.O.F.
       [IRVING]
     4. LOOPER

C   2   2   1859   T16S R4W   S34
Located northwest of Eugene and southeast of Junction City. The gated access driveway (usually locked) is on the east side of Prairie Road opposite the residence at 91184 Prairie Road. This is about one mile south of the Meadowview Road junction with Prairie Road and 0.3 of a mile north of Beacan Drive junction with Prairie Road. It is puzzling why this much-used cemetery has virtually passed out of use. Volunteers are undertaking extensive clearing and restoration which started in 1992; on the Thomas and Elizabeth Baker D.L.C., RB #1652. {22 May 1991} (Not shown on Junction City 1967-86 USGS Quad. map.)

MABEL
AKA: 1. BRETHREN
     2. DUNKARD
       CHURCH
       OF THE
       BRETHREN

B   0.2   5   1886   T16S R1W   S5
Take Marcola Road north past the junction of Shotgun Creek Road on the left; continue on Marcola Road crossing Shotgun Creek. Almost immediately on the right is Mabel Grange Hall. The cemetery is in the woods

Name of Cemetery and also known as	Number of burials	Acres	Condition	Date started or earliest known burial	Township	Range	Section

3. GERMAN
    BAPTIST
    BRETHREN
4. LOWER
    MABEL
5. MABLE

on the right towards the Mohawk River, about 500 feet north of Shotgun Creek Bridge and about 100 yards east of Marcola Road. It is reached by a gravel driveway to the right, the first driveway south of the small cluster of houses near the Mabel Grange Hall. Only about a dozen stones were present in September 1980. The church disbanded in 1950. It is on the William C. Baird D.L.C. #43, RB #1802. (Marcola 1988 USGS Quad. map.)

MADERIS, LYMAN
AKA: 1. MADERA

A   0.01   2   15 Jan 1916   T15S R10W   S29
The grave is located on the southern shoulder of Klickitat Mountain, within the Siuslaw National Forest, at the junction of Forestry Roads #58 and #37. It lies on the southwest side of the road at the foot of a stump. Leave U.S. Hwy. 101 south of Yachats, just north of the Cape Perpetua visitor center and turn inland. After a mile or so continue easterly on Forestry Road #55. At 11.4 miles from U.S. Hwy. 101 is a fork; leave the Forestry Road #55 and take Forestry Road #58 to the right. Continue 2.2 miles to the junction with Forestry Road #37 and the grave. Lyman Maderis was a 20-year old youth who froze to death in a severe snow storm. His body was found 16 April 1916: see *Salem Capital Journal* 28 Nov. 1970 and *Eugene Register-Guard* 10 July 1988. NOTE: Both the USGS Quad. map and the Siuslaw Forestry map use the wrong spelling of Madera. (Cummins Peak 1984 USGS Quad. map.)

MARCOLA
AKA: 1. I.O.O.F.
2. I.O.O.F.
   MOHAWK LODGE
   #200
3. MOHAWK
4. MOHAWK LODGE
5. VALLEY VIEW

C   1.7   2   1881   T16S R2W   S24
Regrettably and confusingly, there are 2 cemeteries in the area which can be called Valley View. This particular cemetery is better called Marcola. See Valley View article for the other cemetery in this vicinity. Going north on Marcola Road from Springfield, this cemetery is about 200 feet north (left) off of Marcola Road and about 1 mile southwest of the junction of Marcola Road with Wendling Road. This cemetery is on a knoll on the George Alkire D.L.C. #44, RB

Name of Cemetery and also known as	Number of burials	Acres	Condition	Date started or earliest known burial	Township	Range	Section

#1961. The plat was filed in 1909 as Mohawk Cemetery, but is more commonly called Marcola. (Marcola 1988 USGS Quad. map.)

MARQUESS, MARK WAYNE

A 0.01 ? 1979 T19S R3W S24
Located on tax lot #3200 or #3201. There are no roads to this burial site; this young man died in a diving accident. NOTE: This site is on private property. (Not shown on Jasper 1986 USGS Quad. map.)

MASONIC [EUGENE]
AKA: 1. EUGENE CITY
LODGE #11
2. GRAND ARMY
OF THE
REPUBLIC

E 10 2 1854 T18S R3W S5
Located in Eugene on University Street, between East 25th and East 26th Avenues. It was first platted in 1859 and includes the Hope Abbey Mausoleum. It is on the Fielding McMurry DLC OC#1580. {17 June 2000} (Eugene East 1967-86 USGS Quad. map.)

McCLANE, THOMAS HENRY

A 0.01 ? 14 Apr 1911 T21S R3E S8
A death certificate reports that Thomas Henry McClane, born 15 July 1826 in Pennsylvania, was buried on his farm at Hazeldell. This was presumably a family burial ground in the vicinity of what is now Westfir. The 1931 *Metsker Landownership Atlas of Lane County* shows that the family still owned land east of Westfir along the county road to Oakridge. The creek here has a variant spelling of McLane Creek. (NOT shown on Westfir East 1986 USGS Quad. map.)

McCOLLUM
AKA: 1. BALL
2. TEAGUE

A 1 5 ? T18S R4W S30
Located at 85105 Lorane Highway, about 700 yards, as the crow flies, west of the road and across a valley on the far slope. The cemetery faces east. The USGS Quad. map shows no driveway access. NOTE: Although the cemetery address is 85105 Lorane Highway, it is necessary to use the driveway of 85086, and please ask permission as the site is on private property. (Fox Hollow 1984 USGS Quad. map.)

Lane County

Name of Cemetery and also known as	Number of burials	Acres	Condition	Date started or earliest known burial	Township	Range	Section

McCULLOCH
AKA: 1. CROW
    2. I.O.O.F.
      [CROW]

B 2 2 1886   T18S R5W   S34

This is not to be confused with the Crow Family Cemetery. Travel about 4 miles south and east of Crow via Territorial Road. Turn left (northeast) onto Briggs Hill Road and go about 0.8 of a mile. The cemetery is on the left, uphill about 0.25 of a mile off of Briggs Hill Road. The cemetery is about 500 feet west of the west line of the Thomas McCulloch D.L.C. #45, RB #1757. (Crow 1984 USGS Quad. map.)

McENROE, PATRICK
AKA: 1. PAT CREEK
     BURIAL

A 0.01 2 8 May 1901 T17S R9W   S36

Leave Route "F" (OR. Hwy. 126) and cross the Siuslaw River on Richardson Road. Turn left onto Old Stagecoach Road and drive the winding road alongside the Siuslaw River, heading downstream. You will cross Pat Creek, a considerable creek flowing down from the north in Township 17 South, Range 8 West, Section 31. Since the grave of Patrick McEnroe is so near, the name Pat Creek is not likely a coincidence. This lone grave is on the right of Pat Creek after going under a railway trestle and then crossing the tracks again. (Greenleaf 1984 USGS Quad. map.)

McFARLAND
AKA: 1. McFARLAND
     FAMILY

B 0.4 3 1863-1971 T20S R3W   S28

Located northwest of Cottage Grove on the slopes of McFarland Butte, above the Hidden Valley Golf Course. Leave North River Road, turning right (west) onto Birch Avenue for a block, then right again onto "G" Street and go to the end. After parking, take the footpath to the right and walk about 0.2 of a mile around the butte and up a gentle slope to the cemetery. It is on the James H. McFarland D.L.C. #58, RB #345. There were 38 known burials in 1977. (Cottage Grove 1984 USGS Quad. map.)

McKENZIE BRIDGE
AKA: 1. BULL FAMILY

A 0.01 ? 1902   T16S R5E   ?

Perhaps located in Section 13 or 14. There is a grave "at Mc Kenzie Bridge." A young girl, aged about 10, of the Bull family was in a party crossing the mountains from Crook County. The child was fatally thrown from

Name of Cemetery and also known as	Number of burials	Acres	Condition	Date started or earliest known burial	Township	Range	Section

her horse somewhere between the lava beds and Mc Kenzie Bridge. *The Dalles Chronicle* reported the tragedy which probbly occurred in the summer or early fall of 1902. Someone forgot to note the date of the newspaper. (Not shown on Mc Kenzie Bridge 1989 USGS Quad. map.)

MEDLEY
AKA: 1. MENDELL *[Sic]*

A   0.01   ?   ?   T20S R3W   S19

The lone grave of a young girl is on Cottage Grove-Lorane Road, on the east side of the power line. (Not shown on Cottage Grove 1984 USGS Quad. map.)

MIDDLE FORK
AKA: 1. LANDAX
2. RUSH ISLAND

C   1   8   1880-1947   T19S R1E   S34

Located near the settlement of Eula, now flooded after the construction of Lookout Point Dam. The cemetery was incorporated in Oct. 1908; the graves were removed in Aug. 1952 to Mt. Vernon Cemetery in Springfield. There were 449 known burials. (Not shown on Fall Creek Lake 1986 USGS Quad. map.)

MILLIRON
AKA: 1. JUNCTION
CITY PIONEER
2. MILLIORN
3. RICKARD
4. WASHBURNE

B   0.25   4   1859-1912   T15S R4W   S31

Leave OR. Hwy. 99 in Junction City and go west on West First Street, which becomes High Pass Road. The cemetery is on the right at 0.6 of a mile from OR. Hwy. 99. It is on the John Milliron D.L.C. #59, OC #682. The family was spelled Milliron at the time of the 1852 emigration from Campbell County, Virginia; it has been altered to Milliorn since. The tallest monument in the cemetery spells the family name is "Milliorn." Nevertheless, a long-time neighbor and caretaker says the name is pronounced "Millir'n." There is no signboard present. {15 August 1990} (Junction City 1967-86 USGS Quad. map.)

MOUNTS FAMILY BURIALS
AKA: 1. MOUNSE
BURIALS
2. MOUNTE *[Sic]*
BURIALS
3. MOUNTS

A   0.01   5   ?   T18S R5W   S7

Two burials (a mother and stillborn child) are south of Veneta on the Lewis Hoiland Farm (1980). The Quad. map shows the grave on a hill 500 yards, as the crow flies, east of Territorial Highway. The nearest driveway,

Name of Cemetery and also known as	Number of burials	Acres	Condition	Date started or earliest known burial	Township	Range	Section

BURIALS — which has no direct access however, leaves Territorial Highway to the east about 1 mile south of the junction with Owens-Fleck Road. It is on the Henry R. Mounte [Sic] D.L.C., OC #3028. NOTE: This site is on private property. (Veneta 1984 USGS Quad. map.)

MT. CALVARY CATHOLIC — C 5 1 1904 T18S R3W S7
Located in Eugene. Go south on South Willamette Street and turn right (west) on Crest Drive for 0.25 of a mile to 226 Crest Drive, on a hill. (Eugene East 1967-86 USGS Quad. map.)

MT. VERNON
 AKA: 1. LANDAX
       2. MIDDLE FORK
       3. NEW MIDDLE
          FORK
       4. THURSTON

C 4 1 1872 T18S R2W S4
Located in the southeast part of Springfield. Leave Main Street (OR. Hwy. 126) and go south on South 58th Street which curves and becomes South 57th Street. The cemetery, is on the right at the junction with Mt. Vernon Road with entrances being on Mt. Vernon Road. In August 1952 burials from Middle Fork Cemetery, AKA: Landax Cemetery, were transferred here before the old sites were flooded by Lookout Point Reservoir. For a time this portion was known as New Middle Fork Cemetery, but all has since been known by the name Mt. Vernon Cemetery. {18 November 2000} (Springfield 1967-86 USGS Quad. map.)

MOXLEY — A 1 5 1883-1894 T19S R4W S12
Proceed about 4 miles northwest of Creswell, via Camas Swale Road, to Tolman Road. Turn right (north) onto Tolman Road and go 1 mile. NOTE: Ask permission at the house. There is a driveway to the right which goes through a field for about 300 yards to the cemetery at the foot of a small hill. In June 1940, the cemetery was advertised for sale for unpaid taxes. The burial ground contained 4 known burials and was reportedly destroyed; it was still there in November of 1980, but badly damaged. (Creswell 1984 USGS Quad. map.)

Name of Cemetery and also known as	Number of burials	Acres	Condition	Date started or earliest known burial	Township	Range	Section

MULHOLLAND FAMILY

A   0.33 5   1854-1879   T19S R2W   S4
Located near Pleasant Hill Cemetery. Leave OR. Hwy. 58, going south on Enterprise Road for 0.93 of a mile; then turn right (west) onto Morningstar Road North and proceed 0.6 of a mile. The cemetery is 100 yards to the right (north) on the edge of a hill on private land. Burials for 5 adults and 4 children are on the Edward Mulholland Sr. D.L.C. #44, RB #1370. The follwing is a list of burials found on an undated D.A.R. list: Edward Mulholland 1799-1858, Infant children of Locke died in 1854 and 1859, Margaret Mulholland 1835-1860, John Mulholland 1836-1866, Margaret, infant daughter of Thomas and Mary died 1866, Martha Jane Spry wife of William died 1866, M. Jane, infant daughter of Wm. & J. died 1866, Martha Mulholland 1806-1879. (Jasper 1986 USGS Quad. map.)

MULKEY

D   2.1 3   1850   T18S R4W   S2
Located in Eugene. Turn southwest off of West 18th Avenue onto Hawkins Lane and up Hawkins Hill to the intersection with Broadview and the cemetery driveway. (Eugene West 1967-86 USGS Quad. map.)

NELSON CREEK
AKA: 1. WHEELER
      BURIAL

A   0.1 5   1887-1894   T17S R8W   S14
Located on the north side of Nelson Mountain-Chickahominy Road, above a sharp curve just east of Leaver Creek. (Not shown on Greenleaf 1984 USGS Quad. map.)

OAK HILL

C   10   1   1853   T17S R5W   S25
Located west of Eugene. Head west off of OR. Hwy. 99 on Royal Avenue, then turn south on Oak Hill Cemetery Road. The cemetery was almost entirely vandalized after having been abandoned, but it has since been rehabilitated and enlarged. {12 June 1996} (Eugene West 1967-86 USGS Quad. map.)

PACIFIC SUNSET MEMORIAL PARK
AKA: 1. CUSHMAN
     2. FLORENCE

D 16.25 1   1893   T18S R12W   S25
This is the principal cemetery for Florence. Enter 0.2 of a mile east of North Fork Bridge on OR. Hwy. 126 and go

Name of Cemetery and also known as	Number of burials	Acres	Condition	Date started or earliest known burial	Township	Range	Section

3. FLORENCE
   LODGE A.F.
   AND A.M.
   #107
4. MASONIC
   [FLORENCE]

uphill. The present name was given in 1960:
There were 1,412 known burials in 1982.
(Florence 1984 USGS Quad. map.)

PIONEER MEMORIAL CEMETERY PARK
AKA: 1. BRIGGS FAMILY, ELISA AND MARY
2. I.O.O.F. SPRINGFIELD LODGE #70
3. OLD SPRINGFIELD
4. SPRINGFIELD PIONEER MEMORIAL PARK

A   0.25   1   1852-1953   T17S R3W   S35
Located in Springfield at South "C" Street
and 4th. This old cemetery is now a city
park. First used as a burial ground for the
family of Elias and Mary Briggs, they deeded
the cemetery on 31 October 1866 to Lane
County. Burials lessened after 1900 and the
cemetery was taken over by the city of
Springfield in 1913: however few
improvements were made until 1973. Most of
the burials were moved to Laurel Grove
Cemetery but 12 monuments remain here, for 13
people, with dates from 1856 to 1953. Nine
markers are cemented into a flooring and 3
fragments are standing against the large
signboard. Originally about 2 acres were
dedicated, but the park is now much smaller:
on the Elias M. Briggs D.L.C. #67, OC #1673.
{14 August 1992} (Eugene East 1967-86 USGS
Quad. map.)

PLEASANT HILL PIONEER
AKA: 1. PLEASANT HILL

C   4   1   1853   T18S R2W   S34
Located on OR. Hwy. 58 about 1 mile east of
the community of Pleasant Hill, on the
(north) side of the highway.   It is on the
Elijah Bristow D.L.C. #69, OC #2634. (Jasper
1986 USGS Quad. map.)

POOLE FAMILY, HAROLD

?   ?   ?   ?   T16S R10W   S29
There have been reported family burials on
the Poole Family place located somewhere out
of Florence. The 1931 *Metsker Landownership
Atlas of Lane County* shows a Monroe Poole
owned land at the-then site of the locale of
Pawn. If this is indeed the site of the
Harold Poole place it is many miles up the
North Fork Road from Florence and is in the
Township, Range and Section indicated here.
(Not shown on the Cummins Peak 1984 USGS
Quad. map.)

Name of Cemetery and also known as	Number of burials	Acres	Condition	Date started or earliest known burial	Township	Range	Section

RENFREW, DOCTOR ALEXANDER

A   0.01   5   Aug. 1876   T16S R4E   S5

A lone grave near Gold Hill Forest Lookout site, on a ridge between the watersheds of the McKenzie and Calapooia Rivers, north of the Blue River Dam. (Blue River 1989 USGS Quad. map. Not shown on the Willamette National Forest 1990 map.)

RENSHAW, MARY JULIA

A   0.01   ?   17 Mar 1858   T18S R3W   ?

This is possibly on Section 32 or 33. Mary Julia Renshaw, daughter of William D. Renshaw and Mary Jane Walker, born 31 May 1855, died 17 March 1858. The diary of 13-year old Elizabeth Maria Jane Renshaw, niece of William who was present at the burial says, "they buried her in Uncle William's pasture, in a grove of trees. There were a good many at little Julia's burying" (18 March 1858). William D. Renshaw came across the plains in 1852 and settled in the north part of Camas Swale, between Creswell and Goshen. The Creswell 1984 USGS Quad. map shows no buildings of any kind within his 320-acre D.L.C.. Take OR. Hwy. 99 south of Goshen parallel to I-5 Freeway for 2 miles, to Dillard Road. Turn right (west) and proceed on Dillard Road for 1.4 miles; turn left (south) on Hideaway Hills Road for 0.75 of a mile, making one turn, to the right (west). Lastly, turn left (south) onto Hideaway Branch Road for 0.5 of a mile. It ends at a house on a ridge. Any further search must be on foot and on private property. On the William Renshaw D.L.C. #55, RB #2075; the prospects for locating this burial would appear slim. (Not shown on Creswell 1984 USGS Quad. map.)

REPSLEGER ROAD
AKA: 1. BUCK
      2. MARTIN

A   0.01   5   Circa 1898   T20S R4W   S23

Located northwest of Cottage Grove via Cottage Grove-Lorane Road, then turn left onto Repsleger Road. The burials are on a hill near Silk Creek Cemetery. Go 0.65 of a mile on Repsleger Road to a 90-degree turn to the left; turn into a driveway on the right, at 79442 Repsleger Road and ask permission to visit this cemetery. One virtually needs a guide to walk to the two graves: one on the southeast slope of the hill and one near the summit, which was for Mrs. Gertrude Martin, who died in 1898. She was reburied in the Fir Grove Cemetery but her vacated grave was filled with a horse named Nellie, buried sometime between 1902 and 1908. (Not shown on Lorane 1984 USGS Quad. map.)

REST HAVEN MEMORIAL PARK

D 76 1 Mar 1930 T18S R3W S5

Located at 3986 Willamette Street, Eugene, it includes a small mausoleum. (Eugene East 1967-86 USGS Quad. map.)

REST LAWN MEMORIAL PARK
AKA: 1. BARROW
2. BEAR CREEK
3. COX BUTTE
4. I.O.O.F. [JUNCTION CITY]
5. LONG TOM
6. MAHON
7. OASIS LODGE #41 I.O.O.F.

E 16 1 1897 T15S R5W S34

Go 4.5 miles west of Junction City via High Pass Road; then right (north) on Territorial Road 0.5 of a mile. It is on the Solomon Cox D.L.C., RB #1427. {15 August 1990} (Cheshire 1984 USGS Quad. map.)

RICHARDSON
AKA: 1. EVERGREEN HILL CAMP
2. MODERN WOODMEN OF THE WORLD: EUGENE CAMP #583
3. RICHARDSON BUTTE

B 2 3 1853 T17S R5W S4

Located about 0.25 of a mile west of Fern Ridge Dam on Clear Creek Road. Turn into the Engineers Office parking lot and drive up the butte to the cemetery which has had vandalism, old and new. It is on the Benjamin Richardson D.L.C. #42, RB #1749. {22 May 1991} (Veneta 1984 USGS Quad. map.)

RICHARDSON FAMILY, GIDEON

A 1 4 1864 T15S R5W S15

This family burial ground has sometimes been confused with the Fergueson Cemetery. The latter is on the summit of a hill; the Richardson family burials are on the northwest slope of the next hill to the east of the Fergueson Cemetery. There is no roadway or pathway connection between the two. The Richardson family burials are on

Name of Cemetery and also known as	Number of burials	Acres	Condition	Date started or earliest known burial	Township	Range	Section

private property and are reached by a quite complicated driveway from Territorial Road. Park by the Long Tom River and walk through a cow pasture to the graves under an oak tree. The present marker is estimated to be only about 40 years old. It names 8 members of the family, of whom the latest date of death is 1932. In addition, 2 boys of the family who drowned in 1892 are buried here. The enclosing fence is now gone but telltale growing Vinca major and an old lilac proclaim a bygone burial ground. Located on the Gideon and Margaret Richardson D.L.C., OC #76. {22 September 1993} (Not shown on Monroe 1969-75 USGS Quad. map.)

SAGINAW

? ? 12 ?   T20S R3W   ?

Probably located in section 15 or 16. This cemetery apparently was on the south side of Saginaw West Road soon after it leaves OR. Hwy. 99. It is reported to have been plowed over; the headstones were supposedly stored in a barn in the 1930's. (Not shown on Cottage Grove 1984 USGS Quad. map.)

SAILOR PIONEER
AKA: 1. BOYD
     2. NOTI
     3. SAYLOR

C 3 2 1859   T17S R6W   S28

Located 1 mile east of Noti or go west from the traffic light at Veneta, at the junction of Territorial Highway and Route "F" (OR. Hwy. 126). It is 4.1 miles over the new alignment of Route "F" to Sailor Cemetery Road on the right, which leads back up the hill to the cemetery. The earliest marker found was 1859 (26 May 1977 *Eugene Register Guard*). This cemetery was severely vandalized in Feburary 1992. {9 August 1991} (Noti 1984 USGS Quad. map.)

SANFORD, JOSIAH

A 0.01 ? 1882   T21S R3E   S9

This was on the grounds of the Circle Bar Golf Club near Oakridge. Josiah Sanford, born in 1801, was the first white settler at Oakridge. This burial has been removed to Pleasant Hill Cemetery (see that entry).

Name of Cemetery and also known as	Number of burials	Acres	Condition	Date started or earliest known burial	Township	Range	Section

SAYLOR
AKA: 1. LLOYD
     2. RAGSDALE

A 0.25 5 1856   T19S R2W   S19

Located east off of Bear Creek Road, 1 mile south of Cloverdale and 0.5 of a mile south of the Cloverdale School, at 82531 Bear Creek Road. Only 2 markers were found in 1981; on the Sydner [Sic] H. Saylor D.L.C. #59, RB #339. NOTE: The owner, without a very good reason did not wish visitors. (Not shown on Jasper 1986 USGS Quad. map.)

SCHRIMPF FAMILY

A 0.1 5 1900   T19S R5W   S2

Located south of Crow, north of Lorane and off of Territorial Road. Henry C. Schrimpf (1823-1900) and Minnie L. Schrimpf (1872-1903) are buried here. Other family members are in McCulloch Cemetery. NOTE: This site is on private property. The landowner wished to protect the gravesite which is, in any event, very difficult to reach and impossible without a guide. (Not shown on Crow 1984 USGS Quad. map.)

SEARS
AKA: 1. MOUNTAIN VIEW

C 10 2 1853   T20S R3W   S35

Located 3 miles east of Cottage Grove via Row River Road. Go 0.5 of a mile east of the Row River Bridge to a driveway on the right (south) and go about 300 yards. The cemetery is on the west side of the road, on a hillside; divided between the Robert Alexander D.L.C. #70, RB #1171 and the Joseph Gale D.L.C. #72, RB #266. (Cottage Grove 1984 USGS Quad. map.)

SHARPLES GRAVES

A 0.01 2 1920-1937   T18S R2W   S29

Located about 3 miles southeast of Goshen Interchange of the I-5 Freeway and OR. Hwy. 58. Leave OR. Hwy. 58, turn left on Brabham Road and left again on Holm Lane. These graves were in a wheat field in 1981. NOTE: This site is on private property. (Jasper 1986 USGS Quad. map.)

SHIELDS
AKA: 1. KNOX HILL

C 5 2 1868   T20S R3W   S33

Located in Cottage Grove. Cross under the I-5 Freeway on 16th Street and go to the right on Shields Road, uphill. The plat was filed

Name of Cemetery and also known as	Number of burials	Acres	Condition	Date started or earliest known burial	Township	Range	Section

in 1933, for 4 acres. This is just outside of the William Shields D.L.C. #56, RB #340. NOTE: The AKA: Knox Hill, properly belongs to Cloverdale Cemetery rather than to Shields Cemetery. (Cottage Grove 1984 USGS Quad. map.)

SHILOH BURIAL
AKA: 1. MACDONALD, SHERIDAN

A 0.01 3 3 June 1972 T19S R1W S29
Sheridan MacDonald was a young woman member of the Shiloh Youth Revival Study Center, who was stricken with cancer and asked to be buried there. The Center is at 81868 Lost Valley Lane. Take OR. Hwy. 58 past Pleasant Hill and in the Dexter area, turn right (south) onto Rattlesnake Road. Drive 3.8 miles on Rattlesnake Road and turn right onto Lost Valley Lane. After 0.8 of a mile on the lane there is the entry and a driveway on the right; go 0.25 of a mile to a shop on the right. The rough road forks and it is best to have a guide for the last 0.25 of a mile to the grave. (Not shown on Lowell 1986 USGS Quad. map.)

SILK CREEK COMMUNITY
AKA: 1. ROYAL GRANGE

B 1 2 Circa 1896 T20S R4W S13
Located west of Cottage Grove, on Cottage Grove-Lorane Road opposite the junction with Repsleger Road; on the Royal H. Hazleton D.L.C. #48, RB #752. (Lorane 1984 USGS Quad. map.)

SMALL D.L.C., GEORGE

A 0.01 1 1855-1863 T20S R3W ?
Possibly located in Sections 30, 31 or 32. This is the burial site of 2 children: Amanda E. Small, died 4 November 1855 and George P. Long, died 22 February 1863 . NOTE: They are buried in what is now the yard of a private residence at Cottage Grove, located at 777 South River Road. The owners would prefer that curiosity seekers not attempt to visit the site. It is on the George Small D.L.C. #60, RB #755. This is not to be confused with the Small Family Cemetery out of London. (Not shown on Cottage Grove 1984 USGS Quad. map.)

Lane County

SMALL FAMILY
AKA: 1. LONE PINE

B   1   2   1883   T22S R3W   S17

Located south of Cottage Grove on the east side of London Road, on a low hill 0.3 of a mile north of London School. There is a driveway to the east, to a house where one must ask to visit the cemetery which is just south of the house, and only 0.1 of a mile from London Road. 31 marked graves were found in December of 1980. The local people refer to the cemetery as the Small Family Cemetery, not Lone Pine: on the Dana J. Parish D.L.C. #43, RB #470. (Cottage Grove Lake 1987 USGS Quad. map.)

SMITH, ELIZA B.

A 0.01 5   1872   T18S R2W   S3

This burial is adjacent to, but separate from, the Emigrant Cemetery. Located at 36191 Jasper Road, southeast of Springfield. Drive southerly along Jasper Road for 0.8 of a mile from the junction with Mt. Vernon Road, turn left (east) onto a driveway, into what was the Mt. June Lumber Company. NOTE: At 0.2 of a mile uphill along this driveway is the house, 36191 Jasper Road, where you must ask permission to visit the site. The Eliza Smith monument is on one side of a fence and the Emigrant Cemetery site is on the other, with the marble monument leaning against a large oak tree; on the John Smith D.L.C. #48, RB #1791. (Not shown on Springfield 1967-86 USGS Quad. map.)

SMITH FAMILY

A 0.01 ?   ?   T15S R6W   ?

This could be in Section 23 or 24, 7.5 miles west of Territorial Road, and north off of Ferguson Road. 2 or 3 children are buried on the Smith Homestead 200-300 yards off of Ferguson Road, uphill. (Not shown on Glenbrook 1984 USGS Quad. map.)

SMITH FAMILY
AKA: 1. WEYERHAEUSER
     DUMP ROAD

A 0.1 5   1876-1891   T18S R2W   ?

In Springfield at 57th Street, south of McKenzie Highway (OR. Hwy. 126), take the private logging road of Weyerhaeuser Co. (permission is needed); go about 0.7 of a mile to the east and south to the mill dump. The cemetery, with 4 known burials, is on the left on a hill top. It is unclear to the compiler if this Smith Family Cemetery has a connection to the Eliza B. Smith burial near by, see that article. (Questionable location on the Springfield 1967-86 USGS Quad. map. The map shows a "grave" in Section 10, not Section 3, and is located about 1.4 miles along the same private logging road-not 0.7 of a mile.)

SMITH, TOM

A   0.01   ?   24 Dec 1991 T15S R12W   S27
Mr. Smith, an educator and environmentalist at Yachats, is buried in the woods behind his home at Tenmile Creek. This is on private property and south of Yachats in Lane County. (Not shown on Heceta Head 1984 USGS Quad. map.)

SPARKS FAMILY

A   0.01   5   1911-1912   T16S R4E   S20
Located in the community of Blue River. The site is at 51467 Blue River Drive, on the north side of the road and about 0.6 of a mile from the Forest Service Office. It is about 100 feet from the main road and no visible trace remains. Only the gravestones were moved to Greenwood Cemetery: S. C. Sparks, 1848-1911; infant Naomi Elaine Sparks, 7 October 1912. (Not shown on Blue River 1989 USGS Quad. map.)

SPRINGFIELD MEMORIAL GARDENS

D   25   1   1963   T17S R2W   S35
Located at the east end of Springfield, east of 72nd Street and on the south side of the McKenzie Highway (OR. Hwy. 126). This also includes 2 small mausoleums; on the James C. Looney D.L.C. #85, RB #1663. (Springfield 1967-86 USGS Quad. map.)

SPRUCE POINT

?   ?   ?   ?   T18S R12W   S27
This burial ground, if it ever existed, should be written off of the books. It was supposedly located on the north bank of the Siuslaw River in Florence a short distance downstream from the U.S. Hwy. 101 bridge. It was supposedly along the big curve where Rhododendron Drive is intersected by the

507

Name of Cemetery and also known as	Number of burials	Acres	Condition	Date started or earliest known burial	Township	Range	Section

Peace Hospital Street. A careful search there and interviews with old-timers found no evidence of a cemetery here. Just possibly this was a long-ago indian burial ground. See *Cemeteries in the Florence Area*, compiled by Eileen H. Gray, Siuslaw Genealogical Society, 1993, page 131. (Not shown on Florence 1984 USGS Quad. map.)

STAFFORD FAMILY

B 1.1 2 1853 T17S R2W S3

Go north of Springfield on Marcola Road about 0.9 of a mile north of the Stafford Creek Bridge and about 0.2 of a mile south of the Mohawk River Bridge. Turn right (east) on a lane and go about 0.25 of a mile; it is on a hillside before you reach the powerlines. Located on the Barnett Ramsey D.L.C. #71, RB #1744. (Springfield 1967-86 USGS Quad. map.)

STAPLETON FAMILY

A 0.2 1 21 Sep 1981 T18S R5W S4

A newly-established family cemetery with only a single burial, as of October 1982. The family owns the land that includes the old Central School Cemetery; the access is the same as for that cemetery, but Stapleton Family is about 200 feet further and in a grove of 3 oak trees. NOTE: This site is on private property. (Not shown on Veneta 1984 USGS Quad. map.)

STEPHENS FAMILY
AKA: 1. STEVENS
     FAMILY

B 1 3 1882 T18S R6W S14

Leave Veneta on Bolton Hill Road and drive to Vaughn Road. Turn left onto Vaughn Road and head for Crow. After about 1.5 miles from Bolton Hill Road junction, the cemetery is about 500 feet off on the left (northwest), on a ridge. Turn off of Vaughn Road at the steep gravel driveway for 24325 Vaughn Road. This private family cemetery is at the top of the hill. Ask for permission to visit at the house next door to the cemetery. It is on the Henry B. Smith D.L.C. #37, RB # 1969. The 4 Stephens children died of typhoid in 1882-3, 1 acre of ground was deeded. (Noti 1984 USGS Quad. map.)

Name of Cemetery and also known as	Number of burials	Acres	Condition	Date started or earliest known burial	Township	Range	Section

SUNDSTROM, BRUCE
AKA: 1. ROCK CREEK
        CANYON
        CO-OP

A   0.5   2   31 Oct 1977   T16S R8W   S18
Turn north off of OR. Hwy. 36 at Deadwood onto Deadwood Creek Road. Between Mileposts 8 and 9, turn right onto Bassonette Road. Please obtain permission at Route 1 Box 26, Bassonette Road. Drive 0.4 of a mile down Bassonette Road to a gateway on the east side of the road and a trail of about 250 feet, to the grave. Daniel Hays reported that as of July 1981, there were plans for a regular cemetery for the Co-op. Robert Bruce Sundstrom (1 July 1948-31 October 1977), killed when struck by a logging truck. (Not shown on Windy Peak 1984 USGS Quad. map.)

SUNSET HILLS MEMORIAL GARDENS
AKA: 1. EUGENE
        MEMORIAL
        GARDENS
     2. GARDEN OF
        THE GOOD
        SHEPHERD

D   16   1   1952   T18S R3W   S18
4374 South Willamette Street, Eugene. (Eugene East 1967-86 USGS Quad. map.)

SWAMP CREEK ROAD BURIALS

A   0.1   5   Circa 1899   T16S R7W   S7
Located on Swamp Creek Road, north off of OR. Hwy. 36 on the Slater Homestead. It is on private property at 93674 Swamp Creek Road, which leaves OR. Hwy. 36 west of Blachly. Drive one mile on Swamp Creek Road; the burial site is just above the road exactly opposite the driveway from the barn. One adult and two or three children are buried at this site, of which no visible trace remained in July of 1981. The family name is variously spelled: Slater, Slayter, or Slaytor. (Not shown on Triangle Lake 1984 USGS Quad. map.)

SWEET CREEK
AKA: 1. POINT
        TERRACE

B   ?   ?   25 Mar 1884   T18S R10W   ?
Point Terrace is on the left (south) bank of the Siuslaw River below Mapleton and at the mouth of Sweet Creek. Leave Mapleton on Route "F" (OR. Hwy. 126) and cross the Siuslaw River Bridge. Just beyond the bridge, turn right onto Sweet Creek Road. Drive westward and downstream along the

Name of Cemetery and also known as	Number of burials	Acres	Condition	Date started or earliest known burial	Township	Range	Section

Siuslaw River for 4.7 miles, to the junction with Bernhardt Creek Road. This is at Point Terrace. From this road junction Sweet Creek Road turns inland (south). The burials are presumably somewhere in the vicinity of Point Terrace on the homestead of Zara and Maria Sweet, possably on Section 16 or 17. There are 22 known burials plus four possible burials at this site. (Not shown on Tiernan 1984 USGS Quad. map.)

SWEET HOME
AKA: 1. BORLAND
     2. CARTER
     3. GOLDSON

A 1   2   1898   T16S R6W   S27
This is not to be confused with the town of Sweet Home, in Linn County, which has 4 cemeteries in or nearby, and none of them named Sweet Home. Drive west of Cheshire on OR. Hwy. 36, to about Milepost 41. NOTE: This site is on private property. The cemetery is on the right (north) side of the highway at 24145 Highway 36. Visitors need permission to visit and a guide through the several roadways to the cemetery. A cemetery plat was filed in April 1898. The earliest dated monument found was 1894. You will find a complete listing of known burials in the Genealogical Forum of Oregon's, *Bulletin*, Volume XLI, Quarterly Number 4 on page 181-183. {5 Feb. 1992} (Horton 1984 USGS Quad. map.)

TAYLOR FAMILY

A 0.2 5   1893-1898 T16S R7W   S9
Located just west of Blachly on OR. Hwy 36. Turn southeasterly on Post Road and go about 0.4 of a mile. NOTE: The burials were on the right. There were 2 stones marking 4 burials found in October 1980. Additional research reported 4 adults and 2 children, all buried before nearby Blachly Cemetery was begun. (This small cemetery is reportedly destroyed, however it is shown on the Triangle Lake 1984 USGS Quad. map.)

TAYLOR-LANE FAMILY
AKA: 1. LANE FAMILY
     2. TAYLOR FAMILY

C 2   2   1867   T21S R3W   S16
Located south of Cottage Grove. Take London Road to the left off of OR. Hwy. 99, about 1.5 miles south of the I-5 Freeway turn right (west) off of London Road onto Harris Drive

| Name of Cemetery and also known as | Number of burials | Acres | Condition | Date started or earliest known burial | Township | Range | Section |

and then right onto Nellie Lane to the cemetery. It is on the Henry Taylor D.L.C. #48, RB #670 and Silas Lane D.L.C. #42, RB #672. (Cottage Grove Lake 1987 USGS Quad. map.)

THOMPSON PLACE
AKA: 1. THOMPSON, MANLEY

A 0.01 ? ? T17S R10W ?
Perhaps located in Section 23 or 26. The Thompson Place was located upstream from Mapleton on the south side of the Siuslaw River across from Rainrock. Manley Thompson was reported buried on the place. (Not shown on Mapleton 1984 USGS Quad. map.)

TOLL FAMILY
AKA: 1. APPLEGATE, SARAH ALMIRA

A 0.1 5 Circa 1880 T19S R4W S2
Said to be in the North 1/2 of the Northwest 1/4 of Section 2 and 25 paces from the south line of the Toll property. The burials are on private land at 30488 Fox Hollow Road; guidance is needed to visit the 4 graves: 3 infant girls of Althea Applegate Toll and their maternal grandmother, Sarah Almira Applegate (1832-1893). (Not shown on Fox Hollow 1984 USGS Quad. map.)

TRAPP GIRL

A 0.01 5 21 Jan 1913 T18S R5W S24
Take Spencer Creek Road southwest out of Eugene; turn right (north) onto Pine Grove, then left (west) onto Erickson Road and drive 0.4 of a mile to the driveway of 27716 Erickson Road. NOTE: This site is on private property. After receiving permission at the house, it is necessary to walk 0.5 of a mile, with guidance, to the gravesite on a hillside in the trees of a girl aged about 1 year. (Not shown on Fox Hollow 1984 USGS Quad. map.)

UNION
AKA: 1. MAYS
2. TURNBOW
3. UNION CEMETERY OF LONG TOM

B 1 3 1856 T16S R5W S5
Proceed a total of 2.5 miles west of Territorial Road on High Pass Road. At 0.4 of a mile past the junction of Smyth Road with High Pass Road on the left, at Milepost 6.2 on High Pass Road, turn right (north) up the driveway to a gate. You must

511

Name of Cemetery and also known as	Number of burials	Acres	Condition	Date started or earliest known burial	Township	Range	Section

walk up to the wooded cemetery. {22 September 1993} (Cheshire 1984 USGS Quad. map.)

UNKNOWN

A 0.01 ? ? T18S R11W S12

This burial is on the old Tilly Thomas homesite at Milepost 8.5 on OR. Hwy. 126. This is at the western edge of the community of Tiernan. NOTE: We do not know if it is on the Siuslaw River side or the inland side of the highway. (Not shown on Tiernan 1984 USGS Quad. map.)

UPPER MABEL
AKA: 1. DRURY
    2. MABEL CHURCH

B 0.9 2 1881 T15S R1W S28

Located about 2 miles north of the site of Mabel. Drive 1 mile on Marcola Road north past the Shotgun Creek Road junction. Turn left off of Marcola Road onto Johnson Creek Road and go 0.75 of a mile to the cemetery on the right. (Marcola 1988 USGS Quad. map.)

UPPER SWEET CREEK
AKA: 1. FLOYD FAMILY

A 0.01 ? Circa 1900 ? R10W ?

Located off of Sweet Creek Road and south of Sweet Creek Cemetery. Point Terrace is on the left (south) bank of the Siuslaw River below Mapleton and at the mouth of Sweet Creek. Leave Mapleton on Route "F" (OR. Hwy. 126) and cross the Siuslaw River Bridge. Just beyond the bridge, turn right onto Sweet Creek Road. Drive westward and downstream along the Siuslaw River for 4.7 miles, to the junction with Bernhardt Creek Road. This is at Point Terrace. From this road junction Sweet Creek Road turns inland (south). The burials are presumably somewhere in the vicinity of Point Terrace. Two girls, names now lost, the daughters of Elwood and Maryanna Floyd died of smallpox and were buried on the family property. (Not shown on Tiernan or Goodwin Peak 1984 USGS Quad. maps.)

VALLEY VIEW
AKA: 1. DONNA
    2. MARCOLA
    3. MOHAWK

D 4 2 1928 T17S R2W S3

From the community of Mohawk, leave Marcola Road onto Hill Road and drive 1.5 miles southwest towards Springfield. The

Name of Cemetery and also known as	Number of burials	Acres	Condition	Date started or earliest known burial	Township	Range	Section

4. MOHAWK COMMUNITY CHURCH

cemetery is on the right in a grove of trees. It is on the A. D. E. Washburn D.L.C. #63, RB #1979. NOTE: Most unfortunately, there are 2 separate cemeteries, each of them called Marcola Cemetery and each of them are called Valley View Cemetery. Please see the article on Marcola Cemetery for the other cemetery in this vicinity. Access to the cemetery must be obtained from the pastor of the Mohawk Community Church, who then notifies the people living across the road from the cemetery. About 40 stones were visible in November of 1980 besides the temporary marked and unmarked burials. (Mohawk 1988 USGS Quad. map.)

VINSON, MRS.

A 0.01 8 ?   T19S R1E   S34
She was originally buried near the Middle Fork Cemetery. The burial was moved before Lookout Point Dam was completed on 11 August 1952, and reburied in the New Middle Fork Cemetery, now Mt. Vernon Cemetery, as with the Fred Gray reburial (see that article). The Vinson marker has since disappeared. (Not shown on Fall Creek Lake 1986 USGS Quad. map.)

WALKER
 AKA: 1. WALKER UNION CHURCH

C 1.5 2 1861   T20S R3W   S10
Located between Creswell and Cottage Grove. Leave OR. Hwy. 99 to the west on England Road. The cemetery is behind the church, on the Anderson Hamilton D.L.C. #45, RB #341. (Cottage Grove 1984 USGS Quad. map.)

WALKER ADDITION

A ? ? ?   T21S R3E   S17
The Walker Addition to Oakridge lay on the north side of the railway between Elder and Portal Streets. There were a number of graves here that were at some time moved to Forest Vale Cemetery. (Not shown on Oakridge 1986 USGS Quad. map.)

WALLACE
 AKA: 1. JASPER

B 0.3 2 1866   T18S R2W   S14
At the community of Jasper southeast of Springfield, turn inland on Wallace Creek Road for about 1 mile. Turn right onto the

private logging road of the Weyerhaeuser Company and drive about 0.3 of a mile to the cemetery on the right. 59 markers were found in October of 1980; on the James A. Wallace D.L.C. #40, OC #1651. NOTE: This site is on private property and permission is required. (Springfield 1967-86 USGS Quad. map.)

WALTON
AKA: 1. CENTRAL CEMETERY ASSOCIATION

C 2 2 1872   T18S R7W   S5

Located along Route "F" Highway, (OR. Hwy. 126) by Milepost 34. This is about 1.3 miles east of the community of Walton and about 0.5 of a mile east of the Lyons School. {9 August 1991} (Walton 1984 USGS Quad. map.)

WARNER, MRS.
AKA: 1. SIMPSON CREEK

A 0.01 ? 1853   T24S R3E   S13

Leave OR. Hwy. 58 just east of Oakridge; turn right (south) onto Willamette Forest Hwy. 21 and go past Hills Creek Reservoir, continuing towards Emigrant Pass. About 20 miles from OR. Hwy. 58 and a mile past Campers Flat Camp Forest Hwy. 21 crosses Simpson Creek. Here in 1853 the first emigrant train to pass this way was making a slow and difficult passage. One wagon overturned in crossing Simpson Creek at its confluence with the Middle Fork Willamette River. A Mrs. Warner was fatally injured and was buried here in a lost grave. (Not shown on Staley Ridge 1986 USGS Quad. map.)

WENDLING

A 0.01 5 ?   T16S R1W   S10

The Booth-Kelly Lumber Company had a community of Wendling from 1895 until 1946, of which only traces remain. Leave Marcola Road and turn east onto Wendling Road, crossing the covered bridge over Mill Creek and almost to the entrance to the Georgia Pacific Land Park. The cemetery was on the slope of the hill across the Wolf Creek tributary flowing south into Mill Creek. The cemetery was about 100 feet up the hill behind the chlorine tank of the ruined water treatment plant. (Not shown on Marcola 1988 USGS Quad. map.)

Name of Cemetery and also known as	Number of burials	Acres	Condition	Date started or earliest known burial	Township	Range	Section

WEST LAWN MEMORIAL PARK
AKA: 1. BETHESDA DANISH EVANGELICAL LUTHERAN
2. I.O.O.F. [NEW: EUGENE]
3. I.O.O.F. SPENCER BUTTE LODGE #9

E   10   1   ?   T17S R4W   S33
Go west from Eugene on West 11th Avenue (OR. Hwy. 126). Turn right (north) onto Danebo Road and drive 0.5 of a mile to the cemetery at 225 Danebo road. This cemetery was formed by the amalgamation of Bethesda Danish Lutheran Cemetery, founded in 1901, with Spencer Butte I.O.O.F. #9, which was established in 1923. (Eugene West 1967-86 USGS Quad. map.)

WHITE D.L.C., WILLIAM
AKA: 1. GRIFFIN
2. LIBERTY
3. WINN, JOHN

A   0.25   8   1891   T15S R5W   S20
Leave Territorial Road and drive 1.25 miles west on Ferguson Road to a mailbox at 26253 Ferguson Road. The cemetery site is on private property, so permission must be obtained at the house on the left (south) side of the road. The driveway to the cemetery is to the right (north) of Ferguson Road; go 0.5 of a mile to the farm, then turn left (west) and drive another 0.35 of a mile in a westerly direction. At the fence line, the cemetery site is to the north, in a wheat field on a slight knoll, where the cemetery was bulldozed out before 1976. The tombstones are gone, but records remain of the 8 burials of the Winn, Griffin, and Browning families. Located on the William White D.L.C., RB #2107 which in not shown on Monroe 1969-75 USGS Quad. maps. Nor is the cemetery shown. Liberty refers to the name of a one-time school in the vicinity.

WILLIS BURIALS
AKA: 1. WILLIS FAMILY

A   0.01   5   1856-1862   T19S R3W   S14
Two "white bronze" (actually zinc) monuments have been salvaged from the gravesites and are held at 83267 North Pacific Highway near Creswell. The residence is reached by leaving the I-5 Freeway at the Creswell Exit, going west to OR. Hwy. 99, then turning right (north) and driving 0.4 of a mile (just north of the north city limits of Creswell) to the driveway on the right (east) of 83267. The gravesites were originally in a pasture about 100 yards east of the house near a fence line. The markers are for Malinda C. Willis (2 December 1854-16 March 1856) and John A.

Name of Cemetery and also known as	Number of burials	Acres	Condition	Date started or earliest known burial	Township	Range	Section

Willis (5 November 1814-10 April 1862). The compiler has seen many "white bronze" markers and suspects this pair replaced the original burial markers perhaps as much as a generation later than their deaths. (Not shown on Creswell 1984 USGS Quad. map.)

WINBERRY CREEK BURIALS
AKA: 1. WINBURRY

A 0.01 8 ? T19S R1E S6
These 3 burials were moved to Mt. Vernon Cemetery when Fall Creek Dam was constructed and Fall Creek Lake covered the site. (Not shown on Fall Creek Lake 1986 USGS Quad. map.)

YOUNG
AKA: 1. LANCASTER
2. NORATON

B 1 2 1853-1950'S T15S R4W S7
Located about 2 miles west of Lancaster, at the junction of Jaeger and Howard Roads behind the house. Ask permission at 28985 Jaeger Lane, as this site is on private property. Lancaster was once a rival of Harrisburg, and this cemetery has some fine monuments testifying to bygone prosperity. The burials are on a barely perceptible rise on this, the highest elevation in the vicinity. Flooding could and did reach the edges of the cemetery. Boy Scout Troop 74 cleaned up this long-neglected cemetery in 1992. {5 February 1992} (Harrisburg 1969 USGS Quad. map.)

Mt. Vernon
Stanley R. Clarke (2000)

ADA	LANE CO.	T20S	R11W	S5
ALEXANDER D.L.C., ROBERT see **SEARS**				
	LANE CO.	T20S	R3W	S35
ALKIRE D.L.C., GEORGE see **MARCOLA**				
	LANE CO.	T16S	R2W	S24
ALLEN, WILLIAM P.	LANE CO.	?	?	?
ALMA	LANE CO.	T19S	R8W	S3
ALPHA	LANE CO.	T16S	R8W	?
AMERICAN BOTTOM see **CENTRAL SCHOOL**				
	LANE CO.	T18S	R5W	S4
ANDERSON, RUTH ROGERS see **ANDERSON'S HAVEN OF REST**				
	LANE CO.	T15S	R5W	S30
ANDERSON'S HAVEN OF REST	LANE CO.	T15S	R5W	S30
APPLEGATE, SARAH ALMIRA see **TOLL FAMILY**				
	LANE CO.	T19S	R4W	S2
BAIRD D.L.C., WILLIAM C. see **MABEL**				
	LANE CO.	T16S	R1W	S5
BAKER see **LUPER**	LANE CO.	T16S	R4W	S34
BAKER D.L.C., THOMAS AND ELIZABETH see **LUPER**				
	LANE CO.	T16S	R4W	S34
BAKER FAMILY see **LUPER**	LANE CO.	T16S	R4W	S34
BALL see **McCOLLUM**	LANE CO.	T18S	R4W	S30
BARROW see **REST LAWN MEMORIAL PARK**				
	LANE CO.	T15S	R5W	S34
BEAR CREEK see **REST LAWN MEMORIAL PARK**				
	LANE CO.	T15S	R5W	S34
BEERS see **INDIAN CREEK**	LANE CO.	T16S	R10W	S36
BEMIS	LANE CO.	T22S	R3W	S32
BETHESDA DANISH EVANGELICAL LUTHERAN				
	LANE CO.	T17S	R4W	S33
BETHESDA DANISH EVANGELICAL LUTHERAN see **WEST LAWN MEMORIAL PARK**				
	LANE CO.	T17S	R4W	S33
BLACHLY	LANE CO.	T16S	R7W	S9
BLUE MOUNTAIN see **BRUMBAUGH**	LANE CO.	T21S	R2W	S18
BOOTH-KELLY LUMBER COMPANY see **WENDLING**				
	LANE CO.	T16S	R1W	S10
BORLAND see **SWEET HOME**	LANE CO.	T16S	R6W	S27
BOYD see **SAILOR PIONEER**	LANE CO.	T17S	R6W	S28
BRAY	LANE CO.	T15S	R12W	S27
BRAY, GEORGIANIA STARR see **BRAY**	LANE CO.	T15S	R12W	S27
BRAY, KATIE MYRTH see **BRAY**	LANE CO.	T15S	R12W	S27
BRETHREN see **MABEL**	LANE CO.	T16S	R1W	S5
BRICE D.L.C., WILLIAM H. see **DOWNS, JAMES**				
	LANE CO.	T16S	R4W	?
BRIGGS D.L.C., ELISA M. see **PIONEER MEMORIAL CEMETERY PARK**				
	LANE CO.	T17S	R3W	S35
BRIGGS FAMILY, ELISA AND MARY see **PIONEER MEMORIAL CEMETERY PARK**				
	LANE CO.	T17S	R3W	S35
BRISTOW D.L.C., ELIJAH see **PLEASANT HILL PIONEER**				
	LANE CO.	T18S	R2W	S34
BROWNING FAMILY see **WHITE DLC, WILLIAM**				
	LANE CO.	T15S	R5W	S20

BRUMBAUGH	LANE CO.	T21S	R2W	S18
BUCK see REPSLEGER ROAD	LANE CO.	T20S	R4W	S23
BULL FAMILY see McKENZIE BRIDGE	LANE CO.	T16S	R5E	?
CALDWELL	LANE CO.	T16S	R5W	S24
CAMP CREEK	LANE CO.	T17S	R1W	S19
CANARY see ADA	LANE CO.	T20S	R11W	S5
CARMELITE NUNNERY see GATES OF HEAVEN				
	LANE CO.	T18S	R4W	S5
CARTER see SWEET HOME	LANE CO.	T16S	R6W	S27
CENTRAL CEMETERY ASSOCIATION see WALTON				
	LANE CO.	T18S	R7W	S5
CENTRAL GRANGE see CENTRAL SCHOOL				
	LANE CO.	T18S	R5W	S4
CENTRAL SCHOOL	LANE CO.	T18S	R5W	S4
CHESHIRE see FRANKLIN	LANE CO.	T16S	R5W	S21
CHICKAHOMINY	LANE CO.	T17S	R7W	S20
CHURCH see FALL CREEK	LANE CO.	T18S	R1W	S33
CHURCH OF THE CHRISTIANS see EVERGREEN HILL				
	LANE CO.	T17S	R3W	S14
CLOVERDALE	LANE CO.	T19S	R2W	S18
COBURG see I.O.O.F. [COBURG]	LANE CO.	T17S	R3W	S4
COGSWELL	LANE CO.	T19S	R3W	S5
COOS see DREW MEMORIAL	LANE CO.	T18S	R12W	S24
COTTAGE GROVE see FIR GROVE	LANE CO.	T20S	R3W	S29
COX BUTTE see REST LAWN MEMORIAL PARK				
	LANE CO.	T15S	R5W	S34
COX D.L.C., JESSE see KIME-BROWN FAMILY				
	LANE CO.	T16S	R5W	S17
COX D.L.C., SOLOMON see REST LAWN MEMORIAL PARK				
	LANE CO.	T15S	R5W	S34
CRAIG, JOHN TEMPLETON see CRAIG MEMORIAL				
	LANE CO.	T15S	R7 1/2E	UNS
CRAIG MEMORIAL	LANE CO.	T15S	R7 1/2E	UNS
CRESWELL PIONEER	LANE CO.	T19S	R3W	S21
CROW see McCULLOCH	LANE CO.	T18S	R5W	S34
CROW D.L.C., JOHN see CROW FAMILY				
	LANE CO.	T20S	R5W	S13
CROW FAMILY	LANE CO.	T20S	R5W	S13
CROWE [Sic] see CROW FAMILY	LANE CO.	T20S	R5W	S13
CULP CREEK	LANE CO.	T21S	R1W	S33
CUSHMAN see PACIFIC SUNSET MEMORIAL PARK				
	LANE CO.	T18S	R12W	S25
DANISH	LANE CO.	T16S	R5W	S4
DANISH LUTHERAN CHURCH see DANISH				
	LANE CO.	T16S	R5W	S4
DEADWOOD	LANE CO.	T17S	R9W	S15
DEADWOOD CHURCH see DEADWOOD	LANE CO.	T17S	R9W	S15
DERKATSCH, JOHANN	LANE CO.	T17S	R12W	S36
DIVIDE see HAWLEY	LANE CO.	T21S	R4W	S12
DONNA see VALLEY VIEW	LANE CO.	T17S	R2W	S3
DOOLITTLE FAMILY	LANE CO.	T20S	R2W	S21
DOWNS, JAMES	LANE CO.	T16S	R4W	?

DREW, CHIEF FRANK see **DREW MEMORIAL**				
	LANE CO.	T18S	R12W	S24
DREW MEMORIAL	LANE CO.	T18S	R12W	S24
DRISKELL see **CENTRAL SCHOOL**	LANE CO.	T18S	R5W	S4
DRURY see **UPPER MABLE**	LANE CO.	T15S	R1W	S28
DUNNING PLACE, CHARLES see **INDIAN BURIALS**				
	LANE CO.	?	?	?
DUNKARD CHURCH OF THE BRETHREN see **MABEL**				
	LANE CO.	T16S	R1W	S5
ELMIRA see **INMAN**	LANE CO.	T17S	R5W	S8
EMIGRANT	LANE CO.	T18S	R2W	S3
EUGENE CITY LODGE #11 see **MASONIC [EUGENE]**				
	LANE CO.	T18S	R3W	S5
EUGENE MEMORIAL GARDENS see **SUNSET HILLS MEMORIAL GARDENS**				
	LANE CO.	T18S	R3W	S18
EUGENE PIONEER	LANE CO.	T17S	R3W	S32
EVERGREEN see **EVERGREEN HILL**	LANE CO.	T17S	R3W	S14
EVERGREEN HILL	LANE CO.	T17S	R3W	S14
EVERGREEN HILL CAMP see **RICHARDSON**				
	LANE CO.	T17S	R5W	S4
FALL CREEK	LANE CO.	T18S	R1W	S33
FALL CREEK CHRISTION see **FALL CREEK**				
	LANE CO.	T18S	R1W	S33
FATHERGILL [Sic], JOHN see **FOTHERGILL, JOHN**				
	LANE CO.	T18S	R1W	S33
FERGUESON D.L.C., JOHN B. see **FERGUESON FAMILY**				
	LANE CO.	T15S	R5W	S22
FERGUESON FAMILY	LANE CO.	T15S	R5W	S22
FERGUSON FAMILY see **FERGUESON FAMILY**				
	LANE CO.	T15S	R5W	S22
FERN RIDGE see **CENTRAL SCHOOL**	LANE CO.	T18S	R5W	S4
FIR GROVE	LANE CO.	T20S	R3W	S29
FIR GROVE see **ADA**	LANE CO.	T20S	R11W	S5
FLORENCE see **PACIFIC SUNSET MEMORIAL PARK**				
	LANE CO.	T18S	R12W	S25
FLORENCE LODGE A. F. AND A. M. #107 see **PACIFIC SUNSET MEMORIAL PARK**				
	LANE CO.	T18S	R12W	S25
FLOYD, ELWOOD see **UPPER SWEET CREEK**				
	LANE CO.	?	R10W	?
FLOYD FAMILY see **UPPER SWEET CREEK**				
	LANE CO.	?	R10W	?
FLOYD, MARYANNA see **UPPER SWEET CREEK**				
	LANE CO.	?	R10W	?
FORD see **JENKINS FAMILY**	LANE CO.	T18S	R5W	S22
FOREST VALE MEMORIAL PARK	LANE CO.	T21S	R3E	S10
FOTHERGILL, JOHN	LANE CO.	T18S	R1W	S33
FRANKLIN	LANE CO.	T16S	R5W	S21
FRANKLIN GRANGE see **FRANKLIN**	LANE CO.	T16S	R5W	S21
GALE D.L.C., JOSEPH see **SEARS**	LANE CO.	T20S	R3W	S35
GARBER NURSING HOME	LANE CO.	T18S	R3W	S5
GARDEN OF THE GOOD SHEPHERD see **SUNSET HILLS MEMORIAL GARDENS**				
	LANE CO.	T18S	R3W	S18

GATES	LANE CO.	T18S	R5W	S19
GATES OF HEAVEN	LANE CO.	T18S	R4W	S5
GAY see **COGSWELL**	LANE CO.	T19S	R3W	S5
GAY D.L.C., MARTIN B. see **COGSWELL**				
	LANE CO.	T19S	R3W	S5
GAY PIONEER, MARY see **COGSWELL**	LANE CO.	T19S	R3W	S5
GAY-MASTERSON see **COGSWELL**	LANE CO.	T19S	R3W	S5
GERMAN BAPTIST BRETHREN see **MABEL**				
	LANE CO.	T16S	R1W	S5
GILESPI [Sic] see **GILLESPIE**	LANE CO.	T17S	R3W	S19
GILLESPIE	LANE CO.	T17S	R3W	S19
GILLESPIE D.L.C., JACOB see **GILLESPIE**				
	LANE CO.	T17S	R3W	S19
GLENWOOD see **GREENWOOD**	LANE CO.	T17S	R1E	S12
GOLDSON see **SWEET HOME**	LANE CO.	T16S	R6W	S27
GOSHEN	LANE CO.	T18S	R3W	S24
GOSHEN GRANGE #561 see **GOSHEN**	LANE CO.	T18S	R3W	S24
GRAIG GRAVE see **CRAIG MEMORIAL**	LANE CO.	T15S	R7 1/2E	UNS
GRAND ARMY OF THE REPUBLIC see **MASONIC [EUGENE]**				
	LANE CO.	T18S	R3W	S5
GRANGE see **LORANE GRANGE**	LANE CO.	T20S	R5W	S2
GRANGER see **LORANE GRANGE**	LANE CO.	T20S	R5W	S2
GRAY, EILEEN H. see **SPRUCE POINT**				
	LANE CO.	T18S	R12W	S27
GRAY, FRED W.	LANE CO.	T19S	R1E	S19
GREENWOOD	LANE CO.	T17S	R1E	S12
GRIFFIN see **WHITE D.L.C., WILLIAM**				
	LANE CO.	T15S	R5W	S20
HAMILTON D.L.C., ANDERSON see **WALKER**				
	LANE CO.	T20S	R3W	S10
HANSEN, DAVID W.	LANE CO.	T15S	R6W	S35
HARING PIONEER	LANE CO.	T18S	R11W	S7
HARPER D.L.C., GEORGE W. see **JACKSON FAMILY**				
	LANE CO.	T19S	R3W	S34
HAWLEY	LANE CO.	T21S	R4W	S12
HAWLEY D.L.C., IRA see **HAWLEY**	LANE CO.	T21S	R4W	S12
HAYS, DANIEL see **FALL CREEK**	LANE CO.	T18S	R1W	S33
HAYS, DANIEL see **SUNDSTROM, BRUCE**				
	LANE CO.	T16S	R8W	S18
HAZLETON D.L.C., ROYAL H. see **SILK CREEK COMMUNITY**				
	LANE CO.	T20S	R4W	S13
HEATHERLY D.L.C., JAMES see **HEATHERLY FAMILY**				
	LANE CO.	T19S	R5W	S10
HEATHERLY FAMILY	LANE CO.	T19S	R5W	S10
HECETA LODGE #111 see **I.O.O.F. [GLENADA]**				
	LANE CO.	T19S	R12W	S2
HELFRICH, PRINCE E.	LANE CO.	T16S	R3E	S31
HIGH PRAIRIE see **FOREST VALE MEMORIAL PARK**				
	LANE CO.	T21S	R3E	S10
HILL MEMORIAL, JOHN	LANE CO.	T21S	R3E	S26
HILLS CREEK see **HILL MEMORIAL, JOHN**				
	LANE CO.	T21S	R3E	S26

HISE see **KIME-BROWN FAMILY**	LANE CO.	T16S	R5W	S17
HOILAND FARM, LEWIS see **MOUNTS FAMILY BURIALS**				
	LANE CO.	T18S	R5W	S7
HOLY CROSS	LANE CO.	T18S	R5W	S3
HOPE ABBEY	LANE CO.	T18S	R3W	S5
HOPELAND see **INDIAN CREEK**	LANE CO.	T16S	R10W	S36
HOWE see **CRESWELL PIONEER**	LANE CO.	T19S	R3W	S21
HOWE see **LOWELL**	LANE CO.	T19S	R1W	S15
HULBERT LAKE BURIALS	LANE CO.	T15S	R4W	?
HUNT see **CULP CREEK**	LANE CO.	T21S	R1W	S33
HUSTON FARM see **CALDWELL**	LANE CO.	T16S	R5W	S24
HYLAND see **LOWELL**	LANE CO.	T19S	R1W	S15
I.O.O.F. see **EUGENE PIONEER**	LANE CO.	T17S	R3W	S32
I.O.O.F. see **GOSHEN**	LANE CO.	T18S	R3W	S24
I.O.O.F. see **MARCOLA**	LANE CO.	T16S	R2W	S24
I.O.O.F. [COBURG]	LANE CO.	T17S	R3W	S4
I.O.O.F. [COTTAGE GROVE] see **FIR GROVE**				
	LANE CO.	T20S	R3W	S29
I.O.O.F. [CROW] see **McCULLOCH**	LANE CO.	T18S	R5W	S34
I.O.O.F. [FLORENCE] see **I.O.O.F. [GLENADA]**				
	LANE CO.	T19S	R12W	S2
I.O.O.F. [GLENADA]	LANE CO.	T19S	R12W	S2
I.O.O.F. [IRVING] see **LUPER**	LANE CO.	T16S	R4W	S34
I.O.O.F. [JUNCTION CITY] see **REST LAWN MEMORIAL PARK**				
	LANE CO.	T15S	R5W	S34
I.O.O.F. [LORANE]	LANE CO.	T20S	R5W	S24
I.O.O.F. [MAPLETON]	LANE CO.	T18S	R10W	S11
I.O.O.F. [NEW; EUGENE] see **WESTLAWN MEMORIAL PARK**				
	LANE CO.	T17S	R4W	S33
I.O.O.F. MOHAWK LODGE #200 see **MARCOLA**				
	LANE CO.	T16S	R2W	S24
I.O.O.F. SPENCER BUTTE LODGE #9 see **EUGENE PIONEER**				
	LANE CO.	T17S	R3W	S32
I.O.O.F. SPENCER BUTTE LODGE #9 see **WEST LAWN MEMORIAL PARK**				
	LANE CO.	T17S	R4W	S33
I.O.O.F. SPRINGFIELD LODGE #70 see **LAUREL GROVE**				
	LANE CO.	T18S	R3W	S3
I.O.O.F. SPRINGFIELD LODGE #70 see **PIONEER MEMORIAL CEMETERY PARK**				
	LANE CO.	T17S	R3W	S35
INDEPENDENT ORDER OF GOOD TEMPLARS see **I.O.O.F. [LORANE]**				
	LANE CO.	T20S	R5W	S24
INDIAN	LANE CO.	T17S	R1W	?
INDIAN BURIAL	LANE CO.	T20S	R2W	S31
INDIAN BURIALS	LANE CO.	?	?	?
INDIAN CREEK	LANE CO.	T16S	R10W	S36
INDIAN LIZA	LANE CO.	T17S	R3W	?
INDIAN TOWN see **DREW MEMORIAL**	LANE CO.	T18S	R12W	S24
INMAN	LANE CO.	T17S	R5W	S8
INMAN D.L.C., JOEL C. see **INMAN**	LANE CO.	T17S	R5W	S8
INMAN FAMILY see **INMAN**	LANE CO.	T17S	R5W	S8
JACKSON FAMILY	LANE CO.	T19S	R3W	S34
JASPER see **WALLACE**	LANE CO.	T18S	R2W	S14

JAY BURIALS see **LITTLE LAKE**	LANE CO.	T16S	R7W	S18
JENKINS D.L.C., STEPHEN see **JENKINS FAMILY**				
	LANE CO.	T18S	R5W	S22
JENKINS FAMILY	LANE CO.	T18S	R5W	S22
JOHNSON FAMILY, GEORGE	LANE CO.	?	?	?
JOHNSON PLACE see **JOHNSON FAMILY, GEORGE**				
	LANE CO.	?	?	?
JONES FAMILY	LANE CO.	T16S	R5W	S16
JONES FAMILY see **CENTRAL SCHOOL**	LANE CO.	T18S	R5W	S4
JONES SCHOOL see **CENTRAL SCHOOL**	LANE CO.	T18S	R5W	S4
JUNCTION CITY PIONEER see **MILLIRON**				
	LANE CO.	T15S	R4W	S31
KAY, MARY see **COGSELL**	LANE CO.	T19S	R3W	S5
KEENEY D.L.C., ELI see **KEENEY FAMILY**				
	LANE CO.	T19S	R2W	S5
KEENEY FAMILY	LANE CO.	T19S	R2W	S5
KERR GIRL	LANE CO.	T21S	R1W	S33
KIME-BROWN FAMILY	LANE CO.	T16S	R5W	S17
KNOWLES	LANE CO.	T18S	R10W	S1
KNOWLES CREEK see **KNOWLES**	LANE CO.	T18S	R10W	S1
KNOWLES FAMILY see **KNOWLES**	LANE CO.	T18S	R10W	S1
KNOX HILL see **CLOVERDALE**	LANE CO.	T19S	R2W	S18
KNOX HILL see **SHIELDS**	LANE CO.	T20S	R3W	S33
LAKEVIEW CEMETERY ASSOCIATION see **BLACHLY**				
	LANE CO.	T16S	R7W	S9
LANCASTER see **YOUNG**	LANE CO.	T15S	R4W	S7
LANDAX see **MIDDLE FORK**	LANE CO.	T19S	R1E	S34
LANDAX see **MT. VERNON**	LANE CO.	T18S	R2W	S4
LANE D.L.C., SILAS see **TAYLOR-LANE FAMILY**				
	LANE CO.	T21S	R3W	S16
LANE FAMILY see **TAYLOR-LANE FAMILY**				
	LANE CO.	T21S	R3W	S16
LANE MEMORIAL GRARDENS	LANE CO.	T17S	R4W	S32
LANE SCHOOL DISTRICT #28J see **CENTRAL SCHOOL**				
	LANE CO.	T18S	R5W	S4
LARKINS D.L.C., JOSIAH M. see **MASONIC [EUGENE]**				
	LANE CO.	T18S	R3W	S5
LAUREL GROVE	LANE CO.	T18S	R3W	S3
LAUREL HILL see **LAUREL GROVE**	LANE CO.	T18S	R3W	S3
LAYNE see **ALMA**	LANE CO.	T19S	R8W	S3
LAYNE, MRS. MINNIE	LANE CO.	T19S	R7W	S22
LEABURG see **GREENWOOD**	LANE CO.	T17S	R1E	S12
LIBERTY see **WHITE DLC, WILLIAM**	LANE CO.	T15S	R5W	S20
LILES	LANE CO.	T18S	R5W	S16
LINSLAW PIONEER	LANE CO.	T18S	R8W	S17
LITTLE LAKE	LANE CO.	T16S	R7W	S18
LLOYD see **SAYLOR**	LANE CO.	T19S	R2W	S19
LOCKE CHILDREN see **MULHOLLAND FAMILY**				
	LANE CO.	T19S	R2W	S4
LOCKE D.L.C., DANIEL see **CLOVERDALE**				
	LANE CO.	T19S	R2W	S18
LONE PINE see **SMALL FAMILY**	LANE CO.	T22S	R3W	S17

LONG, GEORGE P. see **SMALL DLC, GEORGE**

	LANE CO.	T20S R3W	?

LONG TOM see **REST LAWN MEMORIAL PARK**

	LANE CO.	T15S R5W	S34

LOONEY D.L.C., JAMES C. see **SPRINGFIELD MEMORIAL GARDENS**

	LANE CO.	T17S R2W	S35
LOOPER see **LUPER**	LANE CO.	T16S R4W	S34
LORANE GRANGE	LANE CO.	T20S R5W	S2
LOWELL	LANE CO.	T19S R1W	S15
LOWER see **CLOVERDALE**	LANE CO.	T19S R2W	S18
LOWER MABEL see **MABEL**	LANE CO.	T16S R1W	S5
LOWER UMPQUA see **DREW MEMORIAL**	LANE CO.	T18S R12W	S24

LUCAS D.L.C., DANIEL see **I.O.O.F. [LORANE]**

	LANE CO.	T20S R5W	S24
LUPER	LANE CO.	T16S R4W	S34
LYLE see **LILES**	LANE CO.	T18S R5W	S16
MABEL	LANE CO.	T16S R1W	S5
MABEL CHURCH see **UPPER MABEL**	LANE CO.	T15S R1W	S28
MABLE see **MABEL**	LANE CO.	T16S R1W	S5

MACDONALD, SHERIDAN see **SHILOH BURIAL**

	LANE CO.	T19S R1W	S29
MADERA see **MADERIS, LYMAN**	LANE CO.	T15S R10W	S29
MADERIS, LYMAN	LANE CO.	T15S R10W	S29
MAHON see **REST LAWN MEMORIAL PARK**			
	LANE CO.	T15S R5W	S34

MAPLE LODGE #139 see **I.O.O.F. (MAPLETON)**

	LANE CO.	T18S R10W	S11

MAPLETON see **I.O.O.F. [MAPLETON]**

	LANE CO.	T18S R10W	S11

MAPLETON MEMORIAL CEMETERY ASSOCIATION see **KNOWLES**

	LANE CO.	T18S R10W	S1
MARCOLA	LANE CO.	T16S R2W	S24
MARCOLA see **VALLEY VIEW**	LANE CO.	T17S R2W	S3
MARQUESS, MARK WAYNE	LANE CO.	T19S R3W	S24
MARTIN see **REPSLEGER ROAD**	LANE CO.	T20S R4W	S23

MARTIN, MRS. GERTRUDE see **REPSLEGER ROAD**

	LANE CO.	T20S R4W	S23
MASONIC [EUGENE]	LANE CO.	T18S R3W	S5

MASONIC [FLORENCE] see **PACIFIC SUNSET MEMORIAL PARK**

	LANE CO.	T18S R12W	S25

MASONIC LODGE #51 [COTTAGE GROVE] see **FIR GROVE**

	LANE CO.	T20S R3W	S29
MAYS see **UNION**	LANE CO.	T16S R5W	S5

McATEE D.L.C., WILLIAM H. see **JONES FAMILY**

	LANE CO.	T16S R5W	S16
McCLANE, THOMAS HENRY	LANE CO.	T21S R3E	S8
McCOLLUM	LANE CO.	T18S R4W	S30
McCULLOCH	LANE CO.	T18S R5W	S34

McCULLOCH D.L.C., THOMAS see **McCULLOCH**

	LANE CO.	T18S R5W	S34
McENROE, PATRICK	LANE CO.	T17S R9W	S36
McFARLAND	LANE CO.	T20S R3W	S28

McFARLAND D.L.C., JAMES H. see **McFARLAND**				
	LANE CO.	T20S	R3W	S28
McFARLAND FAMILY see **McFARLAND**	LANE CO.	T20S	R3W	S28
McKENZIE BRIDGE	LANE CO.	T16S	R5E	?
McMURRY D.L.C., FIELDING see **MASONIC [EUGENE]**				
	LANE CO.	T18S	R3W	S5
MEDLEY	LANE CO.	T20S	R3W	S19
MENDELL *[Sic]* see **MEDLEY**	LANE CO.	T20S	R3W	S19
MIDDLE FORK	LANE CO.	T19S	R1E	S34
MIDDLE FORK see **MT. VERNON**	LANE CO.	T18S	R2W	S4
MILLER D.L.C., ELIZABETH see **CRESWELL PIONEER**				
	LANE CO.	T19S	R3W	S21
MILLIORN see **MILLIRON**	LANE CO.	T15S	R4W	S31
MILLIRON	LANE CO.	T15S	R4W	S31
MILLIRON D.L.C., JOHN see **MILLIRON**				
	LANE CO.	T15S	R4W	S31
MODERN WOODMEN OF THE WORLD: EUGENE CAMP #583 see **RICHARDSON**				
	LANE CO.	T17S	R5W	S4
MOHAWK see **MARCOLA**	LANE CO.	T16S	R2W	S24
MOHAWK see **VALLEY VIEW**	LANE CO.	T17S	R2W	S3
MOHAWK COMMUNITY CHURCH see **VALLEY VIEW**				
	LANE CO.	T17S	R2W	S3
MOHAWK LODGE see **MARCOLA**	LANE CO.	T16S	R2W	S24
MOSBY see **BRUMBAUGH**	LANE CO.	T21S	R2W	S18
MOUND see **ALMA**	LANE CO.	T19S	R8W	S3
MOUNSE BURIALS see **MOUNTS FAMILY BURIALS**				
	LANE CO.	T18S	R5W	S7
MT. CALVARY CATHOLIC	LANE CO.	T18S	R3W	S7
MT. JUNE LUMBER COMPANY see **EMIGRANT**				
	LANE CO.	T18S	R2W	S3
MT. VERNON	LANE CO.	T18S	R2W	S4
MOUNTAIN VIEW see **SEARS**	LANE CO.	T20S	R3W	S35
MOUNTE *[Sic]* BURIALS see **MOUNTS FAMILY BURIALS**				
	LANE CO.	T18S	R5W	S7
MOUNTE *[Sic]* D.L.C., HENRY R. see **MOUNTS FAMILY BURIALS**				
	LANE CO.	T18S	R5W	S7
MOUNTS BURIALS see **MOUNTS FAMILY BURIALS**				
	LANE CO.	T18S	R5W	S7
MOUNTS FAMILY BURIALS	LANE CO.	T18S	R5W	S7
MOXLEY	LANE CO.	T19S	R4W	S12
MULHOLLAND, EDWARD see **MULHOLLAND FAMILY**				
	LANE CO.	T19S	R2W	S4
MULHOLLAND FAMILY	LANE CO.	T19S	R2W	S4
MULHOLLAND, JOHN see **MULHOLLAND FAMILY**				
	LANE CO.	T19S	R2W	S4
MULHOLLAND, MARGARET see **MULHOLLAND FAMILY**				
	LANE CO.	T19S	R2W	S4
MULHOLLAND, MARGARET [INFANT] see **MULHOLLAND FAMILY**				
	LANE CO.	T19S	R2W	S4
MULHOLLAND, MARTHA see **MULHOLLAND FAMILY**				
	LANE CO.	T19S	R2W	S4

MULHOLLAND, MARY see **MULHOLLAND FAMILY**

	LANE CO.	T19S	R2W	S4

MULHOLLAND SR. D.L.C., EDWARD see **MULHOLLAND FAMILY**

	LANE CO.	T19S	R2W	S4

MULHOLLAND, THOMAS see **MULHOLLAND FAMILY**

Name	Location	Township	Range	Section
	LANE CO.	T19S	R2W	S4
MULKEY	LANE CO.	T18S	R4W	S2
NEET see **FALL CREEK**	LANE CO.	T18S	R1W	S33
NELSON CREEK	LANE CO.	T17S	R8W	S14
NEW MIDDLE FORK see **MT. VERNON**	LANE CO.	T18S	R2W	S4
NORATON see **YOUNG**	LANE CO.	T15S	R4W	S7
NORTH FORK see **HARING PIONEER**	LANE CO.	T18S	R11W	S7
NOTI see **SAILOR PIONEER**	LANE CO.	T17S	R6W	S28
OAK HILL	LANE CO.	T17S	R5W	S25

OAKRIDGE see **FOREST VALE MEMORIAL PARK**

	LANE CO.	T21S	R3E	S10

OASIS LODGE #41 I.O.O.F. see **REST LAWN MEMORIAL PARK**

Name	Location	Township	Range	Section
	LANE CO.	T15S	R5W	S34
ODD FELLOWS see **EUGENE PIONEER**	LANE CO.	T17S	R3W	S32
OLD PIONEER see **CULP CREEK**	LANE CO.	T21S	R1W	S33

OLD SPRINGFIELD see **PIONEER MEMORIAL CEMETERY PARK**

Name	Location	Township	Range	Section
	LANE CO.	T17S	R3W	S35
PACIFIC SUNSET MEMORIAL PARK	LANE CO.	T18S	R12W	S25

PARISH D.L.C., DANA J. see **SMALL FAMILY**

	LANE CO.	T22S	R3W	S17

PAT CREEK BURIAL see **McENROE, PATRICK**

Name	Location	Township	Range	Section
	LANE CO.	T17S	R9W	S36
PEPIOT see **GREENWOOD**	LANE CO.	T17S	R1E	S12
PEPIOT FAMILY see **GREENWOOD**	LANE CO.	T17S	R1E	S12
PETTIT see **ALMA**	LANE CO.	T19S	R8W	S3
PETTY see **CLOVERDALE**	LANE CO.	T19S	R2W	S18
PIONEER see **EUGENE PIONEER**	LANE CO.	T17S	R3W	S32
PIONEER MEMORIAL CEMETERY PARK	LANE CO.	T17S	R3W	S35

PIONEER MEMORIAL PARK see **EUGENE PIONEER**

Name	Location	Township	Range	Section
	LANE CO.	T17S	R3W	S32
PISGAH LODGE see **GOSHEN**	LANE CO.	T18S	R3W	S24

PLEASANT HILL see **PLEASANT HILL PIONEER**

Name	Location	Township	Range	Section
	LANE CO.	T18S	R2W	S34
PLEASANT HILL PIONEER	LANE CO.	T18S	R2W	S34
POINT TERRACE see **SWEET CREEK**	LANE CO.	T18S	R10W	?
POOLE FAMILY, HAROLD	LANE CO.	T16S	R10W	S29

POOLE, MONROE see **POOLE FAMILY, HAROLD**

Name	Location	Township	Range	Section
	LANE CO.	T16S	R10W	S29
RAGSDALE see **SAYLOR**	LANE CO.	T19S	R2W	S19

RAIL CREEK RANCH see **HELFRICH, PRINCE E.**

	LANE CO.	T16S	R3E	S31

RAMSEY D.L.C., BARNETT see **STAFFORD FAMILY**

Name	Location	Township	Range	Section
	LANE CO.	T17S	R2W	S3
RENFREW, DOCTOR ALEXANDER	LANE CO.	T16S	R4E	S5

RENSHAW D.L.C., WILLIAM see **RENSHAW, MARY JULIA**

	LANE CO.	T18S	R3W	?

RENSHAW, ELIZABETH MARIA JANE see **RENSHAW, MARY JULIA**				
	LANE CO.	T18S	R3W	?
RENSHAW, MARY JULIA	LANE CO.	T18S	R3W	?
RENSHAW, WILLIAM D. see **RENSHAW, MARY JULIA**				
	LANE CO.	T18S	R3W	?
REPSLEGER ROAD	LANE CO.	T20S	R4W	S23
REST HAVEN MEMORIAL PARK	LANE CO.	T18S	R3W	S5
REST LAWN MEMORIAL PARK	LANE CO.	T15S	R5W	S34
RICHARDSON	LANE CO.	T17S	R5W	S4
RICHARDSON BUTTE see **RICHARDSON**	LANE CO.	T17S	R5W	S4
RICHARDSON D.L.C., BENJAMIN see **RICHARDSON**				
	LANE CO.	T17S	R5W	S4
RICHARDSON D.L.C., GIDION AND MARGARET see **RICHARDSON FAMILY, GIDEON**				
	LANE CO.	T15S	R5W	S15
RICHARDSON FAMILY, GIDEON	LANE CO.	T15S	R5W	S15
RICKARD see **MILLIRON**	LANE CO.	T15S	R4W	S31
RIGGS D.L.C., MILTON see **GOSHEN**	LANE CO.	T18S	R3W	S24
ROCK CREEK CANYON CO-OP see **SUNDSTROM, BRUCE**				
	LANE CO.	T16S	R8W	S18
ROUSE HOMESTEAD, WILLIAM see **BEMIS**				
	LANE CO.	T22S	R3W	S32
ROWE D.L.C., HIRAM see **GATES**	LANE CO.	T18S	R5W	S19
ROYAL GRANGE see **SILK CREEK COMMUNITY**				
	LANE CO.	T20S	R4W	S13
RUSH ISLAND see **MIDDLE FORK**	LANE CO.	T19S	R1E	S34
SAGINAW	LANE CO.	T20S	R3W	?
SAILOR PIONEER	LANE CO.	T17S	R6W	S28
SANFORD, JOSIAH	LANE CO.	T21S	R3E	S9
SAYLOR	LANE CO.	T19S	R2W	S19
SAYLOR see **SAILOR PIONEER**	LANE CO.	T17S	R6W	S28
SAYLOR D.L.C., SYDNER [Sic] see **SAYLOR**				
	LANE CO.	T19S	R2W	S19
SCHRIMPF FAMILY	LANE CO.	T19S	R5W	S2
SCHRIMPF, HENRY C. see **SCHRIMPF FAMILY**				
	LANE CO.	T19S	R5W	S2
SCHRIMPF, MINNIE L. see **SCHRIMPF FAMILY**				
	LANE CO.	T19S	R5W	S2
SEARS	LANE CO.	T20S	R3W	S35
SELLERS see **KEENEY FAMILY**	LANE CO.	T19S	R2W	S5
SEVERY HILL see **I.O.O.F. [GLENADA]**				
	LANE CO.	T19S	R12W	S2
SHARPLES GRAVES	LANE CO.	T18S	R2W	S29
SHIELDS	LANE CO.	T20S	R3W	S33
SHIELDS D.L.C., WILLIAM see **SHIELDS**				
	LANE CO.	T20S	R3W	S33
SHILOH BURIAL	LANE CO.	T19S	R1W	S29
SILK CREEK COMMUNITY	LANE CO.	T20S	R4W	S13
SIMPSON CREEK see **WARNER, MRS.**	LANE CO.	T24S	R3E	S13
SIUSLAW GRANGE see **LORANE GRANGE**				
	LANE CO.	T20S	R5W	S2
SIUSLAW INDIAN see **DREW MEMORIAL**				
	LANE CO.	T18S	R12W	S24

SIUSLAW PRECINCT see **LORANE GRANGE**

    LANE CO.   T20S   R5W   S2

SLATER see **SWAMP CREEK ROAD BURIALS**

    LANE CO.   T16S   R7W   S7

SLAYTER see **SWAMP CREEK ROAD BURIALS**

    LANE CO.   T16S   R7W   S7

SLAYTOR see **SWAMP CREEK ROAD BURIALS**

    LANE CO.   T16S   R7W   S7

SMALL, AMANDA E. see **SMALL D.L.C., GEORGE**

    LANE CO.   T20S   R3W   ?

SMALL D.L.C., GEORGE   LANE CO.   T20S   R3W   ?

SMALL D.L.C., GEORGE see **FIR GROVE**

    LANE CO.   T20S   R3W   S29

SMALL FAMILY   LANE CO.   T22S   R3W   S17

SMITH D.L.C., HENRY B. see **STEPHENS FAMILY**

    LANE CO.   T18S   R6W   S14

SMITH D.L.C., JOHN see **EMIGRANT** LANE CO.   T18S   R2W   S3

SMITH D.L.C., JOHN see **SMITH, ELIZA B.**

    LANE CO.   T18S   R2W   S3

SMITH, ELIZA B.   LANE CO.   T18S   R2W   S3

SMITH FAMILY   LANE CO.   T15S   R6W   ?

SMITH FAMILY   LANE CO.   T18S   R2W   ?

SMITH FAMILY see **EMIGRANT** LANE CO.   T18S   R2W   S3

SMITH HOMESTEAD see **SMITH FAMILY**

    LANE CO.   T15S   R6W   ?

SMITH, TOM   LANE CO.   T15S   R12W   S27

SMITHFIELD see **FRANKLIN**   LANE CO.   T16S   R5W   S21

SOUTHWORTH D.L.C., JAMES B. see **FRANKLIN**

    LANE CO.   T16S   R5W   S21

SPARKS FAMILY   LANE CO.   T16S   R4E   S20

SPARKS, NAOMI ELAINE see **SPARKS FAMILY**

    LANE CO.   T16S   R4E   S20

SPARKS, S. C. see **SPARKS FAMILY** LANE CO.   T16S   R4E   S20

SPENCER BUTTE I.O.O.F. LODGE #9 LANE CO.   T17S   R4W   S33

SPORES D.L.C., JACOB C. see **I.O.O.F. [COBURG]**

    LANE CO.   T17S   R3W   S4

SPRINGFIELD MEMORIAL GARDENS   LANE CO.   T17S   R2W   S35

SPRINGFIELD PIONEER MEMORIAL PARK see **PIONEER MEMORIAL CEMETERY PARK**

    LANE CO.   T17S   R3W   S35

SPRUCE POINT   LANE CO.   T18S   R12W   S27

SPRY, M. JANE see **MULHOLLAND FAMILY**

    LANE CO.   T19S   R2W   S4

SPRY, MARTHA JANE see **MULHOLLAND FAMILY**

    LANE CO.   T19S   R2W   S4

SPRY, WILLIAM see **MULHOLLAND FAMILY**

    LANE CO.   T19S   R2W   S4

STAFFORD FAMILY   LANE CO.   T17S   R2W   S3

STAPLETON FAMILY   LANE CO.   T18S   R5W   S4

STAPLETON FAMILY see **CENTRAL SCHOOL**

    LANE CO.   T18S   R5W   S4

STEPHENS CHILDREN see **STEPHENS FAMILY**

    LANE CO.   T18S   R6W   S14

STEPHENS FAMILY	LANE CO.	T18S	R6W	S14
STEVENS FAMILY see **STEPHENS FAMILY**				
	LANE CO.	T18S	R6W	S14
STEWART see **FALL CREEK**	LANE CO.	T18S	R1W	S33
STONEFIELD BEACH BURIALS see **BRAY**				
	LANE CO.	T15S	R12W	S27
STUART D.L.C., JOHN see **FOTHERGILL, JOHN**				
	LANE CO.	T18S	R1W	S33
SUNDSTROM, BRUCE	LANE CO.	T16S	R8W	S18
SUNDSTROM, ROBERT BRUCE see **SUNDSTROM, BRUCE**				
	LANE CO.	T16S	R8W	S18
SUNSET HILLS MEMORIAL GARDENS	LANE CO.	T18S	R3W	S18
SWAMP CREEK ROAD BURIALS	LANE CO.	T16S	R7W	S7
SWEET CREEK	LANE CO.	T18S	R10W	?
SWEET D.L.C., ZARA see **LAUREL GROVE**				
	LANE CO.	T18S	R3W	S3
SWEET HOME	LANE CO.	T16S	R6W	S27
SWEET, MARIA see **SWEET CREEK**	LANE CO.	T18S	R10W	?
SWEET, ZARA see **SWEET CREEK**	LANE CO.	T18S	R10W	?
TALOR D.L.C., HENRY see **TAYLOR-LANE FAMILY**				
	LANE CO.	T21S	R3W	S16
TAYLOR FAMILY	LANE CO.	T16S	R7W	S9
TAYLOR FAMILY see **TAYLOR-LANE FAMILY**				
	LANE CO.	T21S	R3W	S16
TAYLOR-LANE FAMILY	LANE CO.	T21S	R3W	S16
TEAGUE see **McCOLLUM**	LANE CO.	T18S	R4W	S30
THOMAS HOMESITE, TILLY see **UNKNOWN**				
	LANE CO.	T18S	R11W	S12
THOMPSON D.L.C., JOHN W. see **LORANE GRANGE**				
	LANE CO.	T20S	R5W	S2
THOMPSON, MANLEY see **THOMPSON PLACE**				
	LANE CO.	T17S	R10W	?
THOMPSON PLACE	LANE CO.	T17S	R10W	?
THURSTON see **MT. VERNON**	LANE CO.	T18S	R2W	S4
TOLL, ALTHEA APPLEGATE see **TOLL FAMILY**				
	LANE CO.	T19S	R4W	S2
TOLL FAMILY	LANE CO.	T19S	R4W	S2
TRAPP GIRL	LANE CO.	T18S	R5W	S24
TRIANGLE LAKE see **BLACHLY**	LANE CO.	T16S	R7W	S9
TUFI CHILDREN see **INDIAN BURIALS**				
	LANE CO.	?	?	?
TUFI, MRS. CHARLES see **INDIAN BURIALS**				
	LANE CO.	?	?	?
TURNBOW see **UNION**	LANE CO.	T16S	R5W	S5
UNION	LANE CO.	T16S	R5W	S5
UNION CEMETERY OF LONG TOM see **UNION**				
	LANE CO.	T16S	R5W	S5
UNKNOWN	LANE CO.	T18S	R11W	S12
UPPER MABEL	LANE CO.	T15S	R1W	S28
UPPER SWEET CREEK	LANE CO.	?	R10W	?
UPPER WILLAMETTE see **FOREST VALE MEMORIAL PARK**				
	LANE CO.	T21S	R3E	S10

UPPER WILLAMETTE see **HILL MEMORIAL, JOHN**				
	LANE CO.	T21S	R3E	S26
VALE MEMORIAL PARK see **FOREST VALE MEMORIAL PARK**				
	LANE CO.	T21S	R3E	S10
VALLEY VIEW	LANE CO.	T17S	R2W	S3
VALLEY VIEW see **MARCOLA**	LANE CO.	T16S	R2W	S24
VEATCH see **HAWLEY**	LANE CO.	T21S	R4W	S12
VINSON, MRS.	LANE CO.	T19S	R1E	S34
WALKER	LANE CO.	T20S	R3W	S10
WALKER ADDITION	LANE CO.	T21S	R3E	S17
WALKER, MARY JANE see **RENSHAW, MARY JULIA**				
	LANE CO.	T18S	R3W	?
WALKER PLACE, DONALD see **ALLEN, WILLIAM P.**				
	LANE CO.	?	?	?
WALKER UNION CHURCH see **WALKER**	LANE CO.	T20S	R3W	S10
WALLACE	LANE CO.	T18S	R2W	S14
WALLACE D.L.C., JAMES A. see **WALLACE**				
	LANE CO.	T18S	R2W	S14
WALTON	LANE CO.	T18S	R7W	S5
WARNER see **FALL CREEK**	LANE CO.	T18S	R1W	S33
WARNER D.L.C., FREDERICK see **FALL CREEK**				
	LANE CO.	T18S	R1W	S33
WARNER, MRS.	LANE CO.	T24S	R3E	S13
WASHBURN D.L.C., A. D. E. see **VALLEY VIEW**				
	LANE CO.	T17S	R2W	S3
WASHBURNE see **MILLIRON**	LANE CO.	T15S	R4W	S31
WENDLING	LANE CO.	T16S	R1W	S10
WEST LAWN MEMORIAL PARK	LANE CO.	T17S	R4W	S33
WEST POINT LODGE #62 see **I.O.O.F. [COBURG]**				
	LANE CO.	T17S	R3W	S4
WEYERHAEUSER DUMP ROAD see **SMITH FAMILY**				
	LANE CO.	T18S	R2W	?
WHEELER BURIAL see **NELSON CREEK**	LANE CO.	T17S	R8W	S14
WHITE D.L.C., WILLIAM	LANE CO.	T15S	R5W	S20
WILDWOOD FALLS see **CULP CREEK**	LANE CO.	T21S	R1W	S33
WILLIS BURIALS	LANE CO.	T19S	R3W	S14
WILLIS FAMILY see **WILLIS BURIALS**				
	LANE CO.	T19S	R3W	S14
WILLIS, JOHN A. see **WILLIS BURIALS**				
	LANE CO.	T19S	R3W	S14
WILLIS, MALINDA C. see **WILLIS BURIALS**				
	LANE CO.	T19S	R3W	S14
WINBERRY see **WINBERRY CREEK BURIALS**				
	LANE CO.	T19S	R1E	S6
WINBERRY CREEK BURIALS	LANE CO.	T19S	R1E	S6
WINN, JOHN see **WHITE DLC, WILLIAM**				
	LANE CO.	T15S	R5W	S20
WORTH D.L.C., JAMES see **CAMP CREEK**				
	LANE CO.	T17S	R1W	S19
YOUNG	LANE CO.	T15S	R4W	S7
ZUMWALT see **HULBERT LAKE BURIALS**				
	LANE CO.	T15S	R4W	?

ZUMWALT FAMILY see **HULBERT LAKE BURIALS**

LANE CO.   T15S   R4W   ?

Laurel Grove
Dean H. Byrd (1992)

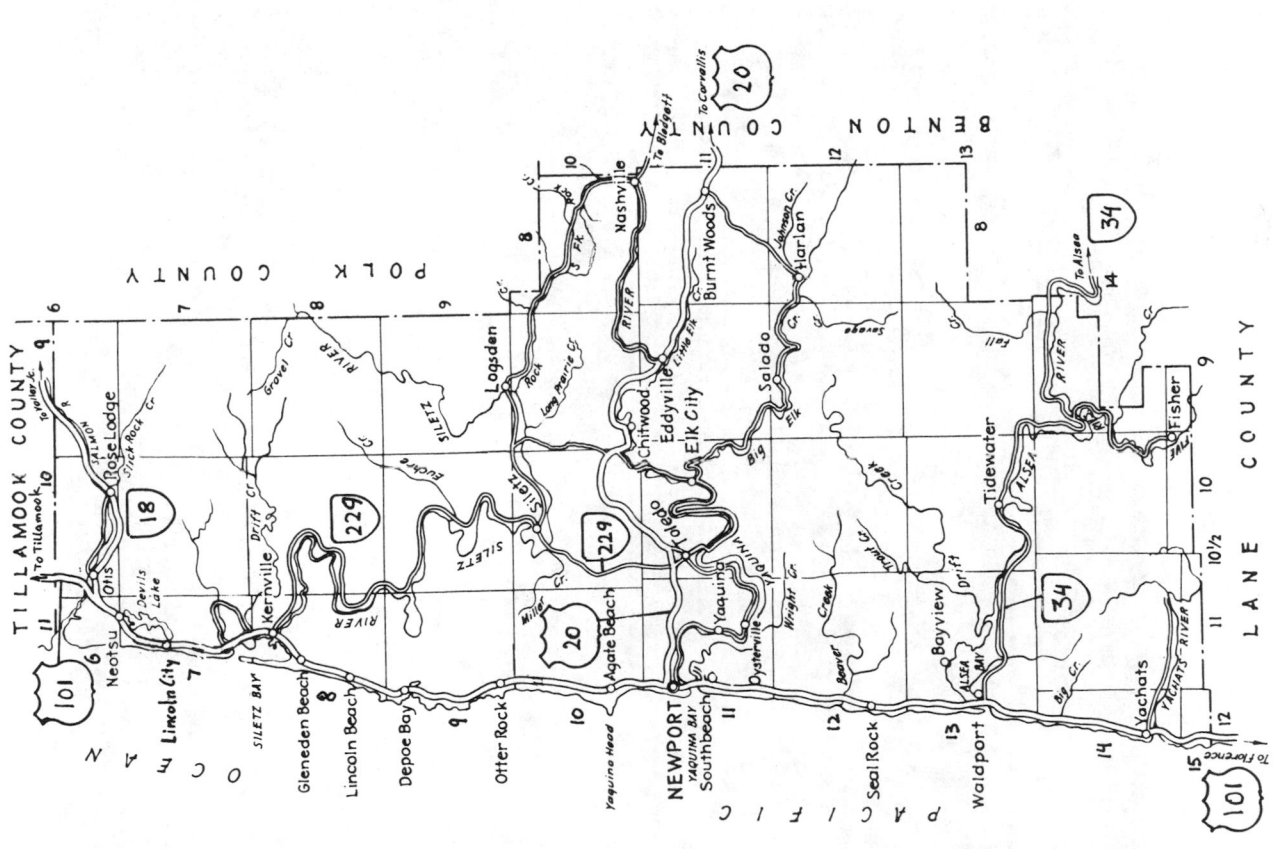

ELK CITY PIONEER CEMETERY
"At Rest in Lincoln County"

Abbey, Charles M. (1858-18??)
Abbey, Francis M. (1851?-1871)
Abbey, daut. of Richard & Rosa
Barber, Mary Ann (1844-1914)
Bevens, Mary S. (1821-1893)
Bevens, Hudson J. (1819-1902)
Bevens, Ruby (1898, infant)
Bevens, Infant son
Bevens, Commodore Perry (1859-1913)
Bly, Hattie M. (1833?-1912)
Cleveland, James C. (1845-1912)
Dixon, James Chester (1871-1932)
Dixon, James Edward (1842-1924)
Dixon, Julia E. (1871-1880)
Dixon, William W. (1873-1881)
Dixon, Bertha (1876-1880)
Dixon, David L. (1878-1881)
Embree, James Benton (1869-1930)
Embree, Orville Lewis (1902-1935)
Endresen, Selma Dorothy (1887-1924)
Gillispie, Hollie R. (1890-1918)
Gillispie, Edward Preston (1864?-1936)
Gillispie, Flora
Graves,
Hagen, Elden Maurice (1924, 16 days)
Heady, Lucy Jane (Babcock) (1874-1937)
Hodges, Nadine Marie (1939, 2 days)
Hodges, Walter (1895-1930)
Hoffman, Frederick C. (1847-1913)
Jacobson, Ann (Styris) (1866-1933)
Jacobson, Jacob E. (1865-1942)
Kruger, William (1863-1942)
Kruger, Anna Elizabeth (1859-1916)
Mays, Ruby (infant)
Miller, Marie (Nelson) (?-1932)

Miller, Paer A. (1854-1915)
Morrison, Chesley L. (1859-1940)
Morrison, Infant son (1914)
Mosier, William R. (1854?-1894)
McDaniel, Ada Ellen (1931, 3 mos.)
McDaniel, Gertrude Caroline (1932, 24 days)
McDonald, Hattie E. (1878-1915)
Owens, Earnest (?-1932)
Palmer, Lottie
Parks, Charles Rice (1820-1911)
Parks, Leander (1853-1935)
Parks, Queen Victoria (Franklin) (1858-1896)
Parks, O.C. (1875-1902)
Parks, Ollie S. (1884-1914)
Ramsdel, David Barclay (1852?-1920)
Ray, James (1892?-1941)
Rochester, Olive A. (1870-1892)
Ross, Victor
Sharp, Lottie (Harding) (1872-1930)
Sharp, Omer Clyde (1904-1932)
Sharp, William (1864-1942)
Simpson, William E. (1881-1920)
Simpson, Joicey Ann (1916-1925)
Smith, Thomas J. (1846-1910)
Timmons, Hettie (1865?-1925)
Timmons, Thomas F. (1858?-1917)
Turnicliff, David (1812?-1885)
Van Orden, Jonathan (1845-1923)
Van Orden, Olive (1850-1928)
Van Orden, Henry
Van Orden, Jessie (Lathrop) (1875-1912)
Van Orden, Marion (1888-1918)
Warren, Bessie (Van Orden) (1884-1917)
Watkins, Frances
Wilson, Jepie (1890?-1906)

DEDICATED MEMORIAL DAY, 1997

Elk City Pioneer
Janice M. Healy (2000)

Area: 992 square miles
Population (1998): 45,368
County seat: Newport, Population: 9,785
County established: 20 February 1893

Lincoln County has a number of Indian cemeteries of which Paul Washington in Siletz is much the most prominent. There was an earlier one at Yachats (pronounced: Ya-hots) and a number of Indian family cemeteries, some still in use. The earliest organized public cemeteries by white settlers were at Elk City (1871), South Beach (1872) and Tidewater (1873).

Elk City Pioneer
Janice M. Healy (2000)

Toledo

Janice M. Healy (2000)

Toledo

Janice M. Healy (2000)

Name of Cemetery and also known as	Number of burials	Acres	Condition	Date started or earliest known burial	Township	Range	Section

AGATE BEACH
AKA: 1. CAPE
        FOULWEATHER
      2. MEGGINSON

A   0.25   5   1873   T10S R11W   S29
These burials are Indian and white graves, located off of the road. Take Lighthouse Drive, then take the first street past the Izzy's Pizza that leads up the hill. Rocky Way was posted No Trespassing (September 1991). It is at the end of this street, on the right. There are 15 known burials, but as of Aug. 1990 only the stones of Mrs. Briggs and a boy could be found. The site is mostly destroyed. (Newport North 1984 USGS Quad. map.)

ALDER GROVE
AKA: 1. ECKMAN CREEK

C   1   2   1895   T13S R11W   S32
Located east of Waldport about 2.5 miles on OR. Hwy. 34. Turn right at the quarry and go 0.5 of a mile uphill to the cemetery. There are at least 122 burials. (Waldport 1984 USGS Quad. map.)

BAYVIEW [NEW]

A   ?   7   1914   T13S R11W   S16
There are several graves located at or near Bayview. There were apparently 2 separate Bayview Cemeteries, one from the 1880's and this later one. (Not shown on Waldport 1984 USGS Quad. map.)

BAYVIEW [OLD]

?   ?   ?   Early 1880   T13S R11W   S18
Located near the north end of the Alsea Bay Bridge. (Not shown on Waldport 1984 USGS Quad. map.)

BENSELL

A   ?   ?   1933-1943   T10S R10W   S4
Located 0.75 of a mile north of Siletz on OR. Hwy. 229, near Fuller Bridge over the Siletz River. Turn right onto a public road along the river bank and go about 0.2 of a mile. The graves are between the road bank and the river; there were 5 known burials (1960). (Toledo North 1984 USGS Quad. map.)

BOONE

A   ?   5   1878   T11S R11W   ?
Located somewhere on Boone Island, Section 25 or 26. (Not shown on Toledo South 1984 USGS Quad. map.)

Name of Cemetery and also known as	Number of burials	Acres	Condition	Date started or earliest known burial	Township	Range	Section

BRIGGS

A ? 5 ? T13S R11W S16

There is a possible small cluster of burials in the vicinity of Shepard's Point, at the north end of the railway trestle for the bygone Galloping Goose Railway, crossing Alsea Bay. These burials have not been well researched. (Not shown on Waldport 1984 USGS Quad. map.)

BURTON FAMILY

A ? 2 1878-1944 T6S R11W S24

Five Burton children who died of diphtheria 12-23 Oct. 1878 are buried here. There are now 17 graves here (1979). This cemetery is 2 or 3 miles northwest of Otis, out on Three Rocks Road. It is on a hill on the right (north) side of the road, in the yard of a house. The cemetery is within the Cascade Head Scenic Research Area, about 60 feet in elevation above the Salmon River estuary. NOTE: This site is on private property. (Not shown on Neskowin 1985 USGS Quad. map.)

CARSON

B 0.25 2 1913 T14S R11W S33

Take Yachats River Road and turn left (north) up Carson Creek Road. The cemetery is about 300 feet on the right from the junction with Yachats River Road. (Yachats 1984 USGS Quad. map.)

CHELAN ABBEY MAUSOLEUM AND COLUMBARIUM

D 3 1 1970 T11S R11W S9

Located at 915 Yaquina Heights Drive, Newport. {August 1991} (Newport North 1984 USGS Quad. map as part of Eureka Cemetery.)

CHITWOOD

C 0.5 5 1890 T10S R9W S32

Go 0.2 of a mile east of Chitwood on U.S. Hwy. 20, near the covered bridge. Turn left (north) off of the highway and go up the hill. There were 117 known burials as of 1978, and at least 4 more have been added since. The cemetery has been "neglected" since 1978. {17 October 2000} (Eddyville 1984 USGS Quad. map.)

Name of Cemetery and also known as	Number of burials	Acres	Condition	Date started or earliest known burial	Township	Range	Section

CURL FAMILY

B 1 3 1880's T6S R11W S25
Located on the west side of U.S. Hwy. 101, at the junction with OR. Hwy. 18, near Otis, off of Kingfisher Road. This Indian family cemetery is on a hill above the right bank of Rowdy Creek. (Not shown on Neskowin 1985 USGS Quad. map.)

DICKENS, JEHU

A 0.01 ? ? T6S R10W ?
Two stones are located on Highland Estates, near Otis. NOTE: No other information was given in the report. (Not shown on Neskowin 1985 USGS Quad. map.)

DOTY FAMILY

A 0.25 ? 1895 T13S R10W S7
From Bayview on the north side of Alsea Bay take Drift Creek Road to its ending at a ford over Drift Creek. The Doty house was on the other side of Drift Creek at what is now the entry into Drift Creek Wilderness Area of the Siuslaw National Forest. The burial or burials were presumably near the Doty house. (Not shown on Tidewater 1984 USGS Quad. map.)

EDDY
AKA: 1. OLD EDDY

A 0.25 4 1875 T11S R9W S4
Located on the riverbank near Eddyville. When heading west from Eddyville, this cemetery is 0.7 of a mile northwest and left off of U.S. Hwy. 20. This is on part of the original Israel Eddy Farm. It is thought that there are 13 graves, but there are only 10 stones remaining now and these are deep in the blackberries. (Eddyville 1984 USGS Quad. map.)

EDDYVILLE
AKA: 1. LITTLE ELK

C 2.3 1 1900 T11S R9W S10
Located 0.15 of a mile east of Eddyville above U.S. Hwy. 20. A "new area" has been added and there are 149 burials listed now (1990). {17 October 2000} (Eddyville 1984 USGS Quad. map.)

ELK CITY

A ? ? Circa 1870 T11S R10W ?
Four known burials are on a hill in an area surveyed for a ball field. NOTE: This site

Name of Cemetery and also known as	Number of burials	Acres	Condition	Date started or earliest known burial	Township	Range	Section

is on private property (Not shown on Elk City or Toledo South 1984 USGS Quad. maps.)

ELK CITY PIONEER　　　B　1　　2　　1871-1942　T11S R10W　　　S11
Located above the Evelyn Schriver (1978) house on the old military road. Go north on Elk City Road about 0.6 of a mile; turn right on Devils Well Road and go about 0.6 of a mile. The records were burned in a 1925 fire. There are 75 known burials, but far more burials are here. {17 October 2000} (Eddyville 1984 USGS Quad. map.)

ENOS　　　A　?　　5　　1886　　T11S R10W　　　?
Found at Depot Slough, just off of OR. Hwy. 229 to Siletz. NOTE: No other information was given in the report. (Not shown on Toledo North or Toledo South 1984 USGS Quad. map.)

EUREKA　　　D　24　　1　　1889　　T11S R11W　　　?
This is on Sections 4 and 5, east of Newport via 3rd Street Northeast and Old Corvallis-Newport Highway. In addition to 19.2 acres for Eureka itself, there are almost 5 acres across the road in the Pacific View Addition. The address is 917 Northeast Yaquina Heights Drive, Newport. {August 1991} (Newport North 1984 USGS Quad. map.)

FAULKNER, T. M.　　　A　0.02　2　21 Aug 1912　T15S R10W　　S1
This small cemetery is located in the bygone community of Fisher, in the Five Rivers country of southern Lincoln County. Take the Alsea Highway (OR. Hwy. 34), from Philomath towards Waldport; drive about 40 miles to the junction of Five Rivers Road on the left (south). Go about 9 miles to the former post office at Fisher. An eighth of a mile beyond is the Fisher School Covered Bridge, which has been set aside as a historical site. Turn right (south) onto Crab Creek Road, cross the replacement bridge and pass the old Fisher School. About 100 yards beyond the school, the road makes a right angle turn; there is a house on the left and the cemetery

Name of Cemetery and also known as	Number of burials	Acres	Condition	Date started or earliest known burial	Township	Range	Section

is on the right about 20 or 30 feet off of Crab Creek Road. Warren Faulkner reports that the cemetery was established after the death of his infant sister Cleora, 10 August 1912. Their father, T. M. Faulkner, gave the small cemetery to the community of Fisher. A Mrs. Vining and a Mr. Miller who died about 1912, a stillborn Faulkner boy about 1920, and an unknown man, who may have been Mr. Wright, are known to be buried here. (Not shown on Five Rivers 1984 USGS Quad. map.)

FERN RIDGE

C   1   2   1901   T12S R11W   S32

Located 2.2 mile east of Seal Rocks on Seal Rock Road. There are more than 165 burials. (Waldport 1984 USGS Quad. map.)

GLENEDEN BEACH

?   ?   5   ?   T8S R11W   ?

This could be in Section 9 or 10. An Indian burial ground located at the north end of Sijota Bluff, at the north end of Gleneden Beach. NOTE: No other information was given in the report. (Not shown on Lincoln City 1984 USGS Quad. map.)

GLENWOOD
AKA: 1. DRIFT CREEK
 2. GLEN

A   1   2   1894   T12S R10W   S13

Located on Drift Creek at the confluence of Gopher Creek at Glen. The visitor should stop at the Big Elk Forest Station and acquire a map of the Siuslaw National Forest. The station is about 1.5 miles west of Harlan. About 1 mile west of Harlan turn right (westerly-southwesterly) onto Forestry Road #31; go about 2.5 miles and turn left (southerly) onto Forestry Road #3125. Go to the cemetery on the right, about 5.5 miles from the starting point 1 mile west of Harlan. These mileages are approximate! The cemetery is on a ridgetop where the road makes a very pronounced curve around the base of this spur. One acre is deeded and there are 20 known burials. In 1988 half of the cemetery was in timber. (Elk City 1984 USGS Quad. map.)

Name of Cemetery and also known as	Number of burials	Acres	Condition	Date started or earliest known burial	Township	Range	Section

GRAHAM FAMILY

? ? 7 1871   T11S R10W   S17

The Graham family originally established a family cemetery in Toledo, at what is now the southwest corner of the Graham Street intersection with Main Street. At some later date the graves were reburied in the present Toledo Cemetery. (Not shown on Toledo South 1984 USGS Quad. map.)

GRUBB FAMILY

? ? ? ?   T10S R11W   S5

Located in the vicinity of Beverly Beach State Park at the mouth of Spencer Creek. This is along U.S. Hwy. 101 north of Newport and immediately south of Otter Crest. The Grubb family settled the first homestead here. Members of the clan and their spouses are reported buried in a private graveyard near the homestead. (Not shown on Newport North 1984 USGS Quad. map.)

HARLAN

B 1.2 2 1880   T12S R8W   S8

At 0.3 of a mile east of Harlan on Harlan Road, turn left and go uphill 0.2 of a mile to the cemetery. (Harlan 1984 USGS Quad. map.)

JACOBSON

A ? 5 Nov 1906   T11S R10W   ?

In Section 2 or 11, on a farm between Elk City and Pioneer on the railroad side of the Yaquina River. NOTE: This site is on private property. (Not shown on Eddyville 1984 USGS Quad. map.)

JANUARY

A 0.01 ?   T12S R8W   S23

This lone grave shows up in the Northeast 1/4 of the Northeast 1/4 of Section 23. It is not situated for the casual visitor. Leave Harlan and travel southeasterly on Harlan Road up the valley of Big Elk Creek. County road jurisdiction ends and the road continues as Siuslaw Forest Road #30. Turn left (east) onto Adams Creek Road. You will need a 4-wheel drive, to turn right (south) off of Adams Creek Road and follow a ditch road along a power ditch that connects Adams Creek

Name of Cemetery and also known as	Number of burials	Acres	Condition	Date started or earliest known burial	Township	Range	Section

with Big Elk Creek. The grave is across the ditch on a hillside a few hundred yards short of Big Elk Creek. January is a family name. (Marys Peak 1984 USGS Quad. mp.)

| KYNISTON FAMILY | A 2 ? | 1906 | T10S R10W | ? |

This family had two separate burial plots. At one, all of the stones have been stolen. At the second, which is near the Everest home (1990) is overgrown and also missing stones. Both plots are virtually lost. It is on the old Siletz Highway, on the Siletz side of the Graves Place. NOTE: This site is on private property. (Not shown on Toledo North 1984 USGS Quad. map.)

| LESLIE FAMILY | A 0.35 ? | 1956 | T11S R8W | S36 |

Located south of Burnt Woods. Go 2.9 miles south of U.S. Hwy. 20 on Shotpouch Road. Four graves are on the west side of the road (1978). (Marys Peak 1984 USGS Quad. Quad. map.)

| LOGAN FAMILY | B ? ? | 1899 | T6S R10W | S30 |

West of Otis, located in the Northwest 1/4 of the Northwest 1/4 of Section 30, off of the south side of Three Rocks Road. It is an Indian family cemetery and still in use. (Not shown on Neskowin 1985 USGS Quad. map.)

| LOGSDEN | ? ? ? ? | | T9S R9W | ? |

Indian burials possibly located in Section 33 or 34.   NOTE: This comes from a 1950 list of cemeteries. (Not shown on Eddyville 1984 USGS Quad. map.

| LOWER SILETZ-EUCHRE MOUNTAIN | ? ? ? ? | | ? ? | ? |

Reportedly, there are burials in this area but no one now knows where they are.

| MATTESON | A ? 5 | 1918 | T11S R10W | S10 |

Located on the John Matteson Homestead. NOTE: No other information was given in the

Name of Cemetery and also known as	Number of burials	Acres	Condition	Date started or earliest known burial	Township	Range	Section

report. This site is on private property. (Not shown on Toledo North Or Toledo South 1984 USGS Quad. maps.)

MORRIS, FAMILY
AKA: 1. WECOMA BEACH

| | A | 0.1 | 2 | 1850-1918 | T7S | R11W | S3 |

Located at the northwest corner of North 30th Street and Port Avenue just west of U.S. Hwy. 101; on Tax Lot #16,000. Most of the burials of this Indian family were removed to the Paul Washington Cemetery in Siletz in 1946. In 1950, 4 markers dating 1901-1918 remained and iron fences were laying around in the dense brush. An article from the *News-Times* of Newport, 2 December 1992, reports that members of the L.D.S. Church in Lincoln City were cleaning up the 50 X 75 foot cemetery after its rediscovery in 1991. They have discovered three headstones. There were also pieces of a wrought iron fence recovered. (Not shown on Lincoln City 1984 USGS Quad. map.)

MULKEY
AKA: 1. BURNT WOODS
2. HENDERSON FARM
3. SHOT POUCH
4. TUM TUM

| | B | 0.25 | ? | 1896 | T11S | R8W | S26 |

Go 2 miles south of Burnt Woods on Shotpouch Road. The cemetery is located on the west side of the road. (Marys Peak 1984 USGS Quad. map.)

NASHVILLE

| | A | 0.01 | ? | ? | T10S | R8W | S36 |

Located in Nashville at the junction of Eddyville-Blodgett Highway with Rock Creek Road, 7.5 miles northwest from Blodgett and U.S. Hwy. 20. The grave is at the westerly corner of the intersection between the highway and the railway. (Summit 1984 USGS Quad. map.)

NORTONS

| | A | ? | ? | 1911 | T10S | R8W | S32 |

Located 0.5 of a mile east of Nortons on Eddyville-Blodgett Highway, on the north side of the road about 1 block from the parking lot. (Nortons Quad. 1984 USGS map.)

Name of Cemetery and also known as	Number of burials	Acres	Condition	Date started or earliest known burial	Township	Range	Section

ONA
AKA: 1. BEAVER CREEK SCHOOLYARD
2. SCHOOL HOUSE

B 1 4 1885-1972 T12S R11W S21
This cemetery is on a hill above Lincoln Grange Hall. Take North Beaver Creek Road from U.S. Hwy. 101 by the Thunder Bay Golf Course. No stones could be found in 1990: the area is now mostly timbered. (Not shown on Newport South 1984 USGS Quad. map.)

OYSTERVILLE

? ? ? 1866 T11S R11W S34
This burial ground was located on McCaffery Island, a 20-acre piece of land which rises above the tidal flats at the mouth of McCaffery Slough on the south side of Yaquina Bay, between Toledo and Newport. Oysterville was a small village settled even before Toledo. It was on the north bank of the bay in Section 27 but later was often called by its postal name of Winant. In February 1866 David Newsom voyaged downstream from Oysterville and noticed a cemetery with one grave on this then-unnamed small island a mile or so from the village. How many additional burials there were and the fate of the cemetery is unknown to the compiler. (The Newport South 1984 USGS Quad. map shows McCaffery Island, but with no graves indicated. Note that the Quad. map now shows Winant on the north bank where the village of Oysterville was located. The same map now shows Oysterville opposite Winant on the south shore of Yaquina Bay. Here is a headache for historians of Lincoln County.)

PACIFIC VIEW

C 5 1 Circa 1980 T11S R11W S9
Located on the south side of Northeast Yaquina Heights Drive, in the 900 Block. Once a separate cemetery, it is now a part of Eureka Cemetery called the Pacific View Addition. {August 1991} (Not shown on Newport North 1984 USGS Quad. map as a separate cemetery.)

Name of Cemetery and also known as	Number of burials	Acres	Condition	Date started or earliest known burial	Township	Range	Section

PACIFIC VIEW MEMORIAL GARDENS AND COLUMBARIUM
AKA: 1. PACIFIC MEMORIAL GARDENS
2. YOUNG MEMORIAL PARK, JOSEPHINE

D 25   1   1968   T7S R11W   S12
Located in Lincoln City on the east side of Devils Lake; 2.3 miles east of U.S. Hwy. 101 off of East Devils Lake Road. {August 1991} (Devils Lake 1984 USGS Quad. map.)

PALMER

A ?   5   ?   T11S R9W   ?
Possibly in Section 19. Located on Bear Creek. NOTE: No other information was given in the report. (Not shown on Elk City 1984 USGS Quad. map.)

PORTER FAMILY

A ?   ?   1881-1898   T10S R8W   S30
A gravestone for a man and his wife is next to a monument for the first school in Lincoln County (1866). Mrs. Porter was the teacher. It is by the Eddyville-Blodgett Highway, where the highway crosses the railway near Nortons. "School Hill" is on north side of the highway where Stony Creek joins the Yaquina River. (Not shown on Nortons 1984 USGS Quad. map.)

RAE

A ?   11   1903   T11S R10W   S15
There was a small cemetery lot deeded to the Adventist Church, but it is now under the Elk City Road. (Not shown on Toledo South 1984 USGS Quad. map.)

RIVERSIDE V.F.W.
AKA: 1. CHARLEY
2. VETERANS OF FOREIGN WARS

D 1.4   1   1898   T10S R10W   S11
Located east of the town of Siletz on the right (south) side of Upper Siletz Road, just west of Milepost 2. The first white burial was Nov. 1918, a death from Spanish flu. This cemetery was originally an Indian cemetery, the original plats and records have been lost. The Indian cemetery was obliterated by a fire and all markers were destroyed. There are 732 known burials (September 1991). {August 1991} (Toledo North 1984 USGS Quad. map.)

Name of Cemetery and also known as	Number of burials	Acres	Condition	Date started or earliest known burial	Township	Range	Section

ROSE LODGE
AKA: 1. SALMON RIVER

A ? ? 1895 T6S R10W S25

Located close to Widow Creek, above a quarry and not far from the Grange Hall (1978). (Not shown on Dolph 1985 USGS Quad. map.)

SCHOONER CREEK

? ? ? 1913 T7S R11W ?

There are several private burial grounds in this region. NOTE: This is the Schooner Creek in the Lincoln City area, not the Schooner Creek in the Newport area. NOTE: No other information was given in the report. (Not shown on Devils Lake 1984 USGS Quad. map.)

SILETZ VALLEY

? ? ? ? ? ? ?

Indian burials. No other information was given in the report.

SOUTH BEACH

B 2 3 1872 T11S R11W S17

Go southbound on U.S. Hwy 101 from Newport, take the Marine Science Center exit and then take the first road to the left. It is now (September 1991) closed by a cable, but there is room to park. Walk about 80 feet and take a trail to the right. The site is at the top of the hill and partially overgrown with salal and huckleberry. There are many lost graves here with a few stones older than Newport. In July 1990, the Depew grandsons replaced the stone for Hiram Depew, a Civil War veteran who died in 1895. {August 1991} (Not shown on Newport South 1984 USGS Quad. map.)

STANTON FAMILY

A ? 5 23 Jun 1878 T10S R10W S32

Located northeast of Toledo. Take Olalla Road north off of U.S. Hwy. 20. The golf course and cemetery border West Olalla Creek on the east side of the road. The burials are above the golf course. Three stones are listed. Cortez Stanton, age 19, was the first burial near the home of F. M. and J. A. Stanton. The burial area is now completely overgrown. (Not shown on Toledo North 1984 USGS Quad. map.)

Name of Cemetery and also known as	Number of burials	Acres	Condition	Date started or earliest known burial	Township	Range	Section

TAFT PIONEER C 0.5 2 1906 T7S R11W S27

Located on the east side of U.S. Hwy. 101 and opposite the Inn at Spanish Head. The cemetery has the finest ocean view in Lincoln City. It was also an Indian burial ground as of 1903. {August 1991} (Lincoln City 1984 USGS Quad. map.)

TEAGUE FAMILY A 0.5 ? 1872 T10S R10W S11

Leave the Upper Siletz Road between Siletz and Logsden and cross the Siletz River on Sam Creek Road. Immediately beyond the bridge turn right (westerly) onto Hamer Road which follows the left bank of the Siletz River. Go about 0.9 of a mile to a "Y" where you leave Hamer Road onto a lesser road to the left going inland. Travel another 0.6 of a mile to the cemetery on the right (west). This cemetery is unnamed on the USGS Quad. map but it is probably the Teague Family Cemetery which was reportedly "along the Siletz River between Siletz and Logsden and consisted of 12 to 14 graves." References: *Salem Capital Journal*, 7 March 1968: *Toledo Lincoln County Leader*, 13 July 1977. (Eddyville 1984 USGS Quad. map.)

THREE ROCKS ? ? ? ? T6S R11W S23

Ruby El Hult in her book *Lost Mines and Treasures*, page 43 has an interesting story. At Three Rocks Beach at the mouth of the Salmon River Indians reported that a boat load of men from a shipwreck landed and buried a large box or chest. Most of them rowed off leaving two behind. One of these was an 8-foot negro: he killed his white companion and then the Indians killed the black man. The story was that a large size skeleton was uncovered later. The compiler confesses to an even larger dose of skepticism. (Not shown on Neskowin 1985 USG Quad. map.)

TIDEWATER C 2 2 1873 T13S R10W S27

Travel 0.75 of a mile east of Tidewater on OR. Hwy. 34, then north off of OR. Hwy. 34 to

Name of Cemetery and also known as	Number of burials	Acres	Condition	Date started or earliest known burial	Township	Range	Section

the ridge top. Many Waldport and Bayview pioneers are buried here. (Tidewater 1984 USGS Quad. map.)

TOLEDO
AKA: 1. I.O.O.F.
    2. ST. JOHNS

D   8   1   1898   **T11S R10W**   **S8**
About 1898 one acre was dedicated in the present cemetery area north of town and deeded to St. Johns Church. The I.O.O.F. area of Toledo Cemetery was surveyed in 1897, but has stones dating from 1886. Additional acreage has been purchased; at present two acres are unused. {17 October 2000} (Toledo North 1984 USGS Quad. map.)

VANSTRUM FAMILY

A   0.01   ?   1 Jan. 1978   **T14S**   ?   ?
Located near Five Rivers. The cremains of four children who burned to death are buried on a farm. NOTE: This site is on private property. (Not shown on Five Rivers 1984 USGS Quad. map.)

WALDPORT MEMORIAL
AKA: 1. CRESTVIEW
    2. MEMORIAL HOME
    3. NEW HOME
    4. WALDPORT

B   3   2   1940   **T13S R11W**   **S30**
Located at Waldport on the west side of Crestline Drive at Salmon Street. {August 1991} (Waldport 1984 USGS Quad. map.)

WASHINGTON, PAUL
AKA: 1. GOVERNMENT
      HILL
    2. INDIAN
    3. SILETZ

D   11   1   1879   **T10S R10W**   **S9**
Located on Government Hill in Siletz. This is an Indian cemetery for the Confederated Tribes of Siletz. {August 1991} (Toledo North 1984 USGS Quad. map.)

WIGLE
AKA: 1. ROCK CREEK

?   0.25   ?   ?   **T10S R9W**   **S12**
Located off of Rock Creek Road. Going from Nortons towards Logsden, it is 1 mile past the junction of North Fork Rock Creek Road. The cemetery is on the right, on the hillside. (Nortons 1984 USGS Quad. Quad. map.)

WOODING

?   ?   ?   1928   **T12S**   ?   ?
This could be in Range 10 or 11 West. "Lost in the brush near Wright Creek at the foot of

Name of Cemetery and also known as	Number of burials	Acres	Condition	Date started or earliest known burial	Township	Range	Section

Dobson Mountain," on a homestead along Wright Creek. NOTE: No other information was given in the report. This is probably a family burial site, but we can not prove it at this time. The USGS does not list a Dobson or Dotson Mountain anywhere in Oregon. (Not shown on Toledo South 1984 USGS Quad. map.)

YACHATS [OLD]
AKA: 1. ALSEA AGENCY

| | B | 1 | 1 | ? | T14S | R12W | S26 |

Located above the Yachats Memorial Park Cemetery in fir timber, off of Agency Drive where it adjoins Yachats Memorial Park: As of 1991 more than 90 burials were known. In May 1996 an informant reported the Old Yachats Cemetery was probably the cemetery for the Alsea Sub-Agency Indian Reservation and furthermore the cemeteries fir trees might be logged off. {August 1991} (Not shown on Yachats 1984 USGS Quad. map.)

YACHATS MEMORIAL PARK
AKA: 1. YACHATS [NEW]

| | C | 2.5 | 1 | 1944 | T14S | R12W | S27 |

This is on Sections 22, 26 and 27, on the east side of U.S. Hwy. 101 at Agency Drive. This cemetery adjoins the Old Yachats Cemetery. {August 1991} (Yachats 1984 USGS Quad. map.)

YAQUINA

| | ? | ? | ? | ? | T11S | R11W | S22 |

At the terminus of the railway from Corvallis, which never reached Newport. No designated cemetery was ever located; but it is known that a baby, an unnamed girl and a Japanese are buried in the west part of Yaquina. There were Japanese laborers at the mill in Toledo and Tokyo Slough in Toledo reflects their stay. (Not shown on Newport South 1984 USGS Quad. map.)

YAQUINA JOHN POINT

| | ? | ? | 5 | ? | T13S | R12W | S24 |

This was on a hillside facing Alsea Bay and the ocean. The burials were mostly destroyed by the construction of U.S. Hwy. 101, circa 1920; some were reburied. At least two known burials remain in a yard above the highway. This was the earliest cemetery at Waldport, named for Yaquina John, an Indian. NOTE: This site is on private property. (Not shown on Waldport 1984 USGS Quad. map.)

Chitwood
The only clue there was a cemetery hidden in the woods.
Janice M. Healy (2000)

Toledo
Janice M. Healy (2000)

Toledo
Janice M. Healy (2000)

AGATE BEACH	LINCOLN CO.	T10S	R11W	S29
ALDER GROVE	LINCOLN CO.	T13S	R11W	S32
ALSEA AGENCY see **YACHATS [OLD]**	LINCOLN CO.	T14S	R12W	S26
BAYVIEW [NEW]	LINCOLN CO.	T13S	R11W	S16
BAYVIEW [OLD]	LINCOLN CO.	T13S	R11W	S18
BEAVER CREEK SCHOOLYARD see **ONA**	LINCOLN CO.	T12S	R11W	S21
BENSELL	LINCOLN CO.	T10S	R10W	S4
BOONE	LINCOLN CO.	T11S	R11W	?
BRIGGS	LINCOLN CO.	T13S	R11W	S16
BRIGS, MRS. see **AGATE BEACH**	LINCOLN CO.	T10S	R11W	S29
BURNT WOODS see **MULKEY**	LINCOLN CO.	T11S	R8W	S26
BURTON CHILDREN see **BURTON FAMILY**				
	LINCOLN CO.	T6S	R11W	S24
BURTON FAMILY	LINCOLN CO.	T6S	R11W	S24
CAPE FOULWEATHER see **AGATE BEACH**				
	LINCOLN CO.	T10S	R11W	S29
CARSON	LINCOLN CO.	T14S	R11W	S33
CHARLEY see **RIVERSIDE V.F.W.**	LINCOLN CO.	T10S	R10W	S11
CHELAN ABBEY MAUSOLEUM AND COLUMBARIUM				
	LINCOLN CO.	T11S	R11W	S9
CHITWOOD	LINCOLN CO.	T10S	R9W	S32
CRESTVIEW see **WALDPORT MEMORIAL**	LINCOLN CO.	T13S	R11W	S30
CURL FAMILY	LINCOLN CO.	T6S	R11W	S25
DEPEW, HIRAM see **SOUTH BEACH**	LINCOLN CO.	T11S	R11W	S17
DICKENS, JEHU	LINCOLN CO.	T6S	R10W	?
DOTY FAMILY	LINCOLN CO.	T13S	R10W	S7
DOTY HOUSE see **DOTY FAMILY**	LINCOLN CO.	T13S	R10W	S7
DRIFT CREEK see **GLENWOOD**	LINCOLN CO.	T12S	R10W	S13
ECKMAN CREEK see **ALDER GROVE**	LINCOLN CO.	T13S	R11W	S32
EDDY	LINCOLN CO.	T11S	R9W	S4
EDDY FARM, ISRAEL see **EDDY**	LINCOLN CO.	T11S	R9W	S4
EDDYVILLE	LINCOLN CO.	T11S	R9W	S10
ELK CITY	LINCOLN CO.	T11S	R10W	?
ELK CITY PIONEER	LINCOLN CO.	T11S	R10W	S11
ENOS	LINCOLN CO.	T11S	R10W	?
EUREKA	LINCOLN CO.	T11S	R11W	?
FAULKNER, CLEORA see **FAULKNER, T. M.**				
	LINCOLN CO.	T15S	R10W	S1
FAULKNER, T. M.	LINCOLN CO.	T15S	R10W	S1
FAULKNER, WARREN see **FAULKNER, T. M.**				
	LINCOLN CO.	T15S	R10W	S1
FERN RIDGE	LINCOLN CO.	T12S	R11W	S32
FISHER SCHOOL COVERED BRIDGE see **FAULKNER, T. M.**				
	LINCOLN CO.	T15S	R10W	S1
GLEN see **GLENWOOD**	LINCOLN CO.	T12S	R10W	S13
GLENEDEN BEACH	LINCOLN CO.	T8S	R11W	?
GLENWOOD	LINCOLN CO.	T12S	R10W	S13
GOVERNMENT HILL see **WASHINGTON, PAUL**				
	LINCOLN CO.	T10S	R10W	S9
GRAHAM FAMILY	LINCOLN CO.	T11S	R10W	S17
GRUBB FAMILY	LINCOLN CO.	T10S	R11W	S5
HARLAN	LINCOLN CO.	T12S	R8W	S8

```
HENDERSON FARM see MULKEY          LINCOLN CO.    T11S   R8W    S26
I.O.O.F. see TOLEDO                LINCOLN CO.    T11S   R10W   S8
INDIAN see WASHINGTON, PAUL        LINCOLN CO.    T10S   R10W   S9
JACOBSON                           LINCOLN CO.    T11S   R10W   ?
JANUARY                            LINCOLN CO.    T12S   R8W    S23
KYNISTON FAMILY                    LINCOLN CO.    T10S   R10W   ?
LESLIE FAMILY                      LINCOLN CO.    T11S   R8W    S36
LITTLE ELK see EDDYVILLE           LINCOLN CO.    T11S   R9W    S10
LOGAN FAMILY                       LINCOLN CO.    T6S    R10W   S30
LOGSDEN                            LINCOLN CO.    T9S    R9W    ?
LOWER SILETZ-EUCHRE MOUNTAIN       LINCOLN CO.    ?      ?      ?
MATTESON                           LINCOLN CO.    T11S   R10W   S10
MATTESON HOMESTEAD, JOHN see MATTESON
                                   LINCOLN CO.    T11S   R10W   S10
MEGGINSON see AGATE BEACH          LINCOLN CO.    T10S   R11W   S29
MEMORIAL HOME see WALDPORT MEMORIAL
                                   LINCOLN CO.    T13S   R11W   S30
MILLER, MR. see FAULKNER, T. M.    LINCOLN CO.    T15S   R10W   S1
MORRIS FAMILY                      LINCOLN CO.    T7S    R11W   S3
MULKEY                             LINCOLN CO.    T11S   R8W    S26
NASHVILLE                          LINCOLN CO.    T10S   R8W    S36
NEW HOME see WALDPORT MEMORIAL     LINCOLN CO.    T13S   R11W   S30
NEWSOM, DAVID see OYSTERVILLE      LINCOLN CO.    T11S   R11W   S34
NORTONS                            LINCOLN CO.    T10S   R8W    S32
OLD EDDY see EDDY                  LINCOLN CO.    T11S   R9W    S4
ONA                                LINCOLN CO.    T12S   R11W   S21
OYSTERVILLE                        LINCOLN CO.    T11S   R11W   S34
PACIFIC MEMORIAL GARDENS see PACIFIC VIEW MEMORIAL GARDENS AND
   COLUMBARIUM                     LINCOLN CO.    T7S    R11W   S12
PACIFIC VIEW                       LINCOLN CO.    T11S   R11W   S9
PACIFIC VIEW MEMORIAL GARDENS AND COLUMBARIUM
                                   LINCOLN CO.    T7S    R11W   S12
PALMER                             LINCOLN CO.    T11S   R9W    ?
PORTER FAMILY                      LINCOLN CO.    T10S   R8W    S30
RAE                                LINCOLN CO.    T11S   R10W   S15
RIVERSIDE V. F. W.                 LINCOLN CO.    T10S   R10W   S11
ROCK CREEK see WIGLE               LINCOLN CO.    T10S   R9W    S12
ROSE LODGE                         LINCOLN CO.    T6S    R10W   S25
ST. JOHNS see TOLEDO               LINCOLN CO.    T11S   R10W   S8
SALMON RIVER see ROSE LODGE        LINCOLN CO.    T6S    R10W   S25
SCHOOL HOUSE see ONA               LINCOLN CO.    T12S   R11W   S21
SCHOONER CREEK                     LINCOLN CO.    T7S    R11W   ?
SCHRIVER, EVELYN see ELK CITY PIONEER
                                   LINCOLN CO.    T11S   R10W   S11
SHOT POUCH see MULKEY              LINCOLN CO.    T11S   R8W    S26
SILETZ see WASHINGTON, PAUL        LINCOLN CO.    T10S   R10W   S9
SILETZ VALLEY                      LINCOLN CO.    ?      ?      ?
SOUTH BEACH                        LINCOLN CO.    T11S   R11W   S17
STANTON, CORTEZ see STANTON FAMILY
                                   LINCOLN CO.    T10S   R10W   S32
STANTON, F. M. see STANTON FAMILY
                                   LINCOLN CO.    T10S   R10W   S32
```

STANTON FAMILY	LINCOLN CO.	T10S	R10W	S32
STANTON, J. A. see **STANTON FAMILY**				
	LINCOLN CO.	T10S	R10W	S32
TAFT PIONEER	LINCOLN CO.	T7S	R11W	S27
TEAGUE FAMILY	LINCOLN CO.	T10S	R10W	S11
THREE ROCKS	LINCOLN CO.	T6S	R11W	S23
TIDEWATER	LINCOLN CO.	T13S	R10W	S27
TOLEDO	LINCOLN CO.	T11S	R10W	S8
TUM TUM see **MULKEY**	LINCOLN CO.	T11S	R8W	S26
VANSTRUM FAMILY	LINCOLN CO.	T14S	?	?
VETERANS OF FOREIGN WARS see **RIVERSIDE V.F.W.**				
	LINCOLN CO.	T10S	R10W	S11
VINING, MRS. see **FAULKNER, T. M.**				
	LINCOLN CO.	T15S	R10W	S1
WALDPORT see **WALDPORT MEMORIAL**	LINCOLN CO.	T13S	R11W	S30
WALDPORT MEMORIAL	LINCOLN CO.	T13S	R11W	S30
WASHINGTON, PAUL	LINCOLN CO.	T10S	R10W	S9
WECOMA BEACH see **MORRIS FAMILY**	LINCOLN CO.	T7S	R11W	S3
WIGLE	LINCOLN CO.	T10S	R9W	S12
WOODING	LINCOLN CO.	T12S	?	?
WRIGHT, MR. see **FAULKNER, T. M.**	LINCOLN CO.	T15S	R10W	S1
YACHATS [NEW] see **YACHATS MEMORIAL PARK**				
	LINCOLN CO.	T14S	R12W	S27
YACHATS [OLD]	LINCOLN CO.	T14S	R12W	S26
YACHATS MEMORIAL PARK	LINCOLN CO.	T14S	R12W	S27
YAQUINA	LINCOLN CO.	T11S	R11W	S22
YAQUINA, JOHN see **YAQUINA JOHN POINT**				
	LINCOLN CO.	T13S	R12W	S24
YAQUINA JOHN POINT	LINCOLN CO.	T13S	R12W	S24
YOUNG MEMORIAL PARK, JOSEPHINE see **PACIFIC VIEW MEMORIAL GARDENS AND**				
COLUMBARIUM	LINCOLN CO.	T7S	R11W	S12

Toledo

Janice M. Healy (2000)

Toledo
Janice M. Healy (2000)

Elk City Pioneer
Janice M. Healy (2000)

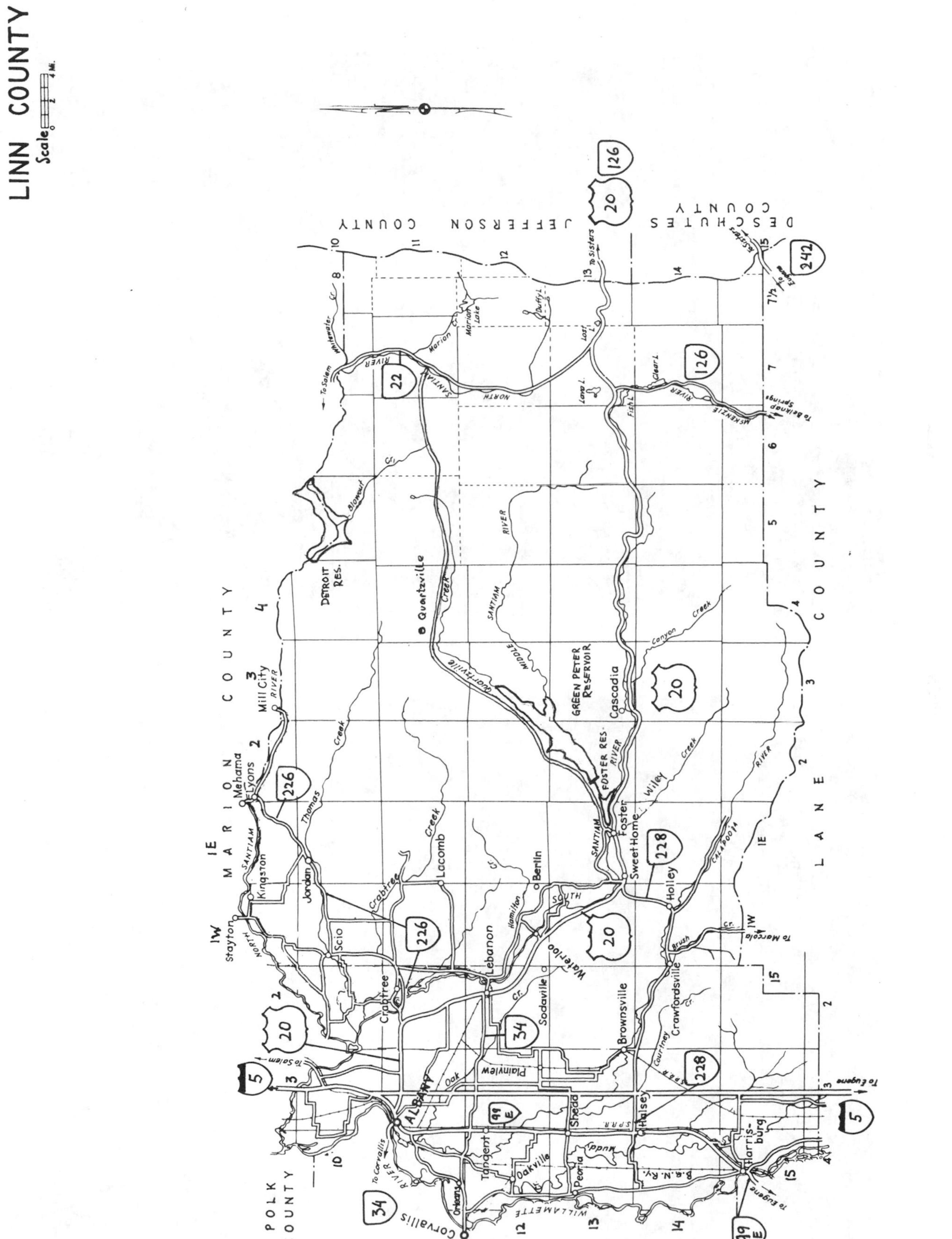

LINN COUNTY
Scale
MARION COUNTY
JEFFERSON COUNTY
DESCHUTES COUNTY
LANE COUNTY
BENTON COUNTY
POLK COUNTY
Albany
Corvallis
Tangent
Oakville
Peoria
Shedd
Halsey
Harrisburg
Orleans
Plainview
Brownsville
Crawfordsville
Holley
Sweet Home
Foster
Cascadia
Lebanon
Sodaville
Waterloo
Berlin
Lacomb
Crabtree
Scio
Jordan
Kingston
Stayton
Lyons
Mehama
Mill City
Quartzville
Detroit Res.
Green Peter Reservoir
Foster Res.

Linn County

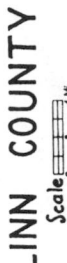

Workman
White Bronze
Dean H. Byrd (1990)

Alford
White Bronze
Dean H. Byrd (1990)

Area: 3,297 square miles
Population (1998): 104,464
County seat: Albany, Population: 37,095
County established: 28 December 1847

Linn County in the Willamette Valley was one of the first areas settled by pioneers seeking farmlands. By 1847 there were at least two public cemeteries; Riverside at Albany and Wisner, a rural burial ground. In the early and mid-1850's numerous cemeteries for public burials were established. Waverly Jewish Cemetery in Albany is the only current Jewish cemetery outside of the Portland Metropolitan area.

Sandridge
Dean H. Byrd (1990)

Gilliland
Dean H. Byrd (1992)

Baptist
Dean H. Byrd (1992)

Name of Cemetery and also known as	Number of burials	Acres	Condition	Date started or earliest known burial	Township	Range	Section

ALFORD

D   4.93   1   1853   T14S R4W   S35
Located 4 miles north of Harrisburg on the northwest side of OR. Hwy. 99E, on the Thomas Alford D.L.C., RB #1301. {11 June 1990} (Harrisburg 1969 USGS Quad. map.)

ALLPHIN FAMILY

A   0.23   12   1848-1876   T10S R3W   S8
Located 0.7 of a mile southeast of where Dever Road crosses the Burlington Northern tracks, on a knoll. There are 3 known graves, and possibly 1 more, of the Allphin family. NOTE: This site is on private property. This cemetery reportedly was bulldozed in 1993 by farming operations. (Albany 1970-75 USGS Quad. map.)

AMES FAMILY

B   0.3   1   1863-1951   T13S R1W   S36
Located at the west edge of Sweet Home, just south of Holley Road (OR. Hwy. 228) up the hill 100 yards. There were 24 known burials of the Ames family in 1958. It is on the Lowell Ames, Sr. D.L.C. #50, OC #2494. (Sweet Home 1984 USGS Quad. map.)

BAPTIST
AKA: 1. BROWNSVILLE BAPTIST
     2. FIRST BAPTIST
     3. PLEASANT BUTTE BAPTIST

C   1.95   2   1854   T13S R3W   S23
Located on the north slope of Powell Hills northwest of Brownsville. Take Seven Mile Lane 2.5 miles northwest of Brownsville. Then turn left at the cemetery signboard and drive 0.3 of a mile up the hill to the cemetery. At certain times of the year, the site of the old Pleasant Butte Baptist Church is visible on the right, part way up the hill. The present-day church is closer to Brownsville. 1855 was the earliest burial date noted. NOTE: The signboard just calls this cemetery "BAPTIST". {1 July 1992} (Halsey 1969 USGS Quad. map.)

BELLINGER
AKA: 1. HAMILTON CREEK
     2. HAPPY HOME

C   1.13   2   5 Nov. 1854   T12S R1W   S15
Leave Lebanon and cross the South Santiam River; at the east end of the bridge turn right onto Berlin Road, go 5.7 miles to the junction with Bellinger Scale Road and turn left (north). Go 1 mile on Bellinger Scale Road, then turn right onto an unsigned road

Name of Cemetery and also known as	Number of burials	Acres	Condition	Date started or earliest known burial	Township	Range	Section

and go 0.7 of a mile to the cemetery. There were 118 known burials in 1955. NOTE: This site is on private property, visitors must check in at the farm house and close all gates. {29 April 1992} (Onehorse Slough 1969-75 USGS Quad. map.)

BILYEU DEN

C 2.52 2 1857 T10S R1E S8

Pronounced "Blue Den", this is just west of Jordan near the Catholic church and 0.9 of a mile east of OR. Hwy. 226 on Camp Morrison Drive, on the south side of the road. It is on the Hubbard Bilyeu D.L.C., OC #4229. {4 August 1991} (Jordan 1985 USGS Quad. map.)

BLACK COUPLE

A ? 5 ? T12S R2W S9

Samuel Arthur Randle reported in 1987 that an elderly black couple came west from Indiana with the Moses Bland family in 1851. The couple reportedly are buried on the Moses Bland D.L.C. #50, OC #1961. (Not shown on Lebanon 1969-86 USGS Quad. map.)

BLACK, MR.

A 0.01 5 1883 T13S R1W S1

Mr. Black is buried on Reeves Hill in the McDowell Creek area. The burial appears to be along McDowell Creek Drive in a saddle between two hills, about 0.75 of a mile east of the bridge over the South Santiam River. The Reeves Place was on the right (south), so presumably the burial is on the lower hill on the right. NOTE: This site is on private property. (Not shown on Waterloo 1988 USGS Quad. map.)

BLAIN
AKA: 1. DINWIDDIE
2. GRAY
3. WILSON

A 0.5 12 1855-1878 T14S R3W S14

Located about 0.25 of a mile west and a bit southwest of Union Point Cemetery which is visible from here. This is now farmed over. It is on the David Gray D.L.C. #43, OC #1808. NOTE: This site is on private property. (Not shown on Indian Head 1969 USGS Quad. map. The USGS mistakenly places the name Blain Cemetery on what is actually Union Point Cemetery.)

Name of Cemetery and also known as	Number of burials	Acres	Condition	Date started or earliest known burial	Township	Range	Section

BOY

A   0.01   ?   ?   T10S R1E   S8
A fenced grave is located on the Fred Zielinski Place about a mile westerly from Jordan, along OR. Hwy. 226 (1972 information). This boy drowned in Thomas Creek. NOTE: This site is on private property. (Not shown on Jordan 1985 USGS Quad. map.)

BRATTAIN FAMILY

A   0.2   3   1854-1916   T12S R4W   S33
This is located north of Peoria, north of Brattain Drive, and east of Peoria Road on the left bank of Muddy Creek. There were 8 known graves in 1938, on the Jonathan H. Brattain D.L.C. #42, OC #803. NOTE: This site is on private property. (Peoria 1969-75 USGS Quad. map.)

BROWNSVILLE PIONEER
 AKA: 1. BROWNSVILLE
        CITY
      2. MASONIC
        [BROWNSVILLE]

D   8.3   1   1851   T13S R2W   S32
Located east of Brownsville on the north side of the Calapooia River, at the east end of Kirk Avenue on a low hill. It is on the William R. Kirk D.L.C. #42, OC #2135. {17 September 2000} (Brownsville 1988 USGS Quad. map.)

BUNKER HILL
 AKA: 1. SAVAGE BUTTE
      2. SAVAGE-MORGAN
         FAMILIES

A   1.5   3   1852-1932   T13S R3W   S9
This cemetery is located on the first knoll east of Shedd via Boston Mill Drive. The knoll is about 0.25 of a mile east of the bridge over the Calapooia River and is just short of the overcrossing over the I-5 Freeway. Savage Butte itself is a large butte just east beyound I-5. The cemetery is on the east side of the knoll on private property and with no ready access. The first burial was of Columbus Savage, the one year-old son of Americus. The child died 5 October 1852. Americus Savage himself committed suicide here 13 August 1876 in despair over his alcoholism. His will donated 10 acres for the cemetery provided the Masons should build a temple on the site. They did not. There were 19 known burials in 1958, on the Americus Savage D.L.C. #50, OC #617. (Halsey 1969 USGS Quad. map.)

Name of Cemetery and also known as	Number of burials	Acres	Condition	Date started or earliest known burial	Township	Range	Section

CALAPOOIA MOUNDS

-	-	-	-	-	-	-

Although the Calapooia Mounds belong in the realm of archeology since they are prehistoric, the compiler provides an article. 87 of these burial mounds were mapped between 1884 and 1924. They are on both sides of the Calapooia River from the mouth of Oak Creek just south of Albany to Brownsville. Since white settlement the mounds have been eroded and flattened by agricultural practices, with only a very few scientifically excavated.

CASCADIA PARK

?	?	?	?	?	R3E	?

We do not know at this time whether this is in Township 13 or 14 South. The burials are across from Cascadia State Park to the south of U.S. Hwy. 20 and the two graves are on a ridge above the road. One is for a little boy named David and the other for a young man, whose name is unknown. (Not shown on Cascadia 1985 USGS Quad. map.)

CHILDS

A	0.9	5	1895-1905	T12S R2W	S36

Located on the old Skeels Place west of Sodaville. From Sodaville, go west 0.4 of a mile on Sodaville Cutoff Road. Turn left (south) on Middle Ridge Drive and cross Oak Creek; at 1 mile from the starting point is a 90 degree turn to the right (south). Do not turn, but continue ahead on a lane 400 feet to a house. Then turn right and go another 800 feet. The cemetery is in open country to the right. There are 3 known graves on the Richard Usher D.L.C. #62, OC #4733. NOTE: This site is on private property. (Brownsville 1988 USGS Quad. map.)

CLAYPOOL FAMILY

B	1	3	1861	T13S R2W	S5

Located southeast of Rock Hill School, northwest of Brownsville and south off of Brownsville Road. There is no access road, it is 0.5 of a mile southeast of the road on a hill that is wooded; on the Reuben Claypool D.L.C. #48, OC #2377. (Brownsville 1988 USGS Quad. map.)

Name of Cemetery and also known as	Number of burials	Acres	Condition	Date started or earliest known burial	Township	Range	Section

COCHRAN, POLLY

A   0.01   5   1854   T13S R2W   S19
One grave of a mother and her child is about 2 miles north of Brownsville. It was obliterated by the mid-1960's; on the William Cochran D.L.C., OC #3838. (Not shown on Brownsville 1988 USGS Quad. map.)

COOPER, MRS.

A   0.01   ?   ?   T12S R1W   S8
Located in the Southeast 1/4 of the Southwest 1/4 of Section 8. Harlan Mastenbrook reports that on the family property there was buried a Mrs. Cooper and some children who died of diphtheria. They are from the 19th century. (Not shown on Onehorse Slough 1969-75 USGS Quad. map.)

CRABTREE FAMILY
AKA: 1. PRIME

A   ?   5   ?   T11S R2W   S13
Located just north and west of Griggs Station, toward Crabtree on Cold Springs Road. There were 5 graves found; on the Job Crabtree D.L.C. #66, OC #4330. NOTE: This site is on private property. (Not shown on Lebanon 1969-86 USGS Quad. map.)

CRAWFORDSVILLE UNION
AKA: 1. UNION
         [CRAWFORDS-
         VILLE]

D   3.69   2   1852   T14S R1W   S17
Located just south of OR. Hwy. 228 about 0.8 of a mile east of the Crawfordsville Bridge on OR. Hwy. 228. Turn right on Cemetery Road, go 0.6 of a mile to the end of this road. The earliest marker found was 1852; but the cemetery is possibly older. There were 728 graves in 1967; on the Timothy Riggs D.L.C. #39, OC #1710. {1 July 1992} (Crawfordsville 1988 USGS Quad. map.)

CURL

?   ?   ?   ?   T10S R2W   ?
This is possibly located on Section 35. A boy is buried near Huffman Bridge at the foot of Hungry Hill on the "upper side of road." NOTE: No other information was given in the report. (Not shown on Crabtree 1970-75 USGS Quad. map.)

563

CUSICK FAMILY
AKA: 1. HOLLENBECK--
     CUSICK FAMILY
   2. HOLLENBECK
     FAMILY, ASA
   3. KIPHART-POINT
   4. PIETROK

A ?   5   1854   T9S R1E   S20
These graves are about 5 miles west of Lyons and north of Kingston-Lyons Road; on a fairly high hill overlooking the North Santiam River in a grove of trees (May 1968), 0.5 of a mile from the road on tax lot #200. There were 21 graves found (May 1968). NOTE: This site is on private property. (Stout Mtn. 1985 USGS Quad. map.)

DARBY, MARTHA S.

A 0.01 ? 11 Jan 1853 T13S R1W   ?
Perhaps located in section 26 or 27. She was the wife of Ben F. Darby and was buried on the Oliver H. Darby D.L.C. #47, OC #4588. The burial is perhaps several hundred feet west of Liberty Road and a third or half mile north of Liberty Road's junction with Fern Ridge Road west of Sweet Home. (Not shown on Waterloo 1988 USGS Quad. map.)

DAVIS FAMILY

A 0.01 5   1860'S-1880 T11S R4W   S24
These burials are located on top of a low rise on the south bank of Oak Creek and on the east side of South Pacific Boulevard (OR. Hwy. 99E). The burials are within the Trust Davis D.L.C. #38, OC #98 and a mile south of Albany. They are now well within the city limits. There was a 1993 interview with an old-time resident and he recalled 4 gravestones leaning against the largest of 4 oak trees in an area about 15 feet square. There were, however, 8 reported burials. (Not shown on Tangent 1969-86 USGS Quad. map.)

DUNDON, CARRIE FRANCES

A 0.01 ? 4 Oct 1909 T13S R2E   S34
A child is buried in the back yard of Robert and Eileen Gourley's farm (old information). This is at Dundon Flat on U.S. Hwy. 20, east of Foster Lake. NOTE: This site is on private property. (Not shown on Green Peter 1984 USGS Quad. map.)

EARL FAMILY
AKA: 1. EAST KNOX
     BUTTE

A 0.01 2   1880'S   T10S R3W   S36
Located on the east side of Knox Butte near Albany and north off of Knox Butte Road.

| Name of Cemetery and also known as | Number of burials | Acres | Condition | Date started or earliest known burial | Township | Range | Section |

There were 3 known graves in 1933 on the John Earl D.L.C. #41, OC #796. NOTE: These burials are on private property. (Not shown on Crabtree or Albany 1970-75 USGS Quad. maps.)

EAST ALBANY
AKA: 1. HOUSTON

B 1.08 1 1851   T11S R3W   S4
Located between Salem Avenue and Waverly Lake, the cemetery adjoins Waverly City Park. The cemetery is also directly across the road from Waverly Memorial and Waverly Jewish Cemeteries. It is on the Anderson Cox D.L.C. #49 OC #97. {26 July 1989} (Albany 1970-75 USGS Quad. map.)

ELDER FAMILY
AKA: 1. ELDER,
       CATHERINE

A 0.01 5 1851   T13S R3W   S8
Located about 0.75 of a mile southwest of Bunker Hill Cemetery, south of Boston Mills and off of Roberts Road (labled Troutman Road on Quad. map). The burial site was described in the deed as 16 feet square and on the south bank of Calapooya Creek (now called Calapooia River). This is apparently the left bank of that stream. Further, the burial site is near the center of the Robert M. and Catherine Elder DLC #51, OC#872. The graves of Mrs. Elder and a daughter are unmarked. NOTE: This site is on private property. (Not shown on Halsey 1969 USGS Quad. map.)

FAIRVIEW
AKA: 1. GATES
     2. KINGS PRAIRIE
     3. MILL CITY
     4. RIVERVIEW

D 3 2 1883   T9S R3E   S34
Located between Mill City and Gates on the south side of the North Santiam River. The road is the Mill City-Gates Road, also called Kingwood Avenue. {11 November 1990} (Mill City South 1985 USGS Quad. map.)

**FAIRVIEW MENNONITE
CHURCH**
AKA: 1. WEST FAIRVIEW
       CHURCH

A 1.4 2 1950'S   T11S R3W   S23
Near Albany off of Spicer Drive and on the west side of Goltra Road, it is on the Martin Payne D.L.C. #43, OC #983. {29 August 1991} (Tangent 1969-86 USGS Quad. map.)

Name of Cemetery and also known as	Number of burials	Acres	Condition	Date started or earliest known burial	Township	Range	Section

FERGUSON
AKA: 1. MARKS RIDGE

A   0.01   12   1886   T13S R1W   S12
Located southeast of Lebanon on the Reeves
Place (1978) and south of McDowell Creek
School. It is along Berlin Road and said to
be farmed over. NOTE: This site is on
private property. (Not shown on Sweet Home
1984 USGS Quad. map.)

FERN RIDGE
AKA: 1. LEWIS,
      FIELDING

A   0.01   5   1854-1866   T13S R1W   S34
Located south of Liberty School and west of
Sweet Home on the Jesse Barr Place (1978) on
Fern Ridge Road. Go west on Fern Ridge Road
from its junction of OR. Hwy. 228. After the
junction with Liberty Road, continue on Fern
Ridge Road another 1.1 mile. Take the road
to the right (north) 300 yards to the house
and grave. Rachel Lewis died in 1854 and her
husband Fielding Lewis died in 1866 on Fern
Ridge. Others in this old cemetery were
reburied in Liberty Cemetery. NOTE: This
site is on private property. (Waterloo 1988
USGS Quad. map shows a "grave".)

FINLEY
  AKA: 1. CALAPOOIA
       I.O.O.F.
       2. I.O.O.F.
       [CRAWFORDS-
       VILLE]

B   1.1   2   1854   T14S R2W   S13
Located midway between the McKercher Park
Bridge and the Crawfordsville Bridge over the
Calapooia River, west of Crawfordsville
and on the north side of OR. Hwy. 228. 27
graves were found in April 1967, on the
Josiah Osborne D.L.C. #53, OC #758.
8 October 1857 was the earliest date found on
a field check (1992). {1 July 1992}
(Crawfordsville 1988 USGS Quad. map.)

FIR GROVE
AKA: 1. THOMPSON

A   2.5   5   1901   T14S R2E   S4
Located 6.5 miles southeast of Sweet Home.
Leave U.S. Hwy. 20 on Wiley Creek Drive and
go 1.6 miles. Turn left onto Whiskey Butte
Road, go about 4.8 miles; then turn right
(southwest) off of Whiskey Butte Road and go
0.15 of a mile. The cemetery is deeded to
the Evangelical United Brethren Church.
Seven graves were found in 1967. The actual
burial area is much smaller than the 2.5 acre
cemetery shown on the assessors' plat map.
(Green Peter 1984 USGS Quad. map.)

Name of Cemetery and also known as	Number of burials	Acres	Condition	Date started or earliest known burial	Township	Range	Section

FISH LAKE
AKA: 1. MARKS, MRS. CHARITY ANN

A   0.01   1   18 Oct 1875   T13S R7E   S30
There is a small fenced plot near the Fish Lake Ranger Station where Mrs. Marks and infant are buried. It is on the north side of the Old Santiam Wagon Road, 0.17 of a mile west of its junction with OR. Hwy. 126. (Echo Mtn. 1984 USGS Quad. map.)

FOX VALLEY
AKA: 1. LYONS

C   3.2   2   1854   T9S R2E   S20
From the junction of OR. Hwy. 226 and Main Street in Lyons, go east 1.6 miles on Lyons-Mill City Drive. The cemetery is on the left (north) side of the road opposite a mill. {25 February 1990} (Lyons 1985 USGS Quad. map.)

FRANKLIN BUTTE
AKA: 1. MASONIC
     2. MASONIC [SCIO]

D   5   2   1859   T10S R1W   S19
Located about 1.5 miles south of Scio on the west side of OR. Hwy. 226. The Cemetery Board has recently purchased 3 more acres (will total 8 acres) for future use (July 1990 information). It is on the John Curl D.L.C., OC #209. {8 July 1990} (Scio 1969-86 USGS Quad. map.)

FRY

A   0.01   5   1856   T11S R3W   S27
All graves except two were moved to Riverside in Albany (1933); they were at the junction of Fry Road and Midway Road. NOTE: This burial site is on private property. (Not shown on Tangent 1969-86 USGS Quad. map.)

GAINES
AKA: 1. GAINES FAMILY
     2. KOTAN

B   0.01   2   1853   T11S R1W   S2
Located west of Larwood Bridge, on the Kotan Farm northwest of Lacomb and east of Crabtree, on a hillside south off of Oupor Drive. It is on the Willis Gaines D.L.C., OC #702. See the map showing the Willis Gaines Farm in the *Historical Atlas of Marion and Linn Counties*, by Edgar Williams Co. 1878, page 69. NOTE: This site is on private property. (Scio 1969-86 USGS Quad. map.)

Name of Cemetery and also known as	Number of burials	Acres	Condition	Date started or earliest known burial	Township	Range	Section

GARRISON
AKA: 1. UPPER SODA

A 0.01 5 1894 T13S R4E ?
This could be on Section 25 or Section 26. A road crew found 3 graves located near Upper Soda, east of Cascadia off of U.S. Hwy. 20. (Not shown on Upper Soda 1985 USGS Quad. map.)

GILLILAND
AKA: 1. SWEET HOME MENNONITE
2. SWEET HOME VALLEY

D 10 1 1854 T13S R1E S34
Located in the eastern part of the town of Sweet Home. Go east on U.S. Hwy. 20 and turn right onto 49th Avenue. Then turn left on Airport Road. At the next fork, 50th Avenue turns right (south), but instead, go left up the hill to the cemetery. Sweet Home Mennonite was established in 1943 as a separate burial ground; see that article. Located on the John W. Gilliland D.L.C. #39, OC #4082. {23 April 1992} (Sweet Home 1984 USGS Quad. map.)

HALSEY PIONEER
AKA: 1. COMMONS
2. RUST
3. SMITH, JOHN P.

B 0.5 3 1855 T14S R4W S11
Directions from Halsey: Leave OR. Hwy. 99E in the south part of Halsey on "D" Street, to the west. At the city limits the name changes to Crook Drive. At 1 mile from OR. Hwy. 99E turn left (south) onto Powerline Road and drive another mile. At that point there is a private driveway, turn right (west) to a farm residence. The cemetery is due west of the barn about 600 feet. You walk that; the cemetery is on the right bank of Muddy Creek, on the James W. Rust D.L.C., RB #1421. This cemetery was deeded 31 October 1883. NOTE: This site is on private property. (Harrisburg 1969 USGS Quad. map.)

HARRIS
AKA: 1. KEENE
2. MANSFIELD
3. MUDDY CREEK
4. SCHOOLING

B 0.3 2 1851-1902 T15S R4W S24
Located east of Powerline Road 0.25 of a mile, and 0.7 of a mile south of Priceboro Road junction. There is no access; it is on an inside bend of Muddy Creek. 46 markers were found in May of 1963. See the map showing the J. R. Harris Farm in the *Historical Atlas of Marion and Linn Counties*, by Edgar Williams Co. 1878, page 88. (Indian Head 1969 USGS Quad. map.)

Name of Cemetery and also known as	Number of burials	Acres	Condition	Date started or earliest known burial	Township	Range	Section

HUMPHREYS FAMILY

A 0.1 3 1865-1890'S T10S R1E S5
Located about 2 miles northwest of Jordan Church and underneath the powerlines. Three burials are on the Thomas M. Humphreys D.L.C., OC #5260. The cemetery was deeded in 1909. There is no ready access. (Jordan 1985 USGS Quad. map.)

I.O.O.F. [ALFORD]
AKA: 1. HARRISBURG I.O.O.F.

C 1.45 2 1851 T14S R4W S35
Located on Powerline Road just south of OR. Hwy. 99E, south of the Alford area and north of Harrisburg. There are two adjoining cemeteries separated by a driveway. The Masons are on the north (see that article); Odd Fellows on the south. {9 April 1990} (Harrisburg 1969 USGS Quad. map.)

I.O.O.F. [LEBANON]
AKA: 1. LEBANON ODD FELLOWS
2. MASONIC [LEBANON]

E 15.42 1 1869 T12S R2W S2
This is in sections 2 and 3. Turn right at the big cemetery sign 0.5 of a mile north of Lebanon on U.S. Hwy. 20. The cemetery was started by the Masons and the I.O.O.F. established one adjacent. The Masons have now withdrawn and the Odd Fellows are the sole owners; on the William B. Gore D.L.C. #38, OC #2516, donated to the I.O.O.F. and Morgan Kees D.L.C. #43, OC #1583 donated to the Masons. {10 August 1990} (Lebanon 1969-86 USGS Quad. map.)

INDIAN

A 0.01 5 ? T13S R6E ?
This Indian grave could be on Section 26 or 27, on Lost Prairie, U.S. Hwy. 20. NOTE: No other information was given in the report. (Not shown on Echo Mtn. 1984 USGS Quad. map.)

KLUM
AKA: 1. BRUCE
2. CLUM
3. KLUM FAMILY
4. SODAVILLE
5. WATERLOO

B 0.62 2 1865 T12S R1W S32
Located 1.4 miles southeast of Sodaville on Sodaville-Waterloo Drive. Turn south on Buckmaster Road from Sodaville-Waterloo Drive and go about 0.15 of a mile. The cemetery is 750 feet up the hill on the driveway to the left. It is on the William Klum D.L.C. #40, OC #3336. (Waterloo 1988 USGS Quad. map.)

Name of Cemetery and also known as	Number of burials	Acres	Condition	Date started or earliest known burial	Township	Range	Section

KNOX BUTTE

C 2 2 1853   T10S R3W   S35
Located on the west slope of Knox Butte, east of Albany and off of Scravel Hill Road. It is on the James Knox D.L.C. #42, OC #131. {29 August 1991} (Albany 1970-75 USGS Quad. map.)

LACOMB
AKA: 1. FERN RIDGE
      2. NAVE

C 1.6 2 1888   T11S R1E   S31
This cemetery is about 0.8 of a mile southeast of Lacomb on the left (east) side of Ford Mill Road. {20 March 1992} (Lacomb 1984 USGS Quad. map.)

LEBANON PIONEER
AKA: 1. METHODIST
         EPISCOPAL
         CHURCH
      2. OLD LEBANON
      3. OLD METHODIST
      4. PIONEER

C 2.8 1 7 Aug 1850 T12S R2W   S11
Located at the end of North Park Street in Lebanon. Burials are from 1850 to 31 August 1927. In 1991 there were extensive repairs made of past vandalism and tumbled markers were re-set. However, many old monuments have been destroyed or stolen in the past. It is on the Luther T. Woodward D.L.C. #45, OC #2172. {26 February 1990} (Lebanon 1969-86 USGS Quad. map.)

LEMASTER

? ? ? ?   T14S R1W   ?
The Lemaster grave is located along Brush Creek southeast of Crawfordsville. NOTE: No other information was given in the report. (Not shown on Crawfordsville 1988 USGS Quad. map.)

LEWIS
AKA: 1. LEWIS CREEK

C 1.5 1 1850   T13S R1E   S23
Located just above Foster Reservoir, off of North River Avenue on the north side of Foster Dam and then 0.5 of a mile east. There were 56 graves in September 1966. {27 February 1991} (Sweet Home 1984 USGS Quad. map.)

LIBERTY [NEW]
AKA: 1. NYE
      2. NYE-LIBERTY

C 5.13 2 1861   T13S R1W   S26
We must deal here with the transfer of the name Liberty Cemetery between what were two separate cemeteries a mile apart. See the article Liberty [old] for the first of the two. It was established in 1860. Meanwhile

Name of Cemetery and also known as	Number of burials	Acres	Condition	Date started or earliest known burial	Township	Range	Section

in 1861 the much larger cemetery called Nye was established about a mile south of Liberty [old] Cemetery. When the latter was obliterated by 1987 the name Liberty was applied to what had been previously known as Nye or Nye-Liberty Cemetery. Obituaries now use the term Liberty for this cemetery. To go to present-day Liberty Cemetery from Sweet Home: at the junction of U.S. Hwy. 20 and OR. Hwy. 228 (Holley Road) go west on OR. Hwy. 228 0.8 of a mile to Fern Ridge Road; continue west on Fern Ridge Road 1.2 miles to Liberty Road. Turn right on Liberty Road and go 1.1 miles. The cemetery is on the left. It is on the Adam Nye D.L.C. #46, OC #2814. {27 February 1991} (Waterloo 1988 USGS Quad. map.)

LIBERTY [OLD]

A   0.01   6   1860   T13S R1W   S23
The original Liberty Baptist Church was founded in 1853 by Joab Powell. They added a small cemetery in 1860. This cemetery was nearly obliterated in 1972 and plowed over in 1987 when the last 2 graves were moved to Nye Cemetery (now called Liberty [new] and the stones to Gilliland. See the article on Liberty [new] Cemetery. On the Jacob Nye D.L.C. #44, OC #2812. (Not shown on Waterloo 1988 USGS Quad. map.)

LINN MEMORIAL
AKA: 1. FAIRVIEW
     MEMORIAL

A   1.41   1   1960   T13S R1W   S4
Located 6.8 miles from the junction of U.S. Hwy. 20 (Santiam Highway) and OR. Hwy. 228, in Sweet Home. It is 6.1 miles from the junction of U.S. Hwy. 20 and Airport Road in Lebanon and 0.40 of a mile southeast from the junction of Ingram Road with U.S. Hwy. 20. The cemetery can readily be seen on the left (west) about 500 feet off the highway and on the south slopes of a ridge, when driving from Sweet Home towards Lebanon. This cemetery was due to be vacated in the summer of 1992 and 7 of the 9 burials in Linn Memorial were due to be reburied in Gilliland Cemetery. (Interview 23 April 1992 with the caretaker of Gilliland) The actual platted

Name of Cemetery and also known as	Number of burials	Acres	Condition	Date started or earliest known burial	Township	Range	Section

area of Linn Memorial only covered about 0.5 of an acre. It is on the John Wible D.L.C. #37, OC #2555. {23 April 1992} (Waterloo 1988 USGS Quad. map.)

MALONE FAMILY

    A   0.01 ? ?   T14S R1W   S24

There are two graves on the Fred Malone Place (1978). The *Historical Atlas of Marion and Linn Counties*, by Edgar Williams Co. 1878, shows F. M. Malone owned land in Sections 12, 13, and 24. The house is shown in Section 24 on the right bank of the Calapooia River about 2 miles or so upstream from Holley, which seems to be the most likely area for the burials to be located. Located off of Upper Calapooia Road to the left over the river, along McClum Road. It is on the James Malone D.L.C., RB #1615. NOTE: This site is on private property. (Not shown on Crawfordsville 1988 USGS Quad. map.)

MASONIC [ALBANY]

    D   5   1   1853   T11S R4W   S12

Located at Southwest Broadway and Southwest 7th Avenue in Albany, on the Harvey Gordon D.L.C. #54, OC #141. {30 July 1989} (Albany 1970-75 USGS Quad. map.)

MASONIC [ALFORD]
  AKA: 1. MASONIC
      [HARRISBURG]

    C 2.05 2 1851   T14S R4W   S35

Located on Powerline Road just south of OR. Hwy. 99E, south of the Alford area and north of Harrisburg. There are 2 adjoining cemeteries separated by a driveway. The Masons are on the north; the Odd Fellows on the south. {30 April 1992} (Harrisburg 1969 USGS Quad. map.)

McHARGUE

    B 0.77 5 1852-1933 T14S R2W   S15

Located west of Crawfordsville and south of OR. Hwy. 228. Go 2 miles east of Brownsville on OR. Hwy. 228. Turn right (south) on Courtney Creek Drive for 3.25 miles, where there is a bridge over Courtney Creek; cross over the bridge. Just past the first house on the left (0.1 of a mile), turn off of the county road, to the left, and back on a driveway over the hillsides for 0.9 of a mile

Name of Cemetery and also known as	Number of burials	Acres	Condition	Date started or earliest known burial	Township	Range	Section

to the cemetery. This is on the James McHargue D.L.C. #48, OC #596. There were 79 known burials in 1938. (Union Point 1988 USGS Quad. map.)

McKNIGHT, JAMES A.
AKA: 1. TOMBSTONE
       PRAIRIE

?   ?   ?   17 Oct 1871 T13S R6E   S31
Tombstone Prairie is just east of the summit of Tombstone Pass, along U.S. Hwy. 20 about 34 miles east of Sweet Home. At Milepost 64 take a foot path on the south side of the highway for 0.25 of a mile to reach this site. It is in the headwaters of Hackleman Creek, a tributary of the McKenzie River. 18 year-old James A. McKnight, his older brother, and several other young men were returning home after a summer along the Deschutes River. James was accidentally shot and killed by knocking over a loaded rifle on 17 October 1871. The party returned to their homes and James was buried in Sandridge Cemetery. In the spring of 1872 his mother commissioned a marble slab in his memory, containing an 8-stanza poem. This marker was erected in the southern part of the prairie and the previous name of Big Prairie became known as Tombstone Prairie Camp, on the old road south of the highway. (Not shown on Harter Mtn. 1984 USGS Quad. map.)

MICHAEL
AKA: 1. TWIN BUTTE

A   0.15   2   1859-1905   T14S R3W   S26
Leave OR. Hwy. 228 on Gap Road at Brownsville and go south and west on Gap Road to Lake Creek Drive and Center School Road, about 4.5 miles, almost to a 90 degree turn to the right in the county road. Near the apex of this angle is a private drive the left to the George Fruit home. With permission, park in yard and walk a mile through a sheep pasture to the cemetery on the summit of a high ridge. Walk under the powerline. Located near the southeast corner of Elijah Michael D.L.C. #45, RB #1551. NOTE: This site is on private property. (Not shown on Indian Head 1969 USGS Quad. map.)

Name of Cemetery and also known as	Number of burials	Acres	Condition	Date started or earliest known burial	Township	Range	Section

MILLER
AKA: 1. SHELBURN

D 3.5 2 1855 T10S R2W S1

This cemetery is about 3 miles northwest of Scio and about 1 mile south of Shelburn, on the west side of Miller Cemetery Road. This location was badly vandalized on Thanksgiving 1982. There were 270 known burials in May 1967; the oldest existing stone is Sept. 1855, for Mrs. Mary Miller, age 33. {28 June 1989} (Scio 1969-86 USGS Quad. map.)

MILLER
AKA: 1. MILLERSBURG

D 2 2 1850 T10S R3W S17

Located about 6 miles north of Albany and west of Old Salem Road, in the Northwest part of Millersburg. The entrance is on Woods Road, 1 mile from Old Salem Road via Morning Star Road and Millersburg Drive. There were 577 graves found in Aug. 1968; on the George Miller Sr. D.L.C. #58, OC #783. {31 May 1989} (Albany 1970-75 USGS Quad. map.)

MILLER
AKA: 1. COON
2. MILLER-COON
3. MILLER-COON
FAMILIES

A 0.1 5 1853-1921 T13S R4W S4

Located on the right bank of Muddy Creek between Fayetteville Drive and Brattain Drive and west of Greenback Road. There is a private road on a farm owned by Jesse Crothers. The cemetery is near the Greenback School. There were 7 known burials (1968), on the James L. Coon D.L.C. # 49, OC #329. NOTE: This site is on private property. (Peoria 1969-75 USGS Quad. map.)

MT. PLEASANT

B 1 2 1854 T9S R1E S30

Located 0.75 of a mile northeast of Mt. Pleasant Community Church, built in 1854 and one of the oldest remaining rural churches in Oregon. Take the driveway on the left (north), uphill off of Mt. Pleasant Drive: on the Robert Irvine D.L.C. #60, OC #4699. {9 August 1990} (Stout Mountain 1985 USGS Quad. map.)

MOUNTAIN HOME
AKA: 1. GUNDERSON
2. NORWEGIAN

B 0.3 2 1893 T13S R1W S20

Located 8 miles south of Sodaville. Leave Sodaville on Sodaville-Mountain Home Road for 6 miles; turn left at the junction of Mountain Home Drive and go 2 miles east to a

Name of Cemetery and also known as	Number of burials	Acres	Condition	Date started or earliest known burial	Township	Range	Section

driveway on the left. The cemetery is 200 yards off the county road. This same cemetery is 9 miles from Brownsville via Kirk Avenue, Northern Drive and Mountain Home Drive. 27 graves were found in May 1967. (Waterloo 1988 USGS Quad. map.)

OAKVILLE

C 3 1 1853 T12S R4W S16

Located west of Tangent, west off Oakville Road and about 0.5 of a mile north of the Oakville Church. {27 May 1989} (Riverside 1969-75 USGS Quad. map.)

ORLEANS
AKA: 1. CIRCLE CITY
2. CUSHMAN
3. CUSHMAN FAMILY

C 1 2 1853 T11S R4W S32

Located on the east side of the Willamette River between Corvallis and Albany, at 34120 Riverside Drive. It is just north of OR. Hwy. 34, at Riverside Drive and Orleans Avenue. Platted in 1911, it is on the Daniel Cushman D.L.C. #68, OC #4900. Orleans Church is directly across the road from the cemetery. {13 July 1989} (Riverside 1969-75 USGS Quad. map.)

OUR LADY OF LOURDES
AKA: 1. CATHOLIC SCHOOL
2. JORDAN
3. JORDAN CATHOLIC CHURCH
4. LOURDES
5. ST. BENEDICT'S

C 0.5 2 1903 T10S R1E S9

Located at Jordan, at the junction of Camp Morrison Drive and Jordan Road. On the John Bryant D.L.C. #50, OC #4370; the burials are behind the church of Our Lady of Lourdes. {4 August 1991} (Jordan 1985 USGS Quad. map.)

PILCHER

? ? ? ? T10S R3W ?

Possibly located in Section 15. Reported to be west of Jefferson. NOTE: No further information was given to the compiler, so location is unknown at this time. (Not shown on Albany 1970-75 USGS Quad. map.)

PINE GROVE
AKA: 1. LONE PINE
2. SHEPHERD

D 4.43 2 1853 T13S R4W S32

Travel south of Peoria 3 miles, then west 0.25 of a mile from the junction with American Drive. A church is at the entrance.

Name of Cemetery and also known as	Number of burials	Acres	Condition	Date started or earliest known burial	Township	Range	Section

It is on the Henry Williams D.L.C. #38, OC #4042 and William Shepherd D.L.C. #39, OC #808. {28 March 1990} (Peoria 1969-75 USGS Quad. map.)

PIONEER [JORDAN]
AKA: 1. BENDER, JOHN
2. JORDAN PIONEER
3. OUR LADY OF LOURDES CATHOLIC
4. SILBERNAGEL

B 0.9 2 1883 T10S R1E S10

Located in the Jordan area, 1 mile east of the church and right (south) off Camp Morrison Drive. The name "Our Lady of Lourdes" has been transferred to the cemetery behind the church about 1 mile away. That was once the Jordan Catholic Cemetery. The name on the gate of this cemetery only says "Pioneer", it is on the George Bilyeu D.L.C. #42, OC #4685. {15 September 1991} (Jordan 1985 USGS Quad. map.)

POE, MARY JANE VANNATTA

A 0.01 ? 21 Oct 1874 T15S R2W S9

This burial is located in the Coburg Hills in Linn County. However it is accessible by roads only from Lane County. There is no certainty of locating the gravesite. Leave Springfield and drive up the Mohawk Valley to Mabel. Turn left (northwest) onto Shotgun Creek Road and head into the Coburg Hills. It would be advisable to acquire maps from the Bureau of Land Management District Office in Eugene as most of the roads off of Shotgun Creek Road are B.L.M. roads. The gravesite is most likely on a broad bench on the west side of the divide and within the William Poe D.L.C., RB #1560 Sections 2 and 8. Mary Jane Vannatta Poe, born 8 May 1836 married William Poe in September 1854. (Not shown on Union Point 1988 USGS Quad. map.)

POWELL
AKA: 1. BERLIN

C 1.5 2 1893 T12S R1E S31

Located off of Berlin Road, a little more than 1 mile north of McDowell Creek Drive junction and just south of Powell Lane. If coming from Lebanon on Berlin Road, go 0.7 of a mile past and southeast of Berlin Junction. The cemetery is about 200 feet east of Berlin Road on a ridge, on the Jason L. Williams D.L.C. #37, OC #4578. {23 January 1992} (Sweet Home 1984 USGS Quad. map.)

Name of Cemetery and also known as	Number of burials	Acres	Condition	Date started or earliest known burial	Township	Range	Section

PROVIDENCE
AKA: 1. PROVIDENCE
BAPTIST CHURCH
2. PROVIDENCE
CHURCH

| | C | 2.5 | 2 | 1856 | T11S | R1W | S10 |

Located 6 miles south of Scio and northwest of Lacomb. The church and cemetery are at the junction of Richardson Gap Road and Providence Drive. {17 March 1991} (Onehorse Slough 1969-75 and Scio 1969-86 USGS Quad. maps.)

QUARTZVILLE

| | ? | ? | ? | ? | T11S | R4E | S22 |

The bygone gold mining settlement of Quartzville reportedly had burials. The site is best reached from the town of Sweet Home. From the north side of Green Peter Dam on Green Peter Reservoir follow the Quartzville Road for 30 miles to the site of Quartzville. This was an active gold mining site from about 1860 to 1902 and was the principal such site in Linn County. (The site of Quartzville is shown but the burials are not indicated on the Quartzville 1985 USGS Quad. map.)

RHODES

| | ? | ? | ? | ? | T10S | R3W | ? |

This could be in Section 19 or 20. Reported to be near Conser (1957 report). NOTE: No further information was given. The compiler at this time does not know the location. (Not shown on Albany 1970-75 USGS Quad. map.)

RICE

| | A | 0.01 | 5 | ? | T13S | R2E | ? |

This grave is thought to be on Section 35. The Rice grave is on Shot Pouch Creek north of U.S. Hwy. 20 between Sweet Home and Cascadia. (Not shown on Green Peter 1984 USGS Quad. map.)

RIVERSIDE

| | C | 10 | 1 | 1847 | T11S | R4W | S12 |

Located on the west end of S.W. 7th Ave. in Albany. The cemetery is at the end of the street, on the Walter Monteith D.L.C. #55, OC #1622. {24 August 1989} (Albany 1970-75 USGS Quad. map.)

Linn County

Name of Cemetery and also known as	Number of burials	Acres	Condition	Date started or earliest known burial	Township	Range	Section

ROBINETT
AKA: 1. ROBINETTE
     2. ROBINETTI
     3. ROBNETT

A   0.01 ? ?   T14S R1W   ?
This could be on Section 16 or perhaps on Section 17. Described in a 1957 report as a daughter of Jim Robinetti buried "On the old Hawk Place up the Calapooia." Could this be in the William Robinett D.L.C. #40, OC #2569 just east (upstream) along the Calapooia River from Crawfordsville? If so, the grave may be on a hillside south of OR. Hwy. 228. (Not shown on Crawfordsville 1988 USGS Quads. map.)

ROCK HILL
AKA: 1. DODGE

C   2.2 2 1877   T12S R2W   S28
Located southwest of Lebanon. Go south on Stoltz Hill Road to Blueberry Hill Road, then 0.6 of a mile southwest on Blueberry Hill Road; turn right on Blueberry Drive for 0.22 of a mile. 111 graves were found in April of 1967. This is on the Henry F. Peterson D.L.C. #59, OC #1594. {10 August 1990} (Brownsville 1988 USGS Quad. map.)

RUSSELL

? ? ? ?   T13S R1E   S33
This is on the Enos Russell Place (1978) in a barn yard. It may be the Newton Russell grave. This is on the Newton Russell D.L.C. #41, OC #2022. Located at 43rd. Avenue south of Long Street, Sweet Home. NOTE: This site is on private property. (Not shown on Sweet Home 1984 USGS Quad. map.)

SALTMARSH, ZERILDA

A   0.01 ? Circa 1856 T12S R1W   S7
Located in the Southwest 1/4 of Southeast 1/4 of Section 7. Harlan Mastenbrook, whose family has owned the property was told of these burials. Zerilda was the first wife of Arthur Saltmarsh; she died before 1857. A male child who died of a rattlesnake bite is also reputed to be buried with her. The site is just east of the east line of the Arthur Saltmarsh DLC #52 and #78, OC #1736. (Not shown on Onehorse Slough 1969-75 USGS Quad. map.)

Name of Cemetery and also known as	Number of burials	Acres	Condition	Date started or earliest known burial	Township	Range	Section

SANDRIDGE
AKA: 1. PETERSON BUTTE
2. SAND RIDGE

C 3.85 2 1850   T12S R3W   S24
Located southwest of Lebanon at the foot of the northwest slope of Peterson Butte, along Sand Ridge Road. Go 0.2 of a mile south on Sand Ridge Road from its junction with Glaser Drive, then turn left (east) for 0.3 of a mile on a driveway to the cemetery. This driveway is on top of the low ridge on Sand Ridge Road, on the Raphael Cheadle D.L.C. #63, OC #1753. NOTE: The plaque on the cemetery gateway spells it "Sandridge." A signboard spells it "Sand Ridge." The county road and nearby school both spell it "Sand Ridge." {26 February 1990} (Lebanon 1969-86 USGS Quad. map.)

SANTIAM CENTRAL
AKA: 1. CENTRAL
2. CENTRAL CHRISTIAN
3. COTTONWOOD
4. EAST KNOX BUTTE

C 1.5 2 1856   T11S R2W   S6
Located about 1 mile southeast of Knox Butte near Albany, on the east side of Harber Road between Knox Butte Road and U.S. Hwy. 20. It is on the Thomas E. Streithoff D.L.C. #37, OC #2560. {25 Aug. 1989} (Crabtree 1970-75 USGS Quad. map.)

SHEA HILL

A ? 5 ?   T13S R1E   ?
Possibly on Section 25, 16, 35, or 36. Located southeast of Foster on Shea Hill Drive. (Not shown on Sweet Home 1984 USGS Quad. map.)

SHEDD
AKA: 1. PUGH FAMILY

C 2.59 2 1853   T13S R4W   S13
Located south and west of Shedd. Go south on OR. Hwy. 99E from the main intersection at Shedd, to Shedd Cemetery Drive; turn right (west) 1 mile to the cemetery. It is on the Francis A. Pugh D.L.C. #68, OC #641. {16 May 1990} (Peoria 1969-75 USGS Quad. map.)

SHELTON, JOHN

A 0.23 5 1866-1907   T9S R1E   S34
Located about 0.5 of a mile southeast of OR. Hwy. 226 on the north slope of a timbered ridge and about 0.2 of a mile from a house. There is no access. There were 19 known graves, with 12 tombstones, in June of 1968;

Name of Cemetery and also known as	Number of burials	Acres	Condition	Date started or earliest known burial	Township	Range	Section

on the James Shelton D.L.C. #53, OC #4442.
NOTE: This site is on private property.
(Jordan 1985 USGS Quad. map.)

SIMISON
AKA: 1. HALE, MILTON
    2. SIMPSON
    3. SIMPSON-HALE
    4. SIMPSON-HALE
       FAMILIES
    5. SYRACUSE

B   0.5   2   1848-1919   **T10S R3W**   **S3**
This cemetery is north off of Santiam Bluffs Road, just east of the I-5 Freeway and just south of the Santiam River. If driving south on the I-5 Freeway, turn off at the Dever-Conner Interchange; double back over the I-5 Freeway onto Santiam Bluffs Road and go 0.5 of a mile to the cemetery. It is on the left, back in the trees 660 feet from the road. It has no official name, hence the numerous confusing designations. It is on the Milton and Susannah Hale D.L.C. #67, OC #130. The Simison family spelled their name Simison, not Simpson. There are some Indian burials also, including old Chief Santiam. (Albany 1970-75 USGS Quad. map.)

SOLDIERS

?   ?   ?   ?   **T13S UNSURVEYED**
Evidence of soldier graves were found on the side of Sand Mountain, east of Tombstone Pass. Probably located alongside the Old Santiam Wagon Road, along the north side of Sand Mountain. NOTE: No other information was given in the report. (Not shown on Santiam Junction 1988 USGS Quad. map.)

SPLAWN FAMILY

A   ?   12   ?   **T14S R1W**   **S11**
Located northwest of Holley along OR. Hwy. 228, perhaps near the junction of Fern Ridge Road or Crawfordsville Drive. In 1930 the *Metsker Land Ownership Atlas* shows Greenberry Splawn owned land on both sides of OR. Hwy. 228. It is on the George W. Splawn D.L.C., RB #1517. This has been farmed over; there were perhaps 3 or more graves at this site. (Not shown on Crawfordsville Quad. 1988 USGS Quad. map.)

SPRING FAMILY

A   0.01   2   1890'S   **T13S R2E**   **S18**
These are north of Foster Reservoir and just east of Sunnyside Road from McDowell to Sunnyside. Just east of Lewis Creek were 3

Name of Cemetery and also known as	Number of burials	Acres	Condition	Date started or earliest known burial	Township	Range	Section

graves (June 1967); also, some Indian graves are nearby. NOTE: This site is on private property. (Green Peter 1984 USGS Quad. map.)

SWALLOW, JOHN

A 0.01 ? Circa 1900 **UNSURVEYED**
Located alongside Skyline Trail near Midget Lake and east of Marion Lake in the Willamette National Forest. It is at the junction of trails #3493 and #3498. The grave is 2 miles north of Marion Lake and 200 yards south of Midget Lake, a few feet off of Trail #3493. Swallow's body and overturned boat were found in what is now Swallow Lake. (Marion Lake 1988 USGS Quad. map.)

SWEET HOME MENNONITE
AKA: 1. GILLILAND

? ? 1 1943 **T13S R1E** S34
This church-related cemetery was established adjacent to or within the existing Gilliland Cemetery at Sweet Home. It was not demarcated separately as of 1992 and the compiler does not know the size or number of burials. Located in the eastern part of the town of Sweet Home. Go east on U.S. Hwy. 20 and turn right onto 49th Avenue. Then turn left on Airport Road. At the next fork, 50th Avenue turns right (south), but instead, go left up the hill to the cemetery. {23 April 1992} (Not named or shown separately from Gilliland Cemetery on Sweet Home 1984 USGS Quad. map.)

THOMPSON, A. K.

A 0.01 ? Nov 1888 **T13S R1W** S18
Located in the southwest 1/4 of Section 18. A single grave and stone on the old Sam Gunderson Place, about 4 miles south of Sodaville. The 1930 *Metsker Land Ownership Atlas* shows the Samuel Gunderson property on both sides of the Sodaville-Mountain Home Road. The 1936 ODOT map of Linn County shows the farm house on the west side of the road. NOTE: This site is on private property. (Not shown on Waterloo 1988 USGS Quad. map.)

TINDALL, MR.

A 0.01 ? 1987 [?] **T14S R2W** S6
A Mr. Tindall is reportedly buried in the backyard of the Foster-Goulard house at 35559

581

Linn County

Name of Cemetery and also known as	Number of burials	Acres	Condition	Date started or earliest known burial	Township	Range	Section

OR. Hwy. 228, Brownsville. From OR. Hwy. 228 in Brownsville at the main intersection near the bridge, drive east not quite a mile. The house is on the left (north) side of the highway. This is on the Henry H. Spalding D.L.C. #56, OC #2418. NOTE: This site is on private property. (Not shown on Brownsville 1988 USGS Quad. map.)

TOWNSEND, JODY CHARLES

| | A | 0.01 | 1 | 2 May 1994 | T15S | R2W | S7 |

This young college student, age 20, died of a brain tumor. He is buried in a meadow on the family property off of Diamond Hill Road, 3 miles east of I-5. (Not shown on Union Point 1988 USGS Quad. map.)

TURNIDGE FAMILY

| | A | ? | ? | ? | T10S | R3W | ? |

Perhaps located in Section 4. An obituary in the *Salem Statesman-Journal*, 22 May 1996 reports that Pauline G. Turnidge, 13 December 1903-21 May 1996, was to be buried in the Turnidge Family Cemetery. She was the widow of Henry who died in 1994. A mortuary spokesman told the compiler that this was a small and old burial ground. Leave I-5 just south of the Santiam River by turning west onto Hoefer Road. To reach the cemetery from Hoefer Road "keep turning to the right, until you are about a mile from I-5." (Not shown on the Albany 1970-75 USGS Quad. map.)

TWIN OAKS MEMORIAL GARDENS
AKA: 1. TWIN OAKS MEMORIAL PARK

| | D | 4.97 | 2 | 1960'S | T11S | R4W | S33 |

Located on the east side of Riverside Drive, and north of Orleans Church at 34275 Riverside Drive Southwest; outside of the Albany city limits. It is on the Wallace Cushman D.L.C. #67, OC #1703. {13 July 1989} (Riverside 1969-75 USGS Quad. map.)

UMPHLETTE, JANE EARL

| | A | 0.01 | 5 | 1846 | T10S | R3W | S15 |

The wife of Stanley Umphlette, she was with the family which crossed the plains in 1845. After wintering in what is now Washington County the family moved to the Knox Butte area east of Albany. There Mrs. Umphlette died. Her daughter, later Mrs. Margaret

Name of Cemetery and also known as	Number of burials	Acres	Condition	Date started or earliest known burial	Township	Range	Section

Powell, was six years old at the time. In June 1932 Mrs. Powell recalled her mother was buried on the western slope of Meeker Hill. The grave was later marked by a rusty iron pipe. The present I-5 Freeway runs at the west base of Meeker Hill. Mrs. Umphlette was the first known burial of a white person in Linn County. This is on the John Meeker D.L.C. #60, OC #785. (Not shown on the Albany 1970-75 USGS Quad. map.)

UNION POINT
AKA: 1. KEENEY
     2. KIRK
     3. OVERTON

B 1.11 4 1862   T14S R3W   S14
Leave OR. Hwy. 228 on Gap Road at Brownsville. Go south nearly 3 miles and turn right (west) onto Ranch Drive. Go about 100 yards past the junction with Stubbs Road. Leave Ranch Drive on a driveway to the left and back about 0.35 of a mile to the top of the ridge. (Indian Head 1969 USGS Quad. map. The cemetery is shown on the USGS Quad. map, but is mislabeled as Blain Cemetery.)

UNKNOWN

A 0.01 ? ?   ?   ?   ?
Located on a shelf south of U.S. Hwy. 20. Three graves that used to have a wooden fence, near Cascadia (1972). NOTE: No other information was given in the report. (Not shown on Cascadia 1985 USGS Quad. map.)

UNKNOWN

A 0.01 ? ?   T14S R2E   S3
1 grave found off of Whiskey Butte Road on the Green Place (1972) near Moss Butte. NOTE: This site is on private property. (Not shown on Green Peter 1984 USGS Quad. map.)

UNKNOWN WOMAN

A 0.01 ? ?   T12S R1W   S7
Located in the Southwest 1/4 of Southeast 1/4 of Section 7. Harlan Mastenbrook reports that on the family property a woman now unknown was buried under a Cherry tree. The tree has since been cut down, but the stump remains to mark the spot. This burial is not to be confused with that of Zerilda Saltmarsh, also in Section 7, or that of Mrs.

Name of Cemetery and also known as	Number of burials	Acres	Condition	Date started or earliest known burial	Township	Range	Section

Cooper in Section 8. See those articles. (Not shown on Onehorse Slough 1969-75 USGS Quad. map.)

WAVERLY JEWISH
AKA: 1. HEBREW

B ? 2 1878 T11S R3W S4
Located in Albany it adjoins Waverly Memorial Park along Salem Avenue. Across the road from these two cemeteries is East Albany Cemetery. It is on the Anderson Cox D.L.C. #49, OC #97. {26 July 1989} (Albany 1970-75 USGS Quad. map.)

WAVERLY MEMORIAL
AKA: 1. ST. JOHN'S
LODGE #17,
MASONS
2. WAVERLY
LAKE
MASONIC

C ? 2 ? T11S R3W S4
Located on the north side of Salem Avenue at Waverly Lake, Albany. This cemetery adjoins the Waverly Jewish Cemetery. Across Salem Avenue from these two cemeteries is East Albany Cemetery. It is on the Anderson Cox D.L.C. #49, OC #97. {26 July 1989} (Albany 1970-75 USGS Quad. map.)

WEGER
AKA: 1. MEEKS

A 0.01 5 1852-1870 T15S R3W S26
Located in the Priceboro area east of the I-5 Freeway, south of Priceboro, and west of Gap Road. Go 8 miles south of Brownsville on Gap Road. Turn hard left, proceeding for 0.25 of a mile, then south for 3 more miles; then go west 0.25 of a mile to the Fred Gates Farm on the south side of the road. Turn south into the Gates barnyard, then go on foot to a single grave. It is on the Thomas M. Meeks D.L.C. #48, RB #1747. NOTE: This site is on private property. (Not shown on Coburg 1967 USGS Quad. map.)

WEST POINT
AKA: 1. WILLOUGHBY

B 1 2 1853 T15S R3W S33
Located in the Priceboro area north of Coburg and west of the I-5 Freeway on the east side of North Coburg Road, and 0.6 of a mile south of Bowers Drive. 91 known graves (1977). NOTE: The name plate on a large marker says "West Point Cemetery 25 April 1885." but there are a number of earlier dates on tombstones. {9 April 1990} (Coburg 1967 USGS Quad. map.)

Name of Cemetery and also known as	Number of burials	Acres	Condition	Date started or earliest known burial	Township	Range	Section

WHITCOMB

A   0.06 ? 1899   **T12S R3E**   **S31**
There are 3 graves of children who died of diphtheria on Whitcomb Island in Green Peter Lake. (Cascadia 1985 USGS Quad. map.)

WHITE, LUTHER

B   0.7 2 1847-1913   **T15S R3W**   **S12**
Located in the Diamond Hill area, south off of Gap Road and 0.5 of a mile east of Diamond Hill Drive and on the south side of White Creek. There are 19 known burials with no access. This is on Luther White D.L.C. #56, RB #1493. NOTE: This site is on private property. (Union Point 1988 USGS Quad. map.)

WIGLE

B   0.15 3 1853-1927   **T14S R3W**   **S35**
Located 5.5 miles southwest of Brownsville, 700 feet west of Tub Run Road. It is 1100 feet north of Belts Drive in a field and visible from the road. There were 25 known burials. On the John M. Wigle D.L.C. #48, RB #1433. NOTE: This site is on private property. (Indian Head 1969 USGS Quad. map.)

WILEY FAMILY

A   0.1 2 1864-1921   **T13S R1E**   **S36**
Located on a hill on the Andrew Wiley D.L.C. #50, OC #4973, which is about 2 miles south of Foster. Head east off Wiley Creek Road 0.5 of a mile and then 200 feet left up the hill, just south of Whiskey Butte Road. (Sweet Home 1984 USGS Quad. map.)

WILLAMETTE MEMORIAL PARK

D   ? 1 ?   **T10S R3W**   **S28**
Located 2 miles north on the Old Salem Road from Albany in Millersburg. NOTE: The obituaries usually refer to this cemetery as being in Albany. It is actually in the separate municipality of Millersburg, on the Isaac Miller Sr. D.L.C. #46, OC #780 and Exum Powell D.L.C. #44, OC #134. {26 July 1989} (Albany 1970-75 USGS Quad. map.)

WISNER
AKA: 1. KINGSTON

C   1.6 2 1847   **T9S R1W**   **S23**
Located southeast of Stayton and about 1.5 miles south of Kingston on Kingston-Jordan Drive. It is on the left (east) side of the

| Name of Cemetery and also known as | Number of burials | Acres | Condition | Date started or earliest known burial | Township | Range | Section |

road.   278 graves were found in May of 1967. {10 October 1988} (Stayton 1969-86 USGS Quad. map.)

WORKMEN
AKA: 1. A. O. U. W.
     2. ALFORD
     3. ANCIENT ORDER
        OF UNITED
        WORKMEN

C   1.53   2   1885   T14S R4W   S36
Located on Powerline Road about 0.5 of a mile south of Alford and just north of Harrisburg. Perhaps no rural area in Oregon is so abundantly supplied with cemetery acreage as is Alford. {30 April 1990} (Harrisburg 1969 USGS Quad. map.)

YARBOROUGH

A   0.01   5   1870'S   T13S R4W   S26
Two miles north of Halsey turn west off of OR. Hwy. 99E onto Oak Plain Drive. Drive about 1.4 miles and then turn left (south) onto Dannen Road. At about 1 mile south, the Fred Dannen Farm is on the right(1977). The cemetery was on the bank of Muddy Creek. No monuments, only sunken grave areas remain in the myrtle (Vinca species). Six burials were known; the cemetery was named for John B. Yarborough, as it is on his D.L.C. #72, OC #333, but none of the Yarborough family is known to be buried here. (Not shown on Peoria 1969-75 USGS Quad. map.)

ZASTROW FAMILY

?   ?   ?   1897   T13S T2E   S19
Located on the east side Foster Lake, along Hufford Road. The graves of the 2 Zastrow children are south of Hufford Road 100 feet. (Not shown on Green Peter 1984 USGS Quad. map.)

A.O.U.W. see **WORKMEN**	LINN CO.	T14S	R4W	S36
ALFORD	LINN CO.	T14S	R4W	S35
ALFORD see **WORKMEN**	LINN CO.	T14S	R4W	S36
ALFORD D.L.C., THOMAS see **ALFORD**				
	LINN CO.	T14S	R4W	S35
ALLPHIN FAMILY	LINN CO.	T10S	R3W	S8
AMES FAMILY	LINN CO.	T13S	R1W	S36
AMES SR. D.L.C., LOWELL see **AMES FAMILY**				
	LINN CO.	T13S	R1W	S36
ANCIENT ORDER OF UNITED WORKMEN see **WORKMEN**				
	LINN CO.	T14S	R4W	S36
BAPTIST	LINN CO.	T13S	R3W	S23
BARR PLACE, JESSE see **FERN RIDGE**				
	LINN CO.	T13S	R1W	S34
BELLINGER	LINN CO.	T12S	R1W	S15
BENDER, JOHN see **PIONEER [JORDAN]**				
	LINN CO.	T10S	R1E	S10
BERLIN see **POWELL**	LINN CO.	T12S	R1E	S31
BILYEU D.L.C., GEORGE see **PIONEER [JORDAN]**				
	LINN CO.	T10S	R1E	S10
BILYEU D.L.C., HUBBARD see **BILYEU DEN**				
	LINN CO.	T10S	R1E	S8
BILYEU DEN	LINN CO.	T10S	R1E	S8
BLACK COUPLE	LINN CO.	T12S	R2W	S9
BLACK, MR.	LINN CO.	T13S	R1W	S1
BLAIN	LINN CO.	T14S	R3W	S14
BLAND D.L.C., MOSES see **BLACK COUPLE**				
	LINN CO.	T12S	R2W	S9
BLAND FAMILY, MOSES see **BLACK COUPLE**				
	LINN CO.	T12S	R2W	S9
BOY	LINN CO.	T10S	R1E	S8
BRATTAIN D.L.C., JONATHAN H. see **BRATTAIN FAMILY**				
	LINN CO.	T12S	R4W	S33
BRATTAIN FAMILY	LINN CO.	T12S	R4W	S33
BROWNSVILLE BAPTIST see **BAPTIST**	LINN CO.	T13S	R3W	S23
BROWNSVILLE CITY see **BROWNSVILLE PIONEER**				
	LINN CO.	T13S	R2W	S32
BROWNSVILLE PIONEER	LINN CO.	T13S	R2W	S32
BRUCE see **KLUM**	LINN CO.	T12S	R1W	S32
BRYANT D.L.C., JOHN see **OUR LADY OF LOURDES**				
	LINN CO.	T10S	R1E	S9
BUNKER HILL	LINN CO.	T13S	R3W	S9
CALAPOOIA I.O.O.F. see **FINLEY**	LINN CO.	T14S	R2W	S13
CALAPOOIA MOUNDS	LINN CO.	-	-	-
CASCADIA PARK	LINN CO.	?	R3E	?
CATHOLIC SCHOOL see **OUR LADY OF LOURDES**				
	LINN CO.	T10S	R1E	S9
CENTRAL see **SANTIAM CENTRAL**	LINN CO.	T11S	R2W	S6
CENTRAL CHRISTIAN see **SANTIAM CENTRAL**				
	LINN CO.	T11S	R2W	S6
CHEADLE D.L.C., RAPHAEL see **SANDRIDGE**				
	LINN CO.	T12S	R3W	S24

CHILDS	LINN CO.	T12S	R2W	S36
CIRCLE CITY see **ORLEANS**	LINN CO.	T11S	R4W	S32
CLAYPOOL D.L.C., REUBEN see **CLAYPOOL FAMILY**				
	LINN CO.	T13S	R2W	S5
CLAYPOOL FAMILY	LINN CO.	T13S	R2W	S5
CLUM see **KLUM**	LINN CO.	T12S	R1W	S32
COCHRAN D.L.C., WILLIAM see **COCHRAN, POLLY**				
	LINN CO.	T13S	R2W	S19
COCHRAN, POLLY	LINN CO.	T13S	R2W	S19
COMMONS see **HALSEY PIONEER**	LINN CO.	T14S	R4W	S11
COON see **MILLER**	LINN CO.	T13S	R4W	S4
COON D.L.C., JAMES L. see **MILLER**				
	LINN CO.	T13S	R4W	S4
COOPER, MRS.	LINN CO.	T12S	R1W	S8
COTTONWOOD see **SANTIAM CENTRAL**	LINN CO.	T11S	R2W	S6
COX D.L.C., ANDERSON see **EAST ALBANY**				
	LINN CO.	T11S	R3W	S4
COX D.L.C., ANDERSON see **WAVERLY JEWISH**				
	LINN CO.	T11S	R3W	S4
COX D.L.C., ANDERSON see **WAVERLY MEMORIAL**				
	LINN CO.	T11S	R3W	S4
CRABTREE D.L.C., JOB see **CRABTREE FAMILY**				
	LINN CO.	T11S	R2W	S13
CRABTREE FAMILY	LINN CO.	T11S	R2W	S13
CRAWFORDSVILLE UNION	LINN CO.	T14S	R1W	S17
CURL	LINN CO.	T10S	R2W	?
CURL D.L.C., JOHN see **FRANKLIN BUTTE**				
	LINN CO.	T10S	R1W	S19
CUSHMAN see **ORLEANS**	LINN CO.	T11S	R4W	S32
CUSHMAN D.L.C., DANIAL see **ORLEANS**				
	LINN CO.	T11S	R4W	S32
CUSHMAN D.L.C., WALLACE see **TWIN OAKS MEMORIAL GARDENS**				
	LINN CO.	T11S	R4W	S33
CUSHMAN FAMILY see **ORLEANS**	LINN CO.	T11S	R4W	S32
CUSICK FAMILY	LINN CO.	T9S	R1E	S20
DANNEN FARM, FRED see **YARBOROUGH**				
	LINN CO.	T13S	R4W	S26
DARBY, BEN F. see **DARBY, MARTHA S.**				
	LINN CO.	T13S	R1W	?
DARBY D.L.C., OLIVER H. see **DARBY, MARTHA S.**				
	LINN CO.	T13S	R1W	?
DARBY, MARTHA S.	LINN CO.	T13S	R1W	?
DAVIS D.L.C., TRUST see **DAVIS FAMILY**				
	LINN CO.	T11S	R4W	S24
DAVIS FAMILY	LINN CO.	T11S	R4W	S24
DINWIDDIE see **BLAIN**	LINN CO.	T14S	R3W	S14
DODGE see **ROCK HILL**	LINN CO.	T12S	R2W	S28
DUNDON, CARRIE FRANCES	LINN CO.	T13S	R2E	S34
EARL D.L.C., JOHN see **EARL FAMILY**				
	LINN CO.	T10S	R3W	S36
EARL FAMILY	LINN CO.	T10S	R3W	S36
EAST ALBANY	LINN CO.	T11S	R3W	S4

EAST KNOX BUTTE see **EARL FAMILY** LINN CO.		T10S	R3W	S36
EAST KNOX BUTTE see **SANTIAM CENTRAL**				
	LINN CO.	T11S	R2W	S6
ELDER, CATHERINE see **ELDER FAMILY**				
	LINN CO.	T13S	R3W	S8
ELDER D.L.C., ROBERT M. AND CATHERINE see **ELDER FAMILY**				
	LINN CO.	T13S	R3W	S8
ELDER FAMILY	LINN CO.	T13S	R3W	S8
ELDER, MRS. see **ELDER FAMILY**	LINN CO.	T13S	R3W	S8
FAIRVIEW	LINN CO.	T9S	R3E	S34
FAIRVIEW MEMORIAL see **LINN MEMORIAL**				
	LINN CO.	T13S	R1W	S4
FAIRVIEW MENNONITE CHURCH	LINN CO.	T11S	R3W	S23
FERGUSON	LINN CO.	T13S	R1W	S12
FERN RIDGE	LINN CO.	T13S	R1W	S34
FERN RIDGE see **LACOMB**	LINN CO.	T11S	R1E	S31
FINLEY	LINN CO.	T14S	R2W	S13
FIR GROVE	LINN CO.	T14S	R2E	S4
FIRST BAPTIST see **BAPTIST**	LINN CO.	T13S	R3W	S23
FISH LAKE	LINN CO.	T13S	R7E	S30
FOSTER-GOULARD HOUSE see **TINDALL, MR.**				
	LINN CO.	T14S	R2W	S6
FOX VALLEY	LINN CO.	T9S	R2E	S20
FRANKLIN BUTTE	LINN CO.	T10S	R1W	S19
FRUIT HOME, GEORGE see **MICHAEL**	LINN CO.	T14S	R3W	S26
FRY	LINN CO.	T11S	R3W	S27
GAINES	LINN CO.	T11S	R1W	S2
GAINES D.L.C., WILLIS see **GAINES**				
	LINN CO.	T11S	R1W	S2
GAINES FAMILY see **GAINES**	LINN CO.	T11S	R1W	S2
GARRISON	LINN CO.	T13S	R4E	?
GATES see **FAIRVIEW**	LINN CO.	T9S	R3E	S34
GATES FARM, FRED see **WEGER**	LINN CO.	T15S	R3W	S26
GILLILAND	LINN CO.	T13S	R1E	S34
GILLILAND see **SWEET HOME MENNONITE**				
	LINN CO.	T13S	R1E	S34
GILLILAND D.L.C., JOHN W. see **GILLILAND**				
	LINN CO.	T13S	R1E	S34
GORDON D.L.C., HARVEY see **MASONIC [ALBANY]**				
	LINN CO.	T11S	R4W	S12
GORE D.L.C., WILLIAM B. see **I.O.O.F. [LEBANON]**				
	LINN CO.	T12S	R2W	S2
GOURLEY'S FARM, ROBERT AND EILEEN see **DUNDON, CARRIE FRANCES**				
	LINN CO.	T13S	R2E	S34
GRAY see **BLAIN**	LINN CO.	T14S	R3W	S14
GRAY D.L.C., DAVID see **BLAIN**	LINN CO.	T14S	R3W	S14
GREEN PLACE see **UNKNOWN**	LINN CO.	T14S	R2E	S3
GUNDERSON see **MOUNTAIN HOME**	LINN CO.	T13S	R1W	S20
GUNDERSON PLACE, SAM see **THOMPSON, A. K.**				
	LINN CO.	T13S	R1W	S18
HALE D.L.C., MILTON AND SUSANNAH see **SIMISON**				
	LINN CO.	T10S	R3W	S3

HALE, MILTON see **SIMISON**	LINN CO.	T10S	R3W	S3
HALSEY PIONEER	LINN CO.	T14S	R4W	S11
HAMILTON CREEK see **BELLINGER**	LINN CO.	T12S	R1W	S15
HAPPY HOME see **BELLINGER**	LINN CO.	T12S	R1W	S15
HARRIS	LINN CO.	T15S	R4W	S24
HARRIS FARM, J. R. see **HARRIS**	LINN CO.	T15S	R4W	S24
HARRISBURG I.O.O.F. see **I.O.O.F.** [ALFORD]				
	LINN CO.	T14S	R4W	S35
HEBREW see **WAVERLY JEWISH**	LINN CO.	T11S	R3W	S4
HOLLENBECK FAMILY, ASA see **CUSICK FAMILY**				
	LINN CO.	T9S	R1E	S20
HOLLENBECK-CUSICK FAMILY see **CUSICK FAMILY**				
	LINN CO.	T9S	R1E	S20
HOUSTON see **EAST ALBANY**	LINN CO.	T11S	R3W	S4
HUMPHREYS, D.L.C., THOMAS M. see **HUMPHREYS FAMILY**				
	LINN CO.	T10S	R1E	S5
HUMPHREYS FAMILY	LINN CO.	T10S	R1E	S5
I.O.O.F. [ALFORD]	LINN CO.	T14S	R4W	S35
I.O.O.F. [CRAWFORDSVILLE] see **FINLEY**				
	LINN CO.	T14S	R2W	S13
I.O.O.F. [LEBANON]	LINN CO.	T12S	R2W	S2
INDIAN	LINN CO.	T13S	R6E	?
IRVINE D.L.C., ROBERT see **MT. PLEASANT**				
	LINN CO.	T9S	R1E	S30
JORDAN see **OUR LADY OF LOURDES**	LINN CO.	T10S	R1E	S9
JORDAN CATHOLIC CHURCH see **OUR LADY OF LOURDES**				
	LINN CO.	T10S	R1E	S9
JORDAN PIONEER see **PIONEER [JORDEN]**				
	LINN CO.	T10S	R1E	S10
KEENE see **HARRIS**	LINN CO.	T15S	R4W	S24
KEENEY see **UNION POINT**	LINN CO.	T14S	R3W	S14
KEES D.L.C., MORGAN see **I.O.O.F.** [LEBANON]				
	LINN CO.	T12S	R2W	S2
KINGS PRAIRIE see **FAIRVIEW**	LINN CO.	T9S	R3E	S34
KINGSTON see **WISNER**	LINN CO.	T9S	R1W	S23
KIPHART-POINT see **CUSICK FAMILY**	LINN CO.	T9S	R1E	S20
KIRK see **UNION POINT**	LINN CO.	T14S	R3W	S14
KIRK D.L.C., WILLIAM R. see **BROWNSVILLE PIONEER**				
	LINN CO.	T13S	R2W	S32
KLUM	LINN CO.	T12S	R1W	S32
KLUM D.L.C., WILLIAAM see **KLUM**	LINN CO.	T12S	R1W	S32
KLUM FAMILY see **KLUM**	LINN CO.	T12S	R1W	S32
KNOX BUTTE	LINN CO.	T10S	R3W	S35
KNOX D.L.C., JAMES see **KNOX BUTTE**				
	LINN CO.	T10S	R3W	S35
KOTAN see **GAINES**	LINN CO.	T11S	R1W	S2
KOTAN FARM see **GAINES**	LINN CO.	T11S	R1W	S2
LACOMB	LINN CO.	T11S	R1E	S31
LEBANON ODD FELLOWS see **I.O.O.F.** [LEBANON]				
	LINN CO.	T12S	R2W	S2
LEBANON PIONEER	LINN CO.	T12S	R2W	S11
LEMASTER	LINN CO.	T14S	R1W	?

LEWIS	LINN CO.	T13S	R1E	S23
LEWIS CREEK see **LEWIS**	LINN CO.	T13S	R1E	S23
LEWIS, FIELDING see **FERN RIDGE**	LINN CO.	T13S	R1W	S34
LEWIS, RACHEL see **FERN RIDGE**	LINN CO.	T13S	R1W	S34
LIBERTY [NEW]	LINN CO.	T13S	R1W	S26
LIBERTY [OLD]	LINN CO.	T13S	R1W	S23
LINN MEMORIAL	LINN CO.	T13S	R1W	S4
LONE PINE see **PINE GROVE**	LINN CO.	T13S	R4W	S32
LOURDES see **OUR LADY OF LOURDES**	LINN CO.	T10S	R1E	S9
LYONS see **FOX VALLEY**	LINN CO.	T9S	R2E	S20
MALONE D.L.C., JAMES see **MALONE FAMILY**				
	LINN CO.	T14S	R1W	S24
MALONE FAMILY	LINN CO.	T14S	R1W	S24
MALONE PLACE, FRED see **MALONE FAMILY**				
	LINN CO.	T14S	R1W	S24
MANSFIELD see **HARRIS**	LINN CO.	T15S	R4W	S24
MARKS, MRS. CHARITY ANN see **FISH LAKE**				
	LINN CO.	T13S	R7E	S30
MARKS RIDGE see **FERGUSON**	LINN CO.	T13S	R1W	S12
MASONIC see **FRANKLIN BUTTE**	LINN CO.	T10S	R1W	S19
MASONIC [ALBANY]	LINN CO.	T11S	R4W	S12
MASONIC [ALFORD]	LINN CO.	T14S	R4W	S35
MASONIC [BROWNSVILLE] see **BROWNSVILLE PIONEER**				
	LINN CO.	T13S	R2W	S32
MASONIC [HARRISBURG] see **MASONIC [ALFORD]**				
	LINN CO.	T14S	R4W	S35
MASONIC [LEBANON] see **I.O.O.F. [LEBANON]**				
	LINN CO.	T12S	R2W	S2
MASONIC [SCIO] see **FRANKLIN BUTTE**				
	LINN CO.	T10S	R1W	S19
MASTENBROOK, HARLAN see **COOPER, MRS.**				
	LINN CO.	T12S	R1W	S8
MASTENBROOK, HARLAN see **SALTMARSH, ZERILDA**				
	LINN CO.	T12S	R1W	S7
MASTENBROOK, HARLAN see **UNKNOWN WOMAN**				
	LINN CO.	T12S	R1W	S7
McHARGUE	LINN CO.	T14S	R2W	S15
McHARGUE D.L.C., JAMES see **McHARGUE**				
	LINN CO.	T14S	R2W	S15
McKNIGHT, JAMES A.	LINN CO.	T13S	R6E	S31
MEEKER D.L.C., JOHN see **UMPHLETTE, JANE EARL**				
	LINN CO.	T10S	R3W	S15
MEEKS see **WEGER**	LINN CO.	T15S	R3W	S26
MEEKS D.L.C., THOMAS M. see **WEGER**				
	LINN CO.	T15S	R3W	S26
METHODIST EPISCOPAL CHURCH see **LEBANON PIONEER**				
	LINN CO.	T12S	R2W	S11
MICHAEL	LINN CO.	T14S	R3W	S26
MICHAEL D.L.C., ELIJAH see **MICHAEL**				
	LINN CO.	T14S	R3W	S26
MILL CITY see **FAIRVIEW**	LINN CO.	T9S	R3E	S34
MILLER	LINN CO.	T10S	R2W	S1

MILLER	LINN CO.	T10S	R3W	S17
MILLER	LINN CO.	T13S	R4W	S4
MILLER-COON see **MILLER**	LINN CO.	T13S	R4W	S4
MILLER-COON FAMILIES see **MILLER**	LINN CO.	T13S	R4W	S4
MILLER, MRS. MARY see **MILLER**	LINN CO.	T10S	R2W	S1
MILLER SR. D.L.C., GEORGE see **MILLER**				
	LINN CO.	T10S	R3W	S17
MILLER SR. D.L.C., ISAAC see **WILLAMETTE MEMORIAL PARK**				
	LINN CO.	T10S	R3W	S28
MILLERSBURG see **MILLER**	LINN CO.	T10S	R3W	S17
MONTEITH D.L.C., WALTER see **RIVERSIDE**				
	LINN CO.	T11S	R4W	S12
MT. PLEASANT	LINN CO.	T9S	R1E	S30
MOUNTAIN HOME	LINN CO.	T13S	R1W	S20
MUDDY CREEK see **HARRIS**	LINN CO.	T15S	R4W	S24
NAVE see **LACOMB**	LINN CO.	T11S	R1E	S31
NORWEGIAN see **MOUNTAIN HOME**	LINN CO.	T13S	R1W	S20
NYE see **LIBERTY [NEW]**	LINN CO.	T13S	R1W	S26
NYE D.L.C., ADAM see **LIBERTY [NEW]**				
	LINN CO.	T13S	R1W	S26
NYE D.L.C., JACOB see **LIBERTY [OLD]**				
	LINN CO.	T13S	R1W	S23
NYE-LIBERTY see **LIBERTY [NEW]**	LINN CO.	T13S	R1W	S26
OAKVILLE	LINN CO.	T12S	R4W	S16
OLD LEBANON see **LEBANON PIONEER**	LINN CO.	T12S	R2W	S11
OLD METHODIST see **LEBANON PIONEER**				
	LINN CO.	T12S	R2W	S11
OLD SKEELS PLACE see **CHILDS**	LINN CO.	T12S	R2W	S36
ORLEANS	LINN CO.	T11S	R4W	S32
OSBORNE D.L.C., JOSIAH see **FINLEY**				
	LINN CO.	T14S	R2W	S13
OUR LADY OF LOURDES	LINN CO.	T10S	R1E	S9
OUR LADY OF LOURDES CATHOLIC see **PIONEER [JORDAN]**				
	LINN CO.	T10S	R1E	S10
OVERTON see **UNION POINT**	LINN CO.	T14S	R3W	S14
PAYNE D.L.C., MARTIN see **FAIRVIEW MENNONITE CHURCH**				
	LINN CO.	T11S	R3W	S23
PETERSON BUTTE see **SANDRIDGE**	LINN CO.	T12S	R3W	S24
PETTERSON D.L.C., HENRY F. see **ROCK HILL**				
	LINN CO.	T12S	R2W	S28
PIETROK see **CUSICK FAMILY**	LINN CO.	T9S	R1E	S20
PILCHER	LINN CO.	T10S	R3W	?
PINE GROVE	LINN CO.	T13S	R4W	S32
PIONEER see **LEBANON PIONEER**	LINN CO.	T12S	R2W	S11
PIONEER [JORDAN]	LINN CO.	T10S	R1E	S10
PLEASANT BUTTE BAPTIST see **BAPTIST**				
	LINN CO.	T13S	R3W	S23
POE D.L.C., WILLIAM see **POE, MARY JANE VANNATTA**				
	LINN CO.	T15S	R2W	S9
POE, MARY JANE VANNATTA	LINN CO.	T15S	R2W	S9
POWELL	LINN CO.	T12S	R1E	S31

POWELL D.L.C., EXUM see **WILLAMETTE MEMORIAL PARK**

	LINN CO.	T10S R3W	S28
POWELL, JOAB see **LIBERTY [OLD]**	LINN CO.	T13S R1W	S23
POWELL, MRS. MARGARET see **UMPHLETTE, JANE EARL**			
	LINN CO.	T10S R3W	S15
PRIME see **CRABTREE FAMILY**	LINN CO.	T11S R2W	S13
PROVIDENCE	LINN CO.	T11S R1W	S10
PROVIDENCE BAPTIST CHURCH see **PROVIDENCE**			
	LINN CO.	T11S R1W	S10
PROVIDENCE CHURCH see **PROVIDENCE**			
	LINN CO.	T11S R1W	S10
PUGH D.L.C., FRANCIS A. see **SHEDD**			
	LINN CO.	T13S R4W	S13
PUGH FAMILY see **SHEDD**	LINN CO.	T13S R4W	S13
QUARTZVILLE	LINN CO.	T12S R4E	S22
RANDLE, SAMUEL ARTHUR see **BLACK COUPLE**			
	LINN CO.	T12S R2W	S9
REEVES PLACE see **BLACK, MR.**	LINN CO.	T13S R1W	S1
REEVES PLACE see **FERGUSON**	LINN CO.	T13S R1W	S12
RHODES	LINN CO.	T10S R3W	?
RICE	LINN CO.	T13S R2E	?
RIGGS D.L.C., TIMOTHY see **CRAWFORDSVILLE UNION**			
	LINN CO.	T14S R1W	S17
RIVERSIDE	LINN CO.	T11S R4W	S12
RIVERVIEW see **FAIRVIEW**	LINN CO.	T9S R3E	S34
ROBINETT	LINN CO.	T14S R1W	?
ROBINETT D.L.C., WILLIAM see **ROBINETT**			
	LINN CO.	T14S R1W	?
ROBINETTE see **ROBINETT**	LINN CO.	T14S R1W	?
ROBINETTI see **ROBINETT**	LINN CO.	T14S R1W	?
ROBINETTI, JIM see **ROBINETT**	LINN CO.	T14S R1W	?
ROBNETT see **ROBINETT**	LINN CO.	T14S R1W	?
ROCK HILL	LINN CO.	T12S R2W	S28
RUSSELL	LINN CO.	T13S R1E	S33
RUSSELL D.L.C., NEWTON see **RUSSELL**			
	LINN CO.	T13S R1E	S33
RUSSELL PLACE, ENOS see **RUSSELL**	LINN CO.	T13S R1E	S33
RUST see **HALSEY PIONEER**	LINN CO.	T14S R4W	S11
ST. BENEDICTS see **OUR LADY OF LOURDES**			
	LINN CO.	T10S R1E	S9
ST. JOHNS LODGE #17, MASONS see **WAVERLY MEMORIAL**			
	LINN CO.	T11S R3W	S4
SALTMARSH, ARTHUR see **SALTMARSH, ZERILDA**			
	LINN CO.	T12S R1W	S7
SALTMARSH D.L.C., ARTHUR see **SALTMARSH, ZERILDA**			
	LINN CO.	T12S R1W	S7
SALTMARSH, ZERILDA	LINN CO.	T12S R1W	S7
SAND RIDGE see **SANDRIDGE**	LINN CO.	T12S R3W	S24
SANDRIDGE	LINN CO.	T12S R3W	S24
SANTIAM CENTRAL	LINN CO.	T11S R2W	S6
SANTIAM, CHIEF see **SIMISON**	LINN CO.	T10S R3W	S3

SAVAGE, AMERICUS see **BUNKER HILL**				
	LINN CO.	T13S	R3W	S9
SAVAGE BUTTE see **BUNKER HILL**	LINN CO.	T13S	R3W	S9
SAVAGE COLUMBUS see **BUNKER HILL**	LINN CO.	T13S	R3W	S9
SAVAGE D.L.C., AMERICUS see **BUNKER HILL**				
	LINN CO.	T13S	R3W	S9
SAVAGE-MORGAN FAMILIES see **BUNKER HILL**				
	LINN CO.	T13S	R3W	S9
SCHOOLING see **HARRIS**	LINN CO.	T15S	R4W	S24
SHEA HILL	LINN CO.	T13S	R1E	?
SHEDD	LINN CO.	T13S	R4W	S13
SHELBURN see **MILLER**	LINN CO.	T10S	R2W	S1
SHELTON D.L.C., JAMES see **SHELTON, JOHN**				
	LINN CO.	T9S	R1E	S34
SHELTON, JOHN	LINN CO.	T9S	R1E	S34
SHEPHERD see **PINE GROVE**	LINN CO.	T13S	R4W	S32
SHEPHERD D.L.C., WILLIAM see **PINE GROVE**				
	LINN CO.	T13S	R4W	S32
SILBERNAGEL see **PIONEER [JORDAN]**				
	LINN CO.	T10S	R1E	S10
SIMISON	LINN CO.	T10S	R3W	S3
SIMISON FAMILY see **SIMISON**	LINN CO.	T10S	R3W	S3
SIMPSON see **SIMISON**	LINN CO.	T10S	R3W	S3
SIMPSON-HALE see **SIMISON**	LINN CO.	T10S	R3W	S3
SIMPSON-HALE FAMILIES see **SIMISON**				
	LINN CO.	T10S	R3W	S3
SMITH, JOHN P. see **HALSEY PIONEER**				
	LINN CO.	T14S	R4W	S11
SODAVILLE see **KLUM**	LINN CO.	T12S	R1W	S32
SOLDIERS	LINN CO.	T13S	UNSURVEYED	
SPALDING D.L.C., HENRY H. see **TINDALL, MR.**				
	LINN CO.	T14S	R2W	S6
SPLAWN D.L.C., GEORGE W. see **SPLAWN FAMILY**				
	LINN CO.	T14S	R1W	S11
SPLAWN FAMILY	LINN CO.	T14S	R1W	S11
SPLAWN, GREENBERRY see **SPLAWN FAMILY**				
	LINN CO.	T14S	R1W	S11
SPRING FAMILY	LINN CO.	T13S	R2E	S18
STREITHOFF D.L.C., THOMAS E. see **SANTIAM CENTRAL**				
	LINN CO.	T11S	R2W	S6
SWALLOW, JOHN	LINN CO.		UNSURVEYED	
SWEET HOME MENNONITE	LINN CO.	T13S	R1E	S34
SWEET HOME MENNONITE see **GILLILAND**				
	LINN CO.	T13S	R1E	S34
SWEET HOME VALLEY see **GILLILAND**	LINN CO.	T13S	R1E	S34
SYRACUSE see **SIMISON**	LINN CO.	T10S	R3W	S3
THOMPSON see **FIR GROVE**	LINN CO.	T14S	R2E	S4
THOMPSON, A. K.	LINN CO.	T13S	R1W	S18
TINDALL, MR.	LINN CO.	T14S	R2W	S6
TOMBSTONE PRAIRIE see **McKNIGHT, JAMES A.**				
	LINN CO.	T13S	R6E	S31
TOWNSEND, JODY CHARLES	LINN CO.	T15S	R2W	S7

TURNIDGE FAMILY	LINN CO.	T10S	R3W	?
TURNIDGE, HENRY see **TURNIDGE FAMILY**				
	LINN CO.	T10S	R3W	?
TURNIDGE, PAULINE G. see **TURNIDGE FAMILY**				
	LINN CO.	T10S	R3W	?
TWIN BUTTE see **MICHAEL**	LINN CO.	T14S	R3W	S26
TWIN OAKS MEMORIAL GARDENS	LINN CO.	T11S	R4W	S33
TWIN OAKS MEMORIAL PARK see **TWIN OAKS MEMORIAL GARDENS**				
	LINN CO.	T11S	R4W	S33
UMPHLETTE, JANE EARL	LINN CO.	T10S	R3W	S15
UMPHLETTE, MRS. see **UMPHLETTE, JANE EARL**				
	LINN CO.	T10S	R3W	S15
UMPHLETTE, STANLEY see **UMPHLETTE, JANE EARL**				
	LINN CO.	T10S	R3W	S15
UNION [CRAWFORDSVILLE] see **CRAWFORDSVILLE UNION**				
	LINN CO.	T14S	R1W	S17
UNION POINT	LINN CO.	T14S	R3W	S14
UNKNOWN	LINN CO.	?	?	?
UNKNOWN	LINN CO.	T14S	R2E	S3
UNKNOWN WOMAN	LINN CO.	T12S	R1W	S7
UPPER SODA see **GARRISON**	LINN CO.	T13S	R4E	?
USHER D.L.C., RICHARD see **CHILDS**				
	LINN CO.	T12S	R2W	S36
WATERLOO see **KLUM**	LINN CO.	T12S	R1W	S32
WAVERLY JEWISH	LINN CO.	T11S	R3W	S4
WAVERLY LAKE MASONIC see **WAVERLY MEMORIAL**				
	LINN CO.	T11S	R3W	S4
WAVERLY MEMORIAL	LINN CO.	T11S	R3W	S4
WEGER	LINN CO.	T15S	R3W	S26
WEST FAIRVIEW CHURCH see **FAIRVIEW MENNONITE CHURCH**				
	LINN CO.	T11S	R3W	S23
WEST POINT	LINN CO.	T15S	R3W	S33
WHITCOMB	LINN CO.	T12S	R3E	S31
WHITE D.L.C., LUTHER see **WHITE, LUTHER**				
	LINN CO.	T15S	R3W	S12
WHITE, LUTHER	LINN CO.	T15S	R3W	S12
WIBLE D.L.C., JOHN see **LINN MEMORIAL**				
	LINN CO.	T13S	R1W	S4
WIGLE	LINN CO.	T14S	R3W	S35
WIGLE D.L.C., JOHN M. see **WIGLE**	LINN CO.	T14S	R3W	S35
WILEY D.L.C., ANDREW see **WILEY FAMILY**				
	LINN CO.	T13S	R1E	S36
WILEY FAMILY	LINN CO.	T13S	R1E	S36
WILLAMETTE MEMORIAL PARK	LINN CO.	T10S	R3W	S28
WILLIAMS D.L.C., HENRY see **PINE GROVE**				
	LINN CO.	T13S	R4W	S32
WILLIAMS D.L.C., JASON L. see **POWELL**				
	LINN CO.	T12S	R1E	S31
WILLOUGHBY see **WEST POINT**	LINN CO.	T15S	R3W	S33
WILSON see **BLAIN**	LINN CO.	T14S	R3W	S14
WISNER	LINN CO.	T9S	R1W	S23

```
WOODWARD D.L.C., LUTHER T. see LEBANON PIONEER
                               LINN CO.        T12S   R2W        S11
WORKMAN                        LINN CO.        T14S   R4W        S36
YARBOROUGH                     LINN CO.        T13S   R4W        S26
YARBOROUGH D.L.C., JOHN B. see YARBOROUGH
                               LINN CO.        T13S   R4W        S26
ZASTROW CHILDREN see ZASTROW FAMILY
                               LINN CO.        T13S   R2E        S19
ZASTROW FAMILY                 LINN CO.        T13S   R2E        S19
ZIELINSKI PLACE, FRED see BOY  LINN CO.        T10S   R1E        S8
```

I.O.O.F. [Lebanon]
Dean H. Byrd (1990)

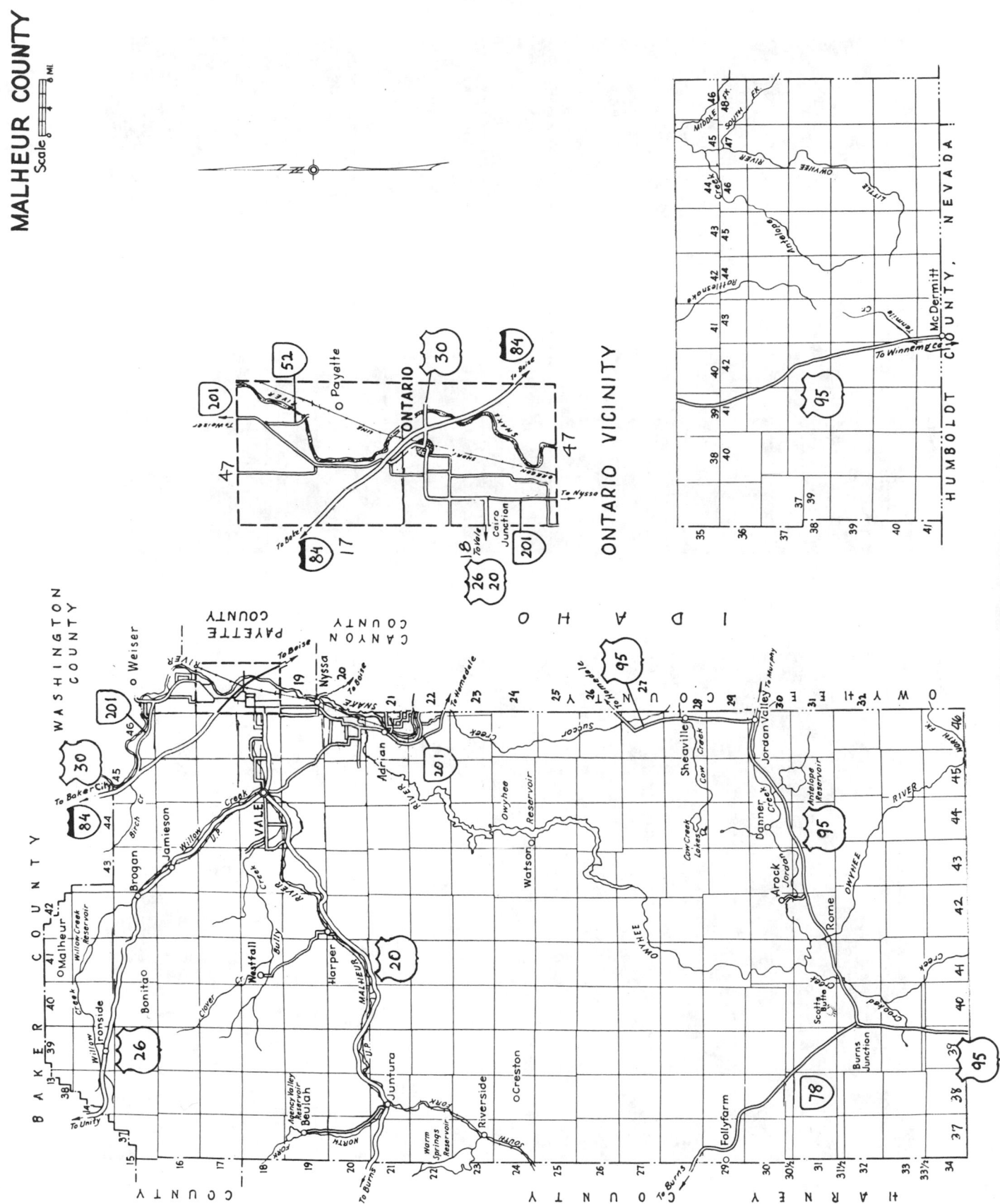

Charbonneau, Jean Baptiste
Janice M. Healy (2000)

Charbonneau, Jean Baptiste
Ruth C. Bishop (2000)

Area: 9,926 square miles
Population (1998): 28,542
County seat: Vale, Population: 1,510
County established: 17 February 1887

This county, considerably larger than the State of Massachusetts, was utilized as a transit area. The Oregon Trail entered what is now Oregon via Malheur County. The cemetery at Arock (1860) appears to have been the earliest organized cemetery in the county. Ironside Cemetery (1873) was the second to be established. There was brief gold mining in the Mormon Basin in the north. But the county was and is largely devoted to livestock ranching but with considerable irrigated agriculture along the Snake River and the lower Malheur River. There is a significant settlement of Spanish Basques ("Bascos") in Malheur County.

Charbonneau, Jean Baptiste
Janice M. Healy (2000)

Charbonneau, Jean Baptiste
Janice M. Healy (2000)

Name of Cemetery and also known as	Number of burials	Acres	Condition	Date started or earliest known burial	Township	Range	Section

APPLEGATE
AKA: 1. PIONEER
    [ONTARIO]

A   0.25   3   1892-1914   T16S R47E   ?
Located in Section 10 or 11. Take OR. Hwy.
201 from Weiser Junction and go about 2 miles
southerly to the Mesquite Road crossing.
Turn right (east) onto Mesquite Road and
continue about another 1.5 miles. The
cemetery site is apparently on one of two
farms on the left (north) between the road
and the Snake River. James Applegate, the
most recent burial, died 2 April 1914, aged
14 years 6 months 21 days, according to the
death certificate #1717. The certificate
states that he was buried on the Clarence
Barker Place. The 1936 *Metsker Land
Ownership Atlas* shows the Barker family owned
considerable acreage along Mesquite Road.
Besides young Applegate, 6 children died in a
diphtheria epidemic in 1892; 3 from the
Erickson family; 2 from the Hopper family;
and 1 from the Duncan family. Billy Randall,
dates unknown, is also reported buried here.
When researched in 1972 there were no
headstones visible but the cemetery had been
fenced. (Not shown on Weiser South 1951 USGS
Quad. map.)

AROCK

A   0.1   5   1860-1885   T30S R42E   ?
Thought to be in Section 26 at Arock, on the
old Sheep Ranch and across the road from the
old stone fort on the old highway. In 1972
the D.A.R. surveyed this cemetery and found
that it had been destroyed. (Not shown on
Arock 1972 USGS Quad. map. The USGS Quad.
calls the ranch Sheep Ranch.)

BARKER, JAMES

A   0.01   ?   10 Nov 1923   T23S R37E   ?
A rancher, James Barker, is reported by the
death certificate to be buried "at
Riverside." However he is not included in
the list of burials at Riverside Cemetery.
His monument, if any, may be lost or he may
be buried somewhere in the vicinity of
Riverside. The compiler cannot say. (Not
shown on Winnemucca Creek 1979 USGS Quad.
map.)

Name of Cemetery and also known as	Number of burials	Acres	Condition	Date started or earliest known burial	Township	Range	Section

BECKER, CHARLES

A 0.01 3 1925-1960 T18S R40E S8
Located about 2 miles east and south off of Bully Creek Road and about 6 miles northwest of Westfall. There are 4 graves here, all Becker family members. Charles Becker, who died in late May 1944, was a Pony Express rider. (Log Creek 1990 USGS Quad. map.)

BECKER RANCH, JIM

A 0.01 4 ? T18S R41E S27
There are 2 unmarked graves on the old Jim Becker Ranch (1978). Take the Old Stage Road easterly from Westfall. John Bouncer was killed by Indians. The other undated burial is for a young girl, Martha Mullins, daughter of Mary Jane Westfall Mullins. (Jim Becker ranch building is shown but not labled, the burials are not shown on Westfall 1990 USGS Quad. map.)

BETTERLY, HAZEL

A 0.01 ? 1890'S T20S R47E ?
This infant was reportedly buried on the old Harris Place sometime between 1890 and 1895. No further information was given. (Not shown on Owyhee 1967 USGS Quad. map.)

BEULAH
AKA: 1. AGENCY
  VALLEY
  2. SCOTT

A 0.8 2 1883-1971 T18S R37E S35
Located north of the north end of Beulah Reservoir. Go northerly 0.34 of a mile from the junction with Beal Ranch Road and then turn left (northwest) off of the county road. Go another 0.26 of a mile to the cemetery, which is off to the right about 500 feet. There were 22 known burials in the D.A.R. survey of 1972. (Beulah 1990 USGS Quad. map.)

BLACK, MRS.

A 0.01 ? 1899 T20S R46E S26
Reportedly buried about 100 yards northwest of Owyhee Junction; OR. Hwy. 201 and Owyhee Avenue. No further information was given in the report. (Not shown on Owyhee 1967 USGS Quad. map.)

Name of Cemetery and also known as	Number of burials	Acres	Condition	Date started or earliest known burial	Township	Range	Section

BROGAN

B   1.7   1   1911   T15S R42E   S26
Travel 23.3 miles north of Vale on U.S. Hwy. 26 to 8th Avenue; turn left (west) and go 1.3 miles on 8th Avenue to the cemetery. There were 41 known burials in 1972. (Brogan 1990 USGS Quad. map.)

CARTER HOMESTEAD, JOE

A   ?   ?   ?   T20S R39E   S29
Located on the Carter Homestead near the site of Peach. Three boys and one girl are in unmarked graves. (Not shown on Jonesboro 1990 USGS Quad. map.)

CEMETERY SPRING

?   ?   ?   ?   T19S R41E   S35
Located in the hills about 2 miles due west of Amick Road, which is in Harper Valley. In the spring of 1958, the compiler was in Malheur County collecting geographic information for a forthcoming State Highway Division map of Malheur County. Some person, now forgotten, informed the compiler of a cemetery here. This unnamed cemetery appears on the subsequent Malheur County Map. The compiler was not especially interested in cemeteries in 1958, and now has no recollection of any story about it. (Cemetery Spring appears on the Westfall 1990 USGS Quad., and a corral is shown about 100 yards to the east downslope, but no burial ground. Nor do any burials show on the adjoining Namorf 1990 USGS Quad. map.)

CHAMBERS, SARAH

A   0.01   2   3 Sept 1845   T18S R37E   S33
Start at the three-way junction of Beulah, Bendire, and Beal Ranch Roads at the north side of Beulah Reservoir. Take Beal Ranch Road to the west and northwest along the North Fork of the Malheur River and go about 3.2 miles. The grave is on the right about 100 feet above the road and was embedded in concrete about 1954. The 22-year-old Mrs. Chambers was the wife of Rowland Chambers and daughter of Nahum King, who settled in Kings Valley, Benton County; they are buried in the cemetery of that name. The death and burial

Name of Cemetery and also known as	Number of burials	Acres	Condition	Date started or earliest known burial	Township	Range	Section

of Sarah Chambers is inextricably tied to the stories, true or otherwise, of the Lost Blue Bucket Mine. (Beulah 1990 USGS Quad. map.)

CHARBONNEAU, JEAN BAPTISTE
AKA: 1. INSKEEP
2. INSKIP RANCHE
3. INSKIP'S STATION

A 0.1 1 1866-1881 T30S R44E S16
Go 17 miles from Jordan Valley, on U.S. Hwy. 95, to the southwest and turn right (north) at Milepost 37 on Danner Road. Go 3.2 miles North on Danner Road. The burials are on the right (east), about 0.2 of a mile north of the Jorden Creek Bridge. Charbonneau who was born 11 February 1805, died 16 May 1866; Jake Dixon died 7 October 1866; Ethan Wright died 13 August 1869; Gertrude Inskeep born 10 May 1872, died 10 December 1873; Emigrant child 1870's; James Doe died 23 March 1881. {11 September 2000} (Danner 1969 USGS Quad. map.)

CHINESE MASSACRE
AKA: 1. CHINAMEN'S MASSACRE

C ? 5 May 1866 T31S R41E ?
Perhaps located in Section 13. See the account compiled by Hazel R. Fretwell-Johnson in her book *In Times Past* (1990) pages 53-54. Varying numbers of Chinese miners who were enroute from Winnemucca to the mines in Idaho are given, perhaps as many as 100. A large band of Paiutes caught them and butchered the Chinese for their few horses, tools, and especially for their long braided queues. One youth escaped. The victims were buried along the Owyhee just upstream from the mouth of Jordan Creek in the area known as Owyhee Crossing or Owyhee Ferry. China Gulch, a short distance further upstream (south) was so named in memory of the slaughter. (Not shown on Rome 1972 USGS Quad. map.)

CORD
AKA: 1. CURTIS
2. SEAWARD
3. SEWARD

A 0.15 4 1907-1912 T28S R38E S7
Located between OR. Hwy. 78 and the Tom Dowell Ranch (1978), 300 feet off of the west side of Crowley-Riverside Road between Turnbull Lakebed and Duck Creek Lakebed. There are three known burials of the Seaward (now Seward) family plus a possible burial of a man named Curtis. Cord was a locale with a post office from 1897 to December 1918. (Dowell Butte 1977 USGS Quad. map.)

Name of Cemetery and also known as	Number of burials	Acres	Condition	Date started or earliest known burial	Township	Range	Section

CRISWELL BOY

A 0.01 ? 1884   T20S R46E   ?
Perhaps located in Section 35 or 36. Fred Criswell's son drowned in the Owyhee River. He is reportedly buried "above OR. Hwy. 201 near the bridge." (Not shown on Owyhee 1967 USGS Quad. map.)

DANNER

A 0.25 12 ?   T30S R44E   S16
This is supposedly a separate cemetery from the Charbonneau burial site. The Danner Cemetery is off of Danner Road. Go 17 miles from Jordan Valley, on U.S. Hwy. 95, to Danner Road. Turn right (north) and go 3.1 miles to Jordan Creek Bridge. The cemetery is 200 yards to the left (west). This site appears to be farmed over or possibly washed out by the creek, no access. {11 September 2000} (Danner 1969 USGS Quad. map.)

DELL
  AKA: 1. JAMIESON
        2. JEMERSON *[Sic]*
        3. WILLOW CREEK

C 2.9 2 1877   T16S R43E   S15
The cemetery is on the right (east), 16 miles north of Vale on U.S. Hwy. 26. (Jamieson 1988 USGS Quad. map.)

EVERGREEN
  AKA: 1. ONTARIO

E 14 1 1886   T18S R47E   S9
Located on South Park Boulevard, Ontario; 3,595 burials were found in the D.A.R. survey of 1972. (Payette 1951-74 USGS Quad. map.)

FAIRVIEW
  AKA: 1. ANNEX
        2. FAIR-VIEW
        3. WEISER
           JUNCTION

C 4.5 1 1875   T15S R47E   S33
Located 15.3 miles northwest of Ontario, via OR. Hwy. 201, to Weiser Junction; turn right (north) onto U.S. Hwy. 95 Spur and go 0.15 of a mile. The cemetery is on the right. Contrariwise, the cemetery is 8 miles south of the bridge over the Snake River at Weiser, Idaho. (Weiser South 1951 USGS Quad. map.)

FIELDS, HAROLD

A 0.01 ? 28 Mar 1916 T19S R47E   S32
Reportedly buried along Main Street in Nyssa. This infant was born and died the same day. He was the son of Archie and Lorena Rambo

Name of Cemetery and also known as	Number of burials	Acres	Condition	Date started or earliest known burial	Township	Range	Section

Fields. No death certificate is on file at the Oregon State Archives. (Not shown on Nyssa 1965 USGS Quad. map.)

GLASCOCK BABY

A 0.01 ? ? ? ? ?

This infant was buried on the Vein Ranch on Willow Creek. The child died of scarlet fever and people were afraid to bury it in the Dell Cemetery at Jamieson. The father was Henry L. "Bulldog" Glascock. (Not shown on Jamieson 1988 USGS Quad. map.)

GOODWIN TOMB

A 0.01 ? 20 Sept. 1963 T17S R37E S19

This miniature mausoleum of concrete and steel was fashioned by Thomas Hugh Goodwin (born 14 April 1895 died 20 Sept 1963) himself. The tomb is reached from Ironside on U.S. Hwy. 26 by going southwest on Rose Creek Road for 15.9 miles. Then turn left (southerly) onto Lost Creek Road, a four-wheel drive track, for another 11 miles. Lastly, there is a gated private driveway to the right (north) to the tomb on the old Goodwin Ranch. The tomb is about 0.75 of a mile from this last junction. Goodwin constructed it about four feet off the ground to be above the spring flood of the Little Malheur River. Goodwin was a colorful character who called himself King of Lost Creek. He died in a bizarre shooting at his residence in Vale while acting the part of a deer for a woman friend whom he was instructing in fire arms. The unloaded gun was loaded. (Castle Rock 1990 USGS Quad. map.)

GRAVEYARD POINT
AKA: 1. ROUND HILL

A ? ? 1891 T23S R47E ?

Possibly located on Section 18. This abandoned graveyard is in Oregon but the geographic feature so named is in Idaho. The long hill rises about 300 feet above the surrounding terrain. Drive from Adrian on OR. Hwy. 201 to the State Line Store. Turn right (south) for a little over a mile along the state line. Turn left (east) into Idaho for a mile to a road right (south). Turn on that road to the south for 2.5 miles to

Name of Cemetery and also known as	Number of burials	Acres	Condition	Date started or earliest known burial	Township	Range	Section

Graveyard Point Road. Turn right (west) and go about 0.6 of a mile to the historical marker on the right. This is not the site of the cemetery however. Continue ahead along the north base of Graveyard Point to a road right (north). This is the state line. Near here is a ditch road following the irrigation canal. Follow this for perhaps 0.6 of a mile to an arroyo that flows north. The old cemetery is somewhere here near an agate bed diggings. There are 6 adults and 2 infants known to have been buried between April 1891 and November 1913. Possibly 2 other infants are also buried here. (Not shown on Graveyard Point 1967 USGS Quad. map.)

HARPER — A 0.1 4 ? T19S R42E S29

Located 1.5 miles north of the Harper School. Go 0.9 of a mile from the school on Harper-Westfall Road. Continue ahead 0.6 of a mile on Old Mail Road to the cemetery on the right. There are 4 known burials. (Little Valley 1990 USGS Quad. map.)

HENDERSON, JOHN D. — A 0.01 ? 9 Aug 1852 T18S R45E S29

Located 0.7 of a mile southeast of Vale and 500 yards from the Malheur River. This grave is outlined with rock. Henderson died of thirst. (Not shown on Vale East 1967-75 USGS Quad. map.)

IRONSIDE — B 1.5 1 1873 T14S R39E S28

This is in Sections 28 and 29 at Ironside, 47.5 miles from Vale on U.S. Hwy. 26. Turn left (south) onto Rose Creek Road and go a short distance. There were 131 known burials in 1972. (Ironside 1990 USGS Quad. map.)

JAMIESON AREA — A 0.01 ? Pre-1880 T16S R43E ?

Somewhere in the vicinity of Jamieson and the Dell Cemetery. On the west (left) side of U.S. Hwy. 26 and about 16 miles north of Vale there is a fenced graveyard with no markers. The first wife of Charles Becker and their 2

Malheur County

| Name of Cemetery and also known as | Number of burials | Acres | Condition | Date started or earliest known burial | Township | Range | Section |

daughters died of typhoid. Becker remarried and moved to the Westfall area. See the article under his name. (Not shown on Jamieson 1988 USGS Quad. map)

JORDAN, MICHAEL M.
AKA 1. CARROLL, JAMES
   2. FOGLE, JOHN

A   0.01 ? 15 Jul 1864 ?   ?   ?
Somewhere along the Owyhee River near the present Idaho-Oregon State line is the site where Michael M. Jordan, John Fogle, and James Carroll were buried. They were killed by Indians. Jordan discovered gold May 1863 along what is now called Jordan Creek. (Not shown on Beaver Charlie Breaks 1982 USGS Quad. map.)

JORDAN VALLEY
AKA: 1. BAXTERVILLE

C 8   1   1875   T30S R46E   S2
Located on a hillside on the west side of U.S. Hwy. 95. As of 1 June 1990 there were 597 known burials, plus 16 more which could not be located. {11 September 2000} (Jordan Valley 1969 USGS Quad. map.)

JUNTURA [NEW]

B 1   2   1918   T21S R38E   S17
Located 0.5 of a mile east of the old cemetery. There were 22 known burials and 8 more unmarked in 1972. (Juntura 1978 and Stemler Ridge 1990 USGS Quad. maps.)

JUNTURA [OLD]

A 0.5 3 1888-1960   T21S R38E   S17
Located in a field near Juntura, on the north side of U.S. Hwy. 20 northwest of town. There were 14 known burials in 1972-1977. (Juntura 1978 and Stemler Ridge 1990 USGS Quad. maps.)

LITTLEFIELD

A 0.01 ? ?   T23S R40E   S35
Drive west from Vale 23 miles, to the Harper Junction on the Central Oregon Highway, U.S. Hwy. 20. Turn left (south) onto Crowley Road; drive about 26.3 miles on Crowley Road to an intersection. Turn left (east) and go 0.25 of a mile. The cemetery is on the left (north), on the lower slope of a ridge above Dry Creek Valley. Five graves for burials

Name of Cemetery and also known as	Number of burials	Acres	Condition	Date started or earliest known burial	Township	Range	Section

from the old Littlefield Home Ranch were reported, but the stones have been carried off. NOTE: This is on private property. (Alder Creek 1972 USGS Quad. map.)

LOCKWOOD RANCH
AKA: 1. BROWN, DAVID P.
2. MOTT, MOSES

A   0.01   ?   1 Mar 1866   ?   ?   ?
See *In Times Past* (1990) by Hazel R. Fretwell-Johnson, page 58, for an acount of the killing of David P. Brown and Moses Mott by Indians. (Not shown on Arock 1972 or Danner 1969 USGS Quad. maps.)

LOWER SUCCOR CREEK
AKA: 1. ALBERTS, CHARLES

A   0.01   ?   29 Mar 1887   T26S R46E   S22
Charles Alberts was killed by Jacob Mussell. The Alberts Ranch is about 4 miles southeast from Rockville on Succor Creek Road via difficult and winding roads. (The ranch which is not named is shown but not the grave on Rockville 1967 USGS Quad. map.)

MALHEUR CITY

C   1   2   1877   T13S R41E   S29
Located on a hill overlooking the site of old Malheur City off of Mormon Basin Road. In August of 1957, a fire burned all of the wooden markers. There were 117 known burials in 1972. (Bridgeport 1990 USGS Quad. map.)

McRAE RANCH

A   0.01   2   1900   T24S R37E   S9
Located 21.5 miles south of U.S. Hwy. 20, on the Juntura-Riverside Road. There is a fenced, single grave south of Riverside and off of the right (west) side of the road. (McEwen Butte 1972 USGS Quad. map.)

MEXICAN PETE

A   0.01   ?   1912   T34S R41E   ?
Hazel R. Fretwell-Johnson in her book *In Times Past* (1990) writes that there is a grave close to the new Bowden Ranch for Pete Juman (spelling?), better known as Mexican Pete. He was killed by a horse about 1912. (page 84.) (Not shown on Bowden Ranch 1979 USGS Quad. map.)

Malheur County

Name of Cemetery and also known as	Number of burials	Acres	Condition	Date started or earliest known burial	Township	Range	Section

MILLER
AKA: 1. SHUCK,
    WILLIAM

A ? ? 25 Oct 1915 T13S R42E S21
Miller was gold mining community in Mormon Bason in northern Malheur County. It had a post office from 18 July 1913 to 31 March 1917. Miller was less than a mile from the Baker County line so a death certificate #5630 was filed in Baker County. William Shuck was 76 years old and killed by an accidental shotgun discharge and was buried by his neighbors. (The site of Miller is shown but not the grave on Mormon Basin 1990 USGS Quad. map.)

MILLIKIN, CARL
  HAMILTON
AKA: 1. MILLIKIN

A 0.01 ? 1888 T21S R46E ?
Located near Adrian, 1 mile west of and 0.25 of a mile north of Adrian Bridge over the Snake River. The 10-month old infant son of John S. and Hanna Millikan or Millikin was reportedly buried in 1888 or 1889. (Not shown on Adrian 1967 USGS Quad. map.)

MORMON BASIN

? ? ? ? T13S R42E ?
The basin itself is located in Sections 17, 20, and 21. Mormon Basin was the scene of extensive gold mining in 1862. (Not shown on Mormon Basin 1990 USGS Quad. map.)

NYSSA
AKA 1. NYSSA
    MUNICIPAL

D 4.6 1 1883 T19S R46E S26
Located 2 miles west of Nyssa on the north side of Alberta Avenue. There were 961 known burials in 1972. (Cairo 1967 USGS Quad. map.)

OWYHEE

D 1.8 1 1883 T20S R46E S27
Drive 8.5 miles southwesterly from Nyssa on OR. Hwy. 201 to the community of Owyhee. Turn right (west) onto Owyhee Avenue and drive 1 mile to the landmark Latter Day Saints Church (Mormon). The cemetery is adjacent to the church. There were 554 known burials in 1988. (Owyhee 1967 USGS Quad. map.)

Name of Cemetery and also known as	Number of burials	Acres	Condition	Date started or earliest known burial	Township	Range	Section

OWYHEE CROSSING
AKA 1. OWYHEE FERRY

A   ?   ?   1860'S   T31S R41E   ?

See *In Times Past* by Hazel R. Fretwell-Johnson (1990), pages 37-38, for an account of at least 3 separate graves near Owyhee Crossing. This was also known as Owyhee Ferry and was just upstream (south) on the Owyhee River from the mouth of Jordan Creek. Also see the article Chinese massacre. (Not shown on Rome 1972 USGS Quad. map.)

OWYHEE PIONEER

A   ?   5   1884-1900   T21S R46E   ?

Perhaps located in Section 3. This, the oldest cemetery along the Owyhee River is "about 2 miles west of OR. Hwy. 201." Drive southerly from the community of Owyhee on OR. Hwy. 201 for 2.1 miles to the intersection of Overstreet and go 0.75 of a mile to the intersection with Willow Avenue; turn right (north) on Willow Avenue and follow to Riverview Drive which runs left (northwesterly) along the edge of the bluff. At the junction with Bob Rice Road one is about 1.3 miles from OR. Hwy. 201. Bob Rice Road is a county road built in 1936, going down the bluff to a bridge over the Owyhee River. This road displaced the small cemetery and the rocks marking the graves. The present marker was erected in 1966 at the edge of the bluff overlooking the valley of the Owyhee to the north. It enumerates the names and dates of the 7 known burials. (Not shown on Owyhee 1967 USGS Quad. map.)

OWYHEE RIVER
AKA: 1. UTTER PARTY

A   ?   ?   Oct 1860   T20S R46E   ?

Apparently these unmarked graves are in Section 25 or Section 36. They are east of the present Owyhee Junction on OR. Hwy. 201 and near the right (east) bank of the Owyhee River. Of the survivors of the Sinker Creek Massacre near present-day Murphy, Idaho, who reached this area, 5 more starved to death and a 10-year old boy was also killed by Indians in October 1860. See also the article on the Utter party, Baker County. (Not shown on Owyhee 1967 USGS Quad. map.)

Name of Cemetery and also known as	Number of burials	Acres	Condition	Date started or earliest known burial	Township	Range	Section

PARKINSON, MR.

A 0.01 ? Pre-1871 T17S R47E ?

A Mr. Parkinson, who left Nebraska on a wagon train, died and was buried near the mouth of the Malheur River. (Not shown on Payette 1951-74 USGS Quad. map.)

RACEY YARD

? ? ? ? T13S R41E ?

Perhaps located in Section 18. There is a report of burials here, but no information was given for the location. (There is a Racey Brothers Spring shown on the Bridgeport 1990 USGS Quad. map, but no cemetery is indicated.)

RIVERSIDE

B 1.1 2 1908 T23S R37E S22

Located at the junction of South and Middle Forks of the Malheur River near Riverside. Leave U.S. Hwy. 20 at Juntura and go south on Juntura-Riverside Road 16.9 miles, to the bridge over the Malheur River. Continue south another 0.2 of a mile, turn right and cross the South Fork of the Malheur River. The cemetery is 0.25 of a mile from the county road. There are 26 known burials with the latest burials being May of 1952, as of the D.A.R. survey in 1972. (Winnemucca Creek 1979 USGS Quad. map.)

ROCKVILLE

A 0.8 3 1885-1918 T26S R46E S2

Leave OR. Hwy. 201 south of Adrian on Succor Creek Road. Leave Succor Creek Road at the old Rockville School and turn left (east) onto McBride Road, towards the Idaho State Line. About 3 miles from the school and a mile east of the Succor Creek Bridge is the cemetery, 100 yards to the right (south) of the road. An undated reading reported 14 marked burials, 5 unmarked, plus 3 possible additional burials. Rudy Wellbrock, in June of 1991, visited and found the fence down and much damage done to the monuments by livestock. One may continue easterly 7 miles from the cemetery to join U.S. Hwy. 95 in Idaho. {17 June 1991} (Rockville 1967 USGS Quad. map.)

Name of Cemetery and also known as	Number of burials	Acres	Condition	Date started or earliest known burial	Township	Range	Section

SCHWEIZER BABY, JOHN — A 0.01 ? ? T20S R46E S33

Located about 1.5 miles west of the large cemetery at Owyhee on the old Otto Schweizer Place. This grave is presumably along the left (south) side of Owyhee Avenue. (Not shown on Owyhee 1967 USGS Quad. map.)

SHEAVILLE — ? 0.1 ? ? T28S R47E S18

Located east of the bygone locale of Sheaville and just west of the site of the military encampment of Camp Lyons. This cemetery is less than 0.5 of a mile from the Idaho State Line. The burials are on the south side of Cow Creek. (Sheaville 1969 USGS Quad. map.)

SHUMWAY, ALFRED J.
AKA: 1. COX, JOHN W.
     2. COX, SALLY
     3. TRIMBALL, BABY

— A ? 2 1908-1917 T23S R37E S34

The grave sites of Alfred J. Shumway, an early pioneer, John W. Cox and Sally Cox about 1910, and a Baby Trimball died 1917 are located south of Riverside, on a hillside off of the Juntura-Riverside Road. (Not shown on Winnemucca Creek 1979 USGS Quad. map.)

SQUAW CREEK
AKA: 1. BROWN, CHARLIE

— A 0.01 ? 1885 T21S R41E ?

Take U.S. Hwy. 20 from Harper Junction and go about 7 miles to the southwest towards Juntura. At that point Squaw Creek enters the Malheur River. A bad road leads to the left (south) up Squaw Creek and somewhere along it is a small monument, placed in 1885, for one Charlie Brown. The site is simply described as Squaw Creek. The USGS Quad. maps show 2 separate Squaw Creeks in Malheur County. One of them flows into the North Owyhee in Township 34 South, Range 46 East, with scarcely 2 miles of the creek within Oregon and therefore seems unlikely to the compiler to be the correct Squaw Creek. (Not shown on Namorf 1990 or Brewster Reservoir 1980 USGS Quad. maps.)

SUNSET
AKA: 1. ST. JOHN'S CATHOLIC

— D 2 1 1913 T18S R47E S8

Located on Sunset Drive off of Southwest 4th, in Ontario. (Payette 1951-74 USGS Quad. map.)

Name of Cemetery and also known as	Number of burials	Acres	Condition	Date started or earliest known burial	Township	Range	Section

UNKNOWN   ? 0.33 ? ?   T14S R42E   S13

Located 5 miles east of Huntington Junction, near Becker Creek on the north side of Huntington Road and west of Becker Creek about 0.5 of a mile short of the Baker County Line. (Becker Creek 1990 USGS Quad. map.)

UNKNOWN   A ? ? ?   T15S R45E   ?

Perhaps in Section 5. A State Highway Department work crew uncovered an unmarked grave containing the remains of an elderly woman and a child. The site was alongside I-84 Freeway about 10 miles south of Huntington and therefore near the Baker County Line. See the Portland *Oregonian* newspaper articles on 16 March and 26 March 1958. (Not shown on Olds Ferry 1952-74 USGS Quad. map.)

UNKNOWN   ? ? ? ?   T21S R38E   ?

Perhaps located in Section 32. There are 2 unmarked and unknown graves on a hillside southwest of Juntura at a bend in the Malheur River and near a small railway tunnel. (Not shown on Juntura 1978 USGS Quad. map.)

UNKNOWN   A 0.01 5 ?   T32S R40E   ?

Perhaps located in Section 12. Hazel R. Fretwell-Johnson in her book *In Times Past* (1990) on page 101 reports: "There are three graves of unknown men, marked once with river rocks at the top of the grade going down into the old Hubble Place. They are between one and two hundred yards east of where the two roads join. In early days the graves were bare of growth but sagebrush and grass have obliterated the spot now." This ranch was downstream on Crooked Creek from the confluence of Palomino and Crooked Creeks. (Not shown on Rome 1972 USGS Quad. map.)

UNKNOWN   A 0.01 2 ?   T34S R41E   ?

Perhaps located in Section 27. Hazel R. Fretwell-Johnson in her book *In Times Past* (1990) writes: "The well-marked grave at the old main Bowden Station is that of a stranger." This stranger was shot by the

Name of Cemetery and also known as	Number of burials	Acres	Condition	Date started or earliest known burial	Township	Range	Section

hostler (page 85). The gravesite is marked on a sketch map on page 78. (Not shown on the Bowden Ranch 1979 USGS Quad. map.)

UNKNOWN

A 0.01 ? ?   T34S R42E   ?

Located about 10 miles east of the Bowden Ranch. A man, aged about 50, with 4 or 5 saddle horses stopped at the Bowden Ranch Station. He then started out for Silver City. Two or three days later his horses were found; the man was dead in his bed roll at what was called Deadman Water Hole. (Not shown on the Jackies Butte 1980 USGS Quad. map.)

UNKNOWN [DEADMAN BUTTE]

A 0.01 ? ?   T34S R42E   S27

An unknown elderly man froze to death on the butte and his body was found much later. See *In Times Past* (1990) by Hazel R. Fretwell-Johnson, pages 83-84. Note: Deadman Butte is shown as Water Hole Butte on the Jackies Butte 1980 USGS Quad. map. (Not shown on Jackies Butte 1980 USGS map.)

UNKNOWN BASQUE SHEEPHERDER

A 0.01 4 ?   T34S R41E   ?

Hazel Fretwell-Johnson in her book *In Times Past* (1990) page 85, mentions the grave of a Basque sheepherder who froze to death and is buried in the vicinity of the old main Bowden Station. (Not shown on the Bowden Ranch 1979 USGS Quad. map.)

VALE PIONEER
AKA: 1. I.O.O.F

C 5 1 1887   T18S R45E   S17

Located 0.75 of a mile north of Vale on U.S. Hwy. 26. Turn left (west) off of U.S. Hwy. 26 and it is on the north side of Cemetery Road. There were 141 known burials in Sept. of 1982. (Henry Gulch and Vale East 1967-75 USGS Quad. maps.)

VALLEY VIEW
AKA: 1. VALE

D 5 1 1882   T18S R45E   S17

Located 1 mile northwest of Vale, left (west) off of U.S. Hwy. 26 and on the south side of

Name of Cemetery and also known as	Number of burials	Acres	Condition	Date started or earliest known burial	Township	Range	Section

Cemetery Road. The 1848 grave was moved in from the Pioneer Cemetery. (Vale East 1967 USGS Quad. map.)

WATSON	A	0.2	3	1915-1929	T26S	R43E	S24

This cemetery was located on the south side of Owyhee Reservoir and about 50 feet above the waterline at the mouth of Juniper Creek. The site of Watson is flooded. There were 10 graves in 1966. (Diamond Butte 1967 USGS Quad. map.)

WESTFALL	C	3.7	2	1884	T18S	R41E	S21

Go 0.6 of a mile east of Westfall on Bully Creek Road and then another 0.4 of a mile to the right (southeast). There were 161 known graves in 1961, but only 121 legible markers in 1972. (Westfall 1990 USGS Quad. map.)

WILSON, BABY	?	?	?	?	T18S	R38E	S8

There has been a report of an unmarked grave of a baby of the Wilson family. The 1935 *Malheur County Metsker Landowner Atlas* names a Wilson Ranch here on the west side of Bendire Creek, northeast of the Beulah Reservoir. (Not shown on Hunter Mountain 1990 USGS Quad. map. The Quad. map shows that no buildings remain on the site.)

AGENCY VALLEY see **BEULAH**	MALHEUR CO.	T18S	R37E	S35
ALBERTS, CHARLES see **LOWER SUCCOR CREEK**				
	MALHEUR CO.	T26S	R46E	S22
ALBERTS RANCH see **LOWER SUCCOR CREEK**				
	MALHEUR CO.	T26S	R46E	S22
ANNEX see **FAIRVIEW**	MALHEUR CO.	T15S	R47E	S33
APPLEGATE	MALHEUR CO.	T16S	R47E	?
APPLEGATE, JAMES see **APPLEGATE**	MALHEUR CO.	T16S	R47E	?
AROCK	MALHEUR CO.	T30S	R42E	?
BARKER, JAMES	MALHEUR CO.	T23S	R37E	?
BARKER PLACE, CLARENCE see **APPLEGATE**				
	MALHEUR CO.	T16S	R47E	?
BAXTERVILLE see **JORDAN VALLEY**	MALHEUR CO.	T30S	R46E	S2
BECKER, CHARLES	MALHEUR CO.	T18S	R40E	S8
BECKER, CHARLES see **JAMIESON AREA**				
	MALHEUR CO.	T16S	R43E	?
BECKER FAMILY see **BECKER, CHARLES**				
	MALHEUR CO.	T18S	R40E	S8
BECKER RANCH, JIM	MALHEUR CO.	T18S	R41E	S27
BETTERLY, HAZEL	MALHEUR CO.	T20S	R47E	?
BEULAH	MALHEUR CO.	T18S	R37E	S35
BLACK, MRS.	MALHEUR CO.	T20S	R46E	S26
BOUNCER, JOHN see **BECKER RANCH, JIM**				
	MALHEUR CO.	T18S	R41E	S27
BOWDEN RANCH see **MEXICAN PETE**	MALHEUR CO.	T34S	R41E	?
BOWDEN STATION see **UNKNOWN BASQUE SHEEPHERDER**				
	MALHEUR CO.	T34S	R41E	?
BROGAN	MALHEUR CO.	T15S	R42E	S26
BROWN, CHARLIE see **SQUAW CREEK**	MALHEUR CO.	T21S	R41E	?
BROWN, DAVID P. see **LOCKWOOD RANCH**				
	MALHEUR CO.	?	?	?
CAMP LYONS see **SHEAVILLE**	MALHEUR CO.	T28S	R47E	S18
CARROLL, JAMES see **JORDAN, MICHAEL M.**				
	MALHEUR CO.	?	?	?
CARTER HOMESTEAD, JOE	MALHEUR CO.	T20S	R39E	S29
CEMETERY SPRING	MALHEUR CO.	T19S	R41E	S35
CHAMBERS, MRS. see **CHAMBERS, SARAH**				
	MALHEUR CO.	T18S	R37E	S33
CHAMBERS, ROWLAND see **CHAMBERS, SARAH**				
	MALHEUR CO.	T18S	R37E	S33
CHAMBERS, SARAH	MALHEUR CO.	T18S	R37E	S33
CHARBONNEAU, JEAN BAPTISTE	MALHEUR CO.	T30S	R44E	S16
CHINAMEN'S MASSACRE see **CHINESE MASSACRE**				
	MALHEUR CO.	T31S	R41E	?
CHINESE MASSACRE	MALHEUR CO.	T31S	R41E	?
CORD	MALHEUR CO.	T28S	R38E	S7
COX, JOHN W. see **SHUMWAY, ALFRED J.**				
	MALHEUR CO.	T23S	R37E	S34
COX, SALLY see **SHUMWAY, ALFRED J.**				
	MALHEUR CO.	T23S	R37E	S34
CRISWELL BOY	MALHEUR CO.	T20S	R46E	?
CRISWELL, FRED see **CRISWELL BOY**	MALHEUR CO.	T20S	R46E	?

CURTIS see **CORD**	MALHEUR CO.	T28S	R38E	S7
DANNER	MALHEUR CO.	T30S	R44E	S16
DELL	MALHEUR CO.	T16S	R43E	S15
DOWELL RANCH, TOM see **CORD**	MALHEUR CO.	T28S	R38E	S7
DUNCAN FAMILY see **APPLEGATE**	MALHEUR CO.	T16S	R47E	?
ERICKSON FAMILY see **APPLEGATE**	MALHEUR CO.	T16S	R47E	?
EVERGREEN	MALHEUR CO.	T18S	R47E	S9
FAIR-VIEW see **FAIRVIEW**	MALHEUR CO.	T15S	R47E	S33
FAIRVIEW	MALHEUR CO.	T15S	R47E	S33
FIELDS, ARCHIE see **FIELDS, HAROLD**				
	MALHEUR CO.	T19S	R47E	S32
FIELDS, HAROLD	MALHEUR CO.	T19S	R47E	S32
FIELDS, LORENA RAMBO see **FIELDS, HAROLD**				
	MALHEUR CO.	T19S	R47E	S32
FOGLE, JOHN see **JORDAN, MICHAEL M.**				
	MALHEUR CO.	?	?	?
GLASCOCK BABY	MALHEUR CO.	?	?	?
GLASCOCK, HENRY L. "BULLDOG" see **GLASCOCK BABY**				
	MALHEUR CO.	?	?	?
GOODWIN RANCH see **GOODWIN TOMB**	MALHEUR CO.	T17S	R37E	S19
GOODWIN, THOMAS HUGH see **GOODWIN TOMB**				
	MALHEUR CO.	T17S	R37E	S19
GOODWIN TOMB	MALHEUR CO.	T17S	R37E	S19
GRAVEYARD POINT	MALHEUR CO.	T23S	R47E	?
HARPER	MALHEUR CO.	T19S	R42E	S29
HARRIS PLACE see **BETTERLY, HAZEL**				
	MALHEUR CO.	T20S	R47E	?
HENDERSON, JOHN D.	MALHEUR CO.	T18S	R45E	S29
HOOPER FAMILY see **APPLEGATE**	MALHEUR CO.	T16S	R47E	?
HUBBLE PLACE see **UNKNOWN**	MALHEUR CO.	T32S	R40E	?
I.O.O.F. see **VALE PIONEER**	MALHEUR CO.	T18S	R45E	S17
INSKEEP see **CHARBONNEAU, JEAN BAPTISTE**				
	MALHEUR CO.	T30S	R44E	S16
INSKIP RANCHE see **CHARBONNEAU, JEAN BAPTISTE**				
	MALHEUR CO.	T30S	R44E	S16
INSKIP'S STATION see **CHARBONNEAU, JEAN BAPTISTE**				
	MALHEUR CO.	T30S	R44E	S16
IRONSIDE	MALHEUR CO.	T14S	R39E	S28
JAMIESON see **DELL**	MALHEUR CO.	T16S	R43E	S15
JAMIESON AREA	MALHEUR CO.	T16S	R43E	?
JEMERSON [Sic] see **DELL**	MALHEUR CO.	T16S	R43E	S15
JORDAN, MICHAEL M.	MALHEUR CO.	?	?	?
JORDAN VALLEY	MALHEUR CO.	T30S	R46E	S2
JUMAN, PETE see **MEXICAN PETE**	MALHEUR CO.	T34S	R41E	?
JUNTURA [NEW]	MALHEUR CO.	T21S	R38E	S17
JUNTURA [OLD]	MALHEUR CO.	T21S	R38E	S17
KING, NAHUM see **CHAMBERS, SARAH**	MALHEUR CO.	T18S	R37E	S33
LITTLEFIELD	MALHEUR CO.	T23S	R40E	S35
LITTLEFIELD HOME RANCH, OLD see **LITTLEFIELD**				
	MALHEUR CO.	T23S	R40E	S35
LOCKWOOD RANCH	MALHEUR CO.	?	?	?
LOWER SUCCOR CREEK	MALHEUR CO.	T26S	R46E	S22

MALHEUR CITY	MALHEUR CO.	T13S	R41E	S29
McRAE RANCH	MALHEUR CO.	T24S	R37E	S9
MEXICAN PETE	MALHEUR CO.	T34S	R41E	?
MILLER	MALHEUR CO.	T13S	R42E	S21
MILLIKIN see **MILLIKIN, CARL HAMILTON**				
	MALHEUR CO.	T21S	R46E	?
MILLIKIN, CARL HAMILTON	MALHEUR CO.	T21S	R46E	?
MILLIKIN, HANNA see **MILLIKIN, CARL HAMILTON**				
	MALHEUR CO.	T21S	R46E	?
MILLIKIN, JOHN S. see **MILLIKIN, CARL HAMILTON**				
	MALHEUR CO.	T21S	R46E	?
MORMON BASIN	MALHEUR CO.	T13S	R42E	?
MOTT, MOSES see **LOCKWOOD RANCH**	MALHEUR CO.	?	?	?
MULLINS, MARTHA see **BECKER RANCH, JIM**				
	MALHEUR CO.	T18S	R41E	S27
MULLINS, MARY JANE WESTFALL see **BECKER RANCH, JIM**				
	MALHEUR CO.	T18S	R41E	S27
MUSSELL, JACOB see **LOWER SUCCOR CREEK**				
	MALHEUR CO.	T26S	R46E	S22
NYSSA	MALHEUR CO.	T19S	R46E	S26
NYSSA MUNICIPAL see **NYSSA**	MALHEUR CO.	T19S	R46E	S26
ONTARIO see **EVERGREEN**	MALHEUR CO.	T18S	R47E	S9
OWYHEE	MALHEUR CO.	T20S	R46E	S27
OWYHEE CROSSING	MALHEUR CO.	T31S	R41E	?
OWYHEE FERRY see **OWYHEE CROSSING**				
	MALHEUR CO.	T31S	R41E	?
OWYHEE PIONEER	MALHEUR CO.	T21S	R46E	?
OWYHEE RIVER	MALHEUR CO.	T20S	R46E	?
PARKINSON, MR.	MALHEUR CO.	T17S	R47E	?
PIONEER [ONTARIO] see **APPLEGATE**				
	MALHEUR CO.	T16S	R47E	?
RACEY YARD	MALHEUR CO.	T13S	R41E	?
RANDALL, BILLY see **APPLEGATE**	MALHEUR CO.	T16S	R47E	?
RIVERSIDE	MALHEUR CO.	T23S	R37E	S22
ROCKVILLE	MALHEUR CO.	T26S	R46E	S2
ROUND HILL see **GRAVEYARD POINT**	MALHEUR CO.	T23S	R47E	?
ST. JOHN'S CATHOLIC see **SUNSET**	MALHEUR CO.	T18S	R47E	S8
SCHWEIZER BABY, JOHN	MALHEUR CO.	T20S	R46E	S33
SCHWEIZER PLACE, OTTO see **SCHWEIZER BABY, JOHN**				
	MALHEUR CO.	T20S	R46E	S33
SCOTT see **BEULAH**	MALHEUR CO.	T18S	R37E	S35
SEAWARD see **CORD**	MALHEUR CO.	T28S	R38E	S7
SEAWARD FAMILY see **CORD**	MALHEUR CO.	T28S	R38E	S7
SEWARD see **CORD**	MALHEUR CO.	T28S	R38E	S7
SHEAVILLE	MALHEUR CO.	T28S	R47E	S18
SHUCK, WILLIAM see **MILLER**	MALHEUR CO.	T13S	R42E	S21
SHUMWAY, ALFRED J.	MALHEUR CO.	T23S	R37E	S34
SQUAW CREEK	MALHEUR CO.	T21S	R41E	?
SUNSET	MALHEUR CO.	T18S	R47E	S8
TRIMBALL, BABY see **SHUMWAY, ALFRED J.**				
	MALHEUR CO.	T23S	R37E	S34
UNKNOWN	MALHEUR CO.	T14S	R42E	S13

UNKNOWN	MALHEUR CO.	T15S	R45E	?
UNKNOWN	MALHEUR CO.	T21S	R38E	?
UNKNOWN	MALHEUR CO.	T32S	R40E	?
UNKNOWN	MALHEUR CO.	T34S	R41E	?
UNKNOWN	MALHEUR CO.	T34S	R42E	?
UNKNOWN [DEADMAN BUTTE]	MALHEUR CO.	T34S	R42E	S27
UNKNOWN BASQUE SHEEPHERDER	MALHEUR CO.	T34S	R41E	?
UTTER PARTY see OWYHEE RIVER	MALHEUR CO.	T20S	R46E	?
VAIN RANCH see GLASCOCK BABY	MALHEUR CO.	?	?	?
VALE see VALLEY VIEW	MALHEUR CO.	T18S	R45E	S17
VALE PIONEER	MALHEUR CO.	T18S	R45E	S17
VALLEY VIEW	MALHEUR CO.	T18S	R45E	S17
WATSON	MALHEUR CO.	T26S	R43E	S24
WEISER JUNCTION see FAIRVIEW	MALHEUR CO.	T15S	R47E	S33
WESTFALL	MALHEUR CO.	T18S	R41E	S21
WILLOW CREEK see DELL	MALHEUR CO.	T16S	R43E	S15
WILSON BABY	MALHEUR CO.	T18S	R38E	S8
WILSON FAMILY see WILSON BABY	MALHEUR CO.	T18S	R38E	S8
WILSON RANCH see WILSON BABY	MALHEUR CO.	T18S	R38E	S8

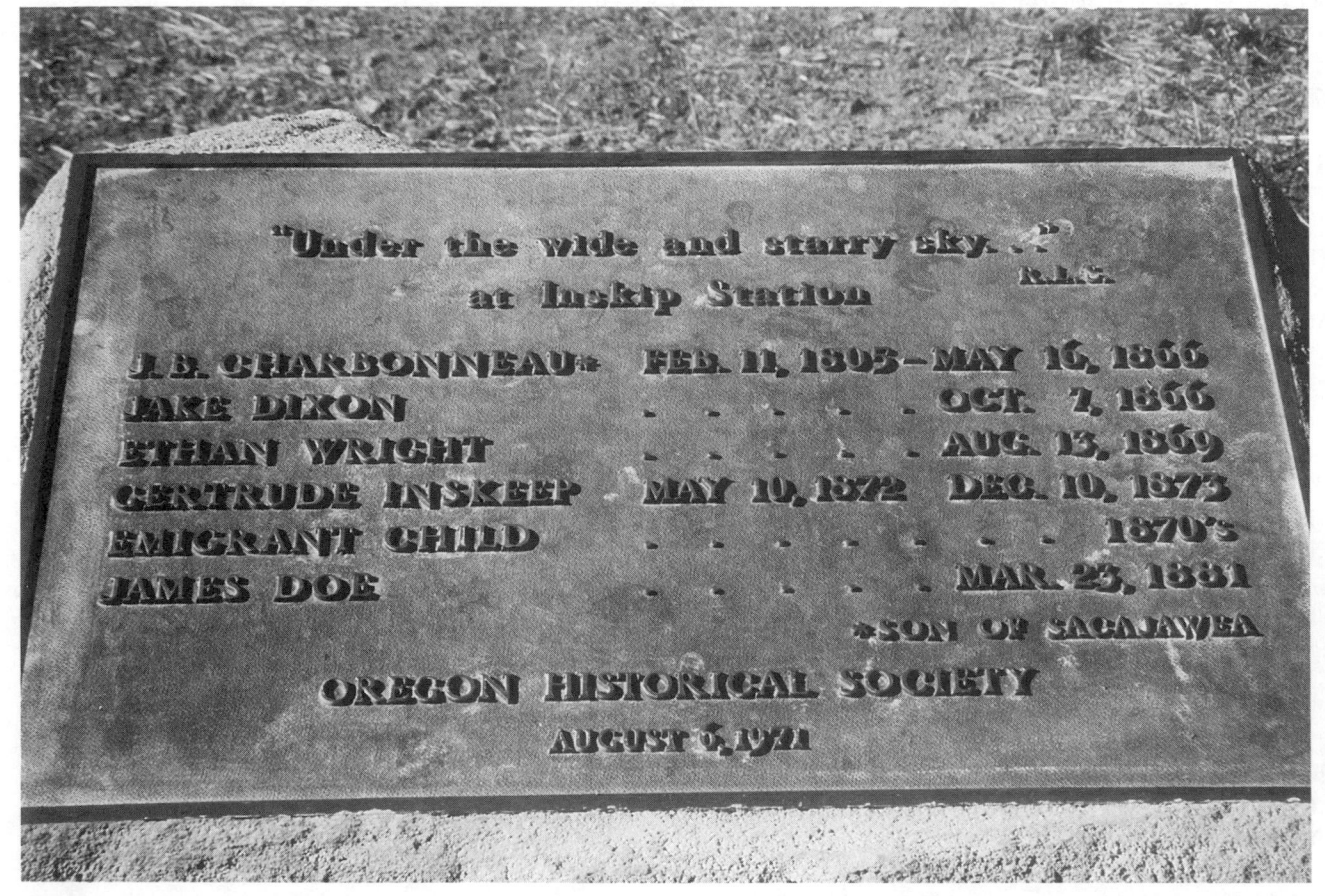

Charbonneau, Jean Baptiste
Janice M. Healy (2000)

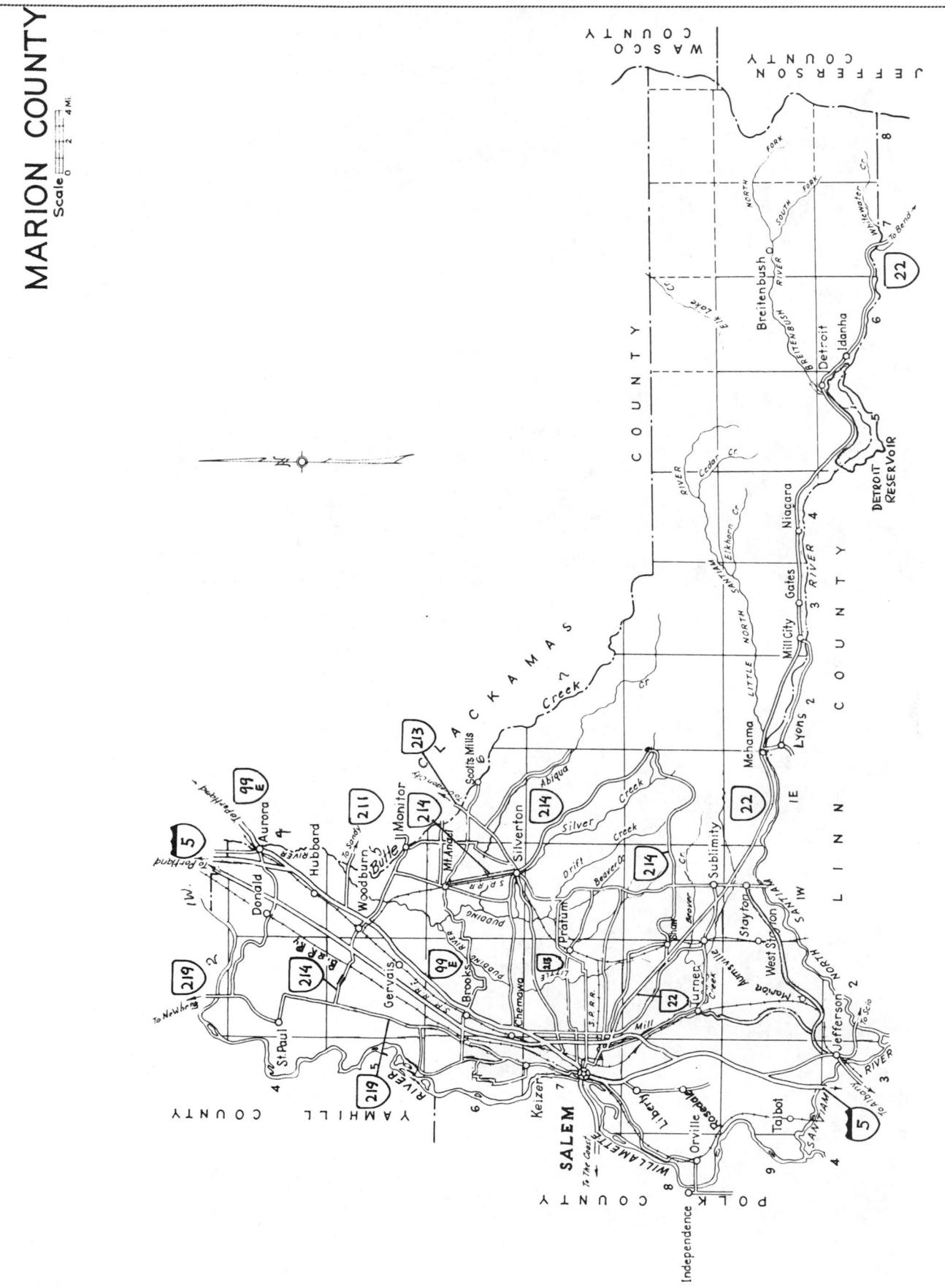

MARION COUNTY

Scale 0 2 4 Mi.

St. Paul's Catholic
Dean H. Byrd (1988)

City View
Ruth C. Bishop (2000)

Oregon Burial Site Guide
Marion County

Area: 1,194 square miles
Population (1998): 268,541
County seat: Salem, Population: 120,835
County established: 5 July 1843

Marion County was the site of the first agricultural settlements of any scale. The settlers at first were Hudsons Bay fur traders whose contracts had expired. They were mostly French Canadians and in the 1830's and early 1840's took up farms on what was soon called French Prairie. Wagon trains of immigrants from the mid-west began arriving in 1843 to occupy the desirable lands suitable for farming. The Willamette Mission was started in 1834 and had a cemetery, mostly for Indians. This seems to be the earliest organized cemetery. French burials at St. Paul's church date from 1837. By 1840 there was a cemetery at the new settlement of Salem and by the mid-1850's there were at least 15 additional organized cemeteries in the county. European settlers (Scandinavians) established Valley View (1893), (Germans and Swiss) Mt. Angel, Mt. Angel Abbey (1860), Apostolic (1866), Pratum (1898), St. Boniface (1880) and Aurora (1886). After World War II there was an influx of Russian Old Believers in and around Woodburn. Still more recently are Mexicans at Woodburn, Mt. Angel and St. Paul. Marion County is also the site of the State institutions. There were many burials and cremations especially of the insane. Marion County also has one Indian Cemetery for the Federal School at Chemawa.

St. Barbara's
Dean H. Byrd (1988)

Marion County

623

Miller

An example why you need to view all sides of stone.

Dean H. Byrd (1989)

Aumsville

Dean H. Byrd (1989)

Old Believer Church

Dean H. Byrd (1990)

St. Luke's Columbarium
Dean H. Byrd (1990)

Mt. Angel
Dean H. Byrd (1990)

Salem Pioneer
Dean H. Byrd (1992)

Name of Cemetery and also known as	Number of burials	Acres	Condition	Date started or earliest known burial	Township	Range	Section

ADAMS FAMILY

A ? 5 1866 T9S R3W S12

Located in the hills south of Salem, south off of Ridgeway Drive Southeast. (Not shown on Turner 1969-86 USGS Quad. map.)

APOSTOLIC
AKA: 1. GERMAN
        CHRISTIAN
        APOSTOLIC
   2. KAUFMAN
   3. KAUFMAN
        ROAD
   4. PUDDING
        RIVER
   5. SWITZERLAND

C 0.5 1 1885 T7S R1W S8

Located about 5.5 or 6 miles southwest of Silverton, on the north side of Kaufman Road Northeast and nearly 2 miles west of Cascade Highway Northeast. It is on the east bank of the Pudding River and on the Hardin and Julia McCallister D.L.C. #49, OC #322. {27 November 1989} (Stayton Northeast 1969 USGS Quad. map.)

ASYLUM
AKA: 1. HOSPITAL
        CREMATORIUM
   2. OREGON STATE
        HOSPITAL
   3. O.S.H.
   4. O.S.I.A.
   5. STATE
        CREMATORIUM

? ? 7 1883-1914 T7S R3W S25

Located in Salem across Asylum Road (now Center Street) from the State Insane Asylum (now the State Hospital) and nearly adjoining Lee Mission Cemetery. The Asylum building was completed in October 1883 and the insane were then brought in from around the state. The first burial is dated 11 November 1883 and the last 12 March 1914. There are indications, however, that there were burials here before the Asylum was built. The *"Illustrated Historical Atlas Map of Marion and Linn Counties,"* by Edgar Williams and Company 1878, on page 38, shows a cemetery symbol just east of the Orphanage. The orphans were housed across the street from the future Asylum. About 1914 the cemetery site was needed for building space so the bodies were exhumed and cremated in a new crematorium at the Asylum. The Asylum Crematorium was in operation from 1914 to 1971 and performed 5,132 cremations. In 1979, 3,809 cremains were placed in burial vaults underneath a drained lily pond near the tennis courts. Families who wish the canister of a relative may apply to the Oregon State Hospital and the canister will be retrieved (4 Nov. 1984 *Oregonian*). (The State Hospital is shown but not the cemetery on Salem West 1969-86 USGS Quad. map.)

Marion County

Name of Cemetery and also known as	Number of burials	Acres	Condition	Date started or earliest known burial	Township	Range	Section

AUMSVILLE
AKA: 1. BUTLER

C 2.4 2 1869 T8S R1W S30
Located northeast of Aumsville. Leave the town and go east on Mill Creek Road about 0.6 of a mile past the railroad crossing; turn left onto Leverman Road, and then left again onto Albus Road, which crosses over the North Santiam Highway (OR. Hwy. 22). On the north side of the overcrossing, turn left onto Steinkamp Road, which leads directly to the cemetery. It is on the John and Elizabeth Taylor D.L.C. #43, OC #21. {6 September 1989} (Stayton 1969-86 USGS Quad. map.)

AURORA COMMUNITY

D 5.76 2 Nov. 1862 T4S R1W S14
Located west of Aurora about 1 mile on Ehlen Road Northeast; turn left (south) on Oak Lane. {29 March 1989} (Woodburn 1956-85 USGS Quad. map.)

BELCREST MEMORIAL PARK AND MAUSOLEUM

E 55 1 1927 T8S R3W S4
This is the largest cemetery in Salem. Located in south Salem. Go south from downtown via Commercial Street, turn right at a curve onto Liberty Road. Leave Liberty Road to the right onto Browning Avenue at the power station. Go up hill on Browning Avenue to the cemetery on the right at 1295 Browning Avenue South, Salem. There were 22,603 interments as of 6 April 1998. {15 September 1989} (Salem West 1969-86 USGS Quad. map.)

BELLE PASSI

E 12 1 1852 T5S R1W S19
Located just off of Hwy. 99E at Woodburn, at 997 Belle Passi Road. It is on the Peter Raymond D.L.C. #58, OC #3374. NOTE: The Belle Passi Memorial Mausoleum across the road is a separate burial site. {20 October 1988} (Woodburn and Silverton 1956-85 USGS Quad. map.)

BELLE PASSI MEMORIAL MAUSOLEUM

C 1 1 1974 T5S R1W S19
Leave OR. Hwy. 99E onto Belle Passi Road at the south edge of Woodburn. Drive 0.2 of a mile to the mausoleum on the left (south) and opposite Belle Passi Cemetery. The two are separate entities. Located on the Joseph

Name of Cemetery and also known as	Number of burials	Acres	Condition	Date started or earliest known burial	Township	Range	Section

Engle D.L.C. #62, OC #2561. (7 June 1993)
(Not shown on Silverton 1956-85 USGS Quad.
map.)

BELLINGER FAMILY

A ? 6 1878   T9S R3W   S35
The graves were a mile north of Jefferson, on
a bluff above Talbot Road and just west of
the Robert Terhune Farm (1980's information).
The Bellinger graves were moved at an unknown
date to the Jefferson Cemetery; on the John
Bellinger D.L.C. #54, OC #1722. (Not shown
on Albany 1970-75 USGS Quad. map.)

BETHANY PIONEER
  AKA: 1. SCANDIA
        2. SCANTY
        3. SILVER CREEK

D 3 2 1850   T6S R1W   S33
Located 2 miles west of Silverton on
Northeast Pine Street and Hazel Green Road.
This was known as Silver Creek from 1850-
1899, and as Bethany Pioneer since 1899.
There are many unidentified gravesites here.
It is on the Elias Cox D.L.C. #43, OC #2192.
{25 August 1988} (Silverton 1956-85 USGS
Quad. map.)

BIELENBERG
  AKA: 1. BEILENBERG

? ? ? ?   T8S R1W   ?
Located "near Sublimity." That is all of the
information given in the report of this
burial site. (Not shown on Stayton 1969-86
USGS Quad. map.)

BLOOR
  AKA: 1. BLOUGHER

? ? ? ?   T8S R2W   S22
Located northeast of Turner, 70th Place
Southeast and Ogle Road. This is in the
midst of a field near the top of a knoll
(June 1982). NOTE: This site is on private
property. (Not shown on Turner 1969-86 USGS
Quad. map.)

BONNEY FAMILY
  AKA: 1. MacLAREN
         SCHOOL

A 0.01 ? 1870   T5S R1W   S9
MacLaren is the state school for delinquent
boys located at Woodburn. The *Statesman-
Journal* issue of 25 September 1995 has an
article on this obscure burial site. The
Bonney family deeded the land to the state in
1927. The known burials are now enclosed in
a 10' X 10' fenced enclosure and had three

markers, two of which are now gone. These were of an adult and a youth. The latter was presumably 13 year-old John Marshall, recorded as buried here on 10 May 1898. There remains a broken marker to John T.: infant son of _____ Bonney, 5 November 1870. The burial ground is east of the water tower and near a walnut orchard. (Not shown on Woodburn 1956-85 USGS Quad. map.)

BOYS
AKA: 1. GATH ROAD
2. STATE REFORM
SCHOOL

A   0.1   1   1908-1910   T8S   R2W   S17
The same block of State-owned land southeast of Salem, which is now the Mill Creek Correction Facility, was purchased as the site of the Oregon Reform School for Boys. It was operated as such from 1908 to 1927, when a fire destroyed the main building. The boys were moved to MacLaren School at Woodburn. A small fenced cemetery is located on the north side of Gath Road Southeast, near its junction with Turner Road Southeast. Located on the John Herren D.L.C. #60, OC #1152 {3 August 1989} (Turner 1969-86 USGS Quad. map.)

BROOKS CATHOLIC
AKA: 1. LABISH CENTER
2. LaFLEMME
3. SKUNK HOLLOW
4. SKUNKVILLE

A   0.75   3   1894   T6S   R2W   S21
Located in Sections 21 and 22, between Brooks and Labish Center at what was once known as Skunkville. It is 1.5 miles east of OR. Hwy. 99E on Brooklake Road and 65th Avenue Northeast, on the Alexander Lapratte D.L.C. #67, OC #1912. {30 August 1988} (Gervais 1957-85 USGS Quad. map.)

BUTTEVILLE [NEW]

D   3   2   1858   T3S   R1W   S32
Located on the east side of Schultz Road, northeast of Butteville. The north portion of this cemetery is on Anton Cone D.L.C. #39, OC #572, but most of this cemetery is on non-D.L.C. land. {22 September 1988} (Sherwood 1961-85 USGS Quad. map.)

BUTTEVILLE [OLD]

?   ?   7   1836-1858   T3S   R1W   S32
The first cemetery was located by the present I.O.O.F. Hall on the right (north) side of Arndt Road Northeast, 0.4 of a mile west of

Name of Cemetery and also known as	Number of burials	Acres	Condition	Date started or earliest known burial	Township	Range	Section

the crossroads with Schultz Road Northeast. This is at the top of the grade before Arndt Road dips down into Butteville, an old river town in the far north of Marion County. The public school, later the I.O.O.F. Hall, was built on the site of the cemetery. Presumably most of burials were transferred to the present Butteville Cemetery on Schultz Road. It is on the Joseph LaForte D.L.C. #39, OC #1734. (Not on Sherwood 1961-85 USGS Quad. map.)

CALVARY — D 3.8 1 ? T6S R1W S3
This is the principal cemetery for Mt. Angel and is located northeast of Mt. Angel on OR. Hwy. 214. (Silverton 1956-85 USGS Quad. map.)

CALVARY BAPTIST CHURCH COLUMBARIUM — ? ? 1 ? T7S R3W S27
Located in Salem at 1230 Liberty Street Southeast between Wilson and Miller Streets. (The church is depicted on the Salem West 1969-86 USGS Quad. map.)

CALVARY LUTHERAN CHURCH COLUMBARIUM [STAYTON] — ? ? 1 ? T9S R1W S10
Located at 198 Fern Ridge Road in Stayton. At the fourway intersection on the ridge at the north edge of Stayton, which is also 1st Avenue and Fern Ridge, turn east onto Fern Ridge Road. The church is on the right (south) before one reaches 3rd Avenue. This is very close to Lone Oak Cemetery. (Not on Stayton 1969-86 USGS Quad. map.)

CAMPBELL-GRIER
AKA: 1. BOEDIGHEIMER
2. LONE OAK [OLD]
3. LONE OAK II
4. STAYTON PIONEER
— C 1 2 1873 T9S R1W S2
Located northeast of Stayton on the east side of Boedigheimer Road, about 0.5 of a mile north of OR. Hwy. 22. {26 February 1989} (Stayton 1969-86 USGS Quad. map.)

CATACOMBS — A 0.01 11 1849-1851 T4S R2W S19
The present Catholic church in St. Paul was built in 1846 superseding a log church erected in 1836. The first burial was on 4

Name of Cemetery and also known as	Number of burials	Acres	Condition	Date started or earliest known burial	Township	Range	Section

April 1849 of Sister Renilde, one of the sisters of Notre Dame De Namur, a native of Belgium. She was later removed to the present Nun's Corner in the main cemetery of St. Paul. There are still 3 known burials underneath the church, all were local young girls buried between 31 December 1849 and 13 April 1851. (The church is shown on the St. Paul 1956-85 USGS Quad. map.)

CHAMPOEG
AKA: 1. CASE
    2. DONALD
    3. OLD MASONIC
    4. SCHOOL
       DIST. #2
    5. YERGEN
    6. YERGENS
       GRAVEYARD
    7. YERGENS',
       WILLIAM
    8. YERGENVILLE
       MISSION

C 2   2   June 1853   T4S R2W   S12
Leave the Champoeg Road by Champoeg State Park and about 0.25 of a mile east of the bridge over Champoeg Creek. Turn right (south) towards Woodburn on Case Road. Drive about one mile to a roadway right (west) lined with fir trees. A short drive brings one to the cemetery on the right bank of Case Creek. The parking lot is the site of the Yergenville Church. The south half of the cemetery was deeded in 1862 and the north half in 1892 by the Masons. {22 September 1988} (St. Paul and Woodburn 1956-85 USGS Quad. maps.)

CHEMAWA

C 0.5 2   1886   T6S R3W   S36
Located at Township 6 South, Range 3 West, Section 36 and Township 7 South, Range 3 West, Section 1. At the Chemawa Indian School on the west side of Indian School Road, as you go south towards Salem. {6 January 1990} (Salem East 1969-86 USGS Quad. map.)

CITY VIEW, MT.
CREST ABBEY
MAUSOLEUM AND
SUNRISE GARDEN
MAUSOLEUM
AKA: 1. FAIRMONT
       HILL

E 42   1   1893   T7S R3W   S33
Go out South Commercial Street from downtown Salem and turn right (west) on Hoyt Street, then go past the Salem Pioneer Cemetery on the right through a gate to the top of the hill. Located at 690 Hoyt Street South, Salem. There are more than 20,000 burials which include 4-5,000 inurnments in the mausoleums as of March 1998. {15 August 1991} (Salem West 1969-86 USGS Quad. map.)

Name of Cemetery and also known as	Number of burials	Acres	Condition	Date started or earliest known burial	Township	Range	Section

CLAGGETT
AKA: 1. CLEAR LAKE
2. SMITH

| C | 3.59 | 2 | | 1841 | T6S | R3W | S26 |

Located in Keizer the top of a low hill, north of the McNary Golf Course, west off of Wheatland Road North and on Bolf Terrace Road. The west portion of the cemetery is within the Alvis Smith D.L.C. #69, OC #2702. Mrs. Isaac Smith who died in 1841 was the first burial. {1 May 1988} (Mission Bottom 1967-93 USGS Quad. map.)

CLOVERDALE
AKA: 1. CORNELIUS
2. I.O.O.F. [MARION]
3. STAPLES

| C | 0.96 | 1 | | 1855 | T9S | R2W | S7 |

Located between Turner and Marion, west off of Parrish Gap Road Southeast and on Cloverdale Cemetery Road. It is on the Simon Smith D.L.C. #37, OC #1028. {3 June 1988} (Turner 1969-86 USGS Quad. map.)

COATES INFANT

| A | ? | ? | | 27 Jan 1914 | T8S | R2W | S19 |

An unnamed male infant born 17 January 1914 is buried "8 miles southwest of Salem" according to Death Certificate #246 for Marion County, 1914. E. S. Coates was the father and _____ Vanderbilt the mother. According to the November 1929 *Metsker Landownership Atlas of Marion County*; E. S. Coates owned land on the east side of what is now Coates Drive Southeast at its junction with what is now Wiltsey Loop Southeast just outside of what is in 1997 the south city limits of Salem. Located on the John Herron [Sic] D.L.C. #60, OC #1152. (Not shown on Turner 1969-86 USGS Quad. map.)

COLBY FARM, J. A.

| ? | ? | ? | | 14 Jan 1921 | ? | ? | ? |

Marion County Death Certificate #29 for 1921 reports the death of Amanda M. Colby, born 29 November 1843, died 14 January 1921. She was the wife of J.A. Colby. She was buried on 16 January 1921 on their farm, described as being along Salem, R. F. D. #3. We have no idea now as to where this would be located.

COX
AKA: 1. ANKENY
2. ANKENY BOTTOM

| B | 1 | 2 | | 22 May 1849 | T9S | R3W | S5 |

Located about 1.5 miles northwest of Buena Vista Road South by way of Sidney Road. At the south edge of the Ankeny Hill Vineyards

Name of Cemetery and also known as	Number of burials	Acres	Condition	Date started or earliest known burial	Township	Range	Section

3. ANKENY SCHOOL
4. SCHOOL
   DISTRICT #36
5. SIDNEY STATION

is a private driveway, which is about 0.25 of a mile from the cemetery up the hill. This is usually blocked by locked gates; on the Joseph and Martha Cox D.L.C. #38, OC #762. NOTE: You must go through private property to get to this cemetery. {15 June 1990} (Sidney 1970-86 USGS Quad. map.)

CROOKED FINGER

A ? 12 1866-1916 T7S R2E S8

Located on Crooked Finger Road 6.7 miles from Scotts Mills, at the 90 degree turn from east to south. A 1978 report indicates that it was destroyed in recent logging operations. After 1978 one visitor said you could still see old plantings of iris, but in May 1989 the compiler visited this site during the iris season and found that there was no sign left of the cemetery. There is now a Christmas tree farm on the site. NOTE: This site is on private property. (Not shown on Elk Prairie 1985 USGS Quad. map.)

CULVER, DAVID

A ? 5 31 Dec 1874 T7S R1W S36

This burial is very close to the intersection of Victor Point Road Northeast and Riches Road Northeast; on the David and Elizabeth Culver D.L.C. #42, OC #17. (Not shown on Stayton Northeast 1969 USGS Quad. map.)

DAVENPORT FAMILY

? ? ? 1860-1870 T7S R1W S22

Here is the grave of the mother of cartoonist Homer Davenport. She died of smallpox, and 2 of her infant children who had died earlier are buried here also. This is on the east side of Cascade Highway and just north of the junction with Sunnyview Road Northeast. NOTE: This site is on private property. (Not shown on Stayton Northeast 1969 USGS Quad. map.)

EOFF

A 0.5 4 1852-1900 T7S R2W S25

Located east of Salem via State Street East. Pass the Howell Prairie Road Southeast junction with State Street and continue east for 0.3 of a mile, then turn right (south) on Sanrodee Drive Southeast. This cemetery is

Name of Cemetery and also known as	Number of burials	Acres	Condition	Date started or earliest known burial	Township	Range	Section

in a subdivision and hidden from Sanrodee Road by a high bank and trees. There were 12 burials noted in 1968. This is on the George and Nancy Eoff D.L.C. #46, OC #309. {3 August 1989} (Salem East 1969-86 USGS Quad. map.)

ESSON MEMORIAL, IDA
AKA: 1. ESSON FAMILY

A   0.5   1   Sept. 1891   T6S   R1W   S5
Located on the old Esson Farm west of Mt. Angel and off of Way Park Drive Northeast. Access is by a driveway through a field from Way Park Drive, then walk to the cemetery on a bluff above the Pudding River bottomlands. There were 21 graves with markers in September of 1989; on the John C. and Sarah Carey D.L.C. #58, OC #257. NOTE: This site is on private property. {7 September 1989} (Not shown on Silverton 1956-85 USGS Quad. map.)

FAIRFIELD

B   1   2   Nov. 1861   T5S   R2W   S19
Located north off of River Road Northeast, near Milepost 9. It is not visible from the road and the access road is gated. This is on the Lorenzo A. Byrd D.L.C. #102, OC #1871, donated by Lorenzo A. Byrd to the community during the high water of 1861. Earlier Fairfield burials remain at the top of the riverbank behind the Durette Farm. {29 May 1989} (St. Paul 1956-85 USGS Quad. map.)

GIBSON FAMILY

?   ?   7   Nov. 1850   T6S   R1W   S14
This is on Sections 14 and 15, on the Randolph C. Gibson D.L.C. #54, OC #1885, on Hook Road Northeast. These were family burials and all of the graves have been relocated. (Not shown on Silverton 1956-85 USGS Quad. map.)

GILKISON, JAMES A.

A   ?   ?   25 Feb 2000   T8S   R3W   S24
An obituary in the Salem Statesman-Journal 28 February 2000 reports this death. James A. "Schatzi" Gilkison, born 16 April 1946, died 25 February 2000 he was to be interred on the family farm. This appears to be located along Fir Tree Drive in southeast Salem which is a

Name of Cemetery and also known as	Number of burials	Acres	Condition	Date started or earliest known burial	Township	Range	Section

short street easterly off of Battle Creek Road Southeast. NOTE: This site is on private property. (Not shown on Turner 1969-86 USGS Quad. map.)

GLEN-OAK ORPHANAGE
AKA: 1. ORPHANS HOME [SALEM]

? 10 ? Circa 1897 T7S R3W S25

According to *Illustrated Historical Atlas Map of Marion and Linn Counties, Oregon* by Edgar Williams and Company, San Francisco 1878, page 23; 10 acres of land was donated in 1866 by Mrs. Elizabeth Parrish for an orphanage. This was on the north side of what is now Center Street Northeast and is now a part of the grounds of the Oregon State Hospital. The same publication on page 38 shows a cemetery symbol next to the orphanage grounds and across the road from what was briefly the Oregon State Penitentiary. The article does not give the year that the orphanage building was constructed but it was still extant in 1878 when seven boys and one girl were residents. At some unknown date after 1883 the orphanage was closed and the grounds taken into the newly established State Hospital. Most are now buried at Lee Mission Cemetery. Located on the Josiah L. Parrish Oregon Provisional Land Claim Notification #46, Claim #61. (Not shown on Salem West 1969-86 USGS Quad. map.)

GLOVER FAMILY

A 0.1 2 1878-1920 T8S R1W S27

A small family burial ground on a dirt road northwest of Sublimity and east off of Anderson Road Southeast. It is on the Philip Glover D.L.C. #65, OC #261. Five children who died of diphtheria and two adults are known to be buried here. NOTE: This site is on private property. (Stayton 1969-86 USGS Quad. map.)

GREEN MOUNTAIN
AKA: 1. DRAKES CROSSING
2. HULLT
3. HULT
4. MOUNTAIN VIEW

C 1 2 1884 T7S R1E S26

Go 9.7 miles from Silverton, to the southeast, on OR. Hwy. 214 to Drake Crossing. Turn left off of OR. Hwy. 214 onto Powers Creek Loop for 0.2 of a mile, then turn right (east) onto Bridge Creek Road for 0.4 of a mile. The cemetery is on the right on a

Name of Cemetery and also known as	Number of burials	Acres	Condition	Date started or earliest known burial	Township	Range	Section

ridgetop. There were 67 known burials May 1968. {4 June 1989} (Drake Crossing 1985 USGS Quad. map.)

HALLS FERRY
AKA: 1. FROHMADER
2. LaFOLLETTE
3. RIVER VIEW
4. SOUTH

A   0.74   5   1875   T8S   R4W   S14
This cemetery is off of South River Road (Salem) near the location of the old Halls Ferry; it is 605 feet along the railroad and lying between the railroad and the county road. {19 January 1992} (Not shown on Monmouth 1970-86 USGS Quad. map.)

HARDING FAMILY

A   ?   4   1866   T4S   R2W   S33
This is between St. Paul and Broadacres, off of West Champoeg Creek. Access is off of OR. Hwy. 214 and French Prairie Road, through private land. It is on the Catharine Challafoix D.L.C. #55, OC #155. There are 5 known burials. The tombstone dates are 1869-1897. NOTE: This site is on private property, please ask permission before going to it. {4 April 1990} (Not shown on St. Paul 1956-85 USGS Quad. map.)

HAYESVILLE
AKA: 1. HALBERT
BAPTIST CHURCH
2. NORTH SALEM
BAPTIST CHURCH
3. STEPHENS
FAMILY

C   0.5   2   1858   T7S   R3W   S12
The Halbert Baptist Church in north Salem is at 4290 Portland Road North East and immediately south of Interchange #258 of Interstate I-5 and OR. Hwy. 99E. The first burial was a daughter of Adam and Lucinda Stephens in 1858. A Baptist church was erected here about 1891, replaced by the present church after 1949. Stephens donated land for the church and cemetery. Located on the Adam and Lucinda Stephens D.L.C., OC #3880. {1 May 1988} (Salem East 1969-86 USGS Quad. map.)

HEATER
AKA: 1. LIPSCOMB
2. OLD DRIFT
CREEK

A   ?   ?   1855-1863   T8S   R1E   S8
This cemetery is on the east side of Drift Creek Road Southeast, about 0.75 of a mile north of OR. Hwy. 214 (Silver Falls Highway). It is in the northwest corner of the Barnet Lipscomb D.L.C. #46, OC #3581, across the

Marion County

Name of Cemetery and also known as	Number of burials	Acres	Condition	Date started or earliest known burial	Township	Range	Section

road from the farm house. NOTE: This site is on private property. (Not shown on Drake Crossing 1985 USGS Quad. map.)

HERREN FAMILY
  AKA: 1. HERRON *[Sic]* FAMILY
       2. PENITENTIARY ANNEX
       3. STATE REFORM SCHOOL

? 0.3 2 1864 T8S R2W S17
Still family-owned, although the surrounding land was long ago sold to the State of Oregon. This cemetery is behind the hog barn of the Penitentiary Annex, now called Mill Creek Corrections Facility. It is on the John Herren D.L.C. #60, OC #1152. (Turner 1969-86 USGS Quad. map. Shows the Annex but NOT the cemetery.)

HOBSON-WHITNEY
  AKA: 1. EAST SUBLIMITY
       2. ETZEL
       3. SUBLIMITY GRAVEYARD

C 1.98 2 1853 T8S R1W S35
Located 1.5 miles east and north of Sublimity. It is off of Boedigheimer Road Southeast and north of Coon Hollow Road; the Sublimity water tank is adjacent to it. It is on the Archibald Rader D.L.C. #68, OC #145. {28 September 1988} (Stayton 1969-86 USGS Quad. map.)

HOLY ROSARY
  AKA: 1. ETTLIN
       2. ST. ROSE
       3. SCOTTS MILLS

A 0.91 2 1910 T6S R1E S36
Located on Ettlin Loop Road towards Holy Rosary Church, southeast of Scotts Mills. Go 3.8 miles from Scotts Mills via Crooked Finger Road to the junction with Ettlin Loop Road Northeast. Turn left on Ettlin Loop Road Northeast and go 0.5 of a mile to the cemetery on the left. {21 May 1989} (Elk Prairie 1985 USGS Quad. map.)

HOPEWELL MENNONITE
  AKA: 1. HOPEWELL CHURCH

C 0.25 2 1894 T4S R1W S36
Located two miles east of Hubbard, behind the Hopewell Mennonite Church on the north side of Whiskey Hill Road; on the Jairus Bonney D.L.C. #53, OC #1174. This cemetery is not to be confused with the better known Hopewell Cemetery in Yamhill County. {27 July 1988} (Woodburn 1956-85 USGS Quad. map.)

Name of Cemetery and also known as	Number of burials	Acres	Condition	Date started or earliest known burial	Township	Range	Section

HOWELL PRAIRIE
AKA: 1. HAZELGREEN
2. HOWELL FAMILY
3. McCORKLE
4. MIDDLEGROVE
5. MUDDY
6. MURPHY FAMILY
7. MURPHY-HOWELL
FAMILIES
8. NEWSOME

C   1.53   2   22 Mar 1848   T7S   R2W   S4
Located east of Salem on 64th Place Northeast 0.25 of a mile north off of Silverton Road. Caretaker Randy Fast told the compiler that the large signboard which says "1843 HOWELL" is in error. The official name of cemetery is Howell Prairie. The Howell family settled here in 1843. This is on the John Howell D.L.C. #47, OC #48. The first death was Temperance Howell, 22 March 1848 (Interview April 1989). {19 April 1989} (Salem East 1969-86 USGS Quad. map.)

HUBBARD
AKA: 1. GRIM
2. HUBBARD
COMMUNITY

D   ?   2   1868   T4S   R1W   S33
Located west of Hubbard on Broadacres Road on the right (north) side of road. {27 July 1988} (Woodburn 1956-85 USGS Quad. map.)

HUMBUG

?   ?   ?   1959   T8S   R2W   S4
28 tombstones from the Asylum Cemetery, dating from 1884 to 1909, were removed and dumped on a hilltop on Cottage Farm (State-owned), southeast of Salem. They were discovered in 1959 by a new superintendent of Cottage Farm, who was horrified at the supposed vandalism. He had them set up in an orderly manner and there they remained; a supposed cemetery with no bodies. They are between Cottage Farm and the more recent Oregon State Correctional Institution (23 Jan. 1958 *Capital Journal*). NOTE: The State Hospital is, of course, on the Salem West Quad. map but the preceding long paragraph is meant to indicate the Cemetery-that-is-not-a-cemetery is NOT on any Quad. map. See the article headed *Oregon State Hospital and Asylum Cemetery, 1883-1913* by Susan N. Bell, 1991. Willamette Valley Genealogical Society, Salem Oregon. {7 January 1992} (Not shown on Salem East 1969-86 USGS Quad. map.)

HUNSAKER FAMILY
AKA: 1. PARRISH GAP
2. PICKARD--
HUNSAKER
FAMILIES

B   2.13   3   1850   T9S   R2W   S17
Located on the west side of the road leading south towards Parrish Gap, in the Jefferson area. It is on Parrish Gap Road, 0.65 of a mile north of Summit Loop. In 1978 there

639

Name of Cemetery and also known as	Number of burials	Acres	Condition	Date started or earliest known burial	Township	Range	Section

were 70 markers. The cemetery was used from Jan. 1862-1939, and there has been a lot of vandalism since. It is on the Joseph Hunsaker D.L.C. #41, OC #1032. {8 September 1989} (Not shown on Turner 1969-86 USGS Quad. map.)

HUNT FAMILY

A 0.16 ? 1858 T8S R1W S23

Located northeast of Sublimity and south off of OR. Hwy. 214. There are supposed to be 2 or 3 burials on the George W. and Elizabeth N. Hunt D.L.C. #58, OC #545. The D.L.C. description sets the site as a burial ground. It is also noted in the *Illustrated Historical Atlas Map of Marion and Linn Counties Oregon*, By Edgar Williams and Co. 1878 reprinted in 1971, on page 48. (Not shown on Stayton 1969-86 USGS Quad. map.)

INDIAN

A 0.1 11 ? T7S R3W S26

"Early Indian Cemetery where Southern Pacific depot now stands" *Capital Journal*, Jan. 1893. (Not shown on Salem West 1969-86 USGS Quad. map.)

JEFFERSON
 AKA: 1. MASONIC
      2. METHODIST

D 9.3 1 1868 T10S R3W S1

This cemetery is above the town of Jefferson on Cemetery Hill, by the city reservoir; There were 1,400 burials as of May 1989. Originally there were two separate cemeteries: Masonic Cemetery, begun in 1868, and the Methodist Cemetery. Both merged in 1935 and were deeded to the town. There are earlier burials than 1868, but these are reburials. It is on the Jos. M. and James M. Bates D.L.C. #65, OC #800. {10 August 1988} (Crabtree 1970-75 USGS Quad. map.)

JORY FAMILY

A 1.52 5 1854 T8S R3W S28

Located south of Salem, 0.3 of a mile west on Cole Road from Liberty Road, and 200 yards north off of Cole Road. The compiler visited this cemetery in July 1991 and found no ready access. The area is overgrown into second-growth forest. Within the small burial area were 9 monuments for 12 people, dating from

Name of Cemetery and also known as	Number of burials	Acres	Condition	Date started or earliest known burial	Township	Range	Section

1870 to 1924. In addition, elderly family members estimate about 6 more relatives are buried here. They also report scattered single burials of other persons, for a total of 34 estimated burials. Located on the James Jory Senior and Mary Jory D.L.C., OC #295. {30 July 1991} (Sidney 1970-86 USGS Quad. map.)

KIMSEY FAMILY
AKA: 1. WALKER FAMILY

A   0.01   2   1859-1879   T8S   R1W   S7
There is one tombstone with the names of the four Kimsey children. The burials approximately two miles Southeast of Macleay, on Jordan Street Southeast in the Waldo Hills, on the southeast foot of a hill in a filbert orchard. This is on the Gilliam H. and Rhoda Walker D.L.C. #50, OC #552. NOTE: This site is on private property. {2 August 1989} (Stayton N.E. 1969 USGS Quad. map.)

LaFOLLETTE FAMILY

A   0.01   5   1879-1882   T6S   R3W   S1
Turn left (west) at the intersection of River Road and Waconda Road Northeast, at a flashing orange light, at Waconda north of Salem. Drive about 1.1 miles, which takes you down into Mission Bottom. A farm is on the right (north) at a sharp turn to the left; this was the old D. H. La Follette Farm, later the C. M. Hall Place. Located well behind the house, away from the road, are 2 tombsones: for D. B. LaFollette, died 28 Febuary 1879 at aged 19, killed in a shotgun accident; S. A. LaFollette, died 6 November 1882, aged 57. Three infants are also known to be buried here; on the Earl Jones D.L.C. #62, OC #627. NOTE: This site is on private property. Reference; *Marion County Historical Society*, Vol XII, 1977-8 page 65. *Illustrated historical Atlas of Marion and Linn Counties 1878*, page 32 by Edgar Williams and Co. (Not shown on Gervais 1957-85 USGS Quad. map.)

LEABO

A   0.5   5   ?   T8S   R4W   S26
Located on the west slopes of the Salem Hills, above River Road South and above the Burlington Northern Railway tracks. There is

Marion County

possible access from Skyline Road South.
NOTE: This site is on private property. (Not
shown on Monmouth 1970-86 USGS Quad. map.)

LEE MISSION
AKA: 1. LEE, JASON
     2. LEE MEMORIAL

D 15   2   1834   T7S R3W   S24
Located on "D" Street between 24th and 19th
Streets in Salem. The date on the lich-gate
says 1834, the dedication plaque says 1835.
The grave of Anna Maria Pittman, wife of
Jason Lee, 26 June 1838 was moved in from the
Willamette Mission Cemetery. {15 April 1990}
(Salem West 1969-86 USGS Quad. map.)

LEWIS
AKA: 1. SILVER CLIFF

B 0.25 2   1871   T7S R1E   S29
Go about 7 miles south of Silverton via
Eureka Avenue, Victor Point Road and Drift
Creek Road, to the junction with Lewis
Cemetery Road on the left (east). The
cemetery is out of sight from Drift Creek
Road and about 0.75 of a mile uphill on the
ridgetop. Entry is usually stopped at a
locked gate at 0.25 of a mile from Drift
Creek Road. It is on the Daniel P. Lewis
D.L.C. #38, OC #3534. {22 August 1990}
(Drake Crossing 1985 USGS Quad. map.)

LONE FIR
AKA: 1. ANDERSON
     2. ANDERSON
        LONE FIR
     3. BEAVER CREEK
     4. DOWNING
     5. ROCK POINT
     6. ROCKY POINT
     7. STONEY POINT

C 2.3 3   1852   T8S R1W   S21
Located about 3 miles northwest of Sublimity,
on the west side of Anderson Road Southeast
and about 0.5 of a mile south of OR. Hwy.
214. The preferred name of this cemetery is
uncertain but USGS labels it Lone Fir. It is
1 or 2 miles from the old locale of Rock
Point and overlooks Beaver Creek Valley. It
is on the James and Eleanor Anderson D.L.C.
#53, OC #267; the Downings were immediate
neighbors. This cemetery has suffered
continuing vandalism. {14 August 1988}
(Stayton 1969-86 USGS Quad. map.)

Name of Cemetery and also known as	Number of burials	Acres	Condition	Date started or earliest known burial	Township	Range	Section

LONE OAK [NEW]
AKA: 1. I.O.O.F.
STAYTON
LODGE #64
2. MASONIC
[STAYTON]
3. SANTIAM
MASONIC
LODGE #1

D 6 2 1888   T9S R1W   S10
Located on the northeast edge of Stayton, on the south side of Fern Ridge Road at the junction with 3rd Avenue. NOTE: St. Marys' cemetery adjoins Lone Oak; they are separated by driveways. {8 October 1989} (Stayton 1969-86 USGS Quad. map.)

LOONEY FAMILY
AKA: 1. STEIWER--
LOONEY

B 0.39 3 1850   T9S R3W   S23
Located off of Jefferson Highway, north of Jefferson and near Looney Butte; north off of Wintercreek Road Southeast, 0.5 of a mile east of Jefferson Highway. It is on the Jesse and Ruby Looney D.L.C. #53, OC #705. {17 June 1988} (Sidney 1970-86 USGS Quad. map.)

LUCIER, MARY

? ? ? Circa 1861 T3S R2W   S33
Here is the grave of Mary Marguerite Tchinouk Lucier, who died after the December 1861 flood and before 1865. Also buried here is a "sister of Etienne Lucier." Both were buried on a knoll in the orchard, near the line between the Lucier and Belleque Farms. This is now cultivated land and the location is known only approximately. It is just east of the present day (1980's) approach to the bridge over the Willamette River to Newberg. (Not shown on Newberg 1961-85 USGS Quad. map.)

MARION COUNTY POOR FARM

? ? ? 13 Feb 1910 T7S R3W   ?
Possibly in Sections 14 or 15. Marion County death certificate #438 for 13 February 1910 reports the death of Patrick Fitzgerald, aged 65, and his burial the following day at the Poor Farm Cemetery. This was then two miles north of Salem on what became North River Road. It was on the east side of the then rural road. The city has long since engulfed the site. Most Poor Farm deaths were interred in Lee Mission Cemetery and Salem Pioneer. The county operated the Poor Farm from 1870 to 1937. (Not shown on Salem West 1969-86 USGS Quad. map.)

| Name of Cemetery and also known as | Number of burials | Acres | Condition | Date started or earliest known burial | Township | Range | Section |

MARION FRIENDS
AKA: 1. FRIENDS
2. I.O.O.F.
3. MARION HILL

C 0.75 1 1891 T9S R2W S29
Located 0.5 of a mile to the west and uphill from the town of Marion, on Marion Hill Road. 1890 is the earliest dated stone remaining. {9 June 1989} (Turner 1969-86 USGS Quad. map)

MASONIC, [GERVAIS]
AKA: 1. GERVAIS
MASONIC

C 1.5 2 1875 T5S R2W S36
Located east of Gervais on the south side of the Gervais-Mt. Angel Road, 0.25 of a mile from OR. Hwy. 99E. There are also many Russian burials here. NOTE: Sacred Heart Cemetery is on the north side of the road. It is on the Theodore C. Poujade D.L.C. #44, OC #2309. {10 April 1988} (Gervais 1957-85 USGS Quad. map.)

MATER DOLOROSA

A 0.2 6 Early 1900 T8S R1W S34
Located in Sublimity on Northeast Starr Street. Drive 0.25 of a mile east from Center Street. The burials were off to the left (north) on a private driveway and behind a screen of arbor vitae shrubs. There were at least 3 burials in 1978. A plat of 0.64 acres was made for the Servite Sisters and filed on 6 April 1964, but it appears that only about a third of that was marked off. It is recorded in Town Plat Book Vol. 21, page 47. The cemetery was closed in the 1970's and the graves were removed to St. Boniface Cemetery. This was on the James M. Denny D.L.C. #69, OC #211. (Not shown on Stayton 1969-86 USGS Quad. map.)

McCOWN, G. W.

A 0.01 4 ? T7S R2E S7
This lone burial is located on private property (please ask for permission to visit) in a brushy fence row and cannot be found without local assistance. It is about a half mile east (left) of Crooked Finger Road. The access driveway is about 5.1 miles from Scotts Mills on Crooked Finger Road. The monument is a standard upright government military monument which states: 1st SGT. G. W. McCown Co. E. 1 ORE. INF., with no date. {30 August 1993} (Not shown on Elk Prairie 1985 USGS Quad. map.)

Name of Cemetery and also known as	Number of burials	Acres	Condition	Date started or earliest known burial	Township	Range	Section

McCULLY
AKA: 1. McCULLEY
     2. PARRISH

?   0.5   5   ?   T9S R2W   S21

This cemetery is near the locale of Marion. The caretaker of Marion Friends Cemetery referred to this as the old Parrish burial ground. It is on a timbered top of a knoll, just south of Pearson Road Southeast and about 0.5 of a mile east of its junction with Parrish Gap Road Southeast. The present landowner has lived here 40 years, during which there have been no burials. No markers were visible at the time of a visit by the compiler 26 March 1990. Jesse Parrish, 1819-1898, owned this land in 1878, perhaps he is buried here see page 40-41 of *Illustrated Historicl Atlas Marion-Linn* 1878, by Edgar Williams and Co. Located on the Isaac McCully D.L.C. #52, OC #1042. {26 March 1990} (Not shown on Turner 1969-86 USGS Quad. map.)

MILLER

D   2   1   Sept. 1852   T6S R1E   S19

Located about 3 miles northeast of Silverton at OR. Hwy. 213 and Herigstad Road Northeast. It was deeded in 1860 and the plaque on the gateway says 1860. Named for Richard Miller who settled here in 1847 on the Richard Miller, D.L.C., OC #4859. He moved to the Shelburn area in Linn County in 1872 and is buried in the Miller Cemetery there. These two Miller Cemeteries must be the only two cemeteries in Oregon named for one person. {15 April 1989} (Scotts Mills 1954-85 USGS Quad. map.)

MT. ANGEL
AKA: 1. HIGHLAND
        PIONEER
     2. ST. MARY'S

C   0.5   2   1860   T6S R1W   S3

Located at the corner of Garfield and Marquam Streets in Mt. Angel, it is on the north side of Marquam Street. {18 January 1990} (Silverton 1956-85 USGS Quad. map.)

MT. HOPE
AKA: 1. HUNT FAMILY
     2. LUTHY
     3. MORRIS
     4. WALDO HILLS
     5. WARREN
     6. WILLARD

D   1.8   2   1858   T7S R1W   S33

Located east of Salem, off of State Street and on 119th Avenue Northeast. It is on the John S. Hunt D.L.C. #39, OC #16. There were 472 recorded burials by 1995. {19 June 1988} (Stayton Northeast 1969 USGS Quad. map.)

Name of Cemetery and also known as	Number of burials	Acres	Condition	Date started or earliest known burial	Township	Range	Section

MUTE SCHOOL
AKA: 1. SCHOOL FOR
 DEAF MUTES
 2. STATE SCHOOL
 FOR THE DEAF

? ? ? 1905 T8S R2W ?

Located in Section 8 or 17. A death record reports the burial of an infant named Halse, on 20 Febuary 1905, at the Mute School Cemetery. This state institution was located 6 miles south of Salem in 1905 but is now within the city limits. The school was located here between 1895 and 1910 when it was moved to its present site in north Salem. The rural site was replaced by the State Tuberculosis Hospital which in turn has been replaced by the present Western Baptist College. It is on Deer Park Drive Southeast, between Turner Road and Aumsville Highway. The compiler does not know if this burial and perhaps others were reburied somewhere else. It was on the William H. Rector D.L.C. #45, OC #52. (Not shown on Salem East 1969-86 USGS Quad. map.)

NEWELL, KITTY

A ? 5 15 Dec 1845 T4S R2W S1

Robert Newell's Nez Perce wife and "another woman" are buried on the right (east) bank of Champoeg Creek at a bend, about halfway between the bridge within Champoeg State Park and the Willamette River. This burial site was abandoned after the flood of Nov. 1861; located on Robert Newell D.L.C. #43, OC #2051. The present marker is not on the exact burial site. {8 September 1994} (Not shown on Newberg 1961-85 USGS Quad. map.)

NEWSOM CAMPGROUND
AKA: 1. McCORKLE
 2. NUSOM *[Sic]*
 3. SCISM

B 1 5 ? T6S R1W S19

Recorded in Marion County Deeds Vol. 20, page 160, and mentioned in David Newsom: *The Western Observer 1805-1882*, page 9. Several burials are mentioned, including a son of David Newsom. Located north off of Nusom Road Northeast and 0.6 of a mile west of the Pudding River. There are 54 known burials. During an August 1989 visit, this compiler and James Nelson could find only one tombstone (broken) for Polly, wife of David Newsom, died 29 Dec. 1877. {3 August 1989} (Not shown on Silverton 1956-85 USGS Quad. map.)

Name of Cemetery and also known as	Number of burials	Acres	Condition	Date started or earliest known burial	Township	Range	Section

OLD BELIEVER CHURCH
AKA: 1. BETHLEHEM
        VILLAGE

C 2.7 2 1976   T5S R1W   S30
Located south of Woodburn in the Russian colony. It is south of Monitor-McKee Road on the George M. Baker D.L.C. #44, OC #2868. {27 September 1990} (Not shown on Silverton 1956-85 USGS Quad. map.)

OLD COLONY
AKA: 1. AURORA COLONY
     2. AURORA PARK
     3. KEIL FAMILY

B 0.25 3 1856   T4S R1W   S12
Located north off of Ehlen Road on Cole Lane northwest of Aurora. Go to the end of the gravelled lane and walk through a yard and a broken gate. Look for the Thuja species "Cedar" tree that is in the cemetery, this is in what was Dr. William Keil's own orchard. In Nov.-Dec. 1862, a son and 3 daughters died of smallpox. The cemetery has had a lot of vandalism. NOTE: This site is on private property. {28 April 1988} (Woodburn 1956-85 USGS Quad. map.)

OLINGER, ABRAM

A 0.01 12 1874   T8S R2W   S3
Located west of 71st Avenue Southeast and south of Gale Street Northeast, in the Macleay area. This is in a cultivated field, all markers are now gone and the burial site is being cultivated as a part of the field. At least 7 burials were known to be on the Abram and Rachel Olinger D.L.C. #57, OC #221. (Not shown on Salem East 1969-86 USGS Quad. map.)

OREGON STATE HOSPITAL

D 0.01 1 1914-1971 T7S R3W   S25
In 1979, 3,809 cremains were placed in vaults beneath a drained lily pond on the west edge of the Oregon State Hospital campus. The circle, planted with evergreens, has a marker dated 27 November 1984. It is located at Center Street Northeast and 24th Street Northeast in Salem; see the article headed "Asylum" for the rest of the story. {7 January 1992} (Not shown on Salem West 1969-86 USGS Quad. map.)

Marion County

| Name of Cemetery and also known as | Number of burials | Acres | Condition | Date started or earliest known burial | Township | Range | Section |

**OREGON STATE
INSTITUTION FOR THE
FEEBLE MINDED**
AKA: 1. O.F.M.I.

? ? ? 1909 T8S R3W S2
This state institution for the mentally retarded was located on Strong Road several miles southeast of Salem. It is now engulfed by the city. The facility was opened in the spring of 1909 and two death certificates report burials on the grounds during that year and 13 were buried in 1910. The compiler does not know the site of the burials, but interments on the grounds evidently were stopped quite soon after this institution opened. The name was changed to Fairview Hospital about 1937 or 1938. (Fairview Hospital is shown on Salem West 1969-86 USGS Quad. map, but the burial site is not shown.)

PATTON FAMILY
AKA: 1. DICKENS
FAMILY

A 0.5 2 1878-1910 T8S R1W S5
Located 3 or 4 miles east of Macleay via Edmunson Drive Southeast and on a private driveway easterly through orchards. There are four known graves on Reuben and Nancy Dickens D.L.C. #48, OC #268. {3 August 1989} (Stayton N.E. 1969 USGS Quad. map.)

PENITENTIARY [NEW]
AKA: 1. O.S.P.

B ? ? 1866 T7S R3W S25
"A small cemetery near the prison not used for a number of years." Reports an 11 Dec. 1923 newspaper article. The notorious pair Tracy and Merrill, killed in 1902 after escaping, were buried in a clump of cottonwoods. There are an estimated 100 burials. "Cemetery was covered with earth for a fill." Reported the 1 April 1956 *Oregonian* article. (Not shown on Salem East or Salem West 1969-86 USGS Quad. maps.)

PENITENTIARY [OLD]

? ? 7 1853-1861 T7S R3W S25
The Oregon State Penitentiary was first located in Salem on what is now the grounds of the Oregon State Hospital. It was on the south side of what is now Center Street Northeast. According to *Illustrated Historical Atlas Map of Marion and Linn Counties, Oregon* 1878, by Edgar Williams and Company , San Francisco 1878 on page 38 this atlas shows a cemetery on the north side of

Name of Cemetery and also known as	Number of burials	Acres	Condition	Date started or earliest known burial	Township	Range	Section

the street opposite the penitentiary. That cemetery is adjacent to an orphanage so the compiler supposes that both convicts and orphans were buried there. A different site for a new penitentiary was purchased in 1864 and a temporary prison was built in 1866 on that site. The site of the first penitentiary was occupied in 1883 for the present Oregon State Hospital. See the respective articles headed Asylum, Orphans Home, and Penitentiary [new]. (Not shown on Salem West 1969-86 USGS Quad. map.)

PIONEER MEMORIAL
AKA: 1. BROOKS
2. BROOKS PIONEER
3. JONES
4. PARKERSVILLE
5. PIONEER [WACONDA]
6. THE NOOK

C 1.4 2 1855 T6S R2W S10
Located west of Parkersville, off of OR. Hwy. 99E on Waconda Road Northeast. Go east to the Pioneer School and turn right (south) on 72nd Avenue Northeast to the Christian Church (1902); the cemetery is on the west side of the road. The signboard simply says: "Pioneer Cemetery." It is on the Daniel Smith D.L.C. #97, OC #2258. {29 September 1988} (Gervais 1957-85 USGS Quad. map.)

PLEASANT GROVE
AKA: 1. CONDIT

B 2.4 2 1856 T9S R2W S11
Located on Pleasant Grove Road Southeast, about 200 yards east of Brick Road Southeast. It is on a gravel road west of Cascade High School. A sign indicates that the church is the "Oldest Presbyterian Church Building on the West Coast." It was founded by Reverend Philip Condit who died 21 Nov. 1856 and is buried here. The actual burial area is only about 0.25 of an acre, on the Philip Condit D.L.C., OC #2536. {20 August 1989} (Turner 1969-86 USGS Quad. map.)

POWELL FAMILY, REVEREND THEOPHILUS

A ? 5 1861 T7S R1W S33
Located a short distance south of State Street East at the junction of 119th Avenue Northeast. All evidence was lost by 1987. A 1966 report listed 4 known burials on the Theophilus Powell D.L.C. #37, OC #18. (Not shown on Stayton N.E. 1969 USGS Quad. map.)

Name of Cemetery and also known as	Number of burials	Acres	Condition	Date started or earliest known burial	Township	Range	Section

PRATUM
AKA: 1. EMMANUEL
        BIBLE CHURCH
     2. McCALISTER
     3. PRATUM
        MENNONITE

B 1 2 1898 T7S R1W S19
Located east of Salem and a mile east of
Pratum. Go east on Sunnyview Road Northeast
and turn right (south) onto 95th Avenue
Northeast for 0.1 of a mile; the cemetery is
on the left (east). {13 December 1988}
(Stayton N.E. 1969 USGS Quad. map.)

PRUNE RIDGE
AKA: 1. DOTY,
        MARY M.

A ? 5 1899 T7S R2E S8
In the Southwest 1/4 of the Southeast 1/4 of
Section 8, located 7 miles southeast of
Scotts Mills on the left (east) side of
Crooked Finger Road. Mary M. Doty is buried
on the site of a church that was in use 1892-
1900. (Not shown on Elk Prairie 1985 USGS
Quad. map.)

PURVINE FARM BURIALS

? ? ? ? ? R1W ?
These could be in Township 4 South, Section
33 or 34, or in Township 5 South, Section 3
or 4; it is unknown which is correct. These
are reportedly near Hubbard on the Ewing
Purvine D.L.C. #38 and #55, OC #1778. Most
of the early burials were later reinterred in
the Zena Cemetery in Polk County. NOTE: No
other information was given in the report.
(Not shown on Woodburn 1956-85 USGS Quad.
map.)

**QUEEN OF ANGELS
CONVENT**
AKA: 1. ST. MARY'S
        CONVENT
     2. SISTERS,
        MT. ANGEL

B 0.36 1 ? T6S R1W S10
Located at the south end of the town of Mt.
Angel at the convent. (Silverton 1956-85
USGS Quad. map.)

QUINABY'S CORNER

A 0.01 1 ? T7S R3W S27
Located at the northwest corner of Mission
Street and University Street Southeast in
Salem. This corner is on the grounds of Bush
Elementary School. Quinaby was a Kalapuya
Indian who lived for many years in Salem.
His death date was given, long after, at
varying dates from Thanksgiving or Christmas
1878 to Christmas of 1883; all the stories
agree that he died of overeating. One of the

Name of Cemetery and also known as	Number of burials	Acres	Condition	Date started or earliest known burial	Township	Range	Section

stories does place his burial somewhere on the grounds of what is now Bush School. In any event, "Quinaby's Corner" on the school grounds is elegantly planted and cared for. {24 April 1992} (Not shown on Salem West 1969-86 USGS Quad. map.)

RICKEY

A ?   ? 19 Jun 1904 T7S R2W   S32

J. C. Caplinger was buried in the Rickey Cemetery off of Macleay Road Southeast. It is thought to be in the James Rickey D.L.C. #81, OC #2515. NOTE: No other information was given in the report. (Not shown on Salem East 1969-86 USGS Quad. map.)

ROSEDALE FRIENDS
  AKA: 1. ROSEDALE

B 0.7 1 1902   T8S R3W   S28

Located south of Salem via Liberty Road. Turn left (east) on Hylo Road South and go 0.5 of a mile to the Friends Church at the intersection with Champion Hill Road. Turn left (north) for 200 yards to the cemetery. 10 January 1899 is the date of the earliest burial. Mr. Alfred Cammack, caretaker, makes the best temporary grave markers this compiler has seen in visiting 300-plus cemeteries. {29 May 1989} (Sidney 1970-86 USGS Quad. map.)

ROWLAND, PATRICK

A 0.01 ? 11 Feb 1847 T4S R2W   S19

"Buried at the edge of the woods opposite the church in St. Paul." This is all that is known of this burial. the church was built in 1846. (The church is shown on the St. Paul 1956-85 USGS Quad. map.)

SACRED HEART
  AKA: 1. BROWN FAMILY
      2. GERVAIS
         CATHOLIC

D 2 2 1850's   T5S R2W   S36

Located east of Gervais from OR. Hwy. 99E on the Gervais-Mt. Angel Road, 0.3 of a mile from 99E on the left (north) side of the road and just past the Gervais Masonic Cemetery. The cemetery was originally a family burial ground for the Samuel and Elizabeth Brown family who arrived here in 1850 and purchased the Peter (Pierre) Depot

Name of Cemetery and also known as	Number of burials	Acres	Condition	Date started or earliest known burial	Township	Range	Section

D.L.C. #54, OC #1839. The cemetery was dedicated on 8 November 1880. {21 January 1990} (Gervais 1957-85 USGS Quad. map.)

ST. BARBARA'S
AKA: 1. ST. JOSEPH
    2. SALEM
       CATHOLIC

E 1   1   Circa 1863 T8S R3W   S3
Drive out South Commercial Street in Salem to where Liberty Street joins Missouri Street. The signboard says: "Established 1867." Reportedly the cemetery is now filled, except for some reserved plots. {30 October 1988} (Salem West 1969-86 USGS Quad. map.)

ST. BENEDICT
AKA: 1. MT. ANGEL
      ABBEY

C 0.4 1   ?   T6S R1W   S11
Located at the Abbey of St. Benedict on Mt. Angel. This is the cemetery for the Brothers and Abbots with one exception noted by the compiler. One monument off to one side was erected to "Mother" and "Father"; Margaret Robl died 30 Jan. 1890 and Andreas Robl died 26 May 1907. Burials of 6 or 7 Abbots, including the founder, Father Adelhelm Odermatt. The cemetery is at the foot of the water tower. {6 September 1990} (Silverton 1956-85 USGS Quad. map.)

ST. BONIFACE

D 1.4 1   1880   T8S R1W   S34
Located in Sublimity on Southeast Church Street, west of the church. {13 January 1990} (Stayton 1969-86 USGS Quad. map. It does show the church and an adjacent unnamed cemetery in Sublimity but erroneously places St. Boniface Cemetery a mile east of town, in what is actually an ordinary farm field.)

ST. LOUIS [NEW]

C 2.3 2   1858   T5S R2W   S21
Located west of Gervais. This old cemetery is under the direction of St. Louis Catholic Church. Go west on Dorion Lane and off of Manning Road Northeast. It is on the Bartholomew Delorme D.L.C. #51, OC #1812. {28 May 1988} (Gervais 1957-85 USGS Quad. map.)

Name of Cemetery and also known as	Number of burials	Acres	Condition	Date started or earliest known burial	Township	Range	Section

ST. LOUIS [OLD]

? ? ? 1840-1858 T5S R2W S21
This old cemetery was directly across Manning Road from the present St. Louis church. The old site is a grassy parking area. There is a record that Marie Ayvoise (Madame Dorion) was buried here 6 Sept. 1850. The present St. Louis Cemetery was dedicated 3 May 1858. See the article on St. Louis. (Not shown on Gervais 1957-85 USGS Quad. Map.)

ST. LUKE'S

D 3 1 1895 T5S R1W S7
The address is 1679 North Front Street, Woodburn. By Mill Creek on Front Street, it is just south of the structure over OR. Hwy. 214; on the Benjamin F. and Mary Ann Hall D.L.C. #51, OC #612. {22 February 1990} (Woodburn 1956-85 USGS Quad. map.)

ST. MARY'S [STAYTON]
AKA: 1. IMMACULATE
CONCEPTION
CHURCH

C 1.7 1 ? T9S R1W S10
This Catholic cemetery at Stayton adjoins Lone Oak Cemetery to the south. It is separated from Lone Oak by the driveway. {8 October 1989} (Stayton 1969-86 USGS Quad. map shows only the name Lone Oak.)

ST. PAUL'S [NEW]

D 3 1 1875 T4S R2W S19
Located on the north side of Church Street (OR. Hwy. 219), at the eastern edge of town. At present, it is the principal cemetery in the town of St. Paul. This includes many reburials from St. Paul [old] Cemetery. {14 January 1990} (St. Paul 1956-85 USGS Quad. map.)

ST. PAUL'S [OLD]
AKA: 1. OLD MISSION

D 1 10 1839-1891 T4S R2W S19
This is on the east side of OR. Hwy. 219; Main Street, on the highway to Newberg. The cemetery was in use from June 1839-1891. This, the oldest white cemetery in Oregon, was destroyed in 1938 after the present St. Paul Cemetery was established. Most burials were interred there, especially after 1888. In due time, the 546 recorded at this St. Paul's site were reburied in the present cemetery. It is impossible to say how many of the old burials were left behind. At

Name of Cemetery and also known as	Number of burials	Acres	Condition	Date started or earliest known burial	Township	Range	Section

present, it is simply a field with a large crucifix dedicated in 1937 and a boulder with a plaque dedicated to early settlers (mostly French-Canadians) in Oct. 1935. {14 January 1990} (The site of this old cemetery is outlined shown on the St. Paul 1956-85 USGS Quad. map.)

ST. PAUL'S CATHOLIC
AKA: 1. HOBART ROAD

C 1 1 1947   T6S R1W   S27
Located north and west of Silverton on Hobart Road, on the Peter Cox D.L.C. #44, OC #1384. {28 January 1989} (Silverton 1956-85 USGS Quad. map.)

ST. PAUL'S EPISCOPAL CHURCH COLUMBARIUM

? ? 1 ?   T7S R3W   S27
Located at 1444 Liberty Street Southeast between Myers and Leffelle Streets in Salem. (The church is depicted on the Salem West 1969-86 USGS Quad. map.)

ST. TIMOTHY'S EPISCOPAL CHURCH MEMORIAL GARDENS

A ? ? ?   T7S R3W   S24
The church is located at 3295 Ladd Ave. Northeast in Salem, it is a new church in a residential area in northeast Salem. Ladd Avenue is a short east-west street off of Savage Road and the church is easterly from the latter. Savage Road itself runs north-south between the arterial streets, 'D' Street and Market Street. (The church is shown on Salem East 1969-86 USGS Quad. map.)

SALEM PIONEER
AKA: 1. I.O.O.F.
        [SALEM]
     2. RURAL

E 16.4 2 1841   T7S R3W   S33
On Sections 33 and 34. Located on Commercial Street South in Salem. Turn right (west) onto Hoyt Street. The present entrance is to the right near the main entrance to City View Cemetery. The 2 cemeteries are separated by a fence. Early records are confused; the property was transferred to the Chemeketa I.O.O.F. Lodge #1 in 1856 and deeded from the Odd Fellows Lodge to the City of Salem in Oct. 1985. Most of the lodge burial records were destroyed in a fire. {25 August 1991} (Salem West 1969-86 USGS Quad. map.)

Name of Cemetery and also known as	Number of burials	Acres	Condition	Date started or earliest known burial	Township	Range	Section

SHAW CATHOLIC
AKA: 1. ST. MARY'S
      CATHOLIC
   2. ST. MARY'S
      [SHAW]

B 0.3 2 1928   T8S R2W   S13
In Shaw southeast of Salem; the cemetery is north across the road from the Catholic church on the south side of OR. Hwy. 214. On the John Bridges D.L.C. #40, OC #1158. {13 January 1990} (Stayton 1969-86 USGS Quad. map.)

SHORT FAMILY

A 0.01 ? ?   T7S R1W   S32
This burial is one male member of the Short family; the John Wesley Short family owned the land by 1870. This is about 0.5 of a mile west of 119th Avenue Southeast, off of State Street East and apparently south of State Street. It is beneath a lone oak tree on the brow of a rather steep field (1987 report). NOTE: This site is on private property. (Not shown on Stayton N.E. 1969 USGS Quad. map.)

SILVERTON
AKA: 1. COOLIDGE AND
      McCLAINE
   2. DeSARTS
      ADDITION
   3. I.O.O.F.
   4. SILVER CREEK

E 3   1   12 Dec 1852 T6S R1W   S34
Located near the western city limits of Silverton on Silverton Road Northeast. The DeSarts Addition, adjacent to the Silverton Cemetery, was established in 1858 and though incorporated into the larger cemetery, it is still marked off by a low wall. It is on the Leander Davis D.L.C. #46, OC #1507. {3 August 1989} (Silverton 1956-85 USGS Quad. map.)

SIMMONS
AKA: 1. SIMMONS HILL

B 2.01 3 1852   T5S R1W   S34
Located north of Mt. Angel on the east side of OR. Hwy. 214 and the north side of Dominic Road. {28 January 1989} (Silverton 1956-85 USGS Quad. map.)

SMALL, REVEREND THOMAS HENDERSON

A ? 5 1867   T7S R1W   S34
Located just east of Cascade Highway and north off of Doerfler Road. There are 5 known burials (1987 visit by Bernita Jones Sharp), on the John S. Hunt D.L.C. #39, OC #16. NOTE: This site is on private property. (Not shown on Stayton N.E. 1969 USGS Quad. map.)

Name of Cemetery and also known as	Number of burials	Acres	Condition	Date started or earliest known burial	Township	Range	Section

STIPP MEMORIAL
AKA: 1. DUNKARD
2. LIBERTY SCHOOL
3. MACLEAY

C 3 2 1849   T8S R2W   S2

This cemetery is west of Macleay on the main road towards Salem, on the corner of Macleay Road and 82nd Avenue Southeast. It is on the John Stipp D.L.C. #51, OC #1872. {13 May 1989} (Salem East 1969-86 USGS Quad. map.)

TERRELL

A ? 5 ?   T9S R1E   S2

There may have been a cemetery along Fern Ridge Road Southeast 2 miles from Mehama. Daraleen Phillips Wade surmises that there were county burials only on the land owned by County Judge G. P. Terrell. There are records for 5 unrelated men buried by the county from August 1900 to February 1903. (*1987 Marion County Cemetery Records*. Vol. 1. by Daraleen Phillips Wade.) A long-time resident east of Stayton, Ralph Siegmund, reported to Rudy Wellbrook in April of 1991 that he, Siegmund, happened upon an abandoned cemetery in the late 1920's or early 1930's. Siegmund was out hunting on the ridge that is the watershed between Mill Creek on the north and Valentine Creek on the south. On the southern slopes of the ridge, in second-growth fir, he found a small cemetery with only 2 sides of picket fencing and 5 or 6 wooden markers, 3 of which were crosses. It was on a flattish section of the ridge. Mr. Siegmund has not returned to it nor heard of any further reports on the cemetery. Using the Stout Mountain 1985 Quad., the two men believe the cemetery was most likely in Township 9 South, Range 1 East, Section 2. (Not shown on Stout Mountain 1985 USGS Quad. map.)

TRINITY LUTHERAN
AKA: 1. GERMAN
LUTHERAN
2. MERIDIAN

C 1 1 1895   T6S R1W   S12

Located 2 miles east of Mt. Angel on Marquam Road Northeast. {25 August 1988} (Silverton 1956-85 USGS Quad. map.)

TWIN OAKS
AKA: 1. I.O.O.F.
[TURNER]

C 3.8 2 1851   T8S R2W   S28

This cemetery is 0.25 of a mile north of Mill Creek Road Northeast on Witzel Road, Turner. {24 September 1989} (Turner 1969-86 USGS Quad. map.)

Name of Cemetery and also known as	Number of burials	Acres	Condition	Date started or earliest known burial	Township	Range	Section

UNION HILL
AKA: 1. KING FAMILY

C 1.5 2 1877 T8S R1E S7
Located between Silverton and Stayton on Union Hill Road Southeast, east of Victor Point Road. The Grange, which used to be a church, is 0.75 of a mile south of the cemetery. It is on the Samuel Kincaid D.L.C. #44, OC #4100. {2 July 1989} (Drake Crossing 1985 USGS Quad. map.)

VALLEY VIEW
AKA: 1. EMANUEL
2. EVANS VALLEY
3. LUTHERAN
4. NORWEGIAN
5. TRINITY

B 3.89 2 Circa 1893 T6S R1W S36
Located just north of Evens Valley Community Center on Valley View Road. NOTE: The community center, an old school house, is spelled "Evens," a Norwegian family name. However, the more familiar Welsh family name of "Evans" has become the most used spelling. {11 September 1988} (Scotts Mills 1954-85 USGS Quad. map.)

VAUGHN BABY

A 0.01 ? 30 Jun 1916 T8S R4W ?
A Marion County death Certificate #344 for 1916 list Unnamed male infant, born 29 June 1916, died 30 June 1916. He was born premature to Sylvester and Bessie Redfiey Vaughn. (Not shown on Rickreall 1969-76 USGS Quad. map.)

WALDO FAMILY

A 0.01 12 1850 T8S R2W S12
This is on Sections 1 or 12, west of Howell Prairie Road and south of Macleay Road at the Portland General Electric Powerline. Behind a power pole on the hill is a pile of rocks. In 1865 Daniel Waldo was incensed when the Methodists refused to bury the body of an executed murderer, George Beale, in the Methodists' Rural Cemetery. Waldo had the body loaded on a wagon and taken from Salem for burial on his own farm. Two young children of the Waldo family are also buried here. It was plowed over by farming equipment in the 1960's or 1970's; on the Daniel and Malinda C. Waldo D.L.C. #41, OC #55. NOTE: This site is on private property. (Not shown on Salem East 1969-86 USGS Quad. map.)

Marion County

Name of Cemetery and also known as	Number of burials	Acres	Condition	Date started or earliest known burial	Township	Range	Section

WELLS FAMILY

A   0.01   3   1850-1929   T10S R2W   S6

Located southwest of Marion on the road to Jefferson. It is on private land near the northwest side of the railway crossing alongside of Jefferson-Marion County Road. There is said to be 20 known burials. This compiler found 9 monuments to 10 burials on 9 June 1989; on the John Wells D.L.C. #48, OC #1043. {9 June 1989} (Not shown on Crabtree 1970-75 USGS Quad. map.)

WESTON FAMILY

A   0.5   3   1855-1896   T4S R2W   S1

Now within Champoeg State Park, it is on the north side of Champoeg Road about 200 feet east of its junction with Case Road Northeast and about 800 feet east of the bridge over Champoeg Creek. There are 11 known burials. This is on David Weston D.L.C. #55, OC #4747. {10 November 1990} (Not shown on St. Paul 1956-85 USGS Quad. map.)

WILLAMETTE MISSION
AKA: 1. MISSION BOTTOM
    2. WILLAMETTE
       METHODIST

B   ?   12   1834   T6S R3W   S3

Led by Jason Lee the Willamette Mission was established in the fall of 1834 by Methodist missionaries. It was the earliest Protestant mission to the Indians in the Willamette Valley. Situated on what was then the right bank of the Willamette River, the cemetery was on a hill above the Mission buildings. In 1840-1841 the main activity was transferred about ten miles to the south to Chemeketa, what is now the city of Salem. By 1844 the Willamette Mission was abandoned; the flood of December 1861 virtually destroyed it. This flood changed the main channel and the site remains on what is now the right bank of an oxbow lake known as Mission Lake. A D.A.R. survey indicated 60+ persons buried here; several of the missionaries were reburied in what is now Lee Mission Cemetery in Salem. There is now no sign of the old Willamette Mission Cemetery which is within Willamette Mission State Park. On the William Matheny D.L.C. #67, OC #2448. {August 1993} (Not shown on Mission Bottom 1967-93 USGS Quad. map.)

Name of Cemetery and also known as	Number of burials	Acres	Condition	Date started or earliest known burial	Township	Range	Section

WILLAMETTE UNIVERSITY MEDICAL SCHOOL

? ? ? 1895-1913 T7S R3W S27

Willamette University in Salem had a medical school for some years. There are death certificates for three deaths in 1911-1912 at the Oregon State Insane Asylum. The cadavers were sent to the Medical School. Another 1912 death at the Salem Hospital was sent to the Medical School. (The University is shown on Salem West 1969-86 USGS Quad. map.)

WOODWORTH CHILDREN
  AKA: 1. NORTH HOWELL

A 0.01 ? ? T7S R2W ?

Probably located in Section 2 or 3. These are the graves of the Woodworth children. The burials are presumably near the old Woodworth home, which was on the north side of Indigo Street Northeast just west of its intersection with 76th Avenue Northeast. It is on the Franklin N. Woodworth D.L.C. #59, OC #2463 and on private land. (Not shown on Salem East 1969-86 USGS Quad. map.)

WORKMEN'S
  AKA: 1. ST. BENEDICT

B 0.1 2 1918 T6S R1W S11

This is a separate small cemetery at the Abbey of St. Benedict on Mt. Angel. This one is for the lay workers, parents of the Brothers and also at least one Oblate. 43 marked graves were noted in September of 1990. The cemetery is about a block northeast, downhill from St. Benedict Cemetery and is shrouded in fir and "cedar" (Thuja) trees. The earliest dated monument: "23 October 1918". {8 September 1990} (Not shown on Silverton 1956-85 USGS Quad. map.)

Marion County

City View

Stanley R. Clarke (2000)

ADAMS FAMILY	MARION CO.	T9S	R3W	S12
ANDERSON see **LONE FIR**	MARION CO.	T8S	R1W	S21
ANDERSON D.L.C., JAMES AND ELEANOR see **LONE FIR**				
	MARION CO.	T8S	R1W	S21
ANDERSON LONE FIR see **LONE FIR**	MARION CO.	T8S	R1W	S21
ANKENY see **COX**	MARION CO.	T9S	R3W	S5
ANKENY BOTTOM see **COX**	MARION CO.	T9S	R3W	S5
ANKENY SCHOOL see **COX**	MARION CO.	T9S	R3W	S5
APOSTOLIC	MARION CO.	T7S	R1W	S8
ASYLUM	MARION CO.	T7S	R3W	S25
AUMSVILLE	MARION CO.	T8S	R1W	S30
AURORA COLONY see **OLD COLONY**	MARION CO.	T4S	R1W	S12
AURORA COMMUNITY	MARION CO.	T4S	R1W	S14
AURORA PARK see **OLD COLONY**	MARION CO.	T4S	R1W	S12
AYVOISE, MARIE [MADAME DORION] see **ST. LOUIS [OLD]**				
	MARION CO.	T5S	R2W	S21
BAKER D.L.C., GEORGE M. see **OLD BELIEVER CHURCH**				
	MARION CO.	T5S	R1W	S30
BATES D.L.C., JOS. M. AND JAMES M. see **JEFFERSON**				
	MARION CO.	T10S	R3W	S1
BEALE, GEORGE see **WALDO FAMILY**	MARION CO.	T8S	R2W	S12
BEAVER CREEK see **LONE FIR**	MARION CO.	T8S	R1W	S21
BEILENBERG see **BIELENBERG**	MARION CO.	T8S	R1W	?
BELCREST MEMORIAL PARK AND MAUSOLEUM				
	MARION CO.	T8S	R3W	S4
BELL, SUSAN N. see **HUMBUG**	MARION CO.	T8S	R2W	S4
BELLE PASSI	MARION CO.	T5S	R1W	S19
BELLE PASSI MEMORIAL MAUSOLEUM	MARION CO.	T5S	R1W	S19
BELLEQUE FARM see **LUCIER, MARY**	MARION CO.	T3S	R2W	S33
BELLINGER D.L.C., JOHN see **BELLINGER FAMILY**				
	MARION CO.	T9S	R3W	S35
BELLINGER FAMILY	MARION CO.	T9S	R3W	S35
BETHANY PIONEER	MARION CO.	T6S	R1W	S33
BETHLEHEM VILLAGE see **OLD BELIEVER CHURCH**				
	MARION CO.	T5S	R1W	S30
BIELENBERG	MARION CO.	T8S	R1W	?
BLOOR	MARION CO.	T8S	R2W	S22
BLOUGHER see **BLOOR**	MARION CO.	T8S	R2W	S22
BOEDIGHEIMER see **CAMPBELL-GRIER**	MARION CO.	T9S	R1W	S2
BONNEY D.L.C., JAIRUS see **HOPEWELL MENNONITE**				
	MARION CO.	T4S	R1W	S36
BONNEY FAMILY	MARION CO.	T5S	R1W	S9
BONNEY, JOHN T. see **BONNEY FAMILY**				
	MARION CO.	T5S	R1W	S9
BOYS	MARION CO.	T8S	R2W	S17
BRIDGES D.L.C., JOHN see **SHAW CATHOLIC**				
	MARION CO.	T8S	R2W	S13
BROOKS see **PIONEER MEMORIAL**	MARION CO.	T6S	R2W	S10
BROOKS CATHOLIC	MARIAN CO.	T6S	R2W	S21
BROOKS PIONEER see **PIONEER MEMORIAL**				
	MARION CO.	T6S	R2W	S10

BROWN, ELIZABETH see **SACRED HEART**

                                                  MARION CO.   T5S   R2W   S36

BROWN, ELIZABETH see **SACRED HEART**				
	MARION CO.	T5S	R2W	S36
BROWN FAMILY see **SACRED HART**	MARION CO.	T5S	R2W	S36
BROWN, SAMUEL see **SACRED HEART**	MARION CO.	T5S	R2W	S36
BUTLER see **AUMSVILLE**	MARION CO.	T8S	R1W	S30
BUTTEVILLE [NEW]	MARION CO.	T3S	R1W	S32
BUTTEVILLE [OLD]	MARION CO.	T3S	R1W	S32
BYRD D.L.C., LORENZO A. see **FAIRFIELD**				
	MARION CO.	T5S	R2W	S19
CALVARY	MARION CO.	T6S	R1W	S3
CALVARY BAPTIST CHURCH COLUMBARIUM				
	MARION CO.	T7S	R3W	S27
CALVARY LUTHERAN CHURCH COLUMBARIUM [STAYTON]				
	MARION CO.	T9S	R1W	S10
CAMMACK, MR. ALFRED see **ROSEDALE FRIENDS**				
	MARION CO.	T8S	R3W	S28
CAMPBELL-GRIER	MARION CO.	T9S	R1W	S2
CAPLINGER, J. C. see **RICKEY**	MARION CO.	T7S	R2W	S32
CAREY D.L.C., JOHN C. AND SARAH see **ESSON MEMORIAL, IDA**				
	MARION CO.	T6S	R1W	S5
CASE see **CHAMPOEG**	MARION CO.	T4S	R2W	S12
CATACOMBS	MARION CO.	T4S	R2W	S19
CHALLAFOIX D.L.C., CATHARINE see **HARDING FAMILY**				
	MARION CO.	T4S	R2W	S33
CHAMPOEG	MARION CO.	T4S	R2W	S12
CHEMAWA	MARION CO.	T6S	R3W	S36
CITY VIEW, MT. CREST ABBEY MAUSOLEUM AND SUNRISE GARDEN MAUSOLEUM				
	MARION CO.	T7S	R3W	S33
CLAGGETT	MARION CO.	T6S	R3W	S26
CLEAR LAKE see **CLAGGETT**	MARION CO.	T6S	R3W	S26
CLOVERDALE	MARION CO.	T9S	R2W	S7
COATES, E. S. see **COATES INFANT**	MARION CO.	T8S	R2W	S19
COATES INFANT	MARION CO.	T8S	R2W	S19
COLBY, AMANDA M. see **COLBY FARM, J. A.**				
	MARION CO.	?	?	?
COLBY FARM, J. A.	MARION CO.	?	?	?
CONDIT see **PLEASANT GROVE**	MARION CO.	T9S	R2W	S11
CONDIT D.L.C., PHILIP see **PLEASANT GROVE**				
	MARION CO.	T9S	R2W	S11
CONDIT, REVEREND PHILIP see **PLEASANT GROVE**				
	MARION CO.	T9S	R2W	S11
CONE D.L.C., ANTON see **BUTTEVILLE [NEW]**				
	MARION CO.	T3S	R1W	S32
COOLIDGE AND McCLAINE see **SILVERTON**				
	MARION CO.	T6S	R1W	S34
CORNELIUS see **CLOVERDALE**	MARION CO.	T9S	R2W	S7
COX	MARION CO.	T9S	R3W	S5
COX D.L.C., ELIAS see **BETHANY PIONEER**				
	MARION CO.	T6S	R1W	S33
COX D.L.C., JOSEPH AND MARTHA see **COX**				
	MARION CO.	T9S	R3W	S5

COX D.L.C., PETER see **ST. PAUL'S CATHOLIC**				
	MARION CO.	T6S	R1W	S27
CROOKED FINGER	MARION CO.	T7S	R2E	S8
CULVER D.L.C., DAVID AND ELIZABETH see **CULVER, DAVID**				
	MARION CO.	T7S	R1W	S36
CULVER, DAVID	MARION CO.	T7S	R1W	S36
DAVENPORT FAMILY	MARION CO.	T7S	R1W	S22
DAVENPORT, HOMER see **DAVENPORT FAMILY**				
	MARION CO.	T7S	R1W	S22
DAVIS D.L.C., LEANDER see **SILVERTON**				
	MARION CO.	T6S	R1W	S34
DELORME D.L.C., BARTHOLOMEW see **ST. LOUIS [NEW]**				
	MARION CO.	T5S	R2W	S21
DENNY D.L.C., JAMES M. see **MATER DOLOROSA**				
	MARION CO.	T8S	R1W	S34
DEPOT, PETER (PIERRE) see **SACRED HEART**				
	MARION CO.	T5S	R2W	S36
DeSARTS ADDITION see **SILVERTON**	MARION CO.	T6S	R1W	S34
DICKENS D.L.C., REUBEN AND NANCY see **PATTON FAMILY**				
	MARION CO.	T8S	R1W	S5
DICKENS FAMILY see **PATTON FAMILY**				
	MARION CO.	T8S	R1W	S5
DONALD see **CHAMPOEG**	MARION CO.	T4S	R2W	S12
DOTY, MARY M. see **PRUNE RIDGE**	MARION CO.	T7S	R2E	S8
DOWNING see **LONE FIR**	MARION CO.	T8S	R1W	S21
DRAKES CROSSING see **GREEN MOUNTAIN**				
	MARION CO.	T7S	R1E	S26
DUNKARD see **STIP MEMORIAL**	MARION CO.	T8S	R2W	S2
DURETTE FARM see **FAIRFIELD**	MARION CO.	T5S	R2W	S19
EAST SUBLIMITY see **HOBSON-WHITNEY**				
	MARION CO.	T8S	R1W	S35
EMANUEL see **VALLEY VIEW**	MARION CO.	T6S	R1W	S36
EMANUEL BIBLE CHURCH see **PRATUM**	MARION CO.	T7S	R1W	S19
ENGLE D.L.C., JOSEPH see **BELLE PASSI MEMORIAL MAUSOLEUM**				
	MARION CO.	T5S	R1W	S19
EOFF	MARION CO.	T7S	R2W	S25
EOFF D.L.C., GEORGE AND NANCY see **EOFF**				
	MARION CO.	T7S	R2W	S25
ESSON FAMILY see **ESSON MEMORIAL, IDA**				
	MARION CO.	T6S	R1W	S5
ESSON FARM see **ESSON MEMORIAL, IDA**				
	MARION CO.	T6S	R1W	S5
ESSON MEMORIAL, IDA	MARION CO.	T6S	R1W	S5
ETTLIN see **HOLY ROSARY**	MARION CO.	T6S	R1E	S36
ETZEL see **HOBSON-WHITNEY**	MARION CO.	T8S	R1W	S35
EVANS VALLEY see **VALLEY VIEW**	MARION CO.	T6S	R1W	S36
FAIRFIELD	MARION CO.	T5S	R2W	S19
FAIRMONT HILL see **CITY VIEW, MT. CREST ABBY MAUSOLEUM AND SUNRISE GARDEN MAUSOLEUM**				
	MARION CO.	T7S	R3W	S33
FAST, RANDY see **HOWELL PRAIRIE**	MARION CO.	T7S	R2W	S4
FITZGERALD, PATRICK see **MARION COUNTY POOR FARM**				
	MARION CO.	T7S	R3W	?

FRIENDS see **MARION FRIENDS**	MARION CO.	T9S	R2W	S29
FROHMADER see **HALLS FERRY**	MARION CO.	T8S	R4W	S14
GATH ROAD see **BOYS**	MARION CO.	T8S	R2W	S17
GERMAN CHRISTIAN APOSTOLIC see **APOSTOLIC**				
	MARION CO.	T7S	R1W	S8
GERMAN LUTHERAN see **TRINITY LUTHERAN**				
	MARION CO.	T6S	R1W	S12
GERVAIS CATHOLIC see **SACRED HART**				
	MARION CO.	T5S	R2W	S36
GERVAIS MASONIC see **MASONIC [GERVAIS]**				
	MARION CO.	T5S	R2W	S36
GIBSON D.L.C., RANDOLPH C. see **GIBSON FAMILY**				
	MARION CO.	T6S	R1W	S14
GIBSON FAMILY	MARION CO.	T6S	R1W	S14
GILKISON, JAMES A.	MARION CO.	T8S	R3W	S24
GLEN-OAK ORPHANAGE	MARION CO.	T7S	R3W	S25
GLOVER D.L.C., PHILIP see **GLOVER FAMILY**				
	MARION CO.	T8S	R1W	S27
GLOVER FAMILY	MARION CO.	T8S	R1W	S27
GREEN MOUNTAIN	MARION CO.	T7S	R1E	S26
GRIM see **HUBBARD**	MARION CO.	T4S	R1W	S33
HALBERT BAPTIST CHURCH see **HAYESVILLE**				
	MARION CO.	T7S	R3W	S12
HALL D.L.C., BENJAMIN F. AND MARY ANN see **ST. LUKE'S**				
	MARION CO.	T5S	R1W	S7
HALL PLACE, C. M. see **LaFOLLETTE FAMILY**				
	MARION CO.	T6S	R3W	S1
HALLS FERRY	MARION CO.	T8S	R4W	S14
HALSE INFANT see **MUTE SCHOOL**	MARION CO.	T8S	R2W	?
HARDING FAMILY	MARION CO.	T4S	R2W	S33
HAYESVILLE	MARION CO.	T7S	R3W	S12
HAZELGREEN see **HOWELL PRAIRIE**	MARION CO.	T7S	R2W	S4
HEATER	MARION CO.	T8S	R1E	S8
HERREN D.L.C., JOHN see **BOYS**	MARION CO.	T8S	R2W	S17
HERREN FAMILY	MARION CO.	T8S	R2W	S17
HERRON D.L.C., JOHN see **HERREN FAMILY**				
	MARION CO.	T8S	R2W	S17
HERRON [Sic] D.L.C., JOHN see **COATES INFANT**				
	MARION CO.	T8S	R2W	S19
HERRON [Sic] FAMILY see **HERREN FAMILY**				
	MARION CO.	T8S	R2W	S17
HIGHLAND PIONEER see **MT. ANGEL**	MARION CO.	T6S	R1W	S3
HOBART ROAD see **ST. PAUL'S CATHOLIC**				
	MARION CO.	T6S	R1W	S27
HOBSON-WHITNEY	MARION CO.	T8S	R1W	S35
HOLY ROSARY	MARION CO.	T6S	R1E	S36
HOPEWELL CHURCH see **HOPEWELL MENNONITE**				
	MARION CO.	T4S	R1W	S36
HOPEWELL MENNONITE	MARION CO.	T4S	R1W	S36
HOSPITAL CREMATORIUM see **ASYLUM**	MARION CO.	T7S	R3W	S25
HOWELL D.L.C., JOHN see **HOWELL PRAIRIE**				
	MARION CO.	T7S	R2W	S4

HOWELL FAMILY see **HOWELL PRAIRIE**				
	MARION CO.	T7S	R2W	S4
HOWELL PRAIRIE	MARION CO.	T7S	R2W	S4
HOWELL, TEMPERANCE see **HOWELL PRAIRIE**				
	MARION CO.	T7S	R2W	S4
HUBBARD	MARION CO.	T4S	R1W	S33
HUBBARD COMMUNITY see **HUBBARD**	MARION CO.	T4S	R1W	S33
HULLT see **GREEN MOUNTAIN**	MARION CO.	T7S	R1E	S26
HULT see **GREEN MOUNTAIN**	MARION CO.	T7S	R1E	S26
HUMBUG	MARION CO.	T8S	R2W	S4
HUNSAKER D.L.C., JOSEPH see **HUNSAKER FAMILY**				
	MARION CO.	T9S	R2W	S17
HUNSAKER FAMILY	MARION CO.	T9S	R2W	S17
HUNT D.L.C., GEORGE W. AND ELIZABETH N. see **HUNT FAMILY**				
	MARION CO.	T8S	R1W	S23
HUNT D.L.C., JOHN S. see **MT. HOPE**				
	MARION CO.	T7S	R1W	S33
HUNT D.L.C., JOHN S. see **SMALL, REVEREND THOMAS HENDERSON**				
	MARION CO.	T7S	R1W	S34
HUNT FAMILY	MARION CO.	T8S	R1W	S23
HUNT FAMILY see **MT. HOPE**	MARION CO.	T7S	R1W	S33
I.O.O.F. see **MARION FRIENDS**	MARION CO.	T9S	R2W	S29
I.O.O.F. see **SALEM PIONEER**	MARION CO.	T7S	R3W	S33
I.O.O.F. see **SILVERTON**	MARION CO.	T6S	R1W	S34
I.O.O.F. [MARION] see **CLOVERDALE**				
	MARION CO.	T9S	R2W	S7
I.O.O.F. [TURNER] see **TWIN OAKS**	MARION CO.	T8S	R2W	S28
I.O.O.F. STAYTON LODGE #64 see **LONE OAK [NEW]**				
	MARION CO.	T9S	R1W	S10
IMMACULATE CONCEPTION CHURCH see **ST. MARY'S [STAYTON]**				
	MARION CO.	T9S	R1W	S10
INDIAN	MARION CO.	T7S	R3W	S26
JEFFERSON	MARION CO.	T10S	R3W	S1
JONES see **PIONEER MEMORIAL**	MARION CO.	T6S	R2W	S10
JONES D.L.C., EARL see **LaFOLLETTE FAMILY**				
	MARION CO.	T6S	R3W	S1
JORY FAMILY	MARION CO.	T8S	R3W	S28
JORY SENIOR D.L.C., JAMES AND MARY see **JORY FAMILY**				
	MARION CO.	T8S	R3W	S28
KAUFMAN see **APOSTOLIC**	MARION CO.	T7S	R1W	S8
KAUFMAN ROAD see **APOSTOLIC**	MARION CO.	T7S	R1W	S8
KEIL, DR. WILLIAM see **OLD COLONY**				
	MARION CO.	T4S	R1W	S12
KEIL FAMILY see **OLD COLONY**	MARION CO.	T4S	R1W	S12
KIMSEY FAMILY	MARION CO.	T8S	R1W	S7
KINCAID D.L.C., SAMUEL see **UNION HILL**				
	MARION CO.	T8S	R1E	S7
KING FAMILY see **UNION HILL**	MARION CO.	T8S	R1E	S7
LABISH CENTER see **BROOKS CATHOLIC**				
	MARION CO.	T6S	R2W	S21
LaFLEMME see **BROOKS CATHOLIC**	MARION CO.	T6S	R2W	S21
LaFOLLETTE see **HALLS FERRY**	MARION CO.	T8S	R4W	S14

LaFOLLETTE, D. B. see **LaFOLLETTE FAMILY**				
	MARION CO.	T6S	R3W	S1
LaFOLLETTE, D. H. see **LaFOLLETTE FAMILY**				
	MARION CO.	T6S	R3W	S1
LaFOLLETTE FAMILY	MARION CO.	T6S	R3W	S1
LaFOLLETTE, S. A. see **LaFOLLETTE FAMILY**				
	MARION CO.	T6S	R3W	S1
LaFORTE D.L.C., JOSEPH see **BUTTEVILLE [OLD]**				
	MARION CO.	T3S	R1W	S32
LAPRATTE D.L.C., ALEXANDER see **BROOKS CATHOLIC**				
	MARIAN CO.	T6S	R2W	S21
LEABO	MARION CO.	T8S	R4W	S26
LEE, JASON see **LEE MISSION**	MARION CO.	T7S	R3W	S24
LEE, JASON see **WILLAMETTE MISSION**				
	MARION CO.	T6S	R3W	S3
LEE MEMORIAL see **LEE MISSION**	MARION CO.	T7S	R3W	S24
LEE MISSION	MARION CO.	T7S	R3W	S24
LEWIS	MARION CO.	T7S	R1E	S29
LEWIS D.L.C., DANIEL P. see **LEWIS**				
	MARION CO.	T7S	R1E	S29
LIBERTY SCHOOL see **STIPP MEMORIAL**				
	MARION CO.	T8S	R2W	S2
LIPSCOMB see **HEATER**	MARION CO.	T8S	R1E	S8
LIPSCOMB D.L.C., BARNET see **HEATER**				
	MARION CO.	T8S	R1E	S8
LONE FIR	MARION CO.	T8S	R1W	S21
LONE OAK [NEW]	MARION CO.	T9S	R1W	S10
LONE OAK [OLD] see **CAMPBELL-GRIER**				
	MARION CO.	T9S	R1W	S2
LONE OAK II see **CAMBELL-GRIER**	MARION CO.	T9S	R1W	S2
LOONEY D.L.C., JESSE AND RUBY see **LOONEY FAMILY**				
	MARION CO.	T9S	R3W	S23
LOONEY FAMILY	MARION CO.	T9S	R3W	S23
LUCIER, ETIENNE see **LUCIER, MARY**				
	MARION CO.	T3S	R2W	S33
LUCIER FARM see **LUCIER, MARY**	MARION CO.	T3S	R2W	S33
LUCIER, MARY	MARION CO.	T3S	R2W	S33
LUCIER, MARY MARGUERITE TCHINOUK see **LUCIER, MARY**				
	MARION CO.	T3S	R2W	S33
LUTHERAN see **VALLEY VIEW**	MARION CO.	T6S	R1W	S36
LUTHY see **MT. HOPE**	MARION CO.	T7S	R1W	S33
MacLAREN SCHOOL see **BONNEY FAMILY**				
	MARION CO.	T5S	R1W	S9
MACLEAY see **STIPP MEMORIAL**	MARION CO.	T8S	R2W	S2
MARION COUNTY POOR FARM	MARION CO.	T7S	R3W	?
MARION FRIENDS	MARION CO.	T9S	R2W	S29
MARION HILL see **MARION FRIENDS**	MARION CO.	T9S	R2W	S29
MARSHALL, JOHN see **BONNEY FAMILY**				
	MARION CO.	T5S	R1W	S9
MASONIC see **JEFFERSON**	MARION CO.	T10S	R3W	S1
MASONIC [GERVAIS]	MARION CO.	T5S	R2W	S36

MASONIC [STAYTON] see **LONE OAK [NEW]**

	MARION CO.	T9S	R1W	S10
MATER DOLOROSA	MARION CO.	T8S	R1W	S34

MATHENY D.L.C., WILLIAM see **WILLAMETTE MISSION**

	MARION CO.	T6S	R3W	S3
McCALISTER see **PRATUM**	MARION CO.	T7S	R1W	S19

McCALLISTER D.L.C., HARDIN AND JULIA see **APOSTOLIC**

	MARION CO.	T7S	R1W	S8
McCORKLE see **HOWELL PRAIRIE**	MARION CO.	T7S	R2W	S4
McCORKLE see **NEWSOM CAMPGROUND**	MARION CO.	T6S	R1W	S19
McCOWN, G. W.	MARION CO.	T7S	R2E	S7
McCULLEY see **McCULLY**	MARION CO.	T9S	R2W	S21
McCULLY	MARION CO.	T9S	R2W	S21

McCULLY D.L.C., ISAAC see **McCULLY**

	MARION CO.	T9S	R2W	S21
MERIDIAN see **TRINITY LUTHERAN**	MARION CO.	T6S	R1W	S12
MERRILL see **PENITENTIARY [NEW]**	MARION CO.	T7S	R3W	S25
METHODIST see **JEFFERSON**	MARION CO.	T10S	R3W	S1
MIDDLEGROVE see **HOWELL PRAIRIE**	MARION CO.	T7S	R2W	S4
MILLER	MARION CO.	T6S	R1E	S19

MILLER D.L.C., RICHARD see **MILLER**

	MARION CO.	T6S	R1E	S19

MISSION BOTTOM see **WILLAMETTE MISSION**

	MARION CO.	T6S	R3W	S3
MORRIS see **MT. HOPE**	MARION CO.	T7S	R1W	S33
MT. ANGEL	MARION CO.	T6S	R1W	S3

MT. ANGEL ABBEY see **ST. BENEDICT**

	MARION CO.	T6S	R1W	S11
MT. HOPE	MARION CO.	T7S	R1W	S33

MOUNTAIN VIEW see **GREEN MOUNTAIN**

	MARION CO.	T7S	R1E	S26
MUDDY see **HOWELL PRAIRIE**	MARION CO.	T7S	R2W	S4

MURPHY FAMILY see **HOWELL PRAIRIE**

	MARION CO.	T7S	R2W	S4

MURPHY-HOWELL FAMILIES see **HOWELL PRAIRIE**

	MARION CO.	T7S	R2W	S4
MUTE SCHOOL	MARION CO.	T8S	R2W	?

NELSON, JAMES see **NEWSOM CAMPGROUND**

	MARION CO.	T6S	R1W	S19

NEWELL D.L.C., ROBERT see **NEWELL, KITTY**

	MARION CO.	T4S	R2W	S1
NEWELL, KITTY	MARION CO.	T4S	R2W	S1
NEWSOME see **HOWELL PRAIRIE**	MARION CO.	T7S	R2W	S4
NEWSOM CAMPGROUND	MARION CO.	T6S	R1W	S19

NEWSOM, DAVID see **NEWSOM CAMPGROUND**

	MARION CO.	T6S	R1W	S19

NEWSOM, POLLY see **NEWSOM CAMPGROUND**

	MARION CO.	T6S	R1W	S19

NORTH HOWELL see **WOODWORTH CHILDREN**

	MARION CO.	T7S	R2W	?

NORTH SALEM BAPTIST CHURCH see **HAYESVILLE**

	MARION CO.	T7S	R3W	S12

Marion County

NORWEGIAN see **VALLEY VIEW**	MARION CO.	T6S	R1W	S36
NUSOM *[Sic]* see **NEWSOM CAMPGROUND**				
	MARION CO.	T6S	R1W	S19
O.F.M.I. see **OREGON STATE INSTITUTION FOR THE FEEBLE MINDED**				
	MARION CO.	T8S	R3W	S2
O.S.H. see **ASYLUM**	MARION CO.	T7S	R3W	S25
O.S.I.A. see **ASYLUM**	MARION CO.	T7S	R3W	S25
O.S.P. see **PENITENTIARY [NEW]**	MARION CO.	T7S	R3W	S25
ODERMATT, FATHER ADELHELM see **ST. BENEDICT**				
	MARION CO.	T6S	R1W	S11
OLD BELIEVER CHURCH	MARION CO.	T5S	R1W	S30
OLD COLONY	MARION CO.	T4S	R1W	S12
OLD DRIFT CREEK see **HEATER**	MARION CO.	T8S	R1E	S8
OLD MASONIC see **CHAMPOEG**	MARION CO.	T4S	R2W	S12
OLD MISSION see **ST. PAUL'S [OLD]**				
	MARION CO.	T4S	R2W	S19
OLINGER, ABRAM	MARION CO.	T8S	R2W	S3
OLINGER D.L.C., ABRAM AND RACHEL see **OLINGER, ABRAM**				
	MARION CO.	T8S	R2W	S3
OREGON STATE HOSPITAL	MARION CO.	T7S	R3W	S25
OREGON STATE HOSPITAL see **ASYLUM**				
	MARION CO.	T7S	R3W	S25
OREGON STATE INSTITUTION FOR THE FEEBLE MINDED				
	MARION CO.	T8S	R3W	S2
ORPHANS HOME [SALEM] see **GLEN-OAK ORPHANAGE**				
	MARION CO.	T7S	R3W	S25
PARKERSVILLE see **PIONEER MEMORIAL**				
	MARION CO.	T6S	R2W	S10
PARRISH see **McCULLY**	MARION CO.	T9S	R2W	S21
PARRISH GAP see **HUNSAKER FAMILY**	MARION CO.	T9S	R2W	S17
PARRISH, JESSE see **McCULLY**	MARION CO.	T9S	R2W	S21
PARRISH, MRS. ELIZABETH see **GLEN-OAK ORPHANAGE**				
	MARION CO.	T7S	R3W	S25
PARRISH OREGON PROVISIONAL LAND CLAIM NOTIFICATION, JOSIAH L. see				
GLEN-OAK ORPHANAGE	MARION CO.	T7S	R3W	S25
PATTON FAMILY	MARION CO.	T8S	R1W	S5
PENITENTIARY [NEW]	MARION CO.	T7S	R3W	S25
PENITENTIARY [OLD]	MARION CO.	T7S	R3W	S25
PENITENTIARY ANNEX see **HERREN FAMILY**				
	MARION CO.	T8S	R2W	S17
PICKARD-HUNSAKER FAMILIES see **HUNSAKER FAMILY**				
	MARION CO.	T9S	R2W	S17
PIONEER [WACONDA] see **PIONEER MEMORIAL**				
	MARION CO.	T6S	R2W	S10
PIONEER MEMORIAL	MARION CO.	T6S	R2W	S10
PITTMAN, ANNA MARIA see **LEE MISSION**				
	MARION CO.	T7S	R3W	S24
PLEASANT GROVE	MARION CO.	T9S	R2W	S11
POUJADE D.L.C., THEODORE C. see **MASONIC [GERVAIS]**				
	MARION CO.	T5S	R2W	S36

POWELL D.L.C., THEOPHILUS see **POWELL FAMILY, REVEREND THEOPHILUS**

	MARION CO.	T7S	R1W	S33
POWELL FAMILY, REVEREND THEOPHILUS				
	MARION CO.	T7S	R1W	S33
PRATUM	MARION CO.	T7S	R1W	S19
PRATUM MENNONITE see **PRATUM**	MARION CO.	T7S	R1W	S19
PRUNE RIDGE	MARION CO.	T7S	R2E	S8
PUDDING RIVER see **APOSTOLIC**	MARION CO.	T7S	R1W	S8
PURVINE D.L.C., EWING see **PURVINE FARM BURIALS**				
	MARION CO.	?	R1W	?
PURVINE FARM BURIALS	MARION CO.	?	R1W	?
QUEEN OF ANGELS CONVENT	MARION CO.	T6S	R1W	S10
QUINABY'S CORNER	MARION CO.	T7S	R3W	S27
RADER D.L.C., ARCHIBALD see **HOBSON-WHITNEY**				
	MARION CO.	T8S	R1W	S35
RAYMOND D.L.C., PETER see **BELLE PASSI**				
	MARION CO.	T5S	R1W	S19
RECTOR D.L.C., WILLIAM H. see **MUTE SCHOOL**				
	MARION CO.	T8S	R2W	?
RENILDE, SISTER see **CATACOMBS**	MARION CO.	T4S	R2W	S19
RICKEY	MARION CO.	T7S	R2W	S32
RICKEY D.L.C., JAMES see **RICKEY**	MARION CO.	T7S	R2W	S32
RIVER VIEW see **HALLS FERRY**	MARION CO.	T8S	R4W	S14
ROBL, ANDREAS see **ST. BENEDICT**	MARION CO.	T6S	R1W	S11
ROBL, MARGARET see **ST. BENEDICT**	MARION CO.	T6S	R1W	S11
ROCK POINT see **LONE FIR**	MARION CO.	T8S	R1W	S21
ROCKY POINT see **LONE FIR**	MARION CO.	T8S	R1W	S21
ROSEDALE see **ROSEDALE FRIENDS**	MARION CO.	T8S	R3W	S28
ROSEDALE FRIENDS	MARION CO.	T8S	R3W	S28
ROWLAND, PATRICK	MARION CO.	T4S	R2W	S19
RURAL see **SALEM PIONEER**	MARION CO.	T7S	R3W	S33
SACRED HEART	MARION CO.	T5S	R2W	S36
ST. BARBARA'S	MARION CO.	T8S	R3W	S3
ST. BENEDICT	MARION CO.	T6S	R1W	S11
ST. BENEDICT see **WORKMAN'S**	MARION CO.	T6S	R1W	S11
ST. BONIFACE	MARION CO.	T8S	R1W	S34
ST. JOSEPH see **ST. BARBARA'S**	MARION CO.	T8S	R3W	S3
ST. LOUIS [NEW]	MARION CO.	T5S	R2W	S21
ST. LOUIS [OLD]	MARION CO.	T5S	R2W	S21
ST. LUKE'S	MARION CO.	T5S	R1W	S7
ST. MARY'S see **MT. ANGEL**	MARION CO.	T6S	R1W	S3
ST. MARY'S [SHAW] see **SHAW CATHOLIC**				
	MARION CO.	T8S	R2W	S13
ST. MARY'S [STAYTON]	MARION CO.	T9S	R1W	S10
ST. MARY'S CATHOLIC see **SHAW CATHOLIC**				
	MARION CO.	T8S	R2W	S13
ST. MARY'S CONVENT see **QUEEN OF ANGELS CONVENT**				
	MARION CO.	T6S	R1W	S10
ST. PAUL'S [NEW; ST. PAUL]	MARION CO.	T4S	R2W	S19
ST. PAUL'S [OLD; ST. PAUL]	MARION CO.	T4S	R2W	S19
ST. PAUL'S CATHOLIC	MARION CO.	T6S	R1W	S27

ST. PAUL'S EPISCOPAL CHURCH COLUMBARIUM

	MARION CO.	T7S	R3W	S27
ST. ROSE see **HOLY ROSARY**	MARION CO.	T6S	R1E	S36

ST. TIMOTHY'S EPISCOPAL CHURCH MEMORIAL GARDENS

	MARION CO.	T7S	R3W	S24
SALEM CATHOLIC see **ST. BARBARA'S**				
	MARION CO.	T8S	R3W	S3
SALEM PIONEER	MARION CO.	T7S	R3W	S33
SANTIAM MASONIC LODGE #1 see **LONE OAK [NEW]**				
	MARION CO.	T9S	R1W	S10
SCANDIA see **BETHANY PIONEER**	MARION CO.	T6S	R1W	S33
SCANTY see **BETHANY PIONEER**	MARION CO.	T6S	R1W	S33
SCHOOL DISTRICT #2 see **CHAMPOEG**	MARION CO.	T4S	R2W	S12
SCHOOL DISTRICT #36 see **COX**	MARION CO.	T9S	R3W	S5
SCHOOL FOR DEAF MUTES see **MUTE SCHOOL**				
	MARION CO.	T8S	R2W	?
SCISM see **NEWSOM CAMPGROUND**	MARION CO.	T6S	R1W	S19
SCOTTS MILLS see **HOLY ROSARY**	MARION CO.	T6S	R1E	S36
SHARP, BERNITA JONES see **SMALL, REVEREND THOMAS HENDERSON**				
	MARION CO.	T7S	R1W	S34
SHAW CATHOLIC	MARION CO.	T8S	R2W	S13
SHORT FAMILY	MARION CO.	T7S	R1W	S32
SIDNEY STATION see **COX**	MARION CO.	T9S	R3W	S5
SIEGMUND, RALPH see **TERRELL**	MARION CO.	T9S	R1E	S2
SILVER CLIFF see **LEWIS**	MARION CO.	T7S	R1E	S29
SILVER CREEK see **BETHANY PIONEER**				
	MARION CO.	T6S	R1W	S33
SILVER CREEK see **SILVERTON**	MARION CO.	T6S	R1W	S34
SILVERTON	MARION CO.	T6S	R1W	S34
SIMMONS	MARION CO.	T5S	R1W	S34
SIMMONS HILL see **SIMMONS**	MARION CO.	T5S	R1W	S34
SISTERS, MT. ANGEL see **QUEEN OF ANGELS CONVENT**				
	MARION CO.	T6S	R1W	S10
SKUNK HOLLOW see **BROOKS CATHOLIC**				
	MARION CO.	T6S	R2W	S21
SKUNKVILLE see **BROOKS CATHOLIC**	MARION CO.	T6S	R2W	S21
SMALL, REVEREND THOMAS HENDERSON				
	MARION CO.	T7S	R1W	S34
SMITH see **CLAGGETT**	MARION CO.	T6S	R3W	S26
SMITH D.L.C., ALVIS see **CLAGGETT**				
	MARION CO.	T6S	R3W	S26
SMITH D.L.C., DANIEL see **PIONEER MEMORIAL**				
	MARION CO.	T6S	R2W	S10
SMITH D.L.C., SIMON see **CLOVERDALE**				
	MARION CO.	T9S	R2W	S7
SMITH, MRS. ISAAC see **CLAGGETT**	MARION CO.	T6S	R3W	S26
SOUTH see **HALLS FERRY**	MARION CO.	T8S	R4W	S14
STAPLES see **CLOVERDALE**	MARION CO.	T9S	R2W	S7
STATE CREMATORIUM see **ASYLUM**	MARION CO.	T7S	R3W	S25
STATE REFORM SCHOOL see **BOYS**	MARION CO.	T8S	R2W	S17
STATE REFORM SCHOOL see **HERREN FAMILY**				
	MARION CO.	T8S	R2W	S17

```
STATE SCHOOL FOR THE DEAF see MUTE SCHOOL
                          MARION CO.      T8S    R2W         ?
STAYTON PIONEER see CAMPBELL-GRIER
                          MARION CO.      T9S    R1W         S2
STEIWER-LOONEY see LOONEY FAMILY
                          MARION CO.      T9S    R3W         S23
STEPHENS D.L.C., ADAM AND LUCINDA see HAYESVILLE
                          MARION CO.      T7S    R3W         S12
STEPHENS FAMILY see HAYESVILLE  MARION CO.      T7S    R3W         S12
STIPP D.L.C., JOHN see STIPP MEMORIAL
                          MARION CO.      T8S    R2W         S2
STIPP MEMORIAL           MARION CO.      T8S    R2W         S2
STONEY POINT see LONE FIR  MARION CO.      T8S    R1W         S21
SUBLIMITY GRAVEYARD see HOBSON-WHITNEY
                          MARION CO.      T8S    R1W         S35
SWITZERLAND see APOSTOLIC  MARION CO.      T7S    R1W         S8
TAYLOR D.L.C., JOHN AND ELIZAABETH see AUMSVILLE
                          MARION CO.      T8S    R1W         S30
TERHUNE FARM, ROBERT see BELLINGER FAMILY
                          MARION CO.      T9S    R3W         S35
TERRELL                  MARION CO.      T9S    R1E         S2
TERRELL, JUDGE G. P. see TERRELL
                          MARION CO.      T9S    R1E         S2
THE NOOK see PIONEER MEMORIAL  MARION CO.      T6S    R2W         S10
TRACY see PENITENTIARY [NEW]  MARION CO.      T7S    R3W         S25
TRINITY see VALLEY VIEW   MARION CO.      T6S    R1W         S36
TRINITY LUTHERAN         MARION CO.      T6S    R1W         S12
TWIN OAKS                MARION CO.      T8S    R2W         S28
UNION HILL               MARION CO.      T8S    R1E         S7
VALLEY VIEW              MARION CO.      T6S    R1W         S36
VANDERBILT, _____ see COATES INFANT
                          MARION CO.      T8S    R2W         S19
VAUGHN BABY              MARION CO.      T8S    R4W         ?
WALDO D.L.C., DANIEL AND MALINDA C. see WALDO FAMILY
                          MARION CO.      T8S    R2W         S12
WALDO FAMILY             MARION CO.      T8S    R2W         S12
WALDO HILLS see MT. HOPE  MARION CO.      T7S    R1W         S33
WALKER D.L.C., GILLIAM H. AND RHODA see KIMSEY FAMILY
                          MARION CO.      T8S    R1W         S7
WALKER FAMILY see KIMSEY FAMILY  MARION CO.      T8S    R1W         S7
WARREN see MT. HOPE       MARION CO.      T7S    R1W         S33
WELLS D.L.C., JOHN see WELLS FAMILY
                          MARION CO.      T10S   R2W         S6
WELLS FAMILY             MARION CO.      T10S   R2W         S6
WESTON D.L.C., DAVID see WESTON FAMILY
                          MARION CO.      T4S    R2W         S1
WESTON FAMILY            MARION CO.      T4S    R2W         S1
WILLAMETTE METHODIST see WILLAMETTE MISSION
                          MARION CO.      T6S    R3W         S3
WILLAMETTE MISSION       MARION CO.      T6S    R3W         S3
WILLAMETTE UNIVERSITY MEDICAL SCHOOL
                          MARION CO.      T7S    R3W         S27
```

WILLARD see **MT. HOPE**	MARION CO.	T7S	R1W	S33
WOODWORTH CHILDREN	MARION CO.	T7S	R2W	?
WOODWORTH D.L.C., FRANKLIN N. see **WOODWORTH CHILDREN**				
	MARION CO.	T7S	R2W	?
WORKMEN'S	MARION CO.	T6S	R1W	S11
YERGEN see **CHAMPOEG**	MARION CO.	T4S	R2W	S12
YERGENS GRAVEYARD see **CHAMPOEG**	MARION CO.	T4S	R2W	S12
YERGENS', WILLIAM see **CHAMPOEG**	MARION CO.	T4S	R2W	S12
YERGONVILLE MISSION see **CHAMPOEG**				
	MARION CO.	T4S	R2W	S12

St. Paul's [Old; St. Paul]
Dean H. Byrd (1991)

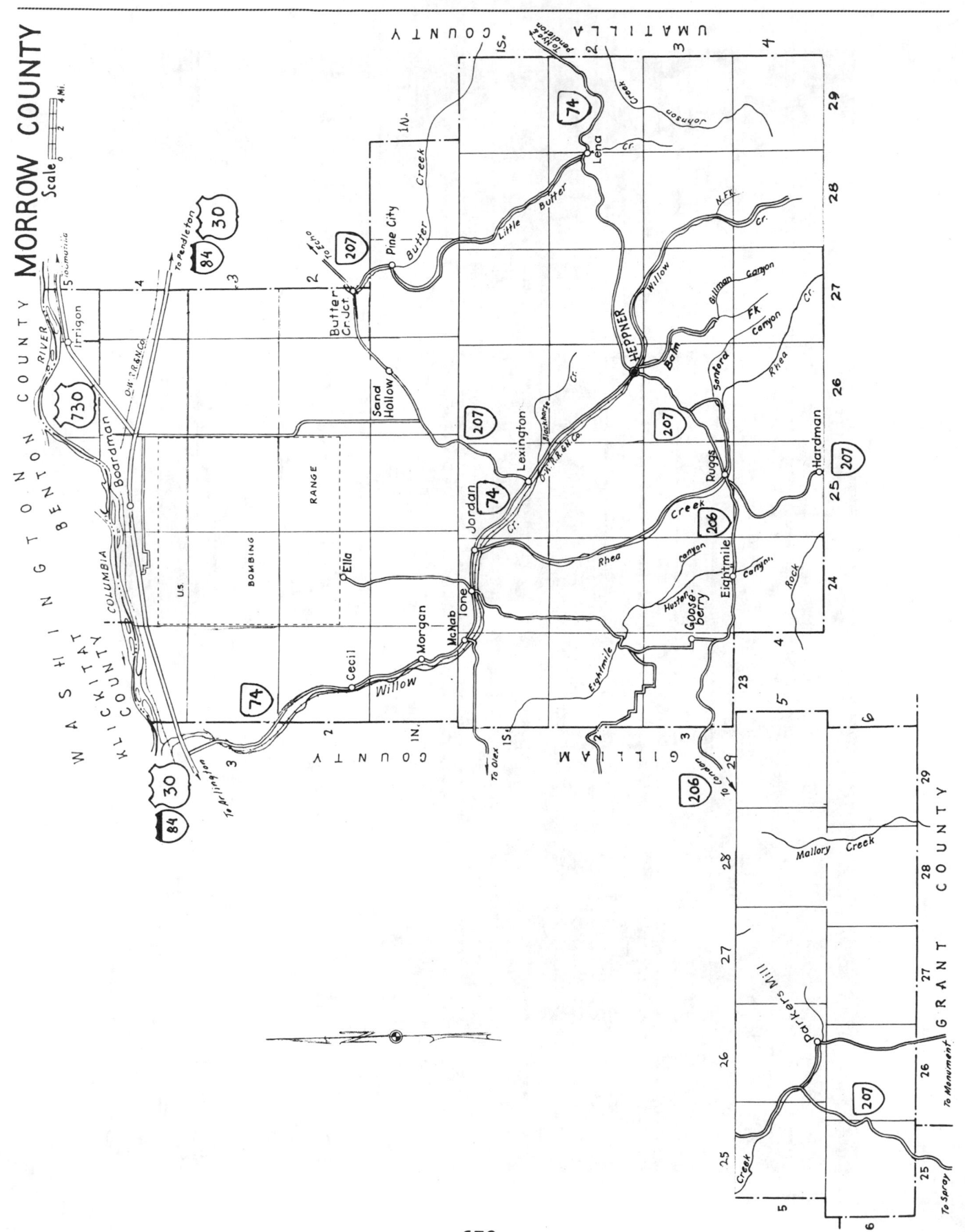

MORROW COUNTY

Hardman [Old]
Janice M. Healy (2000)

Area: 2,049 square miles
Population (1998): 9,985
County seat: Heppner, Population: 1,480
County established: 16 February 1885

A temporary cemetery was established at Well Spring along the Oregon Trail in 1852. Four organized public cemeteries were started in 1868-1870. The county was largely taken over by wheat farmers and livestock ranchers.

Morgan
Janice M. Healy (2000)

Hardman [Old]
Janice M. Healy (2000)

Hardman [Old]
Janice M. Healy (2000)

Name of Cemetery and also known as	Number of burials	Acres	Condition	Date started or earliest known burial	Township	Range	Section

ALLEN FAMILY

A 0.01 ? 1897 T5S R26E S29

Located probably in the Northeast 1/4 of Section 29, near the old buildings on the Allen Homestead. The homestead is in Allen Canyon northwest of Parkers Mill, along a portion of the old road from Heppner to Monument. Reuben and Myria M. Allen settled here in 1878. The burials are for W. Reuben Allen 1832-1897, his wife Myria Mark Allen 1832-1901 and the granddaughter Della Roberts born and died 1902. (The ranch, but not the burial sites are shown on Big Rock Flat 1969-83 USGS Quad. map.)

BAKER
AKA: 1. FAIRVIEW
2. KING
3. TEWS

B 1.4 3 1886-1952 T2S R24E S6

Travel 4 miles south of Ione on the Ione-Gooseberry Road; turn right (west) on Bergevin Road for 0.7 of a mile, then turn left (south) on Tews Road for 1 mile. (Ione South 1968 USGS Quad. map.)

CANTWELL INFANT

A 0.01 ? ? T3S R25E S35

About 1.5 miles east of Ruggs is the burial site for infant Cantwell. No further information was given in the report. (Not shown on Ruggs 1968 USGS Quad. map.)

CHAMBERLIN, MRS. H.

A 0.01 ? ? T4N R24E ?

An early burial was reported in the vicinity of Castle Rock along the Columbia River. The gravesite was probably lost when the Columbia River was dammed. (Not shown on Crow Butte 1962-87 USGS Quad. map.)

CHAPEL, TEDDY ROOSEVELT

A 0.01 ? ? T5S R25E S3

This could be a burial in the old Hardman Cemetery see that article. The report lists only "infant son of Eugene and Ida Chapel, Teddy Roosevelt Chapel burial in Township 5 South, Range 25 East, Section 3." No further information was given in the report. (Not shown on Hardman 1969 USGS Quad. map.)

Morrow County

Name of Cemetery and also known as	Number of burials	Acres	Condition	Date started or earliest known burial	Township	Range	Section

CHILD'S GRAVE

A   0.01   ?   ?   T1N   R23E   ?

There was a child's grave reported at or in the vicinity of Morgan. No further information was given in the report, so perhaps this grave is in the Morgan Cemetery itself. (Not shown on Cecil 1968 USGS Quad. map.)

COPPLE FAMILY

A   0.01   ?   1868   T5S   R27E   S2

A report listing "Charles Wesley Coppel, born 19 August 1861, died 26 November 1879 and William Harvey Copple 4 January 1868 are buried here." This is about three air miles northwest of Copple Butte. No other information was given in the report. (Not shown on Summerfield ridge 1969-83 USGS Quad. map.)

COX CHILDREN

A   ?   ?   1884-1908   T2S   R27E   S36

Two baby girls and a baby boy of F. D. Cox are buried on a knoll on the old F. D. Cox Ranch about 1 mile up Hinton Creek from OR. Hwy. 74, via Hanna Arbuckle (Hinton Creek) Road. NOTE: This site is on private property. (Not shown on Skinners Fork 1968 USGS Quad. map.)

CROW, MRS. ANDREW

A   ?   ?   1852   T1S   R28E   S28

Mrs. Crow and 2 of her 7 children died of cholera and were buried by the Oregon Trail. In 1936 the graves were in a school yard. This is about 4.7 miles north of Lena. NOTE: It is not clear if they are separate from Pleasant Point Cemetery or if this is also some of the same family as in the Crow Cemetery in Lane County. (Not shown on Lena 1968 USGS Quad. map.)

DESERT LAWN MEMORIAL
 AKA: 1. IRRIGON

?   ?   ?   ?   T5N   R27E   S20

Located at the east end of Irrigon. Go east on U.S. Hwy. 730 and turn right (south) on South 15th Street; the cemetery is at South 15th Street and Oregon Avenue. The previous cemetery site is now flooded. NOTE: See

Name of Cemetery and also known as	Number of burials	Acres	Condition	Date started or earliest known burial	Township	Range	Section

article under Irrigon [Old]. (Not shown on Paterson 1993 or Irrigon 1962-70 USGS Quad. maps.)

DURAN CHILD

A 0.01 ? ? ? ? ?

"A child of Edward S. Duran, Morrow County." No further information was given in the report.

ELDER CHILDREN

A ? ? ? T2S R27E S26

About 7 miles east of Heppner along OR. Hwy. 74. Two children of John Elder were buried in a fence corner near the old home. In 1970 Floyd Jones owned the land and a small garage stood over the graves. NOTE: This site is on private property. (Not shown on Skinners Fork 1968 USGS Quad. map.)

FRIEZE CHILDREN

A 0.01 ? ? T3S R28E S15

No further information was given in the report for this site. (Not shown on Freezout Ridge 1967 USGS Quad. map.)

GOOSEBERRY

A 0.2 ? 1896 T3S R23E S14

This cemetery is located 17.4 miles south of Ione. Travel 2.5 miles northwest of OR. Hwy. 206, 0.5 of a mile west of Gooseberry, then 0.5 of a mile north to the junction with Warren Road and the Ione-Gooseberry Road. There were 20 known burials 1972. (Gooseberry 1968 USGS Quad. map.)

HALE FAMILY

A 0.01 ? 1897 T3S R27E S2

A report for this site states that Michael Hale,1819-1879 and Millie Hale, b. 1876 are buried in the above Township, Range and Section. No further information was given in the report. (Not shown on Skinners Fork 1968 USGS Quad. map.)

Name of Cemetery and also known as	Number of burials	Acres	Condition	Date started or earliest known burial	Township	Range	Section

HALLAWAY FAMILY — A 0.01 ? ? T1N R24E S5
This small cemetery contains 5 burials and is northwest of Ione by about five air miles. (Not shown on Ione North 1968 USGS Quad. map.)

HARDMAN [OLD] — B 1 3 1875-1910 T4S R25E S34
Located on a hilltop above the town of Hardman. You now must cross a tilled farm field to reach this site. It is fenced and gated, it is overgrown in tall grass. We found only 5 stones on our visit (2000). It was difficult to bury because of rocky ground, and they needed dynamite to open the graves. There were an estimated 30 known burials 1972. {2 September 2000} (Hardman 1969 USGS Quad. map.)

HENDRIX CHILDREN — A 0.01 ? ? T6S R25E S17
"Two Hendrix children are buried here." No futher information was given in the report. (Not shown on Lefevre Prairie 1969-83 USGS Quad. map.)

HEPPNER
AKA: 1. MASONIC — D 13 1 1874 T2S R26E S35
Located on the south city limits of Heppner. Take Chase Street up the steep hill to the cemetery. (Heppner 1968 USGS Quad. map.)

HIGHVIEW
AKA: 1. I.O.O.F. [IONE]
2. IONE — D 5.7 1 1870 T1S R24E S4
Take Cemetery Road north, up the gulley off of OR. Hwy. 74 onto the hill above the town. There were 415 known burials as of 20 June 1980; Oct. 1898 is the earliest recorded burial. Later, the I.O.O.F. bought more land. 10 acres were fenced as of 1936. (Ione North 1968 USGS Quad. map.)

I.O.O.F. [HARDMAN, NEW] — C 4.4 3 1883 T4S R25E S30
Located 3.5 miles from Hardman in Rood Canyon, on the left side of the road as you leave Hardman toward Eightmile on Ridge Road, then go left 1 mile to the cemetery. It was

Name of Cemetery and also known as	Number of burials	Acres	Condition	Date started or earliest known burial	Township	Range	Section

originally 10 acres, of which 5 acres are fenced. Owned by Lone Balm Lodge #82. There were 122 known burials in 1970. (Hardman 1969 USGS Quad. map.)

I.O.O.F. [LEXINGTON]
AKA: 1. LEXINGTON
[NEW]

?   ?   1   1874   T1S   R25E   S34
Lexington I.O.O.F. is 0.9 of a mile south of Lexington via "B" Street and Cemetery Hill Road. Lexington is noted as south of Penland Cemetery, 2 entrances 0.12 of a mile apart on Cemetery Hill Road. These 2 cemeteries adjoin each other. (Lexington 1968 USGS Quad. map.)

INGRAHAM CHILDREN

A   0.01   ?   ?   T5S   R26E   S35
Two children of William Ingraham are reported to be buried here. No futher information was given in the report. (Not shown on Big Rock Flat 1969-83 USGS Quad. map)

IRRIGON [OLD]

1   ?   9   1919-1967   T5N   R26E   S24
This cemetery was on the south bank of the Columbia River at the north end of 1st Street. An undated list of known burials lists 88, in all, from 1919 to July 1967. After the Columbia River was dammed and Lake Umatilla was created, this cemetery would have been abandoned. Presumably the graves were reburied in Desert Lawn Memorial. (Irrigon 1962-70 and Paterson 1993 USGS Quad. maps. The 1970 editions show the Lake Umatilla water level.)

JUNKINS

A   2.5   3   1885-1902   T3S   R24E   S16
Go 18.45 miles southwest of Heppner on OR. Hwy. 207 and OR. Hwy. 206. Turn right (north) off of OR. Hwy. 206 at Milepost 65.7 onto Valby Road. Go 4 miles on Valby Road. Turn right (east) onto John Bergstrom Road and go 0.7 of a mile and turn off to the right on the driveway across the canyon to the cemetery another 0.3 of a mile. There are 14 known burials, others unknown. NOTE: After leaving Junkins Cemetery the driveway

Name of Cemetery and also known as	Number of burials	Acres	Condition	Date started or earliest known burial	Township	Range	Section

continues and loops back into John Bergstrom Road; at Bergstrom Road Milepost 2.2 you may continue easterly to Eightmile Road. (Eightmile 1968 USGS Quad. map.)

LEXINGTON [OLD]   ?   ?   7   **Circa 1870**   **T1S**   **R25E**   **S27**
The first cemetery occupied 2 city blocks at the corner of "E" Street and Main Street. Mr. Penland donated land for a new cemetery 0.8 of a mile south of town in 1874 and the bodies were moved there. Then in 1904, the I.O.O.F. bought additional land for a second cemetery adjoining the south part of the new Lexington Cemetery. (Not shown on Lexington 1968 USGS Quad. map.)

LONG CHILDREN   A   0.01   ?   **Before 1903**   **T3S**   **R28E**   **S23**
Three babies of the James Long family are buried at the foot of Freezeout Ridge and just above the road. There are no markers. (Not shown on Freezeout Ridge 1967 USGS Quad. map.)

MEDLOCK INFANT   A   0.01   ?   ?   **T6S**   **R25E**   **S3**
The infant of Robert and Minnie Medlock is reported to be buried in this Section. No further information was given in the report. (Not shown on Chapin Creek 1995 USGS Quad. map.)

MORGAN   C   1.1   2   **1905**   **T1N**   **R23E**   **S23**
Morgan was a locale about halfway between Ione and Cecil. From I-84 turn right on OR. Hwy. 74 drive south for about 32 miles turn left on Morgan Road drive about 0.5 of a mile east to a narrow gravel road. Then turn right (south) and travel 0.3 of a mile to the cemetery. It is fenced and gated. {2 September 2000} (Cecil 1968 USGS Quad. map.)

PENLAND   ?   ?   1   **1874**   **T1S**   **R25E**   **S34**
Penland Cemetery is 0.8 of a mile south of Lexington via "B" Street and Cemetery Hill Road. Penland Cemetery is noted as north of

Name of Cemetery and also known as	Number of burials	Acres	Condition	Date started or earliest known burial	Township	Range	Section

Lexington Cemetery. The two entrances are 0.12 of a mile apart on Cemetery Hill Road. These two cemeteries adjoin each other. (Lexington 1968 USGS Quad. map.)

PETTYS
AKA: 1. JORDAN FORD
     2. PETTEYS

| | B | 0.7 | 3 | 1870 | T1S | R25E | S6 |

Located near Ione on Baseline Road. Leave OR. Hwy. 74 at Jordan and turn onto Jordan Grade Road. Go 1.6 miles on Jordan Grade Road to Baseline Road on the right (east) and, finally, 0.3 of a mile on Baseline to the cemetery on the right (south) side of the road. There were 31 graves in 1972. NOTE: USGS Quad. map spells it Petteys, but the 1972 D.A.R. survey says the tombstones always spell it Pettys. (Ione North 1968 USGS Quad. map.)

PINE CITY

| | ? | ? | ? | ? | T1N | R27E | S10 |

It is unclear to the compiler if this is an AKA for Yarlett Cemetery or even Sand Hollow Cemetery. (Pine City is shown on Butter Creek Junction 1968 USGS Quad. map, but no cemetery is indicated there.)

PLEASANT POINT
AKA: 1. LENA

| | B | 0.8 | 2 | 1868 | T1S | R28E | S28 |

Leave OR. Hwy. 74 at Lena on Little Butter Creek Road, go north and northwest 4.7 miles to Pleasant Point Cemetery and an abandoned school. (Lena 1968 USGS Quad. map.)

RHEA CREEK
AKA: 1. DeVORE
     2. MATTESON

| | B | 0.7 | 2 | 1870 | T4S | R26E | S14 |

Leave OR. Hwy. 207 at Ruggs, which is about 11 miles southwest of Heppner. Turn easterly onto Rhea Creek Road and drive 4.7 miles to a road junction from the right. Continue ahead on the road now called Upper Rhea Creek Road for another 4.5 miles to the cemetery on the right (south). (Balm Canyon 1969 USGS Quad. map.)

RICE GIRL

| | A | 0.01 | ? | ? | T2S | R24E | S32 |

This burial site is for the 14 year old daughter of John Rice. This is possibly in the Northeast 1/4 of Section 32 at Eightmile

Morrow County

Canyon. This is about 12 miles south east of Ione and about 3.5 miles north of Valby. (Not shown on Eightmile 1968 USGS Quad map.)

RICKS, JOHN

A 0.01 ? ?   T6S R25E   S2

The only information that we recieved on this burial was John Ricks name and the Township, Range and Section. (Not on Chapin Creek 1995 USGS Quad. map.)

RIVER VIEW
  AKA: 1. BOARDMAN
          [OLD]
       2. RIVERVIEW

? 1 8 1922-1967 T4N R25E   S9

This cemetery was on the bluff between the south bank of the Columbia River and the Union Pacific Railroad. After the Columbia River was dammed and Lake Umatilla was created, a new cemetery was established. (Boardman 1962 USGS Quad. map. The 1970 edition shows the Lake Umatilla water level.)

RIVERVIEW
  AKA 1. BOARDMAN
         [NEW]

C 1.65 1 1967   T4N R25E   S9

Located in the northeast part of town 0.25 of a mile east of the High School; the previous cemetery site is now flooded. See entry on River View Cemetery AKA: Boardman [Old]. (Boardman 1993 USGS Quad. map.)

ROBINSON FAMILY

A 0.01 ? ?   T4S R24E   S34

Two children of C. D. Robinson are buried some where in Section 34. No further information was given in the report. (Not shown on Buttermilk Canyon 1969 USGS Quad. map.)

SAND HOLLOW
  AKA: 1. LONG,
          CHARLIE

B 0.4 5 1884   T1N R26E   S13

Go south off of OR. Hwy. 207 at Milepost 13.2 on Sand Hollow Road for 1.4 miles; turn left (east) on Barclay Road for 1.9 miles. The cemetery is 3.15 miles west of Galloway on the north side of Barclay Road. The stones have been destroyed. There were at least 86 known burials, reported by a D.A.R. survey of 1972. (Strawberry Canyon Southeast 1968 and Butter Creek Junction 1968 USGS Quad. maps.)

Name of Cemetery and also known as	Number of burials	Acres	Condition	Date started or earliest known burial	Township	Range	Section

SCHERZINGER CHILD   A   0.01   ?   ?   T3S   R27E   S28

A child of Ed Scherzinger is reported to be buried in this Section. No further information was given in the report. (Not shown on Skinners Fork 1968 USGS Quad. map.)

SKINNER CHILDREN   ?   ?   ?   ?   T3S   R27E   ?

This is perhaps in Section 12, about 8 miles southeast of Heppner via Willow Creek Road and a private road up Skinner Fork and Willis Creek. The children of John F. M. Skinner were buried on the homestead on Skinner Fork. NOTE: This site is on private property. (Not shown on Skinners Fork 1968 USGS Quad. map.)

SMITH FAMILY   A   0.01   ?   ?   T3S   R26E   S32

"Two children of the Smith family are buried here." No further information was given in the report. (Not shown on Heppner 1968 USGS Quad. map.)

STEWARD FAMILY   A   0.01   ?   ?   ?   ?   ?

We have a report that James Steward and his daughter are buried side by side somewhere in Morrow County. Does any one know about these burials? If so please send some information on them as we have no further information on them.

SWETZER INFANT   A   0.01   ?   ?   T1S   R26E   S35

It has been reported that the infant daughter of William G. Swetzer is buried in this Section. No further information was given in the report. (Not shown on Swaggart Buttes 1968 USGS Quad. map.)

THREE INDIANS   A   0.01   ?   ?   T1S   R26E   S1

Three Indians reported to have been killed during the 1878 Indian war are buried in Section 1. No further information was given in the report. (Not shown on Strawberry Canyon S.E. 1968 USGS Quad. map.)

Morrow County

Name of Cemetery and also known as	Number of burials	Acres	Condition	Date started or earliest known burial	Township	Range	Section

TIPPETT'S FARM
AKA: 1. TIPPETT, CLARK
    2. TIPPITT

A ? ? 1897-1908 T1N R27E ?
Located on the Raymond French Place (1970) along Butter Creek Road and near the Yarlett burials. There are 4 known burials on the Raymond French Place (1970). (Not shown on Butter Creek Junction 1968 USGS Quad. map.)

TURNER CHILDREN

A 0.01 ? ? T1S R26E S26
Two children of James Turner are buried at this site. No further information was given in the report. (Not shown on Swaggart Buttes 1968 USGS Quad. map.)

UNKNOWN

A 0.01 ? ? T2S R27E S34
A skeleton was found of an unknown person. No further information was given in the report. (Not shown on Skinners Fork 1968 USGS Quad. map.)

UNKNOWN

A 0.01 ? ? T4S R27E S1
This is a burial site for 2 children who died of scarlet fever. A large rock marks the site near a fence corner in Carmichael Canyon. There is no access road. (Not shown on Summerfield Ridge 1969-83 USGS Quad. map.)

UNKNOWN

A 0.01 ? ? T4S R27E S12
A report of one unknown person buried on Section 12 in the above Township and Range. No further information was given in the report. (Not shown on Summerfield Ridge 1969-83 USGS Quad. map.)

UNKNOWN CHILD

A 0.01 ? 1878 T2S R26E S25
Located about 1.5 miles east of Heppner on OR. Hwy. 74. A three year old child who was killed by Indians is buried on the old Marlatt Place, which was on the left leaving Heppner. NOTE: This site is on private property. (Not shown on Heppner 1968 USGS Quad. map.)

Name of Cemetery and also known as	Number of burials	Acres	Condition	Date started or earliest known burial	Township	Range	Section

UNKNOWN CHILD

A 0.01 ? ? T3S R24E S24

There is a burial located south of the Liberty School for an unknown child. No further information was given in the report. (Not on Eightmile 1968 USGS Quad. map.)

UNKNOWN CHILD

A 0.01 ? ? T3S R27E S6

"An unknown child is buried on the bluff near a creek." No further information was given in the report. (Not shown on Heppner or Skinners Fork 1968 USGS Quad. map.)

UNKNOWN FAMILY

A 0.01 ? ? T5S R25E S10

"Three children family unknown." Is the cryptic report given on this site. We have no further information. (Not shown on Hardman 1969 USGS Quad. map.)

VALBY
AKA: 1. SWEDE CHURCH

B 0.5 3 1887 T3S R24E S8

Located at Valby, near the Valby Lutheran Church, 18.5 miles from Heppner on OR. Hwys. 206 and 207. Turn right (north) onto Valby Road and go 4.75 miles more to the church and cemetery. There were 46 graves in 1972. (Eightmile 1968 USGS Quad. map.)

VOLLE CHILDREN

A 0.01 ? ? T5S R27E S2

In another cryptic report we have "two children of the Volle family." No other information was given in the report of this family burial site. (Not shown on Madison Butte USGS Quad. map.)

WELL SPRING
AKA: 1. BOARDMAN BOMBING RANGE
2. ELLA
3. EMIGRANT GRAVEYARD
4. WELLS SPRING

B 0.4 5 1852 T2N R25E S20

Located 13 miles east of OR. Hwy. 74 from Cecil at Immigrant and Well Spring Road. It is along the Old Emigrant Road that crosses the county east and west, just south of the Bombing Range. There is a monument to Colonel Cornelius Gilliam, killed here 24 March 1848 and buried in the Dallas Cemetery in 1852. All other burials are unmarked. The headstones are reported to to be in a museum in Ione. (Well Spring 1968 USGS Quad. map.)

Name of Cemetery and also known as	Number of burials	Acres	Condition	Date started or earliest known burial	Township	Range	Section

WILKINSON CHILDREN A 0.01 ? ? T3S R28E S34

A report for the three children of the Wilkinson family has been given, unfortunately the above information is all the compiler received. (Not shown on Freezeout Ridge 1967 USGS Quad. map.)

YARLETT B ? 5 1866-1883 T1N R27E S23

Located about 1.5 miles up Butter Creek Road on a knoll, near the Raymond French Place. The stones have been destroyed. (Not shown on Butter Creek Junction 1968 USGS Quad. map.)

Morgan
Janice M. Healy (2000)

ALLEN FAMILY	MORROW CO.	T5S	R26E	S29
ALLEN, MYRIA M. see **ALLEN FAMILY**				
	MORROW CO.	T5S	R26E	S29
ALLEN, MYRIA MARK see **ALLEN FAMILY**				
	MORROW CO.	T5S	R26E	S29
ALLEN, REUBEN see **ALLEN FAMILY**	MORROW CO.	T5S	R26E	S29
BAKER	MORROW CO.	T2S	R24E	S6
BOARDMAN [NEW] see **RIVERVIEW**	MORROW CO.	T4N	R25E	S9
BOARDMAN [OLD] see **RIVER VIEW**	MORROW CO.	T4N	R25E	S9
BOARDMAN BOMBING RANGE see **WELL SPRING**				
	MORROW CO.	T2N	R25E	S20
CANTWELL INFANT	MORROW CO.	T3S	R25E	S35
CARMICHAEL CANYON see **UNKNOWN**	MORROW CO.	T4S	R27E	S1
CHAMBERLIN, MRS. H.	MORROW CO.	T4N	R24E	?
CHAPEL, TEDDY ROOSEVELT	MORROW CO.	T5S	R25E	S3
CHILD'S GRAVE	MORROW CO.	T1N	R23E	?
COPPLE, CHARLES WESLEY see **COPPLE FAMILY**				
	MORROW CO.	T5S	R27E	S2
COPPLE FAMILY	MORROW CO.	T5S	R27E	S2
COPPLE, WILLIAM HARVEY see **COPPLE FAMILY**				
	MORROW CO.	T5S	R27E	S2
COX CHILDREN	MORROW CO.	T2S	R27E	S36
COX, F. D. see **COX CHILDREN**	MORROW CO.	T2S	R27E	S36
COX, F. D. RANCH see **COX CHILDREN**				
	MORROW CO.	T2S	R27E	S36
CROW, MRS. ANDREW	MORROW CO.	T1S	R28E	S28
DESERT LAWN MEMORIAL	MORROW CO.	T5N	R27E	S20
DeVORE see **RHEA CREEK**	MORROW CO.	T4S	R26E	S14
DURAN CHILD	MORROW CO.	?	?	?
DURAN, EDWARD S. see **DURAN CHILD**				
	MORROW CO.	?	?	?
ELDER CHILDREN	MORROW CO.	T2S	R27E	S26
ELDER, JOHN see **ELDER CHILDREN**	MORROW CO.	T2S	R27E	S26
ELLA see **WELL SPRING**	MORROW CO.	T2N	R25E	S20
EMIGRANT GRAVEYARD see **WELL SPRING**				
	MORROW CO.	T2N	R25E	S20
FAIRVIEW see **BAKER**	MORROW CO.	T2S	R24E	S6
FRENCH PLACE, RAYMOND see **TIPPETT'S FARM**				
	MORROW CO.	T1N	R27E	?
FRENCH PLACE, RAYMOND see **YARLET**				
	MORROW CO.	T1N	R27E	S23
FRIEZE CHILDREN	MORROW CO.	T3S	R28E	S15
GILLIAM, COLONEL CORNELIUS see **WELL SPRING**				
	MORROW CO.	T2N	R25E	S20
GOOSEBERRY	MORROW CO.	T3S	R23E	S14
HALE FAMILY	MORROW CO.	T3S	R27E	S2
HALE, MICHAEL see **HALE FAMILY**	MORROW CO.	T3S	R27E	S2
HALE, MILLIE see **HALE FAMILY**	MORROW CO.	T3S	R27E	S2
HALLAWAY FAMILY	MORROW CO.	T1N	R24E	S5
HARDMAN [OLD]	MORROW CO.	T4S	R25E	S34
HENDRIX CHILDREN	MORROW CO.	T6S	R25E	S17
HEPPNER	MORROW CO.	T2S	R26E	S35

HIGHVIEW	MORROW CO.	T1S	R24E	S4
I.O.O.F. [HARDMAN, NEW]	MORROW CO.	T4S	R25E	S30
I.O.O.F. [IONE] see HIGHVIEW	MORROW CO.	T1S	R24E	S4
I.O.O.F. [LEXINGTON]	MORROW CO.	T1S	R25E	S24
INGRAHAM CHILDREN	MORROW CO.	T5S	R26E	S35
INGRAHAM, WILLIAM see INGRAHAM CHILDREN				
	MORROW CO.	T5S	R26E	S35
IONE see HIGHVIEW	MORROW CO.	T1S	R24E	S4
IRRIGON see DESERT LAWN MEMORIAL				
	MORROW CO.	T5N	R27E	S20
IRRIGON [OLD]	MORROW CO.	T5N	R26E	S24
JONES, FLOYED see ELDER CHILDREN				
	MOOROW CO.	T2S	R27E	S26
JORDAN FORD see PETTYS	MORROW CO.	T1S	R25E	S6
JUNKINS	MORROW CO.	T3S	R24E	S16
KING see BAKER	MORROW CO.	T2S	R24E	S6
LENA see PLEASANT POINT	MORROW CO.	T1S	R28E	S28
LEXINGTON [NEW] see I.O.O.F. [LEXINGTON]				
	MORROW CO.	T1S	R25E	S34
LEXINGTON [OLD]	MORROW CO.	T1S	R25E	S27
LIBERTY SCHOOL see UNKNOWN CHILD				
	MORROW CO.	T3S	R24E	S24
LONG, CHARLIE see SAND HOLLOW	MORROW CO.	T1N	R26E	S13
LONG CHILDREN	MORROW CO.	T3S	R28E	S23
LONG, JAMES see LONG CHILDREN	MORROW CO.	T3S	R28E	S23
MARLATT PLACE, OLD see UNKNOWN CHILD				
	MORROW CO.	T2S	R26E	S25
MASONIC see HEPPNER	MORROW CO.	T2S	R26E	S35
MATTESON see RHEA CREEK	MORROW CO.	T4S	R26E	S14
MEDLOCK INFANT	MORROW CO.	T6S	R25E	S3
MEDLOCK, MINNIE see MEDLOCK INFANT				
	MORROW CO.	T6S	R25E	S3
MEDLOCK, ROBERT see MEDLOCK INFANT				
	MORROW CO.	T6S	R25E	S3
MORGAN	MORROW CO.	T1N	R23E	S23
PENLAND	MORROW CO.	T1S	R25E	S34
PENLAND, MR. see LEXINGTON [OLD]				
	MORROW CO.	T1S	R25E	S27
PETTEYS see PETTYS	MORROW CO.	T1S	R25E	S6
PETTYS	MORROW CO.	T1S	R25E	S6
PINE CITY	MORROW CO.	T1N	R27E	S10
PLEASANT POINT	MORROW CO.	T1S	R28E	R28
RHEA CREEK	MORROW CO.	T4S	R26E	S14
RICE GIRL	MORROW CO.	T2S	R24E	S32
RICE, JOHN see RICE GIRL	MORROW CO.	T2S	R24E	S32
RICKS, JOHN	MORROW CO.	T6S	R25E	S2
RIVER VIEW	MORROW CO.	T4N	R25E	S9
RIVERVIEW	MORROW CO.	T4N	R25E	S9
RIVERVIEW see RIVER VIEW	MORROW CO.	T4N	R25E	S9
ROBERTS, DELLA see ALLEN FAMILY	MORROW CO.	T5S	R26E	S29
ROBINSON, C. D. see ROBINSON FAMILY				
	MORROW CO.	T4S	R24E	S34

ROBINSON FAMILY	MORROW CO.	T4S	R24E	S34
SAND HOLLOW	MORROW CO.	T1N	R26E	S13
SCHERZINGER CHILD	MORROW CO.	T3S	R27E	S28
SCHERZINGER, ED see **SCHERZINGER CHILD**				
	MORROW CO.	T3S	R27E	S28
SKINNER CHILDREN	MORROW CO.	T3S	R27E	?
SKINNER, JOHN F. M. see **SKINNER CHILDREN**				
	MORROW CO.	T3S	R27E	?
SMITH FAMILY	MORROW CO.	T3S	R26E	S32
STEWARD FAMILY	MORROW CO.	?	?	?
STEWARD, JAMES see **STEWARD FAMILY**				
	MORROW CO.	?	?	?
SWEDE CHURCH see **VALBY**	MORROW CO.	T3S	R24E	S8
SWETZER INFANT	MORROW CO.	T1S	R26E	S35
SWETZER, WILLIAM G. see **SWETZER INFANT**				
	MORROW CO.	T1S	R26E	S35
TEWS see **BAKER**	MORROW CO.	T2S	R24E	S6
THREE INDIANS	MORROW CO.	T1S	R26E	S1
TIPPITT see **TIPPETT'S FARM**	MORROW CO.	T1N	R27E	?
TIPPETT, CLARK see **TIPPETT'S FARM**				
	MORROW CO.	T1N	R27E	?
TIPPETT'S FARM	MORROW CO.	T1N	R27E	?
TURNER CHILDREN	MORROW CO.	T1S	R26E	S26
TURNER, JAMES see **TURNER CHILDREN**				
	MORROW CO.	T1S	R26E	S26
UNKNOWN	MORROW CO.	T2S	R27E	S34
UNKNOWN	MORROW CO.	T4S	R27E	S1
UNKNOWN	MORROW CO.	T4S	R27E	S12
UNKNOWN CHILD	MORROW CO.	T2S	R26E	S25
UNKNOWN CHILD	MORROW CO.	T3S	R24E	S24
UNKNOWN CHILD	MORROW CO.	T3S	R27E	S6
UNKNOWN FAMILY	MORROW CO.	T5S	R25E	S10
VALBY	MORROW CO.	T3S	R24E	S8
VOLLE CHILDREN	MORROW CO.	T5S	R27E	S2
WELL SPRING	MORROW CO.	T2N	R25E	S20
WELLS SPRING see **WELL SPRING**	MORROW CO.	T2N	R25E	S20
WILKINSON CHILDREN	MORROW CO.	T3S	R28E	S34
YARLETT	MORROW CO.	T1N	R27E	S23

Morgan
Janice M. Healy (2000)

Hardman [Old]
Janice M. Healy (2000)

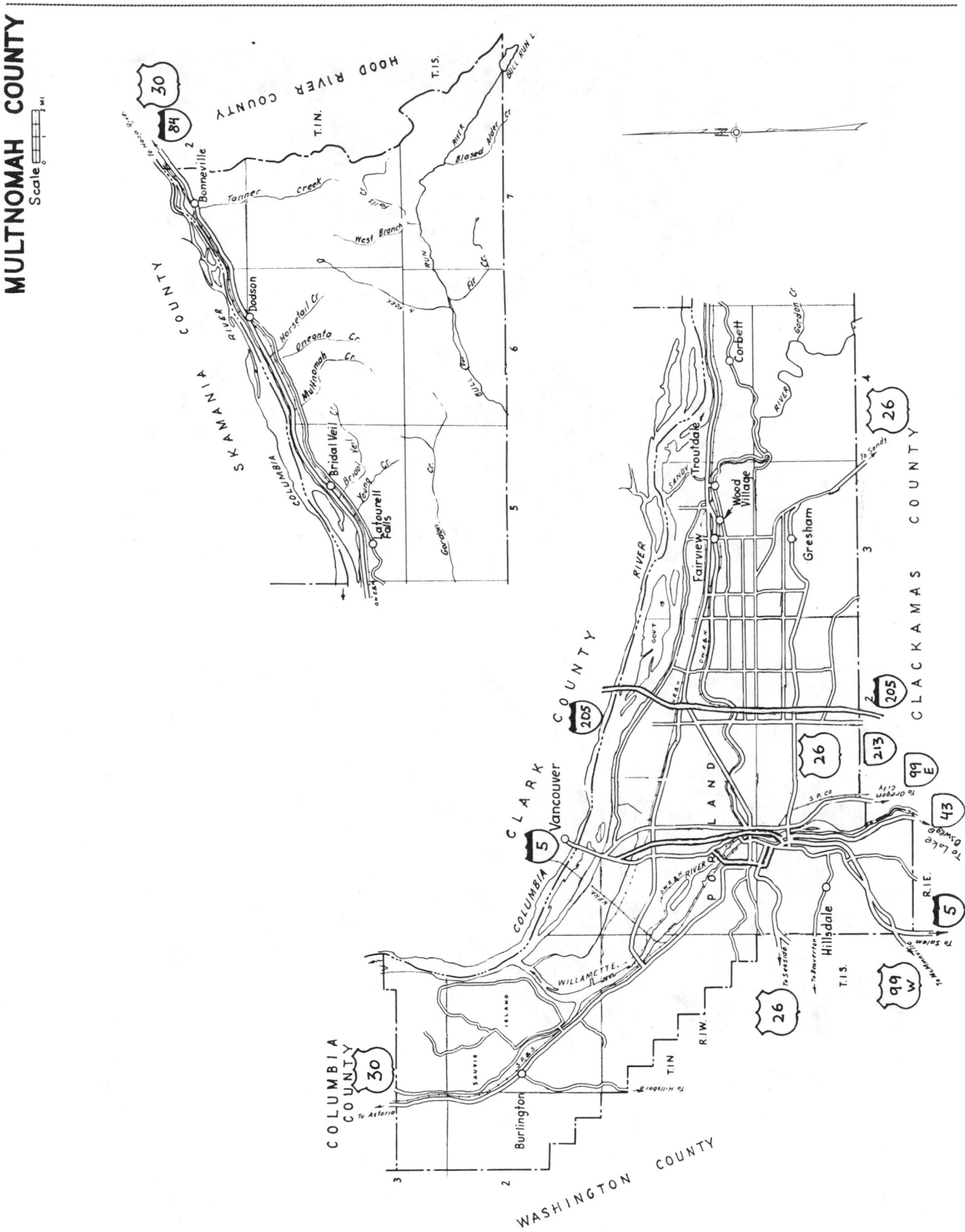

MULTNOMAH COUNTY

Scale

Japanese
Stanley R. Clarke (2000)

Japanese
Stanley R. Clarke (2000)

Area: 465 square miles
Population (1998): 631,082
County seat: Portland, Population: 503,000
County established: 22 December 1854

Portland, founded in 1845, was at the head of tidewater and therefore the head of ocean-going shipping. It was also at the northern end of the Willamette Valley, the principal goal of the early white settlers in Oregon. By 1870 with a population of 8,292 Portland was unchallenged as the state's largest town. The earliest known public cemetery dated from 1847 in Portland. As the city grew and was connected by rail to the east in 1881 and to California in 1883 immigration increased. Portland then received immigrants from eastern and southern Europe to a degree not found in other towns in Oregon. For example there are five Jewish cemeteries at present, Portland also has cemeteries for Chinese and Japanese. Small though Multnomah County is, the eastern third on the far side of the Sandy River is mostly mountainous and timbered.

Lincoln Memorial Park
Stanley R. Clarke (2000)

Ramsey
Stanley R. Clarke (1995)

Servite
Stanley R. Clarke (2000)

Bridal Veil

Showing a finished rubbing done with wax and Pelon.

Jance M. Healy (1992)

Bridal Veil

Stone as found was hard to read.

Jance M. Healy (1992)

Lincoln Memorial Park, Mausoleum
Stanley R. Clarke (2000)

Willamette National, Columbarium
Stanley R. Clarke (2000)

Name of Cemetery and also known as	Number of burials	Acres	Condition	Date started or earliest known burial	Township	Range	Section

PIONEER CEMETERIES
AKA: 1. COUNTY
       CEMETERIES
   2. METRO PIONEER
       CEMETERIES
   3. MULTNOMAH
       COUNTY
       CEMETERIES
   4. MULTNOMAH
       COUNTY
       PIONEER
       CEMETERIES

This article is included to clarify signage on many of the Metro Pioneer Cemeteries. All of them had a sign reading "Pioneer Cemetery" at one time. Some of these cemeteries had another sign giving the actual name of the cemetery, others had no other sign. Metro has replaced the signs with new ones giving the name of the cemetery. Metro operates 14 separate cemeteries in Multnomah County. A 15th is a Jewish consecrated section of one of the 14 and is considered an additional burial site. Please see the articles under the following names: Brainard Pioneer; Columbia Pioneer; Douglass Pioneer; Escobar Pioneer; Gresham Pioneer; Grand Army of the Republic; Havurah Shalom; Jones Pioneer; Lone Fir Pioneer; Mountain View-Corbett Pioneer; Mountain View-Stark Pioneer; Multnomah Park Pioneer; Pleasant Home Pioneer; Powell Grove Pioneer and White Birch Pioneer. The office for the Metro Pioneer Cemeteries is at Lone Fir Pioneer Cemetery, 2115 SE Morrision Street, Portland, OR 97214, phone 503-248-3622.

****

ABRAHAM
AKA: 1. ABRAHAMS
   2. ABRAMS

A   0.7   7   1871   T1S R2E   S6
This was west of Southeast 60th Avenue and south of Southeast Yamhill Street, Portland and is now the site of the Mount Tabor Seventh Day Adventist Church. The cemetery was most likely an early Methodist burial ground with the funerals held at the Mount Tabor Methodist Episcopal Church. There are no known records. It was on the Perry and Elizabeth Prettyman D.L.C. #37 OC #1536. *Multnomah County Deed Records* Book #28 page 119. {9 April 1997} (NOT on Mount Tabor 1990 USGS Quad. map.)

AHAVAI SHOLOM
AKA: 1. AHAVAI SHALOM
   2. AHAVI SHALOM
   3. AHAVI SHALUM
   4. AHAVI SOLEM
   5. AHAVIA SHOLON

E   5   1   1869   T1S R1E   S27
Located at 44 Southwest Alice Street, Portland. It is east of Southwest Boones Ferry Road and south of Southwest Palatine Hill Road at the south end of Southwest 1st Avenue south of Southwest Alice Street. This

---

---

6. B'NAI B'RITH
   OREGON LODGE
   #65
7. CHEBRA AHAVI
   SHOLUM
8. CHEBRA AHIVA
   SHOLUM
9. NEVEH SHOLOM
10. NEVI SHOLOM

cemetery contains B'nai B'rith Cemetery (See article on B'nai B'rith). It is on the John M. Tice D.L.C. OC #3192. *Multnomah County Deed Records* Book 1 page 521 and Book 1 page 537. {10 April 1997} (Lake Oswego 1961-84 USGS Quad. map.)

AMEND, VIRGIL

A 0.01 4 13 May 1941 T1N R5E S22
This burial is a single grave above Bridal Veil State Park, on tax lot #7. Check with the owners of the Bridal Veil Inn for access, then hike up the road from the old Bridal Veil Inn to the deteriorating cabins west of the Upper Bridal Veil Falls. The grave is about halfway between the cabins and the falls and is marked with a bronze plaque on a field stone. The plaque reads: "Virgil Amend 1860-1941." A paper label in a funeral home temporary marker reads: "Virgil Amend died May 13, 1941." This burial is on what was the Amend property, in dense woods with lots of ferns and moss. His wife and daughter are buried in the Bridal Veil Cemetery. {1990} (Not shown on Bridal Veil 1986 USGS Quad. map.)

ASCENSION EPISCOPAL CHAPEL
AKA: 1. ASCENSION
       CHAPEL
       EPISCOPAL
       CHURCH

? ? ? ? T1S R1E S4
Located at 1823 Southwest Spring Street, Portland. An obituary in *The Oregonian* Wednesday, October 1, 1997 listed this as an interment site. No further information is known to the compiler. (Portland 1961-70-71 USGS Quad map.)

ASYLUM

? ? ? ? T1S R1E S2
This was possibly at Southeast 12th Avenue and Southeast Hawthorne Boulevard, Portland. It would have been part of Doctor Hawthorne's Asylum (the first treatment center for the insane in Oregon) although many inmates were interred at Lone Fir. It was on the James B. Stephens D.L.C. #53, OC# 1049. {1997} (Not shown on Portland 1961-70-71 USGS Quad. Map)

Name of Cemetery and also known as	Number of burials	Acres	Condition	Date started or earliest known burial	Township	Range	Section

B'NAI B'RITH
AKA: 1. OREGON LODGE
#65

D 1   1   1875   T1S R1E   S27
Located at 44 Southwest Alice Street, Portland. B'Nai B'rith (#65 I.O.B.B.) is now a part of Ahavai Sholom Cemetery (see article on Ahavai Sholom). It is on the John M. Tice D.L.C. OC #3192. *Multnomah County Deed Records* Book 27 page 294 {1998} (Shown as Ahavai Sholom on Lake Oswego 1961-84 USGS Quad. map.)

BARNARD BABY

? ?   ?   19 May 1908 ?   ?   ?
Premature female born and died 19 May 1908, the child of William N. Barnard and Winnifred Belle Rus Barnard was buried in the family cemetery per Oregon Death Certificate #89, Multnomah County. The child was born and died at 1178 Commericial Street, Portland (1908 address). Where is the family cemetery located and what is its name?

BARNES BABY

A 0.01 ?   13 May 1920 T1S R2E   S20
Premature female born and died 23 May 1920, the child of William Barnes and Elizabeth Baniche Barnes was buried on their own property in the Des Moines Addition to Portland. The 1920 *Polk's City Directory* lists the Barnes address as "Raymond NW Corner Willow." Willow is now Southeast Harney Street and Raymond is either Southeast 65th Avenue, 66th Avenue or 67th Avenue. This burial site is two blocks south of Congregation Keser Israel and Congregation Shaarie Torah Cemeteries in either Block 4, 5, 6, 9, 10, or 11 of Des Moines Addition. The source of this information is an Oregon Death Certificate, Multnomah County, State of Oregon #128. (Not shown on Gladstone 1961-84 USGS Quad. Map.)

BETH ISRAEL [NEW]
AKA: 1. NEW JEWISH
     2. TEMPLE BETH
        ISRAEL

E 14   1   1872   T1S R1E   S21
Located at 426 Southwest Taylors Ferry Road, Portland. It is in the southwest corner of the intersection of Southwest Boones Ferry Road and Southwest Taylors Ferry Road. NOTE: This is the second cemetery of this name and is the oldest continuously operating Jewish cemetery in the nation. The USGS Quad. does

Name of Cemetery and also known as	Number of burials	Acres	Condition	Date started or earliest known burial	Township	Range	Section

not separate Greenwood and Beth Israel Cemeteries though they are on opposite sides of the road, approximately 0.2 of a mile apart. It is on the John M. Tice D.L.C. OC #3192. {10 April 1997} (Lake Oswego 1984 USGS Quad. map.)

BETH ISRAEL [OLD]
AKA: 1. CITY CEMETERY #4
2. GIVOT OLAM
3. JEWISH
4. OLD BETH ISRAEL
5. OLD HEBREW

C	1	7	1858-1873	T1S	R1E	S10

This was on Hood Avenue at the east terminus of Hooker Street. Corbett Avenue passed through a portion at what was Hooker Street prior to the building of the Lake Oswego off-ramp of the Ross Island Bridge. What is left of the property is now 2828 Southwest Corbett Avenue, Portland. A city ordinance 15 February 1871 forbidding burials within the city limits specifically exempted this cemetery for a period of 2 years. A second cemetery of this name was established on Southwest Taylors Ferry Road at Southwest Boones Ferry Road in 1872 (see article under Beth Israel [new]). Located on the Finice Caruthers D.L.C. #43, OC #608. {9 February 1991} (Not shown on Portland 1961-70-77 USGS Quad. map.)

BRADFORD ISLAND

D	?	7	[See below]	T2N	R7E	?

[Pre-white settlement]. Located on Section 21 or 22. During the construction of Bonneville Dam 500 or so human remains were moved in the years 1934-1936 to Greenwood Cemetery in North Bonneville, Klickitat County, Washington. (Not shown on Bonneville Dam 1979 USGS Quad. map.)

BRAINARD PIONEER
AKA: 1. BRAINARD
2. BRAINARY
3. BRAINERD
4. BREYMER
5. MONTAVILLA
6. MT. TABOR VILLA

C	1.1	1	1867	T1N	R2E	S33

Located between Northeast 89th and Northeast 90th Avenues, Northeast Glisan Street on the north and Northeast Flanders Street on the south, in Portland. A Metro Pioneer Cemetery (2115 SE Morrison Street, Portland, OR 97214, phone 503-248-3622) See Chapter 144 *Laws of Oregon* 1951. {13 April 1997} (Mount Tabor 1978, not shown on the Mount Tabor 1990 USGS Quad. maps.)

Name of Cemetery and also known as	Number of burials	Acres	Condition	Date started or earliest known burial	Township	Range	Section

BRIDAL VEIL   B 1   2   1879   T1N   R5E   S22

Located on lot #7 of the First Addition to Bridal Veil. Coming from Portland on the I-84 Freeway, leave the Freeway at Exit 28 to the right (inland). This is a short state-owned connection between the I-84 Freeway and the Scenic Route (Crown Point Highway). As you reach the connection to Westbound I-84 at the end of the viaduct, continue ahead past the church on your left. Ignore the next driveway to the left to some houses, but a very few feet beyond is an obscure unsigned driveway to the left, ahead and downslope. There is a vacant house (1997) here on the left and the cemetery is out of sight. Drive a few hundred feet and the burials are on your left, facing the Columbia River. The cemetery is easily viewed from I-84 and from Amtrak trains as the main line Union Pacific tracks border the north line of the cemetery. There are 57+ graves, with 1934 being the latest dated marker (1999). The transfer of lands in Bridal Veil for future Columbia Gorge Preservation specifically omitted the cemetery from the transfer as there was no known owner. NOTE: Many buildings remaining in Bridal Veil are to be demolished soon. {16 May 1999} (Not shown on Bridal Veil 1986 USGS Quad. map.)

BUTLER FAMILY   A   0.01 1   1880   T1S   R3E   S20

Located on the Clinton Farm, 2212 Southwest Butler Road, Gresham, Tax lot #85; on the Euphemia Butler Homestead. Private property. See the *Gresham Outlook*, 17 July 1981. (Not shown on Damascus 1961-84 USGS Quad. map.)

CHINESE [LONE FIR]   C 1   7   ?   T1S   R1E   S2

This was located north of Southeast Morrison Street and east of 20th Avenue in the southwest corner of Lone Fir Cemetery, Portland. Most burials were returned to China but some burials were relocated to other sections of Lone Fir and some to Lincoln Memorial Park. There are no known records today. The Chinese Benevolent Society had very accurate records at the time

Name of Cemetery and also known as	Number of burials	Acres	Condition	Date started or earliest known burial	Township	Range	Section

of removal. A Metro Pioneer Cemetery (2115 SE Morrison Street, Portland, OR 97214, phone 503-248-3622). It was on the Seldon Murray D.L.C. #54, OC #1413. {30 April 1997} (Portland 1961-70-77 USGS Quad. map.)

CHINESE [MONTAVILLA]   ? ?   11 ?   T1N R2E   S33
Reportedly located between Northeast Glisan Street and Northeast Pacific Street, Northeast 92nd Avenue and Northeast 95th Avenue, Portland. There are no known records. This area has been built over by the I-205 Freeway. (Not shown on Mount Tabor 1990 USGS Quad. map.)

CHINESE [ST. JOHNS]   A 0.01 ? ?   T1N R1E   S18
There are three graves on the bluff above the dry-dock near North Willamette Boulevard, Portland. These are perhaps near the end of North Portsmouth Avenue. (Information was received by the Genealogical Forum of Portland Oregon in 1958.) It is on the John Ward, Jr. (John Waud, or John Wand depending on the source) D.L.C. #47, OC #1350. (Not shown on Portland 1961-70-77 USGS Quad. map.)

CHINESE CEMETERY IN LINCOLN MEMORIAL PARK   D ?   1 1931   T1S R2E   S22
"The Chinese Cemetery on Mount Scott in Lincoln Memorial Park started when two private buyers purchased 2,000 burial sites there in 1931. Burials were initially free so even the poor could get a proper burial, but the Portland Chinese Cemetery Association which manages it now, charges a fee for the 900 plots left. The graves, which are perched on the slope facing Johnson Creek, are supposed to bring good luck to the deceased in their afterlife." See *The Oregonian*, June 28, 1995 Page B 1. (Shown as Lincoln Memorial only on Gladstone 1961-84 USGS Quad. map.)

CITY CEMETERY #1
AKA: 1. STARK   C 2.5 7 1847-1854 T1N R1E   S33
Located on Sections 33 and 34, it was located between Southwest Naito Parkway (formerly Southwest Front Avenue) on the east,

Name of Cemetery and also known as	Number of burials	Acres	Condition	Date started or earliest known burial	Township	Range	Section

Southwest 4th Avenue on the west, Southwest Pine Street on the south and West Burnside Street on the north, Portland. The exact site is unknown today. Most of the bodies were removed circa 1854-1857. Some were removed in 1923 when West Burnside Street was widened. There are no known records. This was on the Benjamin Stark D.L.C. #42, OC #69. {5 February 1992} (Not shown on Portland 1961-70-77 USGS Quad. map.)

CITY CEMETERY #2

C 2.5 7 1854 T1N R1E S33

This cemetery was Lot 255 between Southwest 11th Avenue, Southwest 12th Avenue, Southwest Washington Street and Southwest Stark Street, Portland. See the map on the wall of the manuscript room at Oregon Historical Society in Portland. It was sold to the city of Portland by Daniel H. and Nancy Lownsdale. On the Daniel H. Lownsdale D.L.C. #66, OC #1022. Nancy Gillihan Lownsdale born 1821, died 5 April 1854 may have been buried here. There are no known records. {3 February 1992} (Not shown on Portland 1961-70-77 USGS Quad. map.)

CITY CEMETERY #3
 AKA: 1. CARUTHERS--
        TERWILLIGER
     2. OLD CEMETERY
        CITY OF
        PORTLAND
     3. TERWILLIGER
     4. TERWILLIGER
        PARK

C 10 7 1854-1879 T1S R1E S10

This cemetery contained bodies transferred from City Cemetery #1, and other burials. Southwest Lowell Street, Portland, was the center line of the site. Originally, it extended from about Corbett Avenue on the west to Macadam Avenue on the east from Abernathy Street on the north to Bancroft Street on the south. Three acres are now part of the I-5 Freeway. The city of Portland purchased burial plots in River View Cemetery and moved the bodies to River View and closed this cemetery. The south half was on the James Terwilliger DLC OC #1078 and the north half was on the Elizabeth Caruthers Thomas D.L.C. #43, OC #611. Each sold five acres to the city of Portland. *Multnomah County Deed Records* Book A page 36. {1990} (Not shown on Lake Oswego 1961-84 USGS Quad. map.)

705

Name of Cemetery and also known as	Number of burials	Acres	Condition	Date started or earliest known burial	Township	Range	Section

CITY GARBAGE CREMATORY   ?   5.07   7   1903-1906   T1N   R1E   S29

Located on what was then the south shore of Guild's Lake. It is now reached by a short driveway called Northwest 25th Avenue that leaves Northwest Nicolai Steet to the northwest. It was listed in the city directories under cemeteries during the time period, and is shown in the 1927 *Metsker Land Ownership Atlas*. There are no known records. It was on the Peter Guild D.L.C. #54, OC #1417. {December 1991} (Not shown on the Portland 1961-70-77 USGS Quad. map.)

CLARK FARM   A   0.01   ?   1907   ?   ?   ?

Two known burials of infants in the Gresham area. The premature male child of Frank Clark and Mary Kelly Clark was born and died 11 June 1907 and was buried the same day "upon farm now living on" per Oregon Death Certificate, Multnomah County, #3968. Another male child born 11 June 1907 to George Clark and Bessie Smith Clark died 26 June 1907 and was buried the same day by William Clark on the Clark farm per Oregon Death Certificate, Multnomah County, #4217. Both Frank and George Clark were from Canada thus the compiler is assuming both infants are buried on the same farm. (Not shown on Damascus 1961-84 USGS Quad map.)

CLINE   ?   ?   12   ?   T2N   R1W   ?

This is on Sections 8, 9, 16, and/or 17. It has been abandoned and plowed under, on the Holbrook property (1978) on Sauvie Island. There are no known records. It is on the Jacob Cline D.L.C. #48, OC #1919. NOTE: This site is on private property. (Not shown on Sauvie Island 1990 USGS Quad. map.)

COLUMBIA PIONEER
AKA: 1. COLUMBIA MASONIC
2. COLUMBIA PIONEER MASONIC
3. COLUMBIA SLOUGH LODGE

   E   2.4   1   1877   T1N   R2E   S21

Located on Northeast 99th Avenue and Sandy Boulevard, Portland, on the south side of Sandy Boulevard. It was platted in 1877 but it is thought to be much older. A Metro Pioneer Cemetery (2115 SE Morrison Street, Portland, OR 97214, phone 503-248-3622). See Chapter 7 *Laws of Oregon* 1949. It is on the

Name of Cemetery and also known as	Number of burials	Acres	Condition	Date started or earliest known burial	Township	Range	Section

4. MASONIC SLOUGH
5. PARKROSE MASONIC

Andrew Pullen D.L.C., OC #3715. {10 May 1997} (Mount Tabor 1990 USGS Quad. map.)

COLUMBIAN
AKA: 1. COLUMBIA
2. COLUMBIAN KENTON
3. LOVE
4. LOVEJOY
5. OLD COLUMBIA
6. SLOUGH

| E | 10 | 1 | | 1867 | T1N | R1E | S10 |

Located in the 1100 Block of North Columbia Boulevard, Portland. It is on the north side of Columbia Boulevard, east of the I-5 Freeway and now contains the Love Cemetery (see article on Love, Lewis). Located on the Lewis Love D.L.C. #41, OC #1484. *Multnomah County Deed Records* Book H page 187. {10 May 1997} (Portland 1961-70-77 USGS Quad. map.)

CONGREGATION KESER ISRAEL
AKA: 1. JEWISH
2. KESER ISRAEL
3. PORTLAND HEBREW SICK BENEFIT ASSOCIATION

| C | 2 | 1 | | 1924 | T1S | R2E | S20 |

Located at 6509 Southeast Nehalem Street, Portland. From Southeast Flavel Street travel south on Southeast 65th Avenue. The cemetery is on the east (left) side of 65th Avenue at Nehalem Street. It adjoins Congregation Shaarie Torah Cemetery which lies to the east. NOTE: Congregation Shaarie Torah and Congregation Keser Israel Cemeteries are NOT separately labeled on this USGS map. {11 May 1997} (Gladstone 1961-84 USGS Quad. map.)

CONGREGATION SHAARIE TORAH
AKA: 1. SHAARIE TORAH

| D | 2.6 | 1 | | 1905 | T1S | R2E | S20 |

Located at 8013 Southeast 67th Avenue, Portland. From Southeast Flavel Street travel south on Southeast 67th Avenue to the 8000 block. The cemetery is on the right (west) side of the street. This adjoins Congregation Keser Israel Cemetery which lies to the west. NOTE: Congregation Shaarie Torah and Congregation Keser Israel Cemeteries are not separately labeled on this USGS map. {11 May 1997} (Gladstone 1961-84 USGS Quad. map.)

CORBETT FAMILY

| A | 0.01 | 7 | | ? | T1S | R1E | S3 |

This was located on the southeast corner of their residential property at Southwest 5th Avenue and Southwest Taylor Street, Portland.

Name of Cemetery and also known as	Number of burials	Acres	Condition	Date started or earliest known burial	Township	Range	Section

It was 25 square feet in size. The bodies were moved to River View Cemetery, Portland. {4 February 1992} (Not shown on Portland 1961-70-77 USGS Quad. map.)

COUNTY FARM #1

?	?	7	?		T1S	R1E	S10

This was located between Southwest Meade Street and Southwest Hooker Steet west of Southwest 2nd Avenue, Portland. See the *Oregon Journal*, 7 May, 1957, page 23 and *The Oregonian*, 8 May 1957 page 11. It was on the Finice Caruthers D.L.C. #43, OC #608. {1991} (Not shown on the Portland 1961-70-77 USGS Quad. map.)

COUNTY FARM #2
AKA: 1. POOR FARM

C	?	10	?		T1S	R1E	S5

The County Poor Farm was situated in what is now the Hoyt Aboretum, Oregon Zoo (formerly Washington Park Zoo) and the World Forestry Center. There were two graveyards noted on some of the old maps, with possibly a third of 2.6 acres, as one of that size is shown on one map in a shape not shown on the other maps. Many of the burials were of paupers and unknowns, some of which show up in the Portland death records, but many do not. There are unmarked graves throughout, including that of Wong Luey (See the article under Wong Luey.). Fifteen known burials were moved to Lone Fir Cemetery in 1961 when the zoo was built. {Fall 1991} (The Arboretum and Washington Park are shown on Portland 1961-70-77 USGS Quad. map.)

CROSBY, BABY

?	?	?	8 Jun 1908	?	?		?

Oregon Death Certificate #159 reports that baby Crosby, female child of C. J. Crosby and Nora Reetar Died 8 June 1908 and was buried the same date on the lot at 937 Gantenbein in North Portland. The father was the undertaker. No further information is known by the compiler.

DAVIS FAMILY

A	?	2	?		T1S	R4E	S3

Located in the Southeast 1/4 of Section 3. Leave Crown Point Highway at Springdale to

Name of Cemetery and also known as	Number of burials	Acres	Condition	Date started or earliest known burial	Township	Range	Section

the right (southeasterly) onto Hurlburt Road. Drive about 2 miles and then turn right (south) onto Gordon Creek Road. After about 0.25 of a mile you reach Big Creek - do not cross. A Farm is on the right (west) side of the road. The Davis family markers are on this private property along the right bank of Big Creek just beyond a "neat waterfall" and before the creek descends into a canyon to join the Sandy River. The markers are a couple hundred feet from Gordon Creek Road. {October 1995} (Not shown on Washougal 1961-70-75 USGS Quad. map.)

DOUGLASS
AKA: 1. DOUGLAS

| | E | 9.1 | 1 | 1866 | T1N | R3E | S36 |

Located east of Southeast 257th Avenue on the east side of Southeast Hensley Road (Southeast 262nd Avenue) north of Southeast Stark Street, Troutdale. Turn north off of Southeast Stark Street onto Southeast Troutdale Road then travel 0.9 of a mile north to Southeast 14th Street (unmarked) and make a left. This street ends in the cemetery. If you miss Southeast 14th Street turn left onto Southeast Cherry Park Road and then left onto Southeast Hensley Road (Southeast 262nd Avenue). The cemetery will be on your left. Another route is to turn north off of Southeast Stark Street onto Southeast 257th Avenue and travel north to Southeast Hensley Road. Turn right onto Southeast Hensley Road and proceed east then north to the cemetery which is on the right or east side of Southeast Hensley Road (Southeast 262nd Avenue). A Metro Pioneer Cemetery (2115 SE Morrison Street, Portland, OR 97214, phone 503-248-3622) See Chapter 137 *Laws of Oregon* 1955. It is on the John Douglas D.L.C. #51, OC #5024. {16 May 1999} (Camas 1961-70-75 USGS Quad. map.)

DOUGLASS BABY

| | A | 0.01 | ? | 20 Jan 1908 | T1N | R1E | S14 |

The female child of A. F. Douglass and Ruby Douglass was born and died 20 January 1908 at 1347 E[ast] 10th N[orth], Portland. The father buried the infant 21 January 1908 on private grounds in the Woodlawn subdivision of Portland. Today Woodlawn lies south of

Name of Cemetery and also known as	Number of burials	Acres	Condition	Date started or earliest known burial	Township	Range	Section

Northeast Lombard Street, north of Northeast Holman Street, east of Martin Luther King, Jr. Boulevard and west of Northeast 19th Avenue, Portland. The source of this information is an Oregon Death Certificate #15, Multhomah County. (Not shown on Portland 1960-70-77 USGS Quad map.)

EMANUEL HOSPITAL ? ? ? ? T1N R1E S27

Located at North Commercial Avenue & North Stanton Street in North Portland. The hospital operated its own crematory for children who died within a few hours of birth. (Not shown on Portland 1961-70-75 USGS Quad. map.)

ESCOBAR PIONEER
AKA: 1. ESCOBAR
2. ESCOBAR, FRANK
3. ESCOBAR'S
4. GRESHAM

B 0.66 1 1908 T1S R3E S10

Located in Gresham on Southwest Walters Road. Escobar Cemetery is south of Powell Boulevard (U.S. Hwy. 26) on the east side of Walters Road. It is on the south side of Gresham Pioneer Cemetery and just north of Forest Lawn Cemetery. The abandoned Pepco Railway right-of-way (now Springwater Corridor [Trail]) and Johnson Creek separate Escobar from Forest Lawn. In addition, White Birch Cemetery lies across Walters Road from Escobar. The cemetery is named for Frank Escobar who arrived in Gresham about 1902, and who was considered a "character". He died in 1948 and is buried in Forest Lawn Cemetery. A Metro Pioneer Cemetery (2115 SE Morrison Street, Portland, OR 97214, phone 503-248-3622) See Chapter 277 *Oregon Laws* 1955. It is on the Jacob J. Moore D.L.C., OC #1387. {11 May 1997} (Damascus 1961-84 USGS Quad. map which does not differentiate Escobar from Gresham Pioneer Cemetery.)

FAIRVIEW
AKA: 1. CLEONE

? ? ? ? T1N R3E ?

This could be Section 27 or 28. Stories indicate that there was a cemetery in Fairview. We have been unable to confirm that there was or was not one. (Not shown on Camas 1961-70-75 USGS Quad. map.)

Name of Cemetery and also known as	Number of burials	Acres	Condition	Date started or earliest known burial	Township	Range	Section

FOREST LAWN
AKA: 1. FOREST LAWN
   MEMORIAL PARK

E 40   1   1934   T1S R3E   S10
This cemetery is at 400 Southwest Walters Road, Gresham. Located south of Escobar Cemetery from which it is separated by the abandoned Pepco Railway right-of-way (now Springwater Corridor [Trail]) and Johnson Creek. It is on the east side of Walters Road. Sixteen acres are developed of the 40 acres that are set aside for this cemetery. {11 May 1997} (Damascus 1961-84 USGS Quad. map.)

**FRANCISCAN SISTERS
OF THE EUCHARIST**

A 0.1 1   1981   T1N R5E   S15
Located on the convent grounds at Coopey Falls, east of the locale of Bridal Veil on the south side of the Columbia River Scenic Highway on tax lot #2. (Not shown on Bridal Veil 1986 USGS Quad. map.)

FRIEDMAN, MARKS

A 0.5 ? 1 Jan 1879 T1S R1E   S1
This is a single flat marker in the parking strip in front of 3356 Southeast Main Street (Lot 18 Block 58 Sunnyside Addition), Portland. It is not known if this is a marker placed as a stepping stone or if it is a farm burial. The marker reads "Marks Friedman son of Abraham & Ann Friedman died January 1, 1879 aged 65 years." The marker also contains a four line prayer that is well worn. {October 1997} (Not shown on Portland 1961-70-77 USGS Quad. map.)

GATTON

B 0.5 1 27 Mar 1871 T2N R1W   S36
Located at 12000 North Simmons Road (now North Lombard Street), Portland, on the east side of the road, tax lot #16. See: Snyder, Eugene E. *We Claimed This Land: Portland's Pioneer Settlers* Binford & Mort Publishing, Portland, 1989, pages 84 & 85. It is on the William Gatton D.L.C. #43, OC #1701. {10 May 1997} (Linnton 1961-84 USGS Quad. map.)

GOOD SAMARITAN HOSPITAL

? ?   ?   ?   T1N R1E   S33
The hospital located at Northwest 23rd Avenue and Northwest Marshall Street, Portland,

Name of Cemetery and also known as	Number of burials	Acres	Condition	Date started or earliest known burial	Township	Range	Section

operated its own crematory for children who died within a few hours of birth. (Portland 1961-70-77 USGS Quad. map.)

GRAND ARMY OF THE REPUBLIC
AKA: 1. G.A.R.
2. GREENWOOD

D   2.06   1   1888   T1S   R1E   S27
Located at 9002 Southwest Boones Ferry Road, Portland. An additional 1.24 acres of land lying to the north is owned by Multnomah County which could possibly be used to increase the size of the cemetery. The G.A.R. Cemetery is adjacent to Greenwood Hills Cemetery and the access is via Greenwood Hills Cemetery entrance and roads. The oldest marker is 15 October 1889. Salmon Brown, son of John Brown (of the song "John Brown's Body") is buried here. In 1996 the cemetery was opened to burials of persons other than children and grandchildren of Civil War Veterans. A Metro Pioneer Cemetery (2115 SE Morrsion Street, Portland, OR 97214, phone 248-3622). See Chapter 535 *Oregon Laws* 1955. It is on the John M. Tice D.L.C., OC #3192. {10 April 1997} (Lake Oswego 1961-84 USGS Quad. map. This is not shown separate from Greenwood Cemetery.)

GREENWOOD HILLS
AKA: 1. GREENWOOD
2. GREENWOOD HILL
3. MASONIC
4. PORTLAND MASONIC

E   12.5   2   1884   T1S   R1E   S27
Located at 9002 Southwest Boones Ferry Road, Portland. This originally had 40 acres set aside and dedicated for burial purposes, however portions were sold to create the Grand Army of the Republic and I.O.O.F. Cemeteries. Another portion was sold to River View after a court ruling in favor of the sale as the land was to continue as a burial ground. Still more was removed circa 1987 for residential use. It is on the John M. Tice D.L.C., OC #3192. {10 April 1997} (Lake Oswego 1984 Quad. map.)

GRESHAM PIONEER
AKA: 1. BETHEL
2. GRESHAM
3. GRESHAM SCHOOL
4. OLD PIONEER

D   2   1   1851   T1S   R3E   S10
Located south of Powell Boulevard (U.S. Hwy. 26) on Southwest Walters Road, on the east side of the road and south of the church parking lot, Gresham. The first Japanese person (Miyo Iwakoshi) in Oregon is buried here. A Metro Pioneer Cemetery (2115 SE

Name of Cemetery and also known as	Number of burials	Acres	Condition	Date started or earliest known burial	Township	Range	Section

Morrison Street, Portland, OR 97214, phone 248-3622)   See Chapter 277 *Laws of Oregon* 1955.   It is on the Jacob J. Moore D.L.C., OC #1387.   {11 May 1997}   (Damascus 1961-84 USGS Quad. map.)

HALL, MARY ELIZABETH   A   0.01   ?   1898   T1N   R1E   ?
The infant child of Walter Scott Hall and Sedate E. Hall was born and died July 31, 1898.   The child was buried on their own lot at the head of Northwest Johnson Street in Northwest Portland.   The exact location is not known to the compiler.   A City of Portland Death Certificate shows burial on home place.   (Not shown on Portland 1961-70-77 USGS Quad. map.)

HAVURAH SHALOM   C   0.3   1   1986   T1S   R1E   S6
Located southeast of the intersection of Southwest Hewitt Boulevard and Southwest Scholls Ferry Road just south of the overpass over US Hwy. 26 at Sylvan, Portland.   The entrance is from the church parking lot on the east side of Hewitt Boulevard.   This is a section of the Jones Cemetery which has been consecrated as a holy burial ground for persons of the Jewish faith and which contains 100 grave sites with an option on an additional 300 grave sites.   A Metro Pioneer Cemetery (2115 SE Morrison Street, Portland, OR 97214, phone 248-3622).   It is on the Nathan B. Jones D.L.C., OC #2761.   (see Jones Cemetery for further information)   {10 May 1997}   (Portland 1961-70-77 USGS Quad. map.)

HOLDEN BABY   A   0.01   ?   16 Feb 1910   ?   ?   ?
The stillborn male child of Martin Holden and Minnie Henderson Holden was buried 16 February 1910, the day he was born, in their yard at 43 Kelly Avenue, Portland (1910 address).   This information per Oregon Death Certificate #3, Multnomah County.

I.O.O.F. [CARTERS]   ?   ?   7   Circa 1858   T1S   R1E   S4
AKA: 1. CARTERS
      I.O.O.F.
This was at Canyon Road and Southwest Jefferson Street, Portland.   It was lot #57

713

Name of Cemetery and also known as	Number of burials	Acres	Condition	Date started or earliest known burial	Township	Range	Section

2. SAMARITAN LODGE

of Carter's Addition to the city of Portland and was deeded to Samaritan Lodge #2 in 1858. Samaritan Lodge #2 created I.O.O.F. [Greenwood] in 1884 which would indicate the possibility of the burials being moved to the I.O.O.F. Cemetery at Greenwood Hills circa 1884. Canyon Road crosses over a portion of this location in 1997. The site will probably be marked as a part of the West Side Light Rail Project as the tracks run through the site prior to entering the tunnel. There are no known records. This is on the Thomas Carter D.L.C., #91 OC #4636. *Multnomah County Deed Records* Book A, page 149. {April 1997} (Not shown on Portland 1961-70-77 USGS Quad. map.)

I.O.O.F. [GREENWOOD]
AKA: 1. GREENWOOD
2. GREENWOOD I.O.O.F.
3. SAMARITAN LODGE
4. SUNRISE MEMORIAL PARK

D   2.35 1   Circa 1884   T1S R1E   S27
The entrance is located at 9002 Southwest Boones Ferry Road, Portland via the entrance to Greenwood Hills Cemetery. After entering Greenwood Hills Cemetery follow the left road keeping left at the next fork and right at the third fork. The cemetery is on the right just past the first brick pedestal and row of trees. The row of trees mark the boundary between I.O.O.F. and Greenwood Hills. The road is actually in I.O.O.F. at this point and not in Greenwood Hills. The cemetery is also accessible from River View Cemetery. I.O.O.F. is now part of River View Cemetery but was a part of Greenwood Hills. It probably contains burials from Carters I.O.O.F., Portland (see article on I.O.O.F. [Carters] for additional information). It is on the John M. Tice D.L.C., OC #3192. {10 April 1997} (Lake Oswego 1984 USGS Quad. map.)

I.O.O.F. [KENILWORTH]

?   ?   7   ?   T1S R1E   S12
This was on Sections 12 and 13, on the south side of Southeast Holgate Street across from Kenilworth Park between Southeast 30th and Southeast 33rd Avenues, Portland. The property is now the Friendship Care Center which opperated as an I.O.O.F. retirement home for members of the lodge for many years. There are no known records. It is on the

Name of Cemetery and also known as	Number of burials	Acres	Condition	Date started or earliest known burial	Township	Range	Section

Clinton Kelly D.L.C. #55, OC #1424. {Fall 1991} (Not shown on Lake Oswego 1984 USGS Quad. map.)

JACKSON'S, D. D.

? ? ? ? ? ? ?
Oregon Death Certificate #3842 reports the death of Wm. J. Dwyre at the County Hospital on 17 May 1907. This certificate states Mr. Dwyre was born on Staten Isle, N. Y. and he was a single white male about 40 years of age. Place of burial or removal is listed as D. D. Jackson's. No further information is known by the compiler.

JAPANESE

D 1.04 1 1896 T1N R2E S19
Located at 3743 Northeast 50th Avenue, Portland. This is an independent cemetery in the center of Rose City Cemetery. The entrance is through Rose City Cemetery. The Japanese cemetery is very typical of burial sites in Japan and is well worth a visit to learn more of the culture of the Japanese. {11 November 1991} (Mount Tabor 1990 USGS Quad. map.)

JOHANSON, MRS.

A 0.01 ? ? ? ? ?
A lone grave under a tree on the Handcheck property in East County. NOTE: this site is on private property. No further information was given in *East Multnomah County Pioneer Association Publications* (mid 1980's).

JOHNSON BABY

A 0.01 ? 13 Jan 1909 ? ? ?
The female infant of Hans H. Johnson and Emma Roselund Johnson was born 8 January 1908 and died 13 January 1908. The father buried the infant 7 1/2 miles east of Portland 1/4 mile south of Base Line Road [Stark Street] on 15 January 1909 per Oregon Death Certificate #188, Multhomah County.

JONES PIONEER
AKA: 1. JONES
2. MT. ZION
3. SYLVAN

C 3.5 1 1854 T1S R1E S6
Located southeast of the intersection of Southwest Hewitt Boulevard and Southwest Scholls Ferry Road just south of the overpass

Name of Cemetery and also known as	Number of burials	Acres	Condition	Date started or earliest known burial	Township	Range	Section

over US Hwy. 26 at Sylvan, Portland. Enter from the church parking lot on the east side of Hewitt Boulevard. (In June 1986 a 100-plot parcel was bought by the congregation of Havurah Shalom (see Havurah Shalom article)). See: Snyder, Eugene E., *We Claimed This Land: Portland's Pioneer Settlers*. Binford & Mort Publishing, Portland. 1989. Pages 124-132. It is on the Nathan B. Jones D.L.C., OC #2761. A Metro Pioneer Cemetery (2115 SE Morrison Street, Portland, OR 97214, phone 503-248-3622). See *Multnomah County Deed Book* S page 381. This is the only Metro Pioneer Cemetery that was not placed in the hands of Multnomah County by legislative action. {10 May 1997} (Portland 1960-70-77 USGS Quad. map.)

KELLY, CLINTON
AKA: 1. KEARNS
     2. KELLEY
     3. KELLY

C   0.5   7   Circa 1863   T1S   R1E   S12
This was located in the 4100 block on the north side of Southeast Powell Boulevard, Portland. Clinton Kelly Methodist Episcopal Church was built to the west of the cemetery. In 1923 the City of Portland was ready to sell the cemetery because of a lien against the property for improvements had not been paid. The Methodist Episcopal Church paid the lien. About 1928 some burials were moved to Lincoln Memorial Park. Others were removed to River View Mausoleum (Riverview Abbey?) while still others probably remained. The site is now built over. See the *Oregon Journal*, 29 December 1923 page 11, 31 December 1923 page 3 and *The Telegraph*, 29 December 1923 page 4. This was on the Clinton Kelly D.L.C. #55, OC #1324. {9 February 1992} (Not shown on Gladstone 1961-84 USGS Quad. map.)

KELLY FARM, PLYMPTON

A   0.01   7   7 Sep 1887   T1S   R2E   ?
Clinton Clark Kelly born June 15, 1869 died September 7, 1887 at his parents home and was buried on the farm near Mount Tabor. The farm was on the Plympton Kelly D.L.C. #58, OC #3739 which was bounded by Southeast Lincoln Street on the north, Southeast Powell Boulevard on the south, Southeast 101st

Name of Cemetery and also known as	Number of burials	Acres	Condition	Date started or earliest known burial	Township	Range	Section

Avenue on the east and Southeast 88th Avenue on the west. See the *Pacific Christian Advocate* for obituary. (Not shown on Mount Tabor 1990 or on Gladstone 1961-84 USGS Quad. map.)

KWAN YIN TEMPLE

B ? 1 ? T1N R3E S31

This Chinese Buddhist Temple in Gresham is located at 16525 Northeast Glisan Street, Gresham. There is a "Hall to repay your loved ones" in which there are spaces below the altar for cremains. See *The Oregonian*, 28 June 1995 Sec B, Page 1. (Not shown on Camas 1961-70-75 USGS Quad. map.)

LATOURELL FALLS

? ? ? ? T1N R5E S29

Possible cemetery. It is thought that there should have been a cemetery here, considering the size of the community in the late 1890's and through the early 1900's, but unconfirmed as of 1997. Portland death certificates do indicate bodies shipped to Latourell which was also a railroad station name. (Not shown on Bridal Veil 1986 USGS Quad. map.)

LINCOLN MEMORIAL PARK
AKA: 1. MT. SCOTT

E 443 1 1911 T1S R2E S22

In Sections 22 and 27. Located at 11801 Southeast Mt. Scott Boulevard, Portland. The cemetery is in Multnomah and Clackamas Counties and includes indoor and outdoor mausoleums and a funeral home. The office was in Multnomah County until a new office and funeral home was built about 1995. 90,000 have been interred here (see the 6 February 1992 article in *The Oregonian*.) During the early years of the cemetery a crematory was operated with the cremains going to other locations. See McArthur, Lewis A. *Oregon Geographic Names* 5th Edition, page 522 under Mount Scott. {March 1997} (Gladstone 1961-84 USGS Quad. map.)

LITTLE CHAPEL OF THE CHIMES FUNERAL HOME [GATEWAY]

B ? 1 ? T1N R2E S34

Located on the south side of Northeast Halsey Street and on the west side of Northeast 106th Avenue. The west wall of the funeral

Name of Cemetery and also known as	Number of burials	Acres	Condition	Date started or earliest known burial	Township	Range	Section

home is made of thick stained glass. The interior of this wall is made up of niches with clear glass fronts to form a columbarium. {1995} (Not shown on Mount Tabor 1990 USGS Quad. map.)

LONE FIR PIONEER
AKA: 1. LONE FIR
    2. MT. CRAWFORD
    3. PORTLAND
    4. PORTLAND
       LONE FIR

E 30.5 1 1855   T1S R1E   S1
This is in Sections 1 and 2, at 2115 Southeast Morrison Sreet, Portland. D. A. Lund in *Lone Fir: Silent City of the Dead* states "All nations are represented, all grades of society, all states of wealth and standing. Rich lie here and poor, employer and employee, those with virtue and those without. Death has a way of banishing snobbishness, of cultivating comradeship." The grounds are a wooded, landscaped arboretum in the heart of Portland containing a pioneer rose garden and abundant wildlife. Several areas are sections for groups such as the Masonic Section and the Fireman's section. A Metro Pioneer Cemetery (2115 SE Morrison Street, Portland, OR, phone 248-3622) See Chapter 428 *General Laws of Oregon* 1927. It is on the Seldon Murray D.L.C., #54 OC #1413. {30 May`1999} (Portland 1960-70-77 USGS Quad. map.)

LOOMIS

A 0.5 7 1854-1949 T1N R1W   S2
Located on tax lot #95, this was 98 feet west of North Edison Steet and 557.5 feet north of North Reno Avenue, in the St. Johns area of Portland. It was on the bluff overlooking the Willamette River. The burials of James, Sarah, Charles, Christopher and Edward were removed to River View Cemetery on 11 August 1949. This was on the James Loomis D.L.C. #45, OC #1349. {1987} (Not shown on Linnton 1961-84 USGS Quad. map.)

LOVE, LEWIS

A 0.01 1 ?   T1N R1E   S10
Lewis Love and his family are buried northwest of the northwest corner of the original Columbian Cemetery. Columbian has expanded and now includes and surrounds the Love plot on three sides. The plot has an iron fence around it. See *The Oregonian* for

Name of Cemetery and also known as	Number of burials	Acres	Condition	Date started or earliest known burial	Township	Range	Section

an obituary of Lewis Love who died 3 July 1903. It is on the Lewis Love D.L.C. #410, OC #1484. {10 May 1997} (Not shown on Portland 1960-70-77 USGS Quad. map.)

MASONIC [LONE FIR]
AKA: 1. FREEMASON

C ? 1 Circa 1855 T1S R1E S1
This is now the north central part of Lone Fir Cemetery, and was shown on early maps as a separate cemetery. It is on the Seldon Murray D.L.C. #54, OC #1413. {8 February 1992} (Portland 1960-70-77 USGS Quad. map.)

McCLELLAN, CHARLES

A 0.01 7 23 Aug 1853 T1N R3E S28
This single grave was probably on section 28. The grave was near Main Street in Fairview and was found in 1916 during construction of a roadway. (see *Gresham Outlook*, November 7, 1916, page 1) Charles McClellan was born in 1825 in Ohio and was shot by Ethan Cox and died 23 August 1853 per the *Gresham Outlook*. *Genealogical Material in Oregon Donation Land Claims* Volume II, Genealogical Forum Of Portland Oregon, 1959 gives the year as 1858. He was the first white person buried in the locality of Fairview. (Not shown on Camas 1961-75 USGS Quad. map.)

McGREGOR BABY

A 0.01 ? 15 Jul 1909 ? ? ?
The premature female infant of Donald McGregor and his wife ____ Hills McGregor was born and died 15 July 1909 and was buried in their own yard at 1214 Gladstone Avenue, Portland (1909 address) on the same day. This information is per Oregon Death Certificate #3, Multnomah County.

McNEMEE

0.5 4 11 Oct 1905 T2N R1W S30
Located on tax lot #17 of the Northeast 1/4 of the Southeast 1/4 of Section 30. The north boundary of this cemetery is on the centerline of Section 30 about 150 feet east of the east line of the section. This is 0.5 of a mile north of Pauly Road on McNamee Road, on the north side of the road and in the woods. At the time of a visit (12 January 1991) the only visible burial was

for Moses McNemee, 11 October 1839-12 April 1905. NOTE: The county road is spelled McNamee, but the only tombstone found spells it McNemee. {Summer 1999} (Not shown on Sauvie Island 1990 USGS Quad. map.)

McQUINN

A   1   2   1854   T2N R1W   S6
Located on Sauvie Island, it is on lot #17 of Section 6. Go north on Sauvie Island Road, turn right onto Lucy Reeder Road and go 0.8 of a mile. The cemetery is in a grove of trees 800 feet north off of Lucy Reeder Road. There is no public access. See *The Oregonian*, 25 November 1990, Margie Boule's column. It is on the Alexander H. and Rebecca McQuinn D.L.C. #50, OC #3569. (Not shown on Sauvie Island 1990 USGS Quad. map.)

MELOY FAMILY
AKA: 1. MALLOY FAMILY
     2. MOLLOY FAMILY
     3. NELOY FAMILY

A   0.01 ?   ?   ?   ?   ?
The D.L.C. is located in Township 1 North, Range 3 East, Section 34 and Township 2 South, Range 3 East, Section 3. No further information is known by the compiler. Nathan H. Meloy, Mary W. Meloy Stearns, and an infant were buried near the 12-Mile Corner on Southeast Stark Street. See Chilton, W. R., *Gresham, Stories of our Past*, Gresham Historical Society, 1993, page 28. It is on the Nathan H. Meloy (Widow) and heirs D.L.C. #55, OC #2833. (Not shown on Camas 1961-75 USGS Quad. map.)

MOAR

A   0.25 2   1841-1925 T2N R1W   S7
Located 3 miles to the left on Sauvie Island Road after crossing the bridge from the mainland. It is approximately 850 feet west of the road, on James D. Lyons property (1978). There are 13 known graves in a cultivated field with 2 large oak trees. It is almost fully enclosed by an iron fence. It is on the James Logie D.L.C. #49, OC #1918. NOTE: This site is on private property. {Spring 1996} (Sauvie Island 1990 USGS Quad. map.)

Name of Cemetery and also known as	Number of burials	Acres	Condition	Date started or earliest known burial	Township	Range	Section

MOFFITT BABY

A 0.01 ? 9 Feb 1933 T1N R3E S3

A premature female born and died 9 February 1933, the child of Sterling L. Moffitt and Doris Logan Moffitt was buried on their own property in Troutdale. The exact location is not known by the compiler. The source is an Oregon Death Certificate Multnomah County State #41. (Not shown on Camas 1961-70-75 USGS Quad. map.)

MONASTERY OF THE PRECIOUS BLOOD
AKA: 1. SISTERS OF THE PRECIOUS BLOOD

B ? 7 Circa 1892 T1S R2E S5

This was east of Southeast 76th Avenue at Southeast Main Street, Portland on the grounds of the Monastery of the Sisters Adorers of the Precious Blood Daughters of Mary Immaculate. It was about 30' x 60'. The bodies were moved about 1975 to Gethsemani Cemetery in Clackamas County. The site is now a parking lot and garden for Saint Andrew's Retirement Center, 7617 Southeast Main Street. See the *Oregon Journal*, 7 July 1977 page 3 c3. It was on the Samuel Nelson D.L.C. #50, OC #3982. {April 1997} (Monastery is shown on the Mount Tabor 1990 USGS Quad. map.)

MORGAN FAMILY
AKA: 1. MORDEN

A 1 4 ? T1N R1W S15

A family plot on the west side of Northwest Skyline Boulevard, Portland. It is located across the road from 6140 Northwest Skyline Boulevard and south of Springville Road. It is fenced with a decaying iron fence and overgrown with ivy. Some burials were reportedly removed to other locations. There are no known records, and no markers were visible {12 January 1991}. (Not shown on Linnton 1961-84 USGS Quad. map.)

MT. CALVARY CATHOLIC

E 85 1 1888 T1S R1E S6

This is in Township 1 South Range 1 East Section 6 and in Township 1 North Range 1 East Section 31. Located at 333 Southwest Skyline Boulevard, Portland. There are 135 acres all told, with 85 acres that are developed and approximately 15 acres left to develop. The rest of the site is too steep to be developed. This cemetery is owned by

Name of Cemetery and also known as	Number of burials	Acres	Condition	Date started or earliest known burial	Township	Range	Section

Roman Catholic Archdiocese of Portland in Oregon. {January 1992} (Portland 1960-70-77 USGS Quad. map.)

MOUNTAIN VIEW-CORBETT PIONEER
AKA: 1. CEMETERY HILL
2. CORBETT
3. EVANS
4. EVANS, TOM
5. MT. VIEW--CORBETT

C   2   1   1880   T1S   R4E   S3
Located 1.25 miles southwest of Corbett on Cemetery Road at the intersection of Smith Road and Evans Road. It is on the south side of Smith Road and the west side of Evans Road. From I-84 Freeway take the Corbett exit. At the Crown Point Highway (Historic Columbia River Scenic Highway) turn right then make a left turn at Evans Road and travel south to the intersection of Smith Road. The cemetery is on the right (south) of Smith Road. Coming from Troutdale on the Crown Point Highway make a right turn onto Smith road. Smith Road ends at Evans Road with the cemetery on the right. *The Thomas Guide for the Portland Metro Area* shows the cemetery on the wrong side of the road. A Metro Pioneer Cemetery (2115 SE Morrison Street, Portland, OR 97214, phone 503-248-3622) See Chapter 170 *Laws of Oregon* 1947. {16 May 1999} (Washougal 1961-70-75 USGS Quad. map.)

MOUNTAIN VIEW-STARK PIONEER
AKA: 1. HALL
2. MT. VIEW BASELINE ROAD
3. MT. VIEW--STARK
4. STOTT

C   0.82   1   1881   T1N   R3E   S35
Located on the north side of southeast Stark Street at the end of a dirt frontage road about 150 feet east of 257th Avenue. The entrance to the frontage road is a driveway on the north side of Southeast Stark Street just east of the gas station. A Metro Pioneer Cemetery (2115 SE Morrison Street, Portland, OR, phone 503-248-3622) See chapter 137 *Oregon Laws* 1955. It is on the Benjamin Hall D.L.C. #50, OC #5064. {16 May 1999} (Camas 1961-70-75 USGS Quad. map.)

MULTNOMAH HOSPITAL

?   ?   ?   ?   T1S   R1E   S9
Bodies that were sent to the Multnomah Hospital were most probably used as cadavers as the hospital was associated with the University Of Oregon Medical School. The other possibility is that the hospital operated its own crematory for indigents as

Name of Cemetery and also known as	Number of burials	Acres	Condition	Date started or earliest known burial	Township	Range	Section

it was a county-owned hospital. Multiple Oregon State Death Certificates indicate bodies were sent here. (Not shown on Portland 1960-70-77 USGS Quad. map, University of Oregon Medical School is shown but no graveyard.)

MULTNOMAH PARK PIONEER
AKA: 1. MULTNOMAH PARK

| | E | 9.3 | 1 | 1888 | T1S | R2E | S17 |

Located on the west side of Southeast 82nd Avenue (OR. Hwy. 213) and on the south side of Southeast Holgate Boulevard, Portland. A Metro Pioneer Cemetery (2115 SE Morrison Street, Portland, OR 97214, phone 503-248-3622) See Chapter 88 *Laws of Oregon* 1943. {April 1997} (Gladstone 1961-84 USGS Quad. map.)

NORTH PACIFIC DENTAL COLLEGE
AKA: 1. N. P. DENTAL COLLEGE

| | ? | ? | ? | ? | T1N | R1E | S35 |

Bodies were sent to the college for use as cadavers by the students. *Polk's Portland City Directory* for 1929 lists the school as North Pacific College of Oregon Schools of Dentistry and Pharmacy at "E. 6th N NW Corner Oregon [Street]. A photo of the building appears in the directory. This is presently called the Forum Building. (Not shown on Portland, Oreg.-Wash. 1961 Quad. map.)

ORIENT

| | ? | ? | ? | ? | T1S | R4E | S19 |

Located on the west side of Short Road south of Orient Drive and shown in *Thomas Map guides* 1984, 1988, 1997, 1998 and 2000, and on the 2000 *Rand McNally* map of Gresham and in the *Pittmon Atlas* of Portland 1988. No further information is available. There are no known records. No one in the Gresham/Pleasant Home area knows anything about this cemetery. Thomas Map publishers does not have any record as to where they obtained their information. (Not shown on Sandy 1985 Quad. map.)

PAINTER FAMILY

| | A | 0.25 | 3 | Circa 1880 | T1N | R4E | S25 |

This burial site is on the grounds of Menucha, a retreat center owned by the First Presbyterian Church of Portland. Menucha is on the north side of Crown Point Highway (Historic Columbia River Scenic Highway) between Corbett and the Portland Women's Forum State Scenic Viewpoint at 38711 Crown Point Highway. This is the former estate of Julius L. Meier, former governor of Oregon, located just east of Corbett. The burials are under an old apple tree. The Painter family were refugees from the Sandwich (Hawaiian) Islands, who came to Oregon with some of their native servants. All buried here died of leprosy, with dates of death unknown, the burials are unmarked. It is on the James Deaver Homestead. NOTE: This site is on private property. {18 May 1992} (Not shown on Washougal 1961-70-75 USGS Quad. map.)

PALMER ? ? ? ?   T1N R5E   S24

There may have been a cemetery at the lumbering community of Palmer which was important enough for a post office from February 1898-December 1919. Palmer was on upper Bridal Veil Creek about 3 miles east of the Bridal Veil community. (Not shown on Bridal Veil or Multnomah Falls 1986 USGS Quad. map.)

PARISH OF ST. MARK, THE A ? 1 ?   T1N R1E   S33

The parish of St. Mark (Anglican Church in America) has a columbarium within the church at 1025 Northwest 21st Avenue, Portland Oregon. This information is from an obituary in *The Oregonian* dated 30 September 1999 on page D8 in the obituary of Roger W. 'Bill' Powell. The last paragraph of the obituary states "Private interment will be in the columbarium at the church." (Not shown on Portland, Oreg-Wash 1961 USGS Quad. map.)

PARKS, DAVID A 0.01 7 1875   T1N R3E   ?

This could be in Section 27 or 34. There was one known grave on this farm, but possibly David Parks' five daughters are also buried here, in Wood Village (see the *Gresham Outlook*, 31 May 1976, Section 1, Page 9). The grave was moved to an unknown location

Name of Cemetery and also known as	Number of burials	Acres	Condition	Date started or earliest known burial	Township	Range	Section

because of railroad construction circa 1882. Parks' death notice was reported in the *Pacific Christian Advocate*, which states "died Sandy, 23 June 1875. He was born in Beaver County, Pennsylvania 24 October 1805 and emigrated to Oregon in 1867, being survived by a wife and five daughters". Perhaps located on the Addison C. Dunbar D.L.C. #41, OC #3719. (Not shown on Camas 1961-75 USGS Quad. map.)

PEARSON FAMILY

A 0.01 ? Circa 1856 ? ? ?

This is a private plot near Skyline Boulevard. There are no known records. This may be the same as McNemee, as the last owner of record of McNemee is Rhoda Pearson (address Multnomah County Courthouse per tax records) though McNemee is now a larger site. The W.P.A. map of cemeteries in Multnomah County shows the size to be 20' by 20' but does not give a location.

PLEASANT HOME PIONEER
AKA: 1. KELLEY
    2. KELLY, ARCHON
    3. PLEASANT HOME

C 1.92 1 1884 T1S R4E S20

Located 5 miles southeast of Gresham on the south side of Bluff Road and the west side of Pleasant Home Road, south (in back) of the Pleasant Home United Methodist Church. The center section of the cemetery is reserved for descendants of Archon Kelly. A Metro Pioneer Cemetery (2115 SE Morrison Street, Portland, OR 97214, phone 503-248-3622) See Chapter 126 *Laws of Oregon* 1959. It is on the George W. and Harriet Brown D.L.C., OC #3093. (11 May 1997) (Sandy 1985 USGS Quad. map.)

PORTLAND MEMORIAL AND MAUSOLEUM
AKA: 1. PORTLAND CREMATION ASSOCIATION
    2. PORTLAND INDOOR CEMETERY

E ? 1 1901 T1S R1E S23

Located at 6705 Southeast 14th Avenue, Portland in the Sellwood area. This is a large indoor facility exceeding 100,000 inturements and inurnments. It began as Portland Cremation Association being the first crematorium in the Pacific Northwest. Bodies were shipped here from northern California north to the Canadian Border for cremation. Special funeral streetcars were used to transport bodies and families and

----
| Name of Cemetery and also known as | Number of burials | Acres | Condition | Date started or earliest known burial | Township | Range | Section |
----

friends from all parts of the metropolitan area to the facility. Many people were removed from other sites and brought here as cremation became popular and older cemeteries became run down. A check of their records is worth the effort if you are unable to find an individual or family in the cemetery listed on the death certificate. This facility is filled with artwork and stained glass including windows made by Tiffany. It is well worth a tour to view the artwork. There is a memorial rose garden where cremains are placed rather than spreading elsewhere or being placed in a niche. {10 April 1997} (Lake Oswego 1961-84 USGS Quad. map.)

POTTER FAMILY

A   ?   7   ?   T1N   R1E   S19

This could have been located in Section 19 or 30. W. W. Potter 5 years, I. M. Potter 5 years 10 months, Cora E. Potter 2 years and Minnie Potter 7 months, the children of Levi C. and Hannah M. Potter were buried on D.L.C. OC #566. They were later removed to Greenwood Hills Cemetery to Section 1, Lot 52 on 18 August 1892. (Not shown on Portland 1960-70-77 USGS Quad. map.)

POUNDER
AKA: 1. SUNSET

A   3.4   2   1914   T1N   R4E   S35

Located 1 mile east and south of Corbett. Drive 0.6 of a mile east from Corbett on the Crown Point Highway. Keep ahead and turn to the right onto Grange Hall Road when the main highway veers left. Go 0.2 of a mile to the junction with Littlepage Road, and then turn right (south). Drive 0.2 of a mile more to a dirt road right (west) at 145 Littlepage Road. The cemetery is to the left of the trees and the cattle guard. NOTE: This site is unsigned and all monuments are flat with the ground. The cattle have been roaming through this cemetery and it is reported that a local farmer has been mowing it once in awhile when he has time, otherwise no one seems to be caring for it. It is on tax lot 40. {16 May 1999} (Washougal 1961-70-75 USGS Quad. map.)

Name of Cemetery and also known as	Number of burials	Acres	Condition	Date started or earliest known burial	Township	Range	Section

POWELL GROVE PIONEER
AKA: 1. CENTRAL
        COLUMBIA
     2. CENTRAL GROVE
     3. POWELL
     4. POWELL GROVE

C   0.93   1   1848   T1N   R2E   S23
Located at the southeast corner of Northeast 122nd Avenue and Northeast Sandy Boulevard, Portland, on the David Powell D.L.C. #43, OC #1011. Litigation about moving this cemetery to provide for proposed widening of Northeast 122nd Avenue resulted in the street being routed around the site and to the preservation of other burial sites in the State. A Metro Pioneer Cemetery (2115 SE Morrison Street, Portland, OR 97214, phone 248-3622.). See Chapter 178 *Laws of Oregon* 1949. There were 100 burials with 130 plots available (May 1987). {10 May 1997} (Mount Tabor 1990 USGS Quad. map.)

PULLEN, MARY L.

A   ?   ?   11 Mar 1881   T1S   R2E   S3
Located at 1210 Southeast 112th Avenue, Portland. See the article in *The Oregonian* 18 June 1951 on page 6. The wooden headboard read Mary L. Pullen born March 11, 1845 Died July 13, 1881. This may have been part of a small cemetery at one time. (Not shown on Mt. Tabor 1990 USGS Quad. map.)

PULLINS
AKA: 1. McCARTNEY

?   ?   ?   ?   ?   ?   ?
Oregon Death Certificate #1142, Multnomah County lists Pullins Cemetery as the burial site of Elsworth McCartney born 17 Jan 1910 to Elmer D. McCartney and Marie Warfler McCartney in Linnton, Oregon. This child died 4 April 1910 and was buried 5 April 1910. Where is this cemetery?

QUINN, MARY WHELAN

A   0.01   7   8 Mar 1854   T1N   R1E   S36
In the Laurelhurst District, Portland, this burial is on the Terence Quinn D.L.C. #70, OC #1027, north of Southeast Stark Street, west of Southeast 39th Avenue, east of Southeast 32nd Avenue and south of Northeast Broadway. See: Nichols, M. Leona, *The Mantle of Elias* Binford & Mort Publishers, Portland, 1941 page 334; Snyder, Eugene F., *We Claimed this Land: Portland's Pioneer Settlers*, Binford & Mort Publishing, Portland, 1989, Pages 213-215; Records of Immaculate Conception

Catholic Church, 1854. (Not shown on Portland 1961-70-77 or Mt. Tabor 1990 USGS Quad. maps.)

RAMSEY
AKA: 1. RAMSAY
2. RAMSEY, FRED
3. RAMSEY, FREDERIC H.
4. RAMSEY'S FARM

A 0.12 2 2 Jan 1895 T2N R1W S36
Located on North Columbia Boulevard (formerly Swift Boulevard), on the northeast corner of the intersection of North Burgard Street and North Lombard Street, Portland. There is one large stone here. When Fred Ramsey's grave was dug the skeletons of 4 Indian women were found lending credence to the rumors that he had 4 Indian wives. Known burials are: Frederick H. Ramsey, January 2, 1895; Merrit Titus, February 27, 1899 and John C. Ramsey, July 6, 1901. This is on the James Loomis D.L.C. #45, OC #1349. {10 May 1997} (Linnton 1984 USGS Quad. map.)

RANKIN INFANT

A 0.01 ? Dec. 1900 T1N R5E ?
The infant child of Clark L. and Mary Reutheman Rankin is buried on the Charles Lund Place along the fence row in east county near Palmer. See *East Multnomah County Pioneer Association* publications. (Not shown on Bridal Veil 1986 USGS Quad. map.)

REED, CALVIN

A 0.01 ? 1856 T1N R3E ?
This could be on Section 13, 14, 23, or 24. It is reportedly near the mouth of the Sandy River in the area of the Reynolds Aluminum plant. It is on the Calvin Reed D.L.C. #60, OC #1537. (Not shown on Camas 1961-70-75 USGS Quad. map.)

RIVER VIEW
AKA: 1. RIVERVIEW

E 350 1 1882 T1S R1E S22
This is on Sections 22 and 27. It is at 8421 Southwest Macadam Avenue, Portland. The office and main entrance is on the south side of Southwest Taylors Ferry Road across the road from Riverview Abbey. Many of the city founders are buried here, as well as Virgil Earp the brother of Wyatt Earp. Some of the finest monuments in the state are to be found here. This cemetery contains and now operates I.O.O.F. [Greenwood] Cemetery see

that article. It is on the John M. Tice D.L.C., OC #3192. {10 April 1997} (Lake Oswego 1961-84 USGS Quad. map.)

RIVERVIEW ABBEY MAUSOLEUM
AKA: 1. ABBEY
         RIVERVIEW

E   19.5   1   1916   T1S R1E   S22
Located at 0319 Southwest Taylors Ferry Road, Portland. It is entirely a mausoleum without any ground burials. The Abbey was once part of River View Cemetery but is NOT part of River View Cemetery today. {10 April 1997} (Lake Oswego 1961-84 USGS Quad map.)

ROOSTER ROCK

?   ?   ?   ?   T1N R4E   S25
This may be the same as Bridal Veil Cemetery, but it is also possible that there are a few separate burials at Rooster Rock or above Rooster Rock and below Chanticleer Point. There is a report of 2 or 3 graves between the highway and the cliff below Chanticleer Point. There are death certificates showing Rooster Rock as the burial site/destination. Rooster Rock was also the name of the rail station for Bridal Veil during some years thus these burials may be in Bridal Veil. More information is needed. (Not shown on Washougal 1961-70-75 USGS Quad. map.)

ROSE CITY
AKA: 1. ROSE LAWN

E 80   1   1906   T1N R2E   S19
Located at 5625 Northeast Fremont Street, Portland. The Japanese Cemetery (see article) is an independent cemetery within this cemetery. Rose City has a very large section of ethnic burials with above-ground tombs and extremely interesting markers, many of which have photos on them. {January 1992} (Mount Tabor 1990 USGS Quad. map.)

ROSELAWN MEMORIAL PARK

E   2   *   1932   T1N R2E   S27
This cemetery was platted 4 January 1932 to be built at Northeast 117th Avenue and Northeast Klickitat Street in Portland. *The cemetery was not completed nor was it ever used. (Not shown on Mount Tabor 1990 USGS Quad. map.)

Name of Cemetery and also known as	Number of burials	Acres	Condition	Date started or earliest known burial	Township	Range	Section

ST. JOSEPH
AKA: 1. CATHOLIC
2. GRANT'S
3. GRESHAM
4. KRONENBERG
5. LINNEMANN
6. POWELL VALLEY
7. R. C.
8. ST. AGNES
9. ST. HENRY

C 1.7 1 1880 T1S R3E S8
Now located inside the Gresham city limits on Southeast 198th Avenue and Southeast Powell Boulevard (U.S. Hwy. 26) on the west side of Powell Boulevard. It is owned by the Archdiocese of Portland in Oregon with the records held at Mt. Calvary Cemetery. It is on the Gerhard D. Linnemann D.L.C. #51, OC #4186. {16 May 1999} (Damascus 1961-84 USGS Quad. map.)

ST. MARY'S
AKA: 1. CATHOLIC

E 4 7 1858-1937 T1N R1E S36
It was on the east side of Southeast 26th Avenue and north of Southeast Stark Street (Baseline Road), Portland. There were at least 2,090 burials. Most were reburied in other cemeteries including a St. Mary's section at Mt. Calvary prior to Central Catholic High School being built on the site. It was on the Timothy Sullivan D.L.C. #71, OC #1470. {September 1996} (Not shown on Portland 1960-70-77 USGS Quad. map.)

ST. MARY'S ACADEMY

? ? ? ? T1S R1E S3
A burial site at a convent in Southwest Portland on Southwest Hall Street at 6th Avenue. No further information was given. (Not shown on Portland 1960-70-77 USGS Quad. map.)

SELLWOOD

? ? 7 Circa 1855 T1S R1E S23
Possibly in Sections 23, 24 in Multnomah County, 25 and/or 26 in Clackamas County. This was on Rev. John Sellwood's land. Rev. Sellwood was removed to the Milwaukie Cemetery in Clackamas County, the remainder were removed to other locations. (Not shown on Lake Oswego 1961-84 USGS Quad. map.)

SERVITE

A ? 1 1968 T1N R2E S21
The Order of Servants of Mary popularly know as the "Servites" maintain a small private cemetery on the grounds of their monastery on the upper level of The Grotto, The National Sanctuary of Our Sorrowful Mother. The Grotto is located at Northeast 85th Avenue

Name of Cemetery and also known as	Number of burials	Acres	Condition	Date started or earliest known burial	Township	Range	Section

and Sandy Boulevard in Portland and is a popular tourist attraction with the upper level Meditation Chapel offering a spectacular view of the lower Columbia River Gorge and Mt. St. Helens. The entire 65 acres of The Grotto and Monastery are peaceful and serene, a perfect place to calm oneself of the hustle of everyday life. {9 September 2000} (Not shown on Mt. Tabor 1990 USGS Quad. map.)

SKYLINE MEMORIAL GARDENS
AKA: 1. NORTHWEST MEMORIAL GARDENS
2. SKYLINE MEMORIAL PARK

E 150   1   1951   T1N R1W   S23
Located at 4101 Northwest Skyline Boulevard, Portland. This cemetery has a spectacular view of the Tualatin Valley to the southwest. {5 February 1992} (Linnton 1961-84 USGS Quad. map.)

SMITH

? ?   ? ?   T1N R5E   ?
The site is probably in Section 27 in the area of the old town of Brower. A woman born in New Brunswick was buried on what probably was their own property. The site is reported as sitting on a bluff overlooking the Columbia River. There was an iron fence around the grave at one time. This may have been the homestead of Robert T. Smith who came from New Brunswick, Canada in 1888 with his wife and six children. (Not shown on Bridal Veil 1986 USGS Quad map.)

SMITH BABY

? ?   ? 12 Mar 1906 ?   ?   ?
Oregon Death Certificate #159 reports Baby Smith was born 11 February 1907 in Oregon. The 29 day old male infant of Edward E. Smith of Illinois and Anna Rose ? of Missouri, died 10 March 1906 and was buried by F. S. Dunning at 336 2nd Avenue, Portland, Oregon on 12 March 1906. On 3 October 1907 the infant was moved to Multnomah Cemetery per the same certificate.

SOUTH MT. TABOR [#1]

A ?   7 ?   T1S R2E   S5
Located about Southeast 65th Avenue, north of Division Street (Section Line Road),

731

Name of Cemetery and also known as	Number of burials	Acres	Condition	Date started or earliest known burial	Township	Range	Section

Portland. The exact location is unknown today. There are no known records. This may have been the Prettyman family burials, that were moved to Lone Fir Cemetery and then later moved to Lincoln Memorial Park. This was on the David D. Prettyman D.L.C. #55, OC #5084. SEE: *Oregon Georgraphic Names* by Lewis A. McArthur, 1982 page 569. {9 February 1992} (Not shown on Mount Tabor 1990 USGS Quad. map.)

SOUTH MT. TABOR [#2]	?	?	7	?	T1S	R2E	S8

Reportedly this site was between Southeast Division Street and Southeast Powell Boulevard at about Southeast 65th Avenue. No further information given. (Not shown on Mount Tabor 1990 USGS Quad. map.)

STUMP	B	1	7	1867	T2N	R1E	S6

Portions of blocks 7, 8, 11 and 12, near North Swift Street and North Macrum Avenue of east St. Johns, Portland. Some burials were listed in survey records of 23 July 1911. It is not known if the burials were moved, but the cemetery is shown on maps attached to this survey. See: Snyder, Eugene E. *We Claimed This Land: Portland's Pioneer Settlers*. Binford & Mort Publishing, Portland. 1989, pages 248-249. It was on the Cuthbert Stump D.L.C., OC #2016. (Not shown on Portland 1960-70-77 USGS Quad. map.)

TAYLOR	A	0.20	2	1893	T2N	R1W	S6

Drive 3.5 miles to the left on Sauvie Island Road after crossing the bridge from the mainland. There are 2 marked graves on the highest knoll. This cemetery is visible from Moar Cemetery. No records are known to exist. It is on the James Taylor D.L.C. #57, OC #1977. NOTE: This site is on private property. {Spring 1996} (Not shown on Sauvie Island 1990 USGS Quad. map.)

THOMAS INFANT	?	?	?	1 Sep 1908	?	?	?

The male infant of John Wesley Thomas of Michigan and Kiziy Martin of Indiana was

Name of Cemetery and also known as	Number of burials	Acres	Condition	Date started or earliest known burial	Township	Range	Section

buried on the parents property at 985 East Main in Portland Oregon on 1 September by the father. No further information is known by the compiler.

TRICKEY FAMILY

A 1.1 3 1895-1975 T1S R5E S8

Located on lot #2, on Deverell Road on Larch Mountain in East county between 43190 and 43300 Deverell Road. It is in the Northwest 1/4 of the Northeast 1/4 of Section 8 on the south side of the road. Take the Larch Mountain Road off of the Columbia River Scenic Highway just east of the Portland Women's Forum State Scenic Viewpoint. Drive 3.4 miles to Louden Road and turn right and travel 0.6 of a mile to Deverell Road and turn left and travel 0.5 of a mile. The cemetery is on the right about 200' off the road. "Deep in the Corbett Hills is the tiny family cemetery started by Edward Trickey who hauled logs with horse teams for Bridal Veil Lumber. When he founded the tiny burial plot on his land Trickey had the remains of his wife, Lucy, moved to the site where her towering stone dominates the other graves. Last spring Lloyd Trickey, the last direct descendant of the family was buried there in a grave dug by neighbors and relatives. Since Lloyd Trickey owned his own graveyard no one knows what will happen to the tiny cemetery." *Gresham Outlook*, May 31, 1976, Section 1, Page 9. See also *East Multnomah County Pioneer Association* publications. There are no known records. {3 May 1997} (Not shown on Bridal Veil 1986 USGS Quad. map.)

UNIVERSITY OF OREGON MEDICAL SCHOOL
AKA: 1. OREGON HEALTH SCIENCES CENTER
2. PORTLAND MEDICAL SCHOOL

? ? ? ? T1S R1E S9

There are Oregon State Death Certificates of veterans and others being sent for burial, but the Medical School does not have such records. These were probably used as cadavers. (School is shown on Portland 1977 USGS Quad. map.)

Name of Cemetery and also known as	Number of burials	Acres	Condition	Date started or earliest known burial	Township	Range	Section

UNKNOWN

A 0.01 2 ? T1N R5E S30

A lone unknown burial above Crown Point is marked by a basalt cross. This in on private property in the curve of the private roadway to a residence. {1990} (Not shown on Bridal Veil 1986 USGS Quad. map.)

UNKNOWN PIONEER CHILD

A 0.01 2 1849 T1N R3E S30

An unknown child's grave with a marker, a wagon train burial, is located just east of Northest 169th Avenue and the I-84 Freeway at milepost 12.45 on the north side of the I-84 Freeway about 4 feet north of the pavement between the I-84 Freeway, and the railroad tracks. This burial was marked by a white cross in 1991. No parking is available at this site. In 1990 a bronze marker on a field stone was placed at Wilkes School, at 17020 Northeast Wilkes Road, Portland on the south side of the I-84 Freeway and visible from the freeway directly opposite the actual grave site. It is on the Milton Frazer D.L.C. #46, OC #1674. {3 May 1997} (Not shown on Camas 1961-70-75 USGS Quad. map.)

WALLACE, ARTHUR W.

A 0.01 ? 1898 T1S R1E S10

This is a single burial about 15 feet west of Southwest Barbur Boulevard, in the Southwest Lowell Street right of way. It is marked with a six to eight inch square pillar marker with about the top two feet visible. The inscription reads: "Arthur W. Wallace, born March 6, 1821, died Aug. 26 1898." It is on the Elizabeth Caruthers Thomas DLC #43, OC #611. {April 1999} (Not shown on Lake Oswego 1984 USGS Quad. map.)

WHITE BIRCH PIONEER
AKA: 1. ESCOBAR
    2. GRESHAM
    3. WHITE BIRCH

C 0.9 1 1888 T1S R3E S9

Located on the west side of Southeast Walters Road in Gresham, south of Powell Boulevard (U.S. Hwy. 26) and behind the West Gresham School on Tax Lot 102. It is bounded on the south by the abandoned Pepco Railroad right-of-way (now Springwater Corridor [Trail]). It was once owned by Frank Escobar. A Metro Pioneer Cemetery (2115 SE Morrison Street, Portland, OR 97214, phone

Name of Cemetery and also known as	Number of burials	Acres	Condition	Date started or earliest known burial	Township	Range	Section

248-3622) See Chapter 294 *Laws of Oregon*
1963. It is on the Rev. Alfred Cornutt
D.L.C., OC #1681. {7 February 1991}
(Damascus 1961-84 USGS Quad. map.)

WILLAMETTE NATIONAL

E 336   1   1951   T1S R2E   S22
Located on Sections 22 and 27. Veterans and
veterans families are buried here. There are
in excess of 100,000 burials. It is operated
by the United States Department of Veterans
Affairs. The entrance is north of Southeast
Mt. Scott Boulevard on the east side of
Southeast 112th Avenue. The mailing address
is 11800 Southeast Mt. Scott Boulevard,
Portland. The cemetery is in both Multnomah
and Clackamas counties. {November 1991}
(Gladstone 1961-84 USGS Quad. map.)

WONG LUEY

A   0.01 10 25 Aug 1907 T1S R1E   S5
Located in the Hoyt Aboretum near Southwest
Fisher Avenue, marked by a deodar cedar.
This is the grave of a leper who lived on
this site when it was part of the County Farm
and was cremated in his cabin after his
death, with the ashes being buried here.
NOTE: See the article in the *Oregon Journal*,
1 April 1977 page 3 and the *Oregon Journal* 30
September 1977 page 13. Also Oregon Death
Certificate #4660 dated 25 August 1907
Multnomah County. {Fall 1991} (Not shown on
Portland 1960-70-77 USGS Quad. map.)

Japanese
Stanley R. Clarke (2000)

Mountain View-Corbett
Janice M. Healy (1992)

ABBEY RIVERVIEW see **RIVERVIEW ABBEY MAUSOLEUM**

	MULTNOMAH CO.	T1S	R1E	S22
ABRAHAM	MULTNOMAH CO.	T1S	R2E	S6
ABRAHAMS see **ABRAHAM**	MULTNOMAH CO.	T1S	R2E	S6
ABRAMS see **ABRAHAM**	MULTNOMAH CO.	T1S	R2E	S6
AHAVAI SHALOM see **AHAVAI SHOLOM**	MULTNOMAH CO.	T1S	R1E	S27
AHAVAI SHOLOM	MULTNOMAH CO.	T1S	R1E	S27
AHAVI SHALOM see **AHAVAI SHOLOM**	MULTNOMAH CO.	T1S	R1E	S27
AHAVI SHALUM see **AHAVAI SHOLOM**	MULTNOMAH CO.	T1S	R1E	S27
AHAVI SOLEM see **AHAVAI SHOLOM**	MULTNOMAH CO.	T1S	R1E	S27
AHAVIA SHOLON see **AHAVAI SHOLOM**	MULTNOMAH CO.	T1S	R1E	S27
AMEND, VIRGIL	MULTNOMAH CO.	T1N	R5E	S22

ASCENSION CHAPEL EPISCOPAL CHURCH see **ASCENSION EPISCOPAL CHAPEL**

	MULTNOMAH CO.	T1S	R1E	S4
ASCENSION EPISCOPAL CHAPEL	MULTNOMAH CO.	T1S	R1E	S4
ASYLUM	MULTNOMAH CO.	T1S	R1E	S2
B'NAI B'RITH	MULTNOMAH CO.	T1S	R1E	S27

B'NAI B'RITH OREGON LODGE #65 see **AHAVAI SHOLOM**

	MULTNOMAH CO.	T1S	R1E	S27
BARNARD BABY	MULTNOMAH CO.	?	?	?

BARNARD, WILLIAM N. see **BARNARD BABY**

	MULTNOMAH CO.	?	?	?

BARNARD, WINNIFRED BELLE RUS see **BARNARD BABY**

	MULTNOMAH CO.	?	?	?
BARNES BABY	MULTNOMAH CO.	T1S	R2E	S20

BARNES, ELIZABETH BANCHE see **BARNES BABY**

	MULTNOMAH CO.	T1S	R2E	S20
BARNS, WILLIAM see **BARNES BABY**	MULTNOMAH CO.	T1S	R2E	S20
BETH ISRAEL [NEW]	MULTNOMAH CO.	T1S	R1E	S21
BETH ISRAEL [OLD]	MULTNOMAH CO.	T1S	R1E	S10
BETHEL see **GRESHAM PIONEER**	MULTNOMAH CO.	T1S	R3E	S10
BRADFORD ISLAND	MULTNOMAH CO.	T2N	R7E	?
BRAINARD see **BRAINARD PIONEER**	MULTNOMAH CO.	T1N	R2E	S33
BRAINARD PIONEER	MULTNOMAH CO.	T1N	R2E	S33
BRAINARY see **BRAINARD PIONEER**	MULTNOMAH CO.	T1N	R2E	S33
BRAINERD see **BRAINARD PIONEER**	MULTNOMAH CO.	T1N	R2E	S33
BREYMER see **BRAINARD PIONEER**	MULTNOMAH CO.	T1N	R2E	S33
BRIDAL VEIL	MULTNOMAH CO.	T1N	R5E	S22

BROWN D.L.C., GEORGE W. AND HARRIET see **PLEASANT HOME PIONEER**

	MULTNOMAH CO.	T1S	R4E	S20

BROWN, JOHN see **GRAND ARMY OF THE REPUBLIC**

	MULTNOMAH CO.	T1S	R1E	S27

BROWN, SALMON see **GRAND ARMY OF THE REPUBLIC**

	MULTNOMAH CO.	T1S	R1E	S27
BUTLER FAMILY	MULTNOMAH CO.	T1S	R3E	S20

CARTERS D.L.C., THOMAS see **I.O.O.F. [CARTERS]**

	MULTNOMAH CO.	T1S	R1E	S4

CARTERS I.O.O.F. see **I.O.O.F [CARTERS]**

	MULTNOMAH CO.	T1S	R1E	S4

CARUTHERS D.L.C., FINICE see **BETH ISRAEL [OLD]**

	MULTNOMAH CO.	T1S	R1E	S10

CARUTHERS D.L.C., FINICE see **COUNTY FARM #1**

	MULTNOMAH CO.	T1S	R1E	S10
CARUTHERS-TERWILLIGER see **CITY CEMETERY #3**				
	MULTNOMAH CO.	T1S	R1E	S10
CATHOLIC see **ST. JOSEPH**	MULTNOMAH CO.	T1S	R3E	S8
CATHOLIC see **ST. MARY'S**	MULTNOMAH CO.	T1N	R1E	S36
CEMETERY HILL see **MOUNTAIN VIEW-CORBETT PIONEER**				
	MULTNOMAH CO.	T1S	R4E	S3
CENTRAL COLUMBIA see **POWELL GROVE PIONEER**				
	MULTNOMAH CO.	T1N	R2E	S23
CENTRAL GROVE see **POWELL GROVE PIONEER**				
	MULTNOMAH CO.	T1N	R2E	S23
CHEBRA AHAVI SHOLUM see **AHAVAI SHOLOM**				
	MULTNOMAH CO.	T1S	R1E	S27
CHEBRA AHIVA SHOLUM see **AHAVAI SHOLOM**				
	MULTNOMAH CO.	T1S	R1E	S27
CHILTON, W. R. see **MELOY FAMILY**	MULTNOMAH CO.	?	?	?
CHINESE [LONE FIR]	MULTNOMAH CO.	T1S	R1E	S2
CHINESE [MONTAVILLA]	MULTNOMAH CO.	T1N	R2E	S33
CHINESE [ST. JOHNS]	MULTNOMAH CO.	T1N	R1E	S18
CHINESE BENEVOLENT SOCIETY see **CHINESE [LONE FIR]**				
	MULTNOMAH CO.	T1S	R1E	S2
CHINESE CEMETERY IN LINCOLN MEMORIAL PARK				
	MULTNOMAH CO.	T1S	R2E	S22
CITY CEMETERY #1	MULTNOMAH CO.	T1N	R1E	S33
CITY CEMETERY #2	MULTNOMAH CO.	T1N	R1E	S33
CITY CEMETERY #3	MULTNOMAH CO.	T1S	R1E	S10
CITY CEMETERY #4 see **BETH ISRAEL [OLD]**				
	MULTNOMAH CO.	T1S	R1E	S10
CITY GARBAGE CREMATORY	MULTNOMAH CO.	T1N	R1E	S29
CLARK, BESSIE SMITH see **CLARK FARM**				
	MULTNOMAH CO.	?	?	?
CLARK FARM	MULTNOMAH CO.	?	?	?
CLARK, FRANK see **CLARK FARM**	MULTNOMAH CO.	?	?	?
CLARK, GEORGE see **CLARK FARM**	MULTNOMAH CO.	?	?	?
CLARK, MARY KELLY see **CLARK FARM**				
	MULTNOMAH CO.	?	?	?
CLARK, WILLIAM see **CLARK FARM**	MULTNOMAH CO.	?	?	?
CLEONE see **FAIRVIEW**	MULTNOMAH CO.	T1N	R3E	?
CLINE	MULTNOMAH CO.	T2N	R1W	?
CLINE D.L.C., JACOB see **CLINE**	MULTNOMAH CO.	T2N	R1W	?
CLINTON FARM see **BUTLER FAMILY**	MULTNOMAH CO.	T1S	R3E	S20
COLUMBIA see **COLUMBIAN**	MULTNOMAH CO.	T1N	R1E	S10
COLUMBIA MASONIC see **COLUMBIA PIONEER**				
	MULTNOMAH CO.	T1N	R2E	S21
COLUMBIA PIONEER	MULTNOMAH CO.	T1N	R2E	S21
COLUMBIA PIONEER MASONIC see **COLUMBIA PIONEER**				
	MULTNOMAH CO.	T1N	R2E	S21
COLUMBIA SLOUGH LODGE see **COLUMBIA PIONEER**				
	MULTNOMAH CO.	T1N	R2E	S21
COLUMBIAN	MULTNOMAH CO.	T1N	R1E	S10
COLUMBIAN KENTON see **COLUMBIAN**	MULTNOMAH CO.	T1N	R1E	S10

CONGREGATION KESER ISRAEL	MULTNOMAH CO.	T1S	R2E	S20
CONGREGATION SHAARIE TORAH	MULTNOMAH CO.	T1S	R2E	S20
CORBETT see **MOUNTAIN VIEW-CORBETT PIONEER**				
	MULTNOMAH CO.	T1S	R4E	S3
CORBETT FAMILY	MULTNOMAH CO.	T1S	R1E	S3
CORNUTT D.L.C., REV. ALFRED see **WHITE BIRCH PIONEER**				
	MULTNOMAH CO.	T1S	R3E	S9
COUNTY FARM #1	MULTNOMAH CO.	T1S	R1E	S10
COUNTY FARM #2	MULTNOMAH CO.	T1S	R1E	S5
COX, ETHAN see **McCLELLAN, CHARLES**				
	MULTNOMAH CO.	T1N	R3E	S28
CROSBY, BABY	MULTNOMAH CO.	?	?	?
DAVIS FAMILY	MULTNOMAH CO.	T1S	R4E	S3
DEAVER HOMESTEAD, JAMES see **PAINTER FAMILY**				
	MULTNOMAH CO.	T1N	R4E	S25
DOUGLAS see **DOUGLASS**	MULTNOMAH CO.	T1N	R3E	S36
DOUGLASS	MULTNOMAH CO.	T1N	R3E	S36
DOUGLASS, A. F. see **DOUGLASS BABY**				
	MULTNOMAH CO.	T1N	R1E	S14
DOUGLASS BABY	MULTNOMAH CO.	T1N	R1E	S14
DOUGLASS D.L.C., JOHN see **DOUGLASS**				
	MULTNOMAH CO.	T1N	R3E	S36
DOUGLASS, RUBY see **DOUGLASS BABY**				
	MULTNOMAH CO.	T1N	R1E	S14
DUNBAR D.L.C., ADDISON C. see **PARKS, DAVID**				
	MULTNOMAH CO.	T1N	R3E	?
EARP, VIRGIL see **RIVER VIEW**	MULTNOMAH CO.	T1S	R1E	S22
EARP, WYATT see **RIVER VIEW**	MULTNOMAH CO.	T1S	R1E	S22
EMANUEL HOSPITAL	MULTNOMAH CO.	T1N	R1E	S27
ESCOBAR see **ESCOBAR PIONEER**	MULTNOMAH CO.	T1S	R3E	S10
ESCOBAR see **WHITE BIRCH**	MULTNOMAH CO.	T1S	R3E	S9
ESCOBAR, FRANK see **ESCOBAR PIONEER**				
	MULTNOMAH CO.	T1S	R3E	S10
ESCOBAR PIONEER	MULTNOMAH CO.	T1S	R3E	S10
ESCOBAR'S see **ESCOBAR PIONEER**	MULTNOMAH CO.	T1S	R3E	S10
EVANS see **MOUNTAIN VIEW-CORBETT PIONEER**				
	MULTNOMAH CO.	T1S	R4E	S3
EVANS, TOM see **MOUNTAIN VIEW-CORBETT PIONEER**				
	MULTNOMAH CO.	T1S	R4E	S3
FAIRVIEW	MULTNOMAH CO.	T1N	R3E	?
FOREST LAWN	MULTNOMAH CO.	T1S	R3E	S10
FOREST LAWN MEMORIAL PARK see **FOREST LAWN**				
	MULTNOMAH CO.	T1S	R3E	S10
FRANCISCAN SISTERS OF THE EUCHARIST				
	MULTNOMAH CO.	T1N	R5E	S15
FRAZER D.L.C., MILTON see **UNKNOWN PIONEER CHILD**				
	MULTNOMAH CO.	T1N	R3E	S30
FREEMASON see **MASONIC [LONE FIR]**				
	MULTNOMAH CO.	T1S	R1E	S1
FRIEDMAN, ABRAHAM see **FRIEDMAN, MARKS**				
	MULTNOMAH CO.	T1S	R1E	S1

```
FRIEDMAN, ANN see FRIEDMAN, MARKS
                          MULTNOMAH CO.      T1S    R1E       S1
FRIEDMAN, MARKS           MULTNOMAH CO.      T1S    R1E       S1
G. A. R. see GRAND ARMY OF THE REPUBLIC
                          MULTNOMAH CO.      T1S    R1E       S27
GATTON                    MULTNOMAH CO.      T2N    R1W       S36
GATTON D.L.C., WILLIAM see GATTON
                          MULTNOMAH CO.      T2N    R1W       S36
GIVOT OLAM see BETH ISREAL [OLD]
                          MULTNOMAH CO.      T1S    R1E       S10
GOOD SAMARITAN HOSPITAL   MULTNOMAH CO.      T1N    R1E       S33
GRAND ARMY OF THE REPUBLIC MULTNOMAH CO.     T1S    R1E       S27
GRANT'S see ST. JOSEPH    MULTNOMAH CO.      T1S    R3E       S8
GREENWOOD see GRAND ARMY OF THE REPUBLIC
                          MULTNOMAH CO.      T1S    R1E       S27
GREENWOOD see GREENWOOD HILLS  MULTNOMAH CO. T1S    R1E       S27
GREENWOOD see I.O.O.F. [GREENWOOD]
                          MULTNOMAH CO.      T1S    R1E       S27
GREENWOOD HILL see GREENWOOD HILLS
                          MULTNOMAH CO.      T1S    R1E       S27
GREENWOOD HILLS           MULTNOMAH CO.      T1S    R1E       S27
GREENWOOD I.O.O.F. see I.O.O.F. [GREENWOOD]
                          MULTNOMAH CO.      T1S    R1E       S27
GRESHAM see ESCOBAR PIONEER  MULTNOMAH CO.   T1S    R3E       S10
GRESHAM see GRESHAM PIONEER  MULTNOMAH CO.   T1S    R3E       S10
GRESHAM see ST. JOSEPH    MULTNOMAH CO.      T1S    R3E       S8
GRESHAM see WHITE BIRCH   MULTNOMAH CO.      T1S    R3E       S9
GRESHAM PIONEER           MULTNOMAH CO.      T1S    R3E       S10
GRESHAM SCHOOL see GRESHAM PIONEER
                          MULTNOMAH CO.      T1S    R3E       S10
GUILD D.L.C., PETER see CITY GARBAGE CREMATORY
                          MULTNOMAH CO.      T1N    R1E       S29
GUILD'S LAKE see CITY GARBAGE CREMATORY
                          MULTNOMAH CO.      T1N    R1E       S29
HALL see MOUNTAIN VIEW-STARK PIONEER
                          MULTNOMAH CO.      T1N    R3E       S35
HALL D.L.C., BENJAMIN see MOUNTAIN VIEW-STARK PIONEER
                          MULTNOMAH CO.      T1N    R3E       S35
HALL, MARY ELIZABETH      MULTNOMAH CO.      T1N    R1E       ?
HALL, SEDATE E. see HALL, MARY ELIZABETH
                          MULTNOMAH CO.      T1N    R1E       ?
HALL, WALTER SCOTT see HALL, MARY ELIZABETH
                          MULTNOMAH CO.      T1N    R1E       ?
HANDCHECK PROPERTY see JOHANSON, MRS.
                          MULTNOMAH CO.      ?      ?         ?
HAVURAH SHALOM            MULTNOMAH CO.      T1S    R1E       S6
HOLBROOK PROPERTY see CLINE  MULTNOMAH CO.   T2N    R1W       ?
HOLDEN BABY               MULTNOMAH CO.      ?      ?         ?
HOLDEN, MARTIN see HOLDEN BABY  MULTNOMAH CO. ?     ?         ?
HOLDEN, MINNIE HENDERSON see HOLDEN BABY
                          MULTNOMAH CO.      ?      ?         ?
I.O.O.F. [CARTERS]        MULTNOMAH CO.      T1S    R1E       S4
```

I.O.O.F. [GREENWOOD]	MULTNOMAH CO.	T1S	R1E	S27
I.O.O.F. [KENILWORTH]	MULTNOMAH CO.	T1S	R1E	S12
IWAKOSHI, MIYO see **GRESHAM PIONEER**				
	MULTNOMAH CO.	T1S	R3E	S10
JACKSON'S, D. D.	MULTNOMAH CO.	?	?	?
JAPANESE	MULTNOMAH CO.	T1N	R2E	S19
JEWISH see **BETH ISRAEL [OLD]**	MULTNOMAH CO.	T1S	R1E	S10
JEWISH see **CONGREGATION KESER ISRAEL**				
	MULTNOMAH CO.	T1S	R2E	S20
JOHANSON, MRS.	MULTNOMAH CO.	?	?	?
JOHNSON BABY	MULTNOMAH CO.	?	?	?
JOHNSON, EMMA ROSELUND see **JOHNSON BABY**				
	MULTNOMAH CO.	?	?	?
JOHNSON, HANS H. see **JOHNSON BABY**				
	MULTNOMAH CO.	?	?	?
JONES see **JONES PIONEER**	MULTNOMAH CO.	T1S	R1E	S6
JONES D.L.C., NATHAN B. see **HAVURAH SHALOM**				
	MULTNOMAH CO.	T1S	R1E	S6
JONES D.L.C., NATHAN B. see **JONES PIONEER**				
	MULTNOMAH CO.	T1S	R1E	S6
JONES PIONEER	MULTNOMAH CO.	T1S	R1E	S6
KEARNS see **KELLY, CLINTON**	MULTNOMAH CO.	T1S	R1E	S12
KELLEY see **KELLY, CLINTON**	MULTNOMAH CO.	T1S	R1E	S12
KELLEY see **PLEASANT HOME PIONEER**				
	MULTNOMAH CO.	T1S	R4E	S20
KELLY see **KELLY, CLINTON**	MULTNOMAH CO.	T1S	R1E	S12
KELLY, ARCHON see **PLEASANT HOME PIONEER**				
	MULTNOMAH CO.	T1S	R4E	S20
KELLY, CLINTON	MULTNOMAH CO.	T1S	R1E	S12
KELLY, CLINTON CLARK see **KELLY FARM, PLYMPTON**				
	MULTNOMAH CO.	T1S	R2E	?
KELLY D.L.C., CLINTON see **I.O.O.F. [KENILWORTH PARK]**				
	MULTNOMAH CO.	T1S	R1E	S12
KELLY D.L.C., CLINTON see **KELLY, CLINTON**				
	MULTNOMAH CO.	T1S	R1E	S12
KELLY D.L.C., PLYMPTON see **KELLY FARM, PLYMPTON**				
	MULTNOMAH CO.	T1S	R2E	?
KELLY FARM, PLYMPTON	MULTNOMAH CO.	T1S	R2E	?
KESER ISRAEL see **CONGREGATION KESER ISRAEL**				
	MULTNOMAH CO.	T1S	R2E	S20
KRONENBERG see **ST. JOSEPH**	MULTNOMAH CO.	T1S	R3E	S8
KWAN YIN TEMPLE	MULTNOMAH CO.	T1N	R3E	S31
LATOURELL FALLS	MULTNOMAH CO.	T1N	R5E	S29
LINCOLN MEMORIAL PARK	MULTNOMAH CO.	T1S	R2E	S22
LINNEMANN see **ST. JOSEPH**	MULTNOMAH CO.	T1S	R3E	S8
LINNEMANN D.L.C., GERHARD D. see **ST. JOSEPH**				
	MULTNOMAH CO.	T1S	R3E	S8
LITTLE CHAPEL OF THE CHIMES FUNERAL HOME [GATEWAY]				
	MULTNOMAH CO.	T1N	R2E	S34
LOGIE D.L.C., JAMES see **MOAR**	MULTNOMAH CO.	T2N	R1W	S7
LONE FIR see **LONE FIR PIONEER**	MULTNOMAH CO.	T1S	R1E	S1
LONE FIR PIONEER	MULTNOMAH CO.	T1S	R1E	S1

LOOMIS	MULTNOMAH CO.	T1N	R1W	S2
LOOMIS, CHARLES see **LOOMIS**	MULTNOMAH CO.	T1N	R1W	S2
LOOMIS, CHRISTOPHER see **LOOMIS**	MULTNOMAH CO.	T1N	R1W	S2
LOOMIS D.L.C., JAMES see **LOOMIS**	MULTNOMAH CO.	T1N	R1W	S2
LOOMIS D.L.C., JAMES see **RAMSEY**	MULTNOMAH CO.	T2N	R1W	S36
LOOMIS, EDWARD see **LOOMIS**	MULTNOMAH CO.	T1N	R1W	S2
LOOMIS, JAMES see **LOOMIS**	MULTNOMAH CO.	T1N	R1W	S2
LOOMIS, SARAH see **LOOMIS**	MULTNOMAH CO.	T1N	R1W	S2
LOVE see **COLUMBIAN**	MULTNOMAH CO.	T1N	R1E	S10
LOVE D.L.C., LEWIS see **COLUMBIAN**				
	MULTNOMAH CO.	T1N	R1E	S10
LOVE D.L.C., LEWIS see **LOVE, LEWIS**				
	MULTNOMAH CO.	T1N	R1E	S10
LOVE, LEWIS	MULTNOMAH CO.	T1N	R1E	S10
LOVEJOY see **COLUMBIAN**	MULTNOMAH CO.	T1N	R1E	S10
LOWNSDALE D.L.C., DANIEL H. see **CITY CEMETERY #2**				
	MULTNOMAH CO.	T1N	R1E	S33
LOWNSDALE, DANIEL H. see **CITY CEMETERY #2**				
	MULTNOMAH CO.	T1N	R1E	S33
LOWNSDALE, NANCY see **CITY CEMETERY #2**				
	MULTNOMAH CO.	T1N	R1E	S33
LOWNSDALE, NANCY GILLIHAN see **CITY CEMETERY #2**				
	MULTNOMAH CO.	T1N	R1E	S33
LUEY, WONG see **COUNTY FARM #2**	MULTNOMAH CO.	T1S	R1E	S5
LUND PLACE, CHARLES see **RANKIN INFANT**				
	MULTNOMAH CO.	T1N	R5E	?
LYONS PROPERTY, JAMES D. see **MOAR**				
	MULTNOMAH CO.	T2N	R1W	S7
MALLOY FAMILY see **MELOY FAMILY**	MULTNOMAH CO.	?	?	?
MASONIC see **GREENWOOD HILLS**	MULTNOMAH CO.	T1S	R1E	S27
MASONIC [LONE FIR]	MULTNOMAH CO.	T1S	R1E	S1
MASONIC SLOUGH see **COLUMBIA PIONEER**				
	MULTNOMAH CO.	T1N	R2E	S21
McCARTNEY see **PULLINS**	MULTNOMAH CO.	?	?	?
McCARTNEY, ELMER D. see **PULLINS**	MULTNOMAH CO.	?	?	?
McCARTNEY, ELSWORTH see **PULLINS**	MULTNOMAH CO.	?	?	?
McCARTNEY, MARIE WARFLER see **PULLINS**				
	MULTNOMAH CO.	?	?	?
McCLELLAN, CHARLES	MULTNOMAH CO.	T1N	R3E	S28
McGREGOR, _____ HILLS see **McGREGOR BABY**				
	MULTNOMAH CO.	?	?	?
McGREGOR BABY	MULTNOMAH CO.	?	?	?
McGREGOR, DONALD see **McGREGOR BABY**				
	MULTNOMAH CO.	?	?	?
McNEMEE	MULTNOMAH CO.	T2N	R1W	S30
McNEMEE see **PEARSON FAMILY**	MULTNOMAH CO.	?	?	?
McNEMEE, MOSES see **McNEMEE**	MULTNOMAH CO.	T2N	R1W	S30
McQUINN	MULTNOMAH CO.	T2N	R1W	S6
McQUINN D.L.C., ALEXANDER H. AND REBECCA see **McQUINN**				
	MULTNOMAH CO.	T2N	R1W	S6
MEIER, JULIUS L. see **PAINTER FAMILY**				
	MULTNOMAH CO.	T1N	R4E	S25

```
MELOY D.L.C., NATHAN H. (WIDOW) AND HEIRS see MELOY FAMILY
                              MULTNOMAH CO.    ?      ?         ?
MELOY FAMILY                  MULTNOMAH CO.    ?      ?         ?
MELOY, NATHAN H. see MELOY FAMILY
                              MULTNOMAH CO.    ?      ?         ?
MOAR                          MULTNOMAH CO.    T2N    R1W       S7
MOFFITT BABY                  MULTNOMAH CO.    T1N    R3E       S3
MOFFITT, DORIS LOGAN see MOFFITT BABY
                              MULTNOMAH CO.    T1N    R3E       S3
MOFFITT, STERLING L. see MOFFITT BABY
                              MULTNOMAH CO.    T1N    R3E       S3
MOLLOY FAMILY see MELOY FAMILY  MULTNOMAH CO.  ?      ?         ?
MONASTERY OF THE PRECIOUS BLOOD MULTNOMAH CO.  T1S    R2E       S5
MONTAVILLA see BRAINARD PIONEER MULTNOMAH CO.  T1N    R2E       S33
MOORE D.L.C., JACOB J. see ESCOBAR PIONEER
                              MULTNOMAH CO.    T1S    R3E       S10
MOORE D.L.C., JACOB J. see GRESHAM PIONEER
                              MULTNOMAH CO.    T1S    R3E       S10
MORDEN see MORGAN FAMILY       MULTNOMAH CO.    T1N    R1W       S15
MORGAN FAMILY                 MULTNOMAH CO.    T1N    R1W       S15
MT. CALVARY CATHOLIC          MULTNOMAH CO.    T1S    R1E       S6
MT. CRAWFORD see LONE FIR PIONEER
                              MULTNOMAH CO.    T1S    R1E       S1
MT. SCOTT see LINCOLN MEMORIAL PARK
                              MULTNOMAH CO.    T1S    R2E       S22
MT. TABOR VILLA see BRAINARD PIONEER
                              MULTNOMAH CO.    T1N    R2E       S33
MT. VIEW BASELINE ROAD see MOUNTAIN VIEW-STARK PIONEER
                              MULTNOMAH CO.    T1N    R3E       S35
MT. VIEW-CORBETT see MOUNTAIN VIEW-CORBETT PIONEER
                              MULTNOMAH CO.    T1S    R4E       S3
MT. VIEW-STARK see MOUNTAIN VIEW-STARK PIONEER
                              MULTNOMAH CO.    T1N    R3E       S35
MT. ZION see JONES PIONEER    MULTNOMAH CO.    T1S    R1E       S6
MOUNTAIN VIEW-CORBETT PIONEER MULTNOMAH CO.    T1S    R4E       S3
MOUNTAIN VIEW-STARK PIONEER   MULTNOMAH CO.    T1N    R3E       S35
MULTNOMAH HOSPITAL            MULTNOMAH CO.    T1S    R1E       S9
MULTNOMAH PARK see MULTNOMAH PARK PIONEER
                              MULTNOMAH CO.    T1S    R2E       S17
MULTNOMAH PARK PIONEER        MULTNOMAH CO.    T1S    R2E       S17
MURRAY D.L.C., SELDON see CHINESE [LONE FIR]
                              MULTNOMAH CO.    T1S    R1E       S2
MURRY D.L.C., SELDON see LONE FIR PIONEER
                              MULTNOMAH CO.    T1S    R1E       S1
MURRY D.L.C., SELDON see MASONIC [LONE FIR]
                              MULTNOMAH CO.    T1S    R1E       S1
N. P. DENTAL COLLEGE see NORTH PACIFIC DENTAL COLLEGE
                              MULTNOMAH CO.    T1N    R1E       S35
NELOY FAMILY see MELOY FAMILY  MULTNOMAH CO.   ?      ?         ?
NELSON D.L.C., SAMUEL see MONASTERY OF THE PRECIOUS BLOOD
                              MULTNOMAH CO.    T1S    R2E       S5
NEVEH SHOLOM see AHAVAI SHOLOM MULTNOMAH CO.   T1S    R1E       S27
```

NEVI SHOLOM see **AHAVAI SHOLOM**   MULTNOMAH CO.   T1S   R1E   S27
NEW JEWISH see **BETH ISRAEL [NEW]**
     MULTNOMAH CO.   T1S   R1E   S21
NICHOLS, M. LEONA see **QUINN, MARY WHELAN**
     MULTNOMAH CO.   T1N   R1E   S36
NORTH PACIFIC DENTAL COLLEGE   MULTNOMAH CO.   T1N   R1E   S35
NORTHWEST MEMORIAL GARDENS see **SKYLINE MEMORIAL GARDENS**
     MULTNOMAH CO.   T1N   R1W   S23
OLD BETH ISRAEL see **BETH ISRAEL [OLD]**
     MULTNOMAH CO.   T1S   R1E   S10
OLD CEMETERY CITY OF PORTLAND see **CITY CEMETERY #3**
     MULTNOMAH CO.   T1S   R1E   S10
OLD COLUMBIA see **COLUMBIAN**   MULTNOMAH CO.   T1N   R1E   S10
OLD HEBREW see **BETH ISRAEL [OLD]**
     MULTNOMAH CO.   T1S   R1E   S10
OLD PIONEER see **GRESHAM PIONEER**   MULTNOMAH CO.   T1S   R3E   S10
OREGON HEALTH SCIENCES CENTER see **UNIVERSITY OF OREGON MEDICAL SCHOOL**
     MULTNOMAH CO.   T1S   R1E   S9
OREGON LODGE #65 see **B'NAI B'RITH**
     MULTNOMAH CO.   T1S   R1E   S27
ORIENT   MULTNOMAH CO.   T1S   R4E   S19
PAINTER FAMILY   MULTNOMAH CO.   T1N   R4E   S25
PALMER   MULTNOMAH CO.   T1N   R5E   S24
PARISH OF ST. MARK, THE   MULTNOMAH CO.   T1N   R1E   S33
PARKROSE MASONIC see **COLUMBIA PIONEER**
     MULTNOMAH CO.   T1N   R2E   S21
PARKS, DAVID   MULTNOMAH CO.   T1N   R3E   ?
PEARSON FAMILY   MULTNOMAH CO.   ?   ?   ?
PEARSON, RHODA see **PEARSON FAMILY**
     MULTNOMAH CO.   ?   ?   ?
PLEASANT HOME see **PLEASANT HOME PIONEER**
     MULTNOMAH CO.   T1S   R4E   S20
PLEASANT HOME PIONEER   MULTNOMAH CO.   T1S   R4E   S20
POOR FARM see **COUNTY FARM #2**   MULTNOMAH CO.   T1S   R1E   S5
PORTLAND see **LONE FIR PIONEER**   MULTNOMAH CO.   T1S   R1E   S1
PORTLAND CREMATION ASSOCIATION see **PORTLAND MEMORIAL AND MAUSOLEUM**
     MULTNOMAH CO.   T1S   R1E   S23
PORTLAND HEBREW SICK BENEFIT ASSOCIATION see **CONGRECATION KESER ISRAEL**
     MULTNOMAH CO.   T1S   R2E   S20
PORTLAND INDOOR CEMETERY see **PORTLAND MEMORIAL AND MAUSOLEUM**
     MULTNOMAH CO.   T1S   R1E   S23
PORTLAND LONE FIR see **LONE FIR PIONEER**
     MULTNOMAH CO.   T1S   R1E   S1
PORTLAND MASONIC see **GREENWOOD HILLS**
     MULTNOMAH CO.   T1S   R1E   S27
PORTLAND MEDICAL SCHOOL see **UNIVERSITY OF OREGON MEDICAL SCHOOL**
     MULTNOMAH CO.   T1S   R1E   S9
PORTLAND MEMORIAL AND MAUSOLEUM
     MULTNOMAH CO.   T1S   R1E   S23
POTTER, CORA E. see **POTTER FAMILY**
     MULTNOMAH CO.   T1N   R1E   S19

POTTER D.L.C., LEVI C. AND HANNAH M. see **POTTER FAMILY**

	MULTNOMAH CO.	T1N	R1E	S19
POTTER FAMILY	MULTNOMAH CO.	T1N	R1E	S19

POTTER, HANNAH M. see **POTTER FAMILY**

	MULTNOMAH CO.	T1N	R1E	S19
POTTER, I. M. see **POTTER FAMILY**	MULTNOMAH CO.	T1N	R1E	S19

POTTER, LEVI C. see **POTTER FAMILY**

	MULTNOMAH CO.	T1N	R1E	S19

POTTER, MINNIE see **POTTER FAMILY**

	MULTNOMAH CO.	T1N	R1E	S19
POTTER, W. W. see **POTTER FAMILY**	MULTNOMAH CO.	T1N	R1E	S19
POUNDER	MULTNOMAH CO.	T1N	R4E	S35
POWELL see **POWELL GROVE PIONEER**	MULTNOMAH CO.	T1N	R2E	S23

POWELL D.L.C., DAVID see **POWELL GROVE PIONEER**

	MULTNOMAH CO.	T1N	R2E	S23

POWELL GROVE see **POWELL GROVE PIONEER**

	MULTNOMAH CO.	T1N	R2E	S23
POWELL GROVE PIONEER	MULTNOMAH CO.	T1N	R2E	S23

POWELL, ROGER W. "BILL" see **PARISH OF ST. MARK, THE**

	MULTNOMAH CO.	T1N	R1E	S33
POWELL VALLEY see **ST. JOSEPH**	MULTNOMAH CO.	T1S	R3E	S8

PRETTYMAN D.L.C., DAVID D. see **SOUTH MT. TABOR [#1]**

	MULTNOMAH CO.	T1S	R2E	S5

PRETTYMAN D.L.C., PERRY AND ELIZABETH see **ABRAHAM**

	MULTNOMAH CO.	T1S	R2E	S6

PRETTYMAN FAMILY see **SOUTH MT. TABOR [#1]**

	MULTNOMAH CO.	T1S	R2E	S5

PULLEN D.L.C., ANDREW see **COLUMBIA PIONEER**

	MULTNOMAH CO.	T1N	R2E	S21
PULLEN, MARY L.	MULTNOMAH CO.	T1S	R2E	S3
PULLINS	MULTNOMAH CO.	?	?	?

QUINN D.L.C., TERENCE see **QUINN, MARY WHELAN**

	MULTNOMAH CO.	T1N	R1E	S36
QUINN, MARY WHELAN	MULTNOMAH CO.	T1N	R1E	S36
R. C. see **ST. JOSEPH**	MULTNOMAH CO.	T1S	R3E	S8
RAMSAY see **RAMSEY**	MULTNOMAH CO.	T2N	R1W	S36
RAMSEY	MULTNOMAH CO.	T2N	R1W	S36
RAMSEY, FRED see **RAMSEY**	MULTNOMAH CO.	T2N	R1W	S36
RAMSEY, FREDERICK H. see **RAMSEY**	MULTNOMAH CO.	T2N	R1W	S36
RAMSEY, JOHN C. see **RAMSEY**	MULTNOMAH CO.	T2N	R1W	S36
RAMSEY'S FARM see **RAMSEY**	MULTNOMAH CO.	T2N	R1W	S36

RANKIN, CLARK L. see **RANKIN INFANT**

	MULTNOMAH CO.	T1N	R5E	?
RANKIN INFANT	MULTNOMAH CO.	T1N	R5E	?

RANKIN, MARY REUTHEMAN see **RANKIN INFANT**

	MULTNOMAH CO.	T1N	R5E	?
REED, CALVIN	MULTNOMAH CO.	T1N	R3E	?

REED D.L.C., CALVIN see **REED, CALVIN**

	MULTNOMAH CO.	T1N	R3E	?
RIVER VIEW	MULTNOMAH CO.	T1S	R1E	S22
RIVERVIEW see **RIVER VIEW**	MULTNOMAH CO.	T1S	R1E	S22
RIVERVIEW ABBEY MAUSOLEUM	MULTNOMAH CO.	T1S	R1E	S22

ROOSTER ROCK	MULTNOMAH CO.	T1N	R4E	S25
ROSE CITY	MULTNOMAH CO.	T1N	R2E	S19
ROSE LAWN see **ROSE CITY**	MULTNOMAH CO.	T1N	R2E	S19
ROSELAWN MEMORIAL PARK	MULTNOMAH CO.	T1N	R2E	S27
ST. AGNES see **ST. JOSEPH**	MULTNOMAH CO.	T1S	R3E	S8
ST. HENRY see **ST. JOSEPH**	MULTNOMAH CO.	T1S	R3E	S8
ST. JOSEPH	MULTNOMAH CO.	T1S	R3E	S8
ST. MARY'S	MULTNOMAH CO.	T1N	R1E	S36
ST. MARY'S ACADEMY	MULTNOMAH CO.	T1S	R1E	S3
SAMARITAN LODGE see **I.O.O.F. [CARTERS]**				
	MULTNOMAH CO.	T1S	R1E	S4
SAMARITAN LODGE see **I.O.O.F. [GREENWOOD]**				
	MULTNOMAH CO.	T1S	R1E	S27
SELLWOOD	MULTNOMAH CO.	T1S	R1E	S23
SELLWOOD'S LAND, REV. JOHN see **SELLWOOD**				
	MULTNOMAH CO.	T1S	R1E	S23
SERVITE	MULTNOMAH CO.	T1N	R2W	S21
SHAARIE TORAH see **CONGREGATION SHAARIE TORAH**				
	MULTNOMAH CO.	T1S	R2E	S20
SISTERS OF THE PRECIOUS BLOOD see **MONASTERY OF THE PRECIOUS BLOOD**				
	MULTNOMAH CO.	T1S	R2E	S5
SKYLINE MEMORIAL GARDENS	MULTNOMAH CO.	T1N	R1W	S23
SKYLINE MEMORIAL PARK see **SKYLINE MEMORIAL GARDENS**				
	MULTNOMAH CO.	T1N	R1W	S23
SLOUGH see **COLUMBIAN**	MULTNOMAH CO.	T1N	R1E	S10
SMITH	MULTNOMAH CO.	T1N	R5E	?
SMITH, BABY	MULTNOMAH CO.	?	?	?
SMITH, ROBERT T. see **SMITH**	MULTNOMAH CO.	T1N	R5E	?
SOUTH MT. TABOR [#1]	MULTNOMAH CO.	T1S	R2E	S5
SOUTH MT. TABOR [#2]	MULTNOMAH CO.	T1S	R2E	S8
STARK see **CITY CEMETERY [#1]**	MULTNOMAH CO.	T1N	R1E	S33
STARK D.L.C., BENJAMIN see **CITY CEMETERY #1**				
	MULTNOMAH CO.	T1N	R1E	S33
STEARNS, MARY W. MELOY see **MELOY FAMILY**				
	MULTNOMAH CO.	?	?	?
STEPHENS D.L.C., JAMES B. see **ASYLUM**				
	MULTNOMAH CO.	T1S	R1E	S2
STOTT see **MOUNTAIN VIEW-STARK PIONEER**				
	MULTNOMAH CO.	T1N	R3E	S35
STUMP	MULTNOMAH CO.	T2N	R1E	S6
STUMP D.L.C., CUTHBERT see **STUMP**				
	MULTNOMAH CO.	T2N	R1E	S6
SULLIVAN D.L.C., TIMOTHY see **ST. MARY'S**				
	MULTNOMAH CO.	T1N	R1E	S36
SUNRISE MEMORIAL PARK see **I.O.O.F. [GREENWOOD]**				
	MULTNOMAH CO.	T1S	R1E	S27
SUNSET see **POUNDER**	MULTNOMAH CO.	T1N	R4E	S35
SYLVAN see **JONES PIONEER**	MULTNOMAH CO.	T1S	R1E	S6
TAYLOR	MULTNOMAH CO.	T2N	R1W	S6
TAYLOR D.L.C., JAMES see **TAYLOR**	MULTNOMAH CO.	T2N	R1W	S6
TEMPLE BETH ISRAEL see **BETH ISRAEL [NEW]**				
	MULTNOMAH CO.	T1S	R1E	S21

TERWILLIGER see **CITY CEMETERY [#3]**

      MULTNOMAH CO.   T1S   R1E   S10

TERWILLIGER D.L.C., JAMES see **CITY CEMETERY #3**

      MULTNOMAH CO.   T1S   R1E   S10

TERWILLIGER PARK see **CITY CEMETERY [#3]**

      MULTNOMAH CO.   T1S   R1E   S10

THOMAS D.L.C., ELIZABETH CARUTHERS see **CITY CEMETERY #3**

      MULTNOMAH CO.   T1S   R1E   S10

THOMAS D.L.C., ELIZABETH CARUTHERS see **WALLACE, ARTHUR W.**

      MULTNOMAH CO.   T1S   R1E   S10

THOMAS INFANT   MULTNOMAH CO.   ?   ?   ?

TICE D.L.C., JOHN M. see **AHAVAI SHOLOM**

      MULTNOMAH CO.   T1S   R1E   S27

TICE D.L.C., JOHN M. see **B'NAI B'RITH**

      MULTNOMAH CO.   T1S   R1E   S27

TICE D.L.C., JOHN M. see **BETH ISRAEL [NEW]**

      MULTNOMAH CO.   T1S   R1E   S21

TICE D.L.C., JOHN M. see **GRAND ARMY OF THE REPUBLIC**

      MULTNOMAH CO.   T1S   R1E   S27

TICE D.L.C., JOHN M. see **GREENWOOD HILLS**

      MULTNOMAH CO.   T1S   R1E   S27

TICE D.L.C., JOHN M. see **I.O.O.F. [GREENWOOD]**

      MULTNOMAH CO.   T1S   R1E   S27

TICE D.L.C., JOHN M. see **RIVER VIEW**

      MULTNOMAH CO.   T1S   R1E   S22

TITUS, MERRIT see **RAMSEY**   MULTNOMAH CO.   T2N   R1W   S36

TRICKEY, EDWARD see **TRICKEY FAMILY**

      MULTNOMAH CO.   T1S   R5E   S8

TRICKEY FAMILY   MULTNOMAH CO.   T1S   R5E   S8

TRICKEY, LLOYD see **TRICKEY FAMILY**

      MULTNOMAH CO.   T1S   R5E   S8

TRICKEY, LUCY see **TRICKEY FAMILY**

      MULTNOMAH CO.   T1S   R5E   S8

UNIVERSITY OF OREGON MEDICAL SCHOOL

      MULTNOMAH CO.   T1S   R1E   S9

UNKNOWN   MULTNOMAH CO.   T1N   R5E   S30

UNKNOWN PIONEER CHILD   MULTNOMAH CO.   T1N   R3E   S30

WALLACE, ARTHUR W.   MULTNOMAH CO.   T1S   R1E   S10

WAND D.L.C., JOHN see **CHINESE [ST. JOHNS]**

      MULTNOMAH CO.   T1N   R1E   S18

WARD, JR. D.L.C., JOHN see **CHINESE [ST. JOHNS]**

      MULTNOMAH CO.   T1N   R1E   S18

WAUD D.L.C., JOHN see **CHINESE [ST. JOHNS]**

      MULTNOMAH CO.   T1N   R1E   S18

WHITE BIRCH see **WHITE BIRCH PIONEER**

      MULTNOMAH CO.   T1S   R3E   S9

WHITE BIRCH PIONEER   MULTNOMAH CO.   T1S   R3E   S9

WILKES SCHOOL see **UNKNOWN PIONEER CHILD**

      MULTNOMAH CO.   T1N   R3E   S30

WILLAMETTE NATIONAL   MULTNOMAH CO.   T1S   R2E   S22

WONG LUEY   MULTNOMAH CO.   T1S   R1E   S5

Rose City
Stanley R. Clarke (2000)

Rose City
Stanley R. Clarke (2000)

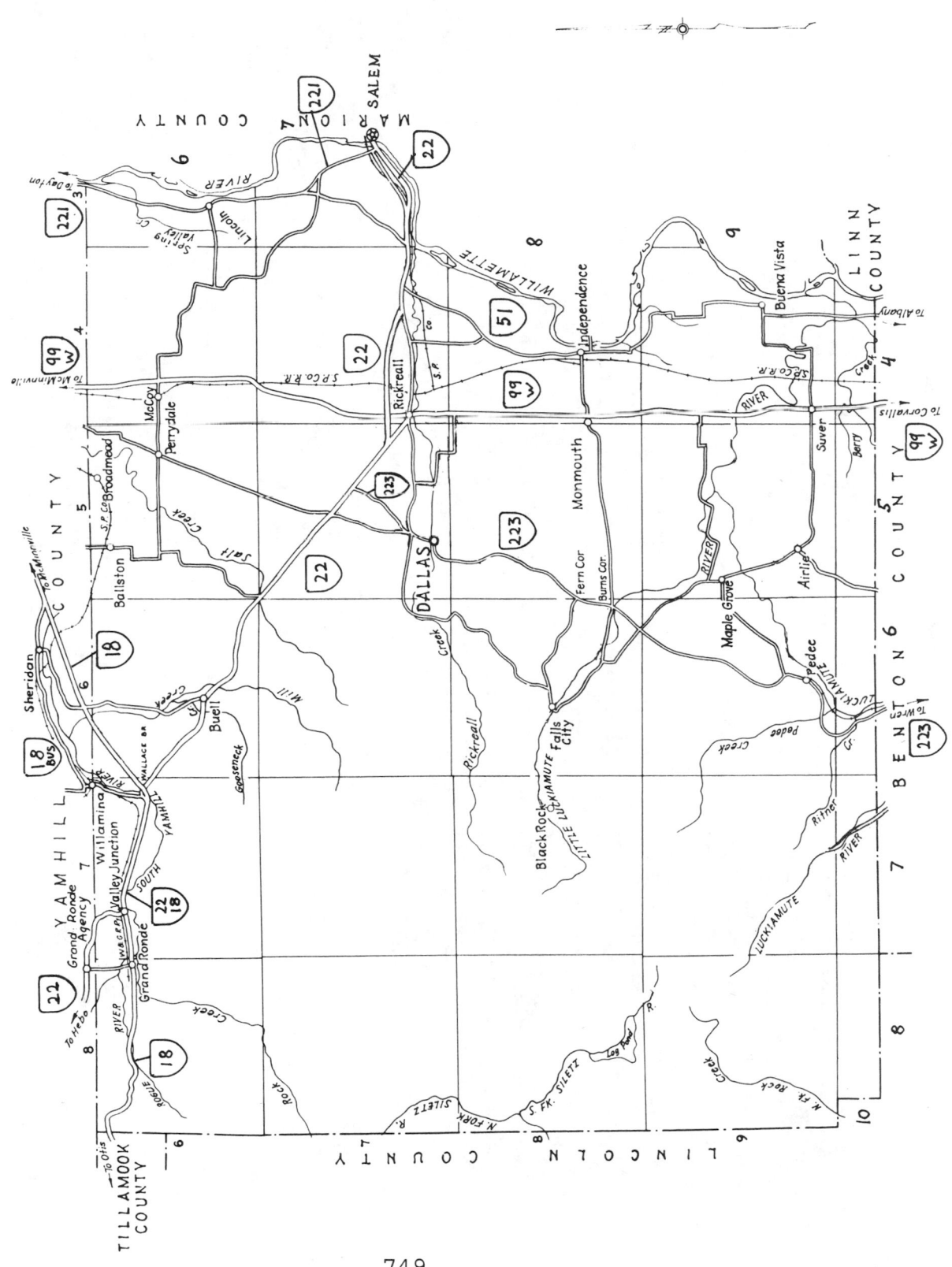

POLK COUNTY

Scale 0 1 2 M.

New Smith
Dean H. Byrd (1988)

Area: 745 square miles
Population (1998): 61,560
County seat: Dallas, Population: 11,360
County established: 22 December 1845

Polk County in the Willamette Valley received American settlers looking for farmlands as early as 1842. After the usual family burials the earliest organized public cemetery was the Pioneer Cemetery at Rickreall (1845). It was followed by cemeteries at Dallas (1847), English and Hart-Riggs (1848), Hilltop (1849) and Salt Creek (1851). By the mid-1850's there were a considerable number of public cemeteries. There is also a sizable Indian cemetery: Consolidated Tribes of Grand Ronde.

Etna, Katherine Johnson
Dean H. Byrd (1997)

Sheridan Mennonite

Dean H. Byrd (1989)

Brown, William C.

Dean H. Byrd (1988)

Womer

Dean H. Byrd (1993)

Womer

Dean H. Byrd (1989)

Name of Cemetery and also known as	Number of burials	Acres	Condition	Date started or earliest known burial	Township	Range	Section

ALDERMAN FAMILY

A 0.16 2 1871   T6S R4W   S13
Located off of Bethel Heights road on the north side of the road and up a steep hillside. Access of 0.25 of a mile is on foot. The first burial was Dec. 1871, with 18 known burials plus "Curly", a dog. NOTE: This site is on private property. {3 January 1990} (Not shown on Mission Bottom 1957-93 USGS Quad. map.)

ANDERSON FAMILY

A 0.23 1 11 Feb 1976 T8S R6W   S16
Access is the same as access to Falls City (Upper) Cemetery. This family cemetery is adjacent to the north boundary of the Falls City Cemetery; they are separated by a fence. There are 4 burials in the Anderson Cemetery. Quite a few family cemeteries have evolved into public cemeteries. Here is the reverse: a family cemetery started immediately adjacent to a public cemetery. {8 May 1989} (Not shown on Falls City 1974 USGS Quad. map.)

BALL
AKA: 1. BALL FAMILY
    2. BALLSTON

B 0.7 2 1853   T6S R5W   S5
Located in Ballston; at the main crossroads of Ballston Road and DeJong Road, go north on DeJong Road for 0.24 of a mile. Turn left onto May Yocum Road and proceed westerly and north to the cemetery driveway on the right. It is on the Isaac Ball D.L.C. #38, OC #194. {20 October 1991} (Ballston 1956-70 USGS Quad. map.)

BASKETT FAMILY

A 0.1 5 1865   T7S R4W   S19
From the crossroads of OR. Hwy. 22 and OR. Hwy. 99W just north of Rickreall, go north on the latter for 0.9 of a mile; turn right (east) on a driveway for 0.8 of a mile; then right again for 100 yards. The old house is adjacent to and west of the railway. The family's slaves were buried just south of the house. Most of the family burials were moved to City View Cemetery in Salem. It is on the George Buskett (*Sic*) D.L.C. #43, OC #3065. NOTE: This site is on private property. (Not shown on Rickreall 1969-76 USGS Quad. map.)

Name of Cemetery and also known as	Number of burials	Acres	Condition	Date started or earliest known burial	Township	Range	Section

BETHEL
AKA: 1. McCOY

D   2   2   1848   T6S R4W   S21
Located at the junction of Zena Road and Oak Grove Road on a low hilltop and 0.5 of a mile south of Bethel. 118 gravestones in this attractive cemetery were toppled in early May 1993. {17 August 1988} (Amity 1957-93 USGS Quad. map.)

BLACK ROCK

?   1   ?   ?   T8S R7W   S14
This cemetery is in the southeast corner of Section 14. Black Rock was a considerable logging community between 1908-1922. Drive about 3.15 miles via Black Rock Road from the west edge of Falls City to the old school house on the left (south). The cemetery was catty-corner to the right across the pond and the bygone railroad yards. There are 3 graves known but surely there are more graves. (Not shown on Falls City 1974 USGS Quad. maps.)

BLAIR FAMILY

B   0.40 2   1853   T6S R6W   S21
This secluded cemetery is located 2 miles north of Buell. Leave OR. Hwy. 22 at the Buell store onto Harmony Road which leads northerly to Sheridan. The Mill Creek Bridge is at 1.5 miles on Harmony Road. Immediately after is the mailbox for 75500 Harmony Road on the left and an unmarked gravel road to the right and back. It is best to have a guide as this road has a number of side roads with several houses and a barn. The cemetery is on top of a knoll surrounded by trees and is 0.4 of a mile from Harmony Road. It is located on the Thomas R. Blair D.L.C. #41, OC #3317. {18 October 1994} (Not shown on Sheridan 1956-70 USGS Quad. map.)

BOISE FAMILY

A   ?   5   Dec. 1865   T7S ?   ?
Thought to be in Range 6 West and Section 25. Ellen Lyon Boise, wife of Reuben Boise, died in December of 1865. She was buried on the Boise farm, and later 2 children were also known to be buried here. The locale of Ellendale about 2 miles west of Dallas was

Name of Cemetery and also known as	Number of burials	Acres	Condition	Date started or earliest known burial	Township	Range	Section

named for her. NOTE: This site is on private property. (Not shown on Dallas 1974-86 USGS Quad. map.)

BOWMAN FAMILY

A   0.01 ?   ?   T9S R5W   ?
Located in Section 5 or 6, Sarah and William Bowman are buried on the Preston Bowman D.L.C. #39, OC #4467 north of Lewisville. NOTE: This site is on private property. (Not shown on the Airlie North 1974 USGS Quad. map.)

BRIGHAM'S GRAVE
 AKA: 1. BURKHART,
      YOUNGABLE

A   0.01 ? 24 Mar 1916 T9S R6W   S35
Located southeast of Pedee. An old man of 87, who was known as "Brigham Young" is buried in a lone grave. In the 1930's there was still a picket fence around the grave, but the marker was no longer legible. "Brigham Young" was Youngable Burkhart, per Oregon State Death Certificate #178 for 1916, Marion County. NOTE: This site is on private property. (Not shown on Kings Valley 1984 USGS Quad. map.)

BROWN, GEORGE

B   0.25 5 1859-1947   T7S R5W   S9
Located north of Dallas, just west of Dolph Corner and on Salt Creek Church Road. Reportedly up hill on the left, immediately after Salt Creek Church Road leaves OR. Hwy. 22. On the George Brown D.L.C. #40, OC #4472. NOTE: This site is on private property. (Not shown on Dallas 1974-86 USGS Quad. map.)

BROWN, WILLIAM C.

C   1   2 1854   T7S R5W   S22
Located 1.25 miles northeast of Dallas on the west side of Kings Valley Highway (OR. Hwy. 223), between Dallas and OR. Hwy. 22. It is on the Ira Smith D.L.C. #54, OC #142. {15 November 1988} (Dallas 1974-86 USGS Quad. map.)

BRUNK FARM
 AKA: 1. McNARY (?)
      2. SHAW

B   0.5   5 1856-1880'S T7S R4W   ?
It is directly north of Oak Knoll Golf Course, which is west of Salem on OR. Hwy.

Name of Cemetery and also known as	Number of burials	Acres	Condition	Date started or earliest known burial	Township	Range	Section

22. Possibly located in Section 22 or 27. It is in a field and has been farmed over; on the Alva C. Shaw D.L.C., #59, OC #4735. (Not shown on Rickreall 1969-76 USGS Quad. map.)

BUENA VISTA
AKA: 1. I.O.O.F.
2. WOODMEN OF
THE WORLD

C 3 2 1846 T9S R4W S23
Located in the northern part of the community of Buena Vista. From Willamette Ferry Street, go north 0.6 of a mile up the hill on Riverview Road; on the John W. Griffith D.L.C. #65, OC #4599. {9 September 1988} (Monmouth 1970-86 USGS Quad. map.)

BUTLER-DAVIDSON FAMILY
AKA: 1. DAVIDSON
FAMILY
2. POWELL FAMILY
3. ROGERS FAMILY

B 0.5 3 1853 T8S R5W S35
This cemetery is 2 miles southwest of Monmouth and south off of the Monmouth Highway. Go 0.4 of a mile west of the bridge over Ash Creek; access is on the left (south) and west over an abandoned county road. Although the cemetery was included in the Camp Adair Military Reservation from 1942 to 1948, the graves were not removed. On a hill and in the trees it has been overgrown for decades and was last cleaned up in 1985. There were 76 known burials, 1853 through June 1940. It is on the James C. Davidson D.L.C. #57, OC #1228. {14 July 1994} (Airlie North 1974 USGS Quad. map.)

CASEY FAMILY

A 0.01 2 16 Jul 1989 T8S R5W S3
This small burial site is for Doctor L. V. Casey 14 February 1916-16 July 1989 and his wife Marion Ethel Pankey Casey 5 January 1928-31 July 1995. The site is on private property. Leave Uglow Street in Dallas and drive southeasterly on Clow Corner Road for 1.3 miles. Then turn right (south) onto Cherry Knoll Road; continue on Cherry Knoll Road uphill for another 0.3 of a mile to a sharp turn right. A gateway ahead leads to the private burial site. Located on the James Harris D.L.C. #44, OC #4197. {26 August 1995} (Not shown on Dallas 1974-86 USGS Quad. map.)

Name of Cemetery and also known as	Number of burials	Acres	Condition	Date started or earliest known burial	Township	Range	Section

CHAMBERLIN FAMILY
AKA: 1. CHAMBERLAIN
       FAMILY
    2. CHAMBERLIN--
       COLLINS FAMILY
    3. HEFFLEY
    4. NEALY FAMILY

B   0.5   5   1859-1923   T9S R5W   S24
This burial ground is located on top of a hill which is about one mile south of the Luckiamute River at Helmick State Park. Take Old Highway 99W, now called Helmick Road, and drive south to Simpson Road and proceed about 0.4 of a mile, just past the first house on the right. The cemetery is out of sight on the hilltop on the left (south) side of the road. It is on private property which has been logged in 1993 as far as the cemetery. The spelling Chamberlin is on the tombstone. Actually, many more of the Smith Collins family are buried here than are Chamberlins. This cemetery, which was on the Camp Adair Military Reservation in World War II, was not dug up and removed. There are 24 known burials on the Aaron C. Chamberlain (variant spelling) D.L.C. #42, OC #1236. The Smith Collins D.L.C. #64, OC #3235 is adjacent to the southwest. {5 October 1993} (Not shown on Monmouth 1970-86 USGS Quad. map.)

CLAREMONT FAMILY

A   0.25 1   14 Oct 1963 T10S R7W   S11
Located in the extreme southwest corner of Polk County, it is best reached from northern Benton County. Take OR. Hwy. 223 (Kings Valley Highway) south from Dallas and past the locale of Kings Valley in Benton County. Turn right (west) onto Hoskins Road. Go west almost 2 miles to Hoskins. There, turn right (north) onto Luckiamute Road and follow it, with the Luckiamute River on your right, to the Benton-Polk County Line, a drive of about 4.3 miles from Hoskins. At the Polk County Line the road name is changed to Wildwood Road. The access to Claremont Cemetery is about 0.25 of a mile north of the county line. The cemetery is on the left (west) about 0.25 of a mile, by a trail. The Benton County Genealogical Society reported 8 burials as of July 1989. NOTE: This site is on private property. (Summit 1984 USGS Quad. map.)

COOPER FAMILY
AKA: 1. COOPER
      HOLLOW

A   ?   ?   3 Dec 1861 T8S R5W   S29
Located in the Cooper Hollow area. James Lindsay Cooper and his wife Hester Ann Moxley

Name of Cemetery and also known as	Number of burials	Acres	Condition	Date started or earliest known burial	Township	Range	Section

are buried here. NOTE: This site is on private property. (Not shown on the Airlie North 1974 USGS Quad. map.)

DALLAS
AKA: 1. I.O.O.F.
    2. MASONIC
    3. OLD PIONEER

E 26 1 1847   T8S R5W   S5
Located 0.5 of a mile south of Dallas on the right (east) side of Or. Hwy. 223 (Kings Valley Highway). It is on the Isaac Levens D.L.C. #37, OC #4143. {30 September 1990} (Dallas 1974-86 USGS Quad. map.)

DOSS FAMILY

A ? ? ?   T6S R8W   ?
An obituary in the Salem *Statesman-Journal* 31 May 1996 reports the death of Judy E. Doss 30 June 1931-27 May 1996 and her burial in the family cemetery. Her husband Lee survives. The Doss Family Cemetery was described as being in the vicinity of Grand Ronde so it could be in either Polk or Yamhill county. (Not shown on Grand Ronde 1979 USGS Quad. map)

EDWARDS FAMILY
AKA: 1. PEDEE
    2. RITNER

B 1.5 2 1859   T9S R6W   S32
This cemetery is on a hill about 0.5 of a mile west of Pedee Schoolhouse, across the road from Womer Cemetery. Womer is on the east, Edwards on the west. It is on the Joseph Edwards D.L.C. #56, OC #4922. {3 May 1989} (Kings Valley 1984 USGS Quad. map.)

EMBREE FAMILY, CAREY D.
AKA: 1. DEMPSEY

B 0.25 2 1863   T7S R5W   S36
Located about 3 miles east of Dallas via East Ellendale Road (formerly OR. Hwy. 223) toward Rickreall and 0.26 of a mile east of the junction with Bowersville Road. The cemetery is about 200 yards on the right (south) of East Ellendale Road (formerly OR. Hwy. 223), on private property. It is fenced with trees surrounding the grounds and has 37 graves; on the Carey Embree D.L.C. #56, OC #4638. {23 February 1995} (Dallas 1974-86 USGS Quad. map.)

Name of Cemetery and also known as	Number of burials	Acres	Condition	Date started or earliest known burial	Township	Range	Section

ENGLISH [NEW]

C 2 1 1942 T9S R5W S1

This cemetery was established in October of 1942 when Camp Adair Military Reservation was created during World War II. The original English Cemetery in the vicinity of Airlie was destroyed, the 75 graves were removed and reburied adjacent to the existing Fir Crest Cemetery; they are separated from it by Fir Crest Road. English Cemetery borders on the south edge of New Smith Cemetery. There are no signboards to guide the visitor and it is especially difficult to tell where English Cemetery ends and New Smith Cemetery begins. Burials continue today, and English is often referred to as Fir Crest. There are 122 burials. {14 December 1988} (Monmouth 1970-86 USGS Quad. map.)

ENGLISH [OLD]
AKA: 1. TARTER

B 1 6 1848-1942 T9S R5W S28

Located on a hill 1.5 miles east of Airlie and on Benjamin English D.L.C. #64, OC #75. It was moved with the establishment of Camp Adair Military Reservation in October of 1942; the 75 graves were removed to the present English Cemetery south of Monmouth. (Not shown on Airlie North 1974 USGS Quad. map.)

ETNA
AKA: 1. AETNA
2. CROWLEY
3. ETNA BAPTIST CHURCH
4. MT. ETNA
5. OAK GROVE
6. PLEASANT HILL BAPTIST
7. WALKER FAMILY

C 1 2 1852 T7S R4W S7

From the crossroads of OR. Hwy. 22 and OR. Hwy. 99W near Rickreall, go north on the latter for 3 miles. The cemetery driveway is on the left (west) of OR. Hwy. 99W and opposite the junction of the highway with Crowley Road. The cemetery driveway is paralleled by a private driveway. Usually a gate blocks access to the cemetery, which is on a hill in the trees and not visible from OR. Hwy. 99W. The Pleasant Hill Baptist Church was established in 1868 and discontinued in the early 1920's. Its site is used for parking. {28 May 1989} (Rickreall 1969-76 USGS Quad. map.)

FALLS CITY
AKA: 1. OLD CITY
2. UPPER

C 1.4 2 1883 T8S R6W S16

Located 0.5 of a mile northeast of Falls City, up the hill off the north side of Falls

---
Name of Cemetery and also known as | Number of burials | Acres | Condition | Date started or earliest known burial | Township | Range | Section

---

City Road; on the Samuel Gothard D.L.C. #48, OC #4748. {8 May 1989} (Falls City 1974 USGS Quad. map.)

FAST
AKA: 1. HARLAND
       FAMILY,
       WILLIAM
     2. POLK
        STATION
     3. QUIRING

A   0.15   2   1893   T7S   R5W   S23
Located northeast of Dallas on the William Harland farm (1967) and east of Polk Station. The cemetery is 0.25 of a mile east of Fir Villa Road and 0.25 of a mile south of OR. Hwy. 22. There were 12 known graves and 2 headstones (1967); on the Asa Shreve D.L.C. #62, OC #4405. There has been some confusion between the Fast and the Robbins Family Cemeteries, as both cemeteries are east of Fir Villa Road. NOTE: This site is on private property. (Dallas 1974-86 USGS Quad. map.)

FIR CREST
AKA: 1. I.O.O.F.
        [MONMOUTH]
     2. K. P.
     3. KNIGHTS OF
        PYTHIAS
     4. MONMOUTH

E   10   2   1848   T9S   R4W   S6
Located on a hill 1.4 miles south of Monmouth, via Knox or Warren Street and continuing on Helmick Road to Fir Crest Road. There has been much confusion here. What is frequently referred to as Fir Crest in obituaries may also refer to New Smith or English Cemeteries. The latter two were constituted in October 1942, during World War II, as the result of the establishment of the military base of Camp Adair and the destruction of several older cemeteries. Fir Crest proper lies between Fir Crest and Helmick Road and has numerous trees. New Smith and English Cemeteries are on the west side of Fir Crest Road and are in open country. There are no signboards to enlighten the unwary; see the separate entries for New Smith and English Cemeteries. {14 December 1988} (Monmouth 1970-86 USGS Quad. map.)

GAY FAMILY

A   ?   5   1870-1882   T6S   R3W   ?
This could be in Section 5 or 8; go north from West Salem on OR. Hwy. 221 (Wallace Road). At the Polk-Yamhill County line, at milepost 9.6, is a granite marker on the left (west) side of the highway about 6 feet into Yamhill County. The site of the Gay House is

Name of Cemetery and also known as	Number of burials	Acres	Condition	Date started or earliest known burial	Township	Range	Section

directly west, on a knoll with a single tree. The family burial ground was about 0.5 of a mile southwesterly in Polk County and has been destroyed by farming. It is on the George Kirby Gay D.L.C. #58, OC #4427. {22 March 1990} (Not shown on Mission Bottom 1957-93 USGS Quad. map.)

GIBSON FAMILY, GEORGE G.

| | ? | ? | 6 | ? | T7S | R3W | S19 |

Located in the Eola Hills west of Salem. The burial grounds as deeded 12 February 1896 were somewhere west of Doaks Ferry Road and north of Eola. The size of the cemetery is not stated in the deed. This area is now in the subdivision tracts of West Salem. Most of the burials were removed to City View in Salem, including George G. Gibson 1806-1882; Mary Bowen Gibson 1808-1861; Benton Gibson 1839-1860; and Douglas Gibson 1850-1906; all were pioneers of 1852. It is on the George G. Gibson D.L.C., OC #3497. (Not shown on Salem West 1969-86 USGS Quad. map.)

GRAND RONDE
AKA: 1. CONFEDERATED TRIBES
2. GRAND RONDE INDIAN TRIBAL
3. TRIBAL

| | ? | 2.3 | ? | 1856 | T6S | R8W | S12 |

This cemetery was established for the Grand Ronde Reservation. It is north of Grand Ronde and south of the old Agency, which is in Yamhill County, 500 feet west of the county road. (Grand Ronde 1979 USGS Quad. map.)

HARMONY
AKA: 1. UNION BAPTIST

| | C | 1 | 2 | 1861 | T6S | R6W | S9 |

The church address is 8805 Harmony Road. It is about 3.5 or 4 miles north of Buell or 1.35 miles south of OR. Hwy. 18, southwest of Sheridan. The sign on the church calls the cemetery Harmony Cemetery; on the William Eades D.L.C. #38, OC #3603. {11 November 1988} (Sheridan 1956-70 USGS Quad. map.)

HART-RIGGS FAMILY
AKA: 1. FERN CORNER
2. HART FAMILY
3. NEALLY FAMILY
4. RIGGS FAMILY

| | B | 0.34 | 4 | 1848-1947 | T8S | R6W | S25 |

Located 0.5 of a mile south of Fern Corner on Kings Valley Highway (OR. Hwy. 223), on the east side of the highway. It is up the bank in the woods and 100 yards south of the house, with private access via a footpath.

Name of Cemetery and also known as	Number of burials	Acres	Condition	Date started or earliest known burial	Township	Range	Section

There are 39 known burials: on the Thomas Hart D.L.C. #39, OC #4354. {19 August 1993} (Airlie North 1974 USGS Quad. map.)

| HIGHLAND | B | 0.1 | 5 | 1870 | T7S | R3W | S17 |

AKA:
1. HIGHLAND METHODIST CHURCH
2. HOSFORD METHODIST CHURCH
3. MOUNTAIN VIEW

This cemetery is at Chapman Corner, on the northeast corner of the intersection of Orchard Heights and Doaks Ferry Road. Reportedly some tombstone fragments are in the gully. There are 22 known burials. Most burials have been removed. On the John Martin D.L.C. #66, OC #1085. NOTE: This site is on private property. (Not shown on Salem West 1969-86 USGS Quad. map.)

| HILLTOP | D | 8 | 2 | 1849 | T9S | R4W | S9 |

AKA:
1. CEMETERY HILL
2. I.O.O.F. [INDEPENDENCE]
3. I.O.O.F. VALLEY LODGE #42
4. PIONEER [INDEPENDENCE]

The principal cemetery for the town of Independence; it is about 3 miles south of town on Corvallis Road. It is on the Benjamin F. Burch D.L.C. #39, OC #319. {9 September 1988} (Monmouth 1970-86 USGS Quad. map.)

| HOLMES, CELI ANN AND HARRIET | A | ? | ? | Pre 1851 | T7S | R4W | S30 |

Harriet Holmes, who died in 1851, and her daughter Celi Ann who died "some years previously" were two of the slaves belonging to Nathaniel Ford. They were buried on the Ford place on the banks of Rickreall Creek just west of the present county fairgrounds. This is on the Nathan Ford D.L.C. #44, OC #85. Reference: Polk County Historical Society publication, *"Historically Speaking"*, Vol 2 page 4. (Not shown on Rickreall 1969-76 USGS Quad. map.)

| HOOKER FAMILY | A | ? | ? | Mar. 1880 | T9S | R6W | ? |

AKA:
1. DANNETTE FARM
2. DUNNETTE

Probably located in Section 23 or 24, north off of Maple Grove Road and since logged over. This is the burial site for 3 children of the Hooker family; on the Ira A.

Name of Cemetery and also known as	Number of burials	Acres	Condition	Date started or earliest known burial	Township	Range	Section

Hooker D.L.C. #48, OC #1657. NOTE: This site is on private property. (Not shown on Airlie North or Falls City 1974 USGS Quad. maps.)

HUBBARD
AKA: 1. BOYDSTON
     2. OAKHURST

A 1 4 1860-1914 T8S R6W S28

Started on 12 April 1860 this cemetery is 1 mile southeast of Falls City via Bridgeport Road. Then turn right (south) onto Frost Road for a short distance. The cemetery is off to the left, out of sight and on a ridgetop driveway. You need permission for access. There are 23 known burials. {19 Aug. 1993} (Falls City 1974 USGS Quad. map.)

HUSSEY FAMILY
AKA: 1. FORT HILL
     2. GOLD CREEK
     3. WALLACE

A 0.5 3 1855 T6S R7W S15

Located about 2 miles west of Wallace Bridge and east of Grand Ronde off of Salmon River Highway (OR. Hwy. 18 and OR. Hwy. 22). The cemetery is just north of the highway, on the north side of the railway tracks; on the Nathan Hussey D.L.C. #45, OC #3273. In 1985, Rudy Wellbrock told the compiler that this cemetery had mostly burials of young people plus one Chinese. At the time of his visit in the early 1950's, Rudy Wellbrock was on a survey crew projecting the present-day highway alignment in the area. Rudy Wellbrock escorted the compiler to this cemetery on 29 March 1991, for his first visit in nearly 40 years. Most markers had disappeared in the interim. We found only 3 intact: Frank Hussey, 24 May 1855, 12 November 1910; John Eldridge, died 8 March 1878, aged 68; Julia Wallace 1848-1936. Two markers were loose: Wm. A. Cox, 15 September 1867, 24 May 1910; Rebecca wife, of S. Edwards, 16 March 1833, 8 November 1855. {29 March 1991} (Grand Ronde 1979 USGS Quad. map.)

I.O.O.F. [FALLS CITY]
AKA: 1. LOWER

C 2.5 2 1907 T8S R6W S21

This is located in Sections 21 and 22. The cemetery is 0.5 of a mile east of Falls City on the south side of Falls City Road. It is almost directly opposite the driveway off of

763

Name of Cemetery and also known as	Number of burials	Acres	Condition	Date started or earliest known burial	Township	Range	Section

Falls City Road up the hill to Falls City Cemetery. On the Samuel Gothard D.L.C. #48, OC #4748. {8 May 1989} (Falls City 1974 USGS Quad. map.)

INDIAN GRAVE HILL

? ? ? ? T9S R6W ?

Located in Section 27 or 33. The late Lena Belle Tartar in *Chronicles from Pedee, Oregon* reported that an Indian medicine man was killed when he failed to cure a sick child. He was said to have been buried on a hill between Pedee and the Luckiamute River "near the site of the Pedee bridge." If the bridge referred to was the Valley and Siletz Railway bridge, that is in Section 27. If she meant the bridge on Ira Hooker Road, that is in Section 33. (Not shown on Falls City 1974 or Kings Valley 1984 USGS Quad. maps.)

JENNINGS
  AKA: 1. EARNEST

B 0.2 4 1862-1942 T6S R4W S13

This cemetery is 5 rods square, about 0.6 of a mile southwest of Alderman Cemetery, as the crow flies, and south off of Bethel Heights Road. NOTE: Access is by permission from the office of the neighboring tree farm. {3 January 1990} (Not shown on Amity 1957-93 USGS Quad. map.)

LEWIS FAMILY

A ? 6 1856 T9S R5W S18

There were 4 graves which were moved on 14 October 1942 to the New Smith Cemetery, following the establishment of Camp Adair Military Reservation. The Lewis Family cemetery was on the John Lewis D.L.C. #54, OC #4534. (Not shown on Airlie North 1974 USGS Quad. map.)

LIGGETT FAMILY

A ? 6 26 Nov 1868 T9S R5W S7

There were 8 graves but only 1 marker when all were moved on 14 October 1942 to New Smith Cemetery, following the establishment of Camp Adair Military Reservation. It was on the Jonathan W. Liggett D.L.C. #53, OC #4495. (Not shown on Airile North 1974 USGS Quad. map.)

Name of Cemetery and also known as	Number of burials	Acres	Condition	Date started or earliest known burial	Township	Range	Section

MARKS FARM

A ? 5 1852 T6S R4W ?

This could be located in Section 28 or 33. There are 2 graves on the crest of a knoll off of Oak Grove Road, south of Bethel Cemetery and in a grove of scrub oaks on private property. (Not shown on Amity 1957-93 USGS Quad. map.)

McGUIRE FARM, WILLIAM

? ? ? ? T9S R5W S13

No other information was given in the report. (Not shown on Monmouth 1970-86 USGS Quad. map.)

McTIMMONDS FAMILY

A ? ? 1857-1878 T9S R6W S10

This is on Sections 10 and 15 off of Kings Valley Highway (OR. Hwy.223), north of Pedee. One cement slab was placed, in the 1940's, for Frances and Lambert McTimmonds. It is on the Lambert McTimmonds D.L.C. #44, OC #4524. NOTE: This site is on private property. (Not shown on Falls City 1974 USGS Quad. map.)

MILLER FAMILY

A ? ? ? T7S R4W S6

Located on the Tree Oaks Farm about 1 mile north of Etna Cemetery, on the west side of OR. Hwy. 99W. The two graves were in the trees surrounded by an iron picket fence. (Not shown on Rickreall 1969-76 USGS Quad. map.)

MILLER, SILAS

A 0.01 5 1861 T7S R5W ?

Perhaps in Section 3, on the Silas Miller D.L.C. #42, OC #1857 at Smithfield. He was buried under an oak tree in the front yard. NOTE: This site is on private property. (Not shown on Dallas 1974-86 USGS Quad. map.)

MONTGOMERY
  AKA: 1. ZUMWALT
       FAMILY

B 0.7 3 Jan. 1850 T9S R6W S23

The cemetery is at the convergence of four sections: 23, 24, 25, and 26. Leave Kings Valley Highway (OR. Hwy. 223) at Milepost 16.8 onto Maple Grove Road and go easterly for about 1.8 miles. The cemetery is on the

Name of Cemetery and also known as	Number of burials	Acres	Condition	Date started or earliest known burial	Township	Range	Section

right (south) 200 yards off of the road. There were 70 burials as of 1987, on the John Zumwalt D.L.C. #49, OC #4969. {19 August 1993} (Falls City 1974 USGS Quad. map.)

NEALY FAMILY — ? ? ? 1867-1882 T9S R5W ?

This is in Section 34 or 35. This cemetery is said to be off of the Airlie Road about 2 miles south and east of Airlie. Presumably therefore, it is on the Samuel Nealy D.L.C. #65, OC #4071. NOTE: This site is on private property. (Not shown on Airlie South 1984 USGS Quad. map.)

NESMITH FAMILY
AKA: 1. DIXIE
2. NESMITH PARK
3. RICKREALL

A 0.1 2 1884-1936 T7S R4W S30

Located at the northeast corner of the Polk County Fairgrounds on the south bank of Rickreall Creek. This was acquired by the Polk County Fair Association in 1969. There are 9 known burials (1982); on the David Goff D.L.C. #45, OC #83. {13 August 1988} (Not shown on Rickreall 1969-76 USGS Quad. map.)

NEW SMITH — C 3 1 Oct. 1942 T9S R5W S1

This cemetery was created in October 1942 during World War II, when the military Camp Adair was established. At least 4 old cemeteries were destroyed and reburials were made in New Smith and the English Cemeteries. These two new cemeteries were placed immediately west of and adjacent to Fir Crest Cemetery, with Fir Crest Road separating the two newer cemeteries from the original Fir Crest cemetery. Sometimes New Smith and English Cemeteries are referred to as Fir Crest in obituaries. New Smith cemetery is bordered on the north by Lamers Road and on the south by English Cemetery. There are no signboards to distinguish these 3 adjoining cemeteries 1.4 miles south of Monmouth via Helmick Road. There were 273 burials (1989). {14 December 1988} (Monmouth 1970-86 USGS Quad. map.)

Name of Cemetery and also known as	Number of burials	Acres	Condition	Date started or earliest known burial	Township	Range	Section

---

OGDEN, DENNIS RAY

A 0.01 ? 11 Feb 1971 T8S R5W S28
One grave of a 21 year-old man, enclosed in a white picket fence, is near the summit of the Monmouth Highway westerly from Monmouth. The compiler does not know on which side of the highway the grave is located. NOTE: This site is on private property. (Not shown on Airlie North 1974 USGS Quad. map.)

PIONEER [RICKREALL]
AKA: 1. BIRCH *[Sic]*
2. BURCH FAMILY
3. THIELSEN

C 0.7 4 1845 T7S R4W S32
This cemetery is about 1 mile southeast of Rickreall as the crow flies. Go east on Rickreall Road from OR. Hwy. 99W for 1.6 miles; turn right (south) onto Morrow Road and go south for 0.25 of a mile. Then turn right (west) onto the unsigned cemetery access road which runs west and then south for 0.55 of a mile to some large sheds. The final 0.25 of a mile to the right (west is through a farm field to the cemetery which is within an oak crove. Located on the Samuel Burch D.L.C. #47, OC #81. {October 1987} (Rickreall 1969-76 USGS Quad. map.)

PLEASANT HILL
AKA: 1. CONNOR FAMILY
2. RED PRAIRIE METHODIST

C 2.5 2 1852 T6S R6W S12
The cemetery is located on Pleasant Hill Road at the junction of Blanchard Road, which is about 4 miles southeast of Sheridan and about 3 miles west of Ballston. It is on the Nathan Conner D.L.C. #59, OC #2663. NOTE: The variant spelling of the family name. {8 December 1988} (Ballston 1956-70 USGS Quad. map.)

PROPES, FRANK FINLEY

A 0.01 1 5 Aug 1993 T6S R7W S35
This burial is at the Mountain Springs Ranch, which is private property. It is located about 5 miles southwest of Buell. (Burial site is not shown on Grand Ronde 1979 USGS Quad. map.)

PUTNAM FARM
AKA: 1. EOLA

A ? ? 1893 T7S R3W ?
Possibly on Section 30. Located off of Doaks Ferry Road, presumably on the west side of the road, in the Eola area. (Not shown on Salem West 1969-86 USGS Quad. map.)

Name of Cemetery and also known as	Number of burials	Acres	Condition	Date started or earliest known burial	Township	Range	Section

REST LAWN MEMORY GARDENS AND MAUSOLEUM

E 15.7 1 1952 T7S R4W S26

This is in Sections 26 and 27, located about 5.5 miles west of the Willamette River Bridges at Salem. This is at 202 Oak Grove Road, at the junction of Oak Grove Road with Salem-Dallas Highway (OR. Hwy. 22.) Turn right (north) off of OR. Hwy. 22. It is on the Alva C. Shaw D.L.C. #59, OC #4735. {17 September 1989} (Rickreall 1969-76 USGS Quad. map.)

ROBBINS FAMILY

A 1 7 1875 T7S R5W S27

Located a short distance northeast of Dallas and off of Fir Villa Road, which runs between Kings Valley Highway and the East Ellendale Road (formerly Dallas-Rickreall Highway, OR. Hwy. 223). The cemetery is in a small grove of fir trees just east of Fir Villa Road. The cemetery was recorded in 1882, and there are 20 known burials, 1875-1906. It is on the Thomas Lovelady D.L.C. #63, OC #4010. NOTE: A 1958 D.A.R. report names a "Robinson Family Cemetery 0.25 of a mile east of Fir Villa Road in Section 23." This report appears to confuse the name Robinson with Robbins and places the location at the Fast Cemetery. (Not shown on Dallas 1974-86 USGS Quad. map.)

ROCK CREEK
AKA: 1. ROCCA-CHANDLER FAMILY
2. ROCK CREEK MEADOWS

A 0.1 5 1878 T9S R8W ?

Perhaps this is located in Section 31. The cemetery is in the extreme southwest of Polk County near the Lincoln County Line, perhaps in the Rock Creek Meadows. A few stones were found here in 1977. Leave the Eddyville-Nashville Highway at Nortons in Lincoln County, going north on Rock Creek Road into Polk County. Good luck! (Not shown on Valsetz 1974 or Nortons 1984 USGS Quad. maps.)

SALT CREEK

C 3.4 1 1851 T7S R5W S6

This is in Sections 6 and 7. The cemetery is northwest of Dallas and off of OR. Hwy. 22. Take the Salt Creek Church Road to the church; continue another 0.25 of a mile to a driveway on the left (southerly) and drive

Name of Cemetery and also known as	Number of burials	Acres	Condition	Date started or earliest known burial	Township	Range	Section

0.3 of a mile up a hill to the cemetery. It is on the James W. Frederick D.L.C. #38, OC #195. {11 November 1988} (Dallas 1974-86 USGS Quad. map.)

SCHRAG FAMILY
AKA: 1. MENNONITE

A 0.15 3 1879-1889 T8S R5W S6

Located 3.5 miles southwest of Dallas. Turn right (west) off of Kings Valley Highway (OR. Hwy. 223) onto Liberty Road and go 1 mile. The cemetery is on the left (south), on top of a hill in thick woods. There were 8 graves visible in 1982. Joseph Schrag and 3 of his children died in the space of 15 days in 1888. NOTE: This site is on private property. (Dallas 1974-86 USGS Quad. map.)

SCHULSON FAMILY

? ? ? May 1990 ? ? ?

Possibly located in Township 6 South, Range 5 West, Section 32 or Township 7 South, Range 5 West, Section 5. Located northwest of Dallas and north of OR. Hwy. 22, on the right (east) side of Van Well Road. NOTE: This site is on private property. (Not shown on Dallas 1974-86 or Ballston 1956-70 USGS Quad. maps.)

SHERIDAN MENNONITE
AKA: 1. MENNONITE
2. MENNONITE CEMETERY AT WALLACE BRIDGE
3. WALLACE BRIDGE MENNONITE
4. WILLAMINA MENNONITE

B 1.7 1 1870 T6S R7W S13

The cemetery is on the southwest side of Wallace Bridge on Sawtell Road, 0.3 of a mile west of OR. Hwy. 22. Turn left off of OR. Hwy. 22 when going west onto Sawtell Road; the cemetery is on the right. The church is located in the town of Sheridan. {25 January 1989} (Sheridan 1956-70 USGS Quad. map.)

SMITH FAMILY
AKA 1. LEWISVILLE

? ? 6 ? T9S R5W S16

This was located on a rise on the north side of Elkins Road, just west of its junction with Smith Road and east of the site of Lewisville. The graves were moved to New Smith Cemetery (see that writeup) in October 1942 with the establishment of the Camp Adair

Name of Cemetery and also known as	Number of burials	Acres	Condition	Date started or earliest known burial	Township	Range	Section

Military Reservation. On the James Smith D.L.C. #56, OC #4250. (Not shown on Airlie North 1974 USGS Quad. map.)

STAATS, ISAAC W.

| | A | ? | ? | 31 Oct 1865 | T9S | R5W | ? |

This was located in Section 32 or 33 on the Isaac Staats D.L.C. #66, OC #4710. As late as 1988 there were reports of a possible family burial site on the Isaac Staats farm. However he and other possible reburials from the family were removed sometime and Isaac Staats is now buried in Fir Crest Cemetery out of Monmouth. (Not shown on Airlie South 1984 USGS Quad. map)

STUMP FARM

| | A | ? | ? | 1882-1888 | T8S | R5W | S27 |

Located southwest of Monmouth and on the north side of the Monmouth Highway and said to be near the north line of the Stump farm. The first burial was 13 December 1882, two known graves were noted in 1988. NOTE: This site is on private property. (Not shown on Airlie North 1974 USGS Quad. map.)

TAYLOR FAMILY

| | A | 0.5 | 2 | 1857-1937 | T9S | R6W | S34 |

Located a short distance south of Pedee. Turn left (south) off of Kings Valley Highway (OR. Hwy. 223) onto Ira Hooker Road and go less than 0.25 of a mile to the first curve left; the cemetery is ahead in a grove of fir trees. There are 11 known burials with 8 markers remaining in June of 1988. It is on the James Taylor D.L.C. #52, OC #4754. {23 January 1995} (Kings Valley 1984 USGS Quad. map.)

UNKNOWN

| | A | ? | ? | ? | T9S | R6W | ? |

Perhaps located in Section 17. An elderly black couple, names now unknown, are buried near an old millsite on the Ronco farm southwest of Pedee. The site is apparently off of Pedee Creek Road. NOTE: This site is on private property. (Not shown on Falls City 1974 USGS Quad. map.)

Name of Cemetery and also known as	Number of burials	Acres	Condition	Date started or earliest known burial	Township	Range	Section

WAYMIRE FAMILY
AKA: 1. CAREY

A   0.1   4   1849   T8S R6W   S15

This old family cemetery is located on a ridgetop in thick woods on private property. Nowadays, it is best reached with local assistance from Falls City Road. It is on the east side of the ridge overlooking the Bridgeport Valley. A newspaper report in the *Dallas Itemizer* of 7 July 1893 say there were "perhaps two dozen graves," the first dating from 1849. A May 1986 reports only 6 known graves marked, one as late as January 1918. Located perhaps 1/4 of a mile north of the Frederick Waymire D.L.C. #47, OC #4585. {5 October 1993} (Not shown on Falls City 1974 USGS Quad. map.)

WHITEAKER FAMILY
AKA: 1. ADAMS

A   0.1   5   1865-1925   T8S R5W   S14

This cemetery is southeast of Dallas and northwest of Monmouth, on private property. Located south off of Whiteaker Road about a mile west of Riddell Road at the first 90-degree turn right of Whiteaker Road. The burials are in a tangle of brush at the south fence line of the Benjamin Whiteaker D.L.C. #65, OC #1241, but is actually on the north edge (on the same fence line) of the James S. Foster D.L.C. #63, OC #1243. Seven stones were found by a group cleaning up this site spring of 1999. {10 February 1995} (Not shown on Dallas 1974-86 USGS Quad. map.)

WHITLEY FAMILY

? ?   ? ?   T7S R5W   ?

Located somewhere on Sections 4, 5, 8 or 9 of their DLC. Located northwest of Dallas in the area of Salt Creek Church Road, on the Andrew H. Whittley [Sic.] D.L.C. #39, OC #3661. NOTE: This site is on private property. (Not shown on Dallas 1974-86 USGS Quad. map.)

WILLAMINA

D   2.4   2   1863   T6S R7W   S1

The town of Willamina straddles the county line between Polk and Yamhill Counties. Most of the town is within the latter, but the cemetery is within Polk County. It is on the

Name of Cemetery and also known as	Number of burials	Acres	Condition	Date started or earliest known burial	Township	Range	Section

hill and briefly visible from the main street (OR. Hwy. 18 Business), when going west. {1 November 1989} (Sheridan 1956-70 USGS Quad. map.)

WILLIAMS FAMILY   A   0.22   5   1865-1939   T9S   R5W   S32
The first burial was 13 March 1865 and the last was 5 Febuary 1939. Located 0.5 of a mile south of Airlie right behind Airlie School in a field. There are 7 known burials, on the James Williams D.L.C. #68, OC #4692. (Airlie South 1984 USGS Quad. map.)

WIMPLE, MARY   A   0.01   5   1 Aug 1852   T8S   R6W   S23
The wife of Adam Wimple was buried here after her husband murdered her and for which he was hung. Located about 2 miles southeast of Falls City in what is described as the Wilson Lee D.L.C. #45, OC #3910. NOTE: This site is on private property. (Not shown on Falls City 1974 USGS Quad. map.)

WOMER   C   1.5   2   1887   T9S   R6W   S32
Go southwest of Pedee on Kings Valley Highway (OR. Hwy. 223); about 0.5 of a mile past the Pedee School turn right (north) up the hill. Edwards Cemetery is on the left side of the driveway, Womer Cemetery is on the right, on the Mary Gilliam D.L.C. #55, OC #5034. {3 May 1989} (Kings Valley 1984 USGS Quad. map.)

ZENA
AKA: 1. SPRING VALLEY PRESBYTERIAN CHURCH   C   1.5   2   1858   T6S   R4W   S36
Go north from West Salem on Wallace Road (OR. Hwy. 221), turning left onto Brush College Road to the northwest and north. The church and cemetery are on a low hill on the right, on the Elias Robbins D.L.C. #49, OC #822. {17 August 1988} (Amity 1957-93 USGS Quad. map.)

ADAMS see **WHITEAKER FAMILY**	POLK CO.	T8S	R5W	S14
AETNA see **ETNA**	POLK CO.	T7S	R4W	S7
ALDERMAN FAMILY	POLK CO.	T6S	R4W	S13
ANDERSON FAMILY	POLK CO.	T8S	R6W	S16
BALL	POLK CO.	T6S	R5W	S5
BALL D.L.C., ISAAC see **BALL**	POLK CO.	T6S	R5W	S5
BALL FAMILY see **BALL**	POLK CO.	T6S	R5W	S5
BALLSTON see **BALL**	POLK CO.	T6S	R5W	S5
BASKETT FAMILY	POLK CO.	T7S	R4W	S19
BETHEL	POLK CO.	T6S	R4W	S21
BIRCH *[Sic]* see **PIONEER [RICKREALL]**				
	POLK CO.	T7S	R4W	S32
BLACK ROCK	POLK CO.	T8S	R7W	S14
BLAIR D.L.C., THOMAS R. see **BLAIR FAMILY**				
	POLK CO.	T6S	R6W	S21
BLAIR FAMILY	POLK CO.	T6S	R6W	S21
BOISE, ELLEN LYON see **BOISE FAMILY**				
	POLK CO.	T7S	?	?
BOISE FAMILY	POLK CO.	T7S	?	?
BOISE, FARM see **BOISE FAMILY**	POLK CO.	T7S	?	?
BOISE, REUBEN see **BOISE FAMILY**	POLK CO.	T7S	?	?
BOWMAN D.L.C., PRESTON see **BOWMAN FAMILY**				
	POLK CO.	T9S	R5W	?
BOWMAN FAMILY	POLK CO.	T9S	R5W	?
BOWMAN, SARAH see **BOWMAN FAMILY**	POLK CO.	T9S	R5W	?
BOWMAN, WILLIAM see **BOWMAN FAMILY**				
	POLK CO.	T9S	R5W	?
BOYDSTON see **HUBBARD**	POLK CO.	T8S	R6W	S28
BRIGHAM'S GRAVE	POLK CO.	T9S	R6W	S35
BROWN D.L.C., GEORGE see **BROWN, GEORGE**				
	POLK CO.	T7S	R5W	S9
BROWN, GEORGE	POLK CO.	T7S	R5W	S9
BROWN, WILLIAM C.	POLK CO.	T7S	R5W	S22
BRUNK FARM	POLK CO.	T7S	R4W	?
BUENA VISTA	POLK CO.	T9S	R4W	S23
BURCH D.L.C., BENJAMIN F. see **HILLTOP**				
	POLK CO.	T9S	R4W	S9
BURCH D.L.C., SAMUEL see **PIONEER [RICKREALL]**				
	POLK CO.	T7S	R4W	S32
BURCH FAMILY see **PIONEER [RICKREAL]**				
	POLK CO.	T7S	R4W	S32
BURKHART, YOUNGABLE see **BRIGHAM'S GRAVE**				
	POLK CO.	T9S	R6W	S35
BUSKETT *[Sic]* D.L.C., GEORGE see **BASKETT FAMILY**				
	POLK CO.	T7S	R4W	S19
BUTLER-DAVIDSON FAMILY	POLK CO.	T8S	R5W	S35
CAREY see **WAYMIRE FAMILY**	POLK CO.	T8S	R6W	S15
CASEY, DOCTOR L. V. see **CASEY FAMILY**				
	POLK CO.	T8S	R5W	S3
CASEY FAMILY	POLK CO.	T8S	R5W	S3
CASEY, MARION ETHEL PANKEY see **CASEY FAMILY**				
	POLK CO.	T8S	R5W	S3

CEMETERY HILL see **HILLTOP**	POLK CO.	T9S	R4W	S9
CHAMBERLAIN D.L.C., AARON C. see **CHAMBERLIN FAMILY**				
	POLK CO.	T9S	R5W	S24
CHAMBERLAIN FAMILY see **CHAMBERLIN FAMILY**				
	POLK CO.	T9S	R5W	S24
CHAMBERLIN FAMILY	POLK CO.	T9S	R5W	S24
CHAMBERLIN-COLLINS FAMILY see **CHAMBERLIN FAMILY**				
	POLK CO.	T9S	R5W	S24
CLAREMONT FAMILY	POLK CO.	T10S	R7W	S11
COLLINS D.L.C., SMITH see **CHAMBERLIN FAMILY**				
	POLK CO.	T9S	R5W	S24
COLLINS, SMITH see **CHAMBERLIN FAMILY**				
	POLK CO.	T9S	R5W	S24
CONFEDERATED TRIBES see **GRAND RONDE**				
	POLK CO.	T6S	R8W	S12
CONNOR D.L.C., NATHAN see **PLEASANT HILL**				
	POLK CO.	T6S	R6W	S12
CONNOR FAMILY see **PLEASANT HILL**	POLK CO.	T6S	R6W	S12
COOPER FAMILY	POLK CO.	T8S	R5W	S29
COOPER, HESTER ANN MOXLEY see **COOPER FAMILY**				
	POLK CO.	T8S	R5W	S29
COOPER HOLLOW see **COOPER FAMILY**	POLK CO.	T8S	R5W	S29
COOPER, JAMES LINDSAY see **COOPER FAMILY**				
	POLK CO.	T8S	R5W	S29
COX, WM. A. see **HUSSEY FAMILY**	POLK CO.	T6S	R7W	S15
CROWLEY see **ETNA**	POLK CO.	T7S	R4W	S7
DALLAS	POLK CO.	T8S	R5W	S5
DANNETTE FARM see **HOOKER FAMILY**	POLK CO.	T9S	R6W	?
DAVIDSON D.L.C., JAMES C. see **BUTLER-DAVIDSON FAMILY**				
	POLK CO.	T8S	R5W	S35
DAVIDSON FAMILY see **BUTLER-DAVIDSON FAMILY**				
	POLK CO.	T8S	R5W	S35
DEMPSEY see **EMBREE FAMILY, CAREY D.**				
	POLK CO.	T7S	R5W	S36
DIXIE see **NESMITH FAMILY**	POLK CO.	T7S	R4W	S30
DOSS FAMILY	POLK CO.	T6S	R8W	?
DOSS, JUDY E. see **DOSS FAMILY**	POLK CO.	T6S	R8W	?
DOSS, LEE see **DOSS FAMILY**	POLK CO.	T6S	R8W	?
DUNNETTE see **HOOKER FAMILY**	POLK CO.	T9S	R6W	?
EADES D.L.C., WILLIAM see **HARMONY**				
	POLK CO.	T6S	R6W	S9
EARNEST see **JENNINGS**	POLK CO.	T6S	R4W	S13
EDWARDS D.L.C., JOSEPH see **EDWARDS FAMILY**				
	POLK CO.	T9S	R6W	S32
EDWARDS FAMILY	POLK CO.	T9S	R6W	S32
EDWARDS, REBECCA see **HUSSEY FAMILY**				
	POLK CO.	T6S	R7W	S15
ELDRIDGE, JOHN see **HUSSEY FAMILY**				
	POLK CO.	T6S	R7W	S15
EMBREE D.L.C., CAREY see **EMBREE FAMILY, CAREY D.**				
	POLK CO.	T7S	R5W	S36

EMBREE FAMILY, CAREY D.	POLK CO.	T7S	R5W	S36
ENGLISH D.L.C., BENJAMIN see **ENGLISH [OLD]**				
	POLK CO.	T9S	R5W	S28
ENGLISH [NEW]	POLK CO.	T9S	R5W	S1
ENGLISH [OLD]	POLK CO.	T9S	R5W	S28
EOLA see **PUTNAM FARM**	POLK CO.	T7S	R3W	?
ETNA	POLK CO.	T7S	R4W	S7
ETNA BAPTIST CHURCH see **ETNA**	POLK CO.	T7S	R4W	S7
FALLS CITY	POLK CO.	T8S	R6W	S16
FAST	POLK CO.	T7S	R5W	S23
FERN CORNER see **HART-RIGGS FAMILY**				
	POLK CO.	T8S	R6W	S25
FIR CREST	POLK CO.	T9S	R4W	S6
FORD D.L.C., NATHAN see **HOLMES, CELI ANN AND HARRIET**				
	POLK CO.	T7S	R4W	S30
FORD, NATHANIEL see **HOLMES, CELI ANN AND HARRIET**				
	POLK CO.	T7S	R4W	S30
FORD PLACE see **HOLMES, CELI ANN AND HARRIET**				
	POLK CO.	T7S	R4W	S30
FORT HILL see **HUSSEY FAMILY**	POLK CO.	T6S	R7W	S15
FOSTER D.L.C., JAMES S. see **WHITEAKER FAMILY**				
	POLK CO.	T8S	R5W	S14
FREDERICK D.L.C., JAMES W. see **SALT CREEK**				
	POLK CO.	T7S	R5W	S6
GAY D.L.C., GEORGE KIRBY see **GAY FAMILY**				
	POLK CO.	T6S	R3W	?
GAY FAMILY	POLK CO.	T6S	R3W	?
GAY HOUSE see **GAY FAMILY**	POLK CO.	T6S	R3W	?
GIBSON, BENTON see **GIBSON FAMILY, GEORGE G.**				
	POLK CO.	T7S	R3W	S19
GIBSON D.L.C., GEORGE G. see **GIBSON FAMILY, GEORGE G.**				
	POLK CO.	T7S	R3W	S19
GIBSON, DOUGLAS see **GIBSON FAMILY, GEORGE G.**				
	POLK CO.	T7S	R3W	S19
GIBSON FAMILY, GEORGE G.	POLK CO.	T7S	R3W	S19
GIBSON, MARY BOWEN see **GIBSON FAMILY, GEORGE G.**				
	POLK CO.	T7S	R3W	S19
GILLIAM D.L.C., MARY see **WOMER**	POLK CO.	T9S	R6W	S32
GOFF D.L.C., DAVID see **NESMITH FAMILY**				
	POLK CO.	T7S	R4W	S30
GOLD CREEK see **HUSSEY FAMILY**	POLK CO.	T6S	R7W	S15
GOTHARD D.L.C., SAMUEL see **FALLS CITY**				
	POLK CO.	T8S	R6W	S16
GOTHARD D.L.C., SAMUEL see **I.O.O.F. [FALLS CITY]**				
	POLK CO.	T8S	R6W	S21
GRAND RONDE	POLK CO.	T6S	R8W	S12
GRAND RONDE INDIAN TRIBAL see **GRAND RONDE**				
	POLK CO.	T6S	R8W	S12
GRIFFITH D.L.C., JOHN W. see **BUENA VISTA**				
	POLK CO.	T9S	R4W	S23
HARLAND FAMILY, WILLIAM see **FAST**				
	POLK CO.	T7S	R5W	S23

HARLAND FARM, WILLIAM see **FAST**	POLK CO.	T7S	R5W	S23
HARMONY	POLK CO.	T6S	R6W	S9
HARRIS D.L.C., JAMES see **CASEY FAMILY**				
	POLK CO.	T8S	R5W	S3
HART D.L.C., THOMAS see **HART-RIGGS FAMILY**				
	POLK CO.	T8S	R6W	S25
HART FAMILY see **HART-RIGGS FAMILY**				
	POLK CO.	T8S	R6W	S25
HART-RIGGS FAMILY	POLK CO.	T8S	R6W	S25
HEFFLEY see **CHAMBERLIN FAMILY**	POLK CO.	T9S	R5W	S24
HIGHLAND	POLK CO.	T7S	R3W	S17
HIGHLAND METHODIST CHURCH see **HIGHLAND**				
	POLK CO.	T7S	R3W	S17
HILLTOP	POLK CO.	T9S	R4W	S9
HOLMES, CELI ANN AND HARRIET	POLK CO.	T7S	R4W	S30
HOOKER D.L.C., IRA A. see **HOOKER FAMILY**				
	POLK CO.	T9S	R6W	?
HOOKER FAMILY	POLK CO.	T9S	R6W	?
HOSFORD METHODIST CHURCH see **HIGHLAND**				
	POLK CO.	T7S	R3W	S17
HUBBARD	POLK CO.	T8S	R6W	S28
HUSSEY D.L.C., NATHAN see **HUSSEY FAMILY**				
	POLK CO.	T6S	R7W	S15
HUSSEY FAMILY	POLK CO.	T6S	R7W	S15
HUSSEY, FRANK see **HUSSEY FAMILY**	POLK CO.	T6S	R7W	S15
I.O.O.F. see **BUENA VISTA**	POLK CO.	T9S	R4W	S23
I.O.O.F. see **DALLAS**	POLK CO.	T8S	R5W	S5
I.O.O.F. [FALLS CITY]	POLK CO.	T8S	R6W	S21
I.O.O.F. [INDEPENDENCE] see **HILLTOP**				
	POLK CO.	T9S	R4W	S9
I.O.O.F. [MONMOUTH] see **FIR CREST**				
	POLK CO.	T9S	R4W	S6
I.O.O.F. VALLEY LODGE #42 see **HILLTOP**				
	POLK CO.	T9S	R4W	S9
INDIAN GRAVE HILL	POLK CO.	T9S	R6W	?
JENNINGS	POLK CO.	T6S	R4W	S13
K. P. see **FIR CREST**	POLK CO.	T9S	R4W	S6
KNIGHTS OF PYTHIAS see **FIR CREST**				
	POLK CO.	T9S	R4W	S6
LEE D.L.C., WILSON see **WIMPLE, MARY**				
	POLK CO.	T8S	R6W	S23
LEVENS D.L.C., ISAAC see **DALLAS**	POLK CO.	T8S	R5W	S5
LEWIS D.L.C., JOHN see **LEWIS FAMILY**				
	POLK CO.	T9S	R5W	S18
LEWIS FAMILY	POLK CO.	T9S	R5W	S18
LEWISVILLE see **SMITH FAMILY**	POLK CO.	T9S	R5W	S16
LIGGETT D.L.C., JONATHAN W. see **LIGGETT FAMILY**				
	POLK CO.	T9S	R5W	S7
LIGGETT FAMILY	POLK CO.	T9S	R5W	S7
LOVELADY D.L.C., THOMAS see **ROBBINS FAMILY**				
	POLK CO.	T7S	R5W	S27
LOWER see **I.O.O.F. [FALLS CITY]**	POLK CO.	T8S	R6W	S21

MARKS FARM	POLK CO.	T6S	R4W	?
MARTIN D.L.C., JOHN see **HIGHLAND**				
	POLK CO.	T7S	R3W	S17
MASONIC see **DALLAS**	POLK CO.	T8S	R5W	S5
McCOY see **BETHEL**	POLK CO.	T6S	R4W	S21
McGUIRE FARM, WILLIAM	POLK CO.	T9S	R5W	S13
McNARY [?] see **BRUNK FARM**	POLK CO.	T7S	R4W	?
McTIMMONDS D.L.C., LAMBERT see **McTIMMONDS FAMILY**				
	POLK CO.	T9S	R6W	S10
McTIMMONDS FAMILY	POLK CO.	T9S	R6W	S10
McTIMMONDS, FRANCES see **McTIMMONDS FAMILY**				
	POLK CO.	T9S	R6W	S10
McTIMMONDS, LAMBERT see **McTIMMONDS FAMILY**				
	POLK CO.	T9S	R6W	S10
MENNONITE see **SCHRAG FAMILY**	POLK CO.	T8S	R5W	S6
MENNONITE see **SHERIDAN MENNONITE**				
	POLK CO.	T6S	R7W	S13
MENNONITE CEMETERY AT WALLACE BRIDGE see **SHERIDAN MENNONITE**				
	POLK CO.	T6S	R7W	S13
MILLER D.L.C., SILAS see **MILLER, SILAS**				
	POLK CO.	T7S	R5W	?
MILLER FAMILY	POLK CO.	T7S	R4W	S6
MILLER, SILAS	POLK CO.	T7S	R5W	?
MONMOUTH see **FIR CREST**	POLK CO.	T9S	R4W	S6
MONTGOMERY	POLK CO.	T9S	R6W	S23
MT. ETNA see **ETNA**	POLK CO.	T7S	R4W	S7
MOUNTAIN VIEW see **HIGHLAND**	POLK CO.	T7S	R3W	S17
NEALLY FAMILY see **HART-RIGGS FAMILY**				
	POLK CO.	T8S	R6W	S25
NEALY D.L.C., SAMUEL see **NEALY FAMILY**				
	POLK CO.	T9S	R5W	?
NEALY FAMILY	POLK CO.	T9S	R5W	?
NEALY FAMILY see **CHAMBERLIN FAMILY**				
	POLK CO.	T9S	R5W	S24
NESMITH FAMILY	POLK CO.	T7S	R4W	S30
NESMITH PARK see **NESMITH FAMILY**				
	POLK CO.	T7S	R4W	S30
NEW SMITH	POLK CO.	T9S	R5W	S1
OAK GROVE see **ETNA**	POLK CO.	T7S	R4W	S7
OAKHURST see **HUBBARD**	POLK CO.	T8S	R6W	S28
OGDEN, DENNIS RAY	POLK CO.	T8S	R5W	S28
OLD CITY see **FALLS CITY**	POLK CO.	T8S	R6W	S16
OLD PIONEER see **DALLAS**	POLK CO.	T8S	R5W	S5
PEDEE see **EDWARDS FAMILY**	POLK CO.	T9S	R6W	S32
PIONEER [INDEPENDENCE] see **HILLTOP**				
	POLK CO.	T9S	R4W	S9
PIONEER [RICKREALL]	POLK CO.	T7S	R4W	S32
PLEASANT HILL	POLK CO.	T6S	R6W	S12
PLEASANT HILL BAPTIST see **ETNA**	POLK CO.	T7S	R4W	S7
POLK STATION see **FAST**	POLK CO.	T7S	R5W	S23
POWELL FAMILY see **BUTLER-DAVIDSON FAMILY**				
	POLK CO.	T8S	R5W	S35

PROPES, FRANK FINLEY	POLK CO.	T6S	R7W	S35
PUTNAM FARM	POLK CO.	T7S	R3W	?
QUIRING see FAST	POLK CO.	T7S	R5W	S23
RED PRAIRIE METHODIST see PLEASANT HILL				
	POLK CO.	T6S	R6W	S12
REST LAWN MEMORY GARDENS AND MAUSOLEUM				
	POLK CO.	T7S	R4W	S26
RICKREALL see NESMITH FAMILY	POLK CO.	T7S	R4W	S30
RIGGS FAMILY see HART-RIGGS FAMILY				
	POLK CO.	T8S	R6W	S25
RITNER see EDWARDS FAMILY	POLK CO.	T9S	R6W	S32
ROBBINS D.L.C., ELIAS see ZENA	POLK CO.	T6S	R4W	S36
ROBBINS FAMILY	POLK CO.	T7S	R5W	S27
ROCCA-CHANDLER FAMILY see ROCK CREEK				
	POLK CO.	T9S	R8W	?
ROCK CREEK	POLK CO.	T9S	R8W	?
ROCK CREEK MEADOWS see ROCK CREEK				
	POLK CO.	T9S	R8W	?
ROGERS FAMILY see BUTLER-DAVIDSON FAMILY				
	POLK CO.	T8S	R5W	S35
RONCO FARM see UNKNOWN	POLK CO.	T9S	R6W	?
SALT CREEK	POLK CO.	T7S	R5W	S6
SCHRAG FAMILY	POLK CO.	T8S	R5W	S6
SCHRAG, JOSEPH see SCHRAG FAMILY				
	POLK CO.	T8S	R5W	S6
SCHULSON FAMILY	POLK CO.	?	?	?
SHAW see BRUNK FARM	POLK CO.	T7S	R4W	?
SHAW D.L.C., ALVA C. see BRUNK FARM				
	POLK CO.	T7S	R4W	?
SHAW D.L.C., ALVA C. see REST LAWN MEMORY GARDENS AND MAUSOLEUM				
	POLK CO.	T7S	R4W	S26
SHERIDAN MENNONITE	POLK CO.	T6S	R7W	S13
SHREVE D.L.C., ASA see FAST	POLK CO.	T7S	R5W	S23
SMITH D.L.C., IRA see BROWN, WILLIAM C.				
	POLK CO.	T7S	R5W	S22
SMITH D.L.C., JAMES see SMITH FAMILY				
	POLK CO.	T9S	R5W	S16
SMITH FAMILY	POLK CO.	T9S	R5W	S16
SPRING VALLEY PRESBYTERIAN CHURCH see ZENA				
	POLK CO.	T6S	R4W	S36
STAATS FARM, ISAAC see STAATS, ISAAC W.				
	POLK CO.	T9S	R5W	?
STAATS, ISAAC W.	POLK CO.	T9S	R5W	?
STUMP FARM	POLK CO.	T8S	R5W	S27
TARTER see ENGLISH [OLD]	POLK CO.	T9S	R5W	S28
TARTER, LENA BELLE see INDIAN GRAVE HILL				
	POLK CO.	T9S	R6W	?
TAYLOR D.L.C., JAMES see TAYLOR FAMILY				
	POLK CO.	T9S	R6W	S34
TAYLOR FAMILY	POLK CO.	T9S	R6W	S34
THIELSEN see PIONEER [RICKREALL]				
	POLK CO.	T7S	R4W	S32

TRIBAL see **GRAND RONDE**	POLK CO.	T6S	R8W	S12
UNION BAPTIST see **HARMONY**	POLK CO.	T6S	R6W	S9
UNKNOWN	POLK CO.	T9S	R6W	?
UPPER see **FALLS CITY**	POLK CO.	T8S	R6W	S16
WALKER FAMILY see **ETNA**	POLK CO.	T7S	R4W	S7
WALLACE see **HUSSEY FAMILY**	POLK CO.	T6S	R7W	S15
WALLACE BRIDGE MENNONITE see **SHERIDAN MENNONITE**				
	POLK CO.	T6S	R7W	S13
WALLACE, JULIA see **HUSSEY FAMILY**				
	POLK CO.	T6S	R7W	S15
WAYMIRE D.L.C., FREDERICK see **WAYMIRE FAMILY**				
	POLK CO.	T8S	R6W	S15
WAYMIRE FAMILY	POLK CO.	T8S	R6W	S15
WHITEAKER D.L.C., BENJAMIN see **WHITEAKER FAMILY**				
	POLK CO.	T8S	R5W	S14
WHITEAKER FAMILY	POLK CO.	T8S	R5W	S14
WHITLEY FAMILY	POLK CO.	T7S	R5W	?
WHITTLEY [Sic] D.L.C., ANDREW H. see **WHITLEY FAMILY**				
	POLK CO.	T7S	R5W	?
WILLAMINA	POLK CO.	T6S	R7W	S1
WILLAMINA MENNONITE see **SHERIDAN MENNENITE**				
	POLK CO.	T6S	R7W	S13
WILLIAMS D.L.C., JAMES see **WILLIAMS FAMILY**				
	POLK CO.	T9S	R5W	S32
WILLIAMS FAMILY	POLK CO.	T9S	R5W	S32
WIMPLE, ADAM see **WIMPLE, MARY**	POLK CO.	T8S	R6W	S23
WIMPLE, MARY	POLK CO.	T8S	R6W	S23
WOMER	POLK CO.	T9S	R6W	S32
WOODMEN OF THE WORLD see **BUENA VISTA**				
	POLK CO.	T9S	R4W	S23
YOUNG, BRIGHAM see **BRIGHAM'S GRAVE**				
	POLK CO.	T9S	R6W	S35
ZENA	POLK CO.	T6S	R4W	S36
ZUMWALT D.L.C., JOHN see **MONTGOMERY**				
	POLK CO.	T9S	R6W	S23
ZUMWALT FAMILY see **MONTGOMERY**	POLK CO.	T9S	R6W	S23

Ball

Dean H. Byrd (1991)

Womer

Dean H. Byrd (1993)

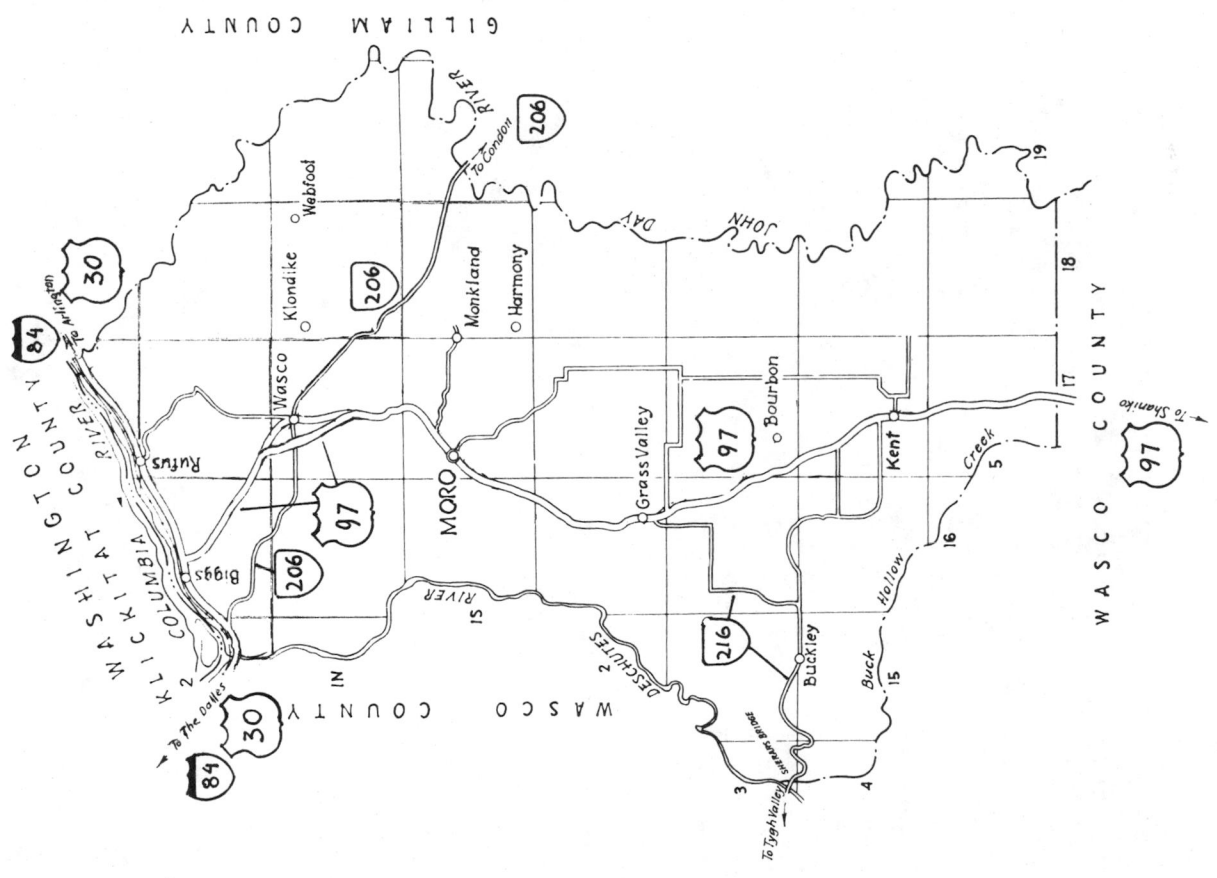

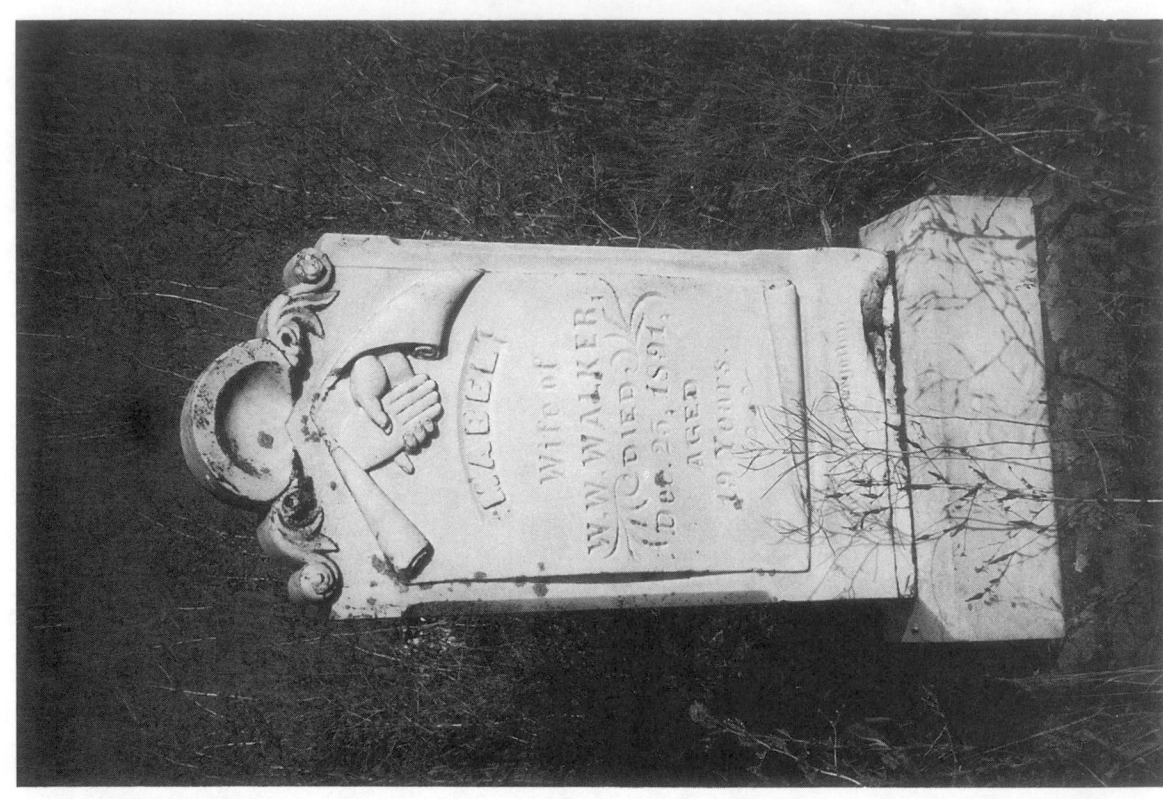

Wasco Methodist
Janice M. Healy (2000)

Wasco Methodist
Janice M. Healy (2000)

Area: 831 square miles
Population (1998): 1,789
County seat: Moro, Population: 295
County established: 25 February 1889

Sherman County was one of the areas of transit and white settlers usually continued west. Sheep ranching flourished briefly in the 1870's but was soon superseded by wheat ranches in the 1880's and so it is to this day. As far as the compiler is aware the first public cemetery was that known as Wasco Methodist Cemetery in 1872.

Wasco Methodist
Janice M. Healy (2000)

Wasco Methodist
Janice M. Healy (2000)

Sun Rise
Janice M. Healy (2000)

Name of Cemetery and also known as	Number of burials	Acres	Condition	Date started or earliest known burial	Township	Range	Section

ALLEN CHILD

A 0.01 5 ? T1N R18E S7

There is a gravestone in the Weedman Farm shop at Klondike which perhaps belonged on the grave of the Allen child. The grave itself was described as near a grain elevator. (Not shown on Klondike 1971 USGS Quad. map.)

BLACKBURNE

A ? 5 1908 T2N R16E ?

Possibly on section 3 or 10. This is on the south side of the I-84 Freeway about 3 miles west of Rufus. Some of these graves were moved due to the construction of The Dalles Dam. They were about 70 feet south of the relocated Interstate I-84 Freeway and in an orchard on the George and Alma Blackburne property (1965). Three known burials, 1 reburial to Sun Rise Cemetery and an undetermined number of other burials are here. (Not shown on Biggs Juction 1977 USGS Quad. map.)

CITY OF MORO
AKA: 1. AMERICAN
        LEGION
     2. BAPTIST
     3. I.O.O.F.
        [MORO]

C 7.6 2 1889 T1S R17E S18

In Moro leave U.S. Hwy. 97 on 4th Street, go 0.4 of a mile to the cemetery entrance on the left. Harris Canyon Road continues on ahead. (Moro 1971 USGS Quad. map.)

DAUGHERTY FAMILY

A ? 5 1888-1933 T5S R17E S12

Located south of Kent and east of Wilcox Station on the road to Wilcox about 1.5 miles as the crow flies east of Decker Road. There is no access road and there are at least 4 burials. NOTE: This site is on private property. (Kent 1970 USGS Quad. map.)

De MOSS
 AKA: 1. DeMOSS SPRINGS

A 0.25 1 1893 T1S R17E S3

Three miles north of Moro and located in Grass Valley Canyon at the foot of a large rock bluff. Go a total of 0.8 of a mile northeast off of U.S. Hwy. 97, crossing Barnum Canyon, pass by the gravel pits and go for another 0.6 of a mile on DeMoss Springs Lane. Then turn right up Grass Valley Canyon

Sherman County

Name of Cemetery and also known as	Number of burials	Acres	Condition	Date started or earliest known burial	Township	Range	Section

for another 0.2 of a mile. There were 10 known burials (1965). (Wasco 1971-87 USGS Quad. map.)

EDWARDS CHILD

A 0.01 5 ?   T3S R16E   ?
There is a record of an unnamed child of LeRoy and Mary Jane Helyer Edwards being buried on Stradley land southwest of Grass Valley. (Not shown on Grass Valley 1962 USGS Quad. map.)

EMIGRANT SPRINGS
AKA: 1. BIGLOW

B 2.5 2 1888-1943 T2N R18E   S34
Located along the side of the Old Oregon Trail 9 miles northeast of Wasco. Leave OR. Hwy. 206 in Wasco and go past the airport. Go 4 miles, then turn left on Klondike Road for 1 mile; turn right on Dehler Road for 3 miles, then turn left (north) for 1 mile. There were 41 known burials and 35 unmarked burials (1965). (Klondike 1971 USGS Quad. map.)

GARLINGTON PLACE

A 0.01 ? ?   T2N R17E   ?
Sherry Kaseberg reports that there was a grave surrounded by a picket fence on the Garlington Place. It is on private property, farmed at one time by L. C. Medler northeast of Wasco. (Not shown on Wasco 1971-87 USGS Quad. map.)

HOGGARD CHILD

A 0.01 5 Circa 1905 T2N R16E   ?
This could be in section 1, 2, 11 or 12. This is on the Allan Tom Ranch (1970) near Rufus. Burials may have been removed to Sun Rise Cemetery. NOTE: This site is on private property. (Not shown on Biggs Junction 1977 or Rufus 1971 USGS Quad. maps.)

I.O.O.F.
 [GRASS VALLEY]
AKA: 1. GRASS VALLEY
       LODGE #131
       I.O.O.F.

C 5.13 2 1887 T2S R16E   S22
Located in Grass Valley on the west side of U.S. Hwy. 97, 1.5 miles north of the center of town and 300 feet off of the highway. There are 406 known burials and 35 unmarked burials (1965). (Erskine 1962 USGS Quad. map.)

Name of Cemetery and also known as	Number of burials	Acres	Condition	Date started or earliest known burial	Township	Range	Section

I.O.O.F. [KENT]

B 5 2 1891   T4S R17E   S21
This cemetery is about 1.5 miles north of
Kent and 200 feet off of U.S. Hwy. 97. There
were 97 known burials and 4 unmarked burials
(1965). (Kent 1970 USGS Quad. map.)

KENNY, CHILDREN

A 0.01 ? ?   T1S R18E   S11
Two unnamed children of William Kenny were
buried in a fenced plot southeast of Wasco
near OR. Hwy. 206. William Kenny himself is
buried in Seneacquoten Cemetery, Bonner
County, Idaho. NOTE: This site is on private
property. (Not shown on Klondike or Harmony
1971 USGS Quad. maps. Kenny Spring is shown
on the Harmony Quad. map.)

MASIKER, GEORGE

A 0.01 5 ?   T2N R16E   S33
There is a grave with no monument located on
the southwest side of OR. Hwy. 206 in Frank
Fulton Canyon and about 2 miles northwest of
the Locust Grove Church. The grave is next
to Sand Spring and on private property.
(Locust Grove 1974 USGS Quad. map.)

McCOY INFANT

A ? 5 1894-1900 T2N R16E   S1
Located on the Harland McDonald property
(1970) in the west part of Rufus. There are
some other unmarked graves on the same ranch.
NOTE: This site is on private property. (Not
shown on Biggs Junction 1977 USGS Quad. map.)

MICHIGAN

A 2.5 3 1887   T3S R16E   S16
Located 3.6 miles southwest of Grass Valley
on OR. Hwy. 216 (Sherars Bridge Highway), on
the left (south) side of the highway. There
were 12 known graves and 1 unknown burial
(1965). (Grass Valley 1962 USGS Quad. map.)

MORAN

A 0.01 ? 1914   T2N R16E   S22
Located along U.S. Hwy. 97 between Wasco and
Biggs Junction and near the confluence of Mud
Hollow and Spanish Hollow. At one time there
was a small stone which was broken up by a
highway construction crew. It is now part of
a pier of the Highway 97 bridge. This

Sherman County

787

Name of Cemetery and also known as	Number of burials	Acres	Condition	Date started or earliest known burial	Township	Range	Section

monument has been replaced by Mr. and Mrs. Ken Hoggatt, Pat McNab and Gordon Hilderbrand 21 October 1999. For the rest of the story see *OHCA Ledger, Volume 8 Issue 3 March 2000.* (Not shown on Biggs Junction 1977 USGS Quad. map.)

ROSE HILL
AKA: 1. ROSE

C   5   2   1885   T1S   R17E   S26
Located 6.75 miles southeast of Moro. Take Lone Rock Road from Moro and go 3.5 miles to Crites Road. Then turn left (east) on Crites Road, and go 2.75 miles to Fraser Road; turn left (north) on Fraser Road for 0.5 of a mile. The cemetery was deeded in June 1905 by William H. Rose. There were 112 known burials (1965). (Moro 1971 USGS Quad. map.)

RUFUS

A   ?   3   1894   T2N   R17E   S6
Located in the Southwest 1/4 of the Northeast 1/4 of Section 6. Due south of Rufus on a bluff overlooking the town and the Columbia River. Perhaps the cemetery is along Vista Drive, up from Main street past the church. There are 11 believed to be buried here, with only 4 stones visible (1965). (Not shown on Rufus 1971 USGS Quad. map.)

SAYRS CHILD

A   0.01   5   Jun 1883   T1S   R16E   ?
An unnamed child of Francis and Emma Powell Sayrs was buried in the field above the Sayrs Homestead west of Moro. Other members of the family are buried in the City of Moro Cemetery. (Not shown on Erskine 1962 USGS Quad. map.)

SUN RISE
AKA: 1. I.O.O.F. [WASCO]
     2. MASONIC [WASCO]
     3. RISING SUN
     4. WASCO
     5. WASCO [NEW]

C   4.63   1   1899   T2N   R17E   S31
Located 2.5 miles northwest of Wasco and approximately 0.3 of a mile south of U.S. Hwy. 97. Take OR. Hwy. 206 west out of Wasco over U.S. Hwy. 97 and go 1.5 miles to the cemetery access road. Turn right (north) on Cemetery Road and go 1 mile. {1 September 2000} (Wasco 1971-87 USGS Quad. map.)

Name of Cemetery and also known as	Number of burials	Acres	Condition	Date started or earliest known burial	Township	Range	Section

UNKNOWN

A 0.01 ? ?   T2N R17E   S20

Leave the town of Wasco on the road to Rufus. Drive 3.3 miles then turn left (northwesterly) onto Gerking Canyon Road. Drive another mile to a driveway on the left which is just short of a house in the canyon. This private driveway leads westerly up the bluff about 300 yards to the lone grave. (Rufus 1971 USGS Quad. map.)

UNKNOWN

A ? ? ?   T1S R17E   ?

There are 5 graves on the Powell Ranch (1970) due east of Moro. NOTE: This site is on private property. (Not shown on Moro 1971 USGS Quad. map.)

UNKNOWN

A ? ? ?   T1S R17E   S3

Said to be south of the Bonneville Power substation (1970), at De Moss Springs and due north of the John "Curly" De Moss home. It is probably farmed over. NOTE: This site is on private property. (Not shown on Wasco 1971-87 USGS Quad. map.)

UNKNOWN

A 0.01 5 1902   T4S R17E   S27

An unidentified man, described as being 5' 4" tall was struck and killed by a train 0.5 of a mile north of Kent. He was buried on the spot where he was killed. (Not shown on Kent 1970 USGS Quad. map.)

WASCO METHODIST
AKA: 1. EATON FAMILY
      2. WASCO [OLD]

C 3.12 3 1872   T2N R17E   S32

Located 2.5. miles northwest of Wasco and across the road from Sun Rise Cemetery, approximately 0.3 of a mile south of U.S. Hwy. 97. Take OR. Hwy. 206 west out of Wasco over U.S. Hwy. 97 and go 1.5 miles to the cemetery access road. Turn right (north) on Cemetery Road and go 1 mile. This was begun as an Eaton Family burial ground. This site was later made public, apparently in 1883. Fenced and gated, overgrown with tall grass and weeds. {1 September 2000} (Wasco 1971-87 USGS Quad. map.)

Name of Cemetery and also known as	Number of burials	Acres	Condition	Date started or earliest known burial	Township	Range	Section

WILCOX-OBSERVER   A   0.35   5   1898   **T5S**   **R17E**   **S10**

AKA: 1. KENT [OLD]
      2. OBSERVER
      3. OBSERVER FARM
      4. WILCOX

A private cemetery. 2.7 miles south of Kent on the east side of U.S. Hwy. 97, 200 feet off of the highway. There were 12 known burials and 12 to 15 unmarked burials (July 1965). D. C. Ireland, publisher of the *Moro Observer* newspaper, owned the land, and he referred to the cemetery as the Observer Cemetery. Wilcox was the name of the nearby railway stop. There are some reburials to the I.O.O.F. [Kent]. An 1891 burial from Wilcox-Observer was reburied at Kent, so an 1898 burial is now the earliest marker at Wilcox-Observer. (Kent 1970 USGS Quad. map.)

Sun Rise
Janice M. Healy (2000)

ALLEN CHILD	SHERMAN CO.	T1N	R18E	S7
AMERICAN LEGION see **CITY OF MORO**				
	SHERMAN CO.	T1S	R17E	S18
BAPTIST see **CITY OF MORO**	SHERMAN CO.	T1S	R17E	S18
BIGLOW see **EMIGRANT SPRINGS**	SHERMAN CO.	T2N	R18E	S34
BLACKBURNE	SHERMAN CO.	T2N	R16E	?
BLACKBURNE PROPERTY, GEORGE AND ALMA see **BLACKBURNE**				
	SHERMAN CO.	T2N	R16E	?
CITY OF MORO	SHERMAN CO.	T1S	R17E	S18
DAUGHERTY FAMILY	SHERMAN CO.	T5S	R17E	S12
De MOSS	SHERMAN CO.	T1S	R17E	S3
De MOSS, JOHN "CURLY" see **UNKNOWN**				
	SHERMAN CO.	T1S	R17E	S3
De MOSS SPRINGS see **De MOSS**	SHERMAN CO.	T1S	R17E	S3
EATON FAMILY see **WASCO METHODIST**				
	SHERMAN CO.	T2N	R17E	S32
EDWARDS CHILD	SHERMAN CO.	T3S	R16E	?
EDWARDS, LEROY see **EDWARDS CHILD**				
	SHERMAN CO.	T3S	R16E	?
EDWARDS, MARY JANE HELYER see **EDWARDS CHILD**				
	SHERMAN CO.	T3S	R16E	?
EMIGRANT SPRINGS	SHERMAN CO.	T2N	R18E	S34
GARLINGTON PLACE	SHERMAN CO.	T2N	R17E	?
GRASS VALLEY LODGE #131 I.O.O.F. see **I.O.O.F. [GRASS VALLEY]**				
	SHERMAN CO.	T2S	R16E	S22
HILDERBRAND, GORDON see **MORAN**	SHERMAN CO.	T2N	R16E	S22
HOGGARD CHILD	SHERMAN CO.	T2N	R16E	?
I.O.O.F. [GRASS VALLEY]	SHERMAN CO.	T2S	R16E	S22
I.O.O.F. [KENT]	SHERMAN CO.	T4S	R17E	S21
I.O.O.F. [MORO] see **CITY OF MORO**				
	SHERMAN CO.	T1S	R17E	S18
I.O.O.F. [WASCO] see **SUN RISE**	SHERMAN CO.	T2N	R17E	S31
IRELAND, D. C. see **WILCOX-OBSERVER**				
	SHERMAN CO.	T5S	R17E	S10
KENNY CHILDREN	SHERMAN CO.	T1S	R18E	S11
KENNY, WILLIAM see **KENNY CHILDREN**				
	SHERMAN CO.	T1S	R18E	S11
KENT [OLD] see **WILCOX-OBSERVER**	SHERMAN CO.	T5S	R17E	S10
MASIKER, GEORGE	SHERMAN CO.	T2N	R16E	S33
MASONIC [WASCO] see **SUN RISE**	SHERMAN CO.	T2N	R17E	S31
McCOY INFANT	SHERMAN CO.	T2N	R16E	S1
McDONALD, HARLAND see **McCOY INFANT**				
	SHERMAN CO.	T2N	R16E	S1
McNAB, PAT see **MORAN**	SHERMAN CO.	T2N	R16E	S22
MEDLER, L. C. see **GARLINGTON PLACE**				
	SHERMAN CO.	T2N	R17E	?
MICHIGAN	SHERMAN CO.	T3S	R16E	S16
MORAN	SHERMAN CO.	T2N	R16E	S22
OBSERVER see **WILCOX-OBSERVER**	SHERMAN CO.	T5S	R17E	S10
OBSERVER FARM see **WILCOX-OBSERVER**				
	SHERMAN CO.	T5S	R17E	S10
POWELL RANCH see **UNKNOWN**	SHERMAN CO.	T1S	R17E	?

RISING SUN see **SUN RISE**	SHERMAN CO.	T2N	R17E	S31
ROSE see **ROSE HILL**	SHERMAN CO.	T1S	R17E	S26
ROSE HILL	SHERMAN CO.	T1S	R17E	S26
ROSE, WILLIAM H. see **ROSE HILL**	SHERMAN CO.	T1S	R17E	S26
RUFUS	SHERMAN CO.	T2N	R17E	S6
SAND SPRING see **MASIKER, GEORGE**	SHERMAN CO.	T2N	R16E	S33
SAYRS CHILD	SHERMAN CO.	T1S	R16E	?
SAYRS, EMMA POWELL see **SAYRS CHILD**				
	SHERMAN CO.	T1S	R16E	?
SAYRS, FRANCIS see **SAYRS CHILD**	SHERMAN CO.	T1S	R16E	?
SAYRS HOMESTEAD see **SAYRS CHILD**	SHERMAN CO.	T1S	R16E	?
STRADLEY LAND see **EDWARDS CHILD**	SHERMAN CO.	T3S	R16E	?
SUN RISE	SHERMAN CO.	T2N	R17E	S31
TOM RANCH, ALLAN see **HOGGARD CHILD**				
	SHERMAN CO.	T2N	R16E	?
UNKNOWN	SHERMAN CO.	T2N	R17E	S20
UNKNOWN	SHERMAN CO.	T1S	R17E	?
UNKNOWN	SHERMAN CO.	T1S	R17E	S3
UNKNOWN	SHERMAN CO.	T4S	R17E	S27
WASCO see **SUN RISE**	SHERMAN CO.	T2N	R17E	S31
WASCO [NEW] see **SUN RISE**	SHERMAN CO.	T2N	R17E	S31
WASCO [OLD] see **WASCO METHODIST**	SHERMAN CO.	T2N	R17E	S32
WASCO METHODIST	SHERMAN CO.	T2N	R17E	S32
WEEDMAN FARM see **ALLEN CHILD**	SHERMAN CO.	T1N	R18E	S7
WILCOX see **WILCOX-OBSERVER**	SHERMAN CO.	T5S	R17E	S10
WILCOX-OBSERVER	SHERMAN CO.	T5S	R17E	S10

De Moss Springs
Janice M. Healy (2000)

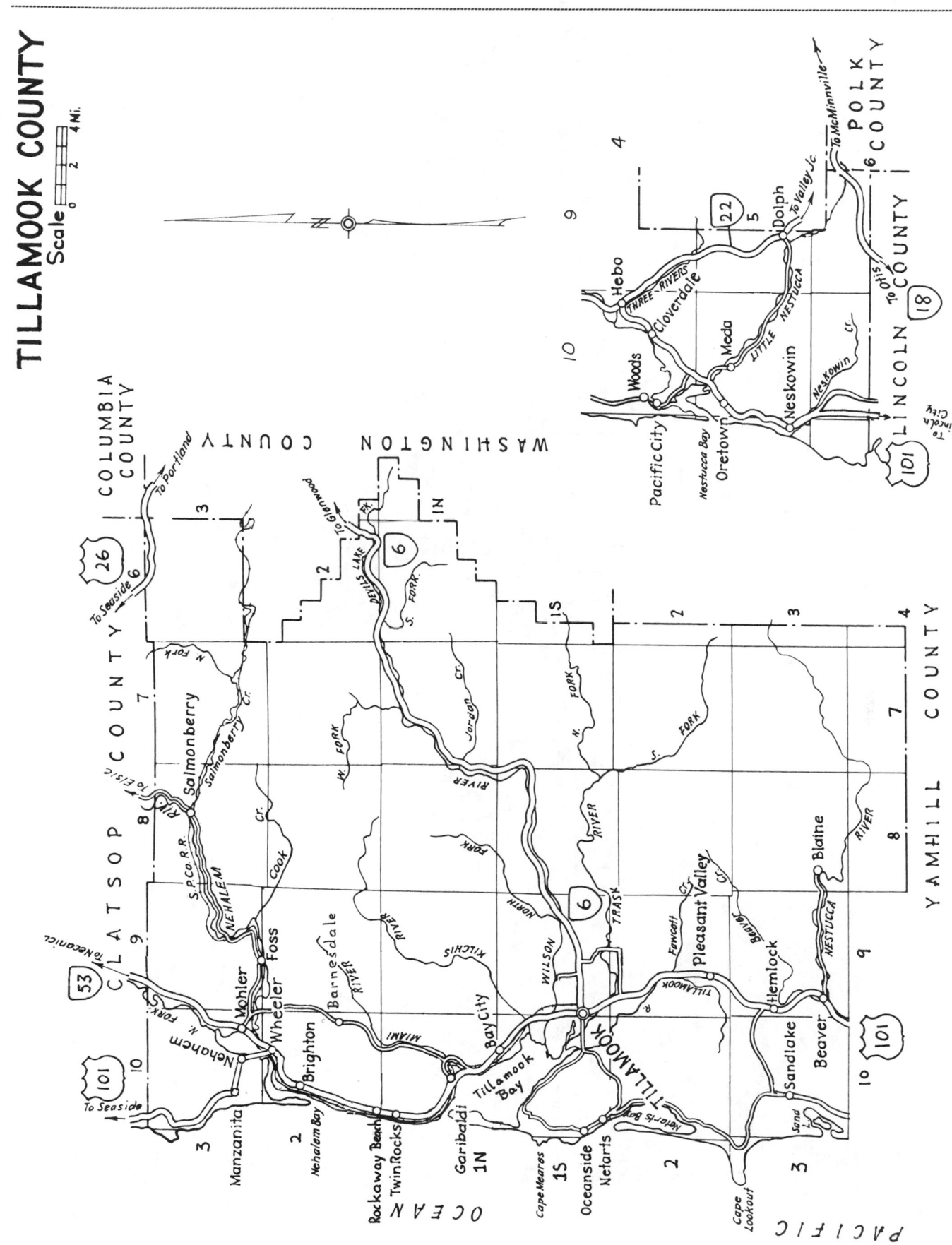

MATILDA C.
PENTER,
BORN
NOV. 15, 1820,
DIED
JAN. 21, 1900,
AGED 79 YEARS.

PENTER

Oretown
Dean H. Byrd (1994)

Area: 1,125 square miles
Population (1998): 24,356
County seat: Tillamook, Population: 4,275
County established: 15 December 1853

Tillamook County attracted settlers for fishing, dairying, and timber. The first organized public cemetery was reportedly the I.O.O.F. Cemetery at Bayview. Since the town was not founded until 1888 this seems a bit too early. Fairview (1861), Trout (1874) and the I.O.O.F. (1864) all near the town of Tillamook seem more likely as the earliest. There were many family burial sites.

Oretown
Dean H. Byrd (1994)

Tillamook County

Oretown

Dean H. Byrd (1994)

Oretown

Dean H. Byrd (1994)

Name of Cemetery and also known as	Number of burials	Acres	Condition	Date started or earliest known burial	Township	Range	Section

ALLEY FAMILY

A ? 3 1885 T3N R9W S18

Seven graves are located on OR. Hwy. 53, 3.6 miles north of Mohler on the John M. Alley Homestead. NOTE: This site is on private property owned by O. F. Knight (1965). (Not shown on Foley Peak or Soapstone Lake 1985 USGS Quad. maps.)

AMERICAN LEGION POST #126
AKA: 1. FRATERNAL UNION
2. KNIGHTS OF PYTHIAS [NEHALEM]
3. NEHALEM AMERICAN LEGION
4. NEHALEM V.F.W.

C 4.3 1 1900 T3N R10W S28

Located about 2 miles west of Nehalem on U.S. Hwy. 101. Turn left onto a side road and go 0.25 of a mile to the cemetery. (Nehalem 1985 USGS Quad. map.)

BAILEY AND MILLER
AKA: 1. MILLER

A ? 5 ? T1S R9W ?

Perhaps this is located in Section 34 or 35, 2 miles east of Tillamook on 3rd Street and then 2 miles south on Trask River Road. Near the Red Clover cheese factory (1965) are the burials: Bailey, mother and 2 babies; Miller, mother and baby. (Not shown on Tillamook 1985 USGS Quad. map.)

BARTNICK

A ? 5 1890 T1S R10W S18

Located near the summit of Cape Meares Loop Road where the road forks: one going to Cape Meares lighthouse; one going to the Tillamook River ferry; and one going to Netarts. At the Cook Place, now called Happy Camp there are 3 graves. (Not shown on Netarts 1986 USGS Quad. map.)

BATTERSON FAMILY

A ? 5 ? T3N R10W ?

This could be in Section 20. Three graves are located on the homestead of William Batterson of Neahkahnie. Later this was the Walter Cain Farm and in 1965 Robert Orcutt had the property. (Not shown on Nehalem 1985 USGS Quad. map.)

Tillamook County

Name of Cemetery and also known as	Number of burials	Acres	Condition	Date started or earliest known burial	Township	Range	Section

BEAVER

? 1 5 1884-1898 T3S R9W ?

The first cemetery for the community of Beaver, it was replaced in 1898 and most were reburied. (Not shown on Beaver 1985 USGS Quad. map.)

BEAVER CREEK
AKA: 1. FOLAND
2. UNITED BRETHREN

C 1 2 1898 T3S R9W S29

Located 16 miles south of Tillamook and 0.2 of a mile east of the community of Beaver; it is on the north (left) side of Blaine Road and 0.25 of a mile uphill. (Beaver 1985 USGS Quad. map.)

BLAINE

B 2 2 1884 T3S R8W S30

This is on the north side of Blaine Road approximately 6.3 miles east of Beaver, on the hill behind the church. (Blaine 1984 USGS Quad. map.)

BOYER FAMILY

? ? ? ? T6S R9W ?

Perhaps located in Section 12, there was no other information given in the report. Boyer was a small locale very near the Polk County Line on the Little Nestucca River. The present-day OR. Hwy. 18 traverses this segment between Grand Ronde and Otis. (Not shown on Midway 1979 USGS Quad. map.)

BROWNING

A 0.01 ? ? T4S R8W S3

One grave is located 4.3 miles above Blaine on the south side of the Nestucca River near the Browning Bridge; turn right (southerly) onto Powder Creek Road which crosses the Nestucca River. (Not shown on Blaine 1984 USGS Quad. map.)

CAPE LOOKOUT

A ? ? 2 Aug 1943 T3S R11W S1

During World War II a B-17 bomber crashed into the side of Cape Lookout, killing 9 of the 10 crew members. A formation of 6 aircraft had left Pendleton Army Air Base bound for Cape Disappointment on a training mission. Lieutenant Wilbur L. Perez, the survivor, had to wait 30 hours before being rescued. There is a bronze plaque by the

Name of Cemetery and also known as	Number of burials	Acres	Condition	Date started or earliest known burial	Township	Range	Section

side of the trail on the south side of the cape. The plaque, misdated to 1 August, is about 0.5 of a mile from the parking lot at the summit of the cape. The crash site itself was about 500 feet farther towards the tip of the cape from the plaque. *Oregon Coast Magazine*. Nov.-Dec. 1990. (Not shown on Sand Lake 1985 USGS Quad. map.)

CHAMBERLAIN FAMILY
AKA: 1. CAMP
MERIWETHER
2. SCOUT CAMP

A 0.01 1 1898   T3S R10W   S7
These burials are on the grounds of Camp Meriwether, owned by the Columbia Pacific Council, Boy Scouts of America. The camp was the homestead of Ezra B. Chamberlain who took up the homestead in 1886. This is the burial site of members of the Chamberlain family and is maintained by the Boy Scouts. NOTE: This site is on private property and permission must be obtained from the Boy Scouts to visit the site. (Camp Meriwether is shown on Sand Lake 1985 USGS Quad. map.)

CHATWOOD BABIES

A 0.01 5 ?   ? ?   ?
Three Chatwood baby burials are located on the Chatwood Place, in south Tillamook County.

CLEMENTS
AKA: 1. CLEMENTS
CORNER

A ? ? 1872   T2S R9W   S16
Located 6 miles south of Tillamook at the 3-way intersection of South Prairie Road with Brickyard and Clements Roads. Leave U.S. Hwy. 101 at Milepost 69.6 onto South Prairie Road and then drive 1.6 miles to the Clements Road junction. On the Leonard Killam D.L.C. #38, OC #5010. (Not shown on Tillamook 1985 USGS Quad. map.)

CONNELL

A 0.01 5 ?   T4S R7W   ?
Perhaps in Section 17, 3 miles southeast of the mouth of Testament Creek Junction on Bible Creek Road is a baby's grave. If it is located in Section 21, this would be in Yamhill County. (Not shown on Springer Mountain 1979 USGS Quad. map.)

Tillamook County

Name of Cemetery and also known as	Number of burials	Acres	Condition	Date started or earliest known burial	Township	Range	Section

DOLPH

| | ? | ? | ? | ? | T5S | R9W | S28 |

The locale of Dolph is in Tillamook County at the junction of Three Rivers Highway (OR. Hwy. 22) and the Little Nestucca Highway. However, the Dolph Cemetery is in Yamhill County. See the entry in the Yamhill County listing. (The Dolph area is shown on the Dolph 1985 USGS Quad. map, but not the cemetery.)

DOUGHERTY, LYDIA

| | A | 0.01 | ? | 1858 | T1S | R9W | ? |

This could be in Sections 21 or 28. Located 2.5 miles east of Tillamook and 0.25 mile north off of OR. Hwy. 6 (Wilson River Highway) on the right (east) side of Olsen Road. Joe Maxwell owned this land in 1965; on the Nathan Dougherty D.L.C. #41, OC #3302. (Not shown on Tillamook 1985 USGS Quad. map.)

EARL

| | A | ? | 3 | ? | T2S | R9W | S4 |

Located 4 miles southeast of Tillamook on Long Prairie Road and just north of the wartime Blimp Base on the Earl Farm. It is near Earl Bridge at Milepost 1.4 on Long Prairie Road. (Not shown on Tillamook 1985 USGS Quad. map.)

EHLSON
 AKA: 1. ELLISON

| | A | ? | ? | 1892 | T3S | R9W | ? |

Located along the Nestucca River near the community of Beaver. (Not shown on Beaver 1985 USGS Quad. map.)

FAWCETT

| | A | ? | ? | ? | T2S | R9W | ? |

This could be in Section 21. Three grave are near the junction of U.S. Hwy. 101 and South Prairie Road at Pleasant Valley, south of Tillamook. (Not shown on Tillamook 1985 USGS Quad. map.)

FISHER BABY

| | A | 0.01 | 5 | ? | ? | ? | ? |

The Fisher baby burial is at the west corner of Shipper Place (1978) on the south side of the road.

Name of Cemetery and also known as	Number of burials	Acres	Condition	Date started or earliest known burial	Township	Range	Section

GIST

B 0.7 2 1887   T4S R10W   S21
Located off of Old Woods Road, which goes on the north side of the Nestucca River, about 2.5 miles northwest of Cloverdale and on the right (north) side of the road. (Nestucca Bay 1985 USGS Quad. map.)

HATCH FAMILY

A 0.01 ? ?   T1N R10W   ?
This could be in Section 22 or Section 23? It is 1 mile east of Garibaldi and 1 mile south across the Miami River on the Winejo Farm (1978). There are 2 family graves. NOTE: This site is on private property. (Not shown on Garibaldi 1985 USGS Quad. map.)

HODGDON

A 0.01 ? 1881   T1S R10W   S32
One known grave overlooks Hodgdon Creek at Netarts in the section where Pearl Street was extended to the Netarts Highway. (Not shown on Netarts 1986 USGS Quad. map.)

HUTCHINS

A 0.01 5 ?   ? ?   ?
Two graves are located 0.75 of a mile west from the Nestucca River on Chris Gableman's place. NOTE: This site is on private property.

I.O.O.F. [BAY CITY]
AKA: 1. KILCHIS
     2. PACIFIC LODGE #105

C 5.1 1 1856   T1S R10W   S1
Travel on Alderbrook Loop Road at the south end of Bay City 1.3 miles southeast of U.S. Hwy. 101 and then left (north) on Doughty Road for 0.15 of a mile. It is on the Hiram and Sarah Jane Smith D.L.C. #37, OC #5165. (Kilchis River 1985 USGS Quad. map.)

I.O.O.F. [TILLAMOOK]
AKA: 1. TILLAMOOK I.O.O.F.
     2. TILLAMOOK ODD FELLOWS

D 10 1 1864   T1S R9W   S29
Located on the north side of East 3rd Street in Tillamook, about 1.5 miles east of downtown: on the John S. Tripp D.L.C. #42 OC #2827. (Tillamook 1985 USGS Quad. map.)

I.O.O.F. [WOODS]
AKA: 1. LAKEVIEW
     2. WOODS

A 0.4 ? 1889   T4S R10W   S18
This cemetery is 0.75 of a mile north of the Nestucca Bridge at the locale of Woods, then

Name of Cemetery and also known as	Number of burials	Acres	Condition	Date started or earliest known burial	Township	Range	Section

0.2 of a mile right (east) to the cemetery on the heights above Town Lake. (Nestucca Bay 1985 USGS Quad. map.)

INDIAN [#1]

| | ? | ? | 5 | ? | T1N | R10W | ? |

This could be in Section 27, across Tillamook Bay from Garibaldi is the site of Squaw Town, later called Hobsonville. (Not shown on Garibaldi 1985 USGS Quad. map.)

INDIAN [#2]

| | ? | ? | 5 | ? | T1S | R10W | ? |

Possibly in Township 1 South or Township 2 South. Located about halfway between Netarts and Bayocean Junction, on the west side of the road. (Not shown on Netarts 1986 USGS Quad. map.)

JENCK
AKA: 1. CLOVERDALE
CATHOLIC
2. ST. JOSEPH
3. ST. MARY'S

| | A | 6 | 5 | 1895 | T4S | R10W | S34 |

Located on the Peter Jenck Homestead, established in 1888, about a mile south of Cloverdale, along Clear Creek. The old burial grounds would be along Jenck Road, the old alignment of U.S. Hwy. 101. Six acres of land were sold to the Archdiocese of Portland in Oregon, in September of 1895 for a Catholic cemetery, but nowhere near that acreage was ever so used. A Jenck and 5 Belleques were known to have been buried; all were removed to Sacred Heart Cemetery sometime between 1946 and 1949. In addition, Anthony and Elizabeth Knoblock, originally buried here, were reburied in Cloverdale Union Cemetery. (Not shown on Nestucca Bay 1985 USGS Quad. map.)

LOCKWOOD

| | A | 0.01 | ? | 1881 & 1924 | T1S | R10W | S31 |

Two known graves overlooking Netarts Bay are above what is now known as Happy Camp. (Not shown on Netarts 1986 USGS Quad. map.)

LOVELL FAMILY

| | A | 0.01 | 5 | 1898 | T3N | R10W | S29 |

In Manzanita are 2 graves of the Lovell family. (Not shown on Nehalem 1985 USGS Quad. map.)

Name of Cemetery and also known as	Number of burials	Acres	Condition	Date started or earliest known burial	Township	Range	Section

LUDTKE FAMILY

A ? 5 1915   T3N R10W   S13
Located in the southeast 1/4 of Section 13, on OR. Hwy. 53 about 2.8 miles from Mohler, at the mouth of the North Fork of the Nehalem River. There are 3 graves on the August Ludtke Homestead which was owned by Andrew Lagler in 1965. (Not shown on Foley Peak 1985 USGS Quad. map.)

McCORMAC

A 0.01 5 1889   T2S R10W   S8
Four graves are located 1.5 miles south of the Netarts boat basin on the back of the Braden Ranch (1978). (Not shown on Netarts 1986 USGS Quad. map.)

McCOWELL

A ? 5 1907   T2S R10W   S6
Located in block 17, lot 5 of the Netarts Bay Park addition. (Not shown on Netarts 1986 USGS Quad. map.)

MOORE

A ? 5 ?   T1S R10W   S5
Located near the intersection of Leonard Street and Bishop Avenue at Netarts. (Not shown on Netarts 1986 USGS Quad. map.)

MUNSON

A 0.01 5 ?   T2S R9W   ?
One grave is located south of Pleasant Valley, south of Tillamook near Basil Tone's house. (Not shown on Beaver 1985 USGS Quad. map.)

NESTUCCA VETERANS OF FOREIGN WARS-ODD FELLOWS
AKA: 1. I.O.O.F. CLOVERDALE
2. I.O.O.F. HEBO
3. NESTUCCA VALLEY
4. NESTUCCA V.F.W.-I.O.O.F.

C 2 2 1889   T4S R10W   S14
Located on the east side of U.S. Hwy. 101, 0.65 of a mile west of Hebo, 21 miles south of Tillamook and 1.8 miles north of Cloverdale. In Dec. 1982, the sign said "Nestucca Valley." (Hebo 1985 USGS Quad. map.)

Name of Cemetery and also known as	Number of burials	Acres	Condition	Date started or earliest known burial	Township	Range	Section

O'HARA FAMILY

A ? ? 1898 T2S R10W S5

Located approximately in the Rice Creek area on the O'Hara Homestead. (Not shown on Netarts 1986 USGS Quad. map.)

ORETOWN

C 1.6 2 1876 T5S R10W S7

Leave U.S. Hwy. 101 at Milepost 93 onto the old highway alignment now called Oretown Road. On the east side of Oretown Road you will see the Oretown Bible Church. Take the one-lane gravel road past the church and up the hill 0.25 of a mile to the cemetery. There were 163 known burials in August, 1956. {31 May 1994} (Nestucca Bay 1985 USGS Quad. map.)

PERRY

A 0.01 5 ? T1S R8W S1

One grave is located near Fox Creek, by the Wilson River, 13 miles east of Tillamook. The Fox Creek Bridge is at Milepost 14.5 on OR. Hwy. 6. (Not shown on Jordan Creek 1984 USGS Quad. map.)

QUICK

A ? 5 1876-1898 T2S R9W S16

This was located on the west side of South Prairie Road. Five graves were on the Isaac Quick Farm; these have been removed to the Tillamook I.O.O.F. Cemetery. NOTE: The origional burial site is on private property. (Not shown on Tillamook 1985 USGS Quad. map.)

RENEKE

A 0.01 5 ? T3S R10W S31

One grave is located on the Beltz Farm (1978) at the south end of Sand Lake. NOTE: This site is on private property. (Not shown on Sand Lake 1985 USGS Quad. map.)

ROOT

A 0.01 5 1920'S T1S R11W S25

One grave is located, at Oceanside approximately across from the community hall. (Not shown on Netarts 1986 USGS Quad. map.)

Name of Cemetery and also known as	Number of burials	Acres	Condition	Date started or earliest known burial	Township	Range	Section

SACRED HEART   C 2   1   1903   T2S   R9W   S5

Leave Tillamook and go south on U.S. Hwy 101 to the junction with Long Prairie Road at Highway Milepost 68.2. Turn left (east) onto Long Prairie Road, drive 1.1 miles to Blimp Boulevard on the right (south) and turn into the old World War II Air Base. Go 0.3 of a mile on Blimp Boulevard and then turn right onto Hangar "B" Road. Drive another 0.15 of a mile, where there is a driveway to the right which leads another 0.25 of a mile to the cemetery. (Tillamook 1985 USGS Quad. map)

SAND LAKE   A   ?   5   ?   T3S   R10W   S17
    AKA: 1. SANDLAKE

Ten known graves are on a hill across from Sand Lake cheese factory (1978). (Not shown on Sand Lake 1985 USGS Quad. map.)

SCHWALNUS FAMILY   A   0.01   5   ?   T3N   R10W   ?

Possibly on Section 1 or 12, on the west side of the North Fork of the Nehalem River, across Market Road from the bridge. There is one grave on the Herman Schollmeyer Farm, now the J. H. Churchill Farm (1965). NOTE: This site is on private property. (Not shown on Soapstone Lake 1985 USGS Quad. map.)

SCOVELL FAMILY   A   ?   5   1889   T3N   R9W   ?

Probably located in Section 6, on OR. Hwy. 53, 5 miles north of Mohler near Three Forks. Five graves are on the James Gray Homestead, now owned by Clifford Scovell (1965). NOTE: This site is on private property. (Not shown on Soapstone Lake 1985 USGS Quad. map.)

SMITH, HIRAM WESLEY   A   0.01   5   28 Nov 1876   T1S   R10W   ?

This could be on Section 1 or 2. On a hill near the Alderbrook Golf Course, west of Bay City I.O.O.F. Cemetery. There are 2 graves on the Hiram Wesley and Sarah Jane Smith D.L.C. #37, OC #5165. (Not shown on Kilchis River 1985 USGS Quad. map.)

Name of Cemetery and also known as	Number of burials	Acres	Condition	Date started or earliest known burial	Township	Range	Section

SNYDER FAMILY A 0.01 5 ? T3N R10W ?

A lone grave is located on U.S. Hwy. 101 east of Manzanita. NOTE: This site is on private property. (Not shown on the Nehalem 1985 USGS Quad. map.)

STRETOFF A ? 5 ? T2S R9W ?

Located 0.5 of a mile south of Long Prairie Road, it is on the old Air Base, 3 miles south of Tillamook on the Earl Homestead (1978). NOTE: This site is on private property. (Not shown on Tillamook 1985 USGS Quad. map.)

SUNSET HEIGHTS MEMORIAL GARDENS C 9.77 1 1941 T1S R9W S28

This is located in Sections 28 and 33. Go 3 miles east of downtown Tillamook on East 3rd Street to Fairview. Turn right (south) onto Trask River Road and go 0.75 of a mile to the cemetery entrance on the left. It is on the Elbridge Trask D.L.C. #37 OC #3926. (Tillamook 1985 USGS Quad. map.)

SUTTON A ? 5 1871 T4S R10W S22

Located on Hill Road at the south edge of Cloverdale. (Not shown on Nestucca Bay Quad. 1985 USGS map.)

TESTAMENT CREEK A 0.01 ? After 1918 T4S R7W S5

Located in the southwest 1/4 of the southeast 1/4 of Section 5. Testament Creek is a tributary to the right (east) bank of Bible Creek which in turn empties into the left (south) bank of the Nestucca River, upstream from Blaine. An article in the *McMinnville News-Register*, 8 August 1965, has a lengthy piece about some lost cinnabar mines. It mentions that on Martin Loban's Homestead (taken up in 1918) are two unmarked graves. One is reportedly a Loban relative, the other a son of Jim Hutchens. The graves are reported "not far from the Loban Homestead." (Not shown on Springer Mtn. 1979 USGS Quad. map.)

806

Name of Cemetery and also known as	Number of burials	Acres	Condition	Date started or earliest known burial	Township	Range	Section

TONE FAMILY

A ? 5 1890   T2S R10W   S3

There was a private family cemetery on the James Tone Homestead in the hills southeast of Netarts. This was about a mile northwest of the present end of Ekloff Road and in the vicinity of an important Crown-Zellerbach logging road. Two infants and 2 adults were known to have been buried; the remains were removed to Sacred Heart Cemetery sometime after 1903. NOTE: This site is on private property. (Not shown on Netarts 1986 USGS Quad. map.)

TRASK PIONEER
AKA: 1. FAIRVIEW
     2. JOHNSON HILL
     3. JOHNSON'S
     4. PIONEER
     5. TRASK

C 1 2 1861   T1S R9W   S27

Located 3 miles east of Tillamook and 0.6 of a mile south on Trask River Road. Turn left (east) off Trask River Road onto Greentree Ridge Road and go 0.4 of a mile to the cemetery; on the Elbridge Trask D.L.C. #37, OC #3926. (Tillamook 1985 USGS Quad. map)

TROUT
AKA: 1. CHAMPION, JOE
     2. HAUXHURST, WEBLEY
     3. HAYNES
     4. PIONEER MEMORIAL PARK

C 0.15 4 1874-1913   T1S R9W   S30

The cemetery is reached by following OR. Hwy. 6 from its junction with U.S. Hwy. 101 in Tillamook; go east 0.75 of a mile and turn left (north) off of OR. Hwy. 6 onto Evergreen Drive North and go 0.13 of a mile. It was described as the first Tillamook cemetery in a 30 May 1938 article in the *Tillamook Headlight Herald*. It was then dedicated as the Pioneer Memorial Park and deeded to the county by the heirs of the Trout family. The Webley Hauxhurst 1874 burial is within the Trout Cemetery. There was estimated to be 300 burials through the 1890's and about 50 stones were left in 1965. This cemetery has been desecrated. It is on the Charles Haynes D.L.C. #43 OC #4160. {September 1991} (Tillamook 1985 USGS Quad. map.)

UNION PIONEER [CLOVERDALE]
AKA: 1. CLOVERDALE BAPTIST

B 1.5 ? 1913   T4S R10W   S33

Drive about 2.6 miles south of Cloverdale on U.S. Hwy. 101. At the church, turn left (east) off of U.S. Hwy. 101 at Milepost 90.2

Name of Cemetery and also known as	Number of burials	Acres	Condition	Date started or earliest known burial	Township	Range	Section

2. CLOVERDALE
   UNION

and onto Hudson Road. Go about 0.1 of a mile to the cemetery. (Nestucca Bay 1985 USGS Quad. map.)

UNKNOWN

| | A | 0.01 | 5 | ? | T3N | R10W | S14 |

Two graves are located on the west side of the North Fork of the Nehalem River, along Anderson Creek, on land homesteaded by Rob Crawford and now owned by Theresa Henderson (1965). (Not shown on Foley Peak 1985 USGS Quad. map.)

UNKNOWN

| | A | 0.01 | 5 | ? | T1S | R10W | S36 |

One grave is located 0.5 of a mile south of Tillamook on Tillamook River Road, then 1 mile west on Matejeck Road. (Not shown on Tillamook 1985 USGS Quad. map.)

WALKER

| | A | ? | 5 | 1887 | T3S | R9W | S26 |

Located 4 miles east of Beaver, on the Beaver-Blaine Road at Boulder Creek at the foot of the hill near an orchard (1978). (Not shown on Beaver 1985 or Blaine 1984 USGS Quad. maps.)

WAUD'S FUNERAL HOME

| | ? | 0.1 | 1 | ? | T1S | R9W | ? |

Located at 1414 3rd Street, Tillamook, Oregon 97141-3408. The funeral home also has niches for inurnments. (Not shown on Tillamook 1985 USGS Quad. map.)

WELLS

| | A | ? | ? | 1897 | T1S | R8W | ? |

This could be in Section 22 or 23? Located 15 miles northeast of Tillamook on the north side of the Trask River, on the left side of the road. This was moved to Tillamook I.O.O.F. (Not shown on The Peninsula 1984 USGS Quad. map.)

WHITE

| | A | ? | 5 | ? | T1S | R9W | ? |

Possibly in Section 33 or 34? Located 2 miles east on 3rd Street in Tillamook and 1 mile south on McCormick Loop Road. (Not shown on Tillamook 1985 USGS Quad. map.)

ALLEY FAMILY	TILLAMOOK CO.	T3N	R9W	S18
ALLEY HOMESTEAD, JOHN M. see **ALLEY FAMILY**				
	TILLAMOOK CO.	T3N	R9W	S18
AMERICAN LEGION POST #126	TILLAMOOK CO.	T3N	R10W	S28
BAILEY AND MILLER	TILLAMOOK CO.	T1S	R9W	?
BARTNICK	TILLAMOOK CO.	T1S	R10W	S18
BATTERSON FAMILY	TILLAMOOK CO.	T3N	R10W	?
BATTERSON, WILLIAM see **BATTERSON FAMILY**				
	TILLAMOOK CO.	T3N	R10W	?
BEAVER	TILLAMOOK CO.	T3S	R9W	?
BEAVER CREEK	TILLAMOOK CO.	T3S	R9W	S29
BELLEQUES see **JENCK**	TILLAMOOK CO.	T4S	R10W	S34
BELTZ FARM see **RENEKE**	TILLAMOOK CO.	T3S	R10W	S31
BLAINE	TILLAMOOK CO.	T3S	R8W	S30
BOYER FAMILY	TILLAMOOK CO.	T6S	R9W	?
BRADEN RANCH see **McCORMAC**	TILLAMOOK CO.	T2S	R10W	S8
BROWNING	TILLAMOOK CO.	T4S	R8W	S3
CAIN FARM, WALTER see **BATTERSON FAMILY**				
	TILLAMOOK CO.	T3N	R10W	?
CAMP MERIWETHER see **CHAMBERLAIN FAMILY**				
	TILLAMOOK CO.	T3S	R10W	S7
CAPE LOOKOUT	TILLAMOOK CO.	T3S	R11W	S1
CHAMBERLAIN FAMILY	TILLAMOOK CO.	T3S	R10W	S7
CHAMBERLAIN HOMESTEAD, EZRA B. see **CHAMBERLAIN FAMILY**				
	TILLAMOOK CO.	T3S	R10W	S7
CHAMPION, JOE see **TROUT**	TILLAMOOK CO.	T1S	R9W	S30
CHATWOOD BABIES	TILLAMOOK CO.	?	?	?
CHATWOOD PLACE see **CHATWOOD BABIES**				
	TILLAMOOK CO.	?	?	?
CHURCHILL FARM, J. H. see **SCHWALNUS FAMILY**				
	TILLAMOOK CO.	T3N	R10W	?
CLEMENTS	TILLAMOOK CO.	T2S	R9W	S16
CLEMENTS CORNER see **CLEMENTS**	TILLAMOOK CO.	T2S	R9W	S16
CLOVERDALE BAPTIST see **UNION PIONEER [CLOVERDALE]**				
	TILLAMOOK CO.	T4S	R10W	S33
CLOVERDALE CATHOLIC see **JENCK**	TILLAMOOK CO.	T4S	R10W	S34
CLOVERDALE UNION see **UNION PIONEER [CLOVERDALE]**				
	TILLAMOOK CO.	T4S	R10W	S33
CONNELL	TILLAMOOK CO.	T4S	R7W	?
COOK PLACE see **BARTNICK**	TILLAMOOK CO.	T1S	R10W	S18
CRAWFORD HOMESTEAD, ROB see **UNKNOWN**				
	TILLAMOOK CO.	T3N	R10W	S14
DOLPH	TILLAMOOK CO.	T5S	R9W	S28
DOUGHERTY D.L.C., NATHAN see **DOUGHERTY, LYDIA**				
	TILLAMOOK CO.	T1S	R9W	?
DOUGHERTY, LYDIA	TILLAMOOK CO.	T1S	R9W	?
EARL	TILLAMOOK CO.	T2S	R9W	S4
EARL FARM see **EARL**	TILLAMOOK CO.	T2S	R9W	S4
EHLSON	TILLAMOOK CO.	T3S	R9W	?
ELLISON see **EHLSON**	TILLAMOOK CO.	T3S	R9W	?
FAIRVIEW see **TRASK PIONEER**	TILLAMOOK CO.	T1S	R9W	S27
FAWCETT	TILLAMOOK CO.	T2S	R9W	?

FISHER BABY	TILLAMOOK CO.	?	?	?
FOLAND see **BEAVER CREEK**	TILLAMOOK CO.	T3S	R9W	S29
FRATERNAL UNION see **AMERICAN LEGION POST #126**				
	TILLAMOOK CO.	T3N	R10W	S28
GABLEMAN, CHRIS see **HUTCHINS**	TILLAMOOK CO.	?	?	?
GIST	TILLAMOOK CO.	T4S	R10W	S21
GRAY HOMESTEAD, JAMES see **SCOVELL FAMILY**				
	TILLAMOOK CO.	T3N	R9W	?
HATCH FAMILY	TILLAMOOK CO.	T1N	R10W	?
HAUXHURST, WEBLEY see **TROUT**	TILLAMOOK CO.	T1S	R9W	S30
HAYNES see **TROUT**	TILLAMOOK CO.	T1S	R9W	S30
HAYNES D.L.C., CHARLES see **TROUT**				
	TILLAMOOK CO.	T1S	R9W	S30
HENDERSON, THERESA see **UNKNOWN**	TILLAMOOK CO.	T3N	R10W	S14
HODGDON	TILLAMOOK CO.	T1S	R10W	S32
HUTCHINS	TILLAMOOK CO.	?	?	?
HUTCHINS, JIM see **TESTAMENT CREEK**				
	TILLAMOOK CO.	T4S	R7W	S5
I.O.O.F. [BAY CITY]	TILLAMOOK CO.	T1S	R10W	S1
I.O.O.F. [TILLAMOOK]	TILLAMOOK CO.	T1S	R9W	S29
I.O.O.F. [WOODS]	TILLAMOOK CO.	T4S	R10W	S18
I.O.O.F. CLOVERDALE see **NESTUCCA VETERANS OF FOREIGN WARS-ODD FELLOWS**				
	TILLAMOOK CO.	T4S	R10W	S14
I.O.O.F. HEBO see **NESTUCCA VETERANS OF FOREIGN WARS-ODD FELLOWS**				
	TILLAMOOK CO.	T4S	R10W	S14
INDIAN [#1]	TILLAMOOK CO.	T1N	R10W	?
INDIAN [#2]	TILLAMOOK CO.	T1S	R10W	?
JENCK	TILLAMOOK CO.	T4S	R10W	S34
JENCK HOMESTEAD, PETER see **JENCK**				
	TILLAMOOK CO.	T4S	R10W	S34
JOHNSON HILL see **TRASK PIONEER**	TILLAMOOK CO.	T1S	R9W	S27
JOHNSON'S see **TRASK PIONEER**	TILLAMOOK CO.	T1S	R9W	S27
KILCHIS see **I.O.O.F. [BAY CITY]**	TILLAMOOK CO.	T1S	R10W	S1
KILLAM D.L.C., LEONARD see **CLEMENTS**				
	TILLAMOOK CO.	T2S	R9W	S16
KNIGHT, O. F. see **ALLEY FAMILY**	TILLAMOOK CO.	T3N	R9W	S18
KNIGHTS OF PYTHIAS [NEHALEM] see **AMERICAN LEGION POST #126**				
	TILLAMOOK CO.	T3N	R10W	S28
KNOBLOCK, ANTHONY see **JENCK**	TILLAMOOK CO.	T4S	R10W	S34
KNOBLOCK ELIZABETH see **JENCK**	TILLAMOOK CO.	T4S	R10W	S34
LAGLER, ANDREW see **LUDTKE FAMILY**				
	TILLAMOOK CO.	T3N	R10W	S13
LAKEVIEW see **I.O.O.F. [WOODS]**	TILLAMOOK CO.	T4S	R10W	S18
LIDTKE HOMESTEAD, AUGUST see **LUDTKE FAMILY**				
	TILLAMOOK CO.	T3N	R10W	S13
LOBAN HOMESTEAD, MARTIN see **TESTAMENT CREEK**				
	TILLAMOOK CO.	T4S	R7W	S5
LOCKWOOD	TILLAMOOK CO.	T1S	R10W	S31
LOVELL FAMILY	TILLAMOOK CO.	T3N	R10W	S29
LUDTKE FAMILY	TILLAMOOK CO.	T3N	R10W	S13
MAXWELL, JOE see **DOUGHERTY, LYDIA**				
	TILLAMOOK CO.	T1S	R9W	?

McCORMAC	TILLAMOOK CO.	T2S	R10W	S8
McCOWELL	TILLAMOOK CO.	T2S	R10W	S6
MILLER see **BAILEY AND MILLER**	TILLAMOOK CO.	T1S	R9W	?
MOORE	TILLAMOOK CO.	T1S	R10W	S5
MUNSON	TILLAMOOK CO.	T2S	R9W	?
NEHALEM AMERICAN LEGION see **AMERICAN LEGION POST #126**				
	TILLAMOOK CO.	T3N	R10W	S28
NEHALEM V. F. W. see **AMERICAN LEGION POST #126**				
	TILLAMOOK CO.	T3N	R10W	S28
NESTUCCA VALLEY see **NESTUCCA VETERANS OF FOREIGN WARS-ODD FELLOWS**				
	TILLAMOOK CO.	T4S	R10W	S14
NESTUCCCA V.F.W.-I.O.O.F. see **NESTUCCA VETERANS OF FOREIGN WARS-ODD FELLOWS**	TILLAMOOK CO.	T4S	R10W	S14
NESTUCCA VETERANS OF FOREIGN WARS-ODD FELLOWS				
	TILLAMOOK CO.	T4S	R10W	S14
O'HARA FAMILY	TILLAMOOK CO.	T2S	R10W	S5
O'HARA HOMESTEAD see **O'HARA FAMILY**				
	TILLAMOOK CO.	T2S	R10W	S5
ORCUTT, ROBERT see **BATTERSON FAMILY**				
	TILLAMOOK CO.	T3N	R10W	?
ORETOWN	TILLAMOOK CO.	T5S	R10W	S7
PACIFIC LODGE #105 see **I.O.O.F. [BAY CITY]**				
	TILLAMOOK CO.	T1S	R10W	S1
PEREZ, LIEUTENANT WILBUR L. see **CAPE LOOKOUT**				
	TILLAMOOK CO.	T3S	R11W	S1
PERRY	TILLAMOOK CO.	T1S	R8W	S1
PIONEER see **TRASK PIONEER**	TILLAMOOK CO.	T1S	R9W	S27
PIONEER MEMORIAL PARK see **TROUT**	TILLAMOOK CO.	T1S	R9W	S30
QUICK	TILLAMOOK CO.	T2S	R9W	S16
QUICK FARM, ISAAC see **QUICK**	TILLAMOOK CO.	T2S	R9W	S16
RENEKE	TILLAMOOK CO.	T3S	R10W	S31
ROOT	TILLAMOOK CO.	T1S	R11W	S25
SACRED HEART	TILLAMOOK CO.	T2S	R9W	S5
ST. JOSEPH see **JENCK**	TILLAMOOK CO.	T4S	R10W	S34
ST. MARY'S see **JENCK**	TILLAMOOK CO.	T4S	R10W	S34
SAND LAKE	TILLAMOOK CO.	T3S	R10W	S17
SANDLAKE see **SAND LAKE**	TILLAMOOK CO.	T3S	R10W	S17
SCHOLLMEYER FARM, HERMAN see **SCHWALNUS FAMILY**				
	TILLAMOOK CO.	T3N	R10W	?
SCHWALNUS FAMILY	TILLAMOOK CO.	T3N	R10W	?
SCOUT CAMP see **CHAMBERLAIN FAMILY**				
	TILLAMOOK CO.	T3S	R10W	S7
SCOVELL, CLIFFORD see **SCOVELL FAMILY**				
	TILLAMOOK CO.	T3N	R9W	?
SCOVELL FAMILY	TILLAMOOK CO.	T3N	R9W	?
SHIPPER PLACE see **FISHER BABY**	TILLAMOOK CO.	?	?	?
SMITH D.L.C., HIRAM AND SARA JANE see **I.O.O.F. [BAY CITY]**				
	TILLAMOOK CO.	T1S	R10W	S1
SMITH D.L.C., HIRAM AND SARA JANE see **SMITH, HIRAM WESLEY**				
	TILLAMOOK CO.	T1S	R10W	?
SMITH, HIRAM WESLEY	TILLAMOOK CO.	T1S	R10W	?
SNYDER FAMILY	TILLAMOOK CO.	T3N	R10W	?

STRETOFF	TILLAMOOK CO.	T2S	R9W	?
SUNSET HEIGHTS MEMORIAL GARDENS	TILLAMOOK CO.	T1S	R9W	S28
SUTTON	TILLAMOOK CO.	T4S	R10W	S22
TESTAMENT CREEK	TILLAMOOK CO.	T4S	R7W	S5
TILLAMOOK I.O.O.F. see **I.O.O.F. [TILLAMOOK]**				
	TILLAMOOK CO.	T1S	R9W	S29
TILLAMOOK ODD FELLOWS see **I.O.O.F. [TILLAMOOK]**				
	TILLAMOOK CO.	T1S	R9W	S29
TONE'S HOUSE, BASIL see **MUNSON**	TILLAMOOK CO.	T2S	R9W	?
TRASK D.L.C., ELBRIDGE see **SUNSET HEIGHTS MEMORIAL GARDENS**				
	TILLAMOOK CO.	T1S	R9W	S28
TRIPP D.L.C., JOHN S. see **I.O.O.F. [TILLAMOOK]**				
	TILLAMOOK CO.	T1S	R9W	S29
TONE FAMILY	TILLAMOOK CO.	T2S	R10W	S3
TONE HOMESTEAD, JAMES see **TONE FAMILY**				
	TILLAMOOK CO.	T2S	R10W	S3
TRASK see **TRASK PIONEER**	TILLAMOOK CO.	T1S	R9W	S27
TRASK D.L.C., ELBRIDGE see **TRASK PIONEER**				
	TILLAMOOK CO.	T1S	R9W	S27
TRASK PIONEER	TILLAMOOK CO.	T1S	R9W	S27
TROUT	TILLAMOOK CO.	T1S	R9W	S30
TROUT FAMILY see **TROUT**	TILLAMOOK CO.	T1S	R9W	S30
UNION PIONEER [CLOVERDALE]	TILLAMOOK CO.	T4S	R10W	S33
UNITED BRETHREN see **BEAVER CREEK**				
	TILLAMOOK CO.	T3S	R9W	S29
UNKNOWN	TILLAMOOK CO.	T3N	R10W	S14
UNKNOWN	TILLAMOOK CO.	T1S	R10W	S36
WALKER	TILLAMOOK CO.	T3S	R9W	S26
WAUD'S FUNERAL HOME	TILLAMOOK CO.	T1S	R9W	?
WELLS	TILLAMOOK CO.	T1S	R8W	?
WHITE	TILLAMOOK CO.	T1S	R9W	?
WINEJO FARM see **HATCH FAMILY**	TILLAMOOK CO.	T1N	R10W	?
WOODS see **I.O.O.F. [WOODS]**	TILLAMOOK CO.	T4S	R10W	S18

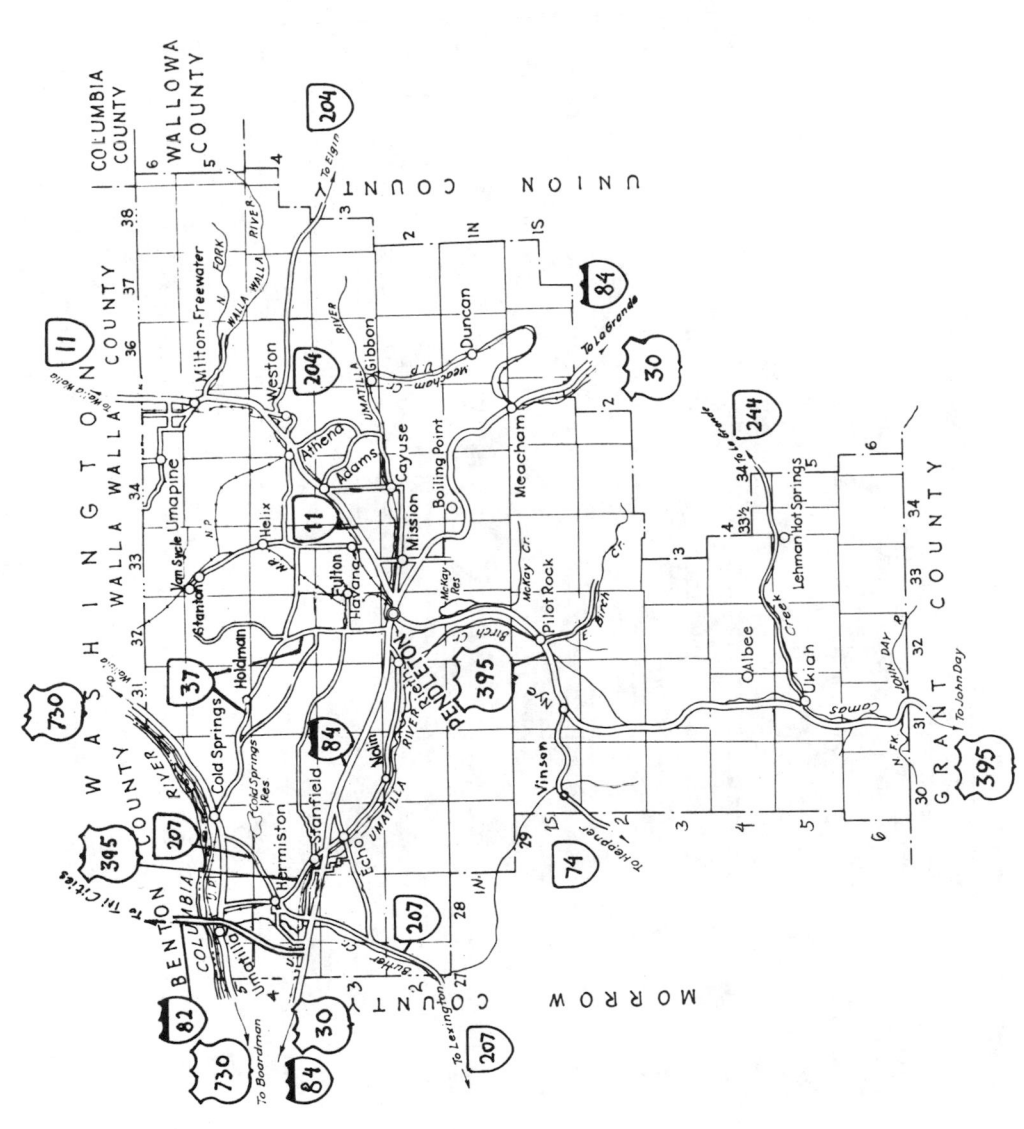

Echo Memorial
Janice M. Healy (2000)

Area: 3,231 square miles
Population (1998): 65,495
County seat: Pendleton, Population: 15,900
County established: 27 September 1862

    The Oregon Trail crossed Umatilla County from the summit of the Blue Mountains down to the Columbia River. The earliest public cemeteries were temporary such as that at Butter Creek Crossing in 1852. By 1861 there was a cemetery at the settlement of Umatilla. By the end of the 1860's there were 8 including one at Pendleton. Wheat ranches and livestock brought more settlers in the 1870's and 1880's. The Umatilla Indian Reservation has eight cemeteries, including Tutuilla Presbyterian Mission dating from 1838 and St. Andrews Catholic from 1847.

Echo Memorial
Janice M. Healy (2000)

Umatilla County

Echo Memorial
Janice M. Healy (2000)

Echo Memorial
Janice M. Healy (2000)

Name of Cemetery and also known as	Number of burials	Acres	Condition	Date started or earliest known burial	Township	Range	Section

AGENCY INDIAN

? 1.13 3 1865   T2N   R33E   S10

Go east out of Pendleton via Southeast Court Avenue (U.S. Hwy. 30); pass the junction with OR. Hwy. 11. At 0.5 of a mile past that junction turn off of U.S. Hwy. 30 onto Mission Road (formerly Mission-Cayuse Road), into the Umatilla Indian Reservation. Drive 3.9 miles on Mission Road (formerly Mission-Cayuse Road) and then turn right (south) on "A" Street for 0.4 of a mile to the cemetery on the bluff. It is about 6 miles out of Pendleton and at the Indian Agency. (Mission 1966-74 USGS Quad. map.)

ALBEE
  AKA: 1. ALBA

B ? ? 1878   T4S   R31E   ?

Possibly on Section 23. Located 2 miles west of Albee, via the virtually impassable unnamed County Road #1428, about 0.25 of a mile off of the road to the right (north) in a swampy area surrounded by timber. There are 43 known burials. 1963 was the latest burial at the time of a 1966 visit. (Not shown on Ukiah Quad. 1967-83 USGS map.)

ATHENA
  AKA: 1. I.O.O.F.
        2. KNIGHTS OF
           PYTHIAS

C 5.1 1 1873   T4N   R34E   S24

Located 0.5 of a mile northwest of Athena on a hill surrounded by a wheat field. Go west on Sherman Street at the north end of town. Originally, said a 1937 report, it was 15 acres in size. (Adams 1966 USGS Quad. map.)

BASKET MOUNTAIN

B ? 3 Circa 1870 T4N   R37E   S18

Drive 10.7 miles east out of Weston on Weston-Elgin Highway (OR. Hwy. 204). Turn left (north) off of OR. Hwy. 204 onto Lower Basket Mtn. Road and drive 1.4 miles to its juction with Basket Mtn. Road (formerly Upper Basket Mtn. Road); turn left again (north) and continue. The cemetery is apparently about 3 miles from OR. Hwy. 204, perhaps near Pole Creek. It was reportedly on the old Hendrickson Ranch (1966) and had no recent burials at that time. (Not shown on Blalock Mountain 1963-83 USGS Quad. map.)

Umatilla County

Name of Cemetery and also known as	Number of burials	Acres	Condition	Date started or earliest known burial	Township	Range	Section

BAUMGARDNER FAMILY
AKA: 1. MEADOWS

A   0.5   ?   1868-1876   T3N   R29E   S7
Located 5 miles northwest of Echo on a small knoll next to the road. This family cemetery is on the south side of Emert Road (formerly Emigrant Road), 100 yards east of the junction with Andrews (formerly Houser Road). There are 6 known graves. (Stanfield 1993 USGS Quad. map.)

BOWLUS

B   2.6   5   1873-1946   T5N   R36E   S3
Located east of Milton-Freewater and on a road south out of Spofford. Leave Main Street (OR. Hwy. 11) in Milton-Freewater on 9th Avenue Southeast to the east, crossing the Walla Walla River onto Milton Cemetery Road. At 0.8 of a mile from Main Street one passes the I.O.O.F. Cemetery. At 2.9 miles from Main Street, turn left (north) onto Spofford Road. At 3.7 miles, turn right (east) off of Spofford Road and onto Whiteman Road; at 5.75 miles turn right (south) onto Powerline Road (formerly Bowlus Hill Road) and continue south to the cemetery on the left (east), about 6.6 miles from the starting point. The cemetery is on a hill, on a farm once owned by Bowlus. There are 74 known burials (1967). (Bowlus Hill 1964-76 USGS Quad. map.)

BOWMAN FAMILY

?   ?   ?   ?   T1N   R29E   ?
This could be on Section 29, 30 or 32, in the Vinson area, on Tony Vey's land (1970). Antone Vey is named as the landowner in the 1932 *Metsker Atlas of Umatilla County*. This is somewhere off of Butter Creek Road. (Not shown on Echo S.W. 1968 USGS Quad. map.)

BUTTER CREEK CROSSING

?   ?   6   1852   T3N   R27E   S25
Drive westerly from Echo for 8.3 miles to the intersection with OR. Hwy. 207. Continue ahead on Madison Road for another mile to the bridge over Butter Creek. The Oregon Trail crossed Butter Creek here; it was a burial site of a number of emigrants. One of these was Lucinda Powell Propst, who died in August 1852 and was buried here. Later, she and other known burials were removed to Echo

Name of Cemetery and also known as	Number of burials	Acres	Condition	Date started or earliest known burial	Township	Range	Section

Cemetery, about 9 miles east of the crossing. NOTE: See the article labelled "Unknown" T3N, R27E, S36. (The Trail Crossing is shown but no graves are shown on Service Buttes 1968 USGS Quad. map.)

BUTTS, SARAH M.

A 0.01 ? 1889   T1S R35E   S15

Located 1 mile southeast of Meacham Lake at a point a few feet east of a fork in the road. There is no enclosure; a small stone is set flush in cement: Sarah M. Butts 1852-1889. (Meacham Lake 1963-83 USGS Quad. map.)

DALE

? ? ? ?   T6S R31E   ?

Several burials are located around the area of the Dale Ranger Station, about 15 miles south of Ukiah Junction along U.S. Hwy. 395. Some or all of these may be in Grant County as is the Ranger Station. (Not shown on Dale 1990 or Bridge Creek 1967-83 USGS Quad. maps.)

DARR FAMILY

A ? 3 1888-1889 T3S R30 1/2E S1

It is 0.33 of a mile west of U.S. Hwy. 395 at Milepost 32.6, on Gurdane Road. The burial site is on the left (south) side of the road in a field. There are 3 known burials. (Gurdane 1968 USGS Quad. map.)

DeSPAIN GULCH

A 1 5 1886-1903 T3N R31E   S10

Located 4.5 miles northwest of Pendleton and 4 miles west of OR. Hwy. 37, on DeSpain Gulch Road. The cemetery is on the right (north) on a hill across DeSpain Gulch, 200 yards from the school and the junction of DeSpain Gulch and Cresswell Roads. (Holdman 1966 USGS Quad. map.)

DOCKWEILER, MARIE VOGLER

A 0.01 ? 3 Apr 1891 T1S R35E   S21

Located on Beaver Creek 3.3 miles southeast of Meacham Lake, just above the road on the left. Enclosed in a wire fence with steel posts; the marker is a metal tag. (Meacham Lake 1963-83 USGS Quad. map.)

Name of Cemetery and also known as	Number of burials	Acres	Condition	Date started or earliest known burial	Township	Range	Section

EASTERN OREGON STATE HOSPITAL
AKA: 1. E.O.S.H.

D ? 6 1913-1984 T2N R32E S9
Located in what is now the Eastern Oregon Correctional Institution on Westgate (U.S. Hwy. 30) in the northwestern part of Pendleton and just west of the bridge over the Umatilla River. While serving as an institution for the insane, deaths were disposed of both by burials and by cremations. Before the buildings were converted to a prison 1,467 cremains were transferred to Olney Cemetery in March 1984. The compiler does not know if this transfer included burials from the Hospital Cemetery. (Pendleton 1966-76 USGS Quad. map shows the institution but not the cemetery.)

ECHO MEMORIAL
AKA: 1. ECHO
2. I.O.O.F.
3. SIPHON

C 4.75 1 1868 T3N R29E S16
Located just north of Echo. From Main and Thielson Streets, go northerly on Thielson towards Stanfield for 0.5 of a mile. Turn right onto Echo Cemetery Road and go uphill 0.2 of a mile to the cemetery. The oldest dated stone is 1868. The city of Echo took over the cemetery from the I.O.O.F. in April, 1922. The name Siphon Cemetery has occasionally been used. This is due to a misplaced word on the USGS Quad. map. {10 October 2000} (Echo 1968 USGS Quad. map.)

FORD
AKA: 1. BALLOU
2. MUD CREEK
3. VALLEY

B 1.8 3 1864 T6N R35E S23
Go about 3 miles north of Milton-Freewater. Leave OR. Hwy. 11, turning left (west) onto Ballou Road and go 1 mile. The cemetery is on the left on a hill overlooking the valley. (Milton-Freewater 1964-78 USGS Quad. map.)

FOSTER PIONEER

B 1.3 5 1862-1913 T3N R29E S5
Located a mile south of Stanfield via U.S. Hwy. 395, on the east side of the Umatilla River and about 500 yards north of the I-84 Freeway Umatilla River Bridge. Turn off of U.S. Hwy. 395 west onto Foster Cemetery Road adjacent to the canal bridge. There are about 50 known burials. (Stanfield 1993 USGS Quad. map.)

Name of Cemetery and also known as	Number of burials	Acres	Condition	Date started or earliest known burial	Township	Range	Section

GALLAHER
AKA: 1. GREASEWOOD

A   0.4   5   1878-1934   T4N R33E   S36
From Pendleton, take OR. Hwy. 11 to Milepost 6.2. Turn left (north) onto Helix Highway and go 4.5 miles; turn right (east) on Reeder Road and go 0.6 of a mile to the cemetery at the top of the hill. There were 28 known burials of Scotch and Irish homesteaders in 1939. *Pendleton East Oregonian* article of 14 Sept. 1976 shows photos of stones, including one for "Millie" dating from Sept. 1887. (Helix 1966 USGS Quad. map.)

GERMAN LUTHERAN
AKA: 1. GERKING FAMILY
     2. GERMAN CHURCH
     3. MYRICK
     4. MYRICK
       STATION
     5. WARREN
       STATION

B   0.75 3   1888   T4N R33E   S29
Located 0.8 of a mile south of Myrick at the northeast corner of the intersection of Myrick Road and Hudemann Road (formerly Jackson Station Road). From Pendleton, take OR. Hwy. 11 to Milepost 6.2. Turn left (north) onto Helix Highway and go 4.5 miles. Turn left (west) onto Hudemann Road (formerly Jackson Station Road) and go 3 miles. There are 24 known burials (no date of report). By 1970 many had been removed and reinterred, but the stones have been left behind. NOTE: Both the German Lutheran Cemetery and Greasewood Cemetery have been confusingly referred to as Warren Station Cemetery and later as Myrick Station Cemetery. (Helix 1966 USGS Quad. map.)

GREASEWOOD FINNISH LUTHERAN
AKA: 1. FINLAND
     2. FINN
     3. GREESEWOOD
     4. LITTLE
       GREASEWOOD

A   0.7 2   1886   T4N R33E   S34
From Pendleton, take OR. Hwy. 11 to Milepost 6.2. Turn left (north) onto Helix Highway and go 5.6 miles to Midway. Turn left on Midway Road (formerly Finn Road) for 0.5 of a mile to the Finnish Church at Embysk Road. On 5 March 1990, Joyce Hales reported that the church had recently been restored. (Helix 1966 USGS Quad. map.)

GURDANE
AKA: 1. MOUNTAIN
       VALLEY

A   0.6 3   1888   T3S R30E   S32
Located about 0.5 of a mile west of Gurdane going from U.S. Hwy. 395, on a hill to the left. Gurdane is 9 miles west of US. Hwy 395

Name of Cemetery and also known as	Number of burials	Acres	Condition	Date started or earliest known burial	Township	Range	Section

via Gurdane Road and 17 miles south of OR. Hwy. 74 at Vinson. The adjacent church is now gone. (Gurdane 1968 USGS Quad. map.)

HANNAH FAMILY
AKA: 1. GERKING RANCH

A   0.23   5   1880-1882   T4N   R34E   S30
Located 1.5 miles from Greasewood Cemetery, between Helix and Adams. This has been plowed over and the stones have been discarded. The original deed reads "a certain plot of ground 100 feet square." Burials for 3 children were last located in 1939. (Not shown on Adams 1966 USGS Quad. map.)

HELIX

C   2   1   1874   T4N   R33E   S11
Located 0.5 of a mile south of Helix. At the school turn south and drive to the cemetery on a bluff overlooking the town. (Helix 1966 USGS Quad. map.)

HERMISTON

?   40   ?   1907   T4N   R28E   S14
Located 0.5 of a mile southwest of U.S. Hwy. 395, on the right (southwest) between Southeast 4th Street and the railway crossing. (Hermiston 1993 USGS Quad. map.)

HOLDMAN

A   1.5   2   1901   T5N   R31E   S33
This cemetery is just west of Holdman on the left (west) on OR. Hwy. 37 and 0.7 of a mile northwest of the grain elevator, on top of the bluff. (Holdman 1966 USGS Quad. map.)

HOMLY
AKA: 1. CAYUSE
      2. HOMELI

?   1   3   1891   T2N   R34E   S2
Located on the Umatilla Reservation. Cross the Umatilla River at Cayuse, go north for 0.6 of a mile on North Cayuse Road (formerly Cayuse-Adams Road), turn right on Johnley Road (formerly Tubbs Road) for another 1.9 miles. Then, turn right on Duff Road, go 1 mile east and turn south onto Homly Road (formerly Curl-Homly Road) for a final 1.2 miles back towards the Umatilla River. The cemetery is just across the railway tracks and usually blocked by a gate. (Cayuse 1966 USGS Quad. map.)

Name of Cemetery and also known as	Number of burials	Acres	Condition	Date started or earliest known burial	Township	Range	Section

HYATT FAMILY

A 0.25 ? 1891-1897 T4N R36E S23
Go 8 miles east of Weston on OR. Hwy. 204;
turn off to the left (north) on Hodgson Road
and go another 0.7 of a mile. Two known
burials are on the right (east) side of the
road. (Weston Mountain 1964-74 USGS Quad.
map.)

I.O.O.F. [MILTON]
AKA: 1. OLD CITY
     2. OLD PIONEER

B 2.5 3 1878 T5N R35E S11
This is in Sections 11 and 12, on a hill
west of Milton-Freewater. Leave Main Street
(OR. Hwy. 11) on Southwest 8th Avenue, go
past city hall and the reservoir 0.55 of a
mile to the cemetery. (Milton-Freewater
1964-78 USGS Quad. map.)

I.O.O.F.
[MILTON-FREEWATER]
AKA: 1. NEW MILTON

D 12.67 1 1886 T5N R35E S12
Located on a hill east of Milton-Freewater,
0.75 of a mile from the intersection of OR.
Hwy. 11 and Southeast 9th Avenue and Milton
Cemetery Road. (Bowlus Hill 1964-76 USGS
Quad. map.)

INDIAN

? ? ? ? ? ? ?
This could be in Township 3 North, Range 35
East, Section 36 or Township 2 North, Range
35 East, Section 1. It is located near
Gibbon on the south side of the Umatilla
River off of Bingham Road, on a high bluff.
(Not shown on Gibbon 1964-83 or Thorn Hollow
1964 USGS Quad. maps.)

JAMES, CALVIN

A 0.01 ? 1888 T4N R33E ?
Located in a grain field near Helix on the
Verne Terjeson Place (1970). Once the site
of a church, this burial site is at the base
of a hill. NOTE: This site is on private
property. (Not shown on Helix 1966 USGS
Quad. map.)

KEES
AKA: 1. BLUE MOUNTAIN
     2. KEY
     3. KEYES

C 1.7 3 1872 T4N R35E S28
Located 0.75 of a mile south via McLean Road
and 1 mile west of Weston, on Kees Cemetery
Road (formerly Rawhide Gulch Road). The

Name of Cemetery and also known as	Number of burials	Acres	Condition	Date started or earliest known burial	Township	Range	Section

family originally spelled this Kees. It was deeded 18 Dec. 1875. (Athena 1974 USGS Quad. map uses the spelling of key.)

KOONTZ, DAVID R.   A 0.01 2 1852   T3N R29E   S16
Located in a grain field on the eastern outskirts of Echo, 0.3 of a mile southeast of Gerome Street (Pendleton cutoff), between the railroad tracks and Rieth Road (formerly Old Pendleton River Road, Old U.S. Hwy. 30). {10 October 2000} (Echo 1968 USGS Quad. map.)

McKAY CREEK   A 0.15 3 1908   T1N R32E   S11
This Indian cemetery is on the southwest end of McKay Reservoir about 8.4 miles south of Pendleton and east of U.S. Hwy. 395. It is 0.4 of a mile off of Frontage Road on a dirt road going to the edge of the reservoir and then another 700 feet on foot (1966). (McKay Reservoir 1966 USGS Quad. map.)

MEACHAM   A 0.5 3 1860-1931 T1S R35E   S3
Located at the Meacham Interchange of the I-84 Freeway between the southwest side of the freeway and Ross Road. It is in a triangular patch of forest between the I-84 Freeway, Meacham Lake Road and Ross Road, 0.25 of a mile southwest of Meacham. Follow Meacham Lake Road from Meacham Store. Go about 100 yards south of the I-84 Freeway and just west of the railway overpass. The cemetery is 100 yards uphill on foot. There were 15 recognizable sites but only 2 readable inscriptions, in 1974. There were few visible traces in 1981. (Not shown on Meacham 1964-83 USGS Quad. map.)

MEACHAM, HARVEY J.   A 0.01 ? 29 May 1872 T1S R35E   S3
Located in the Southeast 1/4 of the Southeast 1/4 of Section 3. The grave is 0.25 of a mile southeast of Meacham off of Hotel Road in a lodgepole pine thicket at the edge of a meadow. Harvey J. Meacham, 1829-1872. (Not shown on Meacham 1964-83 USGS Quad. map.)

Name of Cemetery and also known as	Number of burials	Acres	Condition	Date started or earliest known burial	Township	Range	Section

NOLIN
AKA: 1. NOLAN

B 0.5 2 1867   T2N R30E   S6

Located about 13 miles west of Pendleton on Rieth Road (formerly Old Pendleton River Road, U.S. Hwy. 30). Leave Rieth Road at Milepost 8.4 onto Mac Hoke Road (formerly Two Canyon Road). Cross the Umatilla River, pass one junction with Cunningham Road and then the railway tracks at the locale of Nolin. Turn right (west) and proceed 0.13 of a mile to the second junction with Cunningham Road. Continue ahead on Cunningham Road another 0.2 of a mile to the cemetery on the left (south) on a bluff overlooking the valley of the Umatilla River. {10 October 2000} (Nolin 1968 USGS Quad. map.)

NYE

A ? ? ?   T1S R31E   S19

Nye is a locale at the junction of OR. Hwy. 74 and U.S. Hwy. 395 about 8 miles west of Pilot Rock and 6 miles east of Vinson. The compiler was unaware of any burial here but a 1912 Umatilla County Death Certificate #3688 records the burial at Nye of Mrs. Henry Latimer. She died 12 December 1912 at age 72. (Not shown on Nye 1967 USGS Quad. map.)

OGLE FAMILY

? ? ? ?   ? ?   ?

Possibly located in Township 1 South and Range 32 East. This burial site is outside of Pilot Rock. No other information was given in the report. (Not shown on Pilot Rock 1967 USGS Quad. map.)

OLD AGENCY

A 1.87 3 1898   T2N R33E   S9

Go east out of Pendleton via Southeast Court Avenue, (U.S. Hwy. 30), pass the junction with OR. Hwy. 11 at 0.5 of a mile past that junction turn off U.S. Hwy. 30 onto the Mission Road (formerly Mission-Cayuse Road) into the Umatilla Indian Reservation. Drive 2.7 miles on Mission Road to the cemetery driveway on the right (south). Many were reburied here from times earlier than 1898. (Mission 1966-74 USGS Quad. map.)

Name of Cemetery and also known as	Number of burials	Acres	Condition	Date started or earliest known burial	Township	Range	Section

OLD HALFWAY HOUSE

? ? ? ?   T2S R33E   ?

Possibly on Section 18. Three burials are located 15 miles southeast of Pilot Rock along East Birch Creek Road. Perhaps this is at the confluence of Pearson Creek with East Birch Creek. An 1893 Umatilla county map shows "illegible" House here. (No cemetery is shown on Sevenmile Creek 1967 USGS Quad. map.)

OLNEY
AKA: 1. PENDLETON CITY
     2. SEXTON OLNEY

D 155.56 1 1891   T2N R32E   S15

Located a short distance south of downtown Pendleton off of U.S. Hwy. 395 via Tutuilla Creek Road (formerly Southwest 23rd). This cemetery has many reburials dated earlier than 1891. It also includes a small area for Chinese burials. In addition, 1,467 cremains from Eastern Oregon State Hospital were reburied here in March of 1984. (Pendleton 1966-76 USGS Quad. map.)

PATTERSON, ALEXANDER

A 0.01 ? 9 Dec 1884 T3S R30E   S33

Located on the left (south) side of Gurdane Road as you go into Gurdane from U.S. Hwy. 395 and 8.2 miles from the highway. (Gurdane 1968 USGS Quad. map.)

PILOT ROCK

C 12 1 1865   T1S R32E   S20

Go south on East Birch Creek Road from U.S. Hwy. 395, in town. At 0.7 of a mile turn right (west) and go another 0.4 of a mile up the ridge to the cemetery. (Pilot Rock 1967 USGS Quad. map.)

PIONEER PARK
AKA: 1. PENDLETON

A 2.5 10 1869-1891 T2N R32E   S10

The first cemetery at Pendleton. Most graves were reburied in Olney. This is now a city park, but 4 graves were identified in 1967. This is located on the north bank of the Umatilla River at Northwest 4th and Northwest DeSpain Avenue. (Pendleton 1966-76 USGS Quad. map.)

Name of Cemetery and also known as	Number of burials	Acres	Condition	Date started or earliest known burial	Township	Range	Section

PLEASANT VIEW
AKA: 1. STANFIELD

C 10 1 1914   T4N R29E   S28
Located about 2 miles north of Stanfield on South Edwards Road. (Stanfield 1993 USGS Quad. map.)

RED ELK
AKA: 1. THORN
     HOLLOW

A 0.5 ? 1901   T2N R35E   S3
Located about 18 miles east of Pendleton, 1.25 miles east of the locale of Thorn Hollow and on a bluff south off of Bingham Road (formerly River Road). There is no ready access. This is on the Umatilla Reservation. (Thorn Hollow 1964 USGS Quad. map.)

ST. ANDREWS
AKA: 1. ST. ANDREWS
     MISSION

B 1 ? 1847   T2N R33E   S24
This Indian site is about 12 miles east of Pendleton on the Umatilla Indian Reservation. Leave I-84 Freeway to the right (south) at Exit 216 onto Mission Road. Double back over I-84 Freeway and just beyound this overpass, turn right off of Mission Road onto Kash Kash Road which for a ways runs parallel to Westbound I-84 on the northerly side of the freeway. After 2.25 miles on Kash Kash Road turn left (north) onto Hobby Road and drive 0.25 of a mile. Then turn right (east) onto St. Andrews Road and drive 0.85 of a mile to the cemetery on the left. St. Andrews Church and cemetery briefly operated, 1847-1848, until the Whitman Massacre, both were reactivated in 1887. (Cayuse 1966 USGS Quad. map.)

SKYVIEW MEMORIAL PARK

? 7.5 1 1965   T1N R32E   S10
Located 8 miles south of Pendleton on U.S. Hwy. 395. (McKay Reservoir 1966 USGS Quad. map.)

SOLDIERS

A ? ? 1855-1856   T3N R29E   ?
Two soldiers from Fort Henrietta are buried across the Umatilla River from Echo. (NOT on Echo 1968 USGS Quad. map.)

STURDIVANT
AKA: 1. STURDEVANT

A 0.25 3 1888   T5S R31E   S4
The family prefers the first spelling. Located north of Ukiah Junction on U.S. Hwy.

Name of Cemetery and also known as	Number of burials	Acres	Condition	Date started or earliest known burial	Township	Range	Section

395. The bridge over the North Fork of Owens Creek is at Milepost 47.4 on the highway. The cemetery is west of U.S. Hwy. 395, from this bridge about 0.75 of a mile. It is on a wooded knoll overlooking the valley. (Ukiah 1967-83 USGS Quad. map.)

SUNSET HILLS
AKA: 1. NEW CITY
     2. UMATILLA [NEW]

| | ? | 1.6 | ? | 1954 | T5N | R28E | S19 |

Go south from the Umatilla River Bridge on Powerline Road for 0.75 of a mile; then turn right (west) on Madison Street, then left on Fillmore for one block, then right on Grant Street to the cemetery. It is 0.5 of a mile from Powerline Road. 1951 is the earliest dated marker. (Umatilla 1993 USGS Quad. map.)

TRIBBLE FAMILY

| | A | ? | 5 | 1881-1883 | T3N | R29E | S17 |

Four graves for the Tribble family are located somewere in the vicinity of Echo. These were last recorded in 1941 as about 1 mile west of Echo. Searches in 1961 and 1965 have failed to locate these graves. (Not shown on Echo 1968 USGS Quad. map.)

TUTUILLA PRESBYTERIAN INDIAN MISSION

| | A | 0.5 | 3 | 1838-1847 | T2N | R33E | S29 |

Located on the Umatilla Indian Reservation. Drive east out of Pendleton on I-84 Freeway. Leave I-84 at Exit 216 onto South Market (formerly Mission Road) going south, then turn right (west) at 0.4 of a mile onto Tutuilla Church Road (formerly Shenondoah Road) and drive another 1.5 miles to the church. The cemetery is directly behind the church. It was used for burials 1838-1847 and then interrupted as a result of the Whitman Massacre. Burials were resumed possibly by 1878 when the church was built. (Mission 1966-74 USGS Quad. map.)

UKIAH

| | A | 1 | 3 | 1892 | T5S | R31E | S11 |

Located 0.5 of a mile north of Ukiah on a gravel road beyond the Ranger Station. (Ukiah 1967-83 USGS Quad. map.)

Name of Cemetery and also known as	Number of burials	Acres	Condition	Date started or earliest known burial	Township	Range	Section

UMATILLA [OLD]   B   2   ?   1861   T5N   R28E   S18

Located at the west edge of the town of Umatilla at the corner of U.S. Hwy. 730 and "A" Street, on a hill just east of the Umatilla River Bridge.   (Umatilla 1993 USGS Quad. map.)

UNKNOWN   A   ?   ?   ?   ?   ?   ?

This burial is on a farm between Pendleton and Echo. No other information was given in the report.

UNKNOWN   A   ?   ?   ?   T1N   R29E   ?

Three unmarked graves on the Gaylord Madison Ranch on Butter Creek have been reported. The compiler has no futher information at this time. (Echo S. W. 1968 USGS Quad. map.)

UNKNOWN   B   ?   ?   1878   T3N   R27E   S36

Located in the Northeast 1/4 of the Northwest 1/4 of Section 36 on the Gaylord Madison Ranch (1966). Drive westerly from Echo for 8.3 miles to the intersection of OR. Hwy. 207. Continue ahead on Madison Road for another mile to the bridge over Butter Creek. The Oregon Trail crossed Butter Creek here. There were burials of a number of emigrants and they are written about in the article labelled Butter Creek Crossing, see that artical. From the Butter Creek Bridge upstream 0.8 of a mile are also graves. These are on private property and not accessible by road. There were 64 known burials as of 1966. The compiler wonders if the Butter Creek Crossing graves and these "unknowns" also along Butter Creek are actually a single burial ground. However the former is dated 1852 and the latter as 1878. Let us hope for clarification on these burials. (The graves herein labelled "unknown" are shown on Service Creek NW 1968 USGS Quad. map.)

UNKNOWN   ?   0.2   ?   ?   T1S   R33E   S4

Located 8 miles east of Pilot Rock on upper McKay Creek, 0.5 of a mile east of the

Name of Cemetery and also known as	Number of burials	Acres	Condition	Date started or earliest known burial	Township	Range	Section

junction of McKay Creek Road with Sumac Road (formerly Shaw-Lower McKay Road). It is within the Umatilla Indian Reservation. The cemetery is south across McKay Creek on a ridge. (Table Rock 1966-74 USGS Quad. map.)

VINSON
AKA: 1. VINCENT
2. VINSON
LUTHERAN

B 1 2 1869 T1S R30E S21
Located at Vinson, on a hillside on the west side of OR. Hwy. 74, 0.5 of a mile south of the junction with Butter Creek Road. (Vinson 1968 USGS Quad. map.)

WARNER FAMILY

A ? ? 1891-1892 T2S R32E S30
Located approximately 10 miles south of Pilot Rock. Take U. S. Hwy. 395 south out of Pilot Rock for about 1.5 miles to Milepost 17.1. Turn left off the highway onto Yellowjacket Road and go 5.1 miles to West Birch Creek Road; turn left onto the latter and proceed another 3.4 miles to the graves on the right. (Granite Meadows 1967-83 USGS Quad. map.)

WESTON
AKA: 1. I.O.O.F.
2. MASONIC

C 10.6 1 1871 T4N R35E S22
Located 0.5 of a mile east of Weston on a hill. Take Main Street east past the High School and onto Kirk Road (formerly Old Tollgate Highway), then left (north) on Weston Cemetery Road. The north portion of the cemetery was Masonic; the larger south portion was I.O.O.F. (Athena 1964-74 USGS Quad. map.)

AGENCY INDIAN	UMATILLA CO.	T2N	R33E	S10
ALBA see **ALBEE**	UMATILLA CO.	T4S	R31E	?
ALBEE	UMATILLA CO.	T4S	R31E	?
ATHENA	UMATILLA CO.	T4N	R34E	S24
BALLOU see **FORD**	UMATILLA CO.	T6N	R35E	S23
BASKET MOUNTAIN	UMATILLA CO.	T4N	R37E	S18
BAUMGARDNER FAMILY	UMATILLA CO.	T3N	R29E	S7
BLUE MOUNTAIN see **KEES**	UMATILLA CO.	T4N	R35E	S28
BOWLUS	UMATILLA CO.	T5N	R36E	S3
BOWLUS FARM see **BOWLUS**	UMATILLA CO.	T5N	R36E	S3
BOWMAN FAMILY	UMATILLA CO.	T1N	R29E	?
BUTTER CREEK CROSSING	UMATILLA CO.	T3N	R27E	S25
BUTTS, SARAH M.	UMATILLA CO.	T1S	R35E	S15
CAYUSE see **HOMLY**	UMATILLA CO.	T2N	R34E	S2
DALE	UMATILLA CO.	T6S	R31E	?
DARR FAMILY	UMATILLA CO.	T3S	R30 1/2E	S1
DeSPAIN GULCH	UMATILLA CO.	T3N	R31E	S10
DOCKWEILER, MARIE VOGLER	UMATILLA CO.	T1S	R35E	S21
E.O.S.H. see **EASTERN OREGON STATE HOSPITAL**				
	UMATILLA CO.	T2N	R32E	S9
EASTERN OREGON STATE HOSPITAL	UMATILLA CO.	T2N	R32E	S9
ECHO see **ECHO MEMORIAL**	UMATILLA CO.	T3N	R29E	S16
ECHO MEMORIAL	UMATILLA CO.	T3N	R29E	S16
FINLAND see **GREASEWOOD FINNISH LUTHERAN**				
	UMATILLA CO.	T4N	R33E	S34
FINN see **GREASEWOOD FINNISH LUTHERAN**				
	UMATILLA CO.	T4N	R33E	S34
FORD	UMATILLA CO.	T6N	R35E	S23
FOSTER PIONEER	UMATILLA CO.	T3N	R29E	S5
GALLAHER	UMATILLA CO.	T4N	R33E	S36
GERKING FAMILY see **GERMAN LUTHERAN**				
	UMATILLA CO.	T4N	R33E	S29
GERKING RANCH see **HANNAH FAMILY**	UMATILLA CO.	T4N	R34E	S30
GERMAN CHURCH see **GERMAN LUTHERAN**				
	UMATILLA CO.	T4N	R33E	S29
GERMAN LUTHERAN	UMATILLA CO.	T4N	R33E	S29
GREASEWOOD see **GALLAHER**	UMATILLA CO.	T4N	R33E	S36
GREASEWOOD FINNISH LUTHERAN	UMATILLA CO.	T4N	R33E	S34
GREESEWOOD see **GREASEWOOD FINNISH LUTHERAN**				
	UMATILLA CO.	T4N	R33E	S34
GURDANE	UMATILLA CO.	T3S	R30E	S32
HANNAH FAMILY	UMATILLA CO.	T4N	R34E	S30
HELIX	UMATILLA CO.	T4N	R33E	S11
HENDRICKSON RANCH see **BASKET MOUNTAIN**				
	UMATILLA CO.	T4N	R37E	S18
HENRIETTA, FORT see **SOLDIERS**	UMATILLA CO.	T3N	R29E	?
HERMISTON	UMATILLA CO.	T4N	R28E	S14
HOLDMAN	UMATILLA CO.	T5N	R31E	S33
HOMELI see **HOMLY**	UMATILLA CO.	T2N	R34E	S2
HOMLY	UMATILLA CO.	T2N	R34E	S2
HYATT FAMILY	UMATILLA CO.	T4N	R36E	S23
I.O.O.F. see **ATHENA**	UMATILLA CO.	T4N	R34E	S24

I.O.O.F. see ECHO MEMORIAL	UMATILLA CO.	T3N	R29E	S16
I.O.O.F. see WESTON	UMATILLA CO.	T4N	R35E	S22
I.O.O.F. [MILTON]	UMATILLA CO.	T5N	R35E	S11
I.O.O.F. [MILTON-FREEWATER]	UMATILLA CO.	T5N	R35E	S12
INDIAN	UMATILLA CO.	?	?	?
JAMES, CALVIN	UMATILLA CO.	T4N	R33E	?
KEES	UMATILLA CO.	T4N	R35E	S28
KEY see KEES	UMATILLA CO.	T4N	R35E	S28
KEYES see KEES	UMATILLA CO.	T4N	R35E	S28
KNIGHTS OF PYTHIAS see ATHENA	UMATILLA CO.	T4N	R34E	S24
KOONTZ, DAVID R.	UMATILLA CO.	T3N	R29E	S16
LATIMER, MRS. HENRY see NYE	UMATILLA CO.	T1S	R31E	S19
LITTLE GREASEWOOD see GREASEWOOD FINNISH LUTHERAN				
	UMATILLA CO.	T4N	R33E	S34
MADISON RANCH, GAYLORD see UNKNOWN				
	UMATILLA CO.	T1N	R29E	?
MADISON RANCH, GAYLORD see UNKNOWN				
	UMATILLA CO.	T3N	R27E	S36
MASONIC see WESTON	UMATILLA CO.	T4N	R35E	S22
McKAY CREEK	UMATILLA CO.	T1N	R32E	S11
MEACHAM	UMATILLA CO.	T1S	R35E	S3
MEACHAM, HARVEY J.	UMATILLA CO.	T1S	R35E	S3
MEADOWS see BAUMGARDNER FAMILY	UMATILLA CO.	T3N	R29E	S7
MOUNTAIN VALLEY see GURDANE	UMATILLA CO.	T3S	R30E	S32
MUD CREEK see FORD	UMATILLA CO.	T6N	R35E	S23
MYRICK see GERMAN LUTHERAN	UMATILLA CO.	T4N	R33E	S29
MYRICK STATION see GERMAN LUTHERAN				
	UMATILLA CO.	T4N	R33E	S29
NEW CITY see SUNSET HILLS	UMATILLA CO.	T5N	R28E	S19
NEW MILTON see I.O.O.F. [MILTON-FREEWATER]				
	UMATILLA CO.	T5N	R35E	S12
NOLAN see NOLIN	UMATILLA CO.	T2N	R30E	S6
NOLIN	UMATILLA CO.	T2N	R30E	S6
NYE	UMATILLA CO.	T1S	R31E	S19
OGLE FAMILY	UMATILLA CO.	?	?	?
OLD AGENCY	UMATILLA CO.	T2N	R33E	S9
OLD CITY see I.O.O.F. [MILTON]	UMATILLA CO.	T5N	R35E	S11
OLD HALFWAY HOUSE	UMATILLA CO.	T2S	R33E	?
OLD PIONEER see I.O.O.F. [MILTON]				
	UMATILLA CO.	T5N	R35E	S11
OLNEY	UMATILLA CO.	T2N	R32E	S15
PATTERSON, ALEXANDER	UMATILLA CO.	T3S	R30E	S33
PENDLETON see PIONEER PARK	UMATILLA CO.	T2N	R32E	S10
PENDLETON CITY see OLNEY	UMATILLA CO.	T2N	R32E	S15
PILOT ROCK	UMATILLA CO.	T1S	R32E	S20
PIONEER PARK	UMATILLA CO.	T2N	R32E	S10
PLEASANT VIEW	UMATILLA CO.	T4N	R29E	S28
PROPST, LUCINDA POWELL see BUTTER CREEK CROSSING				
	UMATILLA CO.	T3N	R27E	S25
RED ELK	UMATILLA CO.	T2N	R35E	S3
ST. ANDREWS	UMATILLA CO.	T2N	R33E	S24

```
ST. ANDREWS MISSION see ST. ANDREWS
                            UMATILLA CO.    T2N    R33E    S24
SEXTON OLNEY see OLNEY      UMATILLA CO.    T2N    R32E    S15
SIPHON see ECHO MEMORIAL    UMATILLA CO.    T3N    R29E    S16
SKYVIEW MEMORIAL PARK       UMATILLA CO.    T1N    R32E    S10
SOLDIERS                    UMATILLA CO.    T3N    R29E    ?
STANFIELD see PLEASANT VIEW UMATILLA CO.    T4N    R29E    S28
STURDEVANT see STURDIVANT   UMATILLA CO.    T5S    R31E    S4
STURDIVANT                  UMATILLA CO.    T5S    R31E    S4
SUNSET HILLS                UMATILLA CO.    T5N    R28E    S19
TERJESON PLACE, VERNE see JAMES, CALVIN
                            UMATILLA CO.    T4N    R33E    ?
THORN HOLLOW see RED ELK    UMATILLA CO.    T2N    R35E    S3
TRIBBLE FAMILY              UMATILLA CO.    T3N    R29E    S17
TUTUILLA PRESBYTERIAN INDIAN MISSION
                            UMATILLA CO.    T2N    R33E    S29
UKIAH                       UMATILLA CO.    T5S    R31E    S11
UMATILLA [NEW] see SUNSET HILLS  UMATILLA CO. T5N  R28E    S19
UMATILLA [OLD]              UMATILLA CO.    T5N    R28E    S18
UNKNOWN                     UMATILLA CO.    ?      ?       ?
UNKNOWN                     UMATILLA CO.    T1N    R29E    ?
UNKNOWN                     UMATILLA CO.    T3N    R27E    S36
UNKNOWN                     UMATILLA CO.    T1S    R33E    S4
VALLEY see FORD             UMATILLA CO.    T6N    R35E    S23
VEY, ANTONE see BOWMAN FAMILY    UMATILLA CO. T1N  R29E    ?
VEY'S LAND, TONY see BOWMAN FAMILY
                            UMATILLA CO.    T1N    R29E    ?
VINCENT see VINSON          UMATILLA CO.    T1S    R30E    S21
VINSON                      UMATILLA CO.    T1S    R30E    S21
VINSON LUTHERAN see VINSON  UMATILLA CO.    T1S    R30E    S21
WARNER FAMILY               UMATILLA CO.    T2S    R32E    S30
WARREN STATION see GERMAN LUTHERAN
                            UMATILLA CO.    T4N    R33E    S29
WESTON                      UMATILLA CO.    T4N    R35E    S22
WHITMAN MASSACRE see ST. ANDREWS
                            UMATILLA CO.    T2N    R33E    S24
WHITMAN MASSACRE see TUTUILLA PRESBYTERIAN INDIAN MISSION
                            UMATILLA CO.    T2N    R33E    S29
```

Nolin
Janice M. Healy (2000)

Koontz, David R.

Janice M. Healy (2000)

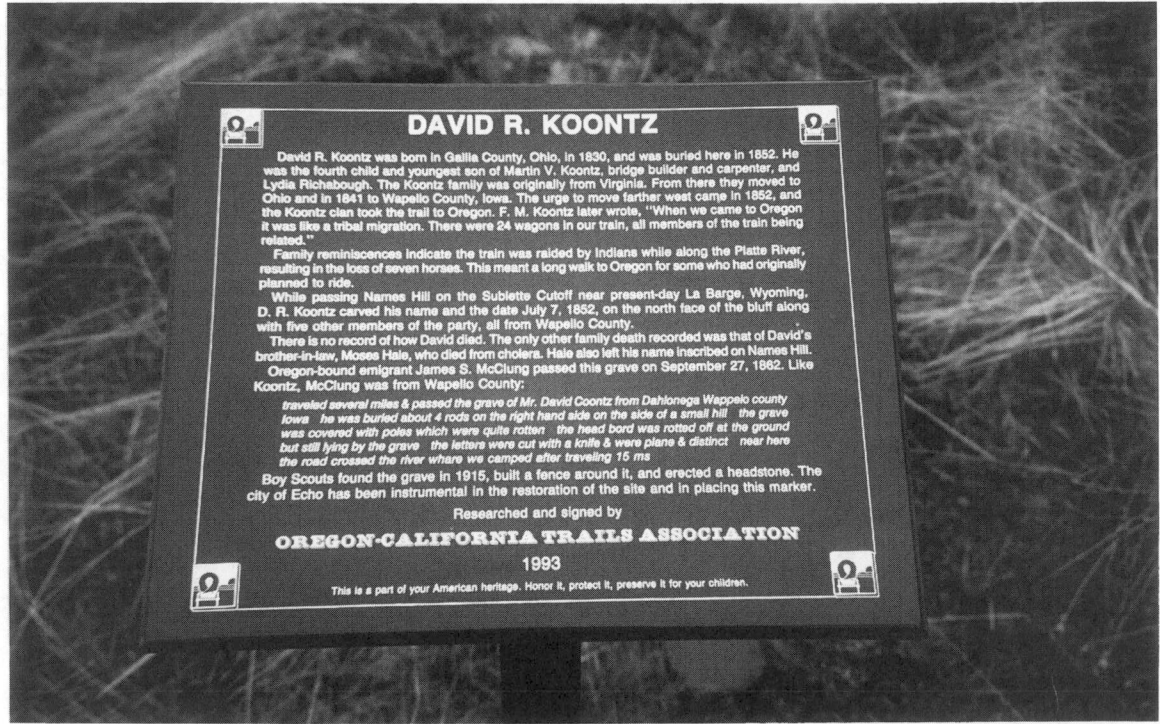

Koontz, David R.

Janice M. Healy (2000)

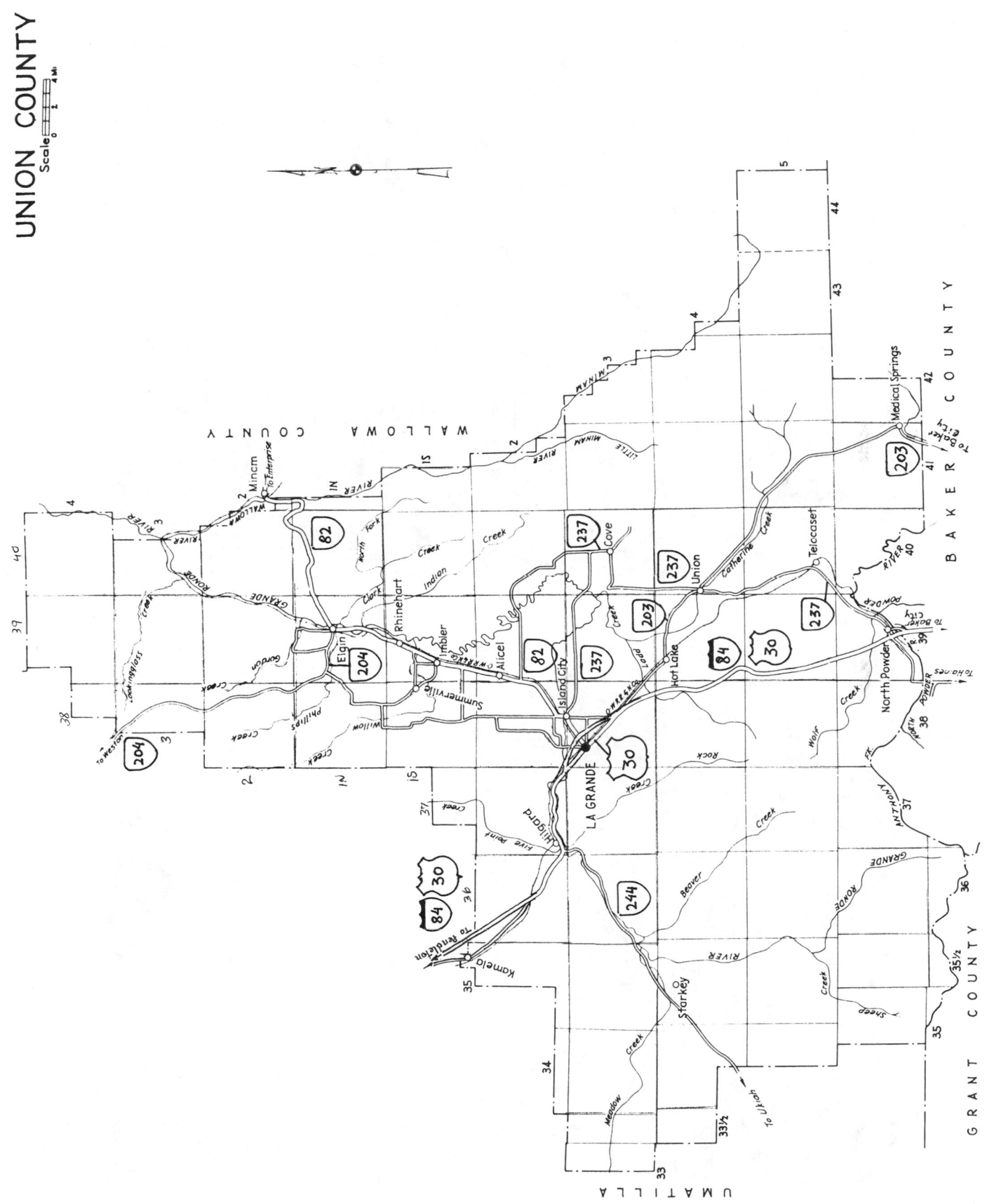

Calvary
Dean H. Byrd (1995)

Hillcrest
Dean H. Byrd (1995)

Area: 2,038 square miles
Population (1998): 24,829
County seat: La Grande, Population: 12,415
County established: 14 October 1864

The Oregon Trail passed through the Grande Ronde River Valley in what became Union County. Explorers and fur traders passed through and in 1842 the first wagon train of settlers came. The earliest organized white cemetery was at the new-founded town of Union in 1862. It was soon followed by a cemetery at La Grande the following year. Settlement in Union County remained closely tied to transit routes after the railways arrived in the mid-1880's.

Grandview
Dean H. Byrd (1995)

Ackles
Dean H. Byrd (1995)

Cove
Dean H. Byrd (1995)

Grandview
Dean H. Byrd (1995)

Name of Cemetery and also known as	Number of burials	Acres	Condition	Date started or earliest known burial	Township	Range	Section

ACKLES
AKA: 1. ACKELS
     2. ECCLES
     3. MT. GLEN
     4. UNION HILL

C 1.8 2 1866   T2S R38E   S21
Take Spruce Street to the north in La Grande and cross the bridge over the Grand Ronde River by Riverside Park. Continue 2.5 miles northerly from the bridge on Mt. Glen Road to the cemetery which is on the right (east), about 800 feet from the road. {28 May 1995} (La Grande 1994 USGS Quad. map.)

**ALLEN, DAVID AND
LeGORE, ARCHIE**

A 0.01 ? 1893   T6S R41E   S18
Located 14.6 miles southeast of Union by an abandoned railway grade 500 yards north of the road between Telocaset and Medical Springs, at a point 1.2 miles east of its junction with Thief Valley Road. Both are named on a single stone; both died of diphtheria. David Allen 1889-1893 and Archie LeGore 1878-1893. (Not shown on Medical Springs 1965-84 USGS Quad. map.)

CALVARY
AKA: 1. CATHOLIC
     [La GRANDE]
     2. HILLCREST
       EAST

D 4 1 1900   T3S R38E   S8
Located on 12th Street and "G" Avenue in La Grande, adjacent to Hillcrest Cemetery. {28 May 1995} (La Grande 1994 USGS Quad. map.)

**CLAY, RUFUS AND
VERNON**

A 0.01 ? June 1890 T2S R37E   S14
Take the Black Hawk Trail at the County Fairgrounds near the I-84 Freeway Overcrossing and go uphill to the landfill where the pavement ends and the name changes to Fox Hill Road. At 3.35 miles from the landfill is a road on the right (Crampton Road) to Rocky Flats. Drive about 0.1 of a mile, to the graves about 200 feet on the left (north); Rufus Clay, born 24 November 1838, died 22 December 1889 and son Vernon, aged 10 who died the same winter. Both were buried the following June. The graves were marked in 1981. (Drumhill Ridge 1964-83 USGS Quad. map.)

COVE

D 15 1 1865   T3S R40E   S22
The cemetery is on a hill about 0.5 of a mile southeast of Main Street and to the right off

Name of Cemetery and also known as	Number of burials	Acres	Condition	Date started or earliest known burial	Township	Range	Section

of Mill Creek Road, and near the water storage tank and a mile from downtown. {29 May 1995} (Cove 1965-84 USGS Quad. map.)

DELANEY, BOBBIE

A   0.01   ?   30 Mar 1908 T1S   R40E   S14
Located 9.3 miles from the junction with OR. Hwy. 82 via Clark Creek Road and Chumos Road. It is along the Middle Fork of Clark Creek and on a hillside within a fenced enclosure; Bobbie Delaney, born 13 Oct. 1907, died 30 Mar. 1908.   (Gasset Bluff 1993 USGS Quad. map.)

DIXIE FLAT
AKA: 1. SHULL INFANT

A   ?   ?   12 Jun 1918 T2S   R37E   ?
Located perhaps in Section 15 or 22. Leave La Grande on I-84 at the junction with U.S. Hwy. 30 at the west edge of town. Drive westerly uphill on I-84 to the Perry interchange. Leave I-84 to the right to the frontage road; turn hard right onto the frontage road and head back parallel to the freeway for about 0.65 of a mile where you cross the railway and head inland up Bear Canyon. About 0.35 of a mile up Bear Canyon turn left (northwesterly) up Robbs Hill Road on a winding route uphill until Dixie Flat is reached. At about 4.5 miles from the Perry Exit is the site of Fox School on the right at the junction of Fox Hill Road. The burial is somewhere in the vicinity. An infant daughter of William and Jessie Rogers Shull died on 12 June 1918 according to Union County death certificate #66. (Not shown on Drumhill Ridge 1964-83 USGS Quad. map.)

DOANE, EMILIE

A   0.01   2   6 Sept 1868 T3S   R37E   S10
In the north 1/2 of Section 10 and about 3 miles west of La Grande. Emilie Doane, born 1831, died 6 September 1868, died in a wagon train and was buried 50-100 yards north of the Oregon Trail. {28 May 1995} (Not shown on Hilgard 1963-84 USGS Quad. map.)

ELGIN

D   10   1   1880   T1N   R39E   S23
Go 0.9 of a mile from OR. Hwy. 82 on Cedar Street, then turn right on Elgin Cemetery

Name of Cemetery and also known as	Number of burials	Acres	Condition	Date started or earliest known burial	Township	Range	Section

Road and go another 0.2 of a mile to the cemetery on the left. (Elgin 1964-83 USGS Quad. map.)

GALLOWAY

| B | 0.2 | 2 | 1876-1911 | T1N | R39E | S3 |

Located 2 miles north of Elgin on Middle Road. There are 46 known burials; 5 others known, but they have been reburied elsewhere. (Elgin 1964-1983 USGS Quad. map.)

GRANDVIEW
AKA: 1. I.O.O.F.

| E | 40 | 1 | 1878 | T3S | R38E | S16 |

Located 0.5 of a mile southeast of La Grande on Foothill Road and 20th Street. On the night of 16/17 May 1993 vandals did an estimated $500,000 worth of damage in knocking over 269 tombstones and opening four crypts in the Mausoleum. There has been much repair since. {27 May 1995} (La Grande 1994 USGS Quad. map.)

HARDSCRABBLE

| A | ? | ? | 30 Sep 1919 | ? | ? | ? |

The compiler is unaware of the site of a cemetery in Union County by the name of Hardscrabble. There is a Union County death certificate #126, 30 September 1919 for John C. Randall, aged 66, a farmer who died in a La Grande hospital. He was buried the following day, 1 October 1919. So this burial site must be quite close to La Grande. Is Hardscrabble a separate cemetery or is it an AKA of a known site?

HIGHLAND
AKA: 1. CRICKET
FLAT

| C | 5 | 2 | 1880 | T1N | R40E | S5 |

Located 0.5 of a mile north of OR. Hwy. 82 on Good Road formerly Cricket Flat Road; the junction is 4.2 miles northeast of Elgin. There were 173 known burials in the fall of 1972. (Cricket Flat 1964-84 USGS Quad. map.)

HILGARD

| B | 1.1 | 2 | 1885 | T2S | R37E | S30 |

Go 6 miles west of La Grande on the I-84 Freeway to the Hilgard Interchange at Mile Post 253 and go onto OR. Hwy. 244. Go 0.2 of a mile on OR. Hwy. 244 to the Five Point Frontage Road on the right and follow the

Name of Cemetery and also known as	Number of burials	Acres	Condition	Date started or earliest known burial	Township	Range	Section

Five Point Frontage Road for 0.3 of a mile to Five Points Creek Road on the left. Follow Five Points Creek Road, crossing the railway tracks; going another 0.6 of a mile and recross the railway. Go another 0.25 of a mile to Hilgard Lane junction; turn right up the hill another 0.34 of a mile on Hilgard Lane to the cemetery. It is in a pine forest on top of the hill. (Hilgard 1963-84 USGS Quad. map.)

HILLCREST
 AKA: 1. MASONIC
   [LA GRANDE]

E 15　1　1895　　T3S R38E　　S8
Located in La Grande, bounded by "E" Avenue, "H" Avenue, 10th Street and 12th Street. The entrance is on 12th Street across from Calvary Cemetery. {27 May 1995} (La Grande 1994 USGS Quad. map.)

INDIAN CREEK

A 0.2　3　1880　　T1N R39E　　S36
Located 5 miles southeast of Elgin via OR. Hwy. 82 to Indian Creek Road. Leave OR. Hwy. 82 at Mile Post 18.3 onto Indian Creek Road. Then go 2.5 miles on Indian Creek Road to the bridge, take the lefthand road at the fork just east of the bridge and go northeast 0.8 of a mile to intersecting Dutton Road. It is on a hill in a wheat field 0.25 of a mile northwest from Dutton Road. There were 10 known burials with 11 more said to be buried here (Fall of 1972); 6 graves are marked, "several unmarked" graves, fenced and "some care" (July of 1983). (Elgin 1964-83 USGS Quad. map.)

ISLAND CITY

D 6.6　1　1890　　T3S R38E　　S3
Located 0.5 of a mile south of Island City on McAlister Lane. {27 May 1995} (La Grande 1994 USGS Quad. map.)

KAMELA
 AKA: 1. DYE, WILLIAM

A 0.01　?　17 Dec 1908 T1S R35E　　S36
Kamela is a railway stop for the Union Pacific in the Blue Mountains just inside of Union County. A skull and upper arm bones were found on 23 and 24 May 1909, 4 miles southwest of Kamela. A coroners' jury at Kamela decided that these were the remains of

Name of Cemetery and also known as	Number of burials	Acres	Condition	Date started or earliest known burial	Township	Range	Section

William Dye, aged about 57, who had lived 3 miles southwest of Kamela and who froze to death on or about 17 December 1908. The burial was at Kamela, all according to death certificate #1553 for Union County, 1908. (Not shown on Meacham Lake 1963-83 USGS Quad. map.)

LA GRANDE

D 10 7 1863-1910 T3S R38E S8

The first white cemetery in Union County and the only one in the county in 1863-1878. It was located between "J" and "L" Avenues and 8th and 10th Streets, and the site is now occupied by Eastern Oregon State College. In disuse as a cemetery by 1910, most burials were removed to Hillcrest Cemetery in 1929. {27 May 1995} (La Grande 1994 USGS Quad. map, but not as a cemetery.)

MEDICAL SPRINGS
AKA: 1. EVELAND, MRS.

A 0.1 ? ? T6S R41E ?

Located off to the east of OR. Hwy. 203 about 0.25 of a mile south of Medical Springs and hard to find (1966). Mrs. Eveland, a little boy of the Butcher family and two little girls of the Tucker and Duncan families are buried on the Gilkenson Farm. NOTE: This site is on private property. No further information was given in this report. (Not shown on Medical Springs 1965-84 USGS Quad. map.)

MT. PLEASANT
AKA: 1. SCOTT
2. SCOTT CHURCH
3. SCOTT GRAVE YARD

A 0.5 2 1900 T2N R40E S15

Drive 7 miles from Elgin on OR. Hwy. 82 to the northeast. At Milepost 27.25, turn left (north) onto Yarrington Road and go another 4.9 miles to the old Scott Baptist Church off to the left (west) of the road. The church is no longer used and the cemetery is 80 yards behind the church. There were 17 marked graves with the latest burial March 1952 (Fall 1972). 15 graves are marked; with "several" unmarked (July 1983). (Rondowa 1964-83 USGS Quad. map.)

Name of Cemetery and also known as	Number of burials	Acres	Condition	Date started or earliest known burial	Township	Range	Section

NIBLEY

A 0.5 12 1898-1910 T3S R39E S1

Located on Cove Road (OR. Hwy. 237) 5 miles west of Cove. Abandoned by 1910 and farmed over after 1950, this was on a bare knoll west of Catherine Creek and about 200 yards south of OR. Hwy. 237. No trace of the cemetery or the town of Nibley was visible in 1981. (Not shown on Conley 1965 USGS Quad. map.)

NORTH POWDER [NEW]

D 15 1 1890 T6S R39E S22

This is in Sections 22 and 23, in the northeast corner of North Powder city limits on OR. Hwy. 237 towards Union. This is the present cemetery for North Powder and was given to the town by I. N. Sanders in 1890. (North Powder 1994 USGS Quad. map.)

NORTH POWDER [OLD]

? ? 5 1875-1890 T6S R39E ?

Perhaps this is in Section 16. This was about 1 mile northwest of town near the foothills and near Wolf Creek. Some graves were moved to the present cemetery, but evidence of others remain. All of these are of unknowns. (Not shown on North Powder 1994 USGS Quad. map.)

PINE GROVE
AKA: 1. ELK FLAT

B 0.3 2 1900 T1N R40E S12

Located about 8 miles east of Elgin. Leave OR. Hwy. 82 at Milepost 27.6 to the right onto Pine Grove Loop and then right (south) onto Follett Road. Pine Grove Church is 0.25 of a mile southeast of OR. Hwy. 82 on a gravel road. Go 0.75 of a mile down Follett Road from the church, in open timber. The cemetery is 0.6 of a mile on the left (east) from the nearest road. There were 30 known graves with October 1955 being the latest known burial (Fall 1972). (Cricket Flat 1964-84 USGS Quad. map.)

**REYNOLDS REST AREA,
C. H.**

? ? ? 1841-1849 T4S R38E S12

There are some unidentified graves at the C. H. Reynolds Rest Area along the I-84 Freeway, 7 miles southeast of La Grande at Milepost

Name of Cemetery and also known as	Number of burials	Acres	Condition	Date started or earliest known burial	Township	Range	Section

269. (The rest area is shown on the Glass Hill 1965-84 USGS Quad. map, but not the graves.)

RIDDELL — A ? ? 25 Mar 1915 ? ? ?

Union County death certificate #1165 reports the death of Benjamin H. Riddell, age about 34 years, on 25 March 1915. He was reported shipped on March 28, to Riddell Cemetery. The compiler does not know the location of this cemetery.

RUGG — A ? ? ? T2S R36E S13

Reportedly there is a burial or burials in the Wallowa-Whitman National Forest in the Blue Mountains. Rugg Spring is in Section 14 and Rugg Cabin is in Section 13. Both the cabin and spring are near Forestry Road #300. (No grave or graves are shown on Huron 1964-83 USGS Quad. map or the Wallowa-Whitman National Forest map.)

STARKEY — A 0.5 5 1882 T4S R35E S3

Located on the homestead of A. T. or John French. On a timbered knoll, and on the fence line, 0.25 of a mile east of McIntyre County Road #1. This is approximately 0.75 of a mile south of OR. Hwy. 244 from the Highway Milepost 33.4 at a point approximately 13 miles southwest of its junction with the I-84 Freeway. There were 7 known burials, 8 more buried here but the graves can no longer be located (1972-1973). (Not shown on Marley Creek 1965-84 USGS Quad. map.)

STARKEY, JOHN B. — A 0.01 ? 1881 T3S R35E S35

This is in the Southwest 1/4 of the Southwest 1/4 of Section 35. This single grave is on the north side of OR. Hwy. 244 between the highway and the old railway grade, 13.5 miles southwest of the junction of OR. Hwy. 244 and the I-84 Freeway. "John B. Starkey 1829-1881." (Not shown on McIntyre Creek 1964-84 USGS Quad. map.)

Name of Cemetery and also known as	Number of burials	Acres	Condition	Date started or earliest known burial	Township	Range	Section

SUMMERVILLE
AKA: 1. SUMMERVILLE--
         IMBLER

D 15   1   1866   T1S R39E   S18
Located 1.5 miles northwest of Imbler on Summerville Road, 0.75 of a mile southeast of Summerville. (Imbler 1994 USGS Quad. map.)

TEDDIE

A   0.01 ?   1923   T5S R41E   S7
Located at the southwest quarter corner of Northwest 1/4 of Northwest 1/4 of Section 7. It is 12.4 miles southeast of Union at an angle of OR. Hwy. 203 and the National Forest Boundary at the boundary sign with Catherine Creek State Forest. There is a small white picket fence enclosure. (Not shown on Little Catherine Creek 1993 USGS Quad. map.)

TELOCASET

A   ?   ?   26 Jun 1918 T5S R40E   S28
Telocaset was a railway stop with a post office in southern Union County. It was about one mile southeast of OR. Hwy. 237 on Telocaset Lane. Baker County Death certificate #85 for 1918 reports the death in Baker City of Maud Elsie Becker, age 30, the divorced wife of P. M. Becker of Telocaset. She was buried at Telocaset, presumably on land owned by her father D. H. Grider. (Not shown on Telocaset 1993 USGS Quad. map.)

THE PARK
AKA: 1. PARK

B   0.5   5   1875   T6S R41E   S2
The death certificates call this Park. It is 16.4 miles southeast of Union on OR. Hwy. 203, in a pine grove 200 feet east of OR. Hwy. 203. There were 37 known graves with 3 more known here but not located; the latest burial on record is 1954 (summer of 1972). NOTE: This site is on private property. (Medical Springs 1965-84 USGS map.)

UNION

D 10   1   1862   T4S R40E   S19
Located 0.5 of a mile east of Main Street (OR. Hwy. 237) on South East Fulton Street. NOTE: There is an abundance of fine monuments on the lower slope of the hillside. {28 May 1995} (Union 1994 USGS Quad. map.)

Name of Cemetery and also known as	Number of burials	Acres	Condition	Date started or earliest known burial	Township	Range	Section

UNKNOWN

A ? ? ?   T3S R33E   S23
A report listing an "unknown infant, Henry Stewart age unknown, infant son of Thomas Davidson and Ludvig aged about 60 years." No further information was given in the report. (Not shown on Tamarack Gulch 1995 USGS Quad. map.)

WEAVER FAMILY

A ? 12 1870   T1N R39E   S26
Located on Indian Creek Road 2.5 miles southeast of Elgin. Leave the main intersection in Elgin and drive south 1.6 miles on OR. Hwy. 82 to about Milepost 18.3. Turn left (easterly) off of the highway onto Indian Creek Road, crossing that creek. About 0.9 of a mile from the highway is the farm on the right (west) with the site uphill in a field above the house. The stones (not burials) were moved to Elgin Cemetery Circa 1950; The plot has been farmed over and there are no remaining visible traces. There were 5 known burials here and probably a few more (1972). NOTE: In 1873-1875 there were 4 burials. (Not shown on Elgin 1964-83 USGS Quad. map.)

WRIGHT FAMILY
 AKA: 1. LOWER COVE

B 2 2 1870   T2S R40E   S18
Located 7 miles east of the junction with OR. Hwy. 82 and Lower Cove Road, on the hillside above the road on the Wright Farm (1978), 100 yards north of Lower Cove Road. A private cemetery with 41 known burials (Summer 1972). This is not to be confused with the other Wright Family Cemetery see that article. (Gasset Bluff 1993 USGS Quad. map.)

WRIGHT FAMILY

A 0.5 5 1899-1964   T6S R41E   S25
Located at Medical Springs on the edge of the bluff immediately above and southeast of the intersection. It is 500 feet southeast of the intersection of Collins Road formerly Big Creek Road with OR. Hwy. 203. The occupants are listed on a large single marker at the intersection. This is for the Dunham Wright family. There were 6 known burials (1972). This is not to be confused with the other Wright Family Cemetery see that article.

Name of Cemetery and also known as	Number of burials	Acres	Condition	Date started or earliest known burial	Township	Range	Section

(Not shown on Medical Springs 1965-84, or
Flagstaff Butte 1993 USGS Quad. maps.)

Ackles
Dean H. Byrd (1995)

ACKELS see **ACKLES**	UNION CO.	T2S	R38E	S21
ACKLES	UNION CO.	T2S	R38E	S21
ALLEN, DAVID AND LeGORE, ARCHIE	UNION CO.	T6S	R41E	S18
BECKER, MAUD ELSIE see **TELOCASET**				
	UNION CO.	T5S	R40E	S28
BECKER, P. M. see **TELOCASET**	UNION CO.	T5S	R40E	S28
BUTCHER FAMILY see **MEDICAL SPRINGS**				
	UNION CO.	T6S	R41E	?
CALVARY	UNION CO.	T3S	R38E	S8
CATHOLIC [LA GRANDE] see **CALVARY**				
	UNION CO.	T3S	R38E	S8
CLAY, RUFUS AND VERNON	UNION CO.	T2S	R37E	S14
COVE	UNION CO.	T3S	R40E	S22
CRICKET FLAT see **HIGHLAND**	UNION CO.	T1N	R40E	S5
DAVIDSON, THOMAS see **UNKNOWN**	UNION CO.	T3S	R33E	S23
DELANEY, BOBBIE	UNION CO.	T1S	R40E	S14
DIXIE FLAT	UNION CO.	T2S	R37E	?
DOANE, EMILIE	UNION CO.	T3S	R37E	S10
DUNCAN FAMILY see **MEDICAL SPRINGS**				
	UNION CO.	T6S	R41E	?
DYE, WILLIAM see **KAMELA**	UNION CO.	T1S	R35E	S36
ECCLES see **ACKLES**	UNION CO.	T2S	R38E	S21
ELGIN	UNION CO.	T1N	R39E	S23
ELK FLAT see **PINE GROVE**	UNION CO.	T1N	R40E	S12
EVELAND, MRS. see **MEDICAL SPRINGS**				
	UNION CO.	T6S	R41E	?
FRENCH, A. T. see **STARKEY**	UNION CO.	T4S	R35E	S3
FRENCH, JOHN see **STARKEY**	UNION CO.	T4S	R35E	S3
GALLOWAY	UNION CO.	T1N	R39E	S3
GILKENSON FARM see **MEDICAL SPRINGS**				
	UNION CO.	T6S	R41E	?
GRANDVIEW	UNION CO.	T3S	R38E	S16
GRIDER, D. H. see **TELOCASET**	UNION CO.	T5S	R40E	S28
HARDSCRABBLE	UNION CO.	?	?	?
HIGHLAND	UNION CO.	T1N	R40E	S5
HILGARD	UNION CO.	T2S	R37E	S30
HILLCREST	UNION CO.	T3S	R38E	S8
HILLCREST EAST see **CALVARY**	UNION CO.	T3S	R38E	S8
I.O.O.F. see **GRANDVIEW**	UNION CO.	T3S	R38E	S16
INDIAN CREEK	UNION CO.	T1N	R39E	S36
ISLAND CITY	UNION CO.	T3S	R38E	S3
KAMELA	UNION CO.	T1S	R35E	S36
LA GRANDE	UNION CO.	T3S	R38E	S8
LeGORE, ARCHIE see **ALLEN, DAVID**	UNION CO.	T6S	R41E	S18
LOWER COVE see **WRIGHT FAMILY**	UNION CO.	T2S	R40E	S18
LUDVIG see **UNKNOWN**	UNION CO.	T3S	R33E	S23
MASONIC [LA GRANDE] see **HILLCREST**				
	UNION CO.	T3S	R38E	S8
MEDICAL SPRINGS	UNION CO.	T6S	R41E	?
MT. GLEN see **ACKLES**	UNION CO.	T2S	R38E	S21
MT. PLEASANT	UNION CO.	T2N	R40E	S15
NIBLEY	UNION CO.	T3S	R39E	S1

NORTH POWDER [NEW]	UNION CO.	T6S	R39E	S22
NORTH POWDER [OLD]	UNION CO.	T6S	R39E	?
PARK see **THE PARK**	UNION CO.	T6S	R41E	S2
PINE GROVE	UNION CO.	T1N	R40E	S12
RANDALL, JOHN C. see **HARDSCRABBLE**				
	UNION CO.	?	?	?
REYNOLDS REST AREA, C. H.	UNION CO.	T4S	R38E	S12
RIDDELL	UNION CO.	?	?	?
RIDDELL, BENJAMIN H. see **RIDDELL**				
	UNION CO.	?	?	?
RUGG	UNION CO.	T2S	R36E	S13
SANDERS, I. N. see **NORTH POWDER [NEW]**				
	UNION CO.	T6S	R39E	S22
SCOTT see **MT. PLEASANT**	UNION CO.	T2N	R40E	S15
SCOTT CHURCH see **MT. PLEASANT**	UNION CO.	T2N	R40E	S15
SCOTT GRAVE YARD see **MT. PLEASANT**				
	UNION CO.	T2N	R40E	S15
SHULL INFANT see **DIXIE FLAT**	UNION CO.	T2N	R37E	?
SHULL, JESSIE ROGERS see **DIXIE FLAT**				
	UNION CO.	T2S	R37E	?
SHULL, WILLIAM see **DIXIE FLAT**	UNION CO.	T2S	R37E	?
STARKEY	UNION CO.	T4S	R35E	S3
STARKEY, JOHN B.	UNION CO.	T3S	R35E	S35
STEWART, HENRY see **UNKNOWN**	UNION CO.	T3S	R33E	S23
SUMMERVILLE	UNION CO.	T1S	R39E	S18
SUMMERVILLE-IMBLER see **SUMMERVILLE**				
	UNION CO.	T1S	R39E	S18
TEDDIE	UNION CO.	T5S	R41E	S7
TELOCASET	UNION CO.	T5S	R40E	S28
THE PARK	UNION CO.	T6S	R41E	S2
TUCKER FAMILY see **MEDICAL SPRINGS**				
	UNION CO.	T6S	R41E	?
UNION	UNION CO.	T4S	R40E	S19
UNION HILL see **ACKLES**	UNION CO.	T2S	R38E	S21
UNKNOWN	UNION CO.	T3S	R33E	S23
WEAVER FAMILY	UNION CO.	T1N	R39E	S26
WRIGHT FAMILY	UNION CO.	T2S	R40E	S18
WRIGHT FAMILY	UNION CO.	T6S	R41E	S25
WRIGHT FAMILY, DUNHAM see **WRIGHT FAMILY**				
	UNION CO.	T6S	R41E	S25

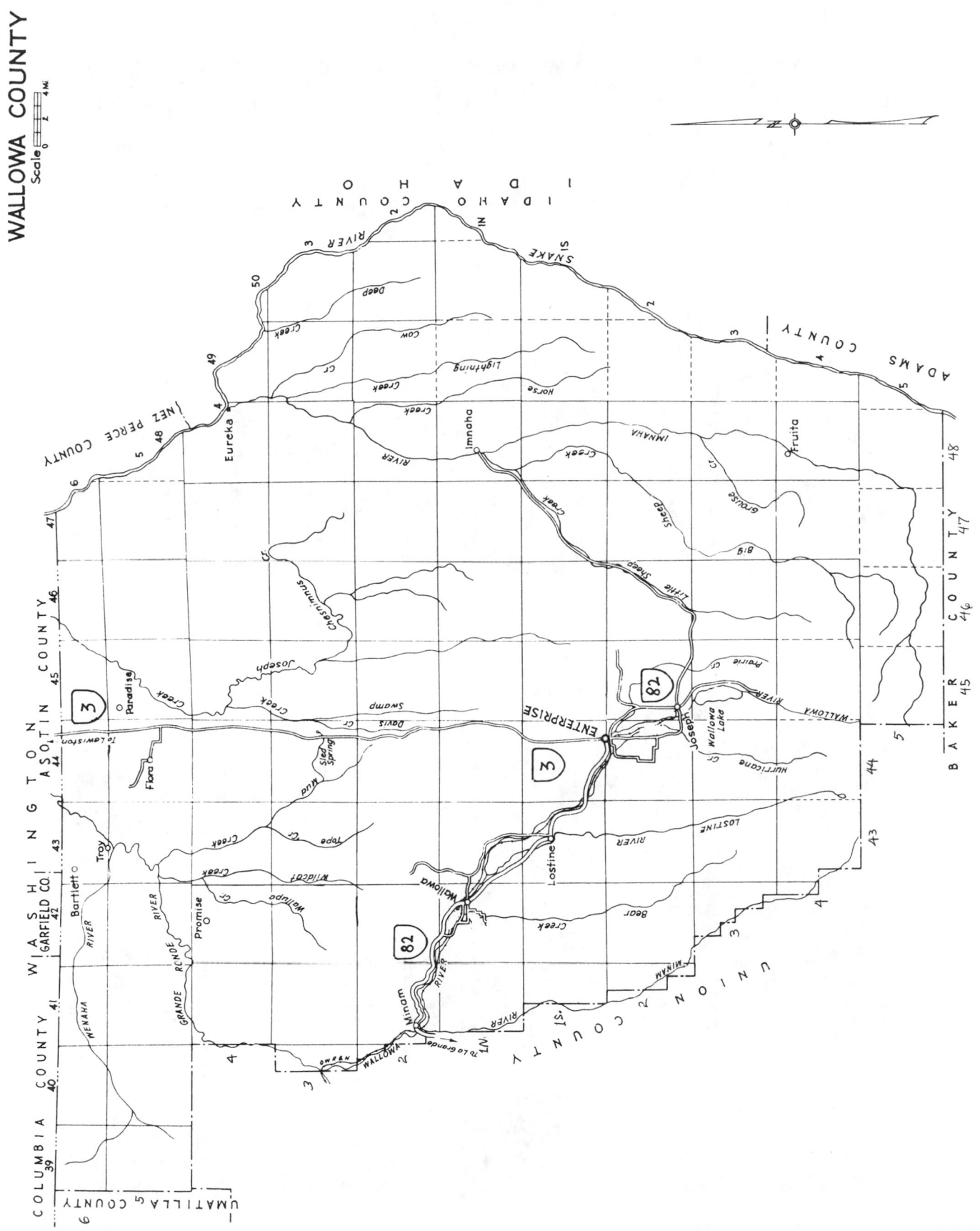

Wallowa
Janice M. Healy (2000)

Chief Joseph Monument
Janice M. Healy taking field notes.
Ruth C. Bishop (2000)

Area: 3,153 square miles
Population (1998): 7,368
County seat: Enterprise, Population: 2,020
County established: 11 February 1887

There is an Indian Cemetery at the outlet of Wallowa Lake. White settlers entered the Wallowa River Valley as early as 1868 (at Lostine) and by the late 1870's there were a number of public cemeteries for the towns in this valley. In the 1880's there were a number of Mormon agricultural settlements to the north of the Wallowa River Valley, but most of these did not thrive despite their optimistic names: Eden, Paradise, Flora, Promise and Utopia.

Chief Joseph Monument
Janice M. Healy (2000)

Wallowa
Janice M. Healy (2000)

Bramlet Memorial
Janice M. Healy (2000)

Name of Cemetery and also known as	Number of burials	Acres	Condition	Date started or earliest known burial	Township	Range	Section

ALDER SLOPE
AKA: 1. ALDER [OLD]

D 3.26 1 Late 1870's T2S R44E S15
Located nearly 3 miles from Enterprise at River Street and OR. Hwy. 82. Go south from Enterprise on Hurricane Creek Road for 1.75 miles to a crossroads. Turn right (west) on Eggleston Lane (County Road #572), go 0.8 of a mile to a junction with an unnamed County Road #807 and turn left (south) for 0.3 of a mile. The cemetery is on the right. It was fenced with granite posts at the time of a June 1968 visit. There are many unmarked and illegible markers. The earliest found date was Oct. 1879. (Enterprise 1990 USGS Quad. map.)

ALIFF, ROSA DANIEL

A 0.01 ? 17 Nov 1910 T4N R43E ?
Rosa Daniel Aliff, born 15 August 1889, died of typhoid. The death certificate states she was buried on the homestead "in the hills 20 miles north of Wallowa." This is in the area of Middle Point, AKA Utopia. Her husband was A. C. Aliff. (Not shown on Wood Butte 1967 USGS Quad. map.)

ARMIN
AKA: 1. HUFFMAN BABY

A 0.01 ? 19 May 1918 T2S R47E S31
Armin was a small settlement with a schoolhouse and a post office from June 1916 to January 1940. Leave Joseph on the Little Sheep Creek Highway towards Imnaha. About 9 miles from Joseph turn right (southerly) onto Armin Road, driving up Rail Canyon to a ridge. The school site is 4.7 miles from the highway. At 5 miles, the junction with Divide Road is to the right. Turn hard left (easterly) down Coyote Creek. At 7 miles is the ranch and site of Armin. A death certificate for an unnamed baby of the Huffman family states a burial somewhere in the vicinity. Are there other burials? (Not shown on Harl Butte 1990 USGS Quad. map.)

BARTLETT
AKA: 1. GROUSE
2. UNION

B 1 3 1883 T6N R43E S21
Located 7.8 miles northwest and north of Troy via Bartlett Road. Go 6.1 miles to a crossroads, then turn east and north going

another 1.75 miles to the site of Bartlett which is very near the Washington State Line. (Troy 1967-83 USGS Quad. map.)

BRAMLET MEMORIAL
AKA: 1. LOWER
VALLEY

C 1.5 1 1870'S T2N R42E S33
Located north of Wallowa. Go 1.5 miles north off of OR. Hwy. 82 on Promise Road, then west on Bramlet Lane for 0.4 of a mile. {13 September 2000} (Wallowa Quad. 1964-84 USGS map.)

BRISCOE, ISAIAH JACKSON

A 0.01 ? 23 Feb 1924 T1N R44E S35
Mr. Briscoe, a widowed laborer aged about 83 was buried on the J. R. White Ranch, according to his death certificate. Perhaps his wife, Elizabeth Rogers Briscoe is also buried there. Drive 6.3 miles north of Enterprise on OR. Hwy. 3, then turn left (west and north) on Dunham Loop Road for 0.9 of a mile. NOTE: This site is on private property. (The ranch house but not the burial is shown on Hicks Spring 1990 USGS Quad. map.)

BUHLER RANCH

A ? ? ? ? ? ?
There are burials reported on this ranch out of Joseph. The compiler has no further information.

CACHE CREEK RANCH

A 0.01 ? Sept 1931 T6N R47E S23
The Cache Creek Ranch is situated at the confluence of that creek with the Snake River. It is about a mile upstream (south) of the Washington State Line. Access is easiest by river boat. Herman Rhodes' was the caretaker of the ranch when a visitor found Rhodes' decomposing body in the cabin. Since Rhodes' horse was found saddled and bridled one theory suggests he had a riding accident. A 10-foot square board fence with a cedar post and granite slab marks the grave on the edge of a field about 100 yards upriver from the ranch buildings. NOTE: This site is private property. (The ranch but not the grave is shown on the Jim Creek Butte 1963 USGS Quad. map.)

Name of Cemetery and also known as	Number of burials	Acres	Condition	Date started or earliest known burial	Township	Range	Section

CEMETERY RIDGE   ?   ?   ?   ?   ?   R48E   ?

This pre-settlement cemetery is possibly in Township 3 North or Township 4 North. Many Indian burials are near the breaks of the Imnaha River above the Snake River at Salmon Bar. (The ridge is shown on Dead Horse Ridge 1963 USGS Quad. map, but no cemetery is shown.)

CHIEF JOSEPH [OLD]   A   ?   6   ?   T1N   R43E   S20

John Harley Horner (1870-1953), a notable collector of Wallowa County history and County Assessor placed the grave of Old Chief Joseph in the Southeast 1/4 of the Southwest 1/4 of Section 20. This is probably on the east side of Baker Road at the foot of a hill and about 0.7 of a mile north of the bridge over the Lostine River. Baker Road leaves OR. Hwy. 82 to the right (north) 4 miles northwest of Lostine. Old Chief Joseph died in the late summer or early fall, perhaps in 1870, and was buried near the forks of the Wallowa and Lostine Rivers. His grave was well marked, amongst other items by the annual sacrifice of a horse until about 1880. This area was homesteaded by V. McAlexander in 1876 who preserved this and 7 other graves. In 1886 a traveling dentist dug up Old Chief Joseph's skull and took it to Baker City, the compiler does not know what became of the skull. On 27 August 1926 Old Chief Joseph's bones were dug up and on 25 September 1926 were reburied in the Wallowa Lake Indian Cemetery. Presumably the 7 adjacent burials were also transferred at the same time. (Not shown on Evans 1990 USGS Quad. map.)

CHIEF JOSEPH MONUMENT   A   5.7   1   1923   T3S   R45E   S5
AKA: 1. NEZ PERCE
     2. WALLOWA LAKE
        INDIAN

Located off of the highway at the north end of Wallowa Lake, it was deeded in 1923. Old Chief Joseph was reburied here on 26 September 1926 from his original burial site. See the article entitled Old Chief Joseph. Also buried here are 5 other marked graves. The burial place of Old Chief Joseph's famous son, (young) Chief Joseph is not known. There is a separate tribal burial ground

Name of Cemetery and also known as	Number of burials	Acres	Condition	Date started or earliest known burial	Township	Range	Section

between the cemetery and the lake. {13 September 2000} (Joseph 1990 USGS Quad. map lumps both cemeteries together.)

CHINESE MINERS MASSACRE B ? ? **26 May 1887 T4N R49E** **UNS**

There was a lengthy article in the *Oregonian* 15 August 1995 page A1 and A9 entitled the *Terrible Secret of Hells Canyon* by reporter R. Gregory Nokes. It relates the story of the massacre of 26-27 May 1887, of 31 unarmed Chinese miners by whites. This is the second of two known massacres of Chinese gold miners in Oregon: the first being that entitled Chinese Massacre in Malheur County. See that article in the Malheur County portion of this book. The Malheur County massacre was perpetrated by Indians whereas the Hells Canyon slaughter was done by whites. Perhaps understandably it is not a widely discussed topic in Wallowa County. In any event at least six men known as horse and livestock thieves and well-armed murdered the unarmed Chinese for any gold the latter may have had. One body washed down the Snake River and was buried in a Lewiston, Idaho Chinese cemetery. What happened to the remaining 30 bodies is unknown. The killings took place mostly along Robinson Gulch or possibly Deep Creek along the Snake River. (Not shown on Cactus Mtn. 1963 USGS Quad. map.)

CROW CREEK
AKA: 1. WARNOCK
        CHILDREN

A 0.01 2 25 Dec 1893 T1N R45E **S13**

Leave OR. Hwy. 82 between Enterprise and Joseph and take the county road towards Chico and Lewis, which follows Crow Creek for many miles. The two graves are in a fenced enclosure alongside the road and near ranch buildings about 16 miles from OR. Hwy. 82. A young daughter and son of D.D. and Eva Warnock are buried here. The latter child died 22 December 1894. (Not shown on Elk Mountain or Elk Mountain S. E. 1990 USGS Quad. map.)

DAVIS, ANNA
AKA: 1. DAUGHERTY
        RANCH

A 0.01 2 17 OCT 1922 T1N R42E **S11**

Anna Davis, a Nez Perce child of about six years from Fort Lapwai, Idaho, died of

Name of Cemetery and also known as	Number of burials	Acres	Condition	Date started or earliest known burial	Township	Range	Section

2. LITTLE INDIAN GIRL

typhoid. She was buried on the "Triple D" Ranch of Bill Daugherty in a grave marked by a heap of stones and surrounded by a small cyclone fence. The grave is on the north side of OR. Hwy. 82 and the north side of the Wallowa River, about halfway between the town of Wallowa and the road to Promise. It is on a flat area on the hillside. NOTE: This site is on private property. (Not shown on Wallowa 1964-84 USGS Quad. map.)

DOBBIN FAMILY

A   0.01   5   ?   T4N   R48E   S34
The Dobbin family site is on Cemetery Ridge. 2 sunken gravesites were found in 1985. It is not easy to locate. No other information was given in the report. (Dead Horse Ridge 1963 USGS Quad. map.)

EDEN
AKA: 1. EDEN RIDGE
     2. HAFER

A   0.25   3   1880   T5N   R42E   S21
Located 10.25 miles southwest of Troy, 800 feet left (south) off of Eden Road, 1.1 miles past Eden School and Eden Grange Hall. (Eden 1967-83 USGS Quad. map.)

ENTERPRISE

E   15.49   1   Late 1880'S   T1S   R44E   S35
Located in Enterprise, at the north end of East Alder Street. (Enterprise 1990 USGS Quad. map.)

FISHER, JOHN D.
AKA: 1. FISCHER, JOHN D.
     2. RATTLESNAKE TREE
     3. SMITH MOUNTAIN

A   0.01   ?   25 Mar 1934   T2N   R41E   ?
Perhaps this is located in Section 21. Wallowa County death certificate #10 for 1934 says he was born in Vienna, Austria, 16 May 1850 and has resided for 34 years in the Minam township, and that he was buried on his "own place". Fisher was buried as he wished and a monument set up under a large pine tree that he called the Rattlesnake Tree, on Smith Mountain. His widow, Elizabeth B. Fisher is buried in Wallowa Cemetery. (Not shown on Howard Butte 1964-84 USGS Quad. map.)

Name of Cemetery and also known as	Number of burials	Acres	Condition	Date started or earliest known burial	Township	Range	Section

FLORA

C   1.5   2   1881   T5N   R44E   S21
Located 0.5 of a mile north of Flora. This cemetery is easy to find. Flora is the most populous locale in the north part of Wallowa County. (Flora 1967 USGS Quad. map.)

FRIDDLES FAMILY

A   0.01   ?   29 Dec 1898   T6N   R43E   S23
Located on the old Friddles place at the east end of Grouse Flat. Go east from Bartlett Cemetery nearly 2 miles to a road junction. Turn right (southeasterly) and go another 1.5 miles. The small fenced cemetery has no direct access. It is perhaps 0.5 of a mile east of the county road in the south edge of a field and overlooking the Grande Ronde River far below. Cordelia B. Friddles, born 13 November 1863, died 20 October 1901; Baby Friddles, born 19 November 1898, died 29 December 1898. (Not shown on Troy 1967-83 USGS Quad. Map.)

GORDON, CHARLES

A   ?   ?   ?   T5N   R45E   ?
The grave of Charles Gordon is cryptically placed somewhere at "Rush Creek-High Trail". The compiler has no further information. (Not shown on Paradise 1967 USGS Quad. map.)

GWYNNE

A   0.01   ?   29 Jan 1915   T1S   R44E   S30
Gwynne was a railway stop for a lumber mill and, according to a railway map of 1926, was then still in use. The station and mill were on the left (south) bank of the Wallowa River between Lostine and Enterprise. OR. Hwy. 10 crosses the river here, 4.5 miles from Lostine and 6 miles from Enterprise. Infant twin girls, Agnes and Alpha Brownlee, died of pneumonia on 29 and 30 January 1915 according to their death certificates. Sites of their burials are not stated, but the probability is they were buried in this vicinity. (Not shown on the Enterprise 1990 USGS Quad. map.)

HAT POINT

A   0.01   ?   ?   T1S   R49E   S35
This is a lone burial of a native american. The grave is located on the left side of the road leading to Hat Point. It is about 0.22

of a mile short of the fork in the road which leads left (north) to Sacajawea Campground or ahead to Hat Point. (Not shown on Hat Point 1990 USGS Quad. map.)

HILTSLEY, FRANK

A 0.01 ? 1911   T1S R50E   UNS

The grave of Frank Hiltsley is reported to be somewhere near where Quartz Creek enters the Snake River in Hells Canyon. This area is unsurveyed. (Not shown on Temperance Creek 1990 USGS Quad. map.)

HORSE CREEK RANCH
AKA: 1. LYDELL, EFFIE MAE
     2. LYDELL-- STUBBLEFIELD, BABIES
     3. STUBBLEFIELD, TINIE

A 0.01 3 1896   T3N R48E   S35

This gravesite is located about 11 miles north of Imnaha on the road heading downstream following the Imnaha River and towards the Trout Creek Guard Station. At the Horse Creek Road junction which leads to the right, continue ahead for about an eighth of a mile to the ranch on the right hand side of the road. Tinie Stubblefield, born 1894, died 1896, and Effie Mae Lydell (also spelled Lightle), born 9 November 1916, died 5 December 1916 are buried here. Possibly an unidentified third person is also buried here. (Haas Hollow 1990 USGS Quad. map.)

HOWARD FAMILY

A ? ? Circa 1900 T3N R41E   ?

There are reported burials of the Howard family at Howard Meadows on upper Howard Creek in Sections 16 or 21. There is a tangle of old logging roads so access to this will not be easy. (NOT shown on Howard Butte 1964-84 USGS Quad. map.)

I.O.O.F. PIONEER [JOSEPH]
AKA: 1. AIRPORT
     2. HURRICANE CREEK
     3. JOSEPH
     4. MASONIC
     5. WEATHERLY

C 3.7 2 1870'S T2S R44E   S36

From the principal intersection on OR. Hwy. 82 in Joseph, go west 1.2 miles to the Joseph airport. The cemetery is 0.1 of a mile beyond. This cemetery has been subject to flooding from Hurricane Creek. There are 30 marked burials and many unmarked burials. (Chief Joseph Mtn. and Joseph 1990 USGS Quad. maps.)

Name of Cemetery and also known as	Number of burials	Acres	Condition	Date started or earliest known burial	Township	Range	Section

IMNAHA

B 2 2 Late 1870'S T1N R48E S21
At Imnaha, go through the feed lots. You need to get permission first. Located off of Little Sheep Creek Highway and across Big Sheep Creek, near its confluence with the Imnaha River. There were 56 known burials and 13 unknown burials (1994). (Imnaha 1990 USGS Quad. map.)

INDIAN GRAVE

? ? ? ? T1S R49E S21
Mainly in Section 21, but also in Section 16 and 20, there is an Indian Grave Creek which is about a mile long. It is a tributary to Horse Creek in the Hells Canyon Recreation Area. Presumably the name of the creek refers to a pre-settlement Indian burial site. (Indian Grave Creek is shown, but the burial is not shown on Hat Point 1990 USGS Quad. map.)

LEAP
AKA: 1. BUNNELL
     FAMILY
   2. LATHROP
     FAMILY

? ? ? ? T1N R44E S8
Leap was a locale about 9 airline miles east of Wallowa. There is a reference to Bunnell and Lathrop family burials at Leap. However the Township, Range, and Section location of Leap Cemetery is given as the same as the Wallowa Cemetery. There are indeed numerous Lathrop burials in Wallowa Cemetery, but Bunnel (sic) burials are listed in Enterprise Cemetery. Is Leap an AKA for Wallowa Cemetery? Was there a cemetery at Leap and the Lathrops and Bunnells reburied at Wallowa and Enterprise? The compiler cannot say. (Not shown on Hicks Spring 1990 USGS Quad. map.)

LIGHTNING CREEK

A 0.01 ? 12 Jul 1908 T3N R48E S12
Reported on the death certificate #7444 as being 55 miles northeast of Enterprise with burial at "Lightning." A. Grover Miller was a cowboy, "aged about 23, family unknown." Miller's foot was caught in a stirrup and he was dragged to death by a runaway horse. This location appears to be in the general vicinity of the confluence of Lightning Creek with the Imnaha River and about three quarters of the way down the Imnaha River

Name of Cemetery and also known as	Number of burials	Acres	Condition	Date started or earliest known burial	Township	Range	Section

from the town of Imnaha towards the Snake River. The Lightning Creek Ranch buildings, although vacant, were still standing in 1954 at the confluence of Lightning Creek and the Imnaha River. (No buildings are shown at the site, nor is the burial shown on the Deadhorse Ridge 1963 USGS Quad. map.)

LOST PRAIRIE

| | B | 0.5 | 2 | **Early 1880** | T6N | R44E | S31 |

Located northwest of Flora, approximately 6.4 miles via Lost Prairie Road, on the left (west) side of the road. (Flora 1967 USGS Quad. map.)

LOSTINE
 AKA: 1. JIM TOWN

| | D | 7.6 | 1 | 1868 | T1S | R43E | S3 |

Located 1.3 miles north of OR. Hwy. 82 at Lostine on Jim Town Road, then left (west) 0.3 of a mile. (Evans 1990 USGS Quad. map.)

MARKS FAMILY

| | A | 0.01 | 5 | **Late 1870'S** | T2S | R48E | S2 |

These two burials are accessible only by a foot bridge over the Imnaha River. Walk downstream 0.5 to 0.75 of a mile; this is about 14 miles south of Imnaha on Upper Imnaha Road and south of College Creek Ranger Station. You will need permission to go here. Two other burials have been removed to Prairie Creek Cemetery. (Not shown on Sheep Creek Divide 1990 USGS Quad. map.)

MARKS, SAM

| | A | 0.01 | ? | ? | ? | ? | ? |

This lone burial is reported to be along Cache Creek, but not specifically identified. If true, this grave could be in the vicinity of the Cache Creek burial site, see that article. On the other hand Marks Cabin on Summit Ridge, Township 3 South, Range 49 East or Marks Creek Township 2 South, Range 50 East are possibilities. Marks Creek is about a mile long and flows into the Snake River in Hells Canyon. (Cache Creek is shown in Jim Creek Butte 1963, Marks Cabin is shown on Squirrel Prairie 1990 , and Marks Creek is shown on Old Timer Mtn. 1990 USGS Quad. maps.)

Name of Cemetery and also known as	Number of burials	Acres	Condition	Date started or earliest known burial	Township	Range	Section

MAXVILLE

? ? ? ?   T3N R42E   S15

Drive about 2 miles north of Wallowa, leave OR. Hwy. 82 and take the road right (north) to Promise. About 13 miles on this road is Maxville, which was a logging camp run by the Bowman-Hicks Lumber company and was the most active during the 1920's and 1930's. There were deaths here, a lot of which were shipped to Arkansas and some were buried in Promise Cemetery according to death certificates. Rumors of one infant burial "by roadside" just may refer to Betty Lou Koon, died 3 December 1925, aged 3 months, 23 days. She smothered in bedclothes. The death certificate only says "died at Maxville" without stating the burial site. (Maxville is shown on the Akers Butte 1964-84 USGS Quad. map, but there are no burials indicated.)

McCUBBIN
AKA: 1. KUHN
     2. WEST SIDE

B   0.125 3 1878   T1S R43E   S5

Leave Lostine on OR. Hwy. 82 going northwest toward Wallowa. 1.7 miles from Lostine turn left onto Allen Canyon Road and proceed 0.85 of a mile to the cemetery which is uphill on the left. Started for 8 or 9 child diphtheria victims. The people at the town of Lostine were fearful of contamination if these were buried in the Lostine Cemetery. (Evans 1990 USGS Quad. map.)

MIDDLE POINT
AKA: 1. UTOPIA

A ?   5 Circa 1900 T4N R43E   S30

This cemetery on Middle Point Ridge was established for a Mormon settlement with the overly optimistic name of Utopia. There was a post office named Utopia from May 1903 to May 1911. About 2 miles north of Wallowa, leave OR. Hwy. 82 and take the road right (north) to Promise. At 11.4 miles from OR. Hwy. 82 leave the Promise Road and turn right (northeast) onto Middle Point Road. After going 5.5 miles on Middle Point Road and 16.9 miles from the highway is a sign: County road closed ahead. The compiler cannot say if you have reached the area of the cemetery. A forest fire years ago burned the grave markers which were all of wood. At least 9 persons, mostly infants, were known to be buried here. (Not shown on Wood Butte 1967 USGS Quad. map.)

MINAM

A   0.01 ? ?   **T2N R41E**   **S19**

Two graves are located on a flat down towards the Wallowa River. Take a private dead-end road north out of Minam. The graves are on the left (west) side of the road and within a mile of Minam. (Not shown on Howard Butte 1964-84 USGS Quad. map.)

NICHOLS, BESSIE

A   0.01 5   **10 Feb 1906 T5N R42E**   **S22**

This lone grave is located in the Southwest 1/4 of the Northwest 1/4 of Section 22. Drive west from Troy towards the Eden Cemetery, but about 1 mile short of that cemetery is the old Eden School. Stop and follow the fence line on foot to the left (south) to the breaks above Cabin Creek and the Grande Ronde River. The grave is said to be easily located from here. It is marked by a large flat rock that was packed up from the river. Bessie Nichols was born and died on the same day. (Not shown on Eden 1967-83 USGS Quad. map.)

NICOSON
  AKA: 1. MARTIN
       2. NICOLSON

A   0.27 1   1890   **T5N R44E**   **S8**

Located 2.9 miles northwest of Flora via Lost Prairie Road, on the left (southwest) side of the road. NOTE: Markers in the cemetery all spell it Nicoson. (Flora 1967 USGS Quad. map.)

ODELL BROTHERS

A   0.01 ? ?   **T3S R45E**   **?**

Two brothers are said to be buried somewhere on the west side of Wallowa Lake. This was talked about but has never been confirmed. (Not shown on Joseph 1990 USGS Quad. map.)

PALLETTE RANCH
  AKA: 1. BUTLER FAMILY
       2. BUTLER RANCH

A ? ? ?   **T4S R48E**   **?**

The ranch buildings straddle Sections 5 and 8. The Pallette Ranch, once the Butler Ranch is about 7 miles farther south in the Upper

Name of Cemetery and also known as	Number of burials	Acres	Condition	Date started or earliest known burial	Township	Range	Section

Imnaha River Valley from Park Cemetery and 25.5 miles south of Imnaha. Three members of the Butler family are buried here. (Ranch buildings but no burial sites are shown on Puderbaugh Ridge 1990 USGS Quad. map.)

PARADISE

B 1.25 2 1880'S T6N R45E S31

Leave OR. Hwy. 3 at Flora Junction and go 5 miles north on Paradise Road. The cemetery is 700 feet off of the road on the right. There were 63 marked graves found in 1986. (Paradise 1967 USGS Quad. map.)

PARK
AKA: 1. FRUITA
2. GROUSE CREEK
3. PARK GRANGE

A 0.66 3 Late 1870'S T3S R48E S3

Take Upper Imnaha Road just south of the mouth of Grouse Creek; the cemetery is 18.4 miles south of Imnaha and west of the road across the river. There are 15 known burials. (Jaynes Ridge 1990 USGS Quad. map.)

PINE CREEK

A 0.01 1 6 Feb 1886 T2N R46E S27

The burials of father and son are located along Pine Creek Road on the west side of Pine Cree about 3 miles northwest of Zumwalt as the crow flies or likewise 3 miles southeast of Greenwood Butte as the crow flies. Thomas Maynard, died 6 Febuary 1886 and son Thomas J. Maynard, died 7 April 1887, are buried here. Rebecca Jane Maynard, the wife and mother, died 20 December 1891, is buried in Prairie Creek Cemetery. (Not shown on Greenwood Butte 1990 USGS Quad. map.)

POWWATKA
AKA: 1. PRINCE

A 0.25 2 Circa 1900 T4N R43E S33

This cemetery was deeded to the public 7 July 1916. It is located in the Southeast 1/4 of the Southeast 1/4 of Section 33. Leave the town of Wallowa and take the road to Troy, to the east and north. Enter the Wallowa-Whitman National Forest, skirting the edge of Wood Butte on the left (west). About 100 yards north of a large waterhole, also on the left, is a crossroads. One is now about 18.6 miles from Wallowa. Turn off the Troy road to the right (east) onto a gated side road which leads about 500 feet to the summit of a ridge and just over the summit and about 250 feet to the right (south) is the cemetery. (Not shown on Wood Butte 1967 USGS Quad. map.)

PRAIRIE CREEK D 13 1 Late 1870'S T2S R45E S34
Located 2.1 miles east of Joseph on Little Sheep Creek Highway, then right (south) 1 mile on Prairie Creek Road. (Joseph 1990 USGS Quad. map.)

PRATT-COLVILLE A ? ? 1901-1902 T3S R43E ?
Located in the Eagle Cap Wilderness of the Wallowa-Whitman National Forest perhaps in Section 22. In the *Northwest Living* section of the *Oregon Journal*, 29 August 1974, Tom McAllister reports that his party found a memorial blazed and carved into a dead spruce. The tree was near a spring on the divide between Wood Lake and Chimney Lake and between the Lostine River on the east and Bear creek on the west. The photo shows "Born in Wallowa, Ore., Ellis Pratt, Nov. 8, 1901, Colville Aug. 20, (Van?) 1902. (Not shown on North Minam Meadows 1990 USGS Quad. map.)

PROMISE C 0.45 2 1880'S T4N R42E S11
This cemetery is at Promise. Go 20 miles north of OR. Hwy. 82 following Promise Road. Then go 1.3 miles north beyond the junction of Sickfoot Road. 82 markers were noted 1893-1961 (1970's report?). NOTE: The new Mormon settlement of Promise had no cemetery until some cowboys rode into town dragging the bodies of 2 Basque sheepherders. The cowboys did not like sheep. Reportedly the cowboys said, "Now you need a cemetery." {October 1986} (Promise 1967 USGS Quad. map.)

RAYMOND, MR. A ? ? ? T2N R50E ?
Perhaps located in Section 14. This is the location of the Somers Ranch. His burial was reported to be on Somers Ranch, along Somers

Creek, a tributary of the Snake River in Hells Canyon. (Not shown on Lord Flat 1990 USGS Quad. map.)

REEL, ROLAND

A   0.01 ? ?   T3N R50E   ?
Perhaps in Section 3, the site of Cat Creek Ranch at the confluence of Cat Creek with the Snake River in Hells Canyon. Roland Bar Rapids is immediately downstream on the Snake River and the confluence of Roland Creek. (Not shown on Wolf Creek 1963 USGS Quad. map.)

RENTFROW, MAY ANN JUDAY
AKA 1. RENFROW

A   0.01 12 1888   T5N R43E   S4
Located in the Northwest corner of the Northeast 1/4 of the Southeast 1/4 of Section 4. In 1971 the lone grave was noted to be within a small fenced enclosure in a field on the east side of the road. In 1982 it was noticed that the area of the grave was cleaned out and plowed over as part of the field. Cross the Grande Ronde River from Troy to the east side, on the county road to Flora. Leave the county road on the first side road to the right to the site which is less than a mile from Troy. Buried here is May Ann Juday, widow of Henry Rentfrow (later Renfrow). (Not shown on Troy 1967-83 USGS Quad. map.)

RUSSELL FAMILY

A ?   5   ?   T6N R42E   ?
This abandoned small cemetery is located in the Wenaha State Wildlife Area, perhaps in Section 35. The Russell Place was bought by the Oregon Game Commission about 1966, the buildings were burnt and the cultivated areas were returned to nature. The cemetery was reported to be about 0.25 of a mile northwest of the old buildings and orchard in the center of what was once a field. One can here look north across the Wenaha River to the Grouse Flat area. Access is mostly blocked. Buried here in the early part of the 20th century are believed to be 3 members of the Russell Family and 3 other persons. (Not shown on Eden 1967-83 USGS Quad. map.)

Name of Cemetery and also known as	Number of burials	Acres	Condition	Date started or earliest known burial	Township	Range	Section

SHIELDS, LOUIS

A 0.01 ? 1895   T1N R50E   UNS
The area is unsurveyed. This single grave is near Temperance Creek at the confluence of the creek with the Snake River in Hells Canyon. The grave is on the Brockman Ranch. (Temperance Creek 1990 USGS Quad. map.)

SILVER FAMILY
  AKA: 1. KOCH FAMILY

A 0.01 2 4 Dec 1895 T6N R43E   S15
This small cemetery is located in the Southwest 1/4 of the Southwest 1/4 of Section 15. Drive east on Grouse Flat about 1.5 miles and the cemetery is on the left (north) on top of the hill behind the Silver home. The original picket fence has been replaced in 1970 by a 20-foot square chain link fence. The original wooden markers have been replaced by a single marble marker. Three persons of the Silver Family and 2 of the Koch Family are known to be buried here, with 8 November 1902 being the most recent date. A small girl of the Knott Family and perhaps a Mr. Sizemore were also buried here. NOTE: This site is on private property. (Not shown on Troy 1967-83 USGS Quad. map.)

TROY

? ? ? ?   T5N R43E   S4
There have been reports of a burial in this location, but the compiler is unaware of any cemetery at Troy itself. Could this be an AKA for the Rentfrow burial less than a mile distant but across the Grande Ronde River from Troy? See the Rentfrow article. (Not shown on Troy 1967-83 USGS Quad. map.)

VICTOR HOMESTEAD

A 0.01 ? 1887   T2N ?   ?
Perhaps the homestead was on Smith Mountain and in Range 41 East or Range 42 East. Three children whose family names are now unknown, are reported to be buried on the Victor homestead. The children died of diphtheria. (Not shown on Howard Butte or Akers Butte 1964-84 USGS Quad. maps.)

WALLOWA
  AKA: 1. CATHOLIC

D 3.28 1 1879   T1N R42E   S13
On Range 42 and 43 East, and on Sections 13 and 18, this cemetery is east of Wallowa 1.2

Name of Cemetery and also known as	Number of burials	Acres	Condition	Date started or earliest known burial	Township	Range	Section

miles and east of OR. Hwy. 82, go east on First, at city limits First becomes Whisky Creek Road, the cemetery will be on your right (south). {13 September 2000} (Evans 1990 and Wallowa 1964-84 USGS Quad. map.)

WILSON TWINS	A	?	?	?	T3N	R41E	S29

These burials are reported at Downards Meadow near Howard Butte. The compiler has no further information. (Not shown on Howard Butte 1964-84 USGS Quad. map.)

ZUMWALT	?	?	?	?	T2N	R47E	?

Zumwalt was a settlement important enough to have a post office from August 1903 until January 1936. Leave OR. Hwy. 82, between Enterprise and Joseph, take the paved county road to the left and back (northeast). At about 5 miles from the highway the pavement ends at a fork. Take the road to the right (easterly) for another 19 miles to the area of Zumwalt. There is a death certificate for the infant Leland Carlson, born 23 January 1918, died 3 February 1918. The report says he is buried at Zumwalt. His parents were Gust and Ellen Carlson. Were there other burials here? (Not shown on Zumwalt 1990 USGS Quad. map.)

Bramlet Memorial
Janice M. Healy (2000)

AIRPORT see **I.O.O.F. PIONEER [JOSEPH]**

	WALLOWA CO.	T2S	R44E	S36
ALDER [OLD] see **ALDER SLOPE**	WALLOWA CO.	T2S	R44E	S15
ALDER SLOPE	WALLOWA CO.	T2S	R44E	S15

ALIFF, A. C. see **ALIFF, ROSA DANIEL**

	WALLOWA CO.	T4N	R43E	?
ALIFF, ROSA DANIEL	WALLOWA CO.	T4N	R43E	?
ARMIN	WALLOWA CO.	T2S	R47E	S31
BARTLETT	WALLOWA CO.	T6N	R43E	S21

BOWMAN-HICKS LUMBER COMPANY LOGGING CAMP see **MAXVILLE**

	WALLOWA CO.	T3N	R42E	S15
BRAMLET MEMORIAL	WALLOWA CO.	T2N	R42E	S33

BRISCOE, ELIZABETH ROGERS see **BRISCOE, ISAIAH JACKSON**

	WALLOWA CO.	T1N	R44E	S35
BRISCOE, ISAIAH JACKSON	WALLOWA CO.	T1N	R44E	S35

BRISCOE, MR. see **BRISCOE, ISAIAH JACKSON**

	WALLOWA CO.	T1N	R44E	S35

BROCKMAN RANCH see **SHIELDS, LOUIS**

	WALLOWA CO.	T1N	R50E	UNS
BROWNLEE, AGNESS see **GWYNNE**	WALLOWA CO.	T1S	R44E	S30
BROWNLEE, ALPHA see **GWYNNE**	WALLOWA CO.	T1S	R44E	S30
BUHLER RANCH	WALLOWA CO.	?	?	?
BUNNELL FAMILY see **LEAP**	WALLOWA CO.	T1N	R44E	S8

BUTLER FAMILY see **PALLETTE RANCH**

	WALLOWA CO.	T4S	R48E	?
BUTLER RANCH see **PALLETTE RANCH**	WALLOWA CO.	T4S	R48E	?
CACHE CREEK RANCH	WALLOWA CO.	T6N	R47E	S23
CARLSON, ELLEN see **ZUMWALT**	WALLOWA CO.	T2N	R47E	?
CARLSON, GUST see **ZUMWALT**	WALLOWA CO.	T2N	R47E	?
CARLSON, LELAND see **ZUMWALT**	WALLOWA CO.	T2N	R47E	?
CATHOLIC see **WALLOWA**	WALLOWA CO.	T1N	R42E	S13
CEMETERY RIDGE	WALLOWA CO.	?	R48E	?
CHIEF JOSEPH [OLD]	WALLOWA CO.	T1N	R43E	S20
CHIEF JOSEPH MONUMENT	WALLOWA CO.	T3S	R45E	S5
CHINESE MINERS MASSACRE	WALLOWA CO.	T4N	R49E	UNS
CROW CREEK	WALLOWA CO.	T1N	R45E	S13
DAUGHERTY, BILL see **DAVIS, ANNA**	WALLOWA CO.	T1N	R42E	S11
DAUGHERTY RANCH see **DAVIS, ANNA**	WALLOWA CO.	T1N	R42E	S11
DAVIS, ANNA	WALLOWA CO.	T1N	R42E	S11
DOBBIN FAMILY	WALLOWA CO.	T4N	R48E	S34
EDEN	WALLOWA CO.	T5N	R42E	S21
EDEN RIDGE see **EDEN**	WALLOWA CO.	T5N	R42E	S21
ENTERPRISE	WALLOWA CO.	T1S	R44E	S35

FISCHER, JOHN D. see **FISHER, JOHN D.**

	WALLOWA CO.	T2N	R41E	?

FISHER, ELIZABETH B. see **FISHER, JOHN D.**

	WALLOWA CO.	T2N	R41E	?
FISHER, JOHN D.	WALLOWA CO.	T2N	R41E	?
FLORA	WALLOWA CO.	T5N	R44E	S21

FRIDDLES BABY see **FRIDDLES FAMILY**

	WALLOWA CO.	T6N	R43E	S23

FRIDDLES, CORDELIA B. see **FRIDDLES FAMILY**				
	WALLOWA CO.	T6N	R43E	S23
FRIDDLES FAMILY	WALLOWA CO.	T6N	R43E	S23
FRUITA see **PARK**	WALLOWA CO.	T3S	R48E	S3
GORDON, CHARLES	WALLOWA CO.	T5N	R45E	?
GROUSE see **BARTLETT**	WALLOWA CO.	T6N	R43E	S21
GROUSE CREEK see **PARK**	WALLOWA CO.	T3N	R48E	S3
GWYNNE	WALLOWA CO.	T1S	R44E	S30
HAFER see **EDEN**	WALLOWA CO.	T5N	R42E	S21
HAT POINT	WALLOWA CO.	T1S	R49E	S35
HILTSLEY, FRANK	WALLOWA CO.	T1S	R50E	UNS
HORNER, JOHN HARLEY see **CHIEF JOSEPH [OLD]**				
	WALLOWA CO.	T1N	R43E	S20
HORSE CREEK RANCH	WALLOWA CO.	T3N	R48E	S35
HOWARD FAMILY	WALLOWA CO.	T3N	R41E	?
HUFFMAN BABY see **ARMIN**	WALLOWA CO.	T2S	R47E	S31
HUFFMAN FAMILY see **ARMIN**	WALLOWA CO.	T2S	R47E	S31
HURRICANE CREEK see **I.O.O.F. PIONEER [JOSEPH]**				
	WALLOWA CO.	T2S	R44E	S36
I.O.O.F. PIONEER [JOSEPH]	WALLOWA CO.	T2S	R44E	S36
IMNAHA	WALLOWA CO.	T1N	R48E	S21
INDIAN GRAVE	WALLOWA CO.	T1S	R49E	S21
JIM TOWN see **LOSTINE**	WALLOWA CO.	T1S	R43E	S3
JOSEPH see **I.O.O.F. PIONEER [JOSEPH]**				
	WALLOWA CO.	T2S	R44E	S36
KNOTT FAMILY see **SILVER FAMILY**	WALLOWA CO.	T6N	R43E	S15
KOCH FAMILY see **SILVER FAMILY**	WALLOWA CO.	T6N	R43E	S15
KOON, BETTY LOU see **MAXVILLE**	WALLOWA CO.	T3N	R42E	S15
KUHN see **McCUBBIN**	WALLOWA CO.	T1S	R43E	S5
LATHROP FAMILY see **LEAP**	WALLOWA CO.	T1N	R44E	S8
LEAP	WALLOWA CO.	T1N	R44E	S8
LIGHTING CREEK	WALLOWA CO.	T3N	R48E	S12
LIGHTING CREEK RANCH see **LIGHTING CREEK**				
	WALLOWA CO.	T3N	R48E	S12
LITTLE INDIAN GIRL see **DAVIS, ANNA**				
	WALLOWA CO.	T1N	R42E	S11
LOST PRAIRIE	WALLOWA CO.	T6N	R44E	S31
LOSTINE	WALLOWA CO.	T1S	R43E	S3
LOWER VALLEY see **BRAMLET MEMORIAL**				
	WALLOWA CO.	T2N	R42E	S33
LYDELL, EFFIE MAE see **HORSE CREEK RANCH**				
	WALLOWA CO.	T3N	R48E	S35
LYDELL-STUBBLEFIELD, BABIES see **HORSE CREEK RANCH**				
	WALLOWA CO.	T3N	R48E	S35
MARKS CABIN see **MARKS, SAM**	WALLOWA CO.	?	?	?
MARKS FAMILY	WALLOWA CO.	T2S	R48E	S2
MARKS, SAM	WALLOWA CO.	?	?	?
MARTIN see **NICOSON**	WALLOWA CO.	T5N	R44E	S8
MASONIC see **I.O.O.F. PIONEER [JOSEPH]**				
	WALLOWA CO.	T2S	R44E	S36
MAXVILLE	WALLOWA CO.	T3N	R42E	S15

MAYNARD, REBECCA JANE see **PINE CREEK**

| | WALLOWA CO. | T2N | R46E | S27 |

MAYNARD, THOMAS see **PINE CREEK**

| | WALLOWA CO. | T2N | R46E | S27 |

MAYNARD, THOMAS J. see **PINE CREEK**

| | WALLOWA CO. | T2N | R46E | S27 |

McALEXANDER HOMESEAD, V. see **CHIEF JOSEPH [OLD]**

| | WALLOWA CO. | T1N | R43E | S20 |

McALLISTER, TOM see **PRATT-COLVILLE**

	WALLOWA CO.	T3S	R43E	?
McCUBBIN	WALLOWA CO.	T1S	R43E	S5
MIDDLE POINT	WALLOWA CO.	T4N	R43E	S30

MILLER, A. GROVER see **LIGHTNING CREEK**

| | WALLOWA CO. | T3N | R48E | S12 |
| **MINAM** | WALLOWA CO. | T2N | R41E | S19 |

NEZ PERCE see **CHIEF JOSEPH MONUMENT**

	WALLOWA CO.	T3S	R45E	S5
NICHOLS, BESSIE	WALLOWA CO.	T5N	R42E	S22
NICOLSON see **NICOSON**	WALLOWA CO.	T5N	R44E	S8
NICOSON	WALLOWA CO.	T5N	R44E	S8

NOKES, R. GREGORY see **CHINESE MINERS MASSACRE**

| | WALLOWA CO. | T4N | R49E | UNS |
| **ODELL BROTHERS** | WALLOWA CO. | T3S | R45E | ? |

OREGON GAME COMMISSION see **RUSSELL FAMILY**

	WALLOWA CO.	T6N	R42E	?
PALLETTE RANCH	WALLOWA CO.	T4S	R48E	?
PARADISE	WALLOWA CO.	T6N	R45E	S31
PARK	WALLOWA CO.	T3S	R48E	S3
PARK GRANGE see **PARK**	WALLOWA CO.	T3S	R48E	S3
PINE CREEK	WALLOWA CO.	T2N	R46E	S27
POWWATKA	WALLOWA CO.	T4N	R43E	S33
PRAIRIE CREEK	WALLOWA CO.	T2S	R45E	S34
PRATT-COLVILLE	WALLOWA CO.	T3S	R43E	?
PRATT, ELLIS see **PRATT-COLVILLE**	WALLOWA CO.	T3S	R43E	?
PRINCE see **POWWATKA**	WALLOWA CO.	T4N	R43E	S33
PROMISE	WALLOWA CO.	T4N	R42E	S11

RATTLESNAKE TREE see **FISHER, JOHN D.**

	WALLOWA CO.	T2N	R41E	?
RAYMOND, MR.	WALLOWA CO.	T2N	R50E	?
REEL, ROLAND	WALLOWA CO.	T3N	R50E	?

RENFROW see **RENTFROW, MAY ANN JUDY**

| | WALLOWA CO. | T5N | R43E | S4 |

RENTFROW, HENRY see **RENTFROW, MAY ANN JUDY**

| | WALLOWA CO. | T5N | R43E | S4 |
| **RENTFROW, MAY ANN JUDY** | WALLOWA CO. | T5N | R43E | S4 |

RHODES, HERMAN see **CACHE CREEK RANCH**

| | WALLOWA CO. | T6N | R47E | S23 |
| **RUSSELL FAMILY** | WALLOWA CO. | T6N | R42E | ? |

RUSSELL PLACE see **RUSSELL FAMILY**

	WALLOWA CO.	T6N	R42E	?
SHIELDS, LOUIS	WALLOWA CO.	T1N	R50E	UNS
SILVER FAMILY	WALLOWA CO.	T6N	R43E	S15

SIZEMORE, MR. see **SILVER FAMILY**	WALLOWA CO.	T6N	R43E	S15
SMITH MOUNTAIN see **FISHER, JOHN D.**				
	WALLOWA CO.	T2N	R41E	?
SOMERS RANCH see **RAYMOND, MR.**	WALLOWA CO.	T2N	R50E	?
STUBBLEFIELD, TINIE see **HORSE CREEK RANCH**				
	WALLOWA CO.	T3N	R48E	S35
TRIPLE D RANCH see **DAVIS, ANNA**	WALLOWA CO.	T1N	R42E	S11
TROY	WALLOWA CO.	T5N	R43E	S4
UNION see **BARTLETT**	WALLOWA CO.	T6N	R43E	S21
UTOPIA see **MIDDLE POINT**	WALLOWA CO.	T4N	R43E	S30
VICTOR HOMESTEAD	WALLOWA CO.	T2N	?	?
WALLOWA	WALLOWA CO.	T1N	R42E	S13
WALLOWA LAKE INDIAN see **CHIEF JOSEPH MONUMENT**				
	WALLOWA CO.	T3S	R45E	S5
WARNOCK CHILDREN see **CROW CREEK**	WALLOWA CO.	T1N	R45E	S13
WARNOCK, D. D. see **CROW CREEK**	WALLOWA CO.	T1N	R45E	S13
WARNOCK, EVA see **CROW CREEK**	WALLOWA CO.	T1N	R45E	S13
WEATHERLY see **I.O.O.F. PIONEER [JOSEPH]**				
	WALLOWA CO.	T2S	R44E	S36
WEST SIDE see **McCUBBIN**	WALLOWA CO.	T1S	R43E	S5
WHITE RANCH, J. R. see **BRISCOE, ISAIAH JACKSON**				
	WALLOWA CO.	T1N	R44E	S35
WILSON TWINS	WALLOWA CO.	T3N	R41E	S29
ZUMWALT	WALLOWA CO.	T2N	R47E	?

Bramlet Memorial
Janice M. Healy (2000)

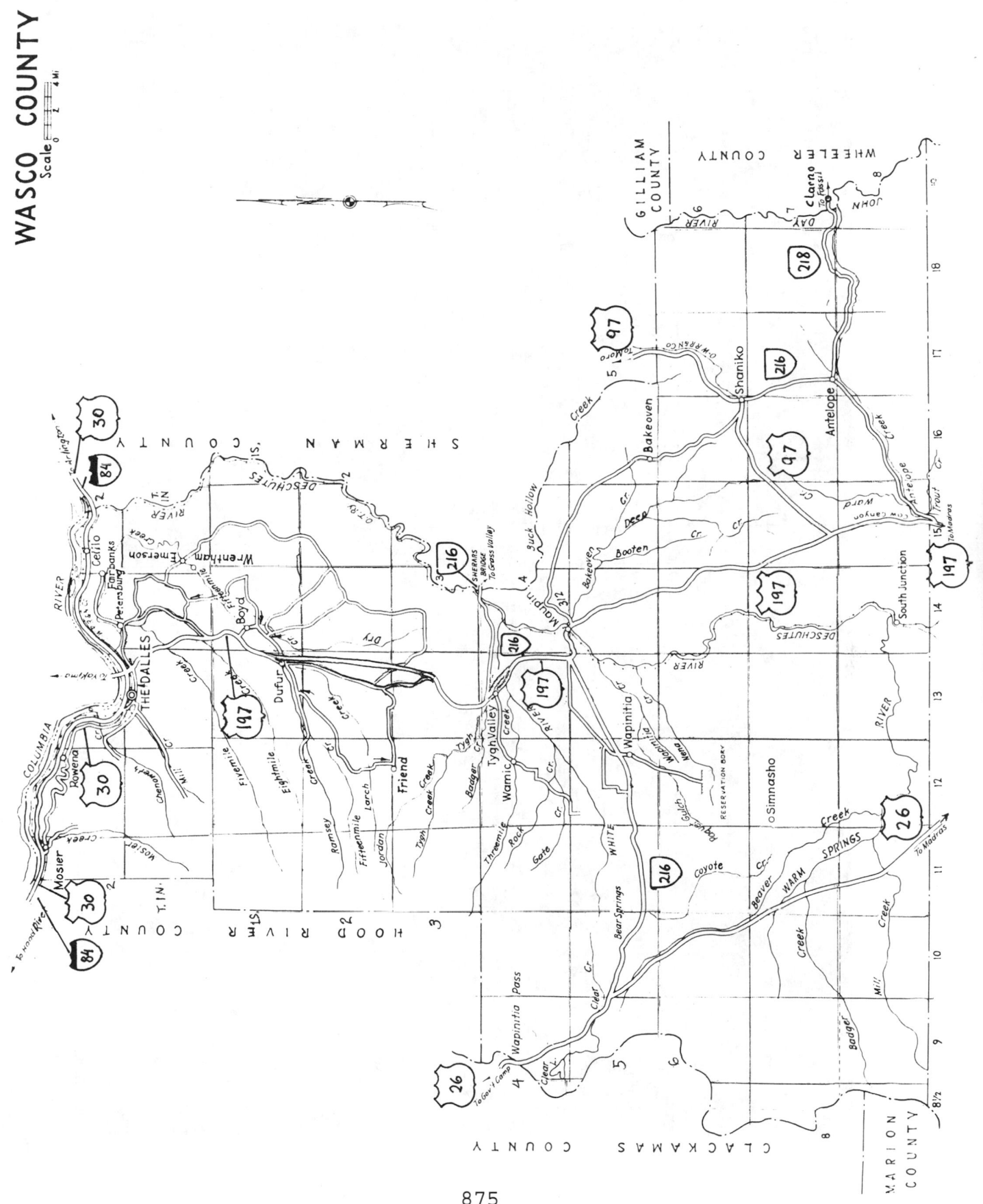

Memaloose Island, Victor Trevitt Monument
Janice M. Healy (2000)

Area: 2,396 square miles
Population (1998): 23,059
County seat: The Dalles, Population: 11,460
County established: 11 January 1854

The Dalles was a trade and transit center long before white settlers arrived and there are still extensive Indian burial grounds in the vicinity which continue to be in use. In addition there is the large Warm Springs Reservation in the southern part of Wasco County. Organized cemeteries established by white settlers began with the Mission Cemetery in The Dalles in 1843 and the Military post of Fort Dalles in 1850. The first "civilian" cemetery was St. Peter's Catholic in 1848. Cemeteries were not organized away from the Columbia River until a generation later.

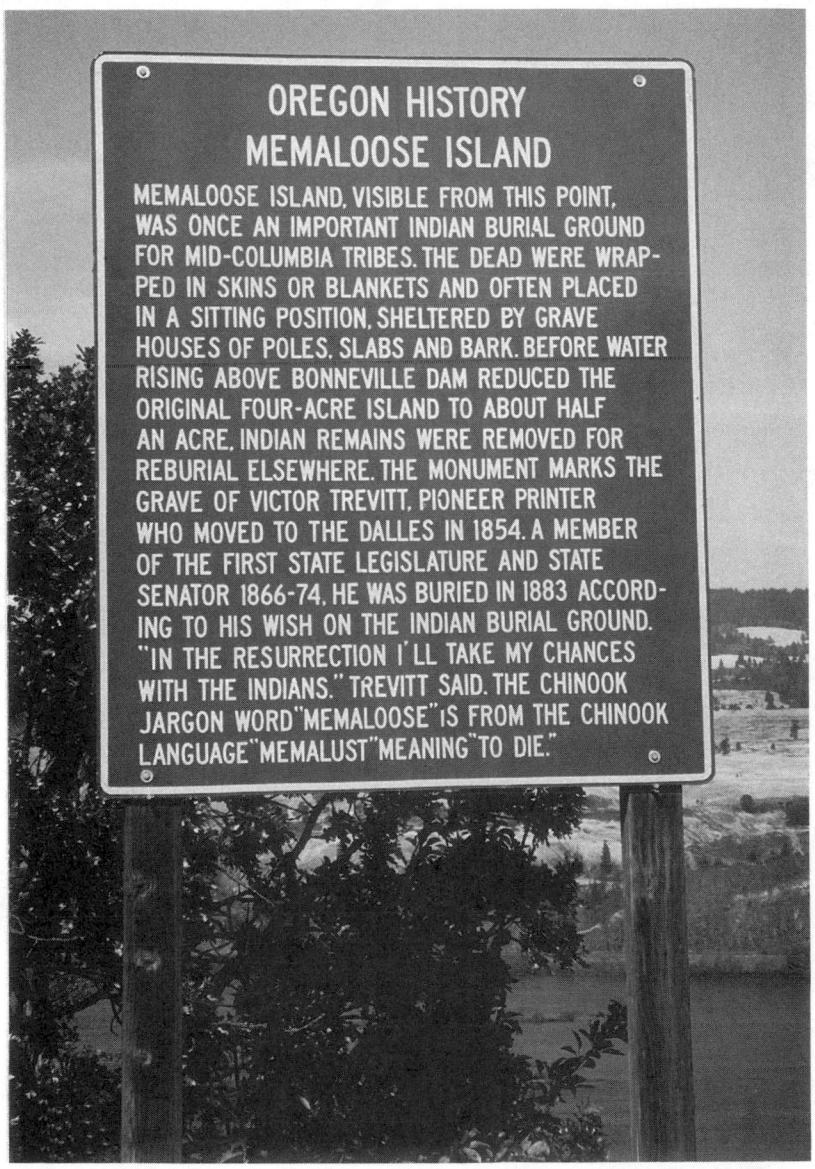

Memaloose Island

Janice M. Healy (2000)

Parklawn
Dean H. Byrd (1997)

I.O.O.F. [The Dalles]
Dean H. Byrd (1997)

Name of Cemetery and also known as	Number of burials	Acres	Condition	Date started or earliest known burial	Township	Range	Section

ALLEN, BILL   A   0.01   3   1884   T4S   R11E   UNS

Located in the Mt. Hood National Forest in projected Section 19 or 30. It is best to use a detailed Forestry Map. Leave White River Road (Forestry Road #48) and turn north onto Grasshopper Road (Forestry Road #4811). After driving 0.2 of a mile on Forestry Road #4811, turn right (easterly) onto Forestry Road #4,811,029 and drive 0.4 of a mile to a "Y" in the road. Walk to the left, downward about 100 paces to another "Y". Keep left again on this abandoned logging road another 200 paces. The grave is marked by a natural stone about 20 feet to the right. It is located above a tributary to the South Fork of Gate Creek. {1 Sept. 1991} (Not shown on Rock Creek Reservoir 1962 USGS Quad. map.)

ANTELOPE [NEW]   C   3   2   1898   T7S   R17E   S32
  AKA: 1. I.O.O.F.

Leave OR. Hwy. 218 in Antelope, driving past the church on Bennett Road; at 0.4 of a mile turn onto a driveway to the left and go 300 yards to the cemetery. {5 June 1990} (Antelope 1987 USGS Quad. map.)

ANTELOPE PIONEER   B   1   3   1874   T7S   R17E   S28
  AKA: 1. WALLACE

Take the same route as to Antelope [New] Cemetery via Bennett Road. Located about 1.8 miles from OR. Hwy 218, the cemetery is off to the right, part way up a butte opposite from Johns Canyon and across Antelope Creek. The bridge washed out so there is no access. NOTE: This site is now on private property. (Antelope 1987 USGS Quad. map.)

BRIGGS GRAVES   A   0.1   2   1861   T4S   R11E   S26
  AKA: 1. GATE CREEK

Located in the Mt. Hood National Forest about 0.25 of a mile south down Gate Creek from White River Road (Forestry Road #48). Jarvis Briggs and his son Newton were returning to the Willamette Valley from Canyon City with a considerable amount of gold. They stopped for the night just short of the Barlow Road Gate, camping on an island in Gate Creek. During the night both were shot and stabbed to death and the gold was taken, never to be found again. Rightly or wrongly, Indians

Wasco County

Name of Cemetery and also known as	Number of burials	Acres	Condition	Date started or earliest known burial	Township	Range	Section

were blamed. This occurred on or about the end of July 1861 or 1 August 1861 (See the *Weekly Oregonian*, Saturday Morning, 24 August 1861, page 3, column 2.) Jarvis Briggs' daughter placed a marker for them on the island about 1918. {7 August 1989} (Not shown on Rock Creek Reservoir 1962 USGS Quad. map.)

BROWN, JOSEPH
AKA: 1. JEWISH

A ? 2 13 Feb 1862 T1N R13E S10
This lone burial is about 100 feet west of the Pioneer Cemetery in The Dalles. It lies at the base of an oak tree at the entrance to what was the Eastern Oregon Tuberculosis Hospital and is now (1995) a community college. Brown had emigrated from Posen, Prussian Poland. See the article in *The Dalles Chronicle* 18 Sept. 1968 in the Barbed Wire column. (Not shown on The Dalles South 1977 USGS Quad. map.)

BUTTS, CATHERINE BONNETT

A 0.02 3 2 Oct 1845 T3S R14E S28
In the Southeast 1/4 of Section 28. Leave U.S. Hwy. 197 at the northern Tygh Valley Junction and turn east onto Sherars Bridge Highway, (OR. Hwy. 216). At milepost 4.7 turn left (north) onto Sand Road, a one-lane county road. Go a mile to the ranch which is at the end of the county maintenance. Continue northerly for about another 1.25 miles to a straight north-south alignment. Just past a fence line on the right are some graves about 500 yards to the right (east). Here are buried a Mrs. Catherine Bonnett Butts and two children who were with the Stephen Meek wagon train. They are believed to be marked by a pile of stones, on private property (the John Conroy Place, 1965) and about two airline miles northwest of Sherars Bridge over the Deschutes River (1989). (Sherars Bridge Quad. 1962 USGS map.)

BUZAN
AKA: 1. FLANAGAN
2. LINDLEY
3. RURAL DALE

C 1 2 1902 T4S R15E S33
Starting in Maupin, cross the Deschutes River Bridge and by the south end, turn off of U.S. Hwy. 197 to the left onto Bakeoven Market Road. Drive past Flanagan (7.2 miles) and at

Name of Cemetery and also known as	Number of burials	Acres	Condition	Date started or earliest known burial	Township	Range	Section

8.9 miles one will find the cemetery on the right. NOTE: People from Shaniko were buried here. {11 June 1990} (Dead Dog Canyon 1971 USGS Quad. map.)

CAMPBELL, BABY GIRL A 0.01 4 24 Apr 1867 T1S R13E S11
Leave U.S. Hwy. 197 at Milepost 7.17, going to the right onto Eightmile Road. Drive about 3 miles to 5745 Eightmile Road. This private property has the grave of Baby Girl Campbell, aged 2 years who drowned in in Eight Mile Creek. {30 May 1992} (Not shown on The Dalles South 1977 or Dufur West 1962-87 USGS Quad. maps.)

CELILO [#1] ? ? ? ? T2N R15E S16
This Indian cemetery is on a bluff above Celilo but can be reached only from the eastern end of Old Moody Road via a 4-wheel drive trail. This site is north of Celilo [#2] by about 0.33 of a mile. Leave OR. Hwy. 206 near the Deschutes River at Milepost 2.77 and turn onto Old Moody Road. Go 1.33 miles to a road on the right and a padlocked gate. Note: this site is on private property. (Wishram 1994 USGS Quad. map.)

CELILO [#2] ? ? ? ? T2N R15E S21
This Indian cemetery is on a bluff above Celilo but can be reached only from the eastern end of Old Moody Road via a 4-wheel drive trail. This site is south of Celilo [#1] by about 0.33 of a mile. Leave OR. Hwy. 206 near the Deschutes River at Milepost 2.77 and turn onto Old Moody Road. Go 1.33 miles to a road on the right and a padlocked gate. Note: this site is on private property. (Wishram 1994 USGS Quad. map.)

CHASTAIN, BESSIE A 0.01 4 9 Feb 1908 T4S R12E S1
Leave the community of Tygh Valley and drive west past the fairgrounds. Cross the Badger Creek Bridge and at the junction on the far side at Milepost 2.45 the pavement ends. Continue ahead (westerly) on Badger Creek Road, through a gate 0.1 of a mile from this

Name of Cemetery and also known as	Number of burials	Acres	Condition	Date started or earliest known burial	Township	Range	Section

junction. Drive about a total of one mile from the junction to a field road with a wooden gate on the left. The field road leads down into Badger Creek Canyon past a wire gate 0.4 of a mile from the wooden gate, 0.1 of a mile past the wire gate is an old corral to the left. Straight out from the corral, at the edge of the field and up against the trees is an iron fence around the overgrown grave. NOTE: this site is on private property. {May 1992} (Not shown on Postage Stamp Butte 1962-87 USGS Quad. map.)

CHINESE [THE DALLES]

?	?	3	?		T1N	R13E	S10

The old Chinese Cemetery, now abandoned, was next to the Pioneer [The Dalles] Cemetery. Presumably most or all of the remains were eventually returned to China as was the custom. (Not shown on The Dalles South 1977 USGS Quad. map.)

CHURCHILL, ELIZABETH J. HUMPHRIES

A	0.01	?	27 Jul 1851	?	?		?

Mrs. Churchill died as a result of childbirth at what was described as a crossing of Bear River "which is now The Dalles." The compiler believes this to be the Bear River in Utah and Idaho as there is no such stream so named near The Dalles. Mrs. Churchill was however buried "at the foot of the Cascade Mountains in Wasco County, Oregon." The grave has been lost, but a stained glass window was placed in her memory in the Plymouth Congregational Church in The Dalles. From *"Memories of Owen Humphrey Churchill and His Family"* by Marion Churchill , Raulston, N.D.

CLARNO

B	1	4	1870		T7S	R19E	S29

Leave OR. Hwy 218 at the Clarno Grange and drive northerly along the John Day River for about 0.75 mile. The cemetery is about 200 yards left (west) of the road on the side of a bluff. There were 13 known burials in 1989, but at least as many more are believed buried here. NOTE: this site is on private property. {7 August 1989} (Clarno 1988 USGS Quad. map.)

Name of Cemetery and also known as	Number of burials	Acres	Condition	Date started or earliest known burial	Township	Range	Section

COGSWELL, JOHN
AKA: 1. COGGSMILL
     2. COGGSWELL
     3. COGSWELL
       GRAVES

A 0.01 ? 1861   T1N R15E   S30
Leave U.S. Hwy. 197 and follow Emerson Loop Road to Wrentham. Then take the Wrentham Cutoff to Emerson. The Cogswell Place was just above the mouth of Standard Hollow. A child is supposedly buried here also. (Not shown on Emerson 1977 USGS Quad. map.)

CONLY

? ? ? ?   T1S R14E   ?
Wasco County Death Certificate #58 for 8 May 1917 reports that infant Loyd D. Carson, son of Dolph and Mary Copland Carson died and was buried the following day in Conly Cemetery. This is reported to be in the area of Boyd. Could this refer to Rice Cemetery? (Not shown on Petersburg 1978 USGS Quad. map.)

COVEY FAMILY

A 0.01 5 1904   T3S R12E   S2
Located at the edge of a field about 0.25 of a mile south and slightly east of Friend. {8 September 1989} (Not shown on Friend 1962-87 USGS Quad. map.)

COX, BEULAH MAY

A 0.01 1 6 Jan 1916 T5S R12E   S24
She is buried on property owned by Dudley Cox, this is somewhere at or in the immediate vicinity of Wapinitia. {Aug. 1991} (Not shown on Maupin S.W. 1962 or Wapinitia 1962-87 USGS Quad. Map.)

CRAMER, MRS.
AKA: 1. KRAMER

A 0.01 ? Circa 1883 T7S R17E   ?
This burial is reportedly on the old Peter Conroy Place near Antelope. Mrs. Cramer was supposedly from a passing wagon train and a field stone was used as a marker. No other information was given in the report. (Not shown on Antelope 1987 USGS Quad. map.)

CRITERION

A 1 4 1918   T6S R15E   S18
Located in the Northwest 1/4 of the Northwest 1/4 of Section 18, on pasture land on the Criterion Ranch between Maupin and Shaniko Junction. This is difficult to find. It is east of U.S. Hwy. 197 and west of the

powerlines. A visit 8 October 1990 disclosed 15 markers, 2 of which were of unknowns. NOTE: This site is on private property. (Criterion 1971 USGS Quad. map.)

CUNNINGHAM GRAVE

A   0.01   5   19 Jul 1894   T5S   R12E   S28
Located in the Northwest 1/4 of the Southeast 1/4 of Section 28. Drive south from Wapinitia towards the Warm Springs Reservation. Turn right (west) onto Back Walters Road and drive about 1.5 miles, passing the gun club on the right (north). Just beyond this is a gated field road to the right (north) with a fence on its left (west).   Drive a short distance to the grave in a field just over this fence, on the west side. The burial is the infant daughter of J.R. and I.C. Cunningham. NOTE: This site is on private property. {August 1991} (Not shown on Wapinitia 1962-87 USGS Quad. map.)

DAFFODIL PATCH

A   0.01   1   7 Jun 1934   T1N   R11E   S12
Located about 10 miles south of Mosier via Mosier Creek Road and Wyss Road, on private property. The daffodils were planted here as a tribute to Miriam Sheldon Ripley who is buried here. The grave is fenced and the daffodils, narcissuses and lupines still bloom. (Not shown on Ketchum Reservoir 1977 USGS Quad. map.)

DARNIELLE, SARAH
  AKA: 1. DARNILLE

A   0.01   5   24 Mar 1884   T1S   R13E   ?
Possibly on Section 25 or 36. This grave is described as being just east of the old highway leading south out of Dufur, and just east of the power station. It is also said to be south of the Dufur City Park. It must be very close to the Roberts-Gray burials. See that article. NOTE: This site is on private property. {28 August 1989} (Not shown on Dufur West 1962-87 USGS Quad. map.)

DOYLE, MRS. C. B.

A   0.01   4   Circa 1916   T6S   R12E   S6
Located in the Northwest 1/4 of the Northwest 1/4 of Section 6, it is thought to be before 1916. Leave OR. Hwy. 216 (Wapinitia Highway)

at Walters Road intersection. Continue ahead to the south for another 0.64 of a mile on a private road. To the left is the driveway to French Cemetery (see that article). Continue to the right past a barn and cattle guard. At 0.5 of a mile from the French Cemetery driveway turn left uphill, keeping to the right, for another 0.9 of a mile to a log cabin and a gate ahead. You are now 1.4 miles from the driveway to the French Cemetery. The grave is another mile beyond the last gate and next to the powerlines. {August 1991} (Not shown on Wapinitia 1962-87 USGS Quad. map.)

DUFUR COMMUNITY
AKA: 1. I.O.O.F.
     2. STAR #23
       REBEKAH
       LODGE
       COMMUNITY

D   5   2   1895   T1S R13E   S24
Located about 1 mile north of Dufur, on the west side of U.S. Hwy. 197. There is a signboard on the cemetery gate which says "Star 23 Rebekah Lodge Community Cemetery". This signboard is long obsolete for proclaiming the cemetery's present name, which is now Dufur Community Cemetery. Because of reburials from earlier cemeteries there are dated monuments preceding 1895. 10 Oct. 1853 is the earliest known. {June 1992} (Dufur East 1967-87 USGS Quad. map.)

EIGHT MILE
AKA: 1. FERGUSON
       FAMILY
     2. JAP HOLLOW
     3. JAPANESE
       HOLLOW

B   1   2   3 Jan 1877 T1S R13E   S1
South of The Dalles, leave U.S. Hwy. 197 at Milepost 7.17, to the right onto Eightmile Road. Drive 1.1 miles to Japanese Hollow Road on the right and then take that road for another 0.63 of a mile to the cemetery on the left. It is on the Eight Mile Place, the homestead of Alfred Ferguson. NOTE: There is and has been much dispute whether the "mile" creeks and roads are to be spelled as one word or as two words. The Wasco County Road Department spells such roads as one word. NOTE: This site is on private property. {1992} (Petersburg Quad. 1978 USGS map.)

ENDERSBY INFANT

A   ?   ?   27 Jan 1912 T1S R13E   S11
Endersby was a locale on Eightmile Creek about 4.25 miles north and west of Dufur. The compiler was unaware of any burials here

Name of Cemetery and also known as	Number of burials	Acres	Condition	Date started or earliest known burial	Township	Range	Section

but there is a Wasco County 1912 death certificate #470 reporting the death of an Endersby infant on 27 January 1912. (Not shown on Dufur West 1962-87 USGS Quad. map.)

FAIRVIEW

? ? ? ?   ? ?   ?

The compiler has located a death certificate in the State Archives for a burial in "Fairview Cemetery near The Dalles." The certificate is #1216 for the 16 April 1909 death of Mary J. McDonald of The Dalles. She was a student, born 29 June 1891, daughter of D.S. and Louisa McDonald and lived on Rural Route 1. Can anyone identify Fairview Cemetery? (Not shown on The Dalles South 1977 USGS Quad. map.)

FORT DALLES

? 0.28 7 1850-1866 T1N R13E S4

The site of the Fort Dalles Cemetery is now beneath the intersection of 16th and Lincoln Streets in what was The Dalles Military Reservation. This Reservation occupied much of what is now the western part of The Dalles. In October 1886 permission was given to disinter and remove the military burials to Fort Vancouver, Washington which was presumably done. The Mission Cemetery was located about two blocks west. See that article. (Not shown on The Dalles South 1977 USGS Quad. map)

FRENCH

A 0.1 5 28 Sep 1872 T5S R12E S33

Located in the West 1/2 of the Southwest 1/4 of Section 33. Leave OR. Hwy. 216 (Wapinitia Highway) at Milepost 15.54 to the south on Walters Road. Go 1 mile to Back Walters Road intersection. Continue ahead to the south for another 0.64 of a mile on a private road, then turn left onto a jeep trail for 200 yards to the graves at a gulch. These were settlers from French Prairie in Marion County but many have been reburied in Kelly Cemetery. There were 6 markers noted during a visit in 1990. NOTE: this site is on private property. {8 October 1990} ("Graves" on Wapinitia 1962-87 USGS Quad. map.)

Name of Cemetery and also known as	Number of burials	Acres	Condition	Date started or earliest known burial	Township	Range	Section

FRIEND [NEW]

B   1   2   1915   T3S R12E   S3

The cemetery is located 0.6 of a mile west of Friend. Go 0.5 of a mile mile south on Clark Mill Road and then 0.1 of a mile right (west) up the hill. {1989} (Friend 1962-87 USGS Quad. map.)

G.A.R. (GRAND ARMY OF THE REPUBLIC)
AKA: 1. VETERANS

C 2.2 1   1883   T1N R13E   S4

Located at the south end of the I.O.O.F., [The Dalles] Cemetery; see the article on that cemetery. The Wasco County Cemetery is at the east end of the G.A.R. Cemetery; see the article on that cemetery. {13 June 1997} (The Dalles South 1977 USGS Quad. map.)

GRAVE ISLAND MEMORIAL

D 3.52 1   1956   T2N R14E   S31

There is a monument located just behind The Dalles Dam Viewpoint parking area. The common grave is only about 20' X 20' in size. Grave Island, in the Columbia River was only about 800 feet from the present The Dalles Dam and therefore is now below water. The island itself was not used for burials after the 1894 flood. Also here are about 624 reburials, moved in 1935 from Lower Memaloose Island. All were Indian. {30 May 1992} (Petersburg 1978 USGS Quad. map.)

GRAVEYARD BUTTE
AKA: 1. ABBOTT

A 0.5 4 1876-1915 T5S R12E   S10

There is a cemetery at the top of Graveyard Butte, AKA: Joe Long Butte. Leave OR. Hwy. 216 at Milepost 15.3 going north on Victor Road. Go 2.5 miles to the junction with White River Road. Continue northerly on White River Road another 0.8 of a mile before the road descends into the White River Canyon. There is no road access so it is necessary to walk about 0.75 of a mile up the butte to reach the cemetery. There are about nine burials. {5 July 1991} NOTE: This site is on private property. (Wamic 1962-87 USGS Quad. map.)

HAIGHT SPRING
AKA: 1. COW CANYON GRADE

A 0.01 ? ?   T8S R15E   S9

Haight Spring is in the Cow Canyon Safety Rest Area at Milepost 71.3 on U.S. Hwy.97.

Name of Cemetery and also known as	Number of burials	Acres	Condition	Date started or earliest known burial	Township	Range	Section

It is to the south of Shaniko Junction. A child is supposedly buried on the left side of the road uphill from the rest area. Presumably there is some connection to Charles Haight, who settled in Cow Canyon in 1880. (The rest area is shown on Shaniko Junction 1987 USGS Quad. map, but no grave.)

HAPPY RIDGE
AKA: 1. OLD TYGH VALLEY
2. TYGH VALLEY PIONEER

B   1   3   1859   T3S   R13E   S32
The current field log of the Wasco County Road Department labels this cemetery as Happy Ridge Cemetery which implies a signboard. The date of the field log is sometime in 1990. Traxtle Cemetery, which is up beyond Happy Ridge itself, is also known by the name of Happy Ridge. See the article on Traxtle Cemetery. Leave U.S. Hwy. 197 at Milepost 33 south of Dufur and north of Tygh Valley; turn west onto Shadybrook Road. Go westerly on Shadybrook Road for 1.1 miles, then turn left onto Fairgrounds Road. The cemetery is on the left, after crossing Tygh Creek, at 1.4 miles from U.S. Hwy. 197. One can return to U.S. Hwy. 197 by continuing southerly to the Badger Creek Road junction (0.4 of a mile), turning left to the town of Tygh Valley, a total of 2.8 miles from the cemetery. NOTE: The past few years this site has been under knee deep water [30 May 1992]. (Postage Stamp Butte 1962-87 USGS Quad. map.)

HAUSER GRAVES

A   0.1   1   1895-1903   T3S   R13E   S32
Located 0.25 of a mile north of the Tygh Valley Fairgrounds and on the Nel Justensen Farm (1992). These burials are separate from the nearby Happy Ridge Cemetery. NOTE: This site is on private property. {8 September 1989} (Not shown on Postage Stamp Butte 1962-87 USGS Quad. map.)

HAWKINS, ALFRED

A   0.01   ?   1982   T5S   R11E   S25
There is a lone grave somewhere northwest of Pine Grove and OR. Hwy. 216. No other information was given in the report. NOTE: This site is on private property. (Not shown on Wapinitia or Foreman Point 1962 USGS Quad. maps.)

Name of Cemetery and also known as	Number of burials	Acres	Condition	Date started or earliest known burial	Township	Range	Section

HEALD, GILBERT SETON

A   0.01 2 6 May 1979 T3S R12E   S22
Located in the Northwest 1/4 of the Northwest 1/4 of Section 22 in the White River Game Management Area. Leave U.S. Hwy. 197 between The Dalles and Tygh Valley at Milepost 33, turning west onto Shadybrook Road. Drive to the end of the county road at milepost 3.93. This is just past the crossing of Tygh Creek. Take the Game Management Road to the right which recrosses Tygh Creek. At the next road on the left (gated) you must leave the vehicle and walk about 0.5 of a mile to the old homestead. It is on the south (right) bank of Tygh Creek. The marker is on the fireplace. The use of a 4-wheel drive vehicle is advisable. {1 September 1991} (Not shown on Friend 1962-87 USGS Quad. map.)

HENDERSON PIONEER
AKA: 1. VANDERPOOL

B   1   2 17 Apr 1875 T1S R13E   S33
Leaving Dufur at Main Street, drive 0.6 of a mile south to the junction with Dufur Valley Road. Turn right (southwesterly) on that road and proceed another 2.4 miles to the cemetery driveway on the left (south). There is a short drive up the ridge to the cemetery. NOTE: This site is now on private property. {1989} (Dufur West Quad. 1962-87 USGS map.)

HINTON
AKA: 1. BAKEOVEN
     2. HINTON-WARD

A 1   5   1874   T5S R16E   S26
In Maupin, cross the Deschutes River Bridge; by the south end, turn off of U.S. Hwy. 197 to the left onto Bakeoven Market Road. Drive past Buzan Cemetery (8.9 miles on Bakeoven Road) to the junction of Hinton Road, on the left at 17.3 miles on Bakeoven Road. Turn onto Hinton Road and go another 3.5 miles to the cemetery on the right. NOTE: This site is on private property. {1989} (Shaniko 1971 USGS Quad. map.)

HOT SPRINGS INDIAN
AKA: 1. WARM SPRINGS
       RIVER

C 4   3   ?   T8S R13E   S27
Located on the Warm Springs Reservation, 3 miles east of Kah-nee-ta Hot Springs resort. (Eagle Butte 1962 USGS Quad. map.)

Wasco County

| Name of Cemetery and also known as | Number of burials | Acres | Condition | Date started or earliest known burial | Township | Range | Section |

I.O.O.F. [THE DALLES]
AKA: 1. COLUMBIA
LODGE #5
2. SUNSET

E 30　　1　1856　　T1N　R13E　　S4
Take Cherry Heights Road up the hill from West 6th Street to West 13th Street (St. Peter's Cemetery on the right). About 400 feet beyond West 13th Street is the driveway, on the left to, the I.O.O.F. Cemetery. It was first called Sunset Cemetery until the Odd Fellows took over on 21 August 1885. The G.A.R. and Wasco County Cemeteries adjoin the I.O.O.F. See the articles under those headings. {13 June 1997} (The Dalles South 1977 USGS Quad. map shows only the I.O.O.F.)

I.O.O.F. [TYGH VALLEY]

C 2　　2　1914　　T4S　R13E　　S10
Leave U.S. Hwy. 197 at Milepost 33.9 onto Tygh Valley Road, which is the old highway alignment. Go 1.3 miles southeasterly, through the town and past the school, almost to the bridge over the White River. The cemetery is on the left. You can continue southerly and rejoin U.S. Hwy. 197 at Milepost 35.6. {August 1992} (Tygh Valley 1962-87 USGS Quad. map.)

INDIAN

?　?　5　?　　T3S　R14E　　S23
This pre-settlement Indian burial ground was listed in the 1978 Oregon Cemetery Survey and described as being 2 miles downstream from Fargher. It is actually about 3 miles downstream on the Deschutes River from Sherars Bridge (OR. Hwy. 216). It is situated about 250 feet above the left bank of the river with no ready access. Nevertheless, this burial ground has been looted and was reportedly destroyed (1988). (Sherars Bridge 1962-87 USGS Quad. map.)

JEWISH [THE DALLES]

?　?　3　?　　T1N　R13E　　S10
An old Jewish cemetery in The Dalles was located next to The Dalles Pioneer Cemetery along with a Chinese burial ground. Probably most of the Jewish burials were eventually reburied in Portland, The exception being Joseph Brown. See that article. (Not shown on The Dalles South 1977 USGS Quad. map.)

Name of Cemetery and also known as	Number of burials	Acres	Condition	Date started or earliest known burial	Township	Range	Section

JOHNSON, ROBERT ROY

? ? ? 1986   T1N   R13E   S1

At 1611 East Lambert Street, The Dalles. (Not shown on The Dalles South Quad. 1977 USGS map.)

KELLY
AKA: 1. JUNIPER FLAT
     2. KELLEY GROVE
     3. KELLY CHURCHYARD
     4. VICTOR

C 5 2 1893   T5S   R13E   S8

Located about 5 miles west of Maupin. Leave U.S. Hwy. 197 at Milepost 42.3 onto Old Wapinitia Road, drive west and southwesterly to the cemetery driveway on the left. It is necessary to go about 0.4 of a mile on this driveway through fields and gates to reach the cemetery. One can continue for 2.75 miles on Old Wapinitia Road to OR. Hwy 216 at Milepost 18.8 and return to Maupin. {1992} (Tygh Valley 1962-87 USGS Quad. map.)

KINGSLEY
AKA: 1. WHITTEN

B 1.2 3 1870   T2S   R13E   S32

Located about 7 miles south of Dufur. Leave U.S. Hwy. 197 to the right at Milepost 16.1, turning onto Dufur Gap Road (the old highway alignment). Continue for 1.8 miles on Dufur Gap Road and then turn right onto Hix Road; go past the Kingsley Catholic Cemetery to a driveway to the right (west) to the cemetery atop the hill. This is about 0.8 of a mile north of the road on the right to Friend. The cemetery is about 1.3 miles north of the old locale of Kingsley. {1989} (Postage Stamp Butte 1962-87 USGS Quad. map.)

KINGSLEY CATHOLIC
AKA: 1. DUFUR CATHOLIC
     2. HENDRICKS

B 0.5 3 21 Apr 1875 T2S   R13E   S28

Located about 6.5 miles south of Dufur. Take the same route as to the Kingsley Cemetery. The Catholic cemetery lies about 0.5 of a mile northeast of the former and is about 100 yards off of Hix Road, on the right when coming from Dufur. There is no ready access. {1989} (Postage Stamp Butte 1962-87 USGS Quad. map.)

LOWER MEMALOOSE
AKA: 1. MEMALOOSE

A 2 5 ?   T3N   R12E   S32

This is an island in the Columbia River between Lyle, Washington and Mosier, Oregon. It had been used as an Indian burial ground for many generations. While the Bonneville

Name of Cemetery and also known as	Number of burials	Acres	Condition	Date started or earliest known burial	Township	Range	Section

Dam was under construction in 1935, about 624 reburials were made from this island to Grave Island Memorial. See that article. A white man, Victor Trevitt, is buried here and his memorial on the island can be seen from the Memaloose Safety Rest Area on the north side of the I-84 Freeway. Also see the article on Upper Memaloose. (Burials are NOT indicated on the Lyle 1978 USGS quad. map.)

MASONIC [THE DALLES]
AKA: 1. WASCO LODGE

B 3.5 6 1864-1983 T1N R13E S10
This cemetery no longer exists as such. It was the north side of East 19th Street in the 1500 and 1600 blocks. 92 of the graves were removed to Parklawn in November, 1983. It is on the John A. Simms D.L.C. #39, The Dalles #3. (The Dalles South 1977 USGS Quad. map.)

McCLURE FAMILY

A 0.1 2 1880 T2N R12E S4
Located 3.5 miles east of Mosier in a field north of U.S. Hwy. 30. (the Old Columbia River Highway and now the Mosier-The Dalles Highway.) NOTE: This site is on private property. (Lyle 1978 USGS Quad. map.)

McCLURE, JAMES

A 0.01 ? 31 Dec 1878 T2N R12E S5
This lone grave is on the east side of Beacon Hill and just west of the fence on the Hudson Place. When the aircraft beacon was erected the wooden enclosure and wooden monument were both destroyed. Take the Mosier-The Dalles Highway, (U.S. Hwy. 30), west from Rowena. A private driveway leads left (south) at the west end of Memaloose Outlook State Park. (the Metsker Land Ownership Atlas identifies Beacon Hill now called Hudson Hill; Not shown on Lyle 1978 USGS Quad. map.)

McQUINN, GEORGE

A 0.01 5 1882 T2N R14E S26
Go east of The Dalles, past Petersburg, onto the Fifteenmile-Fairbanks Road. The grave is at 4472 Fifteenmile Road, before reaching Fairbanks. The lone grave is on the hillside on the south side of Fifteen Mile Creek.

Name of Cemetery and also known as	Number of burials	Acres	Condition	Date started or earliest known burial	Township	Range	Section

NOTE: the usual variants of spelling these "mile" creeks. NOTE: This site is on private property. {30 May 1992} (Not shown on Stacker Butte 1974 USGS Quad. map.)

McRAE RANCH, FARQUHAR
AKA: 1. BETHUNE, MRS. AGNES
2. McRAE, ANNA BELL
3. SCOTT, CHRISSY

A 0.01 5 1905 T6S R19E ?

Perhaps in Section 30. Chrissy Scott was the five-year old daughter of Mr. and Mrs. Jim Scott who lived on Farquhar ("Farker") McRae's ranch about five miles downstream from Clarno. McRae contracted diphtheria, but recovered. Then Chrissy caught the disease and died. McRae had a concrete enclosure around the grave in a hay field in 1911. Farquhar's younger sister Anna Bell McRae was brought from Scotland to her brother's ranch, but died four months later on 1 November 1907 of "paralysis." Presumably she is also buried on the ranch, in addition a Mrs. Agnes Bethune is known to have been buried on Farquhar's Ranch. Mrs. Bethune was a resident of Mitchell in Wheeler County. That town was virtually destroyed in a flash flood on 11 June 1904. Mrs. Bethune's body was swept about 40 miles down Bridge Creek and the John Day River. (Not shown on Chimney Springs 1970 USGS Quad. map.)

MILLER
AKA: 1. FRIEND [OLD]

A 1 4 1888 T2S R12E S34

This is about 0.5 of a mile north of the vacant Friend School and to the west behind a huge garbage dump. It cannot be seen from Old Friend Road. This was the site of the first cemetery for the locale of Friend. Four graves remain here after the present Friend cemetery was opened in 1915. NOTE: this site is on private property. {8 September 1989} (Not shown on Friend 1962-87 USGS Quad. map.)

MISSION [THE DALLES]

? ? 7 1843-1864 T1N R13E S4

This was the earliest cemetery established by whites in what is now Wasco County. The site is about two blocks west of the Fort Dalles Military Cemetery at what is now 16th Street between Garrison and Pentland Streets. After

| Name of Cemetery and also known as | Number of burials | Acres | Condition | Date started or earliest known burial | Township | Range | Section |

the Pioneer Cemetery on Sunset Hill was started in 1864 the Mission Cemetery was abandoned. The compiler does not know how many burials were reburied in the Pioneer Cemetery. (Not shown on The Dalles South 1977 USGS Quad. map)

MOON, JEFF E.

A 0.01 2 ? T2N R13E S32
Take West 10th Street to the west from The Dalles, towards Chenoweth. Beyond Snipes Street intersection go to Pomona Street and turn left (inland) towards the water tower. At 1119 Pomona Street West, on the right hand side, is the owner's house. The grave is in a horse pasture behind a small building. There is a marble replacement for the original broken-off monument; it has no dates. Possibly the original spelling was Moen, as Jeff was the son of Leif and Estelle. On the Charles Shaug D.L.C. #41, The Dalles #4. NOTE: This site is on private property. {15 June 1992} (Not shown on The Dalles South 1977 USGS Quad. map.)

MORTON GRAVES

A 0.1 5 1909 T1N R12E S10
Located southwest of The Dalles and west of Browns Creek Road on the William Ketchum Place (1988). NOTE: This site is on private property. (Not shown on Brown Creek 1974 USGS Quad. map.)

MOSIER
AKA: 1. I.O.O.F.

C 5 2 1882 T2N R11E S1
From the junction at the eastern part of Mosier, off Huskey Road and State Road, take the latter to the left. Cross Mosier Creek and the cemetery is on the right, 0.34 of a mile beyond the bridge, a total of 0.8 of a mile from the Huskey Road fork. {11 June 1990} (White Salmon 1978 USGS Quad. map.)

MOSIER PIONEER
AKA: 1. OAK GROVE
     2. OLD MOSIER

A 1 5 1865-1899 T2N R11E S1
Located atop Graveyard Hill on the right bank of Mosier Creek. There is no road access; take the dirt trail for about 200 yards from the road. Some of the graves were moved to the new cemetery at Mosier. There were 4

Name of Cemetery and also known as	Number of burials	Acres	Condition	Date started or earliest known burial	Township	Range	Section

tombstones visible January 1982. It is on the Jonah H. Mosier D.L.C. #37, OC #3968. {29 March 1992} (White Salmon Quad. 1978 USGS map.)

NEABECK

| | A | 0.1 | 5 | 1909-1910 | T1N | R15E | S20 |

This burial site has been washed out by Fifteen Mile Creek. A temporary hospital was occupied here between July 1909 and November 1910. It was located about 2 miles upstream from Freebridge, on the west bank of the creek and opposite the railway stop of Neabeck. The tracks were removed years ago. The county road, Fifteenmile-Boule Road, passes by. Ten Italian railway workmen were buried here. (Not shown on Emerson 1977 USGS Quad. map.)

OBRIST
AKA: 1. DUTCH FLAT
     2. MT. HOOD
        FLAT
     3. THREE MILE

| | B | 0.4 | 5 | 16 Mar 1890 | T1S | R12E | S2 |

Just south of The Dalles leave Dry Hollow Road to the left (southeast) onto Threemile Road. Stay on Threemile Road as it turns to the right (southwest) at Steel Road, going past Parklawn Cemetery, for a total of 10.1 miles. Here, one is at the intersection of Dutch Flat Road. Turn left (south) onto Dutch Flat Road and go 0.25 of a mile uphill to the junction with Obrist Grade Road on the left (east). Turn onto Obrist Grade Road, a one-lane driveway, and go 0.95 of a mile to the cemetery on the left. Obrist Grade Road is no longer a through road, so you must return the previous route. {6 June 1989} (Brown Creek 1974 USGS Quad. map.)

ORTLEY

| | A | ? | ? | ? | T2N | R12E | ? |

Perhaps located in Section 14. Ortley was a locale important enough to merit a post office between 1911 and 1922. It is located between Mosier and Rowena on Sevenmile Hill between Sevenmile Hill Road and the old Columbia River Highway (U.S. Hwy. 30). There is a 1913 Wasco County death certificate for James S. Hallyburton, a merchant, 20 March

Name of Cemetery and also known as	Number of burials	Acres	Condition	Date started or earliest known burial	Township	Range	Section

1888-26 August 1913 who resided at Ortley and is buried there. The certificate number is illegible on the death certificate. (Not shown on Lyle 1978 USGS Quad. map.)

PARKLAWN
AKA: 1. I.O.O.F
     [THE DALLES]
    2. VETERANS

D 28   1   1955   T1N R13E   S15
Located about 2.5 miles south of The Dalles downtown district. Leave U.S. Hwy. 30 at the east end of the one-way couplet and go up the hill on Brewery Grade to East 9th Street. Continue east a very short distance on East 9th and then turn right (south) onto Dry Hollow Road. Follow Dry Hollow Road for 0.8 of a mile and then turn left onto Threemile Road. Follow Threemile Road for 1.4 miles to the cemetery on the right. In 1975 the cemetery was deeded to the I.O.O.F. and in 1978 one acre was set aside as a burial site for veterans, their wives, and children under age 18. {13 June 1997} (The Dalles South Quad. 1977 USGS map.)

PIONEER [THE DALLES]
AKA: 1. SUNSET HILL

C 2   4   1860-1964   T1N R13E   S10
Located on the south side of Scenic Drive, at The Dalles, just west of Jefferson Street. There is a sign over the gate and a white picket fence. There was much confusion about the use of the word "Sunset" in The Dalles. The Pioneer Cemetery was located on Sunset Hill. The present I.O.O.F. Cemetery was called Sunset Cemetery for several years and the term Sunset has also been wrongly used for Parklawn Cemetery. It is on the Windsor D. Bigelow D.L.C. #40, The Dalles #5. {13 June 1997} (The Dalles South 1977 USGS Quad. map.)

PIONEER GRAVE

A 0.01 ? ?   T2S R14E   ?
There was a single grave marked by a wooden board with the lettering "A Pioneer Grave" on top of Tygh Ridge on what was the Easton Place. No further information was given in the report. (Not shown on Summit Ridge Quad. 1962 USGS map.)

Name of Cemetery and also known as	Number of burials	Acres	Condition	Date started or earliest known burial	Township	Range	Section

PIONEER GRAVES

A 0.01   3   1859   T3S   R13E   S20

Located about 17 miles south of Dufur. Leave U.S. Hwy. 197 south of Dufur at Milepost 16.1 onto Dufur Gap Road for 1.8 miles and then turn right onto Hix Road, passing the Kingsley Catholic Cemetery, but continue ahead to the locale of Kingsley. Continue ahead (south) from Kingsley for another 1.3 miles. The county road ends here as the road enters the White River Game Management Area and the one-lane ahead is now called Postage Stamp Butte Road. When the visitor reaches the James Garfield Easton Homestead cabin on the right (west), which is also marked by a round cement cistern the goal has been reached. There was a single grave on a grassy knoll 30 feet from the road just south of the cabin. Around 1933 the wooden marker said "Emigrant Grave 1859." In 1993 the marker was gone. In addition there are 2 graves about 100 yards west and on the near slope of a ravine. The compiler does not know the names or relationships of these burials. {3 July 1993} (Not shown on Postage Stamp Butte 1962-87 USGS Quad. map.)

PLEASANT RIDGE

A ?   ?   ?   T1S   R12E   ?

Perhaps the cemetery was in the vicinity of Pleasant Ridge School which was in Section 14. Leave The Dalles on Dry Hollow Road at the junction of 19th Street. At 0.4 of a mile turn left (southeast) off of Dry Hollow Road onto Threemile Road. At mile 2.0 you will pass Parklawn Cemetery on the right. At mile 2.7 leave Threemile Road and turn left (southerly) onto Pleasant Ridge Road. Follow Pleasant Ridge Road down into the Fivemile Creek Valley and then ascend onto Pleasant Ridge itself. At 12.2 is the junction with Japanese Hollow Road on the left (east). Continue to follow along the ridge to the southwest past the junction with Omeg Road at mile 14.8 and at 15.2 from the starting point is the Pleasant Ridge School site on the right. The compiler does not know the location of this cemetery which could be anywhere along Pleasant Ridge. (School site is shown on Wolf Run 1962 USGS Quad. map.)

Name of Cemetery and also known as	Number of burials	Acres	Condition	Date started or earliest known burial	Township	Range	Section

PRATT
AKA: 1. WAMIC
PIONEER

A 1 2 25 Apr 1868 T4S R12E S14
Go past the Wamic Store, take the first road to the left by the school, (Emigrant Street) and drive to the end of street. Then walk about 2 blocks down to Three Mile Creek. Wamic was once known as Prattville. The cemetery was fenced in 1993 for use as a combined cemetery and community park. (Not shown on Wamic 1962-87 USGS Quad. map.)

RAINS, BABY
AKA: 1. REINS, BABY

A 0.01 ? ? T5S R12E ?
Perhaps this burial is located in Section 27. The infant was buried on the old Flinn Place just west of the Ben Forman Ranch, later owned by Lloyd Woodside. NOTE: This site is on private property. No further information was given in the report. (Not shown on Wapinitia 1962-87 USGS Quad. map.)

RED LAKE

C 2 3 ? T6S R12E S34
This cemetery is on the Warm Springs Reservation, about 5 miles northeast of Simnasho, on the road to Wapinitia. There is a signboard on the right (east) side of the road. Drive easterly on this side road for 0.5 of a mile and finally turn left (north) another 0.25 of a mile to the cemetery. (Wapinitia 1962-87 USGS Quad. map.)

RICE
AKA: 1. BOLTON
2. BOYD
3. DRY HOLLOW
4. WALDRON

B 1 2 1862 T1S R14E S10
Leave U.S. Hwy. 197 at Milepost 5.83, south of The Dalles. Turn left (east) onto Davis Cutoff, go 0.8 of a mile and then turn; cross Lower Eightmile Road and continue ahead (east) onto Emerson Loop Road. Drive 1.9 miles on Emerson Loop Road and then turn right (south) onto Fax Road; continue on Fax Road for 2.35 miles and just past the grain elevator turn right onto the driveway which goes 0.25 of a mile to the cemetery. This was on the old Absalom Bolton Ranch. Rice was a railway station on the Great Southern Railroad. NOTE: This site is on private property. {30 May 1992} (Petersburg 1978 USGS Quad. map.)

Name of Cemetery and also known as	Number of burials	Acres	Condition	Date started or earliest known burial	Township	Range	Section

ROBERTS-GRAY
AKA: 1. GRAY, MARY E.
     2. ROBERTS,
       DELLA OR
       NELLA

A 0.1 3 1878-1881 T1S R13E S36
Located just south of Dufur. Take U.S. Hwy. 197 which bypasses Dufur. About 0.3 of a mile before U.S. Hwy. 197 joins the old highway which comes south out of Dufur, there is an unmarked roadway on the right, to a gravel pit. The graves are between the gravel pit and a grain field which, in turn, is across the old highway from a substation. There are two stones, badly broken: one is for Della or Nella Roberts, The other is for Mary E. Gray. NOTE: This site is on private property. {16 June 1992} (Not shown on Dufur West 1962-87 USGS Quad. map.)

ST. PETER'S CATHOLIC

D 7 1 1848 T1N R13E S4
Leave West 6th Street at the west end of The Dalles; turn southerly and upslope on Cherry Heights Road. Turn right onto West 13th Street to the cemetery on the right. The earliest dated monument is 1852. It is on the Catholic Mission, St. Peter's D.L.C. #40, The Dalles Spec. Acts box 4. {13 June 1997} (The Dalles South 1977 USGS Quad. map.)

SHAW, BILLY

A 0.01 ? 1901 T1S R11E S11
This lone grave of a child is near Upper Mill Creek Cemetery, but is on the south side of Mill Creek. Both burial sites are within The Dalles Watershed so permission is needed to visit these sites. {1990} (Not shown on Fivemile Butte 1962 USGS Quad. map.)

SIMNASHO

C 5 2 ? T7S R12E S20
Located in the Warm Springs Indian Reservation, 2.5 miles southeast of Simnasho, on the road to Kah-Nee-Ta Hot Springs. (Simnasho 1962 USGS Quad. map.)

SOLDIER'S GRAVE

A 0.01 ? ? T1N R15E ?
Perhaps on Section 4. There is a soldier's grave on upper Fifteen Mile Creek along the Fifteenmile-Boule Road, near the junction

Name of Cemetery and also known as	Number of burials	Acres	Condition	Date started or earliest known burial	Township	Range	Section

with Kloan Road. No further information was given in the report. (Not shown on Emerson 1977 USGS Quad. map.)

STOLLER FAMILY
AKA: 1. PETERSBURG

A   0.1   5   1902   T2N R14E   S33
Leave U.S. Hwy. 30 in the eastern part of The Dalles, taking Lower Eightmile Road to the right. Pass underneath U.S. Hwy. 197, continuing on to Petersburg, a total of 3.2 miles from U.S. Hwy 30. Turn left onto Fifteenmile-Fairbanks Road and go about 0.45 of a mile to the Petersburg School. The burials are about 0.25 of a mile to the left and downstream on the right bank of Fifteen Mile Creek. There is no ready access to the burials of 2 boys of the Stoller family. The grave site is fenced (1992). NOTE: This site is on private property. {30 May 1992} (Petersburg 1978 USGS Quad. map.)

SUTTON, SARAH

A   0.01 5 Sep 1854   T4S R13E   S4
This lone grave is unmarked and is supposed to be at the "foot of the mountains near Tygh Valley." No other information was given in the report. (Not shown on Tygh Valley 1987 or Postage Stamp Butte 1962-87 USGS Quad. maps.)

TEN MILE GRAVEYARD

A   0.01 3   1850   T2N R15E   S31
Leave The Dalles and drive through Petersburg and Fairbanks. Drive 1.23 miles past Fairbanks, from the junction with Old Moody Road and going towards Freebridge, to the driveway on the left, going up the hill. The burial is about 100-150 feet from Fifteenmile-Fairbanks Road and about 50 feet in elevation above that road. There is a bronze plaque on a tall carved stone. An article in the Sunday *Oregon Journal* 1 March 1959 reports that in 1933 road construction workers along Fifteenmile Creek uncovered the skeletons of 17 emigrants slain by Indians. One was of a child of about 12, and one of a baby. Wasco County Coroner C.A. Calloway had the remains reburied on a grassy hillside. Their names and exact dates remain unknown. {6 June 1989} (Emerson 1977 USGS Quad. map.)

Name of Cemetery and also known as	Number of burials	Acres	Condition	Date started or earliest known burial	Township	Range	Section

TILLOTSON FAMILY
AKA: 1. TILLOTSEN

A 1 4 1916   T7S R19E   S19
Leave OR. Hwy. 218 at the Clarno Grange and drive northerly along the John Day River, passing the Clarno Cemetery; see that article. The Tillotson burials are about 2 miles north of Clarno, on the left (west) side of the road. There were 5 graves in 1988. {7 August 1989} (Clarno 1988 USGS Quad. map.)

TRAXTLE
AKA: 1. HAPPY RIDGE
2. LITTLE BADGER CREEK
3. McCORKLE

A 0.1 5 1908   T3S R12E   S27
There is sure to be confusion about the name Happy Ridge Cemetery, which for geographic reasons should belong to this one. However, the name Happy Ridge has now been bestowed on a larger cemetery several miles distant; see the article under that heading. Leave U.S. Hwy. 197 at Milepost 33, south of Dufur and north of Tygh Valley, turning west on Shadybrook Road. Go 1.1 miles on Shadybrook Road, turn left onto Fairgrounds Road and pass the (new) Happy Ridge Cemetery on the left. After 0.7 of a mile on Fairgrounds Road, turn right onto Badger Creek Road. After crossing the stock gate, the road climbs up Happy Ridge and enters the White River Game Management Area. At the Mt. Hood National Forest Boundary, 4.8 miles from Fairgrounds Road and 6.6 miles from U.S. Hwy. 197, turn right (east) onto one-lane McCorkle Grade Road and go about 0.5 of a mile more to the cemetery on the left. There are 6 burials with field stones dating from 1908 to 1926. A lilac bush is planted in the northeast corner of the 40' X 40' plot. {6 June 1989} (Not shown on Friend 1962-87 USGS Quad. map.)

UNKNOWN

A 0.01 ? ?   T1N R12E   ?
Probably located in Section 25 or 36. Mrs. Elkins, now deceased, of the Genealogical Forum of Portland, Oregon Cemetery Committee received a sketchy report from Gordon E.A. Donaldson, apparently in the summer of 1960. Donaldson wrote that "forty or fifty years ago" the body of a man was found on a small wheat field under an uprooted oak tree. The site was given as about 10 miles from The

Dalles up Threemile Creek along the present Skyline Road. The land at the time of the discovery was owned by a homesteader named Harpis, and sold to the Sammis Family in 1910. No further information was given in the report. (Not shown on Brown Creek 1974 USGS Quad. map.)

UNKNOWN

? ? ? ?   **T5S R16E** ?
Probably in Section 32. Anita Drake inquired 4 April 1982 on who was buried here, on a hill above Bakeoven. George Ward knew of the burials, but not who they were. No other information is available at this time. (Not shown on Shaniko 1971 USGS Quad. map.)

UPPER MEMALOOSE
AKA: 1. WISH-HAM

? ? 8 ?   **T2N R13E** S36
This island was used by the Indians for many generations as a burial ground. It is upstream, in the Columbia River, from Lower Memaloose Island which was also a burial site. See that article. Before Upper Memaloose was flooded after construction of The Dalles Dam, there were about 2500 reburials, in 1957-1959, to Wish-Ham in North Dalles, Washington State. Go about 1.25 miles north of The Dalles Bridge (U.S. Hwy. 197) over the Columbia River. (The Dalles North 1974 USGS Quad. map for the Wish-Ham Cemetery.)

UPPER MILL CREEK
AKA: 1. MATNEY

A 0.1 5 1886   **T1S R11E** S11
Located in The Dalles Watershed, which is closed to the public by city ordinance. This was beside the Upper Mill Creek School. {7 August 1990} (Fivemile Butte 1962 USGS Quad. map.)

WAMIC
AKA: 1. FOUR CORNERS
      2. LONE PINE
      3. SMOCK PRAIRIE

C 2 2 1881   **T4S R12E** S22
Located 2 miles south and west from Wamic, on Smock Road. This was originally called Four Corners. The Wasco County field log of the road refers to this cemetery as Wamic, rather than as Lone Pine, the previously preferred name. {June 1992} (Wamic 1962-87 USGS Quad. map.)

Name of Cemetery and also known as	Number of burials	Acres	Condition	Date started or earliest known burial	Township	Range	Section

WAPINITIA

B 1 3 1885 T5S R12E S26

Leave the Wapinitia Highway (OR. Hwy. 216) at Milepost 18.8 and drive south 1.25 miles to the old Wapinitia School, now the community hall. The cemetery is on the left side of the Reservation Road to Simnasho. {August 1991} (Wapinitia 1962-87 USGS Quad. map.)

WARNER
AKA: 1. HARMONY
     2. SHERARS BRIDGE
     3. TYGH RIDGE

A 1.25 3 1880 T3S R14E S16

Located about 15 miles southeast of Dufur. Leave U.S. Hwy. 197 at Milepost 21.12, turn left (southeasterly) onto Tygh Ridge Market Road and go 5.3 miles (0.4 of a mile past the powerlines) to the cemetery. There have been many reburials to other cemeteries and only 9 monuments were present in October of 1981. {1989} (Sherars Bridge 1962-87 USGS Quad. map.)

WASCO COUNTY
AKA: 1. POTTERS FIELD

? 0.25 2 1910-1949 T1N R13E S4

This is at the southeast corner of The Dalles I.O.O.F. Cemetery and just beyond the eastern end of the G.A.R. Cemetery. It lies on the left bank of Mill Creek. See the article on the I.O.O.F. [The Dalles] Cemetery for a description of the access. {13 June 1997} (The Dalles South 1977 USGS Quad. map shows only the I.O.O.F. and G.A.R. Cemeteries.)

YOUNG FAMILY

A 0.01 5 ? T5S R12E S22

The graves of Mr. and Mrs. Young are located on the Scott and Lloyd Woodside Ranch, a short distance west of Wapinitia. From the Wapinitia Junction on OR. Hwy. 216 (milepost 18.8), drive southwesterly 1.5 miles to a field road on the left (south). This field road has a fence on its right (east) and the graves are 300 or 400 yards from the highway, between the field road and the fence. 0.2 of a mile farther west along the highway from the field road, is the entranceway to 2 ranch houses. Mr. Young was called "Colonel" and Mrs. Young's first name may have been Mary. No other information was given in the report. NOTE: This site is on private property. {August 1991} (Graves are NOT shown on Wapinitia 1962-87 USGS Quad. map.)

Wasco County

903

St. Peter's Catholic
Dean H. Byrd (1997)

I.O.O.F. [The Dalles]
Dean H. Byrd (1997)

ABBOTT see **GRAVEYARD BUTTE**	WASCO CO.	T5S	R12E	S10
ALLEN, BILL	WASCO CO.	T4S	R11E	UNS
ANTELOPE [NEW]	WASCO CO.	T7S	R17E	S32
ANTELOPE PIONEER	WASCO CO.	T7S	R17E	S28
BAKEOVEN see **HINTON**	WASCO CO.	T5S	R16E	S26
BETHUNE, MRS. AGNES see **McRAE RANCH, FARQUHAR**				
	WASCO CO.	T6S	R19E	?
BIGELOW D.L.C., WINDSOR D. see **PIONEER [THE DALLES]**				
	WASCO CO.	T1N	R13E	S10
BOLTON see **RICE**	WASCO CO.	T1S	R14E	S10
BOLTON RANCH, ABSALOM see **RICE**	WASCO CO.	T1S	R14E	S10
BOYD see **RICE**	WASCO CO.	T1S	R14E	S10
BRIGGS GRAVES	WASCO.CO.	T4S	R11E	S26
BRIGGS, JARVIS see **BRIGGS GRAVES**				
	WASCO CO.	T4S	R11E	S26
BRIGGS, NEWTON see **BRIGGS GRAVES**				
	WASCO CO.	T4S	R11E	S26
BROWN, JOSEPH	WASCO CO.	T1N	R13E	S10
BUTTS, CATHERINE BONNETT	WASCO CO.	T3S	R14E	S28
BUZAN	WASCO CO.	T4S	R15E	S33
CALLOWAY, C. A. see **TEN MILE GRAVEYARD**				
	WASCO CO.	T2N	R15E	S31
CAMPBELL, BABY GIRL	WASCO CO.	T1S	R13E	S11
CARSON, DOLPH see **CONLY**	WASCO CO.	T1S	R14E	?
CARSON, LOYD D. see **CONLY**	WASCO CO.	T1S	R14E	?
CARSON, MARY COPLAND see **CONLY**	WASCO CO.	T1S	R14E	?
CELILO [#1]	WASCO CO.	T2N	R15E	S16
CELILO [#2]	WASCO CO.	T2N	R15E	S21
CHASTAIN, BESSIE	WASCO CO.	T4S	R12E	S1
CHINESE [THE DALLES]	WASCO CO.	T1N	R13E	S10
CHURCHILL, ELIZABETH J. HUMPHRIES				
	WASCO CO.	?	?	?
CHURCHILL, MRS. see **CHURCHILL, ELIZABETH J. HUMPHRIES**				
	WASCO CO.	?	?	?
CLARNO	WASCO CO.	T7S	R19E	S29
COGGSMILL see **COGSWELL, JOHN**	WASCO CO.	T1N	R15E	S30
COGSWELL see **COGSWELL, JOHN**	WASCO CO.	T1N	R15E	S30
COGSWELL GRAVES see **COGSWELL, JOHN**				
	WASCO CO.	T1N	R15E	S30
COGSWELL, JOHN	WASCO CO.	T1N	R15E	S30
COGSWELL PLACE see **COGSWELL, JOHN**				
	WASCO CO.	T1N	R15E	S30
COLUMBIA LODGE #5 see **I.O.O.F. [THE DALLES]**				
	WASCO CO.	T1N	R13E	S4
CONLY	WASCO CO.	T1S	R14E	?
CONROY PLACE, JOHN see **BUTTS, CATHERINE BONNETT**				
	WASCO CO.	T3S	R14E	S28
CONROY PLACE, PETER see **CRAMER, MRS.**				
	WASCO CO.	T7S	R17E	?
COVEY FAMILY	WASCO CO.	T3S	R12E	S2
COW CANYON GRADE see **HAIGHT SPRING**				
	WASCO CO.	T8S	R15E	S9

COX, BEULAH MAY	WASCO CO.	T5S	R12E	S24
COX, DUDLEY see COX, BEULAH MAY	WASCO CO.	T5S	R12E	S24
CRAMER, MRS.	WASCO CO.	T7S	R17E	?
CRITERION	WASCO CO.	T6S	R15E	S18
CRITERION RANCH see CRITERION	WASCO CO.	T6S	R15E	S18
CUNNINGHAM GRAVE	WASCO CO.	T5S	R12E	S28
CUNNINGHAM, I. C. see CUNNINGHAM GRAVE				
	WASCO CO.	T5S	R12E	S28
CUNNINGHAM, J. R. see CUNNINGHAM GRAVE				
	WASCO CO.	T5S	R12E	S28
DAFFODIL PATCH	WASCO CO.	T1N	R11E	S12
DARNIELLE, SARAH	WASCO CO.	T1S	R13E	?
DARNILLE see DARNIELLE, SARAH	WASCO CO.	T1S	R13E	?
DONALDSON, GORDON E. A. see UNKNOWN				
	WASCO CO.	T1N	R12E	?
DOYLE, MRS. C. B.	WASCO CO.	T6S	R12E	S6
DRAKE, ANITA see UNKNOWN	WASCO CO.	T5S	R16E	?
DRY HOLLOW see RICE	WASCO CO.	T1S	R14E	S10
DUFUR CATHOLIC see KINGSLEY CATHOLIC				
	WASCO CO.	T2S	R13E	S28
DUFUR COMMUNITY	WASCO CO.	T1S	R13E	S24
DUTCH FLAT see OBRIST	WASCO CO.	T1S	R12E	S2
EASTON HOMESTEAD, JAMES GARFIELD see PIONEER GRAVES				
	WASCO CO.	T3S	R13E	S20
EIGHT MILE	WASCO CO.	T1S	R13E	S1
ENDERSBY INFANT	WASCO CO.	T1S	R13E	S11
FAIRVIEW	WASCO CO.	?	?	?
FERGUSON FAMILY see EIGHT MILE	WASCO CO.	T1S	R13E	S1
FERGUSON HOMESTEAD, ALFRED see EIGHT MILE				
	WASCO CO.	T1S	R13E	S1
FLANAGAN see BUZAN	WASCO CO.	T4S	R15E	S33
FLINN PLACE see RAINS, BABY	WASCO CO.	T5S	R12E	?
FORMAN RANCH, BEN see RAINS, BABY				
	WASCO CO.	T5S	R12E	?
FORT DALLES	WASCO CO.	T1N	R13E	S4
FOUR CORNERS see WAMIC	WASCO CO.	T4S	R12E	S22
FRENCH	WASCO CO.	T5S	R12E	S33
FRIEND [NEW]	WASCO CO.	T3S	R12E	S3
FRIEND [OLD] see MILLER	WASCO CO.	T2S	R12E	S34
G.A.R. [GRAND ARMY OF THE REPUBLIC]				
	WASCO CO.	T1N	R13E	S4
GATE CREEK see BRIGGS GRAVES	WASCO CO.	T4S	R11E	S26
GRAVE ISLAND MEMORIAL	WASCO CO.	T2N	R14E	S31
GRAVEYARD BUTTE	WASCO CO.	T5S	R12E	S10
GRAY, MARY E. see ROBERTS-GRAY	WASCO CO.	T1S	R13E	S36
HAIGHT SPRING	WASCO CO.	T8S	R15E	S9
HALLYBURTON, JAMES S. see ORTLEY				
	WASCO CO.	T2N	R12E	?
HAPPY RIDGE	WASCO CO.	T3S	R13E	S32
HAPPY RIDGE see TRAXTLE	WASCO CO.	T3S	R12E	S27
HARMONY see WARNER	WASCO CO.	T3S	R14E	S16
HARPIS see UNKNOWN	WASCO CO.	T1N	R12E	?

HAUSER GRAVES	WASCO CO.	T3S	R13E	S32
HAWKINS, ALFRED	WASCO CO.	T5S	R11E	S25
HEALD, GILBERT SETON	WASCO CO.	T3S	R12E	S22
HENDERSON PIONEER	WASCO CO.	T1S	R13E	S33
HENDRICKS see KINGSLEY CATHOLIC	WASCO CO.	T2S	R13E	S28
HINTON	WASCO CO.	T5S	R16E	S26
HINTON-WARD see HINTON	WASCO CO.	T5S	R16E	S26
HOT SPRINGS INDIAN	WASCO CO.	T8S	R13E	S27
I.O.O.F. see ANTELOPE [NEW]	WASCO CO.	T7S	R17E	S32
I.O.O.F. see DUFUR COMMUNITY	WASCO CO.	T1S	R13E	S24
I.O.O.F. see MOSIER	WASCO CO.	T2N	R11E	S1
I.O.O.F. [THE DALLES]	WASCO CO.	T1N	R13E	S4
I.O.O.F. [THE DALLES] see PARKLAWN				
	WASCO CO.	T1N	R13E	S15
I.O.O.F. [TYGH VALLEY]	WASCO CO.	T4S	R13E	S10
INDIAN	WASCO CO.	T3S	R14E	S23
JAP HOLLOW see EIGHT MILE	WASCO CO.	T1S	R13E	S1
JAPANESE HOLLOW see EIGHT MILE	WASCO CO.	T1S	R13E	S1
JEWISH see BROWN, JOSEPH	WASCO CO.	T1N	R13E	S10
JEWISH [THE DALLES]	WASCO CO.	T1N	R13E	S10
JOE LONG BUTTE see GRAVEYARD BUTTE				
	WASCO CO.	T5S	R12E	S10
JOHNSON, ROBERT ROY	WASCO CO.	T1N	R13E	S1
JUNIPER FLAT see KELLY	WASCO CO.	T5S	R13E	S8
JUSTENSEN FARM, NEL see HAUSER GRAVES				
	WASCO CO.	T3S	R13E	S32
KELLEY GROVE see KELLY	WASCO CO.	T5S	R13E	S8
KELLY	WASCO CO.	T5S	R13E	S8
KELLY CHURCHYARD see KELLY	WASCO CO.	T5S	R13E	S8
KETCHUM PLACE, WILLIAM see MORTON GRAVES				
	WASCO CO.	T1N	R12E	S10
KINGSLEY	WASCO CO.	T2S	R13E	S32
KINGSLEY CATHOLIC	WASCO CO.	T2S	R13E	S28
KRAMER see CRAMER, MRS.	WASCO CO.	T7S	R17E	?
LINDLEY see BUZAN	WASCO CO.	T4S	R15E	S33
LITTLE BADGER CREEK see TRAXTLE	WASCO CO.	T3S	R12E	S27
LONE PINE see WAMIC	WASCO CO.	T4S	R12E	S22
LOWER MEMALOOSE	WASCO CO.	T3N	R12E	S32
MASONIC [THE DALLES]	WASCO CO.	T1N	R13E	S10
MATNEY see UPPER MILL CREEK	WASCO CO.	T1S	R11E	S11
McCLURE FAMILY	WASCO CO.	T2N	R12E	S4
McCLURE, JAMES	WASCO CO.	T2N	R12E	S5
McCORKLE see TRAXTLE	WASCO CO.	T3S	R12E	S27
McDONALD, D. S. see FAIRVIEW	WASCO CO.	?	?	?
McDONALD, LOUISA see FAIRVIEW	WASCO CO.	?	?	?
McDONALD, MARY J. see FAIRVIEW	WASCO CO.	?	?	?
McQUINN, GEORGE	WASCO CO.	T2N	R14E	S26
McRAE, ANNA BELL see McRAE RANCH, FARQUHAR				
	WASCO CO.	T6S	R19E	?
McRAE RANCH, FARQUHAR	WASCO CO.	T6S	R19E	?
MEEK, STEPHEN see BUTTS, CATHERINE BONNETT				
	WASCO CO.	T3S	R14E	S28

MEMALOOSE see **LOWER MEMALOOSE**	WASCO CO.	T3N	R12E	S32
MILLER	WASCO CO.	T2S	R12E	S34
MISSION [THE DALLES]	WASCO CO.	T1N	R13E	S4
MOEN [?] see **MOON, JEFF E.**	WASCO CO.	T2N	R13E	S32
MOON, ESTELLE see **MOON, JEFF E.**	WASCO CO.	T2N	R13E	S32
MOON, JEFF E.	WASCO CO.	T2N	R13E	S32
MOON, LEIF see **MOON, JEFF E.**	WASCO CO.	T2N	R13E	S32
MORTON GRAVES	WASCO CO.	T1N	R12E	S10
MOSIER	WASCO CO.	T2N	R11E	S1
MOSIER D.L.C., JONAH H. see **MOSIER PIONEER**				
	WASCO CO.	T2N	R11E	S1
MOSIER PIONEER	WASCO CO.	T2N	R11E	S1
MT. HOOD FLAT see **OBRIST**	WASCO CO.	T1S	R12E	S2
NEABECK	WASCO CO.	T1N	R15E	S20
OAK GROVE see **MOSIER PIONEER**	WASCO CO.	T2N	R11E	S1
OBRIST	WASCO CO.	T1S	R12E	S2
OLD MOSIER see **MOSIER PIONEER**	WASCO CO.	T2N	R11E	S1
OLD TYGH VALLEY see **HAPPY RIDGE**	WASCO CO.	T3S	R13E	S32
ORTLEY	WASCO CO.	T2N	R12E	?
PARKLAWN	WASCO CO.	T1N	R13E	S15
PETERSBURG see **STOLLER FAMILY**	WASCO CO.	T2N	R14E	S33
PIONEER [THE DALLES]	WASCO CO.	T1N	R13E	S10
PIONEER GRAVE	WASCO CO.	T2S	R14E	?
PIONEER GRAVES	WASCO CO.	T3S	R13E	S20
PLEASANT RIDGE	WASCO CO.	T1S	R12E	?
POTTERS FIELD see **WASCO COUNTY**	WASCO CO.	T1N	R13E	S4
PRATT	WASCO CO.	T4S	R12E	S14
RAINS, BABY	WASCO CO.	T5S	R12E	?
RED LAKE	WASCO CO.	T6S	R12E	S34
REINS, BABY see **RAINS, BABY**	WASCO CO	T5S	R12E	?
RICE	WASCO CO.	T1S	R14E	S10
RIPLEY, MIRIAM SHELDON see **DAFFODIL PATCH**				
	WASCO CO.	T1N	R11E	S12
ROBERTS, DELLA OR NELLA see **ROBERTS-GRAY**				
	WASCO CO.	T1S	R13E	S36
ROBERTS-GRAY	WASCO CO.	T1S	R13E	S36
RURAL DALE see **BUZAN**	WASCO CO.	T4S	R15E	S33
ST. PETER'S CATHOLIC	WASCO CO.	T1N	R13E	S4
ST. PETER'S D.L.C., CATHOLIC MISSION see **ST. PETER'S CATHOLIC**				
	WASCO CO.	T1N	R13E	S4
SAMMIS FAMILY see **UNKNOWN**	WASCO CO.	T1N	R12E	?
SCOTT, CHRISSY see **McRAE RANCH, FARQUHAR**				
	WASCO CO.	T6S	R19E	?
SCOTT, MR. AND MRS. JIM see **McRAE RANCH, FARQUHAR**				
	WASCO CO.	T6S	R19E	?
SHAUG D.L.C., CHARLES see **MOON, JEFF E.**				
	WASCO CO.	T2N	R13E	S32
SHAW, BILLY	WASCO CO.	T1S	R11E	S11
SHERARS BRIDGE see **WARNER**	WASCO CO.	T3S	R14E	S16
SIMMS D.L.C., JOHN A. see **MASONIC [THE DALLES]**				
	WASCO CO.	T1N	R13E	S10
SIMNASHO	WASCO CO.	T7S	R12E	S20

SMOCK PRAIRIE see **WAMIC**	WASCO CO.	T4S	R12E	S22
SOLDIER'S GRAVE	WASCO CO.	T1N	R15E	?
STAR #23 REBEKAH LODGE COMMUNITY see **DUFUR COMMUNITY**				
	WASCO CO.	T1S	R13E	S24
STOLLER FAMILY	WASCO CO.	T2N	R14E	S33
SUNSET see **I.O.O.F. [THE DALLES]**				
	WASCO CO.	T1N	R13E	S4
SUNSET HILL see **PIONEER [THE DALLES]**				
	WASCO CO.	T1N	R13E	S10
SUTTON, SARAH	WASCO CO.	T4S	R13E	S4
TEN MILE GRAVEYARD	WASCO CO.	T2N	R15E	S31
THREE MILE see **OBRIST**	WASCO CO.	T1S	R12E	S2
TILLOTSEN see **TILLOTSON FAMILY**	WASCO CO	T7S	R19E	S19
TILLOTSON FAMILY	WASCO CO.	T7S	R19E	S19
TRAXTLE	WASCO CO.	T3S	R12E	S27
TREVITT, VICTOR see **LOWER MEMALOOSE**				
	WASCO CO.	T3N	R12E	S32
TYGH RIDGE see **WARNER**	WASCO CO.	T3S	R14E	S16
TYGH VALLEY PIONEER see **HAPPY RIDGE**				
	WASCO CO.	T3S	R13E	S32
UNKNOWN	WASCO CO.	T1N	R12E	?
UNKNOWN	WASCO CO.	T5S	R16E	?
UPPER MEMALOOSE	WASCO CO.	T2N	R13E	S36
UPPER MILL CREEK	WASCO CO.	T1S	R11E	S11
VANDERPOOL see **HENDERSON PIONEER**				
	WASCO CO.	T1S	R13E	S33
VETERANS see **G.A.R. [GRAND ARMY OF THE REPUBLIC]**				
	WASCO CO.	T1N	R13E	S4
VETERANS see **PARKLAWN**	WASCO CO.	T1N	R13E	S15
VICTOR see **KELLY**	WASCO CO.	T5S	R13E	S8
WALDRON see **RICE**	WASCO CO.	T1S	R14E	S10
WALLACE see **ANTELOPE PIONEER**	WASCO CO.	T7S	R17E	S28
WAMIC	WASCO CO.	T4S	R12E	S22
WAMIC PIONEER see **PRATT**	WASCO CO.	T4S	R12E	S14
WAPINITIA	WASCO CO.	T5S	R12E	S26
WARD, GEORGE see **UNKNOWN**	WASCO CO.	T5S	R16E	?
WARM SPRINGS RIVER see **HOT SPRINGS INDIAN**				
	WASCO CO.	T8S	R13E	S27
WARNER	WASCO CO.	T3S	R14E	S16
WASCO COUNTY	WASCO CO.	T1N	R13E	S4
WASCO LODGE see **MASONIC [THE DALLES]**				
	WASCO CO.	T1N	R13E	S10
WHITTEN see **KINGSLEY**	WASCO CO.	T2S	R13E	S32
WISH-HAM see **UPPER MEMALOOSE**	WASCO CO.	T2N	R13E	S36
WOODSIDE, LLOYD see **RAINS, BABY**	WASCO CO.	T5S	R12E	?
WOODSIDE RANCH, SCOTT AND LLOYD see **YOUNG FAMILY**				
	WASCO CO.	T5S	R12E	S22
YOUNG FAMILY	WASCO CO.	T5S	R12E	S22
YOUNG, MR. AND MRS. see **YOUNG FAMILY**				
	WASCO CO.	T5S	R12E	S22

Pioneer [The Dalles]
Dean H. Byrd (1997)

Wasco County
Dean H. Byrd (1997)

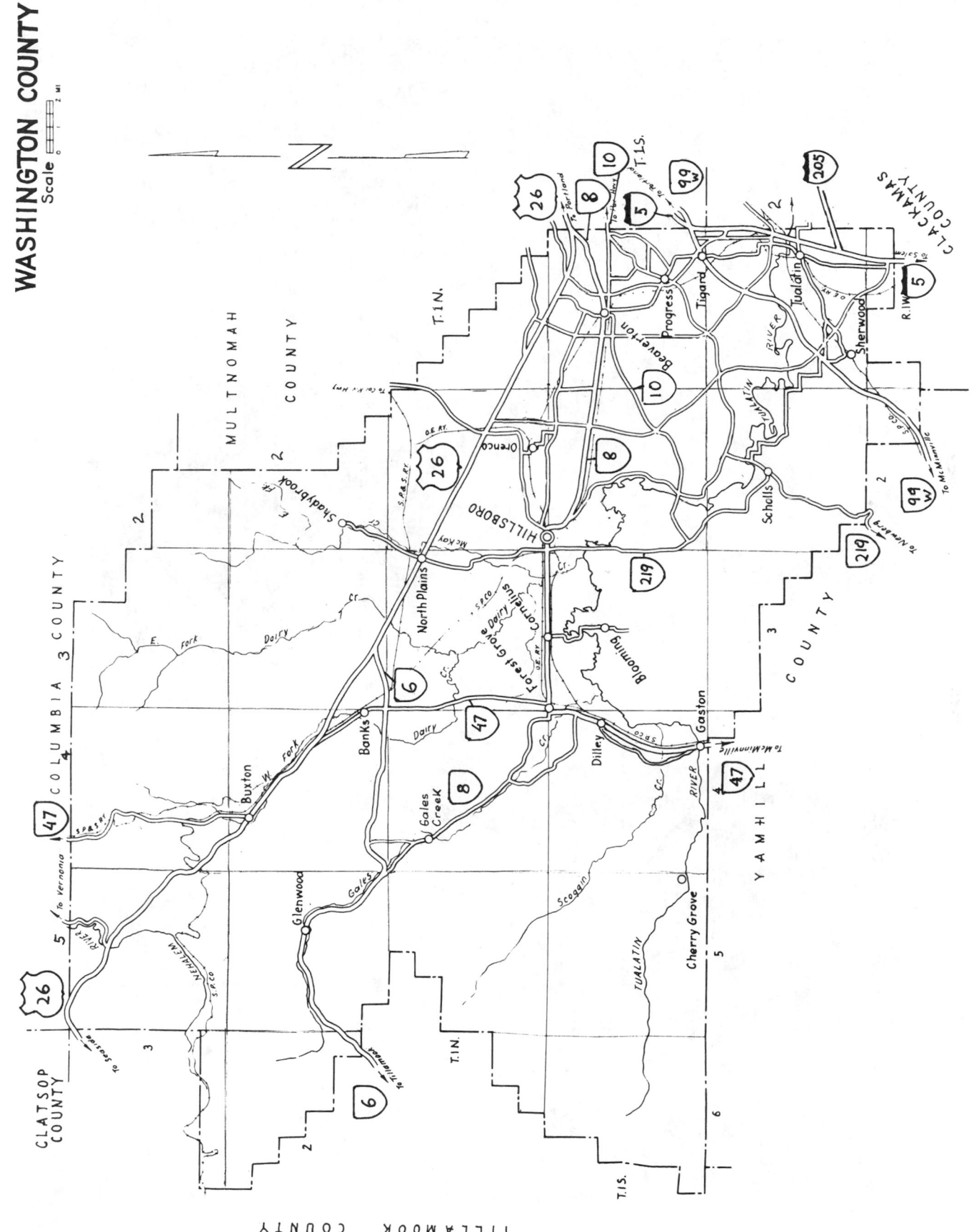

St. Edward's Catholic [New]
Dean H. Byrd (1993)

912

Area: 727 square miles
Population (1998): 399,697
County seat: Hillsboro, Population: 52,105
County established: 5 July 1843

The Tualatin Valley and adjacent hillsides were occupied as desirable farmlands by American wagon train immigrants beginning as early as 1842. Several of the earliest cemeteries have been lost. Of the existing organized cemeteries for the public the earliest may be Forest View (1846), followed by Lewis (1847), Hill (1850), Crescent Grove (1852) and West Union Baptist (1854). Washington County attracted German, Swiss and Dutch settlers, especially in the 1890's so there are a fair number of "ethnic" cemeteries.

Hillsboro Pioneer
Janice M. Healy (1993)

Washington County

913

Buxton Protestant

Dean H. Byrd (1991)

Visitation of the Blessed Virgin Mary

Janice M. Healy (1992)

Name of Cemetery and also known as	Number of burials	Acres	Condition	Date started or earliest known burial	Township	Range	Section

AGGELLES, ALEXIS

13 March 1907
Alexis Aggelles was killed by a dynamite explosion during the construction of a railway tunnel west of Buxton. It has long been assumed that he was buried near the tunnel, but recent research of the death certificate shows that Aggelles was actually buried in Lone Fir Cemetery in Portland (Multnomah County), 15 March 1907. The *Oregon Daily Journal*, 14 March 1907, evening edition, page 10, tells about the accident.

ARCADE
AKA: 1. MILLER
2. PUMPKIN RIDGE

C 1.8 2 9 June 1887 T2N R3W S14
The cemetery is located about 5.5 miles northwest of the town of North Plains, about 500 feet left (north) off of Pumpkin Ridge Road, and 3.7 miles northerly from Shadybrook Road. The first burial was Phoebe Keenon Bennet and baby. {24 August 1993} (Meacham Corner 1979-92 USGS Quad. map.)

BAKER FAMILY

A 0.1 8 1874-1971 T1S R4W S21
The burials were in Scoggins Valley off of Scoggins Valley Road. They were removed to the Forest View Cemetery near Forest Grove on 16 September 1971. The original site was on the Norman Martin D.L.C. #52, OC #2116. (Not shown on Gaston 1956-70 USGS Quad. map.)

BARNUM FAMILY

A ? 2 ? T2S R1W S30
Located north of Sherwood and south of St. Paul Lutheran Church, off of Edy Road, on the Moses R. Barnum D.L.C., OC #1607. There are two burials with one marker according to the report. No other information was given in the report. (Not shown on Sherwood 1961-85 USGS Quad. map.)

BETHANY PIONEER
AKA: 1. BETHANY BIBLE CHURCH
2. BETHANY GERMAN METHODIST
3. BETHANY METHODIST

B 2.26 1 1894 T1N R1W S7
Leave Sunset Highway (U.S. Hwy. 26), at the interchange for Northwest 185th Avenue. Drive north on Northwest 185th for 2.7 miles to its intersection with Northwest Germantown Road. Turn right (east) onto Northwest Germantown Road and drive 0.1 of a mile to the church driveway uphill on the left

915

CHURCH (north). The burial area is not nearly as large as 2.26 acres. {18 July 1998} (Linnton 1961-84 USGS Quad. map.)

BETHANY PRESBYTERIAN
AKA: 1. BETHANY
PRESBYTERIAN
CHURCH
2. BRUGGER
3. GERMAN
PRESBYTERIAN

C 3.23 2 1874 T1N R1W S17
Located north of Beaverton and north of Sunset Highway (U.S. Hwy. 26). Leave the Sunset Highway at the Northwest Cornell Road interchange. Drive east on Northwest Cornell Road for about 0.7 of a mile; turn left (north) onto Northwest 143rd Avenue, passing Union Cemetery on the left (west). After 0.9 of a mile on Northwest 143rd Avenue turn left (west) onto West Union Road. Drive only 0.2 of a mile on West Union Road and then turn right (north) onto Northwest Kaiser Road. Continue on Northwest Kaiser Road for 1.8 miles to the Northwest Springville Road intersection. Here at 3.6 miles from the Sunset Highway is the church itself, at the northwest corner of the intersection. Continue ahead to the north on Northwest Kaiser Road for another 0.6 of a mile to the cemetery on the right (east). The cemetery is outside of but borders the north line of the Jacob Brugger D.L.C. #52, OC #1553. {18 July 1998} (Linnton 1961-84 USGS Quad. map.)

BLOOMING
AKA: 1. BLOOMING
CHURCH
2. BLOOMINGTON [?]
3. ST. PAUL'S
LUTHERAN
4. ST. PETER'S
LUTHERAN

C 3 2 1884 T1S R3W S15
Take OR. Hwy. 219 south out of Hillsboro towards Newberg. Cross the Tualatin River and then turn right (west) onto Tongue Lane, the first county road beyond the bridge. Drive 3.4 miles to the cemetery from OR. Hwy. 219 on Tongue Lane and left (south) on Iowa Hill Road a short distance. The cemetery is at the junction of Iowa Hill and Nursery Roads, south of Cornelius. {20 March 1994} (Laurelwood 1956-92 USGS Quad. map.)

BOOTH FAMILY

A 0.01 1 Circa 1890 T1S R5W S25
Located in Cherry Grove, on the south side of Lee Falls Road west of Cherry Grove and on private property owned by Birgetta Nixon (1991). There are graves of 2 of the Booth children, the grandchildren of Jason Lee, with the possibility of other burials. It is

Name of Cemetery and also known as	Number of burials	Acres	Condition	Date started or earliest known burial	Township	Range	Section

on the Emanuel Horner D.L.C. #38, OC #4717.
(Not shown on Gaston 1956-70 or Turner Creek
1979 USGS Quad. map.)

BRUEHL, EDWARD
AKA: 1. BRUEHL PLACE

A ? 5 27 Mar 1918 T3N R2W S28
Located at the head of Raymond Creek Canyon
near the junction of Washington County with
Columbia and Multnomah Counties. Located 1
to 1.5 miles northwest of the junction of
Dixie Mountain Road with Dixie Road.
Washington County Death Certificate #41 for
27 March 1918, shows Edward Bruehl as a
single man and a rancher died at age 75,
buried on the Bruehl Place near Dixie and
S[c]apoose R. 1, Connell Precinct. (Not
shown on Dixie Mountain 1961-85 USGS Quad.
map.)

BURGDORFER FAMILY
AKA: 1. BURDORFUR

A 0.01 4 1894-1905 T3N R3W S15
Located in the Southwest 1/4 of the Northwest
1/4 of Section 15. This site is northwest of
Mountaindale on the Charles Hanlon Farm, high
on Buck Mountain, east off of Greener Road.
NOTE: There is a Burgdorfer Flat in the
Northeast 1/4 of the Northwest 1/4 of Section
22. (Meacham Corner 1979-92 USGS Quad. map.)

BURRIS FAMILY,
WILLIAM

A 0.01 5 2 Jan 1855 T1N R2W S5
Located at the junction of Jackson Quarry
Road and West Union Road, on the northwest
corner, and on the Joseph Connell Farm, Route
1 Box 80, Hillsboro (1991). This is on the
William Burris D.L.C. #63, OC #1371. Martha
Burris died on the claim 2 January 1855,
William Burris died the winter of 1857. (Not
shown on Hillsboro 1961-85 USGS Quad. map.)

BUXTON CATHOLIC
AKA: 1. ST. THOMAS

C 1.5 2 1901 T2N R4W S4
Driving west on Sunset Highway (U.S. Hwy. 26)
go about 0.5 of a mile beyond the junction
with OR. Hwy. 47. Turn left (south) onto
Strassel Road. After about 400 feet turn
left again onto the first road (Buxton
Cemetery Road; it was not signed). The
cemetery is on the right and 0.8 of a mile
from Strassel Road. There is a driveway

between the Catholic Cemetery on the right and the Protestant Cemetery on the left as one proceeds into the cemetery from Buxton Cemetery Road. See the article for Buxton Protestant Cemetery. {12 November 1991} (Buxton 1979-92 USGS Quad. map.)

BUXTON PROTESTANT

C   1.5   2   1888   T2N   R4W   S5

Driving west on Sunset Highway (U.S. Hwy. 26) go about 0.5 of a mile beyond the junction with OR. Hwy. 47. Turn left (south) onto Strassel Road. After about 400 feet turn left again onto the first road (Buxton Cemetery Road; it was not signed). The cemetery is on the right and 0.8 of a mile from Strassel Road. There is a driveway between the Catholic Cemetery on the right and the Protestant Cemetery on the left as one proceeds into the cemetery from Buxton Cemetery Road. See the article for Buxton Catholic Cemetery. {12 November 1991} (Buxton 1979-92 USGS Quad. map.)

CHERRY GROVE BAPTIST
  AKA: 1. CHERRY GROVE

B   1.83 2   1894   T1S   R4W   S30

Located just east of the locale of Cherry Grove. Leave OR. Hwy. 47 about 0.8 of a mile north of Gaston. Travel due west for 0.4 of a mile to the junction with Patton Valley Road. Turn left (southerly) onto Patton Valley Road and drive 4.7 miles southerly and westerly to the junction with Lee Road on the right (north). Turn onto Lee Road and go 0.1 of mile to the cemetery on the left (west) and 5.2 miles from OR. Hwy. 47. It is on the John J. Gerrish D.L.C. #57, OC #2312. {November 1993} (Gaston 1956-70 USGS Quad. map.)

COOPER MOUNTAIN
  [CATHOLIC]
  AKA: 1. COPPER *[Sic]*
          MOUNTAIN
       2. ST. PAUL
       3. ST. PETER'S

B   1.74 2   1916   T1S   R2W   S25

South of Aloha. Leave Farmington Road (OR. Hwy. 10) and turn south on Southwest Grabhorn Road. Go 0.7 mile and turn left (east) off of Southwest Grabhorn Road onto Southwest Gassner Raod. Continue on Southwest Gassner Road for 0.8 of a mile, then turn right (south) onto Southwest Kemmer Road and drive 0.4 of a mile to a 90-degree left turn. The

Name of Cemetery and also known as	Number of burials	Acres	Condition	Date started or earliest known burial	Township	Range	Section

cemetery is at the northeast corner of this turn. {3 December 1990} (Beaverton 1961-84 USGS Quad. map.)

COOPER MOUNTAIN [PROTESTANT]
AKA: 1. COPPER [Sic] MOUNTAIN
2. EVANGELICAL
3. GASSNER ROAD

C 0.9 4 1899 T1S R2W S25
South of Aloha. Leave Farmington Road (OR. Hwy. 10) and turn south on Southwest Grabhorn Road. Go 0.7 of a mile, turn left (east) off of Southwest Grabhorn Road onto Southwest Gassner Road and drive another 0.5 of a mile. The cemetery is on the right (south) side of Southwest Gassner Road and 400 feet east of Southwest Miller Hill Road. {3 December 1990} (Scholls 1961-85 USGS Quad. map.)

CORNELIUS PIONEER METHODIST
AKA: 1. CORNELIUS METHODIST
2. EMANUEL
3. I.O.O.F.
4. WAPATO LODGE I.O.O.F.

D 1.5 1 1876 T1N R3W S33
Located just north of Cornelius. Turn north off of OR. Hwy. 8 onto North 10th Avenue and drive north just beyond the bridge over Council Creek. The cemetery is on the right (east) side of the road on the hill and 0.7 of mile from OR. Hwy. 8. The first recorded burial was 25 December 1876. The cemetery was sold to the Methodist Episcopal Church 28 May 1887. {13 July 1995} (Forest Grove 1956-92 USGS Quad. map. NOTE: The quad. map mistakenly applies the name Emanuel to this site.)

CRESCENT GROVE
AKA: 1. AMES CHAPEL
2. CRESCENT
3. METZGER
4. PROGRESS

D 21.4 1 1852 T1S R1W S26
Located in Tigard. Turn off onto Greenburg Road from OR. Hwy. 217 towards Washington Square. At the intercange legs on the north side of OR. Hwy 217, continue northerly past the Washington Square shopping mall entry and go 0.3 of a mile from the interchange legs. This brings you to the central and the principal entry to Crescent Grove Cemetery on the left (west). It is on the David Graham D.L.C. #52, OC #3902. {12 May 1993} (Beaverton 1961-84 USGS Quad. map.)

ELLIS, CARRIE ETTA

A 0.01 ? 27 Jun 1915 T1N R5W S25
A lone burial for the daughter of Perry Ellis aged 10 months who died of an accidental skull fracture, is located 6 miles west and 1

Name of Cemetery and also known as	Number of burials	Acres	Condition	Date started or earliest known burial	Township	Range	Section

mile north of Forest Grove in the Gales Peak area. It is on the south 1/2 of Section 25 somewhere off of Soda Springs Road. (Not shown on Gales Creek 1979-92 or Roaring Creek 1979 USGS Quad. map.)

ELLIS FAMILY

| | A | ? | ? | 1909 | T1S | R1W | S12 |

There is a private burial ground of Rachel A. Ellis and members of her family, including A. M. Ellis. The burials are near the Neveh Zedek-Rose City Lodge Cemetery. On the William Pointer D.L.C. #62, OC #3444. A plat map of the ground was filed 9 March 1909 by Perry Ellis and Kitty M. Ellis (both unmarried). (Not shown on Linnton 1961-84 or Portland 1977 USGS Quad. map.)

EMANUEL LUTHERAN
AKA: 1. CORNELIUS
       LUTHERAN
   2. GERMAN
      EVANGELICAL
      LUTHERAN
      EMANUELS
      CHURCH
   3. GERMAN
      LUTHERANER
      [*Sic*] EMANUEL
      CHURCH

| | C | 1 | 1 | 1915 | T1N | R3W | S34 |

In Cornelius go north from eastbound Adair Street (OR. Hwy. 8) or westbound Baseline Street (also OR. Hwy.8) on 9th Street for 0.3 of a mile, 19th Street becomes Susbauer Road ahead. The cemetery is on the left (west) side of Susbauer Road. On the William and Rosana McLin D.L.C. #67, OC #688. {13 July 1995} (Forest Grove 1956-92 USGS Quad. map. NOTE: The Quad. map mistakenly applies the name Emanuel to the Cornelius Methodist Cemetery)

EMERICK FAMILY
AKA: 1. EMERICK,
      SOLOMON
   2. EMRICK
   3. EMRIEK

| | A | 0.01 | 6 | Circa 1899 | T1S | R3W | ? |

This was possibly located in Section 3, 4, or 5. It was on the Solomon Emerick D.L.C. #46, OC #875 south of Cornelius and was moved circa 1916, to an unknown location. (Not shown on Forest Grove 1956-92 USGS Quad. map.)

FERN HILL CATHOLIC
AKA: 1. FERN HILL
   2. HERGERT ROAD
   3. IOWA HILL
      CATHOLIC
   4. ST. JOHN
      THE EVANGELIST

| | B | 1 | 2 | 1891 | T1S | R3W | S16 |

Located 3.5 miles south of Cornelius. Take 10th Avenue south from OR. Hwy. 8, Cross the Tualatin River and then turn right (west) onto LaFollette Road; the road turns left (south) and again crosses the Tualatin River. At the intersection with Blooming-Fern Hill

Name of Cemetery and also known as	Number of burials	Acres	Condition	Date started or earliest known burial	Township	Range	Section

5. SOUTH CORNELIUS CATHOLIC

Road, the road ahead (south) changes name to Hergert Road. The cemetery is on the left (east) side of Hergert Road at the top of the hill. {7 June 1996} (Laurelwood 1956-92 USGS Quad. map.)

FINLEY'S SUNSET HILL MEMORIAL
AKA: 1. SUNSET HILLS MEMORIAL PARK
2. SUNSET MEMORIAL PARK
3. VALKYRIE MEMORIAL PARK
4. WEST HILLS

D 70 1 1936 T1S R1W S1
Located on the north side of Sunset Highway (U.S. Hwy. 26) at 6801 Southwest Sunset Highway: on the William Pointer D.L.C. #62, OC #3444. NOTE: At the time of this writing this area has been undergoing constant road changes due to Westside MAX Light Rail, U.S. Hwy. 26 widening, reconstruction of on and off ramps and the new interchange for OR. Hwy. 8. This will continue for several more years. {January 2000} (Linnton 1961-84 and Portland 1960-70-77 USGS Quad. maps.)

FIR LAWN CEMETERY AND MAUSOLEUM
AKA: 1. HILLSBORO FIR LAWN

E 23.1 1 1929 T1N R3W S36
Located at the west end of West Main Street, at 1070 West Main, Hillsboro. On the Henry and Trijah Davis D.L.C. #68, OC #687. {May 1998} (Forest Grove 1956-92 USGS Quad. map.)

FORD INFANT

A 0.01 ? Ca 1850 T1N R1W S7
Located on section 7 or 8. The one year old child of Reuben W. Ford and Mary Ann Lenox Ford was buried between 1850 and 1855 on their land which is described in their D.L.C. application #5959 which they sold to Joseph Leonard who proved the claim as D.L.C., OC #2844. See *Genealogical Material in Oregon Donation Land Claims*, Volume 4, 1967, page 21. (Not shown on Linnton 1961-84 USGS Quad. map.)

FOREST VIEW MEMORIAL GARDENS
AKA: 1. FOREST VIEW
2. NAYLOR

D 37.86 1 1846 T1N R4W S36
Located just west of Tom McCall Middle School on Ritchey Road, Forest Grove. It is on the Henry Buxton Sr. D.L.C. #44, OC #3781. {10 April 1998} (Gales Creek 1979-92 and Forest Grove 1956-92 USGS Quad. maps.)

Washington County

Name of Cemetery and also known as	Number of burials	Acres	Condition	Date started or earliest known burial	Township	Range	Section

GALES CREEK
AKA: 1. GALES CREEK
       UNION
     2. PIONEER

C   1.3   1   1874   T1N R4W   S18
From Forest Grove, take Gales Creek Road (OR. Hwy. 8) to the village of Gales Creek. Turn left (west) onto Old Wilson River Road, go 0.2 of a mile and then turn left (south) onto Soda Springs Road. Drive about 0.7 of a mile further to the cemetery, which is at a road junction. {27 Sept. 1994} (Gales Creek 1979-92 USGS Quad. map.)

HALL FARM

A   0.01   ?   30 Jan 1916 T1S R4W   ?
This was said to be located somewhere out of Gaston. This is possibly referring to the C. C. Hall property that was located in the South 1/2 of Section 18 as shown on the *Metsker Land Ownership Atlas*, dated 1928. South of West Shore Road formerly Sain Creek Road and west of Shore creek road formerly Hankins Road. NOTE: The Gaston 1956-70 USGS quad. map still shows the original road names and does not show Henry Hagg Lake and Scoggins Dam. A death certificate #20 for the infant William Satterlee, 30 January 1916, the child of Arthur and Ruth Hall Satterlee, states the burial was on the Hall Farm "8 miles up Scoggins Valley." (Not shown on Gaston 1956-70 USGS Quad. map.)

HANEY FAMILY

A   0.01   3   Circa 1900 T1S R4W   S35
Located on the north side of Patton Valley Road and just west of Bates Road, on private property. A daughter of the Haneys is buried here, on the Donald McLeod D.L.C. #49, OC #2300. (Not shown on Gaston 1956-70 USGS Quad. map.)

HARRISON
AKA: 1. TOMPKINS
     2. TOOLEY
     3. VADIS

B   1.74   2   1856-1964   T1N R3W   S3
Located just west of North Plains and 0.5 of a mile south of Sunset Highway (US. Hwy. 26) on Dersham Road. It is 0.3 of a mile west of Vadis Road, on the north side of the Southern Pacific Railway track: on the John Harrison D.L.C. #38, OC #2138. { 28 March 1994} (Forest Grove 1956-92 USGS Quad. map.)

Name of Cemetery and also known as	Number of burials	Acres	Condition	Date started or earliest known burial	Township	Range	Section

HAYWARD

B 1.0 2 1894 T2N R4W S19

Located in Sections 19 and Section 20. At 0.1 of a mile west of Milepost 46 on Wilson River Highway (OR. Hwy. 6), turn right (north) onto Cedar Canyon Road. Proceed 3.3 miles to the junction of Cedar Canyon Road with Hayward Road (ahead) and Parsons Road (left). The cemetery is on the left. {April 1995} (Buxton 1979-92 USGS Quad. map.)

HEARD, SHIRLEY JEAN

A 0.01 ? 3 Dec 1936 ? ? ?

Oregon Death Certificate #323 reports the death of John W. and Marion Richards Heard's infant daughter. She is buried in the home cemetery at Orenco. (Not shown on Hillsboro 1961-85 USGS Quad. map.)

HELVETIA

C 2.18 1 1894 T1N R2W S3

Located about 3.8 miles east of North Plains on the south side of Helvetia Road. Go east out of North Plains on West Union Road, then turn left (north) onto Jackson Quarry Road and then right (east) onto Helvetia Road to the Helvetia Church and its cemetery. {24 August 1993} (Hillsboro 1961-85 USGS Quad. map.)

HESS, BABY BOY
  AKA 1. CALLAHAN FARM

A 0.01 ? 10 Feb 1917 T1S R4W S33

Located on the H. Callahan Farm near Gaston (1990). The 1928 *Metsker Land Ownership Atlas* shows Hess family ownership at the junction of Patton Valley and Hering Roads; on the Christopher Bridgefarmer D.L.C. #50, OC #1587. Washington County Death Certificate #21 for Baby Hess age 9 1/2 hours, gives his father as Wm. F. Hess, and mother as Anna Eliza Callahan Hess. NOTE: This site is on private property. (Not shown on Gaston 1956-70 USGS Quad. map.)

HILL
  AKA: 1. EAST GASTON
       2. HILL, ALMORAN
       3. THE HILL
       4. WAPATO

D 3.48 2 1850 T2S R3W S6

This cemetery is named for a family, not for a topographic feature. Located 2.2 miles southeast of Gaston via Gaston Road East and Spring Hill Road. The cemetery is on the east side of Spring Hill Road and visible on

Name of Cemetery and also known as	Number of burials	Acres	Condition	Date started or earliest known burial	Township	Range	Section

a hill southeast from the junction of LaSalle Road with Spring Hill Road. The cemetery driveway is 0.2 of a mile south of that junction: on the Almoran Hill D.L.C. #42, OC #3443. {13 October 1996} (Laurelwood 1956-92 USGS Quad. map.)

HILLSBORO PIONEER
AKA: 1. HILLSBORO MASONIC
2. I.O.O.F.
3. MASONIC
4. WILKES NORTH ADDTION

D 7.79 1 1856   T1N R3W   S36
Located on the north side of Tualatin Valley Highway (OR. Hwy. 8) at the west edge of Hillsboro. This was originally 3 separate adjoining cemeteries: on the Wheelock Simmons D.L.C. #70, OC #873. (Forest Grove 1956-92 USGS Quad. map.)

HILLSIDE

C 1 1 1887   T1N R4W   S9
Located at the junction of Hillside and Clapshaw Roads, 1.4 miles east of Gales Creek Road (OR. Hwy 8). {25 July 1994} (Gales Creek 1979-92 USGS Quad. map.)

HOOVER FAMILY

A ? ? ?   T1N R3W   S14
This was located on the north side of Zion Church Road about 0.5 miles west of the intersection with Glencoe Road. It was on the east side of Gordon Road and somewhere north of the junction with Zion Church Road. This was on the Jacob and Malinda Hoover D.L.C. #46, OC #32. The burials were moved to the Old Scotch Church and will be found just north of the church building with a tall obelisk, with five smaller stones around the tall obelisk marking the family plot. (Not on Forest Grove 1956-92 USGS Quad. map)

HORNING, RICHARD

A 0.01 1 27 Apr 1985 T2N R3W   S11
This burial is on private property behind the house at 21277 Northwest Brunswick Canyon Road. Drive to Arcade Cemetery on Pumpkin Ridge Road, then continue ahead to the north on Pumpkin Ridge Road for another 1.25 miles to the junction with Northwest Brunswick Canyon Road, which angles off to the right and ahead. Follow Northwest Brunswick Canyon Road to the ridge top and then down the winding road into Brunswick Canyon almost to

Name of Cemetery and also known as	Number of burials	Acres	Condition	Date started or earliest known burial	Township	Range	Section

the bridge. The house is on the left. Richard "Dick" Horning, born 9 June 1929, died 27 April 1985, was a paratrooper who served in the Korean War. (Not shown on Meacham Corner 1979-92 USGS Quad. map.)

HUGHES, ELMER S.

	A	0.01	?	8 Jan 1916	T3N	R5W	?

Perhaps located in Section 35 or 36. A death certificate #21 on file in the State Archives notes the death of Elmer S. Hughes, born 8 April 1876 and died of exposure and exhaustion about 8 January 1916. He was buried on his farm, on 20 Febuary 1916. About 1.5 miles west of Strassel and east of Timber. He was single, the son of John and Sarah Wimple Hughes and was born in Indiana. This area does not appear to be promising farming country. The grave is perhaps located along Strassel Road or Ridge Road. (Not shown on Timber 1979 USGS Quad. map.)

HUNDLEY BURIAL

	A	0.01	?	?	T1N	R5W	S1

There is a grave on the west side of Thornburgh Road, 0.25 mile south of the junction with Gales Creek Road (OR. Hwy. 8). (Not shown on Gales Creek 1979-92 USGS Quad. map.)

INDIAN

	A	?	?	?	T1N	R4W	S34

Located on a ridge about 100 feet above the western side of Gales Creek Valley, jutting out from Gales Peak. It is near Allens Brook and Gales Creek, off of Stringtown Road: on the David Allen D.L.C. #47, OC #2472. (Not shown on Gales Creek 1979-92 USGS Quad. map.)

IOWA HILL

	?	?	5	?	T1S	R3W	S32

Located in the Northeast 1/4 of the Southeast 1/4 of Section 32 and off of the north side of Dixon Mill Road. NOTE: This site was recorded in the 1954 Oregon Department of Transportation field logs and is still shown on the current Oregon Department of Transportation maps. It is on the Cleves S. Silver D.L.C., OC #4080. (Not shown on Laurelwood 1956-92 USGS Quad. map.)

Name of Cemetery and also known as	Number of burials	Acres	Condition	Date started or earliest known burial	Township	Range	Section

JACKSON FAMILY

B   1   2 Circa 1850 T2N R3W   S36

This burial ground is located just north of North Plains east off of Old Pumpkin Ridge Road and north of Mountaindale Road. On private property on the north shore of Lind Reservoir; access only with permission. It is on the Ulysses Jackson D.L.C. #47, OC #3326. (Forest Grove 1956-92 USGS Quad. map.)

JOHNSON FAMILY

? ? ? ?   ? ?   ?

Supposedly in the Beaverton area and believed to have been moved. No other information was given in the report. We suspect that this is possibly a duplicate of the other Johnson Family entry. (Not shown on Beaverton 1961-84 USGS Quad map.)

JOHNSON FAMILY
  AKA: 1. SEVENTH DAY
        ADVENTIST

? ? 6 8 Jan 1895 T1S R1W   S17

Located west of Beaverton in the Northwest 1/4 of the Southwest 1/4 of Section 17. Go west on Farmington Road (OR. Hwy. 10), turn left (south) onto Southwest 149th Avenue and go to Division Street. Turn right (west) onto Division Street and continue to the 150th block, on the right (north) side of the street. It is believed to have been moved; on the John Innes D.L.C. #56, OC #3857. (Not shown on the Beaverton 1961-84 USGS Quad. map.)

JOLLY FAMILY

? ? 6 ?   T1N R3W   S24

This site was north of Hillsboro on Glencoe Road, just after crossing McKay Creek and on the farm of Don Foeler. In 1912, the graves were moved to three different cemeteries: Hillsboro Pioneer, Tualatin Plains Presbyterian and West Union Baptist. This cemetery was on the William Jolly D.L.C. #74, OC #3829. (Not shown on Hillsboro 1961-85 or Forest Grove 1956-92 USGS Quad. map.)

LEWIS
  AKA: 1. FARMINGTON

C 1.77 2 1847   T1S R2W   S30

Located south of Hillsboro on Burkhalter Road, east one mile from OR. Hwy. 219 and on a low hill on the north side of the road. 72

Name of Cemetery and also known as	Number of burials	Acres	Condition	Date started or earliest known burial	Township	Range	Section

markers were vandalized on the night of 4/5 April 1993. It is on the Charles Lewis D.L.C. #51, OC #3996. {28 November 1990} (Scholls 1961-85 USGS Quad. map.)

MAPLE LANE
AKA: 1. BLUETOWN
     2. KRAUSE
     3. LUTHERAN
     4. SHERWOOD
        LUTHERAN

? 1   2 1892   T2S R1W   S30

This cemetery is another one now nearly engulfed by urban development: in this instance the town of Sherwood. The road network in the vicinity has been extensively rebuilt. OR. Hwy. 99W at Sherwood now has two signalized intersections. At the northerly intersection is the road to Scholls to the west. Take that road for about 0.4 of a mile to the cemetery on the left (south). Maple Lane is a Lutheran cemetery resulting from a breakaway with the St. Paul Lutheran congregation. That cemetery and church would be visible to the west except for the new housing development. {6 April 1997} (Sherwood 1961-85 USGS Quad. map.)

McCANN FAMILY

A   0.01 5 ?   T1S R4W   S32

Located about 200 feet north of Patton Valley Road, under an apple tree in a fir forest. North of John & Emily Mulholland's prune orchard (Aug. 1975) are the 2 unmarked graves for Daniel McCann and his wife. The dates of the burials are unknown. NOTE: These are on private property. (Not shown on Gaston 1956-70 USGS Quad. map.)

MERIDIAN

C   1.5 2 1895   T3S R1W   S1

Leave I-5 Freeway at Exit #286 in the northern part of Wilsonville. Turn east on Elligsen Road for about 1 mile to the junction with Southwest 65th Avenue. Turn left (north) onto 65th Avenue and drive an additional 0.4 of a mile and the cemetery is on the left (west) on a hillside. The name Meridian refers to the Willamette Meridian, one of the two meridians used for surveying all properties in Oregon. The present 65th Avenue, once named Meridian Road, follows that survey line. The first Meridian Cemetery was located about 1.5 miles south of the present cemetery and was located adjacent

Washington County

to the Meridian United Church of Christ. Burials dating back to 1882 were moved to the present site. See the article entitled Meridian [Old] in Clackamas County. {7 December 1989} (Canby 1961-85 USGS Quad. map.)

METHODIST CHURCH AT FARMINGTON
AKA: 1. TWIN OAKS

A ? 11 ? T1S R2W ?
Located in Section 28 or 29. There are no visible remains of the church or cemetery. One report puts it just west of the Harris Bridge over the Tualatin River at Twin Oaks, near the intersection of Farmington Road (OR. Hwy. 10) and River Road. Another report puts it in the northeast corner piece of property at the intersection of Farmington (OR. Hwy. 10) and River Road. We have not been able to prove either location. It would have been on the John M. Ritchey D.L.C. #50, OC #631, in Section 29, as the first possible site: or the Phillip Harris D.L.C. #53, OC #4073, in Section 28, as the second possible site. (Not shown on the Scholls 1961-85 USGS Quad. map.)

METHODIST MEETING HOUSE

? ? 5 Pre 1842 T1N R2W S21
On the Northwest 1/4 of the Southeast 1/4 of Section 21. Located on Northwest 253rd off of Evergreen Road about 2 miles north of Hillsboro. This cemetery has not been just vandalized; it has been desecrated. It is on the Edward and Priscilla Constable D.L.C. #71, OC #623. (Not shown on Hillsboro 1961-85 USGS Quad. map.)

MIDDLETON PIONEER

C 4 1 1871 T2S R2W S36
This is actually in both Township 2 South, Range 2 West, Section 36 and Township 3 South, Range 2 West, and Section 1. Go Southwest of Sherwood on OR. Hwy. 99W to the old Hwy. 99W junction; turn left (south) onto Old Hwy. 99W. Go 0.5 of a mile to the cemetery on the right (west) side of the Old Hwy. 99W. {10 May 1996} (Sherwood 1961-85 USGS Quad. map.)

Name of Cemetery and also known as	Number of burials	Acres	Condition	Date started or earliest known burial	Township	Range	Section

MT. OLIVE CEMETERY OF LAUREL
    1. LAUREL
    2. LAURELWOOD
    3. MT. OLIVE BAPTIST

C 4.5 1 1878   T2S R3W   S12
Located 0.7 of a mile south of the Laurel store on the west side of Laurel Road. {26 November 1990} (Misnamed Pleasant Hill Cemetery on Scholls Quad. 1961-85 USG map.)

MT. OLIVE LUTHERAN
  AKA: 1. DETHLEFS
      2. GERMAN LUTHERAN CHURCH
      3. SEGHERS

A 1 2 1902   T1S R4W   S23
Located south of Forest Grove and north of Gaston on Old Highway 47, 0.8 of a mile south of the junction with Spring Hill Road, on a driveway to the left (east) side of road. On the Joshua Dickson D.L.C. #45, OC #4601. {3 June 1996} (1928 Metsker Land Ownership Atlas. Not shown on Gaston 1956-70 USGS Quad. map.)

MOUNTAIN VIEW
  AKA: 1. DIXIE MOUNTAIN

B 2 2 Circa 1880 T3N R2W   S32
Although this cemetery is in Washington County, it is most conveniently reached by taking Skyline Boulevard (from Cornelius Pass Road) for its entire length to the northwest. Where Skyline Boulevard ends at Rocky Point Road, turn left (west) and follow Rocky Point Road into Washington County. At the fork with Dixie Road (right) and Dixie Mountain Road (left and ahead) follow Dixie Mountain Road. Go past the powerlines about 0.3 of a mile, to a pronounced curve; the cemetery is on the left (south) side of the road. The land was originally part of the Arthur W. Wallace Homestead and was developed after 1880. (Dixie Mountain 1961-85 USGS Quad. map.)

MOUNTAIN VIEW MEMORIAL GARDENS
  AKA: 1. CONGREGATIONAL
      2. OLD FOREST GROVE
      3. PIONEER UNION
      4. UNION

D 9.75 1 1858   T1N R4W   S35
Located in Section 26 and Section 35, on Watercrest Road in the northwest part of Forest Grove. It is on the Benjamin Catching D.L.C. #41, OC #3127. {25 July 1994} (Gales Creek 1979-92 USGS Quad. map.)

MOUNTAINSIDE
  AKA: 1. MOUNTAIN TOP
      2. SCHOLLS

C 5.9 1 1886   T2S R2W   S16
Located near Scholls, 0.5 of a mile southwest of the junction of OR. Hwy. 219 and OR. Hwy.

Name of Cemetery and also known as	Number of burials	Acres	Condition	Date started or earliest known burial	Township	Range	Section

**3. SCHOLLS
PIONEER**

210, and just south of Vanderschuere Road. {20 June 1990} (Scholls 1961-85 USGS Quad. map.)

**NEVEH ZEDEK-ROSE
CITY LODGE**
AKA: 1. ROSE CITY
LODGE
2. TORAH TALMUD

D 1   1   Circa 1900   T1S   R1W   S12
Located at 7925 Southwest Canyon Lane in West Slope. The driveway uphill to the cemetery is on the north side of Southwest Canyon Lane next to the cemetery sign and mailbox. This is West of West Slope Drive, Walnut Lane and almost directly north of West Point, and a short distance east from Valley View Court. There is a small mausoleum and a chapel located here also. Nearly all of the monuments have English and Jewish inscriptions on the east and west sides. Located on Anthony W. Hart D.L.C. #60, OC #3564. {18 July 1998} (Shown in the wrong location on the Linnton 1961-84 USGS Quad. map.)

OAK KNOLL
AKA: 1. PARSONS FAMILY
2. RITCHEY FARM

A ?   1   16 Mar 1863   T1S   R4W   S2
Leave Or. Hwy. 47 onto Stringtown Road to the right (west) about 0.5 of a mile south of Forest Grove city limits. Drive about 1 mile on Stringtown Road to Oregon Garden Products wholesale nursery stock growers and dealers. The cemetery is on the knoll on the right (north) on the nursery property, before you reach Ritchey Road. It is on the Horace and Marilda Parsons D.L.C. #40, OC #3376. (Not shown on Gales Creek 1979-92 USGS Quad. map.)

PACIFIC UNIVERSITY
AKA: 1. PACIFIC
UNIVERSITY
MEMORIAL

A ?   10 Circa 1850   T1N   R3W   S31
There was an old burial ground on what is now the western edge of the campus of Pacific University in Forest Grove. Harvey Clark, the University founder was buried here along with a number of persons. Most of these were reburied in the 1870's in Mountain View Memorial Gardens, but a least four remain. These include John Kimzey, an early settler who died in 1849. Located on Elkanah Walker D.L.C. #60, OC #2997. See the *Hillsboro Argus* for 16 June 1994. (The University is shown but not the burials on Forest Grove 1956-92 USGS Quad. map.)

Name of Cemetery and also known as	Number of burials	Acres	Condition	Date started or earliest known burial	Township	Range	Section

PATTON FAMILY
AKA: 1. PATON
2. PORTLAND GOLF COURSE
3. RALEIGH-PATTON FAMILY
4. WELCHES

C 2 1 Circa 1859 T1S R1W S14
Located near Garden Home at 5900 Southwest Scholls Ferry Road. It is on the west side of Scholls Ferry Road across from the Portland Golf Club. {18 July 1998} (Beaverton 1961-84 USGS Quad. map.)

PATTON FAMILY

A 0.01 6 Circa 1894 T1S R4W S36
This was a farm burial at Cherry Grove that has since been removed to Cherry Grove Baptist Cemetery. It was on the Thomas M. Hines D.L.C. #37, OC #3227. (Not shown on Gaston 1956-70 USGS Quad. map.)

PETERSON FAMILY

A 0.01 ? ? T3N R4W S1
Located at the community of Bacona, near the Columbia County line. The July 1928 *Metsker Land Ownership Atlas* shows Fred Peterson owned the Southeast 1/4 of Section 1. Alec and Alice, the children of Fred Peterson, are buried here. (Not shown on Bacona 1979 USGS Quad. map.)

PHILLIPS
AKA: 1. PHILLIPS GERMAN REFORM CHURCH

C 0.87 3 1896 T1N R2W S12
Located 2 miles north of West Union on the west side of Old Cornelius Pass Road, 0.3 of a mile north of the junction with Cornelius Pass Road. The first burial was in 1898. It is maintained by the Helvetia Cemetery Association. {8 October 1990} (Linnton 1961-84 USGS Quad. map.)

PIONEER CATHOLIC OF ST. ANTHONY OF PADUA
AKA: 1. CEDAR MILLS CATHOLIC
2. PIONEER CATHOLIC
3. ST. ANTHONY OF PADUA
4. ST. CECILIA
6. ST. PIUS CATHOLIC
5. ST. PIUS X [10th]

B 4 1 1879 T1S R1W S4
Located on the east side of Southwest Murray Road (Southwest 145th Avenue) between Butner and Rita Roads, in Beaverton. {18 July 1998} (Linnton 1961-84 USGS Quad. map)

Name of Cemetery and also known as	Number of burials	Acres	Condition	Date started or earliest known burial	Township	Range	Section

POINTER FAMILY

B   ?   9   ?   T1S R1W   S1

This family cemetery is now underneath Sunset Highway (U.S. Hwy. 26). The highway was started as a W.P.A. project during the New Deal in the 1930's. After the family lost a lawsuit, 28 bodies were removed in October and November 1936 and reburied in what is now Finley's Sunset Hill Memorial Park. It was on the William Pointer D.L.C. #62, OC #3444. (Not shown on Linnton 1961-84 USGS Quad. map.)

POOR FARM

?   ?   ?   ?   T1S R2W   S8

Located in Hillsboro, south of Tualatin Valley Highway (OR. Hwy. 8) west of where the County Extension Office was located. The building now used for County offices was once the County Hospital on the County Poor Farm. Most or all of the burials were moved about 1923, to Hillsboro Pioneer; on the Henry Noland, Jr. D.L.C. #68, OC #3665. (Not shown on Hillsboro 1961-85 USGS Quad. map.)

PURDIN FAMILY
  AKA: 1. HOLZMEYER

B   0.13 3 1862   T1N R4W   S25

Located north of Forest Grove. Drive north from Gales Creek Road (OR. Hwy. 8), on Thatcher Road for 1.5 miles. The cemetery is on the right (east) and 0.1 of a mile short of the Purdin Road junction. It is on private property; on the Wesley Mulkey D.L.C. #53, OC #4317. {25 July 1994} (Gales Creek 1979-92 USGS Quad. map.)

RAFFETY
  AKA: 1. MOUNTAINDALE
       2. RAFFETY, S. B.
       3. RAFFERTY [*Sic*]

B   3.99 2 1893   T2N R3W   S27

Located 0.5 of a mile north of junction of Dairy Creek Road and Mountaindale Road. The driveway is to the left (west) off of Dairy Creek Road, uphill into the woods to the cemetery. It is on the Samuel B. Raffety D.L.C. #41, OC #1277. {8 October 1990} (Meacham Corner 1979-92 USGS Quad. map.)

ROBISON FAMILY, JAMES
  AKA: 1. ROBERTSON,
         JAMES B.
       2. ROBINSON,

A   ?   12 1850   T1N R3W   S26

Located in the Northwest 1/4 of the Northwest 1/4 of Section 26. This is about 3 miles northwest of Hillsboro and on the inside turn

Name of Cemetery and also known as	Number of burials	Acres	Condition	Date started or earliest known burial	Township	Range	Section

JAMES B. of Hornecker Road, 0.6 of a mile east of Susbauer Road. The compiler does not know which is the correct spelling of the family name. It is on the James B. Robison D.L.C. #50, OC #3264. (Not on Forest Grove 1956-92 USGS Quad. map.)

ROOD FAMILY   ? ? ? ?   T1S R2W   S6
This is said to be located near Reedville but no further information was given in the report. Since then, research has shown that Fred Rood owned land in Section 6, as depicted in the July 1928 *Washington County Metsker Land Ownership Atlas*. Comparing that location with the Hillsboro 1985 USGS Quad. map indicates that Rood's 1928 holdings are now part of Shute Park, with buildings, and also part of Tualatin Valley Highway (OR. Hwy. 8). Were the graves removed to elsewhere? It is on the Michael Moore D.L.C. #41, OC #558. (Not shown on Hillsboro 1961-85 USGS Quad. map.)

RUM AND GUM CHARLEY   A 0.01 5 16 Aug 1884 T2S ?   ?
The burial is possibly in Range 1 West or Range 2 West. This is a single burial on the Charles Delaney farm located near Middleton. Rum and Gum Charlie was buried where his body was found. (Not shown on Sherwood 1961-85 USGS Quad. map.)

ST. ANTHONY CATHOLIC
AKA: 1. ST. ANTHONY'S
    2. TIGARD
       CATHOLIC
    C 3.58 1 1890   T2S R1W   S3
Located at the corner of 115th and Southwest Gaarde Street, Tigard. {3 June 1994} (Beaverton 1961-84 USGS Quad. map.)

ST. BEDE'S MEMORIAL GARDENS   A ? 1 ?   T1S R3W   S5
Located at 1609 Elm Street, Forest Grove. This is about three blocks south of OR. Hwy. 8 east bound, turn right (south) on Elm Street. This is a small area set aside behind the St. Bede's Episcopal Church for cremains. (The church is shown on the Forest Grove 1956-92 USGS Quad. map.)

Name of Cemetery and also known as	Number of burials	Acres	Condition	Date started or earliest known burial	Township	Range	Section

ST. EDWARD'S CATHOLIC [NEW]
AKA: 1. CATHOLIC
2. NORTH PLAINS
3. NORTH PLAINS CATHOLIC
4. ST. EDWARD
5. ST. EDWARD'S

B 3.25 1 1926   T2N R2W   S31
Located north of North Plains. Drive from the junction of Commercial Avenue on Shadybrook Road for 0.6 of a mile. The cemetery is on the left (west) on the hill and is reached by either of two driveways through a farmer's field. It is on the John Johnson D.L.C. #70, OC #3324. {24 August 1993} (Not shown on Hillsboro 1961-85 USGS Quad. map.)

ST. EDWARD'S CATHOLIC [OLD]
AKA: 1. CATHOLIC
2. NORTH PLAINS
3. NORTH PLAINS CATHOLIC
4. ST. EDWARD
5. ST. EDWARD'S

? 1 6 1919   T1N R3W   S1
It is not clear to the compiler exactly where the old Saint Edward's Cemetery was located. Victor Cropp donated an acre in 1919, a short distance north of Saint Edward's Catholic Church. This appears to have been north of North Avenue, now the northern city limits of North Plains, perhaps between the intersections of Main and 4th Streets. The burials were removed to the new Saint Edward's Cemetery on the Joseph Bernard farm in 1926. It was on the Ulysses Jackson D.L.C. #81, OC #3326. (Not shown on Hillsboro 1961-85 USGS Quad. map.)

ST. FRANCIS CATHOLIC
AKA: 1. ROY CATHOLIC
2. ST. FERDINAND
3. ST. FRANCIS OF ASSISI

D 3 1 March 1920 T1N R3W   S5
Located northwest of Roy and 3 miles southeast of Banks. From Sunset Highway (U.S. Hwy. 26), drive 3.5 miles west from the North Plains interchange and then leave U.S. Hwy. 26 at Mountaindale Road. Go left (westerly) 1.4 miles to the cemetery on the left (south) side of Mountaindale Road. It is on the Robert Walker D.L.C. #80, OC #4561. {15 October 1995} (Forest Grove 1956-92 USGS Quad. map.)

ST. MARY'S BOYS HOME

? ? ? ?   T1S R1W   ?
Persistent rumors and two publications refer to burials at or near the current boys home. *These Valiant Women* (1986) By Wilfred P. Schoenberg S.J. on page 196 reports "Twelve year old James Keegan died and was buried beneath the pine trees in the boys' lonely cemetery." In researching this burial and several others reportedly buried here we

Name of Cemetery and also known as	Number of burials	Acres	Condition	Date started or earliest known burial	Township	Range	Section

learned James Keegan was buried at Mt. Calvary Cemetery per Washington County Death Certificate #168, 16 November 1918, aged 10 years, 10 months and 24 days. Further research shows that he is buried in Section M, Lot 31, Block 1, Grave 2. The above quote is also found in *A Test of Time*, (1989), by Wilfred P. Schoenberg, S.J. on page 58. Further research of Washington County Death Certificates gives us the following information. Chester Kashenorof, Certificate #87, 12 April 1920, aged 8 years, 6 months and 9 days, reports that he is buried at "St. Marys' Home". He is not at Mt. Calvary, it is possible that he was buried in the St. Mary's of the Valley [old] Cemetery. The remaining three Certificates found pertaining to the Boys Home are for Richard Hoskinson, Certificate #54, 28 February 1924, aged 15 Years, 2 months, 16 days, lists as place of burial "St. Marys Cem.". Harry Hughes, Certificate #137, 17 June 1927, aged about 73 years, employee of St. Marys Home, place of burial "St. Marys Cem.". Donald Alton, Certificate #182, 30 July 1939, Aged 15 years, 0 months, 27 days, burial at "Mt. Calvary Cem." He is in Section F3, Block 7, Grave 25. Newspaper reports on 4 August 1939 of *The Beaverton Review*, page 1 and *Beaverton Enterprize*, page 1 of Volume 12-#47 state he was killed on the Highway/Tualatin Valley Road. The conclusion that has been reached is that the St. Marys Cemetery is referring to the St. Mary's of the Valley Cemetery [old]. See that article.

Name of Cemetery and also known as	Number of burials	Acres	Condition	Date started or earliest known burial	Township	Range	Section
ST. MARY'S OF THE VALLEY [NEW]	C	2.2	3	Oct 1970	T1S	R1W	S17

Located on the grounds of St. Mary of the Valley convent and school, in Beaverton. It is situated on Southwest 149th Avenue a short distance north, off of Farmington Road (OR. Hwy. 10). This cemetery contains the graves moved from the St. Mary's of the Valley Cemetery [old] and new burials from the convent. See: *These Valiant Women*, by Wilfred P. Schoenberg S. J., pages 295-296. (Beaverton 1961-84 USGS Quad. map shows only the old cemetery, not the present one.)

Name of Cemetery and also known as	Number of burials	Acres	Condition	Date started or earliest known burial	Township	Range	Section

ST. MARY'S OF THE VALLEY [OLD]

B 2.2 6 1891-1972 T1S R1W S7

This was located on the north side of Tualatin Valley Highway (OR. Hwy. 8) at approximately 145th (Murray Road). Most of the burials were nuns, many moved in from Sublimity in 1891, and were removed to the new cemetery by October 1972. The old cemetery site is now occupied by K-Mart. See: *These Valiant Women*, by Wilfred P. Schoenberg S. J., pages 295-296. (Beaverton 1961-84 USGS Quad. map shows only the old cemetery, not the present one.)

ST. MATTHEW'S CATHOLIC

C 1.29 1 1905 T1S R2W S8

Located near Hillsboro High School on Southwest Rood Bridge Road at the junction of Creek Court. It is on the south side of Southwest Rood Bridge Road. {March 1998} (Scholls 1961-85 USGS Quad. map.)

ST. PAUL LUTHERAN CHURCH
AKA: 1. BLUE TOWN
2. BLUETOWN
3. GERMAN CHURCH
4. ST. PAUL'S LUTHERAN

? 0.5 1 1878 T2S R1W S30

This church and cemetery are now inside the city limits of Sherwood. The road network in the vicinity has been extensively rebuilt. OR. Hwy. 99W at Sherwood now has two signalized intersections. At the northerly intersection is the road to Scholls to the west. Take that road to the church and cemetery about 0.6 of a mile from the highway. On the way you will pass the Maple Lane Cemetery. Please see that article. {6 April 1997} (Sherwood 1961-85 USGS Quad. map.)

SCOTT FAMILY

? ? ? ? ? ? ?

Reportedly somewhere near Forest Grove, but no other information was given in the report.

SEIFFERT INFANT

A 0.01 ? 10 Feb 1924 ? ? ?

Oregon Death Certificate #43 reports the death of the infant daughter of Beathold H. and Hilda Fredeen Seiffert. With the burial as "yard of house". (Not show on the Beaverton 1984 USGS Quad. map.)

Name of Cemetery and also known as	Number of burials	Acres	Condition	Date started or earliest known burial	Township	Range	Section

SHADY BROOK
AKA: 1. HICKENBOTTOM
       FAMILY
    2. SHADYBROOK

B   2   2   Circa 1889 T2N R2W   S30
Located about 4 miles north of North Plains, via Shadybrook Road and Dixie Mountain Road. It is on the right (north) side of Dixie Mountain Road 0.3 of a mile from its junction with Shadybrook and Dorland Roads. {30 March 1991} (Not shown on Dixie Mountain 1961-85 USGS Quad. map.)

SMITH, SAM

A   0.01 ?   9 Sept 1946 T2S R2W   S30
Mr. Smith had been missing since 23 August 1946. His body was found in the woods 9 September 1946. He was buried at the spot where he was found. Oregon Death Certificate #6598 states he was single, about 65 years of age and that he was a wood cutter for Kruger Wood Company and died about 23 August 1946. (Not shown on Newberg 1961-85 USGS Quad. map.)

STAEGER, GOTTLIEB

A   ?   5   1 Aug. 1898 T2N R3W   S34
Located somewhere near Mountaindale. No other information was given in the report. (Not shown on Forest Grove 1956-92 USGS Quad. map.)

STEWART FAMILY

A   0.25 2   Circa 1845 T1S R2W   S9
Located on the Southeast 1/4 of the Northeast 1/4 of Section 9 in the Witch Hazel area of Hillsboro. Turn south off of Southeast Witch Hazel Road onto Southeast 49th Avenue and go a short distance into Stewarts Place Subdivision. Turn right (west) into Stewart Court, a culdesac. The wrought-iron fence around the burials is visible from the street. There are 8 known burial; on the Thomas Stewart D.L.C. #43, OC #3823. {29 June 1997} (Not shown on Scholls 1961-85 USGS Quad. map.)

THE OLD SCOTCH CHURCH
AKA: 1. SCOTCH CHURCH
    2. SCOTCH PLAINS
       PRESBYTERIAN

D   1.2 1   1876   T1N R3W   S13
Go north of Hillsboro on Glencoe Road to Starkey Corner. Turn right (east) at that corner onto Scotch Church Road and go

Name of Cemetery and also known as	Number of burials	Acres	Condition	Date started or earliest known burial	Township	Range	Section

3. TUALATIN
   PLAINS
4. TUALATIN
   PLAINS
   PRESBYTERIAN
5. TUALATIN
   PLAINS
   PRESBYTERIAN
   SCOTCH CHURCH

0.5 of a mile to the church and cemetery on the left (north). It is on the Jacob and Malinda Hoover D.L.C. #46, OC #32. {9 March 1996} (Hillsboro 1961-85 USGS Quad. map.)

TIGARD EVANGELICAL   B   0.69   4   1887   T2S   R1W   S10
AKA: 1. EMANUEL
2. EMANUEL
   EVANGELICAL
   UNITED
   BRETHERN
3. EVANGLE
4. LITTLE BULL
   MOUNTAIN
5. THE PIONEER
   SUNSET
6. TIGARD
   EVANGELICAL
   UNITED
   BRETHREN
7. TIGARDVILLE
8. UNITED
   METHODIST

Located southwest of Tigard town center, but now well within the city limits, on tax lot 4,000. It is on the southeast side of OR. Hwy. 99W (Southwest Pacific Higway) and opposite the junction of Bull Mountain Road with OR. Hwy. 99W (Southwest Pacific Highway). You must approach from the south, in the righthand northbound lane. At 14600 Southwest Pacific Highway (OR. Hwy. 99W), go up a steep driveway on the right of OR. Hwy. 99W (Southwest Pacific Highway); take a left where the main driveway makes a sharp turn right. Turn into a little dirt driveway with parking for 1 or 2 small cars. It is on the Wilson M. Tigard D.L.C., OC #3859. {16 March 2000 the drive way is closed and has been for over a year.} (Not shown on Beaverton 1961-84 USGS Quad. map.)

TOLKE FAMILY   A   0.01   ?   ?   T3N   R4W   S34

Located in Tolke Canyon on Whitcher Creek, in a loop on the east side of the creek. Three or four stones were found by a tree planting crew in 1981. The only access is by foot. No other information was given in the report. (Not shown on Buxton 1979-92 USGS Quad. map.)

UNION   D   4.63   2   1878   T1N   R1W   S29
AKA: 1. CEDAR MILLS
2. OLD COMMUNITY
3. OLD UNION
4. UNION
   CEMETERY OF
   CEDAR MILL
5. UNION
   SCHOOL HOUSE

Located north of Beaverton and north of Sunset Highway (U.S. Hwy. 26). Leave Sunset Highway at the Northwest Cornell Road interchange. Drive east on Cornell Road for about 0.7 of a mile; turn left (north) onto Northwest 143rd Avenue and drive about 0.25 of a mile on 143rd Avenue. The cemetery is on the left (west), just short of Northwest

Hunters Drive; on the Francis McGuire
D.L.C. #57, OC #1535. {8 October 1990}
(Linnton 1961-84 USGS Quad. map.)

UNION POINT
AKA: 1. BANKS
     2. BANKS UNION
       POINT
     3. GREENVILLE
     4. UNION HILL
     5. WILKES
       GREENVILLE

D   2.5   3   Circa 1860 T2N R3W   S31
Located on the south (right) side of Banks
Road, 0.5 of a mile east of Banks. {10 May
1992} (Forest Grove 1956-92 USGS Quad. map.)

UNKNOWN

A ?   5   ?   T1S R2W   S13
Located at 19425 Southwest Kinnaman Road,
Aloha. The burial is reported to be under
the large oak tree on the southwest corner,
right next to the road. The home owner does
not know when the burial took place or who
was buried there, it is on private property.
Located on the James H. McMillan D.L.C. #58,
OC #686. (Not shown on Scholls 1961-85 USGS
Quad. maps.)

UNKNOWN

A ?   ?   ?   T1S R2W   S14
Located just south of Reedville, on the Ladd-
Reed Farm. This is on private property and
is farmed over, no one seems to know much
about it today, one report states that the
stones and all were covered over with 2 to 3
feet of soil so that it could be farmed over
without disturbing the 10 or 12 graves. The
1928 *Metsker's Land Ownership Atlas* shows
Kinnaman Road going straight west, from
Tobias Road now Southwest 198th Avenue, to
Churchley Road now Southwest 229th Ave. This
small cemetery was supposed to be on the
north side of Kinnaman Road. Both sides of
Kinnaman road in 1928 are shown to be
subdivided and platted through the south end
of the Ladd-Reed Farm. On the 1937 *Metsker's
Land Ownership Atlas* the land is shown as
being owned by Patrick J. Kelly, plat lines
have been erased, with the road still shown
but again no clue as to where the cemetery
was. On the 1964 *Metsker's Land Ownership
Atlas* the north half is shown as belonging to

the Sisters of Saint Mary's of Oregon, Inc., with the south half belonging to the Sisters of Saint Mary's, with no trace of a road being shown. It is on the Nathan and Mary Robinson D.L.C. #45, OC #736. (Not shown on Scholls 1961-85 USGS Quad. map.)

VALLEY MEMORIAL PARK AND MAUSOLEUM
AKA: 1. HILLSBORO VALLEY MEMORIAL
2. VALLEY MEMORIAL PARK

D 40.86 1 1950 T1S R2W S9
Located at 3809 Southeast Tualatin Valley Highway (OR. Hwy. 8), Hillsboro. It is on the north side of the highway and clearly visible from the highway; on the Thomas Stewart D.L.C. #43, OC #3823. {10 July 1998} (Hillsboro 1961-85 USGS Quad. map.)

VERBOORT CHURCH

A ? 6 26 Jun 1876 T1N R3W S20
The original burial ground was 200 feet north of the first chapel and was the first burial site of Reverend Verboort. All burials were removed to Visitation Cemetery in 1880. See the article for Visitation Cemetery. It is on the Henry Black D.L.C. #51, OC #34. (Forest Grove 1956-92 USGS Quad. map shows a church but not the old cemetery.)

VISITATION OF THE BLESSED VIRGIN MARY
AKA: 1. CATHOLIC CEMETERY AT VERBOORT
2. VERBOORT CATHOLIC
3. VISITATION
4. VISITATION CATHOLIC

D 2.66 3 1880 T1N R3W S17
Located 0.5 of a mile north of Verboort; turn left (west) on Osterman Road to the cemetery on the right (north). It is on the Charles Conklin D.L.C. #53, OC #3571. {5 October 1997} (Forest Grove 1956-92 USGS Quad. map.)

WEDEKING FAMILY
AKA: 1. WEDEKING-- WARNER FAMILIES

? ? ? ? T2S R2W S12
Located west of Beaverton in the Kinton Community. Go westerly about 4 miles on Scholls Ferry Road (OR. Hwy. 210) from OR. Hwy. 217. Turn left (south) off of Scholls Ferry Road onto Pleasant Valley Road and follow it to the junction with Aten Road on the right (west). The July 1928 *Metsker Land*

Name of Cemetery and also known as	Number of burials	Acres	Condition	Date started or earliest known burial	Township	Range	Section

Ownership Atlas shows a Lav. Wedeking owned land on the north side of Aten Road. (Not shown on Scholls 1961-85 USGS Quad. map.)

WEST UNION BAPTIST
AKA: 1. WEST UNION

C   1.78   2   1854   T1N   R2W   S14

Located north of Hillsboro and north of Sunset Highway (U.S. Hwy. 26). The church and cemetery are situated 0.9 of a mile west of the locale of West Union, on West Union Road at the junction of Dick Road. It is on the David T. Lennox D.L.C. #58, OC #38. {8 October 1990} (Hillsboro 1961-85 USGS Quad. map.)

WHITE FAMILY
AKA: 1. TRACHSEL
        VILLAGE

?   0.03   12   ?   T1S   R2W   S11

Located on the Carl Trachsel Farm north of Reedville at Southwest 219th Avenue now Cornelius Pass Road and Johnson Street, on the northeast corner of the intersection. This has been farmed over and is now possibly built over. Located on the Richard White D.L.C. #48, OC #1281. (Not shown on Hillsboro 1961-85 USGS Quad. map.)

WINONA
AKA: 1. TUALATIN

C   4.32   1   June 1900   T2S   R1W   S23

Located northwest of the old center of Tualatin, but now well within the city limits. Leave the I-5 Freeway at Exit 289 on Nyberg Road to the west. Turn left off of Nyberg Road onto Tualatin-Sherwood Road. At the signalized intersection at 0.5 of a mile, turn right (north) onto Boones Ferry Road for 3 blocks. Boones Ferry Road then veers to the right, but keep ahead, now on Tualatin Road, going northerly and northwesterly past the country club. As the road curves from north to west the cemetery is on the left (south). You are 1.6 miles from the western interchange legs of Exit 289. (20 March 1994) (Beaverton 1961-84 USGS Quad. map.)

WOODS BABY

A   0.01   1   1862   T1S   R2W   S10

Located at 22885 Southwest Johnson Street, Hillsboro, which is privte property. Go north on 228th and north from the northeast corner of what is now [1999] Fred Meyer store

Name of Cemetery and also known as	Number of burials	Acres	Condition	Date started or earliest known burial	Township	Range	Section

property. At the four way stop sign contenue north on what has become Southwest Johnson Street it makes a hard left about one block from the four way stop. At this point there is a new road 67th Ave. going north, at this intersection look to your right and the house is on the right (east) side of the street. The small monument was removed about 1995: it said; "2 Yr.-old daughter Woods-1862." A lady informed us that the girls' name may have been Emma. On the Joseph Woods D.L.C. #48, OC #3856. {18 July 1998} (Not shown on Hillsboro 1961-85 USGS Quad. map.)

WUNSCH, ERDMAN

A ? 4 1895 T3N R4W S6

This grave is located west of OR. Hwy. 47 between the junction of Johnson Road and the Columbia County line. Wunsch was buried on the homestead of his son-in-law and daughter, Gust. and Emma Wunsch Schmidlin. Located on private property. (Not shown on Vernonia 1979 USGS Quad. map.)

ZIMMERMAN FAMILY

A 0.13 1 1890 T2N R2W S8

Located 5 or 6 miles north of North Plains, on the homestead of George E. Zimmerman. The plot is fenced, with 19 known burials; all but one are family members. The first burial was for Emmet W. Zimmerman 1883-1890, son of George E. and Sarah Ann Zimmerman. The death certificate for George Zimmerman states that he was born 24 January 1833, died 13 Febuary 1916 and was buried on his own farm. NOTE: This site is on private property and you must obtain permission to visit. (Not shown on Dixie Mountain 1961-85 USGS Quad. map.)

AGGELLES, ALEXIS	WASHINGTON CO.			
ALLEN D.L.C., DAVID see **INDIAN**	WASHINGTON CO.	T1N	R4W	S34
ALTON, DONALD see **ST. MARY'S BOY'S HOME**				
	WASHINGTON CO.	T1S	R1W	?
AMES CHAPEL see **CRESCENT GROVE**	WASHINGTON CO.	T1S	R1W	S26
ARCADE	WASHINGTON CO.	T2N	R3W	S14
BAKER FAMILY	WASHINGTON CO.	T1S	R4W	S21
BANKS see **UNION POINT**	WASHINGTON CO.	T2N	R3W	S31
BANKS UNION POINT see **UNION POINT**				
	WASHINGTON CO.	T2N	R3W	S31
BARNUM D.L.C., MOSES R. see **BARNUM FAMILY**				
	WASHINGTON CO.	T2S	R1W	S30
BARNUM FAMILY	WASHINGTON CO.	T2S	R1W	S30
BENNET, PHOEBE KEENON AND BABY see **ARCADE**				
	WASHINGTON CO.	T2N	R3W	S14
BERNARD FARM, JOSEPH see **ST. EDWARD'S CATHOLIC [OLD]**				
	WASHINGTON CO.	T1N	R3W	S1
BETHANY BIBLE CHURCH see **BETHANY PIONEER**				
	WASHINGTON CO.	T1N	R1W	S7
BETHANY GERMAN METHODIST see **BETHANY PIONEER**				
	WASHINGTON CO.	T1N	R1W	S7
BETHANY METHODIST CHURCH see **BETHANY PIONEER**				
	WASHINGTON CO.	T1N	R1W	S7
BETHANY PIONEER	WASHINGTON CO.	T1N	R1W	S7
BETHANY PRESBYTERIAN	WASHINGTON CO.	T1N	R1W	S17
BETHANY PRESBYTERIAN CHURCH see **BETHANY PRESBYTERIAN**				
	WASHINGTON CO.	T1N	R1W	S17
BLACK D.L.C., HENRY see **VERBOORT CHURCH**				
	WASHINGTON CO.	T1N	R3W	S20
BLOOMING	WASHINGTON CO.	T1S	R3W	S15
BLOOMING CHURCH see **BLOOMING**	WASHINGTON CO.	T1S	R3W	S15
BLOOMINGTON [?] see **BLOOMING**	WASHINGTON CO.	T1S	R3W	S15
BLUE TOWN see **ST. PAUL LUTHERAN CHURCH**				
	WASHINGTON CO.	T2S	R1W	S30
BLUETOWN see **MAPLE LANE**	WASHINGTON CO.	T2S	R1W	S30
BLUETOWN see **ST. PAUL LUTHERAN CHURCH**				
	WASHINGTON CO.	T2S	R1W	S30
BOOTH FAMILY	WASHINGTON CO.	T1S	R5W	S25
BRIDGEFARMER D.L.C., CHRISTOPHER see **HESS, BABY BOY**				
	WASHINGTON CO.	T1S	R4W	S33
BRUEHL, EDWARD	WASHINGTON CO.	T3N	R2W	S28
BRUEHL PLACE see **BRUEHL, EDWARD**	WASHINGTON CO.	T3N	R2W	S28
BRUGGER see **BETHANY PRESBYTERIAN**				
	WASHINGTON CO.	T1N	R1W	S17
BRUGGER D.L.C., JACOB see **BETHANY PRESBYTERIAN**				
	WASHINGTON CO.	T1N	R1W	S17
BURDORFUR see **BURGDORFER FAMILY**	WASHINGTON CO.	T3N	R3W	S15
BURGDORFER FAMILY	WASHINGTON CO.	T3N	R3W	S15
BURRIS D.L.C., WILLIAM see **BURRIS FAMILY, WILLIAM**				
	WASHINGTON CO.	T1N	R2W	S5
BURRIS FAMILY, WILLIAM	WASHINGTON CO.	T1N	R2W	S5

BURRIS, MARTHA see **BURRIS FAMILY, WILLIAM**

        WASHINGTON CO.   T1N   R2W   S5

BUXTON CATHOLIC   WASHINGTON CO.   T2N   R4W   S4

BUXTON PROTESTANT   WASHINGTON CO.   T2N   R4W   S5

BUXTON SR. D.L.C., HENRY see **FOREST VIEW MEMORIAL GARDENS**

        WASHINGTON CO.   T1N   R4W   S36

CALLAHAN FARM see **HESS, BABY BOY**

        WASHINGTON CO.   T1S   R4W   S33

CALLAHAN FARM, H. see **HESS, BABY BOY**

        WASHINGTON CO.   T1S   R4W   S33

CATCHING D.L.C., BENJAMIN see **MOUNTAIN VIEW MEMORIAL GARDENS**

        WASHINGTON CO.   T1N   R4W   S35

CATHOLIC see **ST. EDWARD'S CATHOLIC [NEW]**

        WASHINGTON CO.   T2N   R2W   S31

CATHOLIC see **ST. EDWARD'S CATHOLIC [OLD]**

        WASHINGTON CO.   T1N   R3W   S1

CATHOLIC CEMETERY AT VERBOORT see **VISITATION OF THE BLESSED VIRGIN MARY**

        WASHINGTON CO.   T1N   R3W   S17

CEDAR MILLS see **UNION**   WASHINGTON CO.   T1N   R1W   S29

CEDAR MILLS CATHOLIC see **PIONEER CATHOLIC OF ST. ANTHONY OF PADUA**

        WASHINGTON CO.   T1S   R1W   S4

CHERRY GROVE see **CHERRY GROVE BAPTIST**

        WASHINGTON CO.   T1S   R4W   S30

CHERRY GROVE BAPTIST   WASHINGTON CO.   T1S   R4W   S30

CLARK, HARVEY see **PACIFIC UNIVERSITY**

        WASHINGTON CO.   T1N   R3W   S31

CONGREGATIONAL see **MOUNTAIN VIEW MEMORIAL GARDENS**

        WASHINGTON CO.   T1N   R4W   S35

CONKLIN D.L.C., CHARLES see **VISITATION OF THE BLESSED VIRGIN MARY**

        WASHINGTON CO.   T1N   R3W   S17

CONNELL FARM, JOSEPH see **BURRIS FAMILY, WILLIAM**

        WASHINGTON CO.   T1N   R2W   S5

CONSTABLE D.L.C., EDWARD AND PRISCILLA see **METHODIST MEETING HOUSE**

        WASHINGTON CO.   T1N   R2W   S21

COOPER MOUNTAIN [CATHOLIC]   WASHINGTON CO.   T1S   R2W   S25

COOPER MOUNTAIN [PROTESTANT] WASHINGTON CO.   T1S   R2W   S25

COPPER *[Sic]* MOUNTAIN see **COOPER MOUNTAIN [CATHOLIC]**

        WASHINGTON CO.   T1S   R2W   S25

COPPER *[Sic]* MOUNTAIN see **COOPER MOUNTAIN [PROTESTANT]**

        WASHINGTON CO.   T1S   R2W   S25

CORNELIUS LUTHERAN see **EMANUEL LUTHERAN**

        WASHINGTON CO.   T1N   R3W   S34

CORNELIUS METHODIST see **CORNELIUS PIONEER METHODIST**

        WASHINGTON CO.   T1N   R3W   S33

CORNELIUS PIONEER METHODIST WASHINGTON CO.   T1N   R3W   S33

CRESCENT see **CRESCENT GROVE** WASHINGTON CO.   T1S   R1W   S26

CRESCENT GROVE   WASHINGTON CO.   T1S   R1W   S26

CROP, VICTOR see **ST. EDWARD'S CATHOLIC [OLD]**

        WASHINGTON CO.   T1N   R3W   S1

DAVIS D.L.C., HENRY AND TRIJAH see **FIR LAWN CEMETERY AND MAUSOLEUM**

        WASHINGTON CO.   T1N   R3W   S36

DELANEY FARM, CHARLES see **RUM AND GUM CHARLEY**				
	WASHINGTON CO.	T2S	?	?
DETHLEFS see **MT. OLIVE LUTHERAN**	WASHINGTON CO.	T1S	R4W	S23
DICKSON D.L.C., JOSHUA see **MT. OLIVE LUTHERAN**				
	WASHINGTON CO.	T1S	R4W	S23
DIXIE MOUNTAIN see **MOUNTAIN VIEW**				
	WASHINGTON CO.	T3N	R2W	S32
EAST GASTON see **HILL**	WASHINGTON CO.	T2S	R3W	S6
ELLIS, A. M. see **ELLIS FAMILY**	WASHINGTON CO.	T1S	R1W	S12
ELLIS, CARRIE ETTA	WASHINGTON CO.	T1N	R5W	S25
ELLIS FAMILY	WASHINGTON CO.	T1S	R1W	S12
ELLIS, KITTY M. see **ELLIS FAMILY**				
	WASHINGTON CO.	T1S	R1W	S12
ELLIS, PERRY see **ELLIS, CARRIE ETTA**				
	WASHINGTON CO.	T1N	R5W	S25
ELLIS, PERRY see **ELLIS FAMILY**	WASHINGTON CO.	T1S	R1W	S12
ELLIS, RACHEL A. see **ELLIS FAMILY**				
	WASHINGTON CO.	T1S	R1W	S12
EMANUEL see **CORNELIUS PIONEER METHODIST**				
	WASHINGTON CO.	T1N	R3W	S33
EMANUEL see **TIGARD EVANGELICAL**	WASHINGTON CO.	T2S	R1W	S10
EMANUEL EVANGELICAL UNITED BRETHERN see **TIGARD EVANGELICAL**				
	WASHINGTON CO.	T2S	R1W	S10
EMANUEL LUTHERAN	WASHINGTON CO.	T1N	R3W	S34
EMERICK D.L.C., SOLOMON see **EMERICK FAMILY**				
	WASHINGTON CO.	T1S	R3W	?
EMERICK FAMILY	WASHINGTON CO.	T1S	R3W	?
EMERICK, SOLOMON see **EMERICK FAMILY**				
	WASHINGTON CO.	T1S	R3W	?
EMRICK see **EMERICK FAMILY**	WASHINGTON CO.	T1S	R3W	?
EMRIEK see **EMERICK FAMILY**	WASHINGTON CO.	T1S	R3W	?
EVANGELICAL see **COOPER MOUNTAIN [PROTESTANT]**				
	WASHINGTON CO.	T1S	R2W	S25
EVANGLE see **TIGARD EVANGELICAL**	WASHINGTON CO.	T2S	R1W	S10
FARMINGTON see **LEWIS**	WASHINGTON CO.	T1S	R2W	S30
FERN HILL see **FERN HILL CATHOLIC**				
	WASHINGTON CO.	T1S	R3W	S16
FERN HILL CATHOLIC	WASHINGTON CO.	T1S	R3W	S16
FINLEY'S SUNSET HILL MEMORIAL	WASHINGTON CO.	T1S	R1W	S1
FIR LAWN CEMETERY AND MAUSOLEUM	WASHINGTON CO.	T1N	R3W	S36
FOELER, DON see **JOLLY FAMILY**	WASHINGTON CO.	T1N	R3W	S24
FORD INFANT	WASHINGTON CO.	T1N	R1W	S7
FORD, MARY ANN LENOX see **FORD INFANT**				
	WASHINGTON CO.	T1N	R1W	S7
FORD, REUBEN W. see **FORD INFANT**	WASHINGTON CO.	T1N	R1W	S7
FOREST VIEW see **FOREST VIEW MEMORIAL GARDENS**				
	WASHINGTON CO.	T1N	R4W	S36
FOREST VIEW MEMORIAL GARDENS	WASHINGTON CO.	T1N	R4W	S36
GALES CREEK	WASHINGTON CO.	T1N	R4W	S18
GALES CREEK UNION see **GALES CREEK**				
	WASHINGTON CO.	T1N	R4W	S18

GASSNER ROAD see **COOPER MOUNTAIN [PROTESTANT]**
        WASHINGTON CO.   T1S   R2W   S25
GERMAN CHURCH see **ST. PAUL LUTHERAN CHURCH**
        WASHINGTON CO.   T2S   R1W   S30
GERMAN EVANGELICAL LUTHERAN EMANUELS CHURCH see **EMANUEL LUTHERAN**
        WASHINGTON CO.   T1N   R3W   S34
GERMAN LUTHERAN CHURCH see **MT. OLIVE LUTHERAN**
        WASHINGTON CO.   T1S   R4W   S23
GERMAN LUTHERANER *[Sic]* EMANUEL CHURCH see **EMANUEL LUTHERAN**
        WASHINGTON CO.   T1N   R3W   S34
GERMAN PRESBYTERIAN see **BETHANY PRESBYTERIAN**
        WASHINGTON CO.   T1N   R1W   S17
GERRISH D.L.C., JOHN J. see **CHERRY GROVE BAPTIST**
        WASHINGTON CO.   T1S   R4W   S30
GRAHAM D.L.C., DAVID see **CRESCENT GROVE**
        WASHINGTON CO.   T1S   R1W   S26
GREENVILLE see **UNION POINT**   WASHINGTON CO.   T2N   R3W   S31
HALL FARM   WASHINGTON CO.   T1N   R4W   ?
HALL PROPERTY, C. see **HALL FARM**   WASHINGTON CO.   T1N   R4W   ?
HANEY FAMILY   WASHINGTON CO.   T1S   R4W   S35
HANLON FARM, CHARLES see **BURGDORFER FAMILY**
        WASHINGTON CO.   T3N   R3W   S15
HARRIS D.L.C., PHILLIP see **METHODIST CHURCH AT FARMINGTON**
        WASHINGTON CO.   T1S   R2W   ?
HARRISON   WASHINGTON CO.   T1N   R3W   S3
HARRISON D.L.C., JOHN see **HARRISON**
        WASHINGTON CO.   T1N   R3W   S3
HART D.L.C., ANTHONY W. see **NEVEH ZEDEK-ROSE CITY LODGE**
        WASHINGTON CO.   T1S   R1W   S12
HAYWARD   WASHINGTON CO.   T2N   R4W   S19
HEARD, SHIRLEY JEAN   WASHINGTON CO.   ?   ?   ?
HELVETIA   WASHINGTON CO.   T1N   R2W   S3
HERGERT ROAD see **FERN HILL CATHOLIC**
        WASHINGTON CO.   T1S   R3W   S16
HESS, ANNA ELIZA CALLAHAN see **HESS, BABY BOY**
        WASHINGTON CO.   T1S   R4W   S33
HESS, BABY BOY   WASHINGTON CO.   T1S   R4W   S33
HESS, WM. F. see **HESS, BABY BOY**   WASHINGTON CO.   T1S   R4W   S33
HICKENBOTTOM FAMILY see **SHADY BROOK**
        WASHINGTON CO.   T2N   R2W   S30
HILL   WASHINGTON CO.   T2S   R3W   S6
HILL, ALMORAN see **HILL**   WASHINGTON CO.   T2S   R3W   S6
HILL D.L.C., ALMORAN see **HILL**   WASHINGTON CO.   T2S   R3W   S6
HILLSBORO FIR LAWN see **FIR LAWN CEMETERY AND MAUSOLEUM**
        WASHINGTON CO.   T1N   R3W   S36
HILLSBORO MASONIC see **HILLSBORO PIONEER**
        WASHINGTON CO.   T1N   R3W   S36
HILLSBORO PIONEER   WASHINGTON CO.   T1N   R3W   S36
HILLSBORO VALLEY MEMORIAL see **VALLEY MEMORIAL PARK AND MAUSOLEUM**
        WASHINGTON CO.   T1S   R2W   S9
HILLSIDE   WASHINGTON CO.   T1N   R4W   S9

```
HINES D.L.C., THOMAS M. see PATTON FAMILY
                              WASHINGTON CO.    T1S    R4W       S36
HOLZMEYER see PURDIN FAMILY    WASHINGTON CO.    T1N    R4W       S25
HOOVER D.L.C., JACOB AND MALINDA see HOOVER FAMILY
                              WASHINGTON CO.    T1N    R3W       S14
HOOVER D.L.C., JACOB AND MALINDA see THE OLD SCOTCH CHURCH
                              WASHINGTON CO.    T1N    R3W       S13
HOOVER FAMILY                 WASHINGTON CO.    T1N    R3W       S14
HORNER D.L.C., EMANUEL see BOOTH FAMILY
                              WASHINGTON CO.    T1S    R5W       S25
HORNING, RICHARD              WASHINGTON CO.    T2N    R3W       S11
HOSKINSON, RICHARD see ST. MARY'S BOY'S HOME
                              WASHINGTON CO.    T1S    R1W       ?
HUGHES, ELMER S.              WASHINGTON CO.    T3N    R5W       ?
HUGHES, HARRY see ST. MARY'S BOY'S HOME
                              WASHINGTON CO.    T1S    R1W       ?
HUGHES, JOHN see HUGHES, ELMER S.
                              WASHINGTON CO.    T3N    R5W       ?
HUGHES, SARAH WIMPLE see HUGHES, ELMER S.
                              WASHINGTON CO.    T3N    R5W       ?
HUNDLEY BURIAL                WASHINGTON CO.    T1N    R5W       S1
I.O.O.F. see CORNELIUS PIONEER METHODIST
                              WASHINGTON CO.    T1N    R3W       S33
I.O.O.F. see HILLSBORO PIONEER WASHINGTON CO.   T1N    R3W       S36
INDIAN                        WASHINGTON CO.    T1N    R4W       S34
INNES D.L.C., JOHN see JOHNSON FAMILY
                              WASHINGTON CO.    T1S    R1W       S17
IOWA HILL                     WASHINGTON CO.    T1S    R3W       S32
IOWA HILL CATHOLIC see FERN HILL CATHOLIC
                              WASHINGTON CO.    T1S    R3W       S16
JACKSON D.L.C., ULYSSES see JACKSON FAMILY
                              WASHINGTON CO.    T2N    R3W       S36
JACKSON D.L.C., ULYSSES see ST. EDWARD'S CATHOLIC [OLD]
                              WASHINGTON CO.    T1N    R3W       S1
JACKSON FAMILY                WASHINGTON CO.    T2N    R3W       S36
JOHNSON D.L.C., JOHN see ST. EDWARD'S CATHOLIC [NEW]
                              WASHINGTON CO.    T2N    R2W       S31
JOHNSON FAMILY                WASHINGTON CO.    ?      ?         ?
JOHNSON FAMILY                WASHINGTON CO.    T1S    R1W       S17
JOLLY D.L.C., WILLIAM see JOLLY FAMILY
                              WASHINGTON CO.    T1N    R3W       S24
JOLLY FAMILY                  WASHINGTON CO.    T1N    R3W       S24
K-MART see ST. MARY'S OF THE VALLEY [OLD]
                              WASHINGTON CO.    T1S    R1W       S7
KASHENOROF, CHESTER see ST. MARY'S BOY'S HOME
                              WASHINGTON CO.    T1S    R1W       ?
KEEGAN, JAMES see ST. MARY'S BOY'S HOME
                              WASHINGTON CO.    T1S    R1W       ?
KELLY, PATRICK J. see UNKNOWN  WASHINGTON CO.    T1S    R2W       S14
KIMZEY, JOHN see PACIFIC UNIVERSITY
                              WASHINGTON CO.    T1N    R3W       S31
```

KRAUSE see **MAPLE LANE**	WASHINGTON CO.	T2S	R1W	S30
LAUREL see **MT. OLIVE CEMETERY OF LAUREL**				
	WASHINGTON CO.	T2S	R3W	S12
LAURELWOOD see **MT. OLIVE CEMETERY OF LAUREL**				
	WASHINGTON CO.	T2S	R3W	S12
LEE, JASON see **BOOTH FAMILY**	WASHINGTON CO.	T1S	R5W	S25
LENNOX D.L.C., DAVID T. see **WEST UNION BAPTIST**				
	WASHINGTON CO.	T1N	R2W	S14
LEONARD D.L.C., JOSEPH see **FORD INFANT**				
	WASHINGTON CO.	T1N	R1W	S7
LEWIS	WASHINGTON CO.	T1S	R2W	S30
LEWIS D.L.C., CHARLES see **LEWIS**	WASHINGTON CO.	T1S	R2W	S30
LITTLE BULL MOUNTAIN see **TIGARD EVANGELICAL**				
	WASHINGTON CO.	T2S	R1W	S10
LUTHERAN see **MAPLE LANE**	WASHINGTON CO.	T2S	R1W	S30
MAPLE LANE	WASHINGTON CO.	T2S	R1W	S30
MARTIN D.L.C., NORMAN see **BAKER FAMILY**				
	WASHINGTON CO.	T1S	R4W	S21
MASONIC see **HILLSBORO PIONEER**	WASHINGTON CO.	T1N	R3W	S36
McCANN, DANIEL see **McCANN FAMILY**				
	WASHINGTON CO.	T1S	R4W	S32
McCANN FAMILY	WASHINGTON CO.	T1S	R4W	S32
McGUIRE D.L.C., FRANCIS see **UNION**				
	WASHINGTON CO.	T1N	R1W	S29
McLIN D.L.C., WILLIAM AND ROSANA see **EMANUEL LUTHERAN**				
	WASHINGTON CO.	T1N	R3W	S34
McLEOD D.L.C., DONALD see **HANEY FAMILY**				
	WASHINGTON CO.	T1S	R4W	S35
McMILLAN D.L.C., JAMES H. see **UNKNOWN**				
	WASHINGTON CO.	T1S	R2W	S13
MERIDIAN	WASHINGTON CO.	T3S	R1W	S1
METHODIST CHURCH AT FARMINGTON	WASHINGTON CO.	T1S	R2W	?
METHODIST MEETING HOUSE	WASHINGTON CO.	T1N	R2W	S21
METZGER see **CRESCENT GROVE**	WASHINGTON CO.	T1S	R1W	S26
MIDDLETON PIONEER	WASHINGTON CO.	T2S	R2W	S36
MILLER see **ARCADE**	WASHINGTON CO.	T2N	R3W	S14
MOORE D.L.C., MICHAEL see **ROOD FAMILY**				
	WASHINGTON CO.	T1S	R2W	S6
MT. OLIVE BAPTIST see **MT. OLIVE CEMETERY OF LAUREL**				
	WASHINGTON CO.	T2S	R3W	S12
MT. OLIVE CEMETERY OF LAUREL	WASHINGTON CO.	T2S	R3W	S12
MT. OLIVE LUTHERAN	WASHINGTON CO.	T1S	R4W	S23
MOUNTAIN TOP see **MOUNTIANSIDE**	WASHINGTON CO.	T2S	R2W	S16
MOUNTAIN VIEW	WASHINGTON CO.	T3N	R2W	S32
MOUNTAIN VIEW MEMORIAL GARDENS	WASHINGTON CO.	T1N	R4W	S35
MOUNTAINDALE see **RAFFETY**	WASHINGTON CO.	T2N	R3W	S27
MOUNTAINSIDE	WASHINGTON CO.	T2S	R2W	S16
MULHOLLAND, EMILY see **McCANN FAMILY**				
	WASHINGTON CO.	T1S	R4W	S32
MULHOLLAND, JOHN see **McCANN FAMILY**				
	WASHINGTON CO.	T1S	R4W	S32

MULKEY D.L.C., WESLEY see **PURDIN FAMILY**

	WASHINGTON CO.	T1N	R4W	S25

NAYLOR see **FOREST VIEW MEMORIAL GARDENS**

	WASHINGTON CO.	T1N	R4W	S36

NEVEH ZEDEK-ROSE CITY LODGE WASHINGTON CO. T1S R1W S12

NEXON, BIRGETTA see **BOOTH FAMILY**

	WASHINGTON CO.	T1S	R5W	S25

NOLAND JR. D.L.C., HENRY see **POOR FARM**

	WASHINGTON CO.	T1S	R2W	S8

NORTH PLAINS see **ST. EDWARD'S CATHOLIC [NEW]**

	WASHINGTON CO.	T2N	R2W	S31

NORTH PLAINS see **ST. EDWARD'S CATHOLIC [OLD]**

	WASHINGTON CO.	T1N	R3W	S1

NORTH PLAINS CATHOLIC see **ST. EDWARD'S CATHOLIC [NEW]**

	WASHINGTON CO.	T2N	R2W	S31

NORTH PLAINS CATHOLIC see **ST. EDWARD'S CATHOLIC [OLD]**

	WASHINGTON CO.	T1N	R3W	S1

OAK KNOLL	WASHINGTON CO.	T1S	R4W	S2
OLD COMMUNITY see **UNION**	WASHINGTON CO.	T1N	R1W	S29

OLD FOREST GROVE see **MOUNTAIN VIEW MEMORIAL GARDENS**

	WASHINGTON CO.	T1N	R4W	S35

OLD UNION see **UNION**	WASHINGTON CO.	T1N	R1W	S29
PACIFIC UNIVERSITY	WASHINGTON CO.	T1N	R3W	S31

PACIFIC UNIVERSITY MEMORIAL see **PACIFIC UNIVERSITY**

	WASHINGTON CO.	T1N	R3W	S31

PARSON D.L.C., HORACE AND MARILDA see **OAK KNOLL**

	WASHINGTON CO.	T1S	R4W	S2

PARSONS FAMILY see **OAK KNOLL**	WASHINGTON CO.	T1S	R4W	S2
PATON see **PATTON FAMILY**	WASHINGTON CO.	T1S	R1W	S14
PATTON FAMILY	WASHINGTON CO.	T1S	R1W	S14
PATTON FAMILY	WASHINGTON CO.	T1S	R4W	S36

PETERSON, ALEC see **PETERSON FAMILY**

	WASHINGTON CO.	T3N	R4W	S1

PETERSON, ALICE see **PETERSON FAMILY**

	WASHINGTON CO.	T3N	R4W	S1

PETERSON FAMILY	WASHINGTON CO.	T3N	R4W	S1

PETERSON, FRED see **PETERSON FAMILY**

	WASHINGTON CO.	T3N	R4W	S1

PHILLIPS	WASHINGTON CO.	T1N	R2W	S12

PHILLIPS GERMAN REFORM CHURCH see **PHILLIPS**

	WASHINGTON CO.	T1N	R2W	S12

PIONEER see **GALES CREEK**	WASHINGTON CO.	T1N	R4W	S18

PIONEER CATHOLIC see **PIONEER CATHOLIC OF ST. ANTHONY OF PADUA**

	WASHINGTON CO.	T1S	R1W	S4

PIONEER CATHOLIC OF ST. ANTHONY OF PADUA

	WASHINGTON CO.	T1S	R1W	S4

PIONEER UNION see **MOUNTAIN VIEW MEMORIAL GARDENS**

	WASHINGTON CO.	T1N	R4W	S35

POINTER D.L.C., WILLIAM see **ELLIS FAMILY**

	WASHINGTON CO.	T1S	R1W	S12

POINTER D.L.C., WILLIAM see **FINLEY'S SUNSET HILL MEMORIAL**

	WASHINGTON CO.	T1S	R1W	S1

POINTER D.L.C., WILLIAM see **POINTER FAMILY**				
	WASHINGTON CO.	T1S	R1W	S1
POINTER FAMILY	WASHINGTON CO.	T1S	R1W	S1
POOR FARM	WASHINGTON CO.	T1S	R2W	S8
PORTLAND GOLF COURSE see **PATTON FAMILY**				
	WASHINGTON CO.	T1S	R1W	S14
PROGRESS see **CRESCENT GROVE**	WASHINGTON CO.	T1S	R1W	S26
PUMPKIN RIDGE see **ARCADE**	WASHINGTON CO.	T2N	R3W	S14
PURDIN FAMILY	WASHINGTON CO.	T1N	R4W	S25
RAFFERTY [Sic] see **RAFFETY**	WASHINGTON CO.	T2N	R3W	S27
RAFFETY	WASHINGTON CO.	T2N	R3W	S27
RAFFETY D.L.C., SAMUEL B. see **RAFFETY**				
	WASHINGTON CO.	T2N	R3W	S27
RAFFETY, S. B. see **RAFFETY**	WASHINGTON CO.	T2N	R3W	S27
RALEIGH-PATTON FAMILY see **PATTON FAMILY**				
	WASHINGTON CO.	T1S	R1W	S14
RITCHEY D.L.C., JOHN M. see **METHODIST CHURCH AT FARMINGTON**				
	WASHINGTON CO.	T1S	R2W	?
RICHEY FARM see **OAK KNOLL**	WASHINGTON CO.	T1S	R4W	S2
ROBERTSON, JAMES B. see **ROBISON FAMILY, JAMES**				
	WASHINGTON CO.	T1N	R3W	S26
ROBINSON, D.L.C., NATHAN AND MARY see **UNKNOWN**				
	WASHINGTON CO.	T1S	R2W	S14
ROBINSON, JAMES B. see **ROBISON FAMILY, JAMES**				
	WASHINGTON CO.	T1N	R3W	S26
ROBISON D.L.C., JAMES B. see **ROBISON FAMILY, JAMES**				
	WASHINGTON CO.	T1N	R3W	S26
ROBISON FAMILY, JAMES	WASHINGTON CO.	T1N	R3W	S26
ROOD FAMILY	WASHINGTON CO.	T1S	R2W	S6
ROOD, FRED see **ROOD FAMILY**	WASHINGTON CO.	T1S	R2W	S6
ROSE CITY LODGE see **NEVEH ZEDEK ROSE CITY LODGE**				
	WASHINGTON CO.	T1S	R1W	S12
ROY CATHOLIC see **ST. FRANCIS CATHOLIC**				
	WASHINGTON CO.	T1N	R3W	S5
RUM AND GUM CHARLEY	WASHINGTON CO.	T2S	?	?
ST. ANTHONY CATHOLIC	WASHINGTON CO.	T2S	R1W	S3
ST. ANTHONY OF PADUA see **PIONEER CATHOLIC OF ST. ANTHONY OF PADUA**				
	WASHINGTON CO.	T1S	R1W	S4
ST. ANTHONY'S see **ST. ANTHONY CATHOLIC**				
	WASHINGTON CO.	T2S	R1W	S3
ST. BEDE'S MEMORIAL GARDENS	WASHINGTON CO.	T1S	R3W	S5
ST. CECILIA see **PIONEER CATHOLIC OF ST. ANTHONY OF PADUA**				
	WASHINGTON CO.	T1S	R1W	S4
ST. EDWARD see **ST. EDWARD'S CATHOLIC [NEW]**				
	WASHINGTON CO.	T2N	R2W	S31
ST. EDWARD see **ST. EDWARD'S CATHOLIC [OLD]**				
	WASHINGTON CO.	T1N	R3W	S1
ST. EDWARD'S see **ST. EDWARD'S CATHOLIC [NEW]**				
	WASHINGTON CO.	T2N	R2W	S31
ST. EDWARD'S see **ST. EDWARD'S CATHOLIC [OLD]**				
	WASHINGTON CO.	T1N	R3W	S1
ST. EDWARD'S CATHOLIC [NEW]	WASHINGTON CO.	T2N	R2W	S31

ST. EDWARD'S CATHOLIC [OLD]	WASHINGTON CO.	T1N	R3W	S1
ST. FERDINAND see **ST. FRANCIS CATHOLIC**				
	WASHINGTON CO.	T1N	R3W	S5
ST. FRANCIS CATHOLIC	WASHINGTON CO.	T1N	R3W	S5
ST. FRANCIS OF ASSISI see **ST. FRANCIS CATHOLIC**				
	WASHINGTON CO.	T1N	R3W	S5
ST. JOHN THE EVANGELIST see **FERN HILL CATHOLIC**				
	WASHINGTON CO.	T1S	R3W	S16
ST. MARY'S BOY'S HOME	WASHINGTON CO.	T1S	R1W	?
ST. MARY'S OF THE VALLEY [NEW]	WASHINGTON CO.	T1S	R1W	S17
ST. MARY'S OF THE VALLEY [OLD]	WASHINGTON CO.	T1S	R1W	S7
ST. MATTHEW'S CATHOLIC	WASHINGTON CO.	T1S	R2W	S8
ST. PAUL see **COOPER MOUNTAIN [CATHOLIC]**				
	WASHINGTON CO.	T1S	R2W	S25
ST. PAUL LUTHERAN CHURCH	WASHINGTON CO.	T2S	R1W	S30
ST. PAUL'S LUTHERAN see **BLOOMING**				
	WASHINGTON CO.	T1S	R3W	S15
ST. PAUL'S LUTHERAN see **ST. PAUL LUTHERAN CHURCH**				
	WASHINGTON CO.	T2S	R1W	S30
ST. PETER'S see **COOPER MOUNTAIN [CATHOLIC]**				
	WASHINGTON CO.	T1S	R2W	S25
ST. PETER'S LUTHERAN see **BLOOMING**				
	WASHINGTON CO.	T1S	R3W	S15
ST. PIUS CATHOLIC see **PIONEER CATHOLIC OF ST. ANTHONY OF PADUA**				
	WASHINGTON CO.	T1S	R1W	S4
ST. PIUS X [10TH] see **PIONEER CATHOLIC OF ST. ANTHONY OF PADUA**				
	WASHINGTON CO.	T1S	R1W	S4
ST. THOMAS see **BUXTON CATHOLIC**	WASHINGTON CO.	T2N	R4W	S4
SATTERLEE, ARTHUR see **HALL FARM**	WASHINGTON CO.	T1N	R4W	?
SATTERLEE, RUTH HALL see **HALL FARM**				
	WASHINGTON CO.	T1N	R4W	?
SATTERLEE, WILLIAM see **HALL FARM**				
	WASHINGTON CO.	T1S	R4W	?
SCHMIDLIN, EMMA WUNSCH see **WUNSCH, ERDMAN**				
	WASHINGTON CO.	T3N	R4W	S6
SCHMIDLIN, GUST see **WUNSCH, ERDMAN**				
	WASHINGTON CO.	T3N	R4W	S6
SCHOLLS see **MOUNTAINSIDE**	WASHINGTON CO.	T2S	R2W	S16
SCHOLLS PIONEER see **MOUNTAINSIDE**				
	WASHINGTON CO.	T2S	R2W	S16
SCOTCH CHURCH see **THE OLD SCOTCH CHURCH**				
	WASHINGTON CO.	T1N	R3W	S13
SCOTCH PLAINS PRESBYTERIAN see **THE OLD SCOTCH CHURCH**				
	WASHINGTON CO.	T1N	R3W	S13
SCOTT FAMILY	WASHINGTON CO.	?	?	?
SEGHERS see **MT. OLIVE LUTHERAN**	WASHINGTON CO.	T1S	R4W	S23
SEIFFERT INFANT	WASHINGTON CO.	?	?	?
SEVENTH DAY ADVENTIST see **JOHNSON FAMILY**				
	WASHINGTON CO.	T1S	R1W	S17
SHADY BROOK	WASHINGTON CO.	T2N	R2W	S30
SHADYBROOK see **SHADY BROOK**	WASHINGTON CO.	T2N	R2W	S30

SHERWOOD LUTHERAN see **MAPLE LANE**

               WASHINGTON CO.   T2S   R1W   S30

SILVER D.L.C., CLEVES S. see **IOWA HILL**

               WASHINGTON CO.   T1S   R3W   S32

SIMMONS D.L.C., WHEELOCK see **HILLSBORO PIONEER**

               WASHINGTON CO.   T1N   R3W   S36

SISTERS OF SAINT MARY'S see **UNKNOWN**

               WASHINGTON CO.   T1S   R2W   S14

SISTERS OF SAINT MARY'S OF OREGON INC. see **UNKNOWN**

               WASHINGTON CO.   T1S   R2W   S14

SMITH, SAM   WASHINGTON CO.   T2S   R2W   S30

SOUTH CORNELIUS CATHOLIC see **FERN HILL CATHOLIC**

               WASHINGTON CO.   T1S   R3W   S16

STAEGER, GOTTLIEB   WASHINGTON CO.   T2N   R3W   S34

STEWART D.L.C., THOMAS see **STEWART FAMILY**

               WASHINGTON CO.   T1S   R2W   S9

STEWART D.L.C., THOMAS see **VALLEY MEMORIAL PARK AND MAUSOLEUM**

               WASHINGTON CO.   T1S   R2W   S9

STEWART FAMILY   WASHINGTON CO.   T1S   R2W   S9

SUNSET HILLS MEMORIAL PARK see **FINLEY'S SUNSET HILL MEMORIAL**

               WASHINGTON CO.   T1S   R1W   S1

SUNSET MEMORIAL PARK see **FINLEY'S SUNSET HILL MEMORIAL**

               WASHINGTON CO.   T1S   R1W   S1

THE HILL see **HILL**   WASHINGTON CO.   T2S   R3W   S6

THE OLD SCOTCH CHURCH   WASHINGTON CO.   T1N   R3W   S13

THE PIONEER SUNSET see **TIGARD EVANGELICAL**

               WASHINTON CO.   T2S   R1W   S10

TIGARD CATHOLIC see **ST. ANTHONY CATHOLIC**

               WASHINGTON CO.   T2S   R1W   S3

TIGARD D.L.C., WILSON M. see **TIGARD EVANGELICAL**

               WASHINGTON CO.   T2S   R1W   S10

TIGARD EVANGELICAL   WASHINGTON CO.   T2S   R1W   S10

TIGARD EVANGELICAL UNITED BRETHREN see **TIGARD EVANGELICAL**

               WASHINGTON CO.   T2S   R1W   S10

TIGARDVILLE see **TIGARD EVANGELICAL**

               WASHINGTON CO.   T2S   R1W   S10

TOLKE FAMILY   WASHINGTON CO.   T3N   R4W   S34

TOMPKINS see **HARRISON**   WASHINGTON CO.   T1N   R3W   S3

TOOLEY see **HARRISON**   WASHINGTON CO.   T1N   R3W   S3

TORAH TALMUD see **NEVAH ZEDEK ROSE CITY LODGE**

               WASHINGTON CO.   T1S   R1W   S12

TRACHSEL FARM, CARL see **WHITE FAMILY**

               WASHINGTON CO.   T1S   R2W   S11

TRACHSEL VILLAGE see **WHITE FAMILY**

               WASHNGTON CO.   T1S   R2W   S11

TUALATIN see **WINONA**   WASHNGTON CO.   T2S   R1W   S23

TUALATIN PLAINS see **THE OLD SCOTCH CHURCH**

               WASHINGTON CO.   T1N   R3W   S13

TUALATIN PLAINS PRESBYTERIAN see **THE OLD SCOTCH CHURCH**

               WASHINGTON CO.   T1N   R3W   S13

TUALATIN PLAINS PRESBYTERIAN SCOTCH CHURCH see **THE OLD SCOTCH CHURCH**

               WASHINGTON CO.   T1N   R3W   S13

```
TWIN OAKS see METHODIST CHURCH AT FARMINGTON
                              WASHINGTON CO.    T1S    R2W         ?
UNION                         WASHINGTON CO.    T1N    R1W         S29
UNION see MOUNTAIN VIEW MEMORIAL GARDENS
                              WASHINGTON CO.    T1N    R4W         S35
UNION CEMETERY OF CEDAR MILL see UNION
                              WASHINGTON CO.    T1N    R1W         S29
UNION HILL see UNION POINT    WASHINGTON CO.    T2N    R3W         S31
UNION POINT                   WASHINGTON CO.    T2N    R3W         S31
UNION SCHOOLHOUSE see UNION   WASHINGTON CO.    T1N    R1W         S29
UNITED METHODIST see TIGARD EVANGELICAL
                              WASHINGTON CO.    T2S    R1W         S10
UNKNOWN                       WASHINGTON CO.    T1S    R2W         S13
UNKNOWN                       WASHINGTON CO.    T1S    R2W         S14
VADIS see HARRISON            WASHINGTON CO.    T1N    R3W         S3
VALKYRIE MEMORIAL PARK see FINLEY'S SUNSET HILL MEMORIAL
                              WASHINGTON CO.    T1S    R1W         S1
VALLEY MEMORIAL PARK see VALLEY MEMORIAL PARK AND MAUSOLEUM
                              WASHINGTON CO.    T1S    R2W         S9
VALLEY MEMORIAL PARK AND MAUSOLEUM
                              WASHINGTON CO.    T1S    R2W         S9
VERBOORT CATHOLIC see VISITATION OF THE BLESSED VIRGIN MARY
                              WASHINGTON CO.    T1N    R3W         S17
VERBOORT CHURCH               WASHINGTON CO.    T1N    R3W         S20
VISITATION see VISITATION OF THE BLESSED VIRGIN MARY
                              WASHINGTON CO.    T1N    R3W         S17
VISITATION CATHOLIC see VISITATION OF THE BLESSED VIRGIN MARY
                              WASHINGTON CO.    T1N    R3W         S17
VISITATION OF THE BLESSED VIRGIN MARY
                              WASHINGTON CO.    T1N    R3W         S17
WALKER D.L.C., ELKANAH see PACIFIC UNIVERSITY
                              WASHINGTON CO.    T1N    R3W         S31
WALKER D.L.C., ROBERT see ST. FRANCIS CATHOLIC
                              WASHINGTON CO.    T1N    R3W         S5
WALLACE HOMESTEAD, ARTHUR W. see MOUNTAIN VIEW
                              WASHINGTON CO.    T3N    R2W         S32
WAPATO see HILL               WASHINGTON CO.    T2S    R3W         S6
WAPATO LODGE I.O.O.F. see CORNELIUS PIONEER METHODIST
                              WASHINGTON CO.    T1N    R3W         S33
WEDEKING FAMILY               WASHINGTON CO.    T2S    R2W         S12
WEDEKING, LAV. see WEDEKING FAMILY
                              WASHINGTON CO.    T2S    R2W         S12
WEDEKING-WARNER FAMILIES see WEDEKING FAMILY
                              WASHINGTON CO.    T2S    R2W         S12
WELCHES see PATTON FAMILY     WASHINGTON CO.    T1S    R1W         S14
WEST HILLS see FINLEY'S SUNSET HILL MEMORIAL
                              WASHINGTON CO.    T1S    R1W         S1
WEST UNION see WEST UNION BAPTIST
                              WASHINGTON CO.    T1N    R2W         S14
WEST UNION BAPTIST            WASHINGTON CO.    T1N    R2W         S14
WHITE D.L.C., RICHARD see WHITE FAMILY
                              WASHINGTON CO.    T1S    R2W         S11
```

WHITE FAMILY	WASHINGTON CO.	T1S	R2W	S11
WILKES, GREENVILLE see **UNION POINT**				
	WASHINGTON CO.	T2N	R3W	S31
WILKES NORTH ADDITION see **HILLSBORO PIONEER**				
	WASHINGTON CO.	T1N	R3W	S36
WINONA	WASHINGTON CO.	T2S	R1W	S23
WOODS BABY	WASHINGTON CO.	T1S	R2W	S10
WOODS D.L.C., JOSEPH see **WOODS BABY**				
	WASHINGTON CO.	T1S	R2W	S10
WUNSCH, ERDMAN	WASHINGTON CO.	T3N	R4W	S6
ZIMMERMAN, EMMET W. see **ZIMMERMAN FAMILY**				
	WASHINGTON CO.	T2N	R2W	S8
ZIMMERMAN FAMILY	WASHINGTON CO.	T2N	R2W	S8
ZIMMERMAN, GEORGE see **ZIMMERMAN FAMILY**				
	WASHINGTON CO.	T2N	R2W	S8
ZIMMERMAN, GEORGE E. see **ZIMMERMAN FAMILY**				
	WASHINGTON CO.	T2N	R2W	S8
ZIMMERMAN, SARAH ANN see **ZIMMERMAN FAMILY**				
	WASHINGTON CO.	T2N	R2W	S8

Valley Memorial Park and Mausoleum
Janice M. Healy (2001)

Meridian

A couple of examples of roll style monuments.
Dean H. Byrd (1989)

Cornelius Pioneer Methodist

Dean H. Byrd (1995)

Raffety
Dean H. Byrd (1990)

Neveh Zedek-Rose City Lodge
Stanley R. Clarke (1998)

Union, Janice M. Healy
Dean H. Byrd (1990)

Shady Brook, Dean H. Byrd
Janice M. Healy (1991)

Cornelius Pioneer Methodist
Dean H. Byrd (1995)

Hillsboro Pioneer
Janice M. Healy (1993)

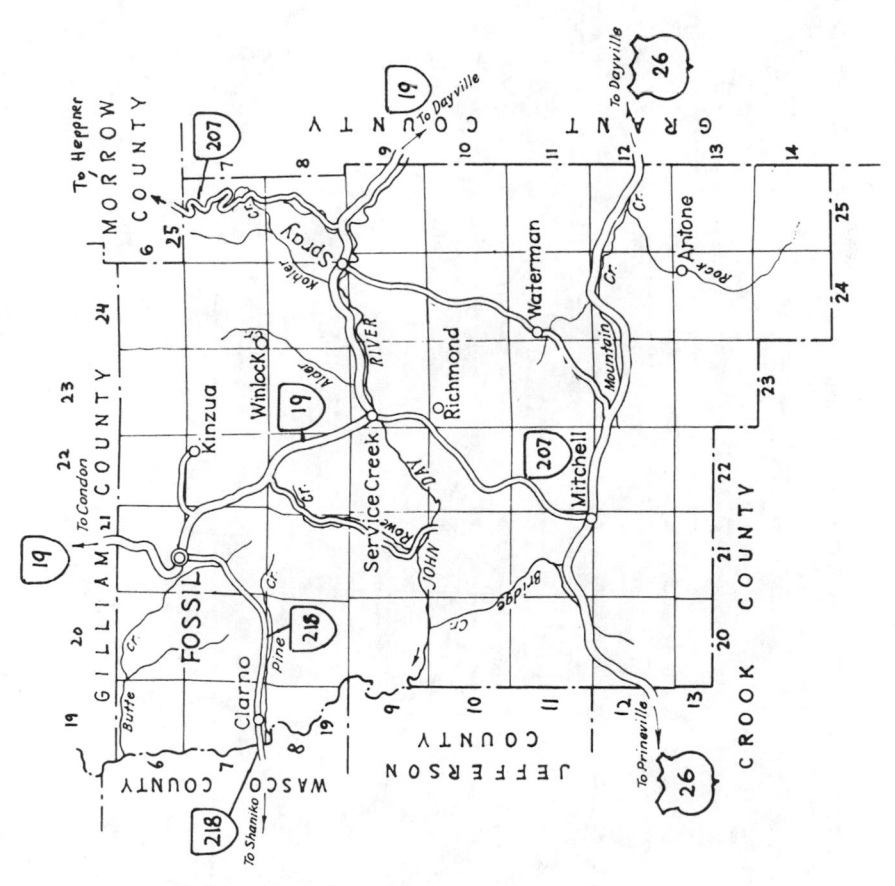

I.O.O.F. [Fossil]
Janice M. Healy (2000)

Area: 1,713 square miles
Population (1998): 1,566
County seat: Fossil, Population: 515
County established: 17 February 1899

Wheeler County was and is predominantly ranching country. It was not settled by whites until the 1870's and the first cemeteries for the public were established in 1881 at Fossil. The 1880's saw the establishment of most of the public cemeteries in the county.

I.O.O.F. [Fossil]
Janice M. Healy (2000)

I.O.O.F. [Fossil]
Janice M. Healy (2000)

Name of Cemetery and also known as	Number of burials	Acres	Condition	Date started or earliest known burial	Township	Range	Section

ARNECKE, FREDERIC

A   0.01   ?   12 Mar 1908   ?   ?   ?

Frederic Arnecke, aged 82 years, is reported buried in a lone grave "northeast of Antone." (Not shown on Antone 1992 USGS Quad. map.)

CALEB

B   1   5   1888-1959   T12S R23E   S14

Go 13.75 miles east of Mitchell on the Ochoco Highway (U.S. Hwy. 26) to the junction with Buck Point Road on the right (south). At this junction turn left (north) off of U.S. Hwy. 26 onto a dirt road. Cross Mountain Creek by fording and then turn left again (west) for 0.5 of a mile to the cemetery. A 1992 map of Wheeler County published by Pittmon Maps shows this cemetery. (Frog Hollow 1990 USGS Quad. map.)

CAMP WATSON

A   0.1   2   1864-1869   T12S R23E   S36

Leave Ochoco Highway (U.S. Hwy. 26) on Antone Road, going southeasterly 1.7 miles. Turn right (south) onto the road to Camp Watson. At 3.2 miles turn right onto a road; the site of Camp Watson is at 3.75 miles. A track leads ahead; go 0.25 of a mile. The cemetery is then due south about 250 feet up a slope in the timber. The camp was named for Lieutenant Stephen Watson who, with a detachment of 26 men, attacked a band of Paulina's men who were ready for them. Watson, two other soldiers and two scouts were killed 18 May 1864. The soldiers' bodies were brought here for burial about 1866 and the place was called Camp Watson. Lieutenant Watson's body was sent to Fort Vancouver for reburial and by the time the army abandoned Camp Watson on 24 May 1869, 6 soldiers were buried here plus an unknown number of civilians. In 1932, marble markers were erected for the soldiers and a marker for Lieutenant Watson, who is not here. (Derr Meadows 1966-85 USGS Quad. map.)

CARROLL FAMILY
AKA: 1. PAINTED HILLS

A   0.2   ?   1870   T10S R21E   S32

Located 5.2 miles northwest of Ochoco Highway (U.S. Hwy. 26) at Milepost 62.6 and on Bridge Creek Road. The cemetery is on the right

Name of Cemetery and also known as	Number of burials	Acres	Condition	Date started or earliest known burial	Township	Range	Section

(east) side of the road on a bench, about 0.5 of a mile short of the road junction to the Painted Hills. (Sutton Mtn. 1987 USGS Quad. map.)

CHAMBERS, JAMES W.

| A | 0.01 | ? | 11 July 1879 | T6S | R21E | S22 |

A single grave is located about 4 miles north of Fossil. Take the John Day Highway (OR. Hwy. 19) north out of Fossil and turn right (northeast) onto the old alignment, now called Hoover Creek Road. At the threeway junction turn right (east) and drive another 0.25 of a mile. The grave is on the left (north), on a knoll above Hoover Creek Valley. Chambers, a nephew of President Andrew Jackson, was the first white settler in the Fossil area in 1869 or 1870. (Fossil North 1970 USGS Quad. map.)

CHINESE HERDSMAN

| A | 0.01 | ? | 1880'S | T10S | R21E | ? |

A member of the Carroll family reported in 1996 that family tradition holds that a Chinese sheepherder was killed by a bear while employed by the family. His remains were buried at the site on Summit Meadow on Sutton Mountain. (Not shown on Sutton Mtn. 1987 USGS Quad. map.)

FOPIANO
AKA: 1. FOPPIANO
2. WATERMAN FLAT

| A | 0.25 | ? | May 1885-1954 | T11S | R23E | S22 |

Leave Ochoco Highway (U.S. Hwy. 26) at Milepost 75.2 on Parrish Creek Road. Go northeasterly 6.5 miles to the ranch on the right side of the road. Continue another 0.16 of a mile to a driveway on the left (northwest); go 0.55 of a mile on this driveway to the junction with a track on the left (southwest). The cemetery is another 0.27 of a mile by this track. NOTE: USGS spells the family name as Fopiano. (Frog Hollow 1990 USGS Quad. map.)

HAYSTACK

| B | 1.6 | 2 | 1901 | T8S | R25E | S16 |

Go east of Spray on OR. Hwy. 19 to the junction with the highway to Heppner (OR. Hwy. 207). Turn left (north) onto OR. Hwy.

207 and go 4.7 miles to the crossing of Haystack Creek. Very soon after that is Milepost 36. At about Milepost 36.2 (0.34 of a mile north of Haystack Creek) is a road on the left (west), off of OR. Hwy. 207. Go on that road almost straight west for 2.1 miles to the cemetery. The land was donated by William Gates. (Whitetail Butte 1990 USGS Quad. map.)

I.O.O.F. [FOSSIL]   C   9.3   2   1881   T7S   R21E   S4

This is on Township 6 South, Range 21 East, Section 33 and Township 7 South, Range 21 East, Section 4. Located at the south edge of Fossil on the east side of OR. Hwy 218. There are 148 known markers (1973), with July 1881 being the earliest identified marker. {1 September 2000} (Fossil South 1987 USGS Quad. map.)

KENNEDY GRAVE   A   0.01   ?   ?   T13S R25E   ?

Perhaps located in Section 14 in Day Basin. This area is southwest of Dayville in Grant County and southeast of Antone in Wheeler County and is difficult to access. Leave U.S. Hwy. 26 about 6 miles west of Dayville and take the Cottonwood Creek Road to the south and upstream. At about another 6 miles and at the south edge of Cottonwood Basin take the Day Basin Road to the right (west) which crosses into Wheeler County. About 3 miles from Cottonwood Creek Road is the Day Basin. The grave is presumabley somewhere in this vicinity. In 1978 it was reportedly along Day Creek on the Carl Shirley Ranch. To confuse the issue still further a Pittmon 1992 map of Wheeler County shows an unnamed cemetery in Township 13 South, Range 25 East, Section 16 on the left bank of East Birch Creek about 2 miles west as the crow flies from Day Basin. Wait! Still more confusion! The Pittmon map shows two separate Day Basins, one along Birch Creek and the other where the USGS Quad. map shows Day Basin. The hapless compiler is simply left guessing. (No grave is shown on Day Basin 1972-85 USGS Quad. map)

Name of Cemetery and also known as | Number of burials | Acres | Condition | Date started or earliest known burial | Township | Range | Section

MASONIC [FOSSIL]
AKA: 1. FOSSIL [OLD]

B   9.3   2   1881   T6S R21E   S33
In Fossil go past the High School on "D"
Street, which is the road to Black Butte.
Turn left (north), up a draw, for 0.25 of a
mile to the cemetery. There are 75 known
markers (1970), with 1881 being the earliest
date. (Fossil North 1970 USGS Quad. map.)

MITCHELL, LOWER
AKA: 1. I.O.O.F.
     2. WEST

C   3   2   1886   T11S R21E   S35
Located just west of Mitchell. Access is off
of Ochoco Highway (U.S. Hwy. 26) on a road
nearly parallel to the highway. The cemetery
is on a hill on the south side of the
highway. Go 0.5 of a mile west from the main
road junction in Mitchell to the cemetery.
(Mitchell 1988 USGS Quad. map.)

MITCHELL, UPPER
AKA: 1. MITCHELL
     [NEW]

B   0.5   2   ?   T12S R21E   S1
This is in Range 21 East, Section 1 and Range
22 East and Section 6. Located just east of
Mitchell. Turn right (south) off of Ochoco
Highway (U.S. Hwy. 26) onto Upper Bridge
Creek Road, cross Keyes Creek, and at 0.32 of
a mile turn left uphill and double back 0.16
of a mile to the cemetery. (Mitchell 1988
USGS Quad. map.)

RICHMOND

B   0.7   3   1881   T10S R23E   S6
Located 17.6 miles northeast of Mitchell via
OR. Hwy. 207. Turn right (east) off of OR.
Hwy. 207, crossing Tamarack Creek, 0.17 of a
mile to a fork. Turn right (south) 500 feet
to the church and cemetery. (Toney Butte
1988 USGS Quad. map.)

ROWLEY

?   0.2   ?   ?   T7S R19E   S35
Located near Lower Pine Creek, off of OR.
Hwy. 218, east of Clarno on the highway to
Fossil. Go on OR. Hwy. 218 0.6 of a mile
east of the entrance to Camp Hancock. The
cemetery is on the right (south), across Pine
Creek on Lee Ranch driveway, 0.25 of a mile
from the highway. This cemetery is referred
to as Rowley, 16 miles southwest of Fossil.

Name of Cemetery and also known as	Number of burials	Acres	Condition	Date started or earliest known burial	Township	Range	Section

See Wheeler County Death Certificate #16 for Linton Saltenstall, died 12 November 1916. (Clarno 1988 USGS Quad. map.)

SPANISH GULCH
AKA: 1. ANTONE

A 0.2 5 1878-1915 T13S R25E S6
Located 2.5 miles east of Antone, in Spanish Gulch, on the old Owens Homestead (1970). It is about 100 feet north of Antone Road, on the left side of the road. There are 11 known graves. (Antone 1992 USGS Quad. map.)

SPRAY

B 1.2 3 **May 1885** T8S R24E S35
Located 1.25 miles southwest of Spray. Take Parrish Creek Road for 1 mile to a driveway, turn right, cross a gulch and go up a low ridge for 0.25 of a mile to the cemetery. (Spray 1990 USGS Quad. map.)

SPRAY [OLD]

? ? ? ? T8S R24E S36
Now located within the city limits of Spray. This cemetery was on the left (west) side of Kahler Basin Road, 0.2 of a mile northwest of its junction with the John Day Highway (OR. Hwy. 19). This cemetery was noted on a field log dated 3 Aug. 1936, taken by a State Highway Department crew. It has presumably been superseded by the newer Spray Cemetery a mile from town. (Not shown on Spray 1990 USGS Quad. map.)

TONEY

A 0.1 ? **After 1870** T11S R22E S3
Go 7 miles north of Mitchell on OR. Hwy. 207 to the old Frizzell Ranch, then 0.85 of a mile to the right (east). The cemetery is on the left (north), 100 yards off of the road. (Toney Butte 1988 USGS Quad. map.)

TWICKENHAM

? 0.1 ? ? T9S R21E S22
Located 2.4 miles north of Twickenham near Rowe Creek. Go north on North Twickenham Road formerly Rowe Creek Road, from Twickenham Bridge, for 3 miles to Rowe Creek Bridge. The cemetery is on the right

Name of Cemetery and also known as	Number of burials	Acres	Condition	Date started or earliest known burial	Township	Range	Section

(northeast), 500 yards behind a small butte. There is no access road. (Rowe Creek 1987 USGS Quad. map.)

UNKNOWN   ?   0.1   ?   ?   T7S R21E   S31

Go 7.6 miles south of Fossil on the Shaniko-Fossil Highway (OR. Hwy. 218) at Milepost 34, then turn left (east) on Pine Creek Road for 1 mile. The cemetery is on the left (north) about 200 feet off of the road. (Porcupine Butte 1988 USGS Quad. map.)

UNKNOWN   ?   0.1   ?   ?   T10S R22E   S32

Located about halfway between Mitchell and Richmond. Go north from Mitchell on OR. Hwy. 207, about 0.7 of a mile short of the junction with South Twickenham Road formerly Girds Creek Road there is a gravel pit on the east side of OR. Hwy. 207. The cemetery is due south of the gravel pit, 0.2 of a mile across Girds Creek. (Toney Butte 1988 USGS Quad. map.)

WATERMAN, MARY E.   A   0.01   ?   11 Sept. 1884 T13S R24E   S2

A lone grave at Antone is located on the east side of Antone Road, at the junction with a road to the west and 7.25 miles south from the junction of Antone Road with the Ochoco Highway (U.S. Hwy. 26). (Antone 1992 USGS Quad. map.)

WEST BRANCH   B   1.5   2   ?   T12S R20E   S15

Go 10 miles west of Mitchell on Ochoco Highway (U.S. Hwy. 26.) at Milepost 56.9. Turn left (south) onto West Branch Road. Go 2.9 miles on West Branch Road, then turn left (east) onto the cemetery access road. It doubles back for a mile to the cemetery which is on a promontory, 100-200 yards from the road. (Lawson Mtn. 1968-85 USGS Quad. map.)

WINLOCK   B   1.2   3   Sept. 1898 T7S R24E   S31

Located southeast of Fossil. Go 0.75 of a mile west of Winlock. Turn right (north)

Name of Cemetery and also known as	Number of burials	Acres	Condition	Date started or earliest known burial	Township	Range	Section

onto Notch Road and go another 0.25 of a mile to the cemetery. There are 39 known graves (1970). (Wheeler Point 1990 USGS Quad. map.)

WOODWARD FAMILY
AKA: 1. GODBOLD, ELLIS
ROBERT

? ? ? ? ? ? ?

There was an obituary in the Salem Statesman-Journal on 1 June 2000. It reported the death of Ellis Robert Godbold, born 18 August 1909, died 29 May 2000. He had resided his last years in Salem. Interment was to be at Woodward Family Cemetery in Mitchell. The compiler was told that this was a private family burial ground somewhere out of Mitchell in Wheeler County.

I.O.O.F. [Fossil]
Janice M. Healy (2000)

I.O.O.F. [Fossil]
Janice M. Healy (2000)

ANTONE see **SPANISH GULCH**	WHEELER CO.	T13S	R25E	S6
ARNECKE, FREDERIC	WHEELER CO.	?	?	?
CALEB	WHEELER CO.	T12S	R23E	S14
CAMP WATSON	WHEELER CO.	T12S	R23E	S36
CARROLL FAMILY	WHEELER CO.	T10S	R21E	S32
CARROLL FAMILY see **CHINESE HERDSMAN**				
	WHEELER CO.	T10S	R21E	?
CHAMBERS, JAMES W.	WHEELER CO.	T6S	R21E	S22
CHINESE HERDSMAN	WHEELER CO.	T10S	R21E	?
FOPIANO	WHEELER CO.	T11S	R23E	S22
FOPPIANO see **FOPIANO**	WHEELER CO.	T11S	R23E	S22
FOSSIL [OLD] see **MASONIC [FOSSIL]**				
	WHEELER CO.	T6S	R21E	S33
FRIZZELL RANCH see **TONEY**	WHEELER CO.	T11S	R22E	S3
GATES, WILLIAM see **HAYSTACK**	WHEELER CO.	T8S	R25E	S16
HAYSTACK	WHEELER CO.	T8S	R25E	S16
I.O.O.F. see **MITCHELL, LOWER**	WHEELER CO.	T11S	R21E	S35
I.O.O.F. [FOSSIL]	WHEELER CO.	T7S	R21E	S4
JACKSON, PRESIDENT ANDREW see **CHAMBERS, JAMES W.**				
	WHEELER CO.	T6S	R21E	S22
KENNEDY GRAVE	WHEELER CO.	T13S	R25E	?
LEE RANCH see **ROWLEY**	WHEELER CO.	T7S	R19E	S35
MASONIC [FOSSIL]	WHEELER CO.	T6S	R21E	S33
MITCHELL [NEW] see **MITCHELL, UPPER**				
	WHEELER CO.	T12S	R21E	S1
MITCHELL, LOWER	WHEELER CO.	T11S	R21E	S35
MITCHELL, UPPER	WHEELER CO.	T12S	R21E	S1
OWENS HOMESTEAD see **SPANISH GULCH**				
	WHEELER CO.	T13S	R25E	S6
PAINTED HILLS see **CARROLL FAMILY**				
	WHEELER CO.	T10S	R21E	S32
RICHMOND	WHEELER CO.	T10S	R23E	S6
ROWLEY	WHEELER CO.	T7S	R19E	S35
SALTENSTALL, LINTON see **ROWLEY**	WHEELER CO.	T7S	R19E	S35
SHIRLEY RANCH, CARL see **KENNEDY GRAVE**				
	WHEELER CO.	T13S	R25E	?
SPANISH GULCH	WHEELER CO.	T13S	R25E	S6
SPRAY	WHEELER CO.	T8S	R24E	S35
SPRAY [OLD]	WHEELER CO.	T8S	R24E	S36
SUMMIT MEADOW see **CHINESE HERDSMAN**				
	WHEELER CO.	T10S	R21E	?
SUTTON MOUNTAIN see **CHINESE HERDSMAN**				
	WHEELER CO.	T10S	R21E	?
TONEY	WHEELER CO.	T11S	R22E	S3
TWICKENHAM	WHEELER CO.	T9S	R21E	S22
UNKNOWN	WHEELER CO.	T7S	R21E	S31
UNKNOWN	WHEELER CO.	T10S	R22E	S32
WATERMAN FLAT see **FOPIANO**	WHEELER CO.	T11S	R23E	S22
WATERMAN, MARY E.	WHEELER CO.	T13S	R24E	S2
WATSON, LIEUTENANT STEPHEN see **CAMP WATSON**				
	WHEELER CO.	T12S	R23E	S36
WEST see **MITCHELL, LOWER**	WHEELER CO.	T11S	R21E	S35

WEST BRANCH	WHEELER CO.	T12S	R20E	S15
WINLOCK	WHEELER CO.	T7S	R24E	S31
WOODWARD FAMILY	WHEELER CO.	?	?	?

I.O.O.F. [Fossil]
Ruth C. Bishop (2000)

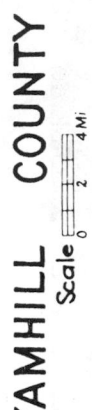

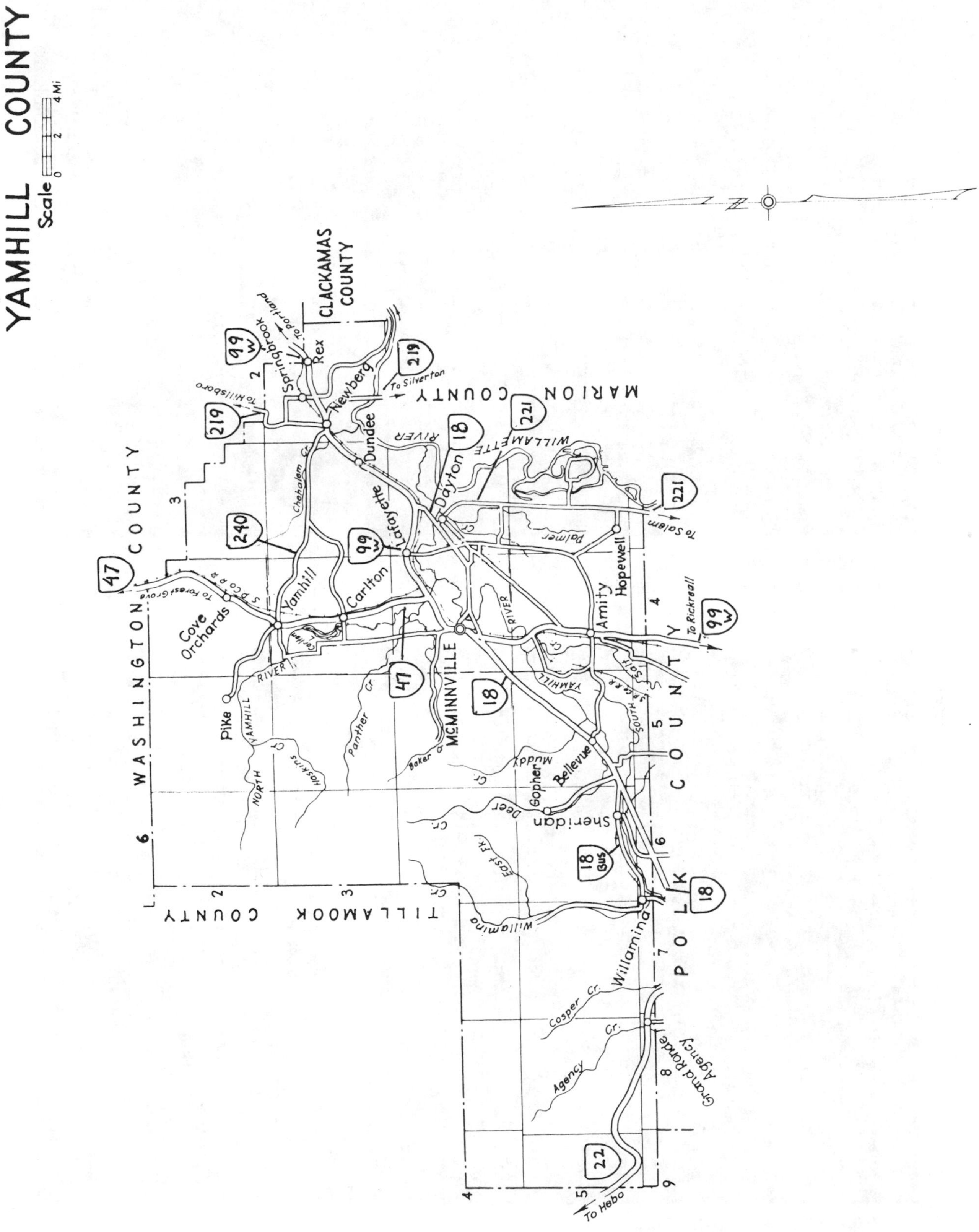
YAMHILL COUNTY
Scale
WASHINGTON COUNTY
CLACKAMAS COUNTY
MARION COUNTY
POLK COUNTY
TILLAMOOK COUNTY
McMINNVILLE
Newberg
Dundee
Dayton
Lafayette
Carlton
Yamhill
Cove Orchards
Pike
Amity
Hopewell
Bellevue
Gopher
Sheridan
Willamina
Grand Ronde Agency
Rex
Springbrook
To Portland
To Hillsboro
To Silverton
To Salem
To Rickreall
To Forest Grove
To Hebo
WILLAMETTE RIVER
YAMHILL RIVER

Yamhill-Carlton
Dean H. Byrd (1990)

Valley View Memorial Park
Dean H. Byrd (1989)

Area: 718 square miles
Population (1998): 82,085
County seat: McMinnville, Population: 22,880
County established: 5 July 1843

Yamhill County was one of the Willamette Valley counties that attracted white settlers desiring farmlands. The earliest cemetery for the public of which the compiler is aware is Brookside in the present town of Dayton. It was established in 1847. By the mid-1850's there were a number of public cemeteries.

Brookside
Dean H. Byrd (1989)

Masonic [McMinnvile]
Dean H. Byrd (1994)

Pike
Dean H. Byrd (1991)

Name of Cemetery and also known as	Number of burials	Acres	Condition	Date started or earliest known burial	Township	Range	Section

AGEE FAMILY
AKA: 1. GOPHER
VALLEY

B 1 3 1883-1941 T4S R6W S36
Located northeast of Sheridan, in Gopher Valley. Leave OR. Hwy. 18, between Sheridan and Bellevue, and go north on Gopher Valley Road. Dupee Valley Road takes off of Gopher Valley Road to the right and back (south) 7.3 miles from OR. Hwy. 18. At this intersection the cemetery is 0.5 of a mile northwest across Gopher Creek and on a hillside. There is no ready access. The location of the cemetery is on the Isaac Agee D.L.C. #37, OC #2265. The D.A.R. survey of Aug. 1951 recorded 18 Agees and 5 Smiths buried here; only one stone was standing upright, that of Cordelia, wife of Isaac, who died Dec. 1893. This is near the Hussey Family Cemetery. NOTE: This site is on private property. (Stony Mountain 1979-92 USGS Quad. map.)

AMITY

D 4 1 1854 T5S R4W S29
Located at the west end of the town of Amity. Leave OR. Hwy. 99W and go west on the highway towards Bellevue. The cemetery is on the left (south) side of the road and on the opposite side is a city park. This is on the John Watt D.L.C. #75, OC #3325. {19 January 1989 and 22 June 1989} (Amity 1957-93 USGS Quad. map.)

BARNUM, NATHAN G.

A 0.01 ? 13 Nov 1913 T2S R4W ?
He was buried on the farm 5 miles north of the town of Yamhill. Death Certificate #4003 reports that Nathan G. Barnum was born 19 May 1837, died 13 November 1913 and was single. (Not shown on Gaston 1956-70 USGS Quad. map.)

BROOKSIDE
AKA: 1. CREEK SIDE
2. DAYTON

C 1.33 2 1847 T4S R3W S17
Located in Dayton, at the south end of town. Access is immediately adjacent to, but not directly connected to OR. Hwy. 221 leading south to Salem. The cemetery is next to the highway bridge over Palmer Creek. Joel Palmer donated the land for 2 grandchildren buried here. It is on the Andrew and Sarah E. Smith D.L.C. #80, OC #258. {12 January 1989} (Dayton 1957-92 USGS Quad. map.)

Name of Cemetery and also known as	Number of burials	Acres	Condition	Date started or earliest known burial	Township	Range	Section

BUCK HOLLOW
AKA: 1. GRUB HOLLOW
2. UPPER WILLAMINA
3. WILLAMINA

C 3.3 2 1866 T5S R7W S13

This cemetery is north from Willamina up Willamina Creek Road. Go 5.4 miles from OR. Hwy. 18 Bus., in Willamina, to the junction with Buck Hollow Road. Then turn right (east) onto Buck Hollow Road and go about 0.25 of a mile to the cemetery on the right. This cemetery is close to Buck Hollow Road but it is difficult to see through the trees. It is partly in the Lucien B. Frazer D.L.C. #73, OC #4894. This cemetery was dedicated on 5 July 1917. NOTE: Although sometimes called Willamina Cemetery this must not be confused with the actual Willamina Cemetery which is located in the town of Willamina, Polk County. {18 June 1990} (Stony Mountain 1979-92 USGS Quad. map.)

BURFORD, WILLIAM

A 0.01 ? 2 Sep 1854 T5S R7W S24

The Memorial Day issue of the *McMinnville News-Register*, 1954 tells the details of this lone burial. It is located on a knoll surrounded by a field on the Mendenhall Farm (1954). Drive 2.5 or 3 miles north out of Willamina on the Willamina Creek Road to the junction with Tindle Creek Road. Turn left onto Tindle Creek Road and cross the creek. The grave is perhaps 1.5 miles north of Tindle Creek Road on private property. In September 1854 several children of Hezekiah Burford were playing in their father's wagon when they noticed a group of Indians approaching. Frightened, the children fled into the house. Two year-old William caught his head between the wagon wheel spokes and strangled. The professionally carved granite monument inscribed with a typical flying dove says "William R.-son of H. and L. Burfords, born 1852, died September 1854." The Burfords moved away a few years later. Located on the Hezekiah Burford D.L.C. #39, OC #2799. (Not shown on Sheridan 1956-70 or Grand Ronde 1979 USGS Quad. maps.)

CARSON, ALEXANDER

A 0.01 ? April 1836 T3S R4W S9

A brother of Christopher "Kit" Carson, Alexander was usually known as Alec. While camping in April or May 1836, on what was

Name of Cemetery and also known as	Number of burials	Acres	Condition	Date started or earliest known burial	Township	Range	Section

later called Alecs Butte, he was shot and killed (while asleep) by an Indian companion. Alecs Butte lies between OR. Hwy. 47 and the North Yamhill River, between the towns of Yamhill and Carlton. There was a rectangular cairn on the butte in 1965. (Carlton 1957-92 USGS Quad. map.)

CATE, J. D.

A   0.01   ?   14 March 1856 T5S R6W   S4
The burial of a 49 year-old man is on private property, perhaps off of the now-impassable portion of Smithville Road and a mile or so east of the Highland Cemetery. (Not shown on Stony Mountain 1979-92 USGS Quad. map.)

DEER CREEK
AKA: 1. THARP

B   1   4   1858   T5S R5W   S28
Located near Bellevue, which is on OR. Hwy. 18, northeast of Sheridan, southwest of McMinnville, and west of Amity. Leave Bellevue and go east on Bellevue-Hopewell Highway towards Amity. At about 0.1 of a mile turn right (south) onto Deer Creek Flats Road and go about 0.75 of a mile to the bridge over Deer Creek. The cemetery is on the right, up a rise in the trees and not visible from the road. Access is on foot, about 100 yards. 1954 was the latest marked burial found in May, 1989 by the compiler. This is on the Joseph Danforth D.L.C. #57, OC #3102. {11 May 1989} (Ballston 1956-70 USGS Quad. map.)

DOLPH

A   ?   5   ?   T5S R9W   S27
This is in the southwest quarter of section 27. The locale of Dolph is in Tillamook County, at the junction of Three Rivers Highway (OR. Hwy. 22) and Nestucca Highway. However, a Metsker map of this township, dated May 1957, shows a cemetery just inside Yamhill County. It is shown north of OR. Hwy. 22 within the Siuslaw National Forest and about 0.5 of a mile from Dolph as the crow flies. Although this is not on the USGS Quad. map, the cemetery would be on a ridge alongside a 4-wheel drive road serving the

Name of Cemetery and also known as	Number of burials	Acres	Condition	Date started or earliest known burial	Township	Range	Section

powerline. Reportedly there are about a dozen graves but only 2 or 3 could be located in 1994. (Not shown on Dolph 1985 USGS Quad. map.)

DUNDEE PIONEER
AKA: 1. DUNDEE
     MEMORIAL
    2. SHUCK

D 10 2 ? T3S R3W S26
Located in Dundee, 1 mile northwest of OR. Hwy. 99W, on a ridgetop. Take Southwest 5th Street by Dundee School, then turn right on Southwest Upland Drive, left on Southwest Dogwood Drive and left on North Viewmont to the cemetery. This is on the Jacob Shuck D.L.C. #57, OC #2335. {5 June 1989} (Dundee 1956-93 USGS Quad. map.)

EBENEZER CHAPEL
AKA: 1. ODELL

D 0.6 5 18 Jan 1848 T5S R3W S7
Located about 3.3 miles north of Hopewell on the left (west) side of Webfoot Road, just before the road descends to cross Holdridge Creek. The cemetery is in thick woods and brush. Ebenezer Chapel was built in 1857 and the present chapel building was dedicated on 5 Sept. 1926. It has been abandoned for some years and has been used for hay storage. There are 104 known burials and 59 unknown burials (Oct 1934). This is on the John Odell D.L.C. #45, OC #913. {14 Sept. 1989} (Dayton 1957-92 USGS Quad. map.)

EVERGREEN MEMORIAL PARK

E 50 1 1922 T4S R4W S10
Located at the northeast end of McMinnville, at the junction of OR. Hwy. 99W and OR. Hwy. 47. It is on the north side of OR. Hwy. 99W and the east side of OR. Hwy. 47. The St. James Cemetery is on the opposite side of OR. Hwy. 47. This is on the Joseph R. Young D.L.C. #68, OC #1510. {29 April 1991} (McMinnville 1957-92 USGS Quad. map.)

FENDALL-ROGERS FAMILY
AKA: 1. FENDALL FAMILY
    2. ROGERS FAMILY
    3. WEST CHEHALEM

A ? 3 1848 T3S R3W S4
Located 7 miles northwest of Newberg. Leave North Valley Road and turn right (north) on Lewis Rogers Lane. Go 0.5 of a mile on Lewis Rogers Road. The cemetery is on the left, 300 feet behind the Fendall house. This is on the Lewis Rogers D.L.C. #39, OC #2740.

Name of Cemetery and also known as	Number of burials	Acres	Condition	Date started or earliest known burial	Township	Range	Section

The D.A.R. survey found 11 graves in Oct. 1934. NOTE: This site is on private property. (Not shown on Dundee 1956-93 USGS Quad. map.)

FERNWOOD PIONEER
AKA: 1. EVEREST
2. FERNWOOD

C 2 2 11 Oct. 1880 T3S R2W S20

This is at the far south end of Everest Street, in the southeast part of Newberg. Everest Street first passes through the Friends Cemetery, and then G.A.R. Cemetery before reaching Fernwood Cemetery. Jane Everest, who died 11 Oct. 1880, wife of Richard, was the first burial. Richard Everest died 29 Aug. 1882; on his own deathbed he donated land for the cemetery. This is on the Richard Everest D.L.C. #52, OC #3971. {4 August 1989} (Newberg 1961-85 USGS Quad. map.)

FRIENDS
AKA: 1. FREE METHODIST CHURCH
2. ROSELAWN

E 15 2 1892 T3S R2W S20

Located in Newberg. Leave East 1st Street (OR. Hwy. 219), go south on Everest Street and enter the cemetery gates. Friends Cemetery is the first and the largest of 3 cemeteries. Next is the G.A.R. Cemetery and at the end of the street is Fernwood Cemetery. This is on the Richard Everest D.L.C. #52, OC #3971. {18 August 1989} (Newberg 1961-85 USGS Quad. map.)

G.A.R. [GRAND ARMY OF THE REPUBLIC]
AKA: 1. KIRKPATRICK POST GRAND ARMY OF THE REPUBLIC

C 2 2 10 May 1892 T3S R2W S20

Located in Newberg. Leave East 1st Street (OR. Hwy. 219), go south on Everest Street and enter the cemetery gates. Friends Cemetery is the first and largest of the 3 cemeteries. Next is the G.A.R. Cemetery and at the end of the street is Fernwood Cemetery. This is on the Richard Everest D.L.C. #52, OC #3971. {4 August 1989} (Newberg 1961-85 USGS Quad. map.)

GIBBS
AKA: 1. CHEHALEM MOUNTAIN
2. DAVID'S

B 1.6 2 1852 T3S R2W S3

Leave Newberg, going north on OR. Hwy. 219 towards Hillsboro. Turn right (east), on Bell Road and follow Bell Road for about 2.75 miles. Turn hard left (north) on Leander

Name of Cemetery and also known as	Number of burials	Acres	Condition	Date started or earliest known burial	Township	Range	Section

Road. The cemetery is about 0.75 of a mile distant on the right (east), at the summit of Chehalem Mountain and almost to the Washington County Line. {22 June 1988} (Newberg 1961-85 USGS Quad. map.)

GOODRICH FAMILY
AKA: 1. GOODRICH--
       WORDEN
    2. WORDEN FAMILY

B   0.2   2   1856   T4S R3W   S21
This family cemetery adjoins the northwest corner of the Odd Fellows Cemetery which was established in 1890. Access is through the Odd Fellows Cemetery. The Goodrich Family Cemetery is not fenced off separately from the Odd Fellows Cemetery. This is on the Carney and Peggy T. Goodrich D.L.C. #49, OC #203. He died 7 Dec. 1860. NOTE: Mr. Goodrich's name is spelled "Carmy" on his monument, but Metsker spells it as "Carney" on their maps. {12 January 1989} (Dayton 1957-92 USGS Quad. map.)

GRAVES FAMILY

A   0.01 ? 1848-1859 T5S R6W   S27
Mr. Graves, an 87-year old descendant, pointed out the burial sites to the compiler from the west edge of the Sheridan Masonic Cemetery. It is about 0.5 of a mile distant, as the crow flies, and up the slope behind the house at the end of Richard Street. Willamina Lumber Company has deeded a 25-foot square plot under the oak trees and the family is fencing it. This is on the James B. Graves D.L.C. #42, OC #3098, just west of Sheridan. It is the burial site of J. B. Graves wife, Dina or Diana, and baby who died 23 March 1848. Also buried was one of their sons, J. M., who died 15 April 1859, age 29. Most of the family are buried in Sheridan Masonic Cemetery. NOTE: This site is on private property. (Not shown on the Sheridan 1956-70 USGS Quad. map.)

GREENCREST MEMORIAL PARK
AKA: 1. GREEN CREST
       MEMORIAL PARK

E 15   1   1945   T5S R6W   S35
Located just outside the south city limits of Sheridan. Leave Sheridan on Bridge Street (OR. Hwy. 18 Bus.), cross the South Yamhill River and the Salmon River Highway (OR. Hwy. 18) on an overcrossing. The cemetery is just beyond and on the left, with Ballston Road

Name of Cemetery and also known as	Number of burials	Acres	Condition	Date started or earliest known burial	Township	Range	Section

continuing ahead. Interchange legs give access to and from Salmon River Highway also. This is on the Charles B. Graves D.L.C. #57, OC #1564. A signboard on the gate says: Greencrest Memorial Park but obituaries use also Green Crest Memorial Park. {2 October 1989} (Sheridan 1956-70 USGS Quad. map.)

HAPPY VALLEY
AKA: 1. BAKER CREEK
     2. HAPPY HOLLOW

B   1   3   1880-1981   T4S R5W   S10
From the north end of McMinnville on Baker Street, turn left (west) onto Baker Creek Road. Go past the golf course on Baker Creek Road and at 4.8 miles turn right (north) onto High Heaven Road. Go another 0.9 of a mile to a driveway, up slope on the left (west), to the cemetery about 0.25 of a mile. The south border of the cemetery borders the northwest corner of the John F. Johnson D.L.C. #54, OC #2039. The cemetery was deeded on 18 October 1886. {12 April 1991} (Muddy Valley 1979-92 USGS Quad. map.)

HEMBREE FAMILY

A   2.2   ?   1854-1919   T3S R4W   S25
Located on the southeast part of Absalom J. Hembree D.L.C. #71, OC #115, 3 miles east of Carlton and 4 miles north of Lafayette. It is 0.16 of a mile north of Bayliss Road, on a knoll. The D.A.R. survey of Oct. 1948 described the cemetery as "a few rods square and with 7 graves," but the Yamhill County Assessors map indicates 2.2 acres is dedicated as a cemetery. NOTE: This site is on private property. (Not shown on Carlton 1957-92 USGS Quad. map.)

HERBER, LEO FERDINAND

A   ?   ?   13 May 1992 ?   ?   ?
Located southwesterly from Sheridan at 3825 Mill Creek Road. His obituary reports that he is buried on the Herber Homestead on Mill Creek Road. NOTE: This site is on private property. (Not shown on the Sheridan 1956-70 USGS Quad. map.)

HESS FAMILY

A   0.01   5   ?   T3S R2W   S8
The D.A.R. survey in June 1948 described this burial ground as "1 mile north of Newberg".

Name of Cemetery and also known as	Number of burials	Acres	Condition	Date started or earliest known burial	Township	Range	Section

It was then "Entirely overgrown with brush. No markers but several stones showing there were graves". The burial ground was one rod square, for 3 children of Tillman L. and Mary L. Hess, in the William T. Wallace D.L.C. #47, OC #3161. The burial ground was described 31 July 1882 as "near the north line of 40 acres sold by Mary L. Hess, widow". Perhaps this is somewhere near Aspen Way. NOTE: This site is on private property. (Not shown on Newberg 1961-85 USGS Quad. map.)

HIGHLAND
AKA: 1. HYLAND
     2. NEWELL

B 0.33 2 1865   T5S R6W   S5
Located about 7.5 miles northwest of Sheridan. Go west on Main Street (OR. Hwy. 18 Bus.) from Bridge Street for 1.6 mile and turn right (north) onto Rock Creek Road. Go through the mill area and past the junction of the road to the Delphian School, for 4.8 miles on Rock Creek Road, to the junction with Buck Hollow Road left. Incidentally, you are now 1.4 miles from Buck Hollow Cemetery, which is to the left (west). Continue northerly on Rock Creek Road for another 1.1 mile to the cemetery on the left (west). {13 March 1992} (Stony Mountain 1979-92 USGS Quad. map.)

HOLMES FAMILY
AKA: 1. HOLMES-McGEE
       FAMILY
     2. McGEE FAMILY
     3. SPIRIT
       MOUNTAIN

B 0.15 3 ?   T5S R8W   S36
Leave Three Rivers Highway (OR. Hwy. 22) at Grand Ronde Agency and go north on Grand Ronde Road for 1.3 miles. This is 200 yards past the junction with Spirit Mountain Road. Turn right (northeast) off of the county road and go uphill on a looping driveway, 0.3 of a mile to the cemetery. (Grand Ronde 1979 USGS Quad. map.)

HOPEWELL
AKA: 1. UNITED
       BRETHREN

D 4.6 2 1856   T5S R3W   S30
The locale of Hopewell is south of Dayton and Lafayette and east of Amity. The church and cemetery are about 0.5 of a mile northwest of Hopewell off of the left (west) side of the Bellevue-Hopewell Highway. The church is readily visible on the easternmost slope of the Eola Hills. The signboard says

| Name of Cemetery and also known as | Number of burials | Acres | Condition | Date started or earliest known burial | Township | Range | Section |

Hopewell Community Church. This is on the Rachel Matheny D.L.C. #66, OC #923. {10 August 1988} (Mission Bottom 1957-93 USGS Quad. map.)

HUSSEY FAMILY
AKA: 1. DOWNING
FAMILY
2. HUSSEY-YOCOM--
PETERSON
FAMILY
3. PETERSON
FAMILY
4. YOCOM
FAMILY

A   0.15   5   1857-1874   T5S   R6W   S1
Located northeast of Sheridan in Gopher Valley. Leave OR. Hwy. 18 between Sheridan and Bellevue, go north on Gopher Valley Road about 6 miles from OR. Hwy. 18 and 0.5 of a mile past the junction of the road on the left to Deer Creek County Park. The cemetery is on the right of Gopher Valley Road. This is on the Stephen Hussey D.L.C. # 51, OC #2928. D.A.R. survey of Dec. 1951 found 10 known burials, but only 1 stone standing upright. The Downings were reburied in Evergreen Memorial Park. Near Agee Family Cemetery. NOTE: 1. This site is on private property. 2. There is another Hussey Family Cemetery located in northern Polk County. See that article in the Polk County section of this book. (Stony Mountain 1979-92 USGS Quad. map.)

I.O.O.F. [DAYTON]
AKA: 1. ODD FELLOWS
[DAYTON]

D   2.6   2   1890   T4S   R3W   S21
Located just south of Dayton. Going south on OR. Hwy. 221 toward Salem, turn right (west) onto Thompson Lane. Go about 0.25 of a mile to the cemetery on the right. This cemetery is only about 0.5 of a mile from the Brookside Cemetery in Dayton. Bordering the northwest corner of the Odd Fellow Cemetery is the Goodrich Family Cemetery, which is older. This is on the Carney and Peggy T. Goodrich D.L.C. #49, OC #203. NOTE: The sign at this cemetery says "Odd Fellow". See Goodrich Family Cemetery. {12 January 1989} (Dayton 1957-92 USGS Quad. map.)

KIMSEY, ALVIS

A   0.01   ?   14 Sept. 1856 T5S R3W   S5
This is south of Dayton between Wallace Road (OR. Hwy. 221) and Webfoot Road and is evidently somewhere near the junction of Webfoot and Kimsey Roads. Presumably, most of the family burials were in the Ebenezer Chapel Cemetery nearby. This burial is on

Name of Cemetery and also known as	Number of burials	Acres	Condition	Date started or earliest known burial	Township	Range	Section

the Alvis Kimsey D.L.C. #43, OC #912; he was aged 40. NOTE: This site is on private property. (Not shown on Dayton 1957-92 USGS Quad. map.)

LAFAYETTE PIONEER
AKA: 1. I.O.O.F.

| | B | 1.7 | 2 | 1850 | T4S | R3W | S6 |

Located 1 mile from OR. Hwy. 99W, on the northeast edge of Lafayette. Leave the highway on Monroe Street and go north; turn right (east) on 7th, going past the school. Turn left (north) on Duniway and go the remaining 0.5 of a mile to the cemetery on the right. The grounds are fairly well kept but the cemetery has been very badly vandalized in the past. {23 May 1989} (Dundee 1956-93 USGS Quad. map.)

MALONE FAMILY

| | A | 0.1 | 2 | 1850 | T4S | R4W | S15 |

This small cemetery is at the northeastern end of McMinnville along OR. Hwy. 99W. Because of the heavy volume of traffic, it is best approached as if from Portland and heading towards downtown McMinnville. The cemetery is on the righthand side of the highway, marked by a flagpole and three large oak trees. Park in the Farmers Market parking. The small burial area is enclosed by a low wall with a pedestrian gate. There is a memorial plaque marking this sad remnant. A 1967 survey recorded 15 known burials but the plaque states that about 25 are believed buried here. The compiler found 5 markers, of which 3 were intact. It is on the Madison Malone D.L.C. #49, OC #106. (23 August 1994) (Not shown on McMinnville 1957-92 USGS Quad. map.)

MASONIC [LAFAYETTE]

| | C | 2.8 | 2 | 1855 | T4S | R4W | S1 |

From the west end of the town of Lafayette, turn right (north) off of OR. Hwy. 99W onto Mineral Springs Road and go 0.64 of a mile, turning hard left. By the cemetery signboard is a gated driveway which leads uphill to the cemetery. {23 May 1989 and 5 June 1989} (Carlton 1957-92 USGS Quad. map.)

Name of Cemetery and also known as	Number of burials	Acres	Condition	Date started or earliest known burial	Township	Range	Section

MASONIC [McMINNVILLE]

E 5 1 1853   T4S R4W   S19

This cemetery is located on Township 4 South, Range 4 West, Section 19 and Township 4 South, Range 5 West, Section 24. From OR. Hwy. 99W in downtown McMinnville, take West 2nd Street and go west about 1.5 miles to the intersection with Hill Road; turn right (north) and go about 0.4 of a mile, then turn left (west) into the cemetery. This is on the Solomon Beary D.L.C. #38 and #54, OC #953. {10 November 1989} (McMinnville 1957-92 USGS Quad. map.)

MASONIC [SHERIDAN]
AKA: 1. SHERIDAN MASONIC LODGE #64

D 4.9 2 1872   T5S R6W   S26

Leave Main Street (OR. Hwy. 18 Bus.) in Sheridan. Taking Lincoln Street to the north, turn left on Van Ostram Street; turn right on Northwest Evans Street and go up the hill toward the water tanks. The cemetery is on the left at Evans and Canyon Road. This is on the Absalom B. Faulconer D.L.C. #43, OC #2564. The Masonic Lodge #64 bought the cemetery 17 Oct. 1882. {29 September 1989} (Sheridan 1956-70 USGS Quad. map.)

McBRIDE
AKA: 1. WHITE CLOUD

C 1.88 2 1857   T3S R4W   S19

This cemetery is 2.5 miles west and 0.7 of a mile north of Carlton. Go west from OR. Hwy. 47 in Carlton on West Main Street which becomes Meadow Lake Road. Turn right (north) onto McBride Cemetery Road and go 0.4 of a mile, turning right (east) on Stout Road for 0.3 of a mile up the hill to the cemetery. The name White Cloud referred to a public school nearby which is now a private residence. This is on the Thomas and Ann McBride D.L.C. #57, OC #128. {24 Oct. 1990} (Carlton 1957-92 USGS Quad. map.)

McMINNVILLE [OLD]

? ? 7 ?   T4S R4W   S21

Turn to the right (east) off of Baker Street which is northbound OR. Hwy. 99W onto East 1st Street. Drive 5 or 6 blocks to Southeast Galloway Street on the right. The old cemetery covered a considerable area: along the righthand (south) side of East 1st Street to the west side of the railway; south to the

Name of Cemetery and also known as	Number of burials	Acres	Condition	Date started or earliest known burial	Township	Range	Section

edge of the bluff above Cozine Creek, including land on both sides of Southeast Washington Street; back north, including land on both sides of block-long Southeast Galloway Street. The area is now built over with houses. An undated map of the 1880's shows an outlined "burial ground" at this site when East 1st Street was "Fifth Street" and Southeast Galloway was "G Street"; what is now Southeast Washington Street was not then platted in this area. The railway, then the O.C.R.R., was present. An adjacent plat of the town of Lafayette shows the Court House in that town, as it was until 1889. McMinnville was founded in 1853. Presumably all or most of the graves were removed to the Masonic Cemetery 2 miles to the west. It is on the William T. and Sarah J. Newby D.L.C. #53, OC #104. (6 August 1994) (Not shown on McMinnville 1957-92 USGS Quad. map.)

MOORES VALLEY
AKA: 1. PUCKERVILLE
[?]

A ? ? ? T3S R5W S9

Located west of the town of Yamhill via Meadow Lake Road, in the vicinity of old Moores Valley School and on W. and R. Wirth property (1978). The school has been torn down. Take Hibbard Road (County Road #235) north from Meadow Lake Road for 0.5 of a mile. The grave is on the left (west), opposite the driveway to the farm. This is on the Marcia Shull, late Marcia Haley D.L.C. #49, OC #3972. NOTE: This site is on private property. (Fairdale 1979 USGS map.)

MORGAREIDGE FAMILY

A 0.21 3 1888 T4S R3W S30

This burial site is on a bluff on the west bank of Palmer Creek about 0.3 of a mile east of Lafayette Highway and north of Palmer Creek Road. This is on the Thomas L. Turner D.L.C. #55, OC #4117. The D.A.R. survey of Oct. 1934 found 5 graves. NOTE: This site is on private property. (Not shown on Dayton 1957-92 USGS Quad. map.)

MURRAY FAMILY

A ? ? 1896 T4S R5W S32

Located in the upper Muddy Valley, north of Bellevue and southwest of McMinnville, off of

Name of Cemetery and also known as	Number of burials	Acres	Condition	Date started or earliest known burial	Township	Range	Section

Eagle Point Road and west of its intersection with Masonville and Muddy Valley Road. The D.A.R. survey in 1948 reported this cemetery as a "small unfenced place at the edge of timber on the Jasper White farm." There are 4 known burials, including Charley Murray and another adult. Several others are probable, including children. There were no markers and no dates. A 1928 *Metsker Land Ownership Atlas* showed Murray land ownership on the western side of the Richard C. Combs D.L.C. #40, OC #3505. NOTE: This site is on private property. (Not shown on Muddy Valley 1979-92 USGS Quad. map.)

NELSON, CORA ALICE　　A　0.01　5　28 Oct 1863　T3S　R3W　S11

This was on the south side of what is now North Valley Road and just west of the junction with Stone Road, about 4 miles northwest of Newberg. The 1948 D.A.R. survey said that all trace of the grave was gone; it was near the farmhouse of Henry Bell. The infant daughter of Josiah C. Nelson and his second wife, Sarah C. Cummins, was buried on the Josiah C. Nelson D.L.C. #45, OC #2938. Cora Alice Nelson was born 27 January 1863. NOTE: This site is on private property. (Not shown on Dundee 1956-93 USGS Quad. map.)

NOBLE　　C　1　2　?　　　T3S　R3W　S3

This is about 5 miles northwest of Newberg. Go north on OR. Hwy. 219 uphill to the junction with North Valley Road. Turn left (west) off of OR. Hwy. 219 and go 3.1 miles on North Valley Road. Then turn right (north) onto Kings Grade Road and go 0.6 of a mile to the cemetery driveway on the left and up a knoll. This is on the Henry Noble D.L.C. #74, OC #3002. {8 June 1988} (Dundee 1956-93 USGS Quad. map.)

OAK GROVE
AKA:　1. DEWEY
　　　2. GUENTHER--
　　　　　PITMAN
　　　　　FAMILY
　　　3. PITMAN FAMILY

B　0.5　3　21 Jun 1892　T2S　R3W　S21

Located northwest of Newberg on Chehalem Mountain. Leave Newberg via OR. Hwy. 219 (North College Street). Turn left (west) onto North Valley Road, go 3.1 miles and then turn right (north) onto Kings Grade Road; go

Name of Cemetery and also known as	Number of burials	Acres	Condition	Date started or earliest known burial	Township	Range	Section

north on Kings Grade Road (past Noble Cemetery on the left) uphill for 3.6 miles to Bald Peak Road and turn left. Almost immediately, go left again, off of Bald Peak Road and onto Guenther Road, going down slope. Go 0.7 of a mile to a road junction of an unnamed road, turn left onto a lane and go 0.4 of a mile to the cemetery. The dedication of 1 acre-plus was recorded 23 Dec. 1893. Half of this is a steep timbered slope. {12 June 1989} (Laurelwood 1956-92 USGS Quad. map.)

OUR LADY OF GUADALUPE TRAPPIST ABBEY
AKA: 1. TRAPPIST ABBEY

A ? 1 1955 T3S R3W S29

Located 3.4 miles north of OR. Hwy. 99W at Lafayette. Take Bridge Street, which changes to Abbey Road, three miles to the north to 9200 Northeast Abbey Road. There are 12 burials here, on the Thomas Hubbard D.L.C. #52, OC #4521. {14 December 1994} (The Abbey is shown on the Dundee 1956-93 USGS Quad. map but not the burials.)

PIKE AND I.O.O.F.
AKA: 1. I.O.O.F. LODGE #56
2. MT. PLEASANT
3. MOUNTAIN BELL
4. OLD PIKE
5. PIKE

D 3.5 2 1854 T2S R5W S25

Leave OR. Hwy. 47 at the north edge of the town of Yamhill and take Pike Road to the northwest. At Milepost 3.94 take Hacker Road to the right (north). Then go 0.25 of a mile to the cemetery driveway on the left (west). This is on the William and Henrietta Dodson D.L.C. #42, OC #2866. The United Brethren Church adjoined the cemetery 1889-1958. There were 575 known graves (Nov. 1974). NOTE: Pike and I.O.O.F. were originally two separate but adjoining cemeteries. {26 September 1991} (Fairdale 1979 USGS Quad. map.)

REST HAVEN MEMORIAL PARK

? ? ? 1942 T6S R6W S3

This ephemeral cemetery just south of Sheridan was scarcely more than a mile southwest of Greencrest Memorial Park. Only one burial was made, and it was disinterred and removed to Greencrest after the latter was opened in 1945. It was located in the William Chapman D.L.C. #86, OC #2837. (Not shown on Sheridan 1956-70 USGS Quad. map.)

Name of Cemetery and also known as	Number of burials	Acres	Condition	Date started or earliest known burial	Township	Range	Section

ST. JAMES

D ? 1 ? T4S R4W S10

This Catholic cemetery is at the northeast edge of McMinnville. It is at the junction of OR. Hwy. 99W and OR. Hwy. 47, on the west side of OR. Hwy. 47, between the highway and the North Yamhill River; on the north side of OR. Hwy. 99W; opposite Evergreen Memorial Park, which is on the east side of OR. Hwy. 47. This is on the Joseph R. Young D.L.C. #68, OC #1510. {12 April 1991} (McMinnville 1957-92 USGS Quad. map.)

ST. PATRICK
AKA: 1. ST. JOE

B 10 5 1871-1895 T5S R5W S4

Located on the west side of Muddy Valley Road, 3.3 miles north of OR. Hwy. 18 at Bellevue. It is on the left (west) side of Muddy Valley Road, on a low hillside facing south and about 200 feet from the road. This is on the site of the oldest Catholic church in Yamhill County, on the James Coleman D.L.C. #40, OC #1830. The *Metsker Land Ownership Atlas* of Sept. 1928 shows the church, which has since been demolished. The County Assessor's map shows 10 acres dedicated to the church and the cemetery but the cemetery itself was very much smaller. NOTE: The area was posted "NO TRESPASSING" 7 October 1991. (Muddy Valley 1979-92 USGS Quad. map.)

SMITH, PETER

A 0.01 1 5 June 1863 T3S R4W S21

Located at 741 West Main Street, in Carlton, next to what was the Methodist church and now is a Bed and Breakfast. It is on the Peter and Ortha Smith D.L.C. #64, OC #121. (Not shown on Carlton 1957-92 USGS Quad. map.)

SOUTH YAMHILL
AKA: 1. McCABE
2. McCABE CHURCH
3. SOUTH YAMHILL BAPTIST CHURCH

C 1.4 2 1862 T5S R5W S3

Leave McMinnville on OR. Hwy. 18 at its junction with OR. Hwy. 99W, at the south end of town. Go southwest on OR. Hwy. 18 for 2 miles to Masonville Road and turn right (west), onto Masonville Road for about 1.75 miles; turn left (south) onto McCabe Chapel Road, then go a very short distance on McCabe Chapel Road and turn right on the driveway up the hill to the cemetery, which

Name of Cemetery and also known as	Number of burials	Acres	Condition	Date started or earliest known burial	Township	Range	Section

is in the timber. This is on the Henry Warren D.L.C. #59, OC #1595. 1.95 acres was dedicated on 2 April 1888 but about 0.5 of an acre is used for parking. This was the site of South Yamhill Baptist Church which was erected in 1850. The present marker on the church site is dated 23 June 1953. {19 April 1989} (Muddy Valley 1979-92 USGS Quad. map.)

SPENCER FAMILY
AKA: 1. GREER FAMILY
2. SPENCER-GREER FAMILY

A ? ? 1884-1930 T3S R3W S22
The D.A.R. survey of 1948 described this cemetery as 1.5 miles northwest of Dundee on the John Spencer D.L.C., OC #2336. The Sept. 1929 *Metsker Land Ownership Atlas* of Yamhill County showed the Spencer family still owned land in Section 22. The cemetery was near the home of Rev. John Spencer, with 5 known graves plus 1 grave containing the ashes of 6. NOTE: This site is on private property. (Not shown on the Dundee 1956-93 USGS Quad. map.)

STEPHENSON FAMILY
AKA: 1. STEVENSON

A ? ? 1876 T3S R5W S22
"On a hill south of Moores Valley, 6 miles west of Carlton and which had 4 or 5 graves." was in a May 1970 report. G. W. Stephenson, son of Edward and Eliza died at age 26. This could be in James Shaw D.L.C. #46, OC #1457, along Panther Creek Road. NOTE: 1. This site is on private property. 2. Another report in 1980 lists G. W. Stephenson (December 24, 1859-1876 aged 17) son of Edward and Eliza as a single burial located in T5S R6W S22. (Not shown on Fairdale 1979 USGS Quad. map.)

TAYLOR
AKA: 1. PHILLIPS
2. WALNUT HILL
3. WHITESON

B 0.6 2 Circa 1848 T5S R4W S10
This is southeast of the community of Whiteson, between Amity and McMinnville, 1.8 miles from Whiteson on OR. Hwy. 99W, via Burns Road and Telegraph Road. It is easier to locate from Amity. Leave Amity on OR. Hwy. 99W and go north to the junction with OR. Hwy. 233, leading to Dayton. Turn right (northeast) onto OR. Hwy. 233 and go 1 mile to Telegraph Road angling off to the right. Turn there and go nearly a mile further on

Name of Cemetery and also known as	Number of burials	Acres	Condition	Date started or earliest known burial	Township	Range	Section

Telegraph Road to an angle in Telegraph Road which turns off to the right onto an unnamed road, uphill through the trees to the cemetery on the left, at the roadside. This is on the Charles M. Johnson D.L.C. #62, OC #2407. There were 41 known burials, with 15 or more unmarked graves (Oct. 1946). {22 June 1989} (McMinnville 1957-92 USGS Quad. map.)

TURNER-TONEY FAMILY
AKA: 1. TONEY
FAMILY

A 0.72 5 1863-1895 T5S R5W S30
Located northeast of Sheridan in Lower Gopher Valley. Leave OR. Hwy. 18 between Sheridan and Bellevue and go north on Gopher Valley Road. The D.A.R. survey in Oct. 1951 described this cemetery as being on a farm in a small grove of oak trees; it is said to be located east of Gopher Valley Road. The Turner D.L.C. is in the southern reaches of Gopher Valley Road and OR. Hwy. 18. Drive about 0.4 of a mile north on Gopher Valley Road to the cemetery, due east about 500 feet, in a grove on a bluff overlooking Deer Creek Valley. Only about 0.4 mile of Gopher Valley Road is within the Owen P. Turner D.L.C. #55, OC #2447. There were 6 known burials but no upright stones. The D.A.R. party could not locate this cemetery without local help. NOTE: This site is on private property. (Not shown on Ballston 1956-70 USGS Quad. map.)

UNKNOWN

? ? ? ? T2S R5W S34
The graves are on the west side of Oak Ridge Road (County Rd. #244), northwest of the town of Yamhill, southeast of Fairdale and about 400 feet north upslope from Turek Reservoir. No other information was given. NOTE: This site is on private property. (Fairdale 1979 USGS Quad. map.)

UNKNOWN

A ? ? ? T3S R5W S9
Located in the Moores Valley area, west of the town of Yamhill, just south of Moores Valley Road. The graves are at the western foot of a steep hill, 600 yards due east of Hibbard Road (County Road # 235) and 50 yards

Name of Cemetery and also known as	Number of burials	Acres	Condition	Date started or earliest known burial	Township	Range	Section

south of the north line of Marcia Shull D.L.C. It is on the Marcia Shull D.L.C. #49, OC #3972. NOTE: This site is on private property. (Fairdale 1979 USGS Quad. map.)

UNKNOWN
[?PLANK FAMILY?]

? ? ? ?   T3S R5W   S8

Located in the hills west of Moores Valley which is west of the town of Yamhill and south of Fairdale. Begin in Moores Valley at the intersection of Moores Valley Road and Hibbard Road. Go southwest on Moores Valley Road 1.3 miles to its junction with Kutch Road. Turn right onto Kutch Road, crossing Haskins Creek Bridge. At the powerlines, turn right off of Kutch Road onto Upper Kutch Road and go 0.3 of a mile to another road junction; keep right. At 0.6 of a mile from Kutch Road there are graves on the left. This is possibly the Plank Family burials, which all we have is the family name for so have no idea where they are located in this general area. NOTE: This site is on private property. (Fairdale 1979 USGS Quad. map.)

VALLEY VIEW MEMORIAL PARK
AKA: 1. HILLCREST
      2. RAMSEY HILL

D 3.6 1 1897   T3S R2W   S19

Located just southwest of Newberg. Take Dayton Avenue from 3rd Street. Dayton Avenue is the old alignment of OR. Hwy. 99W and leads to Dundee. Cross Chehalem Creek Bridge and at about 1 mile from 3rd Street is the driveway, turn right (north) up the hill to the cemetery. This is on the David and Susan Ramsey D.L.C. #40, OC #200. {17 July 1989} (Newberg 1961-85 USGS Quad. map.)

YAMHILL-CARLTON
AKA: 1. CARLTON
      2. CARLTON PIONEER
      3. MERCHANT
      4. NORTH YAMHILL
      5. PIONEER MEMORIAL
      6. YAMHILL-- CARLTON PIONEER MEMORIAL

E 7.5 2 1853   T3S R4W   S10

This cemetery is halfway between the towns of Yamhill and Carlton. Go east off of OR. Hwy. 47 on Fryer Road 0.4 of a mile. The cemetery is on the left. This is on the William D. Clark D.L.C. #84, OC #975. {24 October 1990} (Carlton 1957-92 USGS Quad. map.)

Name of Cemetery and also known as	Number of burials	Acres	Condition	Date started or earliest known burial	Township	Range	Section

7. YAMHILL COUNTY
8. YAMHILL COUNTY
   PIONEER MEMORIAL

YOCOM
AKA: 1. BELLEVUE
2. NORTH
   BELLEVUE
3. YOCUM

| | B | 2.1 | 2 | 1858 | T5S | R5W | S20 |

Bellevue is on OR. Hwy. 18, northeast of Sheridan, west of Amity, and southwest of McMinnville. Leave Bellevue on the northwest side of OR. Hwy. 18, taking Muddy Valley Road, going west. Very soon it turns hard right (north). At about 0.25 of a mile, turn left (west) on Latham Road and go about 0.25 of a mile to an unnamed lane that turns right (north). This lane is between 2 fences and goes uphill about 0.5 of a mile to the cemetery, which is out of sight from below. USGS and Metsker maps spell the name Yocum, but the compiler found only 1 monument with that version. All of the other family markers spell the name Yocom; so do the markers in 4 neighboring cemeteries. There is no signboard in or near the cemetery. This is on the Thomas J. Yokum [sic.] D.L.C. #52, OC #1770. {15 May 1989} (Ballston 1956-70 USGS Quad. map.)

YOUNG, EWING

| | A | 0.01 | ? | 1841 | T3S | R3W | S10 |

The marker is alongside OR. Hwy. 240 on the righthand side, going from Newberg toward Yamhill. It is about at highway Milepost 7.63 but the marker is not readily visible in the brush along the roadside. It is on the Sidney Smith D.L.C. #67, OC #5145. The burial is at Route 1 Box 256 under the "Young" oak. An acorn was planted at the grave in 1846. NOTE: This site is on private property and you must have permission to visit. (Dundee 1956-93 USGS Quad. map.)

Pike
Dean H. Byrd (1991)

Pike
Dean H. Byrd (1991)

AGEE, CORDELIA see **AGEE FAMILY**	YAMHILL CO.	T4S	R6W	S36
AGEE D.L.C., ISAAC see **AGEE FAMILY**				
	YAMHILL CO.	T4S	R6W	S36
AGEE FAMILY	YAMHILL CO.	T4S	R6W	S36
AGEE, ISAAC see **AGEE FAMILY**	YAMHILL CO.	T4S	R6W	S36
AMITY	YAMHILL CO.	T5S	R4W	S29
BAKER CREEK see **HAPPY VALLEY**	YAMHILL CO.	T4S	R5W	S10
BARNUM, NATHAN G.	YAMHILL CO.	T2S	R4W	?
BEARY D.L.C., SOLOMON see **MASONIC [McMINNVILLE]**				
	YAMHILL CO.	T4S	R4W	S19
BELL, HENRY see **NELSON, CORA ALICE**				
	YAMHILL CO.	T3S	R3W	S11
BELLEVUE see **YOCOM**	YAMHILL CO.	T5S	R5W	S20
BROOKSIDE	YAMHILL CO.	T4S	R3W	S17
BUCK HOLLOW	YAMHILL CO.	T5S	R7W	S13
BURFORD D.L.C., HEZEKIAH see **BURFORD, WILLIAM**				
	YAMHILL CO.	T5S	R7W	S24
BURFORD, H. see **BURFORD, WILLIAM**				
	YAMHILL CO.	T5S	R7W	S24
BURFORD, HEZEKIAH see **BURFORD, WILLIAM**				
	YAMHILL CO.	T5S	R7W	S24
BURFORD, L. see **BURFORD, WILLIAM**				
	YAMHILL CO.	T5S	R7W	S24
BURFORD, WILLIAM	YAMHILL CO.	T5S	R7W	S24
BURFORD, WILLIAM R. see **BURFORD, WILLIAM**				
	YAMHILL CO.	T5S	R7W	S24
CARLTON see **YAMHILL-CARLTON**	YAMHILL CO.	T3S	R4W	S10
CARLTON PIONEER see **YAMHILL-CARLTON**				
	YAMHILL CO.	T3S	R4W	S10
CARSON, ALEXANDER	YAMHILL CO.	T3S	R4W	S9
CARSON, CHRISTOPHER "KIT" see **CARSON, ALEXANDER**				
	YAMHILL CO.	T3S	R4W	S9
CATE, J. D.	YAMHILL CO.	T5S	R6W	S4
CHAPMAN D.L.C., WILLIAM see **REST HAVEN MEMORIAL PARK**				
	YAMHILL CO.	T6S	R6W	S3
CHEHALEM MOUNTAIN see **GIBBS**	YAMHILL CO.	T3S	R2W	S3
CLARK D.L.C., WILLIAM D. see **YAMHILL-CARLTON**				
	YAMHILL CO.	T3S	R4W	S10
COLEMAN D.L.C., JAMES see **ST. PATRICK**				
	YAMHILL CO.	T5S	R5W	S4
COMBS D.L.C., RICHARD C. see **MURRAY FAMILY**				
	YAMHILL CO.	T4S	R5W	S32
CREEK SIDE see **BROOKSIDE**	YAMHILL CO.	T4S	R3W	S17
CUMMINS, SARAH C. see **NELSON, CORA ALICE**				
	YAMHILL CO.	T3S	R3W	S11
DANFORTH D.L.C., JOSEPH see **DEER CREEK**				
	YAMHILL CO.	T5S	R5W	S28
DAVID'S see **GIBBS**	YAMHILL CO.	T3S	R2W	S3
DAYTON see **BROOKSIDE**	YAMHILL CO.	T4S	R3W	S17
DEER CREEK	YAMHILL CO.	T5S	R5W	S28
DEWEY see **OAK GROVE**	YAMHILL CO.	T2S	R3W	S21

```
DODSON D.L.C., WILLIAM AND HENRIETTA see PIKE AND I.O.O.F.
                                YAMHILL CO.      T2S     R5W         S25
DOLPH                           YAMHILL CO.      T5S     R9W         S27
DOWNING FAMILY see HUSSEY FAMILY
                                YAMHILL CO.      T5S     R6W         S1
DUNDEE MEMORIAL see DUNDEE PIONEER
                                YAMHILL CO.      T3S     R3W         S26
DUNDEE PIONEER                  YAMHILL CO.      T3S     R3W         S26
EBENEZER CHAPEL                 YAMHILL CO.      T5S     R3W         S7
EVEREST see FERNWOOD PIONEER    YAMHILL CO.      T3S     R2W         S20
EVEREST D.L.C., RICHARD see FERNWOOD PIONEER
                                YAMHILL CO.      T3S     R2W         S20
EVEREST D.L.C., RICHARD see FRIENDS
                                YAMHILL CO.      T3S     R2W         S20
EVEREST D.L.C., RICHARD see G.A.R. [GRAND ARMY OF THE REPUBLIC]
                                YAMHILL CO.      T3S     R2W         S20
EVEREST, JANE see FERNWOOD PIONEER
                                YAMHILL CO.      T3S     R2W         S20
EVEREST, RICHARD see FERNWOOD PIONEER
                                YAMHILL CO.      T3S     R2W         S20
EVERGREEN MEMORIAL PARK         YAMHILL CO.      T4S     R4W         S10
FAULCONER D.L.C., ABSALOM B. see MASONIC [SHERIDAN]
                                YAMHILL CO.      T5S     R6W         S26
FENDALL FAMILY see FENDALL-ROGERS FAMILY
                                YAMHILL CO.      T3S     R3W         S4
FENDALL-ROGERS FAMILY           YAMHILL CO.      T3S     R3W         S4
FERNWOOD see FERNWOOD PIONEER   YAMHILL CO.      T3S     R2W         S20
FERNWOOD PIONEER                YAMHILL CO.      T3S     R2W         S20
FRAZER D.L.C., LUCIEN B. see BUCK HOLLOW
                                YAMHILL CO.      T5S     R7W         S13
FREE METHODIST CHURCH see FRIENDS
                                YAMHILL CO.      T3S     R2W         S20
FRIENDS                         YAMHILL CO.      T3S     R2W         S20
G.A.R. [GRAND ARMY OF THE REPUBLIC]
                                YAMHILL CO.      T3S     R2W         S20
GIBBS                           YAMHILL CO.      T3S     R2W         S3
GOODRICH D.L.C., CARNEY AND PEGGY T. see GOODRICH FAMILY
                                YAMHILL CO.      T4S     R3W         S21
GOODRICH D.L.C., CARNEY AND PEGGY T. see I.O.O.F. [DAYTON]
                                YAMHILL CO.      T4S     R3W         S21
GOODRICH FAMILY                 YAMHILL CO.      T4S     R3W         S21
GOODRICH-WORDEN see GOODRICH FAMILY
                                YAMHILL CO.      T4S     R3W         S21
GOPHER VALLEY see AGEE FAMILY   YAMHILL CO.      T4S     R6W         S36
GRAVES BABY see GRAVES FAMILY   YAMHILL CO.      T5S     R6W         S27
GRAVES D.L.C., CHARLES B. see GREENCREST MEMORIAL PARK
                                YAMHILL CO.      T5S     R6W         S35
GRAVES D.L.C., JAMES B. see GRAVES FAMILY
                                YAMHILL CO.      T5S     R6W         S27
GRAVES, DIANA see GRAVES FAMILY YAMHILL CO.      T5S     R6W         S27
GRAVES, DINA see GRAVES FAMILY  YAMHILL CO.      T5S     R6W         S27
GRAVES FAMILY                   YAMHILL CO.      T5S     R6W         S27
```

```
GRAVES, J. M. see GRAVES FAMILY  YAMHILL CO.      T5S    R6W      S27
GRAVES, MR. see GRAVES FAMILY    YAMHILL CO.      T5S    R6W      S27
GREEN CREST MEMORIAL PARK see GREENCREST MEMORIAL PARK
                                 YAMHILL CO.      T5S    R6W      S35
GREENCREST MEMORIAL PARK         YAMHILL CO.      T5S    R6W      S35
GREER FAMILY see SPENCER FAMILY  YAMHILL CO.      T3S    R3W      S22
GRUB HOLLOW see BUCK HOLLOW      YAMHILL CO.      T5S    R7W      S13
GUENTHER-PITMAN FAMILY see OAK GROVE
                                 YAMHILL CO.      T2S    R3W      S21
HALEY D.L.C., MARCIA see MOORES VALLEY
                                 YAMHILL CO.      T3S    R5W      S9
HAPPY HOLLOW see HAPPY VALLEY    YAMHILL CO.      T4S    R5W      S10
HAPPY VALLEY                     YAMHILL CO.      T4S    R5W      S10
HEMBREE D.L.C., ABSALOM J. see HEMBREE FAMILY
                                 YAMHILL CO.      T3S    R4W      S25
HEMBREE FAMILY                   YAMHILL CO.      T3S    R4W      S25
HERBER HOMESTEAD see HERBER, LEO FERDINAND
                                 YAMHILL CO.      ?      ?        ?
HERBER, LEO FERDINAND            YAMHILL CO.      ?      ?        ?
HESS FAMILY                      YAMHILL CO.      T3S    R2W      S8
HESS, MARY see HESS FAMILY       YAMHILL CO.      T3S    R2W      S8
HESS, TILLMAN L. see HESS FAMILY
                                 YAMHILL CO.      T3S    R2W      S8
HIGHLAND                         YAMHILL CO.      T5S    R6W      S5
HILLCREST see VALLEY VIEW MEMORIAL PARK
                                 YAMHILL CO.      T3S    R2W      S19
HOLMES FAMILY                    YAMHILL CO.      T5S    R8W      S36
HOLMS-McGEE FAMILY see HOLMES FAMILY
                                 YAMHILL CO.      T5S    R8W      S36
HOPEWELL                         YAMHILL CO.      T5S    R3W      S30
HUBBARD D.L.C., THOMAS see OUR LADY OF GUADALUPE TRAPPIST ABBEY
                                 YAMHILL CO.      T3S    R3W      S29
HUSSEY D.L.C., STEPHEN see HUSSEY FAMILY
                                 YAMHILL CO.      T5S    R6W      S1
HUSSEY FAMILY                    YAMHILL CO.      T5S    R6W      S1
HUSSEY-YOCOM-PETERSON FAMILY see HUSSEY FAMILY
                                 YAMHILL CO.      T5S    R6W      S1
HYLAND see HIGHLAND              YAMHILL CO.      T5S    R6W      S5
I.O.O.F. see LAFAYETTE PIONEER   YAMHILL CO.      T4S    R3W      S6
I.O.O.F. [DAYTON]                YAMHILL CO.      T4S    R3W      S21
I.O.O.F. LODGE #56 [PIKE] see PIKE AND I.O.O.F.
                                 YAMHILL CO.      T2S    R5W      S25
JOHNSON D.L.C., CHARLES M. aee TAYLOR
                                 YAMHILL CO.      T5S    R4W      S10
JOHNSON D.L.C., JOHN F. see HAPPY VALLEY
                                 YAMHILL CO.      T4S    R5W      S10
KIMSEY, ALVIS                    YAMHILL CO.      T5S    R3W      S5
KIMSEY D.L.C., ALVIS see KIMSEY, ALVIS
                                 YAMHILL CO.      T5S    R3W      S5
KIRKPATRICK POST GRAND ARMY OF THE REPUBLIC see G.A.R. [GRAND ARMY
   OF THE REPUBLIC]              YAMHILL CO.      T3S    R2W      S20
LAFAYETTE PIONEER                YAMHILL CO.      T4S    R3W      S6
```

MALONE D.L.C., MADISON see **MALONE FAMILY**				
	YAMHILL CO.	T4S	R4W	S15
MALONE FAMILY	YAMHILL CO.	T4S	R4W	S15
MASONIC [LAFAYETTE]	YAMHILL CO.	T4S	R4W	S1
MASONIC [McMINNVILLE]	YAMHILL CO.	T4S	R4W	S19
MASONIC [SHERIDAN]	YAMHILL CO.	T5S	R6W	S26
MATHENY D.L.C., RACHEL see **HOPEWELL**				
	YAMHILL CO.	T5S	R3W	S30
McBRIDE	YAMHILL CO.	T3S	R4W	S19
McBRIDE D.L.C., THOMAS AND ANN see **McBRIDE**				
	YAMHILL CO.	T3S	R4W	S19
McCABE see **SOUTH YAMHILL**	YAMHILL CO.	T5S	R5W	S3
McCABE CHURCH see **SOUTH YAMHILL**	YAMHILL CO.	T5S	R5W	S3
McGEE see **HOLMS FAMILY**	YAMHILL CO.	T5S	R8W	S36
McMINNVILLE [OLD]	YAMHILL CO.	T4S	R4W	S21
MENDENHALL FARM see **BURFORD, WILLIAM**				
	YAMHILL CO.	T5S	R7W	S24
MERCHANT see **YAMHILL-CARLTON**	YAMHILL CO.	T3S	R4W	S10
MOORES VALLEY	YAMHILL CO.	T3S	R5W	S9
MORGAREIDGE FAMILY	YAMHILL CO.	T4S	R3W	S30
MT. PLEASANT see **PIKE AND I.O.O.F.**				
	YAMHILL CO.	T2S	R5W	S25
MOUNTAIN BELL see **PIKE AND I.O.O.F.**				
	YAMHILL CO.	T2S	R5W	S25
MURRY, CHARLEY see **MURRAY FAMILY**				
	YAMHILL CO.	T4S	R5W	S32
MURRAY FAMILY	YAMHILL CO.	T4S	R5W	S32
NELSON, CORA ALICE	YAMHILL CO.	T3S	R3W	S11
NELSON D.L.C., JOSIAH C. see **NELSON, CORA ALICE**				
	YAMHILL CO.	T3S	R3W	S11
NELSON, JOSIAH C. see **NELSON, CORA ALICE**				
	YAMHILL CO.	T3S	R3W	S11
NEWBY D.L.C., WILLIAM T. AND SARAH J. see **McMINNVILLE [OLD]**				
	YAMHILL CO.	T4S	R4W	S21
NEWELL see **HIGHLAND**	YAMHILL CO.	T5S	R6W	S5
NOBLE	YAMHILL CO.	T3S	R3W	S3
NOBLE D.L.C., HENRY see **NOBLE**	YAMHILL CO.	T3S	R3W	S3
NORTH BELLEVUE see **YOCOM**	YAMHILL CO.	T5S	R5W	S20
NORTH YAMHILL see **YAMHILL-CARLTON**				
	YAMHILL CO.	T3S	R4W	S10
OAK GROVE	YAMHILL CO.	T2S	R3W	S21
ODD FELLOWS [DAYTON] see **I.O.O.F. [DAYTON]**				
	YAMHILL CO.	T4S	R3W	S21
ODELL see **EBENEZER CHAPEL**	YAMHILL CO.	T5S	R3W	S7
ODELL D.L.C., JOHN see **EBENEZER CHAPEL**				
	YAMHILL CO.	T5S	R3W	S7
OLD PIKE see **PIKE AND I.O.O.F.**	YAMHILL CO.	T2S	R5W	S25
OUR LADY OF GUADALUPE TRAPPIST ABBEY				
	YAMHILL CO.	T3S	R3W	S29
PALMER, JOEL see **BROOKSIDE**	YAMHILL CO.	T4S	R3W	S17
PETERSON FAMILY see **HUSSEY FAMILY**				
	YAMHILL CO.	T5S	R6W	S1

PHILLIPS see **TAYLOR**	YAMHILL CO.	T5S	R4W	S10
PIKE see **PIKE AND I.O.O.F.**	YAMHILL CO.	T2S	R5W	S25
PIKE AND I.O.O.F.	YAMHILL CO.	T2S	R5W	S25
PIONEER MEMORIAL see **YAMHILL-CARLTON**				
	YAMHILL CO.	T3S	R4W	S10
PITMAN FAMILY see **OAK GROVE**	YAMHILL CO.	T2S	R3W	S21
PLANK FAMILY see **UNKNOWN [?PLANK FAMILY?]**				
	YAMHILL CO.	T3S	R5W	S8
PUCKERVILLE [?] see **MOORES VALLEY**				
	YAMHILL CO.	T3S	R5W	S9
RAMSEY D.L.C., DAVID AND SUSAN see **VALLEY VIEW MEMORIAL PARK**				
	YAMHILL CO.	T3S	R2W	S19
RAMSEY HILL see **VALLEY VIEW MEMORIAL PARK**				
	YAMHILL CO.	T3S	R2W	S19
REST HAVEN MEMORIAL PARK	YAMHILL CO.	T6S	R6W	S3
ROGERS D.L.C., LEWIS see **FENDALL-ROGERS FAMILY**				
	YAMHILL CO.	T3S	R3W	S4
ROGERS FAMILY see **FENDALL-ROGERS FAMILY**				
	YAMHILL CO.	T3S	R3W	S4
ROSELAWN see **FRIENDS**	YAMHILL CO.	T3S	R2W	S20
ST. JAMES	YAMHILL CO.	T4S	R4W	S10
ST. JOE see **ST. PATRICK**	YAMHILL CO.	T5S	R5W	S4
ST. PATRICK	YAMHILL CO.	T5S	R5W	S4
SHAW D.L.C., JAMES see **STEPHENSON FAMILY**				
	YAMHILL CO.	T3S	R5W	S22
SHERIDAN MASONIC LODGE #64 see **MASONIC [SHERIDAN]**				
	YAMHILL CO.	T5S	R6W	S26
SHUCK see **DUNDEE PIONEER**	YAMHILL CO.	T3S	R3W	S26
SHUCK D.L.C., JACOB see **DUNDEE PIONEER**				
	YAMHILL CO.	T3S	R3W	S26
SHULL D.L.C., MARCIA see **UNKNOWN**				
	YAMHILL CO.	T3S	R5W	S9
SMITH D.L.C., ANDREW AND SARAH E. see **BROOKSIDE**				
	YAMHILL CO.	T4S	R3W	S17
SMITH D.L.C., PETER AND ORTHA see **SMITH, PETER**				
	YAMHILL CO.	T3S	R4W	S21
SMITH D.L.C., SIDNEY see **YOUNG, EWING**				
	YAMHILL CO.	T3S	R3W	S10
SMITH, PETER	YAMHILL CO.	T3S	R4W	S21
SOUTH YAMHILL	YAMHILL CO.	T5S	R5W	S3
SOUTH YAMHILL BAPTIST CHURCH see **SOUTH YAMHILL**				
	YAMHILL CO.	T5S	R5W	S3
SPENCER D.L.C., JOHN see **SPENCER FAMILY**				
	YAMHILL CO.	T3S	R3W	S22
SPENCER FAMILY	YAMHILL CO.	T3S	R3W	S22
SPENCER-GREER FAMILY see **SPENCER FAMILY**				
	YAMHILL CO.	T3S	R3W	S22
SPENCER, REV. JOHN see **SPENCER FAMILY**				
	YAMHILL CO.	T3S	R3W	S22
SPIRIT MOUNTAIN see **HOLMES FAMILY**				
	YAMHILL CO.	T5S	R8W	S36
STEPHENSON, EDWARD see **STEPHENSON FAMILY**				

	YAMHILL CO.	T3S	R5W	S22
STEPHENSON, ELIZA see **STEPHENSON FAMILY**				
	YAMHILL CO.	T3S	R5W	S22
STEPHENSON FAMILY	YAMHILL CO.	T3S	R5W	S22
STEPHENSON, G. W. see **STEPHENSON FAMILY**				
	YAMHILL CO.	T3S	R5W	S22
STEVENSON see **STEPHENSON FAMILY**	YAMHILL CO.	T3S	R5W	S22
TAYLOR	YAMHILL CO.	T5S	R4W	S10
THARP see **DEER CREEK**	YAMHILL CO.	T5S	R5W	S28
TONEY FAMILY see **TURNER-TONEY FAMILY**				
	YAMHILL CO.	T5S	R5W	S30
TRAPPIST ABBEY see **OUR LADY OF GUADALUPE TRAPPIST ABBEY**				
	YAMHILL CO.	T3S	R3W	S29
TURNER D.L.C., OWEN P. see **TURNER-TONEY FAMILY**				
	YAMHILL CO.	T5S	R5W	S30
TURNER D.L.C., THOMAS L. see **MORGAREIDGE FAMILY**				
	YAMHILL CO.	T4S	R3W	S30
TURNER-TONEY FAMILY	YAMHILL CO.	T5S	R5W	S30
UNITED BRETHREN see **HOPEWELL**	YAMHILL CO.	T5S	R3W	S30
UNKNOWN	YAMHILL CO.	T2S	R5W	S34
UNKNOWN	YAMHILL CO.	T3S	R5W	S9
UNKNOWN [?PLANK FAMILY?]	YAMHILL CO.	T3S	R5W	S8
UPPER WILLAMINA see **BUCK HOLLOW**	YAMHILL CO.	T5S	R7W	S13
VALLEY VIEW MEMORIAL PARK	YAMHILL CO.	T3S	R2W	S19
WALLACE D.L.C., WILLIAM T. see **HESS FAMILY**				
	YAMHILL CO.	T3S	R2W	S8
WALNUT HILL see **TAYLOR**	YAMHILL CO.	T5S	R4W	S10
WARREN D.L.C., HENRY see **SOUTH YAMHILL**				
	YAMHILL CO.	T5S	R5W	S3
WATT D.L.C., JOHN see **AMITY**	YAMHILL CO.	T5S	R4W	S29
WEST CHEHALEM see **FENDALL-ROGERS FAMILY**				
	YAMHILL CO.	T3S	R3W	S4
WHITE CLOUD see **McBRIDE**	YAMHILL CO.	T3S	R4W	S19
WHITE FARM, JASPER see **MURRAY FAMILY**				
	YAMHILL CO.	T4S	R5W	S32
WHITESON see **TAYLOR**	YAMHILL CO.	T5S	R4W	S10
WILLAMINA see **BUCK HOLLOW**	YAMHILL CO.	T5S	R7W	S13
WIRTH PROPERTY, W. AND R. see **MOORES VALLEY**				
	YAMHILL CO.	T3S	R5W	S9
WORDEN FAMILY see **GOODRICH FAMILY**				
	YAMHILL CO.	T4S	R3W	S21
YAMHILL-CARLTON	YAMHILL CO.	T3S	R4W	S10
YAMHILL-CARLTON PIONEER MEMORIAL see **YAMHILL-CARLTON**				
	YAMHILL CO.	T3S	R4W	S10
YAMHILL COUNTY see **YAMHILL-CARLTON**				
	YAMHILL CO.	T3S	R4W	S10
YAMHILL COUNTY PIONEER MEMORIAL see **YAMHILL-CARLTON**				
	YAMHILL CO.	T3S	R4W	S10
YOCOM	YAMHILL CO.	T5S	R5W	S20
YOCOM FAMILY see **HUSSEY FAMILY**	YAMHILL CO.	T5S	R6W	S1
YOCUM see **YOCOM**	YAMHILL CO.	T5S	R5W	S20
YOKUM [Sic] D.L.C., THOMAS J. see **YOCOM**				

```
                                    YAMHILL CO.      T5S    R5W       S20
YOUNG D.L.C., JOSEPH R. see EVERGREEN MEMORIAL PARK
                                    YAMHILL CO.      T4S    R4W       S10
YOUNG D.L.C., JOSEPH R. see ST. JAMES
                                    YAMHILL CO.      T4S    R4W       S10
YOUNG, EWING                        YAMHILL CO.      T3S    R3W       S10
```

Lafayette Pioneer
Janice M. Healy (1997)

Lafayette Pioneer

Janice M. Healy (1997)

Bibliography

A detailed bibliography would double the size of this publication. Instead we are presenting a bibliography listing a few of the major individual sources along with groups or types of resources used. Extensive research has been done over the past 20-25 years searching through every possible printed material we could obtain. We have depended heavily on local historians to give clues and material. Special thanks to the following organizations: Genealogical Forum of Oregon; Metro Cemeteries (formerly Multnomah County Pioneer Cemeteries); Oregon Historic Cemeteries Association; and the Oregon State Cemetery and Mortuary Board.

AAA (American Automobile Association) maps
A Graveyard Preservation Primer, by Strangstad, Lynette
Bible Records
BLM land records
BLM (Bureau of Land Management) maps
Boy Scout Projects and Camp Maps
Bridge Inspectors
Cemetery Employees, Active and Retired
Cemetery Field Notes
Cemeteries and Gravemarkers: Voices of American Culture, ed. by Meyer, Richard E.
Church Records
City Directories
County Death and Probate Records
County Historical Sociaties
County Land and Survey Records
County Tax Records , etc.
DAR (Daughters of the American Revolution) Cemetery Readings
Diaries
Early American Gravestone Art, by Duval, Francis
Ethnic Groups, Societies and Publications
Family Records
Family Histories
Federal Donation Land Claim Records
Federal Land Surveys
Federal Writers Project Manuscripts and Publications
Fire Departments
Forest Service maps and Records
Funeral homes
Funeral Service Companies
Genealogical Society Publications
Genealogical Forum of Oregon Cemetery Files
Genealogical Material in Oregon Donation Land Claims, Genealogical Forum of Oregon
GNIS (Geographic Names Information System), U.S.G.S.
Grave diggers
LDS (Church of the Latter Day Saints) Cemetery Readings
Local Community Atlases
Local Historians
Local History Publications
Locally Published Maps
Loggers
Memorial Art, Ancient and Modern, by Bliss, Harry A.

Manuscript Collections

Maps of the Oregon Trail, Franswa, Gregory M., The Patrice Press, Gerald, Missouri, 1982

Metro Cemeteries (formerly Multnomah County Pioneer Cemeteries)

Metsker's County Maps

Metsker's County Atlases showing land ownership

Miscellaneous Periodicals

Monument Makers

Morticians, Working and Retired

Newspaper Articles

Obituaries

ODOT (Oregon Department of Transportation) Maps

Oregon Blue Book, State of Oregon

Oregon Cemetery Survey, ODOT, 1978

Oregon Geographic Names, McArthur, Lewis A., Western Imprints

Oregon Historic Cemeteries Association (OHCA)

Oregon Historical Society (OHS) Library, Map Collection and Publications

Oregon Historical Society Map Collection

Oregon Historical Society Publications, etc.

Oregon State Cemetery and Mortuary Board

Oregon State Parks Brochures

Personal Files of the Compilers

Photograph Collections

Pittman Atlases and Maps

Plat Maps

Private Cemetery Publications

Private History Publications

Regional Histories

Road Logs, County

Road Logs, ODOT (Oregon Department of Transportation)

Silent Cities: The Evolution of the American Cemetery, by Jackson, Kenneth T. and Vergara, Camilo Jose

Stranger Stop and Cast an Eye: A Guide to Gravestones and Gravestone Rubbing, by Jacobs, G. Walker

Surveyors' Records

Symbolism on Victorian Grave Markers, by Horton, Loren N., The Palimpsest (Summer 1989) Pg. 62-72, State Historical Society of Iowa, Iowa City.

Television Programs, News and Documentary

Thomas Map Guides

Timber Cruisers

Underfoot: An Everyday Guide to Exploring the American Past, by Weitzman, David.

U. S. Forest Service Maps

USGS Quadrangle maps (United States Department of the Interior Geological Survey 7.5 Minute Topographic), approximately 3,000

Vault Companies (Outer burial container)

With Bodilie Eyes: Eschatological Themes in Puritan Literature and Gravestone Art, by Watters, David H.

WPA (Works Progress Administration) Cemetery Readings and Manuscripts

_____, WILLIE see **HOLLAND**	CLACKAMAS CO.	T1S	R1E	S36
96 RANCH see **LEMCKE RANCH**	GRANT CO.	T16S	R30E	S28
A.O.U.W. see **WORKMEN**	LINN CO.	T14S	R4W	S36
A.O.U.W. RIVERSIDE #68 [HOOD RIVER] see **IDLEWILD**				
	HOOD RIVER CO.	T2N	R10E	S2
ABBEY RIVERVIEW see **RIVERVIEW ABBEY MAUSOLEUM**				
	MULTNOMAH CO.	T1S	R1E	S22
ABBOTT see **GRAVEYARD BUTTE**	WASCO CO.	T5S	R12E	S10
ABBOTT GRAVE	DOUGLAS CO.	?	?	?
ABERT LAKE see **XL RANCH**	LAKE CO.	T33S	R21E	S31
ABRAHAM	MULTNOMAH CO.	T1S	R2E	S6
ABRAHAMS see **ABRAHAM**	MULTNOMAH CO.	T1S	R2E	S6
ABRAMS see **ABRAHAM**	MULTNOMAH CO.	T1S	R2E	S6
ACHILLES D.L.C., SAMUEL C. see **BAYVIEW MEMORIAL**				
	COLUMBIA CO.	T4N	R1W	S17
ACKELS see **ACKLES**	UNION CO.	T2S	R38E	S21
ACKLES	UNION CO.	T2S	R38E	S21
ADA	LANE CO.	T20S	R11W	S5
ADAIR D.L.C., JOHN see **HOLY INNOCENTS EPISCOPAL**				
	CLATSOP CO.	T8N	R9W	S9
ADAMS	CLACKAMAS CO.	T5S	R2E	S22
ADAMS see **MYRTLE CREEK PIONEER**	DOUGLAS CO.	T29S	R5W	S28
ADAMS see **WHITEAKER FAMILY**	POLK CO.	T8S	R5W	S14
ADAMS D.L.C., JOHN see **MYRTLE CREEK PIONEER**				
	DOUGLAS CO.	T29S	R5W	S28
ADAMS D.L.C., MATTHEW see **BOGGESS FAMILY**				
	DOUGLAS CO.	T28S	R5W	S1
ADAMS FAMILY	MARION CO.	T9S	R3W	S12
ADEL [NEW]	LAKE CO.	T39S	R24E	S21
ADEL [OLD]	LAKE CO.	T39S	R24E	?
ADEL AREA	LAKE CO.	T39S	R24E	?
AETNA see **ETNA**	POLK CO.	T7S	R4W	S7
AGATE BEACH	LINCOLN CO.	T10S	R11W	S29
AGEE, CORDELIA see **AGEE FAMILY**	YAMHILL CO.	T4S	R6W	S36
AGEE D.L.C., ISAAC see **AGEE FAMILY**				
	YAMHILL CO.	T4S	R6W	S36
AGEE FAMILY	YAMHILL CO.	T4S	R6W	S36
AGEE, ISAAC see **AGEE FAMILY**	YAMHILL CO.	T4S	R6W	S36
AGENCY INDIAN	UMATILLA CO.	T2N	R33E	S10
AGENCY PLAINS see **GARD, MILO**	JEFFERSON CO.	T10S	R13E	S9
AGENCY VALLEY see **BEULAH**	MALHEUR CO.	T18S	R37E	S35
AGGELLES, ALEXIS	WASHINGTON CO.	-	-	-
AHAVAI SHALOM see **AHAVAI SHOLOM**	MULTNOMAH CO.	T1S	R1E	S27
AHAVAI SHOLOM	MULTNOMAH CO.	T1S	R1E	S27
AHAVI SHALOM see **AHAVAI SHOLOM**	MULTNOMAH CO.	T1S	R1E	S27
AHAVI SHALUM see **AHAVAI SHOLOM**	MULTNOMAH CO.	T1S	R1E	S27
AHAVI SOLEM see **AHAVAI SHOLOM**	MULTNOMAH CO.	T1S	R1E	S27
AHAVIA SHOLON see **AHAVAI SHOLOM**	MULTNOMAH CO.	T1S	R1E	S27
AHLERS, DORTHEA	CLATSOP CO.	T5N	R9W	S22
AHLERS HOUSE see **AHLERS, DORTHEA**				
	CLATSOP CO.	T5N	R9W	S22

AIKEN FAMILY see **AIKIN FAMILY**	JACKSON CO.	T32S	R3E	?
AIKIN FAMILY	JACKSON CO.	T32S	R3E	?
AIMS see **LOWE FAMILY**	CLACKAMAS CO.	T1S	R5E	S30
AIRMEN, 8 see **NAVY MONUMENT**	CURRY CO.	UNSURVEYED		
AIRPORT see **I.O.O.F. PIONEER [JOSEPH]**				
	WALLOWA CO.	T2S	R44E	S36
AKIN D.L.C., JOHN see **STOWEL FAMILY**				
	DOUGLAS CO.	T26S	R6W	S36
AKIN D.L.C., JOHN see **WINCHESTER SCHOOL**				
	DOUGLAS CO.	T26S	R6W	S25
ALBA see **ALBEE**	UMATILLA CO.	T4S	R31E	?
ALBEE	UMATILLA CO.	T4S	R31E	?
ALBERTS, CHARLES see **LOWER SUCCOR CREEK**				
	MALHEUR CO.	T26S	R46E	S22
ALBERTS RANCH see **LOWER SUCCOR CREEK**				
	MALHEUR CO.	T26S	R46E	S22
ALBERTSON, GEORGE see **GREEN, JAMES**				
	COOS CO.	T28S	R13W	S30
ALDER [OLD] see **ALDER SLOPE**	WALLOWA CO.	T2S	R44E	S15
ALDER CREEK	BAKER CO.	T10S	R41E	S35
ALDER GROVE	LINCOLN CO.	T13S	R11W	S32
ALDER SLOPE	WALLOWA CO.	T2S	R44E	S15
ALDERMAN FAMILY	POLK CO.	T6S	R4W	S13
ALDRICH, ELMER OLIVER	GRANT CO.	T13S	R27E	S10
ALDRIDGE, M. C. S. see **LONG FAMILY, JOHN**				
	DOUGLAS CO.	T23S	R5W	?
ALDRIDGE, MARY JANE LONG see **LONG FAMILY, JOHN**				
	DOUGLAS CO.	T23S	R5W	?
ALEXANDER D.L.C., JOSEPH see **CRYSTAL LAKE**				
	BENTON CO.	T12S	R5W	S11
ALEXANDER D.L.C., ROBERT see **SEARS**				
	LANE CO.	T20S	R3W	S35
ALFORD	LINN CO.	T14S	R4W	S35
ALFORD see **WORKMEN**	LINN CO.	T14S	R4W	S36
ALFORD D.L.C., THOMAS see **ALFORD**				
	LINN CO.	T14S	R4W	S35
ALIFF, A. C. see **ALIFF, ROSA DANIEL**				
	WALLOWA CO.	T4N	R43E	?
ALIFF, ROSA DANIEL	WALLOWA CO.	T4N	R43E	?
ALKIRE D.L.C., GEORGE see **MARCOLA**				
	LANE CO.	T16S	R2W	S24
ALL SAINTS COLUMBARIUM see **EMANUAL EPISCOPAL CHURCH COLUMBARIUM**				
	COOS CO.	T25S	R13W	S26
ALLEGANY	COOS CO.	T25S	R11W	S5
ALLEGHANY see **ALLEGANY**	COOS CO.	T25S	R11W	S5
ALLEN, BILL	WASCO CO.	T4S	R11E	UNS
ALLEN CHILD	SHERMAN CO.	T1N	R18E	S7
ALLEN D.L.C., CHARLES see **KINGS VALLEY PIONEER**				
	BENTON CO.	T10S	R6W	S28
ALLEN D.L.C., DAVID see **INDIAN**	WASHINGTON CO.	T1N	R4W	S34

ALLEN D.L.C., NATHAN W. see **GREEN VALLEY**

	DOUGLAS CO.	T24S	R6W	S25
ALLEN, DANIEL see **SPENCE FAMILY**	JOSEPHINE CO.	T40S	R8W	S2
ALLEN, DAVID AND LeGORE, ARCHIE	UNION CO.	T6S	R41E	S18
ALLEN FAMILY	MORROW CO.	T5S	R26E	S29
ALLEN GULCH see **ST. PATRICKS**	JOSEPHINE CO.	T40S	R8W	S34
ALLEN, MYRIA M. see **ALLEN FAMILY**				
	MORROW CO.	T5S	R26E	S29
ALLEN, MYRIA MARK see **ALLEN FAMILY**				
	MORROW CO.	T5S	R26E	S29
ALLEN RANCH	DESCHUTES CO.	T20S	R11E	S8
ALLEN, REUBEN see **ALLEN FAMILY**	MORROW CO.	T5S	R26E	S29
ALLEN, URQUHART see **RIVERTON**	COOS CO.	T28S	R13W	?
ALLEN, WILLIAM P.	LANE CO.	?	?	?
ALLEY FAMILY	TILLAMOOK CO.	T3N	R9W	S18
ALLEY HOMESTEAD, JOHN M. see **ALLEY FAMILY**				
	TILLAMOOK CO.	T3N	R9W	S18
ALLPHIN FAMILY	LINN CO.	T10S	R3W	S8
ALMA	LANE CO.	T19S	R8W	S3
ALPHA	LANE CO.	T16S	R8W	?
ALPINE	BENTON CO.	T14S	R6W	S24
ALSEA	BENTON CO.	T14S	R8W	S1
ALSEA AGENCY see **YACHATS [OLD]**	LINCOLN CO.	T14S	R12W	S26
ALTHOUSE, JAMES see **WALKER GULCH**				
	JOSEPHINE CO.	T40S	R7W	S15
ALTON, DONALD see **ST. MARY'S BOY'S HOME**				
	WASHINGTON CO.	T1S	R1W	?
ALVILLE see **IGO**	GILLIAM CO.	T3S	R20E	S21
AMEND, VIRGIL	MULTNOMAH CO.	T1N	R5E	S22
AMERICAN BOTTOM see **CENTRAL SCHOOL**				
	LANE CO.	T18S	R5W	S4
AMERICAN LEGION see **CITY OF MORO**				
	SHERMAN CO.	T1S	R17E	S18
AMERICAN LEGION POST #126	TILLAMOOK CO.	T3N	R10W	S28
AMES CHAPEL see **CRESCENT GROVE**	WASHINGTON CO.	T1S	R1W	S26
AMES FAMILY	LINN CO.	T13S	R1W	S36
AMES SR. D.L.C., LOWELL see **AMES FAMILY**				
	LINN CO.	T13S	R1W	S36
AMISH see **BLOSSER**	CLACKAMAS CO.	T4S	R1W	S36
AMITY	YAMHILL CO.	T5S	R4W	S29
ANCIENT ORDER OF UNITED WORKMEN see **WORKMEN**				
	LINN CO.	T14S	R4W	S36
ANDERSON see **LONE FIR**	MARION CO.	T8S	R1W	S21
ANDERSON D.L.C., JAMES AND ELEANOR see **LONE FIR**				
	MARION CO.	T8S	R1W	S21
ANDERSON FAMILY	POLK CO.	T8S	R6W	S16
ANDERSON LONE FIR see **LONE FIR**	MARION CO.	T8S	R1W	S21
ANDERSON, RUTH ROGERS see **ANDERSON'S HAVEN OF REST**				
	LANE CO.	T15S	R5W	S30
ANDERSON'S HAVEN OF REST	LANE CO.	T15S	R5W	S30
ANDREWS	HARNEY CO.	T35S	R33E	S22

ANKENY see **COX**	MARION CO.	T9S	R3W	S5
ANKENY BOTTOM see **COX**	MARION CO.	T9S	R3W	S5
ANKENY SCHOOL see **COX**	MARION CO.	T9S	R3W	S5
ANLAUF see **COMSTOCK**	DOUGLAS CO.	T21S	R4W	S20
ANLIKER see **KOBEL**	COLUMBIA CO.	T6N	R2W	S20
ANNEX see **FAIRVIEW**	MALHEUR CO.	T15S	R47E	S33
ANSAMA, MARIE SOPHIA see **JOHANNSEN FAMILY**				
	DOUGLAS CO.	T22S	R11W	S11
ANTELOPE	JACKSON CO.	T36S	R1W	S14
ANTELOPE [NEW]	WASCO CO.	T7S	R17E	S32
ANTELOPE CREEK see **ANTELOPE**	JACKSON CO.	T36S	R1W	S14
ANTELOPE PIONEER	WASCO CO.	T7S	R17E	S28
ANTIOCH	JACKSON CO.	T35S	R2W	S23
ANTONE see **SPANISH GULCH**	WHEELER CO.	T13S	R25E	S6
APIARY	COLUMBIA CO.	T6N	R3W	S14
APOSTOLIC	MARION CO.	T7S	R1W	S8
APPLEGATE	MALHEUR CO.	T16S	R47E	?
APPLEGATE see **MISSOURI FLAT**	JACKSON CO.	T38S	R4W	S6
APPLEGATE CHURCH	JACKSON CO.	T38S	R4W	S22
APPLEGATE D.L.C., JESSE see **APPLEGATE FAMILY**				
	DOUGLAS CO.	T22S	R5W	S28
APPLEGATE FAMILY	DOUGLAS CO.	T22S	R5W	S28
APPLEGATE, JAMES see **APPLEGATE**	MALHEUR CO.	T16S	R47E	?
APPLEGATE, JESSE see **APPLEGATE FAMILY**				
	DOUGLAS CO.	T22S	R5W	S28
APPLEGATE PIONEER	DOUGLAS CO.	T23S	R5W	S4
APPLEGATE, SARAH ALMIRA see **TOLL FAMILY**				
	LANE CO.	T19S	R4W	S2
ARAGO see **FISHTRAP**	COOS CO.	T28S	R13W	S23
ARCADE	WASHINGTON CO.	T2N	R3W	S14
ARCHAMBEAUX D.L.C., FRANCIS see **ARCHAMBEAUX FAMILY**				
	DOUGLAS CO.	T26S	R6W	S31
ARCHAMBEAUX FAMILY	DOUGLAS CO.	T26S	R6W	S31
ARCHER	COOS CO.	T26S	R13W	S1
ARLINGTON	GILLIAM CO.	T3N	R21E	S28
ARMIN	WALLOWA CO.	T2S	R47E	S31
ARMPRIEST FAMILY	CURRY CO.	T36S	R12W	UNS
ARMSTRONG	BENTON CO.	T12S	R5W	S31
ARNECKE, FREDERIC	WHEELER CO.	?	?	?
AROCK	MALHEUR CO.	T30S	R42E	?
ARTHUR see **PLEASANT VIEW [EAST]**	CLACKAMAS CO.	T2S	R3E	S19
ARTHUR D.L.C., WILLIAM see **PLEASANT VIEW [EAST]**				
	CLACKAMAS CO.	T2S	R3E	S19
ASCENSION CHAPEL EPISCOPAL CHURCH see **ASCENSION EPISCOPAL CHAPEL**				
	MULTNOMAH CO.	T1S	R1E	S4
ASCENSION EPISCOPAL CHAPEL	MULTNOMAH CO.	T1S	R1E	S4
ASHBY, BILL see **ASHBY CHILD**	BAKER CO.	?	R47E	?
ASHBY CHILD	BAKER CO.	?	R47E	?
ASHLAND see **ASHLAND CITY**	JACKSON CO	T39S	R1E	S9
ASHLAND CITY	JACKSON CO	T39S	R1E	S9
ASHWOOD see **WOODS**	JEFFERSON CO.	T9S	R16E	S36

```
ASTORIA see CLATSOP PLAINS PIONEER
                                   CLATSOP CO.      T7N    R10W    S4
ASTORIA [OLD]                      CLATSOP CO.      T8N    R9W     S8
ASTORIA PIONEER                    CLATSOP CO.      T8N    R9W     S17
ASYLUM                             MARION CO.       T7S    R3W     S25
ASYLUM                             MULTNOMAH CO.    T1S    R1E     S2
ATHENA                             UMATILLA CO.     T4N    R34E    S24
AUBURN                             BAKER CO.        T10S   R39E    S8
AUDREY see BIG FLAT                BAKER CO.        T12S   R37E    S10
AUMSVILLE                          MARION CO.       T8S    R1W     S30
AUNT POLLY                         BAKER CO.        T12S   R38E    ?
AURORA see ZOAR LUTHERAN [BARLOW ROAD]
                                   CLACKAMAS CO.    T4S    R1E     S7
AURORA COLONY see OLD COLONY       MARION CO.       T4S    R1W     S12
AURORA COMMUNITY                   MARION CO.       T4S    R1W     S14
AURORA MASONIC LODGE #59 see GARDINER
                                   DOUGLAS CO.      T21S   R12W    S22
AURORA MASONIC LODGE #59 see REEDSPORT MASONIC
                                   DOUGLAS CO.      T22S   R12W    S4
AURORA PARK see OLD COLONY         MARION CO.       T4S    R1W     S12
AUSTIN                             GRANT CO.        T11S   R35E    S21
AUSTIN FAMILY see JACKSON FAMILY
                                   CLACKAMAS CO.    T5S    R2E     S7
AYVOISE, MARIE [MADAME DORION] see ST. LOUIS [OLD]
                                   MARION CO.       T5S    R2W     S21
AZALEA                             DOUGLAS CO.      T32S   R5W     S14
AZALEA LODGE see GLENDALE          DOUGLAS CO.      T33S   R6W     S5
B'NAI B'RITH                       MULTNOMAH CO.    T1S    R1E     S27
B'NAI B'RITH OREGON LODGE #65 see AHAVAI SHOLOM
                                   MULTNOMAH CO.    T1S    R1E     S27
BABY [HAY CREEK]                   JEFFERSON CO.    T11S   R15E    S9
BABY'S GRAVE                       HARNEY CO.       T20S   R25E    S9
BACKUS see FRANKTON                HOOD RIVER CO.   T3N    R10E    S27
BAGNELL FERRY see RUMLEY HILL      CURRY CO.        T36S   R14W    S9
BAILEY AND MILLER                  TILLAMOOK CO.    T1S    R9W     ?
BAILEY GULCH                       JACKSON CO.      T37S   R4W     S22
BAILY, DUANE Y. see LOST VALLEY    GILLIAM CO.      T6S    R23E    S4
BAIRD D.L.C., WILLIAM C. see MABEL
                                   LANE CO.         T16S   R1W     S5
BAKEOVEN see HINTON                WASCO CO.        T5S    R16E    S26
BAKER                              MORROW CO.       T2S    R24E    S6
BAKER see LUPER                    LANE CO.         T16S   R4W     S34
BAKER CREEK see HAPPY VALLEY       YAMHILL CO.      T4S    R5W     S10
BAKER D.L.C., GEORGE M. see OLD BELIEVER CHURCH
                                   MARION CO.       T5S    R1W     S30
BAKER D.L.C., THOMAS AND ELIZABETH see LUPER
                                   LANE CO.         T16S   R4W     S34
BAKER, DORSEY                      DOUGLAS CO.      T24S   R5W     S32
BAKER FAMILY                       WASHINGTON CO.   T1S    R4W     S21
BAKER FAMILY see LUPER             LANE CO.         T16S   R4W     S34
```

BAKER, MOSES MATTHEW see **PLEASANT VIEW [WEST]**				
	CLACKAMAS CO.	T3S	R1W	S9
BAKER PRAIRIE	CLACKAMAS CO.	T3S	R1E	S33
BAKERS PRAIRIE see **BAKER PRAIRIE**				
	CLACKAMAS CO.	T3S	R1E	S33
BALD RIDGE	CURRY CO.	T33S	R9W	S8
BALES D.L.C., CHARLES see **MT. UNION**				
	BENTON CO.	T12S	R5W	S7
BALL	POLK CO.	T6S	R5W	S5
BALL see **McCOLLUM**	LANE CO.	T18S	R4W	S30
BALL D.L.C., DAVID see **SISKIYOU MEMORIAL PARK AND MAUSOLEUM**				
	JACKSON CO.	T37S	R1W	S29
BALL D.L.C., ISAAC see **BALL**	POLK CO.	T6S	R5W	S5
BALL FAMILY see **BALL**	POLK CO.	T6S	R5W	S5
BALLOU see **FORD**	UMATILLA CO.	T6N	R35E	S23
BALLSTON see **BALL**	POLK CO.	T6S	R5W	S5
BANCROFT see **MYRTLE CREEK**	COOS CO.	T30S	R11W	S16
BANCROFT see **WATERMAN**	COOS CO.	T30S	R11W	S33
BANDON ODD FELLOWS see **I.O.O.F. [NEW BANDON]**				
	COOS CO.	T28S	R14W	S29
BANDON PIONEER	COOS CO.	T28S	R14W	S30
BANDON PIONEER see **G.A.R. [GRAND ARMY OF THE REPUBLIC] [OLD BANDON]**				
	COOS CO.	T28S	R14W	S30
BANDON PIONEER see **I.O.O.F. [OLD BANDON]**				
	COOS CO.	T28S	R14W	S30
BANKS see **UNION POINT**	WASHINGTON CO.	T2N	R3W	S31
BANKS UNION POINT see **UNION POINT**				
	WASHINGTON CO.	T2N	R3W	S31
BAPTIST	LINN CO.	T13S	R3W	S23
BAPTIST see **CITY OF MORO**	SHERMAN CO.	T1S	R17E	S18
BARBER, DOROTHY see **MARQUAM FAMILY**				
	CLACKAMAS CO.	T6S	R1E	S10
BARCLAY, BABY see **SUMMIT MEADOWS**				
	CLACKAMAS CO.	T3S	R8 1/2E	S25
BARGER, BILL see **SMITH PLACE**	CLACKAMAS CO.	T2S	R4E	S30
BARKER D.L.C., CLEMENT see **EMERICK FAMILY**				
	BENTON CO.	T12S	R6W	S27
BARKER, JAMES	MALHEUR CO.	T23S	R37E	?
BARKER-MORRIS FAMILIES	COOS CO.	T27S	R12W	S14
BARKER PLACE, CLARENCE see **APPLEGATE**				
	MALHEUR CO.	T16S	R47E	?
BARKER ROAD see **BEAVER HOMES**	COLUMBIA CO.	T6N	R2W	?
BARLOW see **BARLOW PIONEER**	CLACKAMAS CO.	T4S	R1E	S6
BARLOW see **ZOAR LUTHERAN [BARLOW ROAD]**				
	CLACKAMAS CO.	T4S	R1E	S7
BARLOW CORNER see **ZOAR LUTHERAN [BARLOW ROAD]**				
	CLACKAMAS CO.	T4S	R1E	S7
BARLOW, JIM	CURRY CO.	T33S	R10W	?
BARLOW PIONEER	CLACKAMAS CO.	T4S	R1E	S6
BARNARD BABY	MULTNOMAH CO.	?	?	?

BARNARD, WILLIAM N. see **BARNARD BABY**				
	MULTNOMAH CO.	?	?	?
BARNARD, WINNIFRED BELLE RUS see **BARNARD BABY**				
	MULTNOMAH CO.	?	?	?
BARNEBURG HILL	JACKSON CO.	T37S	R1W	S32
BARNES	CROOK CO.	T18S	R20E	S35
BARNES BABY	MULTNOMAH CO.	T1S	R2E	S20
BARNES, EDWIN J. see **MERRILL**	COLUMBIA CO.	T5N	R1W	?
BARNES, ELIZABETH BANCHE see **BARNES BABY**				
	MULTNOMAH CO.	T1S	R2E	S20
BARNEY CREEK see **BAYNEY CREEK**	CLATSOP CO.	R6N	R9W	?
BARNS, WILLIAM see **BARNES BABY**	MULTNOMAH CO.	T1S	R2E	S20
BARNUM D.L.C., MOSES R. see **BARNUM FAMILY**				
	WASHINGTON CO.	T2S	R1W	S30
BARNUM FAMILY	WASHINGTON CO.	T2S	R1W	S30
BARNUM LODGE #7 see **I.O.O.F. [CORVALLIS]**				
	BENTON CO.	T11S	R5W	S28
BARNUM, NATHAN G.	YAMHILL CO.	T2S	R4W	?
BARR PLACE, JESSE see **FERN RIDGE**				
	LINN CO.	T13S	R1W	S34
BARRETT FAMILY	DOUGLAS CO.	T21S	R12W	S19
BARROW see **REST LAWN MEMORIAL PARK**				
	LANE CO.	T15S	R5W	S34
BARTLETT	WALLOWA CO.	T6N	R43E	S21
BARTNICK	TILLAMOOK CO.	T1S	R10W	S18
BARTON	CLACKAMAS CO.	T2S	R3E	S14
BASKET MOUNTAIN	UMATILLA CO.	T4N	R37E	S18
BASKETT FAMILY	POLK CO.	T7S	R4W	S19
BASTIAN FAMILY	BAKER CO.	T12S	R45E	?
BASTIAN, MARY D. see **BASTIAN FAMILY**				
	BAKER CO.	T12S	R45E	?
BATES-AUSTIN see **AUSTIN**	GRANT CO.	T11S	R35E	S21
BATES D.L.C., JOS. M. AND JAMES M. see **JEFFERSON**				
	MARION CO.	T10S	R3W	S1
BATTERSON FAMILY	TILLAMOOK CO.	T3N	R10W	?
BATTERSON, WILLIAM see **BATTERSON FAMILY**				
	TILLAMOOK CO.	T3N	R10W	?
BATTLE ROCK	CURRY CO.	T33S	R15W	S4
BATTY FAMILY	CLACKAMAS CO.	T2S	R3E	?
BATY D.L.C., ANDREW J. see **BATY FAMILY**				
	CLACKAMAS CO.	T5S	R2E	S14
BATY FAMILY	CLACKAMAS CO.	T5S	R2E	S14
BAUMGARDNER FAMILY	UMATILLA CO.	T3N	R29E	S7
BAUMGARTNER PLACE see **FERRYDALE**	JOSEPHINE CO.	T36S	R7W	S1
BAXTERVILLE see **JORDAN VALLEY**	MALHEUR CO.	T30S	R46E	S2
BAYNEY CREEK	CLATSOP CO.	T6N	R9W	?
BAYVIEW [NEW]	LINCOLN CO.	T13S	R11W	S16
BAYVIEW [OLD]	LINCOLN CO.	T13S	R11W	S18
BAYVIEW MEMORIAL	COLUMBIA CO.	T4N	R1W	S17
BEAGLE see **ANTIOCH**	JACKSON CO.	T35S	R2W	S23
BEAGLE CREEK see **BIG CREEK**	BAKER CO.	T7S	R41E	S2

BEALE, GEORGE see **WALDO FAMILY**	MARION CO.	T8S	R2W	S12
BEAR CREEK	CLACKAMAS CO.	T5S	R1E	S2
BEAR CREEK	COOS CO.	T28S	R14W	S35
BEAR CREEK see **REST LAWN MEMORIAL PARK**				
	LANE CO.	T15S	R5W	S34
BEARY D.L.C., SOLOMON see **MASONIC [McMINNVILLE]**				
	YAMHILL CO.	T4S	R4W	S19
BEATTIE see **BATY FAMILY**	CLACKAMAS CO.	T5S	R2E	S14
BEAVER	TILLAMOOK CO.	T3S	R9W	?
BEAVER CREEK	CROOK CO.	T16S	R24E	S15
BEAVER CREEK	TILLAMOOK CO.	T3S	R9W	S29
BEAVER CREEK see **LONE FIR**	MARION CO.	T8S	R1W	S21
BEAVER CREEK SCHOOLYARD see **ONA**	LINCOLN CO.	T12S	R11W	S21
BEAVER HILL	COOS CO.	T27S	R13W	S17
BEAVER HOMES	COLUMBIA CO.	T6N	R2W	?
BEAVER VALLEY see **WOODBINE**	COLUMBIA CO.	T7N	R3W	S13
BEAVERCREEK MEMORIAL	CLACKAMAS CO.	T3S	R2E	S26
BEAVERCREEK UNITED CHURCH OF CHRIST see **TEN O'CLOCK**				
	CLACKAMAS CO.	T3S	R2E	S35
BECKER, CHARLES	MALHEUR CO.	T18S	R40E	S8
BECKER, CHARLES see **JAMIESON AREA**				
	MALHEUR CO.	T16S	R43E	?
BECKER FAMILY see **BECKER, CHARLES**				
	MALHEUR CO.	T18S	R40E	S8
BECKER, MAUD ELSIE see **TELOCASET**				
	UNION CO.	T5S	R40E	S28
BECKER, P. M. see **TELOCASET**	UNION CO.	T5S	R40E	S28
BECKER RANCH, JIM	MALHEUR CO.	T18S	R41E	S27
BEDFIELD	KLAMATH CO.	T40S	R11E	S1
BEERS see **INDIAN CREEK**	LANE CO.	T16S	R10W	S36
BEILENBERG see **BIELENBERG**	MARION CO.	T8S	R1W	?
BELCREST MEMORIAL PARK AND MAUSOLEUM				
	MARION CO.	T8S	R3W	S4
BELIEU D.L.C., JAMES see **CIVIL BEND**				
	DOUGLAS CO.	T28S	R6W	S21
BELKNAP D.L.C., JESSE see **ALPINE**				
	BENTON CO.	T14S	R6W	S24
BELKNAP D.L.C., JONAS see **BELLFOUNTAIN**				
	BENTON CO	T14S	R5W	S7
BELL FAMILY	DOUGLAS CO.	T22S	R7W	S29
BELL, HENRY see **NELSON, CORA ALICE**				
	YAMHILL CO.	T3S	R3W	S11
BELL MD., CLEMENTINE see **TULLER**	DOUGLAS CO.	T32S	R7W	?
BELL, SUSAN N. see **HUMBUG**	MARION CO.	T8S	R2W	S4
BELLE PASSI	MARION CO.	T5S	R1W	S19
BELLE PASSI MEMORIAL MAUSOLEUM	MARION CO.	T5S	R1W	S19
BELLEQUE FARM see **LUCIER, MARY**	MARION CO.	T3S	R2W	S33
BELLEQUES see **JENCK**	TILLAMOOK CO.	T4S	R10W	S34
BELLEVUE see **YOCOM**	YAMHILL CO.	T5S	R5W	S20
BELLFOUNTAIN	BENTON CO.	T14S	R5W	S7
BELLINGER	LINN CO.	T12S	R1W	S15

BELLINGER D.L.C., JOHN see **BELLINGER FAMILY**

MARION CO.	T9S	R3W	S35

BELLINGER FAMILY	MARION CO.	T9S	R3W	S35
BELTZ FARM see **RENEKE**	TILLAMOOK CO.	T3S	R10W	S31
BEMIS	LANE CO.	T22S	R3W	S32

BENDER, JOHN see **PIONEER [JORDAN]**

LINN CO.	T10S	R1E	S10

BENHAM see **PIONEER [HARBOR]**	CURRY CO.	T40S	R13W	S9

BENNET, PHOEBE KEENON AND BABY see **ARCADE**

WASHINGTON CO.	T2N	R3W	S14

BENNETT D.L.C., JAMES A. see **OAK LAWN MEMORIAL PARK**

BENTON CO.	T12S	R5W	S10

BENSELL	LINCOLN CO.	T10S	R10W	S4

BENSINGER, A. E. see **BENSINGER, ESSIE**

KLAMATH CO.	T37S	R10E	S19

BENSINGER, CARRIE see **BENSINGER, ESSIE**

KLAMATH CO.	T37S	R10E	S19

BENSINGER, ESSIE	KLAMATH CO.	T37S	R10E	S19

BENSON D.L.C., JAMES M. see **IDLEWILD**

HOOD RIVER CO.	T2N	R10E	S2

BENTON	BENTON CO.	T12S	R5W	S10

BENTON see **OAK LAWN MEMORIAL PARK**

BENTON CO.	T12S	R5W	S10

BENTON COUNTY POOR FARM	BENTON CO.	T14S	R6W	?

BENZINGER, ESSIE see **BENSINGER, ESSIE**

KLAMATH CO.	T37S	R10E	S19

BERLIN see **POWELL**	LINN CO.	T12S	R1E	S31

BERNARD FARM, JOSEPH see **ST. EDWARD'S CATHOLIC [OLD]**

WASHINGTON CO.	T1N	R3W	S1

BERNARD RANCH, HENRY see **DEEDS BABIES**

CROOK CO.	T17S	R25E	S11

BERNEBURG D.L.C., WILLIAM see **I.O.O.F., EASTWOOD [MEDFORD]**

JACKSON CO.	T37S	R1W	S29

BETH ISRAEL [NEW]	MULTNOMAH CO.	T1S	R1E	S21
BETH ISRAEL [OLD]	MULTNOMAH CO.	T1S	R1E	S10

BETHANY BIBLE CHURCH see **BETHANY PIONEER**

WASHINGTON CO.	T1N	R1W	S7

BETHANY GERMAN METHODIST see **BETHANY PIONEER**

WASHINGTON CO.	T1N	R1W	S7

BETHANY MEMORIAL	COLUMBIA CO.	T4N	R1W	S19

BETHANY METHODIST CHURCH see **BETHANY PIONEER**

WASHINGTON CO.	T1N	R1W	S7

BETHANY PIONEER	MARION CO.	T6S	R1W	S33
BETHANY PIONEER	WASHINGTON CO.	T1N	R1W	S7
BETHANY PRESBYTERIAN	WASHINGTON CO.	T1N	R1W	S17

BETHANY PRESBYTERIAN CHURCH see **BETHANY PRESBYTERIAN**

WASHINGTON CO.	T1N	R1W	S17

BETHEL	DOUGLAS CO.	T26S	R7W	S36
BETHEL	POLK CO.	T6S	R4W	S21
BETHEL see **GRESHAM PIONEER**	MULTNOMAH CO.	T1S	R3E	S10

BETHEL MISSION CHURCH see **BETHEL**

	DOUGLAS CO.	T26S	R7W	S36

BETHESDA DANISH EVANGELICAL LUTHERAN

	LANE CO.	T17S	R4W	S33

BETHESDA DANISH EVANGELICAL LUTHERAN see **WEST LAWN MEMORIAL PARK**

	LANE CO.	T17S	R4W	S33

BETHLEHEM VILLAGE see **OLD BELIEVER CHURCH**

	MARION CO.	T5S	R1W	S30

BETHUNE, MRS. AGNES see **McRAE RANCH, FARQUHAR**

	WASCO CO.	T6S	R19E	?
BETTERLY, HAZEL	MALHEUR CO.	T20S	R47E	?
BEULAH	MALHEUR CO.	T18S	R37E	S35
BIELENBERG	MARION CO.	T8S	R1W	?

BIG AGENCY PLAINS see **GARD, MILO**

	JEFFERSON CO.	T10S	R13E	S9
BIG BELLY see **BROWN**	KLAMATH CO.	T36S	R12E	S13
BIG BUTTE see **McBEE FAMILY**	BENTON CO.	T13S	R5W	S23
BIG CAMAS RANGER STATION	DOUGLAS CO.	T27S	R3E	?
BIG CREEK	BAKER CO.	T7S	R41E	S2
BIG FLAT	BAKER CO.	T12S	R37E	S10
BIG MEADOWS	CURRY CO.	T32S	R10W	S36
BIG PLAINS see **GARD, MILO**	JEFFERSON CO.	T10S	R13E	S9

BIGELOW D.L.C., WINDSOR D. see **PIONEER [THE DALLES]**

	WASCO CO.	T1N	R13E	S10
BIGELOW FAMILY see **GREENE**	COOS CO.	T32S	R12W	S8
BIGLOW see **EMIGRANT SPRINGS**	SHERMAN CO.	T2N	R18E	S34
BILLINGS	CURRY CO	T34S	R11W	S7
BILLINGS see **BIG MEADOWS**	CURRY CO.	T32S	R10W	S36
BILLINGS FAMILY see **BILLINGS**	CURRY CO	T34S	R11W	S7
BILLINGS' PLACE see **ILLAHE**	CURRY CO.	T34S	R11W	S18

BILYEU D.L.C., GEORGE see **PIONEER [JORDAN]**

	LINN CO.	T10S	R1E	S10

BILYEU D.L.C., HUBBARD see **BILYEU DEN**

	LINN CO.	T10S	R1E	S8
BILYEU DEN	LINN CO.	T10S	R1E	S8
BINGHAM see **POWERS**	COOS CO.	T31S	R12W	S12

BIRCH *[Sic]* see **PIONEER [RICKREALL]**

	POLK CO.	T7S	R4W	S32
BIRD, ROBERT	CLACKAMAS CO.	T2S	R1E	S31
BITTE see **MOUNTAIN VIEW**	COLUMBIA CO.	T6N	R3W	S2
BITTERLING FAMILY	CLATSOP CO.	T7N	R10W	S24

BITTERLING, JULIUS see **BITTERLING FAMILY**

	CLATSOP CO.	T7N	R10W	S24
BLACHLY	LANE CO.	T16S	R7W	S9
BLACK, CLIFTON	JACKSON CO.	T34S	R1W	S28
BLACK COUPLE	LINN CO.	T12S	R2W	S9

BLACK D.L.C., HENRY see **VERBOORT CHURCH**

	WASHINGTON CO.	T1N	R3W	S20

BLACK, JOHN M. see **BLACK, CLIFTON**

	JACKSON CO.	T34S	R1W	S28

BLACK, MARY LOUISA see **BLACK, CLIFTON**

	JACKSON CO.	T34S	R1W	S28
BLACK, MR.	LINN CO.	T13S	R1W	S1
BLACK, MRS.	MALHEUR CO.	T20S	R46E	S26
BLACK ROCK	POLK CO.	T8S	R7W	S14
BLACKBURNE	SHERMAN CO.	T2N	R16E	?

BLACKBURNE PROPERTY, GEORGE AND ALMA see **BLACKBURNE**

	SHERMAN CO.	T2N	R16E	?

BLACKER'S PLACE, WALT see **HOOPINGGARDNER CHILDREN**

	BAKER CO.	T7S	R45E	?
BLACKFORD see **GARDNER**	DOUGLAS CO.	T22S	R6W	?
BLACKFORD FAMILY see **GARDNER**	DOUGLAS CO.	T22S	R6W	?
BLAIN	LINN CO.	T14S	R3W	S14
BLAINE	TILLAMOOK CO.	T3S	R8W	S30

BLAIR D.L.C., THOMAS R. see **BLAIR FAMILY**

	POLK CO.	T6S	R6W	S21
BLAIR FAMILY	POLK CO.	T6S	R6W	S21
BLALOCK	GILLIAM CO.	T3N	R19E	S36
BLANCHARD, DEAN see **BLANCHARD'S**	COLUMBIA CO.	T7N	R2W	S16

BLANCHARD, MERRILL see **DIBBLEE HOUSE**

	COLUMBIA CO.	T7N	R2W	S16
BLANCHARD'S	COLUMBIA CO.	T7N	R2W	S16
BLAND see **BLAND MOUNTAIN**	DOUGLAS CO.	T30S	R4W	S24

BLAND D.L.C., MOSES see **BLACK COUPLE**

	LINN CO.	T12S	R2W	S9

BLAND FAMILY, MOSES see **BLACK COUPLE**

	LINN CO.	T12S	R2W	S9
BLAND MOUNTAIN	DOUGLAS CO.	T30S	R4W	S24
BLASSER see **BLOSSER**	CLACKAMAS CO.	T4S	R1W	S36
BLODGETT	BENTON CO.	T11S	R7W	S23

BLODGETT D.L.C., ENOCH see **YOUNGS RIVER**

	CLATSOP CO.	T7N	R9W	S10

BLODGETT D.L.C., WILLIAM see **BLODGETT**

	BENTON CO.	T11S	R7W	S23
BLODGETT FAMILY see **BLODGETT**	BENTON CO.	T11S	R7W	S23
BLOOMING	WASHINGTON CO.	T1S	R3W	S15
BLOOMING CHURCH see **BLOOMING**	WASHINGTON CO.	T1S	R3W	S15
BLOOMINGTON [?] see **BLOOMING**	WASHINGTON CO.	T1S	R3W	S15
BLOOR	MARION CO.	T8S	R2W	S22
BLOSSER	CLACKAMAS CO.	T4S	R1W	S36
BLOUGHER see **BLOOR**	MARION CO.	T8S	R2W	S22
BLUE MOUNTAIN see **BRUMBAUGH**	LANE CO.	T21S	R2W	S18
BLUE MOUNTAIN see **KEES**	UMATILLA CO.	T4N	R35E	S28
BLUE MOUNTAIN see **SUMPTER**	BAKER CO.	T9S	R37E	S33

BLUE TOWN see **ST. PAUL LUTHERAN CHURCH**

	WASHINGTON CO.	T2S	R1W	S30
BLUETOWN see **MAPLE LANE**	WASHINGTON CO.	T2S	R1W	S30

BLUETOWN see **ST. PAUL LUTHERAN CHURCH**

	WASHINGTON CO.	T2S	R1W	S30
BLY [NEW]	KLAMATH CO.	T36S	R14E	S28
BLY [OLD]	KLAMATH CO.	?	?	?

BOARDMAN [NEW] see **RIVERVIEW**	MORROW CO.	T4N	R25E	S9
BOARDMAN [OLD] see **RIVER VIEW**	MORROW CO.	T4N	R25E	S9
BOARDMAN BOMBING RANGE see **WELL SPRING**				
	MORROW CO.	T2N	R25E	S20
BOBBINGTON, THOMAS	BAKER CO.	T6S	R45E	S34
BOBBINGTON, THOMAS see **UNKNOWN INFANT**				
	BAKER CO.	T6S	R45E	S34
BOEDIGHEIMER see **CAMPBELL-GRIER**	MARION CO.	T9S	R1W	S2
BOGGESS FAMILY	DOUGLAS CO.	T28S	R5W	S1
BOGGUS see **BOGGESS FAMILY**	DOUGLAS CO.	T28S	R5W	S1
BOISE, ELLEN LYON see **BOISE FAMILY**				
	POLK CO.	T7S	?	?
BOISE FAMILY	POLK CO.	T7S	?	?
BOISE, FARM see **BOISE FAMILY**	POLK CO.	T7S	?	?
BOISE, REUBEN see **BOISE FAMILY**	POLK CO.	T7S	?	?
BOLTON see **RICE**	WASCO CO.	T1S	R14E	S10
BOLTON RANCH, ABSALOM see **RICE**	WASCO CO.	T1S	R14E	S10
BONANZA MEMORIAL PARK	KLAMATH CO.	T39S	R12E	S10
BONNEY	CLACKAMAS CO.	T4S	R3E	S35
BONNEY D.L.C., JAIRUS see **HOPEWELL MENNONITE**				
	MARION CO.	T4S	R1W	S36
BONNEY FAMILY	MARION CO.	T5S	R1W	S9
BONNEY, JOHN T. see **BONNEY FAMILY**				
	MARION CO.	T5S	R1W	S9
BOONE	LINCOLN CO.	T11S	R11W	?
BOOT HILL	BAKER CO.	T8S	R44E	?
BOOT HILL	GRANT CO.	T13S	R31E	S36
BOOT HILL	JOSEPHINE CO.	T38S	R5W	?
BOOTH FAMILY	WASHINGTON CO.	T1S	R5W	S25
BOOTH-KELLY LUMBER COMPANY see **WENDLING**				
	LANE CO.	T16S	R1W	S10
BORLAND see **SWEET HOME**	LANE CO.	T16S	R6W	S27
BOUNCER, JOHN see **BECKER RANCH, JIM**				
	MALHEUR CO.	T18S	R41E	S27
BOUNDS	DOUGLAS CO.	T28S	R6W	S35
BOURNE	BAKER CO.	T8S	R37E	?
BOURNE, CHARLES F.	DOUGLAS CO.	T22S	R9W	S8
BOWDEN RANCH see **MEXICAN PETE**	MALHEUR CO.	T34S	R41E	?
BOWDEN STATION see **UNKNOWN BASQUE SHEEPHERDER**				
	MALHEUR CO.	T34S	R41E	?
BOWLUS	UMATILLA CO.	T5N	R36E	S3
BOWLUS FARM see **BOWLUS**	UMATILLA CO.	T5N	R36E	S3
BOWMAN D.L.C., JOSHUA see **MAPLEWOOD**				
	CLACKAMAS CO.	T6S	R1E	S14
BOWMAN D.L.C., PRESTON see **BOWMAN FAMILY**				
	POLK CO.	T9S	R5W	?
BOWMAN FAMILY	POLK CO.	T9S	R5W	?
BOWMAN FAMILY	UMATILLA CO.	T1N	R29E	?
BOWMAN-HICKS LUMBER COMPANY LOGGING CAMP see **MAXVILLE**				
	WALLOWA CO.	T3N	R42E	S15
BOWMAN, SARAH see **BOWMAN FAMILY**	POLK CO.	T9S	R5W	?

BOWMAN, WILLIAM see **BOWMAN FAMILY**				
	POLK CO.	T9S	R5W	?
BOY	LINN CO.	T10S	R1E	S8
BOYD see **RICE**	WASCO CO.	T1S	R14E	S10
BOYD see **SAILOR PIONEER**	LANE CO.	T17S	R6W	S28
BOYDSTON see **HUBBARD**	POLK CO.	T8S	R6W	S28
BOYER, DUDLEY see **FERN HILL**	CLACKAMAS CO.	T5S	R3E	S21
BOYER FAMILY	BAKER CO.	T12S	R38E	?
BOYER FAMILY	TILLAMOOK CO.	T6S	R9W	?
BOYER FAMILY see **FERN HILL**	CLACKAMAS CO.	T5S	R3E	S21
BOYER RANCH, FRED see **BOYER FAMILY**				
	BAKER CO.	T12S	R38E	?
BOYER RANCH, FRED see **DEVIN, GRANDMA**				
	BAKER CO.	T12S	R38E	?
BOYER, THOMAS see **BOYER FAMILY**	BAKER CO.	T12S	R38E	?
BOYS	MARION CO.	T8S	R2W	S17
BRACK FAMILY	COOS CO.	T29S	R12W	S26
BRACKETT see **IRVIN FAMILY**	CLACKAMAS CO.	T4S	R1E	S18
BRADEN RANCH see **McCORMAC**	TILLAMOOK CO.	T2S	R10W	S8
BRADFORD ISLAND	MULTNOMAH CO.	T2N	R7E	?
BRADLEY FAMILY	JACKSON CO.	?	?	?
BRADLEY, KASS see **UNKNOWN**	COLUMBIA CO.	T4N	R2W	S16
BRADLEY, WM. D. see **BRIGGS, SAMUEL**				
	DOUGLAS CO.	T30S	R5W	S20
BRAINARD see **BRAINARD PIONEER**	MULTNOMAH CO.	T1N	R2E	S33
BRAINARD PIONEER	MULTNOMAH CO.	T1N	R2E	S33
BRAINARY see **BRAINARD PIONEER**	MULTNOMAH CO.	T1N	R2E	S33
BRAINERD see **BRAINARD PIONEER**	MULTNOMAH CO.	T1N	R2E	S33
BRAMLET MEMORIAL	WALLOWA CO.	T2N	R42E	S33
BRATTAIN D.L.C., JONATHAN H. see **BRATTAIN FAMILY**				
	LINN CO.	T12S	R4W	S33
BRATTAIN FAMILY	LINN CO.	T12S	R4W	S33
BRAY	LANE CO.	T15S	R12W	S27
BRAY, GEORGIANIA STARR see **BRAY**	LANE CO.	T15S	R12W	S27
BRAY, KATIE MYRTH see **BRAY**	LANE CO.	T15S	R12W	S27
BREEN, ANNIE WASSON see **BREEN, BABY**				
	COOS CO.	T25S	R13W	?
BREEN, BABY	COOS CO.	T25S	R13W	?
BREESE	DESCHUTES CO.	T21S	R11E	S29
BRELAGE RANCH, ARNOLD see **WHEELER, ANNIE R.**				
	COOS CO.	T25S	R12W	S5
BRETHREN see **MABEL**	LANE CO.	T16S	R1W	S5
BREUER	COOS CO.	T29S	R12W	S36
BREUER, ALBERT see **BREUER**	COOS CO.	T29S	R12W	S36
BREYMER see **BRAINARD PIONEER**	MULTNOMAH CO.	T1N	R2E	S33
BRICE D.L.C., WILLIAM H. see **DOWNS, JAMES**				
	LANE CO.	T16S	R4W	?
BRIDAL VEIL	MULTNOMAH CO.	T1N	R5E	S22
BRIDGEFARMER D.L.C., CHRISTOPHER see **HESS, BABY BOY**				
	WASHINGTON CO.	T1S	R4W	S33
BRIDGEPORT	BAKER CO.	T12S	R41E	S30

BRIDGES D.L.C., JOHN see **SHAW CATHOLIC**

MARION CO.	T8S	R2W	S13

BRIGGS   LINCOLN CO.   T13S   R11W   S16

BRIGGS D.L.C., ELISA M. see **PIONEER MEMORIAL CEMETERY PARK**

LANE CO.	T17S	R3W	S35

BRIGGS D.L.C., GEORGE E. see **FORT BRIGGS**

JOSEPHINE CO.	T39S	R8W	S35

BRIGGS FAMILY see **UNKNOWN**   JOSEPHINE CO.   T36S   R8W   S18

BRIGGS FAMILY, ELISA AND MARY see **PIONEER MEMORIAL CEMETERY PARK**

LANE CO.	T17S	R3W	S35

BRIGGS GRAVES   WASCO CO.   T4S   R11E   S26

BRIGGS, JARVIS see **BRIGGS GRAVES**

WASCO CO.	T4S	R11E	S26

BRIGGS, NEWTON see **BRIGGS GRAVES**

WASCO CO.	T4S	R11E	S26

BRIGGS, SAMUEL   DOUGLAS CO.   T30S   R5W   S20

BRIGHAM'S GRAVE   POLK CO.   T9S   R6W   S35

BRIGS, MRS. see **AGATE BEACH**   LINCOLN CO.   T10S   R11W   S29

BRINGLE, ABSALOM see **CHEWAUCAN**   LAKE CO.   T34S   R19E   S33

BRISCOE, ELIZABETH ROGERS see **BRISCOE, ISAIAH JACKSON**

WALLOWA CO.	T1N	R44E	S35

BRISCOE, ISAIAH JACKSON   WALLOWA CO.   T1N   R44E   S35

BRISCOE, MR. see **BRISCOE, ISAIAH JACKSON**

WALLOWA CO.	T1N	R44E	S35

BRISTO   JACKSON CO.   ?   ?   ?

BRISTOW D.L.C., ELIJAH see **PLEASANT HILL PIONEER**

LANE CO.	T18S	R2W	S34

BROCKMAN RANCH see **SHIELDS, LOUIS**

WALLOWA CO.	T1N	R50E	UNS

BROCKWAY see **CIVIL BEND**   DOUGLAS CO.   T28S   R6W   S21

BROCKWAY see **NICHOLS**   DOUGLAS CO.   T28S   R6W   S20

BROGAN   MALHEUR CO.   T15S   R42E   S26

BROOKS see **PIONEER MEMORIAL**   MARION CO.   T6S   R2W   S10

BROOKS CATHOLIC   MARIAN CO.   T6S   R2W   S21

BROOKS PIONEER see **PIONEER MEMORIAL**

MARION CO.	T6S	R2W	S10

BROOKSIDE   YAMHILL CO.   T4S   R3W   S17

BROUSSARD JR., ELDRIDGE J.   CLACKAMAS CO.   T2S   R5E   ?

BROWN   COOS CO.   ?   ?   ?

BROWN   KLAMATH CO.   T36S   R12E   S13

BROWN, CHARLIE see **SQUAW CREEK**   MALHEUR CO.   T21S   R41E   ?

BROWN D.L.C., GEORGE see **BROWN, GEORGE**

POLK CO.	T7S	R5W	S9

BROWN D.L.C., GEORGE W. AND HARRIET see **PLEASANT HOME PIONEER**

MULTNOMAH CO.	T1S	R4E	S20

BROWN, DAVID P. see **LOCKWOOD RANCH**

MALHEUR CO.	?	?	?

BROWN, ELIZABETH see **SACRED HEART**

MARION CO.	T5S	R2W	S36

BROWN FAMILY   GILLIAM CO.   T3S   R22E   S10

BROWN FAMILY see **SACRED HART**   MARION CO.   T5S   R2W   S36

BROWN FAMILY, H. G.	DOUGLAS CO.	T22S	R8W	S21
BROWN, GEORGE	POLK CO.	T7S	R5W	S9
BROWN, JOHN see **GRAND ARMY OF THE REPUBLIC**				
	MULTNOMAH CO.	T1S	R1E	S27
BROWN, JOHN see **KLAMATH COUNTY POOR FARM**				
	KLAMATH CO.	?	?	?
BROWN, JOSEPH	WASCO CO.	T1N	R13E	S10
BROWN, O. C.	DOUGLAS CO.	T27S	R5W	S24
BROWN RANCH, NEGRO see **SMITH, WHISTLING**				
	JEFFERSON CO.	T10S	R13E	S7
BROWN, SALMON see **GRAND ARMY OF THE REPUBLIC**				
	MULTNOMAH CO.	T1S	R1E	S27
BROWN, SAMUEL see **SACRED HEART**	MARION CO.	T5S	R2W	S36
BROWN, WILLIAM C.	POLK CO.	T7S	R5W	S22
BROWNHILL CHILDREN	JEFFERSON CO.	T9S	R13E	S24
BROWNING	TILLAMOOK CO.	T4S	R8W	S3
BROWNING FAMILY see **WHITE DLC, WILLIAM**				
	LANE CO.	T15S	R5W	S20
BROWNLEE, AGNESS see **GWYNNE**	WALLOWA CO.	T1S	R44E	S30
BROWNLEE, ALPHA see **GWYNNE**	WALLOWA CO.	T1S	R44E	S30
BROWNSBORO	JACKSON CO.	T36S	R1E	S4
BROWNSVILLE BAPTIST see **BAPTIST**	LINN CO.	T13S	R3W	S23
BROWNSVILLE CITY see **BROWNSVILLE PIONEER**				
	LINN CO.	T13S	R2W	S32
BROWNSVILLE PIONEER	LINN CO.	T13S	R2W	S32
BROWNTOWN see **WALKER GULCH**	JOSEPHINE CO.	T40S	R7W	S15
BRUCE see **KLUM**	LINN CO.	T12S	R1W	S32
BRUEHL, EDWARD	WASHINGTON CO.	T3N	R2W	S28
BRUEHL PLACE see **BRUEHL, EDWARD**	WASHINGTON CO.	T3N	R2W	S28
BRUGGER see **BETHANY PRESBYTERIAN**				
	WASHINGTON CO.	T1N	R1W	S17
BRUGGER D.L.C., JACOB see **BETHANY PRESBYTERIAN**				
	WASHINGTON CO.	T1N	R1W	S17
BRUMBAUGH	LANE CO.	T21S	R2W	S18
BRUNK FARM	POLK CO.	T7S	R4W	?
BRUNO	JEFFERSON CO.	T9S	R12E	S23
BRYANT	COLUMBIA CO.	T7N	R4W	S9
BRYANT D.L.C., JOHN see **OUR LADY OF LOURDES**				
	LINN CO.	T10S	R1E	S9
BRYANT, E. G. see **BRYANT**	COLUMBIA CO.	T7N	R4W	S9
BRYANT FAMILY	DOUGLAS CO.	T29S	R4W	S21
BRYANT, NANCY C. see **BRYANT**	COLUMBIA CO.	T7N	R4W	S9
BRYANT RANCH, J. see **BRYANT FAMILY**				
	DOUGLAS CO.	T29S	R4W	S21
BUCK see **REPSLEGER ROAD**	LANE CO.	T20S	R4W	S23
BUCK HOLLOW	YAMHILL CO.	T5S	R7W	S13
BUCKHEAD CAMP	DOUGLAS CO.	T27S	R2E	S31
BUENA VISTA	POLK CO.	T9S	R4W	S23
BUHLER RANCH	WALLOWA CO.	?	?	?
BULL FAMILY see **McKENZIE BRIDGE**	LANE CO.	T16S	R5E	?
BULLARD FAMILY	COOS CO.	T28S	R14W	S7

BULLOCK D.L.C., JESSE see **OSWEGO PIONEER**

	CLACKAMAS CO.	T2S	R1E	S16

BULLOCK D.L.C., JESSE see **SACRED HEART**

	CLACKAMAS CO.	T2S	R1E	S16
BUNKER HILL	LINN CO.	T13S	R3W	S9
BUNNELL FAMILY see **LEAP**	WALLOWA CO.	T1N	R44E	S8
BUNYARD, WILLARD	HARNEY CO.	T37S	R36E	S12

BURCH D.L.C., BENJAMIN F. see **HILLTOP**

	POLK CO.	T9S	R4W	S9

BURCH D.L.C., SAMUEL see **PIONEER [RICKREALL]**

	POLK CO.	T7S	R4W	S32

BURCH FAMILY see **PIONEER [RICKREAL]**

	POLK CO.	T7S	R4W	S32

BURCH FAMILY [?] see **FORTUNE BRANCH GRAVES**

	DOUGLAS CO.	T32S	R5W	S20
BURDORFUR see **BURGDORFER FAMILY**	WASHINGTON CO.	T3N	R3W	S15

BURFORD D.L.C., HEZEKIAH see **BURFORD, WILLIAM**

	YAMHILL CO.	T5S	R7W	S24

BURFORD, H. see **BURFORD, WILLIAM**

	YAMHILL CO.	T5S	R7W	S24

BURFORD, HEZEKIAH see **BURFORD, WILLIAM**

	YAMHILL CO.	T5S	R7W	S24

BURFORD, L. see **BURFORD, WILLIAM**

	YAMHILL CO.	T5S	R7W	S24
BURFORD, WILLIAM	YAMHILL CO.	T5S	R7W	S24

BURFORD, WILLIAM R. see **BURFORD, WILLIAM**

	YAMHILL CO.	T5S	R7W	S24
BURGDORFER FAMILY	WASHINGTON CO.	T3N	R3W	S15
BURKEMONT	BAKER CO.	T7S	R42E	S28

BURKHART, YOUNGABLE see **BRIGHAM'S GRAVE**

	POLK CO.	T9S	R6W	S35

BURNETT D.L.C., JOHN S. see **BURNETT FAMILY**

	DOUGLAS CO.	T29S	R6W	S12
BURNETT FAMILY	DOUGLAS CO.	T29S	R6W	S12
BURNS	HARNEY CO.	T23S	R30E	S13
BURNS PAIUTE see **PAIUTE [OLD]**	HARNEY CO.	T23S	R30E	S14
BURNT RIVER see **UNITY**	BAKER CO.	T13S	R36E	S12
BURNT WOODS see **MULKEY**	LINCOLN CO.	T11S	R8W	S26

BURRIS D.L.C., WILLIAM see **BURRIS FAMILY, WILLIAM**

	WASHINGTON CO.	T1N	R2W	S5
BURRIS FAMILY, WILLIAM	WASHINGTON CO.	T1N	R2W	S5

BURRIS, MARTHA see **BURRIS FAMILY, WILLIAM**

	WASHINGTON CO.	T1N	R2W	S5
BURT	DOUGLAS CO.	T27S	R5W	S14

BURTON CHILDREN see **BURTON FAMILY**

	LINCOLN CO.	T6S	R11W	S24
BURTON FAMILY	LINCOLN CO.	T6S	R11W	S24

BUSKETT *[Sic]* D.L.C., GEORGE see **BASKETT FAMILY**

	POLK CO.	T7S	R4W	S19

BUTCHER FAMILY see **MEDICAL SPRINGS**

	UNION CO.	T6S	R41E	?

BUTLER see **AUMSVILLE**	MARION CO.	T8S	R1W	S30
BUTLER, CHARLES	JOSEPHINE CO.	T39S	R9W	S10
BUTLER FAMILY	MULTNOMAH CO.	T1S	R3E	S20
BUTLER FAMILY see **PALLETTE RANCH**				
	WALLOWA CO.	T4S	R48E	?
BUTLER FARM, CLARENCE see **HILL, RICHARD**				
	COOS CO.	T32S	R11W	?
BUTLER RANCH see **PALLETTE RANCH**	WALLOWA CO.	T4S	R48E	?
BUTLER-DAVIDSON FAMILY	POLK CO.	T8S	R5W	S35
BUTLER-THOMPSON FAMILY see **MYER FAMILY**				
	JACKSON CO.	T38S	R1E	S30
BUTTE see **PINE GROVE BUTTE**	HOOD RIVER CO.	T2N	R10E	S13
BUTTE FALLS	JACKSON CO.	T35S	R2E	S5
BUTTER CREEK CROSSING	UMATILLA CO.	T3N	R27E	S25
BUTTERWORTH, CHARLES E. see **LILYGLEN**				
	JACKSON CO.	T38S	R3E	S14
BUTTEVILLE [NEW]	MARION CO.	T3S	R1W	S32
BUTTEVILLE [OLD]	MARION CO.	T3S	R1W	S32
BUTTS, CATHERINE BONNETT	WASCO CO.	T3S	R14E	S28
BUTTS, SARAH M.	UMATILLA CO.	T1S	R35E	S15
BUXTON CATHOLIC	WASHINGTON CO.	T2N	R4W	S4
BUXTON PROTESTANT	WASHINGTON CO.	T2N	R4W	S5
BUXTON SR. D.L.C., HENRY see **FOREST VIEW MEMORIAL GARDENS**				
	WASHINGTON CO.	T1N	R4W	S36
BUZAN	WASCO CO.	T4S	R15E	S33
BYRD D.L.C., LORENZO A. see **FAIRFIELD**				
	MARION CO.	T5S	R2W	S19
CABBAGE HILL see **REVENUE FAMILY**	CLACKAMAS CO.	T2S	R5E	S7
CABELL CITY	GRANT CO.	T8S	R35 1/2E	S1
CABELL FAMILY see **CABELL CITY**	GRANT CO.	T8S	R35 1/2E	S1
CABELL, FRED see **CABELL CITY**	GRANT CO.	T8S	R35 1/2E	S1
CABELL, JOHANNA CAMILLA see **CABELL CITY**				
	GRANT CO.	T8S	R35 1/2E	S1
CABELL, MRS. see **CABELL CITY**	GRANT CO.	T8S	R35 1/2E	S1
CACHE CREEK RANCH	WALLOWA CO.	T6N	R47E	S23
CAIN FARM, WALTER see **BATTERSON FAMILY**				
	TILLAMOOK CO.	T3N	R10W	?
CALAPOOIA I.O.O.F. see **FINLEY**	LINN CO.	T14S	R2W	S13
CALAPOOIA MOUNDS	LINN CO.	-	-	-
CALDWELL	LANE CO.	T16S	R5W	S24
CALEB	WHEELER CO.	T12S	R23E	S14
CALL MEADOW GRAVE	HARNEY CO.	T20S	R33E	S29
CALLAHAN BABY see **DAIRY**	KLAMATH CO.	T38S	R11 1/2E	?
CALLAHAN D.L.C., CLIFTON R. see **CALLAHAN FAMILY**				
	CLACKAMAS CO.	T5S	R2E	S24
CALLAHAN D.L.C., CLIFTON R. see **FEYRER**				
	CLACKAMAS CO.	T5S	R3E	S19
CALLAHAN FAMILY	CLACKAMAS CO.	T5S	R2E	S24
CALLAHAN FARM see **HESS, BABY BOY**				
	WASHINGTON CO.	T1S	R4W	S33

CALLAHAN FARM, H. see **HESS, BABY BOY**

	WASHINGTON CO.	T1S	R4W	S33

CALLOWAY, C. A. see **TEN MILE GRAVEYARD**

	WASCO CO.	T2N	R15E	S31
CALVARY	MARION CO.	T6S	R1W	S3
CALVARY	UNION CO.	T3S	R38E	S8

CALVARY BAPTIST CHURCH COLUMBARIUM

	MARION CO.	T7S	R3W	S27

CALVARY LUTHERAN CHURCH COLUMBARIUM [STAYTON]

	MARION CO.	T9S	R1W	S10
CAMAS VALLEY	DOUGLAS CO.	T31S	R8W	S5
CAMERON see **UNIONTOWN**	JACKSON CO.	T38S	R3W	S34

CAMMACK, MR. ALFRED see **ROSEDALE FRIENDS**

	MARION CO.	T8S	R3W	S28

CAMP C. F. SMITH see **BUNYARD, WILLARD**

	HARNEY CO.	T37S	R36E	S12
CAMP CREEK	LANE CO.	T17S	R1W	S19
CAMP CREEK see **BARNES**	CROOK CO.	T18S	R20E	S35
CAMP CURREY	HARNEY CO.	T22S	R25E	S25
CAMP LYONS see **SHEAVILLE**	MALHEUR CO.	T28S	R47E	S18

CAMP MERIWETHER see **CHAMBERLAIN FAMILY**

	TILLAMOOK CO.	T3S	R10W	S7
CAMP POLK	DESCHUTES CO.	T14S	R10E	S27
CAMP WARNER	LAKE CO.	T36S	R22E	S33
CAMP WATSON	WHEELER CO.	T12S	R23E	S36
CAMP WRIGHT see **WRIGHT POINT**	HARNEY CO.	T24S	R31E	?
CAMPBELL, BABY GIRL	WASCO CO.	T1S	R13E	S11
CAMPBELL-GRIER	MARION CO.	T9S	R1W	S2
CANARY see **ADA**	LANE CO.	T20S	R11W	S5

CANBY LUTHERAN see **ZION MEMORIAL PARK**

	CLACKAMAS CO.	T3S	R1E	S34
CANBY PIONEER see **BAKER PRAIRIE**	CLACKAMAS CO.	T3S	R1E	S33
CANEMAH	CLACKAMAS CO.	T3S	R1E	S1
CANNON, SARAH	DOUGLAS CO.	T22S	R4W	S20
CANTWELL INFANT	MORROW CO.	T3S	R25E	S35
CANYON CITY	GRANT CO.	T13S	R31E	S35
CANYON CREEK see **BONNEY**	CLACKAMAS CO.	T4S	R3E	S35

CANYON CREEK see **SABASTOPOL FLATS**

	JOSEPHINE CO.	T39S	R9W	S15
CANYONVILLE	DOUGLAS CO.	T30S	R5W	S27

CANYONVILLE BIBLE ACADEMY see **ROSE HILL MEMORIAL**

	DOUGLAS CO.	T30S	R5W	S27
CANYONVILLE PIONEER	DOUGLAS CO.	T30S	R5W	S34

CAPE BLANCO CATHOLIC see **CAPE BLANCO PIONEER**

	CURRY CO.	T31S	R16W	S36
CAPE BLANCO PIONEER	CURRY CO.	T31S	R16W	S36

CAPE FOULWEATHER see **AGATE BEACH**

	LINCOLN CO.	T10S	R11W	S29
CAPE LOOKOUT	TILLAMOOK CO.	T3S	R11W	S1

CAPLES D.L.C., CHARLES C. see **KINDER**

	COLUMBIA CO.	T5N	R1W	S16

CAPLINGER, J. C. see **RICKEY**	MARION CO.	T7S	R2W	S32
CARBERRY see **STEAMBOAT**	JACKSON CO.	T4OS	R4W	S20
CAREY see **WAYMIRE FAMILY**	POLK CO.	T8S	R6W	S15
CAREY, BLYTHE GAITTENS see **MERRILL**				
	COLUMBIA CO.	T5N	R1W	?
CAREY D.L.C., JOHN C. AND SARAH see **ESSON MEMORIAL, IDA**				
	MARION CO.	T6S	R1W	S5
CARLSON, ELLEN see **ZUMWALT**	WALLOWA CO.	T2N	R47E	?
CARLSON, GUST see **ZUMWALT**	WALLOWA CO.	T2N	R47E	?
CARLSON, LELAND see **ZUMWALT**	WALLOWA CO.	T2N	R47E	?
CARLTON see **YAMHILL-CARLTON**	YAMHILL CO.	T3S	R4W	S10
CARLTON PIONEER see **YAMHILL-CARLTON**				
	YAMHILL CO.	T3S	R4W	S10
CARMELITE NUNNERY see **GATES OF HEAVEN**				
	LANE CO.	T18S	R4W	S5
CARMICHAEL CANYON see **UNKNOWN**	MORROW CO.	T4S	R27E	S1
CARPENTER	CURRY CO.	T39S	R14W	?
CARROLL see **KEASEY**	COLUMBIA CO.	T5N	R5W	S27
CARROLL FAMILY	WHEELER CO.	T10S	R21E	S32
CARROLL FAMILY see **CHINESE HERDSMAN**				
	WHEELER CO.	T10S	R21E	?
CARROLL, JAMES see **JORDAN, MICHAEL M.**				
	MALHEUR CO.	?	?	?
CARSON	LINCOLN CO.	T14S	R11W	S33
CARSON, ALEXANDER	YAMHILL CO.	T3S	R4W	S9
CARSON, CHRISTOPHER "KIT" see **CARSON, ALEXANDER**				
	YAMHILL CO.	T3S	R4W	S9
CARSON, DOLPH see **CONLY**	WASCO CO.	T1S	R14E	?
CARSON, LOYD D. see **CONLY**	WASCO CO.	T1S	R14E	?
CARSON, MARY COPLAND see **CONLY**	WASCO CO.	T1S	R14E	?
CARTER see **SWEET HOME**	LANE CO.	T16S	R6W	S27
CARTER D.L.C., TOLBERT see **PALESTINE**				
	BENTON CO.	T10S	R4W	S22
CARTER HOMESTEAD, JOE	MALHEUR CO.	T20S	R39E	S29
CARTER, TOLBERT see **PALESTINE**	BENTON CO.	T10S	R4W	S22
CARTERS D.L.C., THOMAS see **I.O.O.F. [CARTERS]**				
	MULTNOMAH CO.	T1S	R1E	S4
CARTERS I.O.O.F. see **I.O.O.F [CARTERS]**				
	MULTNOMAH CO.	T1S	R1E	S4
CARTWRIGHT PLACE see **BLY [NEW]**	KLAMATH CO.	T36S	R14E	S28
CARUS	CLACKAMAS CO.	T3S	R2E	S27
CARUTHERS D.L.C., FINICE see **BETH ISRAEL [OLD]**				
	MULTNOMAH CO.	T1S	R1E	S10
CARUTHERS D.L.C., FINICE see **COUNTY FARM #1**				
	MULTNOMAH CO.	T1S	R1E	S10
CARUTHERS-TERWILLIGER see **CITY CEMETERY #3**				
	MULTNOMAH CO.	T1S	R1E	S10
CASCADE LOCKS	HOOD RIVER CO.	T2N	R7E	S12
CASCADES see **CASCADE LOCKS**	HOOD RIVER CO.	T2N	R7E	S12
CASCADIA PARK	LINN CO.	?	R3E	?
CASE see **CHAMPOEG**	MARION CO.	T4S	R2W	S12

CASE, CHARLES LAFERTY	CLACKAMAS CO.	T2S	R1E	S36
CASEY, DOCTOR L. V. see **CASEY FAMILY**				
	POLK CO.	T8S	R5W	S3
CASEY FAMILY	KLAMATH CO.	T39S	R11 1/2E	?
CASEY FAMILY	POLK CO.	T8S	R5W	S3
CASEY FAMILY, ROSE	CLATSOP CO.	T7N	R9W	?
CASEY, J. T. see **CASEY FAMILY**	KLAMATH CO.	T39S	R11 1/2E	?
CASEY, JENNIE see **CASEY FAMILY**	KLAMATH CO.	T39S	R11 1/2E	?
CASEY, MARION ETHEL PANKEY see **CASEY FAMILY**				
	POLK CO.	T8S	R5W	S3
CASEY PLACE see **CASEY FAMILY**	KLAMATH CO.	T39S	R11 1/2E	?
CASON D.L.C., FENDALL see **CASON, REBECCA**				
	CLACKAMAS CO.	T2S	R2E	S20
CASON, JOHN see **CASON, REBECCA**	CLACKAMAS CO.	T2S	R2E	S20
CASON, REBECCA	CLACKAMAS CO.	T2S	R2E	S20
CATACOMBS	MARION CO.	T4S	R2W	S19
CATCHING CREEK	COOS CO.	T29S	R13W	S35
CATCHING D.L.C., BENJAMIN see **MOUNTAIN VIEW MEMORIAL GARDENS**				
	WASHINGTON CO.	T1N	R4W	S35
CATE, J. D.	YAMHILL CO.	T5S	R6W	S4
CATHOLIC see **ASTORIA [OLD]**	CLATSOP CO.	T8N	R9W	S8
CATHOLIC see **BANDON PIONEER**	COOS CO.	T28S	R14W	S30
CATHOLIC see **I.O.O.F. [LAKEVIEW]**				
	LAKE CO.	T39S	R20E	S10
CATHOLIC see **JACKSONVILLE**	JACKSON CO.	T37S	R2W	S29
CATHOLIC see **MT. HOPE**	BAKER CO.	T9S	R40E	S21
CATHOLIC see **ST. EDWARD'S CATHOLIC [NEW]**				
	WASHINGTON CO.	T2N	R2W	S31
CATHOLIC see **ST. EDWARD'S CATHOLIC [OLD]**				
	WASHINGTON CO.	T1N	R3W	S1
CATHOLIC see **ST. JOSEPH**	GILLIAM CO.	T4S	R21E	S10
CATHOLIC see **ST. JOSEPH**	MULTNOMAH CO.	T1S	R3E	S8
CATHOLIC see **ST. MARY'S**	HOOD RIVER CO.	T2N	R10E	S2
CATHOLIC see **ST. MARY'S**	MULTNOMAH CO.	T1N	R1E	S36
CATHOLIC see **ST. PATRICKS**	JOSEPHINE CO.	T40S	R8W	S34
CATHOLIC see **WALLOWA**	WALLOWA CO.	T1N	R42E	S13
CATHOLIC [BANDON]	COOS CO.	T28S	R14W	S30
CATHOLIC [LA GRANDE] see **CALVARY**				
	UNION CO.	T3S	R38E	S8
CATHOLIC [OLD] see **HINES**	HARNEY CO.	T23S	R30E	S24
CATHOLIC CEMETERY AT VERBOORT see **VISITATION OF THE BLESSED VIRGIN MARY**				
	WASHINGTON CO.	T1N	R3W	S17
CATHOLIC SCHOOL see **OUR LADY OF LOURDES**				
	LINN CO.	T10S	R1E	S9
CATLOW, JOHN AND MARGARET FINN	HARNEY CO.	T40S	R31E	S4
CATLOW RANCH see **CATLOW, JOHN AND MARGARET FINN**				
	HARNEY CO.	T40S	R31E	S4
CAYUSE see **HOMLY**	UMATILLA CO.	T2N	R34E	S2
CECIL CHILDREN, ANNA LAURA AND WALTER				
	GILLIAM CO.	T3N	R22E	S12

```
CECIL, MARY ELLEN see CECIL CHILDREN, ANNA LAURA AND WALTER
                              GILLIAM CO.       T3N    R22E     S12
CECIL, WILLIAM Y. see CECIL CHILDREN, ANNA LAURA AND WALTER
                              GILLIAM CO.       T3N    R22E     S12
CEDAR CREEK ROAD              COLUMBIA CO.      T4N    R2W      S18
CEDAR HILL                    DOUGLAS CO.       T25S   R5W      S5
CEDAR HILL see BRYANT         COLUMBIA CO.      T7N    R4W      S9
CEDAR MILLS see UNION         WASHINGTON CO.    T1N    R1W      S29
CEDAR MILLS CATHOLIC see PIONEER CATHOLIC OF ST. ANTHONY OF PADUA
                              WASHINGTON CO.    T1S    R1W      S4
CELILO [#1]                   WASCO CO.         T2N    R15E     S16
CELILO [#2]                   WASCO CO.         T2N    R15E     S21
CEMETERY ASSOCIATION see HAZELWOOD
                              CLACKAMAS CO.     T2S    R3E      S13
CEMETERY HILL see HILLTOP     POLK CO.          T9S    R4W      S9
CEMETERY HILL see MOUNTAIN VIEW-CORBETT PIONEER
                              MULTNOMAH CO.     T1S    R4E      S3
CEMETERY RIDGE                WALLOWA CO.       ?      R48E     ?
CEMETERY SPRING               MALHEUR CO.       T19S   R41E     S35
CENTRAL see SANTIAM CENTRAL   LINN CO.          T11S   R2W      S6
CENTRAL CEMETERY ASSOCIATION see WALTON
                              LANE CO.          T18S   R7W      S5
CENTRAL CHRISTIAN see SANTIAM CENTRAL
                              LINN CO.          T11S   R2W      S6
CENTRAL COLUMBIA see POWELL GROVE PIONEER
                              MULTNOMAH CO.     T1N    R2E      S23
CENTRAL GRANGE see CENTRAL SCHOOL
                              LANE CO.          T18S   R5W      S4
CENTRAL GROVE see POWELL GROVE PIONEER
                              MULTNOMAH CO.     T1N    R2E      S23
CENTRAL POINT                 JACKSON CO.       T37S   R2W      S1
CENTRAL SCHOOL                LANE CO.          T18S   R5W      S4
CHALLAFOIX D.L.C., CATHARINE see HARDING FAMILY
                              MARION CO.        T4S    R2W      S33
CHAMBERLAIN D.L.C., AARON C. see CHAMBERLIN FAMILY
                              POLK CO.          T9S    R5W      S24
CHAMBERLAIN FAMILY            TILLAMOOK CO.     T3S    R10W     S7
CHAMBERLAIN FAMILY see CHAMBERLIN FAMILY
                              POLK CO.          T9S    R5W      S24
CHAMBERLAIN HOMESTEAD, EZRA B. see CHAMBERLAIN FAMILY
                              TILLAMOOK CO.     T3S    R10W     S7
CHAMBERLIN-COLLINS FAMILY see CHAMBERLIN FAMILY
                              POLK CO.          T9S    R5W      S24
CHAMBERLIN FAMILY             POLK CO.          T9S    R5W      S24
CHAMBERLIN, MRS. H.           MORROW CO.        T4N    R24E     ?
CHAMBERS, JAMES W.            WHEELER CO.       T6S    R21E     S22
CHAMBERS, MRS. see CHAMBERS, SARAH
                              MALHEUR CO.       T18S   R37E     S33
CHAMBERS, ROWLAND see CHAMBERS, SARAH
                              MALHEUR CO.       T18S   R37E     S33
CHAMBERS, SARAH               MALHEUR CO.       T18S   R37E     S33
```

CHAMPAGNE see **CHAMPAIGN FAMILY**	DOUGLAS CO.	T27S	R6W	S6
CHAMPAIGN D.L.C., JOSEPH see **CHAMPAIGN FAMILY**				
	DOUGLAS CO.	T27S	R6W	S6
CHAMPAIGN FAMILY	DOUGLAS CO.	T27S	R6W	S6
CHAMPION, JOE see **TROUT**	TILLAMOOK CO.	T1S	R9W	S30
CHAMPOEG	MARION CO.	T4S	R2W	S12
CHAPEL, TEDDY ROOSEVELT	MORROW CO.	T5S	R25E	S3
CHAPMAN D.L.C., WILLIAM see **REST HAVEN MEMORIAL PARK**				
	YAMHILL CO.	T6S	R6W	S3
CHARBONNEAU, JEAN BAPTISTE	MALHEUR CO.	T30S	R44E	S16
CHARLEY see **RIVERSIDE V.F.W.**	LINCOLN CO.	T10S	R10W	S11
CHASE BURIAL	CLACKAMAS CO.	T4S	R4E	?
CHASE D.L.C., WILLIAM see **HARGADINE**				
	JACKSON CO.	T39S	R1E	S5
CHASTAIN, BESSIE	WASCO CO.	T4S	R12E	S1
CHATWOOD BABIES	TILLAMOOK CO.	?	?	?
CHATWOOD PLACE see **CHATWOOD BABIES**				
	TILLAMOOK CO.	?	?	?
CHEADLE D.L.C., RAPHAEL see **SANDRIDGE**				
	LINN CO.	T12S	R3W	S24
CHEBRA AHAVI SHOLUM see **AHAVAI SHOLOM**				
	MULTNOMAH CO.	T1S	R1E	S27
CHEBRA AHIVA SHOLUM see **AHAVAI SHOLOM**				
	MULTNOMAH CO.	T1S	R1E	S27
CHEHALEM MOUNTAIN see **GIBBS**	YAMHILL CO.	T3S	R2W	S3
CHELAN ABBEY MAUSOLEUM AND COLUMBARIUM				
	LINCOLN CO.	T11S	R11W	S9
CHEMAWA	MARION CO.	T6S	R3W	S36
CHERRY GROVE see **CHERRY GROVE BAPTIST**				
	WASHINGTON CO.	T1S	R4W	S30
CHERRY GROVE BAPTIST	WASHINGTON CO.	T1S	R4W	S30
CHERRYVILLE	CLACKAMAS CO.	T2S	R6E	S30
CHESHIRE see **FRANKLIN**	LANE CO.	T16S	R5W	S21
CHEWAUCAN	LAKE CO.	T34S	R19E	S33
CHICKAHOMINY	LANE CO.	T17S	R7W	S20
CHIEF CONCOMLY see **COMCOMLY'S GRAVE**				
	CLATSOP CO.	T8N	R9W	S8
CHIEF JOSEPH [OLD]	WALLOWA CO.	T1N	R43E	S20
CHIEF JOSEPH MONUMENT	WALLOWA CO.	T3S	R45E	S5
CHILDS	LINN CO.	T12S	R2W	S36
CHILD'S GRAVE	GRANT CO.	T9S	R31E	S14
CHILD'S GRAVE	MORROW CO.	T1N	R23E	?
CHILTON, W. R. see **MELOY FAMILY**	MULTNOMAH CO.	?	?	?
CHINAMEN'S MASSACRE see **CHINESE MASSACRE**				
	MALHEUR CO.	T31S	R41E	?
CHINESE [BAKER CITY]	BAKER CO.	T9S	R40E	S15
CHINESE [GARDINER ?]	DOUGLAS CO.	T21S	R12W	?
CHINESE [LONE FIR]	MULTNOMAH CO.	T1S	R1E	S2
CHINESE [MONTAVILLA]	MULTNOMAH CO.	T1N	R2E	S33
CHINESE [ST. JOHNS]	MULTNOMAH CO.	T1N	R1E	S18
CHINESE [SPARTA]	BAKER CO.	T8S	R44E	?

CHINESE [THE DALLES]	WASCO CO.	T1N	R13E	S10
CHINESE see **MASONIC [OLD ROSEBURG]**				
	DOUGLAS CO.	T27S	R5W	S19
CHINESE BENEVOLENT SOCIETY see **CHINESE [LONE FIR]**				
	MULTNOMAH CO.	T1S	R1E	S2
CHINESE CEMETERY IN LINCOLN MEMORIAL PARK				
	MULTNOMAH CO.	T1S	R2E	S22
CHINESE HERDSMAN	WHEELER CO.	T10S	R21E	?
CHINESE MASSACRE	MALHEUR CO.	T31S	R41E	?
CHINESE MINERS MASSACRE	WALLOWA CO.	T4N	R49E	UNS
CHITWOOD	LINCOLN CO.	T10S	R9W	S32
CHITWOOD see **DAMASCUS PIONEER**	CLACKAMAS CO.	T2S	R3E	S8
CHRIST CHURCH PARISH	CLACKAMAS CO.	T2S	R1E	S10
CHRISTILDA see **CRISTILLA PIONEER**				
	CLACKAMAS CO.	T1S	R2E	S36
CHRISTMAS VALLEY	LAKE CO.	T27S	R17E	S28
CHURCH see **FALL CREEK**	LANE CO.	T18S	R1W	S33
CHURCH OF BRETHREN see **DUNKARD**	JACKSON CO.	T38S	R1W	S23
CHURCH OF THE CHRISTIANS see **EVERGREEN HILL**				
	LANE CO.	T17S	R3W	S14
CHURCHILL D.L.C., WILLIAM see **COLES VALLEY**				
	DOUGLAS CO.	T25S	R7W	S35
CHURCHILL, ELIZABETH J. HUMPHRIES				
	WASCO CO.	?	?	?
CHURCHILL FARM, J. H. see **SCHWALNUS FAMILY**				
	TILLAMOOK CO.	T3N	R10W	?
CHURCHILL, MRS. see **CHURCHILL, ELIZABETH J. HUMPHRIES**				
	WASCO CO.	?	?	?
CIRCLE CITY see **ORLEANS**	LINN CO.	T11S	R4W	S32
CITIZENS see **DRAIN [NORTH]**	DOUGLAS CO.	T22S	R5W	S8
CITY see **ASTORIA PIONEER**	CLATSOP CO.	T8N	R9W	S17
CITY see **DRAIN [NORTH]**	DOUGLAS CO.	T22S	R5W	S8
CITY see **JACKSONVILLE**	JACKSON CO.	T37S	R2W	S29
CITY see **JUNIPER HAVEN**	CROOK CO.	T14S	R16E	S31
CITY CEMETERY #1	MULTNOMAH CO.	T1N	R1E	S33
CITY CEMETERY #2	MULTNOMAH CO.	T1N	R1E	S33
CITY CEMETERY #3	MULTNOMAH CO.	T1S	R1E	S10
CITY CEMETERY #4 see **BETH ISRAEL [OLD]**				
	MULTNOMAH CO.	T1S	R1E	S10
CITY GARBAGE CREMATORY	MULTNOMAH CO.	T1N	R1E	S29
CITY OF ASHLAND see **HARGADINE**	JACKSON CO.	T39S	R1E	S5
CITY OF MORO	SHERMAN CO.	T1S	R17E	S18
CITY OF OREGON CITY see **MOUNTAIN VIEW**				
	CLACKAMAS CO.	T3S	R2E	S5
CITY OF VERNONIA MEMORIAL see **VERNONIA MEMORIAL**				
	COLUMBIA CO.	T4N	R4W	S5
CITY VIEW, MT. CREST ABBEY MAUSOLEUM AND SUNRISE GARDEN MAUSOLEUM				
	MARION CO.	T7S	R3W	S33
CIVIL BEND	DOUGLAS CO.	T28S	R6W	S21
CLACKAMAS	CLACKAMAS CO.	T2S	R2E	S4
CLACKAMAS PIONEER see **CLACKAMAS**	CLACKAMAS CO.	T2S	R2E	S4

CLAGGETT	MARION CO.	T6S	R3W	S26
CLAREMONT FAMILY	POLK CO.	T10S	R7W	S11
CLARK, BESSIE SMITH see **CLARK FARM**				
	MULTNOMAH CO.	?	?	?
CLARK CHILDREN	BAKER CO.	T8S	R46E	?
CLARK D.L.C., JAMES G. see **CANYONVILLE**				
	DOUGLAS CO.	T30S	R5W	S27
CLARK D.L.C., JAMES G. see **ROSE HILL MEMORIAL**				
	DOUGLAS CO.	T30S	R5W	S27
CLARK D.L.C., WILLIAM D. see **YAMHILL-CARLTON**				
	YAMHILL CO.	T3S	R4W	S10
CLARK FARM	MULTNOMAH CO.	?	?	?
CLARK, FRANK see **CLARK FARM**	MULTNOMAH CO.	?	?	?
CLARK, GEORGE see **CLARK FARM**	MULTNOMAH CO.	?	?	?
CLARK GRAVE	DOUGLAS CO.	?	?	?
CLARK, HARVEY see **PACIFIC UNIVERSITY**				
	WASHINGTON CO.	T1N	R3W	S31
CLARK, MARY KELLY see **CLARK FARM**				
	MULTNOMAH CO.	?	?	?
CLARK, WILLIAM see **CLARK FARM**	MULTNOMAH CO.	?	?	?
CLARKES see **CLARKES PIONEER**	CLACKAMAS CO.	T4S	R3E	S29
CLARKES PIONEER	CLACKAMAS CO.	T4S	R3E	S29
CLARKSVILLE	BAKER CO.	T12S	R41E	S34
CLARNO	WASCO CO.	T7S	R19E	S29
CLARNO AND RALPH BABIES see **RALPH AND CLARNO BABIES**				
	CURRY CO.	T39S	R14W	S2
CLARNO SPRINGS	CURRY CO.	T36S	R14W	S9
CLATSOP see **OCEAN VIEW**	CLATSOP CO.	T8N	R10W	S28
CLATSOP COUNTY see **PAUPER [WARRENTON]**				
	CLATSOP CO.	T8N	R10W	S21
CLATSOP INDIANS	CLATSOP CO.	T6N	R10W	S28
CLATSOP PLAINS PIONEER	CLATSOP CO.	T7N	R10W	S4
CLAUSEN, NICK	CLACKAMAS CO.	T4S	R4E	?
CLAWSON BABIES	BAKER CO.	?	?	?
CLAWSON, ELLIS L. see **CLAWSON BABIES**				
	BAKER CO.	?	?	?
CLAWSON, MARTHA LUCILE STAM see **CLAWSON BABIES**				
	BAKER CO.	?	?	?
CLAY HILL	CURRY CO.	T34S	R11W	S2
CLAY, RUFUS AND VERNON	UNION CO.	T2S	R37E	S14
CLAYPOOL D.L.C., REUBEN see **CLAYPOOL FAMILY**				
	LINN CO.	T13S	R2W	S5
CLAYPOOL FAMILY	LINN CO.	T13S	R2W	S5
CLEAR CREEK see **NORTH CEMETERY OF CLEAR CREEK**				
	COLUMBIA CO.	T4N	R5W	S27
CLEAR LAKE see **CLAGGETT**	MARION CO.	T6S	R3W	S26
CLEAVER see **MT. HOPE**	BAKER CO.	T9S	R40E	S21
CLEM	GILLIAM CO.	T1S	R21E	S32
CLEMENTS	TILLAMOOK CO.	T2S	R9W	S16
CLEMENTS CORNER see **CLEMENTS**	TILLAMOOK CO.	T2S	R9W	S16
CLEONE see **FAIRVIEW**	MULTNOMAH CO.	T1N	R3E	?

CLEVELAND	DOUGLAS CO.	T26S	R7W	S24
CLEVELAND HILL see **CLEVELAND**	DOUGLAS CO.	T26S	R7W	S24
CLIFFSIDE	CLACKAMAS CO.	T2S	R5E	S7
CLIMAX GRAVES	JACKSON CO.	T38S	R2E	S5
CLINE	MULTNOMAH CO.	T2N	R1W	?
CLINE D.L.C., JACOB see **CLINE**	MULTNOMAH CO.	T2N	R1W	?
CLINE RANCH, MONTE see **BLY [NEW]**				
	KLAMATH CO.	T36S	R14E	S28
CLINTON FARM see **BUTLER FAMILY**	MULTNOMAH CO.	T1S	R3E	S20
CLOUTIER see **LATTIE-CLOUTRIE FAMILY**				
	CLATSOP CO.	T6N	R10W	S21
CLOUTRIE, ANTOINE J. see **LATTIE-CLOUTRIE FAMILY**				
	CLATSOP CO.	T6N	R10W	S21
CLOUTRIE, HELEN see **LATTIE-CLOUTRIE FAMILY**				
	CLATSOP CO.	T6N	R10W	S21
CLOVERDALE	LANE CO.	T19S	R2W	S18
CLOVERDALE	MARION CO.	T9S	R2W	S7
CLOVERDALE BAPTIST see **UNION PIONEER [CLOVERDALE]**				
	TILLAMOOK CO.	T4S	R10W	S33
CLOVERDALE CATHOLIC see **JENCK**	TILLAMOOK CO.	T4S	R10W	S34
CLOVERDALE UNION see **UNION PIONEER [CLOVERDALE]**				
	TILLAMOOK CO.	T4S	R10W	S33
CLUM see **KLUM**	LINN CO.	T12S	R1W	S32
COATES, E. S. see **COATES INFANT**	MARION CO.	T8S	R2W	S19
COATES INFANT	MARION CO.	T8S	R2W	S19
COBURG see **I.O.O.F. [COBURG]**	LANE CO.	T17S	R3W	S4
COBURN FAMILY see **JACKSON FAMILY, HENRY**				
	KLAMATH CO.	T36S	R11E	S29
COCHRAN D.L.C., WILLIAM see **COCHRAN, POLLY**				
	LINN CO.	T13S	R2W	S19
COCHRAN, POLLY	LINN CO.	T13S	R2W	S19
COCHRAN, WALLACE	GRANT CO.	T9S	R27E	S5
COFFEE CREEK	DOUGLAS CO.	T30S	R2W	S18
COGGSMILL see **COGSWELL, JOHN**	WASCO CO.	T1N	R15E	S30
COGGSWELL see **COGSWELL, JOHN**	WASCO CO.	T1N	R15E	S30
COGSWELL	LANE CO.	T19S	R3W	S5
COGSWELL GRAVES see **COGSWELL, JOHN**				
	WASCO CO.	T1N	R15E	S30
COGSWELL, JOHN	WASCO CO.	T1N	R15E	S30
COGSWELL PLACE see **COGSWELL, JOHN**				
	WASCO CO.	T1N	R15E	S30
COLBY, AMANDA M. see **COLBY FARM, J. A.**				
	MARION CO.	?	?	?
COLBY FARM, J. A.	MARION CO.	?	?	?
COLE FAMILY, DR. JAMES	DOUGLAS CO.	T25S	R6W	S8
COLEMAN D.L.C., JAMES see **ST. PATRICK**				
	YAMHILL CO.	T5S	R5W	S4
COLES VALLEY	DOUGLAS CO.	T25S	R7W	S35
COLLINGS GRAVES	JACKSON CO.	T40S	R4W	S36
COLLINS D.L.C., SMITH see **CHAMBERLIN FAMILY**				
	POLK CO.	T9S	R5W	S24

```
COLLINS, SMITH see CHAMBERLIN FAMILY
                                POLK CO.         T9S     R5W      S24
COLLVER, BENHAM B.              COOS CO.         T26S    R14W     ?
COLT, ISAAC                     BAKER CO.        T13S    R37E     S5
COLT RANCH, PORTER see COLT, ISAAC
                                BAKER CO.        T13S    R37E     S5
COLTON LUTHERAN                 CLACKAMAS CO.    T5S     R3E      S3
COLUMBIA see COLUMBIAN          MULTNOMAH CO.    T1N     R1E      S10
COLUMBIA LODGE #5 see I.O.O.F. [THE DALLES]
                                WASCO CO.        T1N     R13E     S4
COLUMBIA MASONIC see COLUMBIA PIONEER
                                MULTNOMAH CO.    T1N     R2E      S21
COLUMBIA MEMORIAL GARDENS       COLUMBIA CO.     T4N     R2W      S36
COLUMBIA PIONEER                MULTNOMAH CO.    T1N     R2E      S21
COLUMBIA PIONEER MASONIC see COLUMBIA PIONEER
                                MULTNOMAH CO.    T1N     R2E      S21
COLUMBIA SLOUGH LODGE see COLUMBIA PIONEER
                                MULTNOMAH CO.    T1N     R2E      S21
COLUMBIAN                       MULTNOMAH CO.    T1N     R1E      S10
COLUMBIAN KENTON see COLUMBIAN  MULTNOMAH CO.    T1N     R1E      S10
COLVER D.L.C., SAMUEL see PHOENIX [NEW]
                                JACKSON CO.      T38S    R1W      S9
COLVER, JEMIMA see PHOENIX [NEW]
                                JACKSON CO.      T38S    R1W      S9
COLVER, LEWELLYN see PHOENIX [NEW]
                                JACKSON CO.      T38S    R1W      S9
COLVIN                          DOUGLAS CO.      T22S    R5W      S6
COLVIN GRAVE                    CURRY CO.        T37S    R14W     ?
COLVIN RANCH, G. N. see RICE-MARSH FAMILY
                                DOUGLAS CO.      T23S    R5W      S31
COMBE FARM, D. BUD see UNKNOWN  JOSEPHINE CO.    T37S    R6W      ?
COMBS D.L.C., RICHARD C. see MURRAY FAMILY
                                YAMHILL CO.      T4S     R5W      S32
COMCOMLY'S GRAVE                CLATSOP CO.      T8N     R9W      S8
COMMONS see HALSEY PIONEER      LINN CO.         T14S    R4W      S11
COMSTOCK                        DOUGLAS CO.      T21S    R4W      S20
CONCOMLY see COMCOMLY'S GRAVE   CLATSOP CO.      T8N     R9W      S8
CONDIT see PLEASANT GROVE       MARION CO.       T9S     R2W      S11
CONDIT D.L.C., PHILIP see PLEASANT GROVE
                                MARION CO.       T9S     R2W      S11
CONDIT, REVEREND PHILIP see PLEASANT GROVE
                                MARION CO.       T9S     R2W      S11
CONE D.L.C., ANTON see BUTTEVILLE [NEW]
                                MARION CO.       T3S     R1W      S32
CONFEDERATED TRIBES see GRAND RONDE
                                POLK CO.         T6S     R8W      S12
CONGREGATION KESER ISRAEL       MULTNOMAH CO.    T1S     R2E      S20
CONGREGATION SHAARIE TORAH      MULTNOMAH CO.    T1S     R2E      S20
CONGREGATIONAL see MOUNTAIN VIEW MEMORIAL GARDENS
                                WASHINGTON CO.   T1N     R4W      S35
```

CONINGER D.L.C., DAVID A. see **COLUMBIA MEMORIAL GARDENS**
    COLUMBIA CO.   T4N   R2W   S36
CONKLIN D.L.C., CHARLES see **VISITATION OF THE BLESSED VIRGIN MARY**
    WASHINGTON CO.   T1N   R3W   S17
CONLIFF, FRED see **MASTERS**   COOS CO.   T26S   R12W   S6
CONLY   WASCO CO.   T1S   R14E   ?
CONNELL   TILLAMOOK CO.   T4S   R7W   ?
CONNELL FARM, JOSEPH see **BURRIS FAMILY, WILLIAM**
    WASHINGTON CO.   T1N   R2W   S5
CONNOR CREEK   BAKER CO.   T11S   R45E   S34
CONNOR D.L.C., NATHAN see **PLEASANT HILL**
    POLK CO.   T6S   R6W   S12
CONNOR FAMILY see **PLEASANT HILL** POLK CO.   T6S   R6W   S12
CONROE'S PIG RANCH see **HAMLIN, NATHANIEL**
    BAKER CO.   T7S   R39E   S27
CONROY PLACE, JOHN see **BUTTS, CATHERINE BONNETT**
    WASCO CO.   T3S   R14E   S28
CONROY PLACE, PETER see **CRAMER, MRS.**
    WASCO CO.   T7S   R17E   ?
CONSTABLE D.L.C., EDWARD AND PRISCILLA see **METHODIST MEETING HOUSE**
    WASHINGTON CO.   T1N   R2W   S21
CONYERS D.L.C., ENOCH W. see **MAPLEWOOD**
    COLUMBIA CO.   T7N   R4W   S8
CONYERS D.L.C., ENOCH W. see **MURRAY HILL**
    COLUMBIA CO.   T7N   R4W   S17
COOK, CHRIS   COOS CO.   T30S   R10W   S3
COOK PLACE see **BARTNICK**   TILLAMOOK CO.   T1S   R10W   S18
COOKE, RONALD PETER   CLACKAMAS CO.   ?   ?   ?
COOLEY FAMILY   CURRY CO.   T41S   R13W   S9
COOLIDGE AND McCLAINE see **SILVERTON**
    MARION CO.   T6S   R1W   S34
COON see **MILLER**   LINN CO.   T13S   R4W   S4
COON D.L.C., JAMES L. see **MILLER**
    LINN CO.   T13S   R4W   S4
COOPER FAMILY   POLK CO.   T8S   R5W   S29
COOPER, HESTER ANN MOXLEY see **COOPER FAMILY**
    POLK CO.   T8S   R5W   S29
COOPER HOLLOW see **COOPER FAMILY** POLK CO.   T8S   R5W   S29
COOPER, J. F. J.   BAKER CO.   T12S   R44E   S19
COOPER, JAMES LINDSAY see **COOPER FAMILY**
    POLK CO.   T8S   R5W   S29
COOPER MD., ARTHUR   CURRY CO.   T40S   R14W   S10
COOPER MOUNTAIN [CATHOLIC]   WASHINGTON CO.   T1S   R2W   S25
COOPER MOUNTAIN [PROTESTANT]   WASHINGTON CO.   T1S   R2W   S25
COOPER, MRS.   LINN CO.   T12S   R1W   S8
COOPER'S, DOCTOR see **COOPER MD, ARTHUR**
    CURRY CO.   T40S   R14W   S10
COOS see **DREW MEMORIAL**   LANE CO.   T18S   R12W   S24
COOS RIVER PIONEER   COOS CO.   T25S   R12W   S25
COPPER see **STEAMBOAT**   JACKSON CO.   T40S   R4W   S20

COPPER *[Sic]* MOUNTAIN see **COOPER MOUNTAIN [CATHOLIC]**

	WASHINGTON CO.	T1S	R2W	S25

COPPER *[Sic]* MOUNTAIN see **COOPER MOUNTAIN [PROTESTANT]**

	WASHINGTON CO.	T1S	R2W	S25
COPPERFIELD FAMILY	KLAMATH CO.	?	?	?
COPPERFIELD-HOMESTEAD	BAKER CO.	T6S	R48E	S33

COPPLE, CHARLES WESLEY see **COPPLE FAMILY**

	MORROW CO.	T5S	R27E	S2
COPPLE FAMILY	MORROW CO.	T5S	R27E	S2

COPPLE, WILLIAM HARVEY see **COPPLE FAMILY**

	MORROW CO.	T5S	R27E	S2

COQUILLE PIONEER see **I.O.O.F. [OLD COQUILLE]**

	COOS CO.	T27S	R13W	S36

CORBETT see **MOUNTAIN VIEW-CORBETT PIONEER**

	MULTNOMAH CO.	T1S	R4E	S3
CORBETT FAMILY	MULTNOMAH CO.	T1S	R1E	S3
CORD	MALHEUR CO.	T28S	R38E	S7
CORD, OTTO see **GOLD RIDGE MINE**	BAKER CO.	T12S	R43E	S16
CORNELIUS see **CLOVERDALE**	MARION CO.	T9S	R2W	S7

CORNELIUS LUTHERAN see **EMANUEL LUTHERAN**

	WASHINGTON CO.	T1N	R3W	S34

CORNELIUS METHODIST see **CORNELIUS PIONEER METHODIST**

	WASHINGTON CO.	T1N	R3W	S33
CORNELIUS PIONEER METHODIST	WASHINGTON CO.	T1N	R3W	S33
CORNUCOPIA	BAKER CO.	T6S	R45E	?

CORNUTT D.L.C., REV. ALFRED see **WHITE BIRCH PIONEER**

	MULTNOMAH CO.	T1S	R3E	S9

CORSE, HERMANN see **CORSE, HERMANN HEINRICH**

	JOSEPHINE CO.	T39S	R9W	S10
CORSE, HERMANN HEINRICH	JOSEPHINE CO.	T39S	R9W	S10
CORWIN see **CULVER I.O.O.F.**	JEFFERSON CO.	T12S	R13E	S16
COSTELLOE, EDMOND	CURRY CO.	T41S	R12W	S5
COTTAGE GROVE see **FIR GROVE**	LANE CO.	T20S	R3W	S29
COTTONWOOD see **SANTIAM CENTRAL**	LINN CO.	T11S	R2W	S6
COUNTY see **GRANITE HILL**	JOSEPHINE CO.	T36S	R6W	S13
COUNTY see **PAUPER [WARRENTON]**	CLATSOP CO.	T8N	R10W	S21
COUNTY FARM #1	MULTNOMAH CO.	T1S	R1E	S10
COUNTY FARM #2	MULTNOMAH CO.	T1S	R1E	S5
COUNTY POOR FARM	COOS CO.	T27S	R12W	S29
COVE	UNION CO.	T3S	R40E	S22
COVEY FAMILY	WASCO CO.	T3S	R12E	S2

COW CANYON GRADE see **HAIGHT SPRING**

	WASCO CO.	T8S	R15E	S9
COX	MARION CO.	T9S	R3W	S5
COX, BEULAH MAY	WASCO CO.	T5S	R12E	S24

COX BUTTE see **REST LAWN MEMORIAL PARK**

	LANE CO.	T15S	R5W	S34
COX CHILDREN	MORROW CO.	T2S	R27E	S36

COX D.L.C., ANDERSON see **EAST ALBANY**

	LINN CO.	T11S	R3W	S4

COX D.L.C., ANDERSON see **WAVERLY JEWISH**				
	LINN CO.	T11S	R3W	S4
COX D.L.C., ANDERSON see **WAVERLY MEMORIAL**				
	LINN CO.	T11S	R3W	S4
COX D.L.C., ELIAS see **BETHANY PIONEER**				
	MARION CO.	T6S	R1W	S33
COX D.L.C., JESSE see **KIME-BROWN FAMILY**				
	LANE CO.	T16S	R5W	S17
COX D.L.C., JOHN see **COX, JOHN**	DOUGLAS CO.	T28S	R6W	?
COX D.L.C., JOSEPH AND MARTHA see **COX**				
	MARION CO.	T9S	R3W	S5
COX D.L.C., PETER see **ST. PAUL'S CATHOLIC**				
	MARION CO.	T6S	R1W	S27
COX D.L.C., SOLOMON see **REST LAWN MEMORIAL PARK**				
	LANE CO.	T15S	R5W	S34
COX, DUDLEY see **COX, BEULAH MAY**	WASCO CO.	T5S	R12E	S24
COX, ETHAN see **McCLELLAN, CHARLES**				
	MULTNOMAH CO.	T1N	R3E	S28
COX, F. D. see **COX CHILDREN**	MORROW CO.	T2S	R27E	S36
COX, F. D. RANCH see **COX CHILDREN**				
	MORROW CO.	T2S	R27E	S36
COX FAMILY	DOUGLAS CO.	?	?	?
COX, JOHN	DOUGLAS CO.	T28S	R6W	?
COX, JOHN W. see **SHUMWAY, ALFRED J.**				
	MALHEUR CO.	T23S	R37E	S34
COX PLACE see **COX FAMILY**	DOUGLAS CO.	?	?	?
COX, SALLY see **SHUMWAY, ALFRED J.**				
	MALHEUR CO.	T23S	R37E	S34
COX, SARAH	DOUGLAS CO.	T22S	R4W	S20
COX, WM. A. see **HUSSEY FAMILY**	POLK CO.	T6S	R7W	S15
COZAD D.L.C., JONATHAN see **HARRIS, DR.**				
	DOUGLAS CO.	T24S	R4W	?
CRABTREE D.L.C., JOB see **CRABTREE FAMILY**				
	LINN CO.	T11S	R2W	S13
CRABTREE FAMILY	LINN CO.	T11S	R2W	S13
CRAIG, HENRY CLAY	COLUMBIA CO.	?	?	?
CRAIG, JOHN TEMPLETON see **CRAIG MEMORIAL**				
	LANE CO.	T15S	R7 1/2E	UNS
CRAIG, MARTHA see **CRAIG, HENRY CLAY**				
	COLUMBIA CO.	?	?	?
CRAIG MEMORIAL	LANE CO.	T15S	R7 1/2E	UNS
CRAMER, MRS.	WASCO CO.	T7S	R17E	?
CRANE	HARNEY CO.	T25S	R33E	S12
CRATER	JACKSON CO.	T35S	R2E	?
CRAWFORD HOMESTEAD, ROB see **UNKNOWN**				
	TILLAMOOK CO.	T3N	R10W	S14
CRAWFORDSVILLE UNION	LINN CO.	T14S	R1W	S17
CRAZY VALLEY	CLATSOP CO.	T5N	R9W	?
CREEK SIDE see **BROOKSIDE**	YAMHILL CO.	T4S	R3W	S17
CRESCENT see **CRESCENT GROVE**	WASHINGTON CO.	T1S	R1W	S26
CRESCENT GROVE	WASHINGTON CO.	T1S	R1W	S26

CRESTVIEW see **GREENWOOD**	CLATSOP CO.	T8N	R9W	S33
CRESTVIEW see **WALDPORT MEMORIAL**	LINCOLN CO.	T13S	R11W	S30
CRESWELL PIONEER	LANE CO.	T19S	R3W	S21
CREW FAMILY	CURRY CO.	T32S	R15W	S9
CREW, MR. see **CREW FAMILY**	CURRY CO.	T32S	R15W	S9
CREW, MRS. see **CREW FAMILY**	CURRY CO.	T32S	R15W	S9
CRICKET FLAT see **HIGHLAND**	UNION CO.	T1N	R40E	S5
CRISTESER FAMILY see **BALD RIDGE**	CURRY CO.	T33S	R9W	S8
CRISTILLA PIONEER	CLACKAMAS CO.	T1S	R2E	S36
CRISWELL BOY	MALHEUR CO.	T20S	R46E	?
CRISWELL, FRED see **CRISWELL BOY**	MALHEUR CO.	T20S	R46E	?
CRITERION	WASCO CO.	T6S	R15E	S18
CRITERION RANCH see **CRITERION**	WASCO CO.	T6S	R15E	S18
CRITESER, MAY see **BALD RIDGE**	CURRY CO.	T33S	R9W	S8
CROOK COUNTY see **JUNIPER HAVEN**	CROOK CO.	T14S	R16E	S31
CROOKED FINGER	MARION CO.	T7S	R2E	S8
CROP, VICTOR see **ST. EDWARD'S CATHOLIC [OLD]**				
	WASHINGTON CO.	T1N	R3W	S1
CROSBY, BABY	MULTNOMAH CO.	?	?	?
CROW see **McCULLOCH**	LANE CO.	T18S	R5W	S34
CROW CREEK	WALLOWA CO.	T1N	R45E	S13
CROW D.L.C., JOHN see **CROW FAMILY**				
	LANE CO.	T20S	R5W	S13
CROW FAMILY	LANE CO.	T20S	R5W	S13
CROW, MRS. ANDREW	MORROW CO.	T1S	R28E	S28
CROWE *[Sic]* see **CROW FAMILY**	LANE CO.	T20S	R5W	S13
CROWLEY see **ETNA**	POLK CO.	T7S	R4W	S7
CROXTON PIONEER MEMORIAL PARK	JOSEPHINE CO.	T36S	R5W	S8
CRUME FAMILY	KLAMATH CO.	T36S	R12E	?
CRUMP'S RANCH HOUSE, CHARLIE see **HESS, DOC.**				
	LAKE CO.	T39S	R24E	S16
CRYSTAL	KLAMATH CO.	T34S	R6E	?
CRYSTAL LAKE	BENTON CO.	T12S	R5W	S11
CULBERTSON see **HANSEN**	COOS CO.	T28S	R12W	S25
CULP CREEK	LANE CO.	T21S	R1W	S33
CULTUS MOUNTAIN	DESCHUTES CO.	UNSURVEYED		
CULVER D.L.C., DAVID AND ELIZABETH see **CULVER, DAVID**				
	MARION CO.	T7S	R1W	S36
CULVER, DAVID	MARION CO.	T7S	R1W	S36
CULVER I.O.O.F.	JEFFERSON CO.	T12S	R13E	S16
CUMMINGS	GRANT CO.	T13S	R28E	?
CUMMINGS FIELD	HARNEY CO.	T29S	R33E	S31
CUMMINS, SARAH C. see **NELSON, CORA ALICE**				
	YAMHILL CO.	T3S	R3W	S11
CUNNINGHAM GRAVE	WASCO CO.	T5S	R12E	S28
CUNNINGHAM, I. C. see **CUNNINGHAM GRAVE**				
	WASCO CO.	T5S	R12E	S28
CUNNINGHAM, J. R. see **CUNNINGHAM GRAVE**				
	WASCO CO.	T5S	R12E	S28
CUNNINGHAM RANCH see **DRY LAKE**	CROOK CO.	T20S	R20E	S14
CUPPER FAMILY	GRANT CO.	T8S	R27E	S33

CUPPER, HARRY CHARLES ADAMS see **CUPPER FAMILY**

	GRANT CO.	T8S	R27E	S33
CUPPER, HENRY see **CUPPER FAMILY**	GRANT CO.	T8S	R27E	S33

CUPPER, NORA ALICE see **CUPPER FAMILY**

	GRANT CO.	T8S	R27E	S33
CURL	LINN CO.	T10S	R2W	?

CURL D.L.C., JOHN see **FRANKLIN BUTTE**

	LINN CO.	T10S	R1W	S19
CURL FAMILY	LINCOLN CO.	T6S	R11W	S25

CURRIN D.L.C., GEORGE see **CURRINSVILLE**

	CLACKAMAS CO.	T3S	R4E	S7

CURRIN D.L.C., HUGH see **CURRIN FAMILY**

	CLACKAMAS CO.	T3S	R4E	S8
CURRIN FAMILY	CLACKAMAS CO.	T3S	R4E	S8
CURRINSVILLE	CLACKAMAS CO.	T3S	R4E	S7
CURRINSVILLE see **CURRIN FAMILY**	CLACKAMAS CO.	T3S	R4E	S8
CURTIN see **COMSTOCK**	DOUGLAS CO.	T21S	R4W	S20
CURTIS see **CORD**	MALHEUR CO.	T28S	R38E	S7
CUSHMAN see **ORLEANS**	LINN CO.	T11S	R4W	S32

CUSHMAN see **PACIFIC SUNSET MEMORIAL PARK**

	LANE CO.	T18S	R12W	S25

CUSHMAN D.L.C., DANIAL see **ORLEANS**

	LINN CO.	T11S	R4W	S32

CUSHMAN D.L.C., WALLACE see **TWIN OAKS MEMORIAL GARDENS**

	LINN CO.	T11S	R4W	S33
CUSHMAN FAMILY see **ORLEANS**	LINN CO.	T11S	R4W	S32
CUSHMAN'S PASTURE	HOOD RIVER CO.	T3N	R10E	?
CUSICK FAMILY	LINN CO.	T9S	R1E	S20

CUTSFORTH, DELBERT LEE see **CUTSFORTH FAMILY**

	BENTON CO.	?	?	?
CUTSFORTH FAMILY	BENTON CO.	?	?	?

CUTSFORTH, FLORENCE M. see **CUTSFORTH FAMILY**

	BENTON CO.	?	?	?

CUTSFORTH RANCH see **CUTSFORTH FAMILY**

	BENTON CO.	?	?	?

CUTTING, ABIGAIL see **CUTTING FAMILY**

	CLACKAMAS CO.	T4S	R2E	S36

CUTTING, BABY see **CUTTING FAMILY**

	CLACKAMAS CO.	T4S	R2E	S36

CUTTING, CHARLES see **CUTTING FAMILY**

	CLACKAMAS CO.	T4S	R2E	S36

CUTTING D.L.C., CHARLES see **CUTTING FAMILY**

	CLACKAMAS CO.	T4S	R2E	S36

CUTTING D.L.C., MARY see **REDLAND PIONEER**

	CLACKAMAS CO.	T3S	R3E	S16
CUTTING FAMILY	CLACKAMAS CO.	T4S	R2E	S36

CUTTING FAMILY see **REDLAND PIONEER**

	CLACKAMAS CO.	T3S	R3E	S16
CYRUS CHILDREN	GILLIAM CO.	T1N	R20E	S15

CYRUS, GEORGE W. see **CYRUS CHILDREN**

	GILLIAM CO.	T1N	R20E	S15

CYRUS, LAWSON see **CYRUS CHILDREN**				
	GILLIAM CO.	T1N	R20E	S15
CYRUS, LILLIA MAY see **CYRUS CHILDREN**				
	GILLIAM CO.	T1N	R20E	S15
CYRUS, MARTHA H. MILKEY see **CYRUS CHILDREN**				
	GILLIAM CO.	T1N	R20E	S15
CYRUS, WAYMAN see **CYRUS CHILDREN**				
	GILLIAM CO.	T1N	R20E	S15
DAFFODIL PATCH	WASCO CO.	T1N	R11E	S12
DAGAN, DR. see **RED HILL**	DOUGLAS CO.	T23S	R5W	S34
DAGAN, DOCTOR THEOPHILUS see **RED HILL**				
	DOUGLAS CO.	T23S	R5W	S34
DAGAN, THEOPHILUS see **RED HILL**	DOUGLAS CO.	T23S	R5W	S34
DAIRY	KLAMATH CO.	T38S	R11 1/2E	?
DALE	UMATILLA CO.	T6S	R31E	?
DALE BURIALS	GRANT CO.	T7S	R31E	?
DALLAS	POLK CO.	T8S	R5W	S5
DAMASCUS see **DAMASCUS PIONEER**	CLACKAMAS CO.	T2S	R3E	S8
DAMASCUS PIONEER	CLACKAMAS CO.	T2S	R3E	S8
DANFORTH, BABY GIRL	KLAMATH CO.	T34S	R6E	S23
DANFORTH D.L.C., JOSEPH see **DEER CREEK**				
	YAMHILL CO.	T5S	R5W	S28
DANFORTH, F. J. see **DANFORTH, BABY GIRL**				
	KLAMATH CO.	T34S	R6E	S23
DANFORTH, MARY JANE BROWN see **DANFORTH, BABY GIRL**				
	KLAMATH CO.	T34S	R6E	S23
DANISH	LANE CO.	T16S	R5W	S4
DANISH LUTHERAN CHURCH see **DANISH**				
	LANE CO.	T16S	R5W	S4
DANNEN FARM, FRED see **YARBOROUGH**				
	LINN CO.	T13S	R4W	S26
DANNER	MALHEUR CO.	T30S	R44E	S16
DANNETTE FARM see **HOOKER FAMILY**	POLK CO.	T9S	R6W	?
DANS CREEK	COOS CO.	?	?	?
DAR MAKKAH see **ISLAMIC CEMETERY OF OREGON**				
	BENTON CO.	T12S	R5W	S5
DARBY, BEN F. see **DARBY, MARTHA S.**				
	LINN CO.	T13S	R1W	?
DARBY D.L.C., OLIVER H. see **DARBY, MARTHA S.**				
	LINN CO.	T13S	R1W	?
DARBY, MARTHA S.	LINN CO.	T13S	R1W	?
DARNIELLE, SARAH	WASCO CO.	T1S	R13E	?
DARNILLE see **DARNIELLE, SARAH**	WASCO CO.	T1S	R13E	?
DARR FAMILY	UMATILLA CO.	T3S	R30 1/2E	S1
DART see **MOLALLA MEMORIAL**	CLACKAMAS CO.	T5S	R2E	S20
DAUGHERTY, BILL see **DAVIS, ANNA**	WALLOWA CO.	T1N	R42E	S11
DAUGHERTY FAMILY	SHERMAN CO.	T5S	R17E	S12
DAUGHERTY RANCH see **DAVIS, ANNA**	WALLOWA CO.	T1N	R42E	S11
DAVENPORT FAMILY	MARION CO.	T7S	R1W	S22
DAVENPORT, HOMER see **DAVENPORT FAMILY**				
	MARION CO.	T7S	R1W	S22

DAVID'S see **GIBBS**	YAMHILL CO.	T3S	R2W	S3
DAVIDSON	BENTON CO.	T12S	R7W	S8
DAVIDSON D.L.C., JAMES C. see **BUTLER-DAVIDSON FAMILY**				
	POLK CO.	T8S	R5W	S35
DAVIDSON FAMILY see **BUTLER-DAVIDSON FAMILY**				
	POLK CO.	T8S	R5W	S35
DAVIDSON HOMESTEAD, HARRISON see **DAVIDSON**				
	BENTON CO.	T12S	R7W	S8
DAVIDSON, THOMAS see **UNKNOWN**	UNION CO.	T3S	R33E	S23
DAVIS	COOS CO.	T29S	R10W	S28
DAVIS, ANNA	WALLOWA CO.	T1N	R42E	S11
DAVIS, BETTY see **VETERAN'S GRAVE**				
	COLUMBIA CO.	T6N	R5W	S24
DAVIS D.L.C., HENRY AND TRIJAH see **FIR LAWN CEMETERY AND MAUSOLEUM**				
	WASHINGTON CO.	T1N	R3W	S36
DAVIS D.L.C., LEANDER see **SILVERTON**				
	MARION CO.	T6S	R1W	S34
DAVIS D.L.C., TRUST see **DAVIS FAMILY**				
	LINN CO.	T11S	R4W	S24
DAVIS FAMILY	LINN CO.	T11S	R4W	S24
DAVIS FAMILY	MULTNOMAH CO.	T1S	R4E	S3
DAVIS FAMILY, DANIEL D. see **FOLKS, B. A.**				
	BENTON CO.	T10S	R5W	S10
DAVIS'S PLACE, JIMMY	CURRY CO.	?	?	?
DAVLIN see **NICHOLS**	DOUGLAS CO.	T28S	R6W	S20
DAY D.L.C., WILLIAM P. see **DAY FAMILY**				
	DOUGLAS CO.	T29S	R9W	S26
DAY FAMILY	DOUGLAS CO.	T29S	R9W	S26
DAY, PHOEBE see **DAY FAMILY**	DOUGLAS CO.	T29S	R9W	S26
DAY, WILLIAM P. see **DAY FAMILY**	DOUGLAS CO.	T29S	R9W	S26
DAYS CREEK [?] see **BLAND MOUNTAIN**				
	DOUGLAS CO.	T30S	R4W	S24
DAYTON see **BROOKSIDE**	YAMHILL CO.	T4S	R3W	S17
DAYVILLE	GRANT CO.	T12S	R26E	S34
De MOSS	SHERMAN CO.	T1S	R17E	S3
De MOSS, JOHN "CURLY" see **UNKNOWN**				
	SHERMAN CO.	T1S	R17E	S3
De MOSS SPRINGS see **De MOSS**	SHERMAN CO.	T1S	R17E	S3
DEADMANS POINT	JACKSON CO.	T40S	R2W	S27
DEADWOOD	LANE CO.	T17S	R9W	S15
DEADWOOD CHURCH see **DEADWOOD**	LANE CO.	T17S	R9W	S15
DEAN see **DEEN, TOMMY**	GILLIAM CO.	T1N	R22E	S26
DEAN HILL see **PROSPECT**	JACKSON CO.	T32S	R3E	S31
DEARDORFF D.L.C., JOHN M. see **CRISTILLA PIONEER**				
	CLACKAMAS CO.	T1S	R2E	S36
DEARDORFF FAMILY see **CRISTILLA PIONEER**				
	CLACKAMAS CO.	T1S	R2E	S36
DEAVER HOMESTEAD, JAMES see **PAINTER FAMILY**				
	MULTNOMAH CO.	T1N	R4E	S25
DECKEY see **DICKEY FAMILY**	CLACKAMAS CO.	T5S	R2E	S23
DEEDS BABIES	CROOK CO.	T17S	R25E	S11

DEEDS FAMILY see **DEEDS BABIES**	CROOK CO.	T17S	R25E	S11
DEEN, TOMMY	GILLIAM CO.	T1N	R22E	S26
DEER CREEK	JOSEPHINE CO.	T38S	R7W	S18
DEER CREEK	YAMHILL CO.	T5S	R5W	S28
DEER ISLAND see **KINDER**	COLUMBIA CO.	T5N	R1W	S16
DEER PARK see **GREENE**	COOS CO.	T32S	R12W	S8
DELANEY, BOBBIE	UNION CO.	T1S	R40E	S14
DELANEY FARM, CHARLES see **RUM AND GUM CHARLEY**				
	WASHINGTON CO.	T2S	?	?
DELANEY, JOSEPH see **WALKER GULCH**				
	JOSEPHINE CO.	T40S	R7W	S15
DELL	MALHEUR CO.	T16S	R43E	S15
DELORE	CROOK CO.	T18S	R25E	S13
DELORME D.L.C., BARTHOLOMEW see **ST. LOUIS [NEW]**				
	MARION CO.	T5S	R2W	S21
DEMARIS see **BARNES**	CROOK CO.	T18S	R20E	S35
DEMENT D.L.C., SAMUAL see **DEMENT FAMILY**				
	COOS CO.	T30S	R12W	S7
DEMENT, ELLIS see **JEFFERSON, THOMAS**				
	COOS CO.	T31S	R11W	S31
DEMENT FAMILY	COOS CO.	T30S	R12W	S7
DEMENT HOUSE, SAM see **McGLONE GRAVES**				
	CURRY CO.	T31S	R12W	S31
DEMENT RANCH see **HAINES**	CURRY CO.	T31S	R13W	S36
DEMENT RANCH, WALLACE see **DEMENT FAMILY**				
	COOS CO.	T30S	R12W	S7
DEMPSEY see **EMBREE FAMILY, CAREY D.**				
	POLK CO.	T7S	R5W	S36
DENIO	HARNEY CO.	T41S	R35E	S20
DENMARK	CURRY CO.	T31S	R15W	S10
DENN see **DAY FAMILY**	DOUGLAS CO.	T29S	R9W	S26
DENNY D.L.C., JAMES M. see **MATER DOLOROSA**				
	MARION CO.	T8S	R1W	S34
DEPEW, HIRAM see **SOUTH BEACH**	LINCOLN CO.	T11S	R11W	S17
DEPOT, PETER [PIERRE] see **SACRED HEART**				
	MARION CO.	T5S	R2W	S36
DERKATSCH, JOHANN	LANE CO.	T17S	R12W	S36
DeSARTS ADDITION see **SILVERTON**	MARION CO.	T6S	R1W	S34
DESCHUTES MEMORIAL GARDENS	DESCHUTES CO.	T17S	R12E	S9
DESERT LAWN MEMORIAL	MORROW CO.	T5N	R27E	S20
DeSPAIN GULCH	UMATILLA CO.	T3N	R31E	S10
DETHLEFS see **MT. OLIVE LUTHERAN**	WASHINGTON CO.	T1S	R4W	S23
DEUTSCHE EVANGELISCHE REFORMIETE MERIDIAN CHURCH see **MERIDIAN [OLD]**				
	CLACKAMAS CO.	T3S	R1W	S13
DEVILS GAP see **BROWN FAMILY**	GILLIAM CO.	T3S	R22E	S10
DEVIN, GRANDMA	BAKER CO.	T12S	R38E	?
DeVORE see **RHEA CREEK**	MORROW CO.	T4S	R26E	S14
DEWEY see **OAK GROVE**	YAMHILL CO.	T2S	R3W	S21
DIAMOND see **CUMMINGS FIELD**	HARNEY CO.	T29S	R33E	S31
DIBBLE FAMILY see **JACKSON FAMILY**				
	CLACKAMAS CO.	T5S	R2E	S7

DIBBLEE HOUSE	COLUMBIA CO.	T7N	R2W	S16
DIBBLEE, JOHN see **DIBBLEE HOUSE**	COLUMBIA CO.	T7N	R2W	S16
DIBBLEE, MERRILL see **DIBBLEE HOUSE**				
	COLUMBIA CO.	T7N	R2W	S16
DIBBLEE, SARAH BLANCHARD see **DIBBLEE HOUSE**				
	COLUMBIA CO.	T7N	R2W	S16
DICKENS D.L.C., REUBEN AND NANCY see **PATTON FAMILY**				
	MARION CO.	T8S	R1W	S5
DICKENS FAMILY see **PATTON FAMILY**				
	MARION CO.	T8S	R1W	S5
DICKENS, JEHU	LINCOLN CO.	T6S	R10W	?
DICKERSON RANCH	GRANT CO.	T8S	R30E	S8
DICKEY D.L.C., JOHN K. see **DICKEY FAMILY**				
	CLACKAMAS CO.	T5S	R2E	S23
DICKEY FAMILY	CLACKAMAS CO.	T5S	R2E	S23
DICKSON D.L.C., JOSHUA see **MT. OLIVE LUTHERAN**				
	WASHINGTON CO.	T1S	R4W	S23
DIETRICH, W.	COOS CO.	T33S	R12W	S33
DILLARD see **WILLIS CREEK**	DOUGLAS CO.	T29S	R6W	S9
DIMMICK D.L.C., ZIBA see **DIMMICK FAMILY**				
	DOUGLAS CO.	T23S	R7W	S20
DIMMICK FAMILY	DOUGLAS CO.	T23S	R7W	S20
DINWIDDIE see **BLAIN**	LINN CO.	T14S	R3W	S14
DIVIDE see **HAWLEY**	LANE CO.	T21S	R4W	S12
DIX see **BONNEY**	CLACKAMAS CO.	T4S	R3E	S35
DIXIE see **LIME-DIXIE**	BAKER CO.	T13S	R44E	S22
DIXIE see **NESMITH FAMILY**	POLK CO.	T7S	R4W	S30
DIXIE FLAT	UNION CO.	T2S	R37E	?
DIXIE MOUNTAIN see **MOUNTAIN VIEW**				
	WASHINGTON CO.	T3N	R2W	S32
DIXON see **LIVINGSTON**	DOUGLAS CO.	T27S	R4W	S7
DIXON D.L.C., HIRAM see **DIXON FAMILY**				
	DOUGLAS CO.	T26S	R5W	S26
DIXON FAMILY	DOUGLAS CO.	T26S	R5W	S26
DIXON, WILLIAM see **HENDERSON FAMILY**				
	BENTON CO.	T12S	R6W	S36
DIXONVILLE see **LIVINGSTON**	DOUGLAS CO.	T27S	R4W	S7
DOANE, EMILIE	UNION CO.	T3S	R37E	S10
DOBBIN FAMILY	WALLOWA CO.	T4N	R48E	S34
DOCKWEILER, MARIE VOGLER	UMATILLA CO.	T1S	R35E	S21
DR. DUTCH see **RED HILL**	DOUGLAS CO.	T23S	R5W	S34
DODGE see **ROCK HILL**	LINN CO.	T12S	R2W	S28
DODGE BRIDGE	JACKSON CO.	T35S	R1W	S17
DODSON D.L.C., WILLIAM AND HENRIETTA see **PIKE AND I.O.O.F.**				
	YAMHILL CO.	T2S	R5W	S25
DOG CREEK	JOSEPHINE CO.	T34S	R6W	S8
DOG MOUNTAIN see **SUNSET VALLEY**	HARNEY CO.	T25S	R31E	S27
DOLE see **BURNETT FAMILY**	DOUGLAS CO.	T29S	R6W	S12
DOLPH	TILLAMOOK CO.	T5S	R9W	S28
DOLPH	YAMHILL CO.	T5S	R9W	S27
DONALD see **CHAMPOEG**	MARION CO.	T4S	R2W	S12

DONALDSON, GORDON E. A. see **UNKNOWN**				
	WASCO CO.	T1N	R12E	?
DONNA see **VALLEY VIEW**	LANE CO.	T17S	R2W	S3
DOOLITTLE FAMILY	LANE CO.	T20S	R2W	S21
DORA	COOS CO.	T28S	R11W	S10
DORITY PLACE see **FROZEN CREEK**	DOUGLAS CO.	T28S	R4W	?
DOSS FAMILY	POLK CO.	T6S	R8W	?
DOSS, JUDY E. see **DOSS FAMILY**	POLK CO.	T6S	R8W	?
DOSS, LEE see **DOSS FAMILY**	POLK CO.	T6S	R8W	?
DOTY FAMILY	LINCOLN CO.	T13S	R10W	S7
DOTY HOUSE see **DOTY FAMILY**	LINCOLN CO.	T13S	R10W	S7
DOTY, MARY M. see **PRUNE RIDGE**	MARION CO.	T7S	R2E	S8
DOUGHERTY D.L.C., NATHAN see **DOUGHERTY, LYDIA**				
	TILLAMOOK CO.	T1S	R9W	?
DOUGHERTY, LYDIA	TILLAMOOK CO.	T1S	R9W	?
DOUGLAS see **DOUGLASS**	MULTNOMAH CO.	T1N	R3E	S36
DOUGLAS see **GIBSON**	CLACKAMAS CO.	T3S	R4E	?
DOUGLAS COUNTY see **MASONIC [OLD ROSEBURG]**				
	DOUGLAS CO.	T27S	R5W	S19
DOUGLAS COUNTY BROOKSIDE	DOUGLAS CO.	T27S	R5W	S17
DOUGLAS COUNTY POOR FARM	DOUGLAS CO.	T26S	R6W	S30
DOUGLAS RIDGE see **FORRESTER**	CLACKAMAS CO.	T2S	R4E	S29
DOUGLASS	MULTNOMAH CO.	T1N	R3E	S36
DOUGLASS, A. F. see **DOUGLASS BABY**				
	MULTNOMAH CO.	T1N	R1E	S14
DOUGLASS BABY	MULTNOMAH CO.	T1N	R1E	S14
DOUGLASS D.L.C., JOHN see **DOUGLASS**				
	MULTNOMAH CO.	T1N	R3E	S36
DOUGLASS, RUBY see **DOUGLASS BABY**				
	MULTNOMAH CO.	T1N	R1E	S14
DOW D.L.C., WILLIAM W. see **DOW, OSCAR A.**				
	BENTON CO.	T13S	R5W	S28
DOW, OSCAR A.	BENTON CO.	T13S	R5W	S28
DOW, WILLIAM see **DOW, OSCAR A.**	BENTON CO.	T13S	R5W	S28
DOWELL RANCH, TOM see **CORD**	MALHEUR CO.	T28S	R38E	S7
DOWNING see **I.O.O.F. [CONDON]**	GILLIAM CO.	T4S	R21E	S2
DOWNING see **LONE FIR**	MARION CO.	T8S	R1W	S21
DOWNING FAMILY see **HUSSEY FAMILY**				
	YAMHILL CO.	T5S	R6W	S1
DOWNING-MAYGER FAMILY see **MAYGER-DOWNING FAMILY**				
	COLUMBIA CO.	T8N	R3W	S19
DOWNING PLACE	JACKSON CO.	?	?	?
DOWNS, JAMES	LANE CO.	T16S	R4W	?
DOYLE, MRS. C. B.	WASCO CO.	T6S	R12E	S6
DRAIN [EAST] see **I.O.O.F. [DRAIN]**				
	DOUGLAS CO.	T22S	R4W	S16
DRAIN [NORTH]	DOUGLAS CO.	T22S	R5W	S8
DRAKE, ANITA see **UNKNOWN**	WASCO CO.	T5S	R16E	?
DRAKES CROSSING see **GREEN MOUNTAIN**				
	MARION CO.	T7S	R1E	S26
DRAPER FAMILY	CLACKAMAS CO.	T3S	R1E	S1

DRAPER, GEORGE see **DRAPER FAMILY**

	CLACKAMAS CO.	T3S	R1E	S1

DRAPER, MARTHA see **DRAPER FAMILY**

	CLACKAMAS CO.	T3S	R1E	S1
DREW see **TISON**	DOUGLAS CO.	T31S	R1W	S19

DREW, CHIEF FRANK see **DREW MEMORIAL**

	LANE CO.	T18S	R12W	S24
DREW MEMORIAL	LANE CO.	T18S	R12W	S24
DREWS RANCH see **HODSON**	KLAMATH CO.	T38S	R11 1/2E	?
DREWSEY	HARNEY CO.	T20S	R35E	S23
DREWSEY FIELD	HARNEY CO.	T20S	R35E	?
DRIFT CREEK see **GLENWOOD**	LINCOLN CO.	T12S	R10W	S13
DRISKELL see **CENTRAL SCHOOL**	LANE CO.	T18S	R5W	S4

DRIVER D.L.C., SAMUEL see **DRIVER FAMILY**

	DOUGLAS CO.	T24S	R4W	S22
DRIVER FAMILY	DOUGLAS CO.	T24S	R4W	S22
DRURY see **UPPER MABLE**	LANE CO.	T15S	R1W	S28
DRY CREEK	JEFFERSON CO.	T9S	R12E	S12
DRY HOLLOW see **RICE**	WASCO CO.	T1S	R14E	S10
DRY LAKE	CROOK CO.	T20S	R20E	S14
DRYDEN see **DEER CREEK**	JOSEPHINE CO.	T38S	R7W	S18

DUFUR CATHOLIC see **KINGSLEY CATHOLIC**

	WASCO CO.	T2S	R13E	S28
DUFUR COMMUNITY	WASCO CO.	T1S	R13E	S24

DUMOND, AUGUST see **DUMONT, AUGUST**

	DOUGLAS CO.	T30S	R4W	S9

DUMONT, ALEXANDER see **DUMONT, AUGUST**

	DOUGLAS CO.	T30S	R4W	S9
DUMONT, AUGUST	DOUGLAS CO.	T30S	R4W	S9

DUMONT D.L.C., ALEXANDER see **DUMONT, AUGUST**

	DOUGLAS CO.	T30S	R4W	S9

DUNBAR D.L.C., ADDISON C. see **PARKS, DAVID**

	MULTNOMAH CO.	T1N	R3E	?
DUNCAN FAMILY see **APPLEGATE**	MALHEUR CO.	T16S	R47E	?

DUNCAN FAMILY see **MEDICAL SPRINGS**

	UNION CO.	T6S	R41E	?

DUNDEE MEMORIAL see **DUNDEE PIONEER**

	YAMHILL CO.	T3S	R3W	S26
DUNDEE PIONEER	YAMHILL CO.	T3S	R3W	S26
DUNDON, CARRIE FRANCES	LINN CO.	T13S	R2E	S34
DUNES MEMORIAL MAUSOLEUM	DOUGLAS CO.	T22S	R12W	S4
DUNKARD	JACKSON CO.	T38S	R1W	S23
DUNKARD see **STIP MEMORIAL**	MARION CO.	T8S	R2W	S2

DUNKARD CHURCH OF THE BRETHREN see **MABEL**

	LANE CO.	T16S	R1W	S5
DUNKIN, GEORGE	CLATSOP CO.	T7N	R8W	?
DUNN FAMILY	BENTON CO.	T13S	R6W	S11

DUNN FAMILY see **HILL-DUNN FAMILY**

	JACKSON CO.	T39S	R2E	S30

DUNN-HILL FAMILY see **HILL-DUNN FAMILY**

	JACKSON CO.	T39S	R2E	S30

DUNNETTE see **HOOKER FAMILY**	POLK CO.	T9S	R6W	?
DUNNING PLACE, CHARLES see **INDIAN BURIALS**				
	LANE CO.	?	?	?
DURAN CHILD	MORROW CO.	?	?	?
DURAN, EDWARD S. see **DURAN CHILD**				
	MORROW CO.	?	?	?
DURBIN see **LIME-DIXIE**	BAKER CO.	T13S	R44E	S22
DURETTE FARM see **FAIRFIELD**	MARION CO.	T5S	R2W	S19
DURKEE	BAKER CO.	T11S	R43E	S18
DURNAME, MR. see **WOLF VALLEY**	DOUGLAS CO.	T25S	R7W	S8
DUTCH FLAT see **OBRIST**	WASCO CO.	T1S	R12E	S2
DYE, WILLIAM see **KAMELA**	UNION CO.	T1S	R35E	S36
E.O.S.H. see **EASTERN OREGON STATE HOSPITAL**				
	UMATILLA CO.	T2N	R32E	S9
EADES D.L.C., WILLIAM see **HARMONY**				
	POLK CO.	T6S	R6W	S9
EAGLE CREEK see **SCHEEL FAMILY**	CLACKAMAS CO.	T3S	R5E	S18
EAGLE POINT see **ANTELOPE**	JACKSON CO.	T36S	R1W	S14
EAGLE POINT NATIONAL see **NATIONAL VETERANS ADMINISTRATION**				
	JACKSON CO.	T36S	R1W	S2
EAGLE VALLEY	BAKER CO.	T9S	R45E	S26
EAGLES see **MT. HOPE**	BAKER CO.	T9S	R40E	S21
EAGON D.L.C., JOSEPH see **WISE FAMILY, GEORGE**				
	CLACKAMAS CO.	T2S	R2E	S5
EARL	TILLAMOOK CO.	T2S	R9W	S4
EARL D.L.C., JOHN see **EARL FAMILY**				
	LINN CO.	T10S	R3W	S36
EARL FAMILY	LINN CO.	T10S	R3W	S36
EARL FARM see **EARL**	TILLAMOOK CO.	T2S	R9W	S4
EARL RANCH, LYLE see **NOEL FAMILY**				
	DOUGLAS CO.	T21S	R11W	S3
EARLY I.O.O.F. see **MASONIC [OLD ROSEBURG]**				
	DOUGLAS CO.	T27S	R5W	S19
EARLY MASONIC see **MASONIC [OLD ROSEBURG]**				
	DOUGLAS CO.	T27S	R5W	S19
EARNEST see **JENNINGS**	POLK CO.	T6S	R4W	S13
EARP, VIRGIL see **RIVER VIEW**	MULTNOMAH CO.	T1S	R1E	S22
EARP, WYATT see **RIVER VIEW**	MULTNOMAH CO.	T1S	R1E	S22
EAST see **I.O.O.F. [DRAIN]**	DOUGLAS CO.	T22S	R5W	S16
EAST ALBANY	LINN CO.	T11S	R3W	S4
EAST GARDINER	DOUGLAS CO.	?	?	?
EAST GASTON see **HILL**	WASHINGTON CO.	T2S	R3W	S6
EAST KNOX BUTTE see **EARL FAMILY**	LINN CO.	T10S	R3W	S36
EAST KNOX BUTTE see **SANTIAM CENTRAL**				
	LINN CO.	T11S	R2W	S6
EAST SUBLIMITY see **HOBSON-WHITNEY**				
	MARION CO.	T8S	R1W	S35
EASTERN OREGON STATE HOSPITAL	UMATILLA CO.	T2N	R32E	S9
EASTLAWN MEMORIAL GARDENS see **LITTLE CHAPEL OF THE CHIMES MEMORIAL**				
GARDEN	CLACKAMAS CO.	T1S	R2E	S33
EASTON FAMILY see **JUNGLEBANK**	COOS CO.	T28S	R10W	S6

EASTON HOMESTEAD, JAMES GARFIELD see **PIONEER GRAVES**

	WASCO CO.	T3S	R13E	S20

EASTON, MILDRED NEELY see **JUNGLEBANK**

	COOS CO.	T28S	R10W	S6

EASTON, ROBERT A. see **JUNGLEBANK**

	COOS CO.	T28S	R10W	S6

EASTON, THEODORE see **JUNGLEBANK** COOS CO. T28S R10W S6

EASTWOOD I.O.O.F. see **I.O.O.F., EASTWOOD [MEDFORD]**

	JACKSON CO.	T37S	R1W	S29

EATON FAMILY see **WASCO METHODIST**

	SHERMAN CO.	T2N	R17E	S32
EBENEZER CHAPEL	YAMHILL CO.	T5S	R3W	S7
EBENGER FAMILY	BAKER CO.	T12S	R45E	S14
ECCLES see **ACKLES**	UNION CO.	T2S	R38E	S21
ECHO see **ECHO MEMORIAL**	UMATILLA CO.	T3N	R29E	S16
ECHO MEMORIAL	UMATILLA CO.	T3N	R29E	S16
ECKLEY see **DEMENT FAMILY**	COOS CO.	T30S	R12W	S7
ECKMAN CREEK see **ALDER GROVE**	LINCOLN CO.	T13S	R11W	S32
EDDY	LINCOLN CO.	T11S	R9W	S4
EDDY, FANNY see **EDDY, HARRIET**	CURRY CO.	T30S	R14W	?
EDDY FARM, ISRAEL see **EDDY**	LINCOLN CO.	T11S	R9W	S4
EDDY, FRANK see **EDDY, HARRIET**	CURRY CO.	T30S	R14W	?
EDDY, HARRIET	CURRY CO.	T30S	R14W	?
EDDYVILLE	LINCOLN CO.	T11S	R9W	S10
EDEN	DOUGLAS CO.	T27S	R7W	S2
EDEN	WALLOWA CO.	T5N	R42E	S21
EDEN LUTHERAN CHURCH see **EDEN**	DOUGLAS CO.	T27S	R7W	S2
EDEN RIDGE see **EDEN**	WALLOWA CO.	T5N	R42E	S21
EDEN VALLEY	COOS CO.	T32S	R11W	S12
EDGERTON FAMILY	CURRY CO.	T35S	R12W	S12
EDSALL see **PINEHURST**	JACKSON CO.	T40S	R4E	S5

EDSON, A. J. see **EDSON, HARRIET G.**

	CURRY CO.	T36S	R14W	S6
EDSON, HARRIET G.	CURRY CO.	T36S	R14W	S6
EDWARDS see **REEVES**	BENTON CO.	T14S	R5W	S7
EDWARDS CHILD	SHERMAN CO.	T3S	R16E	?

EDWARDS D.L.C., JOSEPH see **EDWARDS FAMILY**

	POLK CO.	T9S	R6W	S32
EDWARDS FAMILY	POLK CO.	T9S	R6W	S32

EDWARDS, LEROY see **EDWARDS CHILD**

	SHERMAN CO.	T3S	R16E	?

EDWARDS, MARY JANE HELYER see **EDWARDS CHILD**

	SHERMAN CO.	T3S	R16E	?

EDWARDS, REBECCA see **HUSSEY FAMILY**

	POLK CO.	T6S	R7W	S15

EGGERS, C. L. see **SMITH PLACE** CLACKAMAS CO. T2S R4E S30

EGGERS, JANE A. see **SMITH PLACE** CLACKAMAS CO. T2S R4E S30

EGGSMANN	KLAMATH CO.	T36S	R7E	S15
EHLSON	TILLAMOOK CO.	T3S	R9W	?
EIGHT MILE	WASCO CO.	T1S	R13E	S1
EIGHTMILE	GILLIAM CO.	T1N	R22E	S5

```
EILER PEAK see ILERS PEAK          CLACKAMAS CO.     T2S     R3E      S18
EILERS PEAK see ILERS PEAK         CLACKAMAS CO.     T2S     R3E      S18
ELDER, CATHERINE see ELDER FAMILY
                                   LINN CO.          T13S    R3W      S8
ELDER CHILDREN                     MORROW CO.        T2S     R27E     S26
ELDER D.L.C., ROBERT M. AND CATHERINE see ELDER FAMILY
                                   LINN CO.          T13S    R3W      S8
ELDER FAMILY                       LINN CO.          T13S    R3W      S8
ELDER, JOHN see ELDER CHILDREN     MORROW CO.        T2S     R27E     S26
ELDER, MRS. see ELDER FAMILY       LINN CO.          T13S    R3W      S8
ELDRIDGE, JOHN see HUSSEY FAMILY
                                   POLK CO.          T6S     R7W      S15
ELEPHANT ROCK                      CURRY CO.         T32S    R14W     S11
ELGAROSE see EDEN                  DOUGLAS CO.       T27S    R7W      S2
ELGIN                              UNION CO.         T1N     R39E     S23
ELK CITY                           LINCOLN CO.       T11S    R10W     ?
ELK CITY PIONEER                   LINCOLN CO.       T11S    R10W     S11
ELK FLAT see PINE GROVE            UNION CO.         T1N     R40E     S12
ELKHEAD CHURCH see SHOESTRING      DOUGLAS CO.       T23S    R4W      S10
ELKS see HAINES                    BAKER CO.         T7S     R39E     S21
ELKTON                             DOUGLAS CO.       T22S    R7W      S29
ELLA see WELL SPRING               MORROW CO.        T2N     R25E     S20
ELLIOTT FAMILY                     JOSEPHINE CO.     T37S    R7W      ?
ELLIOTT, HENDERSON see NARROWS     HARNEY CO.        T26S    R30E     S26
ELLIOTT, JOHN T. see ELLIOTT FAMILY
                                   JOSEPHINE CO.     T37S    R7W      ?
ELLIOTT, LUTHER see ELLIOTT FAMILY
                                   JOSEPHINE CO.     T37S    R7W      ?
ELLIOTT-PERKINS FAMILIES           DOUGLAS CO.       T21S    R12W     ?
ELLIOTT, THEODOSIA MILLER see NARROWS
                                   HARNEY CO.        T26S    R30E     S26
ELLIS                              DOUGLAS CO.       ?       ?        ?
ELLIS, A. M. see ELLIS FAMILY      WASHINGTON CO.    T1S     R1W      S12
ELLIS, CARRIE ETTA                 WASHINGTON CO.    T1N     R5W      S25
ELLIS FAMILY                       WASHINGTON CO.    T1S     R1W      S12
ELLIS, KITTY M. see ELLIS FAMILY
                                   WASHINGTON CO.    T1S     R1W      S12
ELLIS, PERRY see ELLIS, CARRIE ETTA
                                   WASHINGTON CO.    T1N     R5W      S25
ELLIS, PERRY see ELLIS FAMILY      WASHINGTON CO.    T1S     R1W      S12
ELLIS PROPERTY see ELLIS           DOUGLAS CO.       ?       ?        ?
ELLIS, RACHEL A. see ELLIS FAMILY
                                   WASHINGTON CO.    T1S     R1W      S12
ELLISON see EHLSON                 TILLAMOOK CO.     T3S     R9W      ?
ELMIRA see INMAN                   LANE CO.          T17S    R5W      S8
ELSIE                              CLATSOP CO.       T4N     R7W      S5
ELWOOD see MT. HOME                CLACKAMAS CO.     T4S     R4E      S19
EMANUEL see CORNELIUS PIONEER METHODIST
                                   WASHINGTON CO.    T1N     R3W      S33
EMANUEL see TIGARD EVANGELICAL     WASHINGTON CO.    T2S     R1W      S10
EMANUEL see VALLEY VIEW            MARION CO.        T6S     R1W      S36
```

EMANUEL BIBLE CHURCH see **PRATUM**	MARION CO.	T7S	R1W	S19
EMANUEL EPISCOPAL CHURCH COLUMBARIUM				
	COOS CO.	T25S	R13W	S26
EMANUEL EVANGELICAL UNITED BRETHERN see **TIGARD EVANGELICAL**				
	WASHINGTON CO.	T2S	R1W	S10
EMANUEL HOSPITAL	MULTNOMAH CO.	T1N	R1E	S27
EMANUEL LUTHERAN	WASHINGTON CO.	T1N	R3W	S34
EMBREE D.L.C., CAREY see **EMBREE FAMILY, CAREY D.**				
	POLK CO.	T7S	R5W	S36
EMBREE FAMILY, CAREY D.	POLK CO.	T7S	R5W	S36
EMERICK AND ALLIED FAMILIES see **EMERICK FAMILY**				
	BENTON CO.	T12S	R6W	S27
EMERICK D.L.C., SOLOMON see **EMERICK FAMILY**				
	WASHINGTON CO.	T1S	R3W	?
EMERICK FAMILY	BENTON CO.	T12S	R6W	S27
EMERICK FAMILY	WASHINGTON CO.	T1S	R3W	?
EMERICK, SOLOMON see **EMERICK FAMILY**				
	WASHINGTON CO.	T1S	R3W	?
EMIGRANT	LANE CO.	T18S	R2W	S3
EMIGRANT GRAVES	BAKER CO.	T14S	R45E	S20
EMIGRANT GRAVEYARD see **WELL SPRING**				
	MORROW CO.	T2N	R25E	S20
EMIGRANT SPRINGS	SHERMAN CO.	T2N	R18E	S34
EMPIRE	COOS CO.	T25S	R13W	S17
EMRICK see **EMERICK FAMILY**	WASHINGTON CO.	T1S	R3W	?
EMRIEK see **EMERICK FAMILY**	WASHINGTON CO.	T1S	R3W	?
ENCHANTED PRAIRIE	COOS CO.	T29S	R11W	S35
ENDERSBY INFANT	WASCO CO.	T1S	R13E	S11
ENGLE D.L.C., JOSEPH see **BELLE PASSI MEMORIAL MAUSOLEUM**				
	MARION CO.	T5S	R1W	S19
ENGLEWOOD	COOS CO.	T25S	R13W	?
ENGLISH D.L.C., BENJAMIN see **ENGLISH [OLD]**				
	POLK CO.	T9S	R5W	S28
ENGLISH [NEW]	POLK CO.	T9S	R5W	S1
ENGLISH [OLD]	POLK CO.	T9S	R5W	S28
ENNIS HOMESTEAD, DAVE see **BRIDGEPORT**				
	BAKER CO.	T12S	R41E	S30
ENOS	LINCOLN CO.	T11S	R10W	?
ENSLEY FAMILY	DOUGLAS CO.	T22S	R6W	S2
ENTERPRISE	WALLOWA CO.	T1S	R44E	S35
EOFF	MARION CO.	T7S	R2W	S25
EOFF D.L.C., GEORGE AND NANCY see **EOFF**				
	MARION CO.	T7S	R2W	S25
EOLA see **PUTNAM FARM**	POLK CO.	T7S	R3W	?
ERB see **BLOSSER**	CLACKAMAS CO.	T4S	R1W	S36
ERICKSON FAMILY see **APPLEGATE**	MALHEUR CO.	T16S	R47E	?
ESCOBAR see **ESCOBAR PIONEER**	MULTNOMAH CO.	T1S	R3E	S10
ESCOBAR see **WHITE BIRCH**	MULTNOMAH CO.	T1S	R3E	S9
ESCOBAR, FRANK see **ESCOBAR PIONEER**				
	MULTNOMAH CO.	T1S	R3E	S10
ESCOBAR PIONEER	MULTNOMAH CO.	T1S	R3E	S10

ESCOBAR'S see **ESCOBAR PIONEER**	MULTNOMAH CO.	T1S	R3E	S10
ESSON FAMILY see **ESSON MEMORIAL, IDA**				
	MARION CO.	T6S	R1W	S5
ESSON FARM see **ESSON MEMORIAL, IDA**				
	MARION CO.	T6S	R1W	S5
ESSON MEMORIAL, IDA	MARION CO.	T6S	R1W	S5
ESTACADA see **I.O.O.F. [ESTACADA]**				
	CLACKAMAS CO.	T3S	R4E	S21
ESTACADA ODD FELLOWS see **I.O.O.F. [ESTACADA]**				
	CLACKAMAS CO.	T3S	R4E	S21
ESTOOS see **FITCHA HOMESTEAD**	CLATSOP CO.	T8N	R8W	S31
ETERNAL HILLS MEMORIAL GARDENS	KLAMATH CO.	T39S	R10E	S18
ETERNAL MEMORIAL GARDENS see **LITTLE CHAPEL OF THE CHIMES MEMORIAL**				
GARDEN	CLACKAMAS CO.	T1S	R2E	S33
ETERNITY AT SEA COLUMBARIUM	CLATSOP CO.	T5N	R11W	S-0
ETNA	POLK CO.	T7S	R4W	S7
ETNA BAPTIST CHURCH see **ETNA**	POLK CO.	T7S	R4W	S7
ETTLIN see **HOLY ROSARY**	MARION CO.	T6S	R1E	S36
ETZEL see **HOBSON-WHITNEY**	MARION CO.	T8S	R1W	S35
EUGENE CITY LODGE #11 see **MASONIC [EUGENE]**				
	LANE CO.	T18S	R3W	S5
EUGENE MEMORIAL GARDENS see **SUNSET HILLS MEMORIAL GARDENS**				
	LANE CO.	T18S	R3W	S18
EUGENE PIONEER	LANE CO.	T17S	R3W	S32
EUREKA	LINCOLN CO.	T11S	R11W	?
EUREKA VALLEY see **COLVIN**	DOUGLAS CO.	T22S	R5W	S6
EVANGELICAL see **COOPER MOUNTAIN [PROTESTANT]**				
	WASHINGTON CO.	T1S	R2W	S25
EVANGLE see **TIGARD EVANGELICAL**	WASHINGTON CO.	T2S	R1W	S10
EVANS see **MOUNTAIN VIEW-CORBETT PIONEER**				
	MULTNOMAH CO.	T1S	R4E	S3
EVANS, TOM see **MOUNTAIN VIEW-CORBETT PIONEER**				
	MULTNOMAH CO.	T1S	R4E	S3
EVANS VALLEY	JACKSON CO.	T35S	R4W	?
EVANS VALLEY see **VALLEY VIEW**	MARION CO.	T6S	R1W	S36
EVELAND, MRS. see **MEDICAL SPRINGS**				
	UNION CO.	T6S	R41E	?
EVEREST see **FERNWOOD PIONEER**	YAMHILL CO.	T3S	R2W	S20
EVEREST D.L.C., RICHARD see **FERNWOOD PIONEER**				
	YAMHILL CO.	T3S	R2W	S20
EVEREST D.L.C., RICHARD see **FRIENDS**				
	YAMHILL CO.	T3S	R2W	S20
EVEREST D.L.C., RICHARD see **G.A.R. [GRAND ARMY OF THE REPUBLIC]**				
	YAMHILL CO.	T3S	R2W	S20
EVEREST, JANE see **FERNWOOD PIONEER**				
	YAMHILL CO.	T3S	R2W	S20
EVEREST, RICHARD see **FERNWOOD PIONEER**				
	YAMHILL CO.	T3S	R2W	S20
EVERGREEN	CLATSOP CO.	T6N	R10W	S34
EVERGREEN	MALHEUR CO.	T18S	R47E	S9
EVERGREEN see **EVERGREEN HILL**	LANE CO.	T17S	R3W	S14

EVERGREEN see **MASONIC [ST. HELENS]**

	COLUMBIA CO.	T5N	R1W	S33
EVERGREEN HILL	LANE CO.	T17S	R3W	S14

EVERGREEN HILL CAMP see **RICHARDSON**

	LANE CO.	T17S	R5W	S4

EVERGREEN LODGE #137 see **EVERGREEN**

	CLATSOP CO.	T6N	R10W	S34
EVERGREEN MEMORIAL PARK	YAMHILL CO.	T4S	R4W	S10
EVERTS, J. H. see **PEEL**	DOUGLAS CO.	T27S	R3W	S11
EWING FAMILY	GILLIAM CO.	T3N	R22E	S34
EWING, HARVEY see **EWING FAMILY**	GILLIAM CO.	T3N	R22E	S34
FAIR OAKS	DOUGLAS CO.	T25S	R4W	S7
FAIR VIEW see **MT. HOPE**	BAKER CO.	T9S	R40E	S21
FAIR-VIEW see **FAIRVIEW**	MALHEUR CO.	T15S	R47E	S33
FAIRFIELD	MARION CO.	T5S	R2W	S19

FAIRMONT HILL see **CITY VIEW, MT. CREST ABBY MAUSOLEUM AND SUNRISE GARDEN**
    MAUSOLEUM

	MARION CO.	T7S	R3W	S33
FAIRVIEW	COLUMBIA CO.	T3N	R2W	S24
FAIRVIEW	COOS CO.	T27S	R12W	S26
FAIRVIEW	LINN CO.	T9S	R3E	S34
FAIRVIEW	MALHEUR CO.	T15S	R47E	S33
FAIRVIEW	MULTNOMAH CO.	T1N	R3E	?
FAIRVIEW	WASCO CO.	?	?	?
FAIRVIEW see **BAKER**	MORROW CO.	T2S	R24E	S6
FAIRVIEW see **MT. HOPE**	BAKER CO.	T9S	R40E	S21
FAIRVIEW see **MT. LAKI**	KLAMATH CO.	T40S	R9E	S2
FAIRVIEW see **TRASK PIONEER**	TILLAMOOK CO.	T1S	R9W	S27

FAIRVIEW MEMORIAL see **LINN MEMORIAL**

	LINN CO.	T13S	R1W	S4
FAIRVIEW MENNONITE CHURCH	LINN CO.	T11S	R3W	S23
FALL CREEK	LANE CO.	T18S	R1W	S33

FALL CREEK CHRISTION see **FALL CREEK**

	LANE CO.	T18S	R1W	S33
FALLS CITY	POLK CO.	T8S	R6W	S16

FARMER D.L.C., JAMES see **FARMER FAMILY**

	DOUGLAS CO.	T22S	R6W	S2
FARMER FAMILY	DOUGLAS CO.	T22S	R6W	S2
FARMINGTON see **LEWIS**	WASHINGTON CO.	T1S	R2W	S30
FAST	POLK CO.	T7S	R5W	S23
FAST, RANDY see **HOWELL PRAIRIE**	MARION CO.	T7S	R2W	S4

FATHERGILL [Sic], JOHN see **FOTHERGILL, JOHN**

	LANE CO.	T18S	R1W	S33

FAULCONER D.L.C., ABSALOM B. see **MASONIC [SHERIDAN]**

	YAMHILL CO.	T5S	R6W	S26

FAULKNER, CLEORA see **FAULKNER, T. M.**

	LINCOLN CO.	T15S	R10W	S1
FAULKNER, T. M.	LINCOLN CO.	T15S	R10W	S1

FAULKNER, WARREN see **FAULKNER, T. M.**

	LINCOLN CO.	T15S	R10W	S1
FAWCETT	TILLAMOOK CO.	T2S	R9W	?
FELLOWS	CLACKAMAS CO.	T4S	R3E	S3

FELLOWS D.L.C., HIRAM see **FELLOWS**

CLACKAMAS CO.	T4S	R3E	S3

FENDALL FAMILY see **FENDALL-ROGERS FAMILY**

YAMHILL CO.	T3S	R3W	S4

FENDALL-ROGERS FAMILY YAMHILL CO. T3S R3W S4

FENN RANCH, JOEL R. see **ARCHAMBEAUX FAMILY**

DOUGLAS CO.	T26S	R6W	S31

FERGUESON D.L.C., JOHN B. see **FERGUESON FAMILY**

LANE CO.	T15S	R5W	S22

FERGUESON FAMILY LANE CO. T15S R5W S22

FERGUSON LINN CO. T13S R1W S12

FERGUSON, EPHRAIM see **FERGUSON FAMILY**

CLACKAMAS CO.	T2S	R2E	?

FERGUSON FAMILY CLACKAMAS CO. T2S R2E ?

FERGUSON FAMILY see **EIGHT MILE** WASCO CO. T1S R13E S1

FERGUSON FAMILY see **FERGUESON FAMILY**

LANE CO.	T15S	R5W	S22

FERGUSON HOMESTEAD, ALFRED see **EIGHT MILE**

WASCO CO.	T1S	R13E	S1

FERN CORNER see **HART-RIGGS FAMILY**

POLK CO.	T8S	R6W	S25

FERN HILL CLACKAMAS CO. T5S R3E S21

FERN HILL see **FERN HILL CATHOLIC**

WASHINGTON CO.	T1S	R3W	S16

FERN HILL CATHOLIC WASHINGTON CO. T1S R3W S16

FERN RIDGE LINCOLN CO. T12S R11W S32

FERN RIDGE LINN CO. T13S R1W S34

FERN RIDGE see **CENTRAL SCHOOL** LANE CO. T18S R5W S4

FERN RIDGE see **LACOMB** LINN CO. T11S R1E S31

FERNHILL see **FERN HILL** CLACKAMAS CO. T5S R3E S21

FERNWOOD see **FERNWOOD PIONEER** YAMHILL CO. T3S R2W S20

FERNWOOD see **JOHNSON FAMILY** CLACKAMAS CO. T5S R3E S18

FERNWOOD PIONEER YAMHILL CO. T3S R2W S20

FERRELL, LLOYD see **PAUPER [WARRENTON]**

CLATSOP CO.	T8N	R10W	S21

FERRY, HENRIETTA see **GARRETT** COOS CO. T29S R12W ?

FERRYDALE JOSEPHINE CO. T36S R7W S1

FETTER COOS CO. T29S R10W S28

FETTER CREEK, JOHN see **FETTER** COOS CO. T29S R10W S28

FEYRER CLACKAMAS CO. T5S R3E S19

FIELDS CLACKAMAS CO. T2S R1E S34

FIELDS [#1] HARNEY CO. T38S R34E S24

FIELDS [#2] HARNEY CO. T38S R34E S24

FIELDS see **MOON CREEK** GRANT CO. T13S R29E S20

FIELDS, ARCHIE see **FIELDS, HAROLD**

MALHEUR CO.	T19S	R47E	S32

FIELDS CREEK see **MOON CREEK** GRANT CO. T13S R29E S20

FIELDS D.L.C., JOSEPH A. see **FIELDS**

CLACKAMAS CO.	T2S	R1E	S34

FIELDS, HAROLD MALHEUR CO. T19S R47E S32

FIELDS, LORENA RAMBO see **FIELDS, HAROLD**				
	MALHEUR CO.	T19S	R47E	S32
FINLAND see **GREASEWOOD FINNISH LUTHERAN**				
	UMATILLA CO.	T4N	R33E	S34
FINLEY	LINN CO.	T14S	R2W	S13
FINLEY'S SUNSET HILL MEMORIAL	WASHINGTON CO.	T1S	R1W	S1
FINN see **GREASEWOOD FINNISH LUTHERAN**				
	UMATILLA CO.	T4N	R33E	S34
FINNISH see **SVENSEN PIONEER**	CLATSOP CO.	T8N	R8W	S23
FIR CREST	POLK CO.	T9S	R4W	S6
FIR GROVE	LANE CO.	T20S	R3W	S29
FIR GROVE	LINN CO.	T14S	R2E	S4
FIR GROVE see **ADA**	LANE CO.	T20S	R11W	S5
FIR GROVE see **IRWIN FAMILY**	BENTON CO.	T13S	R5W	S22
FIR HILL	CLACKAMAS CO.	T2S	R4E	S14
FIR LAWN see **FIR HILL**	CLACKAMAS CO.	T2S	R4E	S14
FIR LAWN CEMETERY AND MAUSOLEUM	WASHINGTON CO.	T1N	R3W	S36
FIR MEMORIAL see **FIR HILL**	CLACKAMAS CO.	T2S	R4E	S14
FIRST BAPTIST see **BAPTIST**	LINN CO.	T13S	R3W	S23
FISCHER, BABY	CLACKAMAS CO.	?	?	?
FISCHER, JOHN D. see **FISHER, JOHN D.**				
	WALLOWA CO.	T2N	R41E	?
FISCHER, JOHN G.	HOOD RIVER CO.	T1N	R10E	S31
FISCHER, MR. see **FISCHER, JOHN G.**				
	HOOD RIVER CO.	T1N	R10E	S31
FISH see **MYRTLE CREEK**	COOS CO.	T30S	R11W	S16
FISH LAKE	LINN CO.	T13S	R7E	S30
FISHER BABY	TILLAMOOK CO.	?	?	?
FISHER, ELIZABETH B. see **FISHER, JOHN D.**				
	WALLOWA CO.	T2N	R41E	?
FISHER, JOHN D.	WALLOWA CO.	T2N	R41E	?
FISHER SCHOOL COVERED BRIDGE see **FAULKNER, T. M.**				
	LINCOLN CO.	T15S	R10W	S1
FISHHAWK	COLUMBIA CO.	T6N	R5W	S17
FISHTRAP	COOS CO.	T28S	R13W	S23
FITCHA HOMESTEAD	CLATSOP CO.	T8N	R8W	S31
FITZGERALD, PATRICK see **MARION COUNTY POOR FARM**				
	MARION CO.	T7S	R3W	?
FLANAGAN see **BUZAN**	WASCO CO.	T4S	R15E	S33
FLEETWOOD FAMILY, ASA	BAKER CO.	T12S	R38E	S20
FLEETWOOD FAMILY, JIM	BAKER CO.	T12S	R38E	S25
FLEETWOOD HOMESTEAD, ASA see **FLEETWOOD FAMILY, ASA**				
	BAKER CO.	T12S	R38E	S20
FLEETWOOD RANCH, JIM see **FLEETWOOD FAMILY, JIM**				
	BAKER CO.	T12S	R38E	S25
FLETCHER	GRANT CO.	T13S	R30E	S28
FLETCHER see **INGLE**	GRANT CO.	T13S	R30E	S27
FLETT	GILLIAM CO.	T2S	R22E	S9
FLINN PLACE see **RAINS, BABY**	WASCO CO.	T5S	R12E	?
FLORA	WALLOWA CO.	T5N	R44E	S21
FLORAS CREEK see **DENMARK**	CURRY CO.	T31S	R15W	S10

FLORENCE see **PACIFIC SUNSET MEMORIAL PARK**

                                LANE CO.   T18S   R12W   S25

FLORENCE LODGE A. F. AND A. M. #107 see **PACIFIC SUNSET MEMORIAL PARK**

    LANE CO.   T18S   R12W   S25

Name	County	T	R	S
FLOUNCE ROCK see **NYE FAMILY**	JACKSON CO.	T33S	R2E	S10
FLOYD, ELWOOD see **UPPER SWEET CREEK**				
	LANE CO.	?	R10W	?
FLOYD FAMILY see **UPPER SWEET CREEK**				
	LANE CO.	?	R10W	?
FLOYD, FRANCIS see **BROWN**	COOS CO.	?	?	?
FLOYD, MARYANNA see **UPPER SWEET CREEK**				
	LANE CO.	?	R10W	?
FOELER, DON see **JOLLY FAMILY**	WASHINGTON CO.	T1N	R3W	S24
FOGEL, BERTHA see **STEWART'S POINT**				
	COLUMBIA CO.	T8N	R4W	?
FOGLE, JOHN see **JORDAN, MICHAEL M.**				
	MALHEUR CO.	?	?	?
FOISY D.L.C., AUGUSTINE see **BETHEL**				
	DOUGLAS CO.	T26S	R7W	S36
FOLAND see **BEAVER CREEK**	TILLAMOOK CO.	T3S	R9W	S29
FOLKS, B. A.	BENTON CO.	T10S	R5W	S10
FOOTS	JACKSON CO.	T36S	R4W	S35
FOOTS CREEK CHAPEL see **FOOTS**	JACKSON CO.	T36S	R4W	S35
FOPIANO	WHEELER CO.	T11S	R23E	S22
FOPPIANO see **FOPIANO**	WHEELER CO.	T11S	R23E	S22
FORD	UMATILLA CO.	T6N	R35E	S23
FORD see **JENKINS FAMILY**	LANE CO.	T18S	R5W	S22
FORD D.L.C., NATHAN see **HOLMES, CELI ANN AND HARRIET**				
	POLK CO.	T7S	R4W	S30
FORD INFANT	WASHINGTON CO.	T1N	R1W	S7
FORD, MARY ANN LENOX see **FORD INFANT**				
	WASHINGTON CO.	T1N	R1W	S7
FORD, NATHANIEL see **HOLMES, CELI ANN AND HARRIET**				
	POLK CO.	T7S	R4W	S30
FORD PLACE see **HOLMES, CELI ANN AND HARRIET**				
	POLK CO.	T7S	R4W	S30
FORD, REUBEN W. see **FORD INFANT**	WASHINGTON CO.	T1N	R1W	S7
FOREST CREEK see **LOGTOWN**	JACKSON CO.	T38S	R3W	S14
FOREST HILL see **SVENSEN PIONEER**	CLATSOP CO.	T8N	R8W	S23
FOREST LAWN	MULTNOMAH CO.	T1S	R3E	S10
FOREST LAWN MEMORIAL PARK see **FOREST LAWN**				
	MULTNOMAH CO.	T1S	R3E	S10
FOREST VALE MEMORIAL PARK	LANE CO.	T21S	R3E	S10
FOREST VIEW see **FOREST VIEW MEMORIAL GARDENS**				
	WASHINGTON CO.	T1N	R4W	S36
FOREST VIEW MEMORIAL GARDENS	WASHINGTON CO.	T1N	R4W	S36
FORMAN RANCH, BEN see **RAINS, BABY**				
	WASCO CO.	T5S	R12E	?
FORRESTER	CLACKAMAS CO.	T2S	R4E	S29
FORT ASTORIA	CLATSOP CO.	T8N	R10W	S8
FORT BRIGGS	JOSEPHINE CO.	T39S	R8W	S35

FORT DALLES	WASCO CO.	T1N	R13E	S4
FORT GEORGE see **FORT ASTORIA**	CLATSOP CO.	T8N	R10W	S8
FORT HARNEY	HARNEY CO.	T22S	R32 1/2E	S18
FORT HAYES	JOSEPHINE CO.	T37S	R8W	S35
FORT HILL	CURRY CO.	T32S	R15W	S5
FORT HILL see **HUSSEY FAMILY**	POLK CO.	T6S	R7W	S15
FORT KLAMATH see **MODOC WARRIORS**	KLAMATH CO.	T33S	R7 1/2E	S23
FORT KLAMATH MEMORIAL	KLAMATH CO.	T33S	R7 1/2E	S22
FORT ROCK	LAKE CO.	T25S	R14E	S29
FORT ROCK PIONEER see **FORT ROCK**	LAKE CO.	T25S	R14E	S29
FORT STEVENS see **U.S. ARMY FORT STEVENS**				
	CLATSOP CO.	T8N	R10W	S8
FORT STEVENS [OLD]	CLATSOP CO.	T8N	R10W	S5
FORT UMPQUA [NEW]	DOUGLAS CO.	T21S	R12W	S31
FORT UMPQUA [OLD]	DOUGLAS CO.	T22S	R7W	S30
FORT WARNER see **CAMP WARNER**	LAKE CO.	T36S	R22E	S33
FORTUNE BRANCH GRAVES	DOUGLAS CO.	T32S	R5W	S20
FOSSIL [OLD] see **MASONIC [FOSSIL]**				
	WHEELER CO.	T6S	R21E	S33
FOSTER BAR	CURRY CO.	T34S	R11W	S18
FOSTER CREEK see **ILLAHE**	CURRY CO.	T34S	R11W	S18
FOSTER D.L.C., JAMES S. see **WHITEAKER FAMILY**				
	POLK CO.	T8S	R5W	S14
FOSTER D.L.C., JAMES W. see **SUTER FARM**				
	CLACKAMAS CO.	T2S	R4E	S30
FOSTER D.L.C., PHILIP see **FOSTER PIONEER**				
	CLACKAMAS CO.	T2S	R4E	S31
FOSTER PIONEER	CLACKAMAS CO.	T2S	R4E	S31
FOSTER PIONEER	UMATILLA CO.	T3N	R29E	S5
FOSTER-GOULARD HOUSE see **TINDALL, MR.**				
	LINN CO.	T14S	R2W	S6
FOTHERGILL, JOHN	LANE CO.	T18S	R1W	S33
FOUR CORNERS see **WAMIC**	WASCO CO.	T4S	R12E	S22
FOUR CORNERS see **ZOAR LUTHERAN [BARLOW ROAD]**				
	CLACKAMAS CO.	T4S	R1E	S7
FOX	GRANT CO.	T11S	R30E	S6
FOX BRIDGE	COOS CO.	T28S	R12W	S15
FOX HILL	CURRY CO.	T35S	R14W	S8
FOX VALLEY	LINN CO.	T9S	R2E	S20
FOX VALLEY see **FOX**	GRANT CO.	T11S	R30E	S6
FRANCISCAN SISTERS OF THE EUCHARIST				
	MULTNOMAH CO.	T1N	R5E	S15
FRANKLIN	LANE CO.	T16S	R5W	S21
FRANKLIN BUTTE	LINN CO.	T10S	R1W	S19
FRANKLIN GRANGE see **FRANKLIN**	LANE CO.	T16S	R5W	S21
FRANKTON	HOOD RIVER CO.	T3N	R10E	S27
FRATERNAL UNION see **AMERICAN LEGION POST #126**				
	TILLAMOOK CO.	T3N	R10W	S28
FRAZER D.L.C., LUCIEN B. see **BUCK HOLLOW**				
	YAMHILL CO.	T5S	R7W	S13

FRAZER D.L.C., MILTON see **UNKNOWN PIONEER CHILD**

	MULTNOMAH CO.	T1N	R3E	S30

FREDENBURG see **MT. HOOD COMMUNITY**

	HOOD RIVER CO.	T1N	R10E	S21

FREDERICK D.L.C., JAMES W. see **SALT CREEK**

	POLK CO.	T7S	R5W	S6

FREE METHODIST CHURCH see **FRIENDS**

	YAMHILL CO.	T3S	R2W	S20

FREEMAN D.L.C., JOHN see **FREEMAN FAMILY**

	DOUGLAS CO.	T28S	R7W	?
FREEMAN FAMILY	DOUGLAS CO.	T28S	R7W	?

FREEMASON see **MASONIC [LONE FIR]**

	MULTNOMAH CO.	T1S	R1E	S1
FRENCH	WASCO CO.	T5S	R12E	S33
FRENCH, A. T. see **STARKEY**	UNION CO.	T4S	R35E	S3
FRENCH CREEK	DOUGLAS CO.	T32S	R3W	S4

FRENCH, IKE AND WIFE see **FRENCH CREEK**

	DOUGLAS CO.	T32S	R3W	S4
FRENCH, JOHN see **STARKEY**	UNION CO.	T4S	R35E	S3

FRENCH PLACE, RAYMOND see **TIPPETT'S FARM**

	MORROW CO.	T1N	R27E	?

FRENCH PLACE, RAYMOND see **YARLET**

	MORROW CO.	T1N	R27E	S23
FRENCH SETTLEMENT see **MELROSE**	DOUGLAS CO.	T27S	R7W	S1

FRIDDLES BABY see **FRIDDLES FAMILY**

	WALLOWA CO.	T6N	R43E	S23

FRIDDLES, CORDELIA B. see **FRIDDLES FAMILY**

	WALLOWA CO.	T6N	R43E	S23
FRIDDLES FAMILY	WALLOWA CO.	T6N	R43E	S23

FRIEDENBURG see **MT. HOOD COMMUNITY**

	HOOD RIVER CO.	T1N	R10E	S21

FRIEDENBURG HOMESTEAD, AVERY see **MT. HOOD COMMUNITY**

	HOOD RIVER CO.	T1N	R10E	S21

FRIEDLEY D.L.C., JOSEPH P. see **ST. MARY'S CATHOLIC**

	BENTON CO.	T11S	R5W	S27

FRIEDMAN, ABRAHAM see **FRIEDMAN, MARKS**

	MULTNOMAH CO.	T1S	R1E	S1

FRIEDMAN, ANN see **FRIEDMAN, MARKS**

	MULTNOMAH CO.	T1S	R1E	S1
FRIEDMAN, MARKS	MULTNOMAH CO.	T1S	R1E	S1
FRIEND [NEW]	WASCO CO.	T3S	R12E	S3
FRIEND [OLD] see **MILLER**	WASCO CO.	T2S	R12E	S34
FRIENDS	YAMHILL CO.	T3S	R2W	S20
FRIENDS see **FRIENDSHIP**	KLAMATH CO.	T34S	R7E	S34
FRIENDS see **MARION FRIENDS**	MARION CO.	T9S	R2W	S29
FRIENDS RANCH see **MAUPIN**	JEFFERSON CO.	T9S	R16E	S24
FRIENDSHIP	KLAMATH CO.	T34S	R7E	S34
FRIER FAMILY	DOUGLAS CO.	T22S	R6W	S1
FRIER PLACE, EARL see **COLVIN**	DOUGLAS CO.	T22S	R5W	S6

FRIER RANCH, CARL see **FRIER FAMILY**

	DOUGLAS CO.	T22S	R6W	S1

FRIEZE CHILDREN	MORROW CO.	T3S	R28E	S15
FRINK FAMILY	JACKSON CO.	T36S	R1W	?
FRIZZELL RANCH see **TONEY**	WHEELER CO.	T11S	R22E	S3
FROG POND CHURCH see **MERIDIAN [OLD]**				
	CLACKAMAS CO.	T3S	R1W	S13
FROHMADER see **HALLS FERRY**	MARION CO.	T8S	R4W	S14
FROZEN CREEK	DOUGLAS CO.	T28S	R4W	?
FRUIT HOME, GEORGE see **MICHAEL**	LINN CO.	T14S	R3W	S26
FRUITA see **PARK**	WALLOWA CO.	T3S	R48E	S3
FRY	LINN CO.	T11S	R3W	S27
FRY see **FRYE FAMILY**	CURRY CO.	T33S	R10W	?
FRY FAMILY see **BILLINGS**	CURRY CO	T34S	R11W	S7
FRYE FAMILY	CURRY CO.	T33S	R10W	?
FRYE HOMESTEAD see **RAT HOLE**	CURRY CO.	T35S	R11W	S5
FRYE HOMESTEAD, C. J. see **FRYE FAMILY**				
	CURRY CO.	T33S	R10W	?
G. A. R. see **GRAND ARMY OF THE REPUBLIC**				
	MULTNOMAH CO.	T1S	R1E	S27
G. A. R. [GRAND ARMY OF THE REPUBLIC]				
	WASCO CO.	T1N	R13E	S4
G. A. R. [GRAND ARMY OF THE REPUBLIC]				
	YAMHILL CO.	T3S	R2W	S20
G. A. R. [GRAND ARMY OF THE REPUBLIC] see **BANDON PIONEER**				
	COOS CO.	T28S	R14W	S30
G. A. R. [GRAND ARMY OF THE REPUBLIC; OLD BANDON]				
	COOS CO.	T28S	R14W	S30
G. W. W.	CLACKAMAS CO.	T3S	R2E	S4
GABLEMAN, CHRIS see **HUTCHINS**	TILLAMOOK CO.	?	?	?
GABRIEL FAMILY	KLAMATH CO.	T37S	R9E	S25
GAGE D.L.C., JOSEPH see **NICHOLS**	DOUGLAS CO.	T28S	R6W	S20
GAGE, JOSEPH see **COX, JOHN**	DOUGLAS CO.	T28S	R6W	?
GAGE, TOM see **COX, JOHN**	DOUGLAS CO.	T28S	R6W	?
GAINES	LINN CO.	T11S	R1W	S2
GAINES D.L.C., WILLIS see **GAINES**				
	LINN CO.	T11S	R1W	S2
GAINES FAMILY see **GAINES**	LINN CO.	T11S	R1W	S2
GALE D.L.C., JOSEPH see **SEARS**	LANE CO.	T20S	R3W	S35
GALENA	GRANT CO.	T10S	R32E	S12
GALES CREEK	WASHINGTON CO.	T1N	R4W	S18
GALES CREEK UNION see **GALES CREEK**				
	WASHINGTON CO.	T1N	R4W	S18
GALL see **HAYS**	JACKSON CO.	T36S	R3W	S20
GALLAHER	UMATILLA CO.	T4N	R33E	S36
GALLOWAY	UNION CO.	T1N	R39E	S3
GANIARD, A. JUDD see **HOLLAND SCHOOL**				
	JOSEPHINE CO.	T39S	R7W	S33
GARBER NURSING HOME	LANE CO.	T18S	R3W	S5
GARD, JOHN see **SCHUEBEL**	CLACKAMAS CO.	T3S	R2E	S36
GARD, MILO	JEFFERSON CO.	T10S	R13E	S9
GARDEN OF REVERENCE	CLACKAMAS CO.	T1S	R4E	S28

GARDEN OF THE GOOD SHEPHERD see **SUNSET HILLS MEMORIAL GARDENS**				
	LANE CO.	T18S	R3W	S18
GARDINER	DOUGLAS CO.	T21S	R12W	S22
GARDINER D.L.C., SAMUEL see **WILBUR [NEW]**				
	DOUGLAS CO.	T26S	R5W	S7
GARDNER	DOUGLAS CO.	T22S	R6W	?
GARDNER FAMILY see **GARDNER**	DOUGLAS CO.	T22S	R6W	?
GARDNINER D.L.C., SAMUEL see **REED-HILL FAMILY**				
	DOUGLAS CO.	T26S	R5W	S7
GARFIELD see **MT. ZION**	CLACKAMAS CO.	T3S	R4E	S22
GARLINGTON PLACE	SHERMAN CO.	T2N	R17E	?
GARRETT	COOS CO.	T29S	R12W	?
GARRETT RANCH see **GARRETT**	COOS CO.	T29S	R12W	?
GARRISON	LINN CO.	T13S	R4E	?
GARWOOD GRAVE see **BIG CAMAS RANGER STATION**				
	DOUGLAS CO.	T27S	R3E	?
GARWOOD, MR. see **BIG CAMAS RANGER STATION**				
	DOUGLAS CO.	T27S	R3E	?
GASSNER ROAD see **COOPER MOUNTAIN [PROTESTANT]**				
	WASHINGTON CO.	T1S	R2W	S25
GATE CREEK see **BRIGGS GRAVES**	WASCO CO.	T4S	R11E	S26
GATES	LANE CO.	T18S	R5W	S19
GATES see **FAIRVIEW**	LINN CO.	T9S	R3E	S34
GATES FARM, FRED see **WEGER**	LINN CO.	T15S	R3W	S26
GATES OF HEAVEN	LANE CO.	T18S	R4W	S5
GATES, WILLIAM see **HAYSTACK**	WHEELER CO.	T8S	R25E	S16
GATEWAY see **KAMPFER FAMILY**	JEFFERSON CO.	T9S	R14E	S11
GATH ROAD see **BOYS**	MARION CO.	T8S	R2W	S17
GATTON	MULTNOMAH CO.	T2N	R1W	S36
GATTON D.L.C., WILLIAM see **GATTON**				
	MULTNOMAH CO.	T2N	R1W	S36
GAY see **COGSWELL**	LANE CO.	T19S	R3W	S5
GAY D.L.C., GEORGE KIRBY see **GAY FAMILY**				
	POLK CO.	T6S	R3W	?
GAY D.L.C., MARTIN B. see **COGSWELL**				
	LANE CO.	T19S	R3W	S5
GAY FAMILY	POLK CO.	T6S	R3W	?
GAY HOUSE see **GAY FAMILY**	POLK CO.	T6S	R3W	?
GAY-MASTERSON see **COGSWELL**	LANE CO.	T19S	R3W	S5
GAY PIONEER, MARY see **COGSWELL**	LANE CO.	T19S	R3W	S5
GEER D.L.C., FREDERICK W. see **GEER PIONEER**				
	CLACKAMAS CO.	T3S	R1W	S31
GEER, JOSPH C. see **GEER PIONEER**	CLACKAMAS CO.	T3S	R1W	S31
GEER, MARY see **GEER PIONEER**	CLACKAMAS CO.	T3S	R1W	S31
GEER PIONEER	CLACKAMAS CO.	T3S	R1W	S31
GEISEL FAMILY	CURRY CO.	T36S	R15W	S1
GEISEL, JOHN see **GEISEL FAMILY**	CURRY CO.	T36S	R15W	S1
GENEVA see **GRANDVIEW**	JEFFERSON CO.	T12S	R11E	S36
GEORGE	CLACKAMAS CO.	T3S	R5E	S19
GEORGE PROTESTANT see **GEORGE**	CLACKAMAS CO.	T3S	R5E	S19
GERHARD PLACE, LOREN	DOUGLAS CO.	T21S	R11W	S9

GERHART, CHARLES see **LILYGLEN**	JACKSON CO.	T38S	R3E	S14
GERHART, MARGRET see **LILYGLEN**	JACKSON CO.	T38S	R3E	S14
GERKING FAMILY see **GERMAN LUTHERAN**				
	UMATILLA CO.	T4N	R33E	S29
GERKING RANCH see **HANNAH FAMILY**	UMATILLA CO.	T4N	R34E	S30
GERMAN see **METHODIST HILL**	JEFFERSON CO.	T11S	R13E	S32
GERMAN BAPTIST see **STAFFORD BAPTIST CHURCH**				
	CLACKAMAS CO.	T2S	R1E	S31
GERMAN BAPTIST BRETHREN see **MABEL**				
	LANE CO.	T16S	R1W	S5
GERMAN CHRISTIAN APOSTOLIC see **APOSTOLIC**				
	MARION CO.	T7S	R1W	S8
GERMAN CHURCH see **GERMAN LUTHERAN**				
	UMATILLA CO.	T4N	R33E	S29
GERMAN CHURCH see **ST. PAUL LUTHERAN CHURCH**				
	WASHINGTON CO.	T2S	R1W	S30
GERMAN EVANGELICAL see **ST. JOHANN**				
	CLACKAMAS CO.	T3S	R1E	S36
GERMAN EVANGELICAL LUTHERAN EMANUELS CHURCH see **EMANUEL LUTHERAN**				
	WASHINGTON CO.	T1N	R3W	S34
GERMAN LUTHERAN	UMATILLA CO.	T4N	R33E	S29
GERMAN LUTHERAN see **TRINITY LUTHERAN**				
	MARION CO.	T6S	R1W	S12
GERMAN LUTHERAN CHURCH see **MT. OLIVE LUTHERAN**				
	WASHINGTON CO.	T1S	R4W	S23
GERMAN LUTHERANER [Sic] EMANUEL CHURCH see **EMANUEL LUTHERAN**				
	WASHINGTON CO.	T1N	R3W	S34
GERMAN ORDER OF RED MEN see **JACKSONVILLE**				
	JACKSON CO.	T37S	R2W	S29
GERMAN PRESBYTERIAN see **BETHANY PRESBYTERIAN**				
	WASHINGTON CO.	T1N	R1W	S17
GERMANY HILL see **MASONIC [ST. HELENS]**				
	COLUMBIA CO.	T5N	R1W	S33
GERRISH D.L.C., JOHN J. see **CHERRY GROVE BAPTIST**				
	WASHINGTON CO.	T1S	R4W	S30
GERVAIS CATHOLIC see **SACRED HART**				
	MARION CO.	T5S	R2W	S36
GERVAIS MASONIC see **MASONIC [GERVAIS]**				
	MARION CO.	T5S	R2W	S36
GETHSEMANE see **GETHSEMANI**	CLACKAMAS CO.	T1S	R2E	S33
GETHSEMANI	CLACKAMAS CO.	T1S	R2E	S33
GHIRARDELLI, JOHN see **WALKER GULCH**				
	JOSEPHINE CO.	T40S	R7W	S15
GIBBS	YAMHILL CO.	T3S	R2W	S3
GIBBS FAMILY	CURRY CO.	T31S	R13W	?
GIBBS PROPERTY, RALPH see **MILLER FAMILY**				
	COOS CO.	T29S	R12W	S33
GIBSON	CLACKAMAS CO.	T3S	R4E	?
GIBSON, BENTON see **GIBSON FAMILY, GEORGE G.**				
	POLK CO.	T7S	R3W	S19

GIBSON D.L.C., GEORGE G. see **GIBSON FAMILY, GEORGE G.**

| | POLK CO. | T7S | R3W | S19 |

GIBSON D.L.C., RANDOLPH C. see **GIBSON FAMILY**

| | MARION CO. | T6S | R1W | S14 |

GIBSON, DOUGLAS see **GIBSON FAMILY, GEORGE G.**

	POLK CO.	T7S	R3W	S19
GIBSON FAMILY	MARION CO.	T6S	R1W	S14
GIBSON FAMILY, GEORGE G.	POLK CO.	T7S	R3W	S19

GIBSON, MARY BOWEN see **GIBSON FAMILY, GEORGE G.**

| | POLK CO. | T7S | R3W | S19 |

GILBREATH, J. C. see **GILBREATH-MOECK FAMILY**

	COLUMBIA CO.	T7N	R2W	S18
GILBREATH-MOECK FAMILY	COLUMBIA CO.	T7N	R2W	S18

GILBREATH, SARA ANN see **GILBREATH-MOECK FAMILY**

| | COLUMBIA CO. | T7N | R2W | S18 |

| GILESPI [Sic] see **GILLESPIE** | LANE CO. | T17S | R3W | S19 |

GILHAM D.L.C., JOHN B. see **CLEVELAND**

| | DOUGLAS CO. | T26S | R7W | S24 |

GILKENSON FARM see **MEDICAL SPRINGS**

| | UNION CO. | T6S | R41E | ? |

GILKINSON SAWMILL see **STURGILL CHILDREN, HILDA AND LOUIE**

	BAKER CO.	T8S	R43E	?
GILKISON, JAMES A.	MARION CO.	T8S	R3W	S24
GILLAM see **QUINES CREEK**	DOUGLAS CO.	T32S	R5W	S15
GILLESPIE	LANE CO.	T17S	R3W	S19

GILLESPIE D.L.C., JACOB see **GILLESPIE**

| | LANE CO. | T17S | R3W | S19 |

GILLETT D.L.C., PRESTON W. see **LEWIS AND CLARK**

	CLATSOP CO.	T7N	R9W	S6
GILLIAM see **WINCHESTER SCHOOL**	DOUGLAS CO.	T26S	R6W	S25

GILLIAM, COLONEL CORNELIUS see **WELL SPRING**

	MORROW CO.	T2N	R25E	S20
GILLIAM D.L.C., MARY see **WOMER**	POLK CO.	T9S	R6W	S32
GILLIAMS see **QUINES CREEK**	DOUGLAS CO.	T32S	R5W	S15
GILLILAND	LINN CO.	T13S	R1E	S34

GILLILAND see **SWEET HOME MENNONITE**

| | LINN CO. | T13S | R1E | S34 |

GILLILAND D.L.C., JOHN W. see **GILLILAND**

| | LINN CO. | T13S | R1E | S34 |

GILMORE D.L.C., JAMES P. see **GILMORE FAMILY**

	DOUGLAS CO.	T28S	R5W	S11
GILMORE FAMILY	DOUGLAS CO.	T28S	R5W	S11
GINGLES	BENTON CO.	T10S	R4W	S15

GINGLES D.L.C., JAMES see **GINGLES**

| | BENTON CO. | T10S | R4W | S15 |

GIRGENSON, BERTHA CHRISTINA see **GIRGENSON FAMILY**

	COLUMBIA CO.	T6N	R3W	S14
GIRGENSON FAMILY	COLUMBIA CO.	T6N	R3W	S14

GIRGENSON, JOHN see **GIRGENSON FAMILY**

	COLUMBIA CO.	T6N	R3W	S14
GIST	TILLAMOOK CO.	T4S	R10W	S21

GITHENS FAMILY	CLACKAMAS CO.	T3S	R4E	S5
GIVOT OLAM see **BETH ISREAL [OLD]**				
	MULTNOMAH CO.	T1S	R1E	S10
GLASCOCK BABY	MALHEUR CO.	?	?	?
GLASCOCK, HENRY L. "BULLDOG" see **GLASCOCK BABY**				
	MALHEUR CO.	?	?	?
GLEASON	CLACKAMAS CO.	T4S	R	S
GLEASON, PARSON see **GLEASON**	CLACKAMAS CO.	T4S	R	S
GLEN see **GLENWOOD**	LINCOLN CO.	T12S	R10W	S13
GLEN-OAK ORPHANAGE	MARION CO.	T7S	R3W	S25
GLENDALE	DOUGLAS CO.	T33S	R6W	S5
GLENEDEN BEACH	LINCOLN CO.	T8S	R11W	?
GLENWOOD	LINCOLN CO.	T12S	R10W	S13
GLENWOOD see **GREENWOOD**	LANE CO.	T17S	R1E	S12
GLIDE see **WIMBERLY**	DOUGLAS CO.	T26S	R3W	S19
GLOVER D.L.C., JOHN P. see **SMITH PLACE**				
	CLACKAMAS CO.	T2S	R4E	S30
GLOVER D.L.C., PHILIP see **GLOVER FAMILY**				
	MARION CO.	T8S	R1W	S27
GLOVER FAMILY	MARION CO.	T8S	R1W	S27
GOBLE see **NEER CITY**	COLUMBIA CO.	T6N	R2W	S2
GOFF D.L.C., DAVID see **NESMITH FAMILY**				
	POLK CO.	T7S	R4W	S30
GOFF FAMILY	DOUGLAS CO.	T25S	R5W	S30
GOLD BEACH see **ROGUE RIVER**	CURRY CO.	T37S	R15W	S12
GOLD CREEK see **HUSSEY FAMILY**	POLK CO.	T6S	R7W	S15
GOLD RIDGE MINE	BAKER CO.	T12S	R43E	S16
GOLDEN D.L.C., WILLIAM see **SCOTTSBURG**				
	DOUGLAS CO.	T22S	R9W	S8
GOLDEN RULE I.O.O.F. LODGE #78 [GRANTS PASS] see **I.O.O.F. [GRANTS PASS]**				
	JOSEPHINE CO.	T36S	R5W	S16
GOLDSON see **SWEET HOME**	LANE CO.	T16S	R6W	S27
GOOD SAMARITAN HOSPITAL	MULTNOMAH CO.	T1N	R1E	S33
GOODMAN see **ALPINE**	BENTON CO	T14S	R6W	S24
GOODMAN CHILDREN	KLAMATH CO.	T39S	R12E	?
GOODRICH D.L.C., CARNEY AND PEGGY T. see **GOODRICH FAMILY**				
	YAMHILL CO.	T4S	R3W	S21
GOODRICH D.L.C., CARNEY AND PEGGY T. see **I.O.O.F. [DAYTON]**				
	YAMHILL CO.	T4S	R3W	S21
GOODRICH FAMILY	YAMHILL CO.	T4S	R3W	S21
GOODRICH-WORDEN see **GOODRICH FAMILY**				
	YAMHILL CO.	T4S	R3W	S21
GOODWIN RANCH see **GOODWIN TOMB**	MALHEUR CO.	T17S	R37E	S19
GOODWIN, THOMAS HUGH see **GOODWIN TOMB**				
	MALHEUR CO.	T17S	R37E	S19
GOODWIN TOMB	MALHEUR CO.	T17S	R37E	S19
GOOSE CREEK	BAKER CO.	T8S	R43E	S29
GOOSEBERRY	MORROW CO.	T3S	R23E	S14
GOPHER VALLEY see **AGEE FAMILY**	YAMHILL CO.	T4S	R6W	S36
GORDON see **WORDEN**	KLAMATH CO.	T40S	R8E	S34
GORDON, CHARLES	WALLOWA CO.	T5N	R45E	?

GORDON D.L.C., HARVEY see **MASONIC [ALBANY]**				
	LINN CO.	T11S	R4W	S12
GORDON, FRANK	BAKER CO.	T10S	R36E	?
GORE D.L.C., WILLIAM B. see **I.O.O.F. [LEBANON]**				
	LINN CO.	T12S	R2W	S2
GORE FAMILY	COLUMBIA CO.	T5N	R2W	S10
GORE, HENRY C. see **GORE FAMILY**	COLUMBIA CO.	T5N	R2W	S10
GORE, MARY C. see **GORE FAMILY**	COLUMBIA CO.	T5N	R2W	S10
GOSA, JIM see **JOHNSON PLACE, LOREN**				
	COLUMBIA CO.	T3N	R1W	?
GOSHEN	LANE CO.	T18S	R3W	S24
GOSHEN GRANGE #561 see **GOSHEN**	LANE CO.	T18S	R3W	S24
GOTCHER	JOSEPHINE CO.	T38S	R5W	S22
GOTHARD D.L.C., SAMUEL see **FALLS CITY**				
	POLK CO.	T8S	R6W	S16
GOTHARD D.L.C., SAMUEL see **I.O.O.F. [FALLS CITY]**				
	POLK CO.	T8S	R6W	S21
GOURLEY'S FARM, ROBERT AND EILEEN see **DUNDON, CARRIE FRANCES**				
	LINN CO.	T13S	R2E	S34
GOVERNMENT HILL see **WASHINGTON, PAUL**				
	LINCOLN CO.	T10S	R10W	S9
GRAHAM D.L.C., DAVID see **CRESCENT GROVE**				
	WASHINGTON CO.	T1S	R1W	S26
GRAHAM FAMILY	LINCOLN CO.	T11S	R10W	S17
GRAIG GRAVE see **CRAIG MEMORIAL**	LANE CO.	T15S	R7 1/2E	UNS
GRAND ARMY OF THE REPUBLIC	MULTNOMAH CO.	T1S	R1E	S27
GRAND ARMY OF THE REPUBLIC see **MASONIC [EUGENE]**				
	LANE CO.	T18S	R3W	S5
GRAND RONDE	POLK CO.	T6S	R8W	S12
GRAND RONDE INDIAN TRIBAL see **GRAND RONDE**				
	POLK CO.	T6S	R8W	S12
GRANDVIEW	JEFFERSON CO.	T12S	R11E	S36
GRANDVIEW	UNION CO.	T3S	R38E	S16
GRANGE see **LORANE GRANGE**	LANE CO.	T20S	R5W	S2
GRANGER see **LORANE GRANGE**	LANE CO.	T20S	R5W	S2
GRANGERS see **YOUNGS RIVER**	CLATSOP CO.	T7N	R9W	S10
GRANITE	GRANT CO.	T9S	R35 1/2E	S4
GRANITE HILL	JOSEPHINE CO.	T36S	R6W	S13
GRANT	CROOK CO.	T13S	R19E	S1
GRANT COUNTY POOR FARM	GRANT CO	T12S	R30E	S12
GRANT'S see **ST. JOSEPH**	MULTNOMAH CO.	T1S	R3E	S8
GRASS FLAT see **WALKER GULCH**	JOSEPHINE CO.	T40S	R7W	S15
GRASS VALLEY LODGE #131 I.O.O.F. see **I.O.O.F. [GRASS VALLEY]**				
	SHERMAN CO.	T2S	R16E	S22
GRAVE CREEK	JOSEPHINE CO.	T34S	R6W	?
GRAVE HILL see **STEARNS FAMILY**	JACKSON CO.	T38S	R1W	S34
GRAVE ISLAND MEMORIAL	WASCO CO.	T2N	R14E	S31
GRAVELFORD	COOS CO.	T28S	R12W	S26
GRAVES BABY see **GRAVES FAMILY**	YAMHILL CO.	T5S	R6W	S27
GRAVES D.L.C., CHARLES B. see **GREENCREST MEMORIAL PARK**				
	YAMHILL CO.	T5S	R6W	S35

GRAVES D.L.C., JAMES B. see **GRAVES FAMILY**

	YAMHILL CO.	T5S	R6W	S27
GRAVES, DIANA see **GRAVES FAMILY**	YAMHILL CO.	T5S	R6W	S27
GRAVES, DINA see **GRAVES FAMILY**	YAMHILL CO.	T5S	R6W	S27
GRAVES FAMILY	YAMHILL CO.	T5S	R6W	S27
GRAVES, J. M. see **GRAVES FAMILY**	YAMHILL CO.	T5S	R6W	S27
GRAVES, MR. see **GRAVES FAMILY**	YAMHILL CO.	T5S	R6W	S27
GRAVEYARD BUTTE	WASCO CO.	T5S	R12E	S10
GRAVEYARD POINT	MALHEUR CO.	T23S	R47E	?

GRAVEYARD POINT see **SOUTH SLOUGH**

	COOS CO.	T26S	R14W	S15
GRAY see **BLAIN**	LINN CO.	T14S	R3W	S14
GRAY, ANNA C. see **GORE FAMILY**	COLUMBIA CO.	T5N	R2W	S10
GRAY BUTTE	JEFFERSON CO.	T13S	R14E	S6
GRAY D.L.C., DAVID see **BLAIN**	LINN CO.	T14S	R3W	S14

GRAY D.L.C., JOHN F. see **HILLCREST MEMORIAL PARK AND MAUSOLEUM**

	JACKSON CO.	T38S	R1W	S3

GRAY D.L.C., WILLIAM H. see **OCEAN VIEW**

	CLATSOP CO.	T8N	R10W	S28

GRAY, EILEEN H. see **SPRUCE POINT**

	LANE CO.	T18S	R12W	S27
GRAY, FRED W.	LANE CO.	T19S	R1E	S19

GRAY HOMESTEAD, JAMES see **SCOVELL FAMILY**

	TILLAMOOK CO.	T3N	R9W	?
GRAY, ISAAC see **GORE FAMILY**	COLUMBIA CO.	T5N	R2W	S10
GRAY, MARY E. see **ROBERTS-GRAY**	WASCO CO.	T1S	R13E	S36
GRAY, MRS. ELIZA JANE	CLACKAMAS CO	T6S	R2E	S16
GRAY'S see **GRAY BUTTE**	JEFFERSON CO	T13S	R14E	S6
GREASEWOOD see **GALLAHER**	UMATILLA CO.	T4N	R33E	S36
GREASEWOOD FINNISH LUTHERAN	UMATILLA CO.	T4N	R33E	S34

GREEN CREST MEMORIAL PARK see **GREENCREST MEMORIAL PARK**

	YAMHILL CO.	T5S	R6W	S35
GREEN, JAMES	COOS CO.	T28S	R13W	S30
GREEN MOUNTAIN	COLUMBIA CO.	T7N	R3W	S13
GREEN MOUNTAIN	MARION CO.	T7S	R1E	S26
GREEN MOUNTAIN ROAD	CLATSOP CO.	T6N	R8W	?

GREEN MOUNTAIN [NORTH] see **WOODBINE**

	COLUMBIA CO.	T7N	R3W	S13

GREEN MOUNTAIN SOUTH see **GREEN MOUNTAIN**

	COLUMBIA CO.	T7N	R3W	S13
GREEN PLACE see **UNKNOWN**	LINN CO.	T14S	R2E	S3
GREEN SPRINGS see **PINEHURST**	JACKSON CO.	T40S	R4E	S5
GREEN VALLEY	DOUGLAS CO.	T24S	R6W	S25
GREENCREST MEMORIAL PARK	YAMHILL CO.	T5S	R6W	S35
GREENE	COOS CO.	T32S	R12W	S8

GREENER PLACE, ED see **CLARK CHILDREN**

	BAKER CO.	T8S	R46E	?
GREENHORN	BAKER CO.	T10S	R35E	S9
GREENVILLE see **UNION POINT**	WASHINGTON CO.	T2N	R3W	S31
GREENWOOD	CLATSOP CO.	T8N	R9W	S33
GREENWOOD	LANE CO.	T17S	R1E	S12

GREENWOOD see **GRAND ARMY OF THE REPUBLIC**

	MULTNOMAH CO.	T1S	R1E	S27
GREENWOOD see **GREENWOOD HILLS**	MULTNOMAH CO.	T1S	R1E	S27

GREENWOOD see **I.O.O.F. [GREENWOOD]**

	MULTNOMAH CO.	T1S	R1E	S27

GREENWOOD HILL see **GREENWOOD HILLS**

	MULTNOMAH CO.	T1S	R1E	S27
GREENWOOD HILLS	MULTNOMAH CO.	T1S	R1E	S27

GREENWOOD I.O.O.F. see **I.O.O.F. [GREENWOOD]**

	MULTNOMAH CO.	T1S	R1E	S27
GREENWOOD MEMORIAL	DESCHUTES CO.	T17S	R12E	S33
GREER FAMILY see **SPENCER FAMILY**	YAMHILL CO.	T3S	R3W	S22

GREESEWOOD see **GREASEWOOD FINNISH LUTHERAN**

	UMATILLA CO.	T4N	R33E	S34
GRESHAM see **ESCOBAR PIONEER**	MULTNOMAH CO.	T1S	R3E	S10
GRESHAM see **GRESHAM PIONEER**	MULTNOMAH CO.	T1S	R3E	S10
GRESHAM see **ST. JOSEPH**	MULTNOMAH CO.	T1S	R3E	S8
GRESHAM see **WHITE BIRCH**	MULTNOMAH CO.	T1S	R3E	S9
GRESHAM PIONEER	MULTNOMAH CO.	T1S	R3E	S10

GRESHAM SCHOOL see **GRESHAM PIONEER**

	MULTNOMAH CO.	T1S	R3E	S10
GRIBBLE	CLACKAMAS CO.	T4S	R1E	S21

GRIBBLE D.L.C., ANDREW E. see **GRIBBLE**

	CLACKAMAS CO.	T4S	R1E	S21
GRIDER, D. H. see **TELOCASET**	UNION CO.	T5S	R40E	S28

GRIFFIN see **WHITE D.L.C., WILLIAM**

	LANE CO.	T15S	R5W	S20
GRIFFIN CREEK	JACKSON CO.	T38S	R2W	S9

GRIFFIN D.L.C., EDWARD see **HENDERER FAMILY**

	DOUGLAS CO.	T22S	R8W	S23

GRIFFIN FAMILY see **GRIFFIN CREEK**

	JACKSON CO.	T38S	R2W	S9

GRIFFITH D.L.C., JOHN W. see **BUENA VISTA**

	POLK CO.	T9S	R4W	S23
GRIM see **HUBBARD**	MARION CO.	T4S	R1W	S33
GRISSOM, ANDREW J. see **UNKNOWN**	JACKSON CO.	T37S	R2E	S8
GRIZZLY	JEFFERSON CO.	T12S	R15E	S33
GRONNEL see **GRONNELL FAMILY**	CLATSOP CO.	T4N	R7W	?
GRONNELL FAMILY	CLATSOP CO.	T4N	R7W	?
GROUSE see **BARTLETT**	WALLOWA CO.	T6N	R43E	S21
GROUSE CREEK see **PARK**	WALLOWA CO.	T3N	R48E	S3
GROVE see **RESTLAWN**	GRANT CO.	T13S	R31E	S22
GRUB HOLLOW see **BUCK HOLLOW**	YAMHILL CO.	T5S	R7W	S13
GRUBB FAMILY	LINCOLN CO.	T10S	R11W	S5

GUENTHER-PITMAN FAMILY see **OAK GROVE**

	YAMHILL CO.	T2S	R3W	S21
GUEST, WLLIAM see **DEER CREEK**	JOSEPHINE CO.	T38S	R7W	S18

GUILD D.L.C., PETER see **CITY GARBAGE CREMATORY**

	MULTNOMAH CO.	T1N	R1E	S29

GUILD'S LAKE see **CITY GARBAGE CREMATORY**

	MULTNOMAH CO.	T1N	R1E	S29

GUNDERSON see **MOUNTAIN HOME**   LINN CO.   T13S   R1W   S20
GUNDERSON PLACE, SAM see **THOMPSON, A. K.**
    LINN CO.   T13S   R1W   S18
GUNTER   DOUGLAS CO.   T20S   R7W   S27
GUNTER, CLYDE M. see **GUNTER MEMORIAL, CLYDE M.**
    JOSEPHINE CO.   T36S   R6W   ?
GUNTER MEMORIAL, CLYDE M.   JOSEPHINE CO.   T36S   R6W   ?
GURDANE   UMATILLA CO.   T3S   R30E   S32
GWYNNE   WALLOWA CO.   T1S   R44E   S30
HABELT, MRS.   CLACKAMAS CO.   T4S   R4E   S26
HACKER, BRICE see **KEASEY**   COLUMBIA CO.   T5N   R5W   S27
HAFER see **EDEN**   WALLOWA CO.   T5N   R42E   S21
HAGER, DAN see **IDA MINE**   JOSEPHINE CO.   T35S   R5W   S26
HAHN see **WILLIS FAMILY, WILLIAM A.**
    DOUGLAS CO.   T27S   R4W   S19
HAIGHT, JR. RANCH, DON see **WHEELOCK, HATTIE**
    BAKER CO.   T8S   R46S   ?
HAIGHT SPRING   WASCO CO.   T8S   R15E   S9
HAINES   BAKER CO.   T7S   R39E   S21
HAINES   CURRY CO.   T31S   R13W   S36
HAINES FAMILY   DOUGLAS CO.   T22S   R7W   S32
HALBERT BAPTIST CHURCH see **HAYESVILLE**
    MARION CO.   T7S   R3W   S12
HALE see **CULVER I.O.O.F.**   JEFFERSON CO.   T12S   R13E   S16
HALE D.L.C., MILTON AND SUSANNAH see **SIMISON**
    LINN CO.   T10S   R3W   S3
HALE FAMILY   MORROW CO.   T3S   R27E   S2
HALE I.O.O.F. see **CULVER I.O.O.F.**
    JEFFERSON CO.   T12S   R13E   S16
HALE, MICHAEL see **HALE FAMILY**   MORROW CO.   T3S   R27E   S2
HALE, MILLIE see **HALE FAMILY**   MORROW CO.   T3S   R27E   S2
HALE, MILTON see **SIMISON**   LINN CO.   T10S   R3W   S3
HALE, MINERVA see **CULVER I.O.O.F.**
    JEFFERSON CO.   T12S   R13E   S16
HALE PLACE see **PLUM TREE**   CURRY CO.   T32S   R14W   S3
HALEY D.L.C., MARCIA see **MOORES VALLEY**
    YAMHILL CO.   T3S   R5W   S9
HALF MOON BAR   CURRY CO.   T33S   R11W   S25
HALFWAY see **PINE HAVEN**   BAKER CO.   T8S   R46E   S17
HALL   KLAMATH CO.   T39S   R14E   S32
HALL see **MOUNTAIN VIEW-STARK PIONEER**
    MULTNOMAH CO.   T1N   R3E   S35
HALL D.L.C., BENJAMIN see **MOUNTAIN VIEW-STARK PIONEER**
    MULTNOMAH CO.   T1N   R3E   S35
HALL D.L.C., BENJAMIN F. AND MARY ANN see **ST. LUKE'S**
    MARION CO.   T5S   R1W   S7
HALL FARM   WASHINGTON CO.   T1N   R4W   ?
HALL FARM, GEORGE see **BROWN**   COOS CO.   ?   ?   ?
HALL, J. G.   JOSEPHINE CO.   T35S   R6W   S13
HALL, JESSE "JACK" W. see **HALL, JESSIE W.**
    COLUMBIA CO.   ?   ?   ?

HALL, JESSE W.	COLUMBIA CO.	?	?	?
HALL, MARY ELIZABETH	MULTNOMAH CO.	T1N	R1E	?
HALL PLACE, C. M. see **LaFOLLETTE FAMILY**				
	MARION CO.	T6S	R3W	S1
HALL PROPERTY, C. see **HALL FARM**	WASHINGTON CO.	T1N	R4W	?
HALL, SEDATE E. see **HALL, MARY ELIZABETH**				
	MULTNOMAH CO.	T1N	R1E	?
HALL, WALTER SCOTT see **HALL, MARY ELIZABETH**				
	MULTNOMAH CO.	T1N	R1E	?
HALL-TIPTON FAMILY	COLUMBIA CO.	T4N	R4W	S3
HALLAWAY FAMILY	MORROW CO.	T1N	R24E	S5
HALLS FERRY	MARION CO.	T8S	R4W	S14
HALLYBURTON, JAMES S. see **ORTLEY**				
	WASCO CO.	T2N	R12E	?
HALSE INFANT see **MUTE SCHOOL**	MARION CO.	T8S	R2W	?
HALSEY PIONEER	LINN CO.	T14S	R4W	S11
HAMACHER FAMILY	DOUGLAS CO.	?	?	?
HAMBLOCH see **BULLARD FAMILY**	COOS CO.	T28S	R14W	S7
HAMBLOCK see **BULLARD FAMILY**	COOS CO.	T28S	R14W	S7
HAMILTON	GRANT CO.	T9S	R28E	S35
HAMILTON CREEK see **BELLINGER**	LINN CO.	T12S	R1W	S15
HAMILTON D.L.C., ANDERSON see **WALKER**				
	LANE CO.	T20S	R3W	S10
HAMLET	CLATSOP CO.	T4N	R8W	S6
HAMLIN, NATHANIEL	BAKER CO.	T7S	R39E	S27
HAMMACK RANCH, VERLE see **DRY LAKE**				
	CROOK CO.	T20S	R20E	S14
HAMMACK, VERLE see **DRY LAKE**	CROOK CO.	T20S	R20E	S14
HANDCHECK PROPERTY see **JOHANSON, MRS.**				
	MULTNOMAH CO.	?	?	?
HANEY FAMILY	WASHINGTON CO.	T1S	R4W	S35
HANKINS	GRANT CO.	T18S	R32E	S7
HANLON FARM, CHARLES see **BURGDORFER FAMILY**				
	WASHINGTON CO.	T3N	R3W	S15
HANNAH FAMILY	UMATILLA CO.	T4N	R34E	S30
HANSEN	COOS CO.	T28S	R12W	S25
HANSEN, DAVID W.	LANE CO.	T15S	R6W	S35
HANSON, ANDREW see **BENTON COUNTY POOR FARM**				
	BENTON CO.	T14S	R6W	?
HANZICKER, AL	CURRY CO.	T41S	R11W	S9
HAPPY HOLLOW see **HAPPY VALLEY**	YAMHILL CO.	T4S	R5W	S10
HAPPY HOME see **BELLINGER**	LINN CO.	T12S	R1W	S15
HAPPY RIDGE	WASCO CO.	T3S	R13E	S32
HAPPY RIDGE see **TRAXTLE**	WASCO CO.	T3S	R12E	S27
HAPPY VALLEY	HARNEY CO.	T29S	R33E	S12
HAPPY VALLEY	YAMHILL CO.	T4S	R5W	S10
HAPPY VALLEY RANCH see **HAPPY VALLEY**				
	HARNEY CO.	T29S	R33E	S12
HARDIE RANCH, DAVID see **WASHBURN, ROYAL ARTHUR**				
	GILLIAM CO.	T6S	R23E	S4

HARDIE RANCH, EARL see **LOST VALLEY**

	GILLIAM CO.	T6S	R23E	S4
HARDING FAMILY	MARION CO.	T4S	R2W	S33
HARDMAN [OLD]	MORROW CO.	T4S	R25E	S34

HARDMAN, FRANK see **HARDMAN GIRLS**

	BAKER CO.	T11S	R37E	S31
HARDMAN GIRLS	BAKER CO.	T11S	R37E	S31

HARDMAN, GRACE see **HARDMAN GIRLS**

	BAKER CO.	T11S	R37E	S31

HARDMAN HOMESTEAD, FRANKLIN LINCOLN see **HARDMAN GIRLS**

	BAKER CO.	T11S	R37E	S31

HARDMAN, JOSEPH BART see **HARDMAN GIRLS**

	BAKER CO.	T11S	R37E	S31
HARDSCRABBLE	UNION CO.	?	?	?

HARDY D.L.C., THEOTINE see **HARDY FAMILY, THEOTINE**

	DOUGLAS CO.	T27S	R6W	S6
HARDY FAMILY, THEOTINE	DOUGLAS CO.	T27S	R6W	S6
HARGADINE	JACKSON CO.	T39S	R1E	S5
HARING PIONEER	LANE CO.	T18S	R11W	S7
HARLAN	LINCOLN CO.	T12S	R8W	S8

HARLAND FAMILY, WILLIAM see **FAST**

	POLK CO.	T7S	R5W	S23
HARLAND FARM, WILLIAM see **FAST**	POLK CO.	T7S	R5W	S23
HARLEM see **CATHOLIC [BANDON]**	COOS CO.	T28S	R14W	S30
HARMONY	POLK CO.	T6S	R6W	S9
HARMONY see **WARNER**	WASCO CO.	T3S	R14E	S16
HARNEY	HARNEY CO.	T22S	R32E	S24
HARNEY CITY see **HARNEY**	HARNEY CO.	T22S	R32E	S24
HARPER	MALHEUR CO.	T19S	R42E	S29
HARPER see **ALLEN RANCH**	DESCHUTES CO.	T20S	R11E	S8

HARPER D.L.C., GEORGE W. see **JACKSON FAMILY**

	LANE CO.	T19S	R3W	S34
HARPIS see **UNKNOWN**	WASCO CO.	T1N	R12E	?
HARRINGTON, LEONARD	JOSEPHINE CO.	T38S	R8W	S14
HARRIS	LINN CO.	T15S	R4W	S24
HARRIS CABIN	JOSEPHINE CO.	T35S	R6W	S24

HARRIS D.L.C., JAMES see **CASEY FAMILY**

	POLK CO.	T8S	R5W	S3

HARRIS D.L.C., LEONARD see **UNKNOWN CHILD**

	COLUMBIA CO.	T5N	R1W	?

HARRIS D.L.C., PHILLIP see **METHODIST CHURCH AT FARMINGTON**

	WASHINGTON CO.	T1S	R2W	?
HARRIS, DR.	DOUGLAS CO.	T24S	R4W	?
HARRIS FARM, J. R. see **HARRIS**	LINN CO.	T15S	R4W	S24
HARRIS, GEORGE see **HARRIS CABIN**	JOSEPHINE CO.	T35S	R6W	S24

HARRIS HOUSE, E. B. see **PHILOMATH [OLD]**

	BENTON CO.	T12S	R6W	S12
HARRIS, MR. see **LOST CREEK**	DOUGLAS CO.	T25S	R7W	S12

HARRIS PLACE see **BETTERLY, HAZEL**

	MALHEUR CO.	T20S	R47E	?

```
HARRISBURG I.O.O.F. see I.O.O.F. [ALFORD]
                              LINN CO.        T14S    R4W      S35
HARRISON                      WASHINGTON CO.  T1N     R3W      S3
HARRISON D.L.C., JOHN see HARRISON
                              WASHINGTON CO.  T1N     R3W      S3
HART D.L.C., ANTHONY W. see NEVEH ZEDEK-ROSE CITY LODGE
                              WASHINGTON CO.  T1S     R1W      S12
HART D.L.C., THOMAS see HART-RIGGS FAMILY
                              POLK CO.        T8S     R6W      S25
HART FAMILY see HART-RIGGS FAMILY
                              POLK CO.        T8S     R6W      S25
HART-RIGGS FAMILY             POLK CO.        T8S     R6W      S25
HARTLEY                       JOSEPHINE CO.   T39S    R5W      S4
HARVEY FAMILY                 DOUGLAS CO.     T24S    R4W      S30
HASKELL FAMILY                DOUGLAS CO.     ?       ?        ?
HASKELL PLACE see HASKELL FAMILY
                              DOUGLAS CO.     ?       ?        ?
HASKINS see UNIONTOWN         JACKSON CO.     T38S    R3W      S34
HASKINS YARD                  BAKER CO.       T13S    R37E     ?
HASTINGS D.L.C., HENRY B. see BRYANT
                              COLUMBIA CO.    T7N     R4W      S9
HAT POINT                     WALLOWA CO.     T1S     R49E     S35
HATCH FAMILY                  TILLAMOOK CO.   T1N     R10W     ?
HATFIELD FARM, LAVERN see MT. HOOD COMMUNITY
                              HOOD RIVER CO.  T1N     R10E     S21
HATFIELD, NORMA see STRADER FAMILY
                              DOUGLAS CO.     T27S    R4W      ?
HATFIELD, W. W. see PIONEER [HARBOR]
                              CURRY CO.       T40S    R13W     S9
HAUSER GRAVES                 WASCO CO.       T3S     R13E     S32
HAUXHURST, WEBLEY see TROUT   TILLAMOOK CO.   T1S     R9W      S30
HAVEN OF ST. JOHN MAUSOLEUM see CRYSTAL LAKE
                              BENTON CO.      T12S    R5W      S11
HAVLIK PLACE                  COLUMBIA CO.    T3N     R2W      ?
HAVURAH SHALOM                MULTNOMAH CO.   T1S     R1E      S6
HAWKINS, ALFRED               WASCO CO.       T5S     R11E     S25
HAWKINS, ANGIE see HAWKINS PLACE, ANGIE
                              CURRY CO.       T35S    R13W     S33
HAWKINS PLACE, ANGIE          CURRY CO.       T35S    R13W     S33
HAWLEY                        LANE CO.        T21S    R4W      S12
HAWLEY D.L.C., IRA see HAWLEY LANE CO.        T21S    R4W      S12
HAWTHORNE MEMORIAL GARDENS    JOSEPHINE CO.   T36S    R6W      S13
HAY CREEK PIONEER             JEFFERSON CO.   T11S    R15E     S9
HAY CREEK RANCH see HAY CREEK PIONEER
                              JEFFERSON CO.   T11S    R15E     S9
HAY CREEK RANCH see UNKNOWN   JEFFERSON CO.   T11S    R15E     ?
HAYES                         COOS CO.        T31S    R11W     S19
HAYES RANCH, TOM see JEFFERSON, THOMAS
                              COOS CO.        T31S    R11W     S31
HAYESVILLE                    MARION CO.      T7S     R3W      S12
HAYNES see TROUT              TILLAMOOK CO.   T1S     R9W      S30
```

HAYNES, CHARLES T.	COOS CO.	T26S	R13W	S25
HAYNES D.L.C., CHARLES see **TROUT**				
	TILLAMOOK CO.	T1S	R9W	S30
HAYNESVILLE see **HALL**	KLAMATH CO.	T39S	R14E	S32
HAYS	JACKSON CO.	T36S	R3W	S20
HAYS, DANIEL see **FALL CREEK**	LANE CO.	T18S	R1W	S33
HAYS, DANIEL see **SUNDSTROM, BRUCE**				
	LANE CO.	T16S	R8W	S18
HAYSTACK	WHEELER CO.	T8S	R25E	S16
HAYWARD	WASHINGTON CO.	T2N	R4W	S19
HAZELGREEN see **HOWELL PRAIRIE**	MARION CO.	T7S	R2W	S4
HAZELWOOD	CLACKAMAS CO.	T2S	R3E	S13
HAZLETON D.L.C., ROYAL H. see **SILK CREEK COMMUNITY**				
	LANE CO.	T20S	R4W	S13
HEALD, GILBERT SETON	WASCO CO.	T3S	R12E	S22
HEARD, SHIRLEY JEAN	WASHINGTON CO.	?	?	?
HEARING see **ROCK CREEK**	BAKER CO.	T7S	R38E	S36
HEATER	MARION CO.	T8S	R1E	S8
HEATH, TOM	BAKER CO.	T8S	R47E	?
HEATHERLY D.L.C., JAMES see **HEATHERLY FAMILY**				
	LANE CO.	T19S	R5W	S10
HEATHERLY FAMILY	LANE CO.	T19S	R5W	S10
HEBREW see **WAVERLY JEWISH**	LINN CO.	T11S	R3W	S4
HECETA LODGE #111 see **I.O.O.F. [GLENADA]**				
	LANE CO.	T19S	R12W	S2
HECKARD FAMILY	CLATSOP CO.	T7N	R9W	S18
HEDRICK FAMILY	DOUGLAS CO.	T21S	R6W	S35
HEDRICK FAMILY	DOUGLAS CO.	T22S	R6W	S1
HEFFLEY see **CHAMBERLIN FAMILY**	POLK CO.	T9S	R5W	S24
HEFTY FAMILY	DOUGLAS CO.	T20S	R6W	S34
HELD	CROOK CO.	T19S	R19E	·S4
HELFRICH, PRINCE E.	LANE CO.	T16S	R3E	S31
HELIX	UMATILLA CO.	T4N	R33E	S11
HELVETIA	WASHINGTON CO.	T1N	R2W	S3
HEMBREE D.L.C., ABSALOM J. see **HEMBREE FAMILY**				
	YAMHILL CO.	T3S	R4W	S25
HEMBREE FAMILY	YAMHILL CO.	T3S	R4W	S25
HENDERER FAMILY	DOUGLAS CO.	T22S	R8W	S23
HENDERSON D.L.C., DAVID see **PHILOMATH [OLD]**				
	BENTON CO.	T12S	R6W	S12
HENDERSON, EDNA WAGGONER see **EAST GARDINER**				
	DOUGLAS CO.	?	?	?
HENDERSON FAMILY	BENTON CO.	T12S	R6W	S36
HENDERSON FARM see **MULKEY**	LINCOLN CO.	T11S	R8W	S26
HENDERSON, HARRY see **EAST GARDINER**				
	DOUGLAS CO.	?	?	?
HENDERSON, JOHN D.	MALHEUR CO.	T18S	R45E	S29
HENDERSON, MERVIN DONALD see **EAST GARDINER**				
	DOUGLAS CO.	?	?	?
HENDERSON PIONEER	WASCO CO.	T1S	R13E	S33
HENDERSON, THERESA see **UNKNOWN**	TILLAMOOK CO.	T3N	R10W	S14

HENDRICKS see **KINGSLEY CATHOLIC**	WASCO CO.	T2S	R13E	S28
HENDRICKSON RANCH see **BASKET MOUNTAIN**				
	UMATILLA CO.	T4N	R37E	S18
HENDRIX CHILDREN	MORROW CO.	T6S	R25E	S17
HENDRIX-LOBSTER VALLEY see **LOBSTER VALLEY**				
	BENTON CO.	T15S	R8W	S4
HENDRIX MEMORIAL GARDEN, CHARLES see **LOBSTER VALLEY**				
	BENTON CO	T15S	R8W	S4
HENLEY see **MT. LAKI**	KLAMATH CO.	T40S	R9E	S2
HENNEY see **SUNSET VALLEY**	HARNEY CO.	T25S	R31E	S27
HENRIETTA, FORT see **SOLDIERS**	UMATILLA CO.	T3N	R29E	?
HEPPNER	MORROW CO.	T2S	R26E	S35
HERBER HOMESTEAD see **HERBER, LEO FERDINAND**				
	YAMHILL CO.	?	?	?
HERBER, LEO FERDINAND	YAMHILL CO.	?	?	?
HERBERT, ADAM see **HERBERT PIONEER**				
	BENTON CO.	T13S	R5W	S17
HERBERT D.L.C., ELIZABETH see **HERBERT PIONEER**				
	BENTON CO.	T13S	R5W	S17
HERBERT, ELIZABETH see **HERBERT PIONEER**				
	BENTON CO.	T13S	R5W	S17
HERBERT FAMILY see **HERBERT PIONEER**				
	BENTON CO.	T13S	R5W	S17
HERBERT, JAMES see **HERBERT PIONEER**				
	BENTON CO.	T13S	R5W	S17
HERBERT, JOSHUA see **HERBERT PIONEER**				
	BENTON CO.	T13S	R5W	S17
HERBERT PIONEER	BENTON CO.	T13S	R5W	S17
HERGERT ROAD see **FERN HILL CATHOLIC**				
	WASHINGTON CO.	T1S	R3W	S16
HERMANN	COOS CO.	T30S	R12W	S5
HERMISTON	UMATILLA CO.	T4N	R28E	S14
HERREN D.L.C., JOHN see **BOYS**	MARION CO.	T8S	R2W	S17
HERREN FAMILY	MARION CO.	T8S	R2W	S17
HERRON D.L.C., JOHN see **HERREN FAMILY**				
	MARION CO.	T8S	R2W	S17
HERRON [Sic] D.L.C., JOHN see **COATES INFANT**				
	MARION CO.	T8S	R2W	S19
HERRON [Sic] FAMILY see **HERREN FAMILY**				
	MARION CO.	T8S	R2W	S17
HERWICK HOMESTEAD see **HERWICK JR., FRED WM.**				
	COLUMBIA CO.	T4N	R3W	S35
HERWICK JR., FRED WM.	COLUMBIA CO.	T4N	R3W	S35
HESS, ANNA ELIZA CALLAHAN see **HESS, BABY BOY**				
	WASHINGTON CO.	T1S	R4W	S33
HESS, BABY BOY	WASHINGTON CO.	T1S	R4W	S33
HESS, DOC.	LAKE CO.	T39S	R24E	S16
HESS FAMILY	YAMHILL CO.	T3S	R2W	S8
HESS, MARY see **HESS FAMILY**	YAMHILL CO.	T3S	R2W	S8
HESS PLACE see **HESS, DOC.**	LAKE CO.	T39S	R24E	S16

HESS, TILLMAN L. see **HESS FAMILY**				
	YAMHILL CO.	T3S	R2W	S8
HESS, WM. F. see **HESS, BABY BOY**	WASHINGTON CO.	T1S	R4W	S33
HIATT D.L.C., ISAAC see **HILL-DUNN FAMILY**				
	JACKSON CO.	T39S	R2E	S30
HIBBARD CREEK	BAKER CO.	T12S	R45E	S27
HIBBERT	KLAMATH CO.	T38S	R10E	S8
HICKENBOTTOM FAMILY see **SHADY BROOK**				
	WASHINGTON CO.	T2N	R2W	S30
HIGGINS AND MAHONEY	CURRY CO.	T33S	R10W	S9
HIGGINS, SUSAN see **SPENCE FAMILY**				
	JOSEPHINE CO.	T40S	R8W	S2
HIGGINSON D.L.C., FRANK J. see **NOAH**				
	DOUGLAS CO.	T29S	R8W	S7
HIGH PRAIRIE see **FOREST VALE MEMORIAL PARK**				
	LANE CO.	T21S	R3E	S10
HIGHLAND	POLK CO.	T7S	R3W	S17
HIGHLAND	UNION CO.	T1N	R40E	S5
HIGHLAND	YAMHILL CO.	T5S	R6W	S5
HIGHLAND see **FELLOWS**	CLACKAMAS CO.	T4S	R3E	S3
HIGHLAND METHODIST CHURCH see **HIGHLAND**				
	POLK CO.	T7S	R3W	S17
HIGHLAND PIONEER see **MT. ANGEL**	MARION CO.	T6S	R1W	S3
HIGHVIEW	MORROW CO.	T1S	R24E	S4
HILDERBRAND, GORDON see **MORAN**	SHERMAN CO.	T2N	R16E	S22
HILGARD	UNION CO.	T2S	R37E	S30
HILL	WASHINGTON CO.	T2S	R3W	S6
HILL see **HILL, DAVID**	KLAMATH CO.	T35S	R7E	S32
HILL, ALMORAN see **HILL**	WASHINGTON CO.	T2S	R3W	S6
HILL D.L.C., ALMORAN see **HILL**	WASHINGTON CO.	T2S	R3W	S6
HILL, DAVID	KLAMATH CO.	T35S	R7E	S32
HILL, DOLLIE see **HILL, RICHARD**	COOS CO.	T32S	R11W	?
HILL FAMILY see **HAMLET**	CLATSOP CO.	T4N	R8W	S6
HILL FAMILY see **HILL-DUNN FAMILY**				
	JACKSON CO.	T39S	R2E	S30
HILL MEMORIAL, JOHN	LANE CO.	T21S	R3E	S26
HILL, RICHARD	COOS CO.	T32S	R11W	?
HILL, RUSSEL J. see **HILL, RICHARD**				
	COOS CO.	T32S	R11W	?
HILL-DUNN FAMILY	JACKSON CO.	T39S	R2E	S30
HILLCREST	COLUMBIA CO.	T5N	R2W	S36
HILLCREST	UNION CO.	T3S	R38E	S8
HILLCREST see **VALLEY VIEW MEMORIAL PARK**				
	YAMHILL CO.	T3S	R2W	S19
HILLCREST EAST see **CALVARY**	UNION CO.	T3S	R38E	S8
HILLCREST MEMORIAL PARK AND CREMATORY				
	JOSEPHINE CO.	T36S	R5W	S8
HILLCREST MEMORIAL PARK AND MAUSOLEUM				
	JACKSON CO.	T38S	R1W	S3
HILLS CREEK see **HILL MEMORIAL, JOHN**				
	LANE CO.	T21S	R3E	S26

```
HILLSBORO FIR LAWN see FIR LAWN CEMETERY AND MAUSOLEUM
                              WASHINGTON CO.    T1N    R3W       S36
HILLSBORO MASONIC see HILLSBORO PIONEER
                              WASHINGTON CO.    T1N    R3W       S36
HILLSBORO PIONEER             WASHINGTON CO.    T1N    R3W       S36
HILLSBORO VALLEY MEMORIAL see VALLEY MEMORIAL PARK AND MAUSOLEUM
                              WASHINGTON CO.    T1S    R2W       S9
HILLSIDE                      WASHINGTON CO.    T1N    R4W       S9
HILLSIDE see ASTORIA PIONEER  CLATSOP CO.       T8N    R9W       S17
HILLTOP                       POLK CO.          T9S    R4W       S9
HILLTOP see ASTORIA PIONEER   CLATSOP CO.       T8N    R9W       S17
HILTSLEY, FRANK               WALLOWA CO.       T1S    R50E      UNS
HINDMAN see CAMP POLK         DESCHUTES CO.     T14S   R10E      S27
HINES                         HARNEY CO.        T23S   R30E      S24
HINES see HAVLIK PLACE        COLUMBIA CO.      T3N    R2W       ?
HINES D.L.C., THOMAS M. see PATTON FAMILY
                              WASHINGTON CO.    T1S    R4W       S36
HINTON                        WASCO CO.         T5S    R16E      S26
HINTON-WARD see HINTON        WASCO CO.         T5S    R16E      S26
HISE see KIME-BROWN FAMILY    LANE CO.          T16S   R5W       S17
HOBART ROAD see ST. PAUL'S CATHOLIC
                              MARION CO.        T6S    R1W       S27
HOBSON-WHITNEY                MARION CO.        T8S    R1W       S35
HODGDON                       TILLAMOOK CO.     T1S    R10W      S32
HODGE, ANDREW see HODGE, GERTRUDE
                              CLACKAMAS CO.     T3S    R1E       ?
HODGE, CORA see HODGE, GERTRUDE CLACKAMAS CO.   T3S    R1E       ?
HODGE, GERTRUDE               CLACKAMAS CO.     T3S    R1E       ?
HODSON                        KLAMATH CO.       T38S   R11 1/2E  ?
HOFFMAN                       COOS CO.          T29S   R12W      S22
HOFFMAN HOMESTEAD see HOFFMAN COOS CO.          T29S   R12W      S22
HOG FLAT STAGE STATION see GRANT COUNTY POOR FARM
                              GRANT CO.         T12S   R30E      S12
HOGGARD CHILD                 SHERMAN CO.       T2N    R16E      ?
HOILAND FARM, LEWIS see MOUNTS FAMILY BURIALS
                              LANE CO.          T18S   R5W       S7
HOLBROOK PROPERTY see CLINE   MULTNOMAH CO.     T2N    R1W       ?
HOLDEN BABY                   MULTNOMAH CO.     ?      ?         ?
HOLDEN, MARTIN see HOLDEN BABY MULTNOMAH CO.    ?      ?         ?
HOLDEN, MINNIE HENDERSON see HOLDEN BABY
                              MULTNOMAH CO.     ?      ?         ?
HOLDMAN                       UMATILLA CO.      T5N    R31E      S33
HOLDMAN D.L.C., JOSEPH see GOFF FAMILY
                              DOUGLAS CO.       T25S   R5W       S30
HOLLAND                       CLACKAMAS CO.     T1S    R1E       S36
HOLLAND, ELIZA see HOLLAND    CLACKAMAS CO.     T1S    R1E       S36
HOLLAND SCHOOL                JOSEPHINE CO.     T39S   R7W       S33
HOLLAND, WILLIAM see HOLLAND  CLACKAMAS CO.     T1S    R1E       S36
HOLLENBECK FAMILY, ASA see CUSICK FAMILY
                              LINN CO.          T9S    R1E       S20
```

HOLLENBECK-CUSICK FAMILY see **CUSICK FAMILY**				
	LINN CO.	T9S	R1E	S20
HOLMES, CELI ANN AND HARRIET	POLK CO.	T7S	R4W	S30
HOLMES FAMILY	YAMHILL CO.	T5S	R8W	S36
HOLMS D.L.C., WILLIAM see **I.O.O.F. [OREGON CITY]**				
	CLACKAMAS CO.	T3S	R2E	S5
HOLMS D.L.C., WILLIAM see **MASONIC [OREGON CITY]**				
	CLACKAMAS CO.	T3S	R2E	S5
HOLMS D.L.C., WILLIAM see **MOUNTAIN VIEW**				
	CLACKAMAS CO.	T3S	R2E	S5
HOLMS D.L.C., WILLIAM see **ST. JOHN'S CATHOLIC**				
	CLACKAMAS CO.	T3S	R2E	S5
HOLMS-McGEE FAMILY see **HOLMES FAMILY**				
	YAMHILL CO.	T5S	R8W	S36
HOLTON CREEK	JOSEPHINE CO.	T39S	R8W	S9
HOLY CROSS	LANE CO.	T18S	R5W	S3
HOLY FAMILY CHURCH see **HINES**	HARNEY CO.	T23S	R30E	S24
HOLY INNOCENTS EPISCOPAL	CLATSOP CO.	T8N	R9W	S9
HOLY NAMES see **SISTERS OF THE HOLY NAMES**				
	CLACKAMAS CO.	T2S	R1E	S14
HOLY NEW MARTYRS RUSSIAN ORTHODOX CHURCH				
	CLACKAMAS CO.	T4S	R2E	?
HOLY ROSARY	MARION CO.	T6S	R1E	S36
HOLY TRINITY see **CATHOLIC [BANDON]**				
	COOS CO.	T28S	R14W	S30
HOLZMEYER see **PURDIN FAMILY**	WASHINGTON CO.	T1N	R4W	S25
HOME see **HIBBARD CREEK**	BAKER CO.	T12S	R45E	S27
HOMELI see **HOMLY**	UMATILLA CO.	T2N	R34E	S2
HOMEPLACE see **POWELL FAMILY**	BENTON CO.	T13S	R6W	S3
HOMESTEAD see **COPPERFIELD-HOMESTEAD**				
	BAKER CO.	T6S	R48E	S33
HOMESTEADER GRAVE	HOOD RIVER CO.	T1N	R10E	S21
HOMLY	UMATILLA CO.	T2N	R34E	S2
HOOD LOOP see **FIR HILL**	CLACKAMAS CO.	T2S	R4E	S14
HOOD RIVER COUNTY see **MOUNTAIN VIEW MEMORIAL**				
	HOOD RIVER CO.	T2N	R10E	S2
HOODVIEW see **PLEASANT VIEW [WEST]**				
	CLACKAMAS CO.	T3S	R1W	S9
HOOKER D.L.C., IRA A. see **HOOKER FAMILY**				
	POLK CO.	T9S	R6W	?
HOOKER FAMILY	POLK CO.	T9S	R6W	?
HOOPER FAMILY see **APPLEGATE**	MALHEUR CO.	T16S	R47E	?
HOOPINGGARDNER CHILDREN	BAKER CO.	T7S	R45E	?
HOOVER D.L.C., JACOB AND MALINDA see **HOOVER FAMILY**				
	WASHINGTON CO.	T1N	R3W	S14
HOOVER D.L.C., JACOB AND MALINDA see **THE OLD SCOTCH CHURCH**				
	WASHINGTON CO.	T1N	R3W	S13
HOOVER FAMILY	WASHINGTON CO.	T1N	R3W	S14
HOPE ABBEY	LANE CO.	T18S	R3W	S5
HOPELAND see **INDIAN CREEK**	LANE CO.	T16S	R10W	S36
HOPEWELL	YAMHILL CO.	T5S	R3W	S30

HOPEWELL CHURCH see **HOPEWELL MENNONITE**

	MARION CO.	T4S	R1W	S36
HOPEWELL MENNONITE	MARION CO.	T4S	R1W	S36
HORN, COLUMBIA	BENTON CO.	?	?	?
HORN, J. M. see **HORN, COLUMBIA**	BENTON CO.	?	?	?
HORN, M. J. see **HORN, COLUMBIA**	BENTON CO.	?	?	?

HORNER D.L.C., EMANUEL see **BOOTH FAMILY**

	WASHINGTON CO.	T1S	R5W	S25

HORNER, JOHN HARLEY see **CHIEF JOSEPH [OLD]**

	WALLOWA CO.	T1N	R43E	S20
HORNING, RICHARD	WASHINGTON CO.	T2N	R3W	S11
HORSE CREEK RANCH	WALLOWA CO.	T3N	R48E	S35
HORTON, GUS	HARNEY CO.	T20S	R35E	?
HORTON, GUS see **DREWSEY FIELD**	HARNEY CO.	T20S	R35E	?

HOSFORD METHODIST CHURCH see **HIGHLAND**

	POLK CO.	T7S	R3W	S17

HOSKINS D.L.C., WILLIAM see **FAIR OAKS**

	DOUGLAS CO.	T25S	R4W	S7

HOSKINSON, RICHARD see **ST. MARY'S BOY'S HOME**

	WASHINGTON CO.	T1S	R1W	?
HOSPITAL CREMATORIUM see **ASYLUM**	MARION CO.	T7S	R3W	S25
HOT SPRINGS INDIAN	WASCO CO.	T8S	R13E	S27
HOUSTON see **EAST ALBANY**	LINN CO.	T11S	R3W	S4

HOVEY D.L.C., ALBERT G. see **VALHALLA MEMORIAL PARK**

	BENTON CO.	T12S	R5W	S4
HOWARD	CROOK CO.	T14S	R19E	S8
HOWARD FAMILY	CLACKAMAS CO.	T4S	R2E	S17
HOWARD FAMILY	WALLOWA CO.	T3N	R41E	?
HOWE see **CRESWELL PIONEER**	LANE CO.	T19S	R3W	S21
HOWE see **LOWELL**	LANE CO.	T19S	R1W	S15

HOWELL D.L.C., JOHN see **HOWELL PRAIRIE**

	MARION CO.	T7S	R2W	S4

HOWELL FAMILY see **HOWELL PRAIRIE**

	MARION CO.	T7S	R2W	S4
HOWELL HOMESTEAD	GRANT CO.	T9S	?	?
HOWELL PRAIRIE	MARION CO.	T7S	R2W	S4

HOWELL, TEMPERANCE see **HOWELL PRAIRIE**

	MARION CO.	T7S	R2W	S4
HOWLETT see **GIBSON**	CLACKAMAS CO.	T3S	R4E	?

HOWLETT D.L.C., WILLIAM J. see **GIBSON**

	CLACKAMAS CO.	T3S	R4E	?
HUBBARD	MARION CO.	T4S	R1W	S33
HUBBARD	POLK CO.	T8S	R6W	S28
HUBBARD COMMUNITY see **HUBBARD**	MARION CO.	T4S	R1W	S33

HUBBARD D.L.C., THOMAS see **OUR LADY OF GUADALUPE TRAPPIST ABBEY**

	YAMHILL CO.	T3S	R3W	S29
HUBBLE PLACE see **UNKNOWN**	MALHEUR CO.	T32S	R40E	?

HUBERT, _____ see **WALKER GULCH**

	JOSEPHINE CO.	T40S	R7W	S15

HUCKLEBERRY KNOB see **HUCKLEBERRY KNOLL**

	CURRY CO.	T32S	R13W	S22

HUCKLEBERRY KNOLL	CURRY CO.	T32S	R13W	S22
HUCKTILL	CURRY CO.	?	?	?
HUDSON	COLUMBIA CO.	T7N	R3W	S13
HUDSON [OLD] see **WOODBINE**	COLUMBIA CO.	T7N	R3W	S13
HUDSON PARK see **HUDSON**	COLUMBIA CO.	T7N	R3W	S13
HUDSON, SAMUEL K. see **HUDSON**	COLUMBIA CO.	T7N	R3W	S13
HUDSON, SAMUEL K. see **WOODBINE**	COLUMBIA CO.	T7N	R3W	S13
HUFFMAN BABY see **ARMIN**	WALLOWA CO.	T2S	R47E	S31
HUFFMAN FAMILY see **ARMIN**	WALLOWA CO.	T2S	R47E	S31
HUFFMAN, THOMAS see **SPEAK RANCH**	BAKER CO.	?	R45E	?
HUGHES, ELMER S.	WASHINGTON CO.	T3N	R5W	?
HUGHES FAMILY see **CAPE BLANCO PIONEER**				
	CURRY CO.	T31S	R16W	S36
HUGHES, HARRY see **ST. MARY'S BOY'S HOME**				
	WASHINGTON CO.	T1S	R1W	?
HUGHES, JOHN see **HUGHES, ELMER S.**				
	WASHINGTON CO.	T3N	R5W	?
HUGHES, SARAH WIMPLE see **HUGHES, ELMER S.**				
	WASHINGTON CO.	T3N	R5W	?
HULBERT LAKE BURIALS	LANE CO.	T15S	R4W	?
HULLT see **GREEN MOUNTAIN**	MARION CO.	T7S	R1E	S26
HULT see **GREEN MOUNTAIN**	MARION CO.	T7S	R1E	S26
HULTIN	COOS CO.	T28S	R14W	S3
HUMBUG	MARION CO.	T8S	R2W	S4
HUMPHREYS, D.L.C., THOMAS M. see **HUMPHREYS FAMILY**				
	LINN CO.	T10S	R1E	S5
HUMPHREYS FAMILY	LINN CO.	T10S	R1E	S5
HUNDLEY BURIAL	WASHINGTON CO.	T1N	R5W	S1
HUNGRY HILL	JOSEPHINE CO.	?	?	?
HUNSAKER D.L.C., JOSEPH see **HUNSAKER FAMILY**				
	MARION CO.	T9S	R2W	S17
HUNSAKER FAMILY	MARION CO.	T9S	R2W	S17
HUNT see **CULP CREEK**	LANE CO.	T21S	R1W	S33
HUNT D.L.C., GEORGE W. AND ELIZABETH N. see **HUNT FAMILY**				
	MARION CO.	T8S	R1W	S23
HUNT D.L.C., JOHN S. see **MT. HOPE**				
	MARION CO.	T7S	R1W	S33
HUNT D.L.C., JOHN S. see **SMALL, REVEREND THOMAS HENDERSON**				
	MARION CO.	T7S	R1W	S34
HUNT FAMILY	MARION CO.	T8S	R1W	S23
HUNT FAMILY see **MT. HOPE**	MARION CO.	T7S	R1W	S33
HUNT PLACE, ROY see **STURGILL CHILDREN, HILDA AND LOUI**				
	BAKER CO.	T8S	R43E	?
HUNTINGTON [NEW] see **I.O.O.F. [HUNTINGTON]**				
	BAKER CO.	T14S	R45E	S19
HUNTINGTON [OLD]	BAKER CO.	T14S	R44E	S13
HUNTLY, RUBY see **JEFFERSON, THOMAS**				
	COOS CO.	T31S	R11W	S31
HUNTS MEMORIAL see **FAIR OAKS**	DOUGLAS CO.	T25S	R4W	S7
HURD, SAMUEL see **WALKER GULCH**	JOSEPHINE CO.	T40S	R7W	S15

HURRICANE CREEK see **I.O.O.F. PIONEER** [JOSEPH]				
	WALLOWA CO.	T2S	R44E	S36
HURST D.L.C., DAVID see **HURST FAMILY**				
	DOUGLAS CO.	T25S	R6W	S22
HURST FAMILY	DOUGLAS CO.	T25S	R6W	S22
HUSSEY D.L.C., NATHAN see **HUSSEY FAMILY**				
	POLK CO.	T6S	R7W	S15
HUSSEY D.L.C., STEPHEN see **HUSSEY FAMILY**				
	YAMHILL CO.	T5S	R6W	S1
HUSSEY FAMILY	POLK CO.	T6S	R7W	S15
HUSSEY FAMILY	YAMHILL CO.	T5S	R6W	S1
HUSSEY, FRANK see **HUSSEY FAMILY**	POLK CO.	T6S	R7W	S15
HUSSEY-YOCOM-PETERSON FAMILY see **HUSSEY FAMILY**				
	YAMHILL CO.	T5S	R6W	S1
HUSTON FARM see **CALDWELL**	LANE CO.	T16S	R5W	S24
HUTCHINS	TILLAMOOK CO.	?	?	?
HUTCHINS, JIM see **TESTAMENT CREEK**				
	TILLAMOOK CO.	T4S	R7W	S5
HYATT FAMILY	UMATILLA CO.	T4N	R36E	S23
HYDE, JACQUIE see **JOHANSON FAMILY**				
	CLATSOP CO.	?	?	?
HYDE, JIM see **JOHANSON FAMILY**	CLATSOP CO.	?	?	?
HYLAND see **HIGHLAND**	YAMHILL CO.	T5S	R6W	S5
HYLAND see **LOWELL**	LANE CO.	T19S	R1W	S15
I.O.O.F. see **ANTELOPE** [NEW]	WASCO CO.	T7S	R17E	S32
I.O.O.F. see **ATHENA**	UMATILLA CO.	T4N	R34E	S24
I.O.O.F. see **BUENA VISTA**	POLK CO.	T9S	R4W	S23
I.O.O.F. see **BURNS**	HARNEY CO.	T23S	R30E	S13
I.O.O.F. see **CANYON CITY**	GRANT CO.	T13S	R31E	S35
I.O.O.F. see **CANYONVILLE**	DOUGLAS CO.	T30S	R5W	S27
I.O.O.F. see **CENTRAL POINT**	JACKSON CO.	T37S	R2W	S1
I.O.O.F. see **CORNELIUS PIONEER METHODIST**				
	WASHINGTON CO.	T1N	R3W	S33
I.O.O.F. see **CULVER I.O.O.F.**	JEFFERSON CO.	T12S	R13E	S16
I.O.O.F. see **DALLAS**	POLK CO.	T8S	R5W	S5
I.O.O.F. see **DREWSEY**	HARNEY CO.	T20S	R35E	S23
I.O.O.F. see **DUFUR COMMUNITY**	WASCO CO.	T1S	R13E	S24
I.O.O.F. see **ECHO MEMORIAL**	UMATILLA CO.	T3N	R29E	S16
I.O.O.F. see **EUGENE PIONEER**	LANE CO.	T17S	R3W	S32
I.O.O.F. see **GOSHEN**	LANE CO.	T18S	R3W	S24
I.O.O.F. see **GRANDVIEW**	UNION CO.	T3S	R38E	S16
I.O.O.F. see **HILLSBORO PIONEER**	WASHINGTON CO.	T1N	R3W	S36
I.O.O.F. see **JACKSONVILLE**	JACKSON CO.	T37S	R2W	S29
I.O.O.F. see **KINGS VALLEY PIONEER**				
	BENTON CO.	T10S	R6W	S28
I.O.O.F. see **LAFAYETTE PIONEER**	YAMHILL CO.	T4S	R3W	S6
I.O.O.F. see **LOOKINGGLASS**	DOUGLAS CO.	T27S	R7W	S35
I.O.O.F. see **MARCOLA**	LANE CO.	T16S	R2W	S24
I.O.O.F. see **MARION FRIENDS**	MARION CO.	T9S	R2W	S29
I.O.O.F. see **MITCHELL, LOWER**	WHEELER CO.	T11S	R21E	S35
I.O.O.F. see **MOSIER**	WASCO CO.	T2N	R11E	S1

I.O.O.F. see **PAISLEY**	LAKE CO.	T33S	R18E	S24
I.O.O.F. see **SALEM PIONEER**	MARION CO.	T7S	R3W	S33
I.O.O.F. see **SCOTTSBURG**	DOUGLAS CO.	T22S	R9W	S8
I.O.O.F. see **SILVERTON**	MARION CO.	T6S	R1W	S34
I.O.O.F. see **TOLEDO**	LINCOLN CO.	T11S	R10W	S8
I.O.O.F. see **TUMALO**	DESCHUTES CO.	T16S	R12E	S29
I.O.O.F. see **VALE PIONEER**	MALHEUR CO.	T18S	R45E	S17
I.O.O.F. see **WESTON**	UMATILLA CO.	T4N	R35E	S22
I.O.O.F. see **WINGVILLE**	BAKER CO.	T8S	R39E	S29
I.O.O.F. **[ALFORD]**	LINN CO.	T14S	R4W	S35
I.O.O.F. **[ASHLAND]** see **MOUNTAIN VIEW I.O.O.F. AND MAUSOLEUM**				
	JACKSON CO.	T39S	R1E	S15
I.O.O.F. **[AURORA]** see **YODER, CLAYTON**				
	CLACKAMAS CO.	T4S	R1E	S18
I.O.O.F. **[BAKER CITY]** see **MT. HOPE**				
	BAKER CO.	T9S	R40E	S21
I.O.O.F. **[BAY CITY]**	TILLAMOOK CO.	T1S	R10W	S1
I.O.O.F. **[CARTERS]**	MULTNOMAH CO.	T1S	R1E	S4
I.O.O.F. **[COBURG]**	LANE CO.	T17S	R3W	S4
I.O.O.F. **[CONDON]**	GILLIAM CO.	T4S	R21E	S2
I.O.O.F. **[COOS BAY]**	COOS CO.	T25S	R13W	S34
I.O.O.F. **[CORVALLIS]**	BENTON CO.	T11S	R5W	S28
I.O.O.F. **[COTTAGE GROVE]** see **FIR GROVE**				
	LANE CO.	T20S	R3W	S29
I.O.O.F. **[CRAWFORDSVILLE]** see **FINLEY**				
	LINN CO.	T14S	R2W	S13
I.O.O.F. **[CROW]** see **McCULLOCH**	LANE CO.	T18S	R5W	S34
I.O.O.F. **[DAYTON]**	YAMHILL CO.	T4S	R3W	S21
I.O.O.F. **[DRAIN]**	DOUGLAS CO.	T22S	R5W	S16
I.O.O.F. **[ESTACADA]**	CLACKAMAS CO.	T3S	R4E	S21
I.O.O.F. **[FALLS CITY]**	POLK CO.	T8S	R6W	S21
I.O.O.F. **[FLORENCE]** see **I.O.O.F. [GLENADA]**				
	LANE CO.	T19S	R12W	S2
I.O.O.F. **[FOSSIL]**	WHEELER CO.	T7S	R21E	S4
I.O.O.F. **[GLENADA]**	LANE CO.	T19S	R12W	S2
I.O.O.F. **[GOLD HILL]**	JACKSON CO.	T36S	R3W	S17
I.O.O.F. **[GRANTS PASS]**	JOSEPHINE CO.	T36S	R5W	S16
I.O.O.F. **[GRASS VALLEY]**	SHERMAN CO.	T2S	R16E	S22
I.O.O.F. **[GREENWOOD]**	MULTNOMAH CO.	T1S	R1E	S27
I.O.O.F. **[HARDMAN, NEW]**	MORROW CO.	T4S	R25E	S30
I.O.O.F. **[HUNTINGTON]**	BAKER CO.	T14S	R45E	S19
I.O.O.F. **[INDEPENDENCE]** see **HILLTOP**				
	POLK CO.	T9S	R4W	S9
I.O.O.F. **[IONE]** see **HIGHVIEW**	MORROW CO.	T1S	R24E	S4
I.O.O.F. **[IRVING]** see **LUPER**	LANE CO.	T16S	R4W	S34
I.O.O.F. **[JUNCTION CITY]** see **REST LAWN MEMORIAL PARK**				
	LANE CO.	T15S	R5W	S34
I.O.O.F. **[KENILWORTH]**	MULTNOMAH CO.	T1S	R1E	S12
I.O.O.F. **[KENT]**	SHERMAN CO.	T4S	R17E	S21
I.O.O.F. **[KLAMATH FALLS]** see **LINKVILLE**				
	KLAMATH CO.	T38S	R9E	S29

I.O.O.F. **[LAKEVIEW]**	LAKE CO.	T39S	R20E	S10
I.O.O.F. **[LEBANON]**	LINN CO.	T12S	R2W	S2
I.O.O.F. **[LEXINGTON]**	MORROW CO.	T1S	R25E	S24
I.O.O.F. **[LORANE]**	LANE CO.	T20S	R5W	S24
I.O.O.F. **[MAPLETON]**	LANE CO.	T18S	R10W	S11
I.O.O.F. [MARION] see **CLOVERDALE**				
	MARION CO.	T9S	R2W	S7
I.O.O.F. **[MAYVILLE]**	GILLIAM CO.	T5S	R21E	S28
I.O.O.F. **[MERRILL]**	KLAMATH CO.	T40S	R10E	S33
I.O.O.F. **[MILTON]**	UMATILLA CO.	T5N	R35E	S11
I.O.O.F. **[MILTON-FREEWATER]**	UMATILLA CO.	T5N	R35E	S12
I.O.O.F. [MONMOUTH] see **FIR CREST**				
	POLK CO.	T9S	R4W	S6
I.O.O.F. [MORO] see **CITY OF MORO**				
	SHERMAN CO.	T1S	R17E	S18
I.O.O.F. **[MYRTLE CREEK]**	DOUGLAS CO.	T29S	R5W	S22
I.O.O.F. **[NEW BANDON]**	COOS CO.	T28S	R14W	S29
I.O.O.F. **[NEW COQUILLE]**	COOS CO.	T28S	R13W	S1
I.O.O.F. [NEW; EUGENE] see **WESTLAWN MEMORIAL PARK**				
	LANE CO.	T17S	R4W	S33
I.O.O.F. **[OAKLAND]**	DOUGLAS CO.	T25S	R5W	S4
I.O.O.F. [OAKLAND, 2ND] see **CEDAR HILL**				
	DOUGLAS CO.	T25S	R5W	S5
I.O.O.F. [OLD] see **MOLALLA MEMORIAL**				
	CLACKAMAS CO.	T5S	R2E	S20
I.O.O.F. [OLD] see **RUSSELLVILLE**	CLACKAMAS CO.	T6S	R2E	S2
I.O.O.F. **[OLD BANDON]**	COOS CO.	T28S	R14W	S30
I.O.O.F. [OLD BANDON] see **BANDON PIONEER**				
	COOS CO.	T28S	R14W	S30
I.O.O.F. **[OLD COQUILLE]**	COOS CO.	T27S	R13W	S36
I.O.O.F. **[OREGON CITY]**	CLACKAMAS CO.	T3S	R2E	S5
I.O.O.F. [PARKDALE] see **UPPER VALLEY**				
	HOOD RIVER CO.	T1N	R10E	S33
I.O.O.F. [PRINEVILLE] see **JUNIPER HAVEN**				
	CROOK CO.	T14S	R16E	S31
I.O.O.F. [RICHLAND] see **EAGLE VALLEY**				
	BAKER CO.	T9S	R45E	S26
I.O.O.F. **[ROSEBURG]**	DOUGLAS CO.	T27S	R5W	S19
I.O.O.F. [SCOTTS MILLS] see **MAPLEWOOD**				
	CLACKAMAS CO.	T6S	R1E	S14
I.O.O.F. [ST. HELENS] see **BAYVIEW MEMORIAL**				
	COLUMBIA CO.	T4N	R1W	S17
I.O.O.F. [TERREBONNE] see **PIONEER [TERREBONNE]**				
	DESCHUTES CO.	T14S	R13E	S22
I.O.O.F. **[THE DALLES]**	WASCO CO.	T1N	R13E	S4
I.O.O.F. [THE DALLES] see **PARKLAWN**				
	WASCO CO.	T1N	R13E	S15
I.O.O.F. **[TILLAMOOK]**	TILLAMOOK CO.	T1S	R9W	S29
I.O.O.F. [TURNER] see **TWIN OAKS**	MARION CO.	T8S	R2W	S28
I.O.O.F. **[TYGH VALLEY]**	WASCO CO.	T4S	R13E	S10
I.O.O.F. [WASCO] see **SUN RISE**	SHERMAN CO.	T2N	R17E	S31

I.O.O.F. [WOODS]	TILLAMOOK CO.	T4S	R10W	S18
I.O.O.F. #93 see **OSWEGO PIONEER**				
	CLACKAMAS CO.	T2S	R1E	S16
I.O.O.F. #193 see **CENTRAL POINT**	JACKSON CO.	T37S	R2W	S1
I.O.O.F. #196 see **MT. JEFFERSON MEMORIAL PARK**				
	JEFFERSON CO.	T11S	R14E	S6
I.O.O.F. CLOVERDALE see **NESTUCCA VETERANS OF FOREIGN WARS-ODD FELLOWS**				
	TILLAMOOK CO.	T4S	R10W	S14
I.O.O.F., EASTWOOD [MEDFORD]	JACKSON CO.	T37S	R1W	S29
I.O.O.F. HEBO see **NESTUCCA VETERANS OF FOREIGN WARS-ODD FELLOWS**				
	TILLAMOOK CO.	T4S	R10W	S14
I.O.O.F. IDLEWILDE #107 [HOOD RIVER] see **IDLEWILD**				
	HOOD RIVER CO.	T2N	R10E	S2
I.O.O.F. LODGE #55 OF KERBY see **LAUREL**				
	JOSEPHINE CO.	T39S	R8W	S15
I.O.O.F. LODGE #56 [PIKE] see **PIKE AND I.O.O.F.**				
	YAMHILL CO.	T2S	R5W	S25
I.O.O.F. MOHAWK LODGE #200 see **MARCOLA**				
	LANE CO.	T16S	R2W	S24
I.O.O.F. PIONEER see **I.O.O.F. [OREGON CITY]**				
	CLACKAMAS CO.	T3S	R2E	S5
I.O.O.F. PIONEER [JOSEPH]	WALLOWA CO.	T2S	R44E	S36
I.O.O.F. SPENCER BUTTE LODGE #9 see **EUGENE PIONEER**				
	LANE CO.	T17S	R3W	S32
I.O.O.F. SPENCER BUTTE LODGE #9 see **WEST LAWN MEMORIAL PARK**				
	LANE CO.	T17S	R4W	S33
I.O.O.F. SPRINGFIELD LODGE #70 see **LAUREL GROVE**				
	LANE CO.	T18S	R3W	S3
I.O.O.F. SPRINGFIELD LODGE #70 see **PIONEER MEMORIAL CEMETERY PARK**				
	LANE CO.	T17S	R3W	S35
I.O.O.F. STAYTON LODGE #64 see **LONE OAK [NEW]**				
	MARION CO.	T9S	R1W	S10
I.O.O.F. VALLEY LODGE #42 see **HILLTOP**				
	POLK CO.	T9S	R4W	S9
IDA MINE	JOSEPHINE CO.	T35S	R5W	S26
IDELWILDE see **IDLEWILD**	HOOD RIVER CO.	T2N	R10E	S2
IDLEWILD	HOOD RIVER CO.	T2N	R10E	S2
IDLEWOOD see **IDLEWILD**	HOOD RIVER CO.	T2N	R10E	S2
IGO	GILLIAM CO.	T3S	R20E	S21
IGO GRANGE see **IGO**	GILLIAM CO.	T3S	R20E	S21
ILERS PEAK	CLACKAMAS CO.	T2S	R3E	S18
ILLAHE	CURRY CO.	T34S	R11W	S18
IMMACULATE CONCEPTION CHURCH see **ST. MARY'S [STAYTON]**				
	MARION CO.	T9S	R1W	S10
IMNAHA	WALLOWA CO.	T1N	R48E	S21
IMPROVED ORDER OF REDMEN see **LA PINE COMMUNITY**				
	DESCHUTES CO.	T22S	R11E	S7
INDEPENDENT ORDER OF REDMEN; WICKIUP TRIBE #21 see **SVENSEN PIONEER**				
	CLATSOP CO.	T8N	R8W	S23
INDEPENDENT ORDER OF GOOD TEMPLARS see **I.O.O.F. [LORANE]**				
	LANE CO.	T20S	R5W	S24

INDIAN	DOUGLAS CO.	T22S	R4W	S18
INDIAN	DOUGLAS CO.	T25S	R4W	?
INDIAN	LAKE CO.	T39S	R24E	S20
INDIAN	LANE CO.	T17S	R1W	?
INDIAN	LINN CO.	T13S	R6E	?
INDIAN	MARION CO.	T7S	R3W	S26
INDIAN	UMATILLA CO.	?	?	?
INDIAN	WASCO CO.	T3S	R14E	S23
INDIAN	WASHINGTON CO.	T1N	R4W	S34
INDIAN [#1]	TILLAMOOK CO.	T1N	R10W	?
INDIAN [#2]	TILLAMOOK CO.	T1S	R10W	?
INDIAN see **OAK FLATS**	CURRY CO.	T35S	R11W	S20
INDIAN see **TIPTON, MACE**	DOUGLAS CO.	T26S	R3W	S1
INDIAN see **WASHINGTON, PAUL**	LINCOLN CO.	T10S	R10W	S9
INDIAN [NEW] see **PAIUTE [NEW]**	HARNEY CO.	T23S	R30E	S1
INDIAN [OLD] see **PAIUTE [OLD]**	HARNEY CO.	T23S	R30E	S14
INDIAN BOY	DOUGLAS CO.	T26S	R7W	S13
INDIAN BURIAL	CLACKAMAS CO.	T2S	R2E	S30
INDIAN BURIAL	LANE CO.	T20S	R2W	S31
INDIAN BURIAL GROUNDS	DOUGLAS CO.	T22S	R12W	?
INDIAN BURIALS	LANE CO.	?	?	?
INDIAN BURIALS see **BLANCHARD'S**	COLUMBIA CO.	T7N	R2W	S16
INDIAN CREEK	LANE CO.	T16S	R10W	S36
INDIAN CREEK	UNION CO.	T1N	R39E	S36
INDIAN GEORGE see **DUNKIN, GEORGE**				
	CLATSOP CO.	T7N	R8W	?
INDIAN GRAVE	WALLOWA CO.	T1S	R49E	S21
INDIAN GRAVE HILL	POLK CO.	T9S	R6W	?
INDIAN GRAVES	CLACKAMAS CO.	T5S	R2E	?
INDIAN LIZA	LANE CO.	T17S	R3W	?
INDIAN RANCHERIA TRAIL MASSACRE	JACKSON CO.	T35S	R4E	S18
INDIAN TOWN see **DREW MEMORIAL**	LANE CO.	T18S	R12W	S24
INGLE	GRANT CO.	T13S	R30E	S27
INGLEMAN PLACE, JOHN see **SKOOKUMHOUSE**				
	CURRY CO.	T36S	R13W	?
INGLES see **STEWART CREEK**	COLUMBIA CO.	T7N	R4W	S3
INGLIS see **STEWART CREEK**	COLUMBIA CO.	T7N	R4W	S3
INGRAHAM CHILDREN	MORROW CO.	T5S	R26E	S35
INGRAHAM, WILLIAM see **INGRAHAM CHILDREN**				
	MORROW CO.	T5S	R26E	S35
INMAN	LANE CO.	T17S	R5W	S8
INMAN D.L.C., JOEL C. see **INMAN**	LANE CO.	T17S	R5W	S8
INMAN FAMILY see **INMAN**	LANE CO.	T17S	R5W	S8
INNES D.L.C., JOHN see **JOHNSON FAMILY**				
	WASHINGTON CO.	T1S	R1W	S17
INSKEEP see **CHARBONNEAU, JEAN BAPTISTE**				
	MALHEUR CO.	T30S	R44E	S16
INSKIP RANCHE see **CHARBONNEAU, JEAN BAPTISTE**				
	MALHEUR CO.	T30S	R44E	S16
INSKIP'S STATION see **CHARBONNEAU, JEAN BAPTISTE**				
	MALHEUR CO.	T30S	R44E	S16

IONE see **HIGHVIEW**	MORROW CO.	T1S	R24E	S4
IOWA HILL	WASHINGTON CO.	T1S	R3W	S32
IOWA HILL CATHOLIC see **FERN HILL CATHOLIC**				
	WASHINGTON CO.	T1S	R3W	S16
IRELAND, D. C. see **WILCOX-OBSERVER**				
	SHERMAN CO.	T5S	R17E	S10
IRON MOUNTAIN GRAVE see **DIETRICH, W.**				
	COOS CO.	T33S	R12W	S33
IRONSIDE	MALHEUR CO.	T14S	R39E	S28
IRRIGON see **DESERT LAWN MEMORIAL**				
	MORROW CO.	T5N	R27E	S20
IRRIGON [OLD]	MORROW CO.	T5N	R26E	S24
IRVIN D.L.C., GEORGE AND MARY ANN see **IRVIN FAMILY**				
	CLACKAMAS CO.	T4S	R1E	S18
IRVIN FAMILY	CLACKAMAS CO.	T4S	R1E	S18
IRVINE D.L.C., ROBERT see **MT. PLEASANT**				
	LINN CO.	T9S	R1E	S30
IRWIN D.L.C., RICHARD see **IRWIN FAMILY**				
	BENTON CO.	T13S	R5W	S22
IRWIN FAMILY	BENTON CO.	T13S	R5W	S22
IRWIN FAMILY see **IRVIN FAMILY**	CLACKAMAS CO.	T4S	R1E	S18
ISLAMIC CEMETERY OF OREGON	BENTON CO.	T12S	R5W	S5
ISLAND CITY	UNION CO.	T3S	R38E	S3
IWAKOSHI, MIYO see **GRESHAM PIONEER**				
	MULTNOMAH CO.	T1S	R3E	S10
IZEE	GRANT CO.	T17S	R28E	S29
J-SPEAR RANCH see **CHEWAUCAN**	LAKE CO.	T34S	R19E	S33
JACK CREEK	CURRY CO.	T40S	R13W	?
JACKSON D.L.C., THOMAS J. see **FAIRVIEW**				
	COLUMBIA CO.	T3N	R2W	S24
JACKSON D.L.C., ULYSSES see **JACKSON FAMILY**				
	WASHINGTON CO.	T2N	R3W	S36
JACKSON D.L.C., ULYSSES see **ST. EDWARD'S CATHOLIC [OLD]**				
	WASHINGTON CO.	T1N	R3W	S1
JACKSON FAMILY	CLACKAMAS CO.	T5S	R2E	S7
JACKSON FAMILY	HOOD RIVER CO.	T2N	R11E	S30
JACKSON FAMILY	LANE CO.	T19S	R3W	S34
JACKSON FAMILY	WASHINGTON CO.	T2N	R3W	S36
JACKSON FAMILY, HENRY	KLAMATH CO.	T36S	R11E	S29
JACKSON, HENRY see **JACKSON FAMILY, HENRY**				
	KLAMATH CO.	T36S	R11E	S29
JACKSON, PRESIDENT ANDREW see **CHAMBERS, JAMES W.**				
	WHEELER CO.	T6S	R21E	S22
JACKSON, TOM see **JOHNSON PLACE, LOREN**				
	COLUMBIA CO.	T3N	R1W	?
JACKSON'S, D. D.	MULTNOMAH CO.	?	?	?
JACKSONVILLE	JACKSON CO.	T37S	R2W	S29
JACKSONVILLE PIONEER see **JACKSONVILLE**				
	JACKSON CO.	T37S	R2W	S29
JACOBSON	LINCOLN CO.	T11S	R10W	?
JAMES, CALVIN	UMATILLA CO.	T4N	R33E	?

JAMES, SAMUEL M.	DOUGLAS CO.	T23S	R4W	S22
JAMIESON see **DELL**	MALHEUR CO.	T16S	R43E	S15
JAMIESON AREA	MALHEUR CO.	T16S	R43E	?
JANUARY	LINCOLN CO.	T12S	R8W	S23
JAP HOLLOW see **EIGHT MILE**	WASCO CO.	T1S	R13E	S1
JAPANESE	MULTNOMAH CO.	T1N	R2E	S19
JAPANESE HOLLOW see **EIGHT MILE**	WASCO CO.	T1S	R13E	S1
JASPER see **WALLACE**	LANE CO.	T18S	R2W	S14
JAY BURIALS see **LITTLE LAKE**	LANE CO.	T16S	R7W	S18
JEFFERSON	MARION CO.	T10S	R3W	S1
JEFFERSON, THOMAS	COOS CO.	T31S	R11W	S31
JEMERSON *[Sic]* see **DELL**	MALHEUR CO.	T16S	R43E	S15
JENCK	TILLAMOOK CO.	T4S	R10W	S34
JENCK HOMESTEAD, PETER see **JENCK**				
	TILLAMOOK CO.	T4S	R10W	S34
JENKINS D.L.C., STEPHEN see **JENKINS FAMILY**				
	LANE CO.	T18S	R5W	S22
JENKINS FAMILY	LANE CO.	T18S	R5W	S22
JENNINGS	POLK CO.	T6S	R4W	S13
JENNINGS, L. B. see **FETTER**	COOS CO.	T29S	R10W	S28
JERRYS FLAT see **MERRIMAN**	CURRY CO.	T36S	R14W	S16
JEWELL	CLATSOP CO.	T5N	R7W	S11
JEWELL [OLD]	CLATSOP CO.	T5N	R7W	S12
JEWISH see **BETH ISRAEL [OLD]**	MULTNOMAH CO.	T1S	R1E	S10
JEWISH see **BROWN, JOSEPH**	WASCO CO.	T1N	R13E	S10
JEWISH see **CONGREGATION KESER ISRAEL**				
	MULTNOMAH CO.	T1S	R2E	S20
JEWISH see **JACKSONVILLE**	JACKSON CO.	T37S	R2W	S29
JEWISH [THE DALLES]	WASCO CO.	T1N	R13E	S10
JIM TOWN see **LOSTINE**	WALLOWA CO.	T1S	R43E	S3
JOE LONG BUTTE see **GRAVEYARD BUTTE**				
	WASCO CO.	T5S	R12E	S10
JOHANNSEN, ANDREAS see **JOHANNSEN FAMILY**				
	DOUGLAS CO.	T22S	R11W	S11
JOHANNSEN, ANDREW see **JOHANNSEN FAMILY**				
	DOUGLAS CO.	T22S	R11W	S11
JOHANNSEN FAMILY	DOUGLAS CO.	T22S	R11W	S11
JOHANSON BABIES see **JOHANSON FAMILY**				
	CLATSOP CO.	?	?	?
JOHANSON FAMILY	CLATSOP CO.	?	?	?
JOHANSON, MRS.	MULTNOMAH CO.	?	?	?
JOHN DAY see **RESTLAWN**	GRANT CO.	T13S	R31E	S22
JOHNSON, ANDREAS see **JOHANNSEN FAMILY**				
	DOUGLAS CO.	T22S	R11W	S11
JOHNSON, ANDREW see **JOHANNSEN FAMILY**				
	DOUGLAS CO.	T22S	R11W	S11
JOHNSON, ANDREW see **JOHNSON FAMILY**				
	CLACKAMAS CO.	T5S	R3E	S18
JOHNSON BABY	MULTNOMAH CO.	?	?	?
JOHNSON, CAROLINE see **JOHNSON FAMILY**				
	JACKSON CO.	T34S	R1W	S15

JOHNSON D.L.C., CHARLES M. see **TAYLOR**
    YAMHILL CO.   T5S   R4W   S10
JOHNSON D.L.C., JOHN see **ST. EDWARD'S CATHOLIC [NEW]**
    WASHINGTON CO.   T2N   R2W   S31
JOHNSON D.L.C., JOHN F. see **HAPPY VALLEY**
    YAMHILL CO.   T4S   R5W   S10
JOHNSON, DOCTOR   LAKE CO.   T39S   R24E   ?
JOHNSON, EMMA ROSELUND see **JOHNSON BABY**
    MULTNOMAH CO.   ?   ?   ?
JOHNSON FAMILY   CLACKAMAS CO.   T5S   R3E   S18
JOHNSON FAMILY   JACKSON CO.   T34S   R1W   S15
JOHNSON FAMILY   WASHINGTON CO.   ?   ?   ?
JOHNSON FAMILY   WASHINGTON CO.   T1S   R1W   S17
JOHNSON FAMILY see **JOHANNSEN FAMILY**
    DOUGLAS CO.   T22S   R11W   S11
JOHNSON FAMILY, GEORGE   LANE CO.   ?   ?   ?
JOHNSON, HANS H. see **JOHNSON BABY**
    MULTNOMAH CO.   ?   ?   ?
JOHNSON, HERMAN   DOUGLAS CO.   T27S   R6W   S25
JOHNSON HILL see **TRASK PIONEER**   TILLAMOOK CO.   T1S   R9W   S27
JOHNSON PLACE see **JOHNSON FAMILY, GEORGE**
    LANE CO.   ?   ?   ?
JOHNSON PLACE see **WOLFE VALLEY**   DOUGLAS CO.   T25S   R7W   S8
JOHNSON PLACE, LOREN   COLUMBIA CO.   T3N   R1W   ?
JOHNSON, ROBERT ROY   WASCO CO.   T1N   R13E   S1
JOHNSON, SETH see **SUNNYSIDE PIONEER**
    CLACKAMAS CO.   T2S   R2E   S2
JOHNSON'S see **TRASK PIONEER**   TILLAMOOK CO.   T1S   R9W   S27
JOLLY D.L.C., WILLIAM see **JOLLY FAMILY**
    WASHINGTON CO.   T1N   R3W   S24
JOLLY FAMILY   WASHINGTON CO.   T1N   R3W   S24
JONES see **JONES FAMILY**   COLUMBIA CO.   T6N   R2W   S33
JONES see **JONES PIONEER**   MULTNOMAH CO.   T1S   R1E   S6
JONES see **PIONEER MEMORIAL**   MARION CO.   T6S   R2W   S10
JONES D.L.C., EARL see **LaFOLLETTE FAMILY**
    MARION CO.   T6S   R3W   S1
JONES D.L.C., JACOB see **JONES FAMILY**
    DOUGLAS CO.   T27S   R6W   S10
JONES D.L.C., NATHAN B. see **HAVURAH SHALOM**
    MULTNOMAH CO.   T1S   R1E   S6
JONES D.L.C., NATHAN B. see **JONES PIONEER**
    MULTNOMAH CO.   T1S   R1E   S6
JONES FAMILY   COLUMBIA CO.   T6N   R2W   S33
JONES FAMILY   DOUGLAS CO.   T27S   R6W   S10
JONES FAMILY   LANE CO.   T16S   R5W   S16
JONES FAMILY see **CENTRAL SCHOOL**   LANE CO.   T18S   R5W   S4
JONES, FLOYED see **ELDER CHILDREN**
    MOOROW CO.   T2S   R27E   S26
JONES PIONEER   MULTNOMAH CO.   T1S   R1E   S6
JONES SCHOOL see **CENTRAL SCHOOL**   LANE CO.   T18S   R5W   S4
JORDAN see **OUR LADY OF LOURDES**   LINN CO.   T10S   R1E   S9

JORDAN CATHOLIC CHURCH see **OUR LADY OF LOURDES**				
	LINN CO.	T10S	R1E	S9
JORDAN FORD see **PETTYS**	MORROW CO.	T1S	R25E	S6
JORDAN, MICHAEL M.	MALHEUR CO.	?	?	?
JORDAN PIONEER see **PIONEER [JORDEN]**				
	LINN CO.	T10S	R1E	S10
JORDAN VALLEY	MALHEUR CO.	T30S	R46E	S2
JORY FAMILY	MARION CO.	T8S	R3W	S28
JORY SENIOR D.L.C., JAMES AND MARY see **JORY FAMILY**				
	MARION CO.	T8S	R3W	S28
JOSEPH see **I.O.O.F. PIONEER [JOSEPH]**				
	WALLOWA CO.	T2S	R44E	S36
JOSEPHINE MEMORIAL PARK see **HILLCREST MEMORIAL PARK AND CREMATORY**				
	JOSEPHINE CO.	T36S	R5W	S8
JUDD see **FORRESTER**	CLACKAMAS CO.	T2S	R4E	S29
JUMAN, PETE see **MEXICAN PETE**	MALHEUR CO.	T34S	R41E	?
JUNCTION CITY PIONEER see **MILLIRON**				
	LANE CO.	T15S	R4W	S31
JUNGLEBANK	COOS CO.	T28S	R10W	S6
JUNIPER FLAT see **KELLY**	WASCO CO.	T5S	R13E	S8
JUNIPER HAVEN	CROOK CO.	T14S	R16E	S31
JUNKINS	MORROW CO.	T3S	R24E	S16
JUNTURA [NEW]	MALHEUR CO.	T21S	R38E	S17
JUNTURA [OLD]	MALHEUR CO.	T21S	R38E	S17
JUSTENSEN FARM, NEL see **HAUSER GRAVES**				
	WASCO CO.	T3S	R13E	S32
K-MART see **ST. MARY'S OF THE VALLEY [OLD]**				
	WASHINGTON CO.	T1S	R1W	S7
K. P. see **FIR CREST**	POLK CO.	T9S	R4W	S6
K. P. see **KNIGHTS OF PYTHIAS [RAINIER]**				
	COLUMBIA CO.	T7N	R2W	S21
KALAMA	JEFFERSON CO.	T9S	R12E	S35
KALANDER FAMILY, EMIL see **MAPLEWOOD**				
	CLATSOP CO.	T8N	R7W	S16
KALLIO, ISRAEL see **GREEN MOUNTAIN ROAD**				
	CLATSOP CO.	T6N	R8W	?
KAMELA	UNION CO.	T1S	R35E	S36
KAMPFER, EMMA see **KAMPFER FAMILY**				
	JEFFERSON CO.	T9S	R14E	S11
KAMPFER FAMILY	JEFFERSON CO.	T9S	R14E	S11
KAMPFER, GODFREY see **KAMPFER FAMILY**				
	JEFFERSON CO.	T9S	R14E	S11
KANE CREEK	JACKSON CO.	T36S	R3E	?
KANIPE MEMORIAL COUNTY PARK see **KANIPE, MILDRED**				
	DOUGLAS CO.	T24S	R4W	S18
KANIPE, MILDRED	DOUGLAS CO.	T24S	R4W	S18
KASHENOROF, CHESTER see **ST. MARY'S BOY'S HOME**				
	WASHINGTON CO.	T1S	R1W	?
KAUFMAN see **APOSTOLIC**	MARION CO.	T7S	R1W	S8
KAUFMAN ROAD see **APOSTOLIC**	MARION CO.	T7S	R1W	S8
KAY, MARY see **COGSELL**	LANE CO.	T19S	R3W	S5

KEARNS see **KELLY, CLINTON**	MULTNOMAH CO.	T1S	R1E	S12
KEASEY	COLUMBIA CO.	T5N	R5W	S27
KEATING see **GOOSE CREEK**	BAKER CO.	T8S	R43E	S29
KEEGAN, JAMES see **ST. MARY'S BOY'S HOME**				
	WASHINGTON CO.	T1S	R1W	?
KEENE see **HARRIS**	LINN CO.	T15S	R4W	S24
KEENEY see **UNION POINT**	LINN CO.	T14S	R3W	S14
KEENEY D.L.C., ELI see **KEENEY FAMILY**				
	LANE CO.	T19S	R2W	S5
KEENEY FAMILY	LANE CO.	T19S	R2W	S5
KEES	UMATILLA CO.	T4N	R35E	S28
KEES D.L.C., MORGAN see **I.O.O.F.** [LEBANON]				
	LINN CO.	T12S	R2W	S2
KEIL, DR. WILLIAM see **OLD COLONY**				
	MARION CO.	T4S	R1W	S12
KEIL FAMILY see **OLD COLONY**	MARION CO.	T4S	R1W	S12
KELLEY see **KELLY, CLINTON**	MULTNOMAH CO.	T1S	R1E	S12
KELLEY see **PLEASANT HOME PIONEER**				
	MULTNOMAH CO.	T1S	R4E	S20
KELLEY GROVE see **KELLY**	WASCO CO.	T5S	R13E	S8
KELLOGG	DOUGLAS CO.	T23S	R7W	S29
KELLOGG D.L.C., JOHN see **KELLOGG**				
	DOUGLAS CO.	T23S	R7W	S29
KELLOGG D.L.C., ORRIN see **KELLOGG FAMILY**				
	CLACKAMAS CO.	T2S	R2E	S7
KELLOGG FAMILY	CLACKAMAS CO.	T2S	R2E	S7
KELLY	WASCO CO.	T5S	R13E	S8
KELLY see **KELLY, CLINTON**	MULTNOMAH CO.	T1S	R1E	S12
KELLY, ARCHON see **PLEASANT HOME PIONEER**				
	MULTNOMAH CO.	T1S	R4E	S20
KELLY CHURCHYARD see **KELLY**	WASCO CO.	T5S	R13E	S8
KELLY, CLINTON	MULTNOMAH CO.	T1S	R1E	S12
KELLY, CLINTON CLARK see **KELLY FARM, PLYMPTON**				
	MULTNOMAH CO.	T1S	R2E	?
KELLY D.L.C., CLINTON see **I.O.O.F.** [KENILWORTH PARK]				
	MULTNOMAH CO.	T1S	R1E	S12
KELLY D.L.C., CLINTON see **KELLY, CLINTON**				
	MULTNOMAH CO.	T1S	R1E	S12
KELLY D.L.C., JOHN see **JOHNSON, HERMAN**				
	DOUGLAS CO.	T27S	R6W	S25
KELLY D.L.C., PLYMPTON see **KELLY FARM, PLYMPTON**				
	MULTNOMAH CO.	T1S	R2E	?
KELLY FARM, PLYMPTON	MULTNOMAH CO.	T1S	R2E	?
KELLY, PATRICK J. see **UNKNOWN**	WASHINGTON CO.	T1S	R2W	S14
KENNEDY GRAVE	WHEELER CO.	T13S	R25E	?
KENNEDY, SUSAN	GRANT CO.	T13S	R32E	?
KENNY CHILDREN	SHERMAN CO.	T1S	R18E	S11
KENNY, WILLIAM see **KENNY CHILDREN**				
	SHERMAN CO.	T1S	R18E	S11
KENO	KLAMATH CO.	T40S	R8E	S6
KENT [OLD] see **WILCOX-OBSERVER**	SHERMAN CO.	T5S	R17E	S10

```
KENT FAMILY see COX, JOHN      DOUGLAS CO.      T28S   R6W      ?
KENT, LEWIS see COX, JOHN      DOUGLAS CO.      T28S   R6W      ?
KENTUCK INLET                  COOS CO.         T25S   R12W     ?
KENTUCK SLOUGH see KENTUCK INLET
                               COOS CO.         T25S   R12W     ?
KENTUCKY FLAT                  COLUMBIA CO.     T7N    R2W      S16
KERBY see LAUREL               JOSEPHINE CO.    T39S   R8W      S15
KERBY D.L.C., JAMES see HOLTON CREEK
                               JOSEPHINE CO.    T39S   R8W      S9
KERBY [OLD] see HOLTON CREEK   JOSEPHINE CO.    T39S   R8W      S9
KERBYVILLE see HOLTON CREEK    JOSEPHINE CO.    T39S   R8W      S9
KERR GIRL                      LANE CO.         T21S   R1W      S33
KESER ISRAEL see CONGREGATION KESER ISRAEL
                               MULTNOMAH CO.    T1S    R2E      S20
KETCHUM PLACE, WILLIAM see MORTON GRAVES
                               WASCO CO.        T1N    R12E     S10
KEY see KEES                   UMATILLA CO.     T4N    R35E     S28
KEYES see KEES                 UMATILLA CO.     T4N    R35E     S28
KIGGENS, PATRICK LEROY         CLACKAMAS CO.    T3S    R4E      S5
KIGGENS, TED see GITHENS FAMILY CLACKAMAS CO.   T3S    R4E      S5
KIGGENS, TED see KIGGENS, PATRICK LEROY
                               CLACKAMAS CO.    T3S    R4E      S5
KILCHIS see I.O.O.F. [BAY CITY] TILLAMOOK CO.   T1S    R10W     S1
KILLAM D.L.C., LEONARD see CLEMENTS
                               TILLAMOOK CO.    T2S    R9W      S16
KIME-BROWN FAMILY              LANE CO.         T16S   R5W      S17
KIMSEY, ALVIS                  YAMHILL CO.      T5S    R3W      S5
KIMSEY D.L.C., ALVIS see KIMSEY, ALVIS
                               YAMHILL CO.      T5S    R3W      S5
KIMSEY FAMILY                  MARION CO.       T8S    R1W      S7
KIMZEY, JOHN see PACIFIC UNIVERSITY
                               WASHINGTON CO.   T1N    R3W      S31
KINCAID D.L.C., SAMUEL see UNION HILL
                               MARION CO.       T8S    R1E      S7
KINDER                         COLUMBIA CO.     T5N    R1W      S16
KING see BAKER                 MORROW CO.       T2S    R24E     S6
KING D.L.C., ISAAC see KING FAMILY, ISAAC
                               BENTON CO.       T10S   R6W      S28
KING FAMILY see UNION HILL     MARION CO.       T8S    R1E      S7
KING FAMILY, ISAAC             BENTON CO.       T10S   R6W      S28
KING, NAHUM see CHAMBERS, SARAH MALHEUR CO.     T18S   R37E     S33
KING OF PEACE see I.O.O.F. [CONDON]
                               GILLIAM CO.      T4S    R21E     S2
KINGERY FAMILY                 DOUGLAS CO.      T23W   R5W      ?
KINGERY, JOHN WESLEY see KINGERY FAMILY
                               DOUGLAS CO.      T23W   R5W      ?
KINGS PRAIRIE see FAIRVIEW     LINN CO.         T9S    R3E      S34
KINGS VALLEY PIONEER           BENTON CO.       T10S   R6W      S28
KINGSBURY see HILL-DUNN FAMILY JACKSON CO.      T39S   R2E      S30
KINGSBURY SODA SPRINGS see HILL-DUNN FAMILY
                               JACKSON CO.      T39S   R2E      S30
```

KINGSLEY	WASCO CO.	T2S	R13E	S32
KINGSLEY CATHOLIC	WASCO CO.	T2S	R13E	S28
KINGSTON see WISNER	LINN CO.	T9S	R1W	S23
KIPHART-POINT see CUSICK FAMILY	LINN CO.	T9S	R1E	S20
KIRK see UNION POINT	LINN CO.	T14S	R3W	S14
KIRK D.L.C., WILLIAM R. see BROWNSVILLE PIONEER				
	LINN CO.	T13S	R2W	S32
KIRKPATRICK POST GRAND ARMY OF THE REPUBLIC see G.A.R. [GRAND ARMY OF				
THE REPUBLIC]	YAMHILL CO.	T3S	R2W	S20
KIST see NORTH CEMETERY OF CLEAR CREEK				
	COLUMBIA CO.	T4N	R5W	S27
KITTERMAN CHILDREN see HOLLAND SCHOOL				
	JOSEPHINE CO.	T39S	R7W	S33
KLAMATH COUNTY POOR FARM	KLAMATH CO.	?	?	?
KLAMATH MEMORIAL PARK	KLAMATH CO.	T39S	R9E	S8
KLINGER see KLINGLER MEMORIAL	CLACKAMAS CO.	T4S	R1E	S24
KLINGLER see KLINGLER MEMORIAL	CLACKAMAS CO.	T4S	R1E	S24
KLINGLER D.L.C., JOHN L. see KLINGLER MEMORIAL				
	CLACKAMAS CO.	T4S	R1E	S24
KLINGLER MEMORIAL	CLACKAMAS CO.	T4S	R1E	S24
KLINKER	CLACKAMAS CO.	T3S	R5E	?
KLUM	LINN CO.	T12S	R1W	S32
KLUM D.L.C., WILLIAAM see KLUM	LINN CO.	T12S	R1W	S32
KLUM FAMILY see KLUM	LINN CO.	T12S	R1W	S32
KNAPP, L. see THRIFT RANCH	CURRY CO.	T32S	R15W	?
KNAPPA see KNAPPA PRAIRE	CLATSOP CO.	T8N	R7W	S17
KNAPPA PRAIRIE	CLATSOP CO.	T8N	R7W	S17
KNIGHT D.L.C., HENRIETTA see GITHENS FAMILY				
	CLACKAMAS CO.	T3S	R4E	S5
KNIGHT D.L.C., HENRIETTA see KIGGENS, PATRICK LEROY				
	CLACKAMAS CO.	T3S	R4E	S5
KNIGHT, O. F. see ALLEY FAMILY	TILLAMOOK CO.	T3N	R9W	S18
KNIGHTS OF PYTHIAS see ATHENA	UMATILLA CO.	T4N	R34E	S24
KNIGHTS OF PYTHIAS see FIR CREST				
	POLK CO.	T9S	R4W	S6
KNIGHTS OF PYTHIAS see I.O.O.F. [CONDON]				
	GILLIAM CO.	T4S	R21E	S2
KNIGHTS OF PYTHIAS [BANDON] see VETERANS OF FOREIGN WARS				
	COOS CO.	T28S	R14W	S29
KNIGHTS OF PYTHIAS [HOOD RIVER] see MOUNTAIN VIEW MEMORIAL				
	HOODRIVER CO.	T2N	R10E	S2
KNIGHTS OF PYTHIAS [NEHALEM] see AMERICAN LEGION POST #126				
	TILLAMOOK CO.	T3N	R10W	S28
KNIGHTS OF PYTHIAS [RAINIER]	COLUMBIA CO.	T7N	R2W	S21
KNOBLOCK, ANTHONY see JENCK	TILLAMOOK CO.	T4S	R10W	S34
KNOBLOCK, ELIZABETH see JENCK	TILLAMOOK CO.	T4S	R10W	S34
KNOTT FAMILY see SILVER FAMILY	WALLOWA CO.	T6N	R43E	S15
KNOWLES	LANE CO.	T18S	R10W	S1
KNOWLES CREEK see KNOWLES	LANE CO.	T18S	R10W	S1
KNOWLES FAMILY see KNOWLES	LANE CO.	T18S	R10W	S1
KNOX BUTTE	LINN CO.	T10S	R3W	S35

KNOX D.L.C., JAMES see **KNOX BUTTE**				
	LINN CO.	T10S	R3W	S35
KNOX FAMILY, E. B.	CROOK CO.	T17S	R19E	S8
KNOX HILL see **CLOVERDALE**	LANE CO.	T19S	R2W	S18
KNOX HILL see **SHIELDS**	LANE CO.	T20S	R3W	S33
KNOX RANCH, E. B. see **KNOX FAMILY, E. B.**				
	CROOK CO.	T17S	R19E	S8
KNUTSEN FAMILY see **APPLEGATE CHURCH**				
	JACKSON CO.	T38S	R4W	S22
KOBEL	COLUMBIA CO.	T6N	R2W	S20
KOCH FAMILY see **SILVER FAMILY**	WALLOWA CO.	T6N	R43E	S15
KOLB RANCH see **SRURGILL CHILDREN, EFFIE AND ESTER**				
	BAKER CO.	T9S	R40E	S19
KOON, BETTY LOU see **MAXVILLE**	WALLOWA CO.	T3N	R42E	S15
KOONTZ, DAVID R.	UMATILLA CO.	T3N	R29E	S16
KOONTZ FAMILY	BAKER CO.	T12S	R40E	?
KOTAN see **GAINES**	LINN CO.	T11S	R1W	S2
KOTAN FARM see **GAINES**	LINN CO.	T11S	R1W	S2
KOWALL, THERESA	CLACKAMAS CO.	T3S	R5E	S18
KRAMER see **CRAMER, MRS.**	WASCO CO.	T7S	R17E	?
KRAUSE see **MAPLE LANE**	WASHINGTON CO.	T2S	R1W	S30
KREWSON	DOUGLAS CO.	T22S	R5W	S4
KRONENBERG see **PARKERSBURG**	COOS CO.	T28S	R14W	S15
KRONENBERG see **ST. JOSEPH**	MULTNOMAH CO.	T1S	R3E	S8
KRUEGER FARM, WALTER see **HILL, RICHARD**				
	COOS CO.	T32S	R11W	?
KUHN see **McCUBBIN**	WALLOWA CO.	T1S	R43E	S5
KWAN YIN TEMPLE	MULTNOMAH CO.	T1N	R3E	S31
KYNISTON FAMILY	LINCOLN CO.	T10S	R10W	?
LA GRANDE	UNION CO.	T3S	R38E	S8
LA PINE COMMUNITY	DESCHUTES CO.	T22S	R11E	S7
LABISH CENTER see **BROOKS CATHOLIC**				
	MARION CO.	T6S	R2W	S21
LaBRIE FAMILY	DOUGLAS CO.	T26S	R6W	S30
LACEY, CHARLES S.	COLUMBIA CO.	T3N	R2W	?
LACOMB	LINN CO.	T11S	R1E	S31
LADD HILL see **GEER PIONEER**	CLACKAMAS CO.	T3S	R1W	S31
LAFAYETTE PIONEER	YAMHILL CO.	T4S	R3W	S6
LaFLEMME see **BROOKS CATHOLIC**	MARION CO.	T6S	R2W	S21
LaFOLLETTE see **HALLS FERRY**	MARION CO.	T8S	R4W	S14
LaFOLLETTE, D. B. see **LaFOLLETTE FAMILY**				
	MARION CO.	T6S	R3W	S1
LaFOLLETTE, D. H. see **LaFOLLETTE FAMILY**				
	MARION CO.	T6S	R3W	S1
LaFOLLETTE FAMILY	MARION CO.	T6S	R3W	S1
LaFOLLETTE, S. A. see **LaFOLLETTE FAMILY**				
	MARION CO.	T6S	R3W	S1
LaFORTE D.L.C., JOSEPH see **BUTTEVILLE [OLD]**				
	MARION CO.	T3S	R1W	S32
LAGLER, ANDREW see **LUDTKE FAMILY**				
	TILLAMOOK CO.	T3N	R10W	S13

LAIDLAW see **TUMALO**	DESCHUTES CO.	T16S	R12E	S29
LAIDLAW ODD FELLOWS see **TUMALO**	DESCHUTES CO.	T16S	R12E	S29
LAIRD, KENNETH see **WHITTINGTON**	COOS CO.	T29S	R12W	S32
LAIRD RANCH, KENNETH see **SKAGGS, MARTHA J.**				
	COOS CO.	T28S	R10W	S10
LAKE, RACHEL N. see **SMITH PLACE**	CLACKAMAS CO.	T2S	R4E	S30
LAKECREEK	JACKSON CO.	T37S	R2E	S4
LAKESIDE	COOS CO.	T23S	R13W	S13
LAKEVIEW see **I.O.O.F. [WOODS]**	TILLAMOOK CO.	T4S	R10W	S18
LAKEVIEW CEMETERY ASSOCIATION see **BLACHLY**				
	LANE CO.	T16S	R7W	S9
LAMBERSON D.L.C., TIMOTHY see **LAMBERSON FAMILY**				
	COLUMBIA CO.	T3N	R2W	S1
LAMBERSON FAMILY	COLUMBIA CO.	T3N	R2W	S1
LAMBERSON, SARAH see **LAMBERSON FAMILY**				
	COLUMBIA CO.	T3N	R2W	S1
LAMONTA see **GRIZZLY**	JEFFERSON CO.	T12S	R15E	S33
LAMPA CREEK	COOS CO.	T28S	R13W	?
LANCASTER see **YOUNG**	LANE CO.	T15S	R4W	S7
LANDAX see **MIDDLE FORK**	LANE CO.	T19S	R1E	S34
LANDAX see **MT. VERNON**	LANE CO.	T18S	R2W	S4
LANE D.L.C., SILAS see **TAYLOR-LANE FAMILY**				
	LANE CO.	T21S	R3W	S16
LANE FAMILY see **TAYLOR-LANE FAMILY**				
	LANE CO.	T21S	R3W	S16
LANE FAMILY see **WINCHESTER SCHOOL**				
	DOUGLAS CO.	T26S	R6W	S25
LANE MEMORIAL GRARDENS	LANE CO.	T17S	R4W	S32
LANE SCHOOL DISTRICT #28J see **CENTRAL SCHOOL**				
	LANE CO.	T18S	R5W	S4
LANGLEY see **LIME-DIXIE**	BAKER CO.	T13S	R44E	S22
LANGLOIS see **DENMARK**	CURRY CO.	T31S	R15W	S10
LAPRATTE D.L.C., ALEXANDER see **BROOKS CATHOLIC**				
	MARIAN CO.	T6S	R2W	S21
LARKINS D.L.C., JOSIAH M. see **MASONIC [EUGENE]**				
	LANE CO.	T18S	R3W	S5
LARKINS D.L.C., MONROE AND ELIZABETH V. see **LARKINS, MONROE AND**				
ELIZABETH V.	CLACKAMAS CO.	T4S	R2E	?
LARKINS D.L.C., RACHEL see **JACKSON FAMILY**				
	CLACKAMAS CO.	T5S	R2E	S7
LARKINS FAMILY see **JACKSON FAMILY**				
	CLACKAMAS CO.	T5S	R2E	S7
LARKINS, MONROE AND ELIZABETH V.				
	CLACKAMAS CO.	T4S	R2E	?
LATHROP FAMILY see **LEAP**	WALLOWA CO.	T1N	R44E	S8
LATIMER, MRS. HENRY see **NYE**	UMATILLA CO.	T1S	R31E	S19
LATOURELL FALLS	MULTNOMAH CO.	T1N	R5E	S29
LATOURETTE D.L.C., LYMAN D. see **G. W. W.**				
	CLACKAMAS CO.	T3S	R2E	S4
LATOURETTE WOODS see **KLINGLER MEMORIAL**				
	CLACKAMAS CO.	T4S	R1E	S24

LATTIE, ALEXANDRE see **LATTIE-CLOUTRIE FAMILY**

                                     CLATSOP CO.   T6N   R10W   S21

LATTIE-CLOUTRIE FAMILY   CLATSOP CO.   T6N   R10W   S21

LATTIE D.L.C., ELIZABETH see **CLATSOP INDIANS**

                                       CLATSOP CO.   T6N   R10W   S28

LATTIE D.L.C., ELIZABETH see **LATTIE-CLOUTRIE FAMILY**

                                       CLATSOP CO.   T6N   R10W   S21

LATTIE D.L.C., WILLIAM see **UNKNOWN SAILORS**

                                       CLATSOP CO.   T6N   R10W   S28

LATTIE, ELIZABETH see **LATTIE-CLOUTRIE FAMILY**

                                       CLATSOP CO.   T6N   R10W   S21

LATTIE, WILLIAM see **LATTIE-CLOUTRIE FAMILY**

                                       CLATSOP CO.   T6N   R10W   S21

Name	County	T	R	S
LAUREL	JOSEPHINE CO.	T39S	R8W	S15

LAUREL see **MT. OLIVE CEMETERY OF LAUREL**

                                     WASHINGTON CO.   T2S   R3W   S12

Name	County	T	R	S
LAUREL GROVE	LANE CO.	T18S	R3W	S3
LAUREL GROVE see **LOGTOWN**	JACKSON CO.	T38S	R3W	S14
LAUREL HILL see **LAUREL**	JOSEPHINE CO.	T39S	R8W	S15
LAUREL HILL see **LAUREL GROVE**	LANE CO.	T18S	R3W	S3
LAURELHURST	JACKSON CO.	T33S	?	?

LAURELWOOD see **MT. OLIVE CEMETERY OF LAUREL**

                                     WASHINGTON CO.   T2S   R3W   S12

Name	County	T	R	S
LAVADOURE	DOUGLAS CO.	T30S	R3W	S29
LAYNE see **ALMA**	LANE CO.	T19S	R8W	S3
LAYNE, MRS. MINNIE	LANE CO.	T19S	R7W	S22
LEABO	MARION CO.	T8S	R4W	S26
LEABURG see **GREENWOOD**	LANE CO.	T17S	R1E	S12
LEAP	WALLOWA CO.	T1N	R44E	S8

LEASURE, ROBERT see **HOMESTEADER GRAVE**

                                     HOOD RIVER CO.   T1N   R10E   S21

LEBANON ODD FELLOWS see **I.O.O.F. [LEBANON]**

                                     LINN CO.   T12S   R2W   S2

Name	County	T	R	S
LEBANON PIONEER	LINN CO.	T12S	R2W	S11
LEE see **LEE VALLEY**	COOS CO.	T28S	R12W	S1

LEE D.L.C., PHILANDER see **ZOAR LUTHERAN**

                                     CLACKAMAS CO.   T3S   R1E   S34

Name	County	T	R	S
LEE D.L.C., THOMAS see **MT. ZION**	CLACKAMAS CO.	T3S	R4E	S22

LEE D.L.C., WILSON see **WIMPLE, MARY**

                                     POLK CO.   T8S   R6W   S23

Name	County	T	R	S
LEE, JASON see **BOOTH FAMILY**	WASHINGTON CO.	T1S	R5W	S25
LEE, JASON see **LEE MISSION**	MARION CO.	T7S	R3W	S24

LEE, JASON see **WILLAMETTE MISSION**

                                     MARION CO.   T6S   R3W   S3

Name	County	T	R	S
LEE MEMORIAL see **LEE MISSION**	MARION CO.	T7S	R3W	S24
LEE MISSION	MARION CO.	T7S	R3W	S24
LEE RANCH see **ROWLEY**	WHEELER CO.	T7S	R19E	S35
LEE VALLEY	COOS CO.	T28S	R12W	S1
LEEHMAN COW CAMP see **UNKNOWN**	LAKE CO.	T29S	R23E	S35
LeGORE, ARCHIE see **ALLEN, DAVID**	UNION CO.	T6S	R41E	S18

LEISMAN, ANNIE JACKSON see **LEISMAN, FAMILY**				
	CLACKAMAS CO.	T4S	R3E	?
LEISMAN, FAMILY	CLACKAMAS CO.	T4S	R3E	?
LEISMAN, JOSEPH see **LEISMAN, FAMILY**				
	CLACKAMAS CO.	T4S	R3E	?
LEITH PLACE see **COLVIN GRAVE**	CURRY CO.	T37S	R14W	?
LELAND	JOSEPHINE CO.	T34S	R6W	S32
LEMASTER	LINN CO.	T14S	R1W	?
LEMCKE RANCH	GRANT CO.	T16S	R30E	S28
LEMONS GROVE see **FLETCHER**	GRANT CO.	T13S	R30E	S28
LEMONS RANCH, BYRON see **FLETCHER**				
	GRANT CO.	T13S	R30E	S28
LEMONS RANCH, BYRON see **UNKNOWN**	GRANT CO.	T13S	R30E	?
LEMONS RANCH, DENNIS see **INGLE**	GRANT CO.	T13S	R30E	S27
LENA see **PLEASANT POINT**	MORROW CO.	T1S	R28E	S28
LENNOX D.L.C., DAVID T. see **WEST UNION BAPTIST**				
	WASHINGTON CO.	T1N	R2W	S14
LEONA	DOUGLAS CO.	T21S	R5W	S34
LEONARD D.L.C., JOSEPH see **FORD INFANT**				
	WASHINGTON CO.	T1N	R1W	S7
LEONARD FAMILY	JOSEPHINE CO.	T40S	R7W	S4
LESLIE FAMILY	LINCOLN CO.	T11S	R8W	S36
LETITIA	DOUGLAS CO.	T29S	R3W	S20
LETSOM D.L.C., JOHN see **INDIAN**	DOUGLAS CO.	T22S	R4W	S18
LETT CHILDREN	COOS CO.	T30S	R11W	S9
LETT FARM see **LETT CHILDREN**	COOS CO.	T30S	R11W	S9
LEVENS D.L.C., DANIEL H. see **LEVENS GRAVE, ALBERT**				
	DOUGLAS CO.	T32S	R5W	S21
LEVENS D.L.C., ISAAC see **DALLAS**	POLK CO.	T8S	R5W	S5
LEVENS D.L.C., THOMAS see **HAINES FAMILY**				
	DOUGLAS CO.	T22S	R7W	S32
LEVENS D.L.C., ZACHEUS see **ELKTON**				
	DOUGLAS CO.	T22S	R7W	S29
LEVENS GRAVE, ALBERT	DOUGLAS CO.	T32S	R5W	S21
LEWELLEN D.L.C., ELISON B. see **SPRINGWATER**				
	CLACKAMAS CO.	T4S	R4E	S8
LEWIS	LINN CO.	T13S	R1E	S23
LEWIS	MARION CO.	T7S	R1E	S29
LEWIS	WASHINGTON CO.	T1S	R2W	S30
LEWIS AND CLARK	CLATSOP CO.	T7N	R9W	S6
LEWIS CREEK see **LEWIS**	LINN CO.	T13S	R1E	S23
LEWIS D.L.C., CHARLES see **LEWIS**	WASHINGTON CO.	T1S	R2W	S30
LEWIS D.L.C., DANIEL P. see **LEWIS**				
	MARION CO.	T7S	R1E	S29
LEWIS D.L.C., HEMAN see **ZION LUTHERAN**				
	BENTON CO.	T11S	R5W	S23
LEWIS D.L.C., JOHN see **LEWIS FAMILY**				
	POLK CO.	T9S	R5W	S18
LEWIS FAMILY	POLK CO.	T9S	R5W	S18
LEWIS, FIELDING see **FERN RIDGE**	LINN CO.	T13S	R1W	S34
LEWIS, RACHEL see **FERN RIDGE**	LINN CO.	T13S	R1W	S34

LEWISBURG see **LOCKE**	BENTON CO.	T11S	R5W	S12
LEWISVILLE see **SMITH FAMILY**	POLK CO.	T9S	R5W	S16
LEWMAN, R. F. see **WILLIAMSBURG**	JOSEPHINE CO.	T38S	R5W	S24
LEWTHWAITE	CLACKAMAS CO.	T2S	R2E	S20
LEXINGTON [NEW] see **I.O.O.F. [LEXINGTON]**				
	MORROW CO.	T1S	R25E	S34
LEXINGTON [OLD]	MORROW CO.	T1S	R25E	S27
LIBBY	COOS CO.	T26S	R13W	?
LIBERTY see **WHITE DLC, WILLIAM**	LANE CO.	T15S	R5W	S20
LIBERTY [NEW]	LINN CO.	T13S	R1W	S26
LIBERTY [OLD]	LINN CO.	T13S	R1W	S23
LIBERTY HILL see **MASONIC [ST. HELENS]**				
	COLUMBIA CO.	T5N	R1W	S33
LIBERTY SCHOOL see **STIPP MEMORIAL**				
	MARION CO.	T8S	R2W	S2
LIBERTY SCHOOL see **UNKNOWN CHILD**				
	MORROW CO.	T3S	R24E	S24
LIDTKE HOMESTEAD, AUGUST see **LUDTKE FAMILY**				
	TILLAMOOK CO.	T3N	R10W	S13
LIGGETT D.L.C., JONATHAN W. see **LIGGETT FAMILY**				
	POLK CO.	T9S	R5W	S7
LIGGETT FAMILY	POLK CO.	T9S	R5W	S7
LIGHTING CREEK	WALLOWA CO.	T3N	R48E	S12
LIGHTING CREEK RANCH see **LIGHTING CREEK**				
	WALLOWA CO.	T3N	R48E	S12
LILES	LANE CO.	T18S	R5W	S16
LILLENAS see **FITCHA HOMESTEAD**	CLATSOP CO.	T8N	R8W	S31
LILYGLEN	JACKSON CO.	T38S	R3E	S14
LIME see **LIME-DIXIE**	BAKER CO.	T13S	R44E	S22
LIME-DIXIE	BAKER CO.	T13S	R44E	S22
LINCOLN [?] see **PINEHURST**	JACKSON CO.	T40S	R4E	S5
LINCOLN MEMORIAL PARK	CLACKAMAS CO.	T1S	R2E	S22
LINCOLN MEMORIAL PARK	MULTNOMAH CO.	T1S	R2E	S22
LINDLEY see **BUZAN**	WASCO CO.	T4S	R15E	S33
LINKVILLE	KLAMATH CO.	T38S	R9E	S29
LINN MEMORIAL	LINN CO.	T13S	R1W	S4
LINN, PHILIP E.	CLACKAMAS CO.	T3S	R4E	S21
LINN, PHILIP E. see **I.O.O.F. [ESTACADA]**				
	CLACKAMAS CO.	T3S	R4E	S21
LINNEMANN see **ST. JOSEPH**	MULTNOMAH CO.	T1S	R3E	S8
LINNEMANN D.L.C., GERHARD D. see **ST. JOSEPH**				
	MULTNOMAH CO.	T1S	R3E	S8
LINSLAW PIONEER	LANE CO.	T18S	R8W	S17
LIPSCOMB see **HEATER**	MARION CO.	T8S	R1E	S8
LIPSCOMB D.L.C., BARNET see **HEATER**				
	MARION CO.	T8S	R1E	S8
LISTER see **BEAVER CREEK**	CROOK CO.	T16S	R24E	S15
LISTER RANCH see **BEAVER CREEK**	CROOK CO.	T16S	R24E	S15
LITTLE BADGER CREEK see **TRAXTLE**	WASCO CO.	T3S	R12E	S27
LITTLE BULL MOUNTAIN see **TIGARD EVANGELICAL**				
	WASHINGTON CO.	T2S	R1W	S10

LITTLE CHAPEL OF THE CHIMES MEMORIAL GARDEN
	CLACKAMAS CO.	T1S	R2E	S33

LITTLE CHAPEL OF THE CHIMES FUNERAL HOME [GATEWAY]
	MULTNOMAH CO.	T1N	R2E	S34

LITTLE ELK see **EDDYVILLE**	LINCOLN CO.	T11S	R9W	S10

LITTLE GREASEWOOD see **GREASEWOOD FINNISH LUTHERAN**
	UMATILLA CO.	T4N	R33E	S34

LITTLE INDIAN GIRL see **DAVIS, ANNA**
	WALLOWA CO.	T1N	R42E	S11
LITTLE LAKE	LANE CO.	T16S	R7W	S18
LITTLE PLAINS	JEFFERSON CO.	T11S	R13E	?
LITTLEFIELD	MALHEUR CO.	T23S	R40E	S35

LITTLEFIELD HOME RANCH, OLD see **LITTLEFIELD**
	MALHEUR CO.	T23S	R40E	S35

LIVINGSTON D.L.C., THOMAS see **LIVINGSTON FAMILY**
	DOUGLAS CO.	T27S	R4W	S7
LIVINGSTON FAMILY	DOUGLAS CO.	T27S	R4W	S7
LLOYD see **SAYLOR**	LANE CO.	T19S	R2W	S19

LOBAN HOMESTEAD, MARTIN see **TESTAMENT CREEK**
	TILLAMOOK CO.	T4S	R7W	S5
LOBERT	KLAMATH CO.	T34S	R7E	S31
LOBSTER VALLEY	BENTON CO.	T15S	R8W	S4
LOBSTER VALLEY OLD see **LONE FIR**	BENTON CO.	T15S	R8W	S6

LOCKARD, EARNEST WILLIAM see **MINERAL**
	BAKER CO.	T12S	R45E	S12
LOCKE	BENTON CO.	T11S	R5W	S12

LOCKE CHILDREN see **MULHOLLAND FAMILY**
	LANE CO.	T19S	R2W	S4
LOCKE D.L.C., A. N. see **LOCKE**	BENTON CO.	T11S	R5W	S12

LOCKE D.L.C., DANIEL see **CLOVERDALE**
	LANE CO.	T19S	R2W	S18
LOCKWOOD	TILLAMOOK CO.	T1S	R10W	S31
LOCKWOOD RANCH	MALHEUR CO.	?	?	?

LOEB STATE PARK, ALFRED see **PAYNE FAMILY**
	CURRY CO.	T39S	R12W	?

LOFQUIST, MARGARET UNDERWOOD see **LONG FAMILY, JOHN**
	DOUGLAS CO.	T23S	R5W	?
LOGAN see **PLEASANT VIEW [EAST]**	CLACKAMAS CO.	T2S	R3E	S19
LOGAN FAMILY	LINCOLN CO.	T6S	R10W	S30
LOGDELL	GRANT CO.	T15S	R30E	S33
LOGIE D.L.C., JAMES see **MOAR**	MULTNOMAH CO.	T2N	R1W	S7
LOGSDEN	LINCOLN CO.	T9S	R9W	?
LOGTOWN	JACKSON CO.	T38S	R3W	S14
LOMA [?] see **SUNSET VALLEY**	HARNEY CO.	T25S	R31E	S27
LONE FIR	BENTON CO.	T15S	R8W	S6
LONE FIR	MARION CO.	T8S	R1W	S21
LONE FIR see **LONE FIR PIONEER**	MULTNOMAH CO.	T1S	R1E	S1
LONE FIR PIONEER	MULTNOMAH CO.	T1S	R1E	S1
LONE GRAVE [UNKNOWN]	LAKE CO.	T37S	R28E	S34
LONE OAK see **CURRINSVILLE**	CLACKAMAS CO.	T3S	R4E	S7

LONE OAK see **I.O.O.F.** [ESTACADA]				
	CLACKAMAS CO.	T3S	R4E	S21
LONE OAK [NEW]	MARION CO.	T9S	R1W	S10
LONE OAK [OLD] see **CAMPBELL-GRIER**				
	MARION CO.	T9S	R1W	S2
LONE PINE see **LONE FIR**	BENTON CO.	T15S	R8W	S6
LONE PINE see **PINE GROVE**	LINN CO.	T13S	R4W	S32
LONE PINE see **SMALL FAMILY**	LANE CO.	T22S	R3W	S17
LONE PINE see **WAMIC**	WASCO CO.	T4S	R12E	S22
LONEROCK	GILLIAM CO.	T6S	R24E	S4
LONG, CHARLIE see **SAND HOLLOW**	MORROW CO.	T1N	R26E	S13
LONG CHILDREN	MORROW CO.	T3S	R28E	S23
LONG CREEK	GRANT CO.	T10S	R30E	S11
LONG D.L.C., JOHN see **LONG FAMILY, JOHN**				
	DOUGLAS CO.	T23S	R5W	?
LONG, DOCTOR JAMES see **ST. JOHN THE EVANGELIST**				
	CLACKAMAS CO.	?	?	?
LONG, EMMA M. see **LONG FAMILY, JOHN**				
	DOUGLAS CO.	T23S	R5W	?
LONG FAMILY, JOHN	DOUGLAS CO.	T23S	R5W	?
LONG, GEORGE P. see **SMALL DLC, GEORGE**				
	LANE CO.	T20S	R3W	?
LONG, JAMES see **LONG CHILDREN**	MORROW CO.	T3S	R28E	S23
LONG, JOHN see **LONG FAMILY, JOHN**				
	DOUGLAS CO.	T23S	R5W	?
LONG, MARQUIS see **LONG FAMILY, JOHN**				
	DOUGLAS CO.	T23S	R5W	?
LONG, MINERVA see **LONG FAMILY, JOHN**				
	DOUGLAS CO.	T23S	R5W	?
LONG, MINERVA A. see **LONG FAMILY, JOHN**				
	DOUGLAS CO.	T23S	R5W	?
LONG, MINERVA JANE SMITH see **LONG FAMILY, JOHN**				
	DOUGLAS CO.	T23S	R5W	?
LONG PRAIRIE see **SCOTTSBURG**	DOUGLAS CO.	T22S	R9W	S8
LONG, ROBERT see **LONG FAMILY, JOHN**				
	DOUGLAS CO.	T23S	R5W	?
LONG TOM see **REST LAWN MEMORIAL PARK**				
	LANE CO.	T15S	R5W	S34
LOOKINGGLASS	DOUGLAS CO.	T27S	R7W	S35
LOOMIS	MULTNOMAH CO.	T1N	R1W	S2
LOOMIS, CHARLES see **LOOMIS**	MULTNOMAH CO.	T1N	R1W	S2
LOOMIS, CHRISTOPHER see **LOOMIS**	MULTNOMAH CO.	T1N	R1W	S2
LOOMIS D.L.C., JAMES see **LOOMIS**	MULTNOMAH CO.	T1N	R1W	S2
LOOMIS D.L.C., JAMES see **RAMSEY**	MULTNOMAH CO.	T2N	R1W	S36
LOOMIS, EDWARD see **LOOMIS**	MULTNOMAH CO.	T1N	R1W	S2
LOOMIS, JAMES see **LOOMIS**	MULTNOMAH CO.	T1N	R1W	S2
LOOMIS, SARAH see **LOOMIS**	MULTNOMAH CO.	T1N	R1W	S2
LOONEY D.L.C., JAMES C. see **SPRINGFIELD MEMORIAL GARDENS**				
	LANE CO.	T17S	R2W	S35
LOONEY D.L.C., JESSE AND RUBY see **LOONEY FAMILY**				
	MARION CO.	T9S	R3W	S23

LOONEY FAMILY	MARION CO.	T9S	R3W	S23
LOOPER see **LUPER**	LANE CO.	T16S	R4W	S34
LORANE GRANGE	LANE CO.	T20S	R5W	S2
LORELLA see **HALL**	KLAMATH CO.	T39S	R14E	S32
LOST CREEK	DOUGLAS CO.	T25S	R7W	S12
LOST PRAIRIE	WALLOWA CO.	T6N	R44E	S31
LOST RIVER see **BONANZA MEMORIAL PARK**				
	KLAMATH CO.	T39S	R12E	S10
LOST VALLEY	GILLIAM CO.	T6S	R23E	S4
LOSTINE	WALLOWA CO.	T1S	R43E	S3
LOURDES see **OUR LADY OF LOURDES**	LINN CO.	T10S	R1E	S9
LOVE see **COLUMBIAN**	MULTNOMAH CO.	T1N	R1E	S10
LOVE, AVON S. see **LOVE FAMILY**	BAKER CO.	T8S	R43E	S32
LOVE D.L.C., LEWIS see **COLUMBIAN**				
	MULTNOMAH CO.	T1N	R1E	S10
LOVE D.L.C., LEWIS see **LOVE, LEWIS**				
	MULTNOMAH CO.	T1N	R1E	S10
LOVE FAMILY	BAKER CO.	T8S	R43E	S32
LOVE, LEWIS	MULTNOMAH CO.	T1N	R1E	S10
LOVEJOY see **COLUMBIAN**	MULTNOMAH CO.	T1N	R1E	S10
LOVELADY D.L.C., THOMAS see **ROBBINS FAMILY**				
	POLK CO.	T7S	R5W	S27
LOVELL FAMILY	TILLAMOOK CO.	T3N	R10W	S29
LOWE FAMILY	CLACKAMAS CO.	T1S	R5E	S30
LOWELL	LANE CO.	T19S	R1W	S15
LOWER see **CLOVERDALE**	LANE CO.	T19S	R2W	S18
LOWER see **I.O.O.F. [FALLS CITY]**	POLK CO.	T8S	R6W	S21
LOWER COVE see **WRIGHT FAMILY**	UNION CO.	T2S	R40E	S18
LOWER FISHTRAP see **FISHTRAP**	COOS CO.	T28S	R13W	S23
LOWER HIGHLAND see **FELLOWS**	CLACKAMAS CO.	T4S	R3E	S3
LOWER LOGAN see **PLEASANT VIEW [EAST]**				
	CLACKAMAS CO.	T2S	R3E	S19
LOWER MABEL see **MABEL**	LANE CO.	T16S	R1W	S5
LOWER MEMALOOSE	WASCO CO.	T3N	R12E	S32
LOWER SCHUEBEL see **MOEHNKE**	CLACKAMAS CO.	T3S	R3E	S31
LOWER SILETZ-EUCHRE MOUNTAIN	LINCOLN CO.	?	?	?
LOWER SMITH RIVER see **NORTH FORK**				
	DOUGLAS CO.	T20S	R10W	S31
LOWER SUCCOR CREEK	MALHEUR CO.	T26S	R46E	S22
LOWER UMPQUA see **DREW MEMORIAL**	LANE CO.	T18S	R12W	S24
LOWER VALLEY see **BRAMLET MEMORIAL**				
	WALLOWA CO.	T2N	R42E	S33
LOWER WOLF CREEK	JOSEPHINE CO.	T33S	R6W	S30
LOWERY	CURRY CO.	T36S	R13W`	S1
LOWNSDALE D.L.C., DANIEL H. see **CITY CEMETERY #2**				
	MULTNOMAH CO.	T1N	R1E	S33
LOWNSDALE, DANIEL H. see **CITY CEMETERY #2**				
	MULTNOMAH CO.	T1N	R1E	S33
LOWNSDALE, NANCY see **CITY CEMETERY #2**				
	MULTNOMAH CO.	T1N	R1E	S33

LOWNSDALE, NANCY GILLIHAN see **CITY CEMETERY #2**

	MULTNOMAH CO.	T1N	R1E	S33
LUCAS D.L.C., DANIEL see **I.O.O.F. [LORANE]**				
	LANE CO.	T20S	R5W	S24
LUCAS, MARCELLUS	CURRY CO.	T35S	R11W	S6
LUCIER, ETIENNE see **LUCIER, MARY**				
	MARION CO.	T3S	R2W	S33
LUCIER FARM see **LUCIER, MARY**	MARION CO.	T3S	R2W	S33
LUCIER, MARY	MARION CO.	T3S	R2W	S33
LUCIER, MARY MARGUERITE TCHINOUK see **LUCIER, MARY**				
	MARION CO.	T3S	R2W	S33
LUCKY QUEEN	JOSEPHINE CO.	T34S	R5W	S32
LUDTKE FAMILY	TILLAMOOK CO.	T3N	R10W	S13
LUDVIG see **UNKNOWN**	UNION CO.	T3S	R33E	S23
LUEY, WONG see **COUNTY FARM #2**	MULTNOMAH CO.	T1S	R1E	S5
LUND PLACE, CHARLES see **RANKIN INFANT**				
	MULTNOMAH CO.	T1N	R5E	?
LUPATIA CREW	CLATSOP CO.	T5N	R11W	S1
LUPER	LANE CO.	T16S	R4W	S34
LUTHERAN see **BETHANY MEMORIAL**	COLUMBIA CO.	T4N	R1W	S19
LUTHERAN see **MAPLE LANE**	WASHINGTON CO.	T2S	R1W	S30
LUTHERAN see **VALLEY VIEW**	MARION CO.	T6S	R1W	S36
LUTHERAN-CATHOLIC see **SCHEEL FAMILY**				
	CLACKAMAS CO.	T3S	R5E	S18
LUTHY see **MT. HOPE**	MARION CO.	T7S	R1W	S33
LYDELL, EFFIE MAE see **HORSE CREEK RANCH**				
	WALLOWA CO.	T3N	R48E	S35
LYDELL-STUBBLEFIELD, BABIES see **HORSE CREEK RANCH**				
	WALLOWA CO.	T3N	R48E	S35
LYLE see **LILES**	LANE CO.	T18S	R5W	S16
LYONS see **FOX VALLEY**	LINN CO.	T9S	R2E	S20
LYONS PROPERTY, JAMES D. see **MOAR**				
	MULTNOMAH CO.	T2N	R1W	S7
MABEL	LANE CO.	T16S	R1W	S5
MABLE see **MABEL**	LANE CO.	T16S	R1W	S5
MABEL CHURCH see **UPPER MABEL**	LANE CO.	T15S	R1W	S28
MACDONALD, SHERIDAN see **SHILOH BURIAL**				
	LANE CO.	T19S	R1W	S29
MACEY FAMILY	DOUGLAS CO.	T22S	R11W	S2
MACFARLAND	CURRY CO.	T35S	R13W	S34
MACKEY, JOHN see **WRIGHT POINT**	HARNEY CO.	T24S	R31E	?
MacLAREN SCHOOL see **BONNEY FAMILY**				
	MARION CO.	T5S	R1W	S9
MACLEAY see **STIPP MEMORIAL**	MARION CO.	T8S	R2W	S2
MADERA see **MADERIS, LYMAN**	LANE CO.	T15S	R10W	S29
MADERIS, LYMAN	LANE CO.	T15S	R10W	S29
MADISON RANCH, GAYLORD see **UNKNOWN**				
	UMATILLA CO.	T1N	R29E	?
MADISON RANCH, GAYLORD see **UNKNOWN**				
	UMATILLA CO.	T3N	R27E	S36

MADRAS see **MT. JEFFERSON MEMORIAL PARK**

	JEFFERSON CO.	T11S	R14E	S6

MAHON see **REST LAWN MEMORIAL PARK**

	LANE CO.	T15S	R5W	S34
MAKI FAMILY see **HAMLET**	CLATSOP CO.	T4N	R8W	S6
MALHEUR CITY	MALHEUR CO.	T13S	R41E	S29
MALIN see **MALIN COMMUNITY**	KLAMATH CO.	T41S	R12E	S10
MALIN COMMUNITY	KLAMATH CO.	T41S	R12E	S10
MALLOY FAMILY see **MELOY FAMILY**	MULTNOMAH CO.	?	?	?

MALONE D.L.C., JAMES see **MALONE FAMILY**

	LINN CO.	T14S	R1W	S24

MALONE D.L.C., MADISON see **MALONE FAMILY**

	YAMHILL CO.	T4S	R4W	S15
MALONE FAMILY	LINN CO.	T14S	R1W	S24
MALONE FAMILY	YAMHILL CO.	T4S	R4W	S15

MALONE PLACE, FRED see **MALONE FAMILY**

	LINN CO.	T14S	R1W	S24
MANN GROVE	GRANT CO.	?	?	?
MANSFIELD see **HARRIS**	LINN CO.	T15S	R4W	S24
MAPLE GROVE see **MAPLEWOOD**	CLACKAMAS CO.	T6S	R1E	S14
MAPLE LANE	WASHINGTON CO.	T2S	R1W	S30

MAPLE LODGE #139 see **I.O.O.F. [MAPLETON]**

	LANE CO.	T18S	R10W	S11

MAPLETON see **I.O.O.F. [MAPLETON]**

	LANE CO.	T18S	R10W	S11

MAPLETON MEMORIAL CEMETERY ASSOCIATION see **KNOWLES**

	LANE CO.	T18S	R10W	S1
MAPLEWOOD	CLACKAMAS CO.	T6S	R1E	S14
MAPLEWOOD	CLATSOP CO.	T8N	R7W	S16
MAPLEWOOD	COLUMBIA CO.	T7N	R4W	S8

MARCHINO, MESCHELLE see **MESCHELLE, JENNIE**

	CLATSOP CO.	T6N	R10W	S15
MARCOLA	LANE CO.	T16S	R2W	S24
MARCOLA see **VALLEY VIEW**	LANE CO.	T17S	R2W	S3
MARIAL [OLD]	CURRY CO.	T33S	R10W	S2
MARICK FAMILY	GILLIAM CO.	T1N	R20E	?
MARICK RANCH see **UNKNOWN MAN**	GILLIAM CO.	T1N	R20E	?
MARION COUNTY POOR FARM	MARION CO.	T7S	R3W	?
MARION FRIENDS	MARION CO.	T9S	R2W	S29
MARION HILL see **MARION FRIENDS**	MARION CO.	T9S	R2W	S29

MARK FAMILY see **MARK MEMORIAL PARK**

	CLACKAMAS CO.	T4S	R1E	S20
MARK MEMORIAL PARK	CLACKAMAS CO.	T4S	R1E	S20

MARKHAM D.L.C., DAVID see **INDIAN**

	DOUGLAS CO.	T25S	R4W	?
MARKS see **MARK MEMORIAL PARK**	CLACKAMAS CO.	T4S	R1E	S20
MARKS CABIN see **MARKS, SAM**	WALLOWA CO.	?	?	?

MARKS D.L.C., JOHN AND FANNY see **MARK MEMORIAL PARK**

	CLACKAMAS CO.	T4S	R1E	S20
MARKS FAMILY	WALLOWA CO.	T2S	R48E	S2
MARKS FARM	POLK CO.	T6S	R4W	?

MARKS, MRS. CHARITY ANN see **FISH LAKE**				
	LINN CO.	T13S	R7E	S30
MARKS PRAIRIE see **MARK MEMORIAL PARK**				
	CLACKAMAS CO.	T4S	R1E	S20
MARKS RIDGE see **FERGUSON**	LINN CO.	T13S	R1W	S12
MARKS, SAM	WALLOWA CO.	?	?	?
MARLATT PLACE, OLD see **UNKNOWN CHILD**				
	MORROW CO.	T2S	R26E	S25
MARQUAM D.L.C., ALFRED see **MARQUAM FAMILY**				
	CLACKAMAS CO.	T6S	R1E	S10
MARQUAM FAMILY	CLACKAMAS CO.	T6S	R1E	S10
MARQUESS, MARK WAYNE	LANE CO.	T19S	R3W	S24
MARSH-RICE see **RICE-MARSH FAMILY**				
	DOUGLAS CO.	T23S	R5W	S31
MARSHALL, JOHN see **BONNEY FAMILY**				
	MARION CO.	T5S	R1W	S9
MARSHFIELD	COOS CO.	T25S	R13W	S26
MARSHFIELD see **CLACKAMAS**	CLACKAMAS CO.	T2S	R2E	S4
MARSHLAND	COLUMBIA CO.	T7N	R5W	S11
MARTIN see **NICOSON**	WALLOWA CO.	T5N	R44E	S8
MARTIN see **REPSLEGER ROAD**	LANE CO.	T20S	R4W	S23
MARTIN D.L.C., JOHN see **HIGHLAND**				
	POLK CO.	T7S	R3W	S17
MARTIN D.L.C., NORMAN see **BAKER FAMILY**				
	WASHINGTON CO.	T1S	R4W	S21
MARTIN, MRS. GERTRUDE see **REPSLEGER ROAD**				
	LANE CO.	T20S	R4W	S23
MARTIN'S D.L.C., JACOB AND EVALINE see **ARMSTRONG**				
	BENTON CO.	T12S	R5W	S31
MARTINDALE	DOUGLAS CO.	T29S	R8W	S20
MARTINDALE D.L.C., ALSTON see **MARTINDALE**				
	DOUGLAS CO.	T29S	R8W	S20
MARTINEAU, MICHEL see **MESCHELLE, JENNIE**				
	CLATSOP CO.	T6N	R10W	S15
MARVEL GIRL	GILLIAM CO.	T1N	R22E	S7
MARYLHURST CONVENT see **SISTERS OF THE HOLY NAMES**				
	CLACKAMAS CO.	T2S	R1E	S14
MASCASKET see **BROWN**	KLAMATH CO.	T36S	R12E	S13
MASEKESKET see **BROWN**	KLAMATH CO.	T36S	R12E	S13
MASIKER, GEORGE	SHERMAN CO.	T2N	R16E	S33
MASONIC see **ARLINGTON**	GILLIAM CO.	T3N	R21E	S28
MASONIC see **CANYON CITY**	GRANT CO.	T13S	R31E	S35
MASONIC see **CANYONVILLE**	DOUGLAS CO.	T30S	R5W	S27
MASONIC see **DALLAS**	POLK CO.	T8S	R5W	S5
MASONIC see **FRANKLIN BUTTE**	LINN CO.	T10S	R1W	S19
MASONIC see **GARDINER**	DOUGLAS CO.	T21S	R12W	S22
MASONIC see **GLENDALE**	DOUGLAS CO.	T33S	R6W	S5
MASONIC see **GREENWOOD HILLS**	MULTNOMAH CO.	T1S	R1E	S27
MASONIC see **HEPPNER**	MORROW CO.	T2S	R26E	S35
MASONIC see **HILLSBORO PIONEER**	WASHINGTON CO.	T1N	R3W	S36

```
MASONIC  see I.O.O.F. PIONEER [JOSEPH]
                              WALLOWA CO.      T2S    R44E    S36
MASONIC  see JACKSONVILLE     JACKSON CO.      T37S   R2W     S29
MASONIC  see JEFFERSON        MARION CO.       T10S   R3W     S1
MASONIC  see PORT ORFORD      CURRY CO.        T32S   R15W    S4
MASONIC  see POWERS           COOS CO.         T31S   R12W    S12
MASONIC  see REEDSPORT        DOUGLAS CO.      T22S   R12W    S4
MASONIC  see ROSEBURG MEMORIAL GARDENS
                              DOUGLAS CO.      T27S   R6W     S13
MASONIC  see SUMPTER          BAKER CO.        T9S    R37E    S33
MASONIC  see WESTON           UMATILLA CO.     T4N    R35E    S22
MASONIC [ALBANY]              LINN CO.         T11S   R4W     S12
MASONIC [ALFORD]              LINN CO.         T14S   R4W     S35
MASONIC [BAKER CITY] see MT. HOPE
                              BAKER CO.        T9S    R40E    S21
MASONIC [BROWNSVILLE] see BROWNSVILLE PIONEER
                              LINN CO.         T13S   R2W     S32
MASONIC [CAVE JUNCTION] see LAUREL
                              JOSEPHINE CO.    T39S   R8W     S15
MASONIC [CONDON] see I.O.O.F. [CONDON]
                              GILLIAM CO.      T4S    R21E    S2
MASONIC [COQUILLE]            COOS CO.         T27S   R13W    S36
MASONIC [EUGENE]              LANE CO.         T18S   R3W     S5
MASONIC [FLORENCE] see PACIFIC SUNSET MEMORIAL PARK
                              LANE CO.         T18S   R12W    S25
MASONIC [FOSSIL]              WHEELER CO.      T6S    R21E    S33
MASONIC [GERVAIS]             MARION CO.       T5S    R2W     S36
MASONIC [HARRISBURG] see MASONIC [ALFORD]
                              LINN CO.         T14S   R4W     S35
MASONIC [LA GRANDE] see HILLCREST
                              UNION CO.        T3S    R38E    S8
MASONIC [LAFAYETTE]           YAMHILL CO.      T4S    R4W     S1
MASONIC [LEBANON] see I.O.O.F. [LEBANON]
                              LINN CO.         T12S   R2W     S2
MASONIC [LONE FIR]            MULTNOMAH CO.    T1S    R1E     S1
MASONIC [McMINNVILLE]         YAMHILL CO.      T4S    R4W     S19
MASONIC [OAKLAND]             DOUGLAS CO.      T24S   R5W     S33
MASONIC [OLD ROSEBURG]        DOUGLAS CO.      T27S   R5W     S19
MASONIC [OREGON CITY]         CLACKAMAS CO.    T3S    R2E     S5
MASONIC [PRINEVILLE] see JUNIPER HAVEN
                              CROOK CO.        T14S   R16E    S31
MASONIC [ST. HELENS]          COLUMBIA CO.     T5N    R1W     S33
MASONIC [SCIO] see FRANKLIN BUTTE
                              LINN CO.         T10S   R1W     S19
MASONIC [SEASIDE] see EVERGREEN CLATSOP CO.    T6N    R10W    S34
MASONIC [SHERIDAN]            YAMHILL CO.      T5S    R6W     S26
MASONIC [STAYTON] see LONE OAK [NEW]
                              MARION CO.       T9S    R1W     S10
MASONIC [THE DALLES]          WASCO CO.        T1N    R13E    S10
MASONIC [WASCO] see SUN RISE  SHERMAN CO.      T2N    R17E    S31
MASONIC [YONCALLA]            DOUGLAS CO.      T23S   R5W     S4
```

MASONIC, HOOD RIVER #105 [HOOD RIVER] see **IDLEWILD**

	HOOD RIVER CO.	T2N	R10E	S2

MASONIC LODGE #14 see **CRYSTAL LAKE**

BENTON CO.	T12S	R5W	S11

MASONIC LODGE #51 [COTTAGE GROVE] see **FIR GROVE**

LANE CO.	T20S	R3W	S29

MASONIC LODGE #135 see **CENTRAL POINT**

JACKSON CO.	T37S	R2W	S1

MASONIC, PIONEER [GRANTS PASS]   JOSEPHINE CO.   T36S   R5W   S16

MASONIC SLOUGH see **COLUMBIA PIONEER**

MULTNOMAH CO.	T1N	R2E	S21

MAST FAMILY   COOS CO.   T27S   R11W   ?

MASTEN   DESCHUTES CO.   T22S   R9E   S25

MASTEN HOMESTEAD see **MASTEN**   DESCHUTES CO.   T22S   R9E   S25

MASTENBROOK, HARLAN see **COOPER, MRS.**

LINN CO.	T12S	R1W	S8

MASTENBROOK, HARLAN see **SALTMARSH, ZERILDA**

LINN CO.	T12S	R1W	S7

MASTENBROOK, HARLAN see **UNKNOWN WOMAN**

LINN CO.	T12S	R1W	S7

MASTER [Sic] see **MASTEN**   DESCHUTES CO.   T22S   R9E   S25

MASTERS   COOS CO.   T26S   R12W   S6

MASTERSON, FREDDIE   HOOD RIVER CO.   T2N   R7E   S12

MASTERSON, J. ALFRED see **MASTERSON, FREDDIE**

HOOD RIVER CO.	T2N	R7E	S12

MASTERSON, MARTHA GAY see **MASTERSON, FREDDIE**

HOOD RIVER CO.	T2N	R7E	S12

MATER DOLOROSA   MARION CO.   T8S   R1W   S34

MATHENY D.L.C., RACHEL see **HOPEWELL**

YAMHILL CO.	T5S	R3W	S30

MATHENY D.L.C., WILLIAM see **WILLAMETTE MISSION**

MARION CO.	T6S	R3W	S3

MATLOCK D.L.C., WILLIAM T. see **CLACKAMAS**

CLACKAMAS CO.	T2S	R2E	S4

MATLOCK FAMILY see **CLACKAMAS**   CLACKAMAS CO.   T2S   R2E   S4

MATNEY see **UPPER MILL CREEK**   WASCO CO.   T1S   R11E   S11

MATTESON   LINCOLN CO.   T11S   R10W   S10

MATTESON see **RHEA CREEK**   MORROW CO.   T4S   R26E   S14

MATTESON HOMESTEAD, JOHN see **MATTESON**

LINCOLN CO.	T11S	R10W	S10

MATTHEWS FAMILY   JACKSON CO.   T35S   R1W   S27

MAUPIN   JEFFERSON CO.   T9S   R16E   S24

MAURY see **MAURY MOUNTAIN**   CROOK CO.   T17S   R21E   S11

MAURY MOUNTAIN   CROOK CO.   T17S   R21E   S11

MAUSOLEUM [BAKER CITY] see **MT. HOPE**

BAKER CO.	T9S	R40E	S21

MAUTZ FARM, ALBERT see **SAWTELL FAMILY**

CLACKAMAS CO.	T5S	R2E	S30

MAXVILLE   WALLOWA CO.   T3N   R42E   S15

MAXWELL see **HAINES**   BAKER CO.   T7S   R39E   S21

MAXWELL, JOE see **DOUGHERTY, LYDIA**				
	TILLAMOOK CO.	T1S	R9W	?
MAYGER-DOWNING FAMILY	COLUMBIA CO.	T8N	R3W	S19
MAYNARD, REBECCA JANE see **PINE CREEK**				
	WALLOWA CO.	T2N	R46E	S27
MAYNARD, THOMAS see **PINE CREEK**	WALLOWA CO.	T2N	R46E	S27
MAYNARD, THOMAS J. see **PINE CREEK**				
	WALLOWA CO.	T2N	R46E	S27
MAYS see **MAYS-STROUTS**	BENTON CO.	T11S	R7W	S6
MAYS see **UNION**	LANE CO.	T16S	R5W	S5
MAYS-STROUTS	BENTON CO.	T11S	R7W	S6
MAYVILLE see **I.O.O.F. [MAYVILLE]**				
	GILLIAM CO.	T5S	R21E	S28
McALEXANDER HOMESEAD, V. see **CHIEF JOSEPH [OLD]**				
	WALLOWA CO.	T1N	R43E	S20
McALLISTER, TOM see **PRATT-COLVILLE**				
	WALLOWA CO.	T3S	R43E	?
McATEE D.L.C., WILLIAM H. see **JONES FAMILY**				
	LANE CO.	T16S	R5W	S16
McBEE, ELIZABETH see **McBEE FAMILY**				
	BENTON CO.	T13S	R5W	S23
McBEE FAMILY	BENTON CO.	T13S	R5W	S23
McBEE, WILLIAM see **McBEE FAMILY**	BENTON CO.	T13S	R5W	S23
McBETH, MR. see **INDIAN BOY**	DOUGLAS CO.	T26S	R7W	S13
McBRIDE	YAMHILL CO.	T3S	R4W	S19
McBRIDE D.L.C., THOMAS AND ANN see **McBRIDE**				
	YAMHILL CO.	T3S	R4W	S19
McCABE see **SOUTH YAMHILL**	YAMHILL CO.	T5S	R5W	S3
McCABE CHURCH see **SOUTH YAMHILL**	YAMHILL CO.	T5S	R5W	S3
McCALISTER see **PRATUM**	MARION CO.	T7S	R1W	S19
McCALLISTER D.L.C., HARDIN AND JULIA see **APOSTOLIC**				
	MARION CO.	T7S	R1W	S8
McCANN, DANIEL see **McCANN FAMILY**				
	WASHINGTON CO.	T1S	R4W	S32
McCANN FAMILY	WASHINGTON CO.	T1S	R4W	S32
McCARTNEY see **PULLINS**	MULTNOMAH CO.	?	?	?
McCARTNEY, ELMER D. see **PULLINS**	MULTNOMAH CO.	?	?	?
McCARTNEY, ELSWORTH see **PULLINS**	MULTNOMAH CO.	?	?	?
McCARTNEY, MARIE WARFLER see **PULLINS**				
	MULTNOMAH CO.	?	?	?
McCLANE, THOMAS HENRY	LANE CO.	T21S	R3E	S8
McCLELLAN BURIALS see **STORES FAMILY**				
	DOUGLAS CO.	T22S	R6W	?
McCLELLAN, CHARLES	MULTNOMAH CO.	T1N	R3E	S28
McCLURE FAMILY	WASCO CO.	T2N	R12E	S4
McCLURE, JAMES	WASCO CO.	T2N	R12E	S5
McCOLLUM	LANE CO.	T18S	R4W	S30
McCORKLE see **HOWELL PRAIRIE**	MARION CO.	T7S	R2W	S4
McCORKLE see **NEWSOM CAMPGROUND**	MARION CO.	T6S	R1W	S19
McCORKLE see **TRAXTLE**	WASCO CO.	T3S	R12E	S27
McCORMAC	TILLAMOOK CO.	T2S	R10W	S8

McCOWELL	TILLAMOOK CO.	T2S	R10W	S6
McCOWN, G. W.	MARION CO.	T7S	R2E	S7
McCOY see **BETHEL**	POLK CO.	T6S	R4W	S21
McCOY INFANT	SHERMAN CO.	T2N	R16E	S1
McCUBBIN	WALLOWA CO.	T1S	R43E	S5
McCULLEY see **McCULLY**	MARION CO.	T9S	R2W	S21
McCULLOCH	LANE CO.	T18S	R5W	S34
McCULLOCH D.L.C., THOMAS see **McCULLOCH**				
	LANE CO.	T18S	R5W	S34
McCULLOCH D.L.C., WILLIAM see **McCULLOCH FAMILY**				
	DOUGLAS CO.	T29S	R7W	S6
McCULLOCH FAMILY	DOUGLAS CO.	T29S	R7W	S6
McCULLY	MARION CO.	T9S	R2W	S21
McCULLY D.L.C., ISAAC see **McCULLY**				
	MARION CO.	T9S	R2W	S21
McCURDY, MRS. see **DAIRY**	KLAMATH CO.	T38S	R11 1/2E	?
McDONALD, D. S. see **FAIRVIEW**	WASCO CO.	?	?	?
McDONALD, HARLAND see **McCOY INFANT**				
	SHERMAN CO.	T2N	R16E	S1
McDONALD, LOUISA see **FAIRVIEW**	WASCO CO.	?	?	?
McDONALD, MARY J. see **FAIRVIEW**	WASCO CO.	?	?	?
McENROE, PATRICK	LANE CO.	T17S	R9W	S36
McEWEN	BAKER CO.	T10S	R38E	S18
McEWEN MASONIC LODGE #125 A.F. AND A.M. see **SUMPTER**				
	BAKER CO.	T9S	R37E	S33
McFARLAND	LANE CO.	T20S	R3W	S28
McFARLAND D.L.C., JAMES H. see **McFARLAND**				
	LANE CO.	T20S	R3W	S28
McFARLAND FAMILY see **McFARLAND**	LANE CO.	T20S	R3W	S28
McGEE see **HOLMS FAMILY**	YAMHILL CO.	T5S	R8W	S36
McGLONE GRAVES	CURRY CO.	T31S	R12W	S31
McGLONE, OLD JIMMY see **McGLONE GRAVES**				
	CURRY CO.	T31S	R12W	S31
McGLONE, YOUNG JIMMY see **McGLONE GRAVES**				
	CURRY CO.	T31S	R12W	S31
McGREGOR, _____ HILLS see **McGREGOR BABY**				
	MULTNOMAH CO.	?	?	?
McGREGOR BABY	MULTNOMAH CO.	?	?	?
McGREGOR, DONALD see **McGREGOR BABY**				
	MULTNOMAH CO.	?	?	?
McGREWS PASTURE see **RANGE [OLD]**	GRANT CO.	T8S	R31E	S10
McGUIRE D.L.C., FRANCIS see **UNION**				
	WASHINGTON CO.	T1N	R1W	S29
McGUIRE D.L.C., THOMAS J. see **McGUIRE FAMILY**				
	DOUGLAS CO.	T28S	R7W	S34
McGUIRE FAMILY	DOUGLAS CO.	T28S	R7W	S34
McGUIRE FARM, WILLIAM	POLK CO.	T9S	R5W	S13
McHALEY	GRANT CO.	T13S	R33E	S3
McHALEY, GEORGE see **McHALEY**	GRANT CO.	T13S	R33E	S3
McHARGUE	LINN CO.	T14S	R2W	S15

McHARGUE D.L.C., JAMES see **McHARGUE**				
	LINN CO.	T14S	R2W	S15
McISAAC RANCH	HOOD RIVER CO.	T1N	R10E	S29
McKAMEY see **UPPER VALLEY**	HOOD RIVER CO.	T1N	R10E	S33
McKAY see **FORT UMPQUA [OLD]**	DOUGLAS CO.	T22S	R7W	S30
McKAY CREEK	UMATILLA CO.	T1N	R32E	S11
McKAY D.L.C., MALCOLM see **McKAY, THOMAS**				
	COLUMBIA CO.	T4N	R1W	S31
McKAY, JEAN BAPTISTE DESPORTES see **FORT UMPQUA [OLD]**				
	DOUGLAS CO.	T22S	R7W	S30
McKAY, JONATHAN AND WIFE see **FORT UMPQUA [OLD]**				
	DOUGLAS CO.	T22S	R7W	S30
McKAY, THOMAS	COLUMBIA CO.	T4N	R1W	S31
McKAY, THOMAS see **McPHERSON, JOHN**				
	COLUMBIA CO.	T4N	R1W	S31
McKENZIE BRIDGE	LANE CO.	T16S	R5E	?
McKINLEY see **DORA**	COOS CO.	T28S	R11W	S10
McKINNEY, JEAN see **RYAN FAMILY**	CLATSOP CO.	T7N	R8W	?
McKINNON, PVT. HAROLD J. see **ROBINETTE**				
	BAKER CO.	T9S	R46E	S25
McKNIGHT, JAMES A.	LINN CO.	T13S	R6E	S31
McLAUGHLIN, NETTIE	HARNEY CO.	T28S	R31E	S27
McLEOD D.L.C., DONALD see **HANEY FAMILY**				
	WASHINGTON CO.	T1S	R4W	S35
McLEOD, JACK see **WISE**	COOS CO.	T30S	R12W	S34
McLIN D.L.C., WILLIAM AND ROSANA see **EMANUEL LUTHERAN**				
	WASHINGTON CO.	T1N	R3W	S34
McLOUGHLIN, DOCTOR JOHN see **McLOUGHLIN FAMILY**				
	CLACKAMAS CO.	T2S	R2E	S31
McLOUGHLIN, DOCTOR JOHN see **ST. JOHN THE EVANGELIST**				
	CLACKAMAS CO.	?	?	?
McLOUGHLIN FAMILY	CLACKAMAS CO.	T2S	R2E	S31
McLOUGHLIN, MARGUERITE McKAY see **McLOUGHLIN FAMILY**				
	CLACKAMAS CO.	T2S	R2E	S31
McMILLAN D.L.C., JAMES H. see **UNKNOWN**				
	WASHINGTON CO.	T1S	R2W	S13
McMINNVILLE [OLD]	YAMHILL CO.	T4S	R4W	S21
McMURRY D.L.C., FIELDING see **MASONIC [EUGENE]**				
	LANE CO.	T18S	R3W	S5
McNAB, PAT see **MORAN**	SHERMAN CO.	T2N	R16E	S22
McNARY [?] see **BRUNK FARM**	POLK CO.	T7S	R4W	?
McNEIL, FRED H.	CLACKAMAS CO.	T2S	UNSURVEYED	
McNEMEE	MULTNOMAH CO.	T2N	R1W	S30
McNEMEE see **PEARSON FAMILY**	MULTNOMAH CO.	?	?	?
McNEMEE, MOSES see **McNEMEE**	MULTNOMAH CO.	T2N	R1W	S30
McNULTY D.L.C., JOHN see **McNULTY FAMILY**				
	COLUMBIA CO.	T4N	R1W	S8
McNULTY FAMILY	COLUMBIA CO.	T4N	R1W	S8
McPHERSON, JOHN	COLUMBIA CO.	T4N	R1W	S31
McPHERSON, MRS. see **PEARCE, JOHN**				
	JEFFERSON CO.	T10S	R15E	S32

McPHERSON RANCH, CHAS. see **PEARCE, JOHN**

	JEFFERSON CO.	T10S	R15E	S32
McQUINN	MULTNOMAH CO.	T2N	R1W	S6

McQUINN D.L.C., ALEXANDER H. AND REBECCA see **McQUINN**

	MULTNOMAH CO.	T2N	R1W	S6
McQUINN, GEORGE	WASCO CO.	T2N	R14E	S26

McRAE, ANNA BELL see **McRAE RANCH, FARQUHAR**

	WASCO CO.	T6S	R19E	?
McRAE RANCH	MALHEUR CO.	T24S	R37E	S9
McRAE RANCH, FARQUHAR	WASCO CO.	T6S	R19E	?
McTAVISH, DONALD	CLATSOP CO.	T8N	R9W	S8

McTIMMONDS D.L.C., LAMBERT see **McTIMMONDS FAMILY**

	POLK CO.	T9S	R6W	S10
McTIMMONDS FAMILY	POLK CO.	T9S	R6W	S10

McTIMMONDS, FRANCES see **McTIMMONDS FAMILY**

	POLK CO.	T9S	R6W	S10

McTIMMONDS, LAMBERT see **McTIMMONDS FAMILY**

	POLK CO.	T9S	R6W	S10
MEACHAM	UMATILLA CO.	T1S	R35E	S3
MEACHAM, HARVEY J.	UMATILLA CO.	T1S	R35E	S3
MEADOWS see **BAUMGARDNER FAMILY**	UMATILLA CO.	T3N	R29E	S7
MEADOWS GRAVES	JACKSON CO.	T34S	R3W	S25
MEDICAL SPRINGS	UNION CO.	T6S	R41E	?

MEDLER, L. C. see **GARLINGTON PLACE**

	SHERMAN CO.	T2N	R17E	?
MEDLEY	LANE CO.	T20S	R3W	S19
MEDLOCK INFANT	MORROW CO.	T6S	R25E	S3

MEDLOCK, MINNIE see **MEDLOCK INFANT**

	MORROW CO.	T6S	R25E	S3

MEDLOCK, ROBERT see **MEDLOCK INFANT**

	MORROW CO.	T6S	R25E	S3

MEEK D.L.C., WILLIAM see **MILWAUKIE PIONEER**

	CLACKAMAS CO.	T1S	R1E	S26

MEEK, STEPHEN see **BUTTS, CATHERINE BONNETT**

	WASCO CO.	T3S	R14E	S28

MEEKER D.L.C., JOHN see **UMPHLETTE, JANE EARL**

	LINN CO.	T10S	R3W	S15
MEEKS see **WEGER**	LINN CO.	T15S	R3W	S26

MEEKS D.L.C., THOMAS M. see **WEGER**

	LINN CO.	T15S	R3W	S26
MEGGINSON see **AGATE BEACH**	LINCOLN CO.	T10S	R11W	S29

MEIER, JULIUS L. see **PAINTER FAMILY**

	MULTNOMAH CO.	T1N	R4E	S25
MEINIG PARK	CLACKAMAS CO.	T2S	R4E	S13
MELLIN FAMILY	DESCHUTES CO.	T19S	R15E	?
MELLIN, MRS. see **MELLIN FAMILY**	DESCHUTES CO.	T19S	R15E	?

MELOY D.L.C., NATHAN H. [WIDOW] AND HEIRS see **MELOY FAMILY**

	MULTNOMAH CO.	?	?	?
MELOY FAMILY	MULTNOMAH CO.	?	?	?

MELOY, NATHAN H. see **MELOY FAMILY**

	MULTNOMAH CO.	?	?	?

MELROSE	DOUGLAS CO.	T27S	R7W	S1
MEMALOOSE see **LOWER MEMALOOSE**	WASCO CO.	T3N	R12E	S32
MEMORIAL see **MOLALLA MEMORIAL**	CLACKAMAS CO.	T5S	R2E	S20
MEMORIAL HOME see **WALDPORT MEMORIAL**				
	LINCOLN CO.	T13S	R11W	S30
MEMORY GARDENS MEMORIAL PARK AND MAUSOLEUM				
	JACKSON CO.	T37S	R2W	S34
MENDELL *[Sic]* see **MEDLEY**	LANE CO.	T20S	R3W	S19
MENDENHALL FARM see **BURFORD, WILLIAM**				
	YAMHILL CO.	T5S	R7W	S24
MENNONITE see **BLOSSER**	CLACKAMAS CO.	T4S	R1W	S36
MENNONITE see **SCHRAG FAMILY**	POLK CO.	T8S	R5W	S6
MENNONITE see **SHERIDAN MENNONITE**				
	POLK CO.	T6S	R7W	S13
MENNONITE CEMETERY AT WALLACE BRIDGE see **SHERIDAN MENNONITE**				
	POLK CO.	T6S	R7W	S13
MERCHANT see **YAMHILL-CARLTON**	YAMHILL CO.	T3S	R4W	S10
MERIDIAN	WASHINGTON CO.	T3S	R1W	S1
MERIDIAN [OLD]	CLACKAMAS CO.	T3S	R1W	S13
MERIDIAN see **TRINITY LUTHERAN**	MARION CO.	T6S	R1W	S12
MERIDIAN UNITED CHURCH OF CHRIST see **MERIDIAN [OLD]**				
	CLACKAMAS CO.	T3S	R1W	S13
MERLIN see **PLEASANT VALLEY**	JOSEPHINE CO.	T35S	R6W	S11
MERRIAM see **MERRIMAN**	CURRY CO.	T36S	R14W	S16
MERRILL	COLUMBIA CO.	T5N	R1W	?
MERRILL see **PENITENTIARY [NEW]**	MARION CO.	T7S	R3W	S25
MERRILL D.L.C., JOSEPH see **MERRILL**				
	COLUMBIA CO.	T5N	R1W	?
MERRILL FAMILY see **MERRILL**	COLUMBIA CO.	T5N	R1W	?
MERRILL LAKE see **MERRILL**	COLUMBIA CO.	T5N	R1W	?
MERRILL TOWN see **OLD MERRILL**	KLAMATH CO.	T41S	R10E	S12
MERRIMAN	CURRY CO.	T36S	R14W	S16
MERRIMAN, ARTINECIA [ARTEMISIA?] see **MERRIMAN FAMILY**				
	JACKSON CO.	T38S	R2W	?
MERRIMAN, BABY GIRL	COLUMBIA CO.	T4N	R2W	S35
MERRIMAN FAMILY	JACKSON CO.	T38S	R2W	?
MERRIMAN, WILLIAM H. see **MERRIMAN FAMILY**				
	JACKSON CO.	T38S	R2W	?
MESCASKET see **BROWN**	KLAMATH CO.	T36S	R12E	S13
MESCHELLE, JENNIE	CLATSOP CO.	T6N	R10W	S15
MESERVEY FAMILY	CURRY CO.	T35S	R12W	S16
METHODIST see **HARTLEY**	JOSEPHINE CO.	T39S	R5W	S4
METHODIST see **JEFFERSON**	MARION CO.	T10S	R3W	S1
METHODIST CHURCH AT FARMINGTON	WASHINGTON CO.	T1S	R2W	?
METHODIST EPISCOPAL CHURCH see **LEBANON PIONEER**				
	LINN CO.	T12S	R2W	S11
METHODIST HILL	JEFFERSON CO.	T11S	R13E	S32
METHODIST MEETING HOUSE	WASHINGTON CO.	T1N	R2W	S21
METOLIUS see **METHODIST HILL**	JEFFERSON CO.	T11S	R13E	S32
METZ HILL see **GREEN VALLEY**	DOUGLAS CO.	T24S	R6W	S25
METZGER see **CRESCENT GROVE**	WASHINGTON CO.	T1S	R1W	S26

MEXICAN PETE	MALHEUR CO.	T34S	R41E	?
MEYERS FAMILY see **MYER FAMILY**	JACKSON CO.	T38S	R1E	S30
MICHAEL	LINN CO.	T14S	R3W	S26
MICHAEL D.L.C., ELIJAH see **MICHAEL**				
	LINN CO.	T14S	R3W	S26
MICHIGAN	SHERMAN CO.	T3S	R16E	S16
MICKELSON, EDITH see **MICKELSON FAMILY**				
	CLATSOP CO.	T8N	R7W	S11
MICKELSON FAMILY	CLATSOP CO.	T8N	R7W	S11
MIDDLE FORK	LANE CO.	T19S	R1E	S34
MIDDLE FORK see **MT. VERNON**	LANE CO.	T18S	R2W	S4
MIDDLE POINT	WALLOWA CO.	T4N	R43E	S30
MIDDLEGROVE see **HOWELL PRAIRIE**	MARION CO.	T7S	R2W	S4
MIDDLETON PIONEER	WASHINGTON CO.	T2S	R2W	S36
MILES D.L.C., JESSE see **HAVLIK PLACE**				
	COLUMBIA CO.	T3N	R2W	?
MILES D.L.C., JESSE see **ST. WENCESLAUS**				
	COLUMBIA CO.	T3N	R2W	S13
MILES, JESSE see **HAVLIK PLACE**	COLUMBIA CO.	T3N	R2W	?
MILITARY see **U.S. ARMY FORT STEVENS**				
	CLATSOP CO.	T8N	R10W	S8
MILITARY POST see **MODOC WARRIORS**				
	KLAMATH CO.	T33S	R7 1/2E	S23
MILL CITY see **FAIRVIEW**	LINN CO.	T9S	R3E	S34
MILL CREEK	CROOK CO.	T14S	R17E	S26
MILLER	LINN CO.	T10S	R2W	S1
MILLER	LINN CO.	T10S	R3W	S17
MILLER	LINN CO.	T13S	R4W	S4
MILLER	MALHEUR CO.	T13S	R42E	S21
MILLER	MARION CO.	T6S	R1E	S19
MILLER	WASCO CO.	T2S	R12E	S34
MILLER see **ARCADE**	WASHINGTON CO.	T2N	R3W	S14
MILLER see **BAILEY AND MILLER**	TILLAMOOK CO.	T1S	R9W	?
MILLER see **BLOSSER**	CLACKAMAS CO.	T4S	R1W	S36
MILLER see **MERRIMAN**	CURRY CO.	T36S	R14W	S16
MILLER, A. GROVER see **LIGHTNING CREEK**				
	WALLOWA CO.	T3N	R48E	S12
MILLER, CONRAD see **MILLER FAMILY**				
	COOS CO.	T29S	R12W	S33
MILLER-COON see **MILLER**	LINN CO.	T13S	R4W	S4
MILLER-COON FAMILIES see **MILLER**	LINN CO.	T13S	R4W	S4
MILLER D.L.C., AUGUSTUS F. see **SMITH, SERGEANT**				
	CURRY CO.	T41S	R13W	S7
MILLER D.L.C., ELIZABETH see **CRESWELL PIONEER**				
	LANE CO.	T19S	R3W	S21
MILLER D.L.C., RICHARD see **MILLER**				
	MARION CO.	T6S	R1E	S19
MILLER D.L.C., SILAS see **MILLER, SILAS**				
	POLK CO.	T7S	R5W	?
MILLER FAMILY	COOS CO.	T29S	R12W	S33
MILLER FAMILY	JACKSON CO.	T36S	R1E	S5

MILLER FAMILY	POLK CO.	T7S	R4W	S6
MILLER, FRANK	GILLIAM CO.	T5S	R24E	?
MILLER, HENRY see **JOHNSON PLACE, LOREN**				
	COLUMBIA CO.	T3N	R1W	?
MILLER HOME see **OTEY FAMILY**	DOUGLAS CO.	T26S	R6W	S1
MILLER, J. N. T. see **JACKSONVILLE**				
	JACKSON CO.	T37S	R2W	S29
MILLER, MR. see **FAULKNER, T. M.**	LINCOLN CO.	T15S	R10W	S1
MILLER, MRS. MARY see **MILLER**	LINN CO.	T10S	R2W	S1
MILLER, SILAS	POLK CO.	T7S	R5W	?
MILLER SR. D.L.C., GEORGE see **MILLER**				
	LINN CO.	T10S	R3W	S17
MILLER SR. D.L.C., ISAAC see **WILLAMETTE MEMORIAL PARK**				
	LINN CO.	T10S	R3W	S28
MILLER, WILLIAM M. see **MISSOURI FLAT**				
	JACKSON CO.	T38S	R4W	S6
MILLER'S PLACE, WALTON see **DAVIS'S PLACE, JIMMY**				
	CURRY CO.	?	?	?
MILLERSBURG see **MILLER**	LINN CO.	T10S	R3W	S17
MILLICAN	DESCHUTES CO.	T19S	R15E	S34
MILLIKIN see **MILLIKIN, CARL HAMILTON**				
	MALHEUR CO.	T21S	R46E	?
MILLIKIN, CARL HAMILTON	MALHEUR CO.	T21S	R46E	?
MILLIKIN, HANNA see **MILLIKIN, CARL HAMILTON**				
	MALHEUR CO.	T21S	R46E	?
MILLIKIN, JOHN S. see **MILLIKIN, CARL HAMILTON**				
	MALHEUR CO.	T21S	R46E	?
MILLIORN see **MILLIRON**	LANE CO.	T15S	R4W	S31
MILLIRON	LANE CO.	T15S	R4W	S31
MILLIRON D.L.C., JOHN see **MILLIRON**				
	LANE CO.	T15S	R4W	S31
MILLN HOUSE, RALPH see **INDIAN BURIAL**				
	CLACKAMAS CO.	T2S	R2E	S30
MILWAUKIE see **MILWAUKIE PIONEER**	CLACKAMAS CO.	T1S	R1E	S26
MILWAUKIE PIONEER	CLACKAMAS CO.	T1S	R1E	S26
MINAM	WALLOWA CO.	T2N	R41E	S19
MINERAL	BAKER CO.	T12S	R45E	S12
MINK see **MOEHNKE**	CLACKAMAS CO.	T3S	R3E	S31
MISSION [THE DALLES]	WASCO CO.	T1N	R13E	S4
MISSION BOTTOM see **WILLAMETTE MISSION**				
	MARION CO.	T6S	R3W	S3
MISSOURI FLAT	JACKSON CO.	T38S	R4W	S6
MIST	COLUMBIA CO.	T6N	R5W	S13
MITCHELL [NEW] see **MITCHELL, UPPER**				
	WHEELER CO.	T12S	R21E	S1
MITCHELL, ELSIE see **MITCHELL MONUMENT**				
	LAKE CO.	T36S	R16E	S19
MITCHELL, LOWER	WHEELER CO.	T11S	R21E	S35
MITCHELL MONUMENT	LAKE CO.	T36S	R16E	S19
MITCHELL, MRS. see **MITCHELL MONUMENT**				
	LAKE CO.	T36S	R16E	S19

MITCHELL, REV. ARCHIE see **MITCHELL MONUMENT**

	LAKE CO.	T36S	R16E	S19
MITCHELL, UPPER	WHEELER CO.	T12S	R21E	S1
MO-GHEN-KAS-KET see **BROWN**	KLAMATH CO.	T36S	R12E	S13
MOAR	MULTNOMAH CO.	T2N	R1W	S7

MODERN WOODMEN OF THE WORLD: EUGENE CAMP #583 see **RICHARDSON**

	LANE CO.	T17S	R5W	S4
MODOC WARRIORS	KLAMATH CO.	T33S	R7 1/2E	S23
MOEHNKE	CLACKAMAS CO.	T3S	R3E	S31
MOEHNKE, MICHAEL see **MOEHNKE**	CLACKAMAS CO.	T3S	R3E	S31

MOEK, G. F. see **GILBREATH-MOECK FAMILY**

	COLUMBIA CO.	T7N	R2W	S18

MOEK, LOUISE B. see **GILBREATH-MOECK.FAMILY**

	COLUMBIA CO.	T7N	R2W	S18

MOEK, M. J. see **GILBREATH-MOECK FAMILY**

	COLUMBIA CO.	T7N	R2W	S18
MOEN [?] see **MOON, JEFF E.**	WASCO CO.	T2N	R13E	S32

MOFFIT D.L.C., JOHN W. AND ORRILLA see **WALLUSKI ROAD**

	CLATSOP CO.	T8N	R9W	S34
MOFFITT BABY	MULTNOMAH CO.	T1N	R3E	S3

MOFFITT, DORIS LOGAN see **MOFFITT BABY**

	MULTNOMAH CO.	T1N	R3E	S3
MOFFITT MILL	HARNEY CO.	T19S	R34E	?

MOFFITT, STERLING L. see **MOFFITT BABY**

	MULTNOMAH CO.	T1N	R3E	S3
MOHAWK see **MARCOLA**	LANE CO.	T16S	R2W	S24
MOHAWK see **VALLEY VIEW**	LANE CO.	T17S	R2W	S3

MOHAWK COMMUNITY CHURCH see **VALLEY VIEW**

	LANE CO.	T17S	R2W	S3
MOHAWK LODGE see **MARCOLA**	LANE CO.	T16S	R2W	S24
MOLALLA MEMORIAL	CLACKAMAS CO.	T5S	R2E	S20

MOLALLA PRAIRIE see **MOLALLA MEMORIAL**

	CLACKAMAS CO.	T5S	R2E	S20
MOLLOY FAMILY see **MELOY FAMILY**	MULTNOMAH CO.	?	?	?
MONASTERY OF THE PRECIOUS BLOOD	MULTNOMAH CO.	T1S	R2E	S5
MONMOUTH see **FIR CREST**	POLK CO.	T9S	R4W	S6
MONROE	BENTON CO.	T14S	R5W	S28
MONTAGUE see **EIGHTMILE**	GILLIAM CO.	T1N	R22E	S5
MONTAQUE, C. J. see **G. W. W.**	CLACKAMAS CO.	T3S	R2E	S4
MONTAVILLA see **BRAINARD PIONEER**	MULTNOMAH CO.	T1N	R2E	S33

MONTEITH D.L.C., WALTER see **RIVERSIDE**

	LINN CO.	T11S	R4W	S12
MONTGOMERY	POLK CO.	T9S	R6W	S23
MONTGOMERY PLACE see **WEEVER**	CROOK CO.	T14S	R14E	S23
MONUMENT [NEW]	GRANT CO.	T9S	R27E	S1
MONUMENT [OLD]	GRANT CO.	T9S	R27E	S12
MOON CREEK	GRANT CO.	T13S	R29E	S20
MOON, ESTELLE see **MOON, JEFF E.**	WASCO CO.	T2N	R13E	S32
MOON, JEFF E.	WASCO CO.	T2N	R13E	S32
MOON, LEIF see **MOON, JEFF E.**	WASCO CO.	T2N	R13E	S32
MOORE	TILLAMOOK CO.	T1S	R10W	S5

MOORE see **SAWTELL FAMILY**	CLACKAMAS CO.	T5S	R2E	S30
MOORE D.L.C., JACOB J. see **ESCOBAR PIONEER**				
	MULTNOMAH CO.	T1S	R3E	S10
MOORE D.L.C., JACOB J. see **GRESHAM PIONEER**				
	MULTNOMAH CO.	T1S	R3E	S10
MOORE D.L.C., MICHAEL see **ROOD FAMILY**				
	WASHINGTON CO.	T1S	R2W	S6
MOORE, DR. FRANK see **TIPTON, MACE**				
	DOUGLAS CO.	T26S	R3W	S1
MOORE, MR. T. B. see **DURKEE**	BAKER CO.	T11S	R43E	S18
MOORE PROPERTY see **BELL FAMILY**	DOUGLAS CO.	T22S	R7W	S29
MOORES VALLEY	YAMHILL CO.	T3S	R5W	S9
MORAN	SHERMAN CO.	T2N	R16E	S22
MORDEN see **MORGAN FAMILY**	MULTNOMAH CO.	T1N	R1W	S15
MORGAN	MORROW CO.	T1N	R23E	S23
MORGAN, BABY	CLACKAMAS CO.	T3S	R8 1/2E	S25
MORGAN, DANIEL see **MORGAN, BABY**	CLACKAMAS CO.	T3S	R8 1/2E	S25
MORGAN FAMILY	MULTNOMAH CO.	T1N	R1W	S15
MORGAN, M. D. see **BABY [HAY CREEK]**				
	JEFFERSON CO.	T11S	R15E	S9
MORGAREIDGE FAMILY	YAMHILL CO.	T4S	R3W	S30
MORMON BASIN	MALHEUR CO.	T13S	R42E	?
MORRELL [?] see **EDDY, HARRIET**	CURRY CO.	T30S	R14W	?
MORRELL PLACE, H. E. see **EDDY, HARRIET**				
	CURRY CO.	T30S	R14W	?
MORRILL, HERB see **EDDY, HARRIET**	CURRY CO.	T30S	R14W	?
MORRILL RANCH, HERB	CURRY CO.	?	?	?
MORRIS see **MT. HOPE**	MARION CO.	T7S	R1W	S33
MORRIS FAMILY	COOS CO.	T31S	R12W	S12
MORRIS FAMILY	LINCOLN CO.	T7S	R11W	S3
MORRIS-BARKER FAMILIES see **BARKER-MORRIS FAMILIES**				
	COOS CO.	T27S	R12W	S14
MORRISON D.L.C., ROBERT see **CLATSOP PLAINS PIONEER**				
	CLATSOP CO.	T7N	R10W	S4
MORRISON, RILEY see **MOONVILLE**	JACKSON CO.	?	?	?
MORROW, HONORE WILSON see **RED HILL**				
	DOUGLAS CO.	T23S	R5W	S34
MORSE FAMILY	JACKSON CO.	T38S	R1E	S30
MORTON GRAVES	WASCO CO.	T1N	R12E	S10
MOSBY see **BRUMBAUGH**	LANE CO.	T21S	R2W	S18
MOSHBERGER see **BEAR CREEK**	CLACKAMAS CO.	T5S	R1E	S2
MOSIER	WASCO CO.	T2N	R11E	S1
MOSIER D.L.C., JONAH H. see **MOSIER PIONEER**				
	WASCO CO.	T2N	R11E	S1
MOSIER PIONEER	WASCO CO.	T2N	R11E	S1
MOTT, MOSES see **LOCKWOOD RANCH**	MALHEUR CO.	?	?	?
MOUND see **ALMA**	LANE CO.	T19S	R8W	S3

MOUNSE BURIALS see **MOUNTS FAMILY BURIALS**

	LANE CO.	T18S	R5W	S7
MT. ANGEL	MARION CO.	T6S	R1W	S3
MT. ANGEL ABBEY see **ST. BENEDICT**				
	MARION CO.	T6S	R1W	S11
MT. CALVARY CATHOLIC	LANE CO.	T18S	R3W	S7
MT. CALVARY CATHOLIC	MULTNOMAH CO.	T1S	R1E	S6
MT. CALVARY MEMORIAL PARK	KLAMATH CO.	T39S	R10E	S8
MT. CRAWFORD see **LONE FIR PIONEER**				
	MULTNOMAH CO.	T1S	R1E	S1
MT. ETNA see **ETNA**	POLK CO.	T7S	R4W	S7
MT. GLEN see **ACKLES**	UNION CO.	T2S	R38E	S21
MT. HOME	CLACKAMAS CO.	T4S	R4E	S19
MT. HOMES see **MT. HOME**	CLACKAMAS CO.	T4S	R4E	S19
MT. HOOD see **UPPER VALLEY**	HOOD RIVER CO.	T1N	R10E	S33
MT. HOOD COMMUNITY	HOOD RIVER CO.	T1N	R10E	S21
MT. HOOD FLAT see **OBRIST**	WASCO CO.	T1S	R12E	S2
MT. HOOD LOOP see **FIR HILL**	CLACKAMAS CO.	T2S	R4E	S14
MT. HOOD MEMORIAL see **GARDEN OF REVERENCE**				
	CLACKAMAS CO.	T1S	R4E	S28
MT. HOPE	BAKER CO.	T9S	R40E	S21
MT. HOPE	MARION CO.	T7S	R1W	S33
MT. JEFFERSON MEMORIAL PARK	JEFFERSON CO.	T11S	R14E	S6
MT. JUNE LUMBER COMPANY see **EMIGRANT**				
	LANE CO.	T18S	R2W	S3
MT. LAKI	KLAMATH CO.	T40S	R9E	S2
MT. MORIAH see **POTTER'S**	GILLIAM CO.	T1S	R20E	S29
MT. OLIVE BAPTIST see **MT. OLIVE CEMETERY OF LAUREL**				
	WASHINGTON CO.	T2S	R3W	S12
MT. OLIVE CEMETERY OF LAUREL	WASHINGTON CO.	T2S	R3W	S12
MT. OLIVE LUTHERAN	WASHINGTON CO.	T1S	R4W	S23
MT. PLEASANT	LINN CO.	T9S	R1E	S30
MT. PLEASANT	UNION CO.	T2N	R40E	S15
MT. PLEASANT see **PIKE AND I.O.O.F.**				
	YAMHILL CO.	T2S	R5W	S25
MT. SCOTT see **LINCOLN MEMORIAL PARK**				
	MULTNOMAH CO.	T1S	R2E	S22
MT. SCOTT PARK see **LINCOLN MEMORIAL PARK**				
	CLACKAMAS CO.	T1S	R2E	S22
MT. TABOR VILLA see **BRAINARD PIONEER**				
	MULTNOMAH CO.	T1N	R2E	S33
MT. UNION	BENTON CO.	T12S	R5W	S7
MT. VERNON	LANE CO.	T18S	R2W	S4
	MULTNOMAH CO.	T1N	R3E	S35
MT. VIEW BASELINE ROAD see **MOUNTAIN VIEW-STARK PIONEER**				
	MULTNOMAH CO.	T1N	R3E	S35
MT. VIEW-CORBETT see **MOUNTAIN VIEW-CORBETT PIONEER**				
	MULTNOMAH CO.	T1S	R4E	S3

MT. VIEW-STARK see **MOUNTAIN VIEW-STARK PIONEER**				
	MULTNOMAH CO.	T1N	R3E	S35
MT. ZION	CLACKAMAS CO.	T3S	R4E	S22
MT. ZION see **JONES PIONEER**	MULTNOMAH CO.	T1S	R1E	S6
MT. ZION see **ZION MEMORIAL PARK**	CLACKAMAS CO.	T3S	R1E	S34
MOUNT VIEW see **MOUNTAIN VIEW**	CLACKAMAS CO.	T3S	R2E	S5
MOUNT VIEW see **MOUNTAIN VIEW CREMATORIUM**				
	DOUGLAS CO.	T29S	R5W	S28
MOUNT VIEW see **MOUNTAIN VIEW I.O.O.F. AND MAUSLEUM**				
	JACKSON CO.	T39S	R1E	S15
MOUNTAIN BELL see **PIKE AND I.O.O.F.**				
	YAMHILL CO.	T2S	R5W	S25
MOUNTAIN HOME	LINN CO.	T13S	R1W	S20
MOUNTAIN HOME see **MT. HOME**	CLACKAMAS CO.	T4S	R4E	S19
MOUNTAIN REST STAGE STATION see **GRANT COUNTY POOR FARM**				
	GRANT CO.	T12S	R30E	S12
MOUNTAIN TOP see **MOUNTIANSIDE**	WASHINGTON CO.	T2S	R2W	S16
MOUNTAIN VALLEY see **GURDANE**	UMATILLA CO.	T3S	R30E	S32
MOUNTAIN VIEW	CLACKAMAS CO.	T3S	R2E	S5
MOUNTAIN VIEW	COLUMBIA CO.	T6N	R3W	S2
MOUNTAIN VIEW	WASHINGTON CO.	T3N	R2W	S32
MOUNTAIN VIEW see **GREEN MOUNTAIN**				
	MARION CO.	T7S	R1E	S26
MOUNTAIN VIEW see **HIGHLAND**	POLK CO.	T7S	R3W	S17
MOUNTAIN VIEW see **MT. UNION**	BENTON CO.	T12S	R5W	S7
MOUNTAIN VIEW see **SEARS**	LANE CO.	T20S	R3W	S35
MOUNTAIN VIEW AND RESTHAVEN MAUSOLEUM				
	JACKSON CO.	T39S	R1E	S10
MOUNTAIN VIEW-CORBETT PIONEER	MULTNOMAH CO.	T1S	R4E	S3
MOUNTAIN VIEW CREMATORIUM	DOUGLAS CO.	T29S	R5W	S28
MOUNTAIN VIEW I.O.O.F. AND MAUSOLEUM				
	JACKSON CO.	T39S	R1E	S15
MOUNTAIN VIEW MEMORIAL	HOOD RIVER CO.	T2N	R10E	S2
MOUNTAIN VIEW MEMORIAL GARDENS	WASHINGTON CO.	T1N	R4W	S35
MOUNTAIN VIEW-STARK PIONEER	MULTNOMAH CO.	T1N	R3E	S35
MOUNTAINDALE see **RAFFETY**	WASHINGTON CO.	T2N	R3W	S27
MOUNTAINSIDE	WASHINGTON CO.	T2S	R2W	S16
MOUNTE *[Sic]* BURIALS see **MOUNTS FAMILY BURIALS**				
	LANE CO.	T18S	R5W	S7
MOUNTE *[Sic]* D.L.C., HENRY R. see **MOUNTS FAMILY BURIALS**				
	LANE CO.	T18S	R5W	S7
MOUNTS BURIALS see **MOUNTS FAMILY BURIALS**				
	LANE CO.	T18S	R5W	S7
MOUNTS FAMILY BURIALS	LANE CO.	T18S	R5W	S7
MOXLEY	LANE CO.	T19S	R4W	S12
MUD CREEK see **FORD**	UMATILLA CO.	T6N	R35E	S23
MUDDY see **HOWELL PRAIRIE**	MARION CO.	T7S	R2W	S4
MUDDY CREEK see **HARRIS**	LINN CO.	T15S	R4W	S24

MULE CREEK	CURRY CO.	T33S	R10W	S16
MULHOLLAND, EDWARD see **MULHOLLAND FAMILY**				
	LANE CO.	T19S	R2W	S4
MULHOLLAND, EMILY see **McCANN FAMILY**				
	WASHINGTON CO.	T1S	R4W	S32
MULHOLLAND FAMILY	LANE CO.	T19S	R2W	S4
MULHOLLAND, JOHN see **McCANN FAMILY**				
	WASHINGTON CO.	T1S	R4W	S32
MULHOLLAND, JOHN see **MULHOLLAND FAMILY**				
	LANE CO.	T19S	R2W	S4
MULHOLLAND, MARGARET see **MULHOLLAND FAMILY**				
	LANE CO.	T19S	R2W	S4
MULHOLLAND, MARGARET [INFANT] see **MULHOLLAND FAMILY**				
	LANE CO.	T19S	R2W	S4
MULHOLLAND, MARTHA see **MULHOLLAND FAMILY**				
	LANE CO.	T19S	R2W	S4
MULHOLLAND, MARY see **MULHOLLAND FAMILY**				
	LANE CO.	T19S	R2W	S4
MULHOLLAND SR. D.L.C., EDWARD see **MULHOLLAND FAMILY**				
	LANE CO.	T19S	R2W	S4
MULHOLLAND, THOMAS see **MULHOLLAND FAMILY**				
	LANE CO.	T19S	R2W	S4
MULKEY	LANE CO.	T18S	R4W	S2
MULKEY	LINCOLN CO.	T11S	R8W	S26
MULKEY D.L.C., WESLEY see **PURDIN FAMILY**				
	WASHINGTON CO.	T1N	R4W	S25
MULLALLA *[Sic]* PRAIRIE see **MOLALLA MEMORIAL**				
	CLACKAMAS CO.	T5S	R2E	S20
MULLER	HARNEY CO.	T20S	R34E	S3
MULLINS, MARTHA see **BECKER RANCH, JIM**				
	MALHEUR CO.	T18S	R41E	S27
MULLINS, MARY JANE WESTFALL see **BECKER RANCH, JIM**				
	MALHEUR CO.	T18S	R41E	S27
MULTNOMAH HOSPITAL	MULTNOMAH CO.	T1S	R1E	S9
MULTNOMAH PARK see **MULTNOMAH PARK PIONEER**				
	MULTNOMAH CO.	T1S	R2E	S17
MULTNOMAH PARK PIONEER	MULTNOMAH CO.	T1S	R2E	S17
MUNSEY, COLONEL	CURRY CO.	T37S	R13W	?
MUNSON	TILLAMOOK CO.	T2S	R9W	?
MURPHY FAMILY	DOUGLAS CO.	?	?	?
MURPHY FAMILY see **HOWELL PRAIRIE**				
	MARION CO.	T7S	R2W	S4
MURPHY, MONSIGNOR GEORGE A. see **RANGE [NEW]**				
	GRANT CO.	T8S	R31E	S17
MURPHY PLACE see **MURPHY FAMILY**	DOUGLAS CO.	?	?	?
MURPHY RANCH see **MONUMENT [OLD]**	GRANT CO.	T9S	R27E	S12
MURPHY-HOWELL FAMILIES see **HOWELL PRAIRIE**				
	MARION CO.	T7S	R2W	S4

MURRAY see **MURRY**	DOUGLAS CO.	T29S	R8W	S18
MURRAY D.L.C., SELDON see **CHINESE [LONE FIR]**				
	MULTNOMAH CO.	T1S	R1E	S2
MURRAY FAMILY	YAMHILL CO.	T4S	R5W	S32
MURRAY HILL	COLUMBIA CO.	T7N	R4W	S17
MURRY	DOUGLAS CO.	T29S	R8W	S18
MURRY, CHARLEY see **MURRAY FAMILY**				
	YAMHILL CO.	T4S	R5W	S32
MURRY D.L.C., SELDON see **LONE FIR PIONEER**				
	MULTNOMAH CO.	T1S	R1E	S1
MURRY D.L.C., SELDON see **MASONIC [LONE FIR]**				
	MULTNOMAH CO.	T1S	R1E	S1
MUSLIM see **ISLAMIC CEMETERY OF OREGON**				
	BENTON CO.	T12S	R5W	S5
MUSSELL, JACOB see **LOWER SUCCOR CREEK**				
	MALHEUR CO.	T26S	R46E	S22
MUTE SCHOOL	MARION CO.	T8S	R2W	?
MYER D.L.C., NATHANIEL see **MORSE FAMILY**				
	JACKSON CO.	T38S	R1E	S30
MYER D.L.C., WILLIAM C. see **MYER FAMILY**				
	JACKSON CO.	T38S	R1E	S30
MYER FAMILY	JACKSON CO.	T38S	R1E	S30
MYNOTT D.L.C., CARRICK S. see **QUINES CREEK**				
	DOUGLAS CO.	T32S	R5W	S15
MYRICK see **GERMAN LUTHERAN**	UMATILLA CO.	T4N	R33E	S29
MYRICK STATION see **GERMAN LUTHERAN**				
	UMATILLA CO.	T4N	R33E	S29
MYRTLE CREEK	COOS CO.	T30S	R11W	S16
MYRTLE CREEK PIONEER	DOUGLAS CO.	T29S	R5W	S28
MYRTLE CREST MEMORIAL GARDENS	COOS CO.	T28S	R12W	S7
MYRTLE POINT	COOS CO.	T29S	R12W	S15
N. P. DENTAL COLLEGE see **NORTH PACIFIC DENTAL COLLEGE**				
	MULTNOMAH CO.	T1N	R1E	S35
NARROWS	HARNEY CO.	T26S	R30E	S26
NARROWS see **SUNSET VALLEY**	HARNEY CO.	T25S	R31E	S27
NASHVILLE	LINCOLN CO.	T10S	R8W	S36
NATIONAL VETERANS ADMINISTRATION				
	JACKSON CO.	T36S	R1W	S2
NAVE see **LACOMB**	LINN CO.	T11S	R1E	S31
NAVY MONUMENT	CURRY CO.	UNSURVEYED		
NAYLOR see **FOREST VIEW MEMORIAL GARDENS**				
	WASHINGTON CO.	T1N	R4W	S36
NEABECK	WASCO CO.	T1N	R15E	S20
NEAL	COOS CO.	T30S	R12W	S15
NEAL FAMILY see **PINE GROVE BUTTE**				
	HOOD RIVER CO.	T2N	R10E	S13
NEALLY FAMILY see **HART-RIGGS FAMILY**				
	POLK CO.	T8S	R6W	S25

NEALY D.L.C., SAMUEL see **NEALY FAMILY**

	POLK CO.	T9S	R5W	?

NEALY FAMILY POLK CO. T9S R5W ?

NEALY FAMILY see **CHAMBERLIN FAMILY**

	POLK CO.	T9S	R5W	S24

NECANICUM POST OFFICE see **AHLERS, DORTHEA**

	CLATSOP CO.	T5N	R9W	S22

NEEDY see **ZION MENNONTE** CLACKAMAS CO. T4S R1E S31

NEER see **NEER CITY** COLUMBIA CO. T6N R2W S2

NEER, CALEB see **MASONIC [ST. HELENS]**

	COLUMBIA CO.	T5N	R1W	S33

NEER CITY COLUMBIA CO. T6N R2W S2

NEER D.L.C., ABRAHAM see **MASONIC [ST. HELENS]**

	COLUMBIA CO.	T5N	R1W	S33

NEER FAMILY see **MASONIC [ST. HELENS]**

	COLUMBIA CO.	T5N	R1W	S33

NEET see **FALL CREEK** LANE CO. T18S R1W S33

NEHALEM AMERICAN LEGION see **AMERICAN LEGION POST #126**

	TILLAMOOK CO.	T3N	R10W	S28

NEHALEM V. F. W. see **AMERICAN LEGION POST #126**

	TILLAMOOK CO.	T3N	R10W	S28

NELOY FAMILY see **MELOY FAMILY** MULTNOMAH CO. ? ? ?

NELSON, AMELIA ANN see **NELSON FAMILY**

	COOS CO.	T28S	R12W	S32

NELSON, CORA ALICE YAMHILL CO. T3S R3W S11

NELSON CREEK LANE CO. T17S R8W S14

NELSON D.L.C., JOSIAH C. see **NELSON, CORA ALICE**

	YAMHILL CO.	T3S	R3W	S11

NELSON D.L.C., SAMUEL see **MONASTERY OF THE PRECIOUS BLOOD**

	MULTNOMAH CO.	T1S	R2E	S5

NELSON FAMILY COOS CO. T28S R12W S32

NELSON, FRANK A. see **NELSON FAMILY**

	COOS CO.	T28S	R12W	S32

NELSON, JAMES see **NEWSOM CAMPGROUND**

	MARION CO.	T6S	R1W	S19

NELSON, JOSIAH C. see **NELSON, CORA ALICE**

	YAMHILL CO.	T3S	R3W	S11

NESMITH FAMILY POLK CO. T7S R4W S30

NESMITH PARK see **NESMITH FAMILY** POLK CO. T7S R4W S30

NESTUCCA VALLEY see **NESTUCCA VETERANS OF FOREIGN WARS-ODD FELLOWS**

	TILLAMOOK CO.	T4S	R10W	S14

NESTUCCA V.F.W.-I.O.O.F. see **NESTUCCA VETERANS OF FOREIGN WARS-ODD FELLOWS**

	TILLAMOOK CO.	T4S	R10W	S14

NESTUCCA VETERANS OF FOREIGN WARS-ODD FELLOWS

	TILLAMOOK CO.	T4S	R10W	S14

NEVEH SHOLOM see **AHAVAI SHOLOM** MULTNOMAH CO. T1S R1E S27

NEVEH ZEDEK-ROSE CITY LODGE WASHINGTON CO. T1S R1W S12

NEVI SHOLOM see **AHAVAI SHOLOM** MULTNOMAH CO. T1S R1E S27

NEW CAMP see **PAIUTE [NEW]**	HARNEY CO.	T23S	R30E	S1
NEW CITY see **SUNSET HILLS**	UMATILLA CO.	T5N	R28E	S19
NEW ERA see **ST. JOHANN**	CLACKAMAS CO.	T3S	R1E	S36
NEW ERA CATHOLIC see **ST. PATRICK'S**				
	CLACKAMAS CO.	T3S	R1E	S23
NEW HOME see **WALDPORT MEMORIAL**	LINCOLN CO.	T13S	R11W	S30
NEW JEWISH see **BETH ISRAEL [NEW]**				
	MULTNOMAH CO.	T1S	R1E	S21
NEW MIDDLE FORK see **MT. VERNON**	LANE CO.	T18S	R2W	S4
NEW MILTON see **I.O.O.F. [MILTON-FREEWATER]**				
	UMATILLA CO.	T5N	R35E	S12
NEW PINE CREEK	LAKE CO.	T41S	R21E	S19
NEW SMITH	POLK CO.	T9S	R5W	S1
NEWBY D.L.C., WILLIAM T. AND SARAH J. see **McMINNVILLE [OLD]**				
	YAMHILL CO.	T4S	R4W	S21
NEWELL see **HIGHLAND**	YAMHILL CO.	T5S	R6W	S5
NEWELL D.L.C., ROBERT see **NEWELL, KITTY**				
	MARION CO.	T4S	R2W	S1
NEWELL, KITTY	MARION CO.	T4S	R2W	S1
NEWSOM CAMPGROUND	MARION CO.	T6S	R1W	S19
NEWSOM, DAVID see **NEWSOM CAMPGROUND**				
	MARION CO.	T6S	R1W	S19
NEWSOM, DAVID see **OYSTERVILLE**	LINCOLN CO.	T11S	R11W	S34
NEWSOM, POLLY see **NEWSOM CAMPGROUND**				
	MARION CO.	T6S	R1W	S19
NEWSOME see **HOWELL PRAIRIE**	MARION CO.	T7S	R2W	S4
NEWSOME CREEK see **KNOX FAMILY, E. B.**				
	CROOK CO.	T17S	R19E	S8
NEWTON see **MT. UNION**	BENTON CO.	T12S	R5W	S7
NEWTON D.L.C., ABIATHAR see **ISLAMIC CEMETERY OF OREGON**				
	BENTON CO.	T12S	R5W	S5
NEXON, BIRGETTA see **BOOTH FAMILY**				
	WASHINGTON CO.	T1S	R5W	S25
NEZ PERCE see **CHIEF JOSEPH MONUMENT**				
	WALLOWA CO.	T3S	R45E	S5
NIBLER, WILLIAM J.	BENTON CO.	?	?	?
NIBLEY	UNION CO.	T3S	R39E	S1
NICHOLS	DOUGLAS CO.	T28S	R6W	S20
NICHOLS, BESSIE	WALLOWA CO.	T5N	R42E	S22
NICHOLS D.L.C., JOHN M. see **NICHOLS FAMILY**				
	JACKSON CO.	T35S	R1W	S25
NICHOLS FAMILY	JACKSON CO.	T35S	R1W	S25
NICHOLS, M. LEONA see **QUINN, MARY WHELAN**				
	MULTNOMAH CO.	T1N	R1E	S36
NICKELS FAMILY see **WESTSIDE**	LAKE CO.	T40S	R19E	S6
NICOLSON see **NICOSON**	WALLOWA CO.	T5N	R44E	S8
NICOSON	WALLOWA CO.	T5N	R44E	S8

NIEMI, BABY see **SADDLE MOUNTAIN ROAD**				
	CLATSOP CO.	T6N	R8W	?
NO NAME see **OLD BROOKINGS**	CURRY CO.	T41S	R13W	S5
NOAH	DOUGLAS CO.	T29S	R8W	S7
NOAH FAMILY see **NOAH**	DOUGLAS CO.	T29S	R8W	S7
NOAH, MR.	COOS CO.	T30S	R11W	S9
NOBLE	YAMHILL CO.	T3S	R3W	S3
NOBLE see **HALL**	KLAMATH CO.	T39S	R14E	S32
NOBLE D.L.C., HENRY see **NOBLE**	YAMHILL CO.	T3S	R3W	S3
NOEL FAMILY	DOUGLAS CO.	T21S	R11W	S3
NOFOG	DOUGLAS CO.	T28S	R3W	?
NOKES, R. GREGORY see **CHINESE MINERS MASSACRE**				
	WALLOWA CO.	T4N	R49E	UNS
NOLAN see **NOLIN**	UMATILLA CO.	T2N	R30E	S6
NOLAND JR. D.L.C., HENRY see **POOR FARM**				
	WASHINGTON CO.	T1S	R2W	S8
NOLIN	UMATILLA CO.	T2N	R30E	S6
NONPAREIL see **FAIR OAKS**	DOUGLAS CO.	T25S	R4W	S7
NORATON see **YOUNG**	LANE CO.	T15S	R4W	S7
NORMAN'S HILL	CLATSOP CO.	T7N	?	?
NORMAN'S HOME, LEX see **DUNKIN, GEORGE**				
	CLATSOP CO.	T7N	R8W	?
NORTH see **DRAIN [NORTH]**	DOUGLAS CO.	T22S	R5W	S8
NORTH BELLEVUE see **YOCOM**	YAMHILL CO.	T5S	R5W	S20
NORTH CEMETERY OF CLEAR CREEK	COLUMBIA CO.	T4N	R5W	S27
NORTH FORK	DOUGLAS CO.	T20S	R10W	S31
NORTH FORK see **HARING PIONEER**	LANE CO.	T18S	R11W	S7
NORTH HOWELL see **WOODWORTH CHILDREN**				
	MARION CO.	T7S	R2W	?
NORTH PACIFIC DENTAL COLLEGE	MULTNOMAH CO.	T1N	R1E	S35
NORTH PALESTINE see **PALESTINE**	BENTON CO.	T10S	R4W	S22
NORTH PLAINS CATHOLIC see **ST. EDWARD'S CATHOLIC [NEW]**				
	WASHINGTON CO.	T2N	R2W	S31
NORTH PLAINS CATHOLIC see **ST. EDWARD'S CATHOLIC [OLD]**				
	WASHINGTON CO.	T1N	R3W	S1
NORTH PLAINS see **ST. EDWARD'S CATHOLIC [NEW]**				
	WASHINGTON CO.	T2N	R2W	S31
NORTH PLAINS see **ST. EDWARD'S CATHOLIC [OLD]**				
	WASHINGTON CO.	T1N	R3W	S1
NORTH POWDER [NEW]	UNION CO.	T6S	R39E	S22
NORTH POWDER [OLD]	UNION CO.	T6S	R39E	?
NORTH SALEM BAPTIST CHURCH see **HAYESVILLE**				
	MARION CO.	T7S	R3W	S12
NORTH YAMHILL see **YAMHILL-CARLTON**				
	YAMHILL CO.	T3S	R4W	S10
NORTHWEST MEMORIAL GARDENS see **SKYLINE MEMORIAL GARDENS**				
	MULTNOMAH CO.	T1N	R1W	S23
NORTONS	LINCOLN CO.	T10S	R8W	S32

NORWAY	COOS CO.	T28S	R12W	S32
NORWAY [BARLOW] see **ZOAR LUTHERAN [BARLOW ROAD]**				
	CLACKAMAS CO.	T4S	R1E	S7
NORWEGIAN see **MOUNTAIN HOME**	LINN CO.	T13S	R1W	S20
NORWEGIAN see **VALLEY VIEW**	MARION CO.	T6S	R1W	S36
NORWEGIAN [BARLOW] see **ZOAR LUTHERAN [BARLOW ROAD]**				
	CLACKAMAS CO.	T4S	R1E	S7
NORWEGIAN [CANBY] see **ZOAR LUTHERAN [BARLOW ROAD]**				
	CLACKAMAS CO.	T4S	R1E	S7
NORWEGIAN LUTHERAN see **ZOAR LUTHERAN [BARLOW ROAD]**				
	CLACKAMAS CO.	T4S	R1E	S7
NOTI see **SAILOR PIONEER**	LANE CO.	T17S	R6W	S28
NUSOM *[Sic]* see **NEWSOM CAMPGROUND**				
	MARION CO.	T6S	R1W	S19
NYE	UMATILLA CO.	T1S	R31E	S19
NYE see **LIBERTY [NEW]**	LINN CO.	T13S	R1W	S26
NYE D.L.C., ADAM see **LIBERTY [NEW]**				
	LINN CO.	T13S	R1W	S26
NYE D.L.C., JACOB see **LIBERTY [OLD]**				
	LINN CO.	T13S	R1W	S23
NYE FAMILY	JACKSON CO.	T33S	R2E	S10
NYE-LIBERTY see **LIBERTY [NEW]**	LINN CO.	T13S	R1W	S26
NYSSA	MALHEUR CO.	T19S	R46E	S26
NYSSA MUNICIPAL see **NYSSA**	MALHEUR CO.	T19S	R46E	S26
O.F.M.I. see **OREGON STATE INSTITUTION FOR THE FEEBLE MINDED**				
	MARION CO.	T8S	R3W	S2
O.S.H. see **ASYLUM**	MARION CO.	T7S	R3W	S25
O.S.I.A. see **ASYLUM**	MARION CO.	T7S	R3W	S25
O.S.P. see **PENITENTIARY [NEW]**	MARION CO.	T7S	R3W	S25
O'HARA FAMILY	TILLAMOOK CO.	T2S	R10W	S5
O'HARA HOMESTEAD see **O'HARA FAMILY**				
	TILLAMOOK CO.	T2S	R10W	S5
O'KEEFE RANCH see **ROUSCOE, MRS. DAVE**				
	LAKE CO.	T39S	R24E	S16
OAK CREEK	DOUGLAS CO.	T26S	R4W	S29
OAK FLATS	CURRY CO.	T35S	R11W	S20
OAK GROVE	HOOD RIVER CO.	T2N	R10E	?
OAK GROVE	YAMHILL CO.	T2S	R3W	S21
OAK GROVE see **ETNA**	POLK CO.	T7S	R4W	S7
OAK GROVE see **MOSIER PIONEER**	WASCO CO.	T2N	R11E	S1
OAK GROVE see **OAK FLATS**	CURRY CO.	T35S	R11W	S20
OAK HILL	LANE CO.	T17S	R5W	S25
OAK HILL see **ZOAR LUTHERAN [BARLOW ROAD]**				
	CLACKAMAS CO.	T4S	R1E	S7
OAK KNOLL	WASHINGTON CO.	T1S	R4W	S2
OAK LAWN MEMORIAL PARK	BENTON CO.	T12S	R5W	S10
OAK LAWN MEMORIAL PARK see **BENTON**				
	BENTON CO.	T12S	R5W	S10

OAK RIDGE	BENTON CO.	T13S	R5W	S6
OAKHURST see **HUBBARD**	POLK CO.	T8S	R6W	S28
OAKLAND see **CEDAR HILL**	DOUGLAS CO.	T25S	R5W	S5
OAKLAND CITY see **OLD TOWN OAKLAND**				
	DOUGLAS CO.	T24S	R5W	S33
OAKLAWN MEMORIAL PARK see **BENTON**				
	BENTON CO.	T12S	R5W	S10
OAKRIDGE see **FOREST VALE MEMORIAL PARK**				
	LANE CO.	T21S	R3E	S10
OAKRIDGE see **OAKLAWN MEMORIAL PARK**				
	BENTON CO.	T12S	R5W	S10
OAKRIDGE PRESBYTERIAN CHURCH see **OAK RIDGE**				
	BENTON CO.	T13S	R5W	S6
OAKVILLE	LINN CO.	T12S	R4W	S16
OASIS LODGE #41 I.O.O.F. see **REST LAWN MEMORIAL PARK**				
	LANE CO.	T15S	R5W	S34
OBRIST	WASCO CO.	T1S	R12E	S2
OBSERVER see **WILCOX-OBSERVER**	SHERMAN CO.	T5S	R17E	S10
OBSERVER FARM see **WILCOX-OBSERVER**				
	SHERMAN CO.	T5S	R17E	S10
OCEAN VIEW	CLATSOP CO.	T8N	R10W	S28
OCEAN VIEW	CURRY CO.	T30S	R14W	S21
OCEAN VIEW MEMORIAL GARDENS	COOS CO.	T25S	R13W	S20
OCHOCO see **HOWARD**	CROOK CO.	T14S	R19E	S8
OCUMPAUGH, L. R. see **RUTERS FAMILY**				
	DOUGLAS CO.	T24S	R7W	?
ODD FELLOWS see **EUGENE PIONEER**	LANE CO.	T17S	R3W	S32
ODD FELLOWS see **MOLALLA MEMORIAL**				
	CLACKAMAS CO.	T5S	R2E	S20
ODD FELLOWS CEMETERY OF CORVALLIS see **I.O.O.F. [CORVALLIS]**				
	BENTON CO.	T11S	R5W	S28
ODD FELLOWS [DAYTON] see **I.O.O.F. [DAYTON]**				
	YAMHILL CO.	T4S	R3W	S21
ODELL see **EBENEZER CHAPEL**	YAMHILL CO.	T5S	R3W	S7
ODELL BROTHERS	WALLOWA CO.	T3S	R45E	?
ODELL D.L.C., JOHN see **EBENEZER CHAPEL**				
	YAMHILL CO.	T5S	R3W	S7
ODERMATT, FATHER ADELHELM see **ST. BENEDICT**				
	MARION CO.	T6S	R1W	S11
OFFENBACHER, LANCE see **UNIONTOWN**				
	JACKSON CO.	T38S	R3W	S34
OGDEN, DENNIS RAY	POLK CO.	T8S	R5W	S28
OGLE FAMILY	UMATILLA CO.	?	?	?
OJA, SOPHIA see **MICKELSON FAMILY**				
	CLATSOP CO.	T8N	R7W	S11
OLD AGENCY	UMATILLA CO.	T2N	R33E	S9
OLD BELIEVER CHURCH	MARION CO.	T5S	R1W	S30

OLD BETH ISRAEL see **BETH ISRAEL [OLD]**				
	MULTNOMAH CO.	T1S	R1E	S10
OLD BROOKINGS	CURRY CO.	T41S	R13W	S5
OLD CAMP see **PAIUTE [OLD]**	HARNEY CO.	T23S	R30E	S14
OLD CAMP WARNER	LAKE CO.	T36S	R25E	S24
OLD CANBY see **BAKER PRAIRIE**	CLACKAMAS CO.	T3S	R1E	S33
OLD CEMETERY see **OLD BROOKINGS**	CURRY CO.	T41S	R13W	S5
OLD CEMETERY CITY OF PORTLAND see **CITY CEMETERY #3**				
	MULTNOMAH CO.	T1S	R1E	S10
OLD CITY see **FALLS CITY**	POLK CO.	T8S	R6W	S16
OLD CITY see **I.O.O.F. [MILTON]**	UMATILLA CO.	T5N	R35E	S11
OLD CITY see **MOUNTAIN VIEW**	CLACKAMAS CO.	T3S	R2E	S5
OLD COLONY	MARION CO.	T4S	R1W	S12
OLD COLUMBIA see **COLUMBIAN**	MULTNOMAH CO.	T1N	R1E	S10
OLD COMMUNITY see **UNION**	WASHINGTON CO.	T1N	R1W	S29
OLD COUNTY ROAD see **EMPIRE**	COOS CO.	T25S	R13W	S17
OLD DRIFT CREEK see **HEATER**	MARION CO.	T8S	R1E	S8
OLD EDDY see **EDDY**	LINCOLN CO.	T11S	R9W	S4
OLD EMPIRE see **EMPIRE**	COOS CO.	T25S	R13W	S17
OLD FOREST GROVE see **MOUNTAIN VIEW MEMORIAL GARDENS**				
	WASHINGTON CO.	T1N	R4W	S35
OLD FORT see **CAMP POLK**	DESCHUTES CO.	T14S	R10E	S27
OLD HALFWAY HOUSE	UMATILLA CO.	T2S	R33E	?
OLD HEBREW see **BETH ISRAEL [OLD]**				
	MULTNOMAH CO.	T1S	R1E	S10
OLD INDIAN see **CROXTON PIONEER MEMORIAL PARK**				
	JOSEPHINE CO.	T36S	R5W	S8
OLD LEBANON see **LEBANON PIONEER**	LINN CO.	T12S	R2W	S11
OLD LORELLA see **HALL**	KLAMATH CO.	T39S	R14E	S32
OLD MASONIC see **CHAMPOEG**	MARION CO.	T4S	R2W	S12
OLD MASONIC see **MASONIC [ST. HELENS]**				
	COLUMBIA CO.	T5N	R1W	S33
OLD MERRILL	KLAMATH CO.	T41S	R10E	S12
OLD METHODIST see **LEBANON PIONEER**				
	LINN CO.	T12S	R2W	S11
OLD MISSION see **ST. PAUL'S [OLD]**				
	MARION CO.	T4S	R2W	S19
OLD MIST see **UNITED BRETHREN**	COLUMBIA CO.	T6N	R5W	S36
OLD MOSIER see **MOSIER PIONEER**	WASCO CO.	T2N	R11E	S1
OLD MYRTLE POINT see **MYRTLE POINT**				
	COOS CO.	T29S	R12W	S15
OLD OREGON CITY see **MOUNTAIN VIEW**				
	CLACKAMAS CO.	T3S	R2E	S5
OLD PIKE see **PIKE AND I.O.O.F.**	YAMHILL CO.	T2S	R5W	S25
OLD PIONEER see **CULP CREEK**	LANE CO.	T21S	R1W	S33
OLD PIONEER see **DALLAS**	POLK CO.	T8S	R5W	S5
OLD PIONEER see **FRANKTON**	HOOD RIVER CO.	T3N	R10E	S27
OLD PIONEER see **GRESHAM PIONEER**	MULTNOMAH CO.	T1S	R3E	S10

```
OLD PIONEER see I.O.O.F. [COOS BAY]
                                COOS CO.            T25S    R13W         S34
OLD PIONEER see I.O.O.F. [MILTON]
                                UMATILLA CO.        T5N     R35E         S11
OLD REASE see BREESE            DESCHUTES CO.       T21S    R11E         S29
OLD RED BARN see ARCHER         COOS CO.            T26S    R13W         S1
OLD RICE PLACE see RICE FAMILY  DOUGLAS CO.         T24S    R5W          S5
OLD RITCHEY RANCH see RITCHEY FAMILY
                                DOUGLAS CO.         T21S    R5W          S31
OLD SKEELS PLACE see CHILDS     LINN CO.            T12S    R2W          S36
OLD SOLDIERS see ROSEBURG NATIONAL
                                DOUGLAS CO.         T27S    R6W          S14
OLD SPRINGFIELD see PIONEER MEMORIAL CEMETERY PARK
                                LANE CO.            T17S    R3W          S35
OLD TAYLOR HOUSE see COMCOMLY'S GRAVE
                                CLATSOP CO.         T8N     R9W          S8
OLD THIELE RANCH see THIELE FAMILY
                                DOUGLAS CO.         T24S    R5W          S4
OLD TOWN OAKLAND                DOUGLAS CO.         T24S    R5W          S33
OLD TULELAKE see OLD MERRILL    KLAMATH CO.         T41S    R10E         S12
OLD TYGH VALLEY see HAPPY RIDGE WASCO CO.           T3S     R13E         S32
OLD UNION see UNION             WASHINGTON CO.      T1N     R1W          S29
OLEX                            GILLIAM CO.         T1S     R21E         S11
OLINGER, ABRAM                  MARION CO.          T8S     R2W          S3
OLINGER D.L.C., ABRAM AND RACHEL see OLINGER, ABRAM
                                MARION CO.          T8S     R2W          S3
OLMSTEAD D.L.C., JOHN see McGUIRE FAMILY
                                DOUGLAS CO.         T28S    R7W          S34
OLNEY                           UMATILLA CO.        T2N     R32E         S15
ONA                             LINCOLN CO.         T12S    R11W         S21
ONTARIO see EVERGREEN           MALHEUR CO.         T18S    R47E         S9
ORCUTT, ROBERT see BATTERSON FAMILY
                                TILLAMOOK CO.       T3N     R10W         ?
ORDER OF RED MEN see JACKSONVILLE
                                JACKSON CO.         T37S    R2W          S29
OREGON CITY see MOUNTAIN VIEW   CLACKAMAS CO.       T3S     R2E          S5
OREGON GAME COMMISSION see RUSSELL FAMILY
                                WALLOWA CO.         T6N     R42E         ?
OREGON HEALTH SCIENCES CENTER see UNIVERSITY OF OREGON MEDICAL SCHOOL
                                MULTNOMAH CO.       T1S     R1E          S9
OREGON LODGE #65 see B'NAI B'RITH
                                MULTNOMAH CO.       T1S     R1E          S27
OREGON SOLDIERS HOME see ROSEBURG NATIONAL
                                DOUGLAS CO.         T27S    R6W          S14
OREGON STATE HOSPITAL           MARION CO.          T7S     R3W          S25
OREGON STATE HOSPITAL see ASYLUM
                                MARION CO.          T7S     R3W          S25
```

OREGON STATE INSTITUTION FOR THE FEEBLE MINDED				
	MARION CO.	T8S	R3W	S2
ORETOWN	TILLAMOOK CO.	T5S	R10W	S7
ORIENT	MULTNOMAH CO.	T1S	R4E	S19
ORLEANS	LINN CO.	T11S	R4W	S32
ORPHANS HOME [SALEM] see **GLEN-OAK ORPHANAGE**				
	MARION CO.	T7S	R3W	S25
ORTLEY	WASCO CO.	T2N	R12E	?
OSBORNE D.L.C., JOSIAH see **FINLEY**				
	LINN CO.	T14S	R2W	S13
OSWEGO CATHOLIC see **SACRED HEART**				
	CLACKAMAS CO.	T2S	R1E	S16
OSWEGO PIONEER	CLACKAMAS CO.	T2S	R1E	S16
OTEY D.L.C., EDWIN W. see **OTEY FAMILY**				
	DOUGLAS CO.	T26S	R6W	S1
OTEY FAMILY	DOUGLAS CO.	T26S	R6W	S1
OTLEY FIELD see **CUMMINGS FIELD**	HARNEY CO.	T29S	R33E	S31
OTTINGER, ANNA LOUISE see **BITTERLING FAMILY**				
	CLATSOP CO.	T7N	R10W	S24
OUR LADY OF GUADALUPE TRAPPIST ABBEY				
	YAMHILL CO.	T3S	R3W	S29
OUR LADY OF LOURDES	LINN CO.	T10S	R1E	S9
OUR LADY OF LOURDES CATHOLIC see **PIONEER [JORDAN]**				
	LINN CO.	T10S	R1E	S10
OVERTON see **UNION POINT**	LINN CO.	T14S	R3W	S14
OWEN, LEVI B.	COLUMBIA CO.	?	?	?
OWENS HOMESTEAD see **SPANISH GULCH**				
	WHEELER CO.	T13S	R25E	S6
OWYHEE	MALHEUR CO.	T20S	R46E	S27
OWYHEE CROSSING	MALHEUR CO.	T31S	R41E	?
OWYHEE FERRY see **OWYHEE CROSSING**				
	MALHEUR CO.	T31S	R41E	?
OWYHEE PIONEER	MALHEUR CO.	T21S	R46E	?
OWYHEE RIVER	MALHEUR CO.	T20S	R46E	?
OYSTERVILLE	LINCOLN CO.	T11S	R11W	S34
PACIFIC LODGE #105 see **I.O.O.F. [BAY CITY]**				
	TILLAMOOK CO.	T1S	R10W	S1
PACIFIC MEMORIAL GARDENS see **PACIFIC VIEW MEMORIAL GARDENS AND**				
COLUMBARIUM	LINCOLN CO.	T7S	R11W	S12
PACIFIC SUNSET MEMORIAL PARK	LANE CO.	T18S	R12W	S25
PACIFIC UNIVERSITY	WASHINGTON CO.	T1N	R3W	S31
PACIFIC UNIVERSITY MEMORIAL see **PACIFIC UNIVERSITY**				
	WASHINGTON CO.	T1N	R3W	S31
PACIFIC VIEW	LINCOLN CO.	T11S	R11W	S9
PACIFIC VIEW MEMORIAL GARDENS AND COLUMBARIUM				
	LINCOLN CO.	T7S	R11W	S12
PAINTED HILLS see **CARROLL FAMILY**				
	WHEELER CO.	T10S	R21E	S32

PAINTER FAMILY	MULTNOMAH CO.	T1N	R4E	S25
PAISLEY	LAKE CO.	T33S	R18E	S24
PAIUTE	KLAMATH CO.	T35S	R12E	S35
PAIUTE [NEW]	HARNEY CO.	T23S	R30E	S1
PAIUTE [OLD]	HARNEY CO.	T23S	R30E	S14
PALESTINE	BENTON CO.	T10S	R4W	S22
PALESTINE MEMORIAL CHURCH see **PALESTINE**				
	BENTON CO.	T10S	R4W	S22
PALLASKE FAMILY	COOS CO.	T28S	R13W	S3
PALLETTE RANCH	WALLOWA CO.	T4S	R48E	?
PALM, AUGUST see **PALM PIONEER, AUGUST**				
	COLUMBIA CO.	T7N	R3W	S18
PALM PIONEER, AUGUST	COLUMBIA CO.	T7N	R3W	S18
PALMATEER see **MT. ZION**	CLACKAMAS CO.	T3S	R4E	S22
PALMER	LINCOLN CO.	T11S	R9W	?
PALMER	MULTNOMAH CO.	T1N	R5E	S24
PALMER, JOEL see **BROOKSIDE**	YAMHILL CO.	T4S	R3W	S17
PANKEY see **PANKEY PARK**	JACKSON CO.	T35S	R2W	S30
PANKEY PARK	JACKSON CO.	T35S	R2W	S30
PANNE PLACE, OWEN see **KNOX FAMILY, E. B.**				
	CROOK CO.	T17S	R19E	S8
PANTHER CREEK	DOUGLAS CO.	T20S	R7W	S26
PAPERSACK	GILLIAM CO.	T5S	R22E	S16
PARADISE	WALLOWA CO.	T6N	R45E	S31
PARADISE BAR	CURRY CO.	T33S	R10W	S18
PARDEE see **BRIGGS, SAMUEL**	DOUGLAS CO.	T30S	R5W	S20
PARISH D.L.C., DANA J. see **SMALL FAMILY**				
	LANE CO.	T22S	R3W	S17
PARISH OF ST. MARK, THE	MULTNOMAH CO.	T1N	R1E	S33
PARK	WALLOWA CO.	T3S	R48E	S3
PARK see **THE PARK**	UNION CO.	T6S	R41E	S2
PARK GRANGE see **PARK**	WALLOWA CO.	T3S	R48E	S3
PARK PLACE see **LEWTHWAITE**	CLACKAMAS CO.	T2S	R2E	S20
PARK PLACE see **STRAIGHT FAMILY**	CLACKAMAS CO.	T2S	R2E	S29
PARKDALE see **UPPER VALLEY**	HOOD RIVER CO.	T1N	R10E	S33
PARKER COUNTY PARK, JUDAH see **PARKERSBURG**				
	COOS CO.	T28S	R14W	S15
PARKER PLACE see **BLY [NEW]**	KLAMATH CO.	T36S	R14E	S28
PARKER PLACE see **HODSON**	KLAMATH CO.	T38S	R11 1/2E	?
PARKERSBURG	COOS CO.	T28S	R14W	S15
PARKERSVILLE see **PIONEER MEMORIAL**				
	MARION CO.	T6S	R2W	S10
PARKINSON, JOHN T.	BAKER CO.	T8S	?	?
PARKINSON, MR.	MALHEUR CO.	T17S	R47E	?
PARKLAWN	WASCO CO.	T1N	R13E	S15
PARKROSE MASONIC see **COLUMBIA PIONEER**				
	MULTNOMAH CO.	T1N	R2E	S21
PARKS, DAVID	MULTNOMAH CO.	T1N	R3E	?

PARRISH see **McCULLY**	MARION CO.	T9S	R2W	S21
PARRISH GAP see **HUNSAKER FAMILY**	MARION CO.	T9S	R2W	S17
PARRISH, JESSE see **McCULLY**	MARION CO.	T9S	R2W	S21
PARRISH, MRS. ELIZABETH see **GLEN-OAK ORPHANAGE**				
	MARION CO.	T7S	R3W	S25
PARRISH OREGON PROVISIONAL LAND CLAIM NOTIFICATION, JOSIAH L. see				
GLEN-OAK ORPHANAGE	MARION CO.	T7S	R3W	S25
PARROTT D.L.C., JOSEPH see **ST. PATRICK'S**				
	CLACKAMAS CO.	T3S	R1E	S23
PARSON D.L.C., HORACE AND MARILDA see **OAK KNOLL**				
	WASHINGTON CO.	T1S	R4W	S2
PARSONS FAMILY see **OAK KNOLL**	WASHINGTON CO.	T1S	R4W	S2
PARTIN FAMILY	LAKE CO.	T30S	R16E	S23
PASSLEY, RALPH see **RALPH AND CLARNO BABIES**				
	CURRY CO.	T39S	R14W	S2
PAT CREEK BURIAL see **McENROE, PATRICK**				
	LANE CO.	T17S	R9W	S36
PATON see **PATTON FAMILY**	WASHINGTON CO.	T1S	R1W	S14
PATTERSON, ALEXANDER	UMATILLA CO.	T3S	R30E	S33
PATTERSON D.L.C., ABRAHAM see **PATTERSON FAMILY**				
	DOUGLAS CO.	T29S	R8W	S17
PATTERSON FAMILY	DOUGLAS CO.	T29S	R8W	S17
PATTON FAMILY	MARION CO.	T8S	R1W	S5
PATTON FAMILY	WASHINGTON CO.	T1S	R1W	S14
PATTON FAMILY	WASHINGTON CO.	T1S	R4W	S36
PAULINA see **BEAVER CREEK**	CROOK CO.	T16S	R24E	S15
PAUPER [WARRENTON]	CLATSOP CO.	T8N	R10W	S21
PAUPER'S [ROSEBURG] see **DOUGLAS COUNTY BROOKSIDE**				
	DOUGLAS CO.	T27S	R5W	S17
PAUPER'S [WINSTON]	DOUGLAS CO.	T28S	R6W	S21
PAYNE D.L.C., MARTIN see **FAIRVIEW MENNONITE CHURCH**				
	LINN CO.	T11S	R3W	S23
PAYNE FAMILY	CURRY CO.	T39S	R12W	?
PEAK see **DAVIDSON**	BENTON CO.	T12S	R7W	S8
PEARCE, JOHN	JEFFERSON CO.	T10S	R15E	S32
PEARCE, JOSHUA [Sic] see **PEARCE JOHN**				
	JEFFERSON CO.	T10S	R15E	S32
PEARSON FAMILY	MULTNOMAH CO.	?	?	?
PEARSON, RHODA see **PEARSON FAMILY**				
	MULTNOMAH CO.	?	?	?
PECK FAMILY see **LAKECREEK**	JACKSON CO.	T37S	R2E	S4
PEDEE see **EDWARDS FAMILY**	POLK CO.	T9S	R6W	S32
PEDRO see **FORT HAYES**	JOSEPHINE CO.	T37S	R8W	S35
PEEL	DOUGLAS CO.	T27S	R3W	S11
PENDLETON see **PIONEER PARK**	UMATILLA CO.	T2N	R32E	S10
PENDLETON CITY see **OLNEY**	UMATILLA CO.	T2N	R32E	S15
PENDLETON D.L.C., CHAMPING see **PENDLETON FAMILY**				
	CLACKAMAS CO.	T3S	R1E	S32

PENDLETON, ELIZABETH J. see **FERN HILL**				
	CLACKAMAS CO.	T5S	R3E	S21
PENDLETON FAMILY	CLACKAMAS CO.	T3S	R1E	S32
PENITENTIARY [NEW]	MARION CO.	T7S	R3W	S25
PENITENTIARY [OLD]	MARION CO.	T7S	R3W	S25
PENITENTIARY ANNEX see **HERREN FAMILY**				
	MARION CO.	T8S	R2W	S17
PENLAND	MORROW CO.	T1S	R25E	S34
PENLAND D.L.C., LEVI E. see **POWELL FAMILY**				
	BENTON CO.	T13S	R6W	S3
PENLAND, MR. see **LEXINGTON [OLD]**				
	MORROW CO.	T1S	R25E	S27
PENLAND RANCH see **ANDREWS**	HARNEY CO.	T35S	R33E	S22
PEPIOT see **GREENWOOD**	LANE CO.	T17S	R1E	S12
PEPIOT FAMILY see **GREENWOOD**	LANE CO.	T17S	R1E	S12
PERDUE see **LAVADOURE**	DOUGLAS CO.	T30S	R3W	S29
PEREZ, LIEUTENANT WILBUR L. see **CAPE LOOKOUT**				
	TILLAMOOK CO.	T3S	R11W	S1
PERKINS-ELLIOTT see **ELLIOTT-PERKINS**				
	DOUGLAS CO.	T21S	R12W	?
PERRIN, MARSHALL K.	CLACKAMAS CO.	T3S	R1E	S2
PERRY	TILLAMOOK CO.	T1S	R8W	S1
PERRY D.L.C., FRANCIS see **PERRY FAMILY**				
	COLUMBIA CO.	?	R1W	?
PERRY D.L.C., WILLIAM T. see **DOUGLAS COUNTY BROOKSIDE**				
	DOUGLAS CO.	T27S	R5W	S17
PERRY FAMILY	COLUMBIA CO.	?	R1W	?
PERSHELL, JOSEPH	CLACKAMAS CO.	?	?	?
PETERSBURG see **STOLLER FAMILY**	WASCO CO.	T2N	R14E	S33
PETERSON, ALEC see **PETERSON FAMILY**				
	WASHINGTON CO.	T3N	R4W	S1
PETERSON, ALICE see **PETERSON FAMILY**				
	WASHINGTON CO.	T3N	R4W	S1
PETERSON BUTTE see **SANDRIDGE**	LINN CO.	T12S	R3W	S24
PETERSON FAMILY	WASHINGTON CO.	T3N	R4W	S1
PETERSON FAMILY see **HUSSEY FAMILY**				
	YAMHILL CO.	T5S	R6W	S1
PETERSON, FRED see **PETERSON FAMILY**				
	WASHINGTON CO.	T3N	R4W	S1
PETTERSON D.L.C., HENRY F. see **ROCK HILL**				
	LINN CO.	T12S	R2W	S28
PETTEYS see **PETTYS**	MORROW CO.	T1S	R25E	S6
PETTIT see **ALMA**	LANE CO.	T19S	R8W	S3
PETTY see **CLOVERDALE**	LANE CO.	T19S	R2W	S18
PETTYS	MORROW CO.	T1S	R25E	S6
PHILIPS D.L.C., ROBERT Y. see **WARNER, WILLIAM N.**				
	COOS CO.	T30S	R12W	S34
PHILLIPS	WASHINGTON CO.	T1N	R2W	S12

PHILLIPS see **TAYLOR**	YAMHILL CO.	T5S	R4W	S10
PHILLIPS GERMAN REFORM CHURCH see **PHILLIPS**				
	WASHINGTON CO.	T1N	R2W	S12
PHILOMATH [OLD]	BENTON CO.	T12S	R6W	S12
PHOENIX [NEW]	JACKSON CO.	T38S	R1W	S9
PHOENIX [OLD]	JACKSON CO.	T38S	R1W	S15
PICKARD-HUNSAKER FAMILIES see **HUNSAKER FAMILY**				
	MARION CO.	T9S	R2W	S17
PIETROK see **CUSICK FAMILY**	LINN CO.	T9S	R1E	S20
PIKE see **PIKE AND I.O.O.F.**	YAMHILL CO.	T2S	R5W	S25
PIKE AND I.O.O.F.	YAMHILL CO.	T2S	R5W	S25
PILCHER	LINN CO.	T10S	R3W	?
PILGRIM'S REST	CROOK CO.	T16S	R14E	S11
PILOT BUTTE	DESCHUTES CO.	T17S	R12E	S33
PILOT ROCK	UMATILLA CO.	T1S	R32E	S20
PINE CITY	MORROW CO.	T1N	R27E	S10
PINE CREEK	WALLOWA CO.	T2N	R46E	S27
PINE CREEK see **PINE HAVEN**	BAKER CO.	T8S	R46E	S17
PINE GROVE	LINN CO.	T13S	R4W	S32
PINE GROVE	UNION CO.	T1N	R40E	S12
PINE GROVE see **PINE GROVE BUTTE**	HOOD RIVER CO.	T2N	R10E	S13
PINE GROVE BUTTE	HOOD RIVER CO.	T2N	R10E	S13
PINE HAVEN	BAKER CO.	T8S	R46E	S17
PINE VALLEY see **PINE HAVEN**	BAKER CO.	T8S	R46E	S17
PINEHURST	JACKSON CO.	T40S	R4E	S5
PIONEER see **ASTORIA PIONEER**	CLATSOP CO.	T8N	R9W	S17
PIONEER see **CATHOLIC [BANDON]**	COOS CO.	T28S	R14W	S30
PIONEER see **CROXTON PIONEER MEMORIAL PARK**				
	JOSEPHINE CO.	T36S	R5W	S8
PIONEER see **EUGENE PIONEER**	LANE CO.	T17S	R3W	S32
PIONEER see **GALES CREEK**	WASHINGTON CO.	T1N	R4W	S18
PIONEER see **LEBANON PIONEER**	LINN CO.	T12S	R2W	S11
PIONEER see **OSWEGO PIONEER**	CLACKAMAS CO.	T2S	R1E	S16
PIONEER see **PORT ORFORD**	CURRY CO.	T32S	R15W	S4
PIONEER see **SUMNER [OLD]**	COOS CO.	T26S	R12W	S33
PIONEER see **TEMPLETON**	COOS CO.	T23S	R12W	S26
PIONEER see **TRASK PIONEER**	TILLAMOOK CO.	T1S	R9W	S27
PIONEER [BAKER CITY] see **MT. HOPE**				
	BAKER CO.	T9S	R40E	S21
PIONEER [GOLD BEACH]	CURRY CO.	T36S	R15W	S36
PIONEER [HARBOR]	CURRY CO.	T40S	R13W	S9
PIONEER [INDEPENDENCE] see **HILLTOP**				
	POLK CO.	T9S	R4W	S9
PIONEER [JORDAN]	LINN CO.	T10S	R1E	S10
PIONEER [OAKLAND] see **OLD TOWN OAKLAND**				
	DOUGLAS CO.	T24S	R5W	S33
PIONEER [ONTARIO] see **APPLEGATE**				
	MALHEUR CO.	T16S	R47E	?

```
PIONEER [PRINEVILLE] see JUNIPER HAVEN
                              CROOK CO.          T14S    R16E      S31
PIONEER [RICKREALL]           POLK CO.           T7S     R4W       S32
PIONEER [TERREBONNE]          DESCHUTES CO.      T14S    R13E      S22
PIONEER [THE DALLES]          WASCO CO.          T1N     R13E      S10
PIONEER [WACONDA] see PIONEER MEMORIAL
                              MARION CO.         T6S     R2W       S10
PIONEER [YONCALLA] see APPLEGATE
                              DOUGLAS CO.        T23S    R5W       S4
PIONEER CATHOLIC see PIONEER CATHOLIC OF ST. ANTHONY OF PADUA
                              WASHINGTON CO.     T1S     R1W       S4
PIONEER CATHOLIC OF ST. ANTHONY OF PADUA
                              WASHINGTON CO.     T1S     R1W       S4
PIONEER GRAVE                 WASCO CO.          T2S     R14E      ?
PIONEER GRAVES                WASCO CO.          T3S     R13E      S20
PIONEER MEMORIAL              MARION CO.         T6S     R2W       S10
PIONEER MEMORIAL see LINN, PHILIP E.
                              CLACKAMAS CO.      T3S     R4E       S21
PIONEER MEMORIAL see YAMHILL-CARLTON
                              YAMHILL CO.        T3S     R4W       S10
PIONEER MEMORIAL CEMETERY PARK  LANE CO.         T17S    R3W       S35
PIONEER MEMORIAL PARK see EUGENE PIONEER
                              LANE CO.           T17S    R3W       S32
PIONEER MEMORIAL PARK see TROUT  TILLAMOOK CO.   T1S     R9W       S30
PIONEER PARK                  UMATILLA CO.       T2N     R32E      S10
PIONEER UNION see MOUNTAIN VIEW MEMORIAL GARDENS
                              WASHINGTON CO.     T1N     R4W       S35
PIONEER WOMAN'S GRAVE         CLACKAMAS CO.      T3S     R9E       S29
PISGAH HOME                   COLUMBIA CO.       T4N     R3W       S36
PISGAH LODGE see GOSHEN       LANE CO.           T18S    R3W       S24
PISTOL RIVER                  CURRY CO.          T38S    R14W      S18
PITMAN FAMILY see OAK GROVE   YAMHILL CO.        T2S     R3W       S21
PITTMAN, ANNA MARIA see LEE MISSION
                              MARION CO.         T7S     R3W       S24
PLACER                        JOSEPHINE CO.      T34S    R5W       S8
PLANK FAMILY see UNKNOWN [?PLANK FAMILY?]
                              YAMHILL CO.        T3S     R5W       S8
PLEASANT BUTTE BAPTIST see BAPTIST
                              LINN CO.           T13S    R3W       S23
PLEASANT GROVE                MARION CO.         T9S     R2W       S11
PLEASANT HILL                 COOS CO.           T29S    R12W      S7
PLEASANT HILL                 POLK CO.           T6S     R6W       S12
PLEASANT HILL see PLEASANT HILL PIONEER
                              LANE CO.           T18S    R2W       S34
PLEASANT HILL see PLEASANT VIEW [WEST]
                              CLACKAMAS CO.      T3S     R1W       S9
PLEASANT HILL BAPTIST see ETNA  POLK CO.         T7S     R4W       S7
PLEASANT HILL PIONEER         LANE CO.           T18S    R2W       S34
```

PLEASANT HOME see **PLEASANT HOME PIONEER**				
	MULTNOMAH CO.	T1S	R4E	S20
PLEASANT HOME PIONEER	MULTNOMAH CO.	T1S	R4E	S20
PLEASANT POINT	MORROW CO.	T1S	R28E	R28
PLEASANT RIDGE	WASCO CO.	T1S	R12E	?
PLEASANT VALLEY	BENTON CO.	T12S	R6W	S21
PLEASANT VALLEY	JOSEPHINE CO.	T35S	R6W	S11
PLEASANT VALLEY see **ALDER CREEK**	BAKER CO.	T10S	R41E	S35
PLEASANT VALLEY see **PLEASANT VIEW [EAST]**				
	CLACKAMAS CO.	T2S	R3E	S19
PLEASANT VIEW	UMATILLA CO.	T4N	R29E	S28
PLEASANT VIEW [EAST]	CLACKAMAS CO.	T2S	R3E	S19
PLEASANT VIEW [WEST]	CLACKAMAS CO.	T3S	R1W	S9
PLUM TREE	CURRY CO.	T32S	R14W	S3
PLUM TREES see **PLUM TREE**	CURRY CO.	T32S	R14W	S3
PLUSH	LAKE CO.	T36S	R24E	?
POCAHONTAS	BAKER CO.	T9S	R39E	S5
POE D.L.C., WILLIAM see **POE, MARY JANE VANNATTA**				
	LINN CO.	T15S	R2W	S9
POE, MARY JANE VANNATTA	LINN CO.	T15S	R2W	S9
POE VALLEY see **BEDFIELD**	KLAMATH CO.	T40S	R11E	S1
POINT TERRACE see **SWEET CREEK**	LANE CO.	T18S	R10W	?
POINTER D.L.C., WILLIAM see **ELLIS FAMILY**				
	WASHINGTON CO.	T1S	R1W	S12
POINTER D.L.C., WILLIAM see **FINLEY'S SUNSET HILL MEMORIAL**				
	WASHINGTON CO.	T1S	R1W	S1
POINTER D.L.C., WILLIAM see **POINTER FAMILY**				
	WASHINGTON CO.	T1S	R1W	S1
POINTER FAMILY	WASHINGTON CO.	T1S	R1W	S1
POLAND FAMILY see **ROLAND-POLAND FAMILIES**				
	COOS CO.	T29S	R13W	?
POLAND, JANE see **ROLAND-POLAND FAMILIES**				
	COOS CO.	T29S	R13W	?
POLAND, MRS. PEARL see **ROLAND-POLAND FAMILIES**				
	COOS CO.	T29S	R13W	?
POLK STATION see **FAST**	POLK CO.	T7S	R5W	S23
POLLOCK, EVABELL KENNISTON see **LUCKY QUEEN**				
	JOSEPHINE CO.	T34S	R5W	S32
POLLOCK INFANT see **LUCKY QUEEN**	JOSEPHINE CO.	T34S	R5W	S32
POLLOCK, W. H. see **LUCKY QUEEN**	JOSEPHINE CO.	T34S	R5W	S32
POOLE FAMILY, HAROLD	LANE CO.	T16S	R10W	S29
POOLE, MONROE see **POOLE FAMILY, HAROLD**				
	LANE CO.	T16S	R10W	S29
POOR FARM	WASHINGTON CO.	T1S	R2W	S8
POOR FARM see **COUNTY FARM #2**	MULTNOMAH CO.	T1S	R1E	S5
PORT ORFORD	CURRY CO.	T32S	R15W	S4
PORTER FAMILY	LINCOLN CO.	T10S	R8W	S30
PORTLAND see **LONE FIR PIONEER**	MULTNOMAH CO.	T1S	R1E	S1

```
POWELL D.L.C., THEOPHILUS see POWELL FAMILY, REVEREND THEOPHILUS
                               MARION CO.      T7S    R1W      S33
POWELL FAMILY                  BENTON CO.      T13S   R6W      S3
POWELL FAMILY see BUTLER-DAVIDSON FAMILY
                               POLK CO.        T8S    R5W      S35
POWELL FAMILY, REVEREND THEOPHILUS
                               MARION CO.      T7S    R1W      S33
POWELL GROVE see POWELL GROVE PIONEER
                               MULTNOMAH CO.   T1N    R2E      S23
POWELL GROVE PIONEER           MULTNOMAH CO.   T1N    R2E      S23
POWELL, JOAB see LIBERTY [OLD] LINN CO.        T13S   R1W      S23
POWELL, MRS. MARGARET see UMPHLETTE, JANE EARL
                               LINN CO.        T10S   R3W      S15
POWELL RANCH see UNKNOWN       SHERMAN CO.     T1S    R17E     ?
POWELL, ROGER W. "BILL" see PARISH OF ST. MARK, THE
                               MULTNOMAH CO.   T1N    R1E      S33
POWELL VALLEY see ST. JOSEPH   MULTNOMAH CO.   T1S    R3E      S8
POWERS                         COOS CO.        T31S   R12W     S12
POWRIE, ROBERT E. see HOFFMAN  COOS CO.        T29S   R12W     S22
POWWATKA                       WALLOWA CO.     T4N    R43E     S33
PRAIRIE see KNAPPA PRAIRIE     CLATSOP CO.     T8N    R7W      S17
PRAIRIE CITY                   GRANT CO.       T13S   R33E     S11
PRAIRIE CREEK                  WALLOWA CO.     T2S    R45E     S34
PRATT                          WASCO CO.       T4S    R12E     S14
PRATT, ELLIS see PRATT-COLVILLE WALLOWA CO.    T3S    R43E     ?
PRATT-COLVILLE                 WALLOWA CO.     T3S    R43E     ?
PRATUM                         MARION CO.      T7S    R1W      S19
PRATUM MENNONITE see PRATUM    MARION CO.      T7S    R1W      S19
PRESBYTERIAN see GEORGE        CLACKAMAS CO.   T3S    R5E      S19
PRESCOTT see WELTER FAMILY     COLUMBIA CO.    T6N    R2W      S2
PRESTON D.L.C., WILLIAM see BRIGGS, SAMUEL
                               DOUGLAS CO.     T30S   R5W      S20
PRETTYMAN D.L.C., DAVID D. see SOUTH MT. TABOR [#1]
                               MULTNOMAH CO.   T1S    R2E      S5
PRETTYMAN D.L.C., PERRY AND ELIZABETH see ABRAHAM
                               MULTNOMAH CO.   T1S    R2E      S6
PRETTYMAN FAMILY see SOUTH MT. TABOR [#1]
                               MULTNOMAH CO.   T1S    R2E      S5
PRICE FARM, FRANK see GRAVE CREEK
                               JOSEPHINE CO.   T34S   R6W      ?
PRIME see CRABTREE FAMILY      LINN CO.        T11S   R2W      S13
PRINCE see POWWATKA            WALLOWA CO.     T4N    R43E     S33
PROGRESS see CRESCENT GROVE    WASHINGTON CO.  T1S    R1W      S26
PROMISE                        WALLOWA CO.     T4N    R42E     S11
PROPES, FRANK FINLEY           POLK CO.        T6S    R7W      S35
PROPST, LUCINDA POWELL see BUTTER CREEK CROSSING
                               UMATILLA CO.    T3N    R27E     S25
PROSPECT                       JACKSON CO.     T32S   R3E      S31
```

PROTESTANT see **FAIRVIEW**	COLUMBIA CO.	T3N	R2W	S24
PROVIDENCE	LINN CO.	T11S	R1W	S10
PROVIDENCE BAPTIST CHURCH see **PROVIDENCE**				
	LINN CO.	T11S	R1W	S10
PROVIDENCE CHURCH see **PROVIDENCE**				
	LINN CO.	T11S	R1W	S10
PRUNE RIDGE	MARION CO.	T7S	R2E	S8
PUCKERVILLE [?] see **MOORES VALLEY**				
	YAMHILL CO.	T3S	R5W	S9
PUDDING RIVER see **APOSTOLIC**	MARION CO.	T7S	R1W	S8
PUGH D.L.C., FRANCIS A. see **SHEDD**				
	LINN CO.	T13S	R4W	S13
PUGH FAMILY see **SHEDD**	LINN CO.	T13S	R4W	S13
PUGH'S PLACE, DICK	CURRY CO.	T35S	R13W	S34
PULASKI see **PALLASKE FAMILY**	COOS CO.	T28S	R13W	S3
PULLEN D.L.C., ANDREW see **COLUMBIA PIONEER**				
	MULTNOMAH CO.	T1N	R2E	S21
PULLEN, MARY L.	MULTNOMAH CO.	T1S	R2E	S3
PULLEY-LOWE FAMILY see **LOWE FAMILY**				
	CLACKAMAS CO.	T1S	R5E	S30
PULLINS	MULTNOMAH CO.	?	?	?
PUMPKIN RIDGE see **ARCADE**	WASHINGTON CO.	T2N	R3W	S14
PURDIN FAMILY	WASHINGTON CO.	T1N	R4W	S25
PURVINE D.L.C., EWING see **PURVINE FARM BURIALS**				
	MARION CO.	?	R1W	?
PURVINE FARM BURIALS	MARION CO.	?	R1W	?
PUTNAM D.L.C., JOSEPH see **SUNNYDALE**				
	DOUGLAS CO.	T22S	R6W	S16
PUTNAM FAMILY see **SUNNYDALE**	DOUGLAS CO.	T22S	R6W	S16
PUTNAM FARM	POLK CO.	T7S	R3W	?
PUTZ see **BONNEY**	CLACKAMAS CO.	T4S	R3E	S35
QUARTZVILLE	LINN CO.	T12S	R4E	S22
QUEEN OF ANGELS CONVENT	MARION CO.	T6S	R1W	S10
QUICK	TILLAMOOK CO.	T2S	R9W	S16
QUICK FARM, ISAAC see **QUICK**	TILLAMOOK CO.	T2S	R9W	S16
QUILHAUGH, MAUD	CURRY CO.	T33S	R9W	?
QUINABY'S CORNER	MARION CO.	T7S	R3W	S27
QUINCY see **STEWART CREEK**	COLUMBIA CO.	T7N	R4W	S3
QUINES CREEK	DOUGLAS CO.	T32S	R5W	S15
QUINN, BILLY	DESCHUTES CO.	T21S	R7E	S1
QUINN D.L.C., TERENCE see **QUINN, MARY WHELAN**				
	MULTNOMAH CO.	T1N	R1E	S36
QUINN, MARY WHELAN	MULTNOMAH CO.	T1N	R1E	S36
QUIRING see **FAST**	POLK CO.	T7S	R5W	S23
QUOSATANA CREEK see **MACFARLAND**	CURRY CO.	T35S	R13W	S34
R. C. see **ST. JOSEPH**	MULTNOMAH CO.	T1S	R3E	S8
RACEY YARD	MALHEUR CO.	T13S	R41E	?
RACKLEFF	COOS CO.	T29S	R12W	?

RADER D.L.C., ARCHIBALD see **HOBSON-WHITNEY**

	MARION CO.	T8S	R1W	S35
RAE	LINCOLN CO.	T11S	R10W	S15
RAFFETY	WASHINGTON CO.	T2N	R3W	S27
RAFFERTY *[Sic]* see **RAFFETY**	WASHINGTON CO.	T2N	R3W	S27

RAFFETY D.L.C., SAMUEL B. see **RAFFETY**

	WASHINGTON CO.	T2N	R3W	S27
RAFFETY, S. B. see **RAFFETY**	WASHINGTON CO.	T2N	R3W	S27
RAGSDALE see **SAYLOR**	LANE CO.	T19S	R2W	S19

RAIL CREEK RANCH see **HELFRICH, PRINCE E.**

	LANE CO.	T16S	R3E	S31
RAINS, BABY	WASCO CO.	T5S	R12E	?
RAINVILLE	DOUGLAS CO.	T31S	R2W	S3
RAJNEESH CREMATORIUM	JEFFERSON CO.	T9S	R18E	S1

RALEIGH-PATTON FAMILY see **PATTON FAMILY**

	WASHINGTON CO.	T1S	R1W	S14
RALPH AND CLARNO BABIES	CURRY CO.	T39S	R14W	S2

RAMEY D.L.C., DANIEL C. see **KNAPPA PRAIRIE**

	CLATSOP CO.	T8N	R7W	S17
RAMSAY see **RAMSEY**	MULTNOMAH CO.	T2N	R1W	S36

RAMSAY HOME, DON see **CYRUS CHILDREN**

	GILLIAM CO.	T1N	R20E	S15
RAMSEY	MULTNOMAH CO.	T2N	R1W	S36

RAMSEY D.L.C., BARNETT see **STAFFORD FAMILY**

	LANE CO.	T17S	R2W	S3

RAMSEY D.L.C., DAVID AND SUSAN see **VALLEY VIEW MEMORIAL PARK**

	YAMHILL CO.	T3S	R2W	S19
RAMSEY, FRED see **RAMSEY**	MULTNOMAH CO.	T2N	R1W	S36
RAMSEY, FREDERICK H. see **RAMSEY**	MULTNOMAH CO.	T2N	R1W	S36

RAMSEY HILL see **VALLEY VIEW MEMORIAL PARK**

	YAMHILL CO.	T3S	R2W	S19
RAMSEY, JACK see **RED HEADED MAN**	CLATSOP CO.	?	?	?
RAMSEY, JOHN C. see **RAMSEY**	MULTNOMAH CO.	T2N	R1W	S36
RAMSEY'S FARM see **RAMSEY**	MULTNOMAH CO.	T2N	R1W	S36

RANCHERIA see **INDIAN RANCHERIA TRAIL MASSACRE**

	JACKSON CO.	T35S	R4E	S18
RANDALL, BILLY see **APPLEGATE**	MALHEUR CO.	T16S	R47E	?

RANDALL, JOHN C. see **HARDSCRABBLE**

	UNION CO.	?	?	?

RANDLE, SAMUEL ARTHUR see **BLACK COUPLE**

	LINN CO.	T12S	R2W	S9
RANDOLPH	COOS CO.	T28S	R14W	S3
RANGE [NEW]	GRANT CO.	T8S	R31E	S17
RANGE [OLD]	GRANT CO.	T8S	R31E	S10

RANKIN, CLARK L. see **RANKIN INFANT**

	MULTNOMAH CO.	T1N	R5E	?
RANKIN INFANT	MULTNOMAH CO.	T1N	R5E	?

RANKIN, MARY REUTHEMAN see **RANKIN INFANT**

	MULTNOMAH CO.	T1N	R5E	?
RAT HOLE	CURRY CO.	T35S	R11W	S5
RATH	CLACKAMAS CO.	T3S	R5E	?
RATTLESNAKE TREE see **FISHER, JOHN D.**				
	WALLOWA CO.	T2N	R41E	?
RAYMOND D.L.C., PETER see **BELLE PASSI**				
	MARION CO.	T5S	R1W	S19
RAYMOND, MR.	WALLOWA CO.	T2N	R50E	?
REASE see **BREESE**	DESCHUTES CO.	T21S	R11E	S29
REASE, GUY see **BREESE**	DESCHUTES CO.	T21S	R11E	S29
RECTOR D.L.C., WILLIAM H. see **MUTE SCHOOL**				
	MARION CO.	T8S	R2W	?
RED BARN see **ARCHER**	COOS CO.	T26S	R13W	S1
RED ELK	UMATILLA CO.	T2N	R35E	S3
RED HEADED MAN	CLATSOP CO.	?	?	?
RED HILL	DOUGLAS CO.	T23S	R5W	S34
RED LAKE	WASCO CO.	T6S	R12E	S34
RED PRAIRIE METHODIST see **PLEASANT HILL**				
	POLK CO.	T6S	R6W	S12
RED ROCK CANYON GRAVES	JACKSON CO.	T33S	R2E	?
REDLAND HILLS see **REDLAND PIONEER**				
	CLACKAMAS CO.	T3S	R3E	S16
REDLAND PIONEER	CLACKAMAS CO.	T3S	R3E	S16
REDMEN-LA PINE see **LA PINE COMMUNITY**				
	DESCHUTES CO.	T22S	R11E	S7
REDMOND see **REDMOND MEMORIAL**	DESCHUTES CO.	T15S	R13E	S29
REDMOND MEMORIAL	DESCHUTES CO.	T15S	R13E	S29
REED, CALVIN	MULTNOMAH CO.	T1N	R3E	?
REED D.L.C., CALVIN see **REED, CALVIN**				
	MULTNOMAH CO.	T1N	R3E	?
REED D.L.C., LEWIS see **REESE CREEK**				
	JACKSON CO.	T35S	R1W	S14
REED FAMILY see **REED FAMILY, REASON**				
	DOUGLAS CO.	T25S	R5W	S5
REED FAMILY, REASON	DOUGLAS CO.	T25S	R5W	S5
REED-HILL FAMILY	DOUGLAS CO.	T26S	R5W	S7
REED RANCH see **HARNEY**	HARNEY CO.	T22S	R32E	S24
REEDSPORT	DOUGLAS CO.	T22S	R12W	S4
REEL, ROLAND	WALLOWA CO.	T3N	R50E	?
REES D.L.C., LEWIS see **REESE CREEK**				
	JACKSON CO.	T35S	R1W	S14
REESE D.L.C., LEWIS see **REESE CREEK**				
	JACKSON CO.	T35S	R1W	S14
REEVES D.L.C., THOMAS see **REEVES FAMILY**				
	BENTON CO.	T14S	R5W	S7
REEVES FAMILY	BENTON CO.	T14S	R5W	S7
REEVES PLACE see **BLACK, MR.**	LINN CO.	T13S	R1W	S1

REEVES PLACE see **FERGUSON**	LINN CO.	T13S	R1W	S12
REID [Sic] D.L.C., REASON see **CEDAR HILL**				
	DOUGLAS CO.	T25S	R5W	S5
REID [Sic] D.L.C., REASON see **REED FAMILY, REASON**				
	DOUGLAS CO.	T25S	R5W	S5
REIMER	CLACKAMAS CO.	T3S	R5E	?
REINEMAN CHILD see **NARROWS**	HARNEY CO.	T26S	R30E	S26
REINS, BABY see **RAINS, BABY**	WASCO CO	T5S	R12E	?
REMOTE see **FETTER**	COOS CO.	T29S	R10W	S28
RENEKE	TILLAMOOK CO.	T3S	R10W	S31
RENFREW, DOCTOR ALEXANDER	LANE CO.	T16S	R4E	S5
RENFROW see **RENTFROW, MAY ANN JUDY**				
	WALLOWA CO.	T5N	R43E	S4
RENILDE, SISTER see **CATACOMBS**	MARION CO.	T4S	R2W	S19
RENSHAW D.L.C., WILLIAM see **RENSHAW, MARY JULIA**				
	LANE CO.	T18S	R3W	?
RENSHAW, ELIZABETH MARIA JANE see **RENSHAW, MARY JULIA**				
	LANE CO.	T18S	R3W	?
RENSHAW, MARY JULIA	LANE CO.	T18S	R3W	?
RENSHAW, WILLIAM D. see **RENSHAW, MARY JULIA**				
	LANE CO.	T18S	R3W	?
RENTFROW, HENRY see **RENTFROW, MAY ANN JUDY**				
	WALLOWA CO.	T5N	R43E	S4
RENTFROW, MAY ANN JUDY	WALLOWA CO.	T5N	R43E	S4
REPSLEGER ROAD	LANE CO.	T20S	R4W	S23
REST HAVEN MEMORIAL PARK	LANE CO.	T18S	R3W	S5
REST HAVEN MEMORIAL PARK	YAMHILL CO.	T6S	R6W	S3
REST LAWN MEMORIAL PARK	LANE CO.	T15S	R5W	S34
REST LAWN MEMORY GARDENS AND MAUSOLEUM				
	POLK CO.	T7S	R4W	S26
RESTLAWN	GRANT CO.	T13S	R31E	S22
REVENUE D.L.C., FRANCIS see **REVENUE FAMILY**				
	CLACKAMAS CO.	T2S	R5E	S7
REVENUE FAMILY	CLACKAMAS CO.	T2S	R5E	S7
REXFORD D.L.C., JOHN AND CHARITY ANN see **PLEASANT VALLEY**				
	BENTON CO.	T12S	R6W	S21
REYNOLDS REST AREA, C. H.	UNION CO.	T4S	R38E	S12
RHEA CREEK	MORROW CO.	T4S	R26E	S14
RHODES	LINN CO.	T10S	R3W	?
RHODES D.L.C., CROGHAN see **RIDDERS PIONEER**				
	BENTON CO	T10S	R4W	S9
RHODES, EDWIN A. see **LOGDELL**	GRANT CO.	T15S	R30E	S33
RHODES, ELLA R. DUNCAN see **LOGDELL**				
	GRANT CO.	T15S	R30E	S33
RHODES, HERMAN see **CACHE CREEK RANCH**				
	WALLOWA CO.	T6N	R47E	S23
RICCO	GRANT CO.	T12S	R34E	?
RICCO RANCH, ERNEST see **RICCO**	GRANT CO.	T12S	R34E	?

RICCO RANCH, GENE see **McHALEY**	GRANT CO.	T13S	R33E	S3
RICCO RANCH, HENRY see **AUSTIN**	GRANT CO.	T11S	R35E	S21
RICE	LINN CO.	T13S	R2E	?
RICE	WASCO CO.	T1S	R14E	S10
RICE see **MYRTLE CREEK**	COOS CO.	T30S	R11W	S16
RICE CREEK	DOUGLAS CO.	T29S	R6W	?
RICE FAMILY	DOUGLAS CO.	T24S	R5W	S5
RICE, FRANKLIN see **WOODBINE**	COLUMBIA CO.	T7N	R3W	S13
RICE GIRL	MORROW CO.	T2S	R24E	S32
RICE, JOHN see **RICE GIRL**	MORROW CO.	T2S	R24E	S32
RICE-MARSH FAMILY	DOUGLAS CO.	T23S	R5W	S31
RICE RANCH, ERVIN see **RICE-MARSH FAMILY**				
	DOUGLAS CO.	T23S	R5W	S31
RICHARDS D.L.C., JOHN A. see **RICHARDS FAMILY**				
	DOUGLAS CO.	T28S	R7W	S25
RICHARDS FAMILY	DOUGLAS CO.	T28S	R7W	S25
RICHARDSON	LANE CO.	T17S	R5W	S4
RICHARDSON BUTTE see **RICHARDSON**	LANE CO.	T17S	R5W	S4
RICHARDSON D.L.C., BENJAMIN see **RICHARDSON**				
	LANE CO.	T17S	R5W	S4
RICHARDSON D.L.C., GIDION AND MARGARET see **RICHARDSON FAMILY, GIDEON**				
	LANE CO.	T15S	R5W	S15
RICHARDSON FAMILY see **REDLAND PIONEER**				
	CLACKAMAS CO.	T3S	R3E	S16
RICHARDSON FAMILY, GIDEON	LANE CO.	T15S	R5W	S15
RICHARDSON, MATTHEW see **REDLAND PIONEER**				
	CLACKAMAS CO.	T3S	R3E	S16
RICHMOND	WHEELER CO.	T10S	R23E	S6
RICKARD see **MILLIRON**	LANE CO.	T15S	R4W	S31
RICKERT RANCH	HARNEY CO.	T19S	R33 1/2E	S13
RICKEY	MARION CO.	T7S	R2W	S32
RICKEY D.L.C., JAMES see **RICKEY**	MARION CO.	T7S	R2W	S32
RICKREALL see **NESMITH FAMILY**	POLK CO.	T7S	R4W	S30
RICKS, JOHN	MORROW CO.	T6S	R25E	S2
RIDDELL	UNION CO.	?	?	?
RIDDELL, BENJAMIN H. see **RIDDELL**				
	UNION CO.	?	?	?
RIDDER see **RIDDERS PIONEER**	BENTON CO.	T10S	R4W	S9
RIDDERS POINEER	BENTON CO.	T10S	R4W	S9
RIDDLE	DOUGLAS CO.	T30S	R6W	S23
RIGGS D.L.C., MILTON see **GOSHEN**	LANE CO.	T18S	R3W	S24
RIGGS D.L.C., TIMOTHY see **CRAWFORDSVILLE UNION**				
	LINN CO.	T14S	R1W	S17
RIGGS FAMILY see **HART-RIGGS FAMILY**				
	POLK CO.	T8S	R6W	S25
RILEA FAMILY	CURRY CO.	T35S	R12W	S12
RILEY see **SILVER CREEK**	HARNEY CO.	T23S	R26E	S5
RINGO see **CLARKES PIONEER**	CLACKAMAS CO.	T4S	R3E	S29

RIPLEY, MIRIAM SHELDON see **DAFFODIL PATCH**				
	WASCO CO.	T1N	R11E	S12
RISING SUN see **SUN RISE**	SHERMAN CO.	T2N	R17E	S31
RISLEY D.L.C., JACOB S. see **RISLEY FAMILY**				
	CLACKAMAS CO.	T2S	R1E	S12
RISLEY FAMILY	CLACKAMAS CO.	T2S	R1E	S12
RITCHEY D.L.C., JOHN M. see **METHODIST CHURCH AT FARMINGTON**				
	WASHINGTON CO.	T1S	R2W	?
RITCHEY FAMILY	DOUGLAS CO.	T21S	R5W	S31
RITCHEY FARM see **OAK KNOLL**	WASHINGTON CO.	T1S	R4W	S2
RITNER see **EDWARDS FAMILY**	POLK CO.	T9S	R6W	S32
RITTER	GRANT CO.	T7S	R30E	S31
RIVER BANK FARM see **SLOAN**	JOSEPHINE CO.	T36S	R6W	S30
RIVER VIEW	MORROW CO.	T4N	R25E	S9
RIVER VIEW	MULTNOMAH CO.	T1S	R1E	S22
RIVER VIEW see **HALLS FERRY**	MARION CO.	T8S	R4W	S14
RIVERSIDE	LINN CO.	T11S	R4W	S12
RIVERSIDE	MALHEUR CO.	T23S	R37E	S22
RIVERSIDE V. F. W.	LINCOLN CO.	T10S	R10W	S11
RIVERTON	COOS CO.	T28S	R13W	?
RIVERVIEW	MORROW CO.	T4N	R25E	S9
RIVERVIEW see **FAIRVIEW**	LINN CO.	T9S	R3E	S34
RIVERVIEW see **LEWIS AND CLARK**	CLATSOP CO.	T7N	R9W	S6
RIVERVIEW see **RIVER VIEW**	MORROW CO.	T4N	R25E	S9
RIVERVIEW see **RIVER VIEW**	MULTNOMAH CO.	T1S	R1E	S22
RIVERVIEW ABBEY MAUSOLEUM	MULTNOMAH CO.	T1S	R1E	S22
ROBBINS D.L.C., ELIAS see **ZENA**	POLK CO.	T6S	R4W	S36
ROBBINS FAMILY	COOS CO.	T30S	R12W	S4
ROBBINS FAMILY	POLK CO.	T7S	R5W	S27
ROBERTS	CROOK CO.	T17S	R17E	S22
ROBERTS see **DAIRY**	KLAMATH CO.	T38S	R11 1/2E	?
ROBERTS, BILLY see **DAIRY**	KLAMATH CO.	T38S	R11 1/2E	?
ROBERTS D.L.C., JOSEPH see **CANYONVILLE PIONEER**				
	DOUGLAS CO.	T30S	R5W	S34
ROBERTS, DELLA see **ALLEN FAMILY**	MORROW CO.	T5S	R26E	S29
ROBERTS, DELLA OR NELLA see **ROBERTS-GRAY**				
	WASCO CO.	T1S	R13E	S36
ROBERTS-GRAY	WASCO CO.	T1S	R13E	S36
ROBERTS, HENRY see **DAIRY**	KLAMATH CO.	T38S	R11 1/2E	?
ROBERTSON see **DELORE**	CROOK CO.	T18S	R25E	S13
ROBERTSON, JAMES B. see **ROBISON FAMILY, JAMES**				
	WASHINGTON CO.	T1N	R3W	S26
ROBINETT	LINN CO.	T14S	R1W	?
ROBINETT D.L.C., WILLIAM see **ROBINETT**				
	LINN CO.	T14S	R1W	?
ROBINETTE	BAKER CO.	T9S	R46E	S25
ROBINETTE see **ROBINETT**	LINN CO.	T14S	R1W	?
ROBINETTI see **ROBINETT**	LINN CO.	T14S	R1W	?

ROBINETTI, JIM see **ROBINETT**	LINN CO.	T14S	R1W	?
ROBINSON, BENAIAH see **ROBINSON FAMILY**				
	BENTON CO.	T11S	R5W	S10
ROBINSON, C. D. see **ROBINSON FAMILY**				
	MORROW CO.	T4S	R24E	S34
ROBINSON D.L.C., BENAIAH see **ROBINSON FAMILY**				
	BENTON CO.	T11S	R5W	S10
ROBINSON, D.L.C., NATHAN AND MARY see **UNKNOWN**				
	WASHINGTON CO.	T1S	R2W	S14
ROBINSON FAMILY	BENTON CO.	T11S	R5W	S10
ROBINSON FAMILY	MORROW CO.	T4S	R24E	S34
ROBINSON, JAMES B. see **ROBISON FAMILY, JAMES**				
	WASHINGTON CO.	T1N	R3W	S26
ROBINSON, JANE see **ROBINSON FAMILY**				
	BENTON CO.	T11S	R5W	S10
ROBISON see **FISHTRAP**	COOS CO.	T28S	R13W	S23
ROBISON D.L.C., JAMES B. see **ROBISON FAMILY, JAMES**				
	WASHINGTON CO.	T1N	R3W	S26
ROBISON FAMILY, JAMES	WASHINGTON CO.	T1N	R3W	S26
ROBISON FARM, ITHAMAR see **PALLASKE FAMILY**				
	COOS CO.	T28S	R13W	S3
ROBL, ANDREAS see **ST. BENEDICT**	MARION CO.	T6S	R1W	S11
ROBL, MARGARET see **ST. BENEDICT**	MARION CO.	T6S	R1W	S11
ROBNETT see **ROBINETT**	LINN CO.	T14S	R1W	?
ROCCA-CHANDLER FAMILY see **ROCK CREEK**				
	POLK CO.	T9S	R8W	?
ROCK CREEK	BAKER CO.	T7S	R38E	S36
ROCK CREEK	CLACKAMAS CO.	T5S	R1E	S5
ROCK CREEK	HARNEY CO.	T34S	R30E	S4
ROCK CREEK	KLAMATH CO.	T36S	R11E	S20
ROCK CREEK	POLK CO.	T9S	R8W	?
ROCK CREEK see **VERNONIA PIONEER**	COLUMBIA CO.	T5N	R4W	S33
ROCK CREEK see **WIGLE**	LINCOLN CO.	T10S	R9W	S12
ROCK CREEK CANYON CO-OP see **SUNDSTROM, BRUCE**				
	LANE CO.	T16S	R8W	S18
ROCK CREEK MEADOWS see **ROCK CREEK**				
	POLK CO.	T9S	R8W	?
ROCK CREEK METHODIST CHURCH see **PANKEY PARK**				
	JACKSON CO.	T35S	R2W	S30
ROCK CREEK RANCH see **ROCK CREEK**	HARNEY CO.	T34S	R30E	S4
ROCK HILL	LINN CO.	T12S	R2W	S28
ROCK POINT	JACKSON CO.	T36S	R3W	S17
ROCK POINT see **LONE FIR**	MARION CO.	T8S	R1W	S21
ROCKVILLE	MALHEUR CO.	T26S	R46E	S2
ROCKY POINT see **LONE FIR**	MARION CO.	T8S	R1W	S21
ROGERS D.L.C., LEWIS see **FENDALL-ROGERS FAMILY**				
	YAMHILL CO.	T3S	R3W	S4

ROGERS FAMILY see **BUTLER-DAVIDSON FAMILY**				
	POLK CO.	T8S	R5W	S35
ROGERS FAMILY see **FENDALL-ROGERS FAMILY**				
	YAMHILL CO.	T3S	R3W	S4
ROGUE see **PIONEER [GOLD BEACH]**	CURRY CO.	T36S	R15W	S36
ROGUE RIVER	CURRY CO.	T37S	R15W	S12
ROGUE RIVER see **WOODVILLE**	JACKSON CO.	T36S	R4W	S15
ROLAND D.L.C., WILLIAM see **WISE**	COOS CO.	T30S	R12W	S34
ROLAND FAMILY see **ROLAND-POLAND FAMILIES**				
	COOS CO.	T29S	R13W	?
ROLAND-POLAND FAMILIES	COOS CO.	T29S	R13W	?
ROLAND, WILLIAM see **ROLAND-POLAND FAMILIES**				
	COOS CO.	T29S	R13W	?
RONCO FARM see **UNKNOWN**	POLK CO.	T9S	R6W	?
RONDEAU	DOUGLAS CO.	T30S	R2W	S24
ROOD FAMILY	WASHINGTON CO.	T1S	R2W	S6
ROOD, FRED see **ROOD FAMILY**	WASHINGTON CO.	T1S	R2W	S6
ROOSTER ROCK	MULTNOMAH CO.	T1N	R4E	S25
ROOT	TILLAMOOK CO.	T1S	R11W	S25
ROSE see **ROSE HILL**	SHERMAN CO.	T1S	R17E	S26
ROSE CITY	MULTNOMAH CO.	T1N	R2E	S19
ROSE CITY LODGE see **NEVEH ZEDEK ROSE CITY LODGE**				
	WASHINGTON CO.	T1S	R1W	S12
ROSE HILL	SHERMAN CO.	T1S	R17E	S26
ROSE HILL MEMORIAL	DOUGLAS CO.	T30S	R5W	S27
ROSE LAWN see **ROSE CITY**	MULTNOMAH CO.	T1N	R2E	S19
ROSE LODGE	LINCOLN CO.	T6S	R10W	S25
ROSE, WILLIAM H. see **ROSE HILL**	SHERMAN CO.	T1S	R17E	S26
ROSEBURG	DOUGLAS CO.	T27S	R5W	S18
ROSEBURG CATHOLIC see **ST. JOSEPH CATHOLIC**				
	DOUGLAS CO.	T27S	R5W	S19
ROSEBURG MEMORIAL GARDENS	DOUGLAS CO.	T27S	R6W	S13
ROSEBURG NATIONAL	DOUGLAS CO.	T27S	R6W	S14
ROSEBURG VETERANS see **ROSEBURG NATIONAL**				
	DOUGLAS CO.	T27S	R6W	S14
ROSEDALE see **ROSEDALE FRIENDS**	MARION CO.	T8S	R3W	S28
ROSEDALE FRIENDS	MARION CO.	T8S	R3W	S28
ROSELAWN see **FRIENDS**	YAMHILL CO.	T3S	R2W	S20
ROSELAWN MEMORIAL PARK	MULTNOMAH CO.	T1N	R2E	S27
ROSENBERG HILL	BAKER CO.	T8S	R46E	S13
ROUND BUTTE PIONEER	JEFFERSON CO.	T11S	R13E	S6
ROUND HILL see **GRAVEYARD POINT**	MALHEUR CO.	T23S	R47E	?
ROUSCOE BABY see **ROUSCOE, MRS. DAVE**				
	LAKE CO.	T39S	R24E	S16
ROUSCOE, MRS. DAVE	LAKE CO.	T39S	R24E	S16
ROUSE HOMESTEAD, WILLIAM see **BEMIS**				
	LANE CO.	T22S	R3W	S32
ROWE D.L.C., HIRAM see **GATES**	LANE CO.	T18S	R5W	S19

ROWLAND see **WARNER, WILLIAM N.**	COOS CO.	T30S	R12W	S34
ROWLAND, PATRICK	MARION CO.	T4S	R2W	S19
ROWLEY	WHEELER CO.	T7S	R19E	S35
ROY CATHOLIC see **ST. FRANCIS CATHOLIC**				
	WASHINGTON CO.	T1N	R3W	S5
ROYAL GRANGE see **SILK CREEK COMMUNITY**				
	LANE CO.	T20S	R4W	S13
RUCH see **LOGTOWN**	JACKSON CO.	T38S	R3W	S14
RUFUS	SHERMAN CO.	T2N	R17E	S6
RUGG	UNION CO.	T2S	R36E	S13
RUM AND GUM CHARLEY	WASHINGTON CO.	T2S	?	?
RUMLEY HILL	CURRY CO.	T36S	R14W	S9
RURAL see **SALEM PIONEER**	MARION CO.	T7S	R3W	S33
RURAL DALE see **BUZAN**	WASCO CO.	T4S	R15E	S33
RUSH ISLAND see **MIDDLE FORK**	LANE CO.	T19S	R1E	S34
RUSSELL	COOS CO.	T28S	R14W	S3
RUSSELL	LINN CO.	T13S	R1E	S33
RUSSELL D.L.C., NEWTON see **RUSSELL**				
	LINN CO.	T13S	R1E	S33
RUSSELL FAMILY	WALLOWA CO.	T6N	R42E	?
RUSSELL PLACE see **RUSSELL FAMILY**				
	WALLOWA CO.	T6N	R42E	?
RUSSELL PLACE, ENOS see **RUSSELL**	LINN CO.	T13S	R1E	S33
RUSSELL RANCH see **RUSSELL**	COOS CO.	T28S	R14W	S3
RUSSELLVILLE	CLACKAMAS CO.	T6S	R2E	S2
RUSSELVILLE see **RUSSELLVILLE**	CLACKAMAS CO.	T6S	R2E	S2
RUST see **HALSEY PIONEER**	LINN CO.	T14S	R4W	S11
RUTERS FAMILY	DOUGLAS CO.	T24S	R7W	?
RUU, FREDRICK	CLACKAMAS CO.	?	?	?
RYAN FAMILY	CLATSOP CO.	T7N	R8W	?
RYDELL RANCH see **GARDNER**	DOUGLAS CO.	T22S	R6W	?
RYE VALLEY	BAKER CO.	T13S	R43E	S5
SACCHI	COOS CO.	T26S	R14W	S32
SACCHI RANCH see **SACCHI**	COOS CO.	T26S	R14W	S32
SACRED HEART	CLACKAMAS CO.	T2S	R1E	S16
SACRED HEART	MARION CO.	T5S	R2W	S36
SACRED HEART	TILLAMOOK CO.	T2S	R9W	S5
SACRED HEART CATHOLIC see **COLUMBIA MEMORIAL GARDENS**				
	COLUMBIA CO.	T4N	R2W	S36
SADDLE BUTTE	HARNEY CO.	T25S	R32 1/2E	S1
SADDLE MOUNTAIN ROAD	CLATSOP CO.	T6N	R8W	?
SAGER CHILDREN see **RED HILL**	DOUGLAS CO.	T23S	R5W	S34
SAGINAW	LANE CO.	T20S	R3W	?
SAILOR PIONEER	LANE CO.	T17S	R6W	S28
ST. AGNES see **ST. JOSEPH**	MULTNOMAH CO.	T1S	R3E	S8
ST. AGNES BABY HOME	CLACKAMAS CO.	T2S	R2E	S20
ST. ANDREWS	UMATILLA CO.	T2N	R33E	S24
ST. ANDREWS CATHOLIC	GRANT CO.	T13S	R31E	S35

ST. ANDREWS MISSION see **ST. ANDREWS**				
	UMATILLA CO.	T2N	R33E	S24
ST. ANTHONY CATHOLIC	WASHINGTON CO.	T2S	R1W	S3
ST. ANTHONY OF PADUA see **PIONEER CATHOLIC OF ST. ANTHONY OF PADUA**				
	WASHINGTON CO.	T1S	R1W	S4
ST. ANTHONY'S see **ST. ANTHONY CATHOLIC**				
	WASHINGTON CO.	T2S	R1W	S3
ST. BARBARA'S	MARION CO.	T8S	R3W	S3
ST. BEDE'S MEMORIAL GARDENS	WASHINGTON CO.	T1S	R3W	S5
ST. BENEDICT	MARION CO.	T6S	R1W	S11
ST. BENEDICT see **WORKMAN'S**	MARION CO.	T6S	R1W	S11
ST. BENEDICTS see **OUR LADY OF LOURDES**				
	LINN CO.	T10S	R1E	S9
ST. BONIFACE	MARION CO.	T8S	R1W	S34
ST. CECILIA see **PIONEER CATHOLIC OF ST. ANTHONY OF PADUA**				
	WASHINGTON CO.	T1S	R1W	S4
ST. EDWARD see **ST. EDWARD'S CATHOLIC [NEW]**				
	WASHINGTON CO.	T2N	R2W	S31
ST. EDWARD see **ST. EDWARD'S CATHOLIC [OLD]**				
	WASHINGTON CO.	T1N	R3W	S1
ST. EDWARD'S see **ST. EDWARD'S CATHOLIC [NEW]**				
	WASHINGTON CO.	T2N	R2W	S31
ST. EDWARD'S see **ST. EDWARD'S CATHOLIC [OLD]**				
	WASHINGTON CO.	T1N	R3W	S1
ST. EDWARD'S CATHOLIC [NEW]	WASHINGTON CO.	T2N	R2W	S31
ST. EDWARD'S CATHOLIC [OLD]	WASHINGTON CO.	T1N	R3W	S1
ST. FERDINAND see **ST. FRANCIS CATHOLIC**				
	WASHINGTON CO.	T1N	R3W	S5
ST. FRANCIS CATHOLIC	WASHINGTON CO.	T1N	R3W	S5
ST. FRANCIS DeSALES CATHOLIC	BAKER CO.	T9S	R40E	S8
ST. FRANCIS OF ASSISI see **ST. FRANCIS CATHOLIC**				
	WASHINGTON CO.	T1N	R3W	S5
ST. GEORGE'S EPISCOPAL CHURCH COLUMBARIUM				
	DOUGLAS CO.	T27S	R5W	S19
ST. HELENS PIONEER MASONIC see **MASONIC [ST. HELENS]**				
	COLUMBIA CO.	T5N	R1W	S33
ST. HENRY see **ST. JOSEPH**	MULTNOMAH CO.	T1S	R3E	S8
ST. JAMES	YAMHILL CO.	T4S	R4W	S10
ST. JAMES see **ST. PATRICK'S**	CLACKAMAS CO.	T3S	R1E	S23
ST. JOE see **ST. PATRICK**	YAMHILL CO.	T5S	R5W	S4
ST. JOHANN	CLACKAMAS CO.	T3S	R1E	S36
ST. JOHANN LUTHERAN see **ST. JOHANN**				
	CLACKAMAS CO.	T3S	R1E	S36
ST. JOHN LUTHERAN see **ST. JOHANN**				
	CLACKAMAS CO.	T3S	R1E	S36
ST. JOHN THE APOSTLE see **ST. JOHN'S CATHOLIC**				
	CLACKAMAS CO.	T3S	R2E	S5
ST. JOHN THE EVANGELIST	CLACKAMAS CO.	?	?	?

```
ST. JOHN THE EVANGELIST see FERN HILL CATHOLIC
                                    WASHINGTON CO.    T1S    R3W         S16
ST. JOHN THE EVANGELIST EPISCOPAL CHURCH
                                    CLACKAMAS CO.     T1S    R1E         S36
ST. JOHNS see TOLEDO                LINCOLN CO.       T11S   R10W        S8
ST. JOHNS LODGE #17, MASONS see WAVERLY MEMORIAL
                                    LINN CO.          T11S   R3W         S4
ST. JOHN'S CATHOLIC                 CLACKAMAS CO.     T3S    R2E         S5
ST. JOHN'S CATHOLIC see SUNSET      MALHEUR CO.       T18S   R47E        S8
ST. JOSEPH                          GILLIAM CO.       T4S    R21E        S10
ST. JOSEPH                          MULTNOMAH CO.     T1S    R3E         S8
ST. JOSEPH see JENCK                TILLAMOOK CO.     T4S    R10W        S34
ST. JOSEPH see ST. BARBARA'S        MARION CO.        T8S    R3W         S3
ST. JOSEPH CATHOLIC                 DOUGLAS CO.       T27S   R5W         S19
ST. JOSEPH POLISH CATHOLIC          COLUMBIA CO.      T5N    R3W         S27
ST. LOUIS [NEW]                     MARION CO.        T5S    R2W         S21
ST. LOUIS [OLD]                     MARION CO.        T5S    R2W         S21
ST. LUKE'S                          MARION CO.        T5S    R1W         S7
ST. LUKE'S PARISH COLUMBARIUM       JOSEPHINE CO.     T36S   R5W         S18
ST. MARK THE EVANGELIST CHURCH COLUMBARIUM
                                    HOOD RIVER CO.    T3N    R10E        S36
ST. MARY'S                          HOOD RIVER CO.    T2N    R10E        S2
ST. MARY'S                          MULTNOMAH CO.     T1N    R1E         S36
ST. MARY'S see JENCK                TILLAMOOK CO.     T4S    R10W        S34
ST. MARY'S see MT. ANGEL            MARION CO.        T6S    R1W         S3
ST. MARY'S [SHAW] see SHAW CATHOLIC
                                    MARION CO.        T8S    R2W         S13
ST. MARY'S [STAYTON]                MARION CO.        T9S    R1W         S10
ST. MARY'S ACADEMY                  MULTNOMAH CO.     T1S    R1E         S3
ST. MARY'S BOY'S HOME               WASHINGTON CO.    T1S    R1W         ?
ST. MARY'S CATHOLIC                 BENTON CO.        T11S   R5W         S27
ST. MARY'S CATHOLIC see SHAW CATHOLIC
                                    MARION CO.        T8S    R2W         S13
ST. MARY'S CONVENT see QUEEN OF ANGELS CONVENT
                                    MARION CO.        T6S    R1W         S10
ST. MARY'S OF THE VALLEY [NEW]      WASHINGTON CO.    T1S    R1W         S17
ST. MARY'S OF THE VALLEY [OLD]      WASHINGTON CO.    T1S    R1W         S7
ST. MATTHEW'S CATHOLIC              WASHINGTON CO.    T1S    R2W         S8
ST. PATRICK                         YAMHILL CO.       T5S    R5W         S4
ST. PATRICK see ST. PATRICK'S       CLACKAMAS CO.     T3S    R1E         S23
ST. PATRICK'S                       CLACKAMAS CO.     T3S    R1E         S23
ST. PATRICK'S                       JOSEPHINE CO.     T40S   R8W         S34
ST. PAUL see COOPER MOUNTAIN [CATHOLIC]
                                    WASHINGTON CO.    T1S    R2W         S25
ST. PAUL LUTHERAN CHURCH            WASHINGTON CO.    T2S    R1W         S30
ST. PAUL'S [NEW; ST. PAUL]          MARION CO.        T4S    R2W         S19
ST. PAUL'S [OLD; ST. PAUL]          MARION CO.        T4S    R2W         S19
ST. PAUL'S CATHOLIC                 MARION CO.        T6S    R1W         S27
```

ST. PAUL'S EPISCOPAL CHURCH COLUMBARIUM

	MARION CO.	T7S	R3W	S27

ST. PAUL'S LUTHERAN see **BLOOMING**

| WASHINGTON CO. | T1S | R3W | S15 |

ST. PAUL'S LUTHERAN see **ST. PAUL LUTHERAN CHURCH**

| WASHINGTON CO. | T2S | R1W | S30 |

ST. PETER'S see **COOPER MOUNTAIN [CATHOLIC]**

| WASHINGTON CO. | T1S | R2W | S25 |

ST. PETER'S CATHOLIC   WASCO CO.   T1N   R13E   S4

ST. PETER'S CHURCH see **TEN O'CLOCK**

| CLACKAMAS CO. | T3S | R2E | S35 |

ST. PETER'S D.L.C., CATHOLIC MISSION see **ST. PETER'S CATHOLIC**

| WASCO CO. | T1N | R13E | S4 |

ST. PETER'S LUTHERAN see **BLOOMING**

| WASHINGTON CO. | T1S | R3W | S15 |

ST. PETER'S LUTHERAN CHURCH see **MOEHNKE**

| CLACKAMAS CO. | T3S | R3E | S31 |

ST. PIUS CATHOLIC see **PIONEER CATHOLIC OF ST. ANTHONY OF PADUA**

| WASHINGTON CO. | T1S | R1W | S4 |

ST. PIUS X [10TH] see **PIONEER CATHOLIC OF ST. ANTHONY OF PADUA**

| WASHINGTON CO. | T1S | R1W | S4 |

ST. ROSE see **HOLY ROSARY**   MARION CO.   T6S   R1E   S36

ST. ROSE CATHOLIC   BENTON CO.   T14S   R5W   S32

ST. STEPHENS see **ST. JOSEPH CATHOLIC**

| DOUGLAS CO. | T27S | R5W | S19 |

ST. THOMAS see **BUXTON CATHOLIC**   WASHINGTON CO.   T2N   R4W   S4

ST. TIMOTHY'S EPISCOPAL CHURCH MEMORIAL GARDENS

| MARION CO. | T7S | R3W | S24 |

ST. WENCESLAUS   COLUMBIA CO.   T3N   R2W   S13

SALEM CATHOLIC see **ST. BARBARA'S**

| MARION CO. | T8S | R3W | S3 |

SALEM PIONEER   MARION CO.   T7S   R3W   S33

SALMI, MR. see **MARSHLAND**   COLUMBIA CO.   T7N   R5W   S11

SALMON RIVER see **ROSE LODGE**   LINCOLN CO.   T6S   R10W   S25

SALT CREEK   POLK CO.   T7S   R5W   S6

SALTENSTALL, LINTON see **ROWLEY**   WHEELER CO.   T7S   R19E   S35

SALTMARSH, ARTHUR see **SALTMARSH, ZERILDA**

| LINN CO. | T12S | R1W | S7 |

SALTMARSH D.L.C., ARTHUR see **SALTMARSH, ZERILDA**

| LINN CO. | T12S | R1W | S7 |

SALTMARSH, ZERILDA   LINN CO.   T12S   R1W   S7

SAMARITAN LODGE see **I.O.O.F. [CARTERS]**

| MULTNOMAH CO. | T1S | R1E | S4 |

SAMARITAN LODGE see **I.O.O.F. [GREENWOOD]**

| MULTNOMAH CO. | T1S | R1E | S27 |

SAMMIS FAMILY see **UNKNOWN**   WASCO CO.   T1N   R12E   ?

SAMS, JIM see **BIG CREEK**   BAKER CO.   T7S   R41E   S2

SAMS VALLEY see **PANKEY PARK**   JACKSON CO.   T35S   R2W   S30

SAND HOLLOW	MORROW CO.	T1N	R26E	S13
SAND LAKE	TILLAMOOK CO.	T3S	R10W	S17
SAND RIDGE see **SANDRIDGE**	LINN CO.	T12S	R3W	S24
SAND SPRING see **MASIKER, GEORGE**	SHERMAN CO.	T2N	R16E	S33
SANDERS see **UNIONTOWN**	JACKSON CO.	T38S	R3W	S34
SANDERS FAMILY	CLACKAMAS CO.	T5S	R2E	S4
SANDERS, I. N. see **NORTH POWDER** [NEW]				
	UNION CO.	T6S	R39E	S22
SANDER'S RANCH see **SELDERS, ANTHONY**				
	COLUMBIA CO.	T5N	R5W	S32
SANDLAKE see **SAND LAKE**	TILLAMOOK CO.	T3S	R10W	S17
SANDRIDGE	LINN CO.	T12S	R3W	S24
SANDY HOOD LOOP see **FIR HILL**	CLACKAMAS CO.	T2S	R4E	S14
SANDY PIONEER see **FIR HILL**	CLACKAMAS CO.	T2S	R4E	S14
SANDY RIDGE	CLACKAMAS CO.	T2S	R4E	S27
SANFORD, JOSIAH	LANE CO.	T21S	R3E	S9
SANTIAM CENTRAL	LINN CO.	T11S	R2W	S6
SANTIAM, CHIEF see **SIMISON**	LINN CO.	T10S	R3W	S3
SANTIAM MASONIC LODGE #1 see **LONE OAK** [NEW]				
	MARION CO.	T9S	R1W	S10
SAPP FAMILY HOMESTEAD see **LONE FIR**				
	BENTON CO.	T15S	R8W	S6
SARDINE CREEK see **I.O.O.F.** [GOLD HILL]				
	JACKSON CO.	T36S	R3W	S17
SARDINE CREEK see **ROCK POINT**	JACKSON CO.	T36S	R3W	S17
SATTERLEE, ARTHUR see **HALL FARM**	WASHINGTON CO.	T1N	R4W	?
SATTERLEE, RUTH HALL see **HALL FARM**				
	WASHINGTON CO.	T1N	R4W	?
SATTERLEE, WILLIAM see **HALL FARM**				
	WASHINGTON CO.	T1S	R4W	?
SAUNDERS FAMILY see **SANDERS FAMILY**				
	CLACKAMAS CO.	T5S	R2E	S4
SAVAGE, AMERICUS see **BUNKER HILL**				
	LINN CO.	T13S	R3W	S9
SAVAGE BUTTE see **BUNKER HILL**	LINN CO.	T13S	R3W	S9
SAVAGE COLUMBUS see **BUNKER HILL**	LINN CO.	T13S	R3W	S9
SAVAGE D.L.C., AMERICUS see **BUNKER HILL**				
	LINN CO.	T13S	R3W	S9
SAVAGE-MORGAN FAMILIES see **BUNKER HILL**				
	LINN CO.	T13S	R3W	S9
SAWTELL FAMILY	CLACKAMAS CO.	T5S	R2E	S30
SAYLOR	LANE CO.	T19S	R2W	S19
SAYLOR see **SAILOR PIONEER**	LANE CO.	T17S	R6W	S28
SAYLOR D.L.C., SYDNER [Sic] see **SAYLOR**				
	LANE CO.	T19S	R2W	S19
SAYRS CHILD	SHERMAN CO.	T1S	R16E	?
SAYRS, EMMA POWELL see **SAYRS CHILD**				
	SHERMAN CO.	T1S	R16E	?

SAYRS, FRANCIS see **SAYRS CHILD**	SHERMAN CO.	T1S	R16E	?
SAYRS HOMESTEAD see **SAYRS CHILD**	SHERMAN CO.	T1S	R16E	?
SCANDIA see **BETHANY PIONEER**	MARION CO.	T6S	R1W	S33
SCANDINAVIAN	CLACKAMAS CO.	T2S	R4E	S14
SCANTY see **BETHANY PIONEER**	MARION CO.	T6S	R1W	S33
SCAPPOOSE CATHOLIC see **ST. WENCESLAUS**				
	COLUMBIA CO.	T3N	R2W	S13
SCAPPOOSE PIONEER see **FAIRVIEW**	COLUMBIA CO.	T3N	R2W	S24
SCENIC HILLS MEMORIAL PARK	JACKSON CO.	T39S	R1E	S11
SCHEEL FAMILY	CLACKAMAS CO.	T3S	R5E	S18
SCHERZINGER CHILD	MORROW CO.	T3S	R27E	S28
SCHERZINGER, ED see **SCHERZINGER CHILD**				
	MORROW CO.	T3S	R27E	S28
SCHIEVE, AUGUST	COLUMBIA CO.	T5N	R2W	?
SCHIEVE, JOHN see **SCHIEVE, AUGUST**				
	COLUMBIA CO.	T5N	R2W	?
SCHMIDLIN, EMMA WUNSCH see **WUNSCH, ERDMAN**				
	WASHINGTON CO.	T3N	R4W	S6
SCHMIDLIN, GUST see **WUNSCH, ERDMAN**				
	WASHINGTON CO.	T3N	R4W	S6
SCHMIDT NURSERY see **GARDEN OF REVERENCE**				
	CLACKAMAS CO.	T1S	R4E	S28
SCHNEIDER'S CABIN see **CORNUCOPIA**				
	BAKER CO.	T6S	R45E	?
SCHOLLMEYER FARM, HERMAN see **SCHWALNUS FAMILY**				
	TILLAMOOK CO.	T3N	R10W	?
SCHOLLS see **MOUNTAINSIDE**	WASHINGTON CO.	T2S	R2W	S16
SCHOLLS PIONEER see **MOUNTAINSIDE**				
	WASHINGTON CO.	T2S	R2W	S16
SCHONCHIN, CHIEF AND WINEMA	KLAMATH CO.	T36S	R11E	S25
SCHOOL DISTRICT #1 see **GINGLES**	BENTON CO.	T10S	R4W	S15
SCHOOL DISTRICT #2 see **CHAMPOEG**	MARION CO.	T4S	R2W	S12
SCHOOL DISTRICT #36 see **COX**	MARION CO.	T9S	R3W	S5
SCHOOL FOR DEAF MUTES see **MUTE SCHOOL**				
	MARION CO.	T8S	R2W	?
SCHOOL HOUSE see **ONA**	LINCOLN CO.	T12S	R11W	S21
SCHOOLING see **HARRIS**	LINN CO.	T15S	R4W	S24
SCHOOLMASTER'S GRAVE	COLUMBIA CO.	T7N	R2W	S16
SCHOONER CREEK	LINCOLN CO.	T7S	R11W	?
SCHRAG FAMILY	POLK CO.	T8S	R5W	S6
SCHRAG, JOSEPH see **SCHRAG FAMILY**				
	POLK CO.	T8S	R5W	S6
SCHREIBER, DONALD A. see **SWAILS CEDARS**				
	CLACKAMAS CO.	T3S	R3E	?
SCHRIMPF FAMILY	LANE CO.	T19S	R5W	S2
SCHRIMPF, HENRY C. see **SCHRIMPF FAMILY**				
	LANE CO.	T19S	R5W	S2

SCHRIMPF, MINNIE L. see **SCHRIMPF FAMILY**

	LANE CO.	T19S	R5W	S2

SCHRIVER, EVELYN see **ELK CITY PIONEER**

	LINCOLN CO.	T11S	R10W	S11
SCHUEBEL	CLACKAMAS CO.	T3S	R2E	S36

SCHULKOWSKI, JOSEPH see **SCHIEVE, AUGUST**

	COLUMBIA CO.	T5N	R2W	?
SCHULSON FAMILY	POLK CO.	?	?	?
SCHWALNUS FAMILY	TILLAMOOK CO.	T3N	R10W	?
SCHWEIZER BABY, JOHN	MALHEUR CO.	T20S	R46E	S33

SCHWEIZER PLACE, OTTO see **SCHWEIZER BABY, JOHN**

	MALHEUR CO.	T20S	R46E	S33
SCISM see **NEWSOM CAMPGROUND**	MARION CO.	T6S	R1W	S19

SCOTCH CHURCH see **THE OLD SCOTCH CHURCH**

	WASHINGTON CO.	T1N	R3W	S13

SCOTCH PLAINS PRESBYTERIAN see **THE OLD SCOTCH CHURCH**

	WASHINGTON CO.	T1N	R3W	S13
SCOTT see **BEULAH**	MALHEUR CO.	T18S	R37E	S35
SCOTT see **MT. PLEASANT**	UNION CO.	T2N	R40E	S15

SCOTT, CHRISSY see **McRAE RANCH, FARQUHAR**

	WASCO CO.	T6S	R19E	?
SCOTT CHURCH see **MT. PLEASANT**	UNION CO.	T2N	R40E	S15
SCOTT FAMILY	WASHINGTON CO.	?	?	?

SCOTT GRAVE YARD see **MT. PLEASANT**

	UNION CO.	T2N	R40E	S15

SCOTT, MR. AND MRS. JIM see **McRAE RANCH, FARQUHAR**

	WASCO CO.	T6S	R19E	?
SCOTTS MILLS see **HOLY ROSARY**	MARION CO.	T6S	R1E	S36
SCOTTS MILLS see **MAPLEWOOD**	CLACKAMAS CO.	T6S	R1E	S14
SCOTTSBURG	DOUGLAS CO.	T22S	R9W	S8

SCOUT CAMP see **CHAMBERLAIN FAMILY**

	TILLAMOOK CO.	T3S	R10W	S7

SCOVELL, CLIFFORD see **SCOVELL FAMILY**

	TILLAMOOK CO.	T3N	R9W	?
SCOVELL FAMILY	TILLAMOOK CO.	T3N	R9W	?
SEARS	LANE CO.	T20S	R3W	S35
SEASIDE see **EVERGREEN**	CLATSOP CO.	T6N	R10W	S34
SEAWARD see **CORD**	MALHEUR CO.	T28S	R38E	S7
SEAWARD FAMILY see **CORD**	MALHEUR CO.	T28S	R38E	S7
SEBASTOPOL FLATS	JOSEPHINE CO.	T39S	R9W	S15
SEEKSEEQUA [NORTH]	JEFFERSON CO.	T10S	R12E	S28
SEEKSEEQUA [SOUTH]	JEFFERSON CO.	T10S	R12E	S27
SEGHERS see **MT. OLIVE LUTHERAN**	WASHINGTON CO.	T1S	R4W	S23
SEIDEL FAMILY see **GORE FAMILY**	COLUMBIA CO.	T5N	R2W	S10
SEIFFERT, INFANT	WASHINGTON CO.	?	?	?
SELDERS, ANTHONY	COLUMBIA CO.	T5N	R5W	S32
SELLERS see **KEENEY FAMILY**	LANE CO.	T19S	R2W	S5
SELLWOOD	MULTNOMAH CO.	T1S	R1E	S23

SELLWOOD see **MILWAUKIE PIONEER**	CLACKAMAS CO.	T1S	R1E	S26
SELLWOOD'S LAND, REV. JOHN see **SELLWOOD**				
	MULTNOMAH CO.	T1S	R1E	S23
SELMA [NEW] see **DEER CREEK**	JOSEPHINE CO.	T38S	R7W	S18
SELMA [OLD] see **FORT HAYES**	JOSEPHINE CO.	T37S	R8W	S35
SEVENTH DAY ADVENTIST see **JOHNSON FAMILY**				
	WASHINGTON CO.	T1S	R1W	S17
SEVERY HILL see **I.O.O.F. [GLENADA]**				
	LANE CO.	T19S	R12W	S2
SERVITE	MULTNOMAH CO.	T1N	R2W	S21
SEWARD see **CORD**	MALHEUR CO.	T28S	R38E	S7
SEXTON OLNEY see **OLNEY**	UMATILLA CO.	T2N	R32E	S15
SHAARIE TORAH see **CONGREGATION SHAARIE TORAH**				
	MULTNOMAH CO.	T1S	R2E	S20
SHADY BROOK	WASHINGTON CO.	T2N	R2W	S30
SHADY COVE see **JOHNSON FAMILY**	JACKSON CO.	T34S	R1W	S15
SHADYBROOK see **SHADY BROOK**	WASHINGTON CO.	T2N	R2W	S30
SHAMBROOK D.L.C., GEORGE see **DOUGLAS COUNTY POOR FARM**				
	DOUGLAS CO.	T26S	R6W	S30
SHAMBROOK D.L.C., GEORGE see **LaBRIE FAMILY**				
	DOUGLAS CO.	T26S	R6W	S30
SHARP, BERNITA JONES see **SMALL, REVEREND THOMAS HENDERSON**				
	MARION CO.	T7S	R1W	S34
SHARP D.L.C., THOMAS see **COOLEY FAMILY**				
	CURRY CO.	T41S	R13W	S9
SHARPLES GRAVES	LANE CO.	T18S	R2W	S29
SHAUG D.L.C., CHARLES see **MOON, JEFF E.**				
	WASCO CO.	T2N	R13E	S32
SHAW see **BRUNK FARM**	POLK CO.	T7S	R4W	?
SHAW, BILLY	WASCO CO.	T1S	R11E	S11
SHAW CATHOLIC	MARION CO.	T8S	R2W	S13
SHAW D.L.C., ALVA C. see **BRUNK FARM**				
	POLK CO.	T7S	R4W	?
SHAW D.L.C., ALVA C. see **REST LAWN MEMORY GARDENS AND MAUSOLEUM**				
	POLK CO.	T7S	R4W	S26
SHAW D.L.C., JAMES see **STEPHENSON FAMILY**				
	YAMHILL CO.	T3S	R5W	S22
SHEA HILL	LINN CO.	T13S	R1E	?
SHEARER see **SMITH, JOSEPH**	BENTON CO.	T10S	R5W	S9
SHEAVILLE	MALHEUR CO.	T28S	R47E	S18
SHEDD	LINN CO.	T13S	R4W	S13
SHEEDY, CARL see **KENNEDY, SUSAN**	GRANT CO.	T13S	R32E	?
SHEEL see **SCHEEL FAMILY**	CLACKAMAS CO.	T3S	R5E	S18
SHELBURN see **MILLER**	LINN CO.	T10S	R2W	S1
SHELLEY FAMILY	HOOD RIVER CO.	T2N	R10E	S25
SHELTON D.L.C., JAMES see **SHELTON, JOHN**				
	LINN CO.	T9S	R1E	S34
SHELTON, JOHN	LINN CO.	T9S	R1E	S34

SHEPHARD, MATTIE see **HORN, COLUMBIA**

	BENTON CO.	?	?	?
SHEPHERD see **PINE GROVE**	LINN CO.	T13S	R4W	S32

SHEPHERD D.L.C., WILLIAM see **PINE GROVE**

	LINN CO.	T13S	R4W	S32
SHEPHERD, INA	DOUGLAS CO.	T27S	R5W	?
SHERARS BRIDGE see **WARNER**	WASCO CO.	T3S	R14E	S16

SHERIDAN MASONIC LODGE #64 see **MASONIC [SHERIDAN]**

	YAMHILL CO.	T5S	R6W	S26
SHERIDAN MENNONITE	POLK CO.	T6S	R7W	S13
SHERRETT-LYSTER see **NORTH FORK**	DOUGLAS CO.	T20S	R10W	S31

SHERWOOD LUTHERAN see **MAPLE LANE**

	WASHINGTON CO.	T2S	R1W	S30
SHIELDS	LANE CO.	T20S	R3W	S33

SHIELDS D.L.C., WILLIAM see **SHIELDS**

	LANE CO.	T20S	R3W	S33
SHIELDS, LOUIS	WALLOWA CO.	T1N	R50E	UNS
SHILOH BASIN see **JONES FAMILY**	COLUMBIA CO.	T6N	R2W	S33
SHILOH BURIAL	LANE CO.	T19S	R1W	S29
SHIPLEY see **MT. UNION**	BENTON CO	T12S	R5W	S7
SHIPLEY, REUBEN see **MT. UNION**	BENTON CO	T12S	R5W	S7
SHIPPER PLACE see **FISHER BABY**	TILLAMOOK CO.	?	?	?
SHIRK RANCH	LAKE CO.	T38S	R27E	?

SHIRLEY D.L.C., JAMES see **ZIMMERMAN**

	CLACKAMAS CO.	T4S	R1E	S32

SHIRLEY RANCH, CARL see **KENNEDY GRAVE**

	WHEELER CO.	T13S	R25E	?

SHIVELY D.L.C., JOHN see **ASTORIA [OLD]**

	CLATSOP CO.	T8N	R9W	S8

SHIVELY D.L.C., JOHN see **ASTORIA PIONEER**

	CLATSOP CO.	T8N	R9W	S17

SHIVELY FAMILY see **ASTORIA [OLD]**

	CLATSOP CO.	T8N	R9W	S8

SHIVELY, JOHN M. see **ASTORIA [OLD]**

	CLATSOP CO.	T8N	R9W	S8
SHOESTRING	DOUGLAS CO.	T23S	R4W	S10
SHORT FAMILY	MARION CO.	T7S	R1W	S32
SHOT POUCH see **MULKEY**	LINCOLN CO.	T11S	R8W	S26
SHREVE D.L.C., ASA see **FAST**	POLK CO.	T7S	R5W	S23
SHUBEL see **SCHUEBEL**	CLACKAMAS CO.	T3S	R2E	S36
SHUBEL HILL see **SCHUEBEL**	CLACKAMAS CO.	T3S	R2E	S36
SHUCK see **DUNDEE PIONEER**	YAMHILL CO.	T3S	R3W	S26

SHUCK D.L.C., JACOB see **DUNDEE PIONEER**

	YAMHILL CO.	T3S	R3W	S26
SHUCK, WILLIAM see **MILLER**	MALHEUR CO.	T13S	R42E	S21

SHULL D.L.C., MARCIA see **UNKNOWN**

	YAMHILL CO.	T3S	R5W	S9

```
SHULL FARM, ORAN see SMITH FAMILY
                                 COOS CO.          T28S    R13W     S3
SHULL INFANT see DIXIE FLAT      UNION CO.         T2N     R37E     ?
SHULL, JESSIE ROGERS see DIXIE FLAT
                                 UNION CO.         T2S     R37E     ?
SHULL, WILLIAM see DIXIE FLAT    UNION CO.         T2S     R37E     ?
SHUMWAY, ALFRED J.               MALHEUR CO.       T23S    R37E     S34
SIDNEY STATION see COX           MARION CO.        T9S     R3W      S5
SIEGMUND, RALPH see TERRELL      MARION CO.        T9S     R1E      S2
SILBERNAGEL see PIONEER [JORDAN]
                                 LINN CO.          T10S    R1E      S10
SILETZ see WASHINGTON, PAUL      LINCOLN CO.       T10S    R10W     S9
SILETZ VALLEY                    LINCOLN CO.       ?       ?        ?
SILK CREEK COMMUNITY             LANE CO.          T20S    R4W      S13
SILVA RANCH, see COCHRAN, WALLACE
                                 GRANT CO.         T9S     R27E     S5
SILVER CLIFF see LEWIS           MARION CO.        T7S     R1E      S29
SILVER CREEK                     HARNEY CO.        T23S    R26E     S5
SILVER CREEK see BETHANY PIONEER
                                 MARION CO.        T6S     R1W      S33
SILVER CREEK see SILVERTON       MARION CO.        T6S     R1W      S34
SILVER CREEK VALLEY see SILVER CREEK
                                 HARNEY CO.        T23S    R26E     S5
SILVER D.L.C., CLEVES S. see IOWA HILL
                                 WASHINGTON CO.    T1S     R3W      S32
SILVER FAMILY                    WALLOWA CO.       T6N     R43E     S15
SILVER LAKE                      LAKE CO.          T28S    R14E     S22
SILVERTON                        MARION CO.        T6S     R1W      S34
SILVIES see HANKINS              GRANT CO.         T18S    R32E     S7
SIMISON                          LINN CO.          T10S    R3W      S3
SIMISON FAMILY see SIMISON       LINN CO.          T10S    R3W      S3
SIMMONDS FAMILY see SIMMONS FAMILY
                                 CLATSOP CO.       T7N     R8W      ?
SIMMONS                          MARION CO.        T5S     R1W      S34
SIMMONS D.L.C., WHEELOCK see HILLSBORO PIONEER
                                 WASHINGTON CO.    T1N     R3W      S36
SIMMONS FAMILY                   CLATSOP CO.       T7N     R8W      ?
SIMMONS HILL see SIMMONS         MARION CO.        T5S     R1W      S34
SIMMS D.L.C., JOHN A. see MASONIC [THE DALLES]
                                 WASCO CO.         T1N     R13E     S10
SIMNASHO                         WASCO CO.         T7S     R12E     S20
SIMONDS FARM see SIMMONS FAMILY  CLATSOP CO.       T7N     R8W      ?
                                 LINN CO.          T10S    R3W      S3
SIMPSON see SIMISON              LINN CO.          T10S    R3W      S3
SIMPSON CREEK see WARNER, MRS.   LANE CO.          T24S    R3E      S13
SIMPSON-HALE see SIMISON         LINN CO.          T10S    R3W      S3
SIMPSON-HALE FAMILIES see SIMISON
SIMPSONS CHAPEL see ALPINE       BENTON CO.        T14S    R6W      S24
```

SINE *[Sic]* see **ZION MENNONITE**	CLACKAMAS CO.	T4S	R1E	S31
SINGLETON D.L.C., WILLIAM R. see **SINGLETON FAMILY**				
	DOUGLAS CO.	T26S	R4W	?
SINGLETON FAMILY	DOUGLAS CO.	T26S	R4W	?
SIPHON see **ECHO MEMORIAL**	UMATILLA CO.	T3N	R29E	S16
SISKIYOU MEMORIAL PARK AND MAUSOLEUM				
	JACKSON CO.	T37S	R1W	S29
SISLEY FAMILY	BAKER CO.	T12S	R45E	S15
SISLEY, FRANK see **SISLEY FAMILY**	BAKER CO.	T12S	R45E	S15
SISTERS see **CAMP POLK**	DESCHUTES CO.	T14S	R10E	S27
SISTERS, MT. ANGEL see **QUEEN OF ANGELS CONVENT**				
	MARION CO.	T6S	R1W	S10
SISTERS OF SAINT MARY'S see **UNKNOWN**				
	WASHINGTON CO.	T1S	R2W	S14
SISTERS OF SAINT MARY'S OF OREGON INC. see **UNKNOWN**				
	WASHINGTON CO.	T1S	R2W	S14
SISTERS OF THE HOLY NAMES	CLACKAMAS CO.	T2S	R1E	S14
SISTERS OF THE PRECIOUS BLOOD see **MONASTERY OF THE PRECIOUS BLOOD**				
	MULTNOMAH CO.	T1S	R2E	S5
SIUSLAW GRANGE see **LORANE GRANGE**				
	LANE CO.	T20S	R5W	S2
SIUSLAW INDIAN see **DREW MEMORIAL**				
	LANE CO.	T18S	R12W	S24
SIUSLAW PRECINCT see **LORANE GRANGE**				
	LANE CO.	T20S	R5W	S2
SIXES	CURRY CO.	T32S	R14W	S7
SIZEMORE, MR. see **SILVER FAMILY**	WALLOWA CO.	T6N	R43E	S15
SKAGGS, MARTH J.	COOS CO.	T28S	R10W	S10
SKINNER CHILDREN	MORROW CO.	T3S	R27E	?
SKINNER, JOHN F. M. see **SKINNER CHILDREN**				
	MORROW CO.	T3S	R27E	?
SKOOKUMHOUSE	CURRY CO.	T36S	R13W	?
SKUNK HOLLOW see **BROOKS CATHOLIC**				
	MARION CO.	T6S	R2W	S21
SKUNKVILLE see **BROOKS CATHOLIC**	MARION CO.	T6S	R2W	S21
SKYLINE MEMORIAL GARDENS	MULTNOMAH CO.	T1N	R1W	S23
SKYLINE MEMORIAL PARK see **SKYLINE MEMORIAL GARDENS**				
	MULTNOMAH CO.	T1N	R1W	S23
SKYVIEW MEMORIAL PARK	UMATILLA CO.	T1N	R32E	S10
SLATE CREEK	JOSEPHINE CO.	T37S	R7W	?
SLATE CREEK RANCH see **SLATE CREEK**				
	JOSEPHINE CO.	T37S	R7W	?
SLATER see **SWAMP CREEK ROAD BURIALS**				
	LANE CO.	T16S	R7W	S7
SLAYTER see **SWAMP CREEK ROAD BURIALS**				
	LANE CO.	T16S	R7W	S7
SLAYTOR see **SWAMP CREEK ROAD BURIALS**				
	LANE CO.	T16S	R7W	S7

SLOAN	JOSEPHINE CO.	T36S	R6W	S30
SLOUGH see **COLUMBIAN**	MULTNOMAH CO.	T1N	R1E	S10
SMALL, AMANDA E. see **SMALL D.L.C., GEORGE**				
	LANE CO.	T20S	R3W	?
SMALL BUTTE see **WINKLE FAMILY**	BENTON CO.	T13S	R5W	S22
SMALL D.L.C., GEORGE	LANE CO.	T20S	R3W	?
SMALL D.L.C., GEORGE see **FIR GROVE**				
	LANE CO.	T20S	R3W	S29
SMALL FAMILY	LANE CO.	T22S	R3W	S17
SMALL, REVEREND THOMAS HENDERSON				
	MARION CO.	T7S	R1W	S34
SMALLEY, EVELYN	COOS CO.	T29S	R13W	S11
SMITH	MULTNOMAH CO.	T1N	R5E	?
SMITH see **CLAGGETT**	MARION CO.	T6S	R3W	S26
SMITH BABY	MULTNOMAH CO.	?	?	?
SMITH BURIAL GROUND see **FRANKTON**				
	HOOD RIVER CO.	T3N	R10E	S27
SMITH, CAPTAIN W. H. see **LEWTHWAITE**				
	CLACKAMAS CO.	T2S	R2E	S20
SMITH CLAIM see **DIETRICH, W.**	COOS CO.	T33S	R12W	S33
SMITH D.L.C., ALVIS see **CLAGGETT**				
	MARION CO.	T6S	R3W	S26
SMITH D.L.C., ANDREW AND SARAH E. see **BROOKSIDE**				
	YAMHILL CO.	T4S	R3W	S17
SMITH D.L.C., DANIEL see **PIONEER MEMORIAL**				
	MARION CO.	T6S	R2W	S10
SMITH D.L.C., GREEN B. see **SMITH, JOSEPH**				
	BENTON CO.	T10S	R5W	S9
SMITH D.L.C., HENRY B. see **STEPHENS FAMILY**				
	LANE CO.	T18S	R6W	S14
SMITH D.L.C., HIRAM AND SARA JANE see **I.O.O.F. [BAY CITY]**				
	TILLAMOOK CO.	T1S	R10W	S1
SMITH D.L.C., HIRAM AND SARA JANE see **SMITH, HIRAM WESLEY**				
	TILLAMOOK CO.	T1S	R10W	?
SMITH D.L.C., IRA see **BROWN, WILLIAM C.**				
	POLK CO.	T7S	R5W	S22
SMITH D.L.C., JAMES see **SMITH FAMILY**				
	POLK CO.	T9S	R5W	S16
SMITH D.L.C., JOHN see **EMIGRANT**	LANE CO.	T18S	R2W	S3
SMITH D.L.C., JOHN see **SMITH, ELIZA B.**				
	LANE CO.	T18S	R2W	S3
SMITH D.L.C., NELSON D. see **DUNKARD**				
	JACKSON CO.	T38S	R1W	S23
SMITH D.L.C., PETER AND ORTHA see **SMITH, PETER**				
	YAMHILL CO.	T3S	R4W	S21
SMITH D.L.C., SIDNEY see **YOUNG, EWING**				
	YAMHILL CO.	T3S	R3W	S10

SMITH D.L.C., SIMON see **CLOVERDALE**				
	MARION CO.	T9S	R2W	S7
SMITH D.L.C., THOMAS see **SMITH DAUGHTER**				
	JACKSON CO.	T39S	R1E	S24
SMITH DAUGHTER	JACKSON CO.	T39S	R1E	S24
SMITH, EARL L. see **UNKNOWN**	COLUMBIA CO.	T5N	R4W	S5
SMITH, ELIZA B.	LANE CO.	T18S	R2W	S3
SMITH FAMILY	COOS CO.	T28S	R13W	S3
SMITH FAMILY	CURRY CO.	T35S	R12W	S13
SMITH FAMILY	CURRY CO.	T37S	R14W	S7
SMITH FAMILY	LANE CO.	T15S	R6W	?
SMITH FAMILY	LANE CO.	T18S	R2W	?
SMITH FAMILY	MORROW CO.	T3S	R26E	S32
SMITH FAMILY	POLK CO.	T9S	R5W	S16
SMITH FAMILY see **EMIGRANT**	LANE CO.	T18S	R2W	S3
SMITH HILL see **RED HILL**	DOUGLAS CO.	T23S	R5W	S34
SMITH, HIRAM WESLEY	TILLAMOOK CO.	T1S	R10W	?
SMITH HOMESTEAD see **SMITH FAMILY**				
	LANE CO.	T15S	R6W	?
SMITH, JOHN P. see **HALSEY PIONEER**				
	LINN CO.	T14S	R4W	S11
SMITH, JOSEPH	BENTON CO.	T10S	R5W	S9
SMITH, MARGARET HARRISON see **SMITH DAUGHTER**				
	JACKSON CO.	T39S	R1E	S24
SMITH MOUNTAIN see **FISHER, JOHN D.**				
	WALLOWA CO.	T2N	R41E	?
SMITH, MRS. ISAAC see **CLAGGETT**	MARION CO.	T6S	R3W	S26
SMITH, NORMAN see **OCEAN VIEW**	CURRY CO.	T30S	R14W	S21
SMITH, PETER	YAMHILL CO.	T3S	R4W	S21
SMITH PLACE	CLACKAMAS CO.	T2S	R4E	S30
SMITH RANCH, E. P. see **IZEE**	GRANT CO.	T17S	R28E	S29
SMITH, ROBERT T. see **SMITH**	MULTNOMAH CO.	T1N	R5E	?
SMITH, SAM	WASHINGTON CO.	T2S	R2W	S30
SMITH, SERGEANT	CURRY CO.	T41S	R13W	S7
SMITH, SILVESTER	HARNEY CO.	T28S	R33E	S26
SMITH, THOMAS see **SMITH DAUGHTER**				
	JACKSON CO.	T39S	R1E	S24
SMITH, TILMAN H. see **OAK GROVE**	HOOD RIVER CO.	T2N	R10E	?
SMITH, TOM	LANE CO.	T15S	R12W	S27
SMITH, WHISTLING	JEFFERSON CO.	T10S	R13E	S7
SMITHFIELD see **FRANKLIN**	LANE CO.	T16S	R5W	S21
SMOCK PRAIRIE see **WAMIC**	WASCO CO.	T4S	R12E	S22
SMYRNA	CLACKAMAS CO.	T5S	R1E	S9
SMYRNA UNITED CHURCH OF CHRIST see **SMYRNA**				
	CLACKAMAS CO.	T5S	R1E	S9
SMYTH see **HAPPY VALLEY**	HARNEY CO.	T29S	R33E	S12
SNAKE RIVER see **HIBBARD CREEK**	BAKER CO.	T12S	R45E	S27
SNODGRASS FAMILY see **CARPENTER**	CURRY CO.	T39S	R14W	?

SNODGRASS FARM see **CARPENTER**	CURRY CO.	T39S	R14W	?
SNYDER FAMILY	TILLAMOOK CO.	T3N	R10W	?
SNYDER'S LODGE	CURRY CO.	?	?	?
SODAVILLE see **KLUM**	LINN CO.	T12S	R1W	S32
SOLDIER'S GRAVE	WASCO CO.	T1N	R15E	?
SOLDIERS	LINN CO.	T13S	UNSURVEYED	
SOLDIERS	UMATILLA CO.	T3N	R29E	?
SOLDIERS see **U.S. ARMY FORT STEVENS**				
	CLATSUP CO.	T8N	R10W	S8
SOMERS RANCH see **RAYMOND, MR.**	WALLOWA CO.	T2N	R50E	?
SOUTH see **HALLS FERRY**	MARION CO.	T8S	R4W	S14
SOUTH BEACH	LINCOLN CO.	T11S	R11W	S17
SOUTH CORNELIUS CATHOLIC see **FERN HILL CATHOLIC**				
	WASHINGTON CO.	T1S	R3W	S16
SOUTH DEER CREEK see **BOGGESS FAMILY**				
	DOUGLAS CO.	T28S	R5W	S1
SOUTH FORK see **COOS RIVER PIONEER**				
	COOS CO.	T25S	R12W	S25
SOUTH MT. TABOR [#1]	MULTNOMAH CO.	T1S	R2E	S5
SOUTH MT. TABOR [#2]	MULTNOMAH CO.	T1S	R2E	S8
SOUTH SLOUGH	COOS CO.	T26S	R14W	S15
SOUTH YAMHILL	YAMHILL CO.	T5S	R5W	S3
SOUTH YAMHILL BAPTIST CHURCH see **SOUTH YAMHILL**				
	YAMHILL CO.	T5S	R5W	S3
SOUTHERLIN'S PLACE, BILLY see **LOWERY**				
	CURRY CO.	T36S	R13W`	S1
SOUTHWORTH D.L.C., JAMES B. see **FRANKLIN**				
	LANE CO.	T16S	R5W	S21
SOUTHWORTH RANCH	GRANT CO.	T16S	R31E	S15
SPALDING D.L.C., HENRY H. see **TINDALL, MR.**				
	LINN CO.	T14S	R2W	S6
SPANISH GULCH	WHEELER CO.	T13S	R25E	S6
SPARKS FAMILY	LANE CO.	T16S	R4E	S20
SPARKS, NAOMI ELAINE see **SPARKS FAMILY**				
	LANE CO.	T16S	R4E	S20
SPARKS, S. C. see **SPARKS FAMILY**	LANE CO.	T16S	R4E	S20
SPARLIN	JOSEPHINE CO.	T38S	R5W	S22
SPARLING see **SPARLIN**	JOSEPHINE CO.	T38S	R5W	S22
SPARTA	BAKER CO.	T8S	R44E	S16
SPEAK RANCH	BAKER CO.	?	R45E	?
SPENCE, DR. JAMES C. see **SPENCE FAMILY**				
	JOSEPHINE CO.	T40S	R8W	S2
SPENCE, EVA LOUSE see **SPENCE FAMILY**				
	JOSEPHINE CO.	T40S	R8W	S2
SPENCE FAMILY	JOSEPHINE CO.	T40S	R8W	S2
SPENCE, LAURIE ELDORA see **SPENCE FAMILY**				
	JOSEPHINE CO.	T40S	R8W	S2
SPENCER	KLAMATH CO.	T39S	R7E	S30

SPENCER BUTTE I.O.O.F. LODGE #9	LANE CO.	T17S	R4W	S33
SPENCER D.L.C., JOHN see **SPENCER FAMILY**				
	YAMHILL CO.	T3S	R3W	S22
SPENCER FAMILY	YAMHILL CO.	T3S	R3W	S22
SPENCER-GREER FAMILY see **SPENCER FAMILY**				
	YAMHILL CO.	T3S	R3W	S22
SPENCER, REV. JOHN see **SPENCER FAMILY**				
	YAMHILL CO.	T3S	R3W	S22
SPIRIT MOUNTAIN see **HOLMES FAMILY**				
	YAMHILL CO.	T5S	R8W	S36
SPLAWN D.L.C., GEORGE W. see **SPLAWN FAMILY**				
	LINN CO.	T14S	R1W	S11
SPLAWN FAMILY	LINN CO.	T14S	R1W	S11
SPLAWN, GREENBERRY see **SPLAWN FAMILY**				
	LINN CO.	T14S	R1W	S11
SPORES D.L.C., JACOB C. see **I.O.O.F. [COBURG]**				
	LANE CO.	T17S	R3W	S4
SPRAGUE D.L.C., ALFRED see **SPRAGUE FAMILY**				
	CLACKAMAS CO.	T3S	R3E	S18
SPRAGUE FAMILY	CLACKAMAS CO.	T3S	R3E	S18
SPRAY	WHEELER CO.	T8S	R24E	S35
SPRAY [OLD]	WHEELER CO.	T8S	R24E	S36
SPRING FAMILY	LINN CO.	T13S	R2E	S18
SPRING VALLEY PRESBYTERIAN CHURCH see **ZENA**				
	POLK CO.	T6S	R4W	S36
SPRINGFIELD MEMORIAL GARDENS	LANE CO.	T17S	R2W	S35
SPRINGFIELD PIONEER MEMORIAL PARK see **PIONEER MEMORIAL CEMETERY PARK**				
	LANE CO.	T17S	R3W	S35
SPRINGWATER	CLACKAMAS CO.	T4S	R4E	S8
SPRUCE POINT	LANE CO.	T18S	R12W	S27
SPRY, M. JANE see **MULHOLLAND FAMILY**				
	LANE CO.	T19S	R2W	S4
SPRY, MARTHA JANE see **MULHOLLAND FAMILY**				
	LANE CO.	T19S	R2W	S4
SPRY, WILLIAM see **MULHOLLAND FAMILY**				
	LANE CO.	T19S	R2W	S4
SQUAW CREEK	MALHEUR CO.	T21S	R41E	?
SQUAW CREEK see **COLLINGS GRAVES**	JACKSON CO.	T40S	R4W	S36
STAATS FARM, ISAAC see **STAATS, ISAAC W.**				
	POLK CO.	T9S	R5W	?
STAATS, ISAAC W.	POLK CO.	T9S	R5W	?
STAEGER, GOTTLIEB	WASHINGTON CO.	T2N	R3W	S34
STAFFORD see **STAFFORD BAPTIST CHURCH**				
	CLACKAMAS CO.	T2S	R1E	S31
STAFFORD BAPTIST CHURCH	CLACKAMAS CO.	T2S	R1E	S31
STAFFORD FAMILY	LANE CO.	T17S	R2W	S3
STANFIELD see **PLEASANT VIEW**	UMATILLA CO.	T4N	R29E	S28

```
STANLEY, SUSAN see MERRIMAN FAMILY
                                JACKSON CO.        T38S     R2W          ?
STANTON, CORTEZ see STANTON FAMILY
                                LINCOLN CO.        T10S     R10W         S32
STANTON, F. M. see STANTON FAMILY
                                LINCOLN CO.        T10S     R10W         S32
STANTON FAMILY                  LINCOLN CO.        T10S     R10W         S32
STANTON, J. A. see STANTON FAMILY
                                LINCOLN CO.        T10S     R10W         S32
STAPLES see CLOVERDALE          MARION CO.         T9S      R2W          S7
STAPLETON FAMILY                LANE CO.           T18S     R5W          S4
STAPLETON FAMILY see CENTRAL SCHOOL
                                LANE CO.           T18S     R5W          S4
STAR #23 REBEKAH LODGE COMMUNITY see DUFUR COMMUNITY
                                WASCO CO.          T1S      R13E         S24
STARK see CITY CEMETERY [#1]    MULTNOMAH CO.      T1N      R1E          S33
STARK D.L.C., BENJAMIN see CITY CEMETERY #1
                                MULTNOMAH CO.      T1N      R1E          S33
STARK, ELIZA JANE see DOW, OSCAR A.
                                BENTON CO.         T13S     R5W          S28
STARKEY                         UNION CO.          T4S      R35E         S3
STARKEY, JOHN B.                UNION CO.          T3S      R35E         S35
STATE CREMATORIUM see ASYLUM    MARION CO.         T7S      R3W          S25
STATE REFORM SCHOOL see BOYS    MARION CO.         T8S      R2W          S17
STATE REFORM SCHOOL see HERREN FAMILY
                                MARION CO.         T8S      R2W          S17
STATE SCHOOL FOR THE DEAF see MUTE SCHOOL
                                MARION CO.         T8S      R2W          ?
STAYTON PIONEER see CAMPBELL-GRIER
                                MARION CO.         T9S      R1W          S2
STEAMBOAT                       JACKSON CO.        T40S     R4W          S20
STEARNS D.L.C., DAVID E. see STEARNS FAMILY
                                JACKSON CO.        T38S     R1W          S34
STEARNS FAMILY                  JACKSON CO.        T38S     R1W          S34
STEARNS, MARY W. MELOY see MELOY FAMILY
                                MULTNOMAH CO.      ?        ?            ?
STEIWER-LOONEY see LOONEY FAMILY
                                MARION CO.         T9S      R3W          S23
STEMMERMAN RANCH, LEROY see NORTH FORK
                                DOUGLAS CO.        T20S     R10W         S31
STENNICK FARM see GILBREATH-MOECK FAMILIES
                                COLUMBIA CO.       T7N      R2W          S18
STEPHENS CHILDREN see STEPHENS FAMILY
                                LANE CO.           T18S     R6W          S14
STEPHENS D.L.C., ADAM AND LUCINDA see HAYESVILLE
                                MARION CO.         T7S      R3W          S12
STEPHENS D.L.C., BENJAMIN see BRYANT FAMILY
                                DOUGLAS CO.        T29S     R4W          S21
```

STEPHENS D.L.C., JAMES B. see **ASYLUM**
               MULTNOMAH CO.   T1S   R1E   S2

STEPHENS FAMILY   LANE CO.   T18S R6W   S14

STEPHENS FAMILY see **HAYESVILLE**   MARION CO.   T7S   R3W   S12

STEPHENSON, EDWARD see **STEPHENSON FAMILY**
               YAMHILL CO.   T3S   R5W   S22

STEPHENSON, ELIZA see **STEPHENSON FAMILY**
               YAMHILL CO.   T3S   R5W   S22

STEPHENSON FAMILY   YAMHILL CO.   T3S   R5W   S22

STEPHENSON, G. W. see **STEPHENSON FAMILY**
               YAMHILL CO.   T3S   R5W   S22

STERLING see **STERLINGVILLE**   JACKSON CO.   T38S R2W   S33

STERLINGVILLE   JACKSON CO.   T38S R2W   S33

STEVENS D.L.C., THOMAS see **I.O.O.F. [ROSEBURG]**
               DOUGLAS CO.   T27S R5W   S19

STEVENS D.L.C., THOMAS see **ST. JOSEPH CATHOLIC**
               DOUGLAS CO.   T27S R5W   S19

STEVENS FAMILY see **STEPHENS FAMILY**
               LANE CO.   T18S R6W   S14

STEVENSON see **STEPHENSON FAMILY** YAMHILL CO.   T3S   R5W   S22

STEWARD FAMILY   COOS CO.   T28S R13W   ?

STEWARD FAMILY   MORROW CO.   ?   ?   ?

STEWARD, JAMES see **STEWARD FAMILY**
               MORROW CO.   ?   ?   ?

STEWARD, STEPHEN see **STEWARD FAMILY**
               COOS CO.   T28S R13W   ?

STEWART see **FALL CREEK**   LANE CO.   T18S R1W   S33

STEWART CREEK   COLUMBIA CO.   T7N   R4W   S3

STEWART D.L.C., THOMAS see **STEWART FAMILY**
               WASHINGTON CO. T1S   R2W   S9

STEWART D.L.C., THOMAS see **VALLEY MEMORIAL PARK AND MAUSOLEUM**
               WASHINGTON CO. T1S   R2W   S9

STEWART FAMILY   WASHINGTON CO. T1S   R2W   S9

STEWART, HENRY see **UNKNOWN**   UNION CO.   T3S   R33E   S23

STEWART HILL see **STEWART CREEK** COLUMBIA CO.   T7N   R4W   S3

STEWART, MRS. see **STEWART'S POINT**
               COLUMBIA CO.   T8N   R4W   ?

STEWART'S POINT   COLUMBIA CO.   T8N   R4W   ?

STEWER CREEK see **STEWART CREEK** COLUMBIA CO.   T7N   R4W   S3

STINGER D.L.C., LEONARD see **LAVADOURE**
               DOUGLAS CO.   T30S R3W   S29

STIPP D.L.C., JOHN see **STIPP MEMORIAL**
               MARION CO.   T8S   R2W   S2

STIPP MEMORIAL   MARION CO.   T8S   R2W   S2

STOLLER FAMILY   WASCO CO.   T2N   R14E   S33

STONE D.L.C., ASA see **VIOLA PIONEER**
               CLACKAMAS CO.   T3S   R3E   S23

STONEFIELD BEACH BURIALS see **BRAY**

LANE CO.	T15S	R12W	S27

STONEY POINT see **LONE FIR** | MARION CO. | T8S | R1W | S21

STORES FAMILY DOUGLAS CO. T22S R6W ?

STOTT see **MOUNTAIN VIEW-STARK PIONEER**

MULTNOMAH CO. T1N R3E S35

STOWEL FAMILY DOUGLAS CO. T26S R6W S36

STRADER FAMILY DOUGLAS CO. T27S R4W ?

STRADER, JANE WORTHINGTON see **STRADER FAMILY**

DOUGLAS CO. T27S R4W ?

STRADER, JOHN see **STRADER FAMILY**

DOUGLAS CO. T27S R4W ?

STRADER, MARTHA see **STRADER FAMILY**

DOUGLAS CO. T27S R4W ?

STRADLEY LAND see **EDWARDS CHILD** SHERMAN CO. T3S R16E ?

STRAIGHT D.L.C., HIRAM see **ST. AGNES BABY HOME**

CLACKAMAS CO. T2S R2E S20

STRAIGHT D.L.C., HIRAM see **STRAIGHT FAMILY**

CLACKAMAS CO. T2S R2E S29

STRAIGHT D.L.C., HIRAM AND SUSAN see **LEWTHWAITE**

CLACKAMAS CO. T2S R2E S20

STRAIGHT FAMILY CLACKAMAS CO. T2S R2E S29

STREITHOFF D.L.C., THOMAS E. see **SANTIAM CENTRAL**

LINN CO. T11S R2W S6

STRETOFF TILLAMOOK CO. T2S R9W ?

STRIEBY HOMESTEAD, DR. ULYSSES GRANT see **BIG FLAT**

BAKER CO. T12S R37E S10

STRONG see **SCHOOLMASTER'S GRAVE** COLUMBIA CO. T7N R2W S16

STRONG, CLARENCE see **BROWN** COOS CO. ? ? ?

STRONG, RILEY see **SCHOOLMASTER'S GRAVE**

COLUMBIA CO. T7N R2W S16

STRONG, WILLIAM see **SCHOOLMASTER'S GRAVE**

COLUMBIA CO. T7N R2W S16

STROUTS see **MAYS-STROUTS** BENTON CO. T11S R7W S6

STUART D.L.C., JOHN see **FOTHERGILL, JOHN**

LANE CO. T18S R1W S33

STUBBLEFIELD, TINIE see **HORSE CREEK RANCH**

WALLOWA CO. T3N R48E S35

STUMP MULTNOMAH CO. T2N R1E S6

STUMP D.L.C., CUTHBERT see **STUMP**

MULTNOMAH CO. T2N R1E S6

STUMP FARM POLK CO. T8S R5W S27

STURDEVANT see **STURDIVANT** UMATILLA CO. T5S R31E S4

STURDIVANT UMATILLA CO. T5S R31E S4

STURGILL, ADELINE TALLEY see **STURGILL CHILDREN, EFFIE AND ESTHER**

BAKER CO. T9S R40E S19

STURGILL, CARRIE JONES see **STURGILL CHILDREN, HILDA AND LOUIE**

BAKER CO. T8S R43E ?

STURGILL CHILDREN, EFFIE AND ESTHER
| | BAKER CO. | T9S | R40E | S19 |
STURGILL CHILDREN, HILDA AND LOUIE
| | BAKER CO. | T8S | R43E | ? |
STURGILL, EFFIE LENORA see **STURGILL CHILDREN, EFFIE AND ESTHER**
| | BAKER CO. | T9S | R40E | S19 |
STURGILL, ESTHER ELIZABETH see **STURGILL CHILDREN, EFFIE AND ESTHER**
| | BAKER CO. | T9S | R40E | S19 |
STURGILL, LEWIS see **STURGILL CHILDREN, HILDA AND LOUIE**
| | BAKER CO. | T8S | R43E | ? |
STURGILL, WILLIAM R. see **STURGILL CHILDREN, EFFIE AND ESTHER**
| | BAKER CO. | T9S | R40E | S19 |
STURGIS FAMILY see **UNKNOWN**   JACKSON CO.   T32S R1E   S23
SUBLIMITY GRAVEYARD see **HOBSON-WHITNEY**
| | MARION CO. | T8S | R1W | S35 |
SULLIVAN D.L.C., TIMOTHY see **ST. MARY'S**
| | MULTNOMAH CO. | T1N | R1E | S36 |
SUMMER LAKE   LAKE CO.   T31S R16E   S10
SUMMERS FAMILY see **BATTLE ROCK**   CURRY CO.   T33S R15W   S4
SUMMERS, RALPH see **BATTLE ROCK**   CURRY CO.   T33S R15W   S4
SUMMERVILLE   UNION CO.   T1S   R39E   S18
SUMMERVILLE-IMBLER see **SUMMERVILLE**
| | UNION CO. | T1S | R39E | S18 |
SUMMIT   BENTON CO.   T11S R7W   S8
SUMMIT MEADOW see **CHINESE HERDSMAN**
| | WHEELER CO. | T10S | R21E | ? |
SUMMIT MEADOWS   CLACKAMAS CO. T3S   R8 1/2E S25
SUMNER [OLD]   COOS CO.   T26S R12W   S33
SUMNER PIONEER see **SUMNER [OLD]** COOS CO.   T26S R12W   S33
SUMNER PLOT see **SUMNER SCHOOL**   COOS CO.   T26S R12W   S17
SUMNER SCHOOL   COOS CO.   T26S R12W   S17
SUMPTER   BAKER CO.   T9S   R37E   S33
SUN RISE   SHERMAN CO.   T2N   R17E   S31
SUNDSTROM, BRUCE   LANE CO.   T16S R8W   S18
SUNDSTROM, ROBERT BRUCE see **SUNDSTROM, BRUCE**
| | LANE CO. | T16S | R8W | S18 |
SUNNY HILL CEMETERY OF NEHALEM see **ELSIE**
| | CLATSOP CO. | T4N | R7W | S5 |
SUNNY VALLEY see **GRAVE CREEK**   JOSEPHINE CO. T34S R6W   ?
SUNNYDALE   DOUGLAS CO.   T22S R6W   S16
SUNNYSIDE CHIMES MEMORIAL GARDENS see **LITTLE CHAPEL OF THE CHIMES**
    MEMORIAL GARDEN   CLACKAMAS CO. T1S   R2E   S33
SUNNYSIDE PIONEER   CLACKAMAS CO. T2S   R2E   S2
SUNRISE MEMORIAL PARK see **I.O.O.F. [GREENWOOD]**
| | MULTNOMAH CO. | T1S | R1E | S27 |
SUNSET   LAKE CO.   T39S R20E   S10
SUNSET   MALHEUR CO.   T18S R47E   S8

SUNSET see **I.O.O.F. [THE DALLES]**				
	WASCO CO.	T1N	R13E	S4
SUNSET see **POUNDER**	MULTNOMAH CO.	T1N	R4E	S35
SUNSET see **SUNNYDALE**	DOUGLAS CO.	T22S	R6W	S16
SUNSET HEIGHTS MEMORIAL GARDENS	TILLAMOOK CO.	T1S	R9W	S28
SUNSET HILL see **PIONEER [THE DALLES]**				
	WASCO CO.	T1N	R13E	S10
SUNSET HILLS	UMATILLA CO.	T5N	R28E	S19
SUNSET HILLS MEMORIAL GARDENS	LANE CO.	T18S	R3W	S18
SUNSET HILLS MEMORIAL PARK see **FINLEY'S SUNSET HILL MEMORIAL**				
	WASHINGTON CO.	T1S	R1W	S1
SUNSET MEMORIAL PARK	COOS CO.	T26S	R13W	S2
SUNSET MEMORIAL PARK see **FINLEY'S SUNSET HILL MEMORIAL**				
	WASHINGTON CO.	T1S	R1W	S1
SUNSET PARK see **SUNSET**	LAKE CO.	T39S	R20E	S10
SUNSET VALLEY	HARNEY CO.	T25S	R31E	S27
SUNTEX see **SILVER CREEK**	HARNEY CO.	T23S	R26E	S5
SUPLEE see **DELORE**	CROOK CO.	T18S	R25E	S13
SUSANVILLE see **GALENA**	GRANT CO.	T10S	R32E	S12
SUTER CENTURY FARM see **SUTER FARM**				
	CLACKAMAS CO.	T2S	R4E	S30
SUTER FARM	CLACKAMAS CO.	T2S	R4E	S30
SUTHERLIN [OLD]	DOUGLAS CO.	T25S	R5W	S15
SUTHERLIN see **VALLEY VIEW**	DOUGLAS CO.	T25S	R5W	S13
SUTHERLIN D.L.C., THOMAS see **SUTHERLIN [OLD]**				
	DOUGLAS CO.	T25S	R5W	S15
SUTTER CREEK see **GEORGE**	CLACKAMAS CO.	T3S	R5E	S19
SUTTON	TILLAMOOK CO.	T4S	R10W	S22
SUTTON MOUNTAIN see **CHINESE HERDSMAN**				
	WHEELER CO.	T10S	R21E	?
SUTTON, SARAH	WASCO CO.	T4S	R13E	S4
SVENSEN PIONEER	CLATSOP CO.	T8N	R8W	S23
SWAILS CEDARS	CLACKAMAS CO.	T3S	R3E	?
SWALLOW, JOHN	LINN CO.		UNSURVEYED	
SWAMP CREEK ROAD BURIALS	LANE CO.	T16S	R7W	S7
SWAN LAKE see **HIBBERT**	KLAMATH CO.	T38S	R10E	S8
SWEARINGER D.L.C., ANDREW J. see **HEDRICK FAMILY**				
	DOUGLAS CO.	T21S	R6W	S35
SWEDE see **COLTON LUTHERAN**	CLACKAMAS CO.	T5S	R3E	S3
SWEDE CHURCH see **VALBY**	MORROW CO.	T3S	R24E	S8
SWEET CREEK	LANE CO.	T18S	R10W	?
SWEET D.L.C., ZARA see **LAUREL GROVE**				
	LANE CO.	T18S	R3W	S3
SWEET HOME	LANE CO.	T16S	R6W	S27
SWEET HOME MENNONITE	LINN CO.	T13S	R1E	S34
SWEET HOME MENNONITE see **GILLILAND**				
	LINN CO.	T13S	R1E	S34
SWEET HOME VALLEY see **GILLILAND**	LINN CO.	T13S	R1E	S34

SWEET, MARIA see **SWEET CREEK**	LANE CO.	T18S	R10W	?
SWEET RANCH, PIERCY see **CREW FAMILY**				
	CURRY CO.	T32S	R15W	S9
SWEET, ZARA see **SWEET CREEK**	LANE CO.	T18S	R10W	?
SWEGLE D.L.C., MATTHIAS see **SANDERS FAMILY**				
	CLACKAMAS CO.	T5S	R2E	S4
SWEIGEL FAMILY see **SANDERS FAMILY**				
	CLACKAMAS CO.	T5S	R2E	S4
SWETZER INFANT	MORROW CO.	T1S	R26E	S35
SWETZER, WILLIAM G. see **SWETZER INFANT**				
	MORROW CO.	T1S	R26E	S35
SWICK see **WEBERG FAMILY**	GRANT CO.	T18S	R26E	?
SWIFT, WINIFRED see **McGUIRE FAMILY**				
	DOUGLAS CO.	T28S	R7W	S34
SWITZERLAND see **APOSTOLIC**	MARION CO.	T7S	R1W	S8
SYLVAN see **JONES PIONEER**	MULTNOMAH CO.	T1S	R1E	S6
SYRACUSE see **SIMISON**	LINN CO.	T10S	R3W	S3
TAFT PIONEER	LINCOLN CO.	T7S	R11W	S27
TALENT see **STEARNS FAMILY**	JACKSON CO.	T38S	R1W	S34
TALOR D.L.C., HENRY see **TAYLOR-LANE FAMILY**				
	LANE CO.	T21S	R3W	S16
TARTER see **ENGLISH [OLD]**	POLK CO.	T9S	R5W	S28
TARTER, LENA BELLE see **INDIAN GRAVE HILL**				
	POLK CO.	T9S	R6W	?
TAYLOR	MULTNOMAH CO.	T2N	R1W	S6
TAYLOR	YAMHILL CO.	T5S	R4W	S10
TAYLOR D.L.C., JAMES see **TAYLOR**	MULTNOMAH CO.	T2N	R1W	S6
TAYLOR D.L.C., JAMES see **TAYLOR FAMILY**				
	POLK CO.	T9S	R6W	S34
TAYLOR D.L.C., JOHN AND ELIZAABETH see **AUMSVILLE**				
	MARION CO.	T8S	R1W	S30
TAYLOR D.L.C., LUKE see **YOUNGS RIVER**				
	CLATSOP CO.	T7N	R9W	S10
TAYLOR FAMILY	LANE CO.	T16S	R7W	S9
TAYLOR FAMILY	POLK CO.	T9S	R6W	S34
TAYLOR FAMILY see **TAYLOR-LANE FAMILY**				
	LANE CO.	T21S	R3W	S16
TAYLOR, JOSEPH see **PLEASANT HILL**				
	COOS CO.	T29S	R12W	S7
TAYLOR-LANE FAMILY	LANE CO.	T21S	R3W	S16
TEAGUE see **McCOLLUM**	LANE CO.	T18S	R4W	S30
TEAGUE FAMILY	LINCOLN CO.	T10S	R10W	S11
TEASEL CREEK see **MOLALLA MEMORIAL**				
	CLACKAMAS CO.	T5S	R2E	S20
TEDDIE	UNION CO.	T5S	R41E	S7
TELEGRAPH HILL see **MARSHFIELD**	COOS CO.	T25S	R13W	S26
TELOCASET	UNION CO.	T5S	R40E	S28

TEMPLE BETH ISRAEL see **BETH ISRAEL [NEW]**

	MULTNOMAH CO.	T1S	R1E	S21
TEMPLETON	COOS CO.	T23S	R12W	S26
TEN MILE GRAVEYARD	WASCO CO.	T2N	R15E	S31
TEN O'CLOCK	CLACKAMAS CO.	T3S	R2E	S35

TENBROOK D.L.C., ABRAM see **MEMORY GARDENS MEMORIAL PARK AND MAUSOLEUM**

	JACKSON CO.	T37S	R2W	S34
TENINO	JEFFERSON CO.	T9S	R12E	S27
TENMILE	DOUGLAS CO.	T28S	R7W	S31

TERHUNE FARM, ROBERT see **BELLINGER FAMILY**

	MARION CO.	T9S	R3W	S35

TERJESON PLACE, VERNE see **JAMES, CALVIN**

	UMATILLA CO.	T4N	R33E	?

TERRACE LAWN MEMORIAL PARK see **LITTLE CHAPEL OF THE CHIMES MEMORIAL GARDEN**

	CLACKAMAS CO.	T1S	R2E	S33

TERREBONNE see **PIONEER [TERREBONNE]**

	DESCHUTES CO.	T14S	R13E	S22
TERRELL	MARION CO.	T9S	R1E	S2

TERRELL, JUDGE G. P. see **TERRELL**

	MARION CO.	T9S	R1E	S2

TERWILLIGER see **CITY CEMETERY [#3]**

	MULTNOMAH CO.	T1S	R1E	S10

TERWILLIGER D.L.C., JAMES see **CITY CEMETERY #3**

	MULTNOMAH CO.	T1S	R1E	S10

TERWILLIGER PARK see **CITY CEMETERY [#3]**

	MULTNOMAH CO.	T1S	R1E	S10

TESCH, AARON see **HOLY NEW MARTYRS RUSSIAN ORTHODOX CHURCH**

	CLACKAMAS CO.	T4S	R2E	?
TESTAMENT CREEK	TILLAMOOK CO.	T4S	R7W	S5

TETREAU, ALICE see **FLEETWOOD FAMILY, JIM**

	BAKER CO.	T12S	R38E	S25
TEWS see **BAKER**	MORROW CO.	T2S	R24E	S6
THARP see **DEER CREEK**	YAMHILL CO.	T5S	R5W	S28
THE HILL see **HILL**	WASHINGTON CO.	T2S	R3W	S6
THE NOOK see **PIONEER MEMORIAL**	MARION CO.	T6S	R2W	S10
THE OLD SCOTCH CHURCH	WASHINGTON CO.	T1N	R3W	S13
THE PARK	UNION CO.	T6S	R41E	S2

THE PIONEER SUNSET see **TIGARD EVANGELICAL**

	WASHINTON CO.	T2S	R1W	S10
THIELE FAMILY	DOUGLAS CO.	T24S	R5W	S4

THIELSEN see **PIONEER [RICKREALL]**

	POLK CO.	T7S	R4W	S32

THOMAS D.L.C., ELIZABETH CARUTHERS see **CITY CEMETERY #3**

	MULTNOMAH CO.	T1S	R1E	S10

THOMAS D.L.C., ELIZABETH CARUTHERS see **WALLACE, ARTHUR W.**

	MULTNOMAH CO.	T1S	R1E	S10
THOMAS, ETHEL see **CLAY HILL**	CURRY CO.	T34S	R11W	S2
THOMAS FAMILY see **KENTUCK INLET**	COOS CO.	T25S	R12W	?

```
THOMAS HOMESITE, TILLY see UNKNOWN
                                LANE CO.              T18S      R11W          S12
THOMAS INFANT                   MULTNOMAH CO.         ?         ?             ?
THOMAS, MR. ROBERT M. see GORE FAMILY
                                COLUMBIA CO.          T5N       R2W           S10
THOMAS, ROBERT see BEAVER HOMES COLUMBIA CO.          T6N       R2W           ?
THOMAS, ROBERT M. see ST. JOSEPH POLISH CATHOLIC
                                COLUMBIA CO.          T5N       R3W           S27
THOMPSON see FIR GROVE          LINN CO.              T14S      R2E           S4
THOMPSON, A. K.                 LINN CO.              T13S      R1W           S18
THOMPSON CREEK                  JACKSON CO.           ?         ?             ?
THOMPSON D.L.C., JOHN W. see LORANE GRANGE
                                LANE CO.              T20S      R5W           S2
THOMPSON FAMILY see MYERS FAMILY
                                JACKSON CO.           T38S      R1E           S30
THOMPSON FLAT                   CURRY CO.             T32S      R13W          S22
THOMPSON, MANLEY see THOMPSON PLACE
                                LANE CO.              T17S      R10W          ?
THOMPSON PLACE                  LANE CO.              T17S      R10W          ?
THORN HOLLOW see RED ELK        UMATILLA CO.          T2N       R35E          S3
THREE INDIANS                   MORROW CO.            T1S       R26E          S1
THREE MILE see OBRIST           WASCO CO.             T1S       R12E          S2
THREE ROCKS                     LINCOLN CO.           T6S       R11W          S23
THRIFT RANCH                    CURRY CO.             T32S      R15W          ?
THRUSH                          DOUGLAS CO.           T29S      R8W           S7
THRUSH see HULTIN               COOS CO.              T28S      R14W          S3
THRUSH, ABRAHAM see THRUSH      DOUGLAS CO.           T29S      R8W           S7
THRUSH FARM see HULTIN          COOS CO.              T28S      R14W          S3
THURBER D.L.C., JOHN see PHOENIX [NEW]
                                JACKSON CO.           T38S      R1W           S9
THURSTON see MT. VERNON         LANE CO.              T18S      R2W           S4
TICE D.L.C., JOHN M. see AHAVAI SHOLOM
                                MULTNOMAH CO.         T1S       R1E           S27
TICE D.L.C., JOHN M. see B'NAI B'RITH
                                MULTNOMAH CO.         T1S       R1E           S27
TICE D.L.C., JOHN M. see BETH ISRAEL [NEW]
                                MULTNOMAH CO.         T1S       R1E           S21
TICE D.L.C., JOHN M. see GRAND ARMY OF THE REPUBLIC
                                MULTNOMAH CO.         T1S       R1E           S27
TICE D.L.C., JOHN M. see GREENWOOD HILLS
                                MULTNOMAH CO.         T1S       R1E           S27
TICE D.L.C., JOHN M. see I.O.O.F. [GREENWOOD]
                                MULTNOMAH CO.         T1S       R1E           S27
TICE D.L.C., JOHN M. see RIVER VIEW
                                MULTNOMAH CO.         T1S       R1E           S22
TICHENOR                        CURRY CO.             T33S      R15W          S5
TICHENOR, CAPTAIN WILLIAM see FORT HILL
                                CURRY CO.             T32S      R15W          S5
```

TICHENOR, MARY see **MAPLEWOOD**   COLUMBIA CO.   T7N   R4W   S8
TIDEWATER   LINCOLN CO.   T13S   R10W   S27
TIGARD CATHOLIC see **ST. ANTHONY CATHOLIC**
                                     WASHINGTON CO.   T2S   R1W   S3
TIGARD D.L.C., WILSON M. see **TIGARD EVANGELICAL**
                                     WASHINGTON CO.   T2S   R1W   S10
TIGARD EVANGELICAL   WASHINGTON CO.   T2S   R1W   S10
TIGARD EVANGELICAL UNITED BRETHREN see **TIGARD EVANGELICAL**
                                     WASHINGTON CO.   T2S   R1W   S10
TIGARDVILLE see **TIGARD EVANGELICAL**
                                     WASHINGTON CO.   T2S   R1W   S10
TIGERTOWN see **WALKER GULCH**   JOSEPHINE CO.   T40S   R7W   S15
TILLAMOOK I.O.O.F. see **I.O.O.F. [TILLAMOOK]**
                                     TILLAMOOK CO.   T1S   R9W   S29
TILLAMOOK ODD FELLOWS see **I.O.O.F. [TILLAMOOK]**
                                     TILLAMOOK CO.   T1S   R9W   S29
TILLAMOOK ROCK LIGHTHOUSE see **ETERNITY AT SEA COLUMBARIUM**
                                     CLATSOP CO.   T5N   R11W   S-0
TILLER see **RONDEAU**   DOUGLAS CO.   T30S   R2W   S24
TILLOTSEN see **TILLOTSON FAMILY**   WASCO CO   T7S   R19E   S19
TILLOTSON FAMILY   WASCO CO.   T7S   R19E   S19
TINDALL, MR.   LINN CO.   T14S   R2W   S6
TIPPITT see **TIPPETT'S FARM**   MORROW CO.   T1N   R27E   ?
TIPPETT, CLARK see **TIPPETT'S FARM**
                                     MORROW CO.   T1N   R27E   ?
TIPPETT'S FARM   MORROW CO.   T1N   R27E   ?
TIPTON, MACE   DOUGLAS CO.   T26S   R3W   S1
TISH see **LETITIA**   DOUGLAS CO.   T29S   R3W   S20
TISON   DOUGLAS CO.   T31S   R1W   S19
TISON RANCH see **TISON**   DOUGLAS CO.   T31S   R1W   S19
TITUS, MERRIT see **RAMSEY**   MULTNOMAH CO.   T2N   R1W   S36
TOKAY HEIGHTS see **I.O.O.F. [GRANTS PASS]**
                                     JOSEPHINE CO.   T36S   R5W   S16
TOKAY HEIGHTS see **MASONIC, PIONEER [GRANTS PASS]**
                                     JOSEPHINE CO.   T36S   R5W   S16
TOLEDO   LINCOLN CO.   T11S   R10W   S8
TOLKE FAMILY   WASHINGTON CO.   T3N   R4W   S34
TOLL, ALTHEA APPLEGATE see **TOLL FAMILY**
                                     LANE CO.   T19S   R4W   S2
TOLL FAMILY   LANE CO.   T19S   R4W   S2
TOLO   JACKSON CO.   T36S   R2W   ?
TOM RANCH, ALLAN see **HOGGARD CHILD**
                                     SHERMAN CO.   T2N   R16E   ?
TOMBSTONE PRAIRIE see **McKNIGHT, JAMES A.**
                                     LINN CO.   T13S   R6E   S31
TOMLINSON, ALBERT see **SMALLEY, EVELYN**
                                     COOS CO.   T29S   R13W   S11
TOMPKINS see **HARRISON**   WASHINGTON CO.   T1N   R3W   S3

TOMPKINS FLAT see **THOMPSON FLAT**	CURRY CO.	T32S	R13W	S22
TONE FAMILY	TILLAMOOK CO.	T2S	R10W	S3
TONE HOMESTEAD, JAMES see **TONE FAMILY**				
	TILLAMOOK CO.	T2S	R10W	S3
TONE'S HOUSE, BASIL see **MUNSON**	TILLAMOOK CO.	T2S	R9W	?
TONEY	WHEELER CO.	T11S	R22E	S3
TONEY FAMILY see **TURNER-TONEY FAMILY**				
	YAMHILL CO.	T5S	R5W	S30
TOOLEY see **HARRISON**	WASHINGTON CO.	T1N	R3W	S3
TORAH TALMUD see **NEVAH ZEDEK ROSE CITY LODGE**				
	WASHINGTON CO.	T1S	R1W	S12
TOWNSEND, JODY CHARLES	LINN CO.	T15S	R2W	S7
TRACHSEL FARM, CARL see **WHITE FAMILY**				
	WASHINGTON CO.	T1S	R2W	S11
TRACHSEL VILLAGE see **WHITE FAMILY**				
	WASHNGTON CO.	T1S	R2W	S11
TRACY see **PENITENTIARY [NEW]**	MARION CO.	T7S	R3W	S25
TRAIL	JACKSON CO.	T33S	R1W	S33
TRAIL FORK see **PAPERSACK**	GILLIAM CO.	T5S	R22E	S16
TRAPP GIRL	LANE CO.	T18S	R5W	S24
TRAPPIST ABBEY see **OUR LADY OF GUADALUPE TRAPPIST ABBEY**				
	YAMHILL CO.	T3S	R3W	S29
TRASK see **TRASK PIONEER**	TILLAMOOK CO.	T1S	R9W	S27
TRASK D.L.C., ELBRIDGE see **SUNSET HEIGHTS MEMORIAL GARDENS**				
	TILLAMOOK CO.	T1S	R9W	S28
TRASK D.L.C., ELBRIDGE see **TRASK PIONEER**				
	TILLAMOOK CO.	T1S	R9W	S27
TRASK PIONEER	TILLAMOOK CO.	T1S	R9W	S27
TRAXTLE	WASCO CO.	T3S	R12E	S27
TREVITT, VICTOR see **LOWER MEMALOOSE**				
	WASCO CO.	T3N	R12E	S32
TRIANGLE LAKE see **BLACHLY**	LANE CO.	T16S	R7W	S9
TRIBAL see **GRAND RONDE**	POLK CO.	T6S	R8W	S12
TRIBBLE FAMILY	UMATILLA CO.	T3N	R29E	S17
TRICKEY, EDWARD see **TRICKEY FAMILY**				
	MULTNOMAH CO.	T1S	R5E	S8
TRICKEY FAMILY	MULTNOMAH CO.	T1S	R5E	S8
TRICKEY, LLOYD see **TRICKEY FAMILY**				
	MULTNOMAH CO.	T1S	R5E	S8
TRICKEY, LUCY see **TRICKEY FAMILY**				
	MULTNOMAH CO.	T1S	R5E	S8
TRIMBALL, BABY see **SHUMWAY, ALFRED J.**				
	MALHEUR CO.	T23S	R37E	S34
TRIMBLE FAMILY	BAKER CO.	T12S	R38E	S18
TRIMBLE, JOHN see **TRIMBLE FAMILY**				
	BAKER CO.	T12S	R38E	S18
TRINITY see **VALLEY VIEW**	MARION CO.	T6S	R1W	S36
TRINITY LUTHERAN	MARION CO.	T6S	R1W	S12

TRIPLE D RANCH see **DAVIS, ANNA**	WALLOWA CO.	T1N	R42E	S11
TRIPP D.L.C., JOHN S. see **I.O.O.F. [TILLAMOOK]**				
	TILLAMOOK CO.	T1S	R9W	S29
TROUT	TILLAMOOK CO.	T1S	R9W	S30
TROUT FAMILY see **TROUT**	TILLAMOOK CO.	T1S	R9W	S30
TROY	WALLOWA CO.	T5N	R43E	S4
TRUAX BABY	CURRY CO.	T30S	R14W	S23
TRUAX PLACE see **TRUAX BABY**	CURRY CO.	T30S	R14W	S23
TRULLINGER FAMILY	CLACKAMAS CO.	T4S	R2E	S27
TRUSTY FAMILY see **UNKNOWN**	JACKSON CO.	T32S	R1E	S23
TSIN-IS-TUM see **MESCHELLE, JENNIE**				
	CLATSOP CO.	T6N	R10W	S15
TUALATIN see **WINONA**	WASHINGTON CO.	T2S	R1W	S23
TUALATIN PLAINS see **THE OLD SCOTCH CHURCH**				
	WASHINGTON CO.	T1N	R3W	S13
TUALATIN PLAINS PRESBYTERIAN see **THE OLD SCOTCH CHURCH**				
	WASHINGTON CO.	T1N	R3W	S13
TUALATIN PLAINS PRESBYTERIAN SCOTCH CHURCH see **THE OLD SCOTCH CHURCH**				
	WASHINGTON CO.	T1N	R3W	S13
TUCKER CHILDREN	CLACKAMAS CO.	T4S	R4E	S9
TUCKER D.L.C., BRANCH see **TUCKER CHILDREN**				
	CLACKAMAS CO.	T4S	R4E	S9
TUCKER FAMILY see **MEDICAL SPRINGS**				
	UNION CO.	T6S	R41E	?
TUFI CHILDREN see **INDIAN BURIALS**				
	LANE CO.	?	?	?
TUFI, MRS. CHARLES see **INDIAN BURIALS**				
	LANE CO.	?	?	?
TULLER	DOUGLAS CO.	T32S	R7W	?
TULLER, EDITH see **TULLER**	DOUGLAS CO.	T32S	R7W	?
TULLER, JEREMIAH G. see **TULLER**	DOUGLAS CO.	T32S	R7W	?
TUM TUM see **MULKEY**	LINCOLN CO.	T11S	R8W	S26
TUMALO	DESCHUTES CO.	T16S	R12E	S29
TURKEY HILL	DOUGLAS CO.	T24S	R5W	S17
TURKEY HILL see **MALIN COMMUNITY**	KLAMATH CO.	T41S	R12E	S10
TURNBOW see **UNION**	LANE CO.	T16S	R5W	S5
TURNER CHILDREN	MORROW CO.	T1S	R26E	S26
TURNER D.L.C., OWEN P. see **TURNER-TONEY FAMILY**				
	YAMHILL CO.	T5S	R5W	S30
TURNER D.L.C., THOMAS L. see **MORGAREIDGE FAMILY**				
	YAMHILL CO.	T4S	R3W	S30
TURNER FAMILY	COOS CO.	T30S	R14W	S18
TURNER, JAMES see **TURNER CHILDREN**				
	MORROW CO.	T1S	R26E	S26
TURNER-TONEY FAMILY	YAMHILL CO.	T5S	R5W	S30
TURNIDGE FAMILY	LINN CO.	T10S	R3W	?
TURNIDGE, HENRY see **TURNIDGE FAMILY**				
	LINN CO.	T10S	R3W	?

```
TURNIDGE, PAULINE G. see TURNIDGE FAMILY
                                  LINN CO.         T10S   R3W        ?
TURPIN, ANNIE                     COLUMBIA CO.     T6N    R5W        ?
TURPIN, JOHN S. see TURPIN, ANNIE
                                  COLUMBIA CO.     T6N    R5W        ?
TUTTLE D.L.C., HIRAM see VAN PELT
                                  CURRY CO.        T41S   R13W       S4
TUTUILLA PRESBYTERIAN INDIAN MISSION
                                  UMATILLA CO.     T2N    R33E       S29
TWICKENHAM                        WHEELER CO.      T9S    R21E       S22
TWIN BUTTE see MICHAEL            LINN CO.         T14S   R3W        S26
TWIN OAKS                         MARION CO.       T8S    R2W        S28
TWIN OAKS see METHODIST CHURCH AT FARMINGTON
                                  WASHINGTON CO.   T1S    R2W        ?
TWIN OAKS MEMORIAL GARDENS        LINN CO.         T11S   R4W        S33
TWIN OAKS MEMORIAL PARK see TWIN OAKS MEMORIAL GARDENS
                                  LINN CO.         T11S   R4W        S33
TWO GIRLS see SUTER FARM          CLACKAMAS CO.    T2S    R4E        S30
TWOGOOD D.L.C., JAMES H. see GRAVE CREEK
                                  JOSEPHINE CO.    T34S   R6W        ?
TYGH RIDGE see WARNER             WASCO CO.        T3S    R14E       S16
TYGH VALLEY PIONEER see HAPPY RIDGE
                                  WASCO CO.        T3S    R13E       S32
TYSON see TISON                   DOUGLAS CO.      T31S   R1W        S19
U.S. ARMY FORT STEVENS            CLATSOP CO.      T8N    R10W       S8
UKIAH                             UMATILLA CO.     T5S    R31E       S11
UMATILLA [NEW] see SUNSET HILLS   UMATILLA CO.     T5N    R28E       S19
UMATILLA [OLD]                    UMATILLA CO.     T5N    R28E       S18
UMPHLETTE, JANE EARL              LINN CO.         T10S   R3W        S15
UMPHLETTE, MRS. see UMPHLETTE, JANE EARL
                                  LINN CO.         T10S   R3W        S15
UMPHLETTE, STANLEY see UMPHLETTE, JANE EARL
                                  LINN CO.         T10S   R3W        S15
UMPQUA see UMPQUA CITY            DOUGLAS CO.      T21S   R12W       S31
UMPQUA ACADEMY see WILBUR [OLD]   DOUGLAS CO.      T26S   R5W        S18
UMPQUA CITY                       DOUGLAS CO.      T21S   R12W       S31
UNION                             LANE CO.         T16S   R5W        S5
UNION                             UNION CO.        T4S    R40E       S19
UNION                             WASHINGTON CO.   T1N    R1W        S29
UNION see BARTLETT                WALLOWA CO.      T6N    R43E       S21
UNION see JUNIPER HAVEN           CROOK CO.        T14S   R16E       S31
UNION see MOUNTAIN VIEW MEMORIAL GARDENS
                                  WASHINGTON CO.   T1N    R4W        S35
UNION see YANKTON [OLD]           COLUMBIA CO.     T4N    R2W        S1
UNION BAPTIST see HARMONY         POLK CO.         T6S    R6W        S9
UNION CEMETERY OF CEDAR MILL see UNION
                                  WASHINGTON CO.   T1N    R1W        S29
```

UNION CEMETERY OF LONG TOM see **UNION**				
	LANE CO.	T16S	R5W	S5
UNION [CRAWFORDSVILLE] see **CRAWFORDSVILLE UNION**				
	LINN CO.	T14S	R1W	S17
UNION CREEK	JACKSON CO.	T31S	R3E	?
UNION HILL	MARION CO.	T8S	R1E	S7
UNION HILL see **ACKLES**	UNION CO.	T2S	R38E	S21
UNION HILL see **UNION POINT**	WASHINGTON CO.	T2N	R3W	S31
UNION PIONEER [CLOVERDALE]	TILLAMOOK CO.	T4S	R10W	S33
UNION POINT	LINN CO.	T14S	R3W	S14
UNION POINT	WASHINGTON CO.	T2N	R3W	S31
UNION SCHOOLHOUSE see **UNION**	WASHINGTON CO.	T1N	R1W	S29
UNIONTOWN	JACKSON CO.	T38S	R3W	S34
UNITED BRETHREN	COLUMBIA CO.	T6N	R5W	S36
UNITED BRETHREN see **CLEVELAND**	DOUGLAS CO.	T26S	R7W	S24
UNITED BRETHREN see **BEAVER CREEK**				
	TILLAMOOK CO.	T3S	R9W	S29
UNITED BRETHREN see **HOPEWELL**	YAMHILL CO.	T5S	R3W	S30
UNITED LUTHERAN see **UNITED BRETHREN**				
	COLUMBIA CO.	T6N	R5W	S36
UNITED METHODIST see **TIGARD EVANGELICAL**				
	WASHINGTON CO.	T2S	R1W	S10
UNITY	BAKER CO.	T13S	R36E	S12
UNIVERSITY OF OREGON MEDICAL SCHOOL				
	MULTNOMAH CO.	T1S	R1E	S9
UNKNOWN	BAKER CO.	?	?	?
UNKNOWN	BAKER CO.	T8S	R39E	?
UNKNOWN	BENTON CO.	?	R5W	?
UNKNOWN	CLACKAMAS CO.	T5S	R3E	S5
UNKNOWN	COLUMBIA CO.	T4N	R2W	S16
UNKNOWN	COLUMBIA CO.	T5N	R4W	S5
UNKNOWN	COOS CO.	T26S	R14W	S15
UNKNOWN	CROOK CO.	T14S	R14E	?
UNKNOWN	CROOK CO.	T15S	R25E	S33
UNKNOWN	CURRY CO.	T39S	R14W	S9
UNKNOWN	CURRY CO.	T39S	R14W	S28
UNKNOWN	DOUGLAS CO.	T21S	R11W	S35
UNKNOWN	GILLIAM CO.	T1N	R21E	S18
UNKNOWN	GILLIAM CO.	T5S	R22E	S28
UNKNOWN	GRANT CO.	T13S	R30E	?
UNKNOWN	JACKSON CO.	T32S	R1E	S23
UNKNOWN	JACKSON CO.	T33S	R2E	S10
UNKNOWN	JACKSON CO.	T35S	R2W	?
UNKNOWN	JACKSON CO.	T36S	R2E	S22
UNKNOWN	JACKSON CO.	T37S	R2E	S7
UNKNOWN	JACKSON CO.	T37S	R2E	S8
UNKNOWN	JEFFERSON CO.	T11S	R15E	?
UNKNOWN	JOSEPHINE CO.	T33S	R5W	S29

UNKNOWN		JOSEPHINE CO.	T36S	R8W	S18
UNKNOWN		JOSEPHINE CO.	T37S	R6W	?
UNKNOWN		KLAMATH CO.	T37S	R15E	S8
UNKNOWN		LAKE CO.	T29S	R23E	S35
UNKNOWN		LANE CO.	T18S	R11W	S12
UNKNOWN		LINN CO.	?	?	?
UNKNOWN		LINN CO.	T14S	R2E	S3
UNKNOWN		MALHEUR CO.	T14S	R42E	S13
UNKNOWN		MALHEUR CO.	T15S	R45E	?
UNKNOWN		MALHEUR CO.	T21S	R38E	?
UNKNOWN		MALHEUR CO.	T32S	R40E	?
UNKNOWN		MALHEUR CO.	T34S	R41E	?
UNKNOWN		MALHEUR CO.	T34S	R42E	?
UNKNOWN		MORROW CO.	T2S	R27E	S34
UNKNOWN		MORROW CO.	T4S	R27E	S1
UNKNOWN		MORROW CO.	T4S	R27E	S12
UNKNOWN		MULTNOMAH CO.	T1N	R5E	S30
UNKNOWN		POLK CO.	T9S	R6W	?
UNKNOWN		SHERMAN CO.	T2N	R17E	S20
UNKNOWN		SHERMAN CO.	T1S	R17E	?
UNKNOWN		SHERMAN CO.	T1S	R17E	S3
UNKNOWN		SHERMAN CO.	T4S	R17E	S27
UNKNOWN		TILLAMOOK CO.	T3N	R10W	S14
UNKNOWN		TILLAMOOK CO.	T1S	R10W	S36
UNKNOWN		UMATILLA CO.	?	?	?
UNKNOWN		UMATILLA CO.	T1N	R29E	?
UNKNOWN		UMATILLA CO.	T3N	R27E	S36
UNKNOWN		UMATILLA CO.	T1S	R33E	S4
UNKNOWN		UNION CO.	T3S	R33E	S23
UNKNOWN		WASCO CO.	T1N	R12E	?
UNKNOWN		WASCO CO.	T5S	R16E	?
UNKNOWN		WASHINGTON CO.	T1S	R2W	S13
UNKNOWN		WASHINGTON CO.	T1S	R2W	S14
UNKNOWN		WHEELER CO.	T7S	R21E	S31
UNKNOWN		WHEELER CO.	T10S	R22E	S32
UNKNOWN		YAMHILL CO.	T2S	R5W	S34
UNKNOWN		YAMHILL CO.	T3S	R5W	S9
UNKNOWN	[?PLANK FAMILY?]	YAMHILL CO.	T3S	R5W	S8
UNKNOWN	[DEADMAN BUTTE]	MALHEUR CO.	T34S	R42E	S27
UNKNOWN	[DRAPER?]	JACKSON CO.	T37S	R4W	S15
UNKNOWN	[KEASEY] see **KEASEY**	COLUMBIA CO.	T5N	R5W	S27
UNKNOWN	**BASQUE SHEEPHERDER**	MALHEUR CO.	T34S	R41E	?
UNKNOWN	**CHILD**	COLUMBIA CO.	T5N	R1W	?
UNKNOWN	**CHILD**	MORROW CO.	T2S	R26E	S25
UNKNOWN	**CHILD**	MORROW CO.	T3S	R24E	S24
UNKNOWN	**CHILD**	MORROW CO.	T3S	R27E	S6
UNKNOWN	**FAMILY**	CLATSOP CO.	?	?	?
UNKNOWN	**FAMILY**	MORROW CO.	T5S	R25E	S10

UNKNOWN INFANT	BAKER CO.	T6S	R45E	S34
UNKNOWN MAN	BAKER CO.	T11S	R46E	?
UNKNOWN MAN	GILLIAM CO.	T1N	R20E	?
UNKNOWN PIONEER CHILD	MULTNOMAH CO.	T1N	R3E	S30
UNKNOWN SAILORS	CLATSOP CO.	T6N	R10W	S28
UNKNOWN WOMAN	LINN CO.	T12S	R1W	S7
UPDEGRAVE PLACE see **WELKER GIRLS**				
	DOUGLAS CO.	T26S	R4W	?
UPPER see **FALLS CITY**	POLK CO.	T8S	R6W	S16
UPPER FISH TRAP *[Sic]* see **UPPER FISHTRAP**				
	COOS CO.	T28S	R13W	S34
UPPER FISHTRAP	COOS CO.	T28S	R13W	S34
UPPER MABEL	LANE CO.	T15S	R1W	S28
UPPER MEMALOOSE	WASCO CO.	T2N	R13E	S36
UPPER MILL CREEK	WASCO CO.	T1S	R11E	S11
UPPER SODA see **GARRISON**	LINN CO.	T13S	R4E	?
UPPER SWEET CREEK	LANE CO.	?	R10W	?
UPPER VALLEY	HOOD RIVER CO.	T1N	R10E	S33
UPPER WARM SPRINGS RIVER	JEFFERSON CO.	?	?	?
UPPER WILLAMETTE see **FOREST VALE MEMORIAL PARK**				
	LANE CO.	T21S	R3E	S10
UPPER WILLAMETTE see **HILL MEMORIAL, JOHN**				
	LANE CO.	T21S	R3E	S26
UPPER WILLAMINA see **BUCK HOLLOW**	YAMHILL CO.	T5S	R7W	S13
USHER D.L.C., RICHARD see **CHILDS**				
	LINN CO.	T12S	R2W	S36
UTOPIA see **MIDDLE POINT**	WALLOWA CO.	T4N	R43E	S30
UTTER PARTY	BAKER CO.	T14S	R45E	?
UTTER PARTY see **OWYHEE RIVER**	MALHEUR CO.	T20S	R46E	?
V. F. W. see **VETERANS OF FOREIGN WARS**				
	COOS CO.	T28S	R14W	S29
VADIS see **HARRISON**	WASHINGTON CO.	T1N	R3W	S3
VAIN RANCH see **GLASCOCK BABY**	MALHEUR CO.	?	?	?
VALADE RANCH, EARL see **CUMMINGS**	GRANT CO.	T13S	R28E	?
VALBY	MORROW CO.	T3S	R24E	S8
VALE see **VALLEY VIEW**	MALHEUR CO.	T18S	R45E	S17
VALE MEMORIAL PARK see **FOREST VALE MEMORIAL PARK**				
	LANE CO.	T21S	R3E	S10
VALE PIONEER	MALHEUR CO.	T18S	R45E	S17
VALHALLA MEMORIAL PARK	BENTON CO.	T12S	R5W	S4
VALKYRIE MEMORIAL PARK see **FINLEY'S SUNSET HILL MEMORIAL**				
	WASHINGTON CO.	T1S	R1W	S1
VALLEY see **FORD**	UMATILLA CO.	T6N	R35E	S23
VALLEY MEMORIAL PARK see **VALLEY MEMORIAL PARK AND MAUSOLEUM**				
	WASHINGTON CO.	T1S	R2W	S9
VALLEY MEMORIAL PARK AND MAUSOLEUM				
	WASHINGTON CO.	T1S	R2W	S9
VALLEY VIEW	DOUGLAS CO.	T25S	R5W	S13

VALLEY VIEW	LANE CO.	T17S	R2W	S3
VALLEY VIEW	MALHEUR CO.	T18S	R45E	S17
VALLEY VIEW	MARION CO.	T6S	R1W	S36
VALLEY VIEW see DAYVILLE	GRANT CO.	T12S	R26E	S34
VALLEY VIEW see MARCOLA	LANE CO.	T16S	R2W	S24
VALLEY VIEW MEMORIAL PARK	YAMHILL CO.	T3S	R2W	S19
VAN	HARNEY CO.	T18S	R33 1/2E	S30
VAN CLEAVE, CHARLES AND EDWIN	BAKER CO.	T12S	R38E	?
VAN CLEAVE, TOM see VAN CLEAVE, CHARLES AND EDWIN				
	BAKER CO.	T12S	R38E	?
VAN NORMAN see LAVADOURE	DOUGLAS CO.	T30S	R3W	S29
VAN PELT	CURRY CO.	T41S	R13W	S4
VANDERBILT, _____ see COATES INFANT				
	MARION CO.	T8S	R2W	S19
VANDERPOOL see HENDERSON PIONEER				
	WASCO CO.	T1S	R13E	S33
VANDEVENTER, EZRA see BURKEMONT	BAKER CO.	T7S	R42E	S28
VANDEVERT, GRACE CLARK	DESCHUTES CO.	T20S	R11E	S20
VANDEVERT HOUSE see VANDEVERT, GRACE CLARK				
	DESCHUTES CO.	T20S	R11E	S20
VANDEVERT, KATHERINE GRACE see VANDEVERT, GRACE CLARK				
	DESCHUTES CO.	T20S	R11E	S20
VANNOY	JOSEPHINE CO.	T36S	R6W	?
VANSTRUM FAMILY	LINCOLN CO.	T14S	?	?
VARDIMAN GRAVE, JAMES	GRANT CO.	T10S	?	?
VAUGHN BABY	MARION CO.	T8S	R4W	?
VEATCH see HAWLEY	LANE CO.	T21S	R4W	S12
VERBOORT CATHOLIC see VISITATION OF THE BLESSED VIRGIN MARY				
	WASHINGTON CO.	T1N	R3W	S17
VERBOORT CHURCH	WASHINGTON CO.	T1N	R3W	S20
VERDAMAN see VARDIMAN GRAVE, JAMES				
	GRANT CO.	T10S	?	?
VERNON, MR. see UNKNOWN FAMILY	CLATSOP CO.	?	?	?
VERNONIA	COLUMBIA CO.	T4N	R4W	?
VERNONIA MEMORIAL	COLUMBIA CO.	T4N	R4W	S5
VERNONIA PIONEER	COLUMBIA CO.	T5N	R4W	S33
VETERANS see G.A.R. [GRAND ARMY OF THE REPUBLIC]				
	WASCO CO.	T1N	R13E	S4
VETERANS see NATIONAL VETERANS ADMINISTRATION				
	JACKSON CO.	T36S	R1W	S2
VETERANS see PARKLAWN	WASCO CO.	T1N	R13E	S15
VETERANS ADMINISTRATION see ROSEBURG NATIONAL				
	DOUGLAS CO.	T27S	R6W	S14
VETERANS OF FOREIGN WARS	COOS CO.	T28S	R14W	S29
VETERANS OF FOREIGN WARS see RIVERSIDE V.F.W.				
	LINCOLN CO.	T10S	R10W	S11
VETERAN'S GRAVE	COLUMBIA CO.	T6N	R5W	S24
VEY, ANTONE see BOWMAN FAMILY	UMATILLA CO.	T1N	R29E	?

VEY'S LAND, TONY see **BOWMAN FAMILY**				
	UMATILLA CO.	T1N	R29E	?
VICKERS' CABIN, PERRY see **SUMMIT MEADOWS**				
	CLACKAMAS CO.	T3S	R8 1/2E	S25
VICTOR see **KELLY**	WASCO CO.	T5S	R13E	S8
VICTOR HOMESTEAD	WALLOWA CO.	T2N	?	?
VIENTO	HOOD RIVER CO.	T3N	R9E	S34
VINCENT see **VINSON**	UMATILLA CO.	T1S	R30E	S21
VINING, MRS. see **FAULKNER, T. M.**				
	LINCOLN CO.	T15S	R10W	S1
VINSON	UMATILLA CO.	T1S	R30E	S21
VINSON LUTHERAN see **VINSON**	UMATILLA CO.	T1S	R30E	S21
VINSON, MRS.	LANE CO.	T19S	R1E	S34
VIOLA PIONEER	CLACKAMAS CO.	T3S	R3E	S23
VISITATION see **VISITATION OF THE BLESSED VIRGIN MARY**				
	WASHINGTON CO.	T1N	R3W	S17
VISITATION CATHOLIC see **VISITATION OF THE BLESSED VIRGIN MARY**				
	WASHINGTON CO.	T1N	R3W	S17
VISITATION OF THE BLESSED VIRGIN MARY				
	WASHINGTON CO.	T1N	R3W	S17
VOLLE CHILDREN	MORROW CO.	T5S	R27E	S2
VOLTAGE GRAVES	HARNEY CO.	T27S	R31E	S1
WADE see **LINN, PHILIP E.**	CLACKAMAS CO.	T3S	R4E	S21
WADE D.L.C., WILLIAM N. AND SARAH see **I.O.O.F. [ESTACADA]**				
	CLACKAMAS CO.	T3S	R4E	S21
WADE D.L.C., WILLIAM N. AND SARAH see **LINN, PHILIP E.**				
	CLACKAMAS CO.	T3S	R4E	S21
WADE FAMILY see **LINN, PHILIP E.**	CLACKAMAS CO.	T3S	R4E	S21
WADE MEMORIAL see **LINN, PHILIP E.**				
	CLACKAMAS CO.	T3S	R4E	S21
WADE, SARAH see **LINN, PHILIP E.**	CLACKAMAS CO.	T3S	R4E	S21
WADE, W. H. H. see **LINN, PHILIP E.**				
	CLACKAMAS CO.	T3S	R4E	S21
WADE, WILLIAM N. see **LINN, PHILIP E.**				
	CLACKAMAS CO.	T3S	R4E	S21
WAGNER CREEK see **STEARNS FAMILY**	JACKSON CO.	T38S	R1W	S34
WAGON BOX BURIAL	BAKER CO.	T14S	R45E	S32
WALDO	JOSEPHINE CO.	T40S	R8W	S28
WALDO D.L.C., DANIEL AND MALINDA C. see **WALDO FAMILY**				
	MARION CO.	T8S	R2W	S12
WALDO FAMILY	MARION CO.	T8S	R2W	S12
WALDO HILLS see **MT. HOPE**	MARION CO.	T7S	R1W	S33
WALDPORT see **WALDPORT MEMORIAL**	LINCOLN CO.	T13S	R11W	S30
WALDPORT MEMORIAL	LINCOLN CO.	T13S	R11W	S30
WALDRON see **RICE**	WASCO CO.	T1S	R14E	S10
WALKER	LANE CO.	T20S	R3W	S10
WALKER	TILLAMOOK CO.	T3S	R9W	S26
WALKER ADDITION	LANE CO.	T21S	R3E	S17

WALKER BURIAL PLOT see **MEADOWS GRAVES**

	JACKSON CO.	T34S	R3W	S25

WALKER D.L.C., ELKANAH see **PACIFIC UNIVERSITY**

	WASHINGTON CO.	T1N	R3W	S31

WALKER D.L.C., GILLIAM H. AND RHODA see **KIMSEY FAMILY**

	MARION CO.	T8S	R1W	S7

WALKER D.L.C., ROBERT see **ST. FRANCIS CATHOLIC**

Name	County	Township	Range	Section
	WASHINGTON CO.	T1N	R3W	S5
WALKER FAMILY see **ETNA**	POLK CO.	T7S	R4W	S7
WALKER FAMILY see **KIMSEY FAMILY**	MARION CO.	T8S	R1W	S7
WALKER GULCH	JOSEPHINE CO.	T40S	R7W	S15

WALKER, MARY JANE see **RENSHAW, MARY JULIA**

	LANE CO.	T18S	R3W	?

WALKER PLACE, DONALD see **ALLEN, WILLIAM P.**

Name	County	Township	Range	Section
	LANE CO.	?	?	?
WALKER UNION CHURCH see **WALKER**	LANE CO.	T20S	R3W	S10
WALKEY, EDMUND see **SMITH PLACE**	CLACKAMAS CO.	T2S	R4E	S30
WALLACE	LANE CO.	T18S	R2W	S14
WALLACE see **ANTELOPE PIONEER**	WASCO CO.	T7S	R17E	S28
WALLACE see **HUSSEY FAMILY**	POLK CO.	T6S	R7W	S15
WALLACE, ARTHUR W.	MULTNOMAH CO.	T1S	R1E	S10

WALLACE BRIDGE MENNONITE see **SHERIDAN MENNONITE**

	POLK CO.	T6S	R7W	S13

WALLACE D.L.C., JAMES A. see **WALLACE**

	LANE CO.	T18S	R2W	S14

WALLACE D.L.C., WILLIAM T. see **HESS FAMILY**

	YAMHILL CO.	T3S	R2W	S8

WALLACE HOMESTEAD, ARTHUR W. see **MOUNTAIN VIEW**

	WASHINGTON CO.	T3N	R2W	S32

WALLACE, JULIA see **HUSSEY FAMILY**

	POLK CO.	T6S	R7W	S15

WALLING D.L.C., GABRIEL see **SISTERS OF THE HOLY NAMES**

Name	County	Township	Range	Section
	CLACKAMAS CO.	T2S	R1E	S14
WALLOWA	WALLOWA CO.	T1N	R42E	S13

WALLOWA LAKE INDIAN see **CHIEF JOSEPH MONUMENT**

Name	County	Township	Range	Section
	WALLOWA CO.	T3S	R45E	S5
WALLUSKI AREA	CLATSOP CO.	T8N	R9W	S27
WALLUSKI ROAD	CLATSOP CO.	T8N	R9W	S34
WALNUT HILL see **TAYLOR**	YAMHILL CO.	T5S	R4W	S10
WALTON	LANE CO.	T18S	R7W	S5
WALTON, MRS. see **RANGE [NEW]**	GRANT CO.	T8S	R31E	S17
WALTON PROPERTY see **RANGE [NEW]**	GRANT CO.	T8S	R31E	S17

WALTON RANCH, BEN see **RANGE [NEW]**

Name	County	Township	Range	Section
	GRANT CO.	T8S	R31E	S17
WAMIC	WASCO CO.	T4S	R12E	S22
WAMIC PIONEER see **PRATT**	WASCO CO.	T4S	R12E	S14

WAND D.L.C., JOHN see **CHINESE [ST. JOHNS]**

	MULTNOMAH CO.	T1N	R1E	S18

WAPATO see **HILL**	WASHINGTON CO.	T2S	R3W	S6
WAPATO LODGE I.O.O.F. see **CORNELIUS PIONEER METHODIST**				
	WASHINGTON CO.	T1N	R3W	S33
WAPINITIA	WASCO CO.	T5S	R12E	S26
WARD CREEK see **WOODVILLE**	JACKSON CO.	T36S	R4W	S15
WARD, GEORGE see **UNKNOWN**	WASCO CO.	T5S	R16E	?
WARD, JR. D.L.C., JOHN see **CHINESE [ST. JOHNS]**				
	MULTNOMAH CO.	T1N	R1E	S18
WARD MEMORIAL	CURRY CO.	T40S	R13W	S31
WARM SPRINGS AGENCY see **BRUNO**	JEFFERSON CO.	T9S	R12E	S23
WARM SPRINGS RIVER see **HOT SPRINGS INDIAN**				
	WASCO CO.	T8S	R13E	S27
WARNER	WASCO CO.	T3S	R14E	S16
WARNER see **FALL CREEK**	LANE CO.	T18S	R1W	S33
WARNER see **WARNER, CALVIN**	COOS CO.	T29S	R12W	S28
WARNER, CALVIN	COOS CO.	T29S	R12W	S28
WARNER D.L.C., FREDERICK see **FALL CREEK**				
	LANE CO.	T18S	R1W	S33
WARNER FAMILY	UMATILLA CO.	T2S	R32E	S30
WARNER, MRS.	LANE CO.	T24S	R3E	S13
WARNER, WILLIAM N.	COOS CO.	T30S	R12W	S34
WARNOCK CHILDREN see **CROW CREEK**	WALLOWA CO.	T1N	R45E	S13
WARNOCK, D. D. see **CROW CREEK**	WALLOWA CO.	T1N	R45E	S13
WARNOCK, EVA see **CROW CREEK**	WALLOWA CO.	T1N	R45E	S13
WARREN see **BETHANY MEMORIAL**	COLUMBIA CO.	T4N	R1W	S19
WARREN see **MT. HOPE**	MARION CO.	T7S	R1W	S33
WARREN D.L.C., HENRY see **SOUTH YAMHILL**				
	YAMHILL CO.	T5S	R5W	S3
WARREN FAMILY, DANIEL K.	CLATSOP CO.	T8N	R10W	?
WARREN STATION see **GERMAN LUTHERAN**				
	UMATILLA CO.	T4N	R33E	S29
WASCO see **SUN RISE**	SHERMAN CO.	T2N	R17E	S31
WASCO [NEW] see **SUN RISE**	SHERMAN CO.	T2N	R17E	S31
WASCO [OLD] see **WASCO METHODIST**	SHERMAN CO.	T2N	R17E	S32
WASCO COUNTY	WASCO CO.	T1N	R13E	S4
WASCO LODGE see **MASONIC [THE DALLES]**				
	WASCO CO.	T1N	R13E	S10
WASCO METHODIST	SHERMAN CO.	T2N	R17E	S32
WASHBURN D.L.C., A. D. E. see **VALLEY VIEW**				
	LANE CO.	T17S	R2W	S3
WASHBURN, ROYAL ARTHUR	GILLIAM CO.	T6S	R23E	S4
WASHBURNE see **MILLIRON**	LANE CO.	T15S	R4W	S31
WASHINGTON, PAUL	LINCOLN CO.	T10S	R10W	S9
WASSON	COOS CO.	T26S	R14W	?
WASSON RANCH see **WASSON**	COOS CO.	T26S	R14W	?
WATERLOO see **KLUM**	LINN CO.	T12S	R1W	S32
WATERMAN	COOS CO.	T30S	R11W	S33
WATERMAN FLAT see **FOPIANO**	WHEELER CO.	T11S	R23E	S22

WATERMAN, MARY E.	WHEELER CO.	T13S	R24E	S2
WATKINS see **COLLINGS GRAVES**	JACKSON CO.	T40S	R4W	S36
WATSON	MALHEUR CO.	T26S	R43E	S24
WATSON FARM, LILLI see **CASEY FAMILY, ROSE**				
	CLATSOP CO.	T7N	R9W	?
WATSON, LIEUTENANT STEPHEN see **CAMP WATSON**				
	WHEELER CO.	T12S	R23E	S36
WATT D.L.C., JOHN see **AMITY**	YAMHILL CO.	T5S	R4W	S29
WATTS D.L.C., WILLIAM see **WATTS FAMILY**				
	COLUMBIA CO.	T3N	R2W	?
WATTS FAMILY	COLUMBIA CO.	T3N	R2W	?
WAUD'S FUNERAL HOME	TILLAMOOK CO.	T1S	R9W	?
WAUD D.L.C., JOHN see **CHINESE [ST. JOHNS]**				
	MULTNOMAH CO.	T1N	R1E	S18
WAVERLY see **MILWAUKIE PIONEER**	CLACKAMAS CO.	T1S	R1E	S26
WAVERLY JEWISH	LINN CO.	T11S	R3W	S4
WAVERLY LAKE MASONIC see **WAVERLY MEMORIAL**				
	LINN CO.	T11S	R3W	S4
WAVERLY MEMORIAL	LINN CO.	T11S	R3W	S4
WAY	KLAMATH CO.	T41S	R6E	S8
WAY PLACE, THOMAS see **WAY**	KLAMATH CO.	T41S	R6E	S8
WAYMIRE D.L.C., FREDERICK see **WAYMIRE FAMILY**				
	POLK CO.	T8S	R6W	S15
WAYMIRE FAMILY	POLK CO.	T8S	R6W	S15
WEART, GEORGE W.	HOOD RIVER CO.	T1N	R10E	S8
WEATHERBY	BAKER CO.	T12S	R44E	?
WEATHERLY see **I.O.O.F. PIONEER [JOSEPH]**				
	WALLOWA CO.	T2S	R44E	S36
WEAVER FAMILY	UNION CO.	T1N	R39E	S26
WEBERG FAMILY	GRANT CO.	T18S	R26E	?
WEBERG RANCH see **WEBERG FAMILY**	GRANT CO.	T18S	R26E	?
WEBSTER, EDWARD D. see **KEASEY**	COLUMBIA CO.	T5N	R5W	S27
WECOMA BEACH see **MORRIS FAMILY**	LINCOLN CO.	T7S	R11W	S3
WEDEKING FAMILY	WASHINGTON CO.	T2S	R2W	S12
WEDEKING, LAV. see **WEDEKING FAMILY**				
	WASHINGTON CO.	T2S	R2W	S12
WEDEKING-WARNER FAMILIES see **WEDEKING FAMILY**				
	WASHINGTON CO.	T2S	R2W	S12
WEEDMAN FARM see **ALLEN CHILD**	SHERMAN CO.	T1N	R18E	S7
WEEKS [?] see **JOHNSON FAMILY**	JACKSON CO.	T34S	R1W	S15
WEEKS FAMILY see **GEER PIONEER**	CLACKAMAS CO.	T3S	R1W	S31
WEEVER	CROOK CO.	T14S	R14E	S23
WEGER	LINN CO.	T15S	R3W	S26
WEHRHEIM D.L.C., HENRY see **WEHRHEIM FAMILY**				
	CLACKAMAS CO.	T3S	R4E	S9
WEHRHEIM FAMILY	CLACKAMAS CO.	T3S	R4E	S9
WEISER JUNCTION see **FAIRVIEW**	MALHEUR CO.	T15S	R47E	S33
WELCHES see **PATTON FAMILY**	WASHINGTON CO.	T1S	R1W	S14

WELKER GIRLS	DOUGLAS CO.	T26S	R4W	?
WELL SPRING	MORROW CO.	T2N	R25E	S20
WELLESVILLE see **WELLSVILLE**	JACKSON CO.	T39S	R3W	S15
WELLS	TILLAMOOK CO.	T1S	R8W	?
WELLS D.L.C., GILES see **WELLS FAMILY**				
	JACKSON CO.	T39S	R1E	S13
WELLS D.L.C., IRA see **WELLS FAMILY**				
	DOUGLAS CO.	T22S	R7W	S31
WELLS D.L.C., JOHN see **WELLS FAMILY**				
	MARION CO.	T10S	R2W	S6
WELLS FAMILY	DOUGLAS CO.	T22S	R7W	S31
WELLS FAMILY	JACKSON CO.	T39S	R1E	S13
WELLS FAMILY	MARION CO.	T10S	R2W	S6
WELLS, GRANDMA	CURRY CO.	T31S	R13W	?
WELLS SPRING see **WELL SPRING**	MORROW CO.	T2N	R25E	S20
WELLSVILLE	JACKSON CO.	T39S	R3W	S15
WELTER FAMILY	COLUMBIA CO.	T6N	R2W	S2
WENDLING	LANE CO.	T16S	R1W	S10
WENDT BROTHERS see **BRIDGEEPORT**	BAKER CO.	T12S	R41E	S30
WEST see **MITCHELL, LOWER**	WHEELER CO.	T11S	R21E	S35
WEST BRANCH	WHEELER CO.	T12S	R20E	S15
WEST BUTTEVILLE see **GEER PIONEER**				
	CLACKAMAS CO.	T3S	R1W	S31
WEST CHEHALEM see **FENDALL-ROGERS FAMILY**				
	YAMHILL CO.	T3S	R3W	S4
WEST D.L.C., CALVIN BURNSIDE see **WEST-WINNIFORD FAMILIES**				
	DOUGLAS CO.	T26S	R6W	S7
WEST FAIRVIEW CHURCH see **FAIRVIEW MENNONITE CHURCH**				
	LINN CO.	T11S	R3W	S23
WEST FAMILY BABIES see **SLATE CREEK**				
	JOSEPHINE CO.	T37S	R7W	?
WEST FAMILY, CALVIN B. see **WEST-WINNIFORD FAMILIES**				
	DOUGLAS CO.	T26S	R6W	S7
WEST HILLS see **FINLEY'S SUNSET HILL MEMORIAL**				
	WASHINGTON CO.	T1S	R1W	S1
WEST HOME, WILLIAM see **LAMBERSON FAMILY**				
	COLUMBIA CO.	T3N	R2W	S1
WEST LAWN MEMORIAL PARK	LANE CO.	T17S	R4W	S33
WEST PLACE see **WEST, WILLIAM ROBERT**				
	CURRY CO.	T30S	R14W	?
WEST POINT	LINN CO.	T15S	R3W	S33
WEST POINT LODGE #62 see **I.O.O.F. [COBURG]**				
	LANE CO.	T17S	R3W	S4
WEST SIDE see **McCUBBIN**	WALLOWA CO.	T1S	R43E	S5
WEST UNION see **WEST UNION BAPTIST**				
	WASHINGTON CO.	T1N	R2W	S14
WEST UNION BAPTIST	WASHINGTON CO.	T1N	R2W	S14
WEST, WILLIAM ROBERT	CURRY CO.	T30S	R14W	?

WEST-WINNIFORD FAMILIES	DOUGLAS CO.	T26S	R6W	S7
WESTFALL	MALHEUR CO.	T18S	R41E	S21
WESTON	UMATILLA CO.	T4N	R35E	S22
WESTON D.L.C., DAVID see **WESTON FAMILY**				
	MARION CO.	T4S	R2W	S1
WESTON FAMILY	MARION CO.	T4S	R2W	S1
WESTPORT	CLATSOP CO.	T8N	R6W	S36
WESTSIDE	LAKE CO.	T40S	R19E	S6
WEYERHAEUSER DUMP ROAD see **SMITH FAMILY**				
	LANE CO.	T18S	R2W	?
WHEELER, ANNIE R.	COOS CO.	T25S	R12W	S5
WHEELER BURIAL see **NELSON CREEK**	LANE CO.	T17S	R8W	S14
WHEELER CREEK	CURRY CO.	T41S	R12W	S3
WHEELER, JAMES P.	CURRY CO.	T41S	R12W	S10
WHEELOCK, HATTIE	BAKER CO.	T8S	R46E	?
WHEELOCK, J. B. see **WHEELOCK, HATTIE**				
	BAKER CO.	T8S	R46E	?
WHITCOMB	CLACKAMAS CO.	T1S	R1E	S36
WHITCOMB	LINN CO.	T12S	R3E	S31
WHITCOMB D.L.C., LOT see **HOLLAND**				
	CLACKAMAS CO.	T1S	R1E	S36
WHITCOMB D.L.C., LOT see **WHITCOMB**				
	CLACKAMAS CO.	T1S	R1E	S36
WHITCOMB, LOT see **WHITCOMB**	CLACKAMAS CO.	T1S	R1E	S36
WHITE	TILLAMOOK CO.	T1S	R9W	?
WHITE BIRCH see **WHITE BIRCH PIONEER**				
	MULTNOMAH CO.	T1S	R3E	S9
WHITE BIRCH PIONEER	MULTNOMAH CO.	T1S	R3E	S9
WHITE CITY see **NATIONAL VETERANS ADMINISTRATION**				
	JACKSON CO.	T36S	R1W	S2
WHITE CLOUD see **McBRIDE**	YAMHILL CO.	T3S	R4W	S19
WHITE D.L.C., LUTHER see **WHITE, LUTHER**				
	LINN CO.	T15S	R3W	S12
WHITE D.L.C., RICHARD see **WHITE FAMILY**				
	WASHINGTON CO.	T1S	R2W	S11
WHITE D.L.C., SANFORD see **HENDERSON FAMILY**				
	BENTON CO.	T12S	R6W	S36
WHITE D.L.C., WILLIAM	LANE CO.	T15S	R5W	S20
WHITE FAMILY	WASHINGTON CO.	T1S	R2W	S11
WHITE FAMILY see **PAPERSACK**	GILLIAM CO.	T5S	R22E	S16
WHITE FARM, JASPER see **MURRAY FAMILY**				
	YAMHILL CO.	T4S	R5W	S32
WHITE, LUTHER	LINN CO.	T15S	R3W	S12
WHITE, MRS. see **SNYDER'S LODGE**	CURRY CO.	?	?	?
WHITE RANCH, J. R. see **BRISCOE, ISAIAH JACKSON**				
	WALLOWA CO.	T1N	R44E	S35
WHITE, ROLLY see **SNYDER'S LODGE**	CURRY CO.	?	?	?

WHITEAKER D.L.C., BENJAMIN see **WHITEAKER FAMILY**				
	POLK CO.	T8S	R5W	S14
WHITEAKER FAMILY	POLK CO.	T8S	R5W	S14
WHITEHOURSE RANCH see **BUNYARD, WILLARD**				
	HARNEY CO.	T37S	R36E	S12
WHITESON see **TAYLOR**	YAMHILL CO.	T5S	R4W	S10
WHITLEY FAMILY	POLK CO.	T7S	R5W	?
WHITMAN MASSACRE see **ST. ANDREWS**				
	UMATILLA CO.	T2N	R33E	S24
WHITMAN MASSACRE see **TUTUILLA PRESBYTERIAN INDIAN MISSION**				
	UMATILLA CO.	T2N	R33E	S29
WHITNEY	BAKER CO.	T10S	R36E	S27
WHITSETT, MRS. TOM see **BROWN, O. C.**				
	DOUGLAS CO.	T27S	R5W	S24
WHITTEN see **KINGSLEY**	WASCO CO.	T2S	R13E	S32
WHITTIG	COLUMBIA CO.	T6N	R5W	S20
WHITTIG FAMILY see **WHITTIG**	COLUMBIA CO.	T6N	R5W	S20
WHITTINGTON	COOS CO.	T29S	R12W	S32
WHITTLEY *[Sic]* D.L.C., ANDREW H. see **WHITLEY FAMILY**				
	POLK CO.	T7S	R5W	?
WIBLE D.L.C., JOHN see **LINN MEMORIAL**				
	LINN CO.	T13S	R1W	S4
WIGENT FAMILY	COOS CO.	T29S	?	?
WIGERT FAMILY see **WIGENT FAMILY**	COOS CO.	T29S	?	?
WIGLE	LINCOLN CO.	T10S	R9W	S12
WIGLE	LINN CO.	T14S	R3W	S35
WIGLE D.L.C., JOHN M. see **WIGLE**	LINN CO.	T14S	R3W	S35
WILBUR [NEW]	DOUGLAS CO.	T26S	R5W	S7
WILBUR [OLD]	DOUGLAS CO.	T26S	R5W	S18
WILBER D.L.C., JAMES H. see **WILBUR [OLD]**				
	DOUGLAS CO.	T26S	R5W	S18
WILCOX see **WILCOX-OBSERVER**	SHERMAN CO.	T5S	R17E	S10
WILCOX, MARY E. see **ROBINETTE**	BAKER CO.	T9S	R46E	S25
WILCOX-OBSERVER	SHERMAN CO.	T5S	R17E	S10
WILDERVILLE	JOSEPHINE CO.	T37S	R6W	S6
WILDWOOD FALLS see **CULP CREEK**	LANE CO.	T21S	R1W	S33
WILEY D.L.C., ANDREW see **WILEY FAMILY**				
	LINN CO.	T13S	R1E	S36
WILEY FAMILY	LINN CO.	T13S	R1E	S36
WILKES, GREENVILLE see **UNION POINT**				
	WASHINGTON CO.	T2N	R3W	S31
WILKES NORTH ADDITION see **HILLSBORO PIONEER**				
	WASHINGTON CO.	T1N	R3W	S36
WILKES SCHOOL see **UNKNOWN PIONEER CHILD**				
	MULTNOMAH CO.	T1N	R3E	S30
WILKINSON CHILDREN	MORROW CO.	T3S	R28E	S34
WILKINSON D.L.C., WILLIAM see **DUNN FAMILY**				
	BENTON CO.	T13S	R6W	S11

WILKINSON-DUNN FAMILIES see **DUNN FAMILY**

	BENTON CO.	T13S	R6W	S11
WILLAMETTE MEMORIAL PARK	LINN CO.	T10S	R3W	S28
WILLAMETTE METHODIST see **WILLAMETTE MISSION**				
	MARION CO.	T6S	R3W	S3
WILLAMETTE MISSION	MARION CO.	T6S	R3W	S3
WILLAMETTE NATIONAL	CLACKAMAS CO.	T1S	R2E	S22
WILLAMETTE NATIONAL	MULTNOMAH CO.	T1S	R2E	S22
WILLAMETTE UNIVERSITY MEDICAL SCHOOL				
	MARION CO.	T7S	R3W	S27
WILLAMINA	POLK CO.	T6S	R7W	S1
WILLAMINA see **BUCK HOLLOW**	YAMHILL CO.	T5S	R7W	S13
WILLAMINA MENNONITE see **SHERIDAN MENNENITE**				
	POLK CO.	T6S	R7W	S13
WILLARD see **MT. HOPE**	MARION CO.	T7S	R1W	S33
WILLIAMS see **HARTLEY**	JOSEPHINE CO.	T39S	R5W	S4
WILLIAMS CREEK see **HARTLEY**	JOSEPHINE CO.	T39S	R5W	S4
WILLIAMS CREEK [?] see **MISSOURI FLAT**				
	JACKSON CO.	T38S	R4W	S6
WILLIAMS D.L.C., HENRY see **PINE GROVE**				
	LINN CO.	T13S	R4W	S32
WILLIAMS D.L.C., JAMES see **WILLIAMS FAMILY**				
	POLK CO.	T9S	R5W	S32
WILLIAMS D.L.C., JASON L. see **POWELL**				
	LINN CO.	T12S	R1E	S31
WILLIAMS D.L.C., LEANDER see **GARDEN OF REVERENCE**				
	CLACKAMAS CO.	T1S	R4E	S28
WILLIAMS FAMILY	POLK CO.	T9S	R5W	S32
WILLIAMS, REES AND JANE	BAKER CO.	T8S	R38E	?
WILLIAMSBURG	JOSEPHINE CO.	T38S	R5W	S24
WILLIAMSON FAMILY	BENTON CO.	T10S	R4W	S17
WILLIS BURIALS	LANE CO.	T19S	R3W	S14
WILLIS CREEK	DOUGLAS CO.	T29S	R6W	S9
WILLIS D.L.C., HENRY C. see **SCENIC HILLS MEMORIAL PARK**				
	JACKSON CO.	T39S	R1E	S11
WILLIS D.L.C., STEPHEN D. see **WILLIS CREEK**				
	DOUGLAS CO.	T29S	R6W	S9
WILLIS D.L.C., WILLIAM A. see **WILLIS FAMILY, WILLIAM A.**				
	DOUGLAS CO.	T27S	R4W	S19
WILLIS FAMILY see **WILLIS BURIALS**				
	LANE CO.	T19S	R3W	S14
WILLIS FAMILY see **WILLIS FAMILY, WILLIAM A.**				
	DOUGLAS CO.	T27S	R4W	S19
WILLIS FAMILY, WILLIAM A.	DOUGLAS CO.	T27S	R4W	S19
WILLIS, JOHN A. see **WILLIS BURIALS**				
	LANE CO.	T19S	R3W	S14
WILLIS, MALINDA C. see **WILLIS BURIALS**				
	LANE CO.	T19S	R3W	S14

WILLOUGHBY see **WEST POINT**	LINN CO.	T15S	R3W	S33
WILLOW CREEK	GRANT CO.	T8S	R31E	S28
WILLOW CREEK see **DENMARK**	CURRY CO.	T31S	R15W	S10
WILLOW CREEK see **DELL**	MALHEUR CO.	T16S	R43E	S15
WILLOW CREEK see **GRIZZLY**	JEFFERSON CO.	T12S	R15E	S33
WILSON	CLACKAMAS CO.	T3S	R2E	S1
WILSON	KLAMATH CO.	T35S	R7E	S16
WILSON see **BLAIN**	LINN CO.	T14S	R3W	S14
WILSON BABY	MALHEUR CO.	T18S	R38E	S8
WILSON, BABY see **WILSON FAMILY**	BENTON CO.	T11S	R7W	S34
WILSON, CAPTAIN FREDERICK BACON POWELL see **WILSON FAMILY**				
	BENTON CO.	T11S	R7W	S34
WILSON, CARRIE see **WILSON FAMILY**				
	BENTON CO.	T11S	R7W	S34
WILSON, D. J.	GILLIAM CO.	?	?	?
WILSON FAMILY	BENTON CO.	T11S	R7W	S34
WILSON FAMILY see **SUMNER [OLD]**	COOS CO.	T26S	R12W	S33
WILSON FAMILY see **WILSON BABY**	MALHEUR CO.	T18S	R38E	S8
WILSON GAME MANAGEMENT AREA, E. E. see **WILLLIAMSON FAMILY**				
	BENTON CO.	T10S	R4W	S17
WILSON RANCH see **WILSON BABY**	MALHEUR CO.	T18S	R38E	S8
WILSON RANCH, BEVERLY	CURRY CO.	T14S	R13W	?
WILSON TWINS	WALLOWA CO.	T3N	R41E	S29
WIMBERLY	DOUGLAS CO.	T26S	R3W	S19
WIMPLE, ADAM see **WIMPLE, MARY**	POLK CO.	T8S	R6W	S23
WIMPLE, MARY	POLK CO.	T8S	R6W	S23
WINBERRY see **WINBERRY CREEK BURIALS**				
	LANE CO.	T19S	R1E	S6
WINBERRY CREEK BURIALS	LANE CO.	T19S	R1E	S6
WINCHESTER see **STOWEL FAMILY**	DOUGLAS CO.	T26S	R6W	S36
WINCHESTER SCHOOL	DOUGLAS CO.	T26S	R6W	S25
WINDY POINT	HARNEY CO.	T26S	R33E	S11
WINEJO FARM see **HATCH FAMILY**	TILLAMOOK CO.	T1N	R10W	?
WINGVILLE	BAKER CO.	T8S	R39E	S29
WINKLE BAR	CURRY CO.	T33S	R9W	S18
WINKLE D.L.C., ISAAC W. see **McBEE FAMILY**				
	BENTON CO.	T13S	R5W	S23
WINKLE D.L.C., ISAAC W. see **WINKLE FAMILY**				
	BENTON CO.	T13S	R5W	S22
WINKLE FAMILY	BENTON CO.	T13S	R5W	S22
WINLOCK	WHEELER CO.	T7S	R24E	S31
WINN, JOHN see **WHITE DLC, WILLIAM**				
	LANE CO.	T15S	R5W	S20
WINNIFORD CHILD see **WEST-WINNIFORD FAMILIES**				
	DOUGLAS CO.	T26S	R6W	S7
WINONA	WASHINGTON CO.	T2S	R1W	S23
WINSTON see **CIVIL BEND**	DOUGLAS CO.	T28S	R6W	S21

WIRTH PROPERTY, W. AND R. see **MOORES VALLEY**				
	YAMHILL CO.	T3S	R5W	S9
WISE	COOS CO.	T30S	R12W	S34
WISE FAMILY, GEORGE	CLACKAMAS CO.	T2S	R2E	S5
WISE, GEORGE see **WISE FAMILY, GEORGE**				
	CLACKAMAS CO.	T2S	R2E	S5
WISH-HAM see **UPPER MEMALOOSE**	WASCO CO.	T2N	R13E	S36
WISNER	LINN CO.	T9S	R1W	S23
WITHAM D.L.C., ALFRED M. see **I.O.O.F. [CORVALLIS]**				
	BENTON CO.	T11S	R5W	S28
WITT RANCH, OTTO see **KENTUCK INLET**				
	COOS CO.	T25S	R12W	?
WOLF CREEK	JOSEPHINE CO.	T33S	R6W	S15
WOLFE VALLEY	DOUGLAS CO.	T25S	R7W	S8
WOLLAM, HARRY	HOOD RIVER CO.	T2N	R10E	S3
WOMER	POLK CO.	T9S	R6W	S32
WONDER	JOSEPHINE CO.	T37S	R7W	?
WONG LUEY	MULTNOMAH CO.	T1S	R1E	S5
WOODBINE	COLUMBIA CO.	T7N	R3W	S13
WOODING	LINCOLN CO.	T12S	?	?
WOODLAWN	KLAMATH CO.	T39S	R9E	S5
WOODMEN OF THE WORLD see **BUENA VISTA**				
	POLK CO.	T9S	R4W	S23
WOODRUFF, LYMAN	CURRY CO.	T35S	R14W	S31
WOODS	JEFFERSON CO.	T9S	R16E	S36
WOODS see **I.O.O.F. [WOODS]**	TILLAMOOK CO.	T4S	R10W	S18
WOODS BABY	WASHINGTON CO.	T1S	R2W	S10
WOODS D.L.C., JOSEPH see **WOODS BABY**				
	WASHINGTON CO.	T1S	R2W	S10
WOODSIDE, LLOYD see **RAINS, BABY**	WASCO CO.	T5S	R12E	?
WOODSIDE RANCH, SCOTT AND LLOYD see **YOUNG FAMILY**				
	WASCO CO.	T5S	R12E	S22
WOODVILLE	JACKSON CO.	T36S	R4W	S15
WOODWARD D.L.C., LUTHER T. see **LEBANON PIONEER**				
	LINN CO.	T12S	R2W	S11
WOODWARD FAMILY	WHEELER CO.	?	?	?
WOODWORTH CHILDREN	MARION CO.	T7S	R2W	?
WOODWORTH D.L.C., FRANKLIN N. see **WOODWORTH CHILDREN**				
	MARION CO.	T7S	R2W	?
WOOLLEY see **GUNTER**	DOUGLAS CO.	T20S	R7W	S27
WOOLLEY FAMILY see **COLVIN**	DOUGLAS CO.	T22S	R5W	S6
WOOLLEY RANCH see **HEDRICK FAMILY**				
	DOUGLAS CO.	T21S	R6W	S35
WORDEN	KLAMATH CO.	T40S	R8E	S34
WORDEN FAMILY see **GOODRICH FAMILY**				
	YAMHILL CO.	T4S	R3W	S21
WORKMAN	LINN CO.	T14S	R4W	S36
WORKMEN'S	MARION CO.	T6S	R1W	S11

```
WORTH D.L.C., JAMES see CAMP CREEK
                                LANE CO.          T17S    R1W      S19
WREN                            BENTON CO.        T11S    R6W      S28
WRENN D.L.C., GEORGE P. see WREN
                                BENTON CO.        T11S    R6W      S28
WRENN, GEORGE P. see WREN       BENTON CO.        T11S    R6W      S28
WRENN MEMORIAL, GEORGE P. see WREN
                                BENTON CO.        T11S    R6W      S28
WRIGHT FAMILY                   JACKSON CO.       T41S    R4E      S6
WRIGHT FAMILY                   UNION CO.         T2S     R40E     S18
WRIGHT FAMILY                   UNION CO.         T6S     R41E     S25
WRIGHT FAMILY see LAVADOURE     DOUGLAS CO.       T30S    R3W      S29
WRIGHT FAMILY, DUNHAM see WRIGHT FAMILY
                                UNION CO.         T6S     R41E     S25
WRIGHT, MR. see FAULKNER, T. M. LINCOLN CO.       T15S    R10W     S1
WRIGHT POINT                    HARNEY CO.        T24S    R31E     ?
WRIGHT PROPERTY, RAY see LAVADOURE
                                DOUGLAS CO.       T30S    R3W      S29
WUNSCH, ERDMAN                  WASHINGTON CO.    T3N     R4W      S6
WYETH                           HOOD RIVER CO.    T2N     R8E      S2
WYLAND, DANIEL see WYLAND FAMILY
                                CLACKAMAS CO.     T5S     R1E      S4
WYLAND FAMILY                   CLACKAMAS CO.     T5S     R1E      S4
XL RANCH                        LAKE CO.          T33S    R21E     S31
YACHATS [NEW] see YACHATS MEMORIAL PARK
                                LINCOLN CO.       T14S    R12W     S27
YACHATS [OLD]                   LINCOLN CO.       T14S    R12W     S26
YACHATS MEMORIAL PARK           LINCOLN CO.       T14S    R12W     S27
YAINAX see BROWN                KLAMATH CO.       T36S    R12E     S13
YAINAX AGENCY see ROCK CREEK    KLAMATH CO.       T36S    R11E     S20
YAMHILL-CARLTON                 YAMHILL CO.       T3S     R4W      S10
YAMHILL-CARLTON PIONEER MEMORIAL see YAMHILL-CARLTON
                                YAMHILL CO.       T3S     R4W      S10
YAMHILL COUNTY see YAMHILL-CARLTON
                                YAMHILL CO.       T3S     R4W      S10
YAMHILL COUNTY PIONEER MEMORIAL see YAMHILL-CARLTON
                                YAMHILL CO.       T3S     R4W      S10
YANKTON [OLD]                   COLUMBIA CO.      T4N     R2W      S1
YANKTON-HILLCREST see HILLCREST COLUMBIA CO.      T5N     R2W      S36
YAQUINA                         LINCOLN CO.       T11S    R11W     S22
YAQUINA, JOHN see YAQUINA JOHN POINT
                                LINCOLN CO.       T13S    R12W     S24
YAQUINA JOHN POINT              LINCOLN CO.       T13S    R12W     S24
YARBOROUGH                      LINN CO.          T13S    R4W      S26
YARBOROUGH D.L.C., JOHN B. see YARBOROUGH
                                LINN CO.          T13S    R4W      S26
YARLETT                         MORROW CO.        T1N     R27E     S23
YERGEN see CHAMPOEG             MARION CO.        T4S     R2W      S12
```

YERGENS GRAVEYARD see **CHAMPOEG**	MARION CO.	T4S	R2W	S12
YERGENS', WILLIAM see **CHAMPOEG**	MARION CO.	T4S	R2W	S12
YERGONVILLE MISSION see **CHAMPOEG**				
	MARION CO.	T4S	R2W	S12
YOAKAM FAMILY	COOS CO.	?	R13W	?
YOCOM	YAMHILL CO.	T5S	R5W	S20
YOCOM FAMILY see **HUSSEY FAMILY**	YAMHILL CO.	T5S	R6W	S1
YOCUM	DOUGLAS CO.	T30S	R5W	S19
YOCUM see **YOCOM**	YAMHILL CO.	T5S	R5W	S20
YODER see **SMYRNA**	CLACKAMAS CO.	T5S	R1E	S9
YODER, CLAYTON	CLACKAMAS CO.	T4S	R1E	S18
YODERVILLE see **ZION MENNONITE**	CLACKAMAS CO.	T4S	R1E	S31
YOKUM see **YOCUM**	DOUGLAS CO.	T30S	R5W	S19
YOKUM D.L.C., JOHN see **YOCUM**	DOUGLAS CO.	T30S	R5W	S19
YOKUM *[Sic]* D.L.C., THOMAS J. see **YOCOM**				
	YAMHILL CO.	T5S	R5W	S20
YOUNG	LANE CO.	T15S	R4W	S7
YOUNG, ANDY see **YOUNGS RIVER**	CLATSOP CO.	T7N	R9W	S10
YOUNG, BRIGHAM see **BRIGHAM'S GRAVE**				
	POLK CO.	T9S	R6W	S35
YOUNG D.L.C., JOSEPH R. see **EVERGREEN MEMORIAL PARK**				
	YAMHILL CO.	T4S	R4W	S10
YOUNG D.L.C., JOSEPH R. see **ST. JAMES**				
	YAMHILL CO.	T4S	R4W	S10
YOUNG, EWING	YAMHILL CO.	T3S	R3W	S10
YOUNG FAMILY	WASCO CO.	T5S	R12E	S22
YOUNG MEMORIAL PARK, JOSEPHINE see **PACIFIC VIEW MEMORIAL GARDENS AND COLUMBARIUM**	LINCOLN CO.	T7S	R11W	S12
YOUNG, MR. AND MRS. see **YOUNG FAMILY**				
	WASCO CO.	T5S	R12E	S22
YOUNGS RIVER	CLATSOP CO.	T7N	R9W	S10
ZASTROW CHILDREN see **ZASTROW FAMILY**				
	LINN CO.	T13S	R2E	S19
ZASTROW FAMILY	LINN CO.	T13S	R2E	S19
ZENA	POLK CO.	T6S	R4W	S36
ZIELINSKI PLACE, FRED see **BOY**	LINN CO.	T10S	R1E	S8
ZIMMERMAN	CLACKAMAS CO.	T4S	R1E	S32
ZIMMERMAN, EMMET W. see **ZIMMERMAN FAMILY**				
	WASHINGTON CO.	T2N	R2W	S8
ZIMMERMAN FAMILY	WASHINGTON CO.	T2N	R2W	S8
ZIMMERMAN, GEORGE see **ZIMMERMAN FAMILY**				
	WASHINGTON CO.	T2N	R2W	S8
ZIMMERMAN, GEORGE E. see **ZIMMERMAN FAMILY**				
	WASHINGTON CO.	T2N	R2W	S8
ZIMMERMAN, SARAH ANN see **ZIMMERMAN FAMILY**				
	WASHINGTON CO.	T2N	R2W	S8
ZION [CANBY] see **ZION MEMORIAL PARK**				
	CLACKAMAS CO.	T3S	R1E	S34

ZION [ESTACADA] see **MT. ZION**   CLACKAMAS CO.   T3S   R4E   S22
ZION [HUBBARD] see **ZION MENNONITE**
                                      CLACKAMAS CO.   T4S   R1E   S31
ZION LUTHERAN   BENTON CO.   T11S   R5W   S23
ZION LUTHERAN see **ZION MEMORIAL PARK**
                                      CLACKAMAS CO.   T3S   R1E   S34
ZION LUTHERAN see **ZOAR LUTHERAN [BARLOW ROAD]**
                                      CLACKAMAS CO.   T4S   R1E   S7
ZION MEMORIAL PARK   CLACKAMAS CO.   T3S   R1E   S34
ZION MENNONITE   CLACKAMAS CO.   T4S   R1E   S31
ZOAR see **ZOAR LUTHERAN**   CLACKAMAS CO.   T3S   R1E   S34
ZOAR LUTHERAN   CLACKAMAS CO.   T3S   R1E   S34
ZOAR LUTHERAN [BARLOW ROAD]   CLACKAMAS CO.   T4S   R1E   S7
ZOAR LUTHERAN [EAST] see **ZOAR LUTHERAN**
                                      CLACKAMAS CO.   T3S   R1E   S34
ZOAR LUTHERAN [WEST] see **ZOAR LUTHERAN [BARLOW ROAD]**
                                      CLACKAMAS CO.   T4S   R1E   S7
ZUMWALT   WALLOWA CO.   T2N   R47E   ?
ZUMWALT see **HULBERT LAKE BURIALS**
                                      LANE CO.   T15S   R4W   ?
ZUMWALT D.L.C., JOHN see **MONTGOMERY**
                                      POLK CO.   T9S   R6W   S23
ZUMWALT FAMILY see **HULBERT LAKE BURIALS**
                                      LANE CO.   T15S   R4W   ?
ZUMWALT FAMILY see **MONTGOMERY**   POLK CO.   T9S   R6W   S23

The End